uerbis docu[illegible]
Tu docaor lnaetiu piis
animusas Incelgtaibus
quodpredicusmdogmuae
sucnosatinge ppsrrun
D[illegible] P[illegible] IN Indecollatione sci
Iohannis
Hic Iohannes mise
nuaus desruli
[illegible]sceru . uirae
Iudicem prophetais
quumsua Indigt editais
pirhua nuscendo xpm
pirhua & mortuum
pirhua uino repleais
Hunc aoriumo repleais
sunguinem lubet sui
quise saruprium cedia
auidux coniugalis criminis
[illegible]msuinia coronu

uiau[illegible]
moraum[illegible]
probiu[illegible]
mundi[illegible]
Hunctocam[illegible]
cordumen[illegible]
uasceluf[illegible]
momu[illegible]
consru[illegible]
quum[illegible]
Aiceuo[illegible]
pub[illegible]
puo[illegible]
sio[illegible]
&[illegible]

HISPANIA VETUS

MUSICAL-LITURGICAL MANUSCRIPTS

FROM VISIGOTHIC ORIGINS TO THE

FRANCO-ROMAN TRANSITION (9TH-12TH CENTURIES)

HISPANIA VETUS

MUSICAL-LITURGICAL MANUSCRIPTS
FROM VISIGOTHIC ORIGINS TO THE FRANCO-ROMAN TRANSITION (9TH-12TH CENTURIES)

Susana Zapke (Ed.)

Maria José Azevedo Santos
M.ª Dolores Barrios Martínez
Màrius Bernadó
Susan Boynton
Eva M.ª Castro Caridad
Manuel Cecilio Díaz y Díaz
Marco Daniel Duarte
Maricarmen Gómez
Ramón Gonzálvez Ruiz
Miquel S. Gros
Barbara Haggh
Michel Huglo
Gunilla Iversen
José López-Calo
Shin Nishimagi
M.ª Concepción Peñas García
Elisa Ruiz García
Miguel Carlos Vivancos
Ludwig Vones
Susana Zapke

Foreword
Anscari M. Mundó

Fundación BBVA

CATALOGUING-IN-PUBLICATION DATA

Hispania Vetus : Musical-Liturgical Manuscripts : from Visigothic Origins to the Franco-Roman Transition : 9th-12th Centuries / Susana Zapke (ed.) ; foreword by Anscari M. Mundó. — Bilbao. Fundación BBVA, 2007.
480 p. ; 30 cm
ISBN 978-84-96515-50-5
1. Liturgical Music 2. Manuscripts 3. Iberian Peninsula 4. 9th-12th C. I. Zapke, Susana II. Mundó, Anscari M. III. Fundación BBVA, ed.
783.2:091(46) "09/12"

Hispania Vetus. Musical-Liturgical Manuscripts:
From Visigothic Origins to the Franco-Roman Transition (9th-12th Centuries)

Plaza de San Nicolás, 4. 48005 Bilbao

EDITION AND PRODUCTION: Editorial Nerea, S. A.

TYPESETTING AND LAYOUT: Eurosíntesis Global, S. L.

PRINTED AND BOUND BY: Artes Gráficas Toledo, S. A. U.

ISBN: 978-84-96515-50-5

LEGAL DEPOSIT: TO-1101-2007

Printed in Spain

The books published by the BBVA Foundation are produced with 100% recycled paper made from recovered cellulose fibre (used paper) rather than virgin cellulose, in conformity with the environmental standards required by current legislation.

CONTENTS

Acknowledgments

This work is the fruit of the collective endeavor of a large number of people and institutions to all of which we would like to express our heartfelt thanks. We were offered the greatest of help by the great majority of archives and libraries in Spain and abroad, allowing us to consult the original manuscripts and obtain the many images that illustrate this work. Our special thanks go to the archivists of the ecclesiastical institutions for the painstaking attention and interest with which they helped us consult their rich heritage. Our conversations with specialists from a range of fields were also a source of inspiration and a continuous motivation for the advancement of the work. We would like to thank Anscari M. Mundó, Miquel S. Gros, Michel Huglo, Miguel C. Vivancos, Màrius Bernadó, Elisa Ruiz García, José Manuel Ruiz Asencio, and Manuel C. Díaz y Díaz for their very valuable guidance and their critical judgment, which enabled us to correct some mistakes in time and resolve many of the questions that had arisen during the process of creating the book.

I would also like to express special gratitude to Marta Casares, Marién Nieva, Ruth Salaverría and Beatriz Alday at Editorial Nerea for their meticulous work.

In preparing a scholarly study as formally and materially complex as this one, the Fundación BBVA offered us exceptional conditions which may be unique in the field of research, particularly in the humanities. I would like to thank the Fundación BBVA, as the scholarly publisher of this work, for the trust they placed in the project that resulted in the publication of this book.

We would also like to thank in particular the following institutions and people with whom I have had the privilege of working:

Archivo Capitular, Ávila
Archivo Capitular, Burgos
Archivo Capitular, Burgo de Osma
Archivo Capitular, Córdoba
Archivo Capitular, Huesca
Archivo Capitular, León
Archivo Capitular, Lleida
Archivo Capitular, Ourense
Archivo Capitular, Pamplona
Archivo Capitular, Santiago de Compostela
Archivo Capitular, Santo Domingo de la Calzada
Archivo Capitular, Sigüenza
Archivo de la Corona de Aragón, Barcelona
Archivo Histórico Comarcal, Ripoll
Archivo Histórico Nacional, Madrid
Archivo Histórico Provincial, Huesca
Archivo Real y General de Navarra, Pamplona
Archivo y Biblioteca Episcopal, Vic
Arquivo da Câmara Eclesiástica, Lamego (Portugal)
Arquivo Distrital, Aveiro (Portugal)
Arquivo Distrital, Braga (Portugal)
Arquivo Histórico da Câmara Municipal do Porto (Portugal)
Arquivo da Universidade de Coimbra (Portugal)
Biblioteca de la Abadía de Montserrat
Biblioteca Capitular, Toledo

Biblioteca de Cataluña, Barcelona
Biblioteca General Universitaria, Salamanca
Biblioteca General Universitaria, Santiago de Compostela
Biblioteca General Universitaria, Zaragoza
Biblioteca Nacional de España, Madrid
Biblioteca Nacional de Portugal, Lisbon
Biblioteca Pública Municipal do Porto (Portugal)
Bibliothèque Nationale de France, Paris
British Library, London
Czartorysky Library, Cracow (Poland)
Hispanic Society of America, New York
Instituto dos Arquivos Nacionais da Torre do Tombo, Lisbon
Monastery of Santa Cruz de la Serós, Jaca
Monastery of Santo Domingo de Silos, Silos
Museo de los Concilios y de la Cultura Visigoda, Toledo
Museo de la Real Colegiata de Santa María, Roncevaux
Museo de Santa Cruz, Toledo
Museu de Arte Sacra del Monasterio, Arouca (Portugal)
Patrimonio Nacional, Madrid
Real Academia de la Historia, Madrid
Real Biblioteca de San Lorenzo, El Escorial
Sheffield Galleries & Museums Trust, Collection of the Guild of St. George, Sheffield (Great Britain)
Ramón Abad, Biblioteca de la Universidad de Zaragoza
Pilar Alcalde, Instituto de Estudios Altoaragoneses, Huesca
Fernando Alvira, Huesca
Gonzalo Anes y Álvarez de Castrillón, Real Academia de la Historia, Madrid
José Arranz Arranz, Archivo Capitular, Burgo de Osma
Maria José Azevedo Santos, Arquivo da Universidade de Coimbra (Portugal)
Melchor Bajén Español, Archivo Capitular, Lleida
Georgette Ballez, Bibliothèque Nationale de France, Paris
María Dolores Barrios, Archivo de la Diputación, Huesca
Regine Baumeister, Biblioteca Görres, Madrid
Margarita Becedas, Biblioteca General Universitaria, Salamanca
Nicolas Bell, British Library, London
Màrius Bernadó, University of Lleida
Rogelio Blanco Martínez, Dirección General del Libro, Archivos y Bibliotecas, Ministerio de Cultura
José Antonio Bordallo Huidobro, Patrimonio Nacional
Susan Boynton, Columbia University, New York
Antonio Cabildo Broto, Cathedral of Huesca
Pedro Calahorra, Institución Fernando el Católico, Zaragoza
José Antonio Calixto, Biblioteca Pública de Évora (Portugal)
Christine Campbell, British Library, London
Ana Carles, Archivo Capitular, Lleida
Ilda Carneiro, Arquivo Municipal, Braga (Portugal)
Eva Castro Caridad, University of Santiago de Compostela
Maria Assunçao Chaves, Arquivo Distrital, Braga (Portugal)
Mitchell A Codding, Hispanic Society of America, New York
Marie-Nöel Colette, École Pratique des Hautes Études, Paris
Charlotte Denoël, Département des Manuscrits Occidentaux, Bibliothèque Nationale de France, Paris
Manuel C. Díaz y Díaz, University of Santiago de Compostela
José María Díez Fernández, Cathedral of Santiago de Compostela
Marco Daniel Duarte, University of Coimbra (Portugal)
Henrique Eira, Arquivo da Câmara Eclesiástica, Lamego (Portugal)
Ermelinda Eiras, Biblioteca Pública Municipal do Porto (Portugal)
Ángel Fernández Collado, Biblioteca Capitular, Toledo
Felipe Fernández Ramos, Cathedral of León
Rafael García Serrano, Museo de Santa Cruz, Toledo
Claudio García Turza, Fundación San Millán de la Cogolla
Maria Helena Gil Braga, Arquivo Histórico da Câmara Municipal, Porto (Portugal)
Maricarmen Gómez Muntané, Universidad Autónoma de Barcelona
Miguel Ángel González García, Archivo Capitular, Ourense
Esther González Ibarra, Biblioteca de la Real Academia de la Historia, Madrid
Ramón Gonzálvez, Biblioteca Capitular, Toledo

Julio Gorricho, Archivo Capitular, Pamplona
Miquel S. Gros, Archivo y Biblioteca Episcopal, Vic
Max Haas, University of Zurich (Switzerland)
Barbara Haggh, University of Maryland (USA)
Michel Huglo, Centre National de la Recherque Scientifique, Paris
Gunilla Iversen, University of Stockholm (Sweden)
Jesús Labiano Villanueva, Museo de la Real Colegiata de Santa María, Roncevaux
Silvestre Lacerda, Arquivo Nacional da Torre do Tombo, Lisbon
Dolors Lamarca, Biblioteca de Cataluña, Barcelona
Xosé R. Lema Bendaña, Biblioteca General Universitaria, Santiago de Compostela
Óscar Lilao, Biblioteca General Histórica, Fondo Antiguo, University of Salamanca
Emilio Lizoain, Museo de la Real Colegiata de Santa María, Roncevaux
José López-Calo, University of Santiago de Compostela
Carlos López Rodríguez, Archivo de la Corona de Aragón, Barcelona
Aurora Machado, Biblioteca Nacional de Portugal
Julián Martín Abad, Servicio de Manuscritos, Incunables y Raros, Biblioteca Nacional de España, Madrid
Juan José Martinena Ruiz, Archivo Real y General de Navarra, Pamplona
Jorge Montes Salguero, Biblioteca Nacional de España, Madrid
Anscari M. Mundó, Societat Catalana d'Estudis Litúrgics, Barcelona
José María Nasarre López, Patrimonio Cultural, Bishopric of Huesca
Aires Nascimento, Centro de Estudos Clássicos, University of Lisbon (Portugal)
Manuel Nieto Cumplido, Archivo Capitular, Córdoba
John O'Neill, Department of Manuscripts and Rare Books, The Hispanic Society of America, New York
Shin Nishimagi, École Pratique des Hautes Études, Paris
María Virtudes Pardo Gómez, Biblioteca Universitaria, Colegio de Fonseca, University of Santiago de Compostela
Gilberto Paulo, Biblioteca Nacional de Portugal, Lisbon
M.ª Concepción Peñas García, Universidad Pública de Navarra, Pamplona
Felipe Pérez Rata, Archivo Capitular, Sigüenza
José Miguel Pesqué Lecina, Sección de Cultura, Archivo de Fotografía e Imagen del Alto Aragón, Diputación de Huesca
Arnaldo Pinho, Museu de Arte Sacra del Monasterio de Arouca (Portugal)
Luis Prensa, Institución Fernando el Católico, Zaragoza
Louise Pullen, Ruskin Collection, Sheffield Galleries & Museums Trust, Sheffield (Great Britain)
María Rivas Palá, Archivo Histórico Provincial, Huesca
Carmen Rodríguez Salís, Irun (Spain)
Damià Roure, Biblioteca de la Abadía de Montserrat
Irene Ruiz Albi, University of Valladolid
Gonzalo Ruiz, Archivo Capitular, Santo Domingo de la Calzada
José Manuel Ruiz Asencio, University of Valladolid
Ana Santos Aramburu, Biblioteca Histórica, Universidad Complutense, Madrid
Isabel Santos, Departamento Municipal de Bibliotecas, Câmara Municipal do Porto (Portugal)
Clemente de la Serna, Monastery of Santo Domingo de Silos
Manuel Silva Gonçalves, Arquivo Distrital de Aveiro (Portugal)
Tomás Sobrino Chamón, Patrimonio de la Diócesis de Ávila
Ruth Steiner, Catholic University of America, Washington D. C. (USA)
Marc Taixonera, Biblioteca de la Abadía de Montserrat
Manuel Terrón Bermúdez, Patrimonio Nacional, Madrid
Alberto Torra, Archivo de la Corona de Aragón, Barcelona
Maria da Assunçao Vasconcelos, Arquivo Distrital, Braga (Portugal)
Matías Vicario Santamaría, Archivo Capitular, Burgos
Miguel C. Vivancos, Monastery of Santo Domingo de Silos
Markwardt Zapke Leyhausen, Irun (Spain)

Foreword

Anscari Manuel Mundó

Of all the works I have been asked to introduce throughout my career, few have been as prestigious as *Hispania Vetus,* this study of the early liturgical and musical codices (nearly all of them including contents from both categories) of the Iberian Peninsula. The theme of this book falls within my own academic field—though naturally not encompassing all of it—giving me an incentive to turn my attention, perhaps for the very last time, to the subject of literary, musical, and liturgical codicology and paleography.

I was asked by Susana Zapke, a musicologist with solid Germanic scholarly training who has already done research on subjects closely related to this book. The book has received support from the Fundación BBVA, a sure guarantee not only of perfect presentation, but of scientific rigor, and this is further assured by the quality of the contributors, several of whom are friends of mine. Rather than commenting on the book itself, therefore, I would like to offer a number of remarks. Some may seem obvious; others are intended to remind readers of something which, though fundamental, has not always been properly taken into account by some Iberian and other European medievalists.

This volume will offer considerable help to scholars researching the most diverse period in the history of the Iberian Peninsula: that part of the Middle Ages when the characteristics of the different Iberian cultures were forged and consolidated. To understand this period, it is essential to understand the conditions in which it unfolded.

These cultures were built on a series of substrata which had been superimposed over a period of many centuries. The most obvious of these were the Iberian-Basque, Cantabrian, Celtic, Afro-Berber, Semitico-Jewish, Helleno-Greek and Roman-Latin cultures, with Germanic, Vandal, Swabian and Visigoth additions, and the later emergence of Arab elements. Their respective influence varies from region to region in the Iberian Peninsula.

Broadly speaking, the cultures that arose out of these substrata formed vertical strips running down the Peninsula. From west to east extend Galicia-Portugal, Asturias-León, Rioja-Castile and Catalonia, with Aragón nestling between the last two; to the north lies the Basque-Navarrese enclave, while in the center and south we find the more extensive horizontal Arab strip. Here we need to explain why that superimposition of traditions and cultures led to the formation of political institutions so strong that their respective inhabitants saw themselves as the children of specific motherlands and nations.

While the Moors consolidated their position and resisted incursions from the north, centralising their power in the Córdoba Caliphate, the other regions began the process of political consolidation in the 8th century. Some nuclei—such as Asturias, with its Visigothic royal tradition—stood firm in the north of the peninsula; conscious of their historical past, they soon expanded towards León and Galicia. During the 9th century, the Galician nucleus in the far west spread down towards the future county of Portugal (later to become a kingdom in the 12th century) after it broke away from Asturian-Leonese absorption. The restless kingdom of Navarre resisted the invasion, albeit with difficulty and later inroads from its neighbors. The impregnable Basque nucleus remained isolated. In the northeast of the peninsula, from the end of the 8th century, resistant Hispano-Goths, with the support of their Frankish hosts, formed a county on the banks of the River Aragón which they then extended westward. In the 11th century this county obtained from Navarre the status of a kingdom. At the eastern end of the Pyrenees—an area later conquered by the Moors—Hispano-Goths, with Franco-German support, pushed the borders of the Carolingian kingdom south as far as the *Spanish March*. The various counties were united in what from the 10th century was to be called the *Regnum Barcinonense*[1] by the emirs of Córdoba and its neighbors across the Pyrenees; by the end of the 11th century it had come to be known as *Catalaunia*.[2]

Mozarabia, a Christianized mixture of Arab, Hispanic and Visigothic, had neither the power nor the will to belong to a political structure worthy of its learned ancestors, surviving instead in scattered enclaves within the Caliphate in the south until the 15th century. The Iberian Peninsula was shared, or rather, fragmented into politically distanced homelands, which largely ignored one another.[3]

The first mixes of races and peoples came gradually. Some came about through force, though with the passage of time they became subtly intertwined. One case in particular serves as a good illustration: from the end of the 8th century until long before the country came to be called *Catalaunia*, the local Hispanics, Goths, Jews, Arabs and Franks, came together in a struggle to re-establish the old *ordo christianus*.[4]

The languages of the Iberian Peninsula clearly demonstrate the diversity of independently-developing societies. The different forms of speech—the ways in which the common people (the *plebs, vulgus or rustici*) of a society sharing a common territory over a long period communicated with one another—developed and diversified precisely because of a lack of social and cultural contact with other neighboring communities over several centuries, and the period covered by this book was to be crucial in establishing the cultural and linguistic diversity of the peninsula. These clearly differentiated languages were: Galician-Portuguese, Castilian, Catalonian, Basque (persistent), and a number of intermediary languages and dialects which united and divided these other tongues, as well as the Mozarab Ladino, now almost extinct.[5]

Much of my career has centered on paleographic aspects, both literary (those that use signs to establish words and phrases expressing concepts and ideas) and musical (those which, through signs or neumes, represent sounds in tones and melodies). Given that this wonderful book deals with music and liturgy—art and worship, two very particular themes—which cannot be studied without a solid understanding of the history of the texts used in the Iberian Peninsula and its neighbors, it seems appropriate to introduce some background.

From the first appearance on the peninsula of liturgical texts with musical neumes—antiphonaries of the mass and the holy office, mixed or "mystical" books, plenary missals, pontificals and variety of rites—a clear distinction can be seen between two types. The largest group, in the west, is in a script we call Visigothic, with its own neumes which are commonly called Visigothic and Mozarabic (and we should be careful not to confuse them!) transcribing melodies of the old "Visigothic" or "Toledan" rite. From the 9th century on a second group, no less important in quality, emerged in the east, written in Carolingian script with what are known as "Catalonian" neumes and based on Gregorian melodies.[6]

It is important to remember the initial reasons for the diversity between the Iberian peoples in their liturgical, literary and musical dimensions.

One key factor was the separation of the dioceses and counties of the ecclesiastical province of the *Tarraconensis* from the other territories of the peninsula, which continued to observe the old Visigothic liturgy. This came about as the result of a series of circumstances: the (purportedly temporary) subjugation of the dioceses of Tarragona, liberated by the Carolingian monarchs, to the metropolitan of Narbonne from the end of the 8th century on; and the suspicion of heresy leveled by Carolingian theologians against Visigothic liturgical texts. This was followed by the early acceptance of the rule of St. Benedict in the monasteries and the *ordo canonicorum* of Aachen in the cathedrals. Another important factor was the papal favor enjoyed by Catalonia's ecclesiastical and civic institutions from the end of the 9th century, under Popes Formosus in 892, and Romanus in 897; so strong was this support that according to Paul Fridolin Kehr, between 950 and 1050 Catalonia was the recipient of more papal bulls than any other country in Christendom.[7]

A few examples will suffice to give an idea of the wider picture in the Carolingian bishoprics and counties of the old *Tarraconensis* from the 9th century on. In 874, Frodoin (Frodwin), the Franco-German Bishop of Barcelona, attended the Council of Attigny, which had been called by his friend Emperor Charles the Bald. There he complained to Pope John VIII about certain Mozarabic presbyters, refugees from Córdoba, who wanted to introduce the Visigothic rite inside and outside the city. In another example, at an important ceremony attended by Frodoin and the Archbishop of Narbonne, Sigebod (also Frankish), in Barcelona in 877, it was stated that: "*cum vero quadam die ambo in eadem sede missarum solemnia peragerent*…"; the mass could only be concelebrated in accordance with the Franco-Roman rite observed by the metropolitan prelate.[8]

There are plenty of examples of the new liturgy in the form of fragmentary codices, in palimpsests and documents: the record of the consecration of Tona, dated in Vic in 888, the Tarragona fragment from around 890 and the two Copenhagen palimpsests from the 10th century—the first, from Barcelona's rural *agro* and the remainder from the city of Barcelona—along with several other manuscripts, all reflect a state of liturgical peace that had long existed in the Catalonian area of influence; indeed, it had been achieved two centuries before the "war of the rites" broke out in the interior of the peninsula in the 1070s and 1080s.

There are also examples from the first decades of the 11th century that show the same process in reverse: King Sancho the Great of Navarre was a great admirer of the venerable Oliva (or Oliba), abbot of Ripoll and Bishop of Vic, with whom he struck up a close friendship, requesting his advice on matters of particular importance. At one point, Abbot Oliva wanted to send King Sancho a treatise in the form of a letter on a controversial moral theme. As his envoy, he chose the monk Ponce (*Pontius*, Ponç), a disciple of his at the school of Ripoll and later Abbot of Tabèrnoles (Seu d'Urgell). Sancho was so taken by Ponce's erudition that he kept him on as his tutor (in a letter he calls him *"domne meus magister Poncius abba"*) and later appointed him Bishop of Palencia. The restoring Bishop observed the *mos romanum*. Despite Ponce's good intentions, the liturgical customs he brought from the eastern Pyrenees were not initially welcomed by the members of his congregation, accustomed as they were to the Visigothic rite. However, we must assume that he soon adapted to local customs, given that he ended his ecclesiastical career as the Archbishop of Oviedo. The case of Atón, Bishop of Castile, originally from the east of the peninsula, was similar: in a document associated with Sancho the Great, it is stated that he celebrated the mass according to the Roman rite, causing ill will among his subjects, who were used to the venerable Visigothic rites.[9]

However, such personal contact must have been rare, if we are to judge by the case of the rotuli or *encíclicas mortuorias*. These encyclicals, commonplace in the Pyrenean counties during the 11th century, called for liturgical prayers to be said for important figures who had died. Having made the rounds of the religious communities in the Catalonian sphere of influence, the *tomifer,* who carried the encyclical by hand, visited monasteries and cathedrals in western and central Europe, sometimes going as far afield as Paris or even Flanders and the Rhineland.[10] Yet in the entire 11th century, he never once crossed westward over the Ebro. For the inhabitants of the Catalonian counties this area was *Spania*, the land of Arabs, as many documents and legal texts of the time attest. Such a perspective should come as no surprise, given that much the same idea was held in León and in Galicia.

The case of the Mozarabs of the south who took refuge in Toledo is another example of incomprehension between people from different backgrounds, leading to liturgical intolerance. The Mozarabs ensured the survival of ancient liturgy and melodies from the Visigothic *ordo* in the parishes outside the metropolises. When the new Archbishop of Sahagún, Bernard, imposed the Franco-Roman rite on his diocese (burning any old books containing the Toledan liturgy that were preserved in the cathedral), he confined the southern communities, with their books and their liturgy, to the suburban parishes of the capital. It was Cardinal Cisneros, with his advisor Ortiz, who was to save these codices for posterity, using them for his edition of 1500. Although some of these liturgical codices, also from Toledo, are among the latest examples from the peninsula to contain neumes, and strictly speaking they fall outside the scope of this corpus, in that they date from after the 12th century,[11] I think it is quite reasonable for them to have been included in this volume: as I say, they represent a much earlier tradition, even if the neumes remain mute for us, given the complete absence of any diastematy.

As these examples show, it is very important to approach the medieval culture of the Hispanic peoples with a degree of caution. As the ancients put it "distingue tempora et concordabis iura!"

I would now like to turn my attention to the importance of the copyists' skills. Some of the great scriptoria of cathedrals, monasteries and regular canons were home to men who were expert in a variety of writing arts: calligraphy, draughtsmanship and illumination. It is sometimes assumed that these specialities were exercised by different people. While this may sometimes have been true, it is entirely reasonable to presume that a man with the ability to trace millions of letters with micrometric precision on thousands of pages over many years would also be capable of drawing the great initials at the beginning of the manuscript or its individual sections or chapters; of adding figures or portraits; of illustrating a full-page scene and even of illuminating the drawing. Such a person would be a calligrapher, draughtsman and miniaturist *par excellence*. I have no doubt that in many of the codices included in this collection, the calligrapher who drew the neumes and the copyist of the liturgical text were one and the same.

To illustrate this point, I cite the example of the monk Guifré of Ripoll, the skilful copyist of various codices from the monastery, who worked between 1008 and 1040. Analysing his script, I came to the conclusion that he was responsible for copying at least seven codices and had also worked on several others. The most important of these is the giant Bible, Biblioteca Apostolica Vaticana,

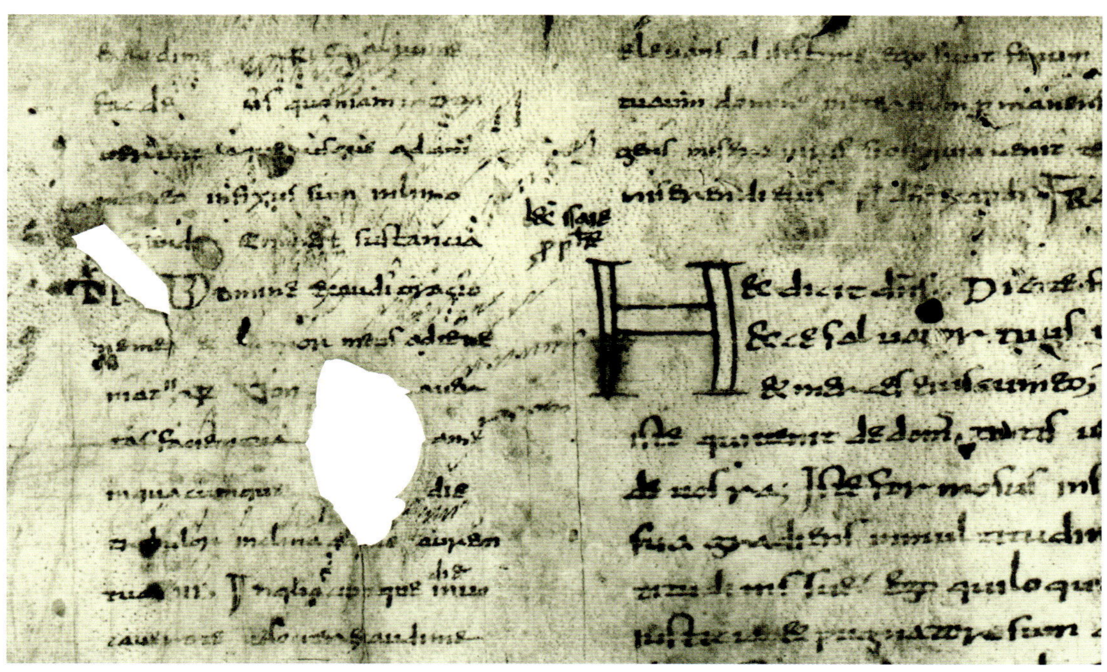

1. Archivo Histórico Archidiocesano, Tarragona, Frag. 22/1, 11th century *ex.*, fol. 1v

ms. Lat. 5729, which is entirely in his hand. A comparative analysis of his writing shows a clear evolution in the penmanship of the letters, signs and abbreviations, allowing us to establish the chronological order of the codices attributed to him. We may deduce, for example, that the great Vatican Bible was on Guifré's lectern between 1015 and 1020. The great initial letters of the books of the Bible—with drawings of plants, animals and humans—are all in his hand, and were drawn before he copied the corresponding text around the edges. Even more important was the discovery that the great illustrations that cover many of the pages, with their wonderful Biblical scenes, are also the fruit of his artistic talent (which I dared to describe as "impressionist"). Among the copies attributed to Guifré there are also two liturgical codices—of the Franco-Roman monastic rite, needless to say—full of Catalonian neumes in his hand.

When the brownish ink and the quill stroke, with its slight wear, in the text and the neumes were compared under the microscope, it was found that the same ink and the same quill had been used to form both the letters and the neumes.[12]

I referred earlier to fragments. One area of codicological research which once seemed to have been ignored—or at least neglected—was the study of fragments of codices or *membra disiecta*. For many years, I have centered my attention on searching out such pieces and describing them.[13] Any fragment, albeit the battered remnant of a single folio, is proof of the existence of a once complete codex, which must have circulated and been known and read by learned figures from the region. Our knowledge of these fragments has greatly extended our understanding, not only of the history of the script, the location of the writing centers and the dissemination of the texts, but to an even greater extent, their cultural implications.

I would like to conclude this foreword with an anecdote which I think may amuse readers, be they palaeographists or liturgists. The setting was the conference on Latin paleography held in 1979 in Switzerland. At the meeting in Saint Gall I presented a study on the fragments of codices preserved in Catalonian libraries or of Catalonian provenance (1980). We were working in collaboration with

2. *Missale mixtum,* Montserrat, Biblioteca de la Abadía, 1254-IV, 11th century *in.*, fol. 3v

Professor Lázsló Mezey (not present at the event), who was in charge of drawing up an inventory of the fragments of codices preserved in the libraries in his home country of Hungary; he had contacts with other "fragmentologists" such as Avelino de Jesús da Coast (not present), an indefatigable searcher of Portuguese fragments, and Manuel C. Díaz y Díaz, a shrewd analyst of the remains of codices, who was present at the event. We considered that in our respective countries, having lost many of the manuscripts to war, invasion and destruction, our only choice was to gather together the fragmentary remains of our old codicological treasures. However, at the end of my paper, one astute colleague asked whether we were founding a new paleographic science: "fragmentology". Of course not! We all know that this is pure codicology: what does it matter whether a codex has five hundred, a hundred, fifty or ten folios, or whether just one, two or five of its folios are still preserved: we must always treat them as the remains of a once-complete codex.

I am convinced that this book will demonstrate the strength of the different Iberian cultures with their respective cultural focuses, the diverse liturgical rites that were introduced at different paces and in very different times in the Iberian Peninsula, and the working methods used in the different scriptoria and the varied work of certain copyists of talent and skill capable of writing, decorating and artistically illustrating a codex and adding musical neumes to the liturgical text, melodically embellishing the public prayers. It will also show the exceptional importance of liturgical-musical fragments to our understanding, given that so few complete codices still remain.

These historical, paleographic and liturgical conclusions have been judiciously applied by Susana Zapke, editor of the work. On certain points she has had to accommodate multiple interpretations, as will be seen in her extensive and erudite concluding chapter to Hispania Vetus. This is nothing other than a demonstration of her exemplary method and of her intelligent and respectful intellectual approach to the opinion of the other contributors, and she should be thanked for it.

Notes

[1] I would like to make a couple of historical and etymological *excursus* on the names given to the area of the Iberian Peninsula to which I belong. On *Regnum Barcinonense*, see Juan Vernet. "*El 'statu quo' internacional de Barcelona en el siglo X*". In Martin Forstner, ed. *Festgabe für Hans-Rudolf Singer. Zum 65. Geburtstag...* Frankfurt, Berne, New York, Paris: Peter Lang, 1991, 509-517, with the Arabic texts that acknowledge it; for the French texts from beginning of the 11th century, see Andreas Floriacensis. *Miracula sancti Benedicti*, Book 4, Prologue and Chaps. 7-9. In Eugène de Certain, ed. *Les miracles de Saint-Benoît, écrits par Adrevald, Aimoin, André, Raoul Tortaire et Hugues de Sainte Marie, moines de Fleury.* Paris: Chez M(adame) V(euve) Jules Renouard librairie de la Societé de l'Institut de France, 1858, 173-174 and 182-191; for the quotes in Catalonian funerary rotuli see note 10; I have used all the accounts in Anscari M. Mundó. "Aportacions de la història local a l'expansió de Catalunya ara fa mil anys". *Annals. Casa-Museu Prat de la Riba. Castelterçol* 5 (1989): 15-25; and *idem.* "Dels Pirineus a Europa, passant per Ripoll". In *Consell d'Europa: una dimensió humana. Dia d'Europa.* Barcelona: Generalitat de Cataluña, 1989, 15-27, especially page 26; summary in *Gran Enciclopèdia Catalana.* Barcelona: Edicions 62, 1973. Vol. 4: 691-692.

[2] My second *excursus* refers to the name *Catalaunia*. A *Cathalanus* appeared for the first time in Besalú in 922, who would have been a native of *Catalaunis* = Chalons-sur-Marne; see *Catalunya carolíngia.* Vol. 5, *Els comtats de Girona, Besalú, Empúries i Peralada.* Barcelona: Institut d'Estudis Catalans, 2003 (Memòries de Secció Històrico-Arqueològica: 61), docs. 183, 185 and 186 and my remark on pages 56-57; mention is made of *Teodoricus Rex francorum dum esset Cathalaunis* in the prologue by the jurist Bonsom to his copies of the *Liber iudicum popularis* written in Barcelona in 1010 and 1011 (edited by Jesús Alturo, et al. *El Liber iudicum popularis ordenat pel jutge Bonsom de Barcelona.* Barcelona: Generalitat de Cataluña, Departament de Justícia i Interior, 2003, 339 and my comments on pages 117 and 228 and note 6, with references to previous works of mine); from approximately 1085 AD, the wife of Zetmar, Lord of Catellterçol bore the name of *Catalana*; when she died in 1125 her heir was a daughter, also called *Catalana* (see "Aportacions de la història local...", cited in note 1). From the same period—around 1100—several citizens of Carcassone, a county recently acquired by Ramon Berenguer III, Count of Barcelona, began to be called *catalani, catalanenses, catelan* and *de Cataluign*; and the count himself and his compatriots are similarly described in the *Liber Maiorichinus,* which describes the help given by the Pisans in the conquest of Majorca and Eivissa in 1114. Accounts written by 12th century Italian and English chroniclers and by the 13th century Hungarian chronicler Simon of Kéza show that legends were already circulating about the coming of Attilla, King of the Huns, from Chalons-sur-Marne, *Cathalaunum*, to the land now known as *Catalaunia,* at the eastern end of the Pyrenees. I therefore consider that of the twenty possible etymologies proposed for *Catalunya*, the most likely origin of the name can undoubtedly be found in *Catalaunum* from Chalons-sur Marne (from 1995, officially called Chalons-en-Champagne). I hope, *Deo volente*, to publish soon a long study under the title *Del "Regnum Barchinonense" a "Catalaunia"* [which has been announced for several years now; for example, in "Los orígenes de la nación catalana". In Club Arnau de Vilanova, ed. *Para entendernos. Los grandes temas del debate España-Cataluña.* 1st ed. Barcelona: Ariel, 1996, especially pages 49-53 and note 32 (2nd ed., 2001, 49-55 and note 32)]. To make it easier to understand the historical discourse, it is common practice to use the terms "*Cataluña*" and "*catalán*" ("Catalonia" and "Catalonian/Catalan") to designate the territory and its adjectives, although these choronyms actually emerged later.

[3] Juan Carrasco, et al. *Historia de las Españas medievales.* Barcelona: Crítica, 2002.

[4] Anscari M. Mundó. *De quan hispans, gots, jueus, àrabs i francs circulaven per Catalunya.* Barcelona: Real Acadèmia de Bones Lletres de Barcelona, Universidad Autónoma de Barcelona, 2001.

[5] I have addressed several of the issues mentioned here in "Los orígenes de la nación catalana". Op. cit., 36-66 (2nd ed., 37-68).

[6] Joaquim Garrigosa I Massana. *Els manuscrits musicals a Catalunya fins al segle XIII. L'evolució de la notació musical.* Lleida: Institut d´Estudis Ilerdencs, 2003, with twenty-six plates.

[7] Paul Fridolin Kehr. *Die älteste Papsturkunden Spaniens.* Berlin: Akademie der Wissenschaften, 1926, 3 (Abhandlungen der Preußischen Akademie der Wissenschaften zu Berlin: Philosophisch-Historische Klasse 2). I give a detailed account in "Notes entorn de les butlles papals catalanes més antigues". In *Homenaje a Johannes Vincke.* Madrid: CSIC, Görresgesellschaft zur Pflege der Wissenschaft, 1962-1963, 113-120 and two plates (republ. in Anscari M. Mundó. *Obres completes. I: Catalunya, 1: De la romanitat a la sobirania.* Barcelona: Curial Edicions Catalanes, Abbey of Montserrat, 1998, 91-100).

[8] For a more extensive study, see my *El Commicus palimpsest Paris 2269. Amb notes sobre litúrgia i manuscrits visigòtics a Septimània i Catalunya.* In *Liturgica, I: Cardinali I. A. Schuster in memoriam.* Montserrat: Abbey of Montserrat, 1956, 84-85, with an interpretation of contemporary sources. The change in the liturgy in the Catalonian counties has been dealt with by other writers on the basis of my work; see particularly Miquel S. Gros on the Catalonian-Narbonnaise *ordines.* More details in Anscari M. Mundó. "El bisbat d'Ègara de l'època tardo-romana a la carolíngia". In *Simposi Internacional sobre les Esglésies de Sant Pere de Terrassa.* Terrasa: Centre d´Estudis Histórics de Terrasa, 1992, 41-49, especially pages 48-49 (now in Anscari M. Mundó. *Obres completes. Ibidem,* especially pages 226-240. The extensive and well-documented work of Ursula Vones-Liebenstein. "Katalonien zwischen Maurenherrschaft und Frankenreich. Probleme um die Ablösung westgotisch-mozarabischer Kirchenstrukturen". In Rainer Berndt, ed. *Das Frankfurter Konzil von 794. Kristallisation Karolingischer Kultur.* Vol. 1, *Politik und Kirche.* Mainz: Mittelrheinische Kirchengeschichte, 1997, 453-505 (Quellen und Abhandlungen zur Mittelrheinische Kirchengeschichte: 80). Vones, in his learned study, touches on the theme of the liturgical change in Catalonia introduced by the Carolingians during the 9th century (citing, among others, "El palimpsest" and "El bisbat d'Égara"; I thank him for his interest in my work). I would like to present two themes discussed on pages 476-78, notes 132, 139, 140, and 142. Certainly there was a kind of war of rites between Bishop Frodo and some of the Mozarabic clerics who had arrived from Córdoba a short time earlier, with some resemblance (albeit limited) to what happened in the center of the peninsula around the second half of the 11th century (see, in my text, the section following note 8). On page 28 of "El bisbat d'Égara," however, I did not refer to "the consecration of bishops" by the Mozarabic presbyter Tirso, but only state that "algú l'empenyia fins al punt d'actuar com a bisbe i així ordenava altres preveres", meaning that he translated them as he pleased, exactly what the capitularies of Charlemagne and Louis the Pious criticized: "de his qui sine consensu episcopi presbyteros in ecclesiis constituunt vel de ecclesiis eiciunt". In the context of another study I intend to return to Baió, who revolted against Frodo, and his fate far from Terrassa.

[9] Justo Pérez de Urbel. *Sancho el Mayor de Navarra.* Navarre: Institución Príncipe de Viana, 1950, 215-217 and 283; see my review in Anscari M. Mundó. "Entorn de Sancho el Mayor de Navarra". *Butlletí de la Societat Catalana d'Estudis Històrics* 1 (1952): 33-42 (reprint in *idem. Obres completes. Ibidem,* 298-307, especially pages 301-303).

[10] Jean Dufour. "Les rouleaux et encycliques mortuaires de Catalogne (1008-1102)". *Cahiers de civilisation médiévale* 20 (1977): 13-48; see also Léopold Delisle. *Les rouleaux des morts du IX au XV siècle.* Paris: Imprimérie Nationale, 1866, 74, 81, 82 and 91, which contains responses from other monasteries which, around 1050, refer to monks from Canigou as *fratres barzolonenses, barcinonenses.*

[11] Anscari M. Mundó. "La datación de los códices litúrgicos visigóticos toledanos". *Hispania Sacra* 18 (1965): 1-25.

[12] *Idem. Les Bíblies de Ripoll.* Vol. 3, *Estudi dels mss. Vaticà, Lat. 5729 i Paris, BNF, Lat.6.* Vatican City: Biblioteca Apostolica Vaticana, 2002, with twenty-seven plates; on Guifré, *passim,* in the text, and also Plates 5, 13a-23b and 25; 16 and 19 show script and neumes in his hand.

[13] Since in 1952, I wrote about "El fragmento bíblico del manuscrito Madrid, BN, ms. 3307". *Estudios bíblicos* 11 (1952): 399-411, and in particular, since I began the study in 1950, published in 1956, of the fragment *El Commicus palimpsest...* Op. cit., a number of works have been published on other fragments: "Les collections de manuscrits en Catalogne et celle du Montserrat en particulier". *Archives, Bibliothèques et Musées en Belgique* 30 (1959): 217-223; "Códices isidorianos de Ripoll". In Manuel C. Díaz y Díaz, ed.

Isidoriana... Estudios... XIV Centenario. Madrid, León: Centro de Estudios e Investigación San Isidoro (CSIC-CECEL), 1961, 389-400; "La col·lecció de papirs de Montserrat". *Studia papyrologica* 2 (1963): 35-42; "Fragments d'un curiós sacramentari-martirologi". In *Gesammelte Aufsätze zur Kulturgeschichte Spaniens.* Münster: Aschendorff, 1963, 12-53 (Spanische Forschungen der Görresgesellschaft: 1/21) (with the collaboration of Alexandre Olivar on the appendix); "Un fragment molt antic de litúrgia romana a Catalunya", followed by "Nous manuscrits amb notació catalana arcaica". In *II Congrés Litúrgic de Montserrat.* Vol. 3, *Secció d'Història.* Montserrat: Abbey of Montserrat, 1967, 173-191; "Documentos visigodos originales en pergamino y su proyección en la época de la reconquista". In *Congresso luso-espanhol de estudos medievais promovido pela Cámara Municipal do Porto.* Porto: Cámara Municipal do Porto, 1968, 200-201; *Los diplomas visigodos originales en pergamino. Transcripción y comentario.* Barcelona: University of Barcelona, 1974; "Les col·leccions de fragments de manuscrits a Catalunya". *Faventia* 2, no. 2 (1980): 115-123; "Fragment del Llibre jutge, versió catalana antiga del *Liber iudiciorum*". In *Miscel·lània Aramon i Serra.* Barcelona: Curial Edicions Catalanes, 1984. Vol. 4: 156-193 + 29 figs. (Estudis Universitaris Catalans: 26); "El fragmento de Celanova de la Hispana reaparecido". *Hispania Sacra* 36, no. 74 (1984): 591-600; "Comment reconnaître la provenance de certains fragments de manuscrits détachés de reliures". In *Codices manuscripti. Zeitschrift für Handschriftenkunde.* Vienna: Brüder Hollinek, 1986. Vol. 11: 116-124; and "Entorn dels papirs de la catedral de Barcelona". In *Miscel·lània papirològica Ramon Roca-Puig.* Barcelona: Fundación Salvador Vives Casajuana, 1986, 221-223; much of "La cultura artística escrita". In Antoni Pladevall i Font, ed. *Catalunya romànica I, Introducció a l'estudi de l'art Romànic Català.* Barcelona: Enciclopèdia Catalana, 1994, 133-162 (republ. "La cultura escrita del segle IX al XII a Catalunya". In Anscari M. Mundó. *Obres completes.* Op. cit., 484-582, is based on the fragments of codices).

Introduction

Susana Zapke

Its geographical situation and the political and cultural circumstances resulting from successive waves of invaders—Romans, Vandals, Visigoths and Moors—have given the Iberian Peninsula a complex, unique history in the context of the general map of Christianity. Located on the periphery of Christian lands and fragmented into political entities that differed widely in their cultures and ideologies, its inclusion in the unifying program drawn up by Pope Gregory VII (1073-1085) was beset by numerous difficulties. The Pope's objective of abolishing the Hispanic liturgical tradition, also known as Visigothic or Mozarabic, and replacing it with a uniform liturgy with a Franco-Roman structure was to result in numerous different scenarios which arose from the political and sociocultural differences between the states that made up the peninsula in the Middle Ages. Indeed, modern historiographers have revived the term *Españas,* which can be found in medieval writings, in preference to the singular form, thus highlighting the diversity of the political entities in the Iberian Peninsula following the decline of the Kingdom of the Visigoths.[1] The North-South divide in Spain that followed the Moorish invasion, the survival of a Visigothic substrate and the Carolingian elements that trickled in over the course of the 8th century laid the foundations of the political edifice that existed in the period under consideration here, at the time of the transition from the Hispanic rite to the Franco-Roman rite. Documentary proof that this transition did not take place to the same degree or at the same time throughout the peninsula appears in the many different forms and structures that can be found in the sources of liturgical music which form the basis of this publication.

The first part of the book presents contributions by nine leading scholars from different disciplines—textual and musical paleography, philology, history and musicology—who raise substantial questions and provide partial solutions to various complex matters which continue to cause controversy. Each of these original articles is a key contribution to the advancement of research in this complicated chapter of the liturgical history of the peninsula, in which many questions remain unanswered. The second part of the book seeks to provide a vision of the vitality of the process of transition, and the diversity of structures of liturgical music that could be found in the Iberian Peninsula, by describing a total of 89 manuscripts representing the various notational systems: Visigothic, Catalonian, transitional modes and Aquitainian, and indicating the cultural areas that provided the backdrop to each of them.

Although the two parts can be viewed as independent documents for consultation, each part of the book complements the other, as the articles in Part One draw from the sources in Part Two.

Historical background

The first contact between the kingdoms of the Iberian Peninsula and the Western Church was made by King Sancho III the Great (1004-1035). As a result of this connection the monasteries of the Pyrenees were annexed into the Benedictine reform, new monasteries were founded, including San Juan de la Peña (1025), and other churches and monasteries were converted, such as San Martín de Albelda, Santa María de Irache, San Salvador de Leyre and the Cathedral of Pamplona, all of which depended personally on the King and his family. Links with Abbot Odilo of Cluny and with Catalonian clerics such as Abbot Oliba of Ripoll and the Bishop of Vic provided the stimuli required to reform the King's domains in an open, progressive spirit driven by the desire to restore Christianity in lands threatened by Moorish incursions. The monastic reform undertaken by the King in the context of a more general political project was to result in the diffusion of the Benedictine rule and the implementation of new liturgical usages stemming not from direct action by Cluny or Rome but from the mediation of such centers as the Abbey at Ripoll and key personages such as the aforesaid Abbot Oliba and Abbot Poncio of San Saturnino de Tavèrnoles. The religious, cultural and economic renewal undertaken by this markedly progressive monarch was to trigger a far-reaching transformation in society over the course of the 11th century.[2]

Papal influence in Catalonia dates back further than in the rest of the peninsula: the first rapprochement took place in the 9th century *ex.* (ca. 892). This turn towards Rome was motivated partly by a desire for independence from the Archbishopric of Narbonne, with which the Bishoprics of Catalonia had been linked since the 8th century *ex.*[3] A case in point is the Monastery of Sant Miquel de Cuixà, which fell under the direct patronage of the Holy See in the year 950. This rapprochement provided the church in Catalonia not only with the assurance of some degree of protection but also with progressively greater autonomy from the Carolingian sovereigns.

Occasional interaction between the papacy and the various political regimes culminated in a plan of action applied to the whole of the peninsula, which was promoted during the pontificate of Gregory VII (1073-1085). A few days after being elected, he established the abolition of the Visigothic heresy and the deviations of the Arianists and Priscillianists in Spain as essential priorities. The absence of any allusion to harmful influences resulting from the Moorish invasion is significant: there was no specific mention of such influences until a papal bull dated 1077, in which the arguments against Arianists and Goths no longer appeared, and all responsibility for corrupting the liturgical rite was heaped upon Muslims and pagans.[4] From then on the program of reform was applied with greater rigor although, as shown repeatedly from various analytical angles in the first part of this book, the absence of a plan of action designed to cover the whole peninsula gave rise to many different scenarios and different rates of transition to the new rite. The first official delegations sent by the Holy See to begin liturgical reforms arrived in the years 1065 and 1071 in the person of Cardinal Hugo Candidus. A journey by Sancho Ramírez to Rome in the year 1069 to enfief the kingdom of Aragón to the Pope was the first direct contact between a Spanish monarch and the Holy See. Its impact was to be felt years later in the reform of the monasteries of San Juan de la Peña and San Victorián de Sobrarbe in 1072, and in the appointment of García, the king's brother, to the Bishopric of Jaca in approximately the year 1076. In a bull dated October 15, 1079, Gregory VII invited Alfonso VI of Castile and León (1040-1109) to carry out *correctionem regni vestri quod diu in herrore perstiterat.* However, political and ecclesiastical centers soon voiced opposition, and the difficulties faced by the Pope are exemplified by the figure of the deposed abbot Robert of the Monastery of Sahagún, reformed in 1079. He had voiced his approval of the Hispanic rite on two previous occasions: once under the pontificate of Pope John X (914-925) and again under Alexander II (1061-1073). However, Gregory VII sought to go further than his predecessors and envisaged an ambitious plan to unify liturgical usage and guarantee the hegemony of Rome throughout Christianity. In this context, the Council of Burgos, held in May 1080, represents a decisive point in the complex relationship of the Spanish kingdoms with the Holy See: This council officially approved the replacement of the Hispanic rite by the Roman rite, and consolidated Spain's definitive subservience to Rome. Liturgical orthodoxy was thus assured in all the kingdoms of Spain, with the elimination of the heretical malformations which Pope Gregory VII believed had risen there because of the region's geographical remoteness from the center of power of Christianity in Rome. Only in Toledo, which had been reconquered by King Alfonso VI in the year 1085, did part of the Visigothic tradition manage to survive in six parishes, in spite of the rigorous sentence by the Pope, who defined the rite as *superstitio toletana*. However, it was to experience a second renaissance centuries later in the context of a Visigothic renovation movement promoted by Cardinal Cisneros (1436-1517). Meanwhile, the primatial see embraced the new rite unreservedly and incorporated French monks into its community. Copies were also commissioned of books of worship belonging to the Franco-Roman tradition by order of the then Archbishop Bernard, who had lived previously as a monk in Cluny and had been abbot of Sahagún.

This ambitious project to Romanize the liturgy entailed political, ideological, social and cultural changes, and was to result in practice in the learning of a new rite and new forms of notation which were unknown to both clergy and congregations, and which were gradually to displace local traditions. This meant that books of worship and copies had to be imported from the centers recently reformed, and that expert calligraphers and annotators had to be enlisted to produce them. The largest collections of manuscripts that survive from the transitional period come from three centers: the abbeys of Santo Domingo de Silos and San Millán de la Cogolla and the Metropolitan See of Toledo. In the process of change, Visigothic manuscripts were relegated to a secondary role, except for consultation in some celebrations under the old rite that survived in the new liturgical order.

Currently, a total of 50 manuscripts of liturgical music from the Hispanic rite survive, some complete and others as fragments, but between them they contain almost the whole of the repertoire. A larger number of complete manuscripts (and an even greater number of fragments) belonging to the Franco-Roman rite survive, dating especially from the 12th century *med.* onwards, when copying was at its height for the many monasteries and cathedrals that had recently switched to the new usage.

Transition

The fast pace of political, social, economic and cultural reform as outlined above was to affect religious expression, aesthetic emotions and the conditions for artistic creation. All this was reflected in both the form and the content of the sources of liturgical music.[5] As in all transitions, there were changes in rules, norms and conventions, so the reform affected not only liturgical practice but also the systems of writing and notation used, the way in which material was organized and even the style of illumination of manuscripts. All these formal elements were linked to a new system of allegorical and symbolic values arising from a transformation of ideological and cultural reality. The sources from which this new liturgical order derived became a way of asserting identity and power, particularly during the transitional period.[6]

The various stages in the transition from the Hispanic rite to the Franco-Roman rite can therefore be recognized directly in the morphology of the sources of liturgical music themselves. A case in point is the unique composition of the calendar of saints and the liturgical calendar, from which significant data can be gleaned on the network of influences and interactions within Spanish centers and between Spanish centers and those elsewhere in Europe, particularly in southeastern France.[7] It is from the latter that various structures containing a hybrid of the Hispanic and Franco-Roman rites derived, and well before them the unique configuration of the Catalonian/Narbonnais rite.[8] However, the gradual assimilation of the new formulae and hagiographic forms of worship took place side by side with two other phenomena: loyalty to autochthonous tradition and the creation of new forms of worship, symptomatic of a desire to reaffirm local identities in the face of pressure to join the reform.[9] The coexistence of elements from different cultural backgrounds and the liberty and individualism reflected in both external and internal manuscript configurations are evidence not only of reluctance to adopt decisions imposed by political power but also of the fact that the reform did not take place systematically and homogeneously. Individual decisions and local cultural contexts acted frequently as variables that determined the survival in some cases and a replacement in others of systems of writing and unique configurations of formulae, liturgical calendars and calendars of saints used in the sources of liturgical music. The transition in the form of the liturgy was thus a long-lasting, diverse process.

The asymmetric configuration of these sources can be explained in part through historical documents which bear witness to the resistance offered by different dioceses and monasteries to an ecclesiastical policy that sought to impose a new liturgical form on them.[10] However, this reluctance should be interpreted within the broader historical context of a country that was constantly striving to defend its borders against Moorish invaders on the one hand and against the reformist policies of Rome—channelled via France—on the other.[11] These two external factors set off a process of change on several levels that affected territorial awareness, the distribution of society, political structure and ideological and cultural identity.

In this sense, the term *frontier*, which has become established as a concept in studies of medieval history, takes on a particular meaning in the description of the new types of source and in discerning the cultural substrates *(Kulturkreise)* from which they stem. The term is a particularly loaded one in the case of Iberian history: it suggests on the one hand an attitude of defence and on the other a process of cultural permeability and tension which served to forge the particular identity that emerges from an analysis of the corpus of sources of liturgical music selected for inclusion in this book.[12]

State of the question

The earliest research on the various liturgical traditions of the Western church in the Middle Ages dates from the 19th century *ex.*, and was conducted for pragmatic reasons: a valid model was being sought for the interpretation of Gregorian chant so that a single, definitive version of choral chant could be established. This goal was approached from a particular ideological orientation, which meant that the scientific approach taken was not exempt from the romantic idealism and the linear, evolution-based vision that pervaded historical studies in the 19th century.

The work of the monks of Solesmes, centered on reconstructing the archetype of Gregorian chant, represents the culmination of a number of attempts made in France over the course of the 17th and 18th centuries.[13] It is to these monks that we are indebted for the earliest studies that have a real impact on the notation and interpretation of sacred monody. It was Prosper Guéranger (1805-

1875), with the publication of his *Institutions liturgiques* (1840-1851)—supported by other specialists working close to him such as Joseph Pothier, Agustín Gontier, and Eugène Cardine—, who established the basis for paleography (*Paléographie musicale,* 1889-1924) and Gregorian semiology (*Semiologie grégorienne*, 1970).

However, the analysis by the monks of Solesmes includes two scientifically controversial points: an attempt to restore a Carolingian archetype—tainted by ideological overtones—and the reading and partial adaptation of semiological methodology. In regard to the latter point, the model of semiology proposed by Cardine has given rise to critical reactions and alternative approaches.[14]

On the other hand, the urgent need for editions that could be put to practical use meant that there was pressure to provide immediate results, which could not be accomplished by scholarly progress conducted at the proper pace. Consequently, even though the *Graduale romanum* (1908) and the *Antiphonale romanum* (1912) date from the early years of the 20th century, certain essential questions still remain to be solved, including points regarding rhythm, the origins of the various forms of melody set down in the sources and even the meaning of the liquescent signs.[15] One may also question the goal of *translating* plainsong notation from one notational language with a rich inventory of graphic variants to another when its limited range is scarcely capable of representing the broad spectrum of nuances of expression contained in the original.

The concept of historiography as evolving towards ever more sophisticated systems of notation stems from an approach that is characteristic of 19th century restoration projects.[16] The concept of medieval notation as a "prelude" or more primitive version of later notations is linked to the way in which the Middle Ages were perceived in the 19th century, but it is a concept that dominated early studies of sacred monophony. In spite of these limitations, however, the material gathered and classified by the monks of Solesmes provided essential impetus for research into the origins and different types of Western notation. In the context of the Iberian Peninsula, the studies by Wagner (1911-1912), Prado (1928), Rojo and Prado (1929), Anglès (1935, 1938) and Sunyol (1935), in particular, are proof of how dynamic a field of research this was in the first few decades of the 20th century.[17]

Research into sacred monophony conducted over the past 25 years reflects a change in orientation, with the subject being tackled from the viewpoints of several different disciplines in an attempt to achieve a broader reflection less centered on purely material analysis.[18] This is an approach that takes into account the general history of the culture in which each of notational language arose, and assumes that there is information not contained in the notational signs themselves that requires a knowledge of the medieval culture from which that notation originates, which knowledge is often hard to access.[19] From a pragmatic viewpoint the difficulties posed by this holistic approach are often insurmountable. In that regard, recent studies have sought to lay down a number of ground rules for the semiological interpretation of notation. Treitler and, more recently, Hass have made notable contributions to this task.[20]

Contents
Part one

The nine studies that make up part one of the book are original contributions from the perspectives of different disciplines that examine some of the key questions regarding knowledge of the sources of liturgical music in the Iberian Peninsula in the period in question.

In the first study, **Ludwig Vones** sums up the historical context underlying the reform project, pointing out various nuances of the process of adopting the new rite and highlighting resistance to it in various circles of the church and the nobility, with particular reference to the complex web of relationships with the Abbey of Cluny in Bourgogne, with various other important centers in southern France such as St. Victor in Marseille and Saint-Pons de Thomières, and with the Holy See in Rome.

The study by **Michel Huglo** provides an approach to the scientific and cultural context in which the Hispanic rite originated, highlighting the origins of *Etimologías* by St. Isidore and its dissemination through the peninsula. In his study of the formal layout of *Etimologías* and its text variants the author differentiates between three sets of manuscripts originating from the south and north of the Iberian Peninsula and two later examples from what is now Portugal. His description of a total of 13 manuscripts representing these traditions provides new data and also corrects errors that have previously slipped into classical reference works. There is an extensive analysis of the harmonic diagrams interpolated into Visigothic manuscripts from the second half of the 8th century onwards. These interpolated diagrams are found only in the Iberian family of manuscripts, and a comparative analysis enables the author to re-establish the original order of the diagrams and identify the ancient Greek theoretical sources on which they are based.

Manuel C. Díaz y Díaz tackles the antiphonary as an early type used to disseminate the Hispanic repertoire, and provides new data concerning the codicological characteristics and the origin and date of the Antiphonary of León (León, AC, ms. 8). The author interprets the much-discussed prologue to the Antiphonary as an expression of the tension caused in the Hispanic church by the controversial attitude of Elipandus of Toledo, against whom Beatus of Liébana, the church of Asturias and various other theological circles of the Carolingian world polemicized. The elegiac couplets found in prologues three and four are seen as further evidence of demand for the continuation of the much-venerated Hispanic liturgy, which was then under threat due to theological and political discrepancies and which was finally to be abolished in the second half of the 11th century. The author also reviews the origin and dating of the miscellaneous codex (Córdoba, AC, ms. 123), situating its production in León in the 11th century *in.* and revealing new data concerning the Book of hours belonging belonging to Ferdinand I (Santiago de Compostela, BXU, ms. 609, Res. 1) and the *Liber canticorum et horarum* (Salamanca, BGU, ms. 2668).

The study by **Maria José Azevedo Santos** provides valuable data on liturgical reform in Portugal based on the paleographical analysis of transitional codices between Visigothic and Carolingian scripts. Data on a large number of fragments preserved in Portuguese archives and libraries helps to complete the topography of Hispanic liturgy and confirms the extensive work done by centers in Coimbra, Braga and Porto during the liturgical transition, which took place there somewhat later than in the rest of the peninsula.

From a philological viewpoint, **Eva Castro Caridad** explores the origins of the texts for the Feast of the Circumcision of Christ, which was widely celebrated in the old Hispanic rite and is of particular importance because it refers to a practice that was abolished by Christians but maintained by the Jewish communities of the Iberian Peninsula. The author studies direct testimonies—sources of liturgical music—and indirect testimonies—such as the *Leges visigothorum*—and shows that most of the Hispanic masses of the *temporale* had been compiled by the 7th century *med.,* including those for the Feast of the Circumcision, which in turn was linked to the celebration of the Nativity. A comparative examination of the sources that describe this feast reveals common structural elements and perceptible differences in a time-frame running from the 11th century to the 16th, i.e. from the earliest testimonies of the *Liber commicus* and the *Liber misticus* to the publication of the *Missale mixtum* by Ortiz and the *Breviarium gothicum* by Lorenzana, and this in turn enables the author to identify the sources from which the various prayers and readings originate.

Gunilla Iversen looks at liturgical poetry produced mainly in Catalonia between the 10th and 13th centuries, and analyses the vocabulary and poetic and compositional structures of a particular group of prosulae, proses and texts linked to the sanctus of the mass. The repertoire of southwestern France makes particular use of the Hebrew word *osanna* as the basis of a whole series of compositions found in numerous copies from Vic, Girona, San Juan de la Peña, Auch, Montserrat, Tortosa, Narbonne and San Martial. The exploration of literary sources enables the author to identify various interpretations of the expression *osanna* that in some cases were used only in these poetic and musical compositions. The uniqueness of the Hispanic repertoire and the creative process of its texts are revealed through a detailed analysis that identifies its formal articulation based on the vowel sounds in the word *osanna*, its unusual selection of vocabulary—vocabulary concerned with the semantic field of music is of particular interest—and an interpretation of the symbolic and allegorical values of the images suggested.

Maricarmen Gómez focuses on the earliest records of what is known as the *Canto de la sibila Eritrea* ("Song of the Erithrean Sybil"), the earliest prophetess of antiquity, whose prophecies were deposited at the Capitol in Rome and were consulted in search of answers on essential matters of state. The reading or performance in song of the sybilline verses was part of the liturgy for matins at Christmas, at the end of Advent, though its exact position is not made absolutely clear in the surviving documentation. Following a comparative analysis of the various literary sources of the texts later used for musical composition, the author looks at the earliest records that contain notation and manages to demonstrate that the tradition was not restricted only to the former territories of the kingdom of Aragón, particularly Catalonia, Majorca and, to a lesser extent, Valencia, but rather extended to a much broader, more complex cultural and geographical context. The musical and literary variants in the records preserved in southern France and in the north and south of the Iberian Peninsula reflect the vitality of an ancient, widespread tradition that was to survive until well into the 18th century at the cathedrals of Toledo and Majorca. The study is illustrated by a number of examples taken from Iberian manuscripts in which the sybilline verses, which were interpreted through a simple choreography, appear mostly in adiastematic and diastematic Aquitainian notation, although copies in Visigothic, Catalonian and Beneventan notation also survive.

Barbara Haggh explores the origins of the texts, melodies and inventory of notational signs used in offices at the Monastery of Santo Domingo de Silos, based on their oldest source: the Antiphonary of Silos (London, BL, Add. ms. 30850). A comparative analysis with other sources from the viewpoint of the structure of the offices and the variety of neumes with which the melodies are is transmitted enables the author to draw new conclusions concerning both the origins and the sources from which the office of St. Dominic was constructed, and the types of Visigothic notation used in the north of the peninsula to transmit the chants for such offices. A comparison of the notations used for this feast in different sources of liturgical music reveals the interaction of the graphic forms of the western and eastern parts of the northern Iberian Peninsula. Some neumes in the Antiphonary of Silos (London, BL, Add. ms. 30850) can also be found in the Antiphonary of León and in the *Liber ordinum* (Silos, AM, Cod. 4), which leads to the hypothesis of a common origin for the two vocabularies, and of contact with parts of France. The author attributes the origin of the *historia* in honor of St. Dominic to a time after the reform of the liturgy at the Monastery of Silos, and suggests that it was composed using models brought from the other side of the Pyrenees. The antiphons and responsories at the end of the Antiphonary of Silos could well, therefore, have been composed after the *historia* was written.

The study by **Susana Zapke** comprises two attempts to construct a select corpus of liturgical musical sources dating from the 9th to 12th centuries, i.e. the Visigothic period, the period of transition to the new Franco-Roman model imposed by Rome and the period of consolidation of the new model, based on two criteria: typology, with the listing of the various modes of writing text and music; and topography, with an attempt to determine the distribution of the sources in the various cultural areas of the peninsula. Using a selection of representative examples taken from 90 liturgical manuscripts, this study looks at the variety of notational systems used in the Iberian Peninsula during the period under consideration: Visigothic notation (northwestern, northeastern, hybrid western/eastern and southern), Catalonian notation, transitional notations and Aquitainian notation. The examples reflect the diversity of writing systems and vocabularies of graphic notation that existed in the various areas and periods considered, the wide range of possible combinations of them during the transitional period from the Hispanic rite to the Franco Roman rite, the wide range of contexts (i.e. types of source) into which musical notation can be placed and the different functions performed by notational signs depending on their context. The main difficulties encountered in both attempts at systematisation lie in the lack of example from some areas and in the lack of a method for bringing together tools for musical paleography with historical and cultural considerations that would offer solutions to the question of the plurality of forms and combinations of writing in the rich corpus of liturgical music manuscripts preserved in the peninsula.

Contents
Part two

The interdisciplinary approach provided by these articles is extended in Part Two with the description of a selective corpus of eighty-nine liturgical musical manuscripts representing the different types and a chronology of the sources and scopes of the ecclesiastical geography of the Iberian Peninsula in the 9th-12th centuries. These manuscripts have been selected for three basic reasons: to bring together representative examples of each of the various types of sources of liturgical music, to compile a corpus characteristic of each region or cultural area of the ecclesiastical life of the peninsula during that time and to compile a set of manuscripts that illustrates the different systems of writing and notation used.

The manuscripts selected are grouped according to their systems of notation—Visigothic, Catalonian, transitional and Aquitainian—and are presented in chronological order within each group.

The types of manuscript featured include six miscellanies (see below), fourteen antiphonaries, twelve breviaries, three sacramentaries, one ritual collectory, two homiliaries, two bibles, six examples of *the liber misticus*, two of the *liber horarum*, three of the *liber ordinum*, one of the *liber canticorum*, eight *collectanea*, two examples of the *liber hymnorum*, three of the *liber psalmorum, canticorum et hymnorum*, one *psalterium et liber canticorum*, one *liber canticorum et horarum*, three lectionaries, five missals, five tropary-prosaries, one *liber responsorialis*, four graduals, three evangeliaries and one pontifical.

The following are also included on an exceptional basis, since they are not liturgical music books *stricto sensu*: a theoretical treatise with additions in Aquitainian notation on some pages (Barcelona, ACA, Ripoll 42), a number of miscellaneous codices (Madrid, BN, ms. 10029; Barcelona, ACA, Ripoll 106, 74 and 40; Montserrat, BM, ms. 72; Lleida, AC, Roda 8) and three manuscripts without notation (Madrid, RAH, Cod. 118 and 14; and London, BL, Add. ms. 30851, although in the latter, there is notation in eight hymns and neumes are used as reference signs). Seven documents from beyond the Pyrenees are also included which were identified at a very early date as liturgical books or exemplars copied at centers in the Iberian Peninsula (Huesca, AC, Cod. 1; some parts of Huesca, AC, Cod. 4; Paris, BNF, Lat. 933, 1871 and 5304; Braga, AD, ms. 1000; and Toledo, BC, 44-1 and 44-2).

Twenty-nine of the manuscripts selected represent the Hispanic rite or come from the Visigothic period, including the two bibles [Burgos, AC, without shelfmark (from now on w./o. s.) and Cracow, Czartorysky, ms. 3.118], seven contain formulae from the Catalonian/Narbonnais tradition and forty-seven are from the Franco-Roman tradition, though formulae from the Hispanic tradition may still be found in them. There are twenty-eight documents with northern Visigothic notation, four manuscripts with southern Visigothic notation, seventeen with Catalonian notation and thirty-seven with Aquitainian notation. Eighteen manuscripts feature combined writing systems characteristic of the transitional period.[21] Not counting certain notated parts of compound manuscripts—e.g. Córdoba, AC, ms. 123—, the corpus contains a total of twenty-one fragments of liturgical music from different periods.

The geographical distribution of the eighty-nine manuscripts selected is as follows:

1. Visigothic period: Toledo group, San Millán/Silos group, Catalonian group, León group, Pyrenees group (Navarre/Aragón).
2. Transitional and Franco-Roman period: San Millán group, Silos group, Catalonian group, Castile group, Toledo group.

The corpus selected provides representative samples of the various liturgical traditions of the peninsula in the period under study. The description that accompanies each codex is guided by reference works by Andrew Hughes and Elisa Ruiz García.[22] The folios shown are chosen in some cases for structural and/ or formal reasons. The rarity of the writing systems used and/ or the repertoire written down have prevailed over considerations of the present state of conservation or aesthetic quality of each document. The selection therefore includes both plainer documents from rural monasteries and superb pieces drawn from royal archives.

Sources. Some clarifications

Not all the material originally envisaged could be presented in the final state of the book. Problems of various kinds, such as the poor condition of some manuscripts, the difficulty of accessing certain archives or obtaining authorisations and, occasionally, problems in locating documents due to changes of catalog number, forced us to abandon our search in some cases.

However, the active efforts of Spanish archives and libraries to catalog material in the past few decades have revealed a considerable number of complete manuscripts and fragments of liturgical music from the Hispanic and Franco-Roman repertoires, mostly in the bindings of notarial records and documents whose contents are not strictly liturgical in nature.[23] The latest such findings are listed below.

The Archivo de la Real Chancillería in Valladolid (parchments, carp. 180, no. 1) contain a fragment of a breviary in Visigothic writing with Aquitainian notation, dated between the last third of the 11th century and the 12th century *in.*[24] The Archivo Histórico Provincial of Huesca contains no less than 84 fragments dated between the 11th and 13th centuries, drawn from the bindings of notarial records.[25]

Other recent findings include the recovery of the Visigothic manuscript *Officia sanctorum* (New York, HS, B2916), located by Susan Boynton and featured in this book, and a fragment of a Visigothic Antiphonary from the 10th and 11th centuries preserved at the Royal Academy of History, Cod. 9/4579.[26]

Along with the increasing number of manuscripts, we must also highlight the fact that there are a number of known manuscripts of the Hispanic rite and others from the transitional period whose whereabouts are currently unknown. Such is the case of the fragment from Cincinnati, Ohio (Hebrew Union College, Klaus Library, a miscellany manuscript with a fragment of a *Liber misticus* dating from the 10th century, listed by Millares Carlo 1999, 1, no. 34, the *Liber misticus* of Santa Cruz de Coimbra (Fernández de la Cuesta 1983) and the Braga fragment (Braga, AD, Registro Geral, Caixa Frag. 280, 3 Coleçao Cronológica. Capa do Tombo de Vilar de Monte), an Antiphonary of the Franco-Roman rite with Visigothic script and Aquitainian notation from the 11th century, ca. 1080-1090) (Millares Carlo 1999, 1, no. 18). In all these cases the most likely explanation is misplacement following a change of catalog number.

Ongoing cataloguing projects of note include those of the Archivo de la Real Chancillería of Valladolid (Ruiz Asencio), the Archivo de la Catedral of Valladolid (López-Calo), that of the Cathedral of Santiago de Compostela (Rey Olleros), numerous archives in Aragón (Institución Fernando el Católico) and the Archivo Diocesano of Burgos (Asensio), from which further study material can be expected to be obtained.

With the exception of the recent findings mentioned above, the documents offered by Janini (1969, 1977a, 1977b),[27] Fernández de la Cuesta (1983, 105-113; 2000, 848-850), Díaz y Díaz (1983) and Millares Carlo (1963, 1999) continue to constitute basic reference material for any systematic listing of sources of liturgical music under the Hispanic rite and the Franco-Roman rite in the Iberian Peninsula. Furthermore, the works by Sablayrolles (1911-1912), Sunyol (1925, French edition 1935), Anglès (1935, 1988), Mundó (1965, 1982), Olivar (1969), Martimort (1982), Mas (1982, 1988) and Garrigosa (1990, 2003) provide substantial data on sources from the Catalonia/ Narbonne region and Septimania.[28] We owe the list of the earliest examples of the Franco-Roman tradition in the Peninsula essentially to Huglo (1985) and Rocha (1982). A selective list of sources from the Franco-Roman repertoire classified by type has also been drawn up by Fernández de la Cuesta and López-Calo (2000, 891-895).

A certain ambiguity in the term "sources of liturgical music" needs to be clarified. As will be seen, notation can be found inserted into documents which are not strictly musical, and in some cases documents intended to contain a melodic repertoire were never notated or provided with only partial notation, as in the case of the *Liber hymnorum* (Madrid, RAH, Cod. 118/ Cod. 14) included in this book, although since this is a hymn repertoire it is possible that it was never intended to include notation. Another case in point is the part of the *hymnarium* comprising the *Liber psalmorum, canticorum et hymnorum* of Silos (London, BL, Add. ms. 30851, 11th century) which contains a limited amount of musical notation but also employs various neumes as references to glosses. Further examples are the breviary of Silos (London,

BL, Add. ms. 30849, 11th century *ex.*), which has no musical notation, although it had at first been planned; the matins Antiphonary of Arles-sur-Tech (Paris, BNF, Lat. 14301), in which the antiphon texts added later were never provided with the notation originally envisaged; the *Liber horarum* (Madrid, RAH, Cod. 118; counterguard, Cod. 14); the *Antiphonarium visigothicum* (Madrid, BN, ms. 10001, fol. 141); the secular Roman breviary (London, BL, Add. ms. 30849), which was also never provided with notation except at the end from fol. 290r onwards—numbering in ink—(fol. 294r: numbering in pencil), not to mention the many examples of partially entered notation in the well-known Glosses of St. Emilianus actually entitled *Sanctorum Cosmae et Damiani passio, missa et orationes* (Madrid, RAH, Cod. 60)—in the *Liber misticus* (Madrid, BN, ms. 10001, flyleaves), in the Sacramentary of Roda (Lleida, AC, Roda 16), in the *Antiphonarium* or *Liber misticus* (Madrid, RAH, Cod. 30) and other documents described in Part Two of this book.

Sources. Geographical range. Centers of production

Manuscripts are ascribed to particular centers of production mainly on the basis of paleographical criteria, in the sense of the techniques applied in their production (preparation of the medium, organisation of material, composition of the page) and the graphic universe deployed in them, ranging from the instruments used to the colors of the inks and even the system of writing, the set of graphic characters used (*ductus,* modules, systems of abbreviation), the illumination, and the types of binding used. All these elements provide valuable indicators for identifying where a particular codex was produced. The catalog descriptions that make up Part Two of the book cover various points, but it has not been possible to determine the exact place of origin of a considerable number of the documents presented. To forestall rash speculation, the various options considered by the specialists involved are given, with question marks against those cases where attribution is not definitive.

Throughout the book, the term "center of production" is preferred to *scriptorium* because the latter is understood to refer to an organized location with a tradition extending over several generations, and there is little documentary evidence that this was the case in the Iberian Peninsula. The only evidence for the existence of a *scriptorium* in the strict sense of the term is a mention of the Tower of Tábara (Madrid, AHN, Cod. 1097 B), in which the term *theca* suggests a room in which codices were produced.[29] In this sense the work carried out at Silos, for instance, by specialists originating from various locations charged with increasing the stock of liturgical (not theological or scientific) works in the library can be better described in terms of a "copying center" than a *scriptorium.*[30] The study by Ruiz Asencio on the various origins of the codices from the Pyrenees and la Rioja held in the library at Silos provides further support for this choice of terminology. Ten codices that entered the monastery in the time of Abbot Domingo seem to have originated from La Rioja and Pamplona: San Millán, Cathedral of Nájera, San Prudencio de Monte Laturce, Albelda and other centers in the kingdom of Pamplona-Nájera, with the *Etimologies* (Paris, BNF, N. A. L. 2169) of 1072 being one of the earliest examples from the school of copyists at Silos.[31] This line of argument is supported by the set of manuscripts, from the transition between the Hispanic and Franco-Roman rites, copied by specialists from a range of different cultural backgrounds. Paleographical analyses by Shailor and Phillips and a mainly historical analysis by Levy find sufficient indicators of situations and procedures characteristic of that period.[32] Moreover, the knowledge provided by Díaz y Díaz of the ways in which royal, cathedral and monastic libraries and collections of books were compiled in the northern Iberian Peninsula from the second half of the 9th century onwards, by copying or by acquisition of copies from various origins, also supports the idea that there was intense interaction between the various centers.[33]

Sources. Chronological scope

The documents selected cover a period of almost four centuries (9th *ex.*-12th *ex.)*, though the exact dating of the manuscripts continues to be a matter of controversy. This is particularly true of the approximately 350 Visigothic manuscripts that survive, including some with false or inaccurate dates, for most of which there is no definitive dating. García Turza estimates that we currently have a total of just 45 documents that can be dated precisely.[34] Mundó's review of Toledan liturgical chant manuscripts of the Hispanic rite proposes dates that differ by several centuries from those attributed by other scholars, as discussed above.[35] García Turza also stresses the lack of consensus on dating and mentions, among others, the representative cases of the glosses of St. Emilianus (Madrid, RAH, Cod. 60), which have been dated anywhere between the 7th and 11th centuries, and the Bible of Quisio (Madrid, RAH, Cod. 20), where there is also a margin of error of almost 4 centuries (7th-11th).[36] In this sense, the article by Díaz y Díaz published here is particularly significant, as it provides new arguments for the precise dating of the Antiphonary of León (León, AC, ms. 8) and the notated fragment from the Cathedral of Córdoba (Córdoba, AC, ms. 123).

Apart from the manuscript corpus of the Visigothic rite, those of the Franco-Roman rite also present us with considerable difficulties in terms of their dating. Textual paleography provides a more sophisticated, more reliable method than musical paleography, partly because of the uniform character of Aquitainian notation and the consequent difficulties of determining precise dates and locations. Nor is the dating of transitional liturgical music documents always clear, since the overlap in writing systems gives rise to anachronisms and archaisms that impede specific dating. In view of these difficulties, the catalog descriptions that make up Part Two of this book include proposals for dating put forward by the author of each description, followed by other dates attributed to each manuscript in the relevant reference literature.

Notes

[1] Concerning the historical revision of the concept of Spain in the Middle Ages, see the opposing positions—now regarded as classic—defended by Américo Castro in *La realidad histórica de España*. México, D. F.: Porrúa, 1980 (1st ed., 1954); by Claudio Sánchez Albornoz in *España. Un enigma histórico*. 2 vols. Barcelona: Edhasa, 1983 (1st ed., 1957); by José Antonio Maravall Casesnoves in *El concepto de España en la Edad Media*. Madrid: Centro de Estudios Constitucionales, 1997 (especially: "De los nombres de España y de sus partes", pp. 53-79); by Julio Caro Baroja. *El mito del carácter nacional. Meditaciones a contrapelo*. Madrid: Seminarios y Ediciones, 1970; and by Juan Carrasco, et al. *Historia de las Españas medievales*. Barcelona: Crítica, 2002.

[2] See Isidro Gonzalo Bango Torviso, dir. *Sancho el Mayor y sus herederos: el linaje que europeizó los reinos hispanos*. (Exhibition catalog.) 2 vols. Pamplona: Fundación para la Conservación del Patrimonio Histórico de Navarra, 2006.

[3] See Manuel Riu y Riu. "La organización eclesiástica" in Ramón Menéndez Pidal, ed. *Historia de España*. Vol. 7**, *La España cristiana de los siglos VIII al XI*. Madrid: Espasa Calpe, 1999, 636-639. There are discrepancies as to the date: Miquel S. Gros puts independence from Narbonne at a later date (ca. 971).

[4] See Ramón Gonzálvez. "The Persistence of the Mozarabic Liturgy in Toledo after A. D. 1080". In Bernard F. Reilly, ed. *Santiago, Saint-Denis and Saint Peter. The Reception of the Roman Liturgy in León-Castile in 1080*. New York: Fordham University Press, 1985, 157-185.

[5] In regard to social changes in the year 1000, marked by the fear of the apocalypse and the change from a ritual, liturgy-based religion to action-based Christianity, see Georges Duby. *L'An Mil,* Paris: Gallimard/ Julliard,1980 (1st ed., 1967). Concerning the transition from the year 1000 to the year 2000 in terms

of *fear* see *idem. An 1000 an 2000. Sur les traces de nos peurs,* Paris: Les Editions Textuel, 1995; see also Manuel C. Díaz y Díaz. "Hispania, año 1000: cultura en declive" in Ramón Villares Paz, Luis Antonio Ribot García and Julio Valdeón Baruque, coord. *Año mil, año dos mil: dos milenios en la historia de España,* Madrid: Sociedad Estatal España Nuevo Milenio, 2001. Vol. 2: 179-198. Concerning the functionality of art and the interaction between art and society in the medieval world see Georges Duby. *Art et société au Moyen Âge.* Paris: Éditions du Seuil, 1997 (1st ed., 1995). On the change of mentality and the origin of a new social class of intellectuals see Jacques Le Goff. *Les intellectuels au Moyen Âge.* 3rd ed. Paris: Éditions du Seuil, 2000 (1st ed., 1957).

[6] The restructuring of society that resulted from the struggle between the nobility and the monarchy, the tension between the new middle-classes and the old nobility and the rebellion against the domination of nobles and ecclesiastics make up the backdrop for the reform of the liturgy, which thus took place in the middle of a complex, prolonged socio-political crisis. The reform of the liturgy was taken in many cases as a pretext for reasserting rights or expanding power, which explains why the process was not homogenous or synchronized in time, and why the very different scenarios alluded to above emerged. On the restructuring of society in the 11th-12th centuries, see Josep Maria Salrach i Marés. "Los grupos sociales" in Ramón Menéndez Pidal, ed. Op. cit., 394-426 and the enlightening summary by José María Mínguez. *La España de los siglos* VI *al* XIII. *Guerra, expansión y transformaciones.* Donostia-San Sebastián: Nerea, 2004, 239-292 (1st ed., 1994).

[7] It must be remembered that this interaction with other lands was not unilateral. Evidence for this phenomenon can be found in the survival of pieces from the Hispanic repertoire in sources from southern France, which can be attributed to the fact that Catalonia and Narbonne belong to the same ecclesiastical area and shared the same liturgical usage. In terms of form, there are various indicators of the survival of old usages. The Visigothic notation was maintained in various cultural circles until well into the 13th century, and the Visigothic system of ruling also continued to be used in some areas. On the other hand, coexistence with Carolingian writing systems denotes the cooperation of experts from different cultural areas. These points are addressed in this book. Regarding the subject at hand, the survival of the *Regula communis* or *Regula abbatum* and the specific section of their *pactum* can be cited as examples of Visigothic rules governing the organisation of monastic communities which remained in force in Portugal, Castile and La Rioja until well into the 11th century. See Ludwig Vones. *Geschichte der Iberischen Halbinsel im Mittelalter (711-1480), Reiche-Kronen-Regionen.* Sigmaringen: Thorbecke, 1993, 20 and subsq.

[8] Below are indicated a few of the studies that deal with: 1) about the interaction between the Visigothic rite and the Catalonian/Narbonnais tradition, see Miquel S. Gros. "El ordo romano-hispánico de Narbona para la consagración de la iglesia". *Hispania Sacra* 19 (1966): 321-401; *idem.* "La liturgie narbonnaise témoin d'un changement rapide de rites liturgiques", in *Liturgie de l'église particulière et liturgie de l'église universelle.* Rome: Edizioni Liturgiche, 1976, 127-154; Alexandre Olivar. "Les supervivències litúrgiques autòctones a Catalunya en els manuscrits dels segles XI-XII" in *II Congrès Litúrgic de Montserrat.* Montserrat: Abbey of Montserrat, 1967. Vol. 3: 21-89; Josep Romà Barriga. *El Sacramentari, Ritual i Pontifical de Roda (Cod. 16 de l'arxiu de la Catedral de Lleida, c. 1000).* Barcelona: Fundació Salvador Vives Casajuana, 1975; 2) about surviving Visigothic forms and structures that mixed the Visigothic and Franco-Roman traditions, see Michel Huglo. "Les *preces* des graduels aquitains empruntées à la liturgie hispanique". *Hispania Sacra* 8 (1955): 361-383; Jean Vezin. "Un calendrier franco-hispanique de la fin du XIème siècle (Madrid, RAH, Cód. 18, fols. 6-11v)", *Bibliothèque de l'École des Chartres* 121 (1963): 5-25; Susana Zapke. "Procesos asimilativos del nuevo repertorio francorromano en el norte de la península" in *Revista de Musicología* 16 (1993): 2257-2267; *idem. Das Antiphonar von Sta. Cruz de la Serós, XII. Jh.* Neuried: Ars Una, 1996: 104-164, 167-215; 3); about the interaction between Languedoc and Moissac with the diocese of Braga, see Pedro Romano Rocha. "Les sources languedociennes du bréviaire de Braga", *Liturgie et Musique (IXe-XIVe s.).* Toulouse: Edouard Privat, 1982, 185-207 (Collection d'Histoire religieuse du langue doc au XIIIe et au début du XIVe siècles: Cahiers de Fanjeaux 17). Finally, readers are referred to the collected volume by Bernard F. Reilly, ed. Op. cit., especially the chapter by Roger E. Reynolds. "The Ordination Rite in Medieval Spain: Hispanic, Roman and Hybrid", pp. 131-155.

[9] Particularly from the 12th century onwards, new hagiographic forms of worship appeared whose formulae stem in part from hagiographic sources—chronicles and judicial protocols—that included certain episodes from the Reconquest. Numerous hagiographic texts bear witness to this procedure, as evidenced by the stories of Sts. Nunilo and Alodia, St. Urbez and St. Eurosia. See Antonio Durán Gudiol. *Los condados de Aragón y Sobrarbe.* Zaragoza: Guara, 1988, 43-49; Susana Zapke. "Procesos asimilativos...". *Ibidem*; and *idem.* "El oficio de san Indalecio en el antifonario de Santa Cruz de la Serós, siglo XII", *Aragonia Sacra* 6 (1991): 181-198.

[10] See Bernard F. Reilly, ed. Op. cit.; Antonio Ubieto Arteta. "La introducción del rito romano en Aragón y Navarra". *Hispania Sacra* 1 (1948): 299-324. Antonio Durán Gudiol. Op. cit.; *idem. Los obispos de Huesca durante los siglos XII y XII.* Zaragoza: Gobierno de Aragón, Centro del Libro de Aragón, 1994; *idem. La Iglesia de Aragón durante los reinados de Sancho Ramírez y Pedro I (1062?-1104).* Rome: Iglesia Nacional Española, 1962; *idem.* "La Santa Sede y los obispados de Huesca y Roda" in *idem. Colección diplomática de la Catedral de Huesca*. Zaragoza: CSIC, Escuela de Estudios Medievales, Instituto de Estudios Pirenaicos, 1969, nos.139, 144, 145 and 181; Paul Kehr. "Das Papsttum und die Königreiche Navarra und Aragón bis zur Mitte des 12. Jahrhunderts". Berlin: Akademie der Wissenschaften, 1928 (Abhandlungen der Preußischen Akademie der Wissenschaften zu Berlin: Philosophisch-Historische Klasse 4); *idem.* "Cómo y cuándo se hizo Aragón feudatario de la Santa Sede". *Estudios de la Edad Media de la Corona de Aragón.* 1 (1955): 285-326; Antonio Ubieto Arteta. *Historia de Aragón.* Zaragoza: Anubar, 1981; José María Lacarra. "A propos de la colonisation franque en Navarre et en Aragón". *Annales du Midi* 65, no. 23 (1953): 331-342; *idem. Historia política del reino de Navarra, desde sus orígenes hasta su incorporación a Castilla.* Vol. 1. Pamplona: Aranzadi for Caja de Ahorros de Navarra, 1972; Anscari M. Mundó. "Moissac, Cluny et les mouvements monastiques de l'Est des Pyrénées du XIe au XIIe siècle" in *Annales du Midi* 75 (1963): 551-573; Peter Segl. *Königtum und Klosterreform in Spanien. Untersuchungen über die Cluniacenserklöster in Kastilien-León vom Beginn des 11. bis zur Mitte des 12. Jahrhunderts.* Kallmünz (Oberpfalz): Michael Lassleben, 1974; Julio Valdeón Baruque, dir. *Historia de Castilla y León,* Valladolid: Ámbito, 1985. (particularly interesting in regard to the topic dealt with here is volume 4, by José Luis Martín. *La afirmación de los reinos (siglos XI-XIII).* In *ibidem.*

[11] See Ursula Vones-Liebenstein. "Katalonien zwischen Maurenherrschaft und Frankenreich. Probleme um die Ablösung westgotisch-mozarabischer Kirchenstrukturen". In Rainer Berndt, ed. *Das Frankfurter Konzil von 794. Kristallisation Karolingischer Kultur.* Vol. 1, *Politik und Kirche*. Mainz: Mittelrheinische Kirchengeschichte, 1977, 453-505 (Quellen und Abhandlungen für Mittelalterliche Kirchengeschichte: 80).

[12] On the concept of "frontier" in the Middle Ages, see Julian Bishko. *Studies in Medieval Spanish Frontier History.* Aldershot: Ashgate, 1980 (Variorum Collected Studies Series). Robert Bartlett, ed. *Medieval Frontier Societies.* Oxford: Clarendon Press, 1989. See also in the same volume Robert Ignatius Burns. "The Significance of the Frontier in the Middle Ages", 307-330.

[13] See Karl Gustav Fellerer. "Choralreform". In Ludwig Finscher, ed. *Die Musik in Geschichte und Gegenwart.* Kassel: Bärenreiter, 1989. Vol. 2: 1323-1331; David Hiley. "The Restoration of Medieval Chant". In *idem. Western Plainchant. A Handbook*. Oxford: Oxford University Press, 1995, 622-629 (1st ed., 1993).

[14] Katherine Bergeron, *Representation, Reproduction, and the Revival of Gregorian Chant at Solesmes*. New York: Ph. D. Cornell University, 1989 (U.M.I. 8924515), published as *Decadent Enchantments: The Revival of Gregorian Chant at Solesmes* (Berkeley and Los Angeles, 1998); Katherine Bergeron and Philipp V. Bohlman eds. *Disciplining Music. Musicology and Its Canons.* Chicago: Chicago University Press 1992; Leo Treitler. "The Early History of Music Writing in the West". *Journal of the American Musicological Society* 35 (1982): 237-279; *idem.* "Reading and Singing: On the Genesis of Occidental Music-Writing". *Early Music History* 4 (1984): 135-208; *idem.* "Paleography and Semiotics". In Michel Huglo, ed. *Musicologie médiévale. Notations et séquences. Actes de la table ronde du C.N.R.S. à IRHT 6-7 septembre 1982.* Paris: CNRS, IRHT, 1987, 17-27; Luigi Agustoni and Johannes B. Göschl. *Einführung in die Interpretation des Gregorianischen Chorals,* Vols. 1-3, Regensburg: Bosse, 1987.

[15] Not counting, in the specific case of the Iberian Peninsula, the lack of criteria for the transcription of the melodies of the Visigothic repertoire and the Catalonian/Narbonnais repertoire in archaic Catalonian notation,

annotated *in campo aperto* with no indications of pitch at all other than in exceptional cases discussed in the study of Hispanic notations in this book (pp. 189 and subsq.). It is equally hard to determine the origin of the three types of Iberian notation prior to the change in the rite: Visigothic notation with its northern (western and eastern zones) and southern variants and Catalonian notation. This formal difficulty is compounded by that fact that there are scarcely any examples of Visigothic notation in the south of the peninsula except for later manuscripts from Toledo. The same goes for northern Portugal, except for a few fragments, and for other areas of the peninsula such as the Pyrenean region of Aragón.

[16] See Max Haas. "Aspekte der Forschungsgeschichte". In *idem. Musikalisches Denken im Mittelalter. Eine Einführung.* Berne: Peter Lang, 2005, 351-361.

[17] See bibliography for Part Two, pp. 429 and subsq.

[18] Among the benchmark studies that provide a new historical view of Gregorian chant must be mentioned Helmut Hucke. "Toward a New Historical View of Gregorian Chant" in *Journal of the American Musicological Society* 33 (1980): 437-467; and David Hiley. Op. cit. Concerning the origins of notation, see Leo Treitler. "The Early History...". Op. cit.; Kenneth Levy. "On the Origin of Neumes". *Early Music History* 7 (1987): 59-90; Harmut Möller. "Institutionen, Musikleben, Musiktheorie". *Neues Handbuch der Musikwissenschaft* 2 (1991): 129-199; Michael Walter. *Grundlagen der Musik des Mittelalters. Schrift-Zeit-Raum.* Stuttgart, Weimar: Metzler, 1994. On the origin of the names of neumes, see Michael Bernhard, ed. "Die Überlieferung der Neumennamen im lateinischen Mittelalter". In *idem. Quellen und Studien zur Musiktheorie des Mittelalters.* Munich: Beck, 1997. Vol. 2: 57-71 (Musikhistorische Kommission: Bayerische Akademie der Wissenschaften, 13). Finally, on the binary of oral tradition/ written tradition see Leo Treitler. "Homer and Gregory: The Transmission of Epic Poetry and Plainchant". *Musical Quarterly* 60 (1974): 333-372; *idem.* "Transmission and the Study of Music History". In *idem,* et al., eds. *Transmission and Form in Oral Traditions. International Musicological Society. Report of the Twelfth Congress Berkeley 1977.* Kassel: Bärenreiter, 1981, 202-211; *idem.* "Reading and Singing...". Op. cit.; Andreas Haug. "Functions of Music Writing in the Early Middle Ages". Lecture on "Musik der Karolingerzeit". Paderborn, 24 and 26 October 1999; Susan Boynton. "Orality, Literacy, and the Early Notation of the Office Hymns". *Journal of the American Musicological Society* 56 (2003): 99-168. On the structure and origins of the Hispanic repertoire, the classic studies by Férotin, Pérez de Urbel, Leclercq, Brou, Cordoliani and Wagner, which are well-known to specialists, are supplemented by new contributions cited in the various chapters of this book and in the bibliography to Part Two.

[19] Max Haas. Op. cit., 365.

[20] Leo Treitler. "Paleography and Semiotics". Op. cit.; *idem.* "Written Music and Oral Music: Improvisation in Medieval Performance". In *idem. With Voice and Pen. Coming to Know Medieval Song and How it Was Made.* Oxford: Oxford University Press, 2003, 39-67. Max Haas. Op. cit., 345-398.

[21] Two schematic diagrams (1 and 2) show the corpus selected in terms of the cultural and political areas from which the documents are drawn and of the types of notation used: see pp. 197 and 201 of this book. An additional table (3) showing the chronological order and indicating the respective writing systems used is given on p. 204.

[22] Andrew Hughes. *Medieval Manuscripts for Mass and Office. A Guide to their Organization and Terminology.* Toronto: University of Toronto Press, 1982 (2nd ed., 1995) and Elisa Ruiz García. *Introducción a la codicología.* 2nd ed. Madrid: Fundación Germán Sánchez Ruipérez, 2002 (1st ed., 1988).

[23] See Carmen Rodríguez Suso. *La monodia litúrgica en el País Vasco. Fragmentos con notación musical de los siglos XII al XVIII.* 3 vols. Bilbao: Bilbao Bizkaia Kutxa, 1993 (Biblioteca Musical del País Vasco). Miguel C. Vivancos. *Catálogo del archivo del Monasterio de Santo Domingo de Silos.* Santo Domingo de Silos: Monastery of Silos, Junta de Castilla y León, 2005. Manuel Rey Olleros. *La música medieval en Ourense.* Vol. 1, *Pergaminos musicales del archivo catedralicio.* Ourense: Xunta de Galicia, 2006.

[24] We are grateful to Prof. Ruiz Asencio for this highly useful information. *Colección Pergaminos, carpeta 180, documento 10.* Bifolio 352 × 463 mm. Ruled with dry point. In highly deteriorated condition.

[25] Susana Zapke. *Fragmentos litúrgico-musicales de la Edad Media en Archivos de Aragón. Siglos XI ex.-XIII ex.* Huesca: IEA, DGA, 2007.

[26] Susan Boynton. "A Lost Mozarabic Liturgical Manuscript Rediscovered: New York, Hispanic Society of America, B 2916, olim Toledo, Biblioteca Capitular 33.2". *Traditio* 57 (2002): 189-219. See also Francesc Xavier Altès i Aguiló. "El retall testimonial d'un full d'Antifoner visigòtic (siglos X-XI) procedent de l'antic arxiu de la Seu de Roda d'Isàvena (Madrid, Real Academia de la Historia, ms. 9/4579)". In *Miscel·lània Litúrgica Catalana* 9 (1999): 33-50. Thanks are due to Miquel S. Gros for drawing my attention to the existence of this document.

[27] José Janini and José Serrano with the collaboration of Anscari M. Mundó. *Manuscritos litúrgicos de la Biblioteca Nacional de Madrid.* Madrid: Dirección General del Libro, Archivos y Bibliotecas, 1969; José Janini and Ramón Gonzálvez. *Catálogo de manuscritos litúrgicos de la Catedral de Toledo.* Toledo: CSIC, Diputación Provincial, 1977a; José Janini. *Manuscritos litúrgicos de las bibliotecas de España*, 2 vols. Burgos: Aldecoa, 1977b, 1980 [Publicaciones de la Facultad de Teología del Norte de España (Sede de Burgos): 38, no. 2], an inventory going up to the 16th century. We must also take into account the earliest attempts of systematically cataloguing the corpus of Hispanic sources by Rudolf Beer. *Die Handschriftenschätze Spaniens. Bibliographische Übersicht der Handschriftenbestände 616 spanischer Bibliotheken und Archive.* Vienna: Kaiserliche Akademie der Wissenschaften, Philosophisch-Historische Klasse, Sitzungsberichte, 1894, 124-131 (2nd ed., 1970). Juan Facundo Riaño. *Critical and biographical notes on early Spanish music.* London: Bernard Quaritch, 1887; Màrius Férotin. "Liber mozarabicus Sacramentorum". *Monumenta Ecclesiae liturgica* 6 (1912) (Rome: Centro Liturgico Vicenziano. Edizioni Liturgiche, 1995) and the study by Jules Tailhan. "Appendice sur les bibliothèques espagnoles du Haut Moyen Âge". In *Nouveaux Mélanges d'Archéologie, d'Histoire et de Littérature sur le Moyen-Âge.* Vol. 4. Paris: Didot, 1887.

[28] "Septimania" refers to the dioceses of Narbonne, Maguelone, Lodève, Béziers, Carcassone, Agde, Nîmes and Elna.

[29] See also "La importancia histórica del *scriptorium* de San Salvador de Tábara". In Fernando Regueras Grande and Hermenegildo García-Aráez Ferrer, eds. *Scriptorium. Tábara visigoda y mozárabe,* Salamanca: Ayuntamiento de Tábara, Centro de Estudios Benaventanos Ledo del Pozo (CECEL-CSIC), Parroquia de Tábara, 2001, 65-83.

[30] José Manuel Ruiz Asencio. "Códices pirenaicos y riojanos en la biblioteca de Silos en el siglo XI". In José A. Fernández Flórez, dir. *Silos. Un milenio. Actas del Congreso Internacional sobre la Abadía de Santo Domingo de Silos.* Vol. 2, *Historia.* Santo Domingo de Silos: Monastery of Silos, University of Burgos, 2003, 177-210 (Studia Silensia: 26).

[31] Barbara Shailor. "The scriptorium of San Sahagún: A Period of Transition". In Bernard F. Reilly. Op. cit., 41-61; see also Nancy Phillips' text: "Nordspanische Neumen" in "Notationen und Notationslehre von Boethius bis zum 12. Jahrhundert". In Thomas Ertelt and Frieder Zaminer, eds. *Geschichte der Musiktheorie,* Vol. 4, *Die Lehre vom einstimmigen liturgischen Gesang.* Darmstadt: Wissenschaftliche Buchgesellschaft, 2000, 445-451; and Kenneth Levy. "Toledo, Rome and the Legacy of Gaul". *Early Music History* 4 (1984): 49-99.

[32] Díaz y Díaz distinguishes between three types of circulation: 1) circulation of manuscripts from the south to the north, driven by the Saracen invasion and coinciding with the establishment of the royal residence in Oviedo during the reigns of Alfonso II (791-842) and Alfonso III (ruled 866-910; 2) circulation of manuscripts between the various northern kingdoms; and 3) circulation between centers in the peninsula and centers beyond the Pyrenees. Finally, the impetus provided by *Visigothic renovation* increased interest in forming select libraries with documents from various sources. Manuel C. Díaz y Díaz. "La circulation des manuscripts dans la Peninsule Ibérique du VIIIe au XIe siècle". *Cahiers de Civilisation Médiévale* 12, nos. 3 and 4 (1969): 219-241 and 383-392.

[33] Claudio García Turza. *Los manuscritos visigóticos: estudio paleográfico y codicológico.* Vol. 1, *Los códices riojanos datados.* Logroño: Fundación San Millán de la Cogolla, 2002, 12.

[34] Anscari M. Mundó. "La datación de los códices litúrgicos visigóticos toledanos". *Hispania Sacra* 18 (1965): 1-25. Solange Corbin takes no account of the review by Mundó; see Solange Corbin. "Neumatic Notations" in *New Grove* 13 (1980): 128-144. Stäblein and Randel cite the article by Mundó but maintain the traditional dating. Dom M. Randel. *The Responsorial Psalm Tones of the Mozarabic Office.* Princeton, New Jersey: Princeton University Press, 1969, 5; Bruno Stäblein. *Schriftbild der einstimmigen Musik.* Leipzig: VEB Deutscher Verlag für Musik, 1975. Vol. 3, part 4: 216 (Musikgeschichte in Bildern). See Agustín Millares Carlo, et al., eds. *Corpus de códices visigóticos.* Vol. 1, *Estudio;* vol. 2, *Álbum*. Las Palmas de Gran Canaria: Gobierno de Canarias, UNED, Centro Asociado de Las Palmas de Gran Canaria, 1999.

[35] Claudio García Turza. Op. cit., 9-10.

PART ONE

Research

The Substitution of the Hispanic Liturgy by the Roman Rite in the Kingdoms of the Iberian Peninsula

Ludwig Vones

For that anonymous chronicler who wrote a book of annals in the 12th century *in.*, which was later included in the *Crónica de San Juan de la Peña*, there was not the slightest doubt: the *lex romana* had been introduced at the Monastery of San Juan on 22 March 1071, a Thursday in the second week of Lent, and from this date onwards it would be strictly followed: "Et tunc intravit lex romana in Sanctum Iohannem de la Penia XI kal. aprilis, secunda septimana quadragesime, feria III, hora Prima et Tertia fuit Tholetana, ora Sexta fuit romana, anno Domini millesimo LXXI et inde fuit servata lex romana".[1] This event is only mentioned once, however, in the line of text giving the date in a forged episcopal document in favor of the monastery. The date given there is 1 August 1071: "primo vero (anno) ingressionis Romani officii in Sancto Iohanne".[2] Nevertheless, the process of replacing the Hispanic liturgy or the Visigothic-Mozarabic rite by the Franco-Roman rite in the kingdom of Aragón, which took place at the same time in the convents of San Victorián de Asán in Sobrarbe, in San Pedro de Loarre, and shortly afterwards under the influence of San Victorián, in Santa María de Alaón as well, cannot be questioned.[3] We must keep two things in mind, however. On the one hand, the change of rite in 1071 did not mean that the new liturgical forms were accepted spontaneously throughout the kingdom of Aragón, but rather that this was the beginning of a gradual process of establishing them that was to last more than two centuries. San Juan de la Peña was the ideal starting point in this process, because it was here, under the reign of Sancho III the Great, where the Cluniac monk, Paterno, had already been named abbot and had introduced the Benedictine reform in 1028.[4] On the other hand, the decision taken in 1071 represented both the result of intensive negotiations between the monarchy and the Papacy and the first conclusion in a long process of evolution that had begun centuries before.

In the Carolingian period, proponents of the various forms of worship had already clashed in the debates on adoptionism. With the decisions approved at the Council of Frankfurt in 794 and at the Synod of Aachen in 816, which advocated the compulsory reforms of the *ordo canonicus* and the *ordo monachorum* that were rigorously inspired by the precepts of the Church Fathers or by the rule of St. Benedict, clearly defined boundaries were established. In the future, this was to trigger intense Carolingian diplomatic activity in the Mozarabic zone, where once again resistance emerged to the advance of the Franks, who favored a Church inspired by Rome and the Papacy.[5]

In the kingdom of Asturias, which saw its political and ecclesiastical autonomy and its very existence threatened, these manoeuvres provoked counter-reactions, including the "discovery" of the tomb of James the Apostle and the creation of a genuinely Hispanic apostolic cult in opposition to the cult of the Roman, Peter.[6] Despite all missionary efforts, the Hispanic liturgy managed to survive in the Christian kingdoms, just as it did in the Mozarabic communities under Muslim rule. Even in Catalonia and in the Pyrenean counties that were exposed to Carolingian influence, from this time onwards, forms of the Hispanic rite are found that later coexisted alongside the Franco-Roman liturgy and often also liturgical forms that mixed both rites.[7] With the disintegration of the Carolingian Empire and the end of expansionist pressure, conflicts over liturgical uses eased, and Christian kingdoms and sovereigns, in particular, practiced—except in the Catalonian counties—an ecclesiastical policy that was further and further removed from Rome and the Pope. The Reconquest spread more as an expansionist political movement than as a war against the infidels and sometimes took on the features of a war in legitimate defence.[8] Only in the 11th century, with the Cluniac and reformist movement of the Church, did the Hispanic kingdoms once again become the focus of papal policy. At that time, the ideas then produced in Rome regarding a

1. Ildephonsus. *De Virginitate. Vitae Sanctorum.* El Escorial, RB, a.II.9, 10th century (part of the codex belongs to the year 954)-11th, fol. 1v

Church subject to the basic supremacy of the Papacy required a purge of Western ecclesiastical structures. This was also due to the reorganisation of the Iberian Peninsula with its new configurations of kingdoms and Christian territories, and—together with the restoration of those dioceses freed from Arab control and their frontiers and property rights—the reestablishment of an ecclestical organisation that was considered to be primitive and inspired by the Roman Curia and St. Peter.[9] The basic conditions for the implementation of the Curia's claims were the incipient relations between the Crown of León and Castile and the Burgundian Order of Cluny, which, because of the latter's close relations with the Papacy, seemed predestined to act as a mediator. The numerous legations that were sent at this time also played an important role. Thanks to these, contacts were initiated and maintained between the Roman Church and the monarchies, the situation on the spot was clarified, and papal decisions were disseminated and adapted to meet pre-existing conditions.

Except for the county of Barcelona, which was basically independent from the end of the 10th century onwards and separate in practice from the Franco-French imperial league, in the 11th century *med.* all of the kingdoms in the Christian north of the Peninsula were ruled by descendents of the ancient Royal Navarrese dynasty.[10] Sancho III the Great of Navarre had unified the counties of Castile, Aragón, Sobrarbe and Ribagorza under his control, had brought them together with the kingdom of Pamplona-Navarre, and had also established his hegemony over the kingdom of León, which allowed him to distribute this zone of influence among his four sons at the end of his life. In this way, the county of Aragón considerably enhanced its status, due to its having been granted the title of royalty. Through a skilful matrimonial policy and a series of dynastic coincidences, León and Castile remained united under Ferdinand I's authority,[11] until they were divided among the King's three sons by inheritance after his death in 1065 and finally reunited again in 1072 under the reign of Alfonso VI. Ultimately, Sancho I Ramírez reigned in Aragón and in the territories of Sobrarbe and Ribagorza, annexed since 1046; in Pamplona-Navarre, Sancho IV Garcés el de Peñalén was destined for the throne, but when he was murdered in 1076, the King of Aragón took his place.

In the eyes of the Curia, the political map of northern Spain was far from representing a homogenous whole, when, in the 1060s, the Curia began to exert its influence there to create an organisational structure for the Church in accordance with its idea of the primacy of the Pope, and especially, to spread the Roman liturgy, with the support of the Benedictine Order as a prerequisite for this integration process. The first attempts to suppress the Hispano-Mozarabic rite, which had dominated previously, and to introduce a liturgical reform that followed ecclesiastical guidelines throughout the Empire, took place during Alexander II's pontificate. To achieve this aim, Cardinal Hugo Candidus deputed a legation to that region from 1065 to 1067-1068 and held two councils in Nájera and in Llantadilla de Pisuerga.[12] At first the results were not at all encouraging, however, because he clearly lacked the political and ecclesiastical support that was needed in Navarre and León, where the Crown, nobility and episcopate were in the midst of a deep crisis. Thanks to a rather tendentious report from

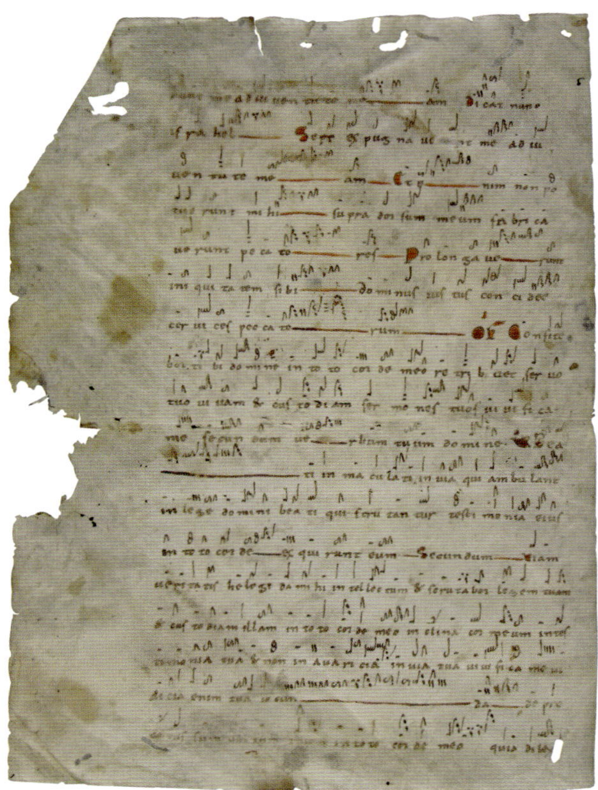

2. Antiphonary for Mass. Barcelona, BC, M. 1408-3, 10th century *in.* (ca. 900), Frag. fol. r

the same period, which appears in the famous *Codex Emilianensis* (from the Monastery of San Millán de la Cogolla and now kept in the Real Biblioteca de San Lorenzo de El Escorial with catalog number I.d.1), we have news about a legation of Spanish Bishops to Rome, possibly between 1065 and 1069, perhaps in late 1066 or early 1067. Once they had arrived there, this legation, which was perhaps accompanied by Hugo Candidus, advocated at a synod in the Pope's presence that their traditional rite should remain in force. It is thought that on this occasion the delegation presented several manuscripts as proof of the orthodoxy of their Hispanic liturgy. These were the Bishops Nuño of Calahorra, Jimeno of Oca de Burgos and Fortún of Álava, and the books that they showed were a *Liber ordinum* from the Monastery of San Martín in Albelda, a *Liber orationum* from Santa María in Irache, a *Liber missarum* from Santa Gemma, near Estella, and a *Liber antiphonarum* also used in Irache. Apparently all of these works were examined in detail by the Pope in person and by the experts expressly brought together there for the occasion. This assembly finally considered the books to be in accordance with orthodoxy, and they were certified as such to the bishops themselves.[13] The same report also alludes to a ratification of the Hispanic liturgy that had already been obtained in the previous century through a Pope named John, presumably Pope John X, and to a papal legate called Zanelo, who may well have been sent to Bishop Sisnando of Santiago de Compostela. Once he had been informed of the situation, the legate went back to Rome, while the Bishop of Santiago and Ordoño II of León encouraged the opening of an investigation on the matter. Shortly afterwards, Zanelo returned to Spain to reform the liturgy. The legate himself was convinced of its orthodoxy, however, and he apparently sent the corresponding report to the Pope, who must have sanctioned the legitimacy of the Hispanic liturgy at that time.[14] This approval, based on a report that was none too rigorous, points more probably to the additional presentation of a false papal document, because only in these circumstances would such a forgery be justified. Despite their bias, the descriptions of 11th century events leave little room for doubt, because their references to the historical context are too precise, their statements are too brief, and no legal validity can be ascribed to their recording in the *Codex*. The report seems to have been more precisely a draft for the development and final conclusion of conversations with the Cardinal's envoy, because neither in León nor in Navarre could they have been sure that the matter had been settled. In any case, the information in the *Codex Emilianensis* provides sound testimony of the stubbornness of noble circles; of their affectations, both spiritual and profane; and of their attachment to ancient traditions. They also represented existing power structures, and ultimately kept them alive.

Only a few years later, the Hispanic kingdoms, dioceses and monasteries understood to what extent the Curia had persisted in introducing the Roman liturgy, when in 1071, Hugo Candidus' new and now successful diplomatic mission introduced the change in the liturgy at the main monasteries in Aragón. This time the papal legate's task was easier, however, because King Sancho Ramírez, unlike the sons of Ferdinand I of León or of Sancho Garcés, favored this change and had even travelled to Rome in spring 1068 to commend his person and his threatened kingdom to the authority of God and St. Peter.[15] A "knight of St.

Peter" was hardly in a position to object fully to the Curia's requests, however, even though these were not restricted to paying a tribute of recognition. With the special protection, legal recognition and the property title granted to the monasteries in Aragón, Alexander II was expressly accepting the act of submission that the King had performed in 1068. The Pope also wanted to stress the total restitution to the Holy See of the monasteries that had been alienated in the past and justify Hugo Candidus' activity on the basis of the prior abandonment by the Hispanic Church of the unity of the faith and its deviation from discipline and worship. In this way, the introduction of the new rite could be presented together with the struggle against simony as items requiring ecclesiastical reform.[16] Since both the King and the abbots concerned openly accepted this line of argument—including the Curia's property rights—the Church of Aragón and the Curia established a close relationship in the following years. In fact, their relationship was not altered when Hugo Candidus was ordered to return and was later condemned at the Roman Lenten synod in 1073, nor did it change with Alexander II's death, particularly when Gerard of Ostia and the Vice-deacon Raimbald's legation ensured contact with the Papacy from 1072-1073.[17]

Nevertheless, the adoption of the Roman rite in the Hispanic kingdoms received a definitive boost with the Cardinal-deacon Hildebrand. It was in 1073—and also partially, on Hugo Candidus' initiative—when this member of the Curia was elected Pope with the name of Gregory VII. The new pontiff, who had been working as a dependable adviser for quite some time, must be considered the real *spiritus rector* of papal policy and, especially, the architect of the change in the rite in Spain. Eight days after being nominated, while still Pope-Elect, he sent two missives to his legates in France and to those members of the nobility, who, following Count Eblo de Roucy, wanted to take the war against the gentiles to Spain. These letters restored Hugo Candidus to his post as papal legate; urged them to support the order of Cluny, lead by its abbot Hugh, to introduce the reforms of the Church; and stressed—now in a clearly programmatic tone—that the "regnum Hyspanie" had been "ab antiquo proprii iuris sancti Petri" and that it could not belong in all fairness to any mortal, but belonged exclusively to the Holy See, as had been agreed with the count,[18] in a *pactio* that Hugh of Cluny and Hugo Candidus, as a legate, were to ensure would be observed. The latter soon fell from grace once again and disappeared from the ecclesiastical political scene, however. His powers were then definitively taken over by Gerard of Ostia and vice-deacon Raimbald,[19] which would not change the broad lines of papal policy in any way. It seems that in 1073 the new legates called a synod, probably somewhere on the frontier between southern Gaul and Hispania, to solve the most urgent problems and insist on the aforementioned canonical rules. Several papal documents dated a year later encourage us to think that at that meeting the question of the rite was also raised and that, to the Curia's satisfaction, it received a new boost, especially in Aragón. Alfonso VI of León and Castile and Sancho IV of Navarre received harsh warnings on 19 March 1074, telling them definitively to impose the Roman liturgy in their kingdoms, while the Pope sent a letter of praise to Sancho Ramírez of Aragón. In this letter, his efforts to introduce the "Romani ordinis officium" were stressed, and the "concordia et amicitia" with the Holy See were also emphasized, as if the Hispanic kings had once been attentive to the Roman Papacy.[20] The actual matter that Sancho had submitted to the Curia on this occasion, which was a request backed up by numerous accusations for Bishop Salomón of Roda to be dismissed, only received time-wasting replies from Gregory VII at first. The Pope argued that neither the competent legate in this case nor the Bishop who was being accused were present, and that, without testimony from his expert legate, canon law did not allow him to deliver a verdict; nevertheless the Bishop should be condemned in the following year or forced to resign, and in this case he was to withdraw to the Monastery of Ripoll.[21] It seems that the new turn taken by the Church of Aragón as far as the liturgy was concerned meant that the Curia had to defend the hegemony of the Crown by purging those characters considered to be awkward, although this was not openly declared. This suspicion fits in with the new allocation of the diocese of Jaca, which was possible thanks to the resignation of Sancho of Aragón, who had, until then, held this post. The filling of the vacancy was delayed by extending the exercise of Sancho's functions, leaving aside other candidates and naming a substitute, until 1076, when the ideal successor was ready: García of Aragón, the King's brother. Raimund Dalmatii's promotion to the diocese of Roda was also organized in 1076 with help from the legate Amado of Olorón, and in this way it was possible to fill the vacancy that Salomón had left in Ribagorza. The Bishop-elect, named in Tierrantona at a synod that brought together the clergy of southern France, above all, and ratified by the legate, immediately went to Rome and appeared before Gregory VII to ask for a privilege for his diocese. This event clearly shows the close relationship that existed at that time between the Church of Aragón and the Papacy, but it also shows the Aragonese Church's subordination to the possibilities of interference by the latter if local churches offered clear resistance, such as in the case of Raimund Dalmattii. In actual fact, the newly elected Bishop could only take possession of his diocese in 1078, thanks to the new papal envoy, Cardinal Richard of Marseille, who was from that moment on the highest-ranking representative of the Roman Church in Spain. Furthermore, the new Bishop immediately tried to have the reform of the rite introduced and took charge of its implementation throughout the diocese.[22]

The year 1076 was also decisive from another point of view, because the unexpected death of Sancho IV of Navarre at the hands of his half-brother Ramón gave Sancho Ramírez of Aragón the chance to unite his kingdom with his cousin's. For the Curia, this meant expanding its sphere of action to a Church which, since Hugo Candidus' legation and the firm refusal of Sancho IV to introduce the Roman rite, had proved to be inaccessible to interference. The acceptance of the government of the monarchy of Aragón also meant that in the long term the adoption of the Roman liturgy was guaranteed, which would allow, in turn, the structure of the Church in Navarre to be supervised. The ideal time to do this came after the death of Bishop Blasco of Pamplona, when his vacant see had to be filled once again. Sancho Ramírez immediately entrusted his brother, Bishop García of Jaca, with leadership of the diocese and of the Monastery of San Salvador de Leyre, which had been led by the same person since Sancho the Great's time as Bishop.[23] This appointment was undoubtedly linked to the task of establishing the Roman rite. The succession in the diocese was not definitively regulated until the arrival of Frotard, the abbot of Saint-Pons de Thomières, who, together with Richard of Marseille, acted as special papal envoy to northern Spain, Aragón and Catalonia, although they did not always share the same opinions. According to a note kept in the Becerro de Leyre, in accordance with the express wishes of the king, his son Peter and the nobility, Pope Gregory VII had entrusted the abbot with the *cura regiminis ecclesiarum* in Sancho Ramírez's kingdoms. This legate made selective use of this prerogative, the only aim of which, most likely, was to ensure the expansion of the orthodox liturgy. In 1083, García had to forgo the diocese of Pamplona when Frotard imposed a candidate of his own, the monk Peter of Roda, which went against the wishes of the Cardinal's legate, Richard of Marseille, who wasted no time to reinforce his position by having French monks placed there and even declaring an interdict.[24] In Leyre, which was now freed from its links with Pamplona, Frotard consecrated an abbot from his order, the monk Raimund of Saint-Pons de Thomières; later on, when Raimund Dalmatii died, he again placed another candidate of his own in the diocese of Roda, the monk Pons of Saint-Pons de Thomières. He also consecrated the Bishop-Elect, Peter, who had been appointed in 1086 to fill the then-vacant see of Jaca, which provoked the wrath of the Archbishop of Narbonne. Nevertheless, in that period the liturgical unity and obedience to Rome of the Churches of Aragón and Navarre was now definitively ensured.[25] Strangely enough, it was later said that Archbishop García of Jaca, at odds with his brother Sancho Ramírez, had claimed to Gregory VII that he and, above all, his father, Ramiro I (d. 1063), deserved credit for having obliged his kingdom to pay tribute to the Holy See and for having introduced the Roman liturgy: "et preeunte divina inspiratione tuo scimus instinctu et alto consilio primus in regno suo quasi alter Moyses abiecta Toletane illusionis supersticione legem ac consuetudines Romanas recepit [...]",[26] and not his brother or Hugo Candidus. It is highly likely that the papal document which appears to establish the boundaries of the diocese as if it would be transferred from Jaca to Huesca is merely a forgery or apocryphal, but, even so, it undoubtedly reflects the ambivalence surrounding the change in the rite and the problems that this caused for Church policy in the kingdom of Aragón.

When in their entry for the year 1078, the *Cronicón Burgense* and the *Cronicón de Cárdena* pointed out "lex Romana intravit in Hispania",[27] they were referring—unlike the chronicler of San Juan de la

Peña—to the reception of the Roman liturgy in the kingdoms of León and Castile.[28] It was here where Alfonso VI had ruled on his own after his brother, Sancho II, was murdered in 1072, but because of his alleged involvement in those bloody events, he had problems with the Castilian nobility led by El Cid, which considerably weakened his position.[29] Although it is true that right from the beginning he seemed to favor the establishment of the Roman rite and decisively supported this option, he nevertheless ran into immediate opposition from a nobility that was not only attached to its inherited traditions but also feared losing its predominant position, because it suspected, justifiably, that any possible interference in the dioceses and monasteries would enable the King to establish his sovereign influence over it. Alfonso VI was not alone in the task of achieving his aims, however. Though he was probably also supported by his wife, Agnès of Aquitaine, he received further support from the widespread Benedictine order of Cluny, which was in the forefront of the reform. This order, which was very closely linked to the Papacy and the traditions of the Roman Church, had already been invited into the kingdom by Alfonso's father Ferdinand I, who had been included in the liturgical "memoria" of the order and had also promised them that they would receive an annual tribute of 1,000 *mancusos*.[30] Alfonso VI kept up a close friendship with abbot Hugh of Cluny throughout his life, although this was tarnished in the end, because earlier the monarch had probably interceded on his behalf to free him after he had been imprisoned by his brother.[31] As soon as he came to power, the Castilian King quickly entrusted several royal monasteries to the Cluniac order: in 1073 San Isidro de las Dueñas, in 1075 San Salvador de Palaz del Rey (León), in 1077 Santiago del Val as well as San Juan de Hérmedes de Cerrato, Santa María la Real de Nájera and Santa Columba (Burgos), which was a measure that in itself favored the expansion of the Roman rite in León and Castile.[32] It is no less true that Alfonso VI came to power at almost the same time as Gregory VII was elected, so that his efforts to introduce the Roman rite were soon subject to the new pontiff's criterion, whose zealous determination to achieve the full integration of Hispania in the Roman Church through a unified liturgy and conformist structures left little room for doubt.[33] In this case it was not so much a question of the Pope being particularly committed to restoring the genuine, original Roman order, since it was very unlikely that this could be rebuilt in any case; it was more about the symbolic value that he placed on the "celebration of the 'Roman' liturgy—which, strictly speaking, should be called Romano-Franco-Germanic—as an expression of obedience to the Church of Rome and the Pope".[34] The missive that he addressed on 19 March 1074 to Alfonso VI of León and Castile and Sancho IV Garcés is well known. He wrote it immediately after a delegation of Spanish bishops explained at the Lenten synod that they were prepared to accept the Roman liturgy. In this letter, Gregory VII accompanied his urgent appeal to accept the *Romanae ecclesiae ordinem et officium,* "non Toletanae vel cuiuslibet aliae, sed istius, quae a Petro et Paulo supra firmam petram per Christum fundata est et sanguine consecrata", with a detailed exposition about the organisation of the Hispanic Church inspired by its Catholic princes and apostolic mission, which included the spreading of its "ordo et officium in divinis cultis agendas", the trials and tribulations that the Christian faith had suffered in those regions throughout history, and the dogmatic foundation established by the popes and councils, especially the Toledanum IV and the Bracarense II.[35] Alfonso VI, unlike the insubordinate Sancho, was favorable to the Pontiff, although he was faced with serious problems. The only purpose of his detailed presentation of the problems with the ritual from the papal point of view could have been to reaffirm him in his efforts, unless in this period the Curia had received totally false information on Hispanic relations. However, this hypothesis does not tally with the connection between the document and the fall of Bishop Nuño of Calahorra ("qui super Symeonem venerabilem fratrem nostrum Ocensem episcopum ordinatus erat"), deposed and excommunicated after being accused of simony by the legates Gerard of Ostia and Raimbald. In the end, in accordance with what had been negotiated at the Lenten synod in 1074, this event was to lead to a reorganisation of the structure of Castilian dioceses.[36]

The *Cronicón Burgense* also provides two mythologizing episodes that also suggest a degree of insecurity on Alfonso VI's part with regard to the liturgy. The first episode reports on a tournament that the Castilian King organized, at which he appealed, so to speak, to a divine judgment in whose execution two individuals were to take part, a Castilian in defence of the Mozarabic liturgy, and, in turn, a Mozarab in defence of the Roman liturgy. This joust, which apparently took place on 9 April 1077, ended with the victory of the Castilian knight, and as a result, of the Mozarabic rite. In the second episode, dissatisfied with the result of the first, Alfonso VI wanted to make a fresh attempt to obtain a divine judgment in accordance with his convictions, which this time consisted of burning some liturgical books with both versions of the rite. Once again, the Mozarabic ritual proved to be stronger and emerged intact from the flames, whereas the Roman manuscript was devoured by the fire; immediately afterwards, the King, who was enraged, also tossed the Mozarabic manuscript into the fire, as he wished to emphasize the superiority of the monarch's will over legal uses.[37] Without needing to accept that there is a historical core here about which there is no doubt, because these episodes must form part of a long polemical oral tradition of rivalry between opposing groups, both episodes and their dating in the late seventies refer to the increasingly difficult situation in which the Castilian King now found himself. In fact, towards 1076, two years before the events mentioned in the *Cronicón Burgense*, the Castilian King had already declared, at Gregory VII's request, that he was openly favorable to the introduction of the Roman liturgy. In the following years he proved to be zealous in imposing the new rite, but he was unable to crush the deeply rooted opposition of the nobility, whose hegemony depended on their spheres of power being kept intact. There are several elements that point in this direction: first of all, the transfer of the royal monasteries to the order of Cluny, which was equivalent to importing the Roman liturgy, and, as a result, canon law; second, the now reinforced collaboration with Hugh of Cluny—which of course his representative, the monk Robert, "noster amicus", encouraged—resulting in doubled interest payments.[38] There was also a rather revealing letter that King Alfonso addressed to the abbot of the Monastery in Burgundy, however, in which he openly admitted the problems that he had experienced up to that time to introduce the Roman office, "quod tua iussione accepimus", and expressly asked him to intervene in Rome to persuade them to send him a legate—he was thinking about Gerard of Ostia—who would support him in the task of adopting the new rite.[39] The papal envoy that Rome sent him, Bishop Cardinal Richard, carried with him a golden key with a relic of St. Peter's chain as an appeal to perform good works. For the chronicler from Burgos, the Cardinal's effectiveness had a clear impact on the introduction of the rite. In the following years, the Cardinal came to Spain on numerous occasions to resolve the problems that were to emerge again and again. His report apparently merited Gregory VII's complete trust.[40] In accordance with Alfonso's wishes, at the same time as the first of these missions, the Pope also consecrated an anonymous abbot as a Bishop, which leads us to think that the monarch had a deliberate influence over the dioceses.[41]

One of the major burdens on Alfonso VI's Church policy—or at the least that was how the Papacy immediately perceived the situation—was the Cluniac monk Robert. The Castilian King had thanked Abbot Hugh of Cluny for sending him to his court in that aforementioned letter, and it seems that Robert soon earned the monarch's trust, whom he had to thank, all in all, for his extraordinary rise as well as his dramatic fall, while Alfonso VI's relations with the Pope—as well as with the Abbot of Cluny—went into a deep crisis. The bone of contention was the appointment of Robert as Abbot of Sahagún in early 1080,[42] without any canonical election process whatsoever, with the total support of the monarch and the subsequent eviction of Abbot Julian, who, until then, had been Superior in the convent. This measure had a clear purpose: with the reform of the venerable monastery inspired by the rules of Cluny, not only was the Roman rite going to be established but also, at the same time, influence would be exerted on the pillars of the power relationships that had been in force until then, to favor the penetration of royal authority. An important result of Robert's appointment was the departure of some of the monks from the monastery. At the same time as this series of changes in the most prestigious of the monasteries of Castile and León, the Council of Burgos was held in May 1080. In addition to instituting other measures of Church policy, this synod declared that the introduction of the Roman liturgy was compulsory;[43] this also meant—let us not forget—that from now on, canon law inspired by the primacy of Rome was to apply, and that this was to be the model for all of the internal decisions of the Church. The importance of this synod in the spread of the Roman rite is also reflected in the *Cronicón Regum Legionensium* by Pelayo of Oviedo, although, given the likely bias of this source, we ought to use it with care:

> Tunc Adefonsus rex uelociter Romam nuntios misit ad Papam Aldebrandum, qui fuit cognomento Septimus Gregorius; ideo hoc fecit, quia romanum misterium habere uoluit in omni regno suo. Memoratus itaque Papa Cardinalem suum Ricardum, abbatem Marsiliensem, in Ispania transmisit. Qui apud Burgensem urbem Concilium celebravit confirmavitque romanum misterium in omni regno regis Adefonsi Era MCXIII.[44]

Despite this apparent triumph of the papal cause, the council was overshadowed by the Sahagún affair.[45] Abbot Robert of Sahagún, as the person in charge of the mission with which he had been specifically entrusted by Hugh of Cluny, did not merely introduce the Roman rite at his monastery and impose the rules of Church reform, but was at first heavily influenced by the powerful conservative groups in the convent which still clung firmly to the Visigothic-Mozarabic liturgy. In the end, he was finally won over for the cause, so that it was no longer possible to talk about the situation evolving in accordance with the interests of the Papacy and the Crown. In these tricky circumstances, Richard of Marseille intervened, probably supported by Alfonso VI, to try to have Robert expelled and replaced by the Cluniac monk, Bernard, who was to lead the reformist measures that were to be implemented without this involving any legal subordination to Cluny.[46] Robert was banished at the very latest at the beginning of May, very probably even before 24 April,[47] and the monarch approved this to prevent this obstacle from affecting the basic decisions taken by the Council of Burgos. News of these events even reached distant Rome, although clearly they arrived with a certain delay. They were of course scandalously distorted, possibly through an apologetic report full of bitter accusations that the Cardinal responsible for this sent in late 1079 to the Abbot of St. Victor in Marseille. Gregory VII reacted harshly, as can be seen in a letter dated 27 June 1080 addressed to the Abbot of Cluny, in which the King of Castile and León did not emerge unscathed either. Robert was branded a "Symonis magi imitator" for having dared to act against the authority of St. Peter and for having led with his "malignitatis astutia" hundreds of thousands of people, who had heeded his insinuations, to lapse once again into the old error, just at the very moment when, thanks to the efforts of the Holy Father, they were to have been brought back to the path of the truth.[48] Although on the whole these declarations have led us to think that he was referring to the struggle against heresy, the historical circumstances seem to confirm that what Gregory VII had in mind when he made them was actually to propagate the Roman rite, which was to be promoted and which, at least for the moment, had clearly come to a standstill—and all this without still having had any news, of course, of Robert's expulsion and of his replacement by Bernard, and of the agreements reached at the Council of Burgos—. On the other hand, the Pope knew considerably more about Alfonso VI's alleged disobedience, the poor way he had behaved towards the Cardinal's legate Richard, and his utter unwillingness to compromise in the matter of the reform because of the *pseudomonachum* Robert's deception, events of which Hugh of Cluny had apparently informed the Pope in writing. Robert was to be forbidden to enter the church and would be relieved of all his responsibilities until Abbot Hugh imposed the corresponding sanction on him, while Alfonso VI, because of the support he had given to Robert and the unpleasant way he had treated the papal envoy, was threatened with excommunication if, disregarding advice, he persisted in his stubborn attitude and did not submit to orthodoxy. In addition, if his supporters were to ignore these warnings and continued to refuse to obey, the Pope himself would travel to Spain to march against the monarch and "beati Petri gladium super te evaginare". Furthermore, the Abbot of Cluny would demand that all of those monks who unjustifiably remained in these kingdoms were to return to the mother house, unless their presence was authorized by the papal envoys. In a parallel letter addressed to Alfonso VI himself, Gregory VII repeated his reproaches and threats, but also added, as a justification for the monarch's fall from grace, an alleged "inceste mulieris amor". He accused him of having had an "illicitum connubium" with an "uxoris tuae consanguinea", which in his judgment had led him astray from the right path.[49] There has been a great deal of speculation about whether this incestuous relationship referred to the marriage that the King had contracted in 1079 with Constanze, the Duke of Burgundy's daughter and Hugh of Cluny's niece a marriage that could well have been encouraged by the Abbot of Cluny himself—or if it referred to another woman from her retinue who was related to her.[50] As far as Constanze is concerned, we know that in the controversy about liturgical reform, she basically supported the French monastic institution's viewpoint, and she worked closely with the miracle-working monk Adelelm of La Chaise-Dieu to re-establish the *apostolica doctrina* in the area south of the Pyrenees. Prayers were later said for her at Cluny.[51] Thus, there is no reason to suspect her of supporting the Mozarabic liturgy. In any case, the problem of the "illicitum connubium" might refer to a concubine, and if it was just a complete misunderstanding, that must have been cleared up immediately, because, in a document written in 1081, Gregory VII declared that he was satisfied that Alfonso VI, in accordance with this claim on *divina clementia*, "quod in ecclesiis regni tui matris omnium sanctae Romanae ecclesiae ordinem recipi et ex antiquo more celebrari effeceris", had returned to the *prisca consuetudo* of the Roman Church, in reference to the decision adopted at Burgos.[52] Because the Pope had also clearly delegated some important decisions to his envoys, Richard of Marseille and Bishop Simeon of Burgos,[53] on matters to do with the Queen, Sahagún and filling the Archbishop's see in newly re-conquered Toledo (for this post he had thought of Bernard of Sahagún as the "persona quae in archiepiscopum fuerat eligenda"[54]), nothing now stood in the way of reconciling differing points of view once any possible sources of controversy had been removed. With the aforementioned reconciliation, the compulsory presence of the Roman liturgy in the churches of León and Castile was guaranteed, and it was now possible to discern the future framework of the Spanish Church represented by the forthcoming Archbishop, Bernard of Toledo.

Gregory VII did not live to see this future, which began for the Spanish Church in 1085 with the reconquest of Toledo from the Muslims by Alfonso VI of León and Castile, because he died on 25 May in the same year in distant Salerno.[55] When the Pope died, the advance of the Roman liturgy in the kingdoms of Spain lost its most ardent champion, at the very time when, thanks to the Reconquest, large areas were being recovered with the church institutions that had survived under Islamic rule. Of course, these institutions were still filled with the spirit of the Mozarabic liturgy, because of among other reasons, the influence of the Mozarabic churches in Toledo—the center of the *superstitio toletana,* as Gregory VII continued to call the Hispanic liturgy—, Coimbra—reconquered in 1064 by Ferdinand I of León—, Braga—one of the oldest metropolitan sees—, and Valencia—the city that fell to El Cid in 1094—.

3. Homiliary Collection of the Guild of St. George, Sheffield Galleries & Museums Trust, ms. 31, 11th century *in.*, fol. CXXX v

Although the decisions adopted at the Council of Burgos in 1080 had endured and were, in theory, still in force, we no longer have any news that in these regions the Roman liturgy overwhelmingly prevailed over the Visigothic-Mozarabic forms, nor that they were later abolished; in fact they seem to have survived.[56] Bernard of Toledo himself and the other Cluniac bishops who came to the episcopal sees in Castile-León at this time[57] stress that the Cluniac order's monastic influence was growing weaker and weaker, and that the personal relationship between Alfonso VI and Abbot Hugh and his order was still clearly marred by the Sahagún controversy. This was despite Hugo's contradictory statements and all of the prayers and promises to pay interest, or an increase in this interest. The fact is that, once it had been reformed, the abbey itself in León ceased to be legally dependent on the Burgundian center, and no other monastery joined the Cluniac federation during the Castilian king's reign.[58] Furthermore, Alfonso VI increasingly tended to favor the monks of Saint Victor of Marseille and seemed to show great tolerance for the traditional rites. Among other factors, this was probably because when they reached the lines along the Tagus and the Ebro, the Christian kings no longer bothered the Mozarabic population settled in the Muslim zone of influence so much with radical measures, and as far as the Christian expansion was concerned, they aimed to remain on the defensive. This does not mean that liturgical unity had been abandoned as a tool for extending power, however, but that from now on this instrument was to be used purposefully and not utterly superficially. They also opted for gradual change. Furthermore, we should not forget that liturgical reform was just one measure among many, and that along with this (or as a result of this), canon law was to replace the Visigothic tradition of jurisprudence, Caroline minuscule would take the place of Visigothic, and the very idea of the struggle against heretics in the religious sense of a *militia sancti Petri* would be transformed, or at the very least completed, by a war of re-conquest that aimed to expand political power.[59] The structures of the Mozarabic Church were wiped out,[60] but its rituals survived all of these adversities in small pockets of resistance. In its traditional centers, especially in Toledo, the Hispanic liturgy was performed together with the other Franco-Roman forms until the 13th century *ex.*, and this was still the case later on, when the Archbishop of Toledo and later Cardinal Gonzalo Pérez Gudiel (he himself a descendent of a Mozarabic family) saw to it that this Hispanic rite survived and gave a boost to the institutions required to ensure this.[61] Even at the end of the 15th century, Cardinal Francisco Jiménez de Cisneros authorized the printing of a Mozarabic breviary and missal and founded a Mozarabic chapel inside the Cathedral of Toledo where the Hispanic liturgy was regularly performed.[62] This situation can only be understood if one bears in mind that the various rites were not as radically different as Gregory VII had claimed with his idea of inner *purity*, which, because of the borrowing of other elements, was impossible to imagine in the case of Catalonia, long characterized by Frankish-Carolingian influence. In fact, from time immemorial there had been numerous points of contact between them, which a comparative analysis of the surviving manuscripts may bring to light. For Gregory VII, the compulsory establishment of the Roman rite inspired by the primacy of the Pope was a tool to ensure that the Spanish Church would remain closely linked to the Papacy in the following years—as an ancient possession belonging to the Church of St. Peter, that according to the Pope had been passed on to him as a gift from Constantine—and that was subordinate to papal centralism imposed through his numerous legations. This reformist Pope finally achieved his aims thanks not just to his tenacious stubbornness, but also to a purposeful course of action that ultimately included deliberate intimidation, as his opinions on Church policy coincided with the personal efforts of the sovereigns of León and Castile, Navarre and Aragón to strengthen their own kingdoms and to consolidate or expand their own authority in them. When Gregory VII died, this fervent reformist spirit vanished from the debate, and inevitably other viewpoints emerged that made it possible in many places for the various rites to coexist in harmony and for religious diversity to be preserved.

Notes

JL = Ph. Jaffé, ed. *Regesta Pontificum Romanorum. Editionem secundam correctam et auctam auspiciis G. Wattenbach curaverunt S. Loewenfeld, F. Kaltenbrunner, P. Ewald.* Leipzig, 1885.

[1] Tomás Ximénez de Embún, ed. *Crónica de San Juan de la Peña*. Zaragoza: Imprenta del Hospicio, 1876, 51. Regarding this source, see Antonio Ubieto Arteta. *Historia de Aragón.* Vol. 1, *Literatura medieval.* Zaragoza: Anubar, 1981, 25, that called "Anales" this introductory part of the *Crónica de San Juan de la Peña* and included it in his

edition of the *Crónica de San Juan de la Peña*. Valencia: Caja de Ahorros y Monte de Piedad de Zaragoza, Aragón y Rioja, 1981, 56-58.

[2] Eduardo Ibarra Rodríguez, ed. *Documentos correspondientes al reinado de Sancho Ramírez*. Zaragoza: Tipografía de Pedro Carra, 1913. Vol. 2: 73, 85 (Colección de Documentos para el Estudio de la Historia de Aragón).

[3] Regarding the introduction of the Roman rite in the kingdom of Aragón, see in particular, Paul Fridolin Kehr. *Wie und wann wurde das Reich Aragón ein Lehen der römischen Kirche?* Berlin: Akademie der Wissenschaften, 1928, 196-223 (Sitzungsberichte der Preuβischen Akademie der Wissenschaften zu Berlin: Philosophisch-Historische Klasse 18). There is a translation into Spanish of this article, "¿Cómo y cuándo se hizo Aragón feudatario de la Santa Sede?". *Estudios de Edad Media de la Corona de Aragón* 1 (1943): 285-326. See also *idem. Das Papsttum und die Königreiche Navarra und Aragón bis zur Mitte des 12. Jahrhunderts*. Berlin: Akademie der Wissenschaften, 1928 (Abhandlungen der Preuβischen Akademie der Wissenschaften zu Berlin: Philosophisch-Historische Klasse 4); Antonio Ubieto Arteta. "La introducción del rito romano en Aragón y Navarra". *Hispania Sacra* 1, no. 2 (1948): 299-324; and Antonio Durán Gudiol. *La Iglesia de Aragón durante los reinados de Sancho Ramírez y Pedro I (1062?-1104)*. Rome: Iglesia Nacional Española, 1962, especially pp. 133 and subsq.

[4] See Peter Segl. *Königtum und Klosterreform in Spanien. Untersuchungen über die Cluniacenserklöster in Kastilien-León vom Beginn des 11. bis zur Mitte des 12. Jahrhunderts*. Kallmünz (Oberpfalz): Michael Lassleben, 1974, 32 and subsq.

[5] The articles compiled in Rainer Berndt's (ed.) work can be consulted regarding this question: *Das Frankfurter Konzil von 794. Kristallisation Karolingischer Kultur.* 2 vols. Mainz: Mittelrheinische Kirchengeschichte, 1997, 453-505 (Quellen und Abhandlungen für Mittelalterliche Kirchengeschichte: 80), and, especially the contribution by Ursula Vones-Liebenstein. "Katalonien zwischen Maurenherrschaft und Frankenreich. Probleme um die Ablösung westgotisch-mozarabischer Kirchenstrukturen". *Ibidem,* 453-505.

[6] See, among others, Odilo Engels. "Die Anfänge des spanischen Jakobusgrabes in kirchenpolitischer Sicht". *Römische Quartalschrift* 75 (1980): 146-170; Jan van Herwaarden. "The origins of the cult of St. James of Compostela". *Journal of Medieval History* 6 (1980): 1-35; and Alexander Pierre Bronisch. "Asturien und das Frankenreich zur Zeit Karls des Großen". *Historisches Jahrbuch* 119 (1999): 1-40.

[7] See Alejandro Olivar. "Les supervivències litúrgiques autòctones a Catalunya en els manuscrits dels segles XI-XII". En *II Congrès Litúrgic de Montserrat.* Montserrat: Abbey of Montserrat, 1967. Vol. 3: 21-89; Roger E. Reynolds. "The Ordination Rite in Medieval Spain: Hispanic, Roman, and Hybrid". In Bernard F. Reilly, ed. *Santiago, Saint-Denis, and Saint-Peter. The Reception of the Roman Liturgy in León-Castille in 1080.* New York: Fordham University Press, 1985, 131-156; and *idem.* "The Visigothic Liturgy in the Realm of Charlemagne". In Rainer Berndt, ed. Op. cit. Vol. 7: 919-945.

[8] The recent research by Alexander Pierre Bronisch on this subject can be consulted: *Reconquista und Heiliger Krieg. Die Deutung des Krieges im christlichen Spanien von den Westgoten bis ins frühe 12. Jahrhundert.* Münster in Westfalen: Aschendorff, 1998; Thomas Deswarte. *De la destruction à la restauration. L'idéologie du royaume d'Oviedo-Léon (VIIIe-XIe siècles).* Turnhout: Brepols, 2003; and Joseph F. O'Callaghan. *Reconquest and Crusade in Medieval Spain.* Philadelphia: University of Pennsylvania Press, 2003.

[9] As a general summary on this question, see Demetrio Mansilla Reoyo. *Geografía eclesiástica de España. Estudio histórico-geográfico de las diócesis.* 2 vols. Rome: Iglesia Nacional Española, 1994.

[10] For a general synthesis on the history of the Iberian Peninsula, the work by Ludwig Vones can be consulted: *Geschichte der Iberischen Halbinsel im Mittelalter, 711-1480. Reiche, Kronen, Regionen.* Sigmaringen: Thorbecke, 1993.

[11] In this respect see: Gonzalo Martínez Díez. *El condado de Castilla (711-1038). La historia frente a la leyenda.* 2 vols. Madrid: Junta de Castilla y León, Consejería de Cultura y Turismo, Marcial Pons Historia, 2005.

[12] Paul Fridolin Kehr. *Das Papsttum und die Königreiche Navarra und Aragón...* Op. cit., 11 and subsq.; Georg Säbekow. *Die päpstlichen Legationen nach Spanien und Portugal bis zum Ausgang des 12. Jahrhunderts.* Ph. D. dissertation. Berlin: Ebering, 1930, 13 and subsq.; Antonio Ubieto Arteta. "La introducción del rito romano...". Op. cit., 306 and subsq.; Stefan Weiss. *Die Urkunden der päpstlichen Legaten von Leo IX bis Coelestin III (1049-1198).* Cologne, Weimar, Vienna: Böhlau, 1995, 24 and subsq. (it includes a compilation of the later bibliography).

[13] Paul Fridolin Kehr. *Ibidem,* 12; Antonio Ubieto Arteta. *Ibidem,* 306 and subsq.

[14] Henrique Flórez. *España sagrada.* 2nd ed. Madrid: Imprenta de José Rodríguez, 1854. Vol. 3: 272-276. Whereas Pierre David *(Études historiques sur la Galice et le Portugal du VIe au XIIe siècle.* Coimbra: Instituto de Estudios Históricos, 1947, 112-116) rejects this report, which he considers

a forgery, Antonio Ubieto Arteta (*ibidem,* 300 and subsq.) tends to accept it as authentic.

[15] Paul Fridolin Kehr. *Das Papsttum und die Königreiche Navarra und Aragón...* Op. cit., 13; *idem. Wie und wann wurde das Reich Aragón...* Op. cit., *passim;* see also Antonio Ubieto Arteta. *Ibidem,* 308. Regarding the legal statute governing these relations, which cannot merely be compared to a feudal situation, and its renewal, see Johannes Fried. *Der päpstliche Schutz für Laienfürsten. Die politische Geschichte des päpstlichen Schutzprivilegs für Laien (11.-13. Jahrhunderts).* Heidelberg: Carl Winter Universitätsverlag, 1980 (particularly pp. 64 and subsq.), which includes a detailed discussion about the transmission of sources.

[16] JL 4691. Paul Fridolin Kehr. *Papsturkunden in Spanien. Vorarbeiten zur Hispania pontificia.* 2 vols. Berlin: Weidmannsche Buchhandlung, 1926-1928, 260 and subsq., nos. 3-4 (ND Göttingen 1970. Abh. Gött. NF 18/2, 22/1)); *idem. Das Papsttum und die Königreiche Navarra und Aragón... Ibidem,* 14 and subsq.; Johannes Fried. *Ibidem,* 65 and subsq., who rejects Antonio Durán Gudiol's doubts about the authenticity of JL 4691. The papal documents on Spanish affairs have been compiled by Demetrio Mansilla Reoyo, ed. *La documentación pontificia hasta Inocencio III, 965-1216.* Rome: Instituto Español de Historia Eclesiástica, 1955.

[17] Paul Fridolin Kehr. *Ibidem,* 16 and subsq.; and also, Stefan Weiss. Op. cit., 28 and subsq.

[18] JL 4777-4778. Erich Caspar, ed. *Das Register Gregors VII.* In *Monumenta Germaniae Historica,* 1920-1923, 8-12 (bk. 1, chaps. 6-7). (Reprinted, Hannover: Hahnsche Buchhandlung, 1990.) See Paul Fridolin Kehr. *Ibidem,* 18; and Antonio Oliver. "'Regnum Hispaniae' in Gregory VII's reform program". *Studi Gregoriani* 14 (1991): 75-82.

[19] Paul Fridolin Kehr. *Ibidem,* 19.

[20] JL 4840-4841. Erich Caspar, ed. Op. cit., 91-94 (bk. 1, chaps. 63-64). See Paul Fridolin Kehr. *Das Papsttum und die Königreiche Navarra und Aragón...* Op. cit., 19 and subsq.

[21] Paul Fridolin Kehr. *Ibidem,* 20 and subsq.; Antonio Ubieto Arteta. "La introducción del rito romano...". Op. cit., 313 and subsq. See also Eladio Gros Bitria. *Los límites diocesanos en el Aragón oriental.* Zaragoza: Guara, 1980, 66 and subsq.

[22] Antonio Ubieto Arteta. *Ibidem,* 311 and subsq.; also Eladio Gros Bitria. *Ibidem,* 71 and subsq.

[23] Antonio Ubieto Arteta. *Ibidem,* 318 and subsq.

[24] Stefan Weiss. Op. cit., 32 and subsq.

[25] Antonio Ubieto Arteta. Op. cit., 318 and subsq.

[26] Antonio Durán Gudiol, ed. *Colección diplomática de la Catedral de Huesca.* Zaragoza: CSIC, Escuela de Estudios Medievales, Instituto de Estudios Pirenaicos, 1969. Vol. 1: 66-68, no. 50. As for the (shifting) criticism of the document, see Paul Fridolin Kehr. *Wie und wann wurde das Reich Aragón...* Op. cit., *passim;* Antonio Durán Gudiol. *La Iglesia de Aragón...* Op. cit., 147 and subsq., 177 and subsq., no. 6.

[27] Henrique Flórez. Op. cit. Vol. 23: 309, 372. Regarding historiography in León and Castile during this period, see Peter Linehan. *History and the Historians of Medieval Spain.* Oxford: Oxford University Press, 1993, particularly 172 and subsq.

[28] Regarding the introduction of the Roman rite in León y Castile, see Demetrio Mansilla Reoyo. *La curia romana y el reino de Castilla en un momento decisivo de su historia.* Burgos: Seminario Metropolitano, 1944; Pierre David. Op. cit., *passim;* Juan Francisco Rivera Recio. "Relaciones de la sede apostólica con los distintos reinos hispanos". In Ricardo García Villoslada, dir. *Historia de la Iglesia en España.* Madrid: Biblioteca de Autores Cristianos, 1982. Vol. 2/1: 259-262; in the latter, see also Javier Faci. "La reforma gregoriana en Castilla y León", 262-275; and Juan Francisco Rivera Recio. "La supresión del rito mozárabe y la introducción del romano", 275-285; and Joseph F. O'Callaghan. "The Integration of Christian Spain into Europe: The Role of Alfonso VI of León-Castile". In Bernard F. Reilly, ed. *Santiago, Saint-Denis, and Saint-Peter...* Op. cit., 101-120.

[29] Regarding Alfonso VI's policy, see Bernard F. Reilly. *The Kingdom of León-Castilla under King Alfonso VI, 1065-1109.* Princeton, New Jersey: Princeton University Press, 1988; and Andrés Gambra. *Alfonso VI: cancillería, curia e imperio.* 2 vols. León: Centro de Estudios e Investigación San Isidoro (CSIC-CECEL), Caja España de Inversiones, Caja de Ahorros y Monte de Piedad, Archivo Histórico Diocesano, 1997.

[30] The following works can be consulted regarding the relations between the kings of León and Castile and Cluny: Charles Julian Bishko. *Spanish and Portuguese Monastic History 600-1300.* London: Variorum Reprints, 1984; and *Studies in Medieval Spanish Frontier History.* Aldershot: Ashgate, 1980 (Variorum Collected Studies Series); Peter Segl. Op. cit. By the same author, see "Cluny in Spanien". *Deutsches Archiv* 33 (1977): 560-569; Antonio Linage Conde. *Los orígenes del monacato benedictino en la Península Ibérica.* León: Centro de Estudios e Investigación San Isidoro (CSIC-CECEL), Patronato José María Quadrado, 1973. Vol. 2: 927-997.

[31] In this regard, see Armin Kohnle's book. *Abt Hugo von Cluny 1049-1109.* Sigmaringen: Thorbecke, 1993.

[32] *Ibidem,* 225; and Peter Segl. *Königtum und Klosterreform...* Op. cit., 1974, 47 and subsq.

[33] Regarding Gregory VII's ideas on the Christian kingdoms in the Peninsula, see Juan Francisco Rivera Recio. "Gregorio VII y la liturgia mozárabe". *Revista Española de Teología* 2 (1942): 3-33; Luciano de la Calzada. "La proyección del pensamiento de Gregorio VII en los reinos de Castilla y León". *Studi Gregoriani* 3 (1948): 1-87; Bernardino Llorca. "Derechos de la Santa Sede sobre España. El pensamiento de Gregorio VII". In *Sacerdozio e Regno da Gregorio VII a Bonifacio VIII.* Rome: Pontificia Università Gregoriana, 1954, 79-105; Antonio García y García. "Reforma gregoriana e idea de la 'Militia sancti Petri' en los reinos ibéricos". *Studi Gregoriani* 13 (1991): 241-262, especially 253 and subsq.; Antonio Oliver. Op. cit., 75-82; and José María Soto Rábanos. "Introducción del rito romano en los reinos de España. Argumentos del papa Gregorio VII". *Studi Gregoriani* 14 (1991): 161-174.

[34] On this subject, see Reinhard Elze. "Gregor VII und die römische Liturgie". *Studi Gregoriani* 13 (1991): 179-188 (the quote is on page 187); F. Pérez. "San Gregorio VII y la liturgia española". *Liturgia* 3 (1948): 229-324; Justo Pérez de Urbel. "El último defensor de la liturgia mozárabe". In *Miscellanea Mohlberg.* Rome: Edizioni Liturgiche, 1949. Vol. 2: 189-197; on the complexity of the Roman liturgy in the 11th century, see Chrysogonus Waddell. "The Reform of the Liturgy from a Renaissance Perspective". In Robert L. Benson y Giles Constable, eds. *Renaissance and Renewal in the Twelfth Century.* Cambridge, Massachusetts: Harvard University Press, 1982, 88-109, particularly pages 92 and subsq.

[35] JL 4840. Erich Caspar, ed. Op. cit., 93 (bk. 1, chap. 64). Detailed analysis of this question is provided in José María Soto Rábanos. Op. cit., 166 and subsq.

[36] JL 4840. Erich Caspar, ed. *Ibidem,* 94. Regarding the case of the Bishop of Calahorra (Oca, Sasamón, Valpuesta) and its background, see Odilo Engels. "Papsttum, Reconquista und spanisches Landeskonzil im Hochmittelalter". *Annuarium Historiae Conciliorum* 1 (1969): 37-49, 241-287, particularly 40 and subsq.; Eliseo Sainz Ripa. *Sedes episcopales de La Rioja. Siglos IV-XIII.* Logroño: Diocese of Calahorra and La Calzada-Logroño, Consejería de Cultura, Deportes y Juventud, Instituto de Estudios Riojanos, 1994, 247 and subsq.; and Georg Gresser. *Die Synoden und Konzilien in der Zeit des Reformpapsttums in Deutschland und Italien von Leo IX bis Calixt II, 1049-1123.* Paderborn: Ferdinand Schöningh, 2006, 121 and subsq.

[37] Henrique Flórez. Op. cit. Vol. 23: 310. See Joseph F. O'Callaghan. "The Integration of Christian Spain...". Op. cit., 107.

[38] Andrés Gambra. Op. cit. Vol. 2: 119-123, nos. 46-47 of 10 July 1077. On interest payments at Cluny and the problems that this led to, see Peter Segl. *Königtum und Klosterreform....* Op. cit., 73 and subsq.; Armin Kohnle. Op. cit., 226 and subsq.

[39] Andrés Gambra. *Ibidem,* 121-123, no. 47. See Armin Kohnle. *Ibidem,* 99, 272, no. 24.

[40] JL 5142. Erich Caspar, ed. Op. cit., 465-467 (bk. 7, chap. 6). See Joseph F. O'Callaghan. "The Integration of Christian Spain...". Op. cit., 108.

[41] JL 5076. Erich Caspar, ed. *Ibidem,* 384-385 (bk. 5, chap. 21). See Armin Kohnle. Op. cit., 97, 272, no. 26.

[42] On 22 January 1080, Robert appears as Abbot of Sahagún in a deed regarding a donation by Alfonso VI (Andrés Gambra. Op. cit., 165-166, no. 66).

[43] Teófilo F. Ruiz. "Burgos and the Council of 1080". In Bernard F. Reilly, ed. *Santiago, Saint-Denis, and Saint-Peter...* Op. cit., 121-130; Andrés Gambra. *Ibidem.* Vol. 1: 541 and subsq.; Fidel Fita. "El concilio nacional de Burgos en 1080. Nuevas ilustraciones". *Boletín de la Real Academia de Historia* 49 (1906): 337-384. The year that this synod was held is highly controversial and researchers' opinions fluctuate between 1080 and 1081. A synthesis on this question can be found (accepting the date 1081) in Antonio García y García. "Concilios y sínodos en el ordenamiento jurídico del reino de León". In *El reino de León en la Alta Edad Media.* Vol. 1, *Cortes, concilios y fueros.* León: Centro de Estudios e Investigación San Isidoro (CSIC-CECEL), Archivo Histórico Diocesano, Caja de Ahorros y Monte de Piedad, 1988, 353-494, especially on pp. 391 and subsq.; and "Legislación de los concilios y sínodos del reino leonés". In *El reino de León en la Alta Edad Media.* Op. cit. Vol. 2, *Ordenamiento jurídico del reino*, 1992, 7-114, particularly 50 and subsq.

[44] Benito Sánchez Alonso, ed. *Crónica del obispo don Pelayo.* Madrid: Centro de Estudios Históricos, 1924, 80. Regarding the date, see Andrés Gambra. *Ibidem,* 541 and subsq.

[45] On this subject the following books can be consulted, among others: Armin Kohnle. Op. cit., 97 and subsq., 225 and subsq.; and Bernard F. Reilly. *The Kingdom of León-Castilla...* Op. cit., 106 and subsq.

[46] See Armin Kohnle. *Ibidem,* 225 and subsq.; also Juan Francisco Rivera Recio. *El arzobispo de Toledo don Bernardo de Cluny (1086-1120).* Rome: Iglesia Nacional Española, 1962, 13 and subsq.; and by the same author, see *La Iglesia de Toledo en el siglo XII (1086-1208).* Rome; Toledo: Instituto Español de Historia Eclesiástica, 1966. Vol. 1: 125 and subsq. In a document by Alfonso VI, dated 8 May 1080, in which he confirmed to Abbot Bernard

that the privileges enjoyed by Monastery of Sahagún were still in force just as they had been during his predecessor, Prior Robert's term of office, it states the following: "decreui [...] prefatum monasterium ad laudem et gloriam Die in honore sanctorum martirum Facundi et Primitiui releuare et in Die seruitio reformare, atque per electionem fratrum ibidem commorantium Bernardo in eodem monasterio prefato abbatem constitui, in presentia Ricardi, Romane aeclesie cardinales". Quoted in Andrés Gambra. Op. cit. Vol. 2: 166-171, no. 67; and Marta Herrero de la Fuente, ed. *Colección diplomática del Monasterio de Sahagún*. León: Centro de Estudios e Investigación San Isidoro (CSIC-CECEL), Caja de Ahorros y Monte de Piedad, Archivo Histórico Diocesano, 1988. Vol. 3: 68-70, no. 781. In this regard, certain problems are raised by a new document by Alfonso VI addressed to Monastery of Sahagún, dated 14 May 1080. This contains some reforming statutes inspired by the Cluniac rules and again mentions Abbot Robert's dispatch, because none of the various explanations provided to date are totally convincing, as pointed out in the prologue to his edition by Andrés Gambra. *Ibidem,* 171-174; and Marta Herrero de la Fuente, ed. *Ibidem,* 71-73, no. 782; see Andrés Gambra. *Ibidem.* Vol. 1: 424, 460-465, and also see Bernard F. Reilly. "The Chancery of Alfonso VI of León-Castile (1065-1109)". In *idem,* ed. *Santiago, Saint-Denis, and Saint-Peter...* Op. cit., 1-40, especially p. 9, and *idem. The Kingdom of León-Castilla... Ibidem,* 111 and subsq.

[47] See Marta Herrero de la Fuente, ed. *Ibidem,* 66-67, no. 779 of 24 April 1080.

[48] JL 5173. Erich Caspar, ed. Op. cit., 517-518 (bk. 8, chap. 2). See Joseph F. O'Callaghan. "The Integration of Christian Spain...". Op. cit., 109 and subsq.; and also José María Soto Rábanos. Op. cit., 163 and subsq.

[49] JL 5174. Erich Caspar, ed. *Ibidem,* 519-520 (bk. 8, chap. 3). See JL 5175. *Ibidem,* 520-521 (bk. 8, chap. 4).

[50] See Luciano de la Calzada. "La proyección del pensamiento de Gregorio VII...". Op. cit., 79 and subsq.; Armin Kohnle. Op. cit., 99 and subsq.; Bernard F. Reilly. *The Kingdom of León-Castilla...* Op. cit., 107 and subsq.; and Andrés Gambra. Op. cit. Vol. 1: 452-469, who again puts forward the interpretations that he knows.

[51] Joseph F. O'Callaghan. "The Integration of Christian Spain...". Op. cit., 110-112; Armin Kohnle. *Ibidem,* 1993, 228; and Peter Segl. *Königtum und Klosterreform...* Op. cit., 183 and subsq.

[52] JL 5205. Erich Caspar, ed. Op. cit., 569-572 (bk. 9, chap. 2).

[53] *Ibidem.*

[54] Andrés Gambra. Op. cit. Vol. 1: 633-636, based on his diplomatic studies, he defends the possibility that the candidate put forward by Alfonso VI, and later Archbishop of Toledo, was Bishop Bernardo of Palencia and not his namesake, the abbot of Sahagún, among other things because the former had already had the title of *archiepiscopus,* as Bishop of Palencia.

[55] For biographical details of Gregorio VII, consult H. E. J. Cowdrey. *Pope Gregory VII, 1073-1085.* Oxford: Oxford University Press, 1998.

[56] Ramón Gonzálvez. "The Persistence of the Mozarabic Liturgy in Toledo after A. D. 1080". In Bernard F. Reilly, ed. *Santiago, Saint-Denis, and Saint-Peter...* Op. cit., 157-185.

[57] See Joachim Mehne. "Cluniazenserbischöfe". *Frühmittelalterliche Studien* 11 (1977): 241-287.

[58] See Peter Segl. *Königtum und Klosterreform...* Op. cit., 47 and subsq., and 69 and subsq. Neither can it be stated for sure that there was any transfer by Alfonso VI with regard to the only monastery in question, Santa María de Villafranca del Bierzo.

[59] See Antonio García y García. "Reforma gregoriana e idea...". Op. cit., 253 and subsq.; and Jean Flori. "Réforme, reconquista, croisade (L'idée de reconquête dans la correspondance pontificale d'Alexandre II à Urbain II)". In *idem. Croisade et chevalerie, XIe-XIIe siècles.* Brussels: De Boeck Université, 1998, 51-80, and especially pages 59 and subsq.

[60] On this question, see Ludwig Vones. "*Reconquista* und *Convivencia*: Die Könige von Kastilien-León und die mozarabischen Organisations-strukturen in den südlichen Grenzzonen im Umkreis der Eroberungen von Coïmbra (1064) und Toledo (1085)". In Odilo Engels and Peter Schreiner, eds. *Die Begegnung des Westens mit dem Osten.* Sigmaringen: Thorbecke, 1993, 221-242.

[61] Ramón Gonzálvez. Op. cit., 179. On the diversity in the lives and activities of the Mozarabs in 13th century Toledo, see Francisco J. Hernández y Peter Linehan. *The Mozarabic Cardinal. The Life and Times of Gonzalo Pérez Gudiel.* Florence: Sismel-Edizioni del Galluzzo, 2004; and on Gonzalo García Gudiel's activities as Archbishop of Toledo, see Peter Linehan. *The Spanish Church and the Papacy in the Thirteenth Century.* Cambridge: Cambridge University Press, 1971, especially pp. 132 and subsq. On the survival of Mozarabic traditions in Toledo, see Julio González. "Los mozárabes toledanos desde el siglo XI hasta el cardenal Cisneros". In *Historia mozárabe. Primer Congreso de Estudios Mozárabes,* 1975. Toledo: Instituto de Estudios Visigótico-Mozárabes de San Eugenio, 1978, 79-90.

[62] Ramón Gonzálvez. *Ibidem*, 179. Juan Meseguer Fernández. "El cardenal Jiménez de Cisneros, fundador de la capilla mozárabe". In *Historia mozárabe*. Toledo: Instituto de Estudios Visigótico-Mozárabes de San Eugenio, 1978, 149-245.

Bibliography

BERNDT, Rainer, ed. *Das Frankfurter Konzil von 794*. 2 vols. Mainz: Mittelrheinische Kirchengeschichte, 1997 (Quellem und Abhandlungen für Mittelalterlichen Kirchengeschichte: 80).

BISHKO, Charles Julian. *Studies in Medieval Spanish Frontier History*. Aldershot: Ashgate, 1980 (Variorum Collected Studies Series).

—. *Spanish and Portuguese Monastic History 600-1300*. London: Variorum Reprints, 1984.

BRONISCH, Alexander Pierre. "Asturien und das Frankenreich zur Zeit Karls des Großen". *Historisches Jahrbuch* 119 (1999): 1-40.

—. *Reconquista und Heiliger Krieg. Die Deutung des Krieges im christlichen Spanien von den Westgoten bis ins frühe 12. Jahrhundert*. Münster in Westfalen: Aschendorff, 1998.

CALZADA, Luciano de la. "La proyección del pensamiento de Gregorio VII en los reinos de Castilla y León". *Studi Gregoriani* 3 (1948): 1-87.

CASPAR, Erich, ed. *Das Register Gregors VII*. In *Monumenta Germaniae Historica*. Berlin: Weidmann 1920-1923. (Reprinted, Hannover: Hahnsche Buchhandlung, 1990.)

COWDREY, H. E. J. *Pope Gregory VII, 1073-1085*. Oxford: Oxford University Press, 1998.

DAVID, Pierre. *Études historiques sur la Galice et le Portugal du VIe au XIIe siècle*. Coimbra: Instituto de Estudios Históricos, 1947.

DESWARTE, Thomas. *De la destruction à la restauration. L'idéologie du royaume d'Oviedo-Léon (VIIIe-XIe siècles)*. Turnhout: Brepols, 2003.

DURÁN GUDIOL, Antonio, ed. *La Iglesia de Aragón durante los reinados de Sancho Ramírez y Pedro I (1062?-1104)*. Rome: Iglesia Nacional Española, 1962.

—, ed. *Colección diplomática de la Catedral de Huesca*. Vol. 1. Zaragoza: CSIC, Escuela de Estudios Medievales, Instituto de Estudios Pirenaicos, 1969.

ELZE, Reinhard. "Gregor VII und die römische Liturgie". *Studi Gregoriani* 13 (1991): 179-188.

ENGELS, Odilo. "Papsttum, Reconquista und spanisches Landeskonzil im Hochmittelalter". *Annuarium Historiae Conciliorum* 1 (1969): 37-49 and 241-287.

—. "Die Anfänge des spanischen Jakobusgrabes in kirchenpolitischer Sicht". *Römische Quartalschrift* 75 (1980): 146-170.

—. *Reconquista und Landesherrschaft. Studien zur Rechts- und Verfassungsgeschichte Spaniens im Mittelalter*. Paderborn: Ferdinand Schöningh, 1989.

FACI, Javier. "La reforma gregoriana en Castilla y León". In Ricardo García Villoslada, dir. *Historia de la Iglesia en España*. Madrid: Biblioteca de Autores Cristianos, 1982. Vol. 2/1: 262-275.

FITA, Fidel. "El concilio nacional de Burgos en 1080. Nuevas ilustraciones". *Boletín de la Real Academia de Historia* 49 (1906): 337-384.

FLORI, Jean. "Réforme, reconquista, croisade (L'idée de reconquête dans la correspondance pontificale d'Alexandre II à Urbain II)". In *idem*. *Croisade et chevalerie, XIe-XIIe siècles*. Brussels: De Boeck Université, 1998, 51-80.

FLÓREZ, Henrique. *España sagrada*. Vol. 3. 2nd ed. Madrid: Imprenta de José Rodríguez, 1854. (1st ed., Madrid: 1799. Vol. 23.)

FRIED, Johannes. *Der päpstliche Schutz für Laienfürsten. Die politische Geschichte des päpstlichen Schutzprivilegs für Laien (XI-XIII Jahrhunderf)*. Heidelberg: Carl Winter Universitätsverlag, 1980.

GAMBRA, Andrés. *Alfonso VI. Cancillería, curia e imperio*. 2 vols. León: Centro de Estudios e Investigación San Isidoro (CSIC-CECEL), Caja España de Inversiones, Caja de Ahorros y Monte de Piedad, Archivo Histórico Diocesano, 1997.

GARCÍA Y GARCÍA, Antonio. "Concilios y sínodos en el ordenamiento jurídico del reino de León". In *El reino de León en la Alta Edad Media*. Vol. 1. *Cortes, concilios y fueros*. León: Centro de Estudios e Investigación San Isidoro (CSIC-CECEL), Archivo Histórico Diocesano, Caja de Ahorros y Monte de Piedad, 1988, 353-494.

—. "Reforma gregoriana e idea de la 'Militia sancti Petri' en los reinos ibéricos". *Studi Gregoriani* 13 (1991): 241-262.

—. "Legislación de los concilios y sínodos del reino leonés". In *El reino de León en la Alta Edad Media*. Op. cit. Vol. 2, *Ordenamiento jurídico del reino*, 1992, 7-114.

GONZÁLEZ, Julio. "Los mozárabes toledanos desde el siglo XI hasta el cardenal Cisneros". In *Historia mozárabe. First Congress of Mozarabic Studies, 1975*. Toledo: Instituto de Estudios Visigótico-Mozárabes de San Eugenio, 1978, 79-90.

GONZÁLVEZ, Ramón. "The Persistence of the Mozarabic Liturgy in Toledo after A. D. 1080". In Bernard F. Reilly, ed. *Santiago, Saint-Denis, and Saint-Peter. The Reception *of the Roman Liturgy in León-Castille in 1080.* New York: Fordham University Press, 1985, 157-185.

Gresser, Georg. *Die Synoden und Konzilien in der Zeit des Reformpapsttums in Deutschland und Italien von Leo IX bis Calixt II, 1049-1123.* Paderborn: Ferdinand Schöningh, 2006.

Gros Bitria, Eladio. *Los límites diocesanos en el Aragón oriental.* Zaragoza: Guara, 1980.

Hernández, Francisco J., and Peter Linehan. *The Mozarabic Cardinal. The Life and Times of Gonzalo Pérez Gudiel.* Florence: Sismel-Edizioni del Galluzzo, 2004.

Herrero de la Fuente, Marta, ed. *Colección diplomática del Monasterio de Sahagún.* Vol. 3. León: Centro de Estudios e Investigación San Isidoro (CSIC-CECEL), Caja de Ahorros y Monte de Piedad, Archivo Histórico Diocesano, 1988.

Herwaarden, Jan van. "The origins of the cult of St. James of Compostela". *Journal of Medieval History* 6 (1980): 1-35.

Ibarra Rodríguez, Eduardo, ed. *Documentos correspondientes al reinado de Sancho Ramírez.* Vol. 2. Zaragoza: Tipografía de Pedro Carra, 1913 (Colección de Documentos para el Estudio de la Historia de Aragón).

Kehr, Paul Fridolin, ed. *Papsturkunden in Spanien. Vorarbeiten zur Hispania Pontificia.* 2 vols. Berlin: Weidmannsche Buchhandlung, 1926-1928 (ND Göttingen 1970. Abh. Gött. NF 18/2, 22/1).

—. *Das Papsttum und die Königreiche Navarra und Aragón bis zur Mitte des 12. Jahrhunderts.* Berlin: Akademie der Wissenschaften, 1928 (Abhandlungen der Preuβischen Akademie der Wissenschaften zu Berlin: Philosophisch-Historische Klasse 4).

—. *Wie und wann wurde das Reich Aragón ein Lehen der römischen Kirche?* Berlin: Akademie der Wissenschaften, 1928 (Sitzungsberichte der preuβischen Akademie der Wissenschaften zu Berlin: Philosophisch-Historische Klasse 18). In Spanish, "¿Cómo y cuándo se hizo Aragón feudatario de la Santa Sede?". *Estudios de Edad Media de la Corona de Aragón* 1 (1943): 285-326.

Kohnle, Armin. *Abt Hugo von Cluny 1049-1109.* Sigmaringen: Thorbecke, 1993.

Linage Conde, Antonio. *Los orígenes del monacato benedictino en la Península Ibérica.* 3 vols. León: Centro de Estudios e Investigación San Isidoro (CSIC-CECEL), Patronato José María Quadrado, 1973.

Linehan, Peter. *The Spanish Church and the Papacy in the Thirteenth Century.* Cambridge: Cambridge University Press, 1971.

—. *History and the Historians of Medieval Spain.* Oxford: Oxford University Press, 1993.

Llorca, Bernardino. "Derechos de la Santa Sede sobre España. El pensamiento de Gregorio VII". In *Sacerdozio e Regno da Gregorio VII a Bonifacio VIII.* Rome: Pontificia Università Gregoriana, 1954, 79-105.

Mansilla Reoyo, Demetrio. *La curia romana y el reino de Castilla en un momento decisivo de su historia.* Burgos: Seminario Metropolitano, 1944.

—, ed. *La documentación pontificia hasta Inocencio III, 965-1216.* Rome: Instituto Español de Historia Eclesiástica, 1955.

—. *Geografía eclesiástica de España. Estudio histórico-geográfico de las diócesis.* 2 vols. Rome: Iglesia Nacional Española, 1994.

Martínez Díez, Gonzalo. *El condado de Castilla (711-1038). La historia frente a la leyenda.* 2 vols. Madrid: Junta de Castilla y León, Consejería de Cultura y Turismo, Marcial Pons Historia, 2005.

Mehne, Joachim. "Cluniazenserbischöfe". *Frühmittelalterliche Studien* 11 (1977): 241-287.

Meseguer Fernández, Juan. "El cardenal Jiménez de Cisneros, fundador de la capilla mozárabe". In *Historia mozárabe.* Toledo: Instituto de Estudios Visigótico-Mozárabes de San Eugenio 1978, 149-245.

O'Callaghan, Joseph F. "The Integration of Christian Spain into Europe: The Role of Alfonso VI of León-Castile". In Bernard F. Reilly, ed. Op. cit., 101-120.

—. *Reconquest and Crusade in Medieval Spain.* Philadelphia: University of Pennsylvania Press, 2003.

Olivar, Alejandro. "Les supervivències litúrgiques autóctones a Catalunya en els manuscrits dels segles xi-xii". In *II Congrés litúrgic de Montserrat.* Montserrat: Abbey of Montserrat, 1967. Vol. 3: 21-89.

Oliver, Antonio. "'Regnum Hispaniae' en el programa de reforma de Gregorio VII". *Studi Gregoriani* 14 (1991): 75-82.

Pérez, F. "San Gregorio VII y la liturgia española". *Liturgia* 3 (1948): 229-324.

Pérez de Urbel, Justo. "El último defensor de la liturgia mozárabe". In *Miscellanea Mohlberg.* Rome: Edizioni Liturgiche, 1949. Vol. 2: 189-197.

Reilly, Bernard F. "The Chancery of Alfonso VI of León-Castile (1065-1109)". In *idem,* ed. Op. cit., 1-40.

—. *The Kingdom of León-Castilla under King Alfonso VI, 1065-1109.* Princeton, New Jersey: Princeton University Press, 1988.

Reynolds, Roger E. "The Ordination Rite in Medieval Spain: Hispanic, Roman, and Hybrid". In Bernard F. Reilly, ed. *Santiago, Saint-Denis, and Saint-Peter...* Op. cit., 131-156.

—. "The Visigothic Liturgy in the Realm of Charlemagne". In Rainer Berndt, ed. Op. cit. Vol. 2: 919-945.

Rivera Recio, Juan Francisco. "Gregorio VII y la liturgia mozárabe". *Revista Española de Teología* 2 (1942): 3-33.

—. *El arzobispo de Toledo don Bernardo de Cluny (1086-1120).* Rome: Iglesia Nacional Española, 1962.

—. *La Iglesia de Toledo en el siglo XII (1086-1208).* Vol. 1. Rome, Toledo: Instituto Español de Historia Eclesiástica, 1966.

—. "Relaciones de la sede apostólica con los distintos reinos hispanos". In Ricardo García Villoslada, dir. Op. cit.

—. "La supresión del rito mozárabe y la introducción del romano". In *ibidem,* 275-285.

Ruiz, Teófilo F. "Burgos and the Council of 1080". In Bernard F. Reilly, ed. Op. cit., 121-130.

Säbekow, Georg. *Die päpstlichen Legationen nach Spanien und Portugal bis zum Ausgang des 12. Jahrhunderts.* Ph. D. dissertation. Berlin: Ebering, 1930.

Sainz Ripa, Eliseo. *Sedes episcopales de La Rioja. Siglos IV-XIII.* Logroño: Diocese of Calahorra and La Calzada-Logroño, Consejería de Cultura, Deportes y Juventud, Instituto de Estudios Riojanos, 1994.

Sánchez Alonso, Benito, ed. *Crónica del obispo don Pelayo.* Madrid: Centro de Estudios Históricos, 1924.

Segl, Peter. *Königtum und Klosterreform in Spanien. Untersuchungen über die Cluniacenserklöster in Kastilien-León vom Beginn des 11. bis zur Mitte des 12. Jahrhunderts.* Kallmünz (Oberpfalz): Michael Lassleben, 1974.

—. "Cluny in Spanien". *Deutsches Archiv* 33 (1977): 560-569.

Smith, Damian. "Sancho Ramírez and the Roman Rite". *Studies in Church History* 31 (1996): 95-105.

Soto Rábanos, José María. "Introducción del rito romano en los reinos de España. Argumentos del papa Gregorio VII". *Studi Gregoriani* 14 (1991): 161-174.

Ubieto Arteta, Antonio. "La introducción del rito romano en Aragón y Navarra". *Hispania Sacra* 1, no. 2 (1948): 299-324.

—, ed. *Crónica de San Juan de la Peña.* Valencia: Caja de Ahorros y Monte de Piedad de Zaragoza, Aragón y Rioja, 1981.

—. *Historia de Aragón.* Vol. 1, *Literatura medieval.* Zaragoza: Anubar, 1981.

Vones, Ludwig. "*Reconquista* und *Convivencia*: Die Könige von Kastilien-León und die mozarabischen Organisationsstrukturen in den südlichen Grenzzonen im Umkreis der Eroberungen von Coïmbra (1064) und Toledo (1085)". In Odilo Engels and Peter Schreiner, eds. *Die Begegnung des Westens mit dem Osten.* Sigmaringen: Thorbecke, 1993, 221-242.

—. *Geschichte der Iberischen Halbinsel im Mittelalter, 711-1480. Reiche, Kronen, Regionen.* Sigmaringen: Thorbecke, 1993.

Vones-Liebenstein, Ursula. "Katalonien zwischen Maurenherrschaft und Frankenreich. Probleme um die Ablösung westgotisch-mozarabischer Kirchenstrukturen". In Rainer Berndt, ed. Op. cit. Vol. 1: 453-505.

Waddell, Chrysogonus. "The Reform of the Liturgy from a Renaissance Perspective". In Robert L. Benson and Giles Constable, eds. *Renaissance and Renewal in the Twelfth Century.* Cambridge, Massachusetts: Harvard University Press, 1982, 88-109.

Weiss, Stefan. *Die Urkunden der päpstlichen Legaten von Leo IX bis Coelestin III (1049-1198).* Cologne, Weimar, Vienna: Böhlau, 1995.

Ximénez de Embún, Tomás, ed. *Crónica de San Juan de la Peña.* Zaragoza: Imprenta del Hospicio, 1876.

The *Musica Isidori* Tradition in the Iberian Peninsula

Michel Huglo

The encyclopedic work that Isidore, Archbishop of Seville (599-636), wrote at the end of his life, entitled *Etymologiarum liber,* is undoubtedly the most copied, widely circulated and best-known book of all the literary and scientific works produced in late Antiquity. This synthesis of the profane and religious knowledge of the 7th century was commissioned and finally edited by Braulio, Archdeacon and later, in 631, Archbishop of Zaragoza. Braulio makes clear what his participation in the long process of preparing the *Etymologiae* involved: first in his *Epistolarium,*[1] which includes his correspondence with Isidore and marks the stages in the development of the great work. He also does so in his *Renotatio*, the bibliography of Isidore's works (see illustration 1):[2]

> *Etymologiarum* codicem nimiae magnitudinis, distinctum ab eo titulis non libris: quem quia rogatu meo fecit, quamvis imperfectum ipse reliquerit, ego in viginti (quindecim: *7 mss.*) libros divisi.
>
> [He had divided the manuscript of the *Etymologiae*, which was extremely long, not into books but into chapters: however, since I had commissioned him to write it, I divided it into twenty (fifteen: *7 mss.*) books, although he left it unfinished.]

In this short fragment, Braulio summarized the long story of the composition of the *Etymologiae* and the story of his later collaboration with Isidore, as the first letters of the *Epistolarium*[3] mention in several places.

Braulio, who had heard rumors about the completion of the *Etymologiae*, immediately reminds Isidore of his old promise to send him the work (*Ep.* II, 4, ll. 27-29).[4] Seven years later, in a long missive to Isidore he again asks him twice for the books of the 'Origins' (*Ep.* IV, 6, ll. 11-17), regretting that his letters have still gone unanswered. A little further on in the same letter, he once again asks him for the books of the *Etymologiae* of which others have received excerpts with mistakes, and asks for a complete, corrected and coherent copy for himself (*ibidem,* 8, ll. 24-28).

Finally, Isidore acknowledges receipt of this letter, which he had read in Toledo, where he had gone to preside over the council in 633: he then sends Braulio a manuscript that he was unable to check because of his health (*Ep.* V, 10, ll. 9-12).

It is remarkable that in this letter Braulio uses the two terms *Originum* and *Etymologiarum,* by which Isidore's final work, *Isidori Hispalensis episcopi Etymologiarum sive Originum libri XX,* would later be known, the division of which into twenty books was due to Braulio. In fact, "[...] for the Ancients, etymological study was [...] a tool for interpreting the origin of words in order to achieve a profound awareness

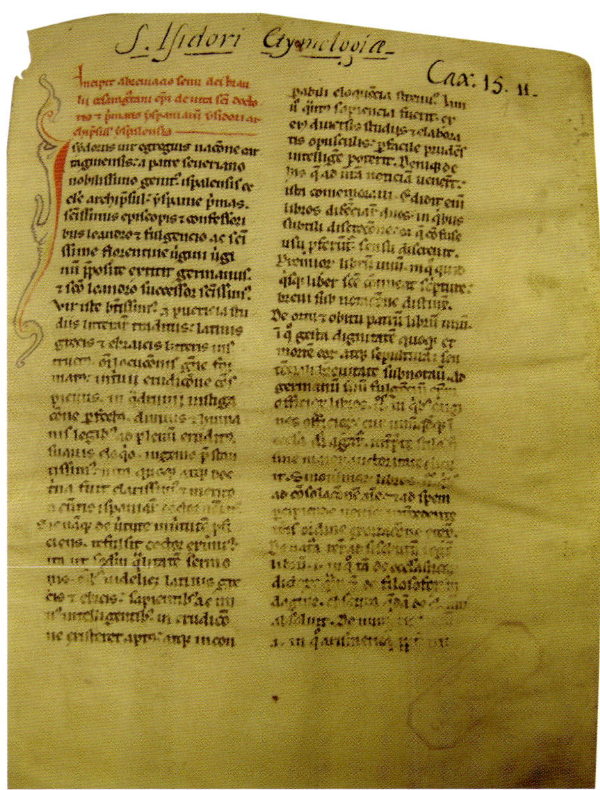

1. Isidorus. *Etymologiae*. Toledo, BC, 15-11, fol. 1r

of the realities designated by these". "Etymologia est origo vocabulorum cum vis verbi vel nominis per interpretationem colligitur", Isidore says (*Orig.* I, 29, 1), when he compiles and presents the tradition of Latin grammarians in his encyclopaedic work of the *Origins* or *Etymologiae.*[5]

In the aforementioned *Renotatio librorum sancti Isidori*, Braulio appears as the forerunner of Isidore's huge work. In fact, in 615 Isidore had dedicated his treatise *De natura rerum*[6] to King Sisebut (612-621), who commissioned the work, so he felt obliged to begin his *Etymologies* with a short dedication to this same king. In 620 he gave him an initial version of the work as a present, which included the first ten books of the definitive edition. However, in the manuscripts in Visigothic script, this same dedication is intended for Braulio, who is very probably responsible for the "change of addressee" and for other modifications that we will touch upon later on.

Isidore's disciple is really the *editor*[7] of the final version of the *Etymologiae*, which remained unfinished. Braulio explains that the manuscript of the *Etymologiae* that he received after 633 was enormous: indeed, the eleven manuscripts in Visigothic script that have survived are almost all over 30 centimetres long, and one of them,[8] written in three columns, is well over 50 centimetres long.

Braulio's remark can also be interpreted in a different sense: the text that he received from his master was of a length, or rather an expanse, that was enormous, accentuated by the fact that the subjects dealt with were not separated into books, but were merely organized by titles (*titulis*) without any numbers. The same procedure is still used today in editions of some of his books, such as Book III, *De mathematica*, where the text is subdivided into four unnumbered *tituli*: *De arithmetica, De geometria, De musica* and *De astronomia.*[9] Thus, Braulio bequeathed a truly personal edition of the *Etymologiae* to posterity.

Braulio's participation in editing the *Etymologiae* does not conceal in any way the prominent role played by Isidore in searching for sources, in selecting them and in its definitive preparation. As Jacques Fontaine wrote, "One can only have access to the genuine originality of Isidore of Seville through a triple strategy. First of all, an appraisal as complete and detailed as possible of his direct and indirect sources. Next, the meticulous study of the deletions, the additions and the modifications to which Isidore subjected each text that he borrowed. Finally, any reference to contemporary reality in all of its aspects...".[10]

As for the liberal arts, especially the *ars musica*, Isidore's source has been studied since 1959 by Paul Lehmann:[11] this is Book II of the *Institutiones,* a text devoted to the study of the liberal arts that Cassiodorus wrote between 551 and 562 for the monks living in his Vivarium Monastery, near the Gulf of Squillace on the southern coast of Calabria.[12]

The text of Cassiodorus's *Institutiones* adopts quite a wide variety of forms in the numerous manuscripts that exist of the work, because before the definitive *edition,* some advance copies of Book II had already been made: the version that Isidore used is not the 'Vulgate' published by Mynors in 1937, but a little-known draft that Louis Holtz[13] identified in 1983.

Furthermore, Isidore removed entire passages from his source: in particular, the extensive list of the modes of ancient Greek music and the bibliography of the *ars musica*'.[14] And, inversely, he added to the question of the secular origins of music a reference to the Bible (Gen. 4:22) regarding Tubal, considered to be the inventor of the *ars musica.*[15]

Among other important additions he made to his sources, we can first mention that "small phrase that has led to rivers of ink being expended" on musical sounds, which, "if they are not learned by memory, fade away for want of a medium for setting them down in writing" [*De musica*, III, i (xv), 2]. There is also the matter of the timbre of singers' voices that Isidore could hear when he presided over the liturgical services in his cathedral: in the tradition of the Visigothic manuscripts of the *Etymologiae,* this passage has *Vocis species multae*[16] as a subtitle. Finally, the list of musical instruments in Chapter VIII (xxij) differs from Cassiodorus's list, because Isidore describes precisely the instruments that he once had the opportunity to hear during his time in southern Spain.

The critique of Isidore's sources concerning the liberal arts in general, and music in particular, must be reconsidered today in light of two studies: the first publishes the interpolated version of the article "Musica" in the *Liber glossarum* of the 8th century, a huge in-folio glossary of 27,000 terms that, mainly by following Isidore's works, develops the articles connected with terms from the liberal arts.[17]

The second study to consider concerns the analysis of the diagram of the scale of Hispanic chant that was interpolated in Visigothic manuscripts during the second half of the 8th century: the present article seeks to go develop this question further in greater depth.

In the *Liber glossarum*, written during the 8th century to support the early Carolingian Renaissance through the study of the liberal arts, the article, "Musica", includes not only the continuous transcription without any subdivisions of Isidore's earlier text in chapters, but also three important excerpts located between what had been Chapters II (xvj) and III (xvij) by Isidore and the eight definitions of *Musica* placed at the end of the article;[18] these additional passages are given here in table 1.

The most important of the two long interpolated passages is undoubtedly the second one, because here we have proof that Isidore used Varro's *De disciplinis libri IX*[19] independently of Augustine,[20] who took the legend of the origin of the Muses from the same source (table 2).

TABLE 2

AUGUSTINE	**LIBER GLOSSARUM**
Non enim audiendi sunt	
errores gentilium	
superstitionum, qui	
novem Musas Jovis	
et Memoriae filias	
esse finxerunt.	
Refellit eos Varro	Hos Varro
quo nescio utrum	
apud eos quisquam	
talium rerum doctior vel	
curiosior esse possit.	
Dicit enim	adferens
civitatem nescio quam	Atheniensium urbem
—non enim nomen recolo—	
locasse apud tres	condidisse apud tres
artifices terna	artifices terna
simulacra Musarum,	simulacra Musarum
quod in templo	quae in templo
Apollinis *donum poneret*,	Apollinis dicarentur
ut, quisquis artificum	ut cui
pulchriora formasset	pulchriora fecisset
ab illo potissimum	ab ipso
electa emerent.	emerentur.
Ita contigisse, ut opera	Sed dum
sua quoque illi	
artifices	omnes vocem
	cunctorum judicio
aeque	
pulchra explicarent,	
et placuisse civitati	placuissent
omnes novem atque	
omnes esse emptas,	emptae sunt
ut in Apollinis templo	et in Apollinis templo
dedicarentur. Quibus	sacratae, quibus
postea dicit Hesiodum	postea Haesiodum
poetam imposuisse	poetam imposuisse
vocabula.	vocabulo.

TABLE 1

ISIDORE			**LIBER GLOSSARUM**
			Music is expressed through the voice (*art. cit.*, p. 28)
I. (xv)	Music; the origin of the term	(*Musica ex Musis)*	
II. (xvj)	The inventors of music	*idem*	
			+ The bucolic origin of music + The mythical origin of the nine muses, according to Varro and Augustine. (*art. cit.*, p. 28-29)
III. (xvij)	The power of music	*idem*	
IV. (xviij)	The three parts of music	*idem*	
V. (xix)	The tripartite division of music	*idem*	
VI. (xx)	The 1st div. of music: harmonics	omitted	
VII. (xxj)	The 2nd div. of music: instrumental	omitted	
VIII. (xxij)	The 3rd div. of music: rhythm	omitted	
IX. (xxiij)	Harmonic numbers	*idem*	
			The eight definitions of music (*art. cit.*, p. 31)

The latter text on the origin of the nine muses poses quite a few problems, especially as far as its origin and provenance are concerned: was it really taken from Varro's *De disciplinis libri IX*, which is now lost, as both authors claim, or is it actually a clever reconstruction by Isidore, following Augustine's text? Do we need to consider this legend to be a text that Isidore reserved with the intention of writing his first paragraph later on about the origin of music? And finally, how could the authors of the *Liber glossarum*, compiled in northern France, have known about these interpolations in the *Musica Isidori*?

This is not the right place to clear up matters like this, because it is more important to deal with the second task concerning the scale of the old Hispanic chant—called *Mozarabic chant*—that properly corresponds to the family of manuscripts in Visigothic script.[21] This appendix of musical theory was to some degree postulated in the ninth and final Chapter IX (xxiij), *De numeris musicis*, as well as in the definition of this art that was provided in the *Etymologiae* (II, xxiv, 15), regarding the purpose of Philosophy. The same definition also appears at the end of the article "Musica" in the *Liber glossarum*: "Musica est disciplina quae de numeris loquitur qui ad aliquid sunt his qui inveniuntur in sonis". ("Music is the science that deals with numbers in connection with those that are contained in sounds.")

Dissemination of the *Etymologiae* in Europe: Manuscripts from the Iberian Peninsula

The number of copies of the *Etymologiae* that have survived has now reached the record figure of 1,100 manuscripts, 29 of which were transcribed before the year 800:[22] nevertheless, we need to bear in mind that some of these manuscripts only include the first ten books, or, on the other hand, the last ten, a circumstance that slightly lowers the initial figure.[23]

The general classification of this set of manuscripts into three families is due to Lindsay. In his 1911 edition of the *Etymologiae,* he presented:

1. The French family (*francica sive integra*, designated with the letter [α]), which is the most widely disseminated not only in the area of the Romance languages but also in German-speaking regions. Lindsay identified 22 manuscripts belonging to this family, eleven of which were dated during or from the end of the 8th century. Among the latter, it is well worth mentioning a manuscript from Corbie in Merovingian script from the end of the 8th century, which probably comes from a Spanish model.[24]

In 1966, Marc Reydellet, in collaboration with Bernhard Bischoff, added seven new items to the list of French manuscripts and subdivided them into two subgroups according to a *stemma codicum*, but he omitted the manuscript from Corbie that I just mentioned.[25]

A set of about fifteen French and German manuscripts that included in their collections of musical theory the nine chapters of the *De musica* with the title of *Musica Isidori*[26] is linked to the Franco-Germanic family.

2. The Italo-Germanic family (*italica sive contracta*, designated by the letter [β]) consists of six very early manuscripts[27] in Lindsay's edition to which Marc Reydellet added the Lombard 8th century manuscript kept in Modena, BC, ms. O. I. 17. This family is characterized by the transfer of the chapter on *De musica* and that on *De astronomia* to Book IV of the *Etymologiae*. Finally, Lindsay judiciously added the Latin manuscript 7530 of Montecassino[28] to the manuscripts in this family, which transmits excerpts from Books I *(De grammatica)* and V *(De legibus)*.

3. The Hispanic family (*hispanica sive interpolata*, designated by the letter [γ]) includes the eleven manuscripts of the *Etymologiae* that were written on the Peninsula in Visigothic minuscule and two Portuguese manuscripts in minuscule from the 12th and 13th centuries, with a few vestiges of the old Visigothic minuscule, but with perfectly drawn diagrams (see table 3).[29]

Lindsay used the term *interpolata* to define this Hispanic family, because it actually includes several interpolations by Braulio, who, thanks to a small team of copyists working in his Bishop's palace, *edited* the *Etymologiarum codex* that Isidore had sent him shortly after 633. Taken together, the five criteria that appear below represent the characteristic tone of this Hispanic family:

TABLE 3: MANUSCRIPTS FROM THE IBERIAN PENINSULA

Manuscripts	Dates	Provenance	Interpolated diagrams		
			Geometric	Musical	Ω 31
Manuscripts from the south of the Iberian Peninsula					
1. El Escorial, &.I.14 [**V**]	VIII-IX	Seville/Córdoba	18-24	// //	//
2. Madrid, BN, glass case 14.3 [**T**]	VIII *ex.*	South of Toledo	18-24	25-30	31
3. El Escorial, P.I.6	X	Andalucía	18-24	25-30	31
4. El Escorial, T.II.24 [**U**]	X	Mozarabic south	18-24	25-30	31
Manuscripts from the north of the Iberian Peninsula					
5. El Escorial, P.I.8	791-812	Septimania	0	0	0
6. El Escorial, P.I.7 [**W**]	IX	by Alfonso of León († 910)	0	0	0
7. Madrid, RAH, Cod. 25	946	San Millán	18-24	25-30	31
8. Madrid, RAH, Cod. 76	954	Cardeña	18-24	25-73	31
9. El Escorial, &.J.3	1047	Oviedo/León	18-24	25-30	31
10. Madrid, BN, 10008	XI	Castile	18-24	25-30	0
11. Paris, BNF, N. A. L. 2169	1072	Silos	19-23	24-27	0
Manuscripts from Portugal					
12. Lisbon, BN, Alcobaça 446	XII	Alcobaça (Santa Maria)	18-24	25-30	31
13. Porto, BPM, 21 (Santa Cruz 17)	XIII	Coimbra (Santa Cruz)	18-24	25-30	31

1. A set of eight letters broken down as follows: the first five, taken from the *Epistolarium* by Braulio,[30] place first of all two letters from Isidore to Braulio, who was then Archdeacon and had not yet been named Bishop of Zaragoza. Dated as a result from between 620 and 631, these two letters are only found in the Hispanic tradition and in a few more recent Spanish manuscripts.[31]

The following five letters (nos. 3-7) appear in all branches of the manuscript tradition. The sixth and final one (no. 8) is a short note by Isidore dedicating the *Etymologiae* to Braulio: it gives the impression that the dedication of the work, initially addressed to Sisebut († 621), which was kept by the manuscripts of the Franco-Germanic family and finally adopted by Lindsay (*lectio difficilior, lectio verior*), must have been reattributed by Braulio to himself. This has led to much confusion in the manuscript tradition and in the printed texts.[32] Sometimes one finds the text of this last letter duplicated, addressed both to Braulio and to Sisebut (as, for example, in the El Escorial manuscript, T.II.24), or even with the title of Preface and with a modified incipit: *En vobis* instead of *En tibi*.

2. Alter the list of 20 books, due explicitly to Braulio, comes the text of the Grammar to which Isidore gives pride of place: but the order and the number of these chapters in the Visigothic manuscript tradition are so confused that they can only be used to differentiate the manuscripts from the south (25 chapters) from the manuscripts from the northern Peninsula. Lindsay avoided the issue by following the order of the oldest manuscript in Visigothic script, which is in Madrid, BN, glass case 14.3 (olim Toledo 15.8) and was reproduced in facsimile by Scato de Vries in 1909.

3. In Book III, between *De geometria* and *De musica,* a considerable number of geometric and musical diagrams were added to the tradition of the Hispanic and Portuguese manuscripts with commentaries: in figure 1, taken—for want of a better source—from the *Patrologia Latina* (vol. LXXXIV: col. 870), figures of plane and solid geometry from Cassiodorus's *Institutiones* (nos. 1-17) were

FIGURE 1: GEOMETRIC AND MUSICAL DIAGRAMS FROM *PATROLOGIA LATINA*

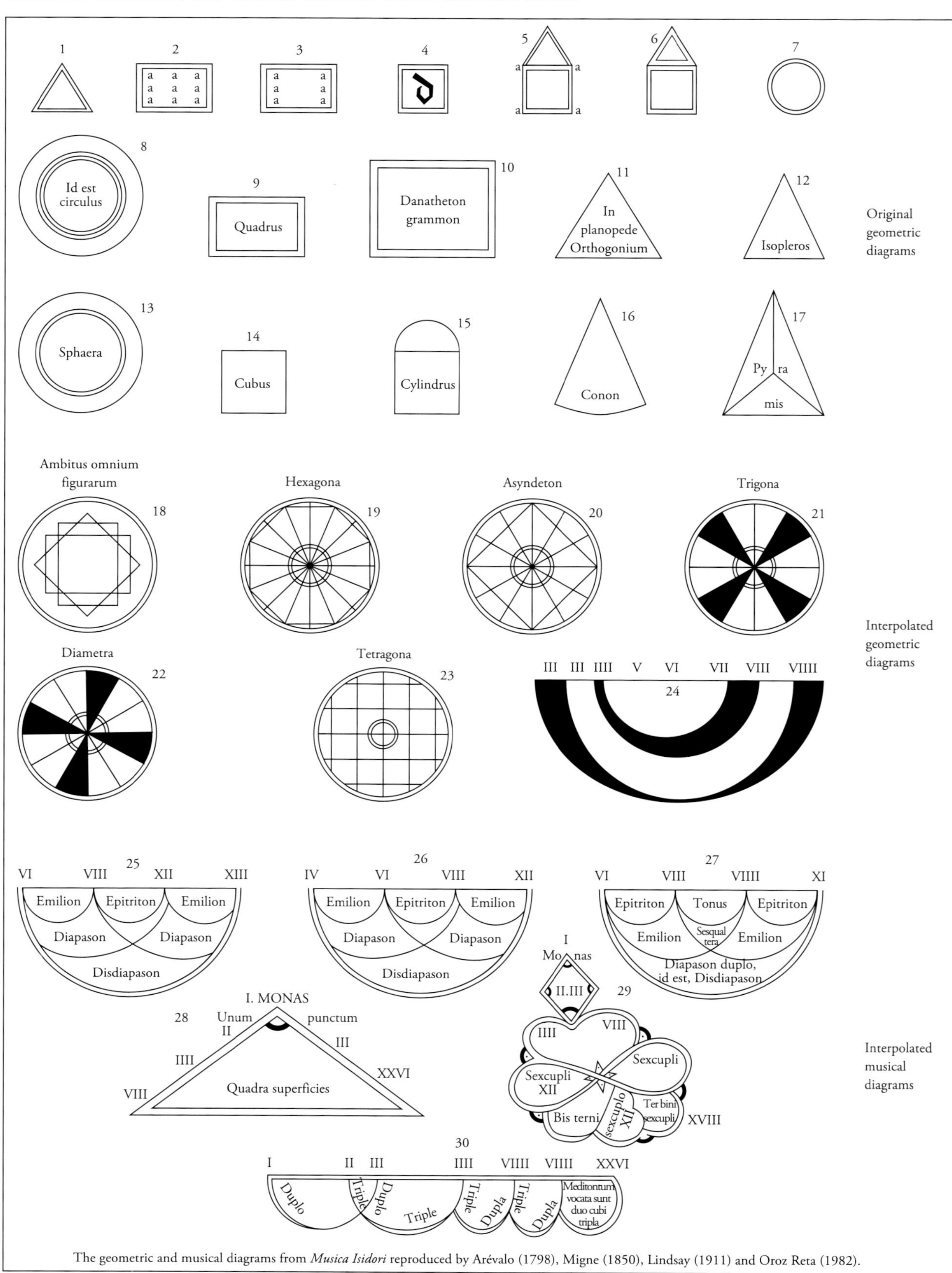

The geometric and musical diagrams from *Musica Isidori* reproduced by Arévalo (1798), Migne (1850), Lindsay (1911) and Oroz Reta (1982).

included; as well as a series of geometric figures (of Arab origin?) applied to astronomy to describe the constellations (nos. 18-23) and the phases of the moon (no. 24). Finally, the small diagrams of harmonics (nos. 25-30), were followed by the large diagram (no. 31), which is finished off by a three-lobed arch shaped like a [Ω], whose purpose was to establish a musical scale.

These important interpolations, which date from the 8th century, seem to have been restricted exclusively to the Iberian Peninsula and have become characteristic of the Visigothic family: we will consider them in the third part of this article.

4. In Chapter VI (xx) *De musica*, Isidore included a significant paragraph about vocal timbres: in the pontifical ceremonies that he attended during his career, he had the opportunity to observe the wide range of vocal qualities that his contemporaries had. In his *De ecclesiasticis officiis*, when it came to selecting a *psalmist*, he also had to reject certain vocal flaws and to prescribe a melodious, gentle, fluid (*liquida*) and yet pure voice, without theatrical effects.[33] In the previous chapter, he formulates a series of more concise prescriptions for the reader's voice and insists above all on a correct accentuation of the Latin used in the readings in the service.

Because these reflections by Isidore on the voice do not refer to the subject of Chapter VI (xx), at the beginning of this paragraph the subtitle *Vocis species multae* was added in the Visigothic and Portuguese manuscripts, and to a lesser extent in others.[34] So it is likely that this addition is due to Braulio, who was personally interested in singing, given that he had composed a hymn to St. Millan.

5. Braulio's most obvious interpolation is the "praise *(laudatio)* of Zaragoza" in Book XV, Chapter I: *De civitatibus*. In fact, Isidore had described this town rather superficially as having been founded by the Scipiones and as the capital of Tarrazona, but Braulio, Archdeacon and later Bishop of the city, wrote a more detailed summary, stressing the mildness of a climate that was better than that of other Spanish towns, and the fact that the town was endowed with numerous graves of martyrs from the early centuries. This note, which aimed to arouse readers' interest, was passed on by several manuscripts from other families;[35] and, more significantly, it furnished a pretext for including other summaries on cities 'forgotten' by Isidore.[36]

According to Walter Porzig,[37] these interpolations were formerly discovered following the comparison of manuscripts belonging to different traditions; Juan López de Velasco, for example, points out in his 1599 edition that there is no trace of the "Elogio de Zaragoza" in a *book* belonging to Cardinal Sirleto and in one of the Toledo books.[38] It needs to be said that the possibility of comparing certain versions with others was favored by the fact that previously the number of manuscripts was—according to Bernhard Bischoff—ten times greater than the number we now have in our libraries.

To these five characteristics of the [γ] family, one must add several passages unique to the "interpolated" family, which Lindsay conveniently printed within square brackets.[39]

There were two continental 9th century manuscripts that Lindsay added to the *hispanica sive interpolata* family:

1. Leiden University, Vossianus Lat. Fol. 74, written in Gaul in the 9th century, with a series of corrections by Loup de Ferrières made in Fulda:[40] clearly, this manuscript adopted several readings of the [γ] family, although the diagrams inserted between *De geometria* and *De musica* do not appear in this manuscript.

2. St. Gall, Stiftsbibliothek, ms. 237: Manuscript produced by two copyists towards 830, in even Caroline minuscule.[41] The first two letters A and B from the [γ] family are missing, and it only contains the five letters (p. 7), that are common to all families, the letter *En tibi* written to Braulio (p. 10) and finally, the "Elogio de Zaragoza" (p. 240). Although Lindsay considered it necessary to keep this manuscript in the [γ] family due to its readings, on the contrary, we have excluded it from our research on the diagrams, which do not appear in Book III.

Bernhard Bischoff pointed out that the oldest surviving copy of the *Etymologiae* on the continent was represented by the fragment in Irish minuscule in St. Gall, Stiftsbibliothek, 1399 a.1, from an insular center on the Continent (Bobbio?):[42] this fragment includes the text of the *Etymologiae* XI, I, 43-46 and 51-53. The *Etymologiae* still appear in the St. Gall manuscripts 231-232 (complete); 233 (*Etymol.* VI-VIII and XII-XX) and 235 (*Etymol.* XII-XX), both from the [β] family; and finally, in ms. 913 (several passages that include *Etymol.* I, iii-iv), all of which were collated in Lindsay's edition.

The example of St. Gall enables us to understand the aforementioned remark by Walter Porzig on the subject of the interpolations that were discovered by medieval readers after they had compared different texts brought together in a single library.

The analysis of the harmonic diagrams inserted into Book III of the *Etymologiae* will, from now on, be based on the manuscripts in Visigothic script and on the two Portuguese manuscripts copied in the 12th century on Visigothic models.

Manuscripts in Visigothic script

The eleven manuscripts of Isidore of Seville's *Etymologiae* written in Visigothic minuscule can be divided into three groups, depending on their textual variants and on the insertion of the diagrams at the beginning of Book III: those from the South of the Peninsula, those from the North, and third, the two Portuguese manuscripts copied in the 12th century on old Visigothic models (see table 3).

In the descriptions that we now provide below the manuscripts are analysed from a codicological and paleographic viewpoint, bearing in mind the studies that we are now going to mention,[43] especially those that deal with the subject of dating Visigothic minuscule, which is usually a cause of debate among specialists.

Description of the manuscripts from the South

1. El Escorial, Real Biblioteca, &.I.14.
168 parchment folios, 515 × 365 mm, in 3 columns <400 × 70/72 mm> with 57 lines. 19 pages at the beginning and 15 later on are missing (see the *Catálogo* by Antolín 1911, 2: 371). The prickings to mark lines are between columns 2 and 3. Gatherings are signed with Roman numerals in majuscule: e.g., Q.LV (fol. 160v).

Binding: wooden panels covered in brown leather, stamped with the coat of arms of St. Lorenzo of El Escorial, here shaped like a grill.

Script: Visigothic minuscule in pale ink dated between the 8th century *ex.* [*CLA (Codices latini antiquiores) XI:* no. 1635] and the 8th-9th centuries (Ewald and Lowe 1920, 11, pl. 13); 8th-9th or 9th century *in.* (Millares Carlo 1999, 2: no. 53). Titles in red; no red or green on the initials. Arabic script on fol. 166v, in the lower margin.

Origin: Its huge size and the arrangement of the texts in three columns of 59-61 lines link this manuscript with others having identical characteristics (listed in *CLA XI:* no. 1635). The Arabic annotations and the reference on fol. 38v to Álvaro de Córdoba († 861) imply a connection with the South.

Provenance: In the 8th century, this manuscript belonged to a church dedicated to St. Romain, near Toledo; in the 17th century, it was owned by the Halls of Residence of Alcalá de Henares (note on fol. 168v). Finally, after 1671, it went on to form part of the Count-Duke of Olivares's collection, which was donated to the Monastery of El Escorial by his nephew, the Marquis of Heliche.

Contents: *Etymologiae* (siglum V, according to Lindsay); *Redemti clerici*, *Obitus sci Isidori*; St. Jerome's letters (they start on fol. 113, in a new gathering); some letters from the correspondence with King Sisebut, etc. (see the *Catálogo* by Antolín 1911, 2: 364-371).

The absence of the first 19 pages deprives us of the beginning of *De musica:* the text starts with the following words *...sicut tonitruum, sicut incudis sonos* from Chapter VI (xx), 12 (on vocal timbres). On the verso of the flyleaf, however, one finds a trace of the first column of fol. 18r (70/72 mm wide), I have been able to reconstruct the first letters in words belonging to the last few chapters of *De geometria:*

Pr[ima autem figura]: III, xij, 7 (p. 136, l. 8).
<space of one line>
Sec[unda linea]: III, xij, 7 (p. 136, l. 9).
R[ecta linea]: III, xij, 7 (p. 136, l. 10).
Su[perficies vero]: III, xij, 7 (p. 136, l. 11).
<space of 8-10 lines>
Nu[merus autem]: III, xiij (p. 136, l. 20).
<space of several lines>
S <red> beginning of the last word in the title *Scripturarum:* III, xiv, 1.
Ali[a ratio]: III, xiv, 1 (p. 136, l. 20).
<space of a dozen lines>
Ite[m secundum]: III, xiv, 2 (p. 136, l. 28).

On the back of fol. 19, you can also read on the flyleaf the end of a series of words or syllables that correspond to chapters VI (xx) 2 to12 and link up with the beginning of fol. 20 ... *sicut tonitruum,* etc.

Thus, fols. 18v and 19r, now lost, once had the space needed for the diagrams nos. 18 to 29 from fig. 1, the larger full-page diagram no. 31 from fig. 3, and finally, chapters I (xv) to VI (xx) 1-12 from the "Musica".

Bibliography: Antolín 1911, 2: 364-371. Millares Carlo 1999, 1: no. 53. Díaz y Díaz 1971, 73-74; 1995, 43.

2. MADRID, Biblioteca Nacional, glass case 14.3 (olim Toledo 15.8).

163 thick parchment folios, 312 × 205 mm <260 × 167 mm>. Some folios are smaller in size, because they were cropped, for example fols. 5-6, 13-14, 21-22, 27v-30), in two columns with 51 lines: the prickings are located between the two columns.

Composition: 21 regular gatherings, except for V (binion) and the XXIst and last one (ternion); gathering signatures at the end (except in Book II made up of folios that are too uneven) with a letter and Roman numeral: for example D.Q.IIII (fol. 32v).

See the codicological analysis in Rudolf Beer's preface to the facsimile of Scato de Vries, Chapter IV (vii-xj) and in *CLA XI:* no. 1638.

Binding: Most likely the manuscript lacked a binding for a long time, because fol. 1 has turned shiny through use; Modern signature: "A. Ménard".

Script: Visigothic minuscule of the 8th century (Ewald and Lowe 1920, pls. 10-12); from the 8th-9th centuries (*CLA XI:* no. 1638); from the 9th century (Millares Carlo 1999, 1: no. 149). Current title in the top margin; titles in small red Visigothic script; subtitles in yellow and green; Small initials with red outlines at the start of chapters, with the inside filled with green or yellow strokes; Signs of scansion (fol. 12).

Numerous Arabic annotations: fols. 27 and 28 ("Musica"); fol. 79v (Millares Carlo 1999, 2: no. 149), 83v (facsimile of the *CLA XI:* no. 1638) and 163v.

Origin: Mérida region, as shown in *Trésors de la Biblioteca Nacional* (Exhibition catalog) (Paris: BNF, 1988), p. 20.

Provenance: Toledo, probably due to the list of Spanish Episcopal sees included on the final folio, 163v in the 9th-10th centuries. The manuscript became part of the collection of the Biblioteca Nacional in 1868.

Contents: only the *Etymologiae*: *Toletanus I* from Arévalo's edition; abbreviation T from the Lindsay's edition.

Fols. 25-27r: all of the geometric figures (fol. 25r-26v) and harmonic diagrams (fol. 26v) that are reproduced in black and white in De Vries's facsimile edition (1909) appear here with a doubly traced edge filled with green or yellow and sometimes both, more rarely with red (the red is used above all for the arches that represent the proportions *tripla* and *dupla*). The titles and subtitles of these drawings are traced in red.

The large diagram on fol. 27r, with a green and yellow edge, fills the entire page. The arches are traced with a raised hand and not a compass (fig. 2); all of the numbers are drawn in red ink, except for those in the bottom row, which are in black.

The nine chapters of *De musica* begin on fol. 27v.

Bibliography: Millares Carlo 1999, 1-2: no. 149. Lowe 1934-1972; Díaz y Díaz 1971, 78.

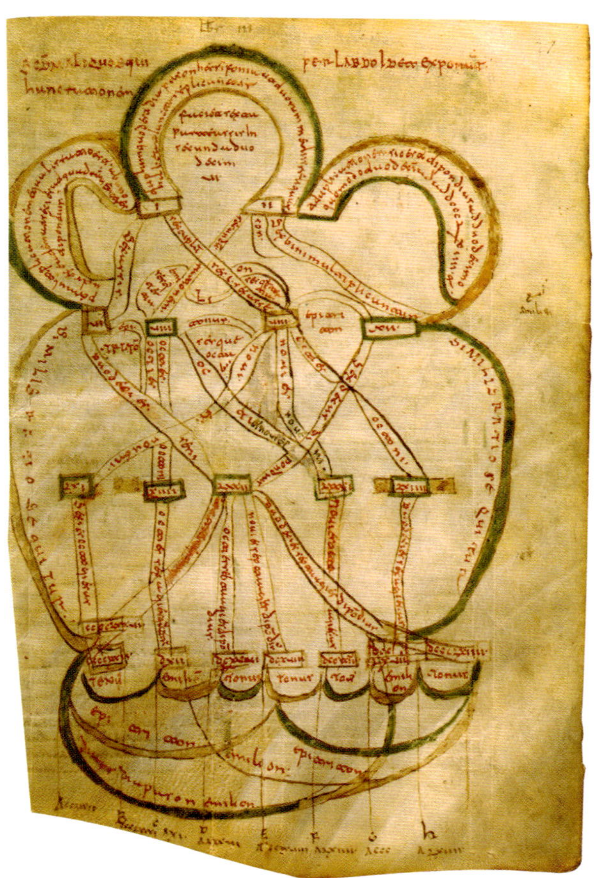

2. Isidorus. *Etymologiae*. Biblioteca Nacional de España, glass case 14.3, 8th century, fol. 27r

3. El Escorial, Real Biblioteca, P.I.6.
118 rigid parchment folios, 360 × 265 mm, folios in two columns, each measuring <264 × 80 mm>. The quaternions are signed at the end: for example III (fol. 16), IIII (fol. 24), etc.

Binding: in brown leather stamped with the coat of arms of El Escorial.

Script: 9th century Visigothic minuscule (Millares Carlo 1999, 1: no. 57); 10th century (Ewald and Lowe 1920, pl. 26); second half of the 10th century (Díaz y Díaz, *Problemas*, p. 78) or 10th to 11th centuries (Antolín 1911, 2: 255). Titles are in medium-sized capital letters. Initials with some colored interlacing begin the twenty books (fols.13, 25v etc.). Arabic annotations on fols. 52 and 74v. Fols. 64v-70, 'continental' 12th century *ex.* minuscule. Fol. 86v, end of Visigothic script. What follows (fols. 87-118) in Book IX and the following ones is written in 'continental' 12th-13th century minuscule, the work of two different hands.

Origin: Andalusian (Díaz y Díaz 1971, 78).

Provenance: a center in La Rioja (?). Count-Duke of Olivares's collection (?).

Contents: only the *Etymologiae* by Isidore of Seville. Due to a gap at the beginning, Book I begins with Chapter XIII *De praepositione*.

Fol. 25v: *Incipit Liber Tertius.* "Praevatio (sic) de quattuor sequentibus disciplinis." *De matematica: Matematica latine dicitur...*

Fol. 29v B: *Expositio Figurarum Infra/scribturarum: Alia ratio...*

["Geometria" III, xiv, 1 (p. 136, l. 20), followed by the musical diagrams, nos. 25, 26 and 27.]

Fol. 30: Figures of the constellations (nos. 18-23).

Fol. 30v: On the left, the diagrams of the phases of the moon (no. 24, deformed) and the musical diagrams nos. 25, 26 and 27 and, taking up the entire page, no. 30. In the column on the right: "Ratio interioris formae" ("Geometria", xiv, 3, p. 136, l. 1).

Fol. 31: The large diagram, 29 cm high, does not take up the entire page—as in the previous manuscript—but only the left-hand part, to the extent that one part of the lobe on the left that encroaches on the interior margin, has ended up in the gap in the binding; on the right-hand side they are superimposed from top to bottom: *Idem secundum aliquos* etc.; diagram 28; a semicircular diagram on the paths followed by the planets; diagram 29 (the four elements); *In planopede sic medium...*, a mention that should have been inscribed under diagram 30 (drawn at the bottom of fol. 30v); and finally, two small diagrams also concerning the four elements (not present in figure 1). Regrettably, to save space on the parchment, the copyist modified the order of the texts and of the interpolated diagrams.

The facsimile given by Jacques Fontaine, *Isidore de Séville et la culture classique dans l'Espagne wisigothique* (Paris, 1959), has disappeared from the second edition (1983).

Fol. 31v: *De musica.* Chapters I-VIIII. Fol. 32 A (in small red capital letters): VOCIS SPECIE[S] MULTE.

Fol. 33v: *De astronomia.*

Bibliography: see the works mentioned in the description Antolín 1913, 3: 255-257. Díaz y Díaz 1971, 78.

4. El Escorial, Real Biblioteca, T.II.24.
257 white but rigid parchment folios: 295 × 205 mm <230 × 158 mm>. The bottom of the folios are in poor condition, the gathering signatures of the quaternions that were placed at the beginning of each gathering are illegible before fol. 86, where gathering XII begins. From fol. 126 onwards, a 14th century hand added a letter before or after the Roman numeral of the gathering signature xvij R (fol. 126), S xviij (fol. 134), T xix (fol. 142), etc.

The catchword signalling the next gathering was added *in French letters* at the end of each gathering.

Binding: cardboard covered in red leather and stamped with the coat of arms of San Lorenzo of El Escorial.

Script: full page, except for fols. 41 and 41A at the top. Ewald and Lowe (pl. 8) suggests the date, 733, which is definitely the date of the model; 9th to 10th centuries (Antolín); 10th century (Millares Carlo 1999, 1: no. 64). Ordinary titles are in small Visigothic capitals highlighted with yellow strokes. Chapter numbers are mossy green (copper oxide?). Initials, and sometimes subtitles, are in turquoise blue.

Arabic annotations on fol. 41 (names of the signs of the zodiac added to the figure of the *Asyndeton* (no. 20) and to fols. 44, 44v and 45 (Chapter VII of "Musica" and following ones).

Origin: probably a Mozarabic environment in southern Spain, different from those that produced one of the manuscripts of the *Etymologiae* that has survived today: nevertheless, the arrangement of the large diagram no. 31 is absolutely identical to that in the previous manuscript (El Escorial, P.I.6), of Andalusian origin. Manuel C. Díaz y Díaz tends to favor the idea that this manuscript and its model are from Córdoba.

Provenance: "De la yglesia de Salamanca" (fol. 1, at the top, 14th century). Count-Duke of Olivares's collection (?)

Contents: fols. 1-3: *Laterculus notarum,* or the table of standard abbreviations in the titles, for example OFFM (Officium). SD (secundum), etc.

Fols. 3v-6v: Correspondence between Braulio and Isidore: Isidore's letter to Braulio (*En tibi*) is separated from the series of seven letters by Braulio's *Praenotatio librorum*, untitled in this case (ed. José Carlos Martín, in CCSL 113 B, p. 183-189: see the Bibliography), and by the list of chapters of Book I of the *Etymologiae*.

The text of this manuscript, collated by Lindsay (abbreviation U), in many cases matches the text of T (El Escorial P.I.6). The nine chapters of *De musica* start on fol. 44: they are preceded by the cycle of diagrams interpolated in the same order as in the previous manuscript, but here, the large diagram no. 31 (280 mm-high), instead of extending into the internal margin, encroaches on the right-hand column and is superimposed on the aforementioned texts. The figures located at the bottom of the diagram have disappeared, because of the destruction of the lower part of the folios. In fol. 43v, the subtitle vocis species *multae* (sic) is in red.

On fol. 190, "Elogio de Zaragoza".

Bibliography: Antolín 1923, 5: 507-510. Díaz y Díaz 1971, 75-76; 1995, 114. Martín 2006, 90-91 (ms. T): 116 and 179.

Description of the manuscripts from the North

5. Escorial, Real Biblioteca, P.I.8.
269 dull parchment folios, ca. 350 × 275 mm in two columns of 33 lines (fols. 8-269). The thick Visigothic script with pointed shafts, which is the work of Juan, Bishop of Maguelonne in Septimania, dates from 791-812 [transcription of the colophon (fol. 269v) in Millares Carlo 1999, 1: no. 59; see *CLA XI,* no. 1630].

The manuscript displays none of the features of Braulio's summary, listed earlier, nor any sign that the page was prepared with the figure and inserted diagrams in mind:

1. The manuscript lacks the two letters from Isidore to Braulio, the Archdeacon (A and B in the Lindsay's edition).

2. The letter *En tibi* is addressed to Braulio (fol. 5), together with the index of the twenty books, and in a second version (fol. 6) to Sisebut as well, as occurs in Lindsay's edition; but in this case it is preceded by a small Oviedo Cross to the left of the dedication.

3. Coming before *De musica*, on fols. 38v-39v, the usual diagrams from "Geometria" (nos. 1-17 in fig. 1) appear. There is no room left to transcribe all the interpolated material about astronomy and music, however. In addition, in Chapter VI (fol. 40v), the characteristic passage in the *Etymologiae* about vocal timbres is not preceded by the subtitle *Vocis species multae*, attributed to Braulio. Finally, at the end of Chapter VIII (fol. 42b), the name of the musical instruments is drawn with minium (an orangish-red color).

4. The "Elogio de Zaragoza" on fol. 204v A makes this manuscript one of the oldest witnesses to the diffusion of this interpolation into Septimania.

On fol. 54v (on a blank page), after Book IV, a "French" 11th century hand wrote a note about the three (not twelve) psalms of the evening service on Easter Sunday, that were the subject of debate in monasteries from the 9th to 12th centuries (see Huglo 2005b, 153-162).

Bibliography: Antolín 1913, 3: 255-257. Clark 1920, no. 530 and pl. 19 (fols. 20v-21). *CLAXI:* no. 1630 (at the end of the volume). Díaz y Díaz 1971, 76-77.

6. ESCORIAL, Real Biblioteca, P.I.7.
322 dull parchment folios, 450 × 260 mm, in two columns, each measuring <280 × 95 mm>. The prickings marking the lines are placed between the columns, less often on the edge of the fols. (see fols. 6-20; 26-29, etc.). The gathering signatures of the quaternions are crowned by a collar beam, as happens in the El Escorial manuscript T.II.25.

Binding: in red leather stamped with the grill-shaped coat of arms of San Lorenzo of El Escorial.

Script: Visigothic minuscule with pointed shafts, 9th century *in.* (Ewald and Lowe 1920, pl. 14; Antolín 1913, 3: 257); 9th-10th century, ca. 900 (Millares Carlo 1999, no. 59; *Les rois bibliophiles*, p. 21, no. 1); no later than 900 (Díaz y Díaz, *Manuscritos*, p. 77). Obelisks and critical marks in the margins. Rare annotations in Visigothic script or French minuscule from the 12th-13th centuries (fols. 168v and 232v); very simple green initials, edged in red.

Fol. 1v is in chessboard-style and made up of alternate letters in red and black, that form the anagram ADEFONSI PRINCIPIS LIBRUM as in Isidore's *Liber sententiarum* (El Escorial, T.II.25: Clark 1920, 145, pl. 18), but with richer colors in this case.

Fol. 6v has an Oviedo Cross before the title with deepset initials in various colors: IN NOMINE DNI/INCIPIUNT LIBRI *Ethimologiarum* [...] (as in ms. T.II.25, fol. 2, but with richer colors in this case).

Origin: this book formed part of King Alfonso III the Great's library, king of Asturias (866-910). In the 16th century, Morales had the chance to examine another three manuscripts from Alfonso III's collection (*Les rois bibliophiles*... p. 21).

Provenance: Oviedo College in Salamanca (16th century). Count-Duke of Olivares's collection, donated to the Monastery of El Escorial by his nephew, the Marquis of Heliche.

Contents: Manuscript W in Lindsay's edition. Fol. 2: Chapters of the twenty books of the *Etymologiae*, written in red and black letters; fols. 5v-6: blank, unused, because they are divided into three columns of the same size; on fol. 6v, the chapters of Book I. This manuscript does not mention the correspondence between Isidore and Braulio.

Fol. 54 B: The figures of plane and (fol. 55v) solid geometry in "Geometria" (nos. 1-17 in fig. 1).

Abruptly on fol. 56, the title DE MU SI CA appears, followed by its nine chapters (not repeated below). On fol. 57 A, on the third from the last line, the subtitle *Vocis species multae* appears in red letters. Fol. 59v A: *De astronomia.* Fol. 222v (*Etymol.* XIV, ij): *Orbis terrae* (the three continents): see Destombes 1964. Finally, fol. 242v (*Etymol.* XV, I, 66): "Elogio de Zaragoza".

Fol. 322: *Explicit feliciter Liber ethimologiarum,* followed by two verses by Virgil: *In freta dum fluvii currunt, dum montibus umbrae* [...] (*Aeneid* I: 607-609), and ending with the names of precious stones: *Nomina* [*lapidum*]: *Zmaragdu(s) qui colores*...(see *Etymol,* XVI, vij, 2).

Bibliography: Antolín 1913, 3: 257-260. Sarriá, Lemaire and Elkhadem 1985, 21-22: no. 1. Díaz y Díaz 1971, 77.

7. MADRID, Real Academia de la Historia, Cod. 25, fol. 64r (illustration 3)
300 yellowed parchment folios; 337 × 236 mm <244 × 172 mm>, in two columns, each measuring 246 × 85 mm. Regarding the ruling of the parchment, see Barbara Shailor (1985, diagrams 2 and 3). Gatherings are numbered at the end with a figure inscribed under a collar beam, followed by a *Q* and a small dash.

Binding: modern cardboard binding.

Script: 10th century Visigothic minuscule script, although the titles appear more recent. The homilies at the beginning (fols. 1-16) are written by an Aquitainian hand from the second half of the 12th century.

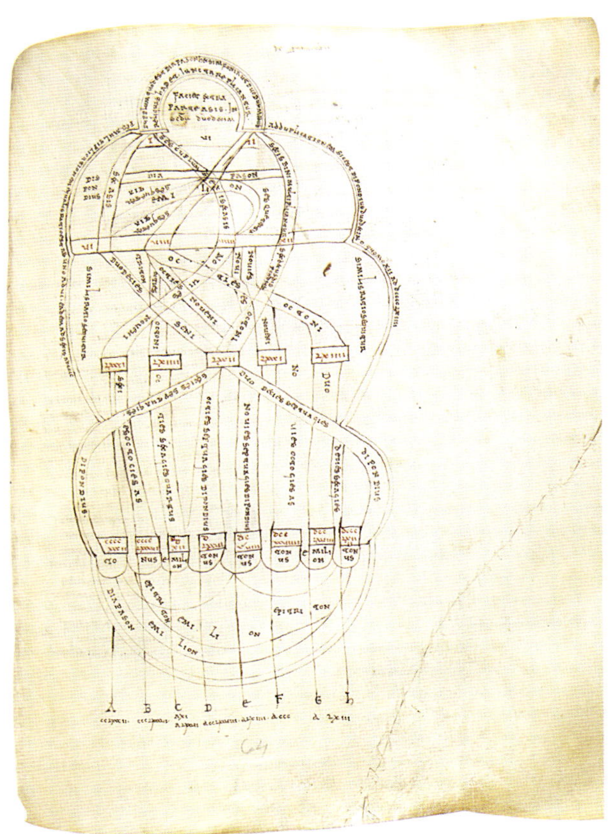

3. Isidorus. *Etymologiae*. Madrid, RAH, Cod. 25, 10th century (946), fol. 64r

Origin: San Millán de la Cogolla. The colophon on fol. 295v gives the date 984 (year 946): see Ewald and Lowe 1920, pl. 22; García Villada 1923, 2: pl. 24, fasc. 31.

Provenance: transferred to the Royal Academy in 1821.

Contents: Fol. 1-16: homilies of St. Bernard; fol. 16v *Capitula Libri Ethimologiarum* (like the El Escorial manuscript, &.I.3, fols. 9v-10r): the title of each book appears in one of the 22 colored circles (circle no. 22 is empty); fols. 18v A-21v: the 7 letters at the beginning of the *Epistolarium* end with the words *Expliciunt epistolae directoriae*; fol. 21v: *Incipit praefatio totius libri... En tibi* (Isidore's letter to Braulio), followed by the chapters in Book I (in identical order to those in Madrid, BN, 10008: the abbreviation *Tl* or *Tls (Toletanus)* appears in red in the margin.

In Book I, the theory regarding metric feet appears beneath some Mozarabic horseshoe arches, as occurs with the canons of Eusebius in the Gospels (identical presentation in the El Escorial manuscript &.I.3).

Fol. 57v: preface of Book III: *Mathematica latine dicitur...*

Fol. 62v EXPOSITIO FIGURARUM INFRA SCRIBTURARUM (rubric in red ink)

Alia ratio... and the geometric figures applied to astronomy (nos. 23, 21, 19 and 22 in fig. 1), the asyndeton (no. 20) has been moved to the top of fol. 63, whereas in the El Escorial manuscript &.I.3, fol. 57v and in RAH, Cod. 76 (Cardeña), fol. 24 these five geometric figures are drawn on a single page.

Under the asyndeton placed at the top of fol. 63, the diagrams about harmonics and the corresponding texts appear, and these finish at the top of fol. 63v, with linear diagram no. 30 in fig. 1.

The large diagram no. 31, which takes up the entire length of the page, is identical to the one in the Cardeña manuscript (RAH, Cod. 76) and the one in El Escorial, &.I.3. Fol. 64v: end of the interpolation, and above column B, beginning of *De musica*. On fol. 65v, the subtitle *Vocis species multae* is written in red ink.

On fol. 211 [?] (*Etymol.* XXII, ij) *Orbis terrae* (see Destombes 1964); fol. 221, in Chapter I (*De civitatibus*) of Book XVI (and not XV), the placenames are written in red: on fol. 221 B (*Etymol.* XV, I, 66): the "Elogio de Zaragoza".

Fol. 295v: colophon (Ewald and Lowe 1920, pl. 22); fol. 296v-300v: fragment of the Venerable Bede's *De natura rerum*, entitled *De celo,* unfinished due to a lack of material. These excerpts are in the manuscript &.I.3 in El Escorial.

Bibliography: Ruiz García 1997, 197. Shailor 1979, 465-467 and figs. 4 and 5. Díaz y Díaz 1971, 73; 1979, 117-122, 175, 264, 284, 323.

8. Madrid, Real Academia de la Historia, Cod. 76, fol. 251 (illustration 4).
162 parchment folios of uneven sizes; approximately 320 × 225 mm in two columns, each measuring <265 × 82 mm>; 44 lines per page. The gatherings are stuck to the flyleaf, but the edges are unevenly trimmed: the gathering signatures at the end are Roman numerals surrounded by four crosses.

Binding: pigskin folder, with a pastedown.

Script: Regular: Visigothic minuscule, which is the work of two copyists, Endura and Diego, dated 990 (Hispanic era; i.e. 952 CE).

Origin: according to the colophon, San Pedro de Cardeña, La Rioja valley.

Provenance: entered the Royal Academy of History in the 19th century.

Contents: a gathering is missing at the beginning, so the *Etymologiae* begin with Book I, Chapter IV *De litteris latinis.*

On fol. 20v: Prologue to Book III: *Mathematica latine dicitur...*

On fol. 23v: *Expositio figurarum infra scripturarum*: the text continues with the following five geometric figures: nos. 23, 21, 19, 22 and 20 (as a result, figure 20 is grouped here—unlike the ms. RAH, Cod. 25—next to the other geometric figures). On fol. 24v, the

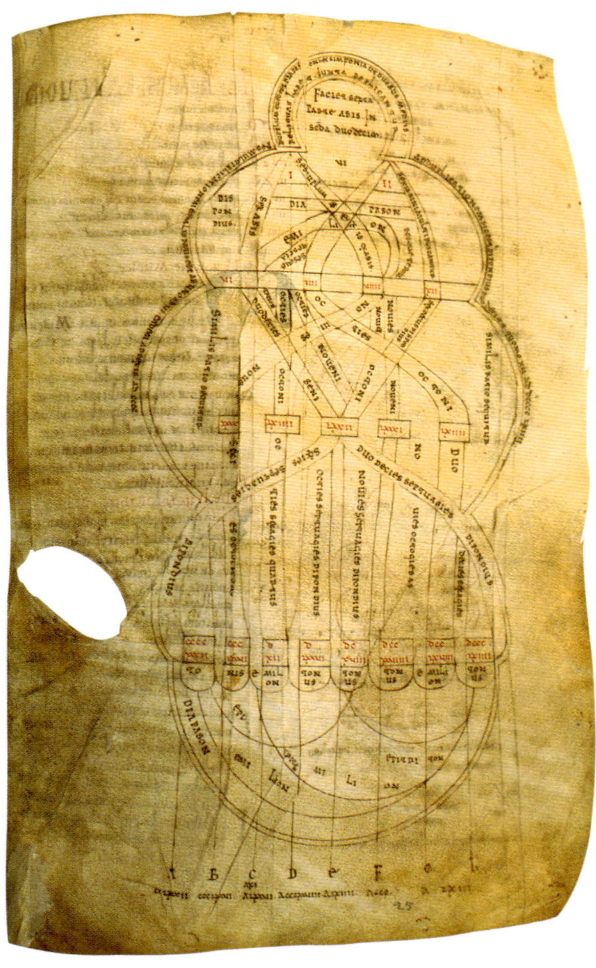

4. Isidorus. *Etymologiae.* Madrid, RAH, Cod. 76, 10th century (954), fol. 25r

five diagrams of harmonics nos. 24, 25, 26 and 27 are regrouped, and, at the bottom of the page, appears no. 30.

On fol. 25: the large diagram no. 31, that is 25 mm larger than the one in El Escorial, &.I.3, although it is 5 mm less than the one in San Millán (RAH Cod. 25). So: RAH Cod. 25 > RAH Cod. 76 > &.I.3.

The nine chapters of *De musica* begin on fol. 25v A (with the subtitle *Vocis species multae* in the middle of Chapter VI).

Fol. 108 (*Etymol.* XIV, ij) *Orbis terrae* (see Marcel Destombes, *Mappemondes, A.D. 1200-1500* (Amsterdam: Israel, 1964). In Book XVI (and not XV, as in the received text), Chapter I (*De civitatibus*), the place names are written in red; "Elogio de Zaragoza" (fol. 117 B).

Bibliography: Ruiz García 1997, 387. Shailor 1979, 444-473. Díaz y Díaz 1979, 120-122; 1971, 73.

9. El Escorial, Real Biblioteca, &.J.3 (olim H 7)
243 parchment folios; 352 × 255 mm in two 273 × 85 (90) mm columns. The pinpricks appear in the outside margins (not between the columns as occurred I in the previous manuscripts).

Binding: Moroccan leather with the El Escorial coat of arms (in the Form of a grille). Count-Duke of Olivares Library (18th century).

Script: Visigothic minuscule script produced in 1047 (1095 era) by Father Dominicus (colophon on fol. 242: see Millares Carlo, no. 52): fol. 243v (final guard): *Ista [scriptura] moçaraba apellatur vel toletana* (15th century). Some initials are ornithomorphic, others are just colored; in the margins of fols. 86-86v, symbol of the four Evangelists (see RAH Cod. 76).

Origin: Toledo, ecclesiastical metropolis of Spain: *liber tholetanus* (fol. I). The selected texts, figure and diagrams in this manuscript are closely linked to the ones in the manuscripts from La Rioja (RAH Cod. 25 and RAH Cod. 76).

Provenance: The Count-Duke of Olivares's collection, donated to the Monastery of El Escorial by his nephew, the Marquis of Heliche.

Contents: fols. 1-5: Correspondence between Ascaricio, Bishop of Asturias, and Tuseredio, published by Arévalo (reproduced in Migne, ed., *PL XCIX:* 1231-1240), according to this manuscript.

Fol. 6v: Full-page Oviedo Cross (*Les rois bibliophiles*, 16); fol. 7: 'labyrinth' with the inscription *Ob honorem sce. Marie virginis*; fols. 7v and 8, blank; fol. 8v: second labyrinth with the inscription *Sancio et Sancia librum* (Sancho II, King of Castile and León).

Fol. 9: title page of the *Etymologiae* (in colored capital letters): *In nomine simplo, trino, divino...* (as in RAH 25); fols.12-15v: the series of Isidore's and Braulio's letters; fol. 15v: chapters in Book I (Clark 1920, pl. 1); fols. 23v-25: under some Mozarabic arches, table of the various prosodic metres (see RAH, Cod. 25).

Fol. 57v: the five applied geometric figures (as in RAH Cod. 76, fol. 24); fol. 58: the five diagrams of harmonics (as in RAH Cod. 76, fol. 24v); fol. 58v: the large diagram of harmonics, 34 cm high; fol. 59 A: the final diagrams of harmonics and the four elements; fols. 59 B-61v: the 9 chapters of *De musica*: the subtitle *Vocis species multae* (fol. 60 A) is in Chapter VI.

Fol. 188: "Elogio de Zaragoza".

Fols. 234-239: seven excerpts from the Venerable Bede, *De natura rerum liber* (Jones 1975, 176, no. 31; excerpt from Chapter VIII of the Venerable Bede, *De temporum ratione* (Jones, 1975, 312-319); fol. 239: *Expositio de Isaiam prophetam* attribuyed to Gregorio Magno; fol. 240: *De Sybillinarum oraculis* and the Sybilline verses, *Judicii signum tellus sudore madescet* (see Anglès 1988, 296-297, table 1; fol. 242: *De septem planetis*).

Bibliography: Antolín 1911, 2: 331-336. García Villada 1923, pl. 27, facs. 36. Díaz y Díaz 1971, 72-73. Cordoliani 1951, 284-285. Sarriá, Lemaire and Elkhadem 1985, 16, 21, no. 2.

10. Madrid, Biblioteca Nacional, 10008 (olim Toledo 15.9).
246 fairly curled-up parchment folios, with holes, 320 × 250 mm. Thirty-one regular gatherings (quaternions); marginal prickings marking 36 horizontal lines in two columns. The catchword at the end of the gathering is often cut off by the binder's guillotine. Regarding the catchword in Visigothic manuscripts, see Vezin 1967.

Binding: wooden boards lined in unwaxed dark brown leather; traces of two seals; spine with three raised bands; title with very open quill: ISIDORUS AETHIMOLOGIARUM GOTHICUM.

Script: Very fine 11th century Visigothic minuscule (Millares Carlo 1999, 1: no. 165), in black ink, 36 lines per page. Initials and titles are in bright red. In the titles, sometimes a single term appears in green ink, with the others in black.

Origin: this manuscript, Arévalo's *Toletanus II*, has quite different origins from *Toletanus I* (Madrid, BN, glass case 14.3): probably Castile.

Provenance: entered the Biblioteca Nacional in 1868.

Contents: only the *Etymologiae*. The list of chapters in Book I differs from the one in *Toletanus I*.

In Book III, the figures and diagrams that appear between "Geometria" and "Musica" are drawn with a quill and are not colored. This also occurs with the five applied geometric diagrams; fol. 41: *Per rationem musicae*... and with the diagrams (facsimile in the catalog, *Trésors de la Biblioteca nacional,* 21): only the figures are written in red. fol. 41v is blank: the large diagram no. 31 has not been drawn.

The "Elogio de Zaragoza" (*Etymol.* XV, I, 66) appears on fol. 180v.

After fol. 246, three fragments have been regrouped that come from the binding reinforcements and contain passages from a short Penitential Psalm.

Bibliography: Díaz y Díaz 1971: 71. *Trésors de la Biblioteca Nacional* (Paris: Bibliothèque Nationale de France, 1988), 20, no. 3, with two facsimiles (fols. 41 and 41v).

11. PARIS, Bibliothèque Nationale de France, N. A. L. 2169.
385 parchment fols., 360 × 267 mm; in two columns each measuring <260 × 180 mm>, the left column with 29 lines (fols. 22-381) and the right column with 34 lines (382-385). Catchword with a cross superimposed at the end of the quaternions (see Vezin, 1967, 19).

Binding: wooden boards lined with fine leather (stuck to the upper back cover is part of the old flexible binding in goatskin with carved edges).

Script: very well formed Visigothic minuscule script, which is the work of two or three alternating copyists, finished on 24 August 1072 (see the facsimile of both scripts in Samaran and Marichel, 1981, pl. 15. The standard titles are in red Visigothic capitals.

Ornamentation: important; it has been analysed in detail by Avril et al. (1982) Initials are ornithomorphic (fols. 66v, 67...), zoomorphic (fols. 67 and subsq., fols. 83 and subsq., fol. 185v), anthropomorphic (fols. 292v, 370v), see examples chosen by Avril et al. (1982). The simple initials traced in black have been highlighted with a colored brushstroke.

Preliminary ornamentation (fols. 1-24v): fol. 2; Visigothic neumes *(probatio pennae)*; fols. 2v-4: *Ordo pascalis*; fols. 4v-5v: *Ratio pascalis*; fols. 5v-9: Calculation treatise (see Goméz Pallarés 1989-1990); fols. 9v-10: on two pages, huge astronomical circle, 170 mm in radius; series of Easter tables (with green and yellow as the predominant colors): Sunday letters (fol. 13), two charts (fols. 14v-15) and two circles to calculate the date of Easter (15v-16); fol. 17: labyrinth that is 172 mm in diameter (reproduced by Kern, 2000, p. 112, no. 183), in the top right-hand corner: *Sphera terrae* (added); fol. 17v: framed table with the signs of the zodiac; fols. 18-18v: Sunday letters; fols. 19v-20 (in four circles): the phases of the moon, reproduced in Avril, 1982, pl. 8) in four circles, table with the hours of sunlight during the four seasons; fol. 20v: *Psallere usum esse primum post Moysen David prophetam*...; fol. 21: *Termini Septuagesimae, Paschae et Pentecosten;* fol. 21v: checkerboard, framed in the four corners by interlacing that ends in a duck's head (facsimile in color: Mentré 1996, pl. 4) that forms the name of the priest Ericone, scribe or donor of this manuscript (see the ms. El Escorial, &.J.3); according to Samaran and Marichal (1981), this must be the donor, because the writing shows the homogenous style of two or three scribes (see further back).

Fols. 22-24v: Calendar: two months a page, each one under a Mozarabic arcade; typical calendar from the Abbey of Silos (Vives and Fábrega 1949, 348 and 374-380).

Origin: Silos, undoubtedly: on fol. 2, ex libris de Silos (18th century). The manuscript was begun between the Council of Jaca (1063) and Council of Burgos (1081), which both prescribed the abolition of the old 'Mozarabic' rite: Díaz y Díaz (1983) also points out that the preliminary ornamentation, that was destined for an antiphonary or a sacramentary, was used in these circumstances as the preface to the *Etymologiae*. Fols. 37-38: note on the consecration of the altars of the Abbey church by Cardinal Richard, papal envoy, in 1088 (see Férotin 1897, 72).

Provenance: sold in Madrid in 1877, the manuscript was purchased in Paris in 1878, by Bachelin Deflorenne and resold to the Biblioteca Nacional (see Delisle 1891).

Contents: The *Etymologiae*: correspondence between Braulio and Isidore; fol. 28v B: "Incipit Praefatio totius libri, Braulioni Isidorus: En tibi sicut pollicitus…"; fol. 29 A: table of chapters in Book I; fol. 77v: the small geometric figures (figure 1, nos. 1-17; fol. 78v: the applied geometic circles (facsimile in Huglo, 1992, 12); fol. 79: the interpolated musical diagrams, as in Madrid, BN, 10008; fol. 79v, at the top of the page: "Secundum Porfyrium et Platonem haec forma exponitur" (see Madrid, BN, glass case 14.3, fol. 27), but in this case the rest of the page is blank; fols. 80 A-83 A: The nine chapters of "Musica": on fol. 80v B, the heading *Vocis specie multe* (sic).

Fol. 193: *stemma* I, on kinship links (*Etymol.* IX, vj, 28); fol. 195, consanguinity tree (*Etymol.* IX, vj, 28, *Stemma* II); fol. 264: *Orbis terrae*: the three parts of the world (Destombes, 1964 pl. 2); fol. 288v, below: the "Elogio de Zaragoza"; fol. 385: Colophon (see transcription and study in Samaran and Marichal 1981).

Bibliography: Samaran and Marichal 1981. Avril et al. 1982, 18-20, no. 26 and plates B (fol. 23, calendar), VI (fol. 77v), VII (initials of fols. 67, 185v, 292v and 315v) and VIII (fol. 19v). Díaz y Díaz 1983, 346, nos. 46 and 453, no. 187; 1971, 70-80. Gómez Pallarés 1989-1990, 133-142. Huglo 1992, 565-578. Mentré 1996, pl. 4, fol. 21v.

THE TWO PORTUGUESE MANUSCRIPTS

The *Inventario dos Codices Illuminados até 1500* (Lisbon, 1994 and 2001) brought to light two manuscripts of the *Etymologiae* that had been unknown until then, written in continental minuscule but copied on manuscripts in Visigothic minuscule, with the texts and interpolated diagrams of harmonics.

12. LISBON, Biblioteca Nacional, Alcobaça 446.
220 parchment folios, 428 × 292 mm <330 × 202 mm>, in two columns; 37 lines per page. The first 25 gatherings are numbered; the following ones (xxvi-xxvij) have a catchword at the end. Standard title in the top margin.

Binding: period binding in white skin; five bosses on the covers.

Origin and provenance: the Cistercian Abbey of Alcobaça, near Lisbon, founded in 1153 by Alfonso I. The 456 Alcobaça manuscripts went to the Biblioteca Nacional de Portugal in 1834, when the religious orders were dissolved.

Script: minuscule from the 12th century that adopts Visigothic spelling; the titles are written in small capitals, as in Visigothic manuscripts.

Content: The manuscript contains the *Etymologiae*, with the interpolations of the [γ] family, followed (fols. 205-219) by Isidore of Seville's *De natura rerum.*

After the seven letters from the correspondence between Isidore and Braulio (fols. 1-3), and the Chapters of the twenty books (fols. 3 B-3v A), the letter to Braulio *En tibi* and the xxv chapters in Book I (fol. 3v) appear.

Fol. 22: Preface to Book III: *Mathematica latine dicitur…*; fol. 32: geometric and (fol. 32v) harmonic diagrams, to which the artist added astronomical figure no. 24 (phases of the moon) and in seven semicircles, the cycle of the seven planets showing their influence on human temperament; fol. 33: the large diagram, drawn with a ruler and compass, flanked in the top left-hand part by the lambda-shaped diagram of the commentary on the *Timaeus* (no. 28) and below on the right, by the figure of the four elements (no. 29).

Fol. 33v: the nine chapters of *De musica*, with the rubric "Vocis species multae" in Chapter VI (fol. 34 A).

Fol. 94: before *stemma* I, on family ties (*Etymol.* IX, vi, 28), the verses *Crux [haec] alma gerit sanctorum corpora fratrum* and the announcement of Isidore's, Leandro's and his sister Florentia's deaths appear (see Paris, BNF, N. A. L. 2169); fol. 96: the consanguinity tree held up by a man without a crown (see illustration 5 and the facsimile in color in the *Inventario*, vol. 1, p. 233). The trees usually appear without any ornamentation: see Schadt 1982).

Fol. 138: the three parts of the world (*Etymol.* XIV, ij: see the following manuscript, fol. 129).

Fol. 205-219: Isidore of Seville, *De natura rerum* (see Fontaine 1960; critical edition based on the oldest manuscripts). Regarding the figures and diagrams, see Gorman (2001).

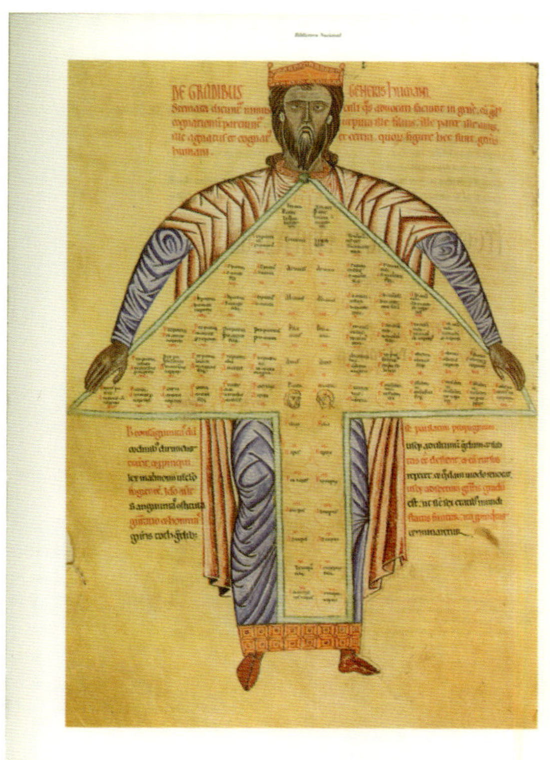

5. Isidorus. *Etymologiae*. Lisbon, BN, Alcobaça 446, 11th century, fol. 96r

Bibliography: Leclercq 1950. Amos 1990, 236-238. Duarte Ferreira 1994, 1: 232, no. 342.

13. PORTO, Biblioteca Pública Municipal, ms. 21 (Santa Cruz, 17).
186 parchment fols., 411 × 293 mm; in two columns with 39 lines.

Binding: in poor condition; wooden boards lined with skin, spine with four raised bands.

Script: standard from the first quarter of the 13th century, with traces of Visigothic minuscule (facsimile in the Nascimento and Merinhos, 453, illustration IX). Titles have red and black deepset initials.

Origin: Santa Cruz de Coimbra, a monastery of canons who followed the rule of St. Augustine, and who came from Saint Ruf of Avignon to settle in Portugal in the early 12th century. When the religious orders were suppressed in Portugal (1834), the Santa Cruz manuscripts were moved to Porto.

Content: The *Etymologiae*, beginning with seven letters from the correspondence between Isidore and Braulio, the chapters of the twenty books (fol. 3A), Isidore's letter to Braulio *En tibi* (fol. 3B), and the chapters in Book I.

Fol. 36v: chapter *De figuris geometriae (Etymol.* III, xij) is followed by (fol. 37 A) five applied geometric figures, the figure of the phases of the moon (no. 24); the diagrams of harmonics nos. 25, 26 and 27; and at the foot of the page, linear diagram no. 30: the semicircles that show the numerical relations that produce double and triple proportions (but not quadruples) are drawn below the number line, while on the following page (37v A), on the same diagram repeated vertically, the semicircles are drawn at the top. In column B, Plato's *lambda* diagram appears, and then, below this, there are seven semicircles that describe the cycle of the planets and their influence on human temperament.

On fol. 38, a large, full-page diagram of the musical scale appears (no. 31): the geometric drawing is in red, and the numbers of the levels are written in black (Reduced facsimile in *Inventario*, II no. 260; Isabel Santos, *Santa Cruz...* p. 256). In short, the use of colors is opposite to that in the Visigothic manuscripts we have described before; fol. 38v is blank.

Fol. 39 A: the nine chapters of "Musica" (fol. 39v A, in red): *Vocis species multae*.

Fol. 91v B: in Book IX, vj, before stemmata I and II (with no character holding up the gráfico): VERSUS IN SEPULCRO DOMNI ISIDORI: *Crux haec alma fulget*. In the middle of the column, in red: DATATIO OBITUUM LEANDRI, ISIDORI ET FLORENTIAE: *Obiit felicis memoriae*. (See Lisbon, BN, Alcobaça 446 and Paris, BNF, N. A. L. 2169.)

On fol. 129: *Orbis terrae (Etymol.* XIV, ij): a 'map of the world' divided into three parts, each of which is attributed to Noah's children (Gen. 5:31): Asia (Sem), Africa (Cham), Europa (Japhet). (See illustration 6 and Destombes 1964.)

Fol. 139 A: at the top, the "Elogio de Zaragoza" (*Etymol.* XV, I, 66).

Fol. 185 B: by a second hand: *Ex concilio apud Theodonis villam* (false capitulary of Thioville: Migne, ed., *PL XCVII:* 677-678).

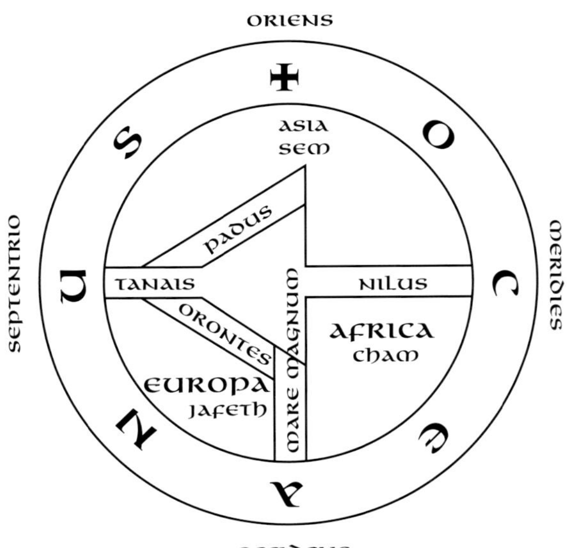

6. Isidorus. *Etymologiae*, Porto, BPM, ms. 21 (Santa Cruz 17), 11th century *ex.*-12th century *in.*, fol. 129r. *Orbis terrae*

Bibliography: Nascimento and Merinhos 1998, 110-112, 453 (illustration IX). Santos 2001, 248, 252, 254, 256 and 270-271. Duarte Ferreira 2001, 2: no. 260.

Ms. 21 is quoted in the review of the *Inventario* published in *Scriptorium* 57 (2003): no. 522.

From this inventary, it can be deduced that, out of the 13 manuscripts of the *Etymologiae* in the Hispanic family, broadly considered, there are only a few pieces of evidence left that help us to restore the diagrams of harmonics in their original order. Of course, we need to reject the El Escorial manuscripts, &.I.14 (incomplete), P.I.6 and T.II.14, as well as the Porto manuscript, BPM, 21 (diagrams are out of order) and finally, the manuscript P.I.8 in El Escorial that, destined for Maguelonne in Septimania, seems to be far removed from the *interpolated* Hispanic family.

Consequently, these diagrams will be reconstructed based on the Madrid manuscript, BN, glass case 14.3, the two La Rioja manuscripts, and the Toledo manuscript, El Escorial, &.I.3, finished in 1047.

Study of the diagrams of harmonics

The first observation that ensues from an analysis of the thirteen manuscripts that contain the diagrams of harmonics is the confusion caused by a deficient page layout. In fact, instead of placing the geometric figures applied to astronomy and the diagrams of harmonics at Book IV *De astronomia*, they were placed at the end of Chapter IX (xxiij) *De numeris musicis*, truly very summarily. The interpolater regrouped all of these additions taken from just after Chapter III (xij) in the Book *De geometria*, which were previously taken, both text and figures, from Cassiodorus's *Institutiones*.

As a result, the first task that needs to be carried out is to untangle the two interpolated treatises, which is something that the editors have carefully avoided, and then to reconstruct the order of the texts and diagrams of harmonics, because the copyists moved these on numerous occasions to regroup these additions in Book III of the *Etymologiae* as well as they possibly could.

The order of the texts and diagrams of harmonics, which has been fairly well maintained in one of the oldest manuscripts as well as in the La Rioja manuscripts, is as follows:

> 1. Per rationem musicae ita fit ut aut septem mensuum nati aut novem vivere possint, octo nunquam, quoniam in septem vel in novem omnes inveniuntur symphoniae, quibus integris firmae stabilitatis crescunt... hoc septies ductis faciunt septimanam et novies faci[unt] novem mensuum.

This text, published by Charles Upson Clark, on the numbers used to create the harmonies[44] and the numbers of months of a pregnancy, is followed by the diagram of the phases of the moon (no. 24): in the ms. in El Escorial, T.II.24, the drawing of the crescent of the moon under the line with the numbers II, III, IIII, V, VI, VII, VIII and VIIII is empty, whereas in the Arévalo's diagram (fig. 1), the crescent is too sloped and blackened.

2. The two following diagrams (nos. 25 and 26) show the numerical ratios that are the basis of the consonances, but these diagrams contains certain lexical as well as graphic errors, i.e., errors in the links between the various numbers that show the two terms in numerical ratios, which form the arithmetic foundation of the consonances. These errors are corrected in fig. 2. This is how the author establishes

the list of the following consonances: 3/2 or *hemiole* (*emilion* in all of the analysed manuscripts, instead of *hemiolion*), the foundation of the consonance of the fifth; *epitriton* (4/3), foundation of the consonance of the fourth; *diplasion*, double ratio (2/1 or its multiples 12/6, 18/9 etc.), foundation of the octave (*diapason*) and not the double octave (*disdiapason*, as in diagram no. 27); the triple ratio (3/1 or its multiples 12/4, 18/6, etc.), foundation of the twelth or octave plus fifth (and not *disdiapason*, as in diagrams nos. 25 and 26).

FIGURE 2: THE INTERPOLATED DIAGRAMS FROM *MUSICA ISIDORI* CORRECTED AND REORGANIZED

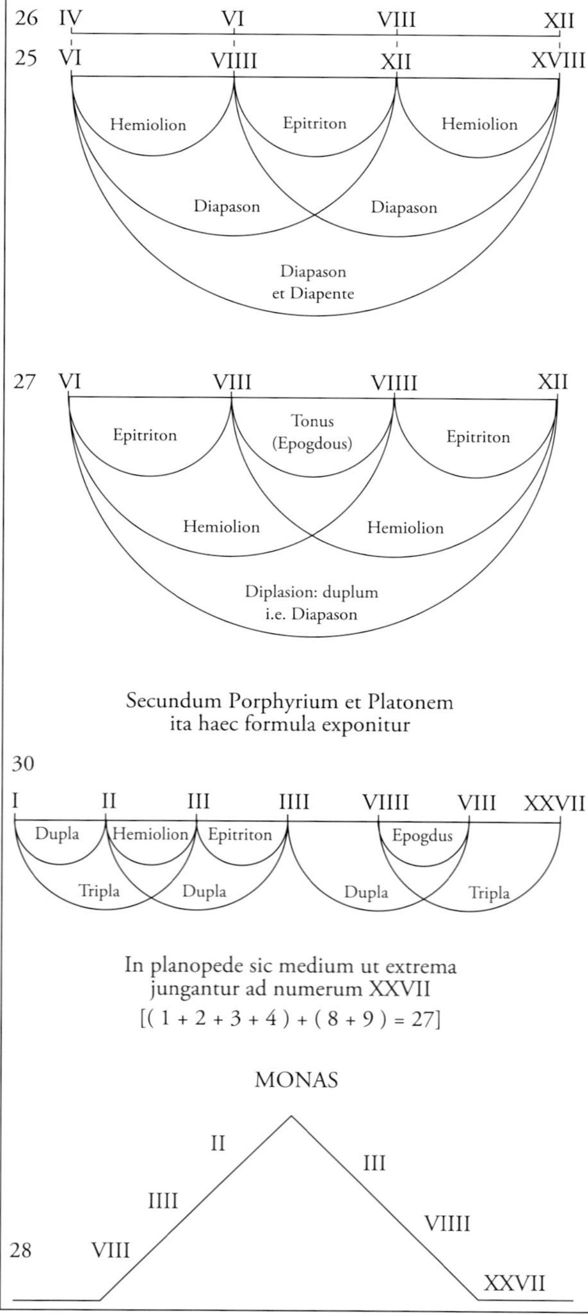

3. Diagram no. 27, made up of the numbers VI, VIII, VIIII and XII, is the most important of the three that form this series, because this is the *Tetraktys*[45] attributed to Pythagoras by Iamblichos, his biographer,[46] that shows the diagram in this way: this diagram established the three main harmonies, as well as the ratio *epogdous* (9/8), the basis of the tone, which is the result of the difference between fifth and fourth (3/2 × 3/4 = 9/8).

ς' η' θ' ιβ'
(6) (8) (9) (12)

Another linear diagram, drawn in the Greek manuscripts, was possibly used as a model for this diagram no. 27:

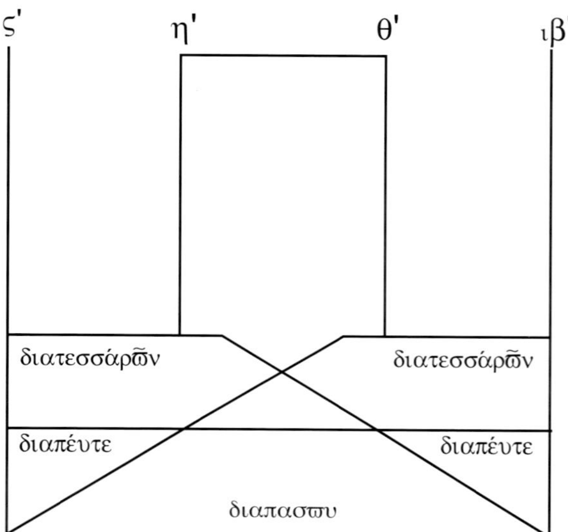

All that was needed was to add the arches linking the various figures translated into Latin: translating Greek numbers into Roman numerals was never a problem for cultured men in late Antiquity and the High Middle Ages: the *Regula formatarum Attici* of the Pontifical Chancery pointed out precisely that “anyone with the slightest notion of Greek knows perfectly well that the letters in the Greek alphabet can also be used to express numbers”.[47]

4. *RATIO INFERIORES FORMAE.* This title, in small capital letters, was read wrongly by copyists and reproduced wrongly by Lindsay;[48] in fact, it should read *inferioris* and not *interioris*, which makes no sense here, because this is the "Evaluation of the diagram located below". *Form* or *formula* are the usual terms used in this treatise to designate a geometric figure or a diagram about musical theory: in this case, the diagram located below is the linear diagram no. 30 in fig. 2.

In this short commentary on the series of figures that Plato lists to expound his theory of the 'composition of the soul of the world',[49] the anonymous author makes numerous remarks on the numbers in this diagram. First, he explains why the VIII goes before the IX in the series of numbers that constitute the *cosmopoeia*: the number 8, because it is the number 2 raised to power of 3, can represent three dimensions, whereas the 9, raised to the power of 2, refers only to a surface, which is less perfect than a three-dimensional figure.

This subtle argument could be refuted by a much simpler observation: when Plato drew the alternate arrangement of even and odd numbers on each side of the *lambda* diagram on the floor of the Academy (fig. 2, no. 28), he inevitably placed the VIIII before the VIII.

A second observation on the numbers in the linear diagram: the number VI is a perfect number for several wellknown reasons from Euclid up to Isidore himself, who took up these same reasons in his work *De numeris*.[50]

To conclude, the author points out that the sum of the Tetrad (I + II + III + IV), plus the sum of the numbers VIIII and VIII, equals XXVII, which is the upper limit of the numbers in the diagram.

This conclusion to the short exposition on the numbers preceding the linear diagram was omitted by Lindsay, who undoubtedly had not seen the heading "Secundum Porphyrium et Platonem ita haec forma exponitur" (according to Porphyrius and Plato, this diagram is shown in this way).

The preceding text refers to to the Commentary by Porphyry on Plato's *Timaeus,* which is now lost but which Macrobius cited twice[51] and used numerous times in his *Commentarii in Somnium Scipionis*:[52] on the basis of these quotes that were reorganized in the order of the chapters of the *Timaeus,* Angelo Sodano reconstructed by conjecture this commentary that is now lost.[53]

The continuation of this paragraph commenting on the linear diagram no. 30 is interrupted by the large full-page diagram no. 31. This is the *lambda* no. 28 drawn for the first time on parchment in Theon of Smyrna's treatise, 'Exposition of questions in mathematics that are useful for reading Plato'.[54] In this work, however, the α [alpha] unit does not appear on the top vertex of the lambda but is replaced by the term *monas,* the monad, the first principle in the various spheres of science: the indivisible unit in arithmetic, the point in geometry, and the indivisable atom in physics. This term *(monas),* which Plato only used on five occasions in his dialogues, was repeated more than 200 times by his commentators: we can find it in Latin in the writings of Ambrosius of Milan, in Macrobius, and also in the final chapter of the *De musica* by Isidore, titled *De numeris musicis*.

In short, all of the texts and small diagrams that we have found up to now are merely a prelude to the construction of the large full-page diagram, commonly found in the manuscripts of the Iberian Peninsula that contain Isidore of Seville's *Etymologiae*.

The large diagram

The large diagram printed in Arévalo's and Lindsay's editions is, of course extraordinarily large, measuring at least 27 × 34.5 cm. Its surprising appearance is explained in another commentary on the *Timaeus*, by Proclus Diadochus († 496):[55] in fact, this learned philosopher distinguishes in his predecessors's work two ways of providing a graphic interpretation of Plato's complicated passage on harmony, 'the soul of the physical world':

1. By means of three triangles fitted together that include the *lambda* (no. 28) with seven numbers at the base; at the top, there is the diagram of harmonic and arithmetical ratios (VI, VIII, VIIII, XII and their equivalents, as in Calcidius's diagram VIII); finally, at the top there is the third triangle that establishes a scale of tones and semitones. This large diagram, attributed to Adrastus of Aphrodisias, was known in the West, because it appears in many Latin manuscripts that show the Latin translation of the *Timaeus* without Calcidius's commentary.[56]

2. Other commentators, Proclus points out, reject the *lambda*-shaped figure and arrange the three categories of numbers in a straight line, just as in the process of dividing the monochord. This is the solution adopted by Porphyry and Severus in their commentaries on the *Timaeus*.

The large diagram in the Visigothic manuscripts is a variant of the first procedure, although it is difficult to read, because all of the operations undertaken to construct the diagram are described in great detail in certain channels that link both terms in the arithmetic operations in question. To simplify things, these operations have been clearly transcribed in figure 3 by placing a Roman numeral at each level that refers back to our commentary.

The figure 3 as a whole is not covered by a triangular "small roof", but by a horseshoe arch, shaped like an omega [Ω], which is typical of the Mozarabic style of architecture. All the numbers in this diagram, except for the ones on level V, are drawn in red ink.

Level I: the diagram starts out from the number 6, the aforementioned *senarius perfectus*.

Level II: consists of the *Tetraktys* (VI, VIII, VIIII and XII) described in diagram no. 27.

FIGURE 3: THE GREAT ISIDORIAN DIAGRAM

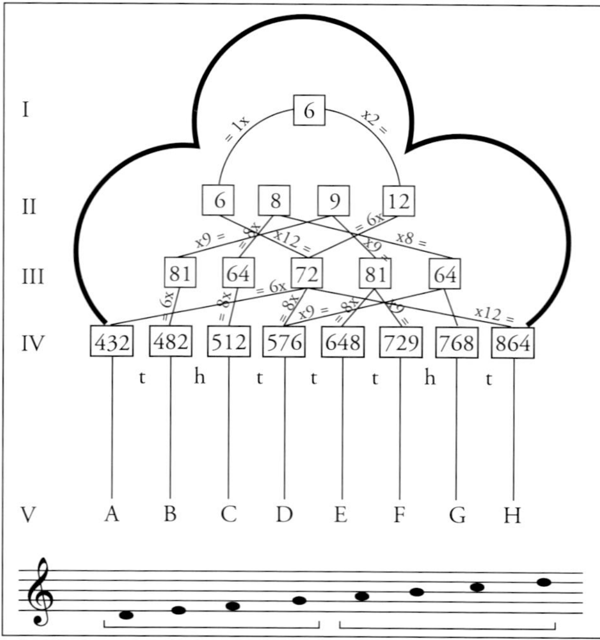

Level III: by multiplying the number 6 by the numbers in the *Tetraktis* or multiplying the latter by each other we obtain a series of five numbers.

Level IV: by using these five numbers once again, we obtain a series of seven numbers, under which the terms *tonus* or *hemilion* appear (instead of *hemitonion*, as on the previous occasion): these notes should be copied between the figures and not below them, because they define the nature of the musical interval between two numbers. In fact, if we move the terms towards the left of the diagram, it is quite clear that a number at the beginning of the series is missing; this number, once restored by the calculation (486 × 8/9), is 432. If we control the remaining numbers in the series, this enables us to discover other small errors, undoubtedly due to a faulty reading of the three-digit numbers written in Greek numerical letters.

This correction leads us to a series of numbers comparable to the ones found in the Timaeus of Locri[57] and in Proclus:

Timaeus of Locri:
384 432 486 512 576 648 729 768 864 972...

Proclus Diadochus:
384 432 486 512 576 648 729 768

Diagram 31:
432 486 512 576 648 729 768 864

The second system for determining the exactitude of the numbers in the diagram is based on *lambda* no. 28, which includes all of the numbers in the large diagram as part of several layers of multiplications (see figure 4).

Level V: Handling the numbers selected in this way results in a musical scale in which notes are the first eight letters in the Latin alphabet (which bears no relationship with medieval alphabetic notation): transcribed into modern notation, this scale is reduced to an octave that includes two symmetrical separate tetrachords, with the semitone in the middle.

Below the alphabetic notation a series of numbers appears that is written in black and not in red as in the previous cases: in our transcription,[58] we have omitted this new series, because it does not correspond to any interpretation attempted through calculations.

FIGURE 4: Expansion of the diagram of the soul of the world

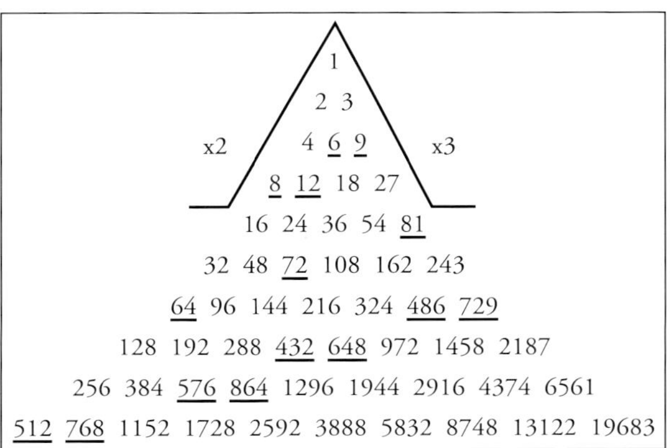

In short, this scale is somewhere between the *tonal system* used in Byzantine chant[59] and the scale of Carolingian chant established in *Musica* and *Scolica enchiriadis*[60] (figure 5). Its central octave is identical to that in the tonal system of Byzantine and Carolingian chant: this similarity is all the more surprising if we bear in mind that the scale in Mozarabic chant never crossed the Pyrenees and that, furthermore, the *Musica* and *Scolica enchiriadis,* probably composed in Werden on the Ruhr river,[61] despite the variety of its sources, gives no evidence whatsoever of contact with the *Musica Isidori.*

FIGURE 5: Comparison of scales from classic Antiquity

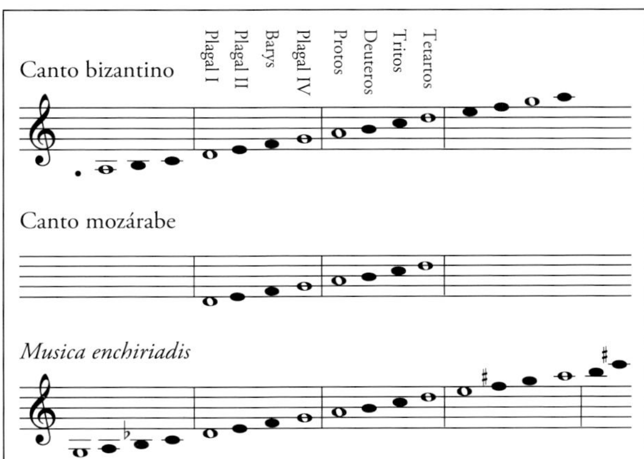

So we need to investigate the common source of these two scales of Latin chant. The common source is clearly Byzantine chant; even more so if we bear in mind that the low *G* (or [γ]), according to Oliver Strunk,[62] appears in some pieces of Byzantine chant (I have represented this using a dot): so that in the low tones we then have a tetrachord that is identical to the tetrachord of the *low notes* in the *Musica enchiriadis.* If the scale described in this treatise includes higher notes than the scale in Byzantine chant, this is because of the wide range of the vocal exercises in certain pieces in the *G* mode, to be more precise, the endless alleluia *melodiae* notated in the Aquitainian manuscripts and in the margins of the Antiphonary of León. Finally, the repertoire of Mozarabic chant, as is also the case with the Carolingian chant that comes from Gallican chant, includes a certain number of pieces sung in Greek that have been transliterated in Latin minuscule or translated from Greek.[63] In short, the scale of Mozarabic chant is closely linked to the scale of Carolingian chant, both of which come from the *octoechos*.

The treatise interpolated between *De geometria* and *De musica* ends with a diagram of the four elements that is quite different from those that Isidore had placed in his *De natura rerum*[64] dedicated to King Sisebut. This philosophical question that Plato tackled in the *Timaeus* (55d-62d) appears both in this anonymous treatise and in the other commentaries on the *Timaeus*.

It is clear that the treatise on harmony in the eleven Visigothic manuscripts and the two Portuguese manuscripts was written in the southern part of the Iberian Peninsula and was copied in a Mozarabic environment, probably before 730, because the model of the El Escorial manuscript, T.II.24, undoubtedly dates from 733. Furthermore, this treatise is not the original, but is a superficial adaptation of a commentary on the *Timaeus*, enriched by commentaries by Porphyry and Proclus.

The errors in reading the numbers written in Greek characters and the lexical errors (*Emilion* instead of *Hemitonion* or *Hemiolion* further back) seem to show that the Greek was translated or adapted into Latin by three authors working together: one reader who read the Greek text aloud, sometimes with mistakes if the model was written in uncial script; a translator who translated the Greek literally into Latin; and a copyist who wrote down what the translator dictated and confused those terms that he had recorded wrongly.[65]

The ideal region in Spain for the spread of Greek texts from southern Italy or North Africa may well have been Cartagena, where Isidore was born. This town, as an exarchate of Byzantium, may well have played a role similar to Ravenna in the cultural sphere, although it was not as important. In any case, a scholar who knew both the *Etymologiae* and Greek literature could have translated this treatise and added diagrams to develop the content in Chapter IX (xxiij) *De numeris musicis* by Isidore. However, unlike the treatises on harmony that remain in the realm of pure theory, this brief treatise had practical consequences, because it led to the definition of the scale used in contemporary chant. To sum up, that this marvellous treatise could reach us, fortunately, was due to the manuscript tradition of the Iberian Peninsula.[66]

Notes

[1] León, AC, ms. 22, fols. 38v-88v. See Agustín Millares Carlo, et al., eds. *Corpus de códices visigóticos*. Vol. 1, *Estudios*; vol. 2, *Álbum*. Las Palmas de Gran Canaria: Gobierno de Canarias, UNED, Centro Asociado de Las Palmas de Gran Canaria, 1999. Reproduction in color of fols. 38v-39r, text of letters A, B, I and II in Lindsay's edition. [Wallace Martin Lindsay, ed. *Isidori Hispalensis episcopi Etymologiarum sive Originum Libri XX*. Oxford: Clarendon Press, 1911 (Oxford Classical Texts).] See José Madoz. *Epistolario de san Braulio de Zaragoza*. Madrid: Imprenta Aldecoa, 1941; and Luis Riesco Terrero. *Epistolario de san Braulio*. Seville: Editorial Católica Española, 1975 (Anales de la Universidad Hispalense: Filosofía y Letras 31).

[2] In five very old manuscripts, including El Escorial, T.II.24 (described below) and Toledo, BC, 15-11 (illustration 1), the number of fifteen books is due to an error of interpretation: see the critical edition by José Carlos Martín, ed. *Scripta de vita Isidori Hispalensis episcopi*. Turnhout: Brepols, 2006, 186-187 (Corpus Christianorum: Series Latina 113B). I would like to thank the author for kindly having sent me the introduction and text of his new edition.

[3] Regarding the history of the manuscript of the *Epistolarium*, copied in Córdoba between 820 and 835, see José Madoz. Op. cit.; and Manuel C. Díaz y Díaz. "La circulation des manuscrits dans la Péninsule Ibérique du VIIIe au XIe siècle". *Cahiers de Civilisation Médiévale* 12 (1969): 224-225.

[4] Letter II is undated: it follows the conclusion to the *Synonyma* that Isidore sent to the Archdeacon Braulio (*Ep.* B, l. 13). It was written seven years before the following request (*Ep.* IV) and also prior to the fourth Council of Toledo in 633, and, as a result, would date from 625-626. Regarding the chronology of these letters, see Luis Riesco Terreiro (op. cit.) and José Carlos Martín (op. cit.).

[5] Dag Ludwig Norberg. "Etymologie et changement de sens". In Ritva Jacobsson and Folke Sandgren, eds. *Au seuil du Moyen Âge*. Vol. 2, *Études linguistiques, métriques et littéraires publiées par ses collègues et élèves à l'occasion de son 65e anniversaire*. Stockholm: Kungliga Vitterhets Historie och Antikvitets Akademien, 1998, 61 (Filologiskt arkiv: 40).

[6] Jacques Fontaine, ed. *Isidore de Séville. Traité de la nature*. Bordeaux: Féret, 1960, 167-169 (Bibliothèque de l'École des Hautes Études Hispaniques: 28). (Reprinted, Turnhout: Brepols, 2002.)

[7] On Braulio's role in the genesis of the *Etymologiae*, see the bilingual edition of St. Isidore of Seville. *Etimologiae*. Manuel C. Díaz y Díaz, Manuel Antonio Marcos Casquero and José Oroz Reta, eds. Madrid: Biblioteca de Autores Cristianos, 1982. Vol. 1 (books 1-10): 4, *La llamada edición brauliana:* 177-180.

[8] The manuscript in El Escorial, &.I.14 measures 515 × 365 cm. See the above description of the manuscripts of the *Etymologiae*.

[9] The various *titles* are subdivided into *capitula* or *chapters*, with a specific numbering for each new *title* instead of continuous numbers for the entire book, as occurs in most editions, especially in those by Wallace Martin Lindsay (1920) and José Oroz Reta (1982): these two editors also add a number for each new phrase.

[10] Jacques Fontaine. "Isidore de Séville et l'astrologie". *Revue des Études Latines* 31 (1953): 300 and no. 1. See also the article by the same author. "Problèmes de méthode dans l'étude des sources isidoriennes". In Manuel C. Díaz y Díaz, ed. *Isidoriana. Colección de estudios sobre Isidoro de Sevilla*. León: Centro de Estudios e Investigación San Isidoro (CSIC-CECEL), 1961, 115-132.

[11] Paul Joachim Georg Lehmann. "*Cassiodor-Studien*". In *idem. Erforschung des Mittelalters: Ausgewählte Abhandlungen und Aufsätze*. 2 vols. Stuttgart: Anton Hiersemann, 1959, 1962. Vol. 2: 38-109. Regarding the dating of the *Institutiones*, see page 41.

[12] Critical edition of the *Institutiones* by Roger Aubrey Baskerville Mynors. *Cassiodori Senatoris Institutiones*. Oxford: Clarendon Press, 1937, 142-150; on p. 193, Mynors provides the list of fragments that Isidore (*Etymol.* I-IV) borrowed from the *Institutiones*. Regarding the Monastery of Vivarium, see Pierre Courcelle. "Le site du monastère de Cassiodore". Article from 1938 published in *Opuscula selecta*. Paris: Études Augustiniennes, 1984, 27-75; and "Nouvelles recherches sur le monastère de Cassiodore". Article from 1957, reproduced in *ibidem*, 137-154. We must not forget that in the age of sailing, Calabria was at least two weeks away from the south-eastern end of the Iberian Peninsula.

[13] Louis Holtz. "Quelques aspects de la tradition et de la diffusion des *Institutiones*". In Sandro Leanza, ed. *Flavio Magno Aurelio Cassiodoro: atti della settimana di studi. Cosenza-Squillace, 19-24 settembre 1983.* Catanzaro: Rubbettino, 1986.

[14] R. A. B. Mynors. *Cassiodori Senatoris Institutiones.* Oxford: Clarendon Press, 1937, 145, l. 22 (bk. II, chap. 8)-148, l. 19 (bk. II, chap. 15) and 149, l. 10 (bk. II, chap. 10)-150, l. 18 (bk. II, chap. 11) of *De musica.* In his *De institutione arithmetica* [140, ls. 17-20 (bk. II, chap. 7)], Cassiodore alludes to the Latin translation by Boethius of Nicomachus's own *De arithmetica.*

[15] In *De musica,* III, xvj, 1, and III, xxij, 2, Isidore establishes a parallel between Tubal, a blacksmith who uses a hammer *(malleator),* and Pythagoras, author of the "law of consonant sounds" discovered while he was listening to blacksmiths working with hammers of various weights. In 615-616, and then in 626, Isidore had formulated in Chapter XIV of his *Crónicas* a different explanation of the origin of music, which he then attributed to Jubal; see José Carlos Martin, ed. *Isidori Hispalensis Chronica.* Turnhout: Brepols, 2003 (Corpus Christianorum: Series Latina 112). I sincerely thank Professor José Carlos Martín for pointing out to me this variant of a story told by Isidore, which until now has gone unnoticed by all musicologists.

[16] See Michel Huglo. "Exercicia vocum". In David Hiley and Janka Szendrei, eds. *Laborare fratres in unum. Festschrift László Dobszay zum 60. Geburtstag.* Hildesheim: Weidmann, 1995, 117-123 (Spolia Berolinensia: 7). On the importance of the vocal qualities of church cantors in Medieval and Renaissance Spain, see François Reynaud. *La polyphonie tolédane et son milieu, des premiers témoignages aux environs de 1600.* Turnhout: Brepols, 1996 (Documents, Études, Recherches: 50).

[17] Michel Huglo. "Les arts libéraux dans le *Liber glossarum*". *Scriptorium* 55 (2001): 3-33, plates 1-4: article reproduced in *idem. La théorie de la musique antique et médiévale.* Aldershot: Ashgate, 2005, art. III + addenda et corrigenda (Variorum Collected Studies Series). The fragment of the Archivo Diocesano de Barcelona, described by Jesús Alturo i Perucho. "Fragment d'un epitom del *Glossarium Ansileubi* de la primera meitat del segle x". *Faventia* 7 (1985): 75-85, must be added to the manuscripts described in this article. Juan Carlos Asensio kindly informed me about this article.

[18] The edition of the interpolated fragments appears in Michel Huglo. *Ibidem,* 28-31.

[19] In this regard, see *ibidem,* 30 and note 38. Remember Isidore's remark (*Etymol.* VI, vij, 1): "Marcus Terentius Varro innumerabiles libros scripsit".

[20] Josef Martin, and Klaus Daur, eds. *Sancti Aurelii Augustini. De doctrina christiana. De vera religione.* Turnhout: Brepols, 1962, 52 (Corpus Christianorum: Series Latina 32).

[21] Michel Huglo. "Les diagrammes d'harmonique interpolés dans les manuscrits hispaniques de la *Musica Isidori*". *Scriptorium* 48 (1994): 171-186. Article reproduced in *idem. Les anciens répertoires de plain-chant.* Aldershot: Ashgate, 2005, art. IX (Variorum Collected Studies Series).

[22] See the list of these 29 manuscripts according to Elias Avery Lowe. *Codices latini antiquiores (CLA)* (Oxford: Clarendon Press, 1934-1972), 12 volumes: 1 (Vatican City), no. 39; 2 (Great Britain), nos. 131 and 144; 3 (Italy), nos. 284, 353 and 370; 5 (Paris) nos. 559, 561 and 647; 7 (Switzerland), nos. 854, 879, 983, 995; 8 (Germany) nos. 1049, 1077, 1189, 1194, 1225; 9 (Germany, 2) nos. 1332, 1380 and 1386; 10 (Austria, Belgium... Holland), nos. 1465, 1554 and 1581; 11 (... Spain...), nos. 1630, 1635 and 1638; 12 (supplement), no. 1674.

[23] Walter Porzig. "Die Rezensionen der *Etymologiae* des Isidorus von Sevilla". *Hermes* 72 (1937): 132-133, takes up Lindsay's list again and uses Charles Henry Beeson's descriptions. *Isidor-Studien.* Munich: C. H. Beck, 1913, 70-80 (Quellen und Untersuchungen zur lateinische Philologie des Mittelalters: 4/2), to rearrange Lindsay's manuscripts (1911) in accordance with his distribution of the 20 Books (I-XX or I-X and XI-XX), regardless of the family to which they belong.

[24] Brussels, Bibliothèque Royale II, 4856 (*CLA X:* no. 1554: "Visigothic and insular symptoms"), facsimile of the title of the nine chapters of the "Musica" in Michel Huglo. "Die Interpolationen von Texten und Diagrammen in der *Musica Isidori*". In Michael Bernhard, ed. *Quellen und Studien zur Musiktheorie des Mittelalters.* 3 vols. Munich: Beck, 2001, 5 (Musikhistorischen Kommission: Bayerische Akademie der Wissenschaften 15). Bernhard Bischoff thinks that this manuscript could have been copied from a Spanish copy: *idem. Mittelalterliche Studien.* Stuttgart: Anton Hiersemann, 1961. Vol. 1: 191. On fol. 1, the title of the work is crowned by a *horseshoe arch* (in the shape of a [Ω], as in Mozarabic architecture). Because Lindsay could not study the manuscript in person, he entrusted Joseph van den Gheyn, the manuscript librarian from the Bibliothèque Royale in Brussels, with the task, and he copied some variants.

[25] Marc Reydellet. "La diffusion des *Origines* d'Isidore de Séville au Haut Moyen-Âge". *Mélanges de l'École française de Rome* 78 (1966): 383-437. The *stemma* includes the four Visigothic manuscripts that Lindsay had already collected in 1911.

[26] The *Musica Isidori* was published by Martin Gerbert. *Scriptores ecclesiastici de Musica Sacra.* Vol. 1. Typis San Blasianis, 1784 (reprinted, Hildesheim: Olms, 1990), 20-24 according to Vienna manuscript, Österreichische

Nationalbibliothek, 2503 (13th century), fols. 32v-33. The list of manuscripts from the 10th to the 13th centuries including this fragment can be found in Michael Bernhard. "Überlieferung und Fortleben der antiken lateinischen Musiktheorie im Mittelalter". In Thomas Ertelt and Frieder Zaminer, eds. *Geschichte der Musiktheorie.* Darmstadt: Wissenschaftliche Buchgesellschaft, 1990. Vol. 3: 33; the manuscripts mentioned in Christian Meyer, ed. *The Theory of Music*. Vol. 6, *Manuscripts from the Carolingian Era up to 1500. Addenda et Corrigenda*. Munich: Henle, 2003, 770 (Index) (Répertoire International des Sources Musicales B. III. 6) need to be added to this list.

[27] K (*CLA IX:* no. 1386) and its *twin brother* L (*CLA I:* no. 39); M (*CLA III:* no. 284), N (*CLA VIII:* no. 1077); two Saint Gall manuscripts, Stiftsbibliothek, 233 and 235, from the 11th century; some excerpts from Paris, BNF, Lat. 7530 (see note 28) and finally, Berlin, Staatsbibliothek Preuβischer Kulturbesitz, Phillipps, 1831 (8th-9th centuries): contains books III (which I have not examined) and XIII. It seems that Lindsay's old catalog number is inaccurate (it is an 11th century calendar) and must be replaced by Lat. Fol. 445: see *CLA,* Suppl. 1674 and Bernhard Bischoff. *Katalog der festländischen Handschriften des neunten Jahrhunderts (mit Ausnahme der wisigothischen).* Part 1, *Aachen-Lambach.* Edited by Birgit Ebersperger. Wiesbaden: Harrassowitz, 1998, 78, no. 372 (and 92, no. 437, Phillipps 1831) (Kommission für die Herausgabe der mittelalterlichen Bibliothekskataloge Deutschlands und der Schweiz: Bayerische Akademie der Wissenschaften).

[28] *CLA V,* no. 569; Louis Holtz, "Le Parisinus Latinus 7530, synthèse cassinienne des arts libéraux". *Studi Medievali,* 3rd Series, 16 (1975): 97-152. Nancy Phillips. "Classical and Late Latin Sources for Ninth-Century Treatises on Music". In André Barbera, ed. *Music Theory and Its Sources. Antiquity and the Middle Ages.* Notre Dame, Indiana: University of Notre Dame Press, 1990, 112.

[29] The first, kept in Porto (BPM, ms. 21 [Santa Cruz, 17] was mentioned in Michel Huglo´s review in the *Bulletin codicologique* of *Scriptorium* 57 (2003): 228*-229, no. 523. The second (Lisbon, BN, Alcobaça 446) was discovered by Susana Zapke in 2005 while preparing this book. I then had the good fortune to examine it on microfilm in the Hill Museum Manuscript Library in Collegeville, Minnesota, in March 2006.

[30] On the order of the letters in this collection, see Ruth Miguel Franco's article, "Posición y relaciones de las epístolas de Braulio de Zaragoza en las *Etymologiae* de Isidoro de Sevilla". In Gregorio Hinojo Andrés and José Carlos Fernández Corte, eds. *Munus quaesitum meritis.* Salamanca: Ediciones Universidad, 2007, 607-616.

[31] For example, in El Escorial, B.I.12 (14th century), but not in the mss. B.I.10 and B.I.11; &.J.2 (same date), Osma; R.III.9 (12th century), with the same origin as the ms. &.I.3 (see below); Paris, Bibliothèque Mazarine, 689 (14th century), Collège de Navarre; Toledo, BC, 15-11 (14th century), but not in the 15-10 of the same period; University Heights, OH, Dr. John Stamitz's collection [s. n.] (13th century), Poblet (?); Vienna, ÖNB, Cpv 683 (14th century); Spanish origin (?); provenance: Salzburg.

[32] For the manuscripts, see Wallace Martin Lindsay. The printed sources by G. Zainer (Augsburg, 1472), Juan López de Velasco (Madrid, 1599) and Faustino Arévalo 1798) keep Braulio as the addressee.

[33] Christopher M. Lawson, ed. *Sancti Isidori Episcopi Hispalensis De ecclesiasticis officiis*. Turnhout: Brepols, 1989, 72 (bk. II, 12) (Corpus Christianorum: Series Latina 113).

[34] It appears, for example, in the fragment of the *Musica Isidori* in Valenciennes, BM, mss. 384-385 (9th century), but not in the complete manuscript of the *Etymologiae* in Valenciennes, BM, ms. 399 (9th century).

[35] Michel Huglo. "Les diagrammes...". Op. cit., 183, list of the numerous manuscripts in which Braulio's summary prevails over Isidore's.

[36] For example, the Balearic Islands, whose note was added in the Poblet manuscript (Dr. John D. Stamitz's collection at University Heights; see note 31). Professor Manuel C. Díaz y Díaz personally explained to me that certain manuscripts included a note to praise their own forgotten city.

[37] Walter Porzig. Op. cit., 133.

[38] *Abest totum hoc a libro Cardinalis Sirleti et uno ex Toletanis:* Juan López de Velasco. *Divi Isidori Hispalensis opera, Philippi II catholici regis jussu e veteribus exemplaribus emendate.* Madrid: Ex Typographia Regia, 1599, 288. The *Toletanus* in question is the ms. 15-11 in the Biblioteca Capitular, fol. 172 A.

[39] For example in *Etymologiae*, in Book XV *(De civitatibus)*, in the section titled *De aedificiis publicis* (XV, II, 1); Lindsay. *Isidori*, 1988. Vol. 2: 159 in the last re-edition (arranged) and of course, the *De geometria* XIV, 1-3, the continuation (4 and 5), belongs to the *De musica*: see the third part.

[40] K. A. de Meyier, ed. *Codices Vossiani Latini.* Vol. 1, *Codices In Folio.* Leiden: Universitaire Pers, 1973, 153-155. This manuscript is not mentioned in Elisabeth Pellegrin. *Bibliothèques retrouvées: manuscrits, bibliothèques et bibliophiles du Moyen Âge et de la Renaissance: Recueil d'études publiées de 1938 à 1985.* Paris: CNRS, 1988.

[41] Albert Bruckner. *Scriptoria medii aevi Helvetica. Denkmäler Schweizerischer Schreibkunst des Mittelalters.* 14

vols. Geneva: Roto-Sadag, 1935-1978. Vol. 3, *Sankt Gallen*. Part 2 (1938): 85. Karl Schmuki (letter dated 12 April 2006) has kindly provided me with this information.

[42] Bernhard Bischoff. "Die europäische Verbreitung der Werken Isidors von Sevilla". In *idem. Mittelalterlichen Studien*. Stuttgart: Anton Hiersemann, 1966. Vol. 1: 180. Description of the fragment in *CLA VII* (Switzerland): no. 995. Another fragment of the *Etymologiae* (I, XXXVII, 5-10) has survived in Anglo-Saxon minuscule in the Saint Gall, Stiftsbibliothek, ms. 1394 (*CLA VII:* no. 983).

[43] *Ibidem,* 171-194.

Elias Avery Lowe. Op. cit. Vol. 11, *Hungary, Luxembourg, Poland, Russia, Spain*. Oxford: Clarendon Press, 1966.

Charles Upson Clark. *Collectanea Hispanica*. Paris: Champion, 1920.

Manuel C. Díaz y Díaz. "La circulation des manuscrits...". Op. cit., 219-241 y 383-392.

—. "Problemas de algunos manuscritos hispánicos de las *Etimologías* de Isidoro de Sevilla". In Johanna Autenrieth and Franz Brunhölzl, eds. *Festschrift Bernhard Bischoff zu seinem 65. Geburtstag*. Stuttgart: Anton Hiersemann, 1971, 70-80.

—. *Manuscritos visigóticos del sur de la Península: ensayo de distribución regional*. Seville: University of Seville, 1995.

Paul Ewald, and Gustav Lowe. *Exempla scripturae visigoticae XL tabulis expressae*. Heidelberg: G. Koester, 1920.

Zacarías García Villada. *Paleografía española: precedida de una introducción sobre paleografía latina*. Madrid: Revista de Filología Española, 1923. (Includes plates.)

Agustín Millares Carlo, et al. Op. cit.

[44] Charles Upson Clark. Op. cit., 218, published this text based on the manuscript in El Escorial, &.J.3, fol. 58: the text published above is based on that in the La Rioja manuscripts, RAH, 25 and RAH, 76. In the manuscript Madrid, BN, glass case 14.3 the conclusion is written differently, which is why a critical edition is needed.

[45] André Barbera. "The Consonant Eleventh and the Expansion of the Musical Tetraktys. A Study of Ancient Pythagoreanism". *Journal of Music Theory* 24 (1980): 191-223.

[46] Iamblichos o Chalkideus, a disciple of Porphyry. See Ludwig Deubner, ed. *Iamblichi De vita Pythagorica liber*. Leipzig: Teubner, 1937; edition revised by the same and Ulrich Klein. *Ibidem*. Stuttgart: Teubner, 1975, 68, no. 26. This edition is based on the following manuscripts: Florence, Biblioteca Medicea Laurenziana, ms. LXXX-VI.3 (14th century) and Paris, BNF, grec 2093 (15th century), fol. 22v.

[47] "Graeca elementa litterarum numeros etiam exprimere potest nullus qui vel tenuiter Graeci sermonis notitiam habet". En Karl Zeumer, ed. *Monumenta Germaniae Historica, Legum, sectio V, Formulae*. Berlin: Weidmann, 1886, 587-588. At the end of this letter a numerical alphabet appears that Latin manuscripts often reproduced in the 9th century. This numerical alphabet was also used to decipher the bills for goods that arrived from Greater Greece.

[48] The copyists mistook the capital F in the title for a T (*interioris*), whose difference is reduced to the central line in the F, which is tiny in small Visigothic majuscule. Lindsay (III, xiv, 3, 139) inserted these three words in the explanatory text for the astronomical figures (III, xiv, 1-2) and the text explaining the following diagram. Arévalo simply rejected this text in the Appendix of his edition (see J.-P. Migne, ed. *PL LXXXII:* col. 753).

[49] Platón. *Timée. Critias*. Edited by Albert Rivaud. Paris: Les Belles Lettres, 1983, 148. See also Jack A. Willis, ed. *Ambrosii Theodosii Macrobii Commentarii in somnium Scipionis*. Stuttgart: Teubner, 1994, I, 6. 2 (p. 18 l.32), C I 12.6 (p. 49 l.2), and and especially, C II 2.1 (p. 99 l.22) (Bibliotheca Scriptorum Graecorum et Romanorum Teubneriana).

[50] Euclid in his *Elementos VII*, definition 22, and Isidore in *De numeris* (ignored by the Peninsular manuscripts); Isidorus Hispalensis. *Le livre des nombres = Liber numerorum*. Edited by Jean-Yves Guillaumin. Paris: Les Belles Lettres, 2005, 34, no. 28. (Auteurs Latins du Moyen Âge). On the *perfect numbers,* see *idem. Boèce. Institution arithmétique*. Paris: Les Belles Lettres, 1995 (Collection des universités de France).

[51] "... auctore Porphyrio, qui in commentariis suis haec... dicit..." (*Commentarii*. I, 3, 17: Jack A. Willis, ed. Op. cit., 12, l. 11); "hanc Platonicorum persuasionem Porphyrius libris inseruit quibus Timaei obscuritatibus non nihil lucis infudit...", *Commentarii*. II, 3, 15: *ibidem,* 107, ll. 1 and 2).

[52] Apart from the Jack Willis edition (Stuttgart: Teubner, 1994), which I mentioned earlier, there is now also the edition by Mireille Armisen-Marchetti (Paris: Les Belles Lettres, 2001 and 2003), that provides a French translation of the Latin text and a commentary on Macrobius's Commentary; see my review of this edition in *Scriptorium* 56 (2002): 75*-76*, no. 198, where I extend the list of manuscripts on which this edition was based, and fill in numerous gaps in the bibliography concerning the question of consonances.

[53] Angelo Raffaele Sodano. *Porphyrii in Platonis Timaeum commentariorum fragmenta*. Naples, 1964; this is a commentary that was evidently been written in Greek,

just like the commentary on the *Harmonica* by Ptolemy, which it very often follows in Greek manuscripts. Proclus († 496) read the commentary on the *Timaeus* by Porphyry and used it for his own commentary on the *Timaeus* (see note 55).

[54] Eduard Hiller, ed. *Theonis Smyrnaei philosophi Platonici Expositio rerum mathematicarum ad legendum Platonem utilium.* Leipzig: Teubner, 1878 (2nd ed., Stuttgart: Teubner, 1995, 95). Translated into French by J. Dupuis. *Théon de Smyrne, philosophe platonicien. Exposition des connaissances mathématiques utiles pour la lecture de Platon.* Paris: Hachette, 1892 (2nd ed., Brussels: Culture et Civilisation, 1966, 156-157).

[55] Ernst Diehl, ed. *Procli Diadochi In Platonis Timaeum commentaria.* Leipzig: Teubner, 1904. Vol. 2: 170-172. Translated into French by A. J. Festugière. *Proclus. Commentaire sur le Timée.* 5 vols. Paris: Vrin, 1966-1968. Bk. 3: 215-217.

[56] See Michel Huglo. "L'étude des diagrammes d'harmonique de Calcidius au Moyen Âge". *Revue de Musicologie* 91 (2005): 311. In this category with 87 manuscripts, only a few show the three *lambda* fitted together. See the list in *idem.* "Les diagrammes". Op. cit., 178 ; see note 18.

[57] Walter Marg. *Timaeus Locri, De natura mundi et animae.* Leiden: Brill, 1972, 72, and Thomas H. Tobin. *Timaios of Locri. On the Nature of the World and the Soul.* Chico, California: Scholars Press, 1985, p. 43.

[58] This final series of numbers, copied in all the Visigothic manuscripts, has been omitted in the Santa Cruz de Coimbra manuscript (Porto, BPM, 21), undoubtedly deliberately.

[59] Oliver Strunk. "The Tonal System of the Byzantine Chant". *Musical Quarterly* 28 (1942): 190-204. See Jørgen Raasted. *The Intonation Formulas and Signatures in Byzantine Musical Manuscripts.* Copenhagen: Munksgaard, 1966, 9 (Monumenta Musicae Byzantinae: Subsidia 7).

[60] Hans Schmid. *Musica et Scolica enchiriadis, una cum aliquibus tractatulis adjunctis.* Munich: Beck, 1981, 6 (Musikhistorische Kommission: Bayerische Akademie der Wissenschaften 3).

[61] Dieter Torkewitz. *Das älteste Dokument zur Entstehung der abendländischen Mehrstimmigkeit.* Stuttgart: Franz Steiner, 1999 (Beihefte zum Archiv für Musikwissenschaft: 44). See Nancy Phillips' review for *Plainsong and Medieval Music* 10 (2001): 77-80.

[62] Oliver Strunk. Op. cit., 199.

[63] Among the latter, we can mention the antiphon *Introeunte te Domine, in sanctam civitatem*, studied by Michel Huglo. "Source hagiopolite d'une antienne hispanique pour le dimanche des Rameaux". *Hispania Sacra* 5, no. 10 (1952): 367-374, article reproduced in *idem. Les anciens répertories...* Op. cit. Aldershot: Ashgate, 2004, article XIX.

[64] Jacques Fontaine. *Isidore de Séville. Traité de la nature.* Op. cit., 212 bis, fig. 4, and 216 bis, fig. 5.

[65] This translation system was suggested by Gabriel Théry. *Études dionysiennes.* Vol. 1, chap. 6, *La traduction de Denys par Hilduin est-elle une traduction phonétique?* Paris: Vrin, 1932, 123-134 (Études de Philosophie Médiévale: 16, 19).

[66] I thank Barbara Haggh for her valuable help with the bibliography, for editing my text and for checking the translation; Dr. José Carlos Martín (Salamanca) for generously informing me of his works on Isidore and Braulio; and also Susana Zapke for illustrating and editing this study on the tradition of the *Musica Isidori* in the Iberian Peninsula.

Bibliography

Alturo i Perucho, Jesús. "Fragment d'un epitom del *Glossarium Ansileubi* de la primera meitat del segle x". *Faventia* 7 (1985): 75-85.

Amos, Thomas Leslie. *The Fundo Alcobaça of the Biblioteca Nacional, Lisbon.* Vol. 3, *Manuscripts 302-456.* Collegeville, Minnesota: Hill Monastic Manuscript Library, 1990.

Anglès, Higini. *La música a Catalunya fins al segle XIII.* Barcelona: Institut d'estudis Catalans, Biblioteca de Cataluña, 1935. (2nd ed., Barcelona: Biblioteca de Cataluña, Universidad Autónoma de Barcelona, 1988.)

Antolín, Guillermo. *Catálogo de los códices latinos de la Real Biblioteca de El Escorial.* 5 vols. Madrid: Imprenta Helénica, 1910-1923.

Avril, François, Jean-Pierre Aniel, Mireille Mentré, Alix Saulnier, and Yolanta Załuska, eds. *Manuscrits enluminés de la Péninsule Ibérique.* Paris: Bibliothèque Nationale de France, 1982.

Barbera, André. "The Consonant Eleventh and the Expansion of the Musical Tetraktys. A Study of Ancient Pythagoreanism". *Journal of Music Theory* 24 (1980): 191-223.

Bede, the Venerable. *De natura rerum.* Charles William Jones and F. Lipp edition. Turnhout: Brepols, 1975 (Corpus Christianorum: Continuatio Mediaevalis: 123 A).

Beer, Rudolf, and Scato de Vries, eds. *Isidori Etymologiae. Codex toletanus (nunc matritensis) 15,8 phototypice editus.* Leiden: Seithoff, 1909 (Códices Graeci et Latini photographice depicti: 13).

BEESON, Charles Henry. *Isidor-Studien*. Munich: C. H. Beck, 1913 (Quellen und Untersuchungen zur lateinische Philologie des Mittelalters: 4/2).

BELLETTINI. Anna. "Il codice del secolo IX di Cesena, Malatestiano, S. XXI. 5: le Etimologiae di Isidoro, testi minori e glosse di età ottoniana". *Italia Medioevale e Umanistica* 65 (2004): 49-114, reviewed by M. Marchiaro in *Scriptorium* 60, no. 1 (2006): 14*, no. 24.

BERNHARD, Michael. "Isidor von Sevilla: Überlieferung und Fortleben der antiken lateinischen Musiktheorie im Mittelalter". In Thomas Ertelt and Frieder Zaminer, eds. *Geschichte der Musiktheorie*. Darmstadt: Wissenschaftliche Buchgesellschaft, 1990, 7-35.

BIBLIOTECA NACIONAL, and BIBLIOTHÈQUE NATIONALE. *Trésors de la Biblioteca Nacional: Bibliothèque Nationale, mars-avril 1988.* Madrid: Biblioteca Nacional de España; Paris: Bibliothèque Nationale de France, 1988.

BISCHOFF, Bernhard. "Die europäische Verbreitung der Werken Isidors von Sevilla". In *idem. Mittelalterliche Studien*. 3 vols. Stuttgart: Anton Hiersemann, 1966.

—. *Katalog der festländischen Handschriften des neunten Jahrhunderts (mit Ausnahme der wisigotischen).* Part 1, *Aachen-Lambach*. Edited by Birgit Ebersperger. Wiesbaden: Harrassowitz, 1998. (Kommission für die Herausgabe der mittelalterlichen Bibliothekskataloge Deutschlands und der Schweiz: Bayerische Akademie der Wissenschaften).

BOYNTON, Susan, and Isabelle COCHELIN, eds. *From Dead of Night to End of Day. The Medieval Customs of Cluny.* Turnhout: Brepols, 2005.

BRUÇKNER, Albert. *Scriptoria medii aevi Helvetica. Denkmäler Schweizerischer Schreibkunst des Mittelalters.* 14 vols. Geneva: Roto-Sadag, 1935-1978.

CARANDE-HERRERO, Rocío, Josep ESCOLA I TUSET, Concepción FERNÁNDEZ MARTÍNEZ, Juan GÓMEZ PALLARÉS, and José Carlos MARTÍN CAMACHO. "Poesía epigráfica latina de transmisión manuscrita: ¿ficción o realidad?" In Walter Berschin, Juan Gómez Pallarés and José Martínez Gásquez, eds. *Mittellateinische Biographie und Epigraphik / Biografía latina medieval y epigrafía.* Heidelberg: Mattes, 2005, 1-45.

CLARK, Charles Upson. *Collectanea Hispanica*. Paris: Champion, 1920.

CORDOLIANI, Alfred. "Les manuscrits de comput ecclésiastiques de la Bibliothèque de l'Escorial". *La Ciudad de Dios* 143 (1951): 284-285.

DELISLE, Léopold. *Manuscrits latins et français ajoutés au fonds des nouvelles acquisitions pendant les années 1875-1891. Inventaire alphabétique.* Paris: Bibliothèque Nationale de France, 1891.

DESTOMBES, Marcel. *Mappemondes, A.D. 1200-1500. Catalogue préparé par la Comission des Cartes Anciennes de l'Union Géographique Internationale.* Amsterdam: N. Israel, 1964.

DEUBNER, Ludwig. *Iamblichi De vita Pythagorica liber.* Leipzig: Teubner, 1937.

DEUBNER, Ludwig, and Ulrich KLEIN, eds. *Iamblichi De vita Pythagorica liber.* Stuttgart: Teubner, 1975.

DÍAZ Y DÍAZ, Manuel C. *Index Scriptorum Latinorum Medii Aevi Hispanorum*. Salamanca: Universidad de Salamanca, 1958.

—, ed. *Isidoriana. Colección de estudios sobre Isidoro de Sevilla, publicados con ocasión del XIV Centenario de su nacimiento*. León: Centro de Estudios e Investigación San Isidoro (CSIC-CECEL), 1961.

—. "La circulation des manuscrits du VIIIe au XIe siècle dans la Péninsule Ibérique". *Cahiers de civilisation médiévale* 12 (1969): 219-241, 383-392.

—. "Problemas de algunos manuscritos hispánicos de las *Etimologías* de Isidoro de Sevilla". In Johanna Authenrieth and Franz Brunhölzl, eds. *Festschrift Bernhard Bischoff zu seinem 65. Geburtstag.* Stuttgart: Anton Hiersemann, 1971, 70-80.

—. *De Isidoro al siglo XI: ocho estudios sobre la vida literaria peninsular*. Barcelona: El Albir, 1976.

—. *Libros y librerías en La Rioja altomedieval.* Logroño: Gobierno de La Rioja, Instituto de Estudios Riojanos, 1979.

—. "Introducción general". In Isidorus de Seville. *Etimologías.* José Oroz Reta and Manuel A. Marcos Casquero's edition. Madrid: Biblioteca de Autores Cristianos, 1982. Vol. 1: 1-257.

—. *Códices visigóticos en la monarquía leonesa.*

León: Centro de Estudios e Investigación San Isidoro (CSIC-CECEL), 1983.

—. *Manuscritos visigóticos del sur de la Península: ensayo de distribución regional.* Seville: University of Seville, 1995.

DIEHL, Ernst, ed. *Procli Diadochi In Platonis Timaeum commentaria.* 3 vols. Leipzig: Teubner, 1903-1906.

DUPUIS, J. *Théon de Smyrne, philosophe platonicien. Exposition des connaissances mathématiques utiles pour la lecture de Platon.* Paris: Hachette, 1892. (Reprinted, Brussels: Culture et Civilisation, 1966.)

EWALD, Paul, and Gustav LOWE. *Exempla scripturae visigoticae XL tabulis expressae*. Heidelberg: G. Koester, 1920.

FERNÁNDEZ CATÓN, José María. *Las* Etimologías *en la tradición manuscrita medieval estudiada por el Profesor Dr.*

Anspach. León: Centro de Estudios e Investigación San Isidoro (CSIC-CECEL), 1966.

Férotin, Màrius. *Histoire de l'Abbaye de Silos*. Paris: Ernest Leroux, 1897.

Festugière, A. J. *Proclus. Commentaire sur le Timée*. 5 vols. Paris: Vrin, 1966-1968.

Fontaine, Jacques. "Isidore de Séville et l'astrologie". *Revue des Études Latines* 31 (1954): 271-300.

—. *Isidore de Séville et la culture classique dans l'Espagne wisigothique*. 2 vols. Paris: Études Augustiniennes, 1959 (Collection des Études Augustiniennes: 7-8). (2nd ed., Paris: Études Augustiniennes, 1983).

—. *Isidore de Sévilla. Traité de la nature*. Bordeaux: Féret, 1960 (Bibliothèque de l'École des Hautes Études Hispaniques: 28). (Reprinted, Turnhout: Brepols, 2002.)

—. "Problèmes de méthode dans l'étude des sources isidoriennes". In Manuel C. Díaz y Díaz, ed. *Isidoriana. Op. cit.*, 115-132.

—. ed. "Compte rendu du Colloque isidorien tenu à l'Institut d'études latines de l'Université de Paris, le 28 juin 1970". *Revue d'Histoire des Textes* 2 (1972): 282-288.

Franco, Ruth Miguel. "Posición y relaciones de las epístolas de Braulio de Zaragoza en las *Etymologiae* de Isidoro de Sevilla". In Gregorio Hinojo Andrés and José Carlos Fernández Corte, eds. *Munus quaesitum meritis*. Salamanca: Ediciones Universidad, 2007, 607-616.

García Villada, Zacarías. *Paleografía española: precedida de una introducción sobre la paleografía latina*. Madrid: Junta para Ampliación de Estudios e Investigaciones Científicas, 1923.

Gerbert, Martin. *Scriptores ecclesiastici de musica sacra potissimum*. Vol. 1. Typis San Blasianis, 1784. (Reprinted, Hildesheim: Olms, 1990.)

Gómez Pallarés, Joan. "Textos latinos de cómputo en manuscritos visigóticos de los siglos x-xi". *Mittellateinisches Jahrbuch (Köln)* 24-25 (1989-90): 133-142.

González Fernández, Julián. *San Isidoro, Doctor de las Españas*. Seville: Caja Duero, 2003.

Gorman, Michael M. "The Diagrams in the Oldest Manuscripts of Isidore's 'De natura rerum', with a Note on the Manuscript Tradition of Isidore's Works". *Studi Medievali*, 3rd series, 42 (2001): 529-545.

Guillaumin, Jean-Yves, ed. *Boèce. Institution arithmétique*. Paris: Les Belles Lettres, 1995 (Collection des universités de France).

Hiller, Eduard, ed. *Theonis Smyrnaei philosophi Platonici exposition rerum mathematicarum ad legendum Platonem utilium*. Leipzig: Teubner, 1878 (2nd ed., Stuttgart: Teubner, 1995).

Holtz, Louis. "Le Parisinus Latinus 7.530, synthèse cassinienne des arts libéraux". *Studi medievali*, 3rd series, 16 (1975): 97-152.

Huglo, Michel. "Le *De musica* de saint Isidore de Séville d'après le manuscrit de Silos, Paris, B.N., N. A. L. 2169". *Revista de Musicología* 15 (1992): 565-578.

—. "Recherches sur les tons psalmodiques de l'ancienne liturgie hispanique". *Revista de musicología* 16, no. 1 (1993): 477-490 *[Actas del XV Congreso de la Sociedad Internacional de Musicología: Culturas Musicales del Mediterráneo y sus Ramificaciones (Madrid, 3-10/IV/1992)]*.

—. "Les diagrammes d'harmonique interpolés dans les manuscrits de la *Musica Isidori*". *Scriptorium* 48 (1994): 171-186. [Article reproduced in *idem*. *Les anciens répertoires de plain-chant*. Aldershot: Ashgate, 2004, art. IX (Variorum Collected Studies Series).]

—. "Exercitia vocum". In David Hiley and Janka Szendrei, eds. *Laborare fratres in unum. Festschrift László Dobszay zum 60. Geburtstag*. Hildesheim: Weidmann, 1995, 117-123 (Spolia Berolinensia: 7).

—. "Isidor von Sevilla, † 636". In Thomas Ertelt and Frieder Zaminer, eds. *Geschichte der Musiktheorie*. Vol. 4, *Die Lehre vom einstimmigen liturgischen Gesang*. Darmstadt: Wissenschaftliche Buchgesellschaft, 1997, 42-47.

—. "Die *Musica Isidori* nach den Handschriften des deutschen Sprachgebietes mit Berücksichtigung der Hds. Wien, ÖNB 683". In Walter Pass and Alexander Rausch, eds. *Mittelalterliche Musiktheorie in Zentraleuropa mit besonderer Berücksichtigung des Bodenseeraumes*. Tutzing: Hans Schneider, 1998, 79-86 (Musica mediaevalis Europae occidentalis: 4).

—. "Les arts libéraux dans le *Liber glossarum*". *Scriptorium* 55 (2001): 3-33, pls. 1-4. (Reprinted in Michel Huglo. *La théorie de la musique antique et medievale*. Aldershot: Ashgate, 2005, art. III + addenda et corrigenda.)

—. "Die Interpolationen von Texten und Diagrammen in der *Musica Isidori*". In Michael Bernhard, ed. *Quellen und Studien zur Musiktheorie des Mittelalters*. Munich: Beck, 2001. Vol. 3: 1-17 (Musikhistorischen Kommission: Bayerische Akademie der Wissenschaften 15).

—. "The Diagrams Interpolated into the *Musica Isidori* and the Scale of the Old Spanish Chant". In Sean Gallagher, James Haar, John Nadas and Timothy Striplin, eds. *Western Plainchant in the First Millenium. Studies in the Medieval Liturgy and its Music*. Aldershot: Ashgate, 2003, 243-260.

—. "Source hagiopolite d'une antienne hispanique pour le dimanche des Rameaux". In *idem*. *Les anciens répertories de plain-chant*. Aldershot: Ashgate, 2004, art. XIX (Variorum Collected Studies Series).

—. "L'étude des diagrammes d'harmonique de Calcidius au Moyen Âge". *Revue de Musicologie* 91 (2005): 305-319.

—. "L'office du dimanche de Pâques à Cluny au Moyen Âge". In Susan Boynton and Isabelle Cochelin, eds. Op. cit., 2005, 153-162.

Kern, Hermann. *Through the Labyrinth. Designs and Meanings over 5000 Years*. Munich: Prestel, 2000.

Lawson, Christopher M., ed. *Sancti Isidori Episcopi Hispalensis De ecclesiasticis officiis*. Turnhout: Brepols, 1989 (Corpus Christianorum: Series Latina 113).

Leanza, Sandro, ed. *Flavio Magno Aurelio Cassiodoro: atti della settimana di studi, Cosenza-Squillace 19-24 settembre 1983*. Catanzaro: Rubbettino, 1986.

Leclercq, Dom Jean. "Les manuscrits d'Alcobaça". *Analecta Sacri Ordinis cisterciensis* 6 (1950): 131-135.

Lehmann, Paul Joachim Georg. "Cassiodor-Studien". In *idem*. *Erforschung des Mittelalters: Ausgewählte Abhandlungen und Aufsätze*. Stuttgart: Anton Hiersemann, 1959, 1962. Vol. 2: 38-109.

Lindsay, Wallace Martin, ed. *Isidori Hispalensis episcopi Etymologiarum sive Originum Libri XX*. Oxford: Clarendon Press, 1911 (Oxford Classical Texts).

López de Velasco, Juan. *Divi Isidori Hispalensis opera, Philippi II catholici Regis jussu e veteribus exemplaribus emendate*. Madrid: Ex Typographia Regia, 1599.

Lowe, Elias Avery. *Codices latini antiquiores. A Palaeographical Guide to Latin Manuscripts Prior to the Ninth Century*. Vol. 11, *Hungary, Luxembourg, Poland, Russia, Spain*. Oxford: Clarendon Press, 1966.

Madoz, José. *Epistolario de San Braulio de Zaragoza*. Madrid: Imprenta Aldecoa, 1941.

Marg, Walter. *Timaeus Locri, De natura mundi et animae*. Leiden: Brill, 1972.

Marshall, Peter K. "Isidore". In L. D. Reynolds, ed. *Texts and Transmission. A Survey of the Latin Classics*. Oxford: Oxford University Press, 1983, 195-196 (2nd ed., 1986, 195-196).

Martín, José Carlos. "El corpus hagiográfico latino en torno a la figura de Isidoro de Sevilla en la Hispania tardoantigua y medieval (siglos VII-XIII)". *Veleia. Revista di Prehistoria Antigua, Arqueologia y Filologia Classicas* 22 (2005): 187-228.

—, ed. *Scripta de vita Isidori Hispalensis episcopi*. Turnhout: Brepols, 2006 (Corpus Christianorum: Series Latina 113B).

Martin, Josef, and Klaus Daur. *Sancti Aurelii Augustini. De doctrina christiana. De vera religione*. Turnhout: Brepols, 1962 (Corpus Christianorum: Series Latina 32).

Martínez Díez, Gonzalo, and Félix Rodríguez. *La colección canónica hispana*. Vol. 5, part 2. Madrid: CSIC, Instituto P. Enrique Flórez, 1992) [pp. 170-274: critical edition of the decisions of the fourth Council of Toledo, at which Isidore, President of the Council, and Braulio of Zaragoza, were present (p. 271, no. 54)].

Mentré, Mireille. *The Illuminated Manuscripts of Medieval Spain*. London: Thames and Hudson, 1996.

Meyer, Christian, ed. *The Theory of Music*. Vol. 6, *Manuscripts from the Carolingian Era up to 1500. Addenda et corrigenda*. Munich: Henle, 2003 (Répertoire International des Sources Musicales B. III. 6).

Meyier, K. A. de, ed. *Codices Vossiani Latini*. Vol. 1, *Codices In-Folio*. Leiden: Universitaire Pers, 1973.

Millares Carlo, Agustín, Manuel C. Díaz y Díaz, Anscari M. Mundó, José Manuel Ruiz Asencio, Blas Casado Quintanilla, and E. Lecuona Ribot, eds. *Corpus de códices visigóticos*. Vol. 1, *Estudios;* vol. 2, *Álbum*. Las Palmas de Gran Canaria: Gobierno de Canarias, UNED, Centro Asociado de Las Palmas de Gran Canaria, 1999. [Michel Huglo´s review in the *Bulletin Codicologique* of *Scriptorium* 53 (1999): 236-237; Barbara A. Shailor´s review in *Speculum* 78 (2003): 1346-1348.]

Mynors, R. A. B. *Cassiodori Senatoris Institutiones*. Oxford: Clarendon Press, 1937.

Nascimento, Aires Augusto, and José Francisco Merinhos. *Catálogo dos Códices da Livraria de Mão do Mosteiro de Santa Cruz de Coimbra na Biblioteca Pública Municipal do Porto*. Porto: Biblioteca Pública Municipal do Porto, 1997.

Norberg, Dag Ludvig. "Étymologie et changement de sens". In Ritva Jacobsson and Folke Sandgren, eds. *Au seuil du Moyen Âge*. Vol. 2, *Études linguistiques, métriques et littéraires publiées par ses collègues et élèves à l'occasion de son 65e anniversaire*. Stockholm: Kungliga Vitterhets, Historie och Antikvitets Akademien, 1998, 61-79 (Filologiskt arkiv: 40).

Pellegrin, Elisabeth. *Bibliothèques retrouvées: manuscrits, bibliothèques et bibliophiles du Moyen Âge et de la Renaissance: Recueil d'études publiées de 1938 à 1985*. Paris: CNRS, 1988.

Phillips, Nancy. "Classical and Late Latin Sources for Ninth-Century Treatises on Music". In André Barbera, ed. *Music Theory and its Sources: Antiquity and the Middle Age*. Notre Dame, Indiana: University of Notre Dame Press, 1990, 100-135.

PHILIPPART, Guy. "*Etymologiarum Liber XVII* d'Isidore de Séville. A propos d'une édition récente". *Scriptorium* 37 (1983): 290-294.

PLATO. *Timée. Critias.* Edited by Albert Rivaud. Paris: Les Belles lettres, 2002.

PORZIG, Walter. "Die Rezensionen der *Etymologiae* des Isidorus von Seville". *Hermes* 72 (1937): 129-170.

RAASTED, Jørgen. *The Intonation Formulas and Modal Signatures in Byzantine Musical Manuscripts.* Copenhagen: Munksgaard, 1966 (Monumenta Musicae Byzantinae: Subsidia 7).

REYDELLET, Marc. "La diffusion des *Origines* d'Isidore de Séville au Haut Moyen Âge". *Mélanges d'Archéologie et d'Histoire de l'École Française de Rome* 78 (1966): 383-487.

REYNAUD, François. *La polyphonie tolédane et son milieu des premiers témoignages aux environs de 1600.* Turnhout: Brepols, 1996 (Documents, Études, Recherches: 50).

RIESCO TERRERO, Luis. *Epistolario de San Braulio.* Seville: Editorial Católica Española, 1975 (Anales de la Universidad Hispalense: Filosofía y Letras 31).

RUIZ GARCÍA, Elisa. *Catálogo de la Sección de Códices de la Real Academia de la Historia.* Madrid: Real Academia de la Historia, 1997.

SAINT ISIDORE OF SEVILLE. *Etimologías.* Manuel C. Díaz y Díaz, José Oroz Reta and Manuel Antonio Marcos Casquero's bilingual edition. 2 vols. Madrid: Biblioteca de Autores Cristianos, 1982.

—. *Le livre des nombres = Liber numerorum.* Edited by Jean-Yves Guillaumin. Paris: Les Belles Lettres, 2005 (Auteurs Latins du Moyen Âge).

SAMARAN, Charles, Robert MARICHAL, Monique-Cécile GARAND, Madeleine MABILLE, Denis MUZERELLE, and Marie-Thérese D'ALVERNY, eds. *Catalogue des manuscrits en écriture latine, portant des indications, de date, de lieu ou de copiste.* Paris: CNRS, 1981.

SANTOS, Isabel. *Santa Cruz de Coimbra. A Cultura Portuguesa Aberta à Europa na Idade Media.* Porto: Biblioteca Pública Municipal do Porto, 2001.

SARRIÁ RUEDA, Amalia, Claudine LEMAIRE, and Hosam ELKHADERN. *Les rois bibliophiles: Europalia 85 España: Bruxelles, Bibliothèque Royale Albert Ier.* Brussels: Bibliothèque Royale Albert Ier, 1985.

SCHADT, Herman. *Die Darstellungen der* Arbores consanguinitatis *und der* Arbores affinitatis. *Bildschemata in juristischen Handschriften.* Tübingen: Wasmuth, 1982.

SCHMID, Hans. *Musica et Scolica enchiriadis, una cum aliquibus tractatulis adjunctis.* Munich: Beck, 1981 (Bayerische Akademie der Wissenschaften: Veröffentlichungen der Musikhistoriche Kommision 3).

SHAILOR, Barbara A. "The Scriptorium of San Pedro de Cardeña". *Bulletin of the John Rylands University Library at Manchester* 61 (1979): 444-473.

—. "The Scriptorium of San Sahagún: A Period of Transition". In Bernard F. Reilly, ed. *Santiago, Saint-Denis and Saint-Peter. The Reception of the Roman Liturgy in León and Castille in 1080.* New York: Fordham University Press, 1985, 41-62.

SODANO, Angelo Raffaele. *Porphyrii in Platonis Timaeum commentariorum fragmenta.* Naples, 1964.

STRUNK, Oliver. "The Tonal System of the Byzantine Chant". *Musical Quarterly* 28 (1942): 190-204.

—. *Essays on Music in the Byzantine World.* New York: Norton, 1977.

THÉRY, Gabriel. *Études dionysiennes.* 2 vols. Paris: Vrin, 1932, 1937 (Études de Philosophie Médiévale: 16, 19).

TOBIN, Thomas H. *Timaios of Locri. On the Nature of the World and the Soul.* Chico, California: Scholars Press, 1985.

TORKEWITZ, Dieter. *Das älteste Dokument zur Entstehung der abendländischen Mehrstimmigkeit.* Stuttgart: Franz Steiner, 1999 (Beihefte zum Archiv für Musikwissenschaft: 44).

VEZIN, Jean. "Observations sur l'emploi des réclames dans les manuscrits latins". *Bibliothèque de l'École des Chartes* 125 (1967): 5-33.

VILARES CEPEDA, Isabel, and Teresa DUARTE FERREIRA. *Inventario dos Códices Illuminados até 1500.* Vol. 1, *Distrito de Lisboa;* vol. 2, *Distrito de Aveiro [...] Coimbra [...] Porto.* Lisbon: Biblioteca Nacional de Portugal, 2001. (Michel Huglo´s review in the *Bulletin Codicologique* of *Scriptorium* 57 (2003): 228*-229*, nos. 522 and 523.)

VIVES, José. *Inscripciones cristianas de la España romana y visigoda.* 2nd ed. Barcelona: A. G. Ponsa, 1969. (1st ed., Barcelona: Balmesiana, 1942.)

WILLIS, Jack A., ed. *Ambrosii Theodosii Macrobii Commentarii in somnium Scipionis.* Stuttgart: Teubner, 1994 (Bibliotheca Scriptorium Graecorum et Romanorum Teubneriana).

ZEUMER, Karl, ed. *Monumenta Germaniae Historica, Legum, Sectio V: Formulae.* Berlin: Weidmann, 1886, 587-588.

Some Incidental Notes on Music Manuscripts

Manuel C. Díaz y Díaz

In the following study, even though it was written with the problems caused by aging documents, which have especially affected the visual analysis of the manuscripts, I have tried to present certain problems regarding musical codices. It seems clear that books like these were already used in the Visigothic period, to which the ones we now have—in various forms—undoubtedly date. They must already have been in use in the 7th century, because otherwise various passages referring to melodic chants in liturgical functions would make no sense, especially with regard to antiphons, which basically constitute the foundation of our musical literature. I do not intend to produce a repertoire of these references here, so it suffices to mention a few phrases by the famous anchorite, Valerio of Bierzo (ca. 620-695), a strict observer of the purity of rites, who found in certain abuses one of the causes of the corruption of mediocre monks. This is what he says in his treatise, which has survived in fragments, *De genere monachorum*, that is, regarding mediocre monks in particular:[1]

> Atque in supradictorum auditum multiplicant diversas crebrasque series officiorum et in sublimi arte attollunt canentes *melodiam* vocum atque crebris genuflexionibus protrahentes copiam orationum et quotidianis *diurnis* atque nocturnis temporibus torporem desidiosum implicant.[2]

We should note in this passage how important chant already was in worship at that time, which was mainly connected with antiphons and, when appropriate, with hymns.

The books that contain this musical writing in early times were usually called antiphonaries, and they continued to be used as separate liturgical books. It is a well-known fact that there were a certain number of them[3] in the Peninsula while the Hispanic rite was in force, which was implacably eliminated beginning in the last third of the 11th century.

I intentionally consider two or three manuscripts of this type that were originally from the northern part of the Peninsula, and I of course make no reference to those from Toledo, because they are from a later period, although they probably partly continued to use old materials.[4]

WERE ANTIPHONARIES COMMON BOOKS?

When we study the progress of these books mentioned in extremely old documents, we can immediately see that when they refer to antiphonaries, they follow two principles: either they are assigned a general value as the common coin of the time or they are made to stand out, their importance always emphasized. In fact, these were not simply any old books, the price of which depended on the number of folios they contained, but were manuscripts written not by a copyist but by a specialist who knew how to draw the neumes and place them properly on the text. Of course, if one person did all this, then his work immediately increased in value many times over.

In this regard, I recall that the first reference, if the document is reliable in this respect, which it seems to be, can already be found in 796, in Villeña in the Liébana area: several books were donated, of which the first is an *antiphonare,* worth three *sueldos,* whereas a orationale and a comic book are each worth two *sueldos*.[5] Another criterion used to understand the esteem in which this type of book was held involves observing that very often they are precisely the ones that head the lists of so-called church books, that is, liturgical codices. It can be no coincidence that these are mentioned first in the magnificent donation of books that Cixila made to Abellar (León) in 927.

When I collected references to books in charters (or in copies of these in cartularies), I could count no fewer than 71 antiphonaries mentioned among 551 altar books of all kinds and in all conditions, including the common compendia that became popular from the

10th century *med.* onwards, that is, the mystical and ritual books that include some of the materials that were previously exclusive to antiphonaries and prayer books.

Were all antiphonaries the same, and, if so, did they nevertheless develop in the same way? In view of some of the fragments that have survived, I would think that there were small antiphonaries, either due to the limited number of services that they contained or, more reasonably, because the systems used to write down music had been simplified.

Furthermore, I have serious doubts about the possibility of reading and interpreting the musical notation system in the harsh 8th to 10th centuries, because it is extremely complex, as specialists in this system are well aware. When many users had problems reading, and understanding, the meaning of phrases and texts at all, reading was the first step towards acquiring a minimum level of culture.

This can be confirmed in the simplified musical versions in certain fragments from different periods, as we will see later with regard to the Córdoba fragment.

My observations made on the basis of codicological evidence, however generic and imprecise they may appear at first sight, may provide suggestions and ideas regarding situations that are generally little known, although they played an important cultural role in León during the 10th century and even later.

Proposal for a new view of codex 8 in Cathedral of León

Fortunately we have an almost complete codex that has always been the basis and starting point for research and investigation. I am referring, of course, to the magnificent Antiphonary that is catalogued under the number 8 among the wonderful manuscripts in Cathedral of León.[6] Because of its condition and quality, as well as the fact that it currently has no colophon, it has given rise to numerous commentaries that cannot be dealt with here in their entirety, despite the fact that, as often happens, most of them have been considered indisputable truths. I will inevitably be providing the reader with my fresh perspectives on the date, the recipient and its period of use, which call previously accepted viewpoints into question, although mine may also be debated and commented on in turn; these critiques would have to be based on fresh elements, however. My efforts aim to free myself of the tyranny of a majority that consider the León antiphoner to date clearly from the second half of the 10th century[7] and of those that resolutely tend to bring its date back far into the 11th century.[8]

I allow myself first to provide a summary of its codicological state, although this may prove rather tedious for readers who are keen to reach conclusions as soon as possible; the discussion might also be considered to be insufficient or to have gone off the point. I propose to study the Antiphonary, as far as possible,[9] by making use of the valuable help that I have had.[10]

The Antiphonary

Basically, the codex of the Antiphonary in its present state consists of the gatherings beginning on fol. 28 and continuing to fol. 308, where it suddenly ends.[11] We can reasonably surmise that what is missing is a small part of the codex. In view of the fact that it currently continues until the first *Dominicum de quotidiano*, it is probably only the final gathering that is missing, which was in fact of a different size[12]—probably not a binion, but more likely a quinion, which was the usual way to finish a long codex—and was damaged for specific reasons.[13]

In the manuscript, as was generally the rule, the right-hand page of fol. 28 is blank.[14] On the back, as is usually the case, the title of the book, *Incipit liber antiphonarium*,[15] is preceded by the standard invocation and followed by the limits of the liturgical year.[16] Then, on fol. 29r, the text begins normally, in this case not just with neumes, but also with beautiful finely and elegantly adorned lettering and initials. So, it looks as if the manuscript, which is certainly complete, to judge from the series of quaternions, the regular nature of the writing, and, except for minor explicable exceptions, by the uniform manner of production of the gatherings and the arrangement of the texts and notation, consisted of fol. 28 until the end, with the aforementioned precise title of the contents. The capitals are decorated and the writing is drawn in a uniform way, to such an extent that it even seems to be the work of a single hand, with certain early features,[17] but definitely written in the first decades of the 10th century.[18] One noteworthy feature (but not at all exclusive to this) is that everything in the manuscript is meticulously placed on the page, from the lines to the letter shapes, with the syllables disposed to match the series of neumes. One detail that is interesting, because it means that a good model was followed precisely, is the text that is often slightly (and always slightly) adapted to match the progression of the neumes. Furthermore, these were drawn after the text was written, as is shown by the frequent overrunning strokes. Almost all of the folios in the codex have 16 lines of text with neumes superimposed on them; only rarely is this arrangement not adhered to, when continuous text appears without the need for musical notation (fols. 126v, 133, 152-153, 267). Incidentally, if the specialists do not claim otherwise, I note that the neumes have enlarged curves and a certain preciosity in the way they are drawn, because they are always agile and executed without any hesitation; the text and music seem to be the meticulous work of an (?) excellent specialist.

As we shall see, the manuscript has been kept in good condition, apart from certain mischievous later changes, and was to be considered to be a beautiful, valuable copy.[19] It is outside my specialization to define the style of the miniatures and decorative elements, but these undoubtedly show significant points of contact with other works of Castilian origin written towards the 10th century *med.*[20]

The set of prolegomena

Let us leave the codex itself aside for a moment and consider the introductory fols. 1-27.[21] This will be interesting, because they seem no different from the rest of the codex and give the impression that they were the original introduction to the manuscript. On this basis, the copy has been dated and the person it was written for has been named, and from this name and quite a bit of speculation, which has sometimes been rather dubious, the historical position of this person has been established. This has basically been used to determine and confirm the date of the manuscript, so I think that we have all created a viscious circle here. To rid ourselves of this fallacy, we need to begin by

1. Antiphonary. León, AC, ms. 8, 10th century *med.*, fol. 198v

realizing that things are not as simple as some have wanted them to be.

I start by taking apart these first 27 folios to find their real meaning and purpose; by following this path, we can reach certain conclusions that I feel are completely fresh. First of all, I emphasize that I have not been satisfied by the currently prevailing points of view on several occasions, but I have probably led some people to cling to their old perspectives[22] with an unjustifiable lack of rigor with respect to the problems posed by this extraordinarily rich manuscript.

Undoubtedly, at this preliminary stage, we can recognize three complete gatherings, as well as other elements. The gatherings, which are quaternions,[23] are as follows:

A: fols. 4-11
B: fols. 12-19
C: fols. 20-27

These gatherings can be considered uniform as far as their current condition is concerned, although as we will soon see, as soon as we analyse them dynamically, that is, in their respective formation processes, they display various problems that will help us in our search.

For a moment I will leave fols. 1, 2 and 3 aside, because they need to be explained separately and meticulously.

I remind readers that we can assume quaternion A[24] has the following content, which I consider to be characteristic and relatively related to the main part of the manuscript. Let me explain this: I deliberately mention the matter of this plausible relationship, because it is only through the circumstances established later in the chapter that I can accept that this section has anything to do with the actual Antiphonary (I will often call it the *basic manuscript*), which has always formed (up to the present day) a closed unit of its own. The first gathering can be broken down and explained as follows:

Fol. 4r: This would initially be blank, in view of the figure on the verso.
Fol. 4v: Like many liturgical or spiritual books, this would have had a large alpha (Christ, according to Apoc. 22:13) that as some experts on the manuscript have noted correctly, seems to include the corresponding omega here.[25]
Fol. 5r: This would also originally be blank, because of the figure on the back.
Fol. 5v: Like so many codices from this period, this page has the so-called cross of Oviedo in one of its forms, with the legends that often appear with this.
Fol. 6r: This would also initially be blank to provide a formal beginning and ensure the drawing and colors of the beginning of the calendar of feast days.

I stress that I believe this is a genuinely old arrangement, which I will later confirm and which will have important consequences.

Fols. 6v-9r are taken up by a calendar, on which we can observe two features. As has long been accepted, and was stressed by the great scholar José Vives Gatell above all, there is an original core that can be isolated for paleographic reasons and, because of this, it tallies with the offices included in the Antiphonary codex itself;[26] in its current form, however, numerous additions were recorded in it with the passing of time and the adventurous travels of our manuscript. All of the mentions of feast days recorded in this liturgical calendar are in columns, as is often the case, under a large horseshoe arch, arranged in months, with two columns per page. In turn, the column for each month is sheltered under another, smaller horseshoe arch, and the two columns for the two consecutive months are covered by the large arch.

This arrangement leads us to think that the person responsible for these folios, who usually began with this section before working on any gathering with the progressive presentation of the feast days of the year,[27] had prepared a quaternion in which he had left the right-hand pages of fols. 4, 5 and 6 blank and in which, moreover, fols. 9v-11v were totally blank. These were undoubtedly intended to receive a relevant text, which would have appeared in the model. It now needs to be pointed out that, although this is not the most common form, the initial blank pages were intended to receive the figures of the alpha-omega and the cross of Oviedo, with the beginning of the liturgical calendar on their versos, perhaps because the manuscript had to be treated in this way because of the quality of the parchment. Thin parchment was treated this way to prevent the ink in the figures from leaking through it. In any case, the arrangement is not strange or surprising, and can be justified by the way in which the calendar of saints' days is organized.

Let us return to fols. 9v-11v, however, which were left blank after the calendar of saints' days had been written. We need to bear in mind that there was a stating ubiquitous rule that parchment cannot be wasted. Furthermore, although this sometimes surprises us, the copyists were such skilled craftsmen in their work that they could calculate, after reading the model, how much space their own copy was going to take up and adapt the folios that they had available to match their plans. It is obvious that fols. 9v-11v were deliberately left blank to receive a specific text. As an annual liturgical book, it cannot be surprising that the text they intended to add was one of the versions in circulation of the so-called *Computus cottonianus,* or a similar text, which was appreciated, despite the complex methods of calculation, because such texts made it easier to locate the date of Easter each year by following the criteria laid down by the Church of Alexandria, which had been imposed in the West thanks to the work of Dionysius Exiguus.

If we take a good look at the magnificent study by Alfred Cordoliani on these computus treatises in the León manuscript,[28] we can bear in mind his extremely sensible conclusions, which refer only to these treatises. I am going to include them in my general speculations.

To receive these computus treatises, which were extremely varied, although they sometimes complemented each other, certain changes in the original plan had to be made. After the folios that were available in the first gathering, a new quaternion with fols. 12-19 was prepared and arranged in the form that we will see, and a separate folio was added, which is now fol. 2, and on its recto page a computus diagram was placed that to, a certain extent, forms part of the same series of texts.[29] It is highly likely that this was how the unit appeared in the 10th century *in.* Remember, as Alfred Cordoliani stresses, that many of these elements also survive in two famous La Rioja manuscripts,[30] in which they are repeated to a certain extent, and basically refer to treatises based on the writings of the Venerable Bede. What we do not know for the moment is what route these texts followed on their way to the Peninsula; almost certainly they came over the Pyrenees, but we do not know how they could have reached the region of León in this form.

All of this additional material, undoubtedly copied during the aforementioned period, in any case seems far removed from the original form of the manuscript, for which these prefaces probably had not been taken into account. In addition, these two bound manuscripts are not written by the same regular, straight and very consistent hand that copied the texts of the Antiphonary.

It is interesting to note Alfred Cordoliani's observation that the computus treatises copied like this come from a manuscript whose *annus praesens* was 806, a circumstance that means it circulated—we do not know exactly how or where—from the 9th century onwards.[31] We will need to keep the date 806 in mind, because it might be useful to us later on.

A quite different matter, from a codicological viewpoint, is posed by gathering C, which consists of fols. 20-27 and is clearly distinct from the rest of the manuscript, thus revealing its properly foreign character. It is rather irregular as far as the writing, support, and preparation of the parchment, yet all of its bifolios, which are sometimes of different origins, are in two columns. The format of the bound manuscript is clearly smaller than the rest of the manuscript in which it is now inserted. In any case it seems probable that it had been initially calculated that four folios would be enough (fols. 20-27 + 21-26), and these have lines with horizontal rulings which run through the middle of column b, corresponding to 42 pricks. When it this binion appeared not to be enough, or when was decided to increase the amount of text to be copied, another two bifolios were inserted, which are now the center of the quaternion (fols. 22-25 + 23-24). They differ in their preparation from the previous two, as the 45 pricks along the edge show, even though there are no more than 42 lines of text, as in the rest of the gathering.

This quaternion has writing that is clearly from the 11th century and can be attributed without the slightest hesitation to Arias,[32] who provides his own name in certain notes on the computus treatises and mentions here *anni praesentes* ranging from 1062 to 1069,[33] the years during which new material was gathered and added to the manuscript.

In this case it can be definitively asserted that this bound set of folios is an addition that was inserted before the main body of what is, strictly speaking, the manuscript, given the time period pointed out by the chronological references.

We still need to clear up the problem of fols. 1-3, which have been the key to the data handled by most of the people who have analysed the codex. Their current state and arrangement result ina remarkable enigma because of their simplicity and presence here. Part of this confusion lies in their actual codicological state, which I now describe.

Contrary to their appearance, each of these folios is actually an independent entity, although fol. 1 is now backstitched,[34] with a poor copy of a marker, to its subsequent folio, fol. 2, whereas fols. 2 + 3 form in turn a false bifolio, because they have been sewn from time immemorial to each other, so that they seem to form the result of a piece of skin folded in the middle, which in truth is not at all the case.

It is not just the fact that they are joined together, but that they are joined (in my opinion, at least since one of the several major manipulations of the introduction of the codex in former times) extremely irregularly, and because they have been linked together without respecting Gregory's Law:[35] in fact, both fols. 2 and 3 have the flesh side on the recto and the hair side on the verso, so that they display an utterly incongruent structure. Nevertheless, this unnatural arrangement is extremely old, as old as the sequence of the text that they contain required.

I pointed out before that fol. 2r has a text that seems to form part of the unit contained on fols. 9v-19. I actually think that the folio was added, either by sticking it or sewing it with its small marker, to fol. 19. In this way, the folio appeared irregularly with its flesh side next to the hair side of the last folio in the second gathering, perhaps because of the very high quality of the parchment, to draw the final computus in the aforementioned series here. However, the text that was added in this way left blank the verso of the folio grafted onto the piece, and the date and meaning of this we will now see.

At this time, the preparers of the manuscript still needed to include the prologue to the antiphonary book on the page that had been left blank, which is the hair side, as is the case with many books, especially, biblical books and less often, liturgical books. There was probably a reason to justify the relevance of this prologue for a codex of this type with this content.

Undoubtedly, this text was already linked, then, to another antiphonary that tallies more precisely with the *annus praesens,* 806, of the above mentioned set of computus treatises. The first prologue was followed by another three, all using different poetic forms:[36]one that is strictly rhythmic with clearly marked cadences, and two that the author himself in his own way calls *elegiac distiches.*

In order that the four texts could be copied in their entirety, yet another new folio was added, with certain dubious characteristics, which was probably obtained opportunistically from somewhere else. This new folio, which is currently fol. 3, was also sewn in an irregular fashion to what is now fol. 2, because the flesh side clashes with the hair side to which it was sewn.

Because of all of these details and working methods, we can assume that these additions were made in a location where they were fairly short of parchment, given that the relevant text was copied in a smaller space on fol. 3 than the text on the previous folio.This is probably because there was once again a lack of space to receive the text that remained to be written. This folio, in fact, has a double series of prickings as a horizontal guide: the first, which is not continuous as far as the lines and writing are concerned and goes along the outer edge; and another, with fewer marks, which is the one that was used for the writing and which is situated in the justified space.[37] Because the lines are narrower, the letters are smaller than the ones on fol. 2v, although the text follows continuously.

Once the prologues to the Antiphonary were finished, the scribe took advantage of a large part of the verso of what is now fol. 3 to add a repertoire that is often used in various liturgical books, namely, the formula that is a result of the *computus* tables for Easter. This is the text *Adnuntiationes festivitatum*, which the Bishop in each diocese used to announce in advance the dates of an entire series of feast days that were linked to the date of Easter.[38]

Let us now take a close look at fol. 1. At present, as we have already mentioned, it is joined to the pseudo-bifolio fols. 2 + 3 and by stitching that is definitely recent. The folio still has a fringe, although it is somewhat spoiled, which is a sign that leads us to presume that at some time it was inserted somewhere else. The flesh side was blank, and it is on the hair side that the poem (!) was placed that functions as a dedication and as a kind of ending at the same time. Underneath is the well-known miniature with the scene in which an *ille,* usually understood as a reference to the copyist, presents a book to the figure called *abba.* That has its distinctive crosier and a hand that, because of the position it is in, seems ready to bless the other character, rather than to receive the book that is being offered.

The fact that this folio now appears as the first one in the book means that it was transferred here at some time from its original position. The style of the piece acceptably concurs with that of the alpha and the cross of Oviedo. Although its codicological form suggests that it was designed and added after the other two large illustrations, it seems that it has a certain unity in its style and the skill used to produce it. I try and test the plausible explanation for these questions later, when I also analyse the poem superimposed on the figures.

HISTORY OF THE GENESIS OF THE MANUSCRIPT

So much for the codicological materials. We now need to resolve two questions that concern the text itself and its content: 1) the initial arrangement of the codex and its oldest configuration and 2) the real meaning of the justification of the form of the manuscript as far as what we might nowadays describe as its literary facets.

From all that has already been said, it can be deduced that there are two main codicological periods (which I would not hesitate to call separate) in the León manuscript. On the one hand, the date of the body of the manuscript itself, which I conclude, on paleographic grounds, to be from the first third of the 10th century and which was then considered, and still is, to be beautiful and extremely striking. On the other hand, there is a following period when they prepared and put the finishing touches on the prefaces to the work. Despite a certain consistency in the artistic style and basic decorative features, I do not think that they are strictly contemporary or were written by the same hands as the main part of the manuscript. I consider it undeniable that neither the quality of the parchment and its treatment nor the rather gradual shape of these prefaces correspond to a single period of production.

To put it another way, I understand that the main body of the codex was produced and finished in a place and time in which there was a fine, highly skilled copyist and, more important, that this copyist had the benefit of a top-quality model. The main body that was prepared in this way was then supplemented by introductory material that was not originally part of the manuscript and was arranged autonomously, although it is understood that this does not mean it might not have appeared in the same model.

So, first of all, that which was strictly speaking the Antiphonary was copied, and perhaps then the preparers of the manuscript thought about providing it with the same preliminary material that the model codex or other similar codices had. Probably, as I have already hinted, this manuscript had a colophon, which may well have been illustrated and used in some way to produce what is now fol. 1. This colophon had to be removed when the codex passed into new hands, owing to a decision taken by the owner for whom it had been written. Perhaps this was the factor that triggered this entire new structure.

The people responsible for providing the Antiphonary with its new frontmatter had the materials that they considered to be appropriate, and they prepared two gatherings (fols. 4-11, 12-19), to which fols. 2-3 had to be added, for various reasons already explained. This unit duplicates and extends to a certain extent what was a single page, fol. 28v, in the original, meticulously prepared manuscript, as has been clearly and adequately described.[39]

A series of elements were to be placed before this first codex, which was basically considered an antiphonary per se, and these were valid in their time, although not essential, such as the alpha-omega on fol. 4v, the cross of Oviedo on fol. 5v and the computus texts that go up to fols. 19 + 2r.

Because this is an antiphonary, the addition of fols. 2v-3v seems to be justified, because let us not forget that they contain a prologue and three items that supplement the main one, as well as a traditional item: the announcement of the feast days related to Easter. However note that only afterwards, in a manner that is not extraordinary but is rather rare, the true present-day title of the book appears.

This new structure gradually leads towards this title, which is based on the elements of a highly significant codex, until we reach the computus texts that this make us consider to be a liturgical book and then the prologues to the book itself, which we must presume were already present in the original manuscript. We cannot know whether the models of the text of the Antiphonary and of the prefaces were the same or whether they had the same date.

Given the previous comments, it is almost certain that there was a model from 806, which perhaps in turn preserved even more archaic elements, those that Pérez de Urbel correctly isolated.[40] However I point out that all of these elements are marginal, despite their importance, as far as the musical and textual body of the Antiphonary are concerned.

The prologues, written here in the aforementioned way, might allow us to continue to see in these a vindication of the Toledo liturgy, specifically of its strict, devout and fervent monastic form; but if I, in 1954, thought that they quite clearly referred[41] to the tensions in the 1160s, I am now forced to correct myself partially and to think of the 8th century *ex.* or the early years of the ninth.[42]

Perhaps this is how the presence of what are expressly described as *elegiac distiches* should be explained, which is a description that marks prologues 3 and 4 as being especially interesting, as the author himself says. The choice of this form, which is familiar in the Latin poetic tradition of any period, must be linked to the predominant feeling in all the compositions: namely, the anger and grief caused by the fact that the legitimacy and orthodoxy of the Hispanic liturgy had been questioned, when this could rely on the Toledo tradition and the sanction of the councils of the Hispanic Church, which were always highly revered and respected both inside and outside Spain because of their sound doctrinal basis. We probably find ourselves here in a religious, monastic and highly orthodox environment that, although it had not taken part in the anti-Elipandus theological debates, felt duty-bound to defend at all costs the doctrinal, traditional purity of the liturgy that it practiced. I wouldn't be surprised if this also led in the same period to the written conservation of the surprisingly varied notes that point out the origin of the texts used to produce the various formulas for the Antiphonary, as the tireless Vives has established, in another sense.[43]

So, the current Antiphonary of León, written in the two aforementioned periods, is a reflection, thanks to the initial texts, of the tensions that the Hispanic Church experienced as a result of the problem caused and supported by Elipandus of Toledo, who Beatus of Liébana and the Asturian Church strongly argued against, as it was asserting itself against Toledo. Theologians in the Carolingian world argued even more strongly against him for various reasons, including, to a large extent, other needs that concerned the world of politics and relations between the Empire and the Church. In the diatribe against Elipandus written by his opponents, there is an evident distrust, and clear insults soon appeared against the Hispanic liturgy (encouraged by the Archbishop of Toledo) that left their mark and would never be forgotten in several key centers of Christendom. They created the ferment that caught on in the raging, destructive movement of the 11th century. In these marginal indications (as an effective, well-known argument) the more than 2,000 quotes from biblical books, including almost 1,500 from the psalms, appear to provide the contents with dignity and with information on the quality and dignity of the Hispanic Passionary, from which the authors of the antiphonal formulas took numerous texts when it suited them.[44]

The main part of the Antiphonary proves that the liturgical texts, in this book at least, have a biblical basis that is unique or that had connections one would not always expect.[45] Where did the music that accompanies these different phases come from? Was it composed when all of the antiphonal formulas were already fixed? Did they apply certain well-known melodies to more than one text, and under what conditions did they do this? Would this musical problem have anything to do with the admiration and sacred respect with which, as we have just seen, the basic manuscript was always held?

The problem with Ikilanus

Up to now, going against the entire bibliographic tradition, I have not devoted a single line to the problem of who was responsible for the manuscript and who it was written for, a topic to which so much philosophising has been devoted since the 19th century, taking for granted the essential role played by Abbot Ikilanus of León. I have nothing against this individual, who remains a mystery to me, because I cannot convince myself that we are dealing with a single supposedly long-lived abbot, who already signs as such in 917[46] and is still an abbot after 960. It is not that I do not believe he could have lived past the age of 80, but rather that I am not sure the León documentation refers to a single Abbot Ikilanus, nor do I totally accept his supposed activity with the manuscript.

It is undeniably true that an *Ikkila abba* became at a certain time the fortunate owner of the codex that we are concerned with here. But let us consider things one at a time.

There are two main pieces of evidence regarding Ikilanus on which his undeniable connection with this antiphonary is based. First of all, he is mentioned on fol. 1v, the form on which have already talked about. In my opinion, this folio, with its blank recto and verso with text and figures, was prepared when its previous owner, probably the unknown (but historically credited) Teodemundo, decided to give him the work as a present, for which he had shown great interest. At this time the folio was added to the manuscript: it was inserted, thanks to its marker, in a prominent position, namely, between fols. 5 and 6, so that an excellent decorative sequence was formed (alpha, cross, dedication and *computus* tables), with a fairly natural appearance. The rectos of these folios, as has already been mentioned, were blank as a sign of respect.

To understand the process of sending the book, we need take another good look at the letters in capitals, which offer adequate limits for dating.[47] My interpretation and its details differ from Pérez de Urbel's, who produced his by correcting Férotin and Serrano in turn.[48] I translate: "Very great merit have you obtained with this gift, O Abbot Teodemundo, you who dwell here with your good monks and will in the future revel with the angels. Shining even brighter thanks to your wishes, O abbot Ikilanus! you can now see that what had been your desire is finished; look again and again at the book prepared for use, illustrated and decorated in gold. May I deserve to be helped by your prayers: remember me, the copyist, for ever, he who has worked so hard out of respect for your name".

So, in this dedication-colophon, in which only the dates and synchronisms are missing that we would have enormously appreciated, I can see how the work took shape: in view of Ikilanus's fervent wishes, Abbot Teodemundo decided to give the book to him as a gift,[49] but completed as we have seen; and it was a copyist who went to all this trouble to fulfill Ikilanus's wishes, helped by Teodemundo's generous attitude.

The codex was probably produced at the monastery run by Teodemundo, which I would place in the eastern part of León owing to the numerous, varied influences provided by its decoration, both northern and southern. Furthermore, its writing displays certain Castilian touches that nevertheless are not essential features. It is impossible to speculate about the origin and the date of the model, because there may have been a copy interposed between the one that we have assumed to be from 806 and ours, just as nothing contradicts this hypothetical manuscript from 806 being from the diocese of Beja,[50] or a copy of one from there. What really matters at this stage is to be able to establish, as seems to be quite clear, a genealogical line that runs from Visigothic times until the unhappy period in which the Hispanic Church was murkily split because of what was known as *Adoptionism.* After this it lapsed into a slow but insuperable tendency to succumb to the uniformity of Romano-Gallican discipline, which would finally and inexorably arrive in the second half of the 11th century.

Having established this, we still need to explain the most important piece of evidence regarding the role played by *Ikkila* in this codex: what really guarantees this, more than the added folio (fol. 1v), is the page tapestry that covers fol. 5r.[51] Before going on, note that it was done in slapdash fashion, without the elegant strokes or the ornamental motifs that characterize the codex, in an opaque blue with which the entire page is smudged rather than painted.[52] The legends and presentation imitate an old form that was quite usual in the kingdom of León and in La Rioja but which is far removed from the grace and quality of almost all of these pieces. The cross is not drawn in a balanced way, and the decorative themes, starting with the swastika that is repeated in the frieze,[53] are crude, although they are sometimes pretentious. This page was left blank deliberately, so that the beginning of the calendar of saints' days and its decorative motifs would stand out.[54] In the end the elegance of the initial work as a whole (without any exceptional qualities, it needs to be said) is spoiled by this eyesore, which did no credit to the owner of the codex when it came to using it.

But there is more. The owner of this rare blue pigment, after spoiling fol. 5r, allowed whoever it was—who thought himself an artist—to make certain retouches and to complete decorations, sometimes just by imitating the existing ones, on the alpha and the cross of Oviedo, which look oddly spoiled; but these abuses did achieve their aim of giving all these folios an apparent sense of unity.

Later on, the codex was subjected to other manipulations, such as the one we can attribute entirely to Arias, gathering C (fols. 20-27).

I have the impression that the old manuscript,[55] without any appendices, that were perhaps from just before the time that this magnificent piece was given to Abbot Ikilanus,[56] remained intact as an venerable object, and in different periods, various people produced *probationes* and all kinds of additions to complement the work, even adding unusual historical news items.

The devices used to add materials, as we have seen, in no way came to an end with the forms that I have pointed out. Even in the 11th century *in.* they were still organising and copying, always by making use of blank pages, the famous office of James the Zebedean, a previously unknown part of the Antiphonary.

As far as this is concerned, I point out that they may well have inserted a bifolio so that the material for the feast of St. James would be integrated into the manuscript at the proper chronological place, with illustrations and a well-presented text and with all its neumes. All of this was respected in some way, even when all noteworthy adulterations had been removed.

Ikilanus's role is not only limited as far as his contribution to this beautiful codex is concerned. All of the speculation about this individual seems utterly worthless with respect to the dating or location of the writing of the manuscript.

I stress this aspect, which is undeniable from a codicological perspective: there is a distinction in the Antiphonary in its oldest form between two different sections: an original, very old section comprising fol. 28 to the end, which Ikilanus merely owned, and another which resulted from Abbot Teodemundo generously deciding to agree to answer Ikilanus' pleas to obtain this magnificent copy. Later on there were people such as Arias or the author of the office of St. James who wanted to complete aspects,[57] not to mention those who copied the royal confirmations of the dynasty of Navarre and those who at all times considered it to be a privilege to print rubbish or nonsense in this extraordinary treasure.

At this point I realize that all of these considerations do not explain the musicological problems posed by the Antiphonary. But I do not have the skills for this. Nevertheless, I do think that I have provided evidence that places the text of the Antiphonary of León in a period well before the date that the beautiful copy we have here was produced.

A NEW KIND OF ANTIPHONARY, OR REPERTORIES OF TEXTS SET TO MUSIC?

I would like to continue to hold the reader's attention with a few more comments. First, I am going to comment on an unusual musical fragment that is kept in Córdoba, AC, ms. 123.[58] I must confess that I do not know what strange oversight led me to overlook this when I published my observations on the manuscript and its various sections in 1983,[59] or when I recognized the contents of the various relevant codicological sections many years before then.[60] I realized I had missed this when I worked together with some eminent paleographers on the materials left by Millares Carlo, many years after his death.[61]

The collection and the arrangement of the two, perhaps three, sections that can be clearly distinguished in the Córdoba manuscript could well be the work of an onlooker, who, when it was produced, collected and joined together two or three manuscripts, all of which were probably the work of a single center or of several closely linked ones. He joined them together as one volume, in which he took great care to highlight the work produced by Álvaro of Córdoba, which meant that the manuscript finally arrived at the homeland of the latter, perhaps in the 16th century *in.*, as a way of honoring that great figure, who, more than anyone else, was the focus of the cultural life and prestige of the Christian community in what was then the capital of the Caliphate.

The codex soon attracted the attention of various scholars, although with varying degrees of fortune. Ewald was the first to appreciate the quality of the scribe, whose name he identified, and to point decisively and precisely to the place of origin of the manuscript.[62] It was then the subject of a critically mediocre monograph, in which there is no reference or data that give any detailed insight.[63] All of those who have mentioned it after this do place it correctly, although they always have doubts about its origin, in view of the works by the writer from Córdoba and its current location.

The first section (fols. 1-164) only contains works by Álvaro, taken directly and in all probability from a highly organized codex,[64] perhaps from Córdoba, by the copyist of our manuscript who referred to himself three times as *Sisuertus presbiter* (fols. 91, 100 and 121) to guarantee his work properly. This was written, it can be said if we take great care, in León, in a center where the Mozarabic tradition was perhaps close and highly important. The text finishes (fol. 164v) with a bound book that was not the last one, as is clearly shown by the mistake in the text and the existence of a catchword that does not match the beginning of the following bound book.

A second section includes fols. 165-207; here, after a series of theological questions and answers, the famous Penitential appears, which is wrongly referred to as being from Córdoba on the basis of its presence in this volume. Millares was the first person to give this part its proper importance. Bezler has studied this in detail, focusing precisely on the Penitential.[65] Later another series of texts appears, which always contains cuts due to errors in preserving the respective gatherings, and the last of these is the one known as *Indiculus de Henoc*, which was so important in Córdoba and Asturias at this time, because it was considered to be a kind of prophecy on the end of Muslim power.[66]

Finally, we may be able to talk about a third sector that runs from fol. 208 to the end, with the sermon on Mary's Assumption, which is followed by a series of various informative texts (geographical and historical news, etc.). If we bear in mind the three or four hands that alternated in turn in these last two sections, it might be stated in almost all probability that from fol. 165 to the end these are the remains of a manuscript whose contents are heterogeneous but, when all is said and done, form a single unit.

In any case, I point out quite firmly that it is highly likely we are talking here about only two manuscripts (Álvaro and final miscellany), and that each one (the latter with its various authors and interests) is the work of an author in León, a region that was strongly influenced by Castilian and Mozarabic trends at the same time. Evidence of the former is provided in the text by the presence of the Penitential[67] and the aforementioned sermon attributed to Jerome[68] but which in actual fact are texts that are clearly from beyond the Pyrenees, the latter, because the direct influence of highly significant Mozarabic elements is quite clear. In my opinion these are part of the same trend that brought the manuscript of St. Augustine's *The City of God* with the Mozarabic nonmusical *notae* that I have had the good fortune to have published at La Cogolla.[69]

Taking advantage of the fact that fol. 208r had been left blank so that the Homily on the Assumption of the Virgin could be honorably included on its verso as a new text, two texts foreign to this one are written, in the same type of script as the one that can be found in this section but which is probably of a slightly later date. I would be bold enough to place this copy in the eastern part of León, but at the end of the 10th century, or more likely, right at the beginning of the 11th century.

These are two sequences, supposedly from the Aquitaine, written without a break with the special feature that the first one is incomplete, because it was undoubtedly begun by taking advantage of a blank ending (not too long, judging by the omitted text)

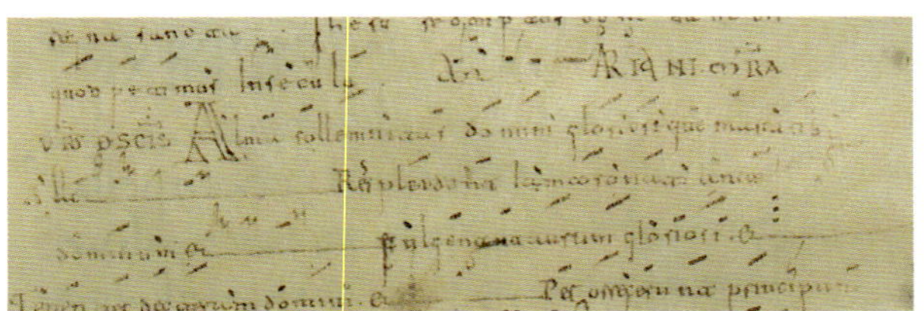

2. *Alvarus Paulus. Opera et alia opuscula.* Córdoba, AC, ms. 123, 10th century, fol. 208r

on the previous folio, which has now been lost. Throughout the codex several quaternions have not survived in complete form. To be more precise, it is undeniable from the form and appearance of the catchwords used here that fol. 207 is not actually the one that went before fol. 208. What remains of the first sequence[70] and of the second contains musical notation, which is always (except by Artiles) correctly attributed to a region in the north of the Peninsula. However I stress that this is not in any way "a lost fragment from another manuscript, but from the same period".[71] We are faced here with the single second part of texts that were copied by taking advantage of blank spaces at the end of the previous bound manuscript (which has now been lost) and at the end of the one that now begins with fol. 208. This is how we can understand why the first sequence is cut short, whereas the second one makes good use of the available space. As a result, I draw attention to certain instances in which codicology might provide firm, reliable data for any later restructuring of a codex.

The person who wrote the aforementioned texts set to music had a model in which the text was already tailored to fit the music, as can be seen from the care taken in the copy to place each word or syllable in accordance with the corresponding melody. To ensure that this did not prevent what we might call the continuous reading of the text, however, the syllables involved were separated properly, and where appropriate a horizontal line was also placed to give the text the right degree of continuity. All this was also done by following the criterion that the lines on the flesh side of the folio should be visible on the hair side, as was normal for preparing the copy of the aforementioned homily. This forced the person who transcribed the text of the sequences to make the letters smaller, so that the line with the text and the corresponding neumes fit on the same lines. As a result, the texts less developed than those in other musical books, such as León or San Juan de la Peña,[72] to give two well-known examples from the 10th century *in.* Furthermore, only certain neumes contain spiral developments, like those so often used in previous periods.

It is clear that we have here a fresh example of an imitation in León of texts and musical forms taken from sources that came from various places. Of course, I can clearly state that the copy is from no later than the 11th century *in.,* as is proved by a series of features in the spelling.

For obvious reasons, given that I live in Santiago de Compostela, I would like to add some more details about another extremely interesting musical text: the so-called *Book of hours belonging to Ferdinand I,* which is kept at the University of Santiago.[73] Copied with all the care and luxury that were possible in its day, it is the work of an exceptional copyist, Pedro, whose origins are unknown. He finished his work in 1055, undoubtedly at the court of León itself, under Queen Sancha's orders, although the paleographical features of the *Hours* lead us to believe that he had received his refined training as a scribe in a center that makes us think more of links with Silos or Cardeña than with La Rioja, even if numerous reminders in his highly refined script show a clear aesthetic debt to Valeránica, as we can recognize in the writing produced by Florencio and his followers. Of course, at no time can he be considered to be from León on the basis of his writing.

The comprehensive preciousness of the writing is in keeping with the techniques employed in the illustrations, which were produced by a man named Fructuoso, who worked on both large, full-page miniatures and on capitals and initials. Specialists have discovered a wide variety of European influences in his work, all of which has a very striking restrained tone. In this way it could form part of an elaborate demonstration of total power in northern Hispania begun by Ferdinand I, along with his immediate claims for a higher status in the West, from the time when he gave himself the title *Imperator Totius Hispaniae.*[74]

This is truly a beautiful psalter with its *liber canticorum,*[75] which totally defines the manuscript. It is enriched with initials and capitals in gold and valuable

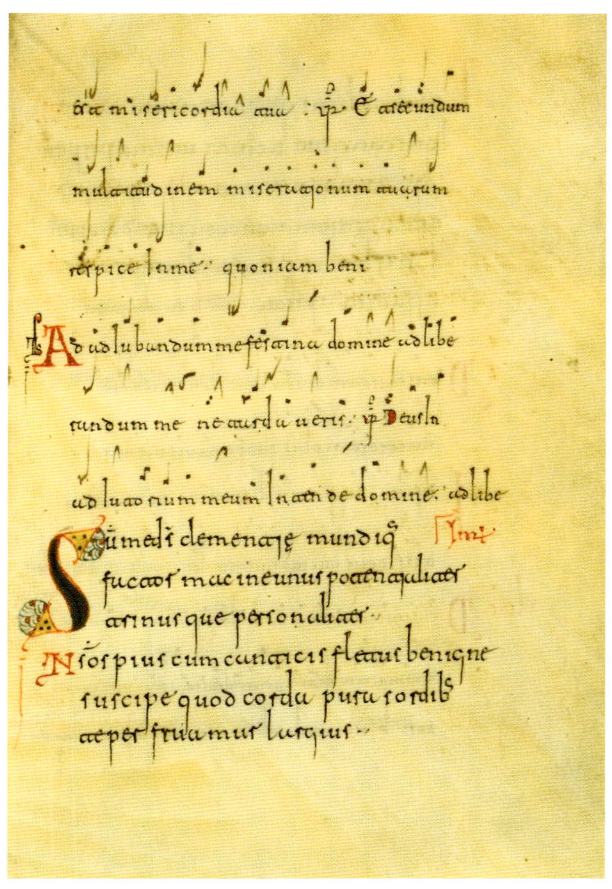

3. *Liber canticorum et horarum.* Salamanca, BGU, ms. 2668, 11th century *med.* (1059), fol. 156r

miniatures, which are the work of the aforementioned Fructuoso. What we are interested in here are the last two quaternions, which were actually added in their day to the book when it was already finished, although it should be borne in mind that they had always been intended to accompany this. In fact they appear after the metric colophon, in which the codex itself speaks to the reader (fol. 208) and only refers to the previous contents, psalms and canticles. In these two bound books the way the parchment is prepared is different yet similar to what has come before. It contains the so-called *Ordo ad medium noctis,* or ritual for the night-time hours, which matches almost completely that in the codex in the British Library in London, Add. ms. 30851. This was published in complete form a century ago by Wilson,[76] once again as an appendix to a psalter and canticles, a text to which the one published for the facsimile edition of our codex can be compared.[77] It is closer, however, to another manuscript, which we might call its twin if it were not for the blatant differences in quality between them. This manuscript, Salamanca, BGU, ms. 2668, is known as the *Breviary of Queen Sancha.*[78]

In our Santiago manuscript, both quaternions (27 and 28)—which we might call devotional (fols. 209-224), although I have not dared to claim that they are not the work of Pedro, the aforementioned scribe of the codex—show certain minute differences in the spelling apart, of course, from their shape when it is compared with the exquisite, balanced and rather nonrounded script of the former. These two gatherings were prepared by individuals who were clearly different from those who prepared the main body of the manuscript, although the writing might be Pedro's. In these folios, one can distinguish quite clearly between the shape of the simple texts and of those accompanied by neumes, although these were traced so carefully with such an apparent reduction in the wealth of spirals and strokes found in other musical manuscripts that at no time (except for the module) can any graphic differences be established between the simple parts and those set to music. Despite this, the final section of the Santiago codex can be distinguished at a glance from the rest.

Was King Ferdinand able to read the music that many of the texts included in this part contained? We have a reference (although it is in a markedly laudatory tone) that is not particularly precise from the *Historia silense,*[79] according to which we know that the King "sometimes enormously enjoyed singing along with the clerics, when the monastic community that looked after the royal church of San Juan in León sang the holy *laudes.*" This church was later called St. Isidore, after the remains of Isidore of Seville arrived there in 1063 to be elevated on its altar.

We cannot know if the book was ever used, but the exceptional state of this beautiful copy seems to rule this out. A comparison of its neumes with the remaining ones that have survived, especially those that accompany identical pieces, might lead specialists to understand once and for all the meaning of the musical richness that lies hidden in our numerous manuscripts.

I am sure that this day will come, if we all make a determined effort.

Notes

[1] I use the text and the version in my recent edition: Manuel C. Díaz y Díaz. *Valerio del Bierzo. Su persona, su obra*. León: Centro de Estudios e Investigación San Isidoro (CSIC-CECEL), 2006, 318 (Fuentes y Estudios de Historia Leonesa: 111).

[2] "Y en los oídos de las gentes multiplican diversas y numerosas series de oficios, y levantan mucho el tono de sus voces y con muchas genuflexiones salmodian multitud de oraciones y en los oficios del día y en las horas de la noche descubren torpeza y desidia y un descuido somnoliento." The terminology, which is sometimes incorrect here, can be completed with the descriptions provided in the last two prologues in the León codex 8, to be discussed later on: *idem*. "Los prólogos del *antiphonale visigothicum* de la Catedral de León (León, Arch. Cat., ms. 8)". *Archivos Leoneses* 8 (1954): 226-257. The terms *melodian* and *diurnis* have been corrected with respect to *melodia* and *diurni* in the original version.

[3] I have made a remarkable list of mentions of liturgical and theological manuscripts in my book: *idem. Códices visigóticos en la monarquía leonesa*. León: Centro de Estudios e Investigación San Isidoro (CSIC-CECEL), 1983 (Fuentes y Estudios de Historia Leonesa: 31) to which I refer. I must point out that the lists are growing almost nonstop, as new sets of documents from that period are discovered and published.

[4] See Anscari M. Mundó. "La datación de los códices litúrgicos visigóticos toledanos". *Hispania Sacra* 18, no. 35 (1965): 1-25. The book has been recognized by critics, as can be seen in Agustín Millares Carlo, et. al., eds. *Corpus de códices visigóticos*. Vol. 1, *Estudio*. Las Palmas: Gobierno de Canarias, UNED, Centro Asociado de Las Palmas de Gran Canaria, 1999, 190-198. Regarding the general problems of the Hispanic liturgy, see the notes by Jordi Pinell in *Diccionario de historia eclesiástica de España*. Vol. 2. Madrid: CSIC, 1972-1987, see *liturgia*.

[5] Manuel C. Díaz y Díaz. *Códices visigóticos…* Op. cit., 157.

[6] It seems almost unnecessary to say that the Benedictine fathers of Silos relatively recently made a study and transcription of this. *Antiphonarium mozarabicum de la Catedral de León*. León, 1928. This transcription is not as flawed as it is often said to be. For the prefaces, it is the only we have. Later the one by Louis Brou, and José Vives, eds., appeared based on new foundations, in *Antifonario visigótico mozárabe de la Catedral de León*. 2 vols. Vol. 1, Barcelona: Centro de Estudios e Investigación San Isidoro (CSIC-CECEL), 1959; vol. 2, Madrid: CSIC, Instituto P. Enrique Flórez, 1953-4 (Monumenta Hispaniae Sacra: Serie Litúrgica 5, no. 2. Facsímiles musicales 1), which is the transcription that accompanies the facsimile edition carefully prepared by the same publishers: *Antifonario visigótico mozárabe de la Catedral de León*. Madrid, Barcelona, León: CSIC, Instituto P. Enrique Flórez, Instituto Español de Musicología, Centro de Estudios e Investigación San Isidoro (CSIC-CECEL), 1953 (Monumenta Hispaniae Sacra: Liturgical Series 5, no. 2. Facsímiles musicales 1). Neither the facsimile nor the transcription provides all of the materials preceding what is, strictly speaking, the Antiphonary.

[7] Certainly most of them, including Louis Brou, and José Vives, eds. *Ibidem*.

[8] The leading authority who decisively tends to favor the 11th century, especially as far as its artistic connections are concerned, is Manuel Gómez Moreno. *Catálogo monumental de España. Provincia de León*. Madrid: Ministerio de Instrucción Pública y Bellas Artes, 1926, 155-158.

[9] I would like to point out that the following study is not always complete because of problems now posed by the rather brutal restoration process that was probably carried out in the 1950s on the facsimile edition, which proved to be really important and productive for paleographic study. The main cause of the codicological changes was the ironing process that certain folios underwent, especially the first few. This also meant that certain information was lost that can sometimes be seen, although always with problems and a degree of uncertainty, thanks to the microfilm of the manuscript that the Photography Service of the Biblioteca Nacional made around that time, which is somewhat inadequate by modern-day standards.

[10] My observations were complemented successfully and with fresh interpretations in the study that my generous friend Professor Ana Suárez of the University of Santiago carried out with great care at my request, to compensate for my poor sight. Most of the results of this work are due to the meticulousness of her notes. I cannot possibly thank her enough here. However, I would like to place her extremely valuable help on record.

[11] Remember that they are folios included in the facsimile edition. Although I have protested on several occasions this decision that deprived us of specific knowledge of the first 27 folios, I now recognize that Louis Brou and José Vives were right to decide this, although the rest is still missing.

[12] It is understood that I mean this was equivalent to a conclusion to a regular series of quaternions.

[13] Although it might be jumping the gun, I think this final item in the codex was perhaps lost, because it contained the colophon and a note about the ownership of the original manuscript, which they felt the need to remove when its destination changed, as we will see.

[14] Although it now contains added texts, various subsequent investigations merely confirm my initial position regarding the folio that the unit contains. I will firmly support this position, both here and later, because the use of a blank page to make *probationes pennae,* to add texts or various types of news, including certain textual supplements, reinforces the idea that at some time, although it would be short from the perspective of the life of the codex, there was a blank page, which was standard practice for all the beginnings of a text or book. The norm was required because this blank page had to serve as a flyleaf and protection for the volume and as the title of each work in particular. This was done to prevent wear and tear from being placed alongside other books and from damaging the title or, in certain cases, the first page of the text. This norm was strictly adhered to in the late Middle Ages, although the use of binding with wooden covers was already starting to spread, which could damage the first page; this was why it was always left without any text or figures, and in this case was especially justified. I would like to stress this principle, because it will be useful as a guide in several stages of my work.

[15] A mediocre reproduction of this title appears in the edition by Louis Brou, and José Vives. Op. cit., which is the published volume of the text, with the addition of certain arbitrary transcriptions of the first few folios that are missing in the facsimile, as already noted.

[16] "De toto anni circulo a festiuitate s. Aciscli usque ad finem."

[17] The scribe himself, or someone who at some time prepares the parchment, uses a technique—that can be seen, for example, in gathering 13 of the manuscript, which starts on fol. 117; in gathering 17, that is, on fol. 146, and on the one that starts on fol. 228—,it has guides for the horizontal lines right along the middle of the folio, which is archaic in the Peninsula. He might have been imitating, perhaps without meaning to, the technique that the model used, more than a century before, depending on certain contents.

[18] Although Lowe's principle does not entirely fulfil the chronological requirements of our Visigothic manuscripts, it is undeniable that the systematic presence of the graphic sequence *V + tj + V* confirms a date after 900, and vice-versa, although the limits are frankly imprecise.

[19] I cannot find an all-embracing reason to explain why in quite a few cases it is necessary to complete the line of text with its corresponding neumes in any of the margins (even the inner ones!) of certain folios.

[20] However, I think that the identification of miniatures and other elements made in the edition by the Benedictines Silos goes too far. Op. cit.

[21] For these folios we have the transcription that the Benedictines made at Silos and, partially, the transcription work by Louis Brou, and José Vives. Op. cit.

[22] Please allow me to make a public apology for two quite different situations: first, the date of the metric prologues that I insisted at the time on attributing to the liturgical struggles of the 11th century, when the campaign against the traditional Hispanic liturgy was at its height (my article in Manuel C. Díaz y Díaz. "Los prólogos del *antiphonale visigothicum…*". Op. cit.). Second, and even more serious, having passed utterly superficially over this manuscript in *idem. Códices visigóticos…* Op. cit., 390-391.

[23] The quaternions are not totally regular because some have added folios that were already arranged in their day as quaternions. On two occasions these are separate folios, provided with a cover, which was folded and sewn properly.

[24] Despite everything, I still have reservations about the real meaning of this entire corpus, which will gradually be revealed in the following pages. I am thinking about the way in which the cross of Oviedo and the alpha and the omega are shown, and even the calendar of saints days, the current form of which we might consider to be normal. But the way that this unit is currently presented already arouses suspicions of serious manipulation. It is odd that the body of the Antiphonary has not been changed at all and that these have piled up at the beginning.

[25] Louis Brou. "Le Joyau des antiphonaires latins". *Archivos Leoneses* 8 (1954): 62-63.

[26] José Vives Gatell, and Ángel Fábrega Grau. "Calendarios hispánicos anteriores al siglo XII". *Hispania Sacra* 2, no. 3 (1949).

[27] I emphasize this because there are books such as the *Ordinum*, in which this chronological sequence does not occur at all [Màrius Férotin, ed. *Le Liber ordinum en usage dans l'Église wisigothique et mozarabe d'Espagne du cinquème, au onzième siècle.* Paris: Librairie Firmin-Didot, 1904 (Monumenta Ecclesiae Liturgica: 5)]. In any case, I would like to draw attention to the fact that this must be an innovation that can probably be attributed to the 8th or 9th centuries, because it does not appear at all, for example, in the famous *Verona Orationale* (Verona, BC, ms. 89), which is from approximately the year 700.

[28] Alfred Cordoliani. "Les Textes et figures de comput de l'Antiphonaire de Léon". *Archivos Leoneses* 8 (1954): 260-283.

[29] I will return to the codicological problem with fols. 1-3 later on.

[30] I am referring from Alfred Cordoliani to what are known as *Albeldense*, from approximately 975, and *Vigilano*, from 992, which are both codicological, paleographic products of San Millán de la Cogolla, as we now know.

[31] Alfred Cordoliani. Op. cit., 286-287.

[32] By this, I merely wish to state that this unusual traveller is responsible for the total or partial addition and for its orientation, which is clearly complementary but with different bases to the treatises and figures in the aforementioned part.

[33] Alfred Cordoliani. Op. cit., recalls that several of the treatises written here by Arias are merely alterations, corrections and adaptations of the ones that made up the previous unit.

[34] What follows might not always show clear proof because of the situation created by the fact that they were rebound in the 1950s, which not only destroyed certain pieces of codicological evidence but also eliminated certain incidental data that the manuscript still displayed at that time.

[35] All of the old manuscripts of the Peninsula, without significant exceptions, comply with this so-called *law*: flesh and hair sides of the parchment always faced each other, not only inside the quaternions, but in any standard additions. Exceptions to this are so rare that they usually indicate foreign, diverse treatment.

[36] This is in contrast to my way of presenting the second text in the article mentioned in note 2, although I speculated that it contained certain rhythmic elements.

[37] This double treatment is what makes me consider a center with limited resources.

[38] This form with quite a few of its variations has been published by Màrius Férotin.

[39] This initial presentation might justify the existence of a colophon, about which I have already speculated, possibly illustrated, at the end, which would round off and complete our original manuscript.

[40] Justo Pérez de Urbel. "El Antifonario de León. El escritor y la época". *Archivos Leoneses* 8 (1954): 138-139.

[41] To be sure of this, I bore two facts in mind: the acceptance of the general date of the Antiphonary in the second half of the 10th century and the fact that the prologues are clearly older than the codex which they came from before.

[42] I recognize that José Vives was right when he disputed my thesis, although I think that he based his arguments more on intuition and a general knowledge of the situation. The solution is now endorsed by trustworthy evidence.

[43] José Vives Gatell. "Fuentes hagiográficas del Antifonario de León". *Archivos Leoneses* 8 (1954).

[44] In any case, I would recall that for various reasons no major conclusions have been reached in the rare attempts to compare the antiphonary formulas that have been preserved here with the references to the incipits of antiphons that we have in other liturgical books.

[45] Celso Rodríguez Fernández. *El antifonario visigótico de León. Estudio literario de sus fórmulas sálmicas*. León: Centro de Estudios e Investigación San Isidoro (CSIC-CECEL), 1985 (Colección Fuentes y Estudios de Historia Leonesa: 35), who, after having studied the origins and ways in which formulas in psalms were joined together and corrupted, reaches conclusions that should not be ignored by musicologists, for he establishes the clearly ancient origin of many formulas, alongside others that he dares to say probably do not date back to before the Arab invasion in 711.

[46] On receiving a substantial endowment in which, among other books, an antiphonary is mentioned.

[47] Without going into superfluous lists, I would like to point out that lettering like this is in capitals and in various colors, in numerous manuscripts.

[48] Justo Pérez de Urbel. Op. cit., 130

[49] I think that I can speculate on the possibility that the codex belonged to Abbot Teodemundo, who appears to be so obscure and who could have joined the monastery run by Iquilanus. Once again, we are dealing here with suppositions that could obviously go on and on.

[50] I think that the news of the saints' calendar, which was shrewdly commented on by Justo Pérez de Urbel. Op. cit., is highly indicative.

[51] Perhaps it fulfilled a function as it faced the page tapestry that covers fol. 5r.

[52] Given that we only have evidence of certain kinds of blue pigment in the second half of the 10th century, maybe it was simply a question of trying out this new color, which they did not yet know how to use with the appropriate, desirable level of skill

[53] As far as I know, various scholars have mentioned this decoration, but I have never see, as far as I remember, an explanation of these forms and strokes.

[54] One might think that the same problem would occur on the following folios, but it does not; the horseshoe arches and their columns appear in almost exactly the same way on both sides of the folio, so that they avoided spoiling these by moving colors from one side to the other.

[55] I recall that this is how I always call and understand the real Antiphonary, fol. 28-end.

[56] I wish to stress that this addition was made, and exquisitely justified, only after all of fols. 4-19 and 2-3 had been placed before the main part of the codex. If it had been written for Iquilanus or directly under his orders, fol. 1v would have formed an integral part of this unit, which did not happen, as we have just seen.

[57] I do not want to miss this opportunity to point out in this regard that the Santiago office, copied on fol. 5r, is a good example of the high regard and esteem in which the Antiphonary was held in at that time, perhaps even greater than the admiration it arouses in us today. The office was added in the 11th century in a manner that was quite advanced for its time, because it relied on two procedures: a conscientious and quite careful imitation of the relevant neumes and a literal text in which a skilful imitation of the writing of the copyist of the Antiphonary can be seen clearly. It only occasionally lets slip certain hints that reveal its situation and period because the cursive features that can be seen at certain points have nothing to do with 10th century writing, or of course with the writing in the codex. Something always gives forgeries away.

[58] This is how it is referred to in Antonio García García, Francisco Cantelar Rodríguez, and Manuel Nieto Cumplido. *Catálogo de los manuscritos e incunables de la Catedral de Córdoba*. Salamanca: Universidad Pontificia de Salamanca, 1976. Before it was simply known as the *Álvaro Codex* [from Córdoba].

[59] I am referring of course to the comprehensive series of observations on its parts that I made in Manuel C. Díaz y Díaz. *Códices visigóticos...* Op. cit.

[60] The resulting texts were described in *idem. Index Scriptorum Latinorum Medii Aevi Hispanorum.* Salamanca: University of Salamanca, 1958-1959. I studied the codex directly in marathon sessions in 1969.

[61] I do not need to tell the expert reader that I am referring to Agustín Millares Carlo's work. Op. cit. (Anscari M. Mundó, José Manuel Ruiz Asencio, Blas Casado and I myself were responsible for reviewing this and making it available to the public.)

[62] Paul Ewald. "Reise nach Spanien in Winter von 1878 auf 1879". *Neues Archiv der Gesellschaft für ältere Deutsche Geschichtskunde* 8 (1884): 359-361.

[63] I am thinking about the article by José Artiles Rodríguez. "El códice visigótico de Álvaro de Córdoba". *Revista de Archivos, Bibliotecas y Museos* 9 (1932): 201-291. In any case, on studying the entire codex, he saw that there were several parts, but he attributed all of them to the 11th century and thought they were from the Andalusian school.

[64] I am assuming this based on the fact that Álvaro's works are distributed in such a way that each new one always begins on a verso, even though he had to leave the corresponding recto blank.

[65] Francis Bezler. *Les Pénitentiels espagnols. Contribution à l'étude de la civilisation de l'Espagne chrétienne du Haut Moyen Âge*. Münster: Aschendorff, 1994 (Forschungen der Görresgesellschaft: 30).

[66] A large part of all of these sometimes incomplete commentaries and texts were published by Jean Leclercq. "Textes et manuscrits de quelques bibliothèques d´Espagne". *Hispania Sacra* 2, no. 3 (1949).

[67] Related, although with numerous variants, to those known as being from Albelda and Silos, because of their origins. In any case, this text, which definitely comes from beyond the Pyrenees, was, as can be seen, widespread in Castile and León, which provides its different versions with a certain degree of unity.

[68] In fact, the work of Pascasius Radbertus (786-865), Abbot of Corbie, a famous writer and theologian.

[69] Manuel C. Díaz y Díaz. "Agustín entre los mozárabes: un testimonio". *Augustinus* 25 (1980): 157-180.

[70] We cannot know if there was another similar text before this or not. The part that has survived corresponds to the sequence *Orbis conditor regressus est*, which is said to be from the Aquitaine.

[71] Agustín Millares Carlo. Op. cit., 45.

[72] With regard to this extremely fragmentary manuscript, I am surprised that neither Susana Zapke's nor Ángel Canellas's studies attempt to locate the origin of the book through its script. I would be bold enough to insinuate, on the basis of the facts narrated in Canellas's study, that this extremely interesting codex is from Navarre, and to be more precise, from a region near Nájera.

[73] Santiago de Compostela, BXU, ms. 609 (Res. 1). There is a splendid facsimile edition: *Libro de horas de Fernando I de León*. Studies by Manuel C. Díaz y Díaz and Serafín Moralejo Álvarez; transcription of the text by M.ª Virtudes Pardo Gómez and M.ª Araceli García Piñeiro. Facsimile edition of manuscript 609 (Res. 1) in the Biblioteca de la Universidad de Santiago de Compostela. Vol. 1, *Facsímile;* vol, 2, *Estudios*. Santiago de Compostela: Testimonio Editorial, Consellería de Educación e Ordenación Universitaria, 1995, 53-63. The edition is accompanied by a volume that includes various studies. In the one by Serafín Moralejo Álvarez on the illustration of the codex certain analogies are recorded not only with the San Millán

book of homilies or the Beatus of Saint-Sever, but there are also signs of an attempt to group together all kinds of artistic trends, perhaps in a desire to give plastic expression to the greatness and unity of the kingdom, freshly consolidated by Ferdinand I, already King of Castile, and now recognized as King of León and Navarre after the defeat of his brother in 1054. The codicological details that I provide here are inspired by the conclusions in my study included in this volume.

[74] Serafín Moralejo Álvarez. *Ibidem.*

[75] A typical combination of the Hispanic liturgy, which at this time became insecure in view of the slanderous rumors spread (not always in public) by Gregory VII and by Cluny, was beginning to establish itself in the Peninsula.

[76] J. P. Gilson. *The Mozarabic Psalter (ms. British Museum, Add. 30851).* London: Harrison and Sons, 1905 (Henry Bradshaw Society: 30).

[77] *Ibidem,* transcription of the text of the *Ordo ad medium noctis,* 183-194.

[78] This is the work of a copyist called Christophorus in 1058. It is far-removed from the quality and meticulousness shown in all the details in the manuscript dedicated to the King.

[79] Francisco Santos Coco. *Historia silense.* Madrid: Centro de Estudios Históricos, 1921, 87; Justo Pérez de Urbel, and Atilano González Ruiz-Zorrilla, eds. *Historia silense.* Madrid, CSIC, 1959, 295.

Bibliography

ARTILES RODRÍGUEZ, José. "El códice visigótico de Álvaro de Córdoba". *Revista de Archivos, Bibliotecas y Museos* 9 (1932): 201-291.

BEZLER, Francis. *Les Pénitentiels espagnols. Contribution à l'étude de la civilisation de l'Espagne chrétienne du Haut Moyen Âge.* Münster: Aschendorff, 1994 (Forschungen der Görresgesellschaft: 30).

BROU, Louis. "Le Joyau des antiphonaires latins". *Archivos Leoneses* 8 (1954): 7-114.

BROU, Louis, and José VIVES, eds. *Antifonario visigótico mozárabe de la Catedral de León.* 2 vols. Vol. 1, Barcelona: Centro de Estudios e Investigación San Isidoro (CSIC-CECEL), 1959; vol. 2, Madrid, CSIC, Instituto P. Enrique Flórez, 1953-4 (Monumenta Hispaniae Sacra: Serie Litúrgica 5, no. 2. Facsímiles musicales 1).

CANELLAS LÓPEZ, Ángel. "Consideraciones paleográficas sobre el antifonario mozárabe de San Juan de la Peña". In *Antiphonale Hispaniae vetus (siglos X-XI).* Facsimile edition. Zaragoza: Institución Fernando el Católico, 1986, 35-40.

CORDOLIANI, Alfred. "Les Textes et figures de comput de l'Antiphonaire de León". *Archivos Leoneses* 8 (1954): 260-283.

DÍAZ Y DÍAZ, Manuel C. "Los prólogos del *antiphonale visigothicum* de la Catedral de León (León, Arch. Cat., 8)". *Archivos Leoneses* 8 (1954): 226-257.

—. "Agustín entre los mozárabes: un testimonio". *Augustinus* 25 (1980): 157-180.

—. *Códices visigóticos en la monarquía leonesa.* León: Centro de Estudios e Investigación San Isidoro (CSIC-CECEL), 1983 (Fuentes y Estudios de Historia Leonesa: 31).

—. *Valerio del Bierzo. Su persona, su obra.* León: Centro de Estudios e Investigación San Isidoro (CSIC-CECEL), 2006, 318. (Fuentes y Estudios de Historia Leonesa: 111).

EWALD, Paul. "Reise nach Spanien in Winter von 1878 auf 1879". *Neues Archiv der Gesellschaft für ältere Deutsche Geschichtskunde* 6 (1881): 217-398.

FÉROTIN, Màrius, ed. *Le Liber ordinum en usage dans l'Église wisigothique et mozarabe d'Espagne du cinquème, au onzième siècle.* Paris: Librairie Firmin-Didot, 1904 (Monumenta Ecclesiae Liturgica: 5).

—. *Le Liber Mozarabicus Sacramentorum et les manuscrits mozarabes (reimpr. de l'édition de Paris 1912 et bibliographie générale de la liturgie hispanique, préparées et présentées par A. Ward et C. Jonson).* Rome: CLV Edizione Liturgiche, 1995 (Bibliotheca Ephemerides Liturgicae 78: Subsidia Instrumenta Liturgica Quarreriensia 4).

GARCÍA Y GARCÍA, Antonio, Francisco CANTELAR RODRÍGUEZ, and Manuel NIETO CUMPLIDO. *Catálogo de los manuscritos e incunables de la Catedral de Córdoba.* Salamanca: Universidad Pontificia de Salamanca, 1976.

GILSON, Julius Parnell, ed. *The Mozarabic Psalter (ms. British Museum, Add. 30851).* London: Harrison and Sons, 1905 (Henry Bradshaw Society: 30).

GÓMEZ MORENO, Manuel. *Catálogo monumental de España. Provincia de León.* Madrid: Ministerio de Instrucción Pública y Bellas Artes, 1926, 155-158.

LECLERCQ, Jean. "Un tratado sobre los nombres divinos en un manuscrito de Córdoba". *Hispania Sacra* 2, no. 4 (1949): 327-338.

Libro de horas de Fernando I de León. Studies by Manuel C. Díaz y Díaz and Serafín Moraleja Álvarez; transcription of the text by M.ª Virtudes Pardo Gómez and M.ª Araceli García Piñeiro. Facsimile edition of manuscript

609 (Res. 1) in the Biblioteca de la Universidad de Santiago de Compostela. Vol. 1, *Facsímile;* vol. 2, *Estudios.* Santiago de Compostela: Consellería de Educación e Ordenación Universitaria, 1995.

MILLARES CARLO, Agustín, Manuel C. DÍAZ Y DÍAZ, Anscari M. MUNDÓ, José Manuel RUIZ ASENCIO, Blas CASADO QUINTANILLA, and E. LECUONA RIBOT, eds. *Corpus de códices visigóticos.* Vol. 1, *Estudios;* vol. 2, *Álbum.* Las Palmas de Gran Canaria: Gobierno de Canarias, UNED, Centro Asociado de Las Palmas de Gran Canaria, 1999.

MORALEJO ÁLVAREZ, Serafín. "Notas a la ilustración del Libro de horas de Fernando I". In *Libro de Horas...* Op. cit., 53-63.

MUNDÓ, Anscari M. "La datación de los códices litúrgicos visigóticos toledanos". *Hispania Sacra* 18, no. 35 (1965): 1-25 [Miscellany in memory of Mario Férotin (1914-1964)].

PADRES BENEDICTINOS DE SILOS, eds. *Antiphonarium mozarabicum de la Catedral de León.* León, 1928.

PÉREZ DE URBEL, Justo. "El Antifonario de León. El escritor y la época". *Archivos Leoneses* 8 (1954): 115-144.

PÉREZ DE URBEL, Justo, and Atilano GONZÁLEZ RUIZ-ZORRILLA, eds. *Historia silense.* Madrid: CSIC, 1959, 295.

PINELL, Jordi. "Liturgia". In Quintín Aldea Vaquero, Tomás Marín Martínez and José Vives Gatell, dirs. *Diccionario de historia eclesiástica de España.* Madrid: CSIC, 1972-1987. Vol. 2: 1303-1320.

RODRÍGUEZ FERNÁNDEZ, Celso. *El antifonario visigótico de León. Estudio literario de sus fórmulas sálmicas.* León: Centro de Estudios e Investigación San Isidoro (CSIC-CECEL), 1985 (Colección Fuentes y Estudios de Historia Leonesa: 35).

SANTOS COCO, Francisco, ed. *Historia silense.* Madrid: Centro de Estudios Históricos, 1921, 87.

VIVES GATELL, José. "Fuentes hagiográficas del Antifonario de León". *Archivos Leoneses* 8 (1954).

VIVES GATELL, José, and Angel FÁBREGA GRAU. "Calendarios hispánicos anteriores al siglo XII". *Hispania Sacra* 2 (1949).

ZAPKE, Susana. *El antifonario de San Juan de la Peña. Estudio litúrgico-musical del rito hispano (siglos X-XI).* Zaragoza: Institución Fernando el Católico, 1995.

Paleographic Tendencies in 10th-12th Century Notated Liturgical Fragments from Portugal

Maria José Azevedo Santos

To write about manuscripts, especially liturgical-musical manuscripts from the space and time in question, is to consider fragments, above all, that is, "parts of a book that have reached us or a set of fragments from a single volume or fragments of different volumes", popularly known by the Latin expression *membra disiecta.*[1]

In fact, there is no trace of a complete manuscript of any kind in Portugal, or of Portuguese origin, before the 12th century. This is why we need to refer to the survival of a highly significant number of medieval fragments, which are now the only material traces of the beautiful books that once constituted the body and soul of important private, ecclesiastical and monastic libraries.

As everyone knows, from the 8th century onwards, and basically as a result of the cultural movement known as the *Carolingian Renaissance,* when centers for the painstaking copy of books by Greco-Latin authors as well as books of the writings of the Church Fathers, liturgical books, Bibles and others proliferated. Such centers would continue their laborious work long after Charlemagne and the Empire that would finally disintegrate politically and administratively in the 9th century. Linked to sacred environments, and especially to the deeply spellbinding place in convents and cathedrals that was the *scriptorium,*[2] the slow, patient transcription of huge numbers of books depended on the training, which was more technical than literary or historical, of scribes who would acquire this in the schools of cathedrals, monasteries or parish churches.

These were the men, mainly unknown clerics or, in certain exceptional cases, lay or religious women,[3] who, provided with certain indispensable working materials including parchment inks, quills, cutting tools and compasses, were gradually to constitute the libraries of their time.[4]

What they all had in common seems to have been the feeling they expressed, through heartfelt words about the harsh nature of this manual work that would tire the entire body, which were accompanied by petitions for divine or earthly rewards.[5]

The scribes considered that to make a book was to produce an asset of incalculable material, spiritual and cultural value. This is why to leaf through or read a book became a ritual act that almost resembled a liturgical ceremony, even including the washing of hands with soap beforehand. In addition, the pages had to be turned extremely carefully, and the fingers were never to come into contact with the letters. We are informed about all of this by the scribe of Paris, BNF, Lat. 3827, from the 13th century, in the following colophon with such beautiful rhetorical devices:

> Bone lector, cum veneris ad legendum lava manus tuas et sic librum istum apprehende, subtiliter volve paginas et longe a littera digitos pone. Quia qui nescit scribere putat se nullum esse laborem, tres sunt digiti qui scribunt sed totum corpus laborat, albosque pressos oculos caliginat. Renes frangit, cervices curvat simul et cetera membra corrumpit. Quia sicut navigator tendit et desiderat venire ad portum salutis, ita et scriptor ad novissimos versus vel paginas. Deo gratias[6].

The language in iconography takes the same direction, as, for example, when on numerous occasions books were represented in the reader's hands, wrapped in a fabric, or kept in leather cases, cabinets, boxes and chests. How far then were scribes, readers and owners of those manuscripts in the late Middle Ages from imagining that centuries later, especially from the 15th century onwards, these treasures of parchment and smoky black ink would mean nothing more to their owners than a decorated canvas in tough resistant material, which, once it had been sold, for a large sum of course, and after it had been taken apart, might at least have had some practical use![7]

In fact, European society in the 15th century, and especially the bureaucratically and progressively complex society of the 16th century, gave rise to a widespread and intensified use of writing that had been unimaginable before then. All public or private services, royal or noble houses, regular religious or secular institutions, schools and guilds, to mention just a few, had begun to consider writing essential for the good management of assets, income and expenditure.

The production of administrative documents and accounts books increased considerably. Property registers and archives, account books showing incomes and expenditures, inventories, books of assessments and evaluations, and property records multiplied; all of these were written on paper, a material that was much cheaper than parchment, but also much more fragile and vulnerable.

At the same time, dozens and dozens of books lay on library shelves in convents and cathedrals, mainly liturgical books or books with sacred music, which had not been read or used for a long time.[8] These were closed books in a difficult language, Latin, or an anachronistic notation, in the case of the music books, and in old letter types, especially the Visigothic script that had become impossible to read. This set of internal factors regarding medieval manuscripts, along with others such as negligence, the devotion to relics, the taste for owning illuminated letters or a page, the spread of printing in the 16th and 17th centuries, or simply the excessive ambition of booksellers or traders who found selling *by the page*, which, as we know, is still the case today, to be an extremely lucrative business, undoubtedly favored the destruction rather than the conservation of a cultural item that few people appreciated anymore.[9]

Thus, taking into account the money earned by selling parchment between the 12th and 15th centuries, the parchment pages of some books came to be re-used as raw material for shoes and clothing.[10] Others were destroyed, on occasion by fire, but most, once their binding had been removed, were to see their entire or trimmed pages turned into covers for handwritten books on paper, especially if these were administrative books. On other occasions, smaller pieces of parchment were used to reinforce bindings, as guard sheets for handwritten books, and even for printed books or as binding and purses for hanging seals. More rarely, but it did happen, the blank versos of these fragments were used to write new documents: this is the case with two letters found in Monastery of Pendorada, dated 1192, something that leads us to recognize that the destruction of the respective manuscript must have occurred, exceptionally, during the 12th century.[11]

Musical manuscripts were destroyed less frequently to reinforce the binding of medieval codices. There is a beautiful missal from Cathedral of Coimbra for pontifical use which has a fragment of a Mozarabic Antiphonary from the 10th *ex.* or 11th century *in.* as a guard sheet on the back cover. With regard to this, Manuel C. Díaz y Díaz wrote that this was "10th century writing and undoubtedly came from the region of the Duero or a little further south".[12] It needs to be stressed that the parchment codex can be dated between the 13th century *ex.* and 14th century *in.*,[13] a fact that points towards an extremely early dismantling of the *Liber misticus* manuscript. This is why, given its great age and value, it is hardly surprising that it would form a part of the anthology of fragments that constituted this study.[14]

This attitude, which is now condemned by anyone who loves and is interested in culture and medieval codices, was naturally a common practice at that time, because, even apart from the reuse of material, it also performed an extremely important function, which was to cover and protect manuscript books written on paper. Judging from the significant number of fragments in books from numerous archival collections, there is no doubt that this type of behavior had not only extended to convents and cathedrals, but also to houses of mercy, town halls, colleges and chancelleries. For these reasons, all of the Portuguese archives, from municipal to provincial archives and from those in houses of mercy to diocesan ones, have quite a significant number of fragments.[15]

Some have survived as book covers in good condition, or, on the contrary, they are badly damaged, worn, stained and torn; others, due to decisions taken by those responsible for them, have been carefully removed from books and can be consulted as separate documents.

In Portugal, based on the information available, the oldest studies on fragments were the work of the illustrious historian and paleographer António de Vasconcelos, who wrote two important pioneering articles on this subject between 1928 and 1929.[16]

Avelino de Jesus da Costa, a distinguished medievalist, gave a decisive boost to the research on fragments in the 1940s. This tireless researcher went to forty-six libraries and national archives and made an inventory of 1,487 fragments, which will always be of incalculable value for the history of medieval culture. Yet even though this is a highly significant number of fragments, it is far from the real number, which is difficult to assess, despite the studies carried out by Pierre David, Agustín Millares Carlo, Solange Corbin, and, more recently, Manuel C. Díaz y Díaz,[17] Anscari M. Mundó,[18] Jesús Alturo i Perucho[19] and José Manuel Ruiz Asencio,[20] all of whom have made an enormous contribution to the development of the subject. As Díaz y Díaz stresses, "The initial search and discovery, and then study of the remains of manuscripts have always been the most productive and exciting fields for codicological researchers. They are interesting from numerous perspectives, as the possibilities of locating them are combined with the chance to reconstruct the codex that the fragments may come from, and to interpret the history of the manuscript until the process of its destruction can be justified or understood".[21]

Another outstanding contribution to the subject was to appear later, in 1993 and 1997, when the first and second parts of the *General Inventory of liturgical fragments of the Coimbra University Archive* were published. These made known seventy-five fragments of codices from the 12th, 13th, 14th and 15th centuries for various kinds of liturgical books (missals, graduals, antiphonaries, psalters and breviaries), which had mainly been used as covers for 16th and 17th century notarial books.[22]

In the meantime, there is great expectation about the systematic inventory of fragments from the Middle Ages that a group of young people, supervised by Saul Gomes from the University of Coimbra, is currently carrying out in all of the archives and libraries in Portugal. In all probability, this inventory will significantly increase the number of fragments of which we currently know.[23]

The study of the liturgy, and as a result of the series of ecclesiastical celebrations that form part of Christian worship, is of course carried out from unwritten sources, such as miniatures, paintings, gold and silver items,or architecture, but the most important contributions to the study of the liturgy are provided by paleographic, epigraphic or sigillographic documents, and especially by books.

In fact, the books not only of the Hispanic rite but also of the Franco-Roman rite, which were adopted on the Peninsula at the end of 11th century, became indispensable for the solemnity, dignity and ritual unity of church services. Some contained only texts, generally taken from the Bible; others contained chant and as a result are called notated liturgical books.[24]

All manuscripts from a codicological and paleographic viewpoint, are the result of methods of producing and writing books unique to scribes at a specific time and place. Leaving aside the codicological aspects of notated liturgical manuscripts for now, which merit special attention because of their specific nature, here we consider in outline the graphic trends in manuscripts and musical fragments from the 10th to 12th centuries kept in Portugal.

It needs to be borne in mind, first of all, that we can only refer to Portugal as a country from 1096 onwards, and as an independent kingdom after 1143. So the 10th century and a large part of the 11th correspond politically to the period of the Reconquest in the Peninsula, because the northern part of what is now Portugal was under the sovereignty of the kingdom of León, and the center and the south of the country was occupied by the Muslims. Nevertheless, in the 11th century *ex.,* there were two important restored dioceses in Braga and

Coimbra and several monastic centers, including those in Guimarães, Santo Tirso, Pendorada and Santa Maria de Lorvão.

Only in the 12th century would the two great symbols of Portuguese medieval culture, Santa Cruz de Coimbra (1131)[25] and Santa Maria de Alcobaça (1152), be founded. As a result, it seems understandable that the cultural environment in the western part of the Peninsula before 1100 was rather unfavorable for the production of music manuscripts, literature or other genres.[26] These activities would gradually become more common, undoubtedly as the kingdom acquired peace and political and social stability. Moreover, the skills of reading and writing were very rare, limited almost exclusively to the lay and regular clergy.

So it needs to be asked what culture the scribes and cleric-notaries had; what method or methods of writing they followed; whether we can talk about writing letters or books; whether the notated liturgical books including chant neumes and texts were written by one or several hands; and wheter it was necessary to know about music and singing to copy notated liturgical manuscripts.

Of course a monastery or a cathedral could not function in any way without monks, canons or books. For this reason, it was not unusual for scribes generally to be members of the very same institution for which they worked, although there were also cases in which books were acquired on commission, on loan or as the result of a donation.

It is a well-known fact that, although it was rare during the period in question, there were female scribes (nuns) and laymen. Despite this, the credit for the copying of books was almost automatically given to men and clerics, which matched the predominant reality throughout Europe. In general, we know little about scribes, because they remain anonymous most of the time. They must have obtained their knowledge of reading, writing, singing and other skills in the teaching centers of that time. Nevertheless, scribes, in particular, would have needed at least two years to achieve a perfect mastery of the quill and the art of copying. In other words, copying was considered to be a complex task that required slow, specialized training, the techniques of which would gradually improve with an increasing number of years of experience and practice.[27]

Because this was the case, it is hardly surprising that after all of this training a scribe was fit to work on all kinds of writings, whether these were books, documents or even inscriptions. On the other hand, it would be less likely that a cleric-notary, who was more used to drawing up or writing a wide variety of diplomatic and legal correspondence, would be able to copy manuscripts. Despite this, what united scribes and clerics-notaries was much greater than what might separate them.[28]

As for the characteristic writing styles used by those who were able to write in Portugal during the 10th-12th centuries, we need to bear in mind that many kinds of writing were in use, both as far as the types of script and the care taken in producing them were concerned.

We are still far from a significant spread of the ability to write in society, and as a result, written expression mainly followed more or less uniform models. Behind these, of course, there was always a hand or a person, but marks or traces of their personality were rarely shown or revealed. It is wellknown that the period between 10th-12th centuries was an age characterized by historical forms of writing that are typical of periods with low or very low levels of literacy. Among these forms of writing, the main ones were the Visigothic, Carolingian and Gothic scripts.

Most of the notated liturgical fragments from Portugal published in this work are written in Carolingian script or in a transitional script moving towards the Gothic, which to a certain extent tallies with the time period to which they have been ascribed after a rigorous critique of external elements, such as the writing, parchment and inks. Characterising the graphic trends in these fragments in this way does not mean that they were copied in these areas at all, because books, just like people, also moved from place to place.

We now consider the Visigothic script, which has an extensive bibliography. It corresponds to a way of writing that was exclusive to Septimania and the Iberian Peninsula, which is where the oldest paleographic

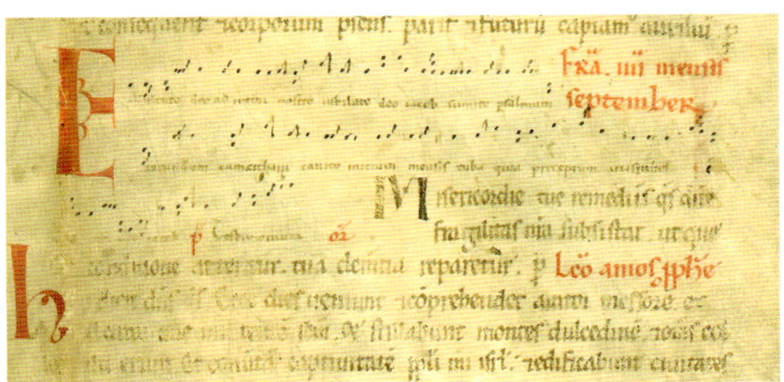

1. Breviary. Braga, AD, Frag. 45, 11th century, fol. r

testimony on slates, dating from the 7th century, comes from.[29]

Furthermore, the oldest original Latin letter that is kept in Arquivo Nacional da Torre do Tombo, dated 27 March 882,[30] comes from the northern region of what is now Portugal, to be more precise, from the church in Lardosa (Penafiel municipality). From this date until 1172, we have a history of the development of writing as far as documents are concerned,[31] but not regarding manuscripts, a study which still needs to be carried out.[32]

In fact, certain very precise periods have been established for categories and types of script. As a result, it is said that until 1014 there are only letters in Visigothic cursive and semi-cursive, because the oldest evidence of rounded Visigothic script dates back to this year and would survive until 1123.

There is a letter from 1054 with the testament of the Matrona and Goda sisters, from the Monastery of Pendorada, however, signed by Ansur: *Ansur scripsit*. This is the oldest documentary proof to provide information about the introduction of abbreviation signs and the morphology of letters that are specific to Carolingian script. This is therefore a unique example of a transitional Visigothic script moving towards the Carolingian, the latter of which persisted until 1172 as part of an extraordinary coexistence between scripts. As a result, it can be claimed that from 1108 onwards, the Carolingian script was being used and, after 1111, the Carolingian-Gothic forms are quite common. In parallel with this, Gothic script would only be adopted after 1123, and Cathedral of Coimbra was an outstanding pioneering center in the practice and diffusion of these new forms of writing, because it definitively eradicated the use of Visigothic script in 1137, almost forty years before it was totally abandoned in 1172, as we have already pointed out, which is the date of a letter regarding a donation given to Monastery of Pedroso.[33]

On the basis of the aforementioned data, we can see how Portugal proved to be conservative as far as the use of the national script was concerned. The fact that it was far removed from the most highly developed *scriptoria*, the progress made by the Reconquest, the limited circulation of people and goods, the traditional reluctancy of people to change, and, finally, the resistance to anything that came from abroad, are the factors, among others, that help us to understand the extremely slow progress from Visigothic to Carolingian and Gothic script.

We are convinced, however, that the trends shown in manuscripts would not have been very different; it is worth stressing that the conservatism in the writing in these letters can be seen above all in small-scale cultural centers, and we have no information whatsoever about any production of manuscripts in these centers. On the contrary, the copying of manuscripts took place in the most economically, culturally and liturgically developed cathedrals and monasteries. Despite this, we cannot rule out the hypothesis that a scribe may have remained faithful to the use of rounded Visigothic writing or a transitional script in an institution in which the use of Carolingian and Gothic script was already predominant. In this regard, it is worth referring here to the fact that the oldest known dated manuscript in Portugal forms part of the *handwritten library* of the Monastery of Santa Cruz in Coimbra, the work of canons belonging to the order of St. Augustine.[34] This is a beautiful parchment copy, in two columns, that contains readings for the daily liturgy, that is, a homiliary: *Liber comicus*. This exemplar is dated from 1139, and contrary to expectations, seems to have been copied at Cathedral of Coimbra in an elegant transitional Visigothic script moving towards a Carolingian script. As we have already pointed out, Cathedral of Coimbra was a highly dynamic cultural center, which provides us with the earliest evidence of the *eradication* of Visigothic script in single documents (1137). However, the discovery of a manuscript from 1139 that was still copied in Visigothic script, even though it shows a strong Carolingian-Gothic

2. Antifonary. Coimbra, AU, Frag. IV-3.ª-Gav. 44 (20) B, 11th century *med.*, fol. r

influence, makes it quite clear that after 1137 scribes at the Cathedral of Coimbra continued to use the old 'national' script when copying manuscripts.

Let us now consider the set of fragments included in this volume. It is clear that these fragments generally belonged to books that had been conceived with an ideological-aesthetic function, and as a result, even if this was not really the case, they were, on the whole, more like luxury books than books for common use. So we need to bear in mind, among other aspects, their size (300 mm long by 220 mm wide on average); the extraordinary care taken in producing their elegant, harmonious script; the decorative elements in the illuminated initials; the meticulously drawn musical notation; and the quality of the ink and the parchment, which was to withstand the widespread abuse that it would suffer over the centuries.

And let us look more specifically at the case of the Visigothic writing that can be seen, for example, in the fragment of the vespers office kept in the Arquivo da Universidade de Coimbra, which comes from its cathedral, as already pointed out. What stands out just by looking at this is the fact that it has two modules. One is very small and is characteristic of texts set to music, whereas the other, which is much larger, is used in the other parts of the manuscript. The hand that wrote the latter was very familiar with Visigothic script in its rounded form, without any influences of cursive or of continental Carolingian writing. It can be said, in all honesty, that this is a pure Visigothic script. However, we do not think that the scribe was a distinguished calligrapher. For example, there are traces of too much ink having been used, and the spaces between words and even between letters are too pronounced. Despite this, the *genetic* characteristics of the morphology of the letters in rounded Visigothic script can still be seen: the open *a* and *g*, the inverted *tau* and *beta*, the tall *i* that is like an *l*, the excessively extended ascenders and descenders of the *p*, *f*, *g* and *i*, as well as the *b*, *l*, *d* and *h*, that are also very long. Another typical feature of this script is the limited use of abbreviation signs. Suspension points and contractions were known but rarely used.

The manuscript, which provides evidence of the Hispanic rite, was copied on Portuguese territory sometime between the 10th century *ex.* and 11th century *in.*[35] Manuel C. Díaz y Díaz placed it, as I have already mentioned, in the Duero region or a bit farther south, which makes sense, given that it was found in a 14th century missal belonging to Cathedral of Coimbra. For this reason, it was probably produced in this city or its surrounding area. This was the Mozarabic period, when mainly churchmen were responsible for the survival of culture and forms of writing in the Hispano-Gothic world. This was the case to such an extent that in an *escurialense* codex from 1047 in rounded Visigothic script, an anonymous but learned hand left the note "littera ista moçarava appellatur" towards the end of the 13th century or the beginning of the 14th, and maybe even the same hand, or another, ended up finishing this off with a "vel toletana".[36] It is well-known that as the years went by, the Visigothic script gradually lost its original characteristics because *Carolingian* script, which had first appeared in the 8th century in Charlemagne's empire, began to exert its influence in the 11th century *med.*, especially among those who could read and write. Traditionally, four factors were considered to have played a decisive role in the introduction of what was known as the Carolingian script. 1) The replacement of the Visigothic or Hispanic rite by the Roman rite, that is, the new rite made it necessary to produce new books, copied at first from manuscripts in Carolingian script. This became a factor that encouraged the introduction of the continental script; 2) The Council of León, which met in 1090 and from which we have no minutes, according to information passed on by later authors, such as Don Lucas of Tuy and Don Rodrigo of Toledo, decided to make the use of Carolingian script in liturgical books compulsory. 3) The influence of monks from Cluny, who brought Carolingian script with them in their writing and books when they came to Portugal, and 4) The arrival in Portugal of individuals of French origin, including Counts Henry and Raymond, as well as various members of the Church. Some time ago, we discussed this subject in greater depth in my doctoral thesis,[37] and we came to the conclusion that none of these factors was decisive, because the oldest traces of knowledge of Carolingian script on Portuguese soil, both in letters and manuscripts, had already appeared in previous decades, before the secondary rather than the leading role played by any of the aforementioned factors could have had any influence.

So what needs to be stressed is that Portugal went through a long period of time when scribes used a script that was between the Visigothic and the Carolingian, a hybrid writing stage that to varying extents contained elements of both scripts; this period has been called *Transitional Visigothic to Carolingian*, and it lasted from the 11th century *med.* to the final quarter of the 12th century. Between 1054 and 1172 we know of about one thousand letters written in this type of transitional script, which is also known as *semi-Visigothic.* In fact, the writing in question had elements that are now minimized of Italian Visigothic and maintained some characteristics of rounded Visigothic, but it differed from these as far as the morphology of the letters and writing movements were concerned. It was still a minuscule script in which the width of letters, in general, was no greater than 2 mm, however.

Some extremely unusual practices emerged from this mixture of tradition and renewal; for example, in the same word the open *a* appears alongside the Carolingian *a*, the *tau* with the *t*, and the open *g* with the closed *g*. The coexistence of Visigothic and Carolingian elements as far as abbreviations are concerned is also significant. As for capital letters, larger lower case letters still appear, and those that are really capitals form part of Roman majuscule or uncial script, even though on occasion unusual tracings can be recognized.

Exceptionally, scribes continued to use monograms, linked and enclosed initials, and, in special cases, cryptography. This occurred in seven cases in 840 letters, as can be seen, for example, in the use of numerals to replace the vowels in the names or the posts of the *scriptores,* who hid behind this kind of *innocent game*: X = *a;* XX = *e;* XXX = *i;* $X^{>}$ = *o;* 1= *u.* It is especially worth mentioning the cryptograms formed by neumes that are equivalent to letters. With regard to this, Louis Brou wrote: "The neumes in the Mozarabic notation in the North of Spain display the special feature that over the centuries they have been assigned various types of meaning that have nothing to do with music. This is what happens in the encoded writing that made use of many of these Northern Mozarabic signs here that were widespread in these regions".[38]

As we have already noted, Visigothic transitional script combined on the one hand, the tradition of maintaining the use of the rounded Visigothic script; and on the other, the future, reflected in the use of Carolingian and even Gothic script. The numerous Portuguese and peninsular manuscripts written in the Visigothic script in transition towards Carolingian script provide solid evidence of this dialectical combination.

So there can be little doubt that at the beginning of the second half of the 11th century, Carolingian script was already known in Portugal. Let us not forget that the oldest piece of documentary evidence for this phenomenon dates back to 1054. In the eyes of the scribes from this remote period, Carolingian script emerged as a revolutionary graphic option that above all required a change of mentality, because, as we have already had the opportunity to state in another piece of work, "changing writing was changing your way of thinking."[39] These changes especially concerned the care scribes needed to take in the abbreviations and in the morphology of the letters, the execution of which from this moment on can generally be considered to be elegant, or even extremely elegant. Created to serve Charlemagne's imperial policy and to eradicate the numerous national scripts that were rough and unpolished, the Carolingian script followed a writing model governed by certain specific rules, with a clearly defined morphology in all its elements, as well as a meticulous and unified approach to its execution, although there were cases of "rural" Carolingian script, which were typical of culturally backward environments, as can be found in Catalonia during the 10th and 11th centuries.[40]

I must emphasize the fact that when Portugal and the other peninsular kingdoms adopted the Carolingian script between the 11th century *ex.* and the 12th century *in.,* they received a script that had already been contaminated by the Gothic, which, in the meantime, had emerged in the Anglo-Norman region. According to Agustín Millares Carlo, it is this "rigid, geometrical and rather mannered" Carolingian script, that corresponds to the so-called Carolingian-Gothic or pre-Gothic forms,[41] of which many of our fragments are good examples.

Even so, in isolated documents as well as in manuscripts, there is evidence of an almost pure Carolingian script. A beautiful copy in Carolingian script is the Mateus Missal, 1130-1150, fol. 8 of which is reproduced in this work. In a comparison, although it is rather brief, between this script and the previous one, the marked difference in the form of all the letters immediately stands out. The inverted beta and tau have disappeared to give rise to the Carolingian *t*; the open *a* and *g* have disappeared and the difference between the sizes of the modules of the letters and of the ascenders and descenders has been reduced; as a result, the strokes finally became somewhat better-proportioned and more harmonious.

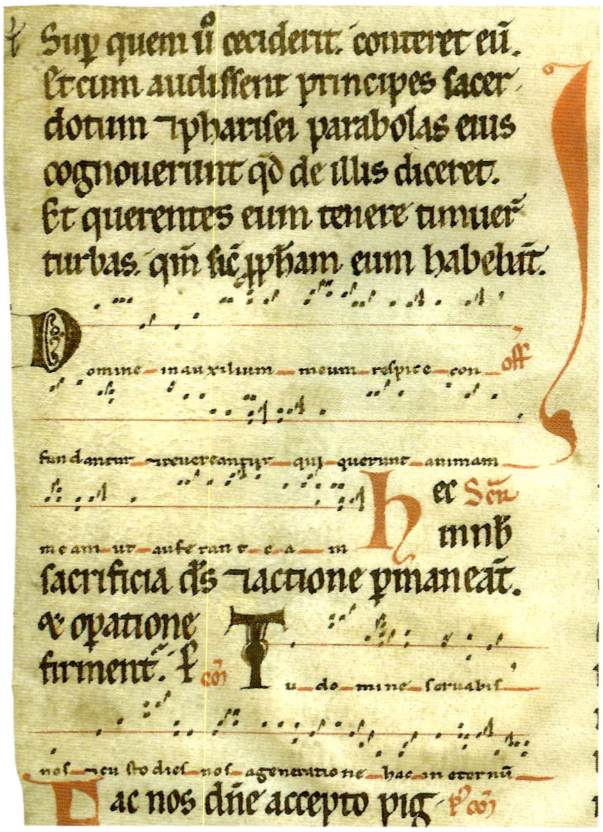

3. Missal/Breviary (?). Braga, AD, Frag. 37, 11th century *ex.*, fol. v

The abbreviation systems were also expanded, despite the fact that they maintained suspension points and contractions, because there were no other solutions. The most emblematic system was the one with superimposed letters, which consisted of placing a vowel with a smaller module over a vowel or a consonant: $\overset{o}{p}$= *pro*; $\overset{a}{a}$= *anima*. Furthermore, various special signs with an absolute value appeared, such as the *ur* and *er,* and they continued to use those with a relative value, such as the one that was shaped like a convex line and at the beginning of a word was equivalent to *con* or *com,* and at the end was equivalent to *us* or *os*. Modifications to letters, such as the strokes attached to the letter *p*, with the meanings *per*, *pro* and *pre,* depending on whether the stroke cuts through the limb horizontally or in undulating fashion, or if it is placed on top, are typical and highly characteristic in Carolingian script. In short, this is a beautiful script that some medieval authors, who were not indifferent to this aspect, described as *good writing* and highly suitable, therefore, for copying manuscripts.

The 12th century *in.* in Portugal was a period of breaks and syntheses in writing. The Visigothic scripts resisted the overpowering introduction of Carolingian, Carolingian-Gothic and finally Gothic as long as they could. In fact, what came to Portugal after 1123 was a new writing model. This was Gothic script, which is a term that refers to the type of writing that was predominant in Europe from the 12th until the 16th centuries *in.* It was originated in the Anglo-Norman region, and its oldest traces date back to the 11th century. The most important changes would be to the technique, however. Gothic script is undeniably the result of a way of carving the quill asymmetrically to the left, which led to alternating thick and fine strokes as well as to certain narrow and thin forms. All of these characteristics were inspired by the numerous artistic forms of expression of the period to which Gothic script aimed to provide a response.[42]

Gothic, just like previous scripts, was also minuscule, but it did now have capitals of its own, many of which were decorated, flourished and even illuminated. In notated liturgical manuscripts we can still identify two modules: a larger one for the text and a smaller one for the antiphons, as occurs in the 12th century Evangeliary readings from the Monastery of Santa Cruz in Coimbra. Its dominant characteristic is the break in the form of all of the letters, especially in the *a*, *g*, *m*, *n* and *o*. This is why there are fewer ligatures, because the more angular strokes are not suitable for joining them together. The monograms, linked initials and enclosed initials are maintained, however.

As for brachygraphy, the Gothic script inherited and reinforced all of the abbreviation processes used in Carolingian script, as well as the aforementioned modifications to letters. This was the script in which medieval codices were written throughout Europe. It proved to be elegant when it was used for books, but later on it became cursive and messy when notaries and scribes recorded a will, a sales contract or an excambion on parchment. It is also called a *university script*, because it was disseminated in the books used by teachers and students in a Europe no longer exclusively restricted to convents and *scriptoria,* it was, as a result, more developed, educated and literate.

To sum up, we have taken a look at the main graphic trends followed by scribes in Portugal in the 10th to 12th centuries. There are still some unanswered questions, however, that we have asked before. Can we talk about writing for letters and writing for books? Yes, we can. There is no doubt that, especially as far as the care taken in carrying out the writing process is concerned, manuscripts never use the cursive or semi-cursive scripts that are characteristic of administrative documents, in which the writing did not have the aesthetic function that was fundamental to codices. Even so, we need to mention the numerous royal, episcopal or private letters with a marked aesthetic value, which is the result, in all probability, of the *vicinity* or very close proximity of the *scriptorium* to the chancery, which would mean that many scribes were also *notatores* or *scriptores*. And what about liturgical books, with their special paleographic features? Were they the work of one or several hands? We will never know. It can be stated, however, that the text and musical notation were most probably written by the same person, but others could take care, as often occurred, of the rubrics, the decorated letters and the miniatures. It would also be interesting to know whether the scribes of notated liturgical manuscripts had to have a knowledge of music. In view of the silence of the sources, we can of course presume that this would have helped them considerably, but it might not have been indispensable for their art.

On the cultural journey from Visigothic to Gothic script, we have witnessed the path followed by many monks and clerics in the arduous task of producing manuscripts. Between tradition and renewal, with skilful hands and well-carved quills, they created some wonderful testimonies of culture and society in the late Middle Ages.

We have left some reflections on these pages on the types of writing that were in use in Portugal from the 10th to 12th centuries and which produced an unknown, but in all probability considerable, number of manuscripts, judging from the number of *golden pages* that have survived and which we can still admire and study today.

Notes

[1] Pilar Ostos, Luisa Pardo, and Elena E. Rodríguez. *Vocabulario de codicología.* Madrid: Arco Libros, 1997, 190.

[2] See Aires Augusto Nascimento. *O scriptorium*. Lisbon: Faculty of Letters of the University of Lisbon, 1999; and María Josefa Sanz Fuentes. "Tiempo de leer y escribir: el 'scriptorium'". *Cuadernos de Investigación del Monasterio de Santa María de la Real* 6 (July 1992): 37-56.

[3] See Regine Pernoud. *La femme au temps des cathédrales.* Paris: Stock, 1980, 34.

[4] See, for further information: Maria José Azevedo Santos. "Technical conditions and materials for copying manuscripts

in the Middle Ages". In *Santa Cruz de Coimbra. Cultura Portuguesa aberta à Europa na Ideda Média. The Portuguese Culture Opened to Europe in the Middle Ages*. Porto: Biblioteca Pública Municipal do Porto, 2001, 29-45.

[5] See Thérèse Glorieux-De Gand. "Formules de copiste: les colophons des manuscrits datés". In *Catalogue (d'exposition, Bruxelles, Bibliothèque Royale Albert Ier, du 7.12.1991 au 25.1.1992)*. Brussels: Bibliothèque Royale Albert Ier,1991.

[6] Antoine Dondaine. "Post-scriptum". *Scriptorium* 32 (1978): 54-55. See also Isaías da Rosa Pereira. *Codicologia. Arqueologia do livro*. Angra do Heroísmo: Instituto Histórico da Ilha Terceira, 1979, 22-23.

[7] It needs to be borne in mind that an identical spirit with regard to reusing materials was also applied to maps from the 15th and 16th centuries that were also cut up and used as book covers in the 16th, 17th and 18th centuries. Consider the case of the fragments found in Viana do Castelo archives—Alfredo Pinheiro Marques. "Alguns fragmentos de mapas encontrados em Viana do Castelo e outras novidades do ano de 1988 para a história da cartografia". *Revista da Universidade de Coimbra* 35 (1989): 309-322. We can also add, for example, that there are several 18th century books of privileges in the Arquivo da Universidade de Coimbra with covers made using 16th century royal letters and bulls.

[8] Consider the case of the obituaries—Mauricio Herrero Jiménez. "Un fragmento de obituario del hospital de San Juan de Duero". In Manuel C. Díaz y Díaz, coord. *Escritos dedicados a José María Fernández Catón*. León: Centro de Estudios e Investigación San Isidoro (CSIC-CESEL), 2004, 689-716.

[9] See Elisabeth Pellegrin. "Fragments et membra disiecta". *Codicologica* 3 (1980): 70-95.

[10] See Ronald Reed. *Ancient Skins, Parchments and Leathers*. London: Seminar Press, 1972, 325-348.

[11] See José Mattoso. *L'abbaye de Pendorada des origines à 1160*. Coimbra: Atlântida, 1962, 88. See also Maria José Azevedo Santos. "Les conditions de conservation des documents et des livres au Portugal (XIIe-XVe siècles)". *Scriptorium* 50 (1996-2), 391-406.

[12] See Manuel C. Díaz y Díaz. *Códices visigóticos en la monarquía leonesa*. León: Centro de Estudios e Investigación San Isidoro (CSIC-CESEL), 1983, 369-370.

[13] Regarding this codex, see Abílio Queirós. "Missal Medieval da Sé de Coimbra". Unpublished doctoral thesis. Coimbra: Faculty of Letters of the University of Coimbra, 1993.

[14] António de Vasconcelos. "Fragmento precioso dum códice visigótico". *Biblos* 5 (1929): 245-273. See Abílio Queirós. "Fragmentos de um códice litúrgico-musical da Sé de Coimbra (séc. X-XI). In *Semente em boa terra: raízes do Cristianismo na Diocese de Coimbra do século IV a 1064*. Coimbra: Gráfica de Coimbra, 2000, 138-140. See Jesús Alturo i Perucho. *El llibre manuscrit a Catalunya. Orígens i esplendor*. Barcelona: Generalitat de Cataluña, 2000.

[15] As an example, we can mention the case of five fragments, all from the same codex, that are kept in the Archivo Municipal of Ceuta and that come from the Santa y Real Casa de la Misericordia in Ceuta [Carmen del Camino Martínez. "Fragmentos bíblicos en escritura carolina". *Boletín Millares Carlo* 13 (1994): 85-94 + 7 plates].

[16] See note 14 and the article by António Vasconcelos. "Fragmentos preciosos de dois códices paleográfico-visigóticos". *Biblos* 4 (1928): 353-369.

[17] Manuel C. Díaz y Díaz. Op. cit.

[18] Anscari M. Mundó. *Obres completes*. Barcelona: Curial Edicions Catalanes, 1998.

[19] Jesús Alturo i Perucho. *Studia in codicum fragmenta*. Barcelona: Universidad Autónoma de Barcelona, 1999.

[20] José Manuel Ruiz Asencio. "La colección de fragmentos latinos de la Chancillería de Valladolid". In *Actas del II Congreso Hispánico de Latín Medieval. León, 11-14 of November 1997*. León: University of León, 1998, 175-185.

[21] Manuel C. Díaz y Díaz. Op. cit., 353.

[22] Abílio Ferreira Queirós. "Fragmentos de pergaminhos litúrgico-musicais. Inventário Geral (1.ª parte)". *Boletim do Arquivo da Universidade de Coimbra* 13-14 (1993-1994): 325-348. *Idem.* "Inventário dos fragmentos litúrgico-musicais existentes no AUC (2.ª parte)". *Ibidem,* 15-16 (1997): 517-547.

[23] See Saul António Gomes. "A codicologia em Portugal: balanço e perspectivas no fim do século XX". In José d'Encarnação, ed. *As Oficinas da História*. Lisbon: Colibri; Coimbra: Faculty of Letters of the University of Coimbra, 2002, 151-174.

[24] We will not devote much space here to the role and importance of music in late medieval Portuguese cathedrals and monasteries, which we leave to specialists. See Éric Palazzo. *Histoire des livres liturgiques: Le Moyen Âge. Des origines au XIIIe siècle*. Paris: Beauchesne, 1993.

[25] Regarding the culture and chancery of this institution, see Saul António Gomes. *In limine conscriptionis. Documentos, chancelaria e cultura no mosteiro de Santa Cruz de Coimbra (séculos XII a XIV)*. Viseu: Palimage, 2007, and Alberto Armando Martins. *O mosteiro de Santa Cruz de*

Coimbra na Idade Média. Lisbon: Center of History of the University of Lisbon, 2003.

[26] José Mattoso. *Religião e Cultura na Idade Média Portuguesa*. Lisbon: INCM, 1982.

[27] See Alphonse Dain. *Les manuscrits*. 3rd ed. Paris: Les Belles Lettres, 1975; Jean Vezin. "La fabrication du manuscrit". In Henri-Jean Martin and Roger Chartier, eds. *Histoire de l'édition française*. Paris: Promodis, 1982, 25-47; and Jesús Alturo i Perucho. *Història del llibre manuscrit a Catalunya*. Barcelona: Generalitat de Cataluña, 2003, 74-142.

[28] Maria José Azevedo Santos. "Os 'clérigos-notários' em Portugal (séculos XI-XII)". In Maria Helena da Cruz Coelho, coord. *Estudos de Diplomática Portuguesa*. Lisbon: Colibri, 2001, 75-91.

[29] See Anscari M. Mundó. "Notas para la historia de la escritura visigótica en su período primitivo". In *Bivium. Homenaje a Manuel C. Díaz y Díaz*. Madrid: Gredos, 1983, 175-196; and Carmen del Camino Martínez. "Los orígenes de la escritura visigótica: ¿otras posibilidades para su estudio?" In *Actas del VIII Coloquio del Comité Internacional de Paleografía Latina. Madrid, Toledo, 29 de septiembre-1 de octubre de 1987*. Madrid: Joyas Bibliográficas, 1990, 29-37; and Jesús Alturo i Perucho. "La escritura visigótica de origen transpirenaico. Una aproximación a sus particularidades". *Hispania Sacra* 46, no. 93 (1994): 33-64.

[30] Avelino de Jesus da Costa. *Álbum de Paleografía e Diplomática Portuguesas*. Coimbra: Faculty of Letters of the University of Coimbra, 1996, doc. 19.

[31] We are referring to the study: Maria José Azevedo Santos. *Da visigótica à carolina. A escrita em Portugal de 882 a 1172. Aspectos técnicos e culturais*. Lisbon: FCG-JNICT, 1994.

[32] See the reference work on Visigothic manuscripts: Claudio García Turza, coord. *Los manuscritos visigóticos: estudio paleográfico y codicológico*. Vol. 1, *Códices riojanos datados*. Logroño: Fundación San Millán de la Cogolla, 2002.

[33] On the production of documents at Cathedral of Coimbra, see Maria do Rosário Morujão. "A Sé de Coimbra: a instituição e a chancelaria (1080-1318)". Unpublished doctoral thesis. University of Coimbra, 2005.

[34] Aires Augusto Nascimento, and José Francisco Meirinhos, coords. *Catálogo dos Códices da Livraria de Mão do Mosteiro de Santa Cruz de Coimbra na Biblioteca Pública Municipal do Porto*. Porto: Biblioteca Pública Municipal do Porto, 1997.

[35] See the Antiphonary of San Juan de la Peña of the same date studied by Susana Zapke. *El Antifonario de San Juan de la Peña (siglos X-XI). Estudio litúrgico-musical del rito hispano*. Zaragoza: Institución Fernando el Católico, 1995.

[36] Maria José Azevedo Santos. *Da visigótica à carolina*... Op. cit., 70-72.

[37] *Ibidem*.

[38] Louis Brou. "Notes de Paléographie Musicale Mozarabe". *Anuario Musical* 10 (1955): 32. See also Maria José Azevedo Santos. *Ibidem*, 108-112.

[39] *Idem*. "Modos de escrever no século XII em Portugal. O caso do Mosteiro de Santa Cruz de Coimbra". *Bibliotheca Portucalensis*, Serie 2, 15-16 (2000-2001): 99-111.

[40] Anscari M. Mundó, and Jesús Alturo i Perucho. "Problemática de les escriptures dels períodes de transició i de les marginals". *Cultura Neolatina* 58 (1998): 129.

[41] Agustín Millares Carlo. *Tratado de paleografía española*. 3rd ed. Madrid: Espasa Calpe, 1983, 110.

[42] Jacques Stiennon. *Paléographie du Moyen Âge*. 2nd ed. Paris: PUF, 1982, 108.

Bibliography

ALTURO I PERUCHO, Jesús. "La escritura visigótica de origen transpirenaico. Una aproximación a sus particularidades". *Hispania Sacra* 46, no. 93 (1994): 33-64.

—. *Studia in codicum fragmenta*. Bellaterra: Universidad Autónoma de Barcelona, 1999.

—. *El llibre manuscrit a Catalunya: orígens i esplendor*. Barcelona: Generalitat de Cataluña, 2000.

—. *Història del llibre manuscrit a Catalunya*. Barcelona: Generalitat de Cataluña, 2003.

BROU, Louis. "Notes de Paléographie Musicale Mozarabe". *Anuario Musical* 10 (1955): 32.

CAMINO MARTÍNEZ, Carmen del. "Los orígenes de la escritura visigótica y otras posibilidades para su estudio". In *Actas del VIII Coloquio del Comité Internacional de Paleografía Latina*. Madrid, Toledo, 29 September-1 October 1987. Madrid: Joyas Bibliográficas, 1990.

—. "Fragmentos bíblicos en escritura carolina". *Boletín Millares Carlo* 13 (1994): 85-94 + 7 plates.

COSTA, Avelino de Jesus da. *Álbum de Paleografía e Diplomática Portuguesas*. Coimbra: Faculty of Letters of the University of Coimbra, 1996.

DAIN, Alphonse. *Les manuscrits*. 3rd ed. Paris: Les Belles Lettres, 1975.

DÍAZ Y DÍAZ, Manuel C. *Códices visigóticos en la monarquía leonesa*. León: Centro de Estudios e Investigación San Isidoro (CSIC-CECEL), 1983.

DONDAINE, Antoine. "Post-scriptum". *Scriptorium* 32 (1978): 54-55.

GARCÍA TURZA, Claudio, coord. *Los manuscritos visigóticos: estudio paleográfico y codicológico.* Vol. 1, *Códices riojanos datados.* Logroño: Fundación San Millán de la Cogolla, 2002.

GLORIEUX DE GAND, Thérèse. "Formules de copiste: les colophons des manuscrits datés". In *Catalogue (d'exposition, Bruxelles, Bibliothèque Royale Albert Ier, du 7.12.1991 au 25.1.1992).* Brussels: Bibliothèque Royale Albert Ier, 1991.

GOMES, Saul António. "A codicologia em Portugal: balanço e perspectivas no fim do século XX". In José d'Encarnação, ed. *As Oficinas da História.* Lisbon: Colibri; Coimbra: Faculty of Letters of the University of Coimbra, 2002.

—. *In limine conscriptionis. Documentos, chancelaria e cultura no mosteiro de Santa Cruz de Coimbra (séculos XII a XIV).* Viseu: Palimage, 2007.

HERRERO JIMÉNEZ, Mauricio. "Un fragmento de obituario del Hospital de San Juan de Duero". In Manuel C. Díaz y Díaz, coord. *Escritos dedicados a José María Fernández Catón.* León: Centro de Estudios e Investigación San Isidoro (CSIC-CECEL), 2004, 689-716.

MARQUES, Alfredo Pinheiro. "Alguns fragmentos de mapas encontrados em Viana do Castelo e outras novidades do ano de 1988 para a história da cartografia". *Revista da Universidade de Coimbra* 35 (1989): 309-322.

MARTINS, Armando Alberto. *O Mosteiro de Santa Cruz de Coimbra na Idade Média.* Lisbon: Center of History of the University of Lisbon, 2003.

MATTOSO, José. *L'abbaye de Pendorada des origines à 1160.* Coimbra: Atlântida, 1962.

—. *Religião e cultura na Idade Média portuguesa.* Lisbon: INCM, 1982.

MILLARES CARLO, Agustín. *Tratado de paleografía española.* 3rd ed. Madrid: Espasa Calpe,1983.

MORUJÃO, Maria do Rosário Barbosa. "A Sé de Coimbra: a instituição e a chancelaria (1080-1318)". Unpublished doctoral thesis. University of Coimbra, 2005.

MUNDÓ, Anscari M. "Notas para la historia de la escritura visigótica en su período primitivo". In *Bivium. Homenaje a Manuel C. Díaz y Díaz.* Madrid: Gredos, 1983.

—. *Obres completes.* Barcelona: Curial Edicions Catalanes, 1998.

MUNDÓ, Anscari M., and Jesús ALTURO I PERUCHO. "Problemàtica de les escriptures dels períodes de transició i de les marginals". *Cultura Neolatina* 58 (1998): 129.

NASCIMENTO, Aires Augusto. *O scriptorium.* Lisbon: Faculty of Letters of the University of Lisbon, 1999.

NASCIMENTO, Aires Augusto, and José Francisco MEIRINHOS, coords. *Catálogo dos códices da Livraria de Mão do Mosteiro de Santa Cruz de Coimbra na Biblioteca Pública Municipal do Porto.* Porto: Biblioteca Pública Municipal do Porto, 1997.

OSTOS, Pilar, María Luisa PARDO, and Elena E. RODRÍGUEZ. *Vocabulario de codicología.* Madrid: Arco Libros, 1997.

PALAZZO, Éric. *Le Moyen Âge: histoire des livres liturgiques: des origines au XIIIe siècle.* Paris: Beauchesne, 1993.

PELLEGRIN, Elisabeth. "Fragments et membra disiecta". *Codicologica* 3 (1980): 70-95.

PEREIRA, Isaías da Rosa. *Codicologia. Arqueologia do livro.* Angra do Heroísmo: Instituto Histórico da Ilha Terceira, 1979.

PERNOUD, Régine. *La femme au temps des cathédrales.* Paris: Stock, 1980.

QUEIRÓS, Abílio Ferreira. "Missal Medieval da Sé de Coimbra". Unpublished doctoral thesis. Coimbra: Faculty of Letters of the University of Coimbra, 1993.

—. "Fragmentos de pergaminhos litúrgico-musicais. Inventário Geral (1.ª parte)". *Boletim do Arquivo da Universidade de Coimbra* 13-14 (1993-1994): 325-348.

—. "Inventário dos Fragmentos litúrgico-musicais existentes no AUC (2.ª parte)". *Boletim do Arquivo da Universidade de Coimbra* 15-16 (1995-1996): 517-547.

—. "Fragmentos de um códice litúrgico-musical da Sé de Coimbra (séc. X-XI)". In *Semente em boa terra: raízes do Cristianismo na Diocese de Coimbra: do século IV a 1064.* Coimbra: Gráfica de Coimbra, 2000.

REED, Ronald. *Ancient Skins, Parchments and Leathers.* London, New York: Seminar Press, 1972.

RUIZ ASENCIO, José Manuel. "La colección de fragmentos latinos de la Chancillería de Valladolid". In *Actas del II Congreso Hispánico de Latín Medieval: León, 11-14 denoviembre de 1997.* León: University of León, 1998. Vol. 1: 175-185.

SANTOS AZEVEDO, Maria José. *Da visigótica à carolina: a escrita em Portugal de 882 a 1172: aspectos técnicos e culturais.* Lisbon: FCG-JNICT, 1994.

—. "Les conditions de conservation des documents et des livres au Portugal (XIIe-XVe siècles)". *Scriptorium* 50 (1996): 391-406.

—. "Modos de escrever no século XII em Portugal. O caso do Mosteiro de Santa Cruz de Coimbra". *Biblio-*

theca Portucalensis, Serie 2, 15-16 (2000-2001): 99-111.

—."Os 'clérigos-notários' em Portugal (séculos XI-XII) ". In Maria Helena da Cruz Coelho, coord. *Estudos de diplomática portuguesa*. Lisbon: Colibri, 2001.

—. "Technical conditions and materials for copying manuscripts in the Middle Ages". In *Santa Cruz de Coimbra. Cultura Portuguesa aberta à Europa na Idade Média. The Portuguese Culture Opened to Europe in the Middle Ages*. Porto: Biblioteca Pública Municipal do Porto, 2001.

SANZ FUENTES, María Josefa. "Tiempo de leer y escribir: el 'scriptorium'". *Cuadernos de Investigación del Monasterio de Santa María de la Real* 6 (July 1992): 37-56.

STIENNON Jacques. *Paléographie du Moyen Âge*. 2nd ed. Paris: PUF, 1982.

VASCONCELOS, António de. "Fragmentos preciosos de dois códices paleográfico-visigóticos". *Biblos* 4 (1928): 353-369.

—. "Fragmento precioso dum códice visigótico". *Biblos* 5 (1929): 245-273.

VEZIN, Jean. "La fabrication du manuscrit". In Henri-Jean Martin and Roger Chartier, eds. *Histoire de l'édition française*. Paris: Promodis, 1982.

ZAPKE, Susana. *El antifonario de San Juan de la Peña (siglos X-XI). Estudio litúrgico-musical del rito hispano.* Zaragoza: Institución Fernando el Católico, Sección de Música Antigua, 1995.

The Hispanic Texts *In Diem Circumcisionis Domini*

Eva Castro Caridad

The first of January gradually came to be filled with a series of religious celebrations in the western liturgical calendar. We need to remember that this day in the calends of January was the day when the cheerful idolatrous festivities of the saturnalia took place. To contrast with such pagan practices, the oldest Christian celebration was a penitential festival with fasting and prayer, known as *Ad prohibendum ab idolis*. This office gradually lost importance during the 6th and 7th centuries, so that the Church of Rome could add the commemoration of the Virginity of Mary, the mother of God, on 1 January. Once 25 December was established as the day of the festivity of the Nativity of the Lord, and since this, together with the celebration of Easter, was one of the two focal points in the Christian liturgical calendar, the Nativity was accompanied by its octave, which coincided exactly with 1 January. In the mass on that day, the Gospel according to St. Luke (2:21-40) was read. The story from the New Testament refers to the evangelical event of Christ's Circumcision, which was considered to be a reason for a special celebration, especially in the Hispanic church, and which only began to be included in books with the Roman rite in the 11th century. The celebration of the festivity of the Holy Name of Jesus is also connected with the reading of the Gospel of St. Luke, which is a second-class feast day that began to establish itself in the 12th century. Finally, it needs to be pointed out that, just as deacons had their feast day on St. Stephen's day, 26 December, priests on the day of St. John the Evangelist, 27 December, and altar boys, on Holy Innocents' Day, 28 of December, subdeacons, especially in northern French churches during the 12th and 13th centuries, had their feast day on 1 January, which gave rise to the so-called *festa stultorum* or *festa asinorum* and led to secular behaviors that were often far removed from any liturgical decorum.[1]

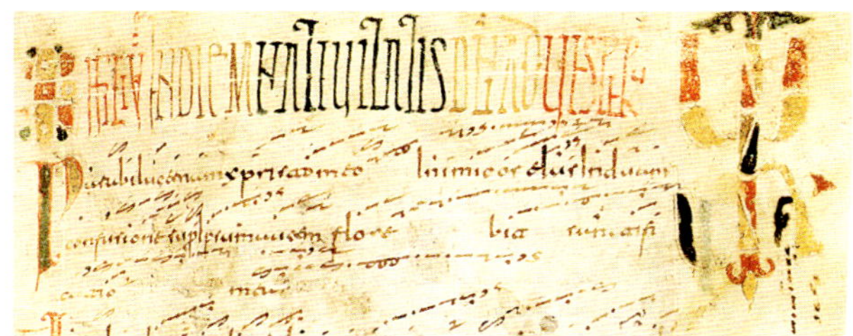

1. *Liber misticus*. Toledo, BC, 35-7, 11th century *ex.*-12th century *in.*, fol. 55r: *Officium in diem nativitatis Domini ad vesperas*

If we now focus on the celebration of the liturgical festivity of the *circumcisionis Domini*, we need to point out that one of the earliest mentions of this commemoration can be found at the II. Council of Tours (567), to be specific in canon 18 (17), where the various fasting periods throughout the year are prescribed:[2]

> Et quia inter natale Domini et epyfania omni die festivitates sunt, idemque prandebunt excepto triduum illud, quod ad calcandam gentilium consuetudinem patris nostri statuerunt, privatas in kalendis Ianuarii fieri letanias, ut in ecclesia psalletur et ora octava in ipsis kalendis circumcissionis missa Deo propitio celebretur; post epyfania vero usque quadragensima ter in septimana ieiunent.

As can be seen, the celebration of this vespers mass of the Lord's Circumcision still falls within the liturgical context of the days of fasting and prayer of the ancient office of the calends of January. This penitential period that contrasted with gentile excesses, established by the early Church Fathers and recalled by St. Augustine in the sermon prepared for this day,[3] still has a significant presence in Hispanic documents from the first half of the 7th century on. One of the most important testimonies is that of St. Isidore, who in his treatise written circa 610-615, titled *De ecclesiasticis officiis*, only describes Christmas and Epiphany as feast days in the Christmas season (*De ecclesiasticis officiis*, bk. I, chaps. 25 and 26). Nevertheless, the day of the calends of January, that is, the first day of the year, is mentioned explicitly as one of the days of fasting in the year that had been created to counteract pagan practices [*De ecclesiasticis officiis*, bk. I, chap. 41 (40): *De ieiunio kalendarum ianuariarum*]:[4]

> Ieiunium kalendarum ianuariarum propter errorem gentilitatis instituit ecclesia. Ianus enim quidam princeps paganorum fuit a quo nomen mensis ianuarii nuncupatur. Quem inperiti homines ueluti deum colentes in religione honoris posteris tradiderunt, diemque ipsum scenis et luxoriae sacrauerunt [...] Proinde ergo sanctipatres considerantes maximam partem generis humani eodem die huiusmodi sacrilegiis ac luxoriis inseruire statuerunt in uniuerso mundo per omnes ecclesias publicum ieiunium, per quod agnoscerent homines in tantum se praue agere ut pro eorum peccatis necesse esset omnibus eclesiis ieiunare.

A few years later, around 615-618, St. Isidore himself mentions the commemoration of the Circumcision of the Lord as one of the most important festivals in the liturgical calendar and consigns fasting to days after this, as can be gathered from two chapters in his *De regula monachorum:*[5]

> Chap. 10: *De feriis [...] Placuit etiam Patribus a die Natalis Domini usque ad diem Circumcisionis solemne tempus efficere, licentiamque vescendi habere.*

> Chap. 11: *De ieiunio... Quartum item quotidianum ieiunium post diem Circumcisionis exoritur, peragiturque usque ad solemnia Pasche.*

In accordance with the aforementioned testimony provided by the Council of Tours, to which the *Benedictio de circumcisione Domini ad Vesperum* in the celebration *De octavas nativitatis Domini kalendas ianuarias* from the Visigothic orationale can be added,[6] it can be said that in the 6th century the celebration of 1 January was the commemoration of the Octave of Christmas, one liturgical themes of which was the Circumcision of the Lord. It was possible for this situation to continue until the IV. Council of Toledo, held in 633, the canon 11 of which, devoted to forbidding the chanting of the halleluja in Lent, clearly shows that the calends of January are a period of penance, and quite directly invokes the previously mentioned text by St. Isidore included in *De ecclesiasticis officiis*, as it recalls how it was created to counteract pagan festivals:[7]

> In temporibus quoque reliquorum calendis ianuariis, propter errorem gentilium aguntur, omnino Alleluia non decantabitur, in quibus etiam praeter piscem et olus, sicut in illis XL diebus, ceteris carnibus abstinetur et a quibusdam etiam nec vinum bibitur.

Nevertheless, in the second half of the 7th century, Visigothic laws already recognized the festivity of the Circumcision as being one of the most special in the annual liturgical calendar, as two laws reveal: one from Recesvinto's time († 672) and another from Ervigio's († 687):[8]

> *Leges visigothorum II, 1, 12:* De diebus festis et feriatis, in quibus non sunt negotia exequenda [...] Nativitatis quoque dominice, Circumcisionis, Epiphanie, Ascensionis et Pentecosten singuli dies simili reverentia venerentur.

> *Leges visigothorum XII, 3, 6:* Ut omnis Iudeus diebus dominicis et in prenotatis festivitatibus ab opere cesset [...] Dies tamen ipsi, qui ab isdem Iudeis sollicita devotione sunt observandi, hii sunt: id est festum virginis sancta Marie, quo gloriosa conceptio eiusdem genitricis Domini celebratur, item natalis Christi vel circumcisionis sive apparitionis sue dies, Pasca quoque sanctum vel dies sacratissimi octavarum, inventionis quoque crucis dominice festum necnon et ascensionis dominice diem vel Pentecosten seu etiam concurrentes per totum annum dies dominicos, religiosa Christi fide venerabiles dies.

This kind of indirect evidence confirms the details passed on directly by manuscript sources because it has been shown that some of the texts in the Circumcision mass in the Hispanic liturgy can be found in codices from the 17th century *med.,* so that it can be confirmed that in the middle of this century most of the Hispanic masses regarding the Tempest had already been written, including the very mass of the festivity that we are concerned with here. With regard to the Christian religious celebration of Christ's Circumcision, the situation was quite complex at that time, however, especially in Hispania, because the Christians, except for the Ethiopians and Syrian Nestorians, were forbidden to practice circumcision, whereas the Jews in the Peninsula maintained it as a sign of their commitment to the Covenant. This clash between a practice applied to Christ and maintained by the Jews yet abolished among Christians explains the highly theological and aesthetic nature of the literary texts for the festivity of the Circumcision in the liturgy of the Hispanic rite.

The pericopes *in diem circumcisionis Domini*

The feast day of the Circumcision, so deeply rooted in the Hispanic liturgy, is a logical extension of the celebration of Christmas because it refers to events that are closely linked to Christ's birth, according to their chronological sequence in the Gospel of Luke, which is the only one to describe them. Bear in mind in this respect that the Gospel at mass *In diem circumcisionis Domini* is Lk 2:21-38, which is the continuation of the Gospel of the mass *In natale Domini* (Lk 2:1-20). We must also point out, however, that many of the liturgical texts for 1 January refer directly to the Lord's Nativity, thus establishing a close relationship and continuity between the two feast days.

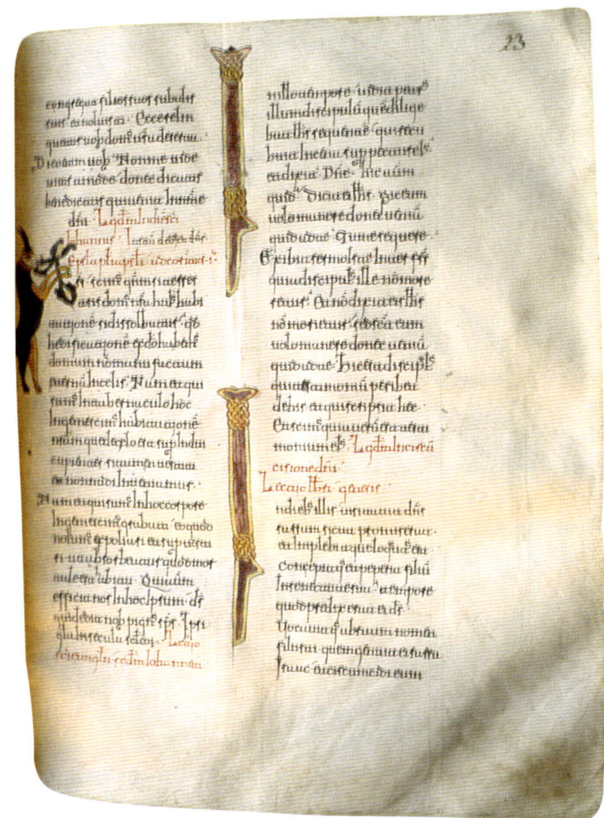

2. *Liber commicus.* Madrid, RAH, Cod. 22, 11th century (1073), fol. 23r

Thanks to a variety of surviving manuscripts, we can know the liturgical texts that shaped the various ceremonies on this day, although here we only focus on the ones that formed part of the mass.[10] To discover the texts of the chants and prayers that made up this mass, we have two very different sources. On the one hand, we inevitably need to turn to the 1500 edition of the *Missale mixtum,* prepared by Ortiz and revised and republished in 1755 by Alejandro Lesley, whose work was reproduced precisely by Migne in his *Patrologia latina LXXXV.*[11] As is wellknown, Ortiz's commendable work displays a series of special features that he himself acknowledges in the dedication to Cardinal Cisneros and which were noted by José Janini.[12] According to this illustrious scholar, Ortiz's Missal is a *liber conflatus*, which uses elements taken from the Toledo missal based on the Roman rite, from manuscripts of the Visigothic-Mozarabic liturgy, and even from creations by Ortiz himself, who changed the position of prayers or rewrote others in imitation of older texts. It needs to be pointed out that the texts for the mass on this feast day have survived in several very old codices. The three readings in the mass are found in two copies of the *Liber commicus*, used by Brother Justo Pérez de Urbel in his edition,[13] whereas the prayers in the mass are known thanks to three codices, used both by Màrius Férotin and by Janini in their scholarship.[14]

If we compare the *Missale mixtum* and the surving liturgical codices, certain differences and significant similarities emerge. The differences in the readings result from comparison of Ortiz's *Missale* to the copies of the *Liber commicus.* There were three readings, as was usually the case on important feast days: first, a reading from the Old Testament prophets *(Prophetia);*[15] second, a reading from the Apostles, normally from St. Paul's letters;[16] and third, the Gospel (*Evangelium*). Both kinds of sources use Lk 2:21-40, as the Gospel reading of mass on the feast day of the Circumcision, given that he is the only Evangelist to tell this story, as we have already noted: "Et postquam consummati sunt dies octo, ut circumcideretur puer, vocatum est nomen eius Iesus, quod vocatum est ab angelo prius quam in utero conciperetur [...]". The Gospel lesson also includes the stories of the purification of Mary, the presentation of Jesus in the temple, the blessing of the old man Simeon and the reference to the prophetess, Anna, and all of these motifs are included in various prayers, antiphons and hymns in the mass and office performed on this feast day.

As far as the other two readings in the mass, from the Prophets and Apostles, the sources differ, however. The first reading in the *Liber commicus*[17] is Gen. 21:1-8, on Sara's conception and the birth of her son, Isaac, who is circumcised on the eighth day and given his name, according to God's command received by his father, Abraham: "Visitavit autem Dominus Sarram, sicut promiserat [...]". Nevertheless, Ortiz's *Missale*[18] includes a passage by the prophet Isaiah (Is 48:12-20), with warnings to Israel about its liberation from Babylon: "Audi me, Iacob, et Israel quem ego voco; ego ipse, ego primus, et ego novissimus [...]". The second reading from the *Liber commicus*[19] is from St. Paul's letters to the romans (Rom. 15:8-13): "Dico enim Christum Iesum ministrum factum circumcisionis propter veritatem Dei, ad confirmandas promissiones patrum", although the *Missale* includes St. Paul's letter to the Philippians (Phil. 3:1-8), where he warns against Judaising practices and claims that the Christians are truly circumcised in spirit: "Gaudete in Domino. Eadem vobis scribere mihi quidem non pigrum, vobis autem necessarium [...]".

A review of the various prayers in the mass and office clearly reveals that, in addition to the Gospel of the day, the readings in the *Liber commicus*, and not the *Missale mixtum*, inspired most of the texts for this feast day. Thus, Abraham is mentioned as the receiver of the covenant, whose sign in the Old Testament was circumcision precisely, as in the prayer *Ad pacem* in the eucharistic celebration on this day:[20] "quem et Abraham in se uno ostendit, quum alios ex circumcisione, alios ex fide sua venire portendit".[21] It was the passage from St. Paul's epistle to the romans, however, that left most traces in several prayers, not just in the mass but also in the office. This is the case with the *Benedictio* in the mass, where we can read: "[...] ad eum perveniatis qui ad confirmandas promissiones patrum minister factus est circumcisionis";[22] or in the prayer from matins, that is joined to the antiphon *Postquam consummati sunt dies octo*, which begins: "Christe Dei filius, qui factus ex muliere, factus sub lege ad confirmandas promissiones patrum minister circumcisionis es factus".[23] St. Paul's epistle is also one of the sources of the prayer *Completuria ad vesperum* on the feast day of the Circumcision in the Visigothic orationale: "Christe, filius Dei patris, qui minister factus circumcisionis et paternarum promissionum es omnimoda plenitudo".[24]

One of the most significant pieces of evidence regarding the pericopes that made up the Eucharistic celebration on the feast day of the Circumcision is the *Benedictio de circumcisionis Domini ad Vesperum* in the celebration *De octavas nativitatis Domini kalendas ianuanias*. As mentioned earlier, this prayer is interesting[25] because it is very old and that it may have been written before the Hispanic feast of the Circumcision was organized, given that it is found precisely in the celebration of the Octave of Christmas, and not on the feast day of 1 January that would become a characteristic feature of the Hispanic liturgical calendar. The blessing, as in any prayer of this type, is a formula consisting of three invocations, to which the congregation would answer *amen*. In it, the gifts they hope to receive are summarized:[26]

> *Benedictio de circumcisione Domini ad Vesperum:*
> Dominus Iesus Christus, qui ad confirmandas promissiones patrum minister circumcisionis voluit esse, ipse cordium vestrorum inmunditias dignetur auferre. Idem, qui precepto legis suae signum desecte carnis accepit, omnes a vobis sordes sui amoris conexione depurget. Et qui vos filios Abrae in se ipso, qui est semen eius, benedicere repromisit, hereditatis beate vos conlatione munificet.

As can be seen, the first prayer is directly inspired by St. Paul's epistle to the romans (Rom. 15:8-13), which establishes the meaning of circumcision in the New Testament based on the figure of Christ in relation to circumcision as a sign in the Old Testament according to Abraham's testimony and his descendents, and this is the meaning of the passage from Genesis (Gen. 21:1-8), chosen as the first reading in the mass of the Circumcision.

The list of pericopes in the *Liber commicus* also explains a well-established typological connection between the New and Old Testament regarding Christ's Circumcision and St. Paul's subsequent spiritual interpretation of this event. In this respect, it needs to be stressed that the Venerable Bede used several chapters both from Genesis, especially those regarding circumcision, as a sign of the new pact between Yahweh and Abraham (Gen. 17), and from St. Paul's epistle to the romans (Rom. 1; 4; 6), in which circumcision in the Old Testament is interpreted as a sign of justice through faith, in his exegetical and homiletic writings.[27] It should nevertheless be borne in mind that the liturgical use of Luke's Gospel in the Venerable Bede's work concerned the Roman rite because the celebrated feast day was the feast of the Octave of Christmas and not of the Circumcision, as was characteristic in Gallican and Hispanic usage. This fact inevitably means that, although Christ's Circumcision plays an important role in the Venerable Bede's reflections, his texts were chosen with the celebration of the Octave of Christmas in mind.

Study of the various pericopes in the first and second reading in the mass on the feast day *(Propheta* and *Apostolus)* as found in the *Missale mixtum* by Ortiz and the *Liber commicus* leads to a final conclusion that whereas the readings in the *Liber* aimed to establish a general typological connection between circumcision in the Old and New Testament, those in Ortiz's *Missale* probably point towards a problem in Visigothic Hispanic Society resulting from the Jewish practice of circumcision of the flesh, which was forbidden by the civil and ecclesiastical authorities.

THE *ORATIONES*

Both types of sources, that is the manuscripts and Ortiz's *Missale mixtum*, show no variation in the nine prayers that make up the typical mass in the Hispanic rite.[28] It has been pointed out on various occasions that it is precisely this set of nine prayers in each mass that helped to give the eucharistic celebration of the Hispanic rite its exuberance and literary and musical splendor, compared with the Roman rite. The prayers that are recited by the officiating priest at various times during the Eucharist form what is called a *canon* in the Roman mass. They are characterized by the fact that they are independent of each other and are specific to each feast day. Their content may be of a general nature, designed more for the specific moment in the liturgy when they are recited, or they may be specific and develop the theological content of the feast day that is being celebrated. In any case, the authors of these texts used a variety of literary sources on numerous occasions and took themes that provided inspiration from them.

The first observation that needs to be made regarding the nine prayers in the mass for the feast day of the Circumcision is that each performs the characteristic function that was traditionally assigned to it.[29] The first prayer in the Circumcision mass is "Deum qui nobis id prospicit" (no. 173), generically called *Missa* or *Oratio admonitionis*, and its aim is to urge the faithful to pray and to celebrate the feast day. The second, "Perfecta ingeniti sapientia patris" (no. 174), known as *Alia*, is characterized by the fact that God is asked here to accept the congregation's requests with benevolence. The third, "Domine Iesu Christe, qui mortalitatis hominem" (no. 175), is the prayer known as *Post nomina*, in which the officiating priest presents the offerings and asks for eternal life for the offerers and the dead. The fourth prayer, *Ad Pacem*, "Christe, finis legis ad iustitiam" (no. 176), asks God to grant peace to those present and absent, and urges the congregation to wish each other peace. The *Inlatio*, "Dignum et iustum est, te ineffabilis inmenseque sapientie deum" (no. 177) is the longest prayer in the mass of the Hispanic rite and is characterized by its theological reflection on the feast day. The prayer *Post Sanctus*, "Vere incomparabiliter te esse sanctum" (no. 178) paraphrases the chants of the ordinary, the sanctus and hosanna. The seventh prayer, "Deus, auctor omnium te conditor" (no. 179), is called *Post pridie* and consists of a prayer to God for him to bless the eucharistic offering and grant spiritual blessings to those members of the congregation who will take part in the communion. The penultimate prayer, *Ad orationem dominicam*, "Unigenite dei filius, qui nos non carne" (no. 180), is an introduction to the Lord's Prayer, which reflects on the reasons for praying. The final prayer in the Hispanic system is called *Benedictio*, and in this case the text "Dominus Iesus Christus, qui ut legem adimpleret" (no. 181) is characterized by its three parts addressed to members of the congregation, who reply *amen* after each one. Each part summarizes the themes expressed in the other prayers.

The second observation that needs to be made regarding the nine prayers for the feast day of the Circumcision, is that all refer to the celebration of this day and its theological meaning, except the first, "Deum qui nobis id prospicit convenire" (no. 173). This text contains the oldest Hispanic functional and thematic characteristics of the *Missa* or *Oratio admonitionis*, because it is addressed to the entire congregation *(tota poscamus, dilectissimi fratres, mentis intentione)*, which extolls the joy of taking part in the celebration, as shown by the use of certain verbs and nouns such as *collaudare, exultare, preconiis* or *gaudia*, and God is asked to enable the congration to achieve eternal life ("ut dum officiis impensius mancipamur, celestium sacramentorum participium consequi mereamur"). One of the themes in this *oratio* is precisely the festivities on this day, but in this case it is not referring to the Lord's Circumcision but to Christmas, which reveals not only the close connection between both festivities, but also the fact that 1 January was also celebrated as the Octave of Christmas ("ut mysterium incarnationis eius [Iesu Christi] pro nostre salutis redemptione celebratum, augeat in nobis gaudia numquam ulterius finienda").

The other prayers refer to the Circumcision both as liturgical celebration and as a symbol of the New Covenant and use biblical passages that are taken not only from the readings of the mass of that day. Among these it is especially worth mentioning not only the lovely *Inlatio,* "Dignum et iustum est, te ineffabilis inmenseque sapientie" (no. 177), but also the second prayer, "Perfecta ingeniti sapientia" (no. 174).[30] It is divided into two well-defined sections as far as its content and form are concerned. The first section is a beautiful prayer addressed to Christ, which is structured around two formulas:

> a) Perfecta ingeniti sapientia patris, mentibus celesti munere inlabere nostris, contemnendo quod offendimus, et condonando te inspirante quod querimus.
>
> b) Abscide, quesumus, cordium nostrorum auriumque preputia, qui pro nobis dignatus es infantie gestare crepundia, ut quod in tua carne secundum legis litteram fieri circumcisione voluisti corporea, id nostre saluti competenter impendens, ab omni superstitione voluptatum absterge nostra precordia.

The first formula asks for the purification of our sins. The second focuses on the theme of the celebration, the circumcision of the flesh, *circumcisione corporea,* as a part of the Christmas cycle, to which it alludes at the text "qui pro nobis dignatus es infantie gestare crepundia" ("you, who for us has deigned to bear the nappies used in childhood"). With all of this, this circumcision to which Christ submits to fulfil the letter of the law, *secundum legis litteram,* has a symbolic nature, in accordance with the new reading from the New Testament: "Abscide, quesumus, cordium nostrorum auriumque preputia" ("Cut, we beg of you, the foreskins of our hearts and ears"). The circumcision of the heart is already mentioned in the Old Testament, specifically in Deuteronomy (Dt. 10:16: "Circumcidite igitur praeputium cordis vestri"; Dt. 30:6: "Circumcidet Dominus Deus tus cor tuum et cor seminis tui"), just as is the circumcision of the ears in a passage from the Prophet Jeremiah (Jer. 6:10: "Cui loquar et quem contestabor ut audita? Ecce incircumcisae aures eorum et audire non possunt"). The text of the Hispanic *oratio* is directly inspired by the exclamation of the protomartyr Stephen included in the New Testament (Acts. 7:51), however: "Dura cervice et incircumcisis cordibus et auribus, vos semper Spiritu sancto resistitis" ("Yet stiffnecked and uncircumcised in heart and ears, you do always resist the Holy Ghost").

As far as the form of the text is concerned, it is worth noting the prose with assonance by means of the use of *cola* with rhymed endings (*pa*tris / *nos*tris; *offend*imus / *quer*imus; *preput*ia / *crepund*ia / *precord*ia; *circumcis*ione / *superstit*ione), and the use of certain stereotypical expressions, such as *ingeniti patris.*[31] As Janini has shown,[32] these two formulas, that is, from *Perfecta* up to *competenter*, are not originally from the Hispanic liturgy but can already be found in a Roman sacramentary from the year 700, kept in Milan.[33] With all this, it is worth pointing out the elegant process used to adapt these formulas to the Hispanic prayer, since the second one is completed by a plea of Hispanic origin that is joined to what has gone before by means of the formal procedure of assonance, as the new text *superstitione* is made to rhyme with the previous *circumcisione,* and *precordia* with *crepundia* and *preputia.*

This new added phrase is not just an *amplificatio* with the aim of embellishing the old prayer but is highly significant insofar as it explains its symbolic value, which is merely the value of purity, with which the Jewish practice of circumcision should be interpreted by Christians.[34] On the other hand, the lexical formulation of this last phrase would evoke among the faithful the Visigothic legislative regulations against the Jews, especially the laws passed by King Ervigio, given that the Jewish religion was often considered to be a *superstitio* by Christian lawmakers.[35] In this body of law the practice of circumcision of the flesh by the Jews, *carnis circumcisio*, is often also contrasted with the circumcision of hearts by Christians, as pointed out in the *Lex visigothorum* XII, 3, 4, titled *Ne Iudei more suo celebrent Pasca vel carnis circumcisiones exerceant ac ne christianum quemquam a fide Christi dimoveant*, where it says: "Et si cordis nobis circumcisione gauderet, adumbratam illam corporis expoliationem nullo modo in carne exprimeret".

The second section of the *oratio* (no. 174) that we are analysing is of Hispanic origin and inspired by the epistles of St. Paul, from which it takes various elements.

> Lac tuum nutriat parvulos, qui fieri dignatus es pro nostra redemptione pusillus. Ut sicut in te quum ista prestares nullum sensit omnipotentia detrimentum, ita et FIDES nostra tuo munere confortata, nullum patiatur aliquando defectum, sed ad solidum gratie tue perveniat fundamentum.

So, the *lac tuum nutriat* syntagm is based on the text in 1 Cor. 3, 1, 2: "Lac vobis potum dedi, non escam"; in the same way that *nullum detrimentum* is on Phil. 3:8: "Verumtamen existimo omnia detrimentum esse propter eminentem scientiam Iesu Christi Domini mei: propter quem omnia detrimentum feci [...]". The author of the Hispanic text also imitates the compositional procedures of the Roman formula by using assonance at the ends of the *cola* by rhyming *detrimentum / defectum / fundamentum*. Furthermore it is possible that the Hispanic liturgist might have remembered the St. Augustine's sermon on the Circumcision of the Lord in which certain elements from the peninsular text can also be found:

> Altissimi namque Salvatoris humilitas non ipsi aliquod intulit detrimentum, sed incrementum nobis contulit magnum [...] dignatus est Creador [...] et Deus factus hominis homo verus ex homine fieri, quinetiam pannis involvi in angustissimo praesepio.

The prayer, which is the first in this mass to refer to the reason for the liturgical celebration of this day, Christ's Circumcision, stresses the close link to the Christmas cycle. On at least two occasions, two themes are restated that are used in prayers from the Christmas mass:[36]

> a) *Dignatus es infantie gestare crepundia* about Circumcision evokes the text *Per illam crepundia gestavit per istam regna subjecit* from the prayer of the *Inlatio* from the Christmas mass.
>
> b) *Lac tuum nutriat parvulos* on Circumcision refers directly to *Lac tuum Eclessie tue parvulos* from the prayer *Alia* from the Christmas mass.

The hymns on the feast day of the Lord's Circumcision

Depending on the sources that one consults, there were two hymns sung at Vespers of the Lord's Circumcision. The famous Antiphonary of León[37] mentions in the incipit, that is, through the first words of the hymn, *A solis ortu cardine,*[38] inspired by the poem of the priest Sedulius (5th century *in.*),[39] which is a hymn of praise for Christmas that mentions Mary's virginity.

The contents of the hymn *Sacer octavarum dies* (published in *Analecta hymnica medii aevi XXVII*: no. 8), refers more specifically to the feast day that we are concerned with here and takes three sources as references,[40] to which we now need to add another one from the 12th century *in.* from Toledo.[41] The poem has seven verses, each of three rhythmic lines with fifteen syllables, with an 8p + 7 pp structure, that imitates the rhythm of the classical trochaic septenary.[42] As far as its content is concerned, the piece is an excellent example of the theological work produced by the Hispano-Visigothic Church,[43] on account of its structure and its inclusion of biblical,

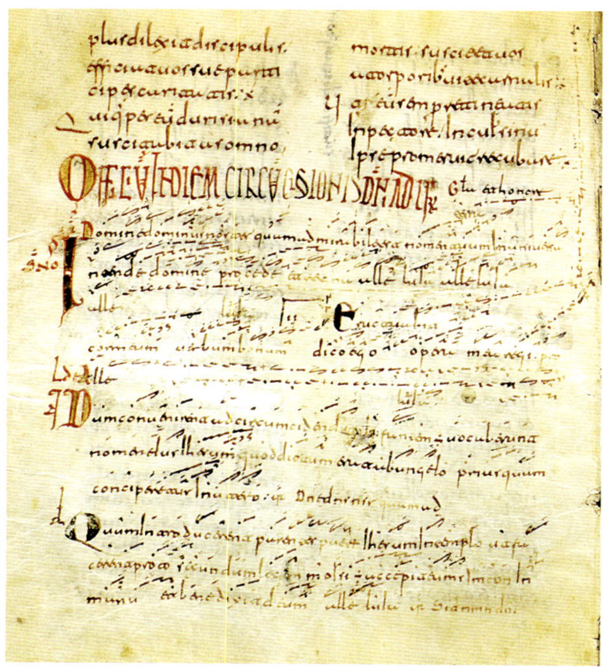

3. *Liber misticus*. Toledo, BC, 35-7, 11th century *ex.*-12th century *in.*, fol. 94v: *Officium in diem circuncisionis Domini ad vesperas*

liturgical and even political references, but these always fall within the themes of the feast day that is being celebrated. The first verse is a good example of what has just been explained:

> 1) Sacer octavarum dies hodiernus rutilat,
> quo secundum carnem Christus circumcisus traditur
> Patri, non adoptione, coaeternus genere.

Each one of the lines elegantly and subtly provides information. The first points out the *hic et nunc* of the feast day and refers to the very old liturgical celebration of the Octave of Christmas; the second is based on the Gospel story itself and stresses the Hispanic liturgical theme; finally, the third restates church dogma by clearly referring to the adoptionist heresy, championed by Elipandus of Toledo[44] in the 8th century *ex.* The hymn is used in this way, just like other liturgical texts, to explain the dogmas of the Catholic faith.

The second verse refers to one of the themes that is dealt with most often in the Christmas liturgical cycle: Mary's virginity. Let us not forget that this theme was included in the original expiatory celebration of 1 January from the 7th century onwards. Thus, the Hispanic text recalls one of the oldest and most traditional contents of this celebration:

> 2) Spiritu completur alvus incorruptae virginis,
> pariens quae mansit caelebs virgoque puerpera.
> Illibatam genetricem proles casta eligit.

The third, *Inde Simeon grandaevus*, and fourth verse, *Sed nec illa impar Anna*, describe the episodes in the New Testament involving the recognition of the Son of God by the elderly Simeon and Anna (Lk 2:25-32; 36-38). These themes were also included in the extensive *Inlatio* in the mass, in the *Oratio ad vesperum* and in the *Completuria ad matutinum* in the celebration *De octavas Nativitatis Domini kalendas ianuarias* in the *Verona Orationale*, and in various antiphons from the office for this day.[45]

The fifth verse is also a literary description of an episode contained in the reading of the Gospel for this day; to be more precise, the story of the offering of a pair of turtle doves or pigeons (Lk 2:24), according to the Lord's Law, for the purification of a woman who has just given birth (Lev. 12:8; 5:11). Whereas the Church Fathers interpreted the birds offered in sacrifice allegorically and symbolically,[46] the Hispanic text sticks scrupulously to the aforementioned biblical meaning, as does the text of the *Inlatio* in the mass for this day:[47]

> 5) Veneranda tunc ex lege offeruntur munera
> Turturum columbarumque bina in sacrificia
> Corporis quae animaeque puritatem doceant.

The sixth verse has a profound evangelical content, since Christ's circumcision is one of the signs that confirm the words that Jesus would say at the beginning of his public life (Mt 5:17): "I am not come to destroy, but to fulfil". His circumcision entails Christ's compliance with and obedience to the Old Law and at the same time has a new meaning. The overlap between Old and New Testament represented by Christ's circumcision is constantly stressed by St. Paul in his epistles and by later homiletic literature.[48] The verse also ends with a line in which the dogma of the Trinity is reasserted, not just to combat the heretical ideas of that time to which it refers, as we have already seen in the third line of the first verse, but also to make way for the final verse, *Gloria et honor*, which is a doxology in praise of the Trinity:

6) Impleta est priscae in eo legis circumcisio,
utriusque ut testamenti se auctorem ostenderet
qui manens in Trinitate universa condidit.

In the same way that the Christmas hymn *A solis ortu cardine* was adapted for performance on certain Marian feast days, such as the Annunciation,[49] *Sacer octavarum dies* was also adapted, possibly very recently, for the Marian feast day of the Purification.[50] The changes consist of omitting verse 6, *Impleta est pricae in eo*, and modifying verse 1 in the following way:

1) *Sacer puritatum dies hodiernus rutilat*
quo secundum carnem Cristus templo Simeon traditur
Patri, non adoptione, coaeternus genere.

The close link between the Christmas celebration of the Lord's Circumcision and the Marian feast day of the Purification is apparent in the constant exchange and adaptation of prayers, antiphons and hymns, as we have just pointed out. However, the fact that many of the Marian texts modelled on Christological compositions only appear in Oritz's *Missale mixtum* and in Lorenzana's *Breviarium gothicum* leads us to suspect that they were pieces that were recreated by 16th century publishers in their eagerness to round off all of the feast days in the liturgical calendar of the Hispanic rite with artistry.

Notes

[1] One of the latest studies on the celebrations for subdeacons is by Wulf Arlt. "The Office for the Feast of the Circumcision from Le Puy". In Margot E. Fassler and Rebecca A. Baltzer, eds. *The Divine Office in the Latin Middle Ages*. New York: Oxford University Press, 2000, 324-343.

[2] *Concilium Turonense (a. 567).* In Carles de Clercq, ed. *Concilia Galliae (a. 511-695).* Turnhout: Brepols, 1963, 182 (Corpus Christianorum: Series Latina 148a).

[3] Augustinus. *Sermones de Tempore. Sermo 198: De calendis januariis*. In J.-P. Migne, ed. *Patrologia Latina*. Paris: Garnier, 1844-1889. Vol. XXXVIII: col. 1024: "Currunt illi ad theatrum, uos ad ecclesiam, inebriantur illi, uos ieiunate".

[4] Isidorus. *De ecclesiasticis officiis*. Turnhout: Brepols, 1989, 46-47 (Corpus Christianorum: Series Latina 113); and J.-P. Migne, ed. *Ibidem,* col. 752. To write this chapter, St. Isidore was inspired by sermon 192 by Cesarius, titled *De kalendis ianuariis.* Turnhout: Brepols, 1953, 779-782 (Corpus Christianorum: Series Latina 104).

[5] Isidorus. *Opera Omnia.* En J.-P. Migne, ed. *Ibidem.* Vol. LXXXIII: cols. 880-881.

[6] José Vives, ed. *Oracional visigótico*. Madrid: CSIC, 1946, 119-120, no. 359: "Dominus Iesus Christus, qui ad confirmandas promissiones patrum minister circumcisionis voluit esse ...".

[7] *Idem,* ed. *Concilios visigóticos e hispano-romanos*. Barcelona, Madrid: CSIC, 1963, 195-196.

[8] Karl Zeumer, ed. *Leges visigothorum*. En *Monumenta Germaniae Historica: Legum sectio I.* Vol. 1. Hannover, Leipzig: Weidmann, 1902, 59, 434-435.

[9] José Janini, ed. *Liber missarum de Toledo y libros místicos*. Toledo: Instituto de Estudios Visigótico-Mozárabes, 1983. Vol. 2: xxxvi, points out that in the Irish palimpsest, from the 7th century *med.* (Munich: Staatsbibliothek, Clm 14429), prayers are kept for the masses for Circumcision, Innocents, Easter and the second Sunday after the Octave of Easter, which were still being copied in the *Liber missarum de Toledo* and in the mystical books of Silos many centuries later.

[10] The different kinds of liturgical books with the Hispanic rite have been listed and described by Jordi Pinell. "Los textos de la antigua liturgia hispana. Fuentes para su estudio". In Juan Francisco Rivera Recio, dir. *Estudios sobre la liturgia mozárabe*. Toledo: Instituto Provincial de Investigaciones y Estudios Toledanos, 1965, 109-164.

[11] J.-P. Migne, ed. Op. cit. Vol. LXXXV: cols. 217-222, *In Circumcisione Domini. Ad missam*. To understand the selection method for pericopes in the *Missale mixtum,* Jordi Gibert-Tarruell's work. "El sistema de lecturas de la cincuentena pascual de la liturgia hispánica, según la tradición B" is very interesting. In *Liturgia y música mozárabes. I Congreso Internacional de Estudios Mozárabes*. Toledo: Diputación de Toledo. Instituto de Estudios Visigótico-Mozárabes, 1975, 111-124.

[12] José Janini, ed. Op. cit. Vol. 2: lxiii-lxviii.

[13] The codices mentioned are: Paris, BNF, N. A. L. 2177, 1067 (from Silos), and Madrid, RAH, Cod. 22, 1073 (from San Millán de la Cogolla). The edition that must be consulted is by Justo Pérez de Urbel, and Atilano González Ruiz-Zorrilla, eds. *Liber commicus*. 2 vols. Madrid: Bermejo, 1950.

[14] José Janini, ed. Op. cit. Vol. 1: 59-62, nn. 173-181, where the *Missa in diem Circumcisionis Domini* is published. The manuscripts that have survived are: Toledo, BC, ms. 35-3, 11th century (which has been used as the

basic text by the previously mentioned author); London: BL, Add. ms. 30844, 11th century; and Toledo, BC, Cod. 35-7, 12th century. The descriptions of these codices can be consulted in *ibidem.* Vol. 2: xvii-xxii. It is also published in Toledo, BC, Cod. 35-7, that contains the offices for this feast day. *Ibidem.* Vol. 2: 233-272, especially pages 264-265. The mass, published on the basis of the three aforementioned codices, is also found In Màrius Férotin, ed. *Le Liber mozarabicus sacramentorum et les manuscrits mozarabes (reimpr. de l'édition de Paris 1912 et bibliographie générale de la liturgie hispanique, préparées et présentées par A. Ward y C. Jonson).* Rome: CLV Edizioni Liturgiche, 1995, 220-222, nn. 173-181 (hereafter *LM*). The celebration of the feast day of the Circumcision, as included in Toledo, BC, ms. 35-7, is found in *LM,* 561-563, and in London, BL, Add. ms. 30844, in *LM,* 587-588.

15 *LM,* 13: "*Prophetia:* La Première des trois lectures bibliques habituelles. Pendant la Carème, elle était tirée du Pentateuque et des Livres historiques de l'Ancient Testament, et dans des traditions variantes on ajoutait des textes tirées des Livres sapientiaux. Au temps de Pâques la lecture était extraite de l'Apocalyse".

16 *Ibidem*: "*Apostolus*: Lecture des Épitres de saint Paul, remplacée pendant le Carême par des textes tirées des Épitres Catholiques, et, dans le temps de Pâques, des Actes des Apôtres".

17 Justo Pérez de Urbel, and Atilano González Ruiz-Zorrilla, eds. Op. cit. Vol. 1: 38-39.

18 J.-P. Migne, ed. Op. cit. Vol. LXXXV: cols. 217-218.

19 Justo Pérez de Urbel, and Atilano González Ruiz-Zorrila, eds. Op. cit. Vol. 1: 39.

20 Regarding the system of prayers in the Hispanic mass and the typical characteristics of each of them, see the bibliographic references contained in note 28.

21 *LM,* 220, no. 176; José Janini, ed. Op. cit. Vol. 1: 60, no. 176.

22 *LM,* 221, no. 181; José Janini, ed. *Ibidem.* Vol. 1: 62, no. 181.

23 José Vives, ed. *Oracional visigótico.* Op. cit., 120, no. 361.

24 *Ibidem,* 126, no. 379. The *completuria* is the most important prayer in each hour of the Hispanic office and is precisely the one that each hour finishes with and includes the theological significance of the mystery being celebrated and the supplications of the community gathered in prayer; see Mauricio Ferro Calvo. *La celebración de la venida del Señor en el oficio hispánico.* Madrid: Instituto Superior de Pastoral, 1972, 32.

25 See note 6.

26 On the meaning of this prayer in the offices, see Mauricio Ferro Calvo. Op. cit., 32. The text of the prayer is in José Vives, ed. *Oracional visigótico.* Op. cit., 119-120, no. 359. It was also included in the office *Ad Vesperum* in the *Breviarium gothicum* prepared by Francisco Antonio de Lorenzana and later published by J.-P. Migne, ed. Op. cit. Vol. LXXXVI: col. 141, where it displays some variations, such as the change of the second person pronoun in the *Oracional visigótico (vobis, vos)* to the first person pronoun in the breviary *(nobis, nos).*

27 Beda Venerabilis. *In Lucae evangelium expositio.* Turnhout: Brepols, 1960, 56 and subsq. (Corpus Christianorum: Series Latina 120); *idem.* "Homelia 11. In octava Nativitatis Domini (Luke 2:21)". In *idem. Opera Homiletica.* Turnhout: Brepols, 1955, 73-79 (Corpus Christianorum: Series Latina 122). A selection of texts of his own, which differs from that in the Hispanic *Liber commicus* and in Beda Venerabilis, and in the *Missale,* is in the very short sermon on Christ's circumcision by Cesarius. *Sermo 191: De circumcisione Domini.* Turnhout: Brepols, 1953: 778-779 (Corpus Christianorum: Series Latina 104).

28 Isidorus. *De ecclessiasticis officiis.* Bk. 1, chap. 15, *De missa et orationibus.* He only described seven prayers in the mass, which implies that the system of nine was still not fixed in his day. The summaries that include the outline of the Hispanic mass prepared by Màrius Férotin are very useful. *LM,* 12-15, and by Ismael Fernández de la Cuesta. *Historia de la música española.* Vol. 1, *Desde los orígenes hasta el Ars Nova.* Madrid: Alianza Editorial, 1983, 123-125. On the general characteristics of these prayers, see Arturo Pascual Pérez. *La imagen de la Iglesia en la liturgia española.* Madrid: Instituto Superior de Pastoral, 1971, 24-30, especially, 26-27.

29 The texts for the prayers in the Circumcision mass are found in: Alfonso Ortiz. *Missale mixtum.* In J.-P. Migne, ed. Op. cit. Vol. 85: cols. 220-222, that followed the edition by Alfonso Ortiz and used manuscript sources; in *LM,* 220 and subsq., nos. 173-181; and José Janini. Op. cit. Vol. 1: 59-62, nos. 173-181.

30 The general function of the second prayer in the mass is described by St. Isidore: *De ecclesiasticis officiis.* Bk. I, chap. 15, *Secunda invocationis ad Deum est, ut clementer suscipiat preces fidelium oblaciones que eorum.*

31 Georg Manz. *Ausdrucksformen der lateinischen Liturgiesprache bis ins elfte Jahrhundert.* Beuron: Erzabtei, 1941; and José Janini. Op. cit. Vol. 2: 349.

32 José Janini. *Ibidem.* Vol. 2: 329.

[33] Milan, Biblioteca Ambrosiana, Cod. M. 12 sup. Alban Dold, ed. *Das Sacramentar im Schabkodex M. 12 sup. der Biblioteca Ambrosiana.* Beuron: Erzabtei, 1952 (Texte und Arbeiten: 43).

[34] This is how St. Cesarius, for example, explained circumcision in Caesarius. Op. cit., 778: "Circumcisio Christi quid est, fratres carissimi, nisi castitas nostra, qua deus delectatur in nobis? Quoniam nos oportet circumcidi non corpore sed spiritu, id est, omne vitium a nobis excidi". For his part, Beda Venerabilis insists on the same explanation in *Opera Homiletica.* Op. cit., 79: "Quae et ipsa cotidiana nostra circumcisio, id est continua cordis mundatio".

[35] A review of the Hispanic legislative corpus reveals that the noun *superstitio* was always accompanied by a modifier. The adjectives used were: *superstitio profana* (*Lex visigothorum* XII, 2, 14), *superstitio diabolica* (*Concilium Toletanum* XVI) and *superstitio judaica* (*Lex visigothorum* XII, 3, 7, and XII, 3, 14).

[36] The reference to the sermon by St. Augustine is "Opusculum quartum, sive sermo in Circumcisione Domini". In J.-P. Migne, ed. Op. cit. Vol. XLVII: col. 1135. The texts for the Christmas mass are also published in *ibidem.* Vol. 85: col. 188 (for the *Inlatio*) and col. 187 (for *Alia*).

[37] Louis Brou, and José Vives, eds. *Antifonario visigótico mozárabe de la Catedral de León.* Barcelona: Centro de Estudios e Investigación San Isidoro (CSIC-CECEL), 1959. Vol. 1: 105 (Monumenta Hispaniae Sacra: Serie Litúrgica 5, no. 2. Facsímiles musicales 1).

[38] The Antiphonary of León also used this hymn in *Officium in diem Sanctae Mariae*, where it was performed no less than three times (*ad Vesperum*, fol. 57; *ad Matutinum*, fol. 60; y *eodem diem ad Vesperum*, fol. 62); *Officium in diem Nativitatis Domini*, sung on two occasions (*ad Vesperum*, fol. 68v; and *ad Matutinum*, fol. 71v); *Officium in diem Apparitionis Domini* (*ad Vesperum*, fol. 84); *Officium in diem Allisionis Infantium*, which is the Hispanic counterpart to the Slaughter of the Innocents in the Gallic-Roman calendar (*ad Vesperum*, fol. 90v); and *In Cena Domini ad Matutinum*, fol. 162.

[39] Sedulio. *Hymnus 2.* In Paolo Mastandrea and Luigi Tessarolo, eds. *Poetria Nova. A CD-Rom of Latin Medieval Poetry (650-1250 a. D.) with a Gateway to Classical and Late Antiquity Texts.* Florence: Edizioni del Galluzzo, 2001. The Hispanic versions can be consulted in the collection *Analecta hymnica medii aevi.* Leipzig: O. R. Reisland, 1897. Vol. XXVII: 117-119, no. 82 (hereafter *AH*).

[40] *MT.* Madrid, BN, ms. 10001 (olim 1005; olim Toledo 35.1), fragment of a *liber misticus* copied in the 11th century *med.; MC.* Madrid, RAH, *Codex Aemilianensis* 30, *Liber misticus*, written in the 10th century, from Monastery of St. Millan; *X.* Francisco Antonio de Lorenzana. Op. cit., cols. 140-141. On the manuscript sources quoted, see *LM*, 523-524, 627-629; and José Janini. Op. cit. Vol. 2: xxiv.

[41] Toledo, BC, ms. 35-7. *Liber misticus*, written around 1100 by the copyist Sebastianus; see José Janini. *Ibidem,* xxi and 233 and subsq.

[42] Dag Norberg. *Introduction à l'étude de la versification latine médiévale.* Stockholm: Almqvist & Wiksell, 1958, 112-113. The oldest example is the primer hymn from the 5th century *med.,* organized in four-line verses, *Audite omnes amantes.*

[43] Mauricio Ferro Calvo. Op. cit., 29: "The Hispanic liturgy arouses researchers' curiosity as they find in it a significant part of the theological production of the golden age of the Hispanic-Visigothic church. If the liturgical texts are analysed, then it is to discover the living theology of a Church in them".

[44] Adoptionism was a heresy about the dogma of the Trinity, according to which Christ, as a man, would only be the Father's adoptive son from his baptism onwards. This philosophy appeared in Hispania in the 8th century *ex.,* advocated by Elipandus of Toledo but once its supporters had died, the heresy soon lost strength (ca. 780-808); see Marcelino Menéndez Pelayo. *Historia de los heterodoxos españoles.* Santander: CSIC, 1947. Vol. 2: 7-58.

[45] The text of the *Inlatio, Dignum et iustum est, te ineffabilis inmenseque sapientie,* has been published by José Janini. Op. cit. Vol. 1: 60-61, no. 179. Both the texts of the *oratio, Iesu domine, cuius admirabile nomen angelus predixit,* and the *completuria, Notum factum est salutare Domini,* in which Simeon and Anna are mentioned can be read in José Vives, ed. Op. cit., 119, no. 358; and 125-126, no. 377. The antiphons *Quum introducerent parentes* and *Simeon in templo elevabit* can be found in the Antiphonary of León, Luis Brou, and José Vives, eds. Op. cit., 105 and subsq.

[46] Agustín de Hipona. *Sermo in circumcisione Domini.* In J.-P. Migne, ed. Op. cit. Vol. XLVII: col. 1138: "In hoc genere avium, dilectissimi fratres, magnum nobis commendatur catholicae fidei sacramentum; in columba enim charitas agnoscitur et in turture castitas invenitur". A different interpretation appears in Beda the Venerable. *In Lucae evangelium expositio.* Op. cit., 63-65, especially p. 63: "Quia enim volucres hae pro cantu gemitus habent non immerito lacrimas humilium designant quibus plurimum in ipsis etiam bonis operibus indigemus". On the symbolic value of these birds, Manfred Lurker. *Diccionario de imágenes y símbolos de la Biblia.* Córdoba: El Almendro, 1994, 160-161.

[47] See José Janini, Op. cit., 61, no. 179: "Offeruntur deinde in sacrificio par turturum vel pulli gemini columbarum, ut in combinatione mundissimarum avium, tam anime quam corporis puritatem litandam deo exemplis evidentibus doceremur".

[48] Cesarius. Op. cit., 778-779; Quodvultdeus. *Liber promissionum I*, cap. 14, *Praedictio figurata*. Turnhout: Brepols, 1976, 29-30 (Corpus Christianorum: Series Latina 60); and Beda Venerabilis. *Opera homiletica, homelia 2, in octavas nativitatis Domini*. Op. cit., 73-79, especially page 74.

[49] *AH XXVII:* 116-117, no. 82.

[50] *AH XXVII:* 67, no. 8 (Circumcision); as well as 116, no. 81 (Purification of the Virgin Mary), whose only testimony comes from the *Breviarium gothicum* compiled by Francisco Antonio de Lorenzana in the 16th century *in.* and collected by J.-P. Migne, ed. Op. cit. Vol. LXXXVI: col. 1088.

Bibliography

I. Sources

AUGUSTINUS. *Sermones.* In J.-P. Migne, ed. *Patrologia Latina XXXVIII.* Paris: Garnier, 1844-1889 (Patrologiae cursus completus: Series Latina).

BEDA VENERABILIS. *Opera Homiletica.* Turnhout: Brepols, 1955 (Corpus Christianorum: Series Latina 122).

—. *In Lucae evangelium expositio.* Turnhout: Brepols, 1960 (Corpus Christianorum: Series Latina 120).

BLUME, Clemens, and Guido Maria DREVES, eds. *Hymnodia Gotica. Die Mozarabischen Hymnen.* In *Analecta hymnica medii aevi XXVII.* Leipzig: O. R. Reisland, 1897. (Reprinted, Frankfurt: Minerva GmbH, 1961.)

BROU, Louis, and José Vives, eds. *Antifonario visigótico mozárabe de la Catedral de León.* 2 vols. Vol. 1, Barcelona: Centro de Estudios e Investigación San Isidoro (CSIC-CECEL), vol. 2, Madrid: CSIC, Instituto P. Enrique Flórez, 1953-1954 (Monumenta Hispaniae Sacra: Serie Litúrgica 5, no. 2. Facsímiles musicales 1)

CAESARIUS. *Opera.* Turnhout: Brepols, 1953 (Corpus Christianorum: Series Latina 104).

CLERCQ, Carles de, ed. *Concilia Galliae (a. 511-695).* Turnhout: Brepols, 1963 (Corpus Christianorum: Series Latina 148a).

DOLD, Alban, ed. *Das Sacramentar im Schabkodex M. 12 sup. der Biblioteca Ambrosiana.* Beuron: Erzabtei, 1952 (Texte und Arbeiten: 43).

FÉROTIN, Màrius, ed. *Le Liber mozarabicus sacramentorum et les manuscrits mozarabes (reimpr. de l'édition de Paris 1912 et bibliographie genérale de la liturgie hispanique, préparées et présentées par A. Ward et C. Jonson).* Rome: CLV Edizioni Liturgiche, 1995 (Monumenta Ecclesiae Liturgica: 6).

ISIDORUS. *De ecclesiasticis officiis.* Turnhout: Brepols, 1989 (Corpus Christianorum: Series Latina 113).

—. *Opera Omnia.* In J.-P. Migne, ed. Op. cit. Vol. LXXXIII.

JANINI, José, ed. *Liber missarum de Toledo y libros místicos.* 2 vols. Toledo: Instituto de estudios visigótico-mozárabes, 1983.

LORENZANA, Francisco Antonio de. *Breviarium gothicum.* In J.-P. Migne, ed. Op. cit. Vol. LXXXVI.

MASTANDREA, Paolo, and Luigi TESSAROLO, eds. *Poetria Nova. A CD-Rom of Latin Medieval Poetry (650-1250 a. D.) with a Gateway to Classical and Late Antiquity Texts.* Florence: Edizioni del Galluzzo, 2001.

ORTIZ, Alfonso. *Missale mixtum.* In J.-P. Migne, ed. Op. cit. Vol. LXXXV.

PÉREZ DE URBEL, Justo, and Atilano GONZÁLEZ RUIZ-ZORRILLA, eds. *Liber commicus.* 2 vols. Madrid: Bermejo, 1950.

QUODVULTDEUS. *Liber promissionum I.* In *Opera tributa.* Turnhout: Brepols, 1976 (Corpus Chistianorum: Series Latina 60).

VIVES, José, ed. *Oracional visigótico.* Madrid: CSIC, 1946.

—, ed. *Concilios visigóticos e hispano-romanos.* Barcelona, Madrid: CSIC, 1963.

ZEUMER, Kart, ed. *Leges visigothorum.* En *Monumenta Germaniae Historica. Legum sectio I.* Vol. 1. Hannover, Leipzig: Weidmann, 1902.

II. Studies

ARLT, Wulf. "The Office for the Feast of the Circumcision from Le Puy". In Margot E. Fassler and Rebecca A. Baltzer, eds. *The Divine Office in the Latin Middle Ages.* New York: Oxford University Press, 2000, 324-343.

FERNÁNDEZ DE LA CUESTA, Ismael. *Historia de la música española.* Vol. 1, *Desde los orígenes hasta el Ars Nova.* Madrid: Alianza Editorial, 1983.

FERRO CALVO, Mauricio. *La celebración de la venida del Señor en el oficio hispánico.* Madrid: Instituto Superior de Pastoral, 1972.

GIBERT-TARRUEL, Jordi. "El sistema de lecturas de la cincuentena pascual de la liturgia hispánica, según la tradición B". In *Liturgia y música mozárabes. I Interna-*

tional Congress of Mozarabic Studies. Toledo: Diputación de Toledo. Instituto de Estudios Visigótico-Mozárabes, 1975, 111-124.

Lurker, Manfred. *Diccionario de imágenes y símbolos de la Biblia*. Córdoba: El Almendro, 1994.

Manz, Georg. *Ausdrucksformen der lateinischen Liturgiesprache bis ins elfte Jahrhundert*. Beuron: Erzabtei, 1941.

Menéndez Pelayo, Marcelino. *Historia de los heterodoxos españoles*. Vol. 2. Santander: CSIC, 1947.

Norberg, Dag. *Introduction à l'étude de la versification latine médiévale*. Stockholm: Almqvist & Wiksell, 1958.

Pascual Pérez, Arturo. *La imagen de la Iglesia en la liturgia española*. Madrid: Instituto Superior de Pastoral, 1971.

Pinell, Jordi. "Los textos de la antigua liturgia hispana. Fuentes para su estudio". In Juan Francisco Rivera Recio, dir. *Estudios sobre la liturgia mozárabe*. Toledo: Instituto Provincial de Investigaciones y Estudios Toledanos, 1965, 109-164.

Osanna Vox Laudabilia. Vocabulary and Compositional Forms in Sanctus Tropes in Iberian Liturgical Manuscripts

Gunilla Iversen

New and fascinating poetic and musical compositions are found in numerous Iberian liturgical manuscripts from the 10th through the 12th and 13th centuries. Among these are a number of prosulas, tropes, and proselike compositions that were performed in connection with the *Sanctus* chant during the celebration of the mass. In the following study we observe that in some of these texts the interpretation of Hebrew words occupies a central place.[1]

As a general preliminary remark, let us just recall the evident fact that liturgical creations such as hymns, and especially proses and tropes, represent not only a new musical world, but also a totally new literary sphere in the monastic culture of the Middle Ages. This biblical poetry, based on Hebrew poetry and Christian authors, had, as we know, dramatic effects on the Latin language. "Christianity gave the Latin tongue an opportunity to free itself, by making possible new use of certain words which the rules did not exclude, but which common usage did not include, since the occasion for the introduction of such usage had not risen," as Jean Leclercq once put it in his classic study *The Love of Learning and the Desire for God.*[2] In this scriptural culture based on a daily liturgy, we see how the most brilliant minds devoted their time to the composition and interpretation of liturgical texts and ceremonies. In this period "literature assumes a place of unparalleled importance. In other words, everything is governed by the art of writing, whether in verse or prose. Everything is taught according to the *artes,* which are inspired by the best models, and to which all production must conform".[3]

It seems that the medieval division between the textual genres in *libri divini* and *libri seculares* has partly determined and formed the research tradition on medieval Latin literature from the 8th to the 13th century, with the result that research on texts in the *libri divini* and related to the liturgy in general has been separated from studies on texts by the Latin authors defined as *auctores.* It is clear that the quantity of texts in liturgical manuscripts that can best be defined as liturgical poetry—tropes, prosulas, sequences or proses—is enormous when compared to the amount of secular poetry. [4] Whereas this circumstance is naturally regarded as a self-evident condition for scholars in the field of medieval music, the liturgical manuscripts have usually been more or less neglected as sources for scholars of medieval Latin literature in general.

Using the *Sanctus* chant as the basis in the present study, we will investigate a few central themes and formal characteristics that might be seen as typical for the *Sanctus* repertories in the Iberian Peninsula.[5] There seem to be certain characteristic compositional forms and themes, and particular preferences can be noticed in the vocabulary of the repertories from places such as Vic and Girona, San Juan de la Peña, Santiago de Compostela, Montserrat, San Millán de la Cogolla, as well as in the 13th century repertories in Tortosa. Generally, but not always, these repertories are closely related to those in southern French sources, such as those from Moissac, Auch or Narbonne.

In the repertories of tropes added to the *Sanctus* chant, a striking innovation can be seen in the Iberian and especially the Catalonian repertories already in the 10th century. Whereas the two angelic hymns, the *Sanctus* and *Gloria*, are normally expanded by trope verses inserted into the parallel invocations in the first part of the chants—*Laudamus te, Benedicimus te, Adoramus te, Glorificamus* and *Sanctus, sanctus, sanctus*—in the early repertories in all regions, the word *osanna* becomes the basis for a number of new compositions in southwest Frankish regions.

Osanna, vox laudabilia

The function and performance of the holy Hebrew word *osanna* and its melisma is treated in a way that is parallel to that of the Hebrew word *alleluia* interpreted as *laudes deo.*

One of these is *Osanna vox laudabilia,* found in the early tropary from the Cathedral of Vic in Catalonia in the manuscript 105, and indicated as well by its incipit in the later manuscript Vic, ABEV, ms. 106.

1 *Osanna,* vox laudabilia,
2 Invenimus te in Hebrea lingua.
3 Interpretat 'rex regum, deus, salvum fac seu salvifica'.
4a Magna es in patria.
4b Canunt te in gloria
5 Vox clara *Osanna*
in excelsis.

> (*Osanna,* laudable word, we have found you in the Hebrew tongue. It means 'King of Kings, God, make us safe or save us'. You are great in [the heavenly] Fatherland. They sing praises in your glory, O brilliant word *osanna* in the highest.)

In the opening words—"Osanna, vox laudabilia"—the author makes the singers address directly not the Lord but precisely the laudable word *osanna.* The address continues in the explanation that we, the Christian Church, have found you, that is, the word, in the Hebrew tongue. The long central line provides the interpretation of the word: "it means King of Kings, God, make us safe or save us". This interpretation, "salvum fac" or "salvifica", recalls, of course, the biblical interpretation within Psalm 117: 25-26: "O domine salvum fac o domine properare benedictus qui venturus est in nomine domini", with the evident reference to the words of the chant taken from the prophet Isaiah: "Osanna benedictus qui venit in nomine domini" (Is 6:3), and repeated by the Evangelists describing the people welcoming Christ as he enters Jerusalem (Mc 11:8-9; Lk 19:37-38; Jn 12:12-13) and in Revelations (Apoc. 4:8).

At the same time, however, the author here continues a long tradition of varying interpretations of the word *osanna* as expressed by the Church Fathers. Thus, St. Jerome, for instance, divides *osanna* into *osi* and *anna*, and explains that *osi* means 'save', whereas *Anna* is the interjection of supplication, and he explains the form *osanna* is the result of an elision like those we find in Virgil, for instance, reading *mane incepto* as *manincepto*:

> OSI ergo 'salvifica' interpretatur; ANNA interiectio deprecantis est. Si ex duobus his velis compositum verbum facere, dices OSIANNA, sive ut nos loquimur, OSANNA, media vocali littera elisa; sicut facere solemus in versibus Virgilii, quando pro "mene incoepto desistere victam", scandimus "men incoepto".[6]

> (Thus, OSI means 'save'. ANNA is the interjection of the supplicant. If you want to make one word of these two you will say OSIANNA, or as when we talk, OSANNA, with elision of the middle vowel, just as we usually do in the verses of Virgil, when we pronounce "men incepto" instead of "mene incoepto desistere victam".)

Isidore of Seville gives a similar explanation of *osanna* as a contraction resulting from elision, and adds the comment that by 'salvifica' we should understand 'save your people' or 'save the whole world':

> OSI enim 'salvifica' interpretatur; ANNA interiectio est, motum animi significans sub deprecantis affectu. Integre autem dicitur OSIANNA, quod nos, corrupta media vocabuli littera, et elisa, dicimus OSANNA sicut fit in versibus cum scandimus. Littera enim prima verbi sequentis extremam prioris verbi veniens excludit, et dicitur Hebraice OSIANNA, quod interpretatur salvifica subaudiendo vel populum tuum vel totum mundum.[7]

> (Thus, OSI means 'save' ANNA is an interjection signifying the spiritual emotion under the affect of the supplicant. Yet as an entity it reads OSIANNA, which we pronounce OSANNA, with the middle letter of the word corrupted and elided as is done in verses when we scan. Thus, the first letter of the following word excludes the last letter of the first

> word. In Hebrew it is pronounced OSIANNA, which means 'save', supplying 'your people' or 'the whole world'.)

Isidore's explanation is repeated in the early exposition *Quotiens contra se* with the addition that through the expression "in excelsis" the song is to be understood as the hymn uniting terrestrial and celestial singers:

> Et *Osanna* interpretatur 'salvifica' subaudiendo vel 'populum tuum', vel 'totum mundum', cui idcirco additur *in excelsis,* quod adventus Christi non tantum hominum salus, sed totius mundi sit, terrena iungens cum coelestibus, ut omne genu ei flectatur coelestium, terrestrium et infernorum.[8]

> (And *Osanna* means 'save' supplementing 'your people', or 'the whole word'. To this is added *in excelsis*, since the Coming of Christ is not only the salvation of mankind, but of the whole world, joining the terrestrial to the heavenly ones. So that all those who are on earth, in heaven and all those buried are kneeling together in front of him.)

In the prosula *Osanna vox laudabilia* this interpretation is expressed in the line where the singers continue to address the holy word *osanna* directly*:* "You are great in the heavenly Fatherland—'Magna es in patria'—where the angels and saints sing praises in your glory, o glorious word *osanna in the highest*".

A notable trait in *Osanna* prosulas like this one is that the vowels of the beginning and the end of *osanna*, *o-* and *-a,* determine the form, the vocabulary, and even the grammar. The desire to end all lines with these vowels even makes the author reject the rules of grammar to obtain this result. Thus, without hesitation, he changes the expected, correct feminine singular *laudabilis* into the form of neuter plural *laudabilia* in order to make the word end in *-a*.

OSANNA VOCE HARMONICA

Structured in the same way is a similar text in the same manuscript, *Osanna voce harmonica:*

1 *Osanna* v**o**ce harm**o**nic**a**
2 Te pert**o**nat in altis c**o**h**o**rs angelic**a**.
3 Regi Christ**o** cr**u**cifix**o** s**u**rgenti a m**o**rte fract**o** barathr**o**
4a Eia, v**o**ce tinnul**a**
4b Psallat ecclesi**a**
5 Et dicant *Osann**a***
in excelsis.[9]

> (*Osanna*, in harmonic voice the host of angels sing you in the highest to Christ, the King, who rises from death after having destroyed the abyss. Eia, in high-sounding voice may the Church sing and may they pronounce *Osanna in the highest.*)

The two opening lines recall the theme of the preface *Per quem maiestatem* introducing the *Sanctus* as the hymn sung by the hosts of angels. Again we see how the author combines this with the address to the holy expression *osanna. Osanna* is the word that the angels make resound in harmonious voice in the highest.[10] To the angelic hosts is now being added the singing Church, so that the heavenly and terrestrial singers sing *osanna* in high-sounding voice to the King, the crucified Christ, who rises from death after having destroyed the abyss. Then follows the interjection *eia* and the exhortation: "Eia, let them—that is the angels and the singers of the Church—sing *osanna in the highest*". Thus, the composition ends with the final words "in excelsis" of the chant. Again, the dominating vowels are *o-* and *-a*, with the long line in the middle sung on repeated *o-* sounds.

These two prosulas are the first and the last items added to the *Sanctus* in the manuscript Vic, ABEV, ms. 105, but, as a matter of fact, all additions to the *Sanctus* chant are formed in the same way in this early Catalonian repertory, that is, as prosulas and even prose, but not as tropes.

OSANNA DULCIS EST CANTICA

The earliest and most frequently used composition following this model is *Osanna dulcis est cantica,* found as well in Aquitainian sources.[11] The earliest version seems to be that presented in the manuscript from Auch, Paris, BNF, Lat. 1118:

1 *Osanna* dulcis est cantic**a**
2 Melliflua, nimisque laudabili**a**,
3 Organica trina una deprecemur omnes in hac aul**a**:
4a Suscipiat cum agmin**a**
4b Angelorum carmin**a**
5 Dicat nunc: *Osann**a***
in excelsis.[12]

> (*Osanna* is a sweet song, fluent with honey and most laudable, let us all in this hall with one and threefold voice pray and beseech that it be perceived together with the songs of the hosts of angels. "Let it now make resound the hymn of the angels in the highest.")

Osanna itself is a song or "cantica" (treated here as singular form). It is sweet and flows with honey and glory—"melliflua", "laudabilia"—. It is sung with the instrument of the voice, "organica", "trina" and "una", in that it combines the Latin, Greek, and Hebrew. The singing together of angels and the church is taken up again in the final exhortation let it, the church, "in hac aula", sing the hymns of the angels in the highest.

Structured in various ways, the prosula is part of Aquitainian and Iberian repertories such as those of Vic, Girona and San Juan de la Peña (Huesca, AC, Cod. 4), and present in Benevento in Italy as well.[13] This is the version of the early repertory in Vic:

1 *Osanna* dulcia cantica, mellifl**ua**
2 Nimisque laudabilia, organic**a**.
3 Trinum et unum laudemus omnes in hac aul**a**.
4 Suscipiat cum agminibus angelorum carmin**a**
5 Dicant nunc: *Osann**a***
in excelsis.[14]

> (*Osanna*, o sweet songs, fluent with honey and most laudable, performed in singing. Let us all in this hall praise the Threefold and One. May he perceive it together with the songs of the hosts of angels. Let them now make resound *osanna in the highest.*)

In the version in Vic, the prosula is, as can be seen here, structured in a slightly different way with the four-syllable words "melliflua" and "organica" placed in the ends of the phrases. All phrases end in the vowel *-a*. We can follow how different redactors try to correct the Latin grammar in several instances. Thus, the phrase "dulcis est cantica" is rendered as "dulcia cantica" in Vic, ABEV, ms. 105, and as "dulcia sunt" in the tropary from Girona (Paris, BNF, Lat. 495). Likewise, the expression "cum agmina" is corrected in the version from Vic into "cum agminibus", and to "cum agmine" in Modena, BC, ms. 7, which is grammatically correct, but destroys the series of final a-sounds. Of the grammatically distorted forms "melliflua" and "laudabilia", "laudabilia" is corrected into *laudabillima* in Huesca, AC, Cod. 4, and to "laudabilis est" in Benevento, BC, ms. 40. What we witness in these various solutions is a conflict between the ambition to create a text resting on a desired vowel and the likewise understandable wish to create a text that is grammatically correct. It seems that in this conflict it is the sound of the desired vowel that generally takes priority. However, the redactor in Vic insists on the correct form. Thus, he also changes "trina una", referring to a way of singing, into "Trinum et unum", transforming the text into a praise of the Trinity, in which the "Threefold and One" is the direct object of the song of praise.

We can note that the four-syllable words "melliflua" and "organica" recall the vocabulary cultivated by the poets around Charles the Bald, such as Sedulius Scotus and John Scotus.[15] Also the expression "in hac aula" is that used in the verses "ad sequentias modulati" in the Antiphonary of Charles the Bald in sequences such as "Letetur et concrepet" or "Gloriosa dies" and "Claris vocibus".[16]

In his study of the notion of *organum* in the medieval theory of music, Fritz Reckow discusses the place of four-syllable words, using as examples "dulcifluus", "harmonicus", "mellifluus", "mellaticus", and "suavisonus" and presenting them in their masculine form. In liturgical poetry, such as these tropes and prosulas, however, they generally end as here, in *-a*, such as "dulciflua".[17]

Osanna plasmatum populum

Whereas *Osanna dulcis est cantica* is tied to the second and final "osanna" at the end of the *Sanctus,* the interpretation of *osanna* as 'salva', 'salvifica' lies behind the text of a shorter prosula tied to the first "osanna" in the repertories from Auch, Vic, Girona, Narbonne and St. Martial, and found as well as in Modena and Benevento.[18] This is the version from Auch:

1 *Osanna* plasmatum populum,
2 Te qui verum fore promit ore Christum,
3 Te cosmi satorem permanentem
in excelsis.[19]

> [*Osanna* ('save') the people you created professing in song that you are the true Christ, that you are the creator of the world remaining forever *in the highest.*]

It is noteworthy that here the author implies that the Hebrew word *osanna* functions as a verbal form interpreted as the imperative form 'save', that is, 'salva' or 'salvifica', before the object "plasmatum populum" ("the people you created"). Thus, he does not add a Latin word. Here we notice that the author uses the form *fore* to mean *esse* in a way similar to that used in Mozarabic hymns.[20]

OSANNA, PATRIS VERBIGENA; OSANNA, UNA SUMMAQUE SOPHIA

A similar combination involves two prosulas—one added to the first and another to second "osanna". It is repeated in the tropary-prosary from Girona:

1 *Osanna*, Patris Verbigen**a**.
2 Voce pura clemens exaudi carmin**a**
3 Ecclesia tua quae boant agmin**a**
in excelsis.[21]

1 *Osanna*, una summaque sophi**a**,
2 Tuum plasma prostratum fraude subdol**a**.
3 Salvifica hac die clara barathri claustra frangens dir**a**.
4a Suscipe precamin**a**
4b Plebis modulamin**a**
5 Spiritum cum glori**a**
in excelsis.[22]

> (*Osanna,* You, who are born through the word of the Father, listen, mildly, to the songs sung in a pure voice in your church, songs that the hosts of angels sing *in the highest.*
>
> *Osanna,* You who are the one and highest wisdom, save your creation, thrown down to the earth through the cunning fraud. On this glorious day, when you break the hard fences off of the abyss, receive the prayers of your people, the melodies, together with the Spirit in the Glory *in the Highest.*)

Here, the words tied to the first "osanna", address the One who is the Word born from the Father, "Patris Verbigena" with the prayer to listen to the songs that the hosts are singing in your Church, and the hosts (of angels) sing in the highest. In this way, the prosula tied to the first "osanna" is about the singing, whereas the other prosula, tied to the second "osanna", takes up the theme of *salvifica*.

The second prosula is then addressed to the one and highest wisdom, "una summaque sophia", tied to the interpretation of *osanna* as "salvifica" and followed by the exhortation to receive the prayers—"precamina" —and the melodies—"modulamina"—with glory in the highest: "gloria in excelsis". The meaning of the word "spiritum" is not clear. Either it is the same as *spirituum*, a genitive form in plural meaning—'of the holy spirits' or 'of the angels'—or else it should be read as *spiritu*: 'together with the Spirit', or even in the sense of *pneuma, neuma,* interpreted as 'in song'.

OSANNA, NUNC TUUM PLASMA

Just as in *Osanna plasmatum populum* above, the interpretation of *osanna* as 'save', 'salvifica', is expressed as well in a number of proselike compositions in which the short prosula format is further extended. This takes place in the same Iberian repertories, in Septimania, Catalonia, as well as in Aquitania.[23] In the repertories from Vic, Tortosa, and San Juan de la Peña, and Narbonne there is such a prose—*Osanna, nunc tuum plasma*—with the interpretation of *osanna* expressed in the final words of the first strophe "tu salva":

1a	*Osanna,* nunc tuum plasma, rex deus, tu salva,	1b	Solus qui sapientia numeras sidera.
2a	Cui luna paret et arva solisque rota,	2b	Plebem serva, gregem visita frequenti cura.
3a	Nunc tibi odas pangimus omnes, trinitas sancta,	3b	Ore quem laudat contio sacra et benedicta

in excelsis.[24]

(*Osanna,* O king and God, now save your creation, you who alone know the number of the stars. You whom the moon, the earth and the wheel of the sun obey, save your people, visit your herd with constant care. Now let us all sing praises to You, O holy Trinity, whom the sacred and blessed troop praises in singing *in the highest.*)

Osanna salvifica

Another similar *Osanna-prose*, *Osanna salvifica*, found its way from Limoges, Narbonne, Moissac, Vic, Girona, Montserrat, San Millán de la Cogolla, San Juan de la Peña, all the way to Santiago de Compostela and the *Codex Calixtinus,* as well as to Tortosa.[25] The following is the version in the earlier tropary from Vic:

Sanctus, sanctus, sanctus,
Dominus deus sabaoth,
Pleni sunt caeli et terra gloria tua,
Osanna in excelsis.
Benedictus qui venit in nomine domini.

1a	*Osanna,* salvific**a** tuum plasm**a** qui creasti simul omni**a.**	1b	Temet laus decet, honor et glori**a**, rex eterne, in secul**a**,
2a	Qui de patris gremi**o** genitus advenisti summ**o**	2b	Redimere perdit**um** hominem sanguine propri**o**.
3a	Quem deceperat Lucif**er** fraude nequam calidissim**e** serpentino coniugis dent**e**,	3b	Quem expulerat proper**e** hoc innexum crimin**e** paradisi cardine atque limit**e**,
4a	Tu dignare salvar**e**	4b	Iesu Christe supern**e**

in excelsis.[26]

(*Osanna,* save your creation, you who once who created all. To you, eternal King, be praise, honor and glory forever. You came from the Father's most high heart to with your own blood redeem the fallen man. The man that Lucifer had deceived with the woman's most evil fraud through the tooth of the serpent, and had thrown out of the doors of paradise, since he was involved in the same crime, we beseech you to deign to save him, O heavenly Jesus Christ *in the highest.*)

In terms recalling the expositions of Sts. Jerome and Isidore on the interpretation of *osanna* as "salva salvifica tuum plasma", the prayer is directed to the eternal King, to whom are due all praise, honor, and glory. In this case, the author puts the interpretation of *osanna* as "salvifica" into the text. The prosula is full of biblical references, recalling, as in 1b: "regi [...] honor et gloria in saecula saeculorum" (1 Tm 1:17; Ps. 95:7); in 2a: "de patris gremio" (Jn 1:18); in 3a-b: "Sed serpens erat callidior cunctis animantibus terrae" (Gen. 3:1); and "et dixit Dominus Deus ad mulierem / quare hoc fecisti quae respondit serpens decepit me et comedi" (Gen. 3:13 and Gen. 3:4-6), or "emisit eum Dominus Deus de paradiso voluptatis; eiecit Adam et conlocavit ante paradisum voluptatis" (Gen. 3:23-24).[27]

Consequently, this way of focusing on the word *osanna* and its interpretations, and this way of adding a prosula, or even of adding proselike texts to the melisma of the *osanna*, is particularly frequent in Catalonian, Iberian, and Aquitainian repertories. There is nothing like this in the East-Frankish repertories, where all additions are formed as trope verses inserted between the phrases of the chant.

1. Prosary-Tropary. Huesca, AC, Cod. 4, 11th century *in.*, fols. 145v-146r: *Osanna salvifica tuum plasma*

Osanna, Carmina plebs sedula

A central theme developed in these texts, as is generally the case in the early repertories, is the act of singing. Musical terms, such as *organa, vox, melodia, alternando voce, consona voce,* are frequently used in these texts.[28] The theme involves the notion of the entire *Sanctus* as the angelic hymn to be sung by celestial and terrestrial singers together in one voice. In the liturgical manuscripts, the *Sanctus* is richly glossed with sequence-like additions to the second "osanna", in which the concept of music occupies an important place. The terrestrial singers are present in the texts as "chorus iste", "coetus iste", "haec plebicula", "vox nostra", "musicorum chorea" or "fidelium turma", whereas the heavenly singers are frequently described as "agmina caelica", "agmina angelorum", "contio angelica" or "virtus uranica". Often, the choir of mankind, the singing Church is presented in the a strophe and paired with the singing celestial choir in the b strophe.[29]

So, for instance, in *Carmina plebs sedula,* God's faithful people—"plebs sedula"—is paired with "contio angelica" as they sing together to the Lord in one voice—"consona voce"—loudly singing—"clangentes"—, with the Spirit—"cum neuma" —again with this double meaning of "inspired singing". The piece is found in the repertories in Girona, Vic, San Millán de la Cogolla, Montserrat, and Tortosa, as well as in Narbonne and in the tropary-prosary from Catania.[30] Here is the version from San Millán de la Cogolla:

1a	*Osanna* Carmina plebs sedula concinat in sede regnanti politica,	1b	Quem tremunt cuncta contio angelica, Cherubim ac Seraphim necne ardentia,
2a	Trinum et unum ecclesia hunc iure colit catholica,	2b	Nostra qui sumpsit mortalia larga misertus clementia.
3a	Natus homo pertulit opprobria; haerens ligno iugia; mundi tersit crimina; obiens tartarea destruxit prorsus imperia.	3b	Morte victa die surgens tertia, plura nempe contulit mundo vitae gaudia; rediens stelligera suis concessit palatia.
4a	Nunc iubilemus illi omnes una	4b	Consona voce clangentes cum neuma

5 Cui semper sit virtus et gloria
in excelsis.[31]

(*Osanna*, may the people sing sincere songs to the One who reigns from his heavenly throne, in front of whom all the angelic hosts, the Cherubim and burning Seraphim are trembling. To the Threefold and One our universal Church justly sing praises. In his great mercy he pitifully took on our mortal flesh. Born as man he bore the disgraces; when he was hanging on the yokes of the cross he took away the crimes of the world; when he died he utterly destroyed the powers of Death. When he had conquered death as he raised on the third day he brought more joys of life to the world; when he returned too heaven he opened his starry palace to his people. Now let us all together sing in jubilation making the voice sound out with the spirit, the word with the neum: to Him be forever virtue and glory *in the highest.*)

2. Antiphonary-Tropary. Madrid, RAH, Cod. 51, 11th century *in.*, fols. 243v-244r

Fidelium turma

In *Fidelium turma,* another prose in the repertory of San Millán de la Cogolla as well as of Tortosa, the choir of the faithful church—"fidelium turma" —is singing together with the "contio sacra" in strophe b. It is notable that the sacred word *osanna* is further stressed by its repetition at the end of each strophe:

(*Osanna,* Let the choir of the faithful ones now joyfully sing in a sonorous voice, and sound out *Osanna!* Let

Osanna,

1a	Fidelium turma iubilet nunc voce sonora et dicat *Osanna*.	1b	Divina clementia regenti omnia concrepet haec contio sacra et dicat *Osanna*.
2a	His fruitur vocibus laude digna plebs Hebrea clamans *Osanna*.	2b	Sic dominum sequitur mente pia dum triplicat clamans *Osanna*.
3a	Angelica nempe factori iugiter agmina concinant nunc tinnula: 'Sancte, sancte rex, semper sit tibi *Osanna*'.	3b	Cuius summa fulget per mundi quattuor climata virtus, honor et gloria. Semper, semper, rex sancte, sit tibi, *Osanna*.

4 Carminibus quorum assiduis
valeat, o deus, tuum plasma
coniungi perpetim
in excelsis.[32]

the host sing as well to the One who mercifully reigns over all, and make resound *Osanna!* The Hebrew people use this word when in worthy praise it exclaims *Osanna!* In this way it follows the Lord when with pious mind it exclaims *Osanna!* And without end the angelic hosts now sing to the Creator: "Saint, saint, o King, to you be forever *Osanna*!" To you, whose most high virtue, honor and glory shines forth over all parts of the world, o saint King, to you be forever and ever *osanna*!' May your creation be joining the never-ending songs of the angels *in the highest*!)

Te laudant agmina

In *Te laudant agmina* belonging to the repertories of San Millán de la Cogolla, Montserrat, Vic, and Narbonne, the theme is expressed in a similar way. In 4a, the creation is again referred to as "tuum plasma" in the vocabulary specific to this region.

Osanna,

1a	Te laudant agmina iugiter caelica,	1b	Sol, luna, sidera, humus et maria.
2a	Supera et infima qui regis tua potentia, nostra dilue contagia.	2b	O dei clementia, refove nos tua gratia, redimis morte quos pro- pria.
3a	Pande superna rex nobis alme, spes qui es nostra, salus aeterna paxque vera.	3b	O quam beata est caeli vita, quae carens meta quae carens meta per saecula.
4a	Illuc tuum plasma, o Iesu bone, tendere praesta.	4b	Innumera namque capere queat ut tua dona.

5 Atque iocunda
iubilet voce domino
in excelsis.[33]

(*Osanna*, The heavenly hosts sing praises without end to you, the sun, the moon, the stars *the* earth and the sees. You who reign over the high and the low delete our stains with your power. O with God's mercy help us in your grace, you who redeems us with your own dead. O mild King, who are our hope, eternal salvation and true peace, open the heaven to us. O how blessed is the life in heaven where without end all rejoice forever. Let your creation come therein, o mild Jesus, so that it can receive your innumerable gifts, and jubilate with joyful voice in front of the Lord *in the highest*!)

Clangat hodie vox nostra

One of the most intriguing proselike compositions of this kind—tied to the *osanna* and expressing the wish to join the angels in praise—is *Clangat hodie*:

Sanctus, sanctus, sanctus,
Dominus deus sabaoth,
Pleni sunt caeli et terra gloria tua.
Osanna in excelsis.
Benedictus qui venit in nomine domini.
Osanna

1a	Clangat hodie vox nostra melodum symphonia,	1b	Instant annua iam quia preclara sollemnia.
2a	Personet nunc tinnula harmoniae organa musicorum chorea;	2b	Tonorum quam dulcia alternatim concrepet necne modulamina!
3a	Diapason altisona per vocum discrimina tetracordis figurarum alta conscendens culmina	3b	Sustollat nostra carmina ad caeli fastigia hymnis angelicis coherenda patri melodia,
4a	Quo nos mereamur ampla capere promissa,	4b	Sine fruituri meta anctorum gloria,

5 Ad quorum collegia
pia nos ducant merita
in excelsis.[34]

Tied to the melisma of the second "osanna" of the *Sanctus* melody 190, this text is found in manuscripts dating from around 1100 and the 12th century from places on both sides of the Pyrenees: Moissac, San Millán de la Cogolla, San Juan de la Peña (Huesca, AC, Cod. 4), and Vic; and the same melody is also given without text in the manuscript Paris, BNF, N. A. L. 1871 from Moissac.[35] Tied to another *Sanctus* melody, 112, *Clangat hodie* is also found in the manuscript Paris, BNF, Lat. 1139 from Limoges, in manuscripts from Narbonne, and from the Norman colony in Sicily, but also in later polyphonic manuscripts from England and northern Spain. Still, the closest concordances of *Clangat hodie* are in repertories from Moissac and San Millán de la Cogolla, where *Clangat hodie* with melody 190 is presented together with the *Osanna* prose *Osanna salvifica* (138) in the same way. [36]

The text operates on several levels and plays with the multiple meanings of the words. Still, at first glance, *Clangat hodie* seems to follow the model of an ordinary Aquitainian prose of transitional type, both in form and content.[37] We immediately recognize the general form of such a sequence: parallel pairs of strophes or couplets, each pair of different length increasing from the first couplet to culminate in the third, and the ending in one short single strophe, with all strophes ending on the final vowel *-a*. The proparoxytone verse of seven syllables—that is, the second hemistich of the rhythmic trochaic septenary—dominates the structure of the versification.

The varied length of the couplets as well as the alternation between paroxytone and proparoxytone verses is observed in a typical way. Not only the strophes, but also their inner lines end on the vowel *-a*. Again, the wish to obtain endings in *-a* leads to a certain number of grammatical anomalies that are perfectly normal in this type of sequence, as we have seen in several proses and prosulas studied earlier in the chapter. The fluctuation between singular and plural forms—"instant/instat" in connection with "festa solemnia" in 1b, "personet/personent" or "resonent" with "chorea" in 2a, "concrepet/concrepent" in 2b and "sustollat/sustollant" in 3b—is found even within the readings of the same manuscript, and the different forms do not divide the manuscripts into significantly different versions.

This text is explicitly focusing on the musical performance of the chant, however. Already in the opening words the essential content of the text is being presented: "Clangat / hodie / vox nostra / melodum symphonia". The musical aspect is underlined in its first word, in the exhortation "Clangat"—"let sound out"—; *clangere* is used particularly often in the Aquitainian sequence vocabulary to express the act of singing in jubilation. We can note that the verb *to sing* is often expressed in verbs such as *clangere*, *pangere*, *personare*, *concrepare*, *resonare*, and so on, in tropes and sequences in these West-Frankish regions, whereas in East-Frankish regions *dicere*, *canere*, and *cantare* remain predominant.[38]

"Our voice"—"vox nostra"—sounds out in a "symphony of songs", or "a symphony of melodies", "melodum symphonia" in 1a. This voice is the voice of the singers on earth. It is the voice of the part of the *Ecclesia* that is placed on earth. The musical

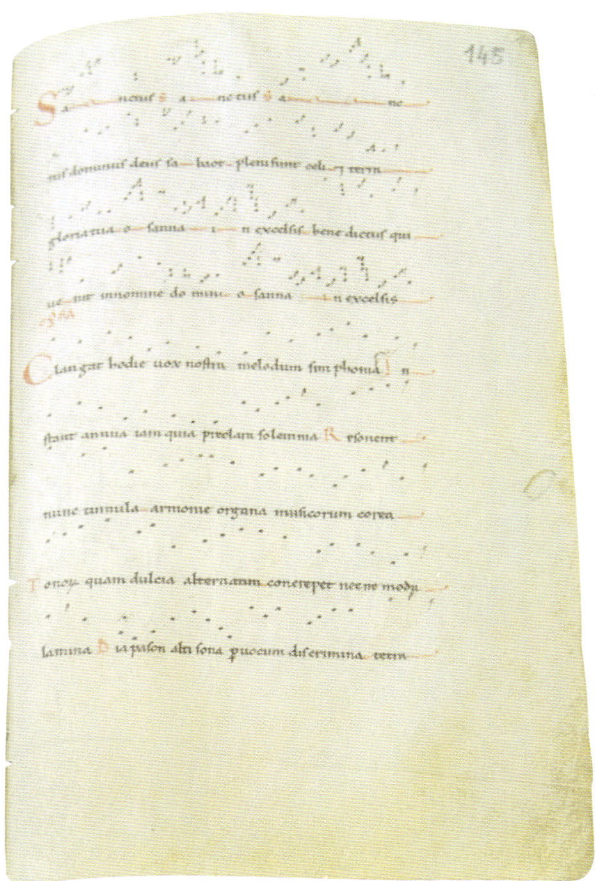

3. Prosary-Tropary. Huesca, AC, Cod. 4, 11th century *in.*, fol. 145r

theme is further expanded in the following two longest couplets, 2a-b and 3a-b, strophes that are filled with musical terms. The text is entirely focused on the act of singing, which is represented by expressions such as "tinnula harmoniae organa", "musicorum chorea", "tonorum [...] modulamina", "alternatim", "carmina" or "melodia". In particular, we recognize *diapason* and *tetrachordum*, like *symphonia* and *harmonia*.

The ring of musicians "is sounding out on high"—*altisona*—spreading its voices over the octave, and this is expressed in the Virgilian phrase "per vocum discrimina". The following phrase—"tetrachordis figurarum alta conscendens culmina" ("ascending in tetrachords to the high summits of the figures of the melody", or "in figures of four notes")—was not without complications for the medieval singers either. The songs—"nostra carmina"—are lifted up by means of the ring of musicians, "musicorum chorea", and at the same time by means of the ascending movements of the melody itself. This is expressed in the words "alta conscendens culmina" in 3a, and "sustollat [...] ad caeli fastigia" in 3b.

Like incense ascending together with the prayers, so does the music that ascends on high lift up the prayer and praise, so that the terrestrial voices join the voices of the heavenly hosts. The resonance of musicians lifts up the songs "echoing of harmony" to make them join the angelic hymns—"hymnis angelicis coherenda"—in 3b; the intensity of the prayer of absolute coherence with the angels is underlined through the gerundive form *coherenda*, "which are to be cohering to" the hymns of the angels.

Concerning the words *harmonia* and *symphonia* in 1a and 2a, it is important to underline that *harmonia* in strophe 1a primarily refers to the perfect concordance of the celestial harmony, to the harmony of spheres. In a similar way, *symphonia* in 2a is not just to be understood as the consonance of the singing assembly, nor even of two half choirs performing the a and b strophes in alternation—"alternatim"—in 3b. Rather, or at the same time, *symphonia* has to be understood as the con-sonance of the voice and the heart *(voce-corde):* a topos constantly repeated in this kind of sequence.

Above all, however, *symphonia* in our text must be understood as a symbol of the ideal "singing together", "con-sonance" of angels and mankind. This idea is underlined by the connected expressions "nostra carmina" and "hymnis angelicis coherenda" in strophe 3b. The word *alternatim* in strophe 2b might also refer to such a con-sonance, *symphonia*, in which celestial and terrestrial singers sing in alternation: the order of the angels singing one part of the *Sanctus* chant, the order of mankind the other.

Another symbolic aspect is represented in the references to musicians and organs. The word *organum* primarily belongs to a vocabulary close to that of the psalms of King David, as "Laudate eum in chordis et organo" (Ps. 150). We recall how Amalar, for instance, expressed the symbolic interpretation that the singers are themselves the instruments, "Our singers do not hold cymbal, or lyre, or cithara in their hands, or any kind of musical instrument, but in their hearts. The singers themselves are the tuba, they are themselves the psalterion, the choir, the strings, the organ and the cymbal" ("Ipsi cantores sunt tuba, ipsi psalterium, ipsi tympanum, ipsi chorus, ipsi cordae, ipsi organum, ipsi cymbala").[39]

The image of the circle of musicians—"musicorum chorea"—in *Clangat hodie* recalls then the biblical imagery of the Psalms, but at the same time the passages in the Apocalypse describing the circle of musicians with instruments in their hands—"habentes singuli citharas"—surrounding the throne and praising (Apoc. 5:8; 14:2 and 15:2). Still, the imagery in *Clangat hodie* seems to be related not only to other sequences from the same area, but to the musical imagery in other works of art from the same places and the same period. Thus, we can observe that the image of the circle of musicians in *Clangat hodie* corresponds to the imagery found in illuminations of the Beatus Apocalypse. And at the same time it seems to be related to the imagery in the sculptured representations of the *Maiestas Domini,* such as the one on the tympanum of Saint Pierre in Moissac, and hence in all of the similar representations on cathedrals from southern France over to San Juan de la Peña and all the way to Santiago de Compostela. There, we see the twenty-four elders from the Apocalypse, all with musical instruments, surrounding the enthroned Lord, and King David himself playing and dancing. As Emile Mâle has pointed out, this new form of monumental sculpture, which was represented in the *Maiestas Domini* on the tympanum of Saint Pierre in Moissac, was inspired precisely by the illuminations of the Beatus Apocalypse in copies found in this area. Describing the illumination in one of these Beatus copies (which he claims to have been the model for the Moissac sculptor), Mâle writes:

One of the most beautiful pages of the manuscript represents Christ in Majesty, surrounded by four beasts. Around Christ, the four and twenty elders form a great circle: seated on thrones and with crowns on their heads, they hold a chalice in one hand and a viol in the other; they turn their gaze toward the resplendent vision and endure its brilliance; around them angels fly in the heavens [...]. This was the Moissac sculptor's model. From a manuscript closely resembling it he borrowed the new type of the elders of the Apocalypse. In fact it is only in the Beatus manuscripts that we find them with their crowns, chalices, viols like Spanish guitars.[40]

The version of *Clangat hodie* tied to melody 190 in manuscripts from Moissac, San Millán de la Cogolla, Vic and San Juan de la Peña (Huesca, AC, Cod. 4) may be better understood in the light of the Apocalyptic representations in illuminations and sculptures in the same places as an exponent of a related symbolic imagery.

Clangat cetus

Finally, let us notice that in the rich *Sanctus*-repertory written for the Cathedral of Tortosa in the 13th century, we find a number of the prosulas and proses observed earlier, but here we also find proses made according to the taste of a new time. Thus, there are new strophic rhymed hymn like tropes and proses. For instance there is the new proselike *Osanna* sequence *Clangat cetus*, found only in this region. In its content, it follows the earlier *Osanna* proses, such as *Clangat hodie,* describing the singing together of mankind and angels. It also follows Iberian preferences in the vocabulary, such as, in 3a, a reference to "Osanna plasma tuum" in the definition of the father as "plasmator".

In its format, however, this composition is unlike the earlier proselike creations, such as *Clangat hodie*. This new *Osanna* prose is versified according to the taste of a new time, in rhyming phrases of 4p + 4p and 7pp. The strophes are rhymed according to a varying pattern (1a, 1b: a a b, a a b; 2a, 2b: a b a, a b a; 3a, 3b: a a a a, a a b a):

Sanctus, sanctus, sanctus,
Dominus deus sabaoth,
Pleni sunt caeli et terra gloria tua.
Osanna in excelsis.
Benedictus qui venit in nomine domini.
Osanna,

1a	Clangat cetus iste letus gloriosa carmina,	1b	Angelorum supernorum quae decantant agmina.
2a	Felix festum, felix dies, in quo datur omni mundo gaudium et magna quies.	2b	Felix partus, felix natus ad salvandum omne genus est a patre nobis datus.
3a	O plasmator, pater pie, mitte filium Marie, ut primeve matris culpe condonetur in hac die.	3b	Et, precamur, sic descendat et a morte nos defendat, ut cantando trina voce sanctus chorus iste pangat

in excelsis.[41]

(Let the joyful troop sing the glorious songs that the hosts of angels sing heaven. Blessed feast and blessed day when joy and great peace is given to the whole world. Blessed birth and blessed child given to us from the Father to save all mankind. O Creator, mild Father, send the son of Mary so that the first mother's guilt might be forgiven today. And, we pray that he may descend and save us from death so that this holy choir in singing in threefold tongues might sound forth *in the highest.*)

Tu super omnia

In the repertory of Tortosa we find the unique strophic *Sanctus* trope *Tu super omnia*, which is inserted between the phrases of the entire chant. All strophes consist of four lines of 6pp ending in the word *omnia* and of one concluding line of 7p ending in the rhyming words addressing the Father in "regnas cum potestate", the Son in "facta in veritate", and the Holy Spirit in "trinus in unitate", and concluding in "unum in trinitate" (a a a a b).

Sanctus,
Tu super omnia
et subtus omnia,
tu infra omnia
et extra omnia
regnas cum potestate.

Sanctus,
Tu regis omnia,
per quem sunt omnia,
ex quo sunt omnia,
in quo sunt omnia
facta in veritate.

Sanctus,
Tu reples omnia,
illustras omnia,
penetras omnia,
accendis omnia
numinis claritate.
Dominus deus «sabaoth.
Pleni sunt caeli et terra gloria tua».
Osanna.

Tu creas omnia,
sustines omnia,
retines omnia
contines omnia,
trinus in unitate
In excelsis.
Benedictus qui venit in nomine domini

Te credant omnia,
te quaerant omnia,
te colant omnia,
te dicant omnia
unum in trinitate.
Osanna in excelsis.[42]

(*Sanctus,* Over all, under all, within all, outside all, you reign in power. *Sanctus,* You govern all, and through you, from you, in you, all is made in truth. *Sanctus,* You fill all, you illuminate all, you penetrate all. You ascend all with the clarity of your divinity. *Dominus deus "sabaoth. Pleni sunt caeli et terra gloria tua". Osanna.* You create all, you sustain all, you hold all, you contain all, o Trine in Unity. In excelsis. All believe in you, all search for you, all venerate you, all call you One in Trinity. *Osanna in excelsis.*)

Thus, in *Tu super omnia,* the author creates a highly theological text by means of a minimum of variations.

Veni redemptor gentium

Finally, another unique strophic composition in the repertory of Tortosa is *Veni redemptor gentium.* Here, the author plays with many earlier Pentecost hymns and sequences. He constructs this work of versified rhymed strophes in a regular meter of 8pp. Although this composition is inserted between *osanna* and *in excelsis,* there is no ambition to find endings in the vowel *-a,* as seen in the early *osanna-prosulas* and proses, and there are no grammatical anomalies caused by the wish to end the phrase in the sound of the desired vowel. Instead, each strophe has eight lines ending in rich two-syllable rhymes following the same pattern (a b a b b a a b):

Sanctus, sanctus, sanctus,
Dominus deus sabaoth,
Pleni sunt caeli et terra gloria tua.
Osanna in excelsis.
Benedictus qui venit in nomine domini,
Osanna,

1. Veni redemptor gentium,
veni creator spiritus,
veni vita viventium,
nostros solari gemitus.
Verus nobis paraclitus,
in fide firma mentium,
in fine morientium,
te laudat omnis exitus.

2. Nostrum regens exilium
rorem infunde caelitus,
quo furor persequentium
non nos seducat ambitus,
sed amor tibi debitus
fervens corde fidelium
nobis ad vitae praemium
sit tibi soli deditus.

3. Tu, qui salvasti saeculum
mirando partu virginis,
ut confundas incredulum,
vires infunde numinis
et contra virum sanguinis
tuum exaltet populum,
qui gerit Christi titulum
ad laudem tui nominis.

4. O quam beata servitus,
qua servit et est libera,
qua mundi miserabitur
dum mutatur in prospera.
O quam libertas misera,
per quam liber sit subditus
et dives inter prospera
vivit Gehenne perditus.
In excelsis.[43]

(Come, redeemer of the peoples, come, creator Holy Spirit, come life of the living. You our true Helper, in the firm faith in our souls, in the end of the dying all, every end praise you. Governing our end infuse your heavenly dew, so that the furious desire of the persecutors may not seduce us, but may due fervent love be rendered to you alone from the heart of the faithful ones, bringing us to the reward of life. / You, who saved the world through the virgin's wonderful birth giving, to confuse the incredulous ones, infuse the strengths of your divinity and against the force of the blood exalt your people that bears the title of Christ to the glory of your name. / O what a blessed servitude in which he serves and is free, feels pity for the world while servitude is rendered prosperous. O what a miserable liberty, in which the free is dominated and the rich in the middle of his prosperity lives as ruined in Gehenna.)

Conclusion

Within the framework of one single chant, the *Sanctus*, we have found new forms of prosulas, proses, and texts built around the *-o* and *-a* sounds of the *wonderful sound* of the Hebrew word *osanna* often in forms that reject the rules of grammar in order to obtain endings in the vowels *-a* or *-o*. In a manner that is typical in this southwest Frankish liturgical poetry, the new pieces are formed as proses and inserted between the second "osanna" and the words "in excelsis". In the 13th century repertory of the Cathedral of Tortosa we have also met hymnlike strophic compositions inserted either between *osanna* and *in excelsis* or between the lines of the entire *Sanctus* chant. It is evident that further studies of the entire corpus of tropes and sequences in Iberian repertories will give us new and interesting insights into musical and poetic creativity of the Iberian regions in the Middle Ages.

Manuscripts

Apt, Bibl. Basil. Sta. Ana, ms. 17
Apt, Bibl. Basil. Sta. Ana, ms. 18
Barcelona, BC, M. 1147
Barcelona, BC, M. 1408-9a
Benevento, BC, ms. 34
Benevento, BC, ms. 35
Benevento, BC, ms. 40
Huesca, AC, Cod. 4
Madrid, BN, ms. 289
Madrid, BN, ms. 19421
Madrid, RAH, Cod. 51
Modena, BC, ms. 7
Montpellier, Bibliothèque de l'École de Médecine, ms. 20
Montserrat, BM, ms. 73
Rome, Bibl. Apostolica Vaticana, Urb. Lat. 602
Paris, BNF, Lat. 778
Paris, BNF, Lat. 887
Paris, BNF, Lat. 903
Paris, BNF, Lat. 909
Paris, BNF, Lat. 1086
Paris, BNF, Lat. 1118
Paris, BNF, Lat. 1120
Paris, BNF, Lat. 1137
Paris, BNF, Lat. 1139
Paris, BNF, N. A. L. 495
Paris, BNF, N. A. L. 1177
Paris, BNF, N. A. L. 1871
Santiago de Compostela, AC, *Codex Calixtinus*
Tortosa, AC, ms. 135
Vic, ABEV, ms. 105
Vic, ABEV, ms. 106
Vic, ABEV, ms. V 40

Notes

[1] I would like to express my deep gratitude to Manuel Ferreira, who first generously invited me to discuss Iberian liturgical repertories and manuscripts in Lisbon, and to Susana Zapke who invited me to pursue this topic further in a wider Iberian perspective.

[2] Jean Leclercq. *L'Amour des lettres et le désir de Dieu.* Paris: Cerf, 1957, 44-45. English translation: *The Love of Learning and the Desire for God.* New York: Fordham University Press, 1985 (1st ed., 1961).

[3] *Ibidem,* 46.

[4] As we know, there are, for instance, more than 5,000 sequences, many thousands of trope verses, large collections of processional antiphons, hymns, and different compositions that are commonly called *liturgical drama.* See the editions of *Corpus Troporum (CT):* Ritva Jonsson, ed. *CT I. Tropes du propre de la messe 1. Cycle de Noël.* Stockholm: Almquist & Wiksell International, 1975 [Acta Universitatis Stockholmiensis (AUS): Studia Latina Stockholmiensia (SLS) 21]; Olof Marcusson, ed. *CT II. Prosules de la messe 1. Tropes de l'Alleluia.* Stockholm: Almquist & Wiksell International, 1976 (AUS: SLS 22); Gunilla Björkvall, Gunilla Iversen and Ritva Jonsson, eds. *CT III. Tropes du propre de la messe 2. Cycle de Pâques.* Critical edition. Stockholm: Almquist & Wiksell International, 1982 (AUS: SLS 25); Gunilla Iversen, ed. *CT IV. Tropes de l'Agnus Dei.* Critical edition and analytical study. Stockholm: Almquist & Wiksell International, 1980 (AUS: SLS 26); Gunilla Björkvcall, ed. *CT V. Les deux tropaires d'Apt mss. 17 et 18.* Selection of the manuscripts and edition of the texts realized by this authoress. Stockholm: Almquist & Wiksell International, 1986 (AUS: SLS 32); Eva Odelman, ed. *CT VI. Prosules de la messe 2. Les prosules limousines de Wolfenbüttel. Edition critique des prosules d'alleluia du ms. Wolfenbüttel, Herzog August Bibliothek Cod. Guelf. 79 Gud. Lat.* Stockholm: Almquist & Wiksell International, 1986 (AUS: SLS 31); Gunilla Iversen, ed. *CT VII. Tropes de l'ordinaire de la messe. Tropes du Sanctus.* Introduction and critical edition of the above mentioned authors. Estocolmo: Almquist & Wiksell International, 1990 (AUS: SLS 34); Ann-Katrin Johansson, ed. *CT IX. The Tropes for the Feasts of the Blessed Virgin.* Stockholm: Almquist & Wiksell International, 1998; and *Analecta hymnica medii aevi (AH),* vols. VII and LIII; and Miguel S. Gros. *Els tropers prosers de la Catedral de Vic. Estudi i edició.* Barcelona: Institut d'Estudis Catalans, 1999.

[5] Vic, ABEV, ms. 105, fol. 44v; see *CT VII,* no. 174.

[6] St. Jerome. *Epistola. PL XXII:* cols. 378-379.

[7] Isidorus. *Etymologiae. PL LXXXII:* col. 254.

[8] *Quotiens contra se. PL XCVI:* col. 1496.

[9] *CT VII,* no. 172. Vic, ABEV, mss. 105 and 106.

[10] See Lars Elfving. *Étude lexicographique sur les Sequences Limousines.* Stockholm: Almquist & Wiksell International, 1972, *passim* (AUS: SLS 7); see Gunilla Iversen. "Music as *Ancilla Verbi* and Words as *Ancilla Musicae.* On the Interpretation of the Musical and Textual forms of two Tropes to *Osanna in excelsis: Laudes deo* and *Trinitas, unitas, deitas*". In Gabriel Silagi, ed. *Liturgische Tropen. Referate zweier Colloquien des Corpus Troporum in München (1983) und Canterbury (1984).* Munich: Arbeo-Gesellschaft, 1985, 45-66; and Charles M. Atkinson. "Music as Mistress of the Words: *Laudes deo ore pio*". In *ibidem,* 67-82. See Pierre-Marie Gy. "Le Sanctus romain et les anaphores orientales". In *Mélanges liturgiques offerts au R. P. Bernard Botte, O.S.B.* Louvain: Abbey of Mont Cesar, 1972, 167-174.

[11] The prosula is found in Paris, BNF, Lat. 909, 1120, 1137, 887, 903, 1118, 778, and 495, Apt, Bibl. Basil. Sta. Ana, mss. 17 and 18; Vic, ABEV, ms. 105; Huesca, AC, Cod. 4; Modena, BC, ms. 7; and Benevento, BC, mss. 34, 35 and 40; see edition in *CT VII,* 48; *AH XLVII:* 343 and subsq.; and Peter Josef Thannabaur. *Das einstimmige Sanctus der römischen Messe in der handschriftlichen Überlieferungen des 11. bis 16. Jahrhunderts.* Munich: Ricke, 1962, mél. 89, 111 and 197 (Erlanger Arbeiten zur Musikwissenschaft: 1). See Gunilla Iversen. "Osanna dulcis est cantica: On a Group of Compositions added to the *Osanna*". In László Dobszay, ed. *IMS Study Session on "Cantus Planus", Tihány, Hungary, 19-24 September 1988.* Budapest: Studia Musicologica Academiae Scientiarum Ungaricae, 1989, 275-296; and Charles M. Atkinson. "Text, Music, and the Persistence of Memory in *Dulcis est cantica*". In Wulf Arlt and Gunilla Björkvall, eds. *Recherches nouvelles sur les tropes liturgiques. (CT.)* Stockholm: Almquist & Wiksell International, 1993b, 95-117 (AUS: SLS 36).

[12] Paris, BNF, Lat. 1118, fol. 21v.

[13] *CT VII,* 48; Paris, BNF, Lat. 909, 1120, 1137, 887, 903, 1118, 778 and 495; Apt, Bibl. Basil. Sta. Ana, mss. 17 and 18; Huesca, AC, Cod. 4; Modena, BC, ms. 7; and Benevento, BC, mss. 34, 35 and 40.

[14] Vic, ABEV, ms. 105, fol. 45.

[15] Fritz Reckow. "Organum-Begriff und frühe Mehrstimmigkeit. Zugleich ein Beitrag zur Bedeutung des 'instrumentalen' in der spätantiken und mittelalterlichen Musiktheorie". In Wulf Arlt, ed. *Basler Studien zur Musikgeschichte.* Bern: Franke, 1975. Vol. 1: 31-167, *passim* (Forum musicologicum: 1). Reckow points out the parallel use of the words *mellifluus* and *organicus* as metaphorical epithets, in the poetry of Sedulius Scotus and overtaken in sequences: "Die Tatsache, dass *organicus* viersilbig ist wie viele der wertenden Epitheta (beispielsweise *angelicus, dulcifluus, dulcisonus, harmonicus, mellifluus,*

mellaticus, suavisonus) und deshalb die gleiche metrische Position einnehmen konnte wie diese, mag seine Beliebtheit, damit aber wohl auch das Abschleifen zum mitunter nur noch unspezifischen Gebrauch gefördert haben. Dass *organicus* auch in der geistlichen Dichtung im wertenden Sinne gebraucht und verstanden worden ist, sei an einem letzten Beispiel gezeigt. Die 'organica cantica' in der Sequenz *Benedicta semper sancta sit trinitas: Et nos voce praecelsa nunc / omnes modulemur/ organica cantica/ dulci melodia*". (Op. cit., 88-89).

[16] On the texts of these proses, see further Gunilla Iversen. "Rex in hac aula. Réflexions sur les séquences de l'Antiphonaire de Charles le Chauve". *Revue de Musicologie* 89 (2003): 31-45; and *idem* and Nicolas Bell, eds. *Sapientia et eloquentia*. Turnhout: Brepols. (In press.)

[17] See *CT VII, passim;* and Lars Elfving. Op. cit., *passim*.

[18] This is the case in Paris, BNF, Lat. 1120, 1118, 778 and 495; Vic, ABEV, ms. 105; Modena, BC, ms. 7; Benevento, BC, mss. 34, 35 and 40.

[19] Paris, BNF, Lat. 1118, fol. 21v; *CT VII*, 111. See Peter Josef Thannabaur. Op. cit., mél. 89, 111 and 197.

[20] See Birgitta Thorsberg. *Étude sur l'hymnologie mozarabe*. Stockholm: Almquist & Wiksell International, 1962, 29, 159 (AUS: SLS 8).

[21] Paris, BNF, Lat. 495, fol. 46v; *CT VII*, 103; *AH XLVII:* 383; Thannabaur. Op. cit., mel. 89.

[22] Paris, BNF, Lat. 495, fol. 46v; *CT VII*, 166; *AH XLVII:* 376; *ibidem,* mel. 43.

[23] Texts containing the word *osanna* in the sense 'salva', 'salvifica', in *CT VII*: *Osanna, agie altissime domine* (Italian); *Osanna plasmatum populum* (Iberian, Aquitainian, Italian); *Osanna, salva, salvifica* (Apt); *Osanna nunc tuum plasma* (Iberian, Aquitainian); *Osanna omnes tua gratia* (West. Frankish, Italian); *Osanna, pater per omnia* (Iberian, Aquitainian); *Osanna, patris sapientia* (Iberian, Aquitainian); *Osanna salvifica tuum plasma* (Iberian, Aquitainian, Italian); *Osanna, una summaque sophia* (Iberian); *Osanna tuum plasma* (Iberian); and *Osanna, vox laudabilia* (Iberian).

[24] Vic, ABEV, ms. 105, fol. 45r-v; *CT VII,* 78; Paris, BNF, Lat. 778; Vic, ABEV, ms. 106, Tortosa, AC, ms. 135; and Huesca, AC, Cod. 4.

[25] *CT VII,* 138; Paris, BNF, Lat. 1139, 1086, 1871, 1177, 778 y 495; Montserrat, BM, ms. 73; Vic, ABEV, mss. 106 and 105; Tortosa, AC, ms. 135; Huesca, AC, Cod. 4; Madrid, RAH, Cod. 51; and Santiago de Compostela, AC, *Codex Calixtinus;* see Rome, Bibl. Apostolica Vaticana, Urb. Lat. 602 from Montecassino; see Thannabaur, mel. 214, 224 var. and 226; *AH XVII:* 205-206; Peter Wagner. *Die Gesänge der Jacobusliturgie zu Santiago de Compostela aus dem sog. Codex Calixtinus*. Freiburg: Kommissionsverlag. Universitæts-Buchhandlung, 1931, 46; and Manuel C. Díaz y Díaz, ed. *El Códice Calixtino de la Catedral de Santiago. Estudio codicológico y de contenido*. Santiago de Compostela: Centro de Estudios Jacobeos, 1988.

[26] Vic, ABEV, ms. 105, fol. 45r-v.

[27] The same vocabulary is found in Aquitainian proses: "Olim deceperat hostis subdola et callida fraude Adam" (*AH VII:* 252, 3a), or "Evae crimen nobis limen paradisi clauserat, haec dum credit et oboedit, caeli claustra reserat" (see *AH I:* 428; and *AH VII:* 75, 4a-b).

[28] Among *Osanna* proses expositing the act of singing in musical metaphors can be mentioned: *CT VII*: *Caeleste praeconium* (no. 10), *Carmina plebs* (no. 12), *Christo digna* (no. 13), *Clangat coetus* (no. 15), *Clangat hodie* (no. 16), *Osanna dulciflua* (no. 47), *Dulcis est cantica* (no. 48), *Fidelium turma* (no. 53), *Laude canora* (no. 67), *Laudes deo* (no. 68), *Nunc tuum plasma* (no. 78), *Ortus occasus* (no. 89), *Patris dextera* (no. 101), *Plebs tibi mente* (no. 112), *Rex gubernans omnia* (no. 132), *Te laudant agmina* (no. 159), *Voce dulcisona* (no. 171) and *Voce harmonica* (no. 172).

[29] See Gunilla Iversen. *Chanter avec les anges. Poésie dans la messe médiévale. Interprétations et commentaires*. Paris: Cerf, 2001.

[30] Madrid, BN, ms. 19421, Paris, BNF, Lat. 778 y N. A. L. 495; Madrid, RAH, Cod. 51; Tortosa, AC, ms. 135; Montserrat, BM, ms. 73; and Vic, ABEV, mss. V 40 and 106 (four times).

[31] Madrid, RAH, Cod. 51, fols. 243v-244r. See further *CT VII*, 12.

[32] *CT VII,* 53; Paris, BNF, Lat. 778; Barcelona, BC, M. 1408-9a; Tortosa, AC, ms. 135; and Madrid, RAH, Cod. 51.

[33] *CT VII,* 159; Monserrat, BM, ms. 73; Paris, BNF, Lat. 778; Vic, ABEV, ms. 106; and Madrid, RAH, Cod. 51.

[34] *CT VII,* 16; Madrid, BN, mss. 289 and 19421; Paris, BNF, Lat. 1139 and 778; Vic, ABEV, ms. 106; Huesca, AC, Cod. 4; Madrid, RAH, Cod. 51; and *AH XLVII:* 341; see Gunilla Iversen. "Music as *Ancilla Verbi*...". Óp. cit., 45-66; and Charles M. Atkinson. "Music as Mistress of the Words...". Op. cit.

[35] According to Eva Castro, the manuscript RAH, Cod. 51 from San Millán de la Cogolla was a result of a number of small number of *libelli* originating from Moissac as well as Narbonne and Toulouse. *Idem.* "Le long chemin de Moissac à S. Millán (Le troparium de la Real Acad.

Hist., Aemil. 51". In Claudio Leonardi and Enrico Menesto, eds. *La Tradizione dei tropi liturgici*. Spoleto: Centro italiano di studi sull'alto medievo di Spoleto, 1991, 245-263.

[36] Gunilla Iversen. "The Mirror of Music. Symbol and Reality in the Text of *Clangat hodie*". *Revista de Musicologia* 16, no. 2 (1993): 771-789; and Charles M. Atkinson. "Music and Meaning in *Clangat Hodie*". *Revista de Musicologia* 17 (1993a): 790-806.

[37] In the manuscripts, *Clangat hodie* is presented in a fascicle of *Sanctus* chant without any specific indication or festal rubric. Only the late manuscript Montpellier, Bibliothèque de l'École de Médecine, ms. 20 has the rubric "Pasquale". In *AH XL:* 132, where *Clangat hodie* is given as a separate sequence from later manuscripts, it is labelled "De omnibus sanctis".

[38] See Gunilla Iversen. "Verba canendi in Tropes and Sequences". In Michael W. Herren, C. J. McDonough and Ross G. Arthur, eds. *Latin Culture in the Eleventh Century*. Publication of *The Journal of Medieval Latin*. Turnhout: Brepols, 2002. Vol. 5: 444-473; see also Gunilla Iversen. *Chanter avec les anges...*, Op. cit.

[39] Jean Michel Hanssens, eds. *Amalari episcopi opera liturgica omnia*. 3 vols. Vatican City: Biblioteca Apostolica Vaticana, 1938-1950. Vol. 2: 267-268. Studi e testi: 138-140).

[40] Émile Mâle. *Religious Art in France. The Twelfth Century. A Study of the Origins of Medieval Iconography.* Princeton, New Jersey: Princeton University Press, 1986, 3-6. (*Art religieux du XIIe siècle*. Paris: Libraire Armand Colin, 1928). The *Commentary on the Apocalypse* composed in Spain by Beatus, abbot of Liebana in 784. His book was adopted by the Church of Spain and recopied for centuries.

[41] Tortosa, AC, ms. 135, fols. 18v-19v; also in Barcelona, BC, M. 1147. *CT VII*, 15; *AH XLVII:* 378.

[42] Tortosa, AC, ms. 135, fol. 29r-v. *CT VII*, 164.

[43] Tortosa, AC, ms. 135, fols. 26-27. *CT VII*, 167.

Bibliography

Atkinson, Charles M. "Music as Mistress of the Words: *Laudes deo ore pio*". In Gabriel Silagi, ed. *Liturgische Tropen. Referate zweier Colloquien des Corpus Troporum in München (1983) und Canterbury (1984)*. Munich: Arbeo-Gesellschaft, 1985, 67-82.

—. "Music and Meaning in *Clangat Hodie*". *Revista de Musicología* 16, no. 2 (1993): 790-806.

—. "Text, Music, and the Persistence of Memory in *Dulcis est cantica*". In Wulf Arlt and Gunilla Björkvall, eds. *Recherches nouvelles sur les tropes liturgiques. (Corpus Troporum.)* Stockholm: Almquist & Wiksell Internacional, 1993, 95-117 (Acta Universitatis Stockholmiensis: Studia Latina Stockholmiensia 36).

Björkvall, Gunilla, ed. *Corpus Troporum V. Les deux tropaires d'Apt mss. 17 et 18.* Stockholm: Almquist & Wiksell International, 1986 (Acta Universitatis Stockholmiensis: Studia Latina Stockholmiensia 32).

Björkvall, Gunilla, Gunilla Iversen, and Ritva Jonsson, eds. *Corpus Troporum III. Tropes du propre de la messe 2. Cycle de Pâques.* Stockholm: Almquist & Wiksell International, 1982 (Acta Universitatis Stockholmiensis: Studia Latina Stockholmiensia 25).

Castro, Eva. "Le long chemin de Moissac à S. Millan (Le troparium de la Real Akad. Hist., Aemil 51". In Claudio Leonardi and Enrico Menesto, eds. *La Tradizione dei tropi liturgici*. Spoleto: Centro italiano di studi sull'alto medievo di Spoleto, 1991, 245-263.

Díaz y Díaz, Manuel C. *El Códice Calixtino de la Catedral de Santiago. Estudio codicológico y de contenido*. Santiago de Compostela: Centro de Estudios Jacobeos, 1988.

Dreves, Guido Maria, Clemens Blume, and Henry Marriott Bannister, eds. *Analecta hymnica medii aevi.* Vols. I, VII, XL, XLVII, LIII. Leipzig: Riesland, 1886-1922.

Elfving, Lars. *Étude lexicographique sur les Sequences Limousines*. Stockholm: Almquist & Wiksell International, 1972 (Acta Universitatis Stockholmiensis: Studia Latina Stockholmiensia 7).

Gros, Miguel S. *Els tropers prosers de la Catedral de Vic. Estudi i edició.* Barcelona: Institut d'Estudis Catalans, 1999 (Biblioteca Litúrgica Catalana: 2).

Gy, Pierre-Marie. "Le Sanctus romain et les anaphores orientales". In *Mélanges liturgiques offerts au R. P. Bernard Botte, O. S. B.* Louvain: Abbey of Mont Cesar, 1972, 167-174.

Hanssens, Jean Michel, ed. *Amalari episcopi opera liturgica omnia.* 3 vols. Vatican City: Biblioteca Apostolica Vaticana, 1938-1950 (Studi e testi: 138-140).

Isidorus. *Etymologiae*. In J.-P. Migne, ed. *Patrologia Latina LXXXII.* Paris: Garnier, 1844-89 (Patrologiae cursus completus: Series Latina).

Iversen, Gunilla, ed. *Corpus Troporum IV. Tropes de l'Agnus Dei.* Stockholm: Almquist & Wiksell International, 1980 (Acta Universitatis Stockholmiensis: Studia Latina Stockholmiensia 26).

—. "Music as *Ancilla Verbi* and Words as *Ancilla Musicae.* On the Interpretation of the Musical and Textual forms of two Tropes to *Osanna in excelsis*: *Laudes deo* and *Trinitas, unitas, deitas*". In Gabriel Silagi, ed. *Liturgische Tropen. Referate zweier Colloquien des Corpus Troporum in München (1983) und Canterbury (1984*). Munich: Arbeo-Gesellschaft 1985, 45-66.

—. "Osanna dulcis est cantica: On a Group of Compositions added to the Osanna". In László Dobszay, ed. *IMS Study Session on "Cantus Planus", Tihány, Hungary, 19-24 September 1988.* Budapest: Hungarian Academy of Sciences, Institute for Musicology, 1989, 275-296.

—, ed. *Corpus Troporum VII. Tropes de l'ordinaire de la messe. Tropes du Sanctus.* Stockholm: Almquist & Wiksell International, 1990 (Acta Universitatis Stockholmiensis: Studia Latina Stockholmiensia 34).

—. "The Mirror of Music. Symbol and Reality in the Text of *Clangat hodie*". *Revista de Musicología* 16, no. 2 (1993): 771-789.

—. *Chanter avec les anges. Poésie dans la messe médiévale. Interprétations et commentaires.* Paris: Cerf, 2001.

—. "Verba canendi in Tropes and Sequences". In Michael W. Herren, Christopher James McDonough, and Ross Gilbert Arthur, eds. *Latin Culture in the Eleventh Century.* Publication of *The Journal of Medieval Latin.* Turnhout: Brepols, 2002. Vol. 5: 444-473.

—. "Rex in hac aula. Réflexions sur les séquences de l'Antiphonaire de Charles le Chauve". *Revue de Musicologie* 89 (2003): 31-45.

Iversen, Gunilla, and Nicolas Bell, eds. *Sapientia et eloquentia. Meaning and Function in Liturgical Poetry, Music, Drama, and Biblical Commentary in the Middle Ages.* Turnhout: Brepols. (In press.)

Johansson, Ann-Katrin, ed. *Corpus Troporum IX. The Tropes for the Feasts of the Blessed Virgin.* Stockholm: Almquist & Wiksell International, 1998.

Jonsson, Ritva, Gunilla Björkvall, and Gunilla Iversen, eds. *Corpus Troporum I. Tropes du propre de la messe 1. Cycle de Noël.* Stockholm: Almquist & Wiksell International, 1975 (Acta Universitatis Stockholmiensis: Studia Latina Stockholmiensia 21).

Leclercq, Jean. *L'amour des lettres et le désir de Dieu.* Paris: Cerf, 1957. [English translation: *The love of learning and the desire for God.* New York: Fordham University Press, 1985 (1st ed., 1961)].

Mâle, Émile. *Religious Art in France. The Twelfth Century. A Study of the Origins of Medieval Iconography.* Princeton, New Jersey: Princeton University Press, 1986, 3-6. (*L'art réligieux du XIIe siècle. Étude sur les origines de l'iconographie du Moyen Âge.* Paris: Libraire Armand Colin, 1928).

Marcusson, Olov, ed. *Corpus Troporum II. Prosules de la messe 1. Tropes de l'Alleluia.* Stockholm: Almquist & Wiksell International, 1976 (Acta Universitatis Stockholmiensis: Studia Latina Stockholmiensia 22).

Odelman, Eva, ed. *Corpus Troporum VI. Prosules de la messe 2. Les prosules limousines de Wolfenbüttel.* Stockholm: Almquist & Wiksell International, 1986 (Acta Universitatis Stockholmiensis: Studia Latina Stockholmiensia 31).

Quotiens contra se. In J.-P. Migne, ed. Op. cit. Vol. XCVI.

Reckow, Fritz. "Organum-Begriff und frühe Mehrstimmigkeit. Zugleich ein Beitrag zur Bedeutung des 'instrumentalen' in der spätantiken und mittelalterlichen Musiktheorie". In Wulf Arlt, ed. *Basler Studien zur Musikgeschichte*. Vol. 1. Bern: Franke, 1975 (Forum musicologicum: 1).

Silagi, Gabriel, ed. *Liturgische Tropen. Referate zweier Colloquien des Corpus Troporum in München (1983) und Canterbury (1984).* Munich: Arbeo-Gesellschaft, 1985, 45-66.

St. Jerome. *Epistola*. In J.-P. Migne, ed. Op. cit. Vol. XXII: cols. 378-379.

Thannabaur, Peter-Josef. *Das einstimmige Sanctus der römischen Messe in der handschriftlichen Überlieferungen des 11. bis 16. Jahrhunderts.* Munich: Ricke, 1962 (Erlanger Arbeiten zur Musikwissenschaft: 1).

Thorsberg, Birgitta. *Étude sur l'hymnologie mozarabe.* Stockholm: Almquist & Wiksell International, 1962 (Acta Universitatis Stockholmiensis: Studia Latina Stockholmiensia 8).

Wagner, Peter. *Die Gesänge der Jacobusliturgie zu Santiago de Compostela aus dem sog. Codex Calixtinus.* Freiburg, 1931.

From the *Iudicii Signum* to the Song of the Sybil: Early Testimony

Maricarmen Gómez

At this time, preparations are in progress as part of the UNESCO project "Oral Heritage of Humanity" for a brief performance that takes place each year on Christmas Eve in the Cathedral in Palma de Majorca, and, according to this model, in numerous churches on the island. The performance is of what is known today as the *Song of the Sybil*, which remained popular for several centuries, although its meaning has now been distorted to a certain extent: it become an expression of culture that is closer to the world of folklore than to the sphere of which it truly is a part, that of art music. With the resurgence of nationalism in Spain in the 21st century *in.*, certain media have convinced people that the Sybil belongs to a specific musical heritage that may include the former territories of the Crown of Aragón, and especially Catalonia, Majorca, and, to a lesser extent, Valencia, but the reality is rather more complex. This should not take credit away from the Cathedral of Majorca for having kept the tradition of performing the Sybil alive after the Cathedral of Toledo decided to eliminate it towards the end of the 18th century or perhaps in the 19th century *in.*[1]

The Sybil is the only figure from pagan antiquity that managed to establish a niche for itself in Christian liturgy, not just because of the song concerning us here, the status of which would be rather insignificant if it were compared to what is probably the most famous of all sequences, the *Dies irae* of the Requiem mass (*LU* 1810-1813), attributed to Thomas of Celano († ca. 1250). Turned into a musical symbol of death in Western culture,[2] this sequence, which is one of the very few to survive the selection process carried out by the Council of Trent (1545-1563), expressly refers to the Sybil in the first and most penetrating of its sentences: "The day of wrath! That special day will dissolve this age into ash: as David and the Sybil bear witness".

The Sybil that the *Dies irae* refers to is the Eritrean sybil, whose prophesies are closely associated with the verses of the *Iudicii signum* from which the sybilline chant came into being.

The Eritrean sybil was the first and most famous of the sybils or prophetesses of Antiquity. Her oracles, collected in writing, were deposited in the Roman Capitol, where they were apparently used to answer important questions of state. A line from the sybilline writings selected at random would become acrostic in certain verses that included the response of the priestly class to the question they had been posed, depending on what was said to have been inspired by the Sybil's prophetic voice.[3]

The prestige of the sybilline oracles meant that they became widely known, especially from the 2nd century BC onwards, having the specific aim of spreading the Jewish and later Christian faith, by using their authority. Up to twelve books compiled at the dawn of the Renaissance have survived that contain manuscript copies of sybilline oracles from a broad geographic area that ranges from Iraq—the former Babylon—to Egypt. Without rhyme or reason, materials of three kinds are intermingled with these texts: fragments of oracles from remote antiquity, others of Jewish origin regarding historical, doctrinal, and eschatological matters, and finally Christian writings on the figure of Christ.

Out of the twelve books of oracles by the Sybil, the third and the eighth are particularly important in our case. The third book, the main body of which seems to date

Di-es i-rae, di-es i-lla, Sol-vet sæ - clum in fa-vi-lla: Tes-te Da-vid cum Si - by-lla

back to the 2nd century BC, is markedly monotheistic; it contains several eschatological oracles that are later mentioned by the Latin historian Lactantius (ca. 250-ca. 317) in his *Divinae institutiones*, which he directly or indirectly attributes to the Eritrean sybil. In bk. 7, chap. 16, which he entitles "De mundi vastatione, eiusque prodigiis" ("Of the devastation of the world and its prophetic omens"), Lactantius refers, for example, to the signs or signals that were to precede the destruction of the Roman Empire in the following terms:

> Sol in perpetuum fuscabitur, ut vix inter noctem diemque discernatur. Luna iam non tribus deficiet horis, sed perpetuo sanguine obfusa, meatus extraordinarios peraget, ut non sit homini promptum, aut siderum cursus, aut rationem temporum agnoscere: fiet enim vel aestas in hyeme, vel hyems in aestate. Tunc annus breviabitur, et mensis minuetur, et dies in angustum coarctabitur. Stellae vero creberrimae cadent, ut caelum omne caecum sine ullis luminibus appareat. Montes quoque altissimi decident, et planis aequabuntur: mare innavigabile constituetur. Ac ne quid malis hominum terraeque desit, audietur e caelo tuba; quod hoc modo Sibylla denuntiat, dicens: Σαλπιγξ ουρανοθεν φωνην πολυθρηνον αφησει. Itaque trepidabunt omnes, et ad luctuosum illum sonitum contremiscent. (*PL VI:* 791-92)[4]

The words Lactantius quotes from the Sybil strangely enough match one of the verses regarding the second coming of Christ that is attributed to the Eritrean sybil in the eighth book of the sybilline oracles, which is of Christian origin (lines 217-250). Written in Greek and with contents that are similar to those in the paragraph taken from the *Divinae institutiones*, they form the famous acrostic ΙΗΣΟΥΣ ΧΡΕΙΣΤΟΣ ΘΕΟΥ ΥΙΟΣ ΣΩΤΗΡ ΣΤΑΥΡΟΣ, in Latin IESUS CHRISTUS DEI FILIUS SALVATOR CRUX.[5] The initials of the six words in the acrostic in turn form another one, ΙΧΘΥΣ (fish), a well-known symbol of Christ. We can sense that the similarity between this acrostic and the manner of manipulating the sybilline texts in the Roman Capitol cannot have come about by chance.

Unlike Lactantius, who merely quoted them, Eusebius of Cesarea (ca. 260-ca. 339), the famous historian of Christian Antiquity, reproduces word by word the aforementioned verses by the Sybil in the *Oratio Constatini ad Sanctorum Coetum*, in the chapter that refers to the prophecies on the coming of Christ.[6] Years later, they reappear in *De civitate Dei,* by St. Augustine (354-430), this time translated from Greek into Latin.

In his bk. 18, chap. 23, which deals with "De Sibylla Erytrea, quae inter alias Sibyllas cognoscitur de Christo evidentia multa cecinisse" ("With the Eritrean sybil, who, among other sybils, is known to have prophesized clear and evident things about Jesus Christ"), St. Augustine tells how the proconsul Flavian spoke to him one day and showed him a book that contained the Sybil's verses with the acrostic in Greek. He then reproduces them in Latin and points out that this is an imperfect version, given the problems posed by translating them, in which the thirty-four hexameters of the original are reduced to twenty-seven, a number that forms a ternary squared integer (3^3) in his own words.[7] St. Augustine's version of the Sybil's verses is as follows:

> **I**udicii signum: tellus sudore madescet.
> **E** caelo Rex adveniet per saecla futurus,
> **S**cilicet in carne praesens, ut iudicet orbem.
> **U**nde Deum cernent incredulus atque fidelis
> **C**elsum cum sanctis, aevi iam termino in ipso.
> **S**ic animae cum carne aderunt, quas iudicat ipse,
> **C**um iacet incultus densis in vepribus orbis.
> **R**eicient simulacra viri, cunctam quoque gazam,
> **E**xurent terras ignis, pontumque polumque
> **I**nquirens, taetri portas effringet Averni.
> **S**anctorum sed enim cunctae lux libera carni
> **T**radetur, sontes aeterna flamma cremabit.
> **O**ccultos actus retegens tunc quisque loquetur
> **S**ecreta, atque Deus reserabit pectora luci.
> **T**unc erit et luctus, stridebunt dentibus omnes.
> **E**ripitur solis iubar, et chorus interit astris.
> **V**olvetur caelum, lunaris splendor obibit.
> **D**eiciet colles, valles extollet ab imo.
> **N**on erit in rebus hominum sublime vel altum.
> **I**am aequantur campis montes, et caerula ponti
> **O**mnia cessabunt, tellus confracta peribit.
> **S**ic pariter fontes torrentur, fluminaque igni.
> **S**ed tuba tum sonitum tristem demittet ab alto
> **O**rbe, gemens facinus miserum variosque labores,
> **T**artareumque chaos monstrabit terra dehiscens.
> **E**t coram hic Domino reges sistentur ad unum.
> **R**ecidet e caelis ignisque et sulphuris amnis.
> (*PL XLI:* 579.)[8]

The fact that St. Augustine includes these verses in one of his most important books meant that during the Middle Ages, the *Sermo de symbolo* addressed "against Jews, pagans and arrians",[9] was attributed to him, when in fact it must have been written by Quodvultdeus, who was Bishop of Carthage between 431 and 439. The sermon has twenty-two chapters, of which the first six are addressed to Christians, whom he urges to remain strong in their faith. Chapters 7-9 attack heretics, and the tenth, Herod and the Jews. In the following eight chapters, he aims to convince the latter of their supposed error by providing various pieces of evidence on the coming of the Messiah. Chapter 19 again attacks heretics, and the last three attempt to prepare the faithful for eternal life.

The section of the sermon that covers chapters 11-18 begins with the words: "Vos inquam convenio, o Iudei, qui usque in hodiernum diem negatis Filium Dei" ("I address you, Jews, who until now denied the Son of God"), after which its author, stressing the scepticism of the people he is addressing, calls upon the prophet Isaiah to furnish his personal testimony on the coming of the Messiah: "Dic, Isaia, testimonium Christo". This is then followed by the passage from the Old Testament that provides his prophecy: "Ecce virgo concipiet, et pariet filium. Et vocabitur nomen eius Emmanuel". ("Behold, a virgin shall conceive and bear a son, and shall call his name Immanuel") (Is 7:14). After Isaiah's testimony, he invokes Jeremiah, whose messianic prophecy is also quoted, and this is followed by testimony from Daniel, Moses, David, and Habakkuk. Next follows testimony from four characters from the New Testament, Simeon, Zacharias, Isabel, and John the Baptist, and testimony by two gentiles, Virgil and Nebuchadnezzar.

The sermon quotes the seventh verse of the *Eclogue IV* by Virgil, dated 40 BC, when the peace of Brundisium was being negotiated. The eclogue refers to a newborn child or one still to be born, perhaps the son of one of the leaders of Rome. The poet, who says he is following a prediction of the Cumean sybil, focuses his hopes on the child as a future leader.[10] Virgil's ambiguous language, inspired by materials from the third book of the sybilline Oracles and perhaps by the Book of Isaiah, meant that the verses in this eclogue acquired a special meaning in the Christian world, which thought it saw in these the expression of a sybilline prophecy about the coming of the Messiah that differed from that by the Eritrean sybil. This is why there is a reference to them in the pseudo-Augustinian sermon, which quotes the verse that says: "iam nova progenies caelo demittitur alto" ("then a new lineage shall be sent from on high").

The last of the prophecies that the *Sermo de symbolo* includes is by the Eritrean sybil, which reproduces the texts of the hexameters of St. Augustine's *De civitate Dei,* and is preceded by the following introduction:

> Quid Sibylla vaticinando etiam de Christo clamaverit in medium proferamus, ut ex uno lapide utrorumque frontes percutiantur, iudaeorum scilicet atque paganorum, atque suo gladio, sicut Golias, Christi omnes percutiantur inimici: audite quid dixerit. (*PL XLII:* 1126.)[11]

Three centuries later, the same hexameters were to reappear in a quite different context. This time it was in a probably apocryphal sermon or speech by the English monk and writer, the Venerable Bede (672-735), whose writings titled *Sibyllinorum verborum interpretatio,*[12] were highly influential in the Carolingian Renaissance. After studying the sybilline oracles, nature and history as far as the Christian faith is concerned, Bede refers to the end of the Roman Empire and the coming of the Antichrist in apocalyptic terms:

> Et cum cessaverit imperium Romanum, tunc revelabitur manifeste Antichristus, et sedebit in domo Domini in Jerusalem. [...] Tunc erit persecutio magna, qualis non fuit antea, nec postea subsequetur. Abbreviavit autem Dominus dies illos, propter electos, et occidetur virtute Domini Antichristus a Michaele archangelo in monte Oliveti. (*PL XC:* 1185-1186.)[13]

According to the first epistle of St. John, the Antichrist must appear shortly before the end of the world (1st epistle John 2:18) and is destroyed by Christ in his second coming. What could be more fitting, then, than to continue the speech in the *interpretatio* with the prophetic verses of the Eritrean sybil, preceded by some introductory words, just as they are in the *Sermo de symbolo.* The speech ends with the promise of eternal life for the righteous and eternal damnation for the wicked, once the Last Judgment has taken place.

The verses by the Eritrean sybil reproduced by St. Augustine, the author of the *Sermo de symbolo,* and the Venerable Bede are not the only late medieval texts to refer to the signs or signals of the end of the world, something that is hardly surprising if we bear in mind that this is a recurring theme in biblical writings. So, certain doctors and prelates of the Church—such as St. Peter Damian (1007-1072), Peter Comestor († 1178) or St. Thomas Aquinas (1225-1274)—attribute to St. Jerome (340-420) a writing in which it is established that there are fifteen signs of the Last Judgment. If it ever existed, the original presumed to be by St. Jerome has been lost, although the aforementioned writers and several others copy or sum up St. Jerome's supposed text.[14] As a result, St. Peter Damian includes it in the final chapter of a brief treatise *De novissimis et Antichristo.*[15] After relating the death of the Antichrist, its author refers to those signs "praecedentia iudicii diem ex S. Hieronymi sententia", which he distributes over fifteen days:

> Signum, inquit, primi diei: Maria omnia in altitudinem exaltabuntur quindecim cubitorum supra montes excelsos orbis terrae, non affluentia, sed sicut muri aequora stabunt.
> Signum secundi diei: Omnia aequora prosternentur in imum profundi, ita ut vix queant ab humanis obtutibus conspici.
> Signum tertii diei: Maria omnia redigentur in pristinum statum, qualiter ab exordio creata fuerant.
> Signum quarti diei: Belluae omnes, et omnia quae moventur in aquis marinis congregabuntur super pelagus, more contentionis, invicem mugientes et rugientes; nescientque homines quid cantent, vel quid cogitent, sed tantum scit Deus, cui omnia vivunt, officio gerendi.
> Signum quinti diei: Omnia volatilia caeli concinabuntur in campis, unumquodque genus in ordine suo; eaedem volucres invicem colloquentes et plorantes erunt, non gustantes, neque bibentes, adventum judicis timentes.
> Signum sexti diei: Flumina ignea ab occasu solis surgent, contra faciem firmamenti, usque ad ortum currentia.
> Signum septimi diei: Errantia sidera, et stationaria spargent ex se igneas comas, qualiter in cometis apparet, orbi et eius habitatoribus.
> Signum octavi diei: Terraemotus erit magnus, ita ut nullus homo stare possit, aut nullum animal, sed solo sternentur omnia.
> Signum noni diei: Omnes lapides tam parvi quam magni scindentur in quatuor partes, et unaquaeque pars collidet alteram partem, nescietque ullus homo sonum illum, nisi solus Deus.
> Signum decimi diei: Omnia ligna silvarum, et olera herbarum sanguineum fluent rorem.
> Signum undecimi diei: Omnes montes, et celles, et omnia aedificia humana arte constructa, in pulverem redigeatur.
> Signum duodecimi diei: Omnia animalia terrae de silvis et montibus venient ad campos rugientia et mugientia, non gustantia et non bibentia.
> Signum decimitertii diei: Omnia ab ortu solis sepulcra usque ad occasum patebunt, cadaveribus surgentibus, usque ad horam judicii.
> Signum decimiquarti diei: Omne humanum genus, quod inventum fuerit, de habitaculis et de locis in quibus erunt velociter abscedent, non intelligentes neque loquentes, sed discurrent ut amentes.
> Signum decimi quinti diei: Vivi homines morientur, ut resurgant cum mortuis longe ante defunctis. (*PL CXLV:* 888.)[16]

The variations between St. Peter Damian's text and the one that other authors transmit are more a question of form than content, so that it is highly likely that they come from the same source. A quite different matter is whether it was St. Jerome who established that there were fifteen signs before the Last Judgment and distributed them over fifteen days, or if he took them from an unknown source. The only certainty is that the sign corresponding to the first day comes from the passage from Genesis about the Flood that reads: "Quindecim cubitis altior fuit aqua super montes, quos operuerat" ("Fifteen cubits upward did the waters prevail; and the mountains were covered") (Gen. 7:20). The number recording the height of the waters in the biblical passage and the number of catastrophes before the Judgment might not match merely by chance, because there are also fifteen steps in the temple in Ezekiel's vision (Ez. 40: 26-31), the same as the number of psalms in the *Canticum graduum* (Ps. 119-133); as a result this number was a symbol in the Middle Ages of the passage from earthly life to eternal life, which is clearly appropriate for a text about the Last Judgment.[17]

Wherever the fifteen signs of the Judgment came from, the text attributed to St. Jerome and the eschatological verses by the Eritrean sybil do not clearly match, except in developing a common theme. The fragments seem to come from different traditions that converge in the Middle Ages.

If the fears of the end of the millenium provided an obvious impetus for the development of eschatological literature,[18] they also definitely helped to attract renewed attention to the Sybil's verses. Certain *Versus de die iudicii* must have resulted from the atmosphere that prevailed especially in ecclesiastical circles, in view of the supposedly impending end of the world. These were copied in a miscellaneous codex from the 9th and 10th centuries from a monastery dedicated to St. Martin. The codex was acquired by the Monastery of St. Martial of Limoges in the 13th century (Paris, BNF, Lat. 1154, fols. 121-122).[19] The verses that I present below (see p. 164) are provided with early Aquitainian adiastematic musical notation, which was added once the text had been written.

No less dramatic than the verses in the Limoges manuscript are others that were added with music at the end of a 10th century collection of letters from the Abbey of Aniane in Languedoc (Montpellier: Bibliothèque de la ville, ms. 6, fols. 133v-134). This is a prose with a refrain that sums up the text of the Apocalypse, and each of its twenty-four stanzas begins with a different letter, in alphabetical order. The last stanza (AΩ) ends with a Gloria to the Trinity. The notation in the piece is Aquitainian and is arranged around a dry point line.[20] Its tune, which is extremely sober, changes slightly from one stanza to the next and is tailored to fit the length of the prepared lines.

The *Aniane Primer* begins with a sombre warning: "Earth, pay heed! Strip of immense sea, pay heed! / Mankind, pay heed! All that live under the sun, pay heed! / The day of supreme wrath draws near. / Hateful day, bitter day / on which the sky will fade away, the sun will turn red, / the moon will change its face, the day will be darkened, / the stars will fall to earth. / Oh wretches! Mankind, why do you persist in your foolish joy?"

We know of two other copies of this *Primer* with music, which nevertheless merely reproduce its first stanza with certain variants in the lyric. The oldest one belongs to an 11th century manuscript from Karlsruhe (Badische Landesbibliothek, ms. 504, fol. 26v) and the other to the famous *Las Huelgas Codex* (fols. 167v, 157), both extremely important copies insofar as that they prove the popularity and survival of apocalyptic prose beyond the year 1000, close to when it must have been written. If there is no clear correspondence between the tunes from Aniane and Karlsruhe, the tune from Las Huelgas manuscript is quite melismatic and is linked to the Aniane version.[21]

Although neither the Aniane manuscript nor those from Karlsruhe and Las Huelgas show where the verses of the *Audi tellus* should go in the liturgy, one of the possible reasons for their survival must have been the fact that they fited to the Office for the Dead, where the fears of mankind in the face of the final judgment could continue to be evoked without the subject falling out of the public eye, at least during the Middle Ages. In this sense it is worth mentioning the existence of a sequence that was widely disseminated between the 13th and 15th centuries, the first two lines of which match those in the Aniane manuscript (the lyric not the music), where they are glossed in seven stanzas that develop the theme of the *ubi sunt;* some of the manuscripts that transmit the composition, including a 15th century *Collectaneum* from the Abbey of St. Victor (Paris, BNF, Lat. 15163, fol. 231), show that this is a prose or sequence, "in officio mortuorum".[22] It did not survive the Council of Trent, which abolished all of the sequences in the Christian liturgy, except for four, one of which was the *Dies irae* in the Requiem Mass.

Versus de die iudicii

I. Quique de morte redempti estis,
Et per crucem liberati,
Precioso comparati
Sanguine filii Dei,
Sursum corda preparate
Et Ihesum desiderate.

II. Diem illum formidate,
Quando mundum iudicare
Christus imperator caeli
Venerit, fulgens in virtute,
Et in magna claritate,
Regnum sanctis preparare.

III. Cum aperta caeli arca,
Fulgorans ab oriente
Lucet vultus Ihesu Christi:
Apparebit mundus omnis;
Obviam volabunt sancti
Ante pium redemptorem.

IV. Cum aperta caeli astra,
Usque ad terminos terrae
Caeperit tuba canere,
Sancti archangeli Dei
Voce magna proclamare,
Et electos congregare.

V. Tunc ad vocem regis magni
Resurgent omnes defuncti;
Recepturus unusquisque
Non solum de pravo facto,
Sed de verbo ocioso
Prout iessit in corpore.

VI. Cum ab igne rota mundi
Tota ceperit ardere,
Saeva flamma concremare,
Caelum ut liber plicare,
Sidera tota cadere,
Finis saeculi venire.

VII. Dies irae, dies illa,
Dies nebulae et caliginis,
Dies tubae et clangoris,
Dies luctus et tremoris,
Quando pondus tenebrarum
Cadet super peccatores.

VIII. Qualis pavor tunc caderit
Quando rex iratus venerit,
Et infernus apparebit,
Qui impios absorbebit.
Sulfur, flamma atque vermes
Cruciabunt peccatores.

IX. Quid dicturi erunt pravi
Quando ipsi trement sancti
Ante tantam maiestatem
Ihesu Christi, filii Dei.
Et si iustus vix evadet,
Impius ubi parebit.

X. Non est locus evadendi
Nec inducias petendi,
Sed est tempus discutendi,
Amara districtione,
Ubi mente accusante
Torquebuntur puniendi.

XI. Ihesu Christe, salus mundi,
Tunc succurre pie nobis
Qui cum Patre nunc te unum
Atque cum Sancto Spiritu,
Adoramus verum Deum,
Salvatorem saeculorum.
Amen.[23]

It is thought that the lyric and music of the *Dies irae* come from a fragment of the responsory for the dead, *Libera me, Domine* (*LU* 1767-1768), which reads: "Dies illa, dies irae, calamitatis et miseriae, dies magna et amara valde" ("That day! Day of wrath, calamity and misery! Day of great bitterness!") The lyric is also linked to certain verses by the prophet Zephaniah that describe the Day of Judgment (Zeph. I, 15-16), that in turn are similar to those in the seventh stanza of the *Versus de die iudicii*, whose author must have taken them from the biblical prophet.

As noted at the beginning of this essay, it is precisely in the *Dies irae* where the only mention appears of the character of the Sybil in all post-Tridentine Christian liturgy in a brief reference to the eschatological verses of the Eritrean sybil, whose prophetic testimony is linked by Thomas of Celano, the disciple and first biographer of St. Francis of Assisi, to King David's 17th Psalm (Ps. 17:5-16).[24]

If the characteristic fears at the end of the first millennium are perfectly reflected in the *Versus de die iudicii* or in the verses of the *Audi tellus*, this is equally true in the *Versus sibille de die iudicii*, one of whose oldest musical witness can be found in the miscellany of St. Martial of Limoges from the 9th-10th centuries (fols. 122-123), following the *Versus de die iudicii* and preceding others *De nativitate Domini*. Among the first copies of the sybilline verses of the *Iudicii signum* after St. Augustine and Bede of which we have news, three belong to three other miscellanies from the 9th century. In two of these, the verses appear without music (Paris, BNF, Lat. 2772, fols. 55v-56 and Lat. 2773, fol. 24), whereas in the third, which is from the Abbey of Saint-Oyan (Jura), where it was received as a donation from the priest Mannon († 880), an anonymous hand from Benevento, some time after the original was written, added notation to it (*ibidem*, Lat. 2832, fols. 123v-124).[25] Both in this one and in the manuscript Lat. 2772, the verses of the Eritrean sybil are preceded by the fragment from the *Divinae institutiones* by Lactantius (bk. 4, chap. 18) that St. Augustine reproduces at the end of the chapter where he provides the Sybil's verses. According to both writers, the fragment in question may include another of her prophecies, this particular one about the passion and death of Jesus Christ.

The main novelty in the version of the sybilline verses in the St. Martial manuscript, when it is compared to the version from Saint-Oyan, lies in the manner of their reproduction. In the latter, they appear exactly like the versions by St. Augustine or Bede, except for the neumes, but in the St. Martial manuscript the verses are turned into a composition with a refrain, as in the *Audi tellus*. The first line functions as a refrain, "Iudicii signum: tellus sudore madescet", which alternates with the thirteen stanzas that result from the grouping into pairs of the following twenty-six lines. Moreover, the adiastematic notation in both versions makes it difficult to compare them musically, but we can still deduce from this that they are quite similar and that the same melodic design in all of the verses is repeated, the details of which vary depending on the number of syllables in each line.

The copies of the Sybil's verses that are contained in four manuscripts from Spain are also from a very early period. Two of these belonged to the Benedictine Monastery of Santa María de Ripoll (Girona), founded in 879, which soon became an important cultural center. The oldest of these manuscripts is an original scientific and sacred miscellany from the 10th century, which includes the lines of the *Iudicii signum* under the rubric: "Metrum iretream sibille mirifice

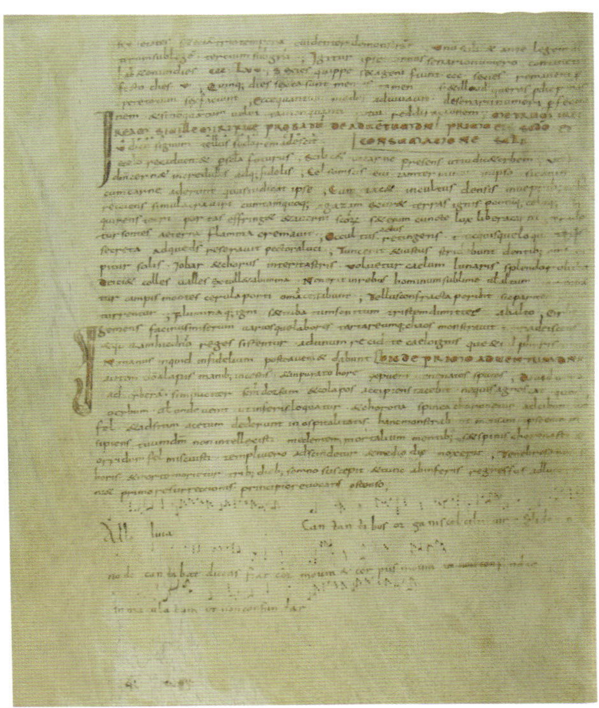

1. Miscellaneous codex. Barcelona, ACA, Ripoll 106, 10th century *in.*, fol. 92v

probatuerit de adventum Domini primo et secundo et consumatione saeculi" ("Verses of the sybil Eritrea that prove the first and second coming of the Lord and the end of the world") (Barcelona, ACA, Ripoll 106, fol. 92v).

The lines are horizontally copied, one after the other. They are followed on the same folio by Lactantius's fragment on the passion, death and resurrection of Christ, which precedes the Sybil's verses in the manuscripts Lat. 2772 and Lat. 2832 in the Bibliothèque Nationale de France. In the space left empty at the bottom, a later hand, perhaps in the 11th century, added the antiphon *Alleluia. Cantantibus organis* with its corresponding Catalonian adiastematic neumes; in passing, this scribe took advantage of the opportunity to add music to the first line of the Sybil's poem; fourteen neumes altogether, one per syllable. Perhaps the limited amount of space left between lines explains why the unknown copyist interrupted his work and left the rest of the poem without music.

The second Ripoll manuscript that reproduces the Sybil's verses is from the 10th and 11th centuries and includes a collection of sermons by the Church Fathers and several letters by Pope Urban II. Bede's *Sibyllinorum verborum interpretatio* appears among the sermons, with the verses of the *Iudicii signum* (Barcelona, ACA, Ripoll 151, fol. 37), which are followed by a sermon on the Nativity of the Virgin Mary.

If Bede's text was known from a very early period onwards in the territory of the former Marca Hispanica, today Catalonia, this is equally the case with the *Sermo de symbolo*. This is suggested by a miscellaneous Tarragona codex from circa 800, in which the Sybil's verses are accompanied by the paragraph that precedes them in the sermon by the Bishop of Carthage (Paris, BNF, Lat. 8093, fols. 35v-36).

Unlike the three previous ones, the fourth manuscript in the Hispanic group that reproduces the *Iudicii signum* is from Castile. This is a *Homiliarium* copied by Florentius at the monastery—now the chapel—of San Baudelio de Berlanga (Burgos), one of the jewels of Mozarabic art (Córdoba, AC, ms. 1); Florentius finished the copy in 953, when he was 35 years old. In the manuscript, the verses form part of the *Sermo de symbolo*, which begins in the eleventh chapter with the words "Vos inquam convenio"; continues with the testimony of the prophets and gentiles until it reaches the Sybil's text, and ends, just as in most later liturgical manuscripts, with the following paragraph, which abbreviates the end of Chapter 16, after the lines of the *Iudicii* and the beginning of Chapter 17 of the aforementioned sermon:

> Haec de Christi nativitate, passione et resurrectione, atque secundo eius adventu ita dicta sunt, ut si quis in graeco capita horum versuum discernere voluerit, inveniat Ιησουζ Χρειστοζ Θεου Υιοζ Σωτηρ. Quod

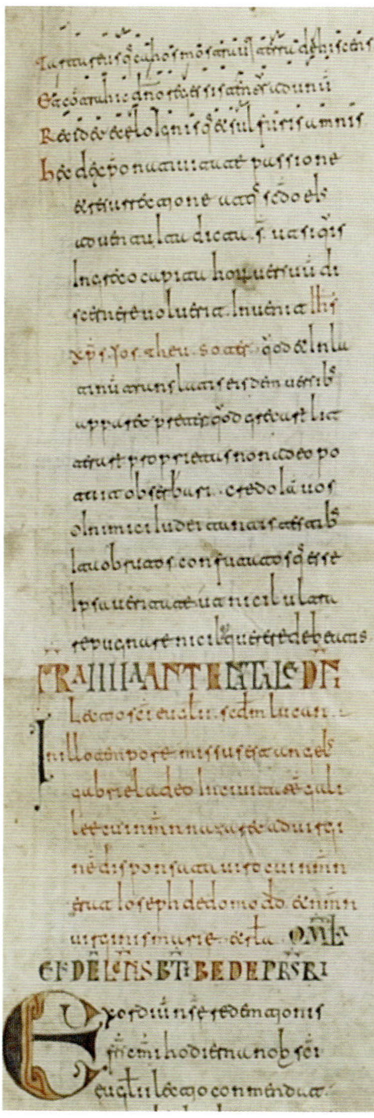

2. Homiliary. Córdoba, AC, ms. 1, 10th century *med.*, fol. 327v

et in latinum translatis eisdem versibus apparet, praeter quod graecarum litterarum propietas non adeo potuit observari. Credo iam vos, o inimici iudaei, tantis testibus ita obrutos confutatosque esse, ipsa veritate ut nihil ultra repugnare, nihil quaerere debeatis.[26]

In the Berlanga manuscript the lesson from the Gospels for the "III Feria ante natale Domini" follows after these words. It can also be read in the Tarragona miscellany after the Sybil's verse.

In the Burgos codex the sybilline verses have adiastematic Aquitainian notation, which was added once the copy of the lyric was already finished; because of the small amount of space available between lines, the melodic inflexion in the composition has regrettably been altered.

In the Berlanga and the Ripoll manuscripts, notation was added to some or all of the Sybil's verses after they were copied. We can deduce that until then they did not include music, and as a result, the melody that accompanies them, which is perhaps the work of a Benedictine monk, may be no earlier than the 9th century *ex.* or 10th century *in.*

If the time and place when the *Iudicii signum* was set to music are unknown, we also do not know when the *Sermo de symbolo* became part of the liturgy either, which it did to a greater extent than the Bede's sermon did, although both events may correspond. Of course the *Sermo,* with its prophetic testimony about the coming of Christ and the Sybil's regarding the second coming, was just right for Advent, a period of penitence considered in the Roman rite to be a preparation for Christmas and for the second coming of Christ before the Last Judgment.[27]

No matter how, an *Ordo romanus* from before 1143 says in allusion to the papal liturgy for Christmas: "In vigilia Natalis Domini ad Matutinum [...] Quarta lectio sermo sancti Augustini *Vos inquam convenio, o iudaei,* in quarta cantantur sibyllini versus *Iudicii signum: tellus sudore madescet"* (*PL LXXVIII:* 1031). This means that in the second third of the 12th century the *Sermo de symbolo*, with the Sybil's verses being sung, had become one of the

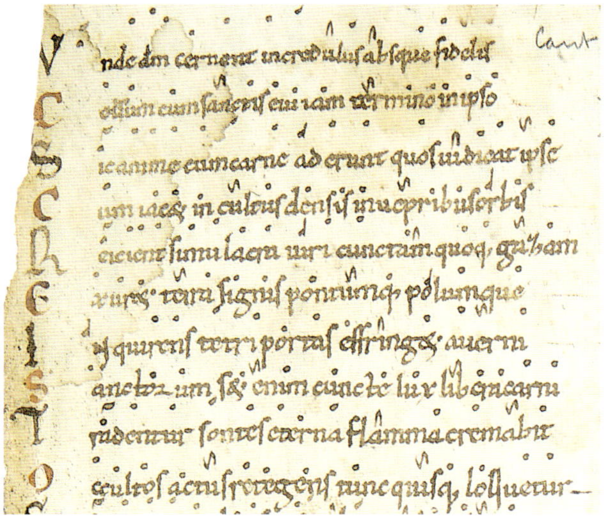

3. Breviary. Vic, ABEV, ms. Frag. XI/1, 11th century *med.*

lessons for Christmas matins in the Pope's chapel, which with slight variations began to become the standard practice at this time. This is proved by the fact that from the 11th century onwards, several lectionaries and books of homilies begin to appear that included the *Sermo de symbolo* either right from the start—"Inter presuras"—, starting from the "Vos, inquam" (chap. 11), or just as a small fragment—"Quid Sibylla [...] quaerere debeatis" (chaps. 16 and 17)—, with the Sybil's verses with or without music, in the liturgy of Christmas matins once Advent was over.[28] In this sense the Berlanga book of homilies represents a precedent for this practice, as does a lectionary from Compiègne, which is also from the 10th century (Paris, BNF, Lat. 16819), in which the sybilline verses are copied without music as part of the Bishop of Carthage's sermon.[29] Of course, neither of the two points out their exact position in the liturgy, nor do the 11th century manuscripts that transmit the sermon.

Among the latter, at least four are of Hispanic origin: a Catalonian book of lessons (Paris, BNF, Lat. 5302, fols. 80-82v); another from Cathedral of Sigüenza (AC, Cod. 20, fols. 28v-35v); a book of homilies written in Spain in the 11th century in Visigoth minuscule, which might have belonged to a Benedictine monastery (Sheffield, Collection of the Guild of St. George, Galleries and Museum Trust, ms. 31, fols. 11v-13. Olim Ruskin Museum 7),[30] and a separate folio from a very old breviary from Cathedral of Vic (ABEV, ms. Frag. XI/1).

Except on the separate folio with Catalonian neumes, in the other three manuscripts the verses of the Eritrean Sybil have Aquitainian notation; in the Sigüenza manuscript the neumes take a drypoint line as a reference, which is not found in the others. The latter manuscript is the only one to show where the sermon was placed; it served as the sixth lesson at Christmas matins in the Castilian cathedral.

An important novelty in these versions of the 11th century *Iudicii signum* compared with other previous ones is that in three of them the sentence "Audite quid dixerit" that precedes the Sybil's verses is set to music (the beginning of the Vic version has not survived). This is a characteristic that they share with a lectionary from circa 1000, where the *Sermo de symbolo* appears as the sixth lesson in the aforementioned matins (Paris, BNF, Lat. 5304, fols. 109v-113);[31] the notation of the verses in this case is still Aquitainian and adiastematic. On the other hand, in a book of homilies from the same period from the Benedictine Abbey of Montecassino, the introduction of the sybilline verses has no music; its Beneventan notation, lacking lines or clef, and the corresponding sermon appear as the last lesson in the second Christmas nocturn (Montecassino 99, fols. 97-99).[32] Among the 11th century manuscripts that copy Quodvultdeus's sermon with the Sybil's verses without music, we can mention a *Lectionarium officii ad usum ecclesiae Arelatensis*, which nevertheless leaves enough room so that notation can be added (Paris, BNF, Lat. 793),[33] and a monastic book of homilies (*ibidem,* Lat. 1646).

The musical transcription of the verses of the *Iudicii signum* in the manuscripts from Sheffield, Vic and Paris (Lat. 5304) proves to be confusing, because the neumes that accompany them are copied with little, insufficient, or non accuracy at all as far as their relative height is concerned. In fact, only the versions of manuscripts Lat. 5302, whose beginning I provide below, and Abbey of Montecassino 99 can be transcribed with any significant

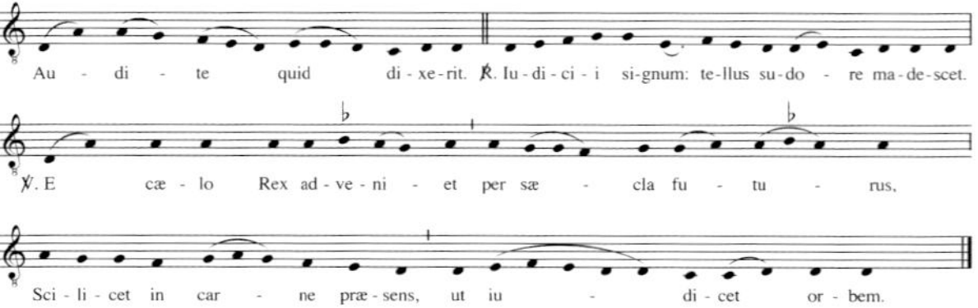

degree of reliability. All this can be extended with reservations to the Sigüenza version, because of a odd error by the copyist. The latter, instead of using the same music for lines 4-5 (stanza III), 6-7 (stanza IV), and so on, as for lines 2-3 (stanza I), as usually happens, applies the music of the refrain to the fourth line, the music that should be in the fourth to the fifth, and so on, so that the entire composition is spoiled, because the music of the refrain is made to alternate with the music in the stanzas without a parallel alternation in the text, the incipit of which—*Iudicii*—is only repeated at the end of the last line, as happens in the Vic version.[34] It is obvious that whoever added music to the version of the Sigüenza Sybil was utterly unfamiliar with the composition, at least in the version that prevailed. From this result, one can assume that its original was similar to the one in the miscellany from the 9th-10th centuries from St. Martial of Limoges, which is the only version that we know of prior to the 12th century in which the text and music of the stanzas of the *Iudicii signum* alternate with the refrain.

A final version of the 11th century Sybil´s verses comes from the Monastery of St. Martial in Limoges or from another in its area. It belongs to the oldest version set to music of a performance in the making, known as *Ordo Prophetarum*—Procession of the prophets—(Paris, BNF, Lat. 1139, fols. 55v-58), which resulted first from featuring and later from dramatising all those characters who in the *Sermo de symbolo* provide their testimony on the coming of the Messiah.[35] Although its study goes beyond the limits of these pages, it is essential to stress that it existed at least from the end of the 11th century—the folios of the manuscript Lat. 1139 that include the *Ordo* are dated 1096/9, which is decisive proof that some verses of those lacking any clear evidence of recitation or singing by anyone other than the reader of the sermon until that time, were then performed by one or more soloists. The aforementioned stanzas of the *Iudicii signum* of the manuscript Lat. 1154 are halfway between the singing or reciting of the Sybil´s verses and the Procession of the prophets of Limoges. Their alternating refrain hints at the involvement of a second soloist or a choir, just as in the hypothetical Sigüenza's original, a kind of performance which can perhaps be extended to the Vic version.

The tradition of including the *Sermo de symbolo* with the Sybil´s verses set to music—whether they formed part of an *Ordo Prophetarum* or not—in the Christmas Eve liturgy took root both in France, Spain and Italy from the 12th century onwards, judging by the number of liturgical manuscripts—especially lectionaries and homilaries—that include it from these three Latin countries, which do not always show its place in the liturgy, at least at first. There is also no evidence about their dramatisation; in fact, it is quite the opposite, because these verses seem to have been performed by one or more soloists and a choir, before they were translated or, to be more precise, adapted to romance languages. This is something we did not know was happening before the 14th century *med.-ex.,* at a time when the aforementioned tradition had begun to decline almost everywhere except in the ecclesiastical provinces further to the south and west of Europe, which are all of those in the Iberian Peninsula and the province of Narbonne. However, it cannot be ruled out that it had already been translated in the 13th century, at the same time as the versions of the fifteen signs of the Last Judgment that began to spread to a great many European countries; an example of which is the one called *Of the signs that will appear before the Judgment,* by Gonzalo de Berceo (1195?-1274?).[36]

The first version of the sybilline verses that we know was translated from Latin is in Occitan, and it is copied in the margins of the folios that include the *Iudicii signum* with music, as a part of the *Sermo de symbolo*, in a 12th century *ex.* lectionary from the Abbey of Aniane (Montpellier: Archives de l'Hérault, ms. 58 H 6, fols. 51v-52v).[37] This is followed by several versions in Catalan, the first of which, included in the *Constitutiones synodales ecclesiae barchinonensis* from 1415, also lacks music (Barcelona, ACA, ms. s. n. fol. 75),[38] and others in Spanish of which the oldest must be that from a Toledan ceremonial from 1585 (New York, Hispanic Society, ms. HC: 380/897), which includes the use of the cathedral from the previous century.[39] Although the sybilline verses were still performed in Portugal until the 20th century *med.,*[40] we are not aware of any version translated or adapted into Portuguese.

We know that most of the versions in romance languages that have been preserved with music and others that we have news of, but which have not survived, were performed by a boy—in exceptional circumstances by a girl—who was dressed up as a Sybil.[41] These are the versions that match what has traditionally been known as the *Song of the Sybil.* Perhaps this form is later than the Council of Trent, which, by eliminating the *Sermo de symbolo* from the readings during Christmas matins, ended an age-old tradition. The tradition survived in Toledo until at least the 18th century *ex.* for reasons which have still not been explained, and also in the Cathedral of Palma de Majorca, modelled on this Toledan practice and even with a similar choreography, despite the fact that its council was one of the first to take the initiative of banning the song´s performance once the Council of Trent had been held.[42] What happened in Majorca from that moment on and its causes would require another essay in itself.

Abbreviations

AH = *Analecta hymnica medii aevi*
LU = *Liber Usualis*
PG = *Patrologia Graeca*
PL = *Patrologia Latina*

Notes

[1] According to Francisco Asenjo Barbieri. "El Canto de la Sibila". *Ilustración Musical Hispano-Americana* 1, no. 7 (1888): 50-51, the Sybil continued to be *done* in Cathedral of Toledo throughout the 18th century and then fell into disuse, despite the effort one of its deans made to restore it in the 19th century *med.*

[2] In this regard, we only need to recall the references to the *Dies irae* that appear in works such as the *Symphonie fantastique* by Hector Berlioz, Camille Saint-Saëns' *Dance macabre,* or Gustav Mahler's *2nd Resurrection Symphony.*

[3] Herbert Newel Bate. *The Sibylline Oracles. Books III-V.* London, New York: Society for Promoting Christian Knowledge, 1918, 12-13.

[4] "The sun will be perpetually darkened, so that there will scarcely any distinction between the night and the day. The moon will now fail; not for three hours only, but overspread with perpetual blood, will go through extraordinary movements, so that it will not be easy for man to

ascertain the courses of the heavenly bodies or the system of the times; for there will either be summer in the winter or winter in the summer. The year will be shortened and the month diminished, and the day contracted into a short space. And stars shall fall in great numbers, so that all the heavens will appear dark without any lights. The loftiest mountains also will fall and be leveled with the plains; the sea will be rendered un-navigable. And that nothing may be wanting to the evils of men and the Earth, the trumpet shall be heard from heaven, which the Sybil foretells in this manner: 'The trumpet from heaven shall its wailing voice´. And then all shall tremble and quake at that mournful sound."

[5] Johannes Geffaken. *Die Oracula Sibyllina*. Leipzig: J. C. Hinrichs, 1902, 153-157.

[6] *PG* 20: 1285-1290.

[7] For the meaning of the number twenty-seven, see especially, Heinz Meyer and Rudolf Suntrup. *Lexikon der mittelalterlichen Zahlenbedeutungen*. Munich: Institut für Frühmittelalterforschung, 1987, 687-689 (Münstersche Mittelalter-Schriften: 56). The authors of the *Lexikon* note that the unique feature of the so-called *tertia progressio* ($3^3 = 27$) "in a mathematical sense is the geometrical relationship to it of a solid three-dimensional body".

[8] Judgment shall moisten the Earth with the sweat of its standard. / Ever enduring, behold the King shall come through the ages, / Sent to be here in the flesh and Judge at the last of the world, / O God, the believing and faithless alike shall behold you, / Uplifted with saints, when at last the ages are ended, / Seated before him are souls in the flesh for his judgment. / Hid in thick vapors, the while desolate lies the earth; / Rejected by men are the idols and long hidden treasures; / Earth is consumed by the fire and it searches the ocean and heaven / Issuing forth, it destroys the terrible portals of hell. / Saints in their body and souls, freedom and light shall inherit, / and those who are guilty shall burn in fire and brimstone forever. / Occult actions revealing, each one shall publish his secrets, Secrets of every man's heart God shall reveal in the light. / Then shall be weeping and wailing, yea, and gnashing of teeth. / Eclipsed is the sun and silenced the stars in their chorus; / Over and gone is the splendor of moonlight, melted the heaven; / Uplifted by him are the valleys and cast down the mountains. / Utterly gone among men are distinctions of lofty and lowly. / Into the plains rush the hills, the skies and oceans are mingled / Oh, what an end of all things! Earth broken in pieces shall perish; / Swelling together at once shall the waters and flames flow in rivers. / Sounding the Archangel's trumpet shall peal down from heaven / Over the wicked who groan in their guilt and manifold sorrows / Trembling, the earth shall be opened, revealing chaos and hell. / Every King before God shall stand on that day to be judged. / Rivers of fire and brimstone shall fall from the heavens.

[9] *PL XLII:* 1117-1130.

[10] J. Conington, and H. Nettleship, eds. *The Works of Virgil*. 2nd ed. Hildesheim, New York, 1979. Vol. 1: 55 (footnotes to *Eclogue IV's* edition).

[11] "Let us proclaim what the Sybil prophesized about Christ, so that the foreheads of the Jews and of the pagans shall be struck by a stone and so that all the enemies of Christ, just like Goliath, shall be cut down by his sword. Listen to what she said."

[12] *PL XC:* 1181-1186.

[13] "And with the fall of the Roman Empire, the Antichrist shall appear and sit in the house of the Lord in Jerusalem [...]. Then a great persecution shall take place, as has never been seen before and shall never be seen again. The Lord shall shorten those days for the sake of the chosen ones and the Archangel Michael shall kill the Antichrist on the Mount of Olives, by the Lord's grace."

[14] As Carolina Michaëlis notes. See "Quindecim Signa ante Judicium". *Archiv für das Studium der neueren Sprachen und Literaturen* 46 (1870): 54-55, which then reproduces the versions transcribed by Peter Comestor and Thomas Aquinas.

[15] *PL CXLV:* 885-888.

[16] The sign on the first day shall say: All the seas will rise fifteen cubits above the high mountains on the surface of the earth, and remain like walls of water that do not flow. / The sign on the second day: All the waters shall be plunged into the depths, so that scarcely will they be visible to the human eye. / The sign on the third day: All the seas will be restored to their original condition, just as they were created in the beginning. / The sign on the fourth day: All the great fishes and everything that moves in the sea will gather together and raising their heads above the sea, roar at one another contentiously, and men will not know what they are screaming or planning; only God will know, by whose action everything lives. / The sign on the fifth day: All the birds of the air will gather together in the fields, each species in its own way, wailing to one another, with neither bite nor sup, for fear of the coming of the Judgment. / The sign on the sixth day: Rivers of fire will arise towards the firmament rushing together from the west to the east. / The sign on the seventh day: All the stars both planets and fixed will throw out fiery tales like comets onto the Earth and its inhabitants. / The sign on the

eighth: There will be a great earthquake, so that all men and animals will be laid low. / The sign on the ninth: All stones, little and great, will be split into four parts, dashing against one another, and no man shall be able to recognize that sound, only God. / The sign on the tenth: All the trees in the forests and plants will be bedewed as it were with blood. / The sign on the eleventh: All the mountains and hills and buildings made by man will be reduced to dust. / The sign on the twelfth: All the animals on the earth will come from forest and mountain to the fields, roaring and bellowing, without bite nor sup. / The sign on the thirteenth: All graves from east to west will open to allow the bodies to rise again, until the hour of Judgment. / The sign on the fourteenth: All men will leave their abode, neither understanding nor speaking, but rushing hither and thither like madmen. / The sign on the fifteenth: All the living will die, to rise again with those who died long before.

[17] On the meaning of the number fifteen, see Heinz Meyer and Rudolf Suntrup. Op. cit., 654-658.

[18] The two benchmark studies on the subject of millenarianism are by Georges Duby. *L'An mil.* Paris: Gallimard/Julliard, 1967, and Henri Focillon. *L'An mil.* Paris: Colin, 1952. There is a compilation of eschatological medieval writings in Claude Carozzi and Huguette Taviani-Carozzi. *La fin des temps. Terreurs et prophéties au Moyen Âge.* Paris: Flammarion, 1999.

[19] For the description of the manuscript, Paris, BNF, Lat. 1154 and its dating, see Jacques Chailley. *L'école musicale de Saint Martial de Limoges jusqu'à la fin du XIe siècle.* Paris: Les Livres Essentiels, 1960, 73-78.

[20] Edition of the lyric and facsimile in Paulin Blanc. "Nouvelle Prose sur le Dernier Jour, composée, avec le Chant noté, vers l'An Mille, et publié pour la première fois d'après un antique manuscrit de l'Abbaye d'Aniane". *Mémoires de la Société Archéologique de Montpellier.* Montpellier: Société Archéologique de Montpellier, 1841. Vol. 2: 451-509. A musical edition is in *AH XLIX:* 778.

[21] Musical transcription of the verses of the *Audi tellus*, according to the version in the *Las Huelgas* Codex, in Higini Anglès. *El códex musical de Las Huelgas.* Barcelona: Institut d'Estudis Catalans, 1931. Vol. 3: 381-382, no. 161, which reproduces the Karlsruhe version in facsimile (vol. 1: 349); Gordon A. Anderson. "The Las Huelgas Manuscript". *Corpus Mensurabilis Musicae* 79, vol. 2 (1982): 115, no. 84; and Juan Carlos Asensio and Josemi Lorenzo. *El códice de las Huelgas.* Madrid: Alpuerto, 2001, 526-527, no. 161.

[22] For the edition with the text of this prose and its variants, see *AH XLIX:* 779.

[23] Verses on the Day of Judgment: I. Those who are redeemed by death and freed by the Cross, thanks to the precious blood of the Son of God, lift up your hearts and desire Jesus. II. Fear the day when Christ, lord of the heavens, resplendent in virtue and dazzling, comes to judge the world and prepare for the kingdom of the saints. III. When the celestial ark opens, the shining face of Jesus Christ will gleam in the East. The entire universe will be revealed. The saints will come to meet the pious Redeemer. IV. When the heavenly bodies open up, the trumpets will sound until the ends of the earth; and the holy archangels of God will be heard and the chosen ones will gather together. V. Then at a shout from the great King, all the dead will rise again. Each will receive the punishment they deserve not only for their wicked actions but also for words taken in vain. VI. All the wheels of the world will start to burn at the same time and the raging flames will reduce everything to ashes. The sky will fold up like a book and the firmament will fall: the end of the world will come. VII. Day of wrath! That day! Day of mist and darkness! Day of trumpets and clamour! Day of suffering and trembling on which the full weight of the darkness shall fall on sinners! VIII. What fear will there be then, when the irate king comes and hell will appear that will gobble up the godless. Brimstone, fire and worms shall torment sinners. IX. What will the wicked say when the very saints tremble before the glorious majesty of Jesus Christ, the Son of God. If the just shall manage to escape, the godless shall appear there. X. There will be nowhere to escape to nor to ask for indulgence; it will be a time of collapse and bitter constriction, where those who are worthy of punishment shall be tormented by the accusatory mind. XI. Take pity on us then, Jesus Christ, savior of the world, at one with the Father and the Holy Ghost, who we worship as the one true God, savior of the world. Amen.

[24] Unhappy about the reference to the Sybil in the third line of the *Dies irae*, the Jansenists in the 18th century suggested changing it to another: "Crucis expandens vexilla" ("unfurling the standards of the cross"); a suggestion that fortunately came to nothing. A brief historical vision of this composition is in Robin Gregory, "Dies irae". *Music & Letters* 34 (1953): 133-139.

[25] According to Solange Corbin. "Le *cantus sibyllae:* origine et premiers textes". *Revue de Musicologie* 31 (1952): 5; and Nicole Sevestre. "La tradition mélodique du *Cantus sibyllae*". Vienna: K. M. Halosar, 1982, 269-280 (Wiener Arbeiten zur germanischen Altertumskunde und Philologie: 20), that includes the version of the Paris, BNF, Lat. 1154 and Lat. 2832 manuscripts with neumes.

[26] "These things have been said about the Nativity, Passion and Resurrection of Christ, as well as about his second coming. If anyone wishes to know the initials of those lines in Greek, they will find that they are 'Iesus Christus Dei Filius Salvador', translated into Latin, in which case the property of the Greek letters cannot be totally preserved. I think that you, Jewish enemies, have been overwhelmed and refuted by so much evidence that you should not continue to reject or search for the truth itself."

[27] Pamela Sheingorn. "For God is such a Doomsman: Origins and Development of the Theme of Last Judgement". In David M. Bevington, ed. *Homo, Memento Finis: The Iconography of Just Judgment In Medieval Art and Drama*. Kalamazoo: Western Michigan University, Medieval Institute, 1985, 29.

[28] Although the coincidence could be by chance, the well-known Christmas sequence, *Laetabundus*, which appeared on French soil in the 11th century, according to Friedrich Gennrich—"Internationale mittelalterliche Melodien". *Zeitschrift für Musikwissenschaft* 11 (1929): 273—, refers to the *sibyllinis versibus* in one of its verses. Transcription in *ibidem,* 274-278.

[29] Solange Corbin. Op. cit., 5-6.

[30] For the description of this manuscript, see Louis Brou. "Un nouvel homiliare en écriture wisigothique: le codex Sheffield, Ruskin Museum 7". *Hispania Sacra* 2, no. 3 (1949): 147-191.

[31] Facsimile edition of fol. 112v, with the beginning of the Sybil, in Higini Anglés. *La música a Catalunya fins al segle XIII*. Barcelona: Institut d'Estudis Catalans, Biblioteca de Cataluña, 1935, fig. 76.

[32] Transcription of the version of the *Iudicii signum* according to Cod. 99 from Montecassino in Agostino Latil. "Spigolatura Cassinesi: Il Canto della Sibilla". *Rassegna Gregoriana* 2 (1903): 530-531.

[33] According to Solange Corbin. Op. cit., 6-7.

[34] Transcription of the version of the *Iudicii signum* according to the Sigüenza codex in Maricarmen Gómez. *El Canto de la Sibila*. Madrid: Alpuerto, 1996-1997. Vol. 1: 51-54, no. 1. Oddly enough, the same mistake in the Sigüenza copy is repeated in a 12th century tropary from Montecassino, which stresses that the verses of the *Iudicii* were performed in this Benedictine abbey in the second nocturn of Christmas matins (Rome: Bibl. Apostolica Vaticana, Urb. Lat. 602, fols. 96v-99v). Given that the quality of the copy of the cassinese tropary, with Beneventan neumes, is excellent, it is difficult to explain the mistake, especially bearing in mind the standard version of the 11th century book of homilies that belonged to the Abbey. Facsimile of fols. 96v-97 in Higini Anglès. *La música a Catalunya...* Op. cit., fig. 80.

[35] For the description of the manuscript Lat. 1139, see Guy de Poerck. "Le Ms Paris, B. N., lat. 1139. Étude codicologique d'un recueil factice de pièces paraliturgiques". *Scriptorium* 23 (1969): 298-312. A transcription of the *Ordo Prophetarum* based on this same manuscript is in Charles-Edmond-Henri de Coussemaker. *Drames liturgiques du Moyen Âge*. Rennes: Vatar, 1860, 11-15, no. 2.

[36] Critical edition in Gonzalo de Berceo. *Signos que aparecerán antes del Juicio final. Duelo de la Virgen. Martirio de San Lorenzo.* Madrid: Castalia, 1980, 127-157. It can be pointed out in this respect that one of the *Cantigas de Santa María* by Alfonso X the Wise (1221-1284), *Madre de Deus*, is merely a personal version of the *Iudicii signum*, as a *contrafactum* in Galician-Portuguese, which ended the first collection of Alfonsine *Cantigas.* For the transcription of this canticle, see, among others: Maricarmen Gómez. Op. cit. Vol. 1: 63 and 64, no. 4A/B.

[37] For the description of this Aniane lectionary and the transcription of the Sybil´s verses in Occitan, see Félix Raugel. "Le chant de la Sibylle d'après un manuscrit du XIIIe siècle conservé aux archives de l'Hérault". In *Actes du Congrès d'Histoire de l'Art. Paris 26 Septembre-5 Octobre 1921.* Paris, 1923-1924. Vol. 3: 774-783.

[38] For the description of the sources that include the verses with music of the *Iudicii signum* in Catalan *(Al jorn del judici)* and its transcription, see Maricarmen Gómez. Op. cit. Vol. 2: 91-103, nos. 7-11: and the related commentaries.

[39] Transcription in *ibidem.* Vol. 1: 71-72, no. 6.

[40] According to Solange Corbin. *Essai sur la musique religieuse portugaise au Moyen Âge (1199-1385).* Paris: Les Belles Lettres, 1952, 288-289, who claims that when the book was written, the tradition of performing the Sybil´s verses still survived at Cathedral of Braga.

[41] In the convent of nuns of the Concepción in Pollença, which moved in 1577 to the town of Palma de Majorca—it is the place of provenance of a choir book with the oldest copy of the Sybil´s verses set to music in Catalan that has survived on the island of Majorca (Palma de Majorca, Museo Diocesano, ms. s. n., fols. 84v-86v)—, the performer was a *bona cantora*. On this point and for the description of the Palma manuscript, see Maricarmen Gómez. "Una fuente desatendida con repertorio sacro mensural de fines del medioevo: el cantoral del convento de la Concepción de Palma de Mallorca [E-Pm]". *Nassarre* 14 (1998): 333-372.

[42] The chapter certificate that orders "quod non fiat Sibilla in matutinis Nativitatis" is dated 5 December 1572.

Bibliography

ANDERSON, Gordon Athol. "The Las Huelgas Manuscript". *Corpus Mensurabilis Musicae* 79, vol. 2 (1982).

ANGLÈS, Higini. *El códex musical de Las Huelgas*. Barcelona: Institut d'Estudis Catalans, Biblioteca de Cataluña, 1931.

—. *La música a Catalunya fins al segle XIII*. Barcelona: Institut d'Estudis Catalans, 1935.

ASENSIO, Juan Carlos, and Josemi LORENZO. *El códice de las Huelgas*. Madrid: Alpuerto, 2001.

BARBIERI, Francisco Asenjo. "El canto de la Sibila". *Ilustración Musical Hispano-Americana* 1, no. 7 (1888): 50-51.

BATE, Herbert Newell. *The Sibylline Oracles. Books III-V.* London, New York: Society for Promoting Christian Knowledge, 1918.

BERCEO, Gonzalo de. *Signos que aparecerán antes del Juicio final. Duelo de la Virgen. Martirio de San Lorenzo.* Madrid: Castalia, 1980.

BLANC, Paulin. "Nouvelle Prose sur le Dernier Jour, Composée, avec le Chant noté, vers l'An Mille, et publié pour la première fois d'après un antique manuscrit de l'Abbaye d'Aniane". *Mémoires de la Société Archéologique de Montpellier.* Montpellier: Societé Archéologique de Montpellier, 1841. Vol. 2: 451-509

BROU, Louis. "Un nouvel homiliare en écriture wisigothique: the Sheffield codex, `Ruskin Museum´ 7". *Hispania Sacra* 2, no. 3 (1949): 147-191.

CAROZZI, Claude, and Huguette TAVIANNI-CAROZZI. *La fin des temps. Terreurs et prophéties au Moyen Âge*. Paris: Flammarion, 1999.

CHAILLEY, Jacques. *L'école musicale de Saint Martial de Limoges jusqu'à la fin du XIe siècle*. Paris: Les Livres Essentiels, 1960.

CORBIN, Solange. "Le *cantus sibyllae:* origine et premiers textes". *Revue de Musicologie* 31 (1952a): 1-10.

—. *Essai sur la musique religieuse portugaise au Moyen Âge (1199-1385).* Paris: Les Belles Lettres, 1952b.

COUSSEMAKER, Charles-Edmond-Henri de. *Drames liturgiques du Moyen Âge*. Rennes: Vatar, 1860.

DUBY, Georges. *L'An mil*. Paris: Gallimard/Julliard, 1967.

FOCILLON, Henri. *L'An mil*. Paris: Colin, 1952.

GEFFAKEN, Johannes. *Die Oracula Sibyllina*. Leipzig: J. C. Hinrichs, 1902.

GENNRICH, Friedrich. "Internationale mittelalterliche Melodien". *Zeitschrift für Musikwissenschaft* 11 (1929): 259-296, 321-348.

GÓMEZ, Maricarmen. *El Canto de la Sibila*. Madrid: Alpuerto, 1996-1997.

—. "Una fuente desatendida con repertorio sacro mensural de fines del medioevo: el cantoral del convento de la Concepción de Palma de Mallorca [E-Pm]". *Nassarre* 14 (1998): 333-372.

GREGORY, Robin. "Dies irae". *Music & Letters* 34 (1953): 133-139.

LATIL, Agostino. "Spigolatura Cassinesi: Il Canto della Sibilla". *Rassegna Gregoriana* 2 (1903): 529-534.

MEYER, Heinz, and Rudolf SUNTRUP. *Lexikon der mittelalterlichen Zahlenbedeutungen*. Munich: Institut für Frühmittelalterforschung, 1987 (Münstersche Mittelalter-Schriften: 56).

MICHAËLIS, Carolina. "Quindecim Signa ante Judicium". *Archiv für das Studium der neueren Sprachen und Literaturen* 46 (1870): 33-60.

POERCK, Guy de. "Le Ms Paris, B. N., lat 1139. Étude codicologique d'un recueil factice de pièces paraliturgiques". *Scriptorium* 23 (1969): 298-312.

RAUGEL, Félix. "Le chant de la Sibylle d'après un manuscrit du XIIIe siècle conservé aux archives de l'Hérault". In *Actes du Congrès d'Histoire de l'Art. Paris 26 Septembre-5 Octobre 1921*. Paris, 1923-24. Vol. 3: 774-783.

SEVESTRE, Nicole. "La tradition mélodique du *Cantus sibyllae*". Vienna: K. M. Halosar, 1982, 269-283 (Wiener Arbeiten zur germanischen Altertumskunde und Philologie: 20).

SHEINGORN, Pamela. "For God is such a Doomsman: Origins and Development of the Theme of Last Judgement". In David M. Bevington, ed. *Homo, Memento Finis: The Iconography of Just Judgment In Medieval Art and Drama.* Kalamazoo: Western Michigan University, Medieval Institute, 1985, 15-58.

The *Historia* for St. Dominic of Silos in British Library, Add. ms. 30850

Barbara Haggh

The earliest *historia* of St. Dominic of Silos († 20 December 1073) is of interest for a number of reasons.[1] It was composed soon after the death of this influential abbot, who gave his name to what would become one of Spain's most significant monasteries. Thus the *historia* dates from a period of time when the Roman (Gregorian) chant was becoming established in Spain, and the regional Mozarabic (Old Hispanic) chant was actively and, by the next century, successfully suppressed.[2] (The Council of Burgos in 1080 had repercussions for Silos, although there was a French presence in Castile and León in the 1470s, and the Mozarabic Rite and script persisted in some locations into the 12th century *in.*)[3] Furthermore, the first surviving copy of the *historia* for St. Dominic is in one of the earliest complete monastic antiphoners, London, BL, Add. ms. 30850 (René-Jean Hesbert's *S* in *CAO*)[4] a manuscript written at Silos with texts in Visigothic script and with a unique notation showing the meeting of the Mozarabic and Gregorian traditions.[5] In short, an analysis of this *historia* in this manuscript allows us to observe its anonymous creator(s) at work in a remarkable time of transition.

The *historia* for the *dies natalis* of St. Dominic of Silos (celebrated on 20 December) is loosely based on the *Life* and *Miracles* of the saint. They were written by Grimald, a monk at Silos, at the request of Dom Fortunius, Dominic's successor as abbot.[6] The request is said to have come in 1073, after Dominic's death. Indeed, Dom Férotin and Vitalino Valcárcel both date Grimald's *Life* from circa 1088 to 1091.[7] This was after 1076, when Dominic's relics were translated, with King Alfonso VI's consent and in the presence of Jimeno, Bishop of Burgos († 17 March 1082), before the altar of St. Martin in the abbey's church. There a new altar for St. Dominic was built, and on 20 September 1088, the Monastery of St. Sebastian was renamed after St. Dominic and dedicated by Cardinal Richard, Abbot of St. Victor of Marseille and papal legate.[8] Thus if the *Life* dates from after 1088, the *historia* for Dominic's *natalis* must date from after 1088, by which time the Roman liturgy had been accepted at Silos.[9]

The content and structure of the *historia* for the *dies natalis* of St. Dominic of Silos as it appears in Hesbert's *S* is summarized in the Appendix to this article, which provides the text incipits of the chant, citing related texts, chant, and modern editions. First Vespers, monastic Matins, Lauds, Prime, and Second Vespers are unremarkable. But on fols. 237v and 239r-240r seven antiphons and seven responsories appear with a tonary and other chant surrounding them and are there merely listed under the rubric "De s[an]c[t]i Dominici c[on]f[essor]". The liturgical purpose of the seven antiphons and seven responsories is not clear. The texts, whose incipits are also given in the Appendix, are not historical but praise St. Dominic and are thus liturgically neutral. They may either have been exchanged with the earlier chant, used for the Octave, or sung during processions to the tomb of the saint during the Octave. The many borrowings in this series of antiphons and responsories without a specific liturgical destination by comparison with few borrowings in the *historia* for the *dies natalis*, suggest that these two groups of chant were compiled in very different circumstances.

Grimald may have composed the first *historia* as well as the *Life,* but no attribution survives in any liturgical or documentary source. The relationship between the text of the *historia* for Dominic's *dies natalis* and Grimald's *Life*, which Miguel C. Vivancos recognized, is minimal and certainly less close than in other *historia* of the time. The author summarizes the *Life,* occasionally using words that are emphasized in it but never quoting more than a phrase. As was the convention by this time, the antiphons and responsories of Vespers and Matins recall the life of the saint in chronological order: Vespers takes Dominic from birth to the priesthood, Matins through his monastic existence and to his death. Born about 1000, Dominic became a monk, spent eighteen months in solitude, and then became the grand prior of the Benedictine monastery at San Millán de la Cogolla. Exiled to Castile by the King of Navarre, Dominic eventually arrived at the Benedictine abbey originally founded in 954, then named after St. Sebastian. Dominic was installed as its abbot on 24 January 1041. At this date, the Mozarabic chant was still sung.[10] Dominic was reputed to have restored the abbey's manuscripts, *scriptorium,* and chant, so presumably the Mozarabic chant, before his death in 1073.[11]

Dominic was said to have produced many miracles—told in books two and three of the *Life*—and they are summarized and counted in the antiphons for Lauds in the *historia*. The miracles were selected carefully; those about the vices of women and gruesome illnesses or wounds were omitted. Instead, Dominic cures fifteen blind men, seven deaf and dumb men and women, and twenty persons possessed by the Devil.

The miracle story (*Life,* Book I, Chapter 10, pp. 258-260) telling of Dominic's cure of the blind Juan from Salas who visited Silos, has been the subject of discussion. It is of interest, because it provides a clue to the date of the office. According to this story, Dominic held mass in the presence of all of the monks, and when the ministers began the communion, *Gustate et videte,* the blind man recovered his sight.[12] Notice the use of the word 'communion' in the *Life.*[13] The miracle is recalled in the tenth responsory of Matins in the *historia* for St. Dominic, *Quidam cecus*, but there a context, but no rubric, is provided for the chant.[14] It is significant that the text *Gustate et videte*, from Psalm 33:9, was sung both in the Mozarabic and Gregorian liturgies from very early on. It functions as the communion for the eighth Sunday after Pentecost in the antiphoners of Rheinau, Mont Blandin, Corbie, and Senlis.[15] In the antiphoner of León, dating from 1066-1070, it appears on fol. 152r under the rubric "Ordo psallendi in Ramos palmarum ad vesperum" as the verse to the third antiphon, *Accedite ad Dominum*. Then, on fol. 154v after the Lesson for Palm Sunday, the *psallendum* follows, with "Gustate et videte" as its sixth and last verse. The Mozarabic text varies slightly from the Gregorian (in brackets): "Gustate et videte quam (not *quoniam*) suavis est dominus beatus homo (not *vir*) qui sperat in eum (not *eo*)", because it follows the Mozarabic psalter.[16]

Vivancos argued that the chant in this miracle story is Mozarabic, but repeats Férotin in stating that *Gustate* was commonly used in the Old Hispanic rite as a chant "ad accedentes". Férotin gives *ad accedentes* as the Mozarabic rubric for *Gustate*, but this rubric is not found in early Mozarabic sources, only in the 16th century *Missale mixtum* (*PL LXXXV:* 564-565) that he cites, which was a newly created compromise between the discontinued Mozarabic rite and the Roman rite.[17] According to Vivancos, because the affluence of monks and of visitors to the tomb as described in the *Life* corresponds exactly to the rubrics of the Visigothic *Liber ordinum*, this must have been be the correct context for the chant, which was therefore Visigothic.[18] Yet the chant is called a *communion* in the miracle story, which also quotes the Gregorian text of the chant. It thus seems more likely that the miracle story was deliberately written, or perhaps rewritten, to acknowledge the newly imported Gregorian chant. In its known state, the miracle story, the office, and its responsory must therefore postdate the *Reconquista.*

The texts of this early *historia* for St. Dominic have been edited several times and studied, most recently by Vivancos, but the chant and its notation have received little attention and are only accessible in the black and white facsimile of the antiphoner of Silos.[19] In fact, other sources not considered here reveal the existence of a different, later office and of several sets of mass propers and numerous hymns.[20] A recent office for the saint that was in use at the Monastery of Silos in 1949 was composed by Dom Pothier from the neumed manuscripts of the abbey.[21]

The earliest source for the office of St. Dominic of Silos and the only source to be considered here, is the antiphoner London, BL, Add. ms. 30850. Its main book block was dated 1081-1088 by Ismael Fernández de la Cuesta (see illustrations 1 and 2).[22] On preceding folios a scribe added the office of the Dedication of the Church. At the end of the manuscript, a scribe added offices for St. Dominic, Sts. John and Paul, St. Mary Magdalene, St. Germain of Auxerre, St. Bartholomew, St. Hippolytus, and St. Thomas, Apostle. A tonary follows, which includes chant from the offices for St. Martin, St. Mary Magdalene, and St. Millan de la Cogolla. Intermingled one finds seven antiphons and seven responsories for St. Dominic, nearly all of which Hesbert passed over. According to Fernández de la Cuesta, the added material dates from before 1116.

The remarkable features of this manuscript are its Visigothic script and neumes, disproportionate redundancy when it is compared with contempora neous antiphoners, the inclusion of some Mozarabic chant, the incorrect placement of the office of St. Andrew at 22 November (as in the Compiègne antiphonary), and the inclusion of several significative letters and episemas. Psalm tone intonations and *differentiae* appear throughout most of the manuscript

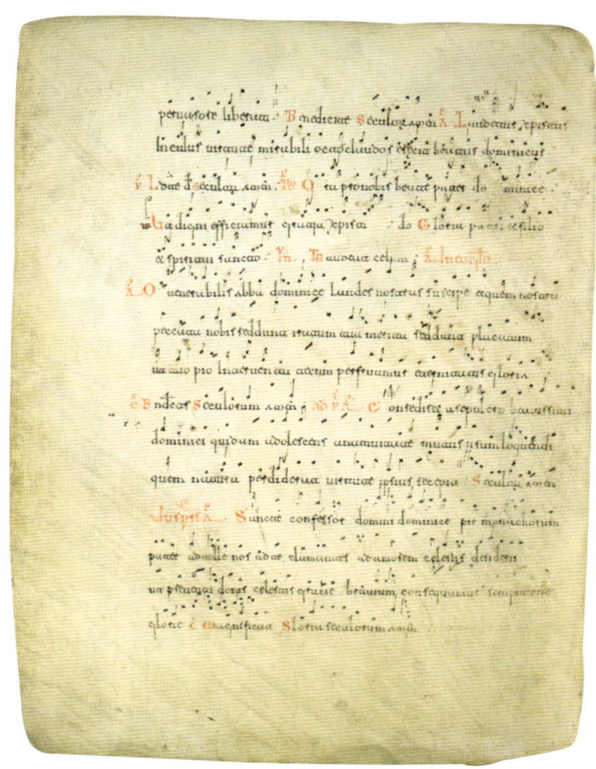

2. Antiphoner. London, BL, Add. ms. 30850, 11th century *ex.*, fol. 226v. Antiphons: *Ora pro nobis, O venerabilis abba Dominice, Con* (sic) *rediret a sepulcro* and *Sancte confessor domini Dominice*

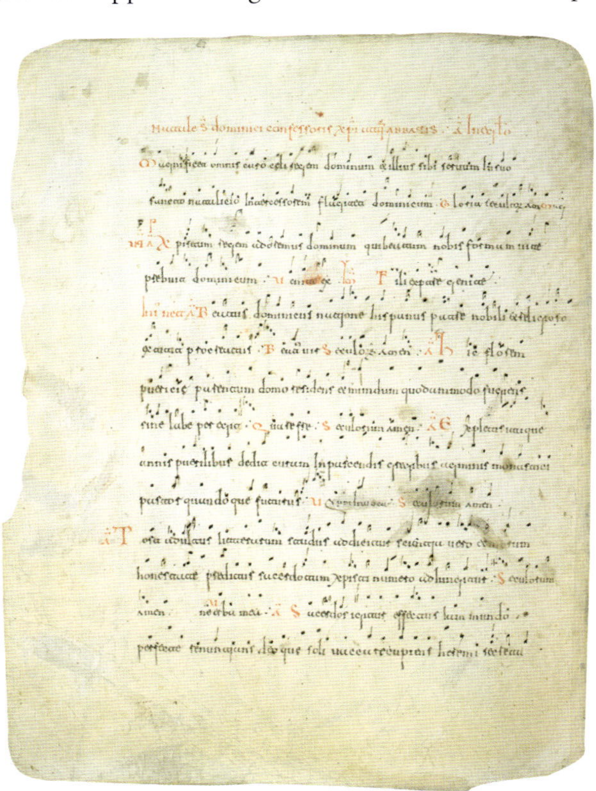

1. Antiphoner. London, BL, Add. ms. 30850, 11th century *ex.*, fol. 223v. Office of St. Dominic of Silos

but were sometimes added in the margins. The manuscript only has occasional marginalia, which also include melismas for which there was not enough room, omitted chant, and the previously noted differentia or responsory doxologies.

Whereas the chant for Dominic's *natalis* in this manuscript is newly composed, with only three possibly derivative texts—those of the invitatory, a responsory, and of the antiphon to the Magnificat of second Vespers—the seven antiphons and seven responsories of uncertain use have texts of which a number were borrowed from eastern, 'Gregorian' offices. These must have been available at the Monastery of Silos and suggest that the additional chant was compiled and written down after the 'Roman' chant had reached Silos.

Two antiphons share texts with antiphons for Sts. Martin and Philibert. There was an altar to St. Martin at Silos at which Dominic cured a leper, and the Silos antiphoner cites chant from the office of St. Martin in its tonary.[23] The concordance with an antiphon for St. Philibert, who was venerated at the Abbey of St. Germain of Auxerre is of interest, because an office for St. Germain of Auxerre is part of the section of the Silos antiphoner that includes the office of St. Dominic.[24]

Moreover, another concept was borrowed from Auxerre around the time of the dedication of the abbey church of Silos, that of the 'Christianized' labyrinth, which symbolized Christ's Harrowing in Hell and Resurrection.[25] Paris, BNF, N. A. L. 2169 is a beautiful manuscript of Isidore of Seville's *Etymologiae* that was written between 1063 and 1081 at the Monastery of Silos. It includes a note on the consecration of the altars in the Silos church written by Cardinal Richard, the pontifical legate, in 1088, on fols. 37r-38r.[26] On fol. 17r, we find a table for calculating the date of Easter and a drawing of a labyrinth, the earliest of this design to survive in any Iberian manuscript.[27] This labyrinth has the circular and symmetrical design that is visible today on the floor of Cathedral of Chartres but was also drawn in manuscripts from the Auxerrois region and has been traced to the Abbey of St. Germain of Auxerre by Craig Wright.[28]

Auxerre is northwest of Cluny in the region of Burgundy, and the Abbey of St. Germain, which dates from before the 9th century, had strong ties with Cluny in the 10th century.[29] Maiolus, Abbot of Cluny, reformed the Abbey of St. Germain from 987 to 989 (it had become Cluniac in 972), and installed his pupil, Heldricus, as abbot in 989.[30] A *Life* of St. Maiolus (*BHL* 5179) centonizes the metrical *Life* of St. Germain of Auxerre, of which a copy was in the Cluny library,[31] and an anonymous sermon about St. Maiolus centonizes excerpts from John Scot's *Periphyseon*, an anonymous sermon in honor of St. Jean of Réôme, works by St. Augustine, and Henric of Auxerre's miracles of St. Germain.[32] Thus a Cluniac intermediary for the transmission of the antiphon for St. Philibert and of the labyrinth design to Silos seems as possible as an Auxerrois intermediary.[33]

More surprising is the fact that the text and music of the responsory *Consilium et opus suum* for St. Dominic are borrowed from the Vespers responsory for St. Lambert, patron saint of Liège, attributed to Bishop Stephen of Liège († 920), the latter whose body was deposed in a crypt dedicated to that saint.[34] Another source for a responsory can be determined precisely and still survives: the texts and chant of the fifth responsory, *O princeps egregie,* were borrowed from a responsory for St. Martial that a scribe from the Monastery of Silos wrote down and neumed on a blank folio, fol. 236v, preceding a *Life* of St. Martial in Visigothic script, on fols. 237r-255r) in Paris, BNF, N. A. L. 2170 (see illustration 3).[35]

Whereas the neumes of Cluny bear no resemblance to those of the antiphoner of Silos, those of other Burgundian abbeys whose histories intersect with Cluny's share some notational features.[36] Hesbert observed points of contact between the antiphonary of Silos and the Antiphonary of Compiègne, which shares added 9th century *sequelae* with Autun, Bibliothèque Municipale, ms. Séminaire 28, a Burgundian manuscript if it is not from Autun itself, as I have argued elsewhere.[37] The neumes above the *sequelae* in Autun, Bibliothèque Municipale, ms. Séminaire 28 include the significative letter for *sursum* and many puncta, as in the Silos manuscript, though they are slanted like the later neumes of Cluny, but unlike those of Silos. Later manuscripts from Autun use the pes with a line descending slightly below the note and the angular porrectus found here as well as the liquescent clivis beginning with a small circle, the angular torculus and scandicus, and the pes stratus, all which are found again in the antiphoner of Silos.[38] The Dijon tonary (Montpellier, Bibliothèque de l'École de Médecine, ms. H 159) includes trigons and frequent puncta and has a vertical ductus.[39] It is odd that the Silos antiphoner includes no quilismas, but it does use liquescence, the earliest known north Spanish manuscript to do so.[40]

Some neumes in the Silos antiphoner also appear in the Mozarabic Antiphoner of León: both use the same forms of pes, the climacus with connected points, the trigon with a line drawn downwards to the right (Silos antiphoner, fols. 42r, 59v), the pes stratus (Silos antiphoner, several on fol. 225v), and the vertical bivirga (Silos, fol. 226r), as well as the angular gestures and vertical ductus. There are a greater number and variety of Mozarabic neumes in the León antiphonary than in the Silos antiphonary, however.

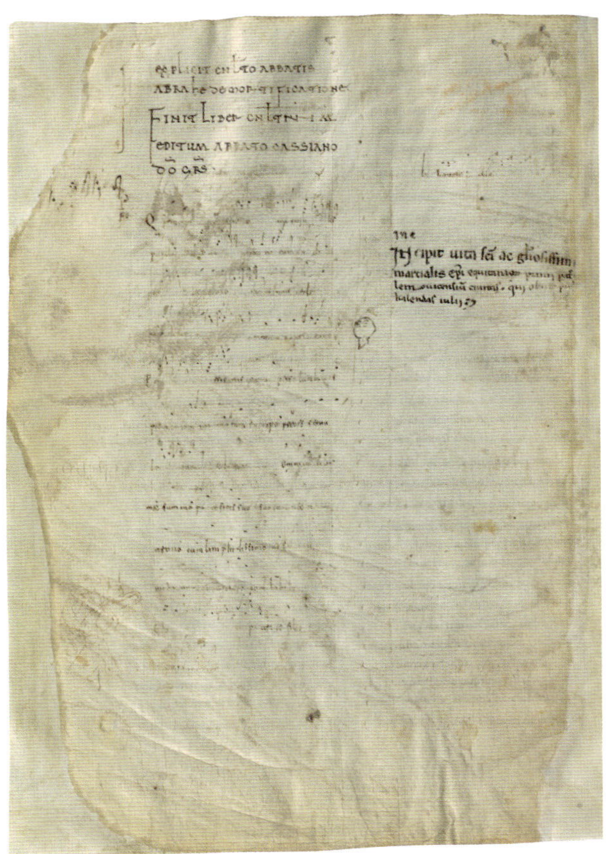

3. Cassianus. *Collationes et alia. Vita Sancti Martialis.* Paris, BNF, N. A. L. 2170, 11th century, fol. 236v

The Silos antiphoner also shares some neume shapes with the earlier *Liber ordinum*, Silos, AM, Cod. 4: the trigon (*Liber ordinum*, fols. 71r-v), the pes, the angular porrectus, and the vertical bivirgae (as in the León antiphoner). But the ^ in the *Liber ordinum* is not found in the Silos antiphonary nor are the Mozarabic forms of pes that are also found in the León antiphoner, AC, ms. 8. (The ^ is used in Autun, Bibliothèque Municipale, ms. Séminaire 20 on the back flyleaf and in Autun, Bibliothèque Municipale, ms. Séminaire 28, fol. 87r.) Fol. 146r in *Liber ordinum* has several oriscus followed by a lower punctum, a use of the oriscus that is not found in the east.

Some neumes in the Silos antiphoner are thus found in east and west: significative letters, the climacus with linked elements, the oriscus (although not its placement), and trigons, the latter also in the León antiphoner. That the so-called *Mozarabic* neumes in the Silos antiphoner include neumes used further east raises questions about a common origin of the eastern and western neumes that are beyond the scope of this study.[41]

When the notation of the *historia* for St. Dominic in the Silos antiphoner is examined, certain musical features come to the fore and the consistent applications of some neumes can be identified. The musical setting of the antiphons is syllabic. All antiphons of Vespers and Lauds, except for the first, end with a short melisma, which is usually a four-note climacus and may function as a kind of *neuma*. Many responsories end with melismas, but only one consists of a repeated phrase.[42] The letters *C* and *F* appear occasionally but not consistently among the neumes to mark pitch.

The climacus is frequent in melismas, where it is often repeated or extended, as in the responsories M-R5 *Procedente* (as many as five notes); M-R7 *Comperto autem* (four notes); M-R8 *Garsie igitur* (repeated four-note patterns); and M-R12 *His et aliis virtutibus* (four notes in final melisma). It may be used to begin or end words or to reflect the stress of accented syllables.

Trigons are used at ends of words and to punctuate melismas. On rare occasions, on accented syllables, they are repeated. The most widely used trigon has a comma to the right, which signifies a longer skip, but a few have the comma below. Trigons appear in the responsories M-R1 *Confessor Cristi*, M-R2 *Hic in adolescentia*, M-R4 *In sacerdocio*, M-R8 *Garsie igitur*, its verse *Fredelandi,* M-R9 *Abbas vero*, its verse *Tres coronas,* M-R11 *Monasterii sui*, M-R12 *His et aliis virtutibus*, L-R *Ora pro nobis*; in the *Gloria patri*'s in the margins of fol. 225v; and in the Magnificat antiphon of Second Vespers *Sancte confessor domini Dominice.*

The *pes stratus* generally appears in chant imported to Hispanic regions from the east. Here it is used in the responsories: M-R8 *Garsie igitur* (and its verse, *Fredelandi*); in M-R9 *Abbas vero* at *visitAcione* (capitalization marks the location of the *pes stratus*), and M-R10 *Quidam cecus* at *oblaciOne.*

The liquescent clivis beginning with a small circle is used in the responsory M-R2 *Hic in adolescentia* at *DEum* and at the beginning of the responsory, *In sacERdocio.*

The scandicus is absent from melismas and appears mostly on accented syllables or, rarely, on a single syllable. It can fall on a final syllable, as at the top of fol. 224r on "pecuniA". It is repeated in the responsory M-R11 *Monasterii* at "MURMURantibus".

Also used are the bivirga, drawn vertically, and the oriscus, in the second antiphon of Lauds, *Quindecim ceci*, where it precedes a punctum and virga, instead of being sandwiched between them, as in the Winchester tropary.

In short, we conclude that the *historia* for the *dies natalis* of St. Dominic of Silos dates from before the antiphons and responsories that follow it in the Silos antiphoner. The *historia* probably dates from after the introduction of 'Gregorian' chant to Silos, given the explanation offered above for responsory 10, which recounts the *Gustate et videte* miracle. That the antiphons and responsories borrow liturgical material from the east confirms their later date. Most likely their compiler(s) learned of the borrowed texts and music from manuscripts brought west by the reformers.

The notation of the *historia* in the Silos antiphoner also reflects a scribe at work in a period of transition. By this time, he had a repertory of notational signs coming from east and west: that it was not possible to separate them suggests that the imposition of norms after the *Reconquista* was a disorderly process marked by some confusion, if not by the reluctance of some local scribes to adopt outright the new practices, particularly in Silos with regard to their most venerated new saint.[43]

APPENDIX[44]

Office of the *dies natalis:* London, BL, Add. ms. 30850, fols. 223v-226v (new foliation in facsimile ed.)

First Vespers
Am. *Magnificet omnis caro celi* (*CAO* 3675)

Matins
Inv. *Christum regem* (*CAO* 1049, see *CAO* 1051 for St. Peter and St. Andrew, and *CAO* 1053 for the Exaltation of the Cross), all with *Christum regem ... adoremus Dominum* in their texts, but different continuations)
Hymn. *Fili ex Patre genite* (*AH XVI:* 109, attributed to Philipp of Huesca; *RH,* no. 6321, in 1524 Breviary of Córdoba).

First Nocturn
A1. *Beatus Dominicus* (*CAO* 1621)
A2. *Hic florem* (*CAO* 3059)
A3. *Expletis itaque* (*CAO* 2799)
A4. *Post adultus* (*CAO* 4323)
A5. *Sacerdos igitur* (*CAO* 4674)
A6. *Anno autem* (*CAO* 1422)
V. *Amavit eum dominus* (not neumed)
R1. *Confessor C[h]risti Dominicus* (*CAO* 6309)
R2. *Hic in adolescentia* (*CAO* 6834; similarity only to text incipit of *CAO* 6835, from the office of St. Gregory in *B, H, D, L: Hic in annis adolescentiae*).
R3. *Tum vero Dei famulus* (*CAO* 7799, see *Dum vero invisibilia Dei* for St. Augustine on fol. 327v of the 14th century *in.* Paris, BNF, Lat. 15182. The text begins *Dum vero invisibilia Dei per ea quae facta sunt intellecta conspexit*, thus emphasizing learning as does the responsory for St. Dominic of Silos)
R4. *In sacerdocio suo* (*CAO* 6934)

Second Nocturn
A7. *Inspirante vero* (*CAO* 3357)
A8. *Suscepto vir* (*CAO* 5090)
A9. *Temptatur a fratribus* (not in *CAO*)
A10. *Celle cuiusdam* (*CAO* 1778)
A11. *Cognita autem* (*CAO* 1845)
A12. *Filius obedientie* (*CAO* 2881)
V. *Justum deduxit* (not neumed)
R5. *Procedente vero tempore* (*CAO* 7436)
R6. *Qui prius instruendus* (*CAO* 7482)

Third Nocturn
R7. *Comperto autem a fratribus* (*CAO* 6303, where the text published by Vergara is corrected)[45]
R8. *Garsie igitur regis persecutione* (*CAO* 6758)
R9. *Abbas vero ordinatus* (*CAO* 6008)
R10. *Quidam cecus, Iohannes nomine* (*CAO* 7493)
R11. *Monasterii sui fratribus* (*CAO* 7173)
R12. *His et aliis virtutibus* (*CAO* 6842)
A. *Ad cantica Obedientiam viri sancti* (*CAO* 4098)

Lauds
A1. *De multis pauca* (*CAO* 2113)
A2. *Quindecim ceci* (*CAO* 4540)
A3. *Septem surdi* (*CAO* 4867)
A4. *Viginti energumini* (*CAO* 5422)
A5. *Laudetur Christus* (*CAO* 3596)
R. *Ora pro nobis, beate pater Dominice* (*CAO* 7327)

Hymn. *Gaudeat celum* (*AH XVI:* 106; not in *RH,* but see *RH* 7070 for St. Gabriel and *RH* 7071 St. Anthony Hermit)
Ab. *O venerabilis abbas Dominice* (*CAO* 4084)

Prime
A. *Con* (sic) *rediret a sepulcro* (not in *CAO*)

Second Vespers
Am. *Sancte confessor domini Dominice* (*CAO* 4708; see the antiphon to the Magnificat of second Vespers of St. Martial on fol. 66r in Paris, BNF, Lat. 1240)

De sancti Dominici: London, BL, Add. ms. 30850, fols. 237v, 239r-240r
A1. *O quam venerandus es* (*CAO* 4071; presence in Silos antiphoner not recognized; in EHRF for St. Maur and St. Vincent)
A2. *Intercede pro nobis* (not in *CAO;* shares most of its text, but no music, with antiphon for St. Martin on fol. 196v in Utrecht, Universiteitsbibliotheek, ms. 406 and in other sources: the full text there is: *Intercede pro nobis beate pontifex Martinus ad Dominum Iesum Christum apud quem est misericordia in perpetuum.*)
A3. *Eius sollemnia* (not in *CAO;* text borrowed from the Office of St. Philibert, a saint venerated at the Abbey of St. Germain of Auxerre (see fol. 71v in Rouen, Bib. Mun., ms. 248).
A4. *Beatus vir Dominicus* (not in *CAO*).
A5. *Beatus Dominicus* (not in *CAO*).
A6 *Sancte confessor Dominice* (not in *CAO*).
A7. *Exemplar especulum* [sic] (not in *CAO*).
R1. *Sanctus Dominicus paruipendebat presentia* (not in *CAO*).
R2. *Ora pro nobis [...] decus excelsum* (not in *CAO*).
R3. *Consilium et opus suum* (not in *CAO;* the text of the responsory only and not of the verse, and not of the music, is borrowed from the responsory of Vespers in the office of St. Lambert: see Antoine Auda. *L'École musicale liégeoise au Xe siècle. Étienne de Liege.* Brussels: M. Hayez, 1922, 187; see Utrecht, Universiteitsbibliotheek, ms. 406, fol. 171r).
R4. *Milex* (sic) *C[h]risti gloriosus Dominicus* (not in *CAO;* see *CAO* 7155, *Miles Christi gloriose*, for St. Eugenius in D and the common of a confessor in F. The rest of the text and the music differs.)
R5. *O princeps egregie* [not in *CAO;* the text and the chant of responsory and verse borrowed from the office of St. Martial, most likely directly from Paris, BNF, N. A. L. 2170, fol. 236v (see I.II.3)]. The responsory and verse can be transcribed from F-CA, Impr. XVI C 4, fol. 147v.
R6. *Beatissimi viri* (not in *CAO*).
R7. *[O] sacer almiflue* (not in *CAO*).

Notes

[1] A *historia* is an office consisting of texts and chant for first Vespers, Matins, Lauds, and second Vespers, in which the antiphons, lessons, and responsories recall the life of a saint. *Historiae* may or may not be rhymed or follow the order of the modes.

[2] The suppression of the Old Hispanic chant was accomplished during the pontificates of Alexander II (1061-1073) and Gregory VII (1073-1085). Cluniac monks played a major role in the introduction of Gregorian chant to Spain. See Ismael Fernández de la Cuesta, "La irrupción del canto gregoriano en España. Bases para un replanteamiento". *Revista de Musicología* 8, no. 2 (1985b): 239-248.

[3] Màrius Férotin. *Histoire de l'Abbaye de Silos*. Paris: Ernest Leroux, 1897a, 276. Also see Bernard F. Reilly, ed. *Santiago, Saint-Denis and Saint Peter: The Reception of the Roman Liturgy in León-Castile in 1080.* New York: Fordham University Press, 1980. I thank Lila Collamore for this reference.

[4] Abbreviations used: *AH* = Guido Maria Dreves and Clemens Blume. *Analecta hymnica medii aevi.* 55 vols. Leipzig: Reisland, 1886-1992; *AMS* = René-Jean Hesbert. *Antiphonale missarum sextuples.* Rome: Herder, 1935, repr. 1985; *BHL* = *Bibliotheca hagiographica latina.* Brussels: Société des Bollandistes, 1898-1899, repr. 1992; *CAO* = René Jean Hesbert. *Corpus antiphonalium officii.* 6 vols. Rome: Herder, 1963-1979; and *RH* = Ulysse Chevalier. *Repertorium hymnologicum.* 6 vols. Louvain: Lefever and Polleunis & Ceuterick; Brussels: Société des Bollandistes, 1892-1920.

[5] The facsimile edition is in Ismael Fernández de la Cuesta, ed. *Antiphonale Silense (British Library, Add. ms. 30850).* Madrid: Sociedad Española de Musicología, 1985a.

[6] The association of the *historia* to the *Life* is discussed briefly by Miguel C. Vivancos in "Officia propria sancti Dominici de Silos ex veteribus codicibus collecta". *Ecclesia Orans* 19 (2002): 68, n. 4.

[7] Grimald's *Life* (*BHL*. Brussels: Société des Bollandistes, 1898-1899, no. 2.238; repr. 1992), survives in Silos, AM, Cod. 12 (13-14th centuries; see Màrius Férotin. Op. cit. 59-62) together with the *Life* by Gonzalo de Berceo

and *Miracles* by Pedro Marín. These last two works date from 1236 and from the 13th century. On the three authors, their writings, and the sources, see Ángeles García de la Borbolla García de Paredes, *"La praesentia" y la "virtus": la imagen y la función del santo a partir de la hagiografía castellano-leonesa del siglo XIII*. Santo Domingo de Silos: Monastery of Silos, 2002, 34-37. On Grimald's *Life* and others, their historical value, and the cult of Domingo, see Miguel C. Vivancos, "Domingo de Silos: historia y leyenda de un santo". In Saturnino López Santidrian and José Antonio Fernández Florez, eds. *Silos. Un milenio. Actas del Congreso Internacional sobre la Abadía de Santo Domingo de Silos (1000-2001)*. Vol. 2, *Historia*. Burgos: University of Burgos, Monastery of Silos, 2003, 223-263 (Studia Silensia: 26). Grimald's *Life* was most recently edited by Vitalino Valcárcel. *La "Vita Dominici Siliensis" de Grimaldo. Estudio, edición crítica y traducción*. Logroño: Servicio de Cultura de la Excma. Diputación Provincial, 1982. According to *ibidem,* 98 and subsq. Grimald wrote the first book and the first forty chapters of the second book between 1088 and 1091; the other material was added in the 12th century. See Miguel C. Vivancos. *Ibidem,* 224-225, where he notes that the *Life* existed in Visigothic script and must therefore date from before the end of the use of the script at Silos *circa* 1100-1120.

[8] Màrius Férotin. *Ibidem,* 63-65; Miguel C. Vivancos. *Ibidem,* 256; and see note 25 below.

[9] The feast for St. Dominic of Silos was celebrated throughout Spain in the Middle Ages, but disappeared after the Council of Trent in some locations. When the last translation of the relics took place in 1733, St. Dominic's name was formally inserted into the Roman martyrology, and a decree of the Congregation of Sacred Rites reestablished his feast in Spain. See Màrius Férotin. *Ibidem,* 65-66.

[10] *Ibidem,* 39-40.

[11] On the possibility that St. Dominic brought a scribe from San Millán to establish the new scriptorium at the Monastery of Silos, see *ibidem,* 47, 183-184. A charter recording a donation of liturgical books, including a neumed antiphoner, orationale, manual, *comicum, ordinum,* hymnary, and others is transcribed on pp. 17-18 of *idem,* ed. *Recueil des chartes de l'Abbaye de Silos*. Paris: Imprimerie Nationale, 1897b. On the *scriptorium* of Silos, see *idem*. *Histoire de l'Abbaye de Silos.* Op. cit., 184-185. On the library of Silos, *ibidem,* 239-288, especially the list of books in the library in the 13th century, 262-263; José Manuel Ruiz Asencio. "Códices pirenaicos y riojanos en la biblioteca de Silos en el siglo XI". In Saturnino López Santidrián y José Antonio Fernández Flórez, eds. Op. cit., 177-210; and Walter Muir Whitehill, Jr., and Justo Pérez de Urbel. *Los manuscritos del Real Monasterio de Santo Domingo de Silos*. Madrid: Tipografía de la *Revista de Archivos*, 1930. The library of Silos still has the *Liber ordinum* (Cod. 4, written in 1052).

[12] *Gustate et videte* is recorded on track 12 of *The Mystery of Santo Domingo de Silos. Gregorian Chant from Spain*. Directed by Ismael Fernandez de la Cuesta and monks of the Abbey of Santo Domingo of Silos. Hamburg: Deutsche Grammophon, Stereo 445 399-2, © 1969, Polydor International, 1994.

[13] Vitalino Valcárcel. Op. cit., Book 1, Chapter 10: "At ubi more ecclesiastico est completum divinum officium uentumque est ad percipiendum corporis et sanguinis Domini sacramentum et ministris officium inchoantibus communionem *Gustate et uidete quoniam suauis est Dominus* que eo die (the specific date is not given in the *Life*) acciderat, repente et insperate oculi ceci, longa cecitate pressi, sunt aperti, omnis alia infirmitas fugata".

[14] *CAO* 7493: *R[esponsorium]: Quidam caecus, Joannes nomine, intolerabili etiam orbium dolore gravatus, peracta pro eo a viro Dei sacrosancta oblatione, desideratae saluti est restitutus. V[ersus]: Dum communicasset vir beatus et* Gustate et videte *pro complendo cantaretur.*

[15] *AMS,* 182-183. The third-mode communion melody is edited in Moines de Solesmes. *Liber Usualis*. Tournai: Desclée, 1962; the eighth-mode tract melody to the same text is edited in Eugène Cardine. *Graduale neumé.* Solesmes: Abbey of Saint-Pierre, 1966, 317-318.

[16] Text as in Louis Brou and José Vives, eds. *Antifonario visigótico mozárabe de la Catedral de León*. 2 vols. Vol. 1, Barcelona: Centro de Estudios e Investigación San Isidoro (CSIC-CECEL), 1959; vol. 2, Madrid: CSIC, Instituto P. Enrique Flórez, 1953-1954 (Monumenta Hispaniae Sacra: Serie Litúrgica 5, no. 2. Facsímiles musicales 1). See Julius Parnell Gilson, ed. *The Mozarabic Psalter (ms. British Museum, add. 30851)*. London: Harrison and Sons, 1905 (Henry Bradshaw Society: 30).

[17] Màrius Férotin. Op. cit., 50.

[18] See Miguel C. Vivancos. "Domingo de Silos: historia y leyenda...". Op. cit., 246.

[19] Editions of the text only are: Sebastián de Vergara. *Vida y milagros de el thaumaturgo español [...] Sto. Domingo Manso [...]*. Madrid: Herederos de Francisco del Hierro, 1736; *CAO*. Vol. 2: 761, 763 (*incipits* only; the full texts appear in volumes 3 and 4, but some chant for St. Dominic in the Silos antiphoner does not receive a *CAO* number from Hesbert); and Miguel C. Vivancos. "Officia propria sancti Dominic...". Op cit.,

63-84. Andrew Hughes did not include the office in his repertory of *historie* (*Late Medieval Liturgical Offices.* 2 vols. Toronto: Pontifical Institute of Mediæval Studies, 1994-1996) because it is not rhymed; but see Anon. "Oficio propio del siervo de Dios'. In José Gil Dorregaray, ed. *Museo español de antigüedades bajo la direccion [de] [...] Juan de Dios de La Rada y Delgado.* 11 vols. Madrid: T. Fortanet, 1872-1880. Vol. 8: 62-110, cited by Juan del Álamo. *Vida histórico-crítica del taumaturgo español, Santo Domingo de Silos*. Madrid: J. Sanchez Ocaña, 1953. Pages 427-429 include discussion of the earliest references in manuscripts to the liturgical veneration of St. Dominic. Also see Miguel C. Vivancos, "El oficio litúrgico de Santo Domingo de Silos". In Saturnino López Santidrián and José Antonio Fernández Flórez, eds. Op. cit. Vol. 1, *Espiritualidad:* 81-88; an abbreviated version of his study published in *Ecclesia Orans*. Màrius Férotin. Op. cit., 276-277, lists the manuscript sources with the office for St. Dominic of Silos.

[20] Their texts are edited in Miguel C. Vivancos, "Officia propria sancti Dominici...". Op. cit. 74-81, and in *AH* XVI: 106-111. The hymns are cited in *RH:* numbers 2.344, 3.014, 4.818-4.820, 5.732, 8.308, 9.056, 27.250, also the processional hymns with numbers 3.828, 12.800, 19.530.

[21] Communication to Michel Huglo from Don Alarcia of Silos in July 1949.

[22] Other sources are listed in Miguel C. Vivancos. "Officia propria sancti Dominici...". Op. cit. On this manuscript, see *CAO*. Vol. 2: XVII-XIX, and the introduction to Ismael Fernández de la Cuesta, ed. *Antiphonale Silense...,* op. cit. It was at Silos until 1835, when it was brought to Madrid, where it was listed in a sale catalog of 1877 and sold to Bernard Quaritch (the page from the sale catalog is reproduced in Màrius Férotin. Op. cit., 252-264), who sold it to to the British Museum in 1878.

[23] Màrius Férotin. *Ibidem,* 49. The library of Silos also had a copy of an office of St. Martin of Tours (in ms. 5, written in 1009).

[24] The remains of St. Philibert were translated to Tournous in Burgundy. On the office for St. Germain of Auxerre, see Barbara Haggh. "The Office of St. Germain, Bishop of Auxerre". *Études Grégoriennes* 26 (1998): 111-134, with an edition of the secular office in Paris, BNF, Lat. 1028, fols. 219v-222r.

[25] It is notable that the antiphoner of Silos includes chant for the *Visitatio Sepulchri* (see Ismael Fernández de la Cuesta, *Antiphonale Silense...*, op. cit., XIV), as does the Breviary of Silos, GB-Lbl add. 30848 (see Walther Lipphardt. *Lateinische Osterfeiern und Osterspiele.* Berlin: De Gruyter, 1981. Vol. 6: 319).

[26] See Màrius Férotin. Op. cit., 72; and Ismael Fernández de la Cuesta. *Ibidem,* XV.

[27] See Hermann Kern. *Through the Labyrinth. Designs and Meanings over 5000 Years.* Munich: Prestel, 2000, 112, no. 183. On the manuscript, see Michel Huglo. "La tradición de la *Musica Isidori* en la Península Ibérica", in this volume, pp 61-92.

[28] Craig Wright, *The Maze and the Warrior.* Cambridge, Massachusetts: Harvard University Press, 2001, 23.

[29] These are explored in Barbara Haggh, "The Office of St. Jean of Réôme: Its Notation, Music and Message". In Terence Bailey and László Dobszay, eds. *Studies in Medieval Chant and Liturgy in Honour of David Hiley*. Budapest: Hungarian Academy of Sciences; Ottawa: Institute of Mediæval Music, 2007: 247-274; and *idem,* and Michel Huglo. "Réôme, Cluny, Dijon". In Terence Bailey and Alma Santosuosso, eds. *Music in Medieval Europe. Festschrift for Bryan Gillingham*. Aldershot: Ashgate, 2007, 49-64.

[30] Niethard Bulst. *Untersuchungen zu den Klosterreformen Wilhelms von Dijon (962-1031).* Bonn: Ludwig Röhrscheid, 1973, 62 and note 235 (Pariser Historische Studien: 11).

[31] Leopold Delisle. *Le cabinet des manuscrits de la Bibliothèque Impériale*. Vol. 2. Paris: Imprimerie Nationale, 1874 (reprint, Hildesheim: Olms, 1978, 475, no. 426.)

[32] See Christian Sapin, ed. *Abbaye Saint-Germain d'Auxerre: Intellectuels et artistes dans l'Europe carolingienne, IXe-XIe siècles.* Auxerre: Musée d'Art et d'Histoire, 1990, 277-283.

[33] See Charles Julian Bishko. "Fernando I and the origins of the Leonese-Castilian Alliance with Cluny". In *Studies in Medieval Spanish Frontier History.* Aldershot: Ashgate, 1980. Art. 2: 1-136. I thank Lila Collamore for this reference.

[34] Antoine Auda. *L'École musicale liégeoise au Xe siècle. Étienne de Liége*. Brussels: M. Hayez, 1922, 34.

[35] On Paris, BNF, N. A. L. 2170, which dates from the 11th century, see Société des Bollandistes, ed. *Catalogus codicum hagiographicorum Parisiense*. Paris: Picard; Brussels: Schepens, 1893. Vol. 3: 473-474; François Avril, et al., eds. *Manuscrits enluminés de la Péninsule Ibérique*. Paris: Bibliothèque Nationale de France, 1983, 20, no. 27 (see no. 17) and plate B (fol. 23r); and Agustín Millares Carlo, et al., eds. *Corpus de códices visigóticos.* Vol. 1, *Estudio;* vol. 2, *Álbum.* Las Palmas de Gran Canaria: Gobierno de Canarias, UNED, Centro Asociado de

Las Palmas de Gran Canaria, 1999. Vol. 1: 167-168, and vol. 2: 239 (plate no. 262 of fol. 20v). The text for St. Martial reads: "O princeps egregie, O Marcialis pastor et dux acquitanorum audi preces servulorum. Et intercede pro salute omnium populorum. V[ersus:] Persistens gemma presulum in conspectu domini tuorum suscipe preces servulorum".

[36] On the neumes of Cluny, see Manuel Pedro Ferreira. *Music at Cluny: The Tradition of Gregorian Chant for the Proper of the Mass. Melodic Variants and Microtonal Nuances.* Ph. D. diss. Princeton, New Jersey: Princeton University, 1997, 167-174. On the web of relationships between Burgundian churches and Cluny, see Barbara Haggh and Michel Huglo. Op. cit.

[37] Marie-Noël Colette. "Séquences et *versus ad sequentias* dans l'antiphonaire de Charles le Chauve (Paris, BNF, Lat. 17.436)". *Revue de Musicologie* 89, no. 1 (2003): 31-45; and Barbara Haggh. "The Office of St. Jean of Réôme". Op. cit.

[38] Autun, Bibliothèque Municipale, ms. Séminaire 10 (clivis with small circle throughout the manuscript); S 13, fol. 2v; S 20, fol. 23r; S 24, fol. 34v, and S 167, fol. 14r (angular torculus and/or scandicus); S 30, fol. 2v (pes stratus). The manuscripts of Autun are described in Claire Maître. *Catalogue des manuscrits conservés à Autun.* Turnhout: Brepols, 2004.

[39] On the trigon, see David G. Hughes. "An Enigmatic Neume". In Bell Yung and Joseph Lam, eds. *Themes and Variations. Writings on Music in Honor of Rulan Chao Pian.* Cambridge, Massachusetts: Harvard University Press; Hong Kong: The Chinese University, 1994, 8-30. On the Dijon tonary, see *H. 159, Montpellier: Tonary of St. Bénigne of Dijon*, transcribed and annotated by Finn Egeland Hansen. Copenhagen: Dan Fog, 1974; *idem.* "Editorial problems connected with the transcription of H 159, Montpellier: Tonary of St. Bénigne of Dijon". *Études Grégoriennes* 16 (1977): 161-172; *idem. The Grammar of Gregorian Tonality: An Investigation Based on the Repertory in Codex H 159, Montpellier.* 2 vols. Copenhagen: Dan Fog, 1979; Michel Huglo. "Grundlage und Ansätze der mittelalterlichen Musiktheorie". In Thomas Eltert and Frieder Zaminer, eds. *Geschichte der Musiktheorie.* Darmstadt: Wissenschaftliche Buchhandlung, 2000. Vol. 4: 98-100 (especially table 5); *idem.* "Le tonaire de Saint-Bénigne de Dijon (Montpellier H. 159) ". *Annales Musicologiques* 4 (1956): 7-18, especially page 9 and note 2, and the facsimile across from page 17; Moines de Solesmes. *Le Graduel romain: Les sources.* Solesmes: Abbey of Saint-Pierre, 1957, 75; *idem. Les tonaires.* Paris: Heugel, 1971, 328-333; Nancy Phillips. "Notationen und Notationslehren von Boethius bis zum 12. Jahrhundert". In Thomas Eltert and Frieder Zaminer, eds. *Ibidem.* Vol. 4, especially 352, 468-469 and 565-572; Moines de Solesmes. *Vatican City, ms. Vat. Lat. 10673.* Tournai: Desclée, 1931, 9 (Paléographie musicale: 14); Moines de Solesmes. *Antiphonarium tonale missarum, XIe siècle: Codex H. 159 de la Bibliothèque de l'École de Médecine de Montpellier.* Solesmes: Abbey of Saint-Pierre, 1901 (Paléographie musicale: 8).

[40] On north Spanish neumes see the very useful tables in Ismael Fernández de la Cuesta. "Mozarabischer Gesang". In Ludwig Finscher, ed. *Die Musik in Geschichte und Gegenwart, Sachteil.* Kassel: Bärenreiter, 1997. Vol. 6: cols. 567-570; Nancy Phillips. *Ibidem,* 445-451, especially page 446, note 353, and page 451. On the significance of liquescence in the Silos antiphoner, see Michel Huglo. *Les anciens répertoires de plain-chant.* Aldershot: Ashgate, 2005, article X: "La notation wisigothique est-elle plus ancienne que les autres notations européennes?". In Emilio Casares, et al., eds. *España en la música de Occidente.* Madrid: Instituto Nacional de las Artes Escénicas y de la Música, Ministerio de Cultura, 1987. Vol. 1: 24.

[41] Michel Huglo. *Ibidem;* and *idem,* and Barbara Haggh. "Écritures et notations wisigothiques hors d'Espagne. I: La notation, le chant, la liturgie et la culture wisigothique: les contacts avec le sud de la France [M. H.], II: Semur-en-Auxois, ms. 1: Témoin franc d'écriture wisigothique [B. H.]". In Robert Stevenson, ed. *Festschrift for Ismael Fernández de la Cuesta.* (In press.)

[42] Compare the responsory for St. Jean of Réôme added in a Hispanic script to Semur-en-Auxois Bibliotheque Municipale, ms. 1, with a repeated melisma indicated by the sign for *duplicatur.* See Haggh. "The Office of St. Jean of Réôme...". Op. cit., and *ibidem*: "II. Semur-en-Auxois".

[43] I am most grateful to Susana Zapke for providing the xeroxes that made this article possible; to the staff of the Hill Monastic Manuscript Library, who facilitated my research on St. Dominic of Silos during my visit in March 2006; to Miguel C. Vivancos for copies of his articles that were not available to me; to the Interlibrary Loan office of the University of Maryland, College Park; and to the University of Maryland, College Park for the GRB Semester Research Award that permitted me to complete this article.

[44] See Miguel C. Vivancos. "Officia propria sancti Dominici...". Op. cit., 70-74, and *CAO* (as indicated), where the texts are given in full.

[45] Sebastián de Vergara. *Vida y milagros de el thaumaturgo español...* Op. cit., 309-452.

Bibliography

Álamo, Juan del. *Vida histórico-crítica del taumaturgo español, Santo Domingo de Silos.* Madrid: J. Sanchez de Ocaña, 1953.

Anon. "Oficio propio del siervo de Dios". In José Gil Dorregaray, ed. *Museo español de antigüedades bajo la dirección [de] [...] Juan de Dios de La Rada y Delgado.* 11 vols. Madrid: T. Fortanet, 1872-1880. Vol. 8: 62-110.

Auda, Antoine. *L'École musicale liégeoise au Xe siècle. Étienne de Liège.* Brussels: M. Hayez, 1922.

Avril, François, Jean-Pierre Aniel, Mireille Mentré, Alix Saulnier, and Yolanta Załuska. *Manuscrits enluminés de la péninsule Ibérique.* Paris: Bibliothèque Nationale de France, 1983.

Bishko, Charles Julian. "Fernando I and the Origins of the Leonese-Castilian Alliance with Cluny". In *Studies in Medieval Spanish Frontier History.* Aldershot: Ashgate, 1980. Art. II: 1-136 (Variorum Collected Studies Series).

Brou, Louis, and José Vives, eds. *Antifonario visigótico mozárabe de la Catedral de León.* 2 vols. Vol. 1, Barcelona: Centro de Estudios e Investigación San Isidoro (CSIC-CECEL), 1959; vol. 2, Madrid: CSIC, Instituto P. Enrique Flórez, 1953-1954 (Monumenta Hispaniae Sacra: Serie Litúrgica 5, no. 2. Facsímiles musicales 1).

Bulst, Niethard. *Untersuchungen zu den Klosterreformen Wilhelms von Dijon (962-1031).* Bonn: Ludwig Röhrscheid, 1973 (Pariser Historische Studien: 11).

Cardine, Eugène, ed. *Graduel neumé.* Solesmes: Abbey of Saint-Pierre, 1966.

Casares, Emilio, Ismael Fernández de la Cuesta, José López-Calo, and José M. Llorens. *España en la música de Occidente. Actas del congreso internacional celebrado en Salamanca, 29 de octubre-5 de noviembre de 1985: Año Europeo de la Música.* Madrid: Instituto de las Artes Escénicas y de la Música, Ministerio de Cultura, 1987.

Chevalier, Ulysse. *Repertorium hymnologicum.* 6 vols. Louvain: Lefever and Polleunis & Ceuterick; Brussels: Société des Bollandistes, 1892-1920.

Colette, Marie-Noël. "Séquences et *versus ad sequentias* dans l'antiphonaire de Charles le Chauve (Paris, BNF, Lat. 17436)". *Revue de Musicologie* 89 (2003): 31-45.

Delisle, Léopold. *Le cabinet des manuscrits de la Bibliothèque Impériale.* 3 vols. Paris: Imprimerie Nationale, 1874 (reprinted, Hildesheim: Olms, 1978.)

Dreves, Guido Maria, and Clemens Blume. *Analecta hymnica medii aevi.* 55 vols. Leipzig: Reisland, 1886-1992.

Fernández de la Cuesta, Ismael, ed. *Antiphonale Silense, British Library, Add. ms. 30850.* Madrid: Sociedad Española de Musicología, 1985.

—. "La irrupción del canto gregoriano en España. Bases para un replanteamiento". *Revista de Musicología* 8 (1985): 239-248.

—, dir., and Choir of the Monks of the Monastery of Santo Domingo de Silos. *The Mystery of Santo Domingo de Silos. Gregorian Chant from Spain.* CD. Hamburg: Deutsche Grammophon, Stereo 445 399-2, © 1969, Polydor International, 1994.

—. "Mozarabischer Gesang". In Ludwig Finscher, ed. *Die Musik in Geschichte und Gegenwart. Sachteil.* Kassel: Bärenreiter, 1997. Vol. 6: cols. 567-570.

Férotin, Màrius. *Histoire de l'Abbaye de Silos.* Paris: Ernest Leroux, 1897a.

—, ed. *Recueil des chartes de l'Abbaye de Silos.* Paris: Imprimerie Nationale, 1897b.

Ferreira, Manuel Pedro. *Music at Cluny: The Tradition of Gregorian Chant for the Proper of the Mass. Melodic Variants and Microtonal Nuances.* Ph.D. diss. Princeton, New Jersey: Princeton University, 1997.

García de la Borbolla García de Paredes, Ángeles. *"La praesentia" y la "virtus": la imagen y la función del santo a partir de la hagiografía castellano-leonesa del siglo* XIII. Santo Domingo de Silos: Monastery of Silos, 2002 (Studia Silensia: 24).

Gilson, Julius Parnell, ed. *The Mozarabic Psalter (ms. British Museum, add. 30851).* London: Harrison and Sons, 1905 (Henry Bradshaw Society: 30).

Haggh, Barbara. "The Office of St. Germain, Bishop of Auxerre". *Études grégoriennes* 26 (1998): 111-134.

—. "The Office of St. Jean of Réôme: Its Notation, Music and Message". In Terence Bailey and László Dobszay, eds. *Studies in Medieval Chant and Liturgy in Honour of David Hiley.* Budapest: Hungarian Academy of Sciences; Ottawa: Institute of Mediæval Music, 2007: 247-274.

Haggh, Barbara, and Michel Huglo. "Réôme, Cluny, Dijon". In Terence Bailey and Alma Santosuosso, eds. *Music in Medieval Europe. Studies in Honour of Bryan Gillingham.* Aldershot: Ashgate, 2007, 49-64.

Hansen, Finn Egeland, ed. *H. 159, Montpellier: Tonary of St. Bénigne of Dijon.* Copenhagen: Dan Fog, 1974.

—. "Editorial Problems connected with the transcription of H 159, Montpellier: Tonary of St. Bénigne of Dijon". *Études Grégoriennes* 16 (1977): 161-172.

—. *The Grammar of Gregorian Tonality: An Investigation Based on the Repertory in Codex H 159, Montpellier*. 2 vols. Copenhagen: Dan Fog, 1979.

Hesbert, René-Jean. *Antiphonale missarum sextuplex*. Brussels: Vromant, 1935 (reprinted, Rome: Herder, 1985.)

—. *Corpus antiphonalium officii*. 6 vols. Rome: Herder, 1963-1979.

Hughes, Andrew. *Late Medieval Liturgical Offices*. 2 vols. Toronto: Pontifical Institute of Mediæval Studies, 1994-1996.

Hughes, David G. "An Enigmatic Neume". In Bell Yung and Joseph Lam, eds. *Themes and Variations. Writings on Music in Honor of Rulan Chao Pian*. Cambridge, Massachusetts: Harvard University; Hong Kong: The Chinese University, 1994, 8-30.

Huglo, Michel. "Le tonaire de Saint-Bénigne de Dijon Montpellier H. 159". *Annales Musicologiques* 4 (1956): 7-18.

—. *Les tonaires*. Paris: Heugel, 1971.

—. "La notation wisigothique est-elle plus ancienne que les autres notations européennes?" Reprinted from Emilio Casares, Ismael Fernández de la Cuesta, José López-Calo and José Llorens, eds. *España en la música de Occidente*. Vol. 1. Madrid: Instituto Nacional de las Artes Escénicas y de la Música, Ministerio de Cultura, 1987. [Article reprinted in Michel Huglo. *Les anciens répertoires de plain-chant*. Art. X. Aldershot: Ashgate, 2005 (Variorum Collected Studies Series).]

—. "Grundlage und Ansätze der mittelalterlichen Musiktheorie". In Thomas Ertelt and Frieder Zaminer, eds. *Geschichte der Musiktheorie*. Darmstadt: Wissenschaftliche Buchgesellschaft, 2000. Vol. 4: 98-100.

—. "La tradición de la *Musica Isidori* en la Península Ibérica". In Susana Zapke, ed. *Hispania Vetus. Manuscritos litúrgico-musicales: de los orígenes visigóticos a la transición francorromana (siglos IX-XII)*. Madrid: Fundación BBVA, 2007, 59-92).

Huglo, Michel, and Barbara Haggh. "Écritures et notations wisigothiques hors d'Espagne. I: La notation, le chant, la liturgie et la culture wisigothique: les contacts avec le sud de la France [M. H.]; II: Semur-en-Auxois, ms. 1: Témoin franc d'écriture wisigothique [B. H.]". In Robert Stevenson, ed. *Festschrift for Ismael Fernández de la Cuesta*. (In press.)

Kern, Hermann. *Through the Labyrinth. Designs and Meanings over 5000 Years*. Munich: Prestel, 2000.

Lipphardt, Walther. *Lateinische Osterfeiern und Osterspiele*. Vol. 6. Berlin: De Gruyter, 1981.

Maître, Claire. *Catalogue des manuscrits conservés à Autun*. Turnhout: Brepols, 2004.

Millares Carlo, Agustín, Manuel C. Díaz y Díaz, Anscari M. Mundó, José Manuel Ruiz Asencio, Blas Casado Quintanilla, and E. Lecuona Ribot, eds. *Corpus de códices visigóticos*. Vol. 1, *Estudio*; vol. 2, *Álbum*. Las Palmas de Gran Canaria: Gobierno de Canarias, UNED, Centro Asociado de Las Palmas de Gran Canaria, 1999.

Moines de Solesmes, eds. *Antiphonarium tonale missarum, XIe siècle: Codex H. 159 de la Bibliothèque de l'École de Médecine de Montpellier*. Solesmes: Abbey of Saint-Pierre, 1901 (Paléographie musicale: 8).

—. *Vatican City, ms. Vat. Lat. 10.673*. Tournai: Desclée, 1931 (Paléographie musicale: 14).

—. *Le Graduel Romain*. Vol. 2, *Les sources*. Edited by Michel Huglo. Solesmes: Abbey of Saint-Pierre, 1957.

—. *Liber usualis*. Tournai: Desclée, 1962.

Phillips, Nancy. "Notationen und Notationslehre von Boethius bis zum 12. Jahrhundert. Nordspanische Neumen". In Thomas Eltert and Frieder Zaminer, eds. Op. cit., 445-451.

Reilly, Bernard F., ed. *Santiago, Saint-Denis and Saint Peter: The Reception of the Roman Liturgy in León-Castile in 1080*. New York: Fordham University Press, 1980.

Ruiz Asencio, José Manuel. "Códices pirenaicos y riojanos en la biblioteca de Silos en el siglo XI". In Saturnino López Santidrián and José Antonio Fernández Flórez, eds. *Silos. Un milenio. Actas del Congreso Internacional sobre la Abadía de Santo Domingo de Silos 1000-2001*. Vol. 2, *Historia*. Burgos: University of Burgos, Monastery of Silos, 2003, 177-210 (Studia Silensia: 26).

Sapin, Christian. *Abbaye Saint-Germain d'Auxerre: Intellectuels et artistes dans l'Europe carolingienne, IXe-XIe siècles*. Auxerre: Musée d'Art et d'Histoire, 1990.

Société des Bollandistes, ed. *Catalogus Codicum Hagiographicorum Parisiense*. Vol. 3. Paris: Picard; Brussels: Schepens, 1893.

—. *Bibliotheca hagiographica latina*. Brussels: Société des Bollandistes, 1898-1899, reprinted in 1992.

Stevenson, Robert, ed. *Festschrift for Ismael Fernández de la Cuesta*. (In press.)

Valcárcel, Vitalino. *La "Vita Dominici Siliensis" de Grimaldo. Estudio, edición crítica y traducción*. Logroño: Servicio de Cultura de la Excma. Diputación Provincial, 1982.

VERGARA, Sebastián de. *Vida y milagros de el thaumaturgo español [...] Sto. Domingo Manso [...]*. Madrid: Herederos de Francisco del Hierro, 1736.

VIVANCOS, Miguel C. "Officia propria sancti Dominici de Silos ex veteribus codicibus collecta". *Ecclesia Orans* 19 (2002): 63-84.

—. "Domingo de Silos: historia y leyenda de un santo". In Saturnino López Santidrián and José Antonio Fernández Flórez, eds. Op. cit., 223-263.

—. "El oficio litúrgico de Santo Domingo de Silos". In *ibidem.* Vol. 1, *Espiritualidad:* 81-88.

WHITEHILL, JR., Walter Muir, and Justo PÉREZ DE URBEL. *Los manuscritos del Real Monasterio de Santo Domingo de Silos.* Madrid: Tipografía de la *Revista de Archivos,* 1930.

WRIGHT, Craig. *The Maze and the Warrior.* Cambridge, Massachusetts: Harvard University Press, 2001.

Notation Systems in the Iberian Peninsula: From Spanish Notations to Aquitainian Notation (9th-12th Centuries)

Susana Zapke

Nisi enim ab homine memoria teneantur, soni pereunt, quia scribi non possunt

St. Isidore of Seville, *Etymol.* III, 15

The long process of replacing the Visigothic rite with the Franco-Roman rite, occupying a vast expanse of time from the 9th century *in.* to the 13th century *ex.*,[1] is reflected by two evolving formal characteristics of the musical liturgical sources: their structure (classification of contents) and their script (reflecting the progressive assimilation of the new types of writing and notation). The process of transition in structure and script was not necessarily concurrent, however.

In the following pages, we shall look at the gradual replacement of the different morphological variants of Spanish, Catalonian and Visigothic notations by a uniform system—Aquitainian notation—that was more functional and more pragmatic. Essential issues, such as the keys to interpreting the systems of notation and the models and process used for copying and learning the new repertory lie outside the limited scope of this study, which aspires to offer an overview of the chronology of the process and its uneven evolution, resulting from the varied assimilation of the new repertory in the different cultural areas of the Iberian Peninsula during this period.[2]

From a methodological perspective, we make flexible use of a notational semiology, examining—to differing extents—the three canonical dimensions in the study of *signs* postulated by Charles. W. Morris in *Foundations of the Theory of Signs* (1938). In addition to setting out the graphic inventory (which might be seen as being the equivalent of a *syntactic study* of the sign), we shall examine its significance (the *semantic* significance of the sign) and the function of the diversity of signs seen as it evolved (comparable to a *pragmatic* dimension of the sign).

The first step in applying this semiologic orientation will be to list the different script systems with their typology and to show how they were distributed in the different cultural spaces or areas. For each sign, we will sort the selected manuscript sources chronologically. The purpose will be to obtain an overview of the various systems that coexisted in the peninsula during this period, incorporating the specific analyses made in the area of musical paleography by a series of leading researchers. We will pay particular attention to the asymmetries that arose within the framework of a characteristically Spanish coexistence between the various, constantly evolving, systems of notation across the space of almost four centuries.

The second section offers an outline for a classification of the different notational systems as they are represented by a selection of liturgical and musical sources from different parts of the Iberian Peninsula. These sources are described in the second part of this volume (see pp. 249 and subsq.). The period under study (the 9th-12th centuries) extends from the time of the first conservative examples of Visigothic and Catalonian notation to the phase of consolidation of Aquitainian notation, and includes the period of transition, when different combinations of notations were in use.

I offer two diagrams of the sources: one based on topographical criteria, representing cultural areas (diagram 1), and the other a formal or typological arrangement, based on the systems of notation represented by the sources (diagram 2). In an appendix to this chapter, I offer an additional list of sources, using a more limited, exclusively chronological criterion, for quick reference.

The third section examines the following aspects, which are illustrated by representative elements from the selected corpus: 1) the variability of the systems of writing and notation from the different areas and chronological periods established; 2) the diversity of contexts, or typologies, of the sources, where both melodic notes and certain neumatic signs are found; and 3) the variety of functions adopted by these notational signs, depending on the context in which they occur. This three-pronged approach will make it possible to visualise the plurality of graphic inventories developed in the different Iberian systems of notation in the period under consideration.

Attempts at a systematic classification of the corpus of manuscripts

This attempt to classify the corpus of liturgical-musical manuscripts dating from such a broad and unusual period as the transition from the Spanish, or Hispano-Visigothic rite, to the Franco-Roman rite, requires the use of some very diverse criteria: historical, paleographic, codicological, semiological and chronological.[3] In addition to this complexity of disciplinary approaches (with their corresponding formal objects and methodological orientation), we also face some purely material difficulties, touched on in the general introduction. Any attempt to classify Visigothic musical-liturgical sources today is hindered by an absence of sources for certain geographic areas (we have almost no idea of the sources used in the south of the Peninsula,[4] the Aragonese region, or even in Catalonia itself before the 10th century), by the fragmentary preservation and the fact that some specimens, previously mentioned in several publications, are now impossible to locate.

The classifications of medieval Iberian literary, liturgical and liturgical-musical manuscript sources that have been proposed to date were based on a range of different criteria. Millares Carlo (1999) classified the Visigothic corpus simply by sorting it in alphabetical order by the current location of the source, whereas Fernández de la Cuesta (1983, 2000),[5] working exclusively with the musical-liturgical sources, classified the corpus according to various typologies, drawing attention to the difficulties posed by chronological and geographical classification. The same author, in his catalog (1980),[6] covering the 9th to the 15th centuries, opted for the alphabetical order of the present sites of conservation. Janini (1977, 1980)[7] also sorts all of the liturgical sources from the 9th to the 17th centuries in alphabetical order of the site of conservation, making no distinction between musical and nonmusical sources, or between those pertaining to the Spanish rite and the Franco-Roman rite.

Without wishing to downplay the value to the researcher of those two cataloguing criteria (site of conservation and typology of the sources), they nevertheless do not represent the chronological or geographical distribution that is essential for the purposes of observation and analysis, nor do they address the script systems of text and notation. Don Randel was the first to propose a classification of the musical-liturgical corpus of the Spanish rite based on melodic structure, which distinguished three traditions corresponding to the areas of León, La Rioja and Toledo.[8] This classification was based not so much on paleographic criteria but on the differentiated application of the psalm tones. His classification does not include sources from the area of Catalonia/Narbonne.

Classifications based on the alphabetical order of the current place of conservation or even chronological classifications are workable and offer solid results, yet because they do not examine the more outstanding attributes of the contents, they are not particularly helpful for scholars tackling issues of theoretical and substantive interest. Moreover, in the latter case, the final result is not entirely free of problems, given the difficulty at this time of dating many specimens.

Any attempt to offer a classification or, at least, to organize and present the manuscripts in a way that goes beyond the minimalist option of their place of conservation and seeks to deal with issues of content, poses difficulties that are hard to ignore. For this reason, I opted to use a key principle in statistics and methodology, parsimonious classification. To put it another way, we have maintained a broad level of initial segregation, but in subsequent steps several elements were collapsed into a more inclusive category, if general reasons (or specific ones related to the elements being classified) made this action advisable. It is well known that although major classifications of empirical material into a small number of categories or sets may be elegant, in the absence of some powerful theory or conceptual outline to justify such an operation, the result can reveal almost as much internal variability between the elements in each category as there is external variability between categories. In other words, such a classification has a high rate of error in assigning elements to the various categories. The transition from broad segregation to more compact classification is certainly complex, and needs to be backed by theorical and/or methodological considerations. This is only possible if studies into the period in question are sufficiently advanced and obviously entails cooperation between a considerable number of scholars from different disciplines interested in the same material object. The purpose of this work is to take a few asymptotic steps towards a larger classification, to help reveal fresh theoretical and interpretative issues.

Our first proposed classification takes as its base the area of origin or use of the sources, which can be geographically and culturally delimited with an acceptable degree of precision (congruous with or confirmable by the general historiographic literature on the period).[9] The second classification is based on the different typologies of notation. These two diagrams, referred to here as 1 and 2, take as their base the corpus of musical-liturgical sources from the Spanish, Catalonian-Narbonnaise, and Franco-Roman traditions, a technical description of which is given in the second part of this work.

One of the main difficulties in building a map of Iberian centers of production[10] of liturgical-musical manuscripts—distinguishing between those of Spanish tradition, Catalonian-Narbonnaise tradition with an autonomous profile and a particular subset confined to Septimania, and the Franco-Roman or Aquitainian tradition—lies in combining the basic political/institutional and cultural criteria with strictly formal (codicological, paleographic, philological, and artistic) and structural ones. Indeed, this is a common issue in methodology: the classification or relationship between differentiated levels of the analysis, one *exogenous* or contextual (the political and cultural framework), the other *endogenous* (the formal properties of the sources). For this reason, the material object concerning us here should ideally be viewed from various disciplinary angles ranging from a purely material analysis of the manuscripts to a consideration of the historical, political, social, and cultural context to which they belong.[11]

As shown in Sections 2 and 3 of this chapter, the group of sources selected reveals a complex combination of script systems, with overlapping and/or coexistence of different inventories, for both writing and annotating, in some cases within the same space and period, in others in different spaces, at the same or different times. The lack of a methodology for precisely establishing the typology and chronology of the different systems of notation is one of the main obstacles to building a model for classifying all of the sources selected.

A rigorous interpretation is needed of the formal asymmetries that arise in the transition to the new Franco-Roman repertory in the different cultural areas *(Kulturkreise)*, asymmetries which are also reflected in the diversity of liturgical traditions or practices, which, combined with the nonexistence of preserved sources for some geographical areas, make the exegesis of notation (or notations) particularly complex in the peninsular area.

The researcher faces another kind of difficulty when drawing up a list of the centers where the codices were produced and, more abstractly, of the cultural environments to which they belong.[12]

First, the continuously fluctuating political borders make it difficult to apply stable and consistent geopolitical terminology. Assigning each manuscript to a given political area or nucleus is a complex task not only because of this variability in the political identity of the territory—which might change over the space of a few years or decades—but also, as Mundó has shown, because the episcopal sees did not always follow a uniform course of action but often followed their own particular dynamic, removed from the more general political context.[13] A distinction must also be drawn between the main monastic, cathedral and rural parishes, with the latter generally assimilating new contents and script forms at a slower pace.

In the case of the Catalonian-Narbonnaise ambit, Mundó highlights these asymmetries and the phenomenon of the early transition marked by hybrid forms, whereby the Catalonian system of notation was associated with a Carolingian script with reminiscences of the Visigothic. He concludes that by around 900, the Visigothic culture was in clear retreat in Catalonia before a Carolingian culture that had already been almost fully assimilated.[14] In contrast to this scenario of early influence and acceptance of Carolingian culture in Catalonia, not entirely unrelated to phenomena of resistance, a series of spaces and enclaves grew up in other areas of the peninsula that were unenthusiastic about the imposition of the new repertory. This reflected the dissonance between the policies promoted by the lay powers and the conservative attitude of the ecclesiastical centers, which would leave its mark on the formal and structural characteristics of the sources listed here. The problems of shifting political borders, especially in the territories of Pamplona, Navarre, and the kingdom-county of Aragón, and the extreme case of the on-and-off union of the kingdoms of Castile and León, illustrates the difficulty of ascribing given manuscripts within a precise and stable geopolitical framework.[15]

Second, the phenomenon of the traffic in manuscripts poses an additional problem for the construction of a topographical diagram or map, in that it tends to obscure the traces of original provenance. In this regard, the cases of interaction between the monasteries of San Millán de la Cogolla and Santo Domingo de Silos are paradigmatic, as is the multiple provenance of the manuscripts in the library at Silos, where it is estimated that only 21 percent come from the center itself, another 50 percent coming from Valeránica, Cardeña, and San Millán and the remaining 29 percent from other centers.[16] Other illustrative cases of the same phenomenon of trafficking in specimens between different Iberian and ultra-Pyrenean centers can be seen in the corpus of codices from the kingdom of León and in the process of creating the libraries of La Rioja.[17]

The third difficulty, which is related to the previous one, is that formal criteria have yet to be established for distinguishing between original manuscripts from a Spanish center of production and manuscripts from centers on the other side of the Pyrenees. As we shall see, this difficulty particularly affects sources from the Catalonian-Narbonnaise area and those with Franco-Roman repertory dating from the 11th century *ex.* to 12th century *med.*, that is, the initial phase of introduction of the new rite, when there was a greater call for ultra-Pyrenean codices to be imported and copied.

Having noted these considerations, let us now address the general direction and architecture of each of the two classification diagrams or proposals. Diagram 1 (see pp. 197 and subsq.) classifies the sources selected here by geographical areas and in chronological order.[18] The four areas covered coincide with the political nuclei of medieval Spain, with the leading centers of manuscript production or copying of the period under consideration identified.[19] The resulting geopolitical spaces were 1) Catalonia, 2) Aragón, 3) Castile and León, 4) Navarre, and 5) Toledo. Within these regions, there were other smaller areas, an expression of the political evolution and the development of the ecclesiastical organisation of the territory. These crystallised into culturally referential centers, such as the monasteries of San Millán and Silos in Castile, Roda de Isábena, Montserrat, La Seu d'Urgell, Vic and Ripoll in Catalonia, and San Juan de la Peña and Huesca in Aragón. We can also distinguish between two separate areas of the peninsula: the western area, comprising Castile and Navarre, and the eastern area, initially called the *Marca Hispánica* and subsequently assimilated under the crown of Aragón, as a result of the appropriation in the 12th century *med.* of a previous march encompassing the county of Barcelona and the kingdom of Aragón. The crown of Castile was constituted from the 13th century, when it came to integrate a culturally diverse group, consisting of the kingdom of Galicia and the kingdom of León (with its original heartland the kingdom of Asturias). The position of the kingdom of Navarre was the most variable. United with the county-kingdom of Aragón until the latter's independence in 1054, its expansion was curbed by Castile on one side and Aragón on the other, with the result that it tended to look north to the Frankish kingdom. Toledo, embedded in Moslem territory, which came to form part of the Christian topography following its annexation to the kingdom of Castile at the end of the 11th century. Finally, the dioceses of Braga and Coimbra, originally associated with the monarchy of León, joined the kingdom of Portugal from the 12th century.

Diagram 1 was created using these categories, defined here as political nuclei. It also incorporates the influential cultural centers within each area, such as, inter alia, Santo Domingo de Silos, San Millán de la Cogolla, Nájera, Ripoll, Vic, San Juan de la Peña, Santa Cruz de la Serós, Huesca, Toledo, Braga, Coimbra, and Aveiro.

In the case of the Castile-León group, a distinction should be drawn between, on the one hand, the set of Visigothic manuscripts from the Leonese monarchy, which encompassed the regions of León, Galicia, and Portugal under the reign of Ferdinand I, and, on the other, the county of Castile, with its formal links to the kingdom of León.[20] But from the codicological and structural point of view of the manuscripts, this distinction is unworkable, given the dense network of relations that existed between these groups. I have therefore chosen to retain the generic category of Castile and León, listing the main centers of manuscript production within it. Portuguese Visigothic manuscripts from the region of the Duero, Lamego, Braga, and Coimbra [AU, IV-3.ª-Gav. 44 (22)] are grouped in an additional set, although they are understood to be politically associated with the kingdom of León and in formal terms show affiliations with either Castilian or Toledan traditions, whereas manuscripts dating from after the 12th century come under the Frankish sphere of influence, and are associated with the reforming dynamic that was at work in Castile.[21] At the same time, the fragments of transition (Santiago de Compostela, AC, Frag. 1, and Ourense, Frag. 3 and 6), although belonging to the new Castilian political framework, formally reflect the conservatism of the Compostellan periphery, that is the Leonese cultural context. The only examples from Sigüenza and Burgo de Osma are two late manuscripts, also from the Castilian area. Silos and San Millán offer two extensive corpuses traversing the 9th to 12th centuries, with representative specimens from the three phases: Visigothic, Transition and Franco-Roman. The origin of the Toledo specimen (BC, 35-6) has not been identified, and it has been attributed both to the northern peninsula and to Toledo itself (Mundó).[22] From the production centers of Albelda and San Prudencio de Monte Laturce, two Visigothic specimens from the Rioja area (eventually incorporated into Castile under Alfonso VI) are worthy of mention. In addition to a few late Visigothic specimens, the Toledo group contains specimens from the Franco-Roman rite copied or imported during the reform process after the city was reconquered by the King of Castile. The political strip dividing these different groups was therefore marked by the transition from the *Leonese Empire* to the nascent *Hispanic Empire.*[23]

As for the Aragonese group, there is some disagreement as to where it should be classified, with some authors using solid arguments to include it in the Catalonian group.[24] The diagram 1 nonetheless keeps the two nuclei separate: Catalonia and Aragón.

Finally, under the heading "Unknown Origin" and "Disputed Origin", contains specimens with locations continue to be the subject of controversy. One group particularly affected by this question includes a number of specimens preserved in the Silos collection.[25] Within the framework of this publication, Díaz y Díaz has corrected the traditional attribution of the Antiphonary of San Juan de la Peña, speculating that it might come from somewhere near the area of Nájera,[26] whereas Ruiz Asencio has proved that the fragment from Santo Domingo de la Calzada was originally from Albelda.

The selection given in diagram 1 also presents some exceptional manuscripts of ultra-Pyrenean provenance, which are underlined in italics. These are the Antiphonary of Toledo (BC, 44-2) and the Tropary-Sequentiary-Prosary-Prosulary of St. Pierre de Moissac (Paris, BNF, N. A. L. 1871). The former is attributed to a *scriptorium* in the south of France, and the second is, without doubt, from Moissac, although it appears to have been used from a very early date as an exemplar in Toledo. Also worthy of mention are the Huesca hymnary (Huesca, AC, Cod. 1),[27] almost certainly from Saint Pierre de Moissac; the tropary-prosary (Huesca, AC, Cod. 4), comprising various sections of diverse ultra-Pyrenean provenance, among which some are from the center in Huesca[28] and, the Missal of Mateus (Braga, AD, ms. 1000), from Saint Martial of Limoges. These ultra-Pyrenean specimens are included as an illustration of the first exemplars from southeast France that were circulating at the beginning of the liturgical reform in the respective Iberian areas.[29] The diagram places these sources in the areas or centers for which they were destined.

A map showing the centers of origin and provenance of the manuscripts set out in the diagram is given at the beginning of the second part of this work.[30]

The topographical classification is seen as a provisional instrument, intended for pragmatic purposes. Attributing the sources to a given cultural, or political-cultural area, some confirmed and others hypothetical,[31] allows us to take on a second objective: defining the typological profile of the sources for each of the subsets established, diagram 2 (see pp. 201 and subsq.) shows the same corpus as the previous diagram, here classified by typology of notation: Visigothic, Catalonian and Aquitainian, with their respective variants of transition, indicating, in addition, the liturgical rite to which the sources belong.

The list allows us to distinguish between three groups that are differentiated by the use of formal criteria—script systems—and structural criteria—the rite to which they belong—which serve to test an archeology of Iberian systems of notation, as does the third part of this study.

From a structural point of view, the diagram is classified as follows:

1) Musical-liturgical manuscripts from the Spanish tradition.
2) Musical-liturgical manuscripts from the Catalonian-Narbonnaise tradition.
3) Musical-liturgical manuscripts from the Franco-Roman tradition: period of transition.
4) Musical-liturgical manuscripts from the Franco-Roman tradition.

Whereas the first two sections involve mostly homogeneous script systems, the third section covers a greater diversity of combinatory models, a result of the period of liturgical change, and the fourth section reflects a consolidation of the reform, during which the generalised implementation of Carolingian script and Aquitainian notation can be observed.

1) Musical-liturgical manuscripts from the Spanish tradition

The repertory from the old Spanish rite is preserved in the following sources: musical-liturgical manuscripts from the 9th to the 13th centuries illustrating different script systems and combinations; hymnaries from the end of the 15th century copied on the initiative of Cardinal Cisneros in an attempt to restore the old rite and, finally, various literary and theoretical sources on the Spanish liturgy.[32] Of particular interest for our study is the first category of sources indicated, which limits the chronology of the musical-liturgical manuscripts to the 9th to 12th centuries—although a brief mention will be made of the Toledan sources, late copies from the 13th to 14th centuries—.[33]

This first group can in turn be used to develop a classification based on formal criteria, divided into the following subsets in an inventory of characteristic neumatic signs:

- Manuscripts in Visigothic script and Visigothic notation. Spanish liturgy. Northern tradition-southern tradition.
- Manuscripts in Visigothic script and forms of notation close to pitch or ekphonetic notation. Spanish liturgy.

2) Musical-liturgical manuscripts from the Catalonian-Narbonnaise tradition

- Manuscripts in Carolingian script and archaic Catalonian notation, 10th century.[34]

3) Musical-liturgical manuscripts from the Franco-Roman tradition: period of transition[35]

The third set includes sources from the transition from the Spanish rite to the Franco-Roman rite, that is, those that reflect the mutation, interaction, or coexistence of the different systems of musical script and notation from each of the traditions.[36] The repertory they transmit belongs to the new Franco-Roman usage, even though they partially maintain formulae typical of the old Spanish rite or of the Catalonian-Narbonnaise tradition. On a formal plane we can distinguish between the following combinatory models resulting from the process of assimilation of the new liturgical usage in the different cultural and political contexts of the Iberian Peninsula:

- Manuscripts in Visigothic script and notation with Aquitainian influence.[37] Franco-Roman liturgy (London, BL, Add. ms. 30850 and Add. ms. 30848).
- Manuscripts in Visigothic script and coexistence of notational systems: Visigothic and Aquitainian notations/Catalonian and Aquitainian notations. Franco-Roman liturgy (Madrid, RAH, Cod. 56; Silos, AM, Cod. 4; and Lleida, AC, Roda 18).
- Manuscripts in Visigothic script and Aquitainian notation. Franco-Roman liturgy (Madrid, RAH, Cod. 18).
- Manuscripts in Carolingian script and Catalonian notation. Catalonian-Narbonnaise/Franco-Roman liturgy (Barcelona, ACA, Ripoll 106).
- Manuscripts in Carolingian script and showing the coexistence of notational systems: Catalonian notation and Aquitainian notation, or Catalonian notation and square notation. Franco-Roman liturgy (Barcelona, ACA, Ripoll 74; Paris, BNF, N. A. L. 495; Lleida, AC, Roda 16 Catalonian and Aquitainian notation with a mixed Visigothic and Franco-Roman formulary).

The second model includes both specimens copied in Visigothic script and notation, to which parts in Carolingian script and Aquitainian notation were subsequently added, and specimens in which the original notation, Visigothic or Catalonian, was scraped to insert in its place the new Aquitainian notation. In most cases, these are books from the Spanish rite that continued to be used for celebrating with specific formularies, or remnants of the Catalonian-Narbonnaise tradition, reflecting an overlapping phase between the different liturgical practices and notational systems. The situation also confirms the celebrant or singer's familiarity with different script systems. An illustrative example can be seen in the breviary of the Spanish rite from the 11th century *med.* (New York, HS, B 2916) in Visigothic script and notation, with later additions in Carolingian script and Aquitainian notation. Other additional examples with Visigothic notation and *addendas* in Aquitainian notation are also shown in diagram 2:[38] the Bibles of Silos (Cracow, Czartorysky Library, ms. 3.118) and Cardeña (Burgos, AC, w./o. s.) with occasional additions, the *Liber ordinum* (Madrid, RAH, Cod. 56), in which the Visigothic notation was scraped to insert the Aquitainian notation and, in an equivalent case from the Catalonian area, the lectionary-antiphonary (Lleida, AC, Roda 18) where the Catalonian notation was scraped in the 12th century *med.* to insert the Aquitainian notation.[39] The *Liber glossarum* (Barcelona, BC, Ripoll 74), with additions in Aquitainian notation *in campo aperto* from the 12th century in some folios; the *Liber ordinum* (Silos, AM, Cod. 4), where a few pieces in Aquitainian notation were inserted in the margin of the folio, respecting the version in Visigothic notation in the body of the text, and the *Liber comicus* (Paris, BNF, N. A. L. 2171), also with some added pieces in Aquitainian notation, attest to the dynamic process of transition and the multiple formal structures through which it was consolidated.

These subsets reflect a progression which, beginning with the local Visigothic tradition, goes through a phase during which the systems are combined with the involvement of copyists from different locations, to finally crystallise in the new Aquitainian model assumed in both fields, script and notation.[40]

The selection of transitional manuscripts shown in diagram 2 might be further extended by adding a group of sources partially included in Millares Carlo's corpus, listed subsequently, on the grounds that—although limited in number and largely preserved in fragments—they are particularly illustrative of the typological, chronological, and cultural asymmetries that can be seen in the dynamic and heterogeneous process of liturgical reform. One of the basic tools for reconstructing the complex process of transition; for casting light on questions such as the intervention of the number of copyists and the origin and provenance of the sources; and for determining the specific practices of each geocultural area indicated is to analyse formal peculiarities, albeit not in their entirety.

To help situate the examples, where applicable, we show the reference number assigned in Volume I of Millares Carlo's catalog:

- Braga, AD, Materiais inúteis, no. 23 (formerly Registro Geral, Caixa Frag. 244, 1). Capa do Tombo de Silvares. *Fragmentum*. Franco-Roman missal. Visigothic script (abbreviated Carolingian system), Aquitainian notation. 12th century. [Millares 17.][41]
- Braga, AD, Registro Geral, Caixa Frag. 280, 3. *Fragmentum*. Franco-Roman Antiphonary. Visigothic script, Aquitainian notation. 11th century. [Millares 18.][42]
- Braga, AD, Registro Geral, Caixa Frag. 284, 12 (Capa do Tombo de Barbeita). *Fragmentum*. Franco-Roman missal. Carolingian script with reminiscences of Visigothic, Carolingian, Aquitainian notation. 12th century. [Millares 19.]
- Lisbon, BN [w./o. s.]. *Fragmentum*. Franco-Roman missal. Visigothic script, Aquitainian notation. 12th century. [Díaz y Díaz 1983, no. 114.]
- Cambridge, UL. Add. ms. 5905. Franco-Roman breviary. *Fragmentum*. Visigothic script, Aquitainian notation (two antiphons). 10th-11th centuries. [Millares 32.]
- León, AC, Frag. III. Franco-Roman breviary. Visigothic script, Aquitainian notation. 11th century *ex.* [Millares 93.]
- Paris, BNF, N. A. L. 235. *Fragmentum*. Franco-Roman breviary. Visigothic script, Aquitainian notation (one responsory). 10th century *ex.* [Millares 253.]
- Paris, BNF, N. A. L. 2170. Cassianus, *Collationes et al.* Visigothic script, Aquitainian notation. 11th century. [Millares 262.][43]
- Paris, BNF, Lat. 2855. Three fragments of manuscripts collected in one volume. Frag. II (fols. 73v-159r + 159v-160v) was copied in Albelda, 950-951. Visigothic script and notation. 10th century. [Millares 244.][44]
- Toledo, BC, 10-5. Franco-Roman Antiphonary. Visigothic script, Aquitainian notation (2 fols.). 12th century *in.* [Millares 313.]
- Venice, BNM, 14th century, ms. 232 (4257). Visigothic script, Aquitainian notation. Franco-Roman repertory. Fragment of *Exultet*. 12th century *in.*[45]
- Valladolid, ARCH. Fragment of a folio in Visigothic script, Aquitainian notation. Currently illegible. 11th century *ex.*-12th century *in.*[46]
- Zamora, AHP. "Musical Parchments" section. Frag. 15, *Liber misticus* from the late 11th century and Frag. 202, mass from the 11th century *ex.* to 12th century *in.*[47] Fragments of a folio in Visigothic script with Carolingian influences and Aquitainian notation.

4) Musical-liturgical manuscripts from the Franco-Roman tradition

Finally, the forth group includes specimens of the Franco-Roman rite in Carolingian script and Aquitainian notation, reflecting the complete assimilation of the new usages, even when the contents may still include forms or celebrations from local traditions.

As diagram 2 shows, the chronology of the three sections does not develop in a linear fashion: in other words, there is no diachronic continuity, but instead a clear asymmetry between the different sets, which can only be attributed to various cultural and geopolitical factors specific to the respective historical contexts to which the specimens belong. Finally, diagram 3 shows the various typologies of the selected examples, in this case in chronological order.

Exegesis of notation: Asymmetries, anachronisms and coexistences

In the context of Iberian studies, greater advances have been made in the area of textual paleography than in musical paleography and semiology.[48] Thanks to the former, we now have a database and a methodological approach which, though it does not address all of the problems, nevertheless offers an equally valid theoretical model for the analysis of the different Iberian notational systems. The perceptible gap between the developments

DIAGRAM 1:[49] CHRONOLOGICAL LIST OF SOURCES BY GEO-POLITICAL AREA AND CULTURAL CENTER

Archive / Library	Catalog number	Source / Provenance	Date	Typology of the script / Typology of the notation
		CATALONIA **Ripoll**		
Barcelona, ACA	Ripoll 106	Ripoll	10th c. *in.*	Carolingian / Catalonian notation
Barcelona, ACA	Ripoll 74	Ripoll	10th c. *ex.*-11th c. *in.*	Carolingian / Catalonian notation and Aquitainian
Barcelona, ACA	Ripoll 42	Ripoll	11th c. *in.*	Visigothic. Theoretical treat., s. n.
Barcelona, ACA	Ripoll 40	Ripoll	11th c. *ex.*	Carolingian / Catalonian notation
		La Seu d'Urgell		
Lleida, AC	Roda 16	La Seu d'Urgell (?) / Ribagorza (?)	11th c. *in.* (1000-18)	Carolingian / archaic Catalonian notation, Visig. infl.
Montserrat, BM	ms. 73	La Seu d'Urgell	12th c. *ex.*	Carolingian / Aquitainian notation
		Vic		
Vic, ABEV	ms. 67	Vic	11th c. *med.*	Carolingian / Catalonian notation
Vic, ABEV	XI/I	Vic	11th c. *ex.*	Visigothic / Catalonian notation
Vic, ABEV	ms. 105	Vic	12th c. *in.*	Carolingian / Catalonian notation and Aquitainian
		Elna/Moissac		
Paris, BNF	*Lat. 5304*[1]	*Saint Pierre de Moissac (?) / Elna (?)*	11th c. *med.*	Carolingian / Catalonian notation
		Roda de Isábena		
Lleida, AC	Roda 18	Roda	11th c. *ex.*	Carolingian Visigothic influence / Catalonian and Aquitainian notation
Lleida, AC	Roda 14	Roda	12th c. *med.*	Carolingian / Aquitainian notation
Lleida, AC	Roda 11	Roda	12th c. *ex.* (1191)	Carolingian / Catalonian notation and Aquitainian
Lleida, AC	Roda 8	Roda	12th c. *ex.*	Carolingian / Aquitainian notation
Montserrat, BM	ms. 822	(Catalonian-Narbonnaise ambit)	12th c. *in.*	Carolingian / Catalonian notation
Montserrat, BM	ms. 794-I	Solsona	12th c. *in.*	Carolingian / Catalonian notation
Montserrat, BM	ms. 72	St. Romá de les Bons	12th c. *ex.*	Carolingian / Catalonian notation
Paris, BNF	Lat. 933	Lagrasse	11th c. *ex.*-12th c. *in.*	Carolingian / Catalonian notation
Paris, BNF	N. A. L. 495	Girona	12th c. *in.*	Carolingian / Aquitainian notation
Barcelona, BC	M. 1147	St. Pere d'Ager	12th c. *ex.*	Carolingian / Aquitainian notation
		ARAGÓN **Huesca**		
Huesca, AC	Cod. 1	*Huesca / Southern France*	11th c. *ex.*	Carolingian / Aquitainian notation
Huesca, AC	Cod. 4	*Huesca / France*	12th c. *in.*	Carolingian / Aquitainian notation
Huesca, AC	Cod. 2	Huesca	12th c. *med.*	Carolingian / Aquitainian notation
Madrid, BN	ms. 9719	(Aragón)	12th c. *ex.* (1169)	Carolingian / Aquitainian notation
Huesca, AHP	12030/36	Huesca	12th c. *ex.*	Carolingian / Aquitainian notation
		Santa Cruz de la Serós		
Jaca, Santa Cruz de la Serós, AM	w./o. s.	Santa Cruz de la Serós	12th c. *ex.*	Carolingian / Aquitainian notation

[1] Codices of ultra-Pyrenean origin are given in italics.

DIAGRAM 1 *(cont.)*: CHRONOLOGICAL LIST OF SOURCES BY GEO-POLITICAL AREA AND CULTURAL CENTER

Archive / Library	Catalog number	Source / Provenance	Date	Typology of the script / Typology of the notation
		San Juan de La Peña		
El Escorial, RB	ms. L.III.3	San Juan de La Peña	12th c. *ex.*	Carolingian / Aquitainian notation
El Escorial, RB	ms. L.III.4	San Juan de La Peña	12th c. *ex.*	Carolingian / Aquitainian notation
El Escorial, RB	ms. Q.III.10	San Juan de La Peña	12th c. *ex.*	Carolingian / Aquitainian notation
		NAVARRE **Santa María la Real de Nájera**		
Zaragoza, BGU	M-418	Santa María La Real de Nájera (Díaz y Díaz) / San Juan de la Peña / La Rioja (Gudiol)	10th c. *ex.*	Visigothic / Visigothic notation
Silos, AM	Cod. 3	Sta. María la Real de Nájera	11th c. *in.* (1039)	Visigothic / Visigothic notation
Silos, AM	Cod. 6	Sta. María la Real de Nájera	11th c. *med.*	Visigothic / Visigothic notation
Silos, AM	Cod. 7	Sta. María la Real de Nájera	11th c. *med.*	Visigothic / Visigothic notation
		PYRENEAN ZONE		
Roncevaux, Museo Colegiata	w./o. s.	(Navarre)	12th c. *ex.*	Carolingian / Aquitainian notation
Pamplona, AC	w./o. s.	(Navarre)	12th c. *ex.*	Carolingian / Aquitainian notation
Pamplona, ARGN	K. 6	Fitero	12th c. *ex.*-13th c. *in.*	Carolingian / Aquitainian notation
		CASTILE-LEÓN **San Pedro de Cardeña**		
Burgos, AC	w./o. s.	San Pedro de Cardeña	10th c. *in.*	Visigothic / Visigothic notation
		San Pedro de Valeránica		
Córdoba, AC	ms. 1	San Pedro de Valeránica	10th c. *med.* (953)	Visigothic / Aquitainian notation (add. 11th c. *med.*)
León, AC	ms. 8	Beja	10th c. *med.*	Visigothic / Visigothic notation
Córdoba, AC	ms. 123	(León)	10th c. *ex.*-11th c. *in.*	Visigothic / Visigothic notation
Sheffield Galleries & Museums Trust	ms. 31	(León?)	11th c. *in.*	Visigothic / Visigothic notation
Santiago de Compostela, BXU	ms. 609 (Res. 1)	(León)	11th c. *med.* (1055)	Visigothic / Visigothic notation
Santiago de Compostela, AC	Frag. 1	Santiago de Compostela	12th c. *in.*	Visigothic / Aquitainian notation
Ourense, AC	Frag. 3 and 6	Ourense	12th c. *in.*	Visigothic / Aquitainian notation
Sigüenza, AC	w./o. s.	(Sigüenza)	12th c. *med.*	Carolingian / Aquitainian notation
Burgo de Osma, AC	ms. 94	Burgo de Osma	12th c. *ex.*	Carolingian / Aquitainian notation
		Santo Domingo de Silos		
London, BL	Add. ms. 30852	Silos / Aragón / Cardeña (?)	9th c. *ex.*	Visigothic / Visigothic notation
Paris, BNF	N. A. L. 2199	Silos / León (?)	10th c. *in.*	Visigothic / Visigothic notation
London, BL	Add. ms. 11695	Silos	10th c. *ex.*	Visigothic / Visigothic notation
Cracow, Czartorysky	ms. 3.118	Silos (?)	10th c. *ex.*	Visigothic / Aquitainian notation
London, BL	Add. ms. 30851	Silos	11th c. *med.*	Visigothic-Reference marks (Visigothic neumes)

DIAGRAM 1 *(cont.)*: CHRONOLOGICAL LIST OF SOURCES BY GEO-POLITICAL AREA AND CULTURAL CENTER

Archive / Library	Catalog number	Source / Provenance	Date	Typology of the script / Typology of the notation
		Santo Domingo de Silos		
Paris, BNF	N. A. L. 2171	Silos	11th c. *med.*	Visigothic / Aquitainian notation (add.)
Silos, AM	Cod. 5	La Rioja / Aragón (?)	11th c. *med.* (1059)	Visigothic / Visigothic notation
London, BL	Add. ms. 30850	Silos	11th c. *ex.*	Visigothic / Visigothic and Aquitainian notation (add.)
London, BL	Add. ms. 30848	Silos	11th c. *ex.*	Visigothic / Aquitainian notation
London, BL	Add. ms. 30847	Silos	11th c. *ex.*	Visigothic / Visigothic notation of Aquitainian influence
		San Millán		
Madrid, RAH	Cod. 30	San Millán	10th c. *ex.*	Visigothic / Visigothic notation
Madrid, RAH	Cod. 56	San Millán	10th c. *ex.*	Visigothic / Visigothic notation (scrapings: Aquitainian)
Madrid, RAH	Cod. 118 / Cod. 14	San Millán	11th c. *in.*	Visigothic s. n. (exception)
New York, HS	B 2916 (To. 33.2)	San Millán	11th c. *med.*	Visigothic / Visigothic, Aquitainian and Alphabetical notation.
Madrid, RAH	Cod. 18	San Millán	11th c. *ex.* (1090)	Visigothic / Aquitainian notation
Madrid, RAH	Cod. 51	San Millán	12th c. *in.*	Carolingian / Aquitainian notation
Madrid, RAH	Cod. 45	San Millán	12th c. *ex.*	Carolingian / Aquitainian notation
Salamanca, BGU	ms. 2668	Silos / San Millán (?)	11th c. *med.* (1059)	Visigothic / Visigothic notation
Salamanca, BGU	ms. 2637	Silos / San Millán (?)	12th c. *ex.*	Carolingian / Aquitainian notation
		San Martín de Albelda		
Santo Domingo la Calzada, AC	Frag. w./o. s.	Albelda	10th c. *ex.*-11th c. *in.*	Visigothic / Visigothic notation
		San Prudencio de Monte Laturce		
Silos, AM	Cod. 4	San Prudencio de Monte Laturce	11th c. *med.* (1052)	Visigothic / Visigothic notation
		PORTUGAL **Coimbra**		
Coimbra, AU	IV-3ª-Gav. 44	Coimbra (Cathedral)	11th c. *in.*	Visigothic / Visigothic notation
Porto, BPM	Santa Cruz 76	Coimbra	12th c. *ex.*	Carolingian / Aquitainian notation
Porto, BPM	Santa Cruz 83	Coimbra	12th c. *ex.*	Carolingian / Aquitainian notation
Lisbon, Torre do Tombo	Frag. Cx 20, no. 14	Coimbra	12th c. *ex.*-13th c. *in.*	Carolingian / Aquitainian notation
		Braga		
Coimbra, AU	IV-3.ª S-Gav. 44 (20)	San Fins de Friestas (Braga)	11th c. *med.*	Visigothic / Aquitainian notation
Braga, AD	*ms. 1000, Mattheus*	*Parish of San Mateo (copied in St. Martial of Limoges)*	12th c. *med.*	Carolingian / Aquitainian notation
Braga, AD	Frag. 49	(Braga)	12th c. *med.*	Carolingian / Aquitainian notation
Braga, AD	Frag. 243	(Braga)	12th c. *med.*	Carolingian / Aquitainian notation
Braga, AD	Frag. 244	(Braga)	12th c. *ex.*	Carolingian / Aquitainian notation
Braga, AD	Frag. 210	(Braga)	12th c. *ex.*	Carolingian / Aquitainian notation

DIAGRAM 1 *(cont.)*: CHRONOLOGICAL LIST OF SOURCES BY GEO-POLITICAL AREA AND CULTURAL CENTER

Archive / Library	Catalog number	Source / Provenance	Date	Typology of the script / Typology of the notation
		Aveiro		
Aveiro, AD	Frag., w./o. s.	San Miguel de Aveiro (?)	12th c. *ex.*	Carolingian / Aquitainian notation
		TOLEDO		
Madrid, BN	ms. 10029	Toledo / Aragón (?)	9th c. *ex.*-10th c. *in.* (11th c. *in.* Mundó)	Visigothic / Visigothic notation
Toledo, BC	*ms.44-1*	*Toledo*	11th c. *ex.*	Carolingian / Aquitainian notation
Paris, BNF	*N. A. L. 1871*	*St. Pierre de Moissac*	11th c. *ex.*	Carolingian / Aquitainian notation
Toledo, BC	*ms. 35-7*	Santa Eulalia (Toledo)	11th c. *ex.*-12th c. *in.*	Visigothic / Visigothic notation
Toledo, BC	*ms. 44-2*	*Toledo*	12th c. *in.*	Carolingian / Visigothic notation
Madrid, BN	ms. 10001 (To. 35-1)	Toledo/León (?)	12th c. *ex.*-13th c. *in.*	Visigothic / Visigothic notation
		UNKNOWN ORIGIN **Northern Iberian tradition**		
London, BL	Add. ms. 30844	? (Silos / La Rioja)	10th c. *in.*	Visigothic / Visigothic notation
London, BL	Add. ms. 30846	?	11th c. *in.*	Visigothic / Visigothic notation
London, BL	Add. ms. 30845	?	11th c. *med.*	Visigothic / Visigothic notation
London, BL	Add. ms. 30849	?	11th c. *ex.*	Carolingian / Aquitainian notation
Toledo, BC	ms. 35-6	?	10th c. *ex.*-11th c. *in.*	Visigothic / Northern Visigothic notation
		ORIGIN DISPUTED		
Silos, AM	Cod. 30852	Silos (?) / Aragón (?) / Cardeña (?)	9th c. *ex.*	
Madrid, BN	ms. 10029 (To. 14-22)	Toledo (Mundó, Ruiz)/ Aragón (Janini)	9th c. *ex.*-10th c. *in.* (11th c. *in.*, Mundó)	Visigothic / Northern Visigothic notation
Madrid, BN	ms. 10001 (To. 35-1)	Toledo (?)/ León (?)	10th c. *ex.*-11th c. *in.* (Millares), 12th c. *ex.*-13th c. *in.* (Mundó)	Visigothic / Visigothic notation (South and North)
Salamanca, BGU	ms. 2668	San Millán (?) / (Silos (?)	11th c. *med.* (1059)	Visigothic / Northern Visigothic notation
Silos, AM	Cod. 5	La Rioja (?) (Vivancos) / Aragón (?)	11th c. *med.* (1059)	Visigothic / Visigothic notation
Salamanca, BGU	ms. 2637	Silos (?) / San Millán (?)	12th c. *ex.*	Carolingian / Aquitainian notation
Paris, BNF	N. A. L. 2199	Silos (?) / León (?)	10th c. *in.*	Visigothic / Northern Visigothic notation
Sheffield Galleries & Museums Trust	ms. 31	León (?)	11th c. *in.*	Visigothic / Visigothic notation
Cracow, Czartorysky	ms. 3.118	Silos (?)	10th c. *ex.*	Visigothic / Aquitainian notation

DIAGRAM 2: SYSTEMS OF NOTATION IN THE IBERIAN PENINSULA IN CHRONOLOGICAL ORDER

Catalog number	Date	Rite[1]
VISIGOTHIC NOTATION: NORTH		
León		
Paris, BNF, N. A. L. 2199	10th c. *in.* (9th c. *ex.*-10th c. *in.*, Gros)	H
León, AC, ms. 8	10th c. *med.*	H
Córdoba, AC, ms. 123	10th c. *ex.*-11th c. *in.*	FR
Santiago, BXU, ms. 609 (Res. 1)	11th c. *med.* (1055)	H
Silos-San Millán		
London, BL, Add. ms. 30852	9th c. *ex.*-10th c. *in.*	H (s. n.)
Madrid, RAH, Cod. 56	10th c. *ex.*	H-Transition* (add.)
Cracow, Czartorysky, ms. 3.118	10th c. *ex.*	H
Madrid, RAH, Cod. 30	10th c. *ex.*	H
London, BL, Add. ms. 11695	10th c. *ex.*	H
Madrid, RAH, Cod. 118 / Cod. 14	11th c. *in.*	H (s. n.)
New York, HS, B 2916 (To. 33-2)	11th c. *med.*	H-Transition (add.)
London, BL, Add. ms. 30851	11th c. *med.*	H (8 notated hymns)
Salamanca, BGU, ms. 2668	11th c. *med.* (1059)	H
Silos, AM, Cod. 5	11th c. *med.* (1059)	H
London, BL, Add. ms. 30850	11th c. *ex.*	FR-Transition (Aquitainian add.)
London, BL, Add. ms. 30847	11th c. *ex.*	FR-Transition (Visigothic Aquitainian influence)
San Prudencio de Monte Laturce		
Silos, AM, Cod. 4	11th c. *med.* (1052)	H-Transition* (add.)
San Martín de Albelda		
Santo Domingo de La Calzada, AC, w./o. s.	10th c. *ex.*-11th c. *in.*	H
Santa María la Real de Nájera		
Zaragoza, BGU, M-418	10th c. *ex.*	H
Silos, AM, Cod. 3	11th c. *in.* (1039)	H
Silos, AM, Cod. 6	11th c. *med.* (Mundó); 10th c. *ex.*-11th c. *in.* (Millares)	H
Silos, AM, Cod. 7	11th c. *med.*	H
San Pedro de Cardeña		
Burgos, AC, w./o. s.	9th c.-10th c.	H (Visigothic add.)
Unknown / Disputed Origin		
Madrid, BN, ms. 10029	9th c. *ex.*-10th c. *in.* (11th c. *in.*, Mundó)	H
London, BL, Add. ms. 30844	10th c. *in.*	H
Toledo, BC, ms. 35-6	10th c. *ex.*-11th c. *in.*	H Insertions of Aquitainian influence (fol. 123v)
Sheffield Galleries & Museums Trust, ms. 31	11th c. *in.*	FR-Transition
London, BL, Add. ms. 30846	11th c. *in.*	H
London, BL, Add. ms. 30845	11th c. *med.*	H
VISIGOTHIC NOTATION: SOUTH		
Toledo		
Toledo, BC, ms. 35-7	11th c. *ex.*-12th c. *in.* (Mundó); 10th c. (Millares Carlo)	H
Madrid, BN, ms. 10001 (To. 35-1)	12th c. *ex.*-13th c. *in.* (Mundó); 9th c. (Millares Carlo)	H

[1] H: Hispanic; FR: Franco-Roman; CN: Catalonian-Narbonnaise; s. n.: *sine neumae;* w./o. s.: without shelfmark.

DIAGRAM 2 *(cont.)*: SYSTEMS OF NOTATION IN THE IBERIAN PENINSULA IN CHRONOLOGICAL ORDER

Catalog number	Date	Rite
Portugal		
Coimbra, AU, IV-3ª-Gav. 44 (22)	11th c. *in.*	H
CATALAN NOTATION		
CATALONIA		
Ripoll		
Barcelona, ACA, Ripoll 106	10th c. *in.* (*add.* 10th c. *med.-ex.*, 11th c. *in.*)	CN
Barcelona, ACA, Ripoll 74	10th c. *ex.*-11th c. *in.*	CN-Transition*
Barcelona, ACA, Ripoll 40	11th c. *ex.*	FR
Roda de Isábena		
Lleida, AC, Roda 16	11th c. *in.* (1000-1018)	FR
Lleida, AC, Roda 18	11th c. *ex.*	FR-Transition* (Aquitainian add.)
Lleida, AC, Roda 11	12th c. (1191)	FR-Transition
Vic		
Vic, ABEV, ms. 67	11th c. *med.*	FR-Transition
Vic, ABEV, Frag. XI/1	11th c. *med.*	CN
Vic, ABEV, ms. 105	12th c. *in.*	FR-Transition
Elna / Moissac		
Paris, BNF, Lat. 5304	11th c. *med.*	FR-Transition
Paris, BNF, Lat. 933	11th c. *ex.*-12th c. *in.*	FR (with Hispanic forms)
Paris, BNF, N. A. L. 495	12th c. *in.*	FR-Transition (Catalonian and square notation)
Montserrat		
Montserrat, BM, ms. 822	12th c. *in.*	FR
Montserrat, BM, ms. 794-I	12th c. *in.*	FR-CN
Montserrat, BM, ms. 72	12th c. *ex.*	CN
Montserrat, BM, ms. 73	12th c. *ex.*	FR
Barcelona, BC, M. 1147	12th c. *ex.*	CN
AQUITAINIAN NOTATION		
CATALONIA		
Ripoll		
Barcelona, ACA, Ripoll 42	11th c. *in.* (1040, Mundó)	(add. Aquitainian notation)
Roda de Isábena		
Lleida, AC, Roda 14	12th c. *med.*	FR-CN
Lleida, AC, Roda 8	12th c. *med.*	FR
ARAGÓN		
Huesca		
Huesca, AC, Cod. 1	11th c. *ex.*	FR
Huesca, AC, Cod. 4	12th c. *in.*	FR
Huesca, AC, Cod. 2	12th c. *med.*	FR
Huesca, AHP, 12030/36	12th c. *ex.*	FR
Santa Cruz de La Serós (Jaca)		
Jaca, AM, w./o. s.	12th c. *ex.*	FR
San Juan de La Peña		
El Escorial, RB, ms. L.III.3	12th c. *ex.*	FR
El Escorial, RB, ms. L.III.4	12th c. *ex.*	FR

DIAGRAM 2 *(cont.)*: SYSTEMS OF NOTATION IN THE IBERIAN PENINSULA IN CHRONOLOGICAL ORDER

Catalog number	Date	Rite
El Escorial, RB, ms. Q.III.10	12th c. *ex.*	FR
Madrid, BN, ms. 9719	12th c. *ex.*	FR
CASTILE-LEÓN		
San Pedro de Valeránica		
Córdoba, AC, ms. 1	10th c. *med.* (953)	H
Santo Domingo de Silos		
Paris, BNF, N. A. L. 2171	11th c. *med.*	FR-Transition* (add.)
London, BL, Add. ms. 30848	11th c. *ex.*	FR-Transition
Salamanca, BGU, ms. 2637	12th c. *ex.*	FR
San Millán		
Madrid, RAH, Cod. 18	11th c. *ex.* (1090)	FR-Transition
Madrid, RAH, Cod. 51	12th c. *in.*	FR
Madrid, RAH, Cod. 45	12th c. *ex.*	FR
Santiago de Compostela, AC, Frag. 1	12th c. *in.*	FR-Transition
Ourense, AC, Frag. 3	12th c. *in.*	FR-Transition
Sigüenza, AC, Frag. w./o. s.	12th c. *med.*	FR
Burgo de Osma, AC, ms. 94	12th c. *ex.*	FR
NAVARRE		
Roncevaux		
Roncevaux, Museo Coleg., w./o. s.	12th c. *ex.*	FR
Pamplona		
Pamplona, AC, w./o. s.	12th c. *ex.*	FR
Fitero		
Pamplona, ARGN, K. 6	12th c. *ex.*-13th c. *in.*	FR
TOLEDO		
Toledo, BC, 44-1	11th c. *ex.*	FR
Paris, BNF, N. A. L. 1871	11th c. *ex.*	FR
Toledo, BC, 44-2	12th c. *in.*	FR
PORTUGAL		
Coimbra (Cathedral)		
Coimbra, AU, IV-3.ª S-Gav. 44 (20)	11th c. *med.*	FR-Transition
Lisbon, IAN, Torre do Tombo, Frag. Cx 20, no. 14	12th c. *ex.*-13th c. *in.* (1172-1200)	FR
Braga		
Braga, AD, ms. 1000	12th c. *med.* (1130-1150)	FR
Braga, AD, Frag. 49	12th c. *med.*	FR
Braga, AD, Frag. 243	12th c. *med.*	FR
Braga, AD, Frag. 244	12th c. *ex.*	FR
Braga, AD, Frag. 210	12th c. *ex.*	FR
Santa Cruz de Coimbra		
Porto, BPM, Santa Cruz 76, General no. 350	12th c. *ex.*	FR
Porto, BPM, Santa Cruz 83, General no. 1134	12th c. *ex.*	FR
Aveiro		
Aveiro, AD, Frag. w./o. s.	12th c. *ex.*	FR
Unknown origin		
London, BL, Add. ms. 30849	11th c. *ex.*	FR
Total: 89		

DIAGRAM 3: LIST OF SOURCES IN CHRONOLOGICAL ORDER

Typology	Provenance	Source	Dating	Script typology / script notation	Transition
Orationale	London, BL, Add. ms. 30852	(Silos) Aragón (Díaz y Díaz) / Cardeña (?)	9th c. *ex.*-10th c. *in.* (Ruiz Asencio)	Visigothic / Northern Visigothic notation	
Anthologia hispana, Azagra Codex	Madrid, BN, ms. 10029	(Toledo), Pyrenean (?)	9th c. *ex.*-10th c. *in.* (11th c. *in,* Mundó)	Visigothic / Northern Visigothic notation	
***Liber canticorum* (Frag.)**	London, BL, Add. ms. 30844	(Silos) (?)	10th c. *in.*	Visigothic / Northern Visigothic notation	
Antiphonary (Frag.)	Paris, BNF, N. A. L. 2199	(Silos), León (?)	10th c. *in.* (9th c. *ex.*-10th c. *in.,* Gros)	Visigothic / Northern Visigothic notation	
Bible	Burgos, AC, w./o. s.	S. Pedro de Cardeña	10th c. *in.* (9th c. *ex.*-10th c. *in.,* Millares Carlo)	Visigothic / Aquitainian notation	
Antiphonary	León, AC, ms. 8	S. Cipriano de las Riberas del Porma, Beja (?)	10th c. *med.*	Visigothic / Northern Visigothic notation	
Homiliary	Córdoba, AC, ms. 1	S. Pedro de Valeránica	10th c. *med.* (953)	Visigothic / Aquitainian notation	
Antiphonary (Frag.)	London, BL, Add. ms. 11695	(Silos)	10th c. *ex.*	Visigothic / Northern Visigothic notation	
Antiphonary (Frag.)	Zaragoza, BGU, M-418	Aragón / La Rioja (?)	10th c. *ex.*	Visigothic / Northern Visigothic notation	
Liber ordinum	Madrid, RAH, Cod. 56	San Millán de La Cogolla	10th c. *ex.*	Visigothic / Northern Visigothic and Aquitainian notation *(add.)*	Transition*
Bible	Cracow, Czartorysky, ms. 3.118	(Silos)	10th c. *ex.*	Visigothic / Aquitainian notation	
Liber misticus	Madrid, RAH, Cod. 30	San Millán de La Cogolla	10th c. *ex.* (Gros)	Visigothic / Northern Visigothic notation	
Collectaneum	Barcelona, ACA, Ripoll 106	Ripoll	10th c. *in.* (add. 10th c. *med.-ex.,* 11th c. *in.*)	Carolingian / Catalonian notation (later add., 10th c. *med.-ex.*-11th c. *in.*)	
***Liber horarum* (Frag.)**	Santo Domingo de La Calzada, AC, w./o. s.	Albelda	10th c. *ex.*-11th c. *in.*	Visigothic / Northern Visigothic notation	
Alvarus Paulus. Opera et alia opuscula	Córdoba, AC, ms. 123	León / Sahagún-Eslonza	10th c. *ex.*-11th c. *in.*	Visigothic / Northern Visigothic notation	
Liber misticus	Toledo, BC, 35-6	Toledo	10th c. *ex.*-11th c. *in.*	Visigothic / Northern Visigothic notation	
Liber glossarum et t[...]logiarum	Barcelona, ACA, Ripoll 74	Santa María de Ripoll	10th c. *ex.*-11th c. *in.* (Mundó, *post quem* 1020)	Carolingian / Catalonian and Aquitainian notation (*add.* 12th c.)	Transition*
Liber misticus	London, BL, Add. ms. 30846	Santo Domingo de Silos	11th c. *in.*	Visigothic / Northern Visigothic notation	
Sacramentary, Ritual and Pontifical	Lleida, BC, Roda 16 (RC 0036)	La Seu d'Urgell / Ribagorza	11th c. *in.* (1000-1018)	Carolingian / archaic Catalonian notation, Visigothic influence	
Musica cum rethorica	Barcelona, ACA, Ripoll 42	Santa María de Ripoll	11th c. *in.* (1040, Mundó)	Visigothic. Theoretical treat., s. n.	
Homiliary	Sheffield Galleries and Museum Trust, ms. 31	(León) (?)	11th c. *in.*	Visigothic / Visigothic notation	Transition
***Liber hymnorum* (Frag.)**	Madrid, RAH, Cod. 118 /Cod. 14	San Millán de La Cogolla	11th c. *in.*	Visigothic s. n.	
Antiphonary (Frag.)	Coimbra, AU, IV-3.ª-Gav. 44 (22)	Cathedral of Coimbra	11th c. *in.*	Visigothic / Southern Visigothic notation	
Liber ordinum	Silos, AM, Cod. 3	Santa María la Real de Nájera (?)	11th c. *in.* (1039)	Visigothic / Northern Visigothic notation	

DIAGRAM 3 *(cont.)*: LIST OF SOURCES IN CHRONOLOGICAL ORDER

Typology	Provenance	Source	Dating	Script typology and notation	Transition
Liber psalmorum, canticorum et hymnorum	London, BL, Add. ms. 30851	Sto. Domingo de Silos	11th c. *med.*	Visigothic-Reference marks (Visigothic neumes)	
Liber misticus	Silos, AM, Cod. 6	Sta. María la Real de Nájera (?)	11th c. *med.* (Mundó) (10th c. *ex.*-11th c. *in.* Millares)	Visigothic / Northern Visigothic notation	
Liber horarum	Silos, AM, Cod. 7	Sta. María la Real de Nájera (?)	11th c. *med.*	Visigothic / Northern Visigothic notation	
Liber misticus	London, BL, Add. ms. 30845	(?)	11th c. *med.*	Visigothic / Northern Visigothic notation	
Officia sanctorum	New York, HS, B 2916 (To. 33-2)	San Millán de La Cogolla	11th c. *med.*	Visigothic / Northern Visigothic, Aquitainian (add.) (and alphabetical) notation	Transition*
Antiphonary (Frag.)	Coimbra, AU, IV-3.a S.-Gav. 44 (20)	San Fins de Friestas	11th c. *med.*	Visigothic / Aquitainian notation	Transition
Liber comicus	Paris, BNF, N. A. L. 2171	Sto. Domingo de Silos	11th c. *med.*	Visigothic / Aquitainian notation (add.)	Transition*
Sacramentary	Vic, ABEV, ms. 67	Sta. María de Ripoll	11th c. *med.*	Carolingian / Catalonian notation	Transition
Breviary (Frag.)	Vic, ABEV, Frag. XI/1	Cathedral of Vic	11th c. *med.*	Visigothic / Catalonian notation (Anglès, Aquitainian influence)	
Lectionary	Paris, BNF, Lat. 5304	Moissac / Elna (?)	11th c. *med.*	Carolingian / Catalonian notation	
Liber ordinum	Silos, AM, Cod. 4	San Prudencio de Monte Laturce	11th c. *med.* (1052)	Visigothic / Northern Visigothic and Aquitainian notation (add.)	Transition*
Psalterium et Liber canticorum. Diurnal of Ferdinand I / Santiago de Compostela, Bibl. General Univ.	Santiago, BGU, ms. 609 (Res. 1)	Sahagún / León / La Rioja / Eastern Castile	11th c. *med.* (1055)	Visigothic / Northern Visigothic notation	
Liber canticorum et horarum	Salamanca, BGU, ms. 2668	Sto. Domingo de Silos	11th c. *med.* (1059)	Visigothic / Northern Visigothic notation	
St. Ildefonsus, De virginitate Sanctae Mariae / St. Domingo de Silos, Arch. Abadía	Silos, AM, Cod. 5	La Rioja (?)	11th c. *med.* (1059)	Visigothic / Northern Visigothic notation	
Missal	Madrid, RAH, Cod. 18	San Millán de La Cogolla	11th c. *ex.* (1090)	Visigothic / Aquitainian notation	Transition
Antiphonary	London, BL, Add. ms. 30850	Sto. Domingo de Silos	11th c. *ex.*	Visigothic / Northern Visigothic and Aquitainian notation (add.)	Transition
Breviary	London, BL, Add. ms. 30847	Sto. Domingo de Silos	11th c. *ex.*	Visigothic / Northern Visigothic notation of Aquitainian influence	Transition
Antiphonary	Toledo, BC, 44-1	Toledo	11th c. *ex.*	Carolingian / Aquitainian notation	
Tropary, Sequentiary, Prosary, Prosulary	Paris, BNF, N. A. L. 1871	St. Pierre de Moissac	11th c. *ex.*	Carolingian / Aquitainian notation	
Breviary	London, BL, Add. ms. 30849	(Silos)	11th c. *ex.*	Carolingian / Aquitainian notation	
Breviary	London, BL, Add. ms. 30848	Sto. Domingo de Silos	11th c. *ex.*	Visigothic / Aquitainian notation	Transition
Hymnary	Huesca, AC, Cod. 1	(Huesca) / Ultrapyrenean	11th c. *ex.*	Carolingian / Aquitainian notation	

DIAGRAM 3 *(cont.)*: LIST OF SOURCES IN CHRONOLOGICAL ORDER

Typology	Provenance	Source	Dating	Script typology and notation	Transi-tion
Miscellaneous codex	Barcelona, ACA, Ripoll 40	Ripoll	11th c. *ex.*	Carolingian / Catalonian notation	
Lectionary. Homiliary of the Office	Lleida, AC, Roda 18	Roda de Isábena	11th c. *ex.*	Carolingian with influence. Visigothic / Catalonian and Aquitainian notation	Transi-tion*
Liber misticus	Toledo, BC, 35-7	Toledo	11th c. *ex.*-12th c. *in.* (Mundó), 10th c. (Millares Carlo)	Visigothic / Southern Visigothic notation	
Collectarium, Ritual	Paris, BNF, Lat. 933	Sta. María de Lagrasse	11th c. *ex.*-12th c. *in.*	Carolingian / Catalonian notation	
Prosary, Tropary	Paris, BNF, N. A. L. 495	Girona	12th c. *in.*	Carolingian / Catalonian notation and square	Transi-tion
Antiphonary	Toledo, BC, 44-2	Toledo	12th c. *in.*	Carolingian / Aquitainian notation	
Antiphonary, Tropary	Madrid, RAH, Cod. 51	San Millán de La Cogolla	12th c. *in.*	Carolingian / Aquitainian notation	
Missal (Frag.)	Santiago de Compostela, AC, Frag. 1	(Santiago de Compostela)	12th c. *in.*	Visigothic / Aquitainian notation	Transi-tion
Breviary (Frag.)	Ourense, AC, Frag. 3.	Ourense	12th c. *in.*	Visigothic / Aquitainian notation	Transi-tion
Prosary, Tropary	Huesca, AC, Cod. 4	(Huesca / San Juan de La Peña)	12th c. *in.*	Carolingian / Aquitainian notation	
Breviary (Frag.)	Montserrat, BM, ms. 822	(Catalonian-Narbonnaise)	12th c. *in.*	Carolingian / Catalonian notation	
Prosary, Tropary	Vic, ABEV, ms. 105	Vic	12th c. *in.*	Carolingian / Catalonian notation and Aquitainian	Transi-tion
***Liber responsorialis* (Frag.)**	Montserrat, BM, ms. 794-I	Solsona (Lleida)	12th c. *in.*-11th c. *in.* (Garrigosa)	Carolingian / Catalonian notation	
Breviary, Matutinary	Huesca, AC, Cod. 2	Huesca	12th c. *med.*	Carolingian / Aquitainian notation	
Missal	Braga, AD, ms. 1000	St. Martial de Limoges	12th c. *med.*	Carolingian / Aquitainian notation	
Collectaneum	Lleida, AC, Roda 8	Roda	12th c. *med.*	Carolingian / Aquitainian notation	
Lectionary	Lleida, AC, Roda 14	Roda	12th c. *med.*	Carolingian / Aquitainian notation	
Breviary (Frag.)	Sigüenza, AC, Frag. w./o. s.	Sigüenza	12th c. *med.*	Carolingian / Aquitainian notation	
Gradual (Frag.)	Braga, AD, Frag. 243	(?)	12th c. *med.*	Carolingian / Aquitainian notation	
Gradual (Frag.)	Braga, AD, Frag. 49	(?)	12th c. *med.*	Carolingian / Aquitainian notation	
Sacramentary, Evangeliary	Madrid, BN, ms. 9719	Aragón	12th c. *ex.* (1169)	Carolingian / Aquitainian notation	
Antiphonary	Barcelona BC, M. 1147	St. Pere d'Ager (La Noguera, Lleida)	12th c. *ex.*	Carolingian / Aquitainian notation	
Prosar, Tropary	Montserrat, BM, ms. 73	La Seu d'Urgell	12th c. *ex.*	Carolingian / Aquitainian notation	
Evangeliary	Burgo de Osma, AC, ms. 94	(?)	12th c. *ex.*	Carolingian / Aquitainian notation	
Missal, Tropary	Salamanca, BGU, ms. 2637	Silos / San Millán (?)	12th c. *ex.*	Carolingian / Aquitainian notation	
Antiphonary (Frag.)	Jaca, AM, w./o. s.	Sta. Cruz de la Serós	12th c. *ex.*	Carolingian / Aquitainian notation	
Antiphonary (Frag.)	Huesca, AHP, 12030/36	Huesca (province)	12th c. *ex.*	Carolingian / Aquitainian notation	

DIAGRAM 3 *(cont.)*: LIST OF SOURCES IN CHRONOLOGICAL ORDER

Typology	Provenance	Source	Dating	Script typology and notation	Transition
Breviary	El Escorial, RB, ms. L.III.3	San Juan de La Peña (?)	12th c. *ex.*	Carolingian / Aquitainian notation	
Breviary	El Escorial, RB, ms. L.III.4	San Juan de La Peña (?)	12th c. *ex.*	Carolingian / Aquitainian notation	
S. Gregorii Magni dialogorum Libri IV, Vita Sanctae Euphrosynae	El Escorial, RB, ms. Q.III.10	San Juan de La Peña (?)	12th c. *ex.*	Carolingian / Aquitainian notation	
Evangeliary	Roncevaux, Museo Colegiata w./o. s.	(?)	12th c. *ex.*	Carolingian / Aquitainian notation	
Evangeliary	Pamplona, AC, w./o. s.	(?)	12th c. *ex.*	Carolingian / Aquitainian notation	
Antiphonary	Madrid, RAH, Cod. 45	San Millán de La Cogolla	12th c. *ex.*	Carolingian / Aquitainian notation	
Antiphonary (Frag.)	Braga, AD, Frag. 244	(Diocese of Braga)	12th c. *ex.*	Carolingian / Aquitainian notation	
Gradual (Frag.)	Braga, AD, Frag. 210	(?)	12th c. *ex.*	Carolingian / Aquitainian notation	
Gradual	Porto, BPM, Santa Cruz 76, general no. 350	Santa Cruz de Coimbra	12th c. *ex.*	Carolingian / Aquitainian notation	
Pontifical	Porto, BPM, Santa Cruz 83, general no. 1134	Santa Cruz de Coimbra	12th c. *ex.*	Carolingian / Aquitainian notation	
Breviary (Frag.)	Aveiro, AD, Frag. w./o. s.	San Miguel de Aveiro	12th c. *ex.*	Carolingian / Aquitainian notation	
Miscellaneous codex	Montserrat, BM, ms. 72	St. Romá de les Bons	12th c. *ex.*	Carolingian / Catalonian notation	
Psalter, Hymnary and rhyming Office of St. Raymond	Lleida, AC, Roda 11	Roda	12th c. *ex.* (1191)	Carolingian / Catalonian notation and Aquitainian	Transition
Psalterium, Liber canticorum, Liber hymnorum	Madrid, BN, ms. 10001 (To. 35-1)	Toledo	12th c. *ex.*-13th c. *in.* (Mundó), 9th c. (Millares Carlo)	Visigothic / Visigothic notation (northern and southern)	
Antiphonary (Frag.)	Lisbon, IAN, Torre do Tombo. Cx 20, no. 14	Coimbra	12th c. *ex.*-13th c. *in.* (1172-1200)	Carolingian / Aquitainian notation	
Missal, Sacramentary	Pamplona, ARGN, K. 6	Fitero	12th c. *ex.*-13th c. *in.*	Carolingian / Aquitainian notation	

in paleography, codicology and textual criticism on the one hand, and in musical paleography on the other, is partly due to the fact that both the Catalonian notation, in its archaic form, and the Visigothic notation present a basic interpretative problem in that they are adiastematic, making it impossible to transcribe them into modern notation. At the same time, a paleographic analysis of the Aquitainian notation does not furnish sufficient information to allow a typological classification based on the different geographic areas or cultural spheres, as shown later, using a series of specific examples.

The selection of musical-liturgical manuscripts shown in diagram 2 offers a sufficiently representative basis to allow us to make a number of summary evaluations: 1) diversity of notational systems, 2) diversity of contexts to which the musical notation belongs, 3) diversity of functions belonging to notational signs, and 4) diversity of periods for each system or the coexistence of different systems.

Diversity of systems

Script systems-systems of notation

An analysis of the corpus of musical-liturgical manuscripts shows that in the case of both Visigothic and Carolingian script, the morphology generally remains more constant and uniform than the notation. The latter is more liable to develop individualised forms, sometimes corrupting the *original* scripts to such an extent that one sign may be mistaken for another even though the graphic variation does not affect its significance but is a result of an individual stylistic feature of the copyist. In the case of the Spanish notations—Visigothic and Catalonian—it is more common to see singular practices, either specific to the copyist or related to the tradition to which the manuscript belongs and a larger number of graphic variants than in text script.[50] The same range of variability is also seen in the transmission of the melodic repertory, even in cases in which the sources pertain to a common model or tradition. There are many reasons for this variability, which can be seen both in the graphic representation of the notational sign and in the melodic transmission. The difference is partly due to the intangible nature of music, as opposed to the more material nature of literary text. Whereas the latter can be traced back to a written tradition, the former is sound-based, thus relating to an abstract dimension. However, this oral aspect can only partly explain these variations. Another important factor was the differentiated topography of political nuclei and cultural centers, which tended to favor the development of local forms. If we further take into account the fact that no document exists to substantiate the basic inventory of signs for the Visigothic and Catalonian notations—as is the case in other Western systems of notation—and bear in mind the type of training received by the copyists of the neumes, we need to look further afield for the reasons for the multiplicity of graphic forms to be found in Spanish notations. Aware of this problem, Rojo and Prado (1929) finally opted for a classification based on the particular neumatic scripts of each codex.

The wealth of notational typologies in the Iberian Peninsula—north, south, and Catalonian—is further extended by graphic mutations throughout their respective histories and is one of the most characteristic and complex features of this family of notation.[51] There is no comparable profusion of forms in the field of writing, where the relative constancy and morphological continuity of the letters contrasts with the morphological variability or freedom of notation. It is well known that the transition from Visigothic to Carolingian script occurred more progressively and over a greater number of intermediary phases than the transition from Visigothic to Aquitainian notation, for which the change was more dramatic throughout most of the peninsula—with the exception of the area of Catalonia and the exceptional cases of Toledo and Coimbra, where Visigothic notation survived until well into the 13th century—.[52] Proof of this can be seen in cases in which the Visigothic script already took on Carolingian features, whereas Visigothic notation remained almost unchanged; and other cases, even more abundant, in which Visigothic script survived in combination with the new Aquitainian notational system.[53]

To identify this variability, I now illustrate the different evolutionary stages of the various notational typologies (diagrams 1 and 2), using a series of examples taken from the codices selected for diagrams 1 and 2, with particular stress on individual graphic forms and exceptional practices. This study encompasses Visigothic notation, Catalonian notation, the transitional notations and, finally, Aquitainian notation.

For Visigothic notation it is traditional to distinguish between two types of graphic representation, one applying to manuscripts from the north, covering the areas of Aragón, Castile and León and Navarre, and the other embracing manuscripts from the south, represented by a more limited corpus of sources from Toledo—where nonetheless both typologies were practiced, as we shall see—and from the north of Portugal, especially represented by the centers at Braga and Coimbra.[54] Recall the essential distinguishing features of the two typologies: 1) the direction of the axis of the script, vertical for the north and horizontal for the south; 2), the *ductus,*[55] is more careful in northern codices; 3) the degree of intended diastemacy in northern codices, which is absent in those from the south; and 4) the greater graphic diversity to be seen in the codices from the north.[56]

Examples with notation from the south: Toledo-Coimbra group

The corpus of Toledan manuscripts encompasses a period ranging from the 11th century *ex.* to the 12th century *in.,* for the oldest copy (Toledo, BC,

35-7), to the second half of the 12th century and well into the 13th for the latest copies (Museo de los Concilios y de la Cultura Visigoda, 1325-1/2 from the 13th century, 1326 from the 12th century *med.* and Toledo BC, 35-5 from the 13th century *med.*). Over the course of this time, a clear mutation can be seen in the musical paleography, which develops to a point where notational signs have a practically symbolic value. In the late manuscripts, hardly any sign is clearly recognisable, the profiles are blurred and the hurried penmanship only manages to sketch the outline of a melody, which would be unrecognisable were it not for the supposed survival of an oral tradition. As the Toledan script evolved, the graphic shapes became ever less clear, to the point where one might wonder whether the copies kept in the Museo de los Concilios y de la Cultura Visigoda were ever really intended to offer a melodic representation or whether they were the product of a pro-Visigothic movement, which championed the old rite then threatened with extinction, well into the 13th century. Aside from these exceptional late examples, not included in the selection, diagram 2 shows a small number of manuscripts from the south, the most significant features of which are illustrated below.

The case of Toledo, BC, 35-7 is surprising, in that a second copyist superimposed another line of notation in a smaller module on the original notation in some folios in a probable attempt to interpret the neumes drawn by the first hand. The additions to some extent gloss the basic musical text, possibly with a view to clarifying its meaning (fig. 1).

It is also worth noting the two-tiered arrangement of the prolonged melisma on the final alleluia. In the example in fol. 100r, a second hand inserts unusual signs within the Visigothic notational inventory, such as an alpha-like sign placed on certain neumes, mainly on the *virgae*. The same sign also appears in other places in the manuscript (fig. 2).

This second hand, intervening in the musical notation to superimpose its own interpretation, reflects a continuous need for reinterpretation of a non-unified graphic system throughout the peninsula and for a melodic repertory based essentially on oral tradition.

Among the earliest manuscripts with Visigothic notation from the south is the fragment from Coimbra (fig. 3).

To complete the chronology of the Toledan sources, we offer four examples originally dated around the 11th century *ex.* to 12th century *in.* and dated by Mundó to the 13th century (figs. 4, 5, 6 and 7).

The fragment of *Liber misticus* kept in Madrid, BN, ms. 10001 (olim Toledo, BC, 35.1) and dated by

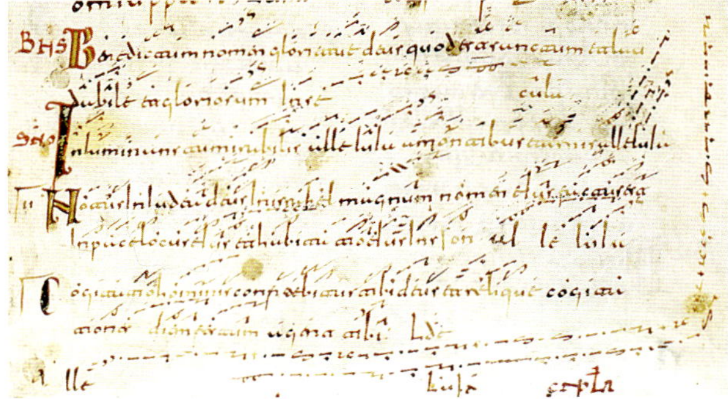

1. Toledo, BC, 35-7, 11th century *ex.*- 12th century *in.*, fol. 100r

Mundó to the 11th century is a particular case. With notation from the northern peninsula, the example contains additions by a second hand, in 12th century Toledan notation (fig. 8).

The coexistence of notational systems of different typology would lead one to think that the codex, of which only two folios are extant, came to

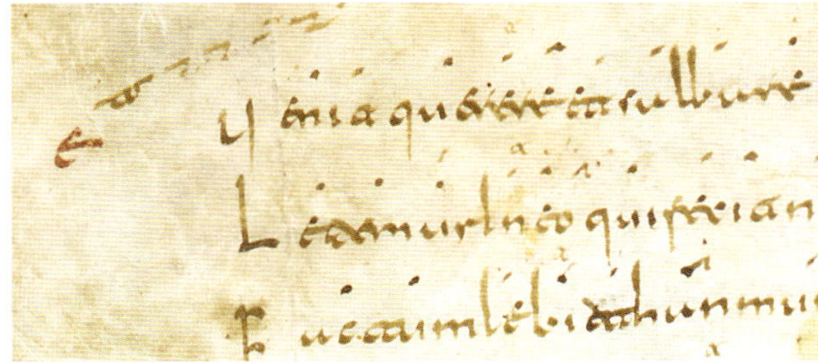

2. Toledo, BC, 35-7, fol. 45v, alfa signs

Toledo from a center in the northern peninsula, probably from the sphere of San Millán or Albelda, where some pieces were later added in the Visigothic notation of the south after the original notation had been scraped off. From the same codex comes the psalter, which comprises the first

152 pages and is dated by Millares Carlo to the 9th century and by Mundó and Ruiz García to the 12th century *ex.* or 13th century *in.* The notation

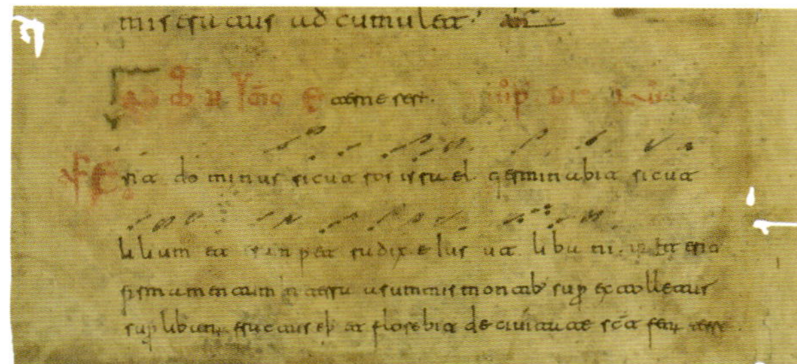

3. Coimbra, AU, IV-3.ª-Gav. 44, 11th century *in.*, Frag.

in dextrogyrate inclination is drawn with a sharper profile than in the previous sample from the Museo de los Concilios y de la Cultura Visigoda in Toledo (fig. 9).

4. Toledo, BC, 35-5, 11th century *med.*, fol. 150r

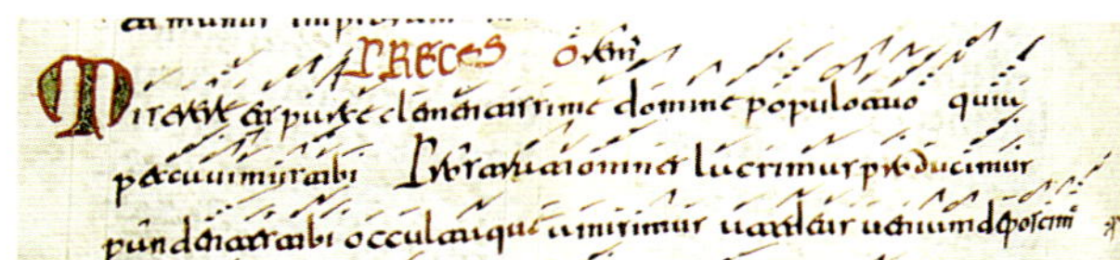

5. Toledo, BC, 35-5, fol. 22v

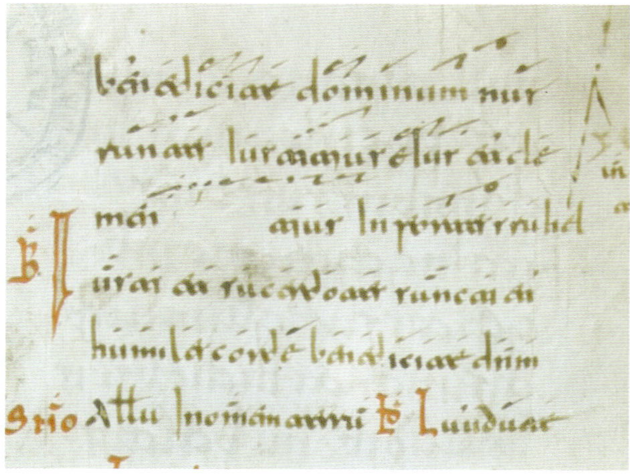

6. Toledo, Museo de los Concilios y de la Cultura Visigoda, 1325-1, 13th century, fol. XIX

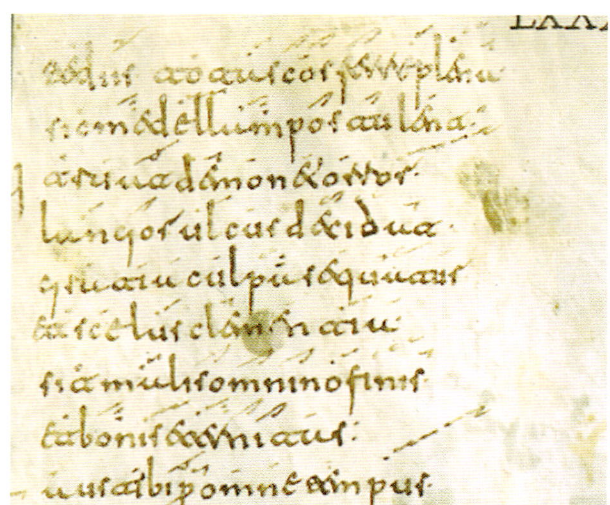

7. Biblioteca Nacional de España, ms. 10001, 12th-13th centuries (Mundó), fol. LXIX (Frag. from the Hymnary)

Specimens with notation from the north

The examples of northern Visigothic notation contain more elaborately drawn neumatic signs with a wider variation of graphic variations than those seen in the southern notation. The specific charac-

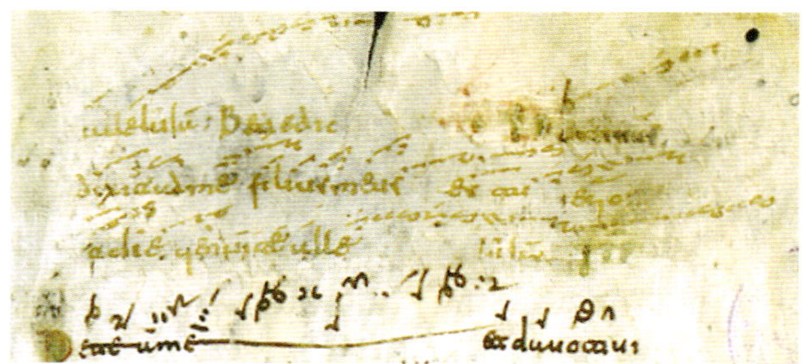

8. Biblioteca Nacional de España, ms. 10001, fol. 2r

teristics, which vary depending on the period and cultural area from which the sources come, still require joint classification and interpretation. The examples selected include some of the more noteworthy aspects.[58]

The set of sources from the northern Peninsula allows us to draw a distinction by groups, based on the graphic quality of the drawing of the neumes, the greater or lesser degree of sophistication of their notational system, and the functional diversity of the different neumatic signs.

An even *ductus* of notation and exquisite workmanship, with a broad inventory of neumatic signs, is

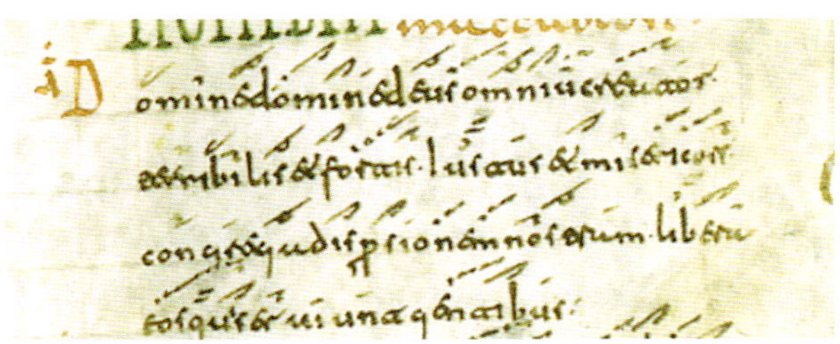

9. Biblioteca Nacional de España, ms. 10001, fol. 178r

represented by León, AC, ms. 8; Madrid, RAH, Cod. 30 and Cod. 56; Zaragoza, BGU, M-418; Santiago de Compostela, BXU, ms. 609 (Res. 1); Salamanca, BGU, ms. 2668; Silos, AM, Cod. 4; and London, BL, Add. ms. 11695.

The example Madrid, RAH, Cod. 56, with a strictly vertical notation, perfect drawing of the neumes with regular alternation of thick and fine lines, and a diastematy that is more suggested than implicit above all in its relationship to melismatic groups, has a *ductus* which is very close to that of the notation represented by Zaragoza, BGU, M-418 (Figs. 10 and 11).[59]

In the Antiphonary of León, representative of an extensive neumatic inventory, the drawing is less accentuated and has a partial inclination to the right (fig. 12).

The lines or stems seen to the side of some neumes are also found in Zaragoza, M-418.

Of particular interest is the early knowledge of the drypoint line, corresponding to the ruling of the writing frame, as a tonal reference in the *Liber misticus*, Madrid, RAH, Cod. 30 from the last quarter of the 10th century. The Carolingian influence on the ruling method allowed Visigothic notation to take on a diastematic dimension, which was in principle atypical. Just as Carolingian features can be seen in the script,[60] this influence can also be seen in the notation. The fact that the use of the drypoint line as a melodic reference

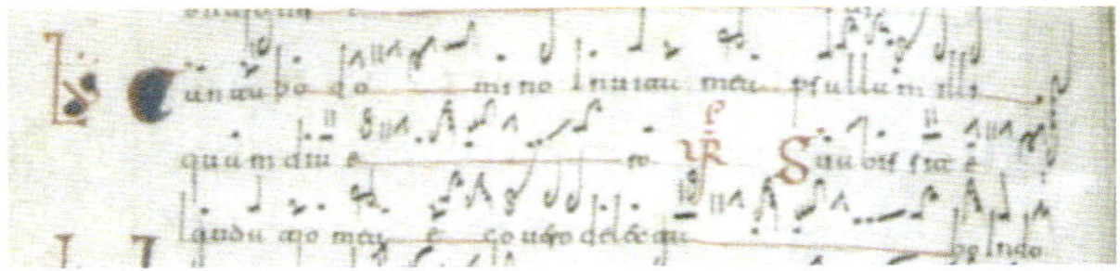

10. Madrid, RAH, Cod. 56, 10th century *ex.*, fol. 48v

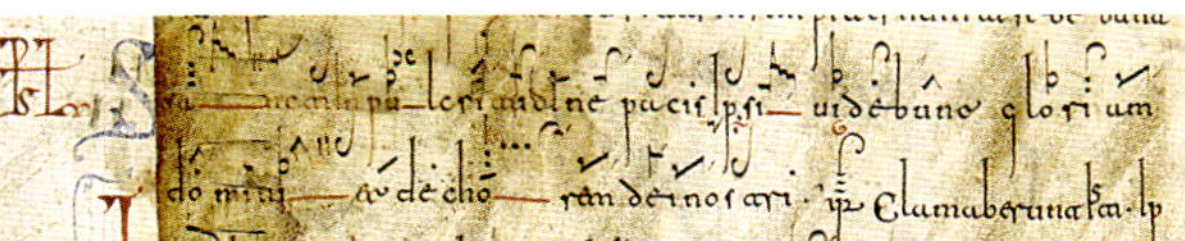

11. Zaragoza, BGU, M-418, 10th century *ex.*, fol. 7v

consists of a single isolated example from the 10th century *ex.* indicates that the Carolingian ruling method did not spread uniformly but instead

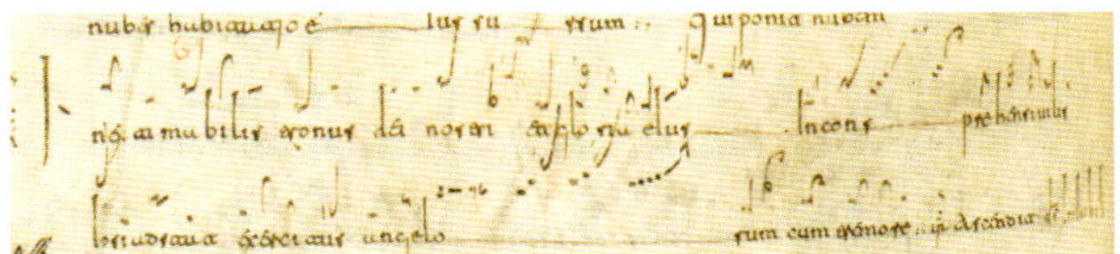

12. León, AC, ms. 8, 10th century *med.*, fol. 198v

resulted from the occasional interaction of certain Iberian centers with the Carolingian cultural sphere (fig. 13).

A similar case, reflecting a knowledge of this ruling system, in which the line of the writing frame is used as a tonal reference, can be seen in the *Liber canticorum*, Salamanca, BGU, ms. 2668 (fig. 14).

A later copy, the London breviary, BL, Add. ms. 30847, in Visigothic transitional notation, uses the drypoint line, typical of the ruling of the page to position the neumes. Here the use of this line is more plausible, given that this is a copy of a Franco-Roman model.

The less elaborate Visigothic notation of *ductus* is illustrated by the following set of sources: New York, HS, B 2916, the fragment from Santo Domingo de la Calzada, AC, w./o. s.; London, BL, Add. ms. 30845 and Add. ms. 30846; Madrid,

13. Madrid, RAH, Cod. 30, 10th century *ex.*, fol. 17r

RAH, Cod. 60 and Silos, AM, cods. 3 and 5. In the case of the two *Liber misticus* (London, BL, Add. ms. 30846 and Add. ms. 30845) the notation is inserted in interlinear spaces not originally provided for this. In the latter, the same hand retouched the

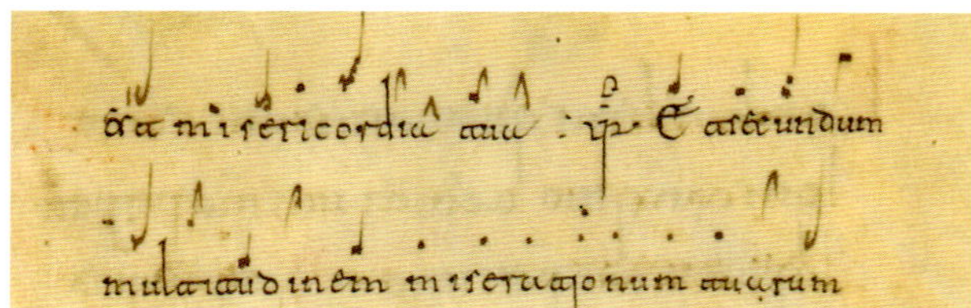

14. Salamanca, BGU, ms. 2668, 11th century *med.*, fol. 156r

initials and some ascenders of the letters *d, l,* and *b* (figs. 15 and 16).

The *Liber misticus* Toledo, BC, 35-6, which was not fully set to music, is an exceptional case illustrating a series of examples with additions in northern notation, the work of at least three different hands from different stages. One of them, in lighter ink than the rest of the notation, is distinguished by its angular strokes and the alternation of thick and fine in the drawing of the neumes.

On fol. 133r neumatic signs were added on a second level to continue a melisma for which the text scribe did not leave enough space (fig. 17).

A careless stroke with thick outlines can be seen in fol. 151v, whereas in fols. 167v-168v a careful *ductus*

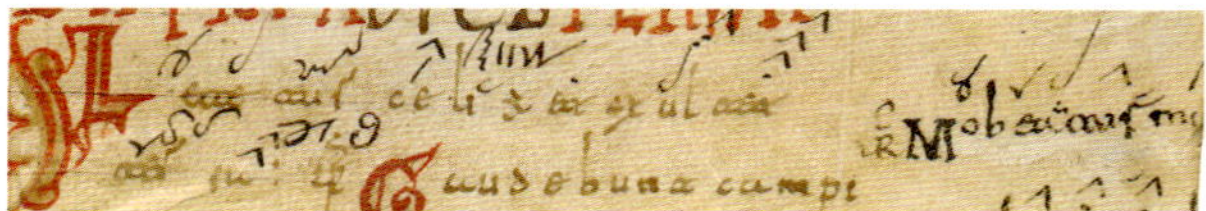

15. London, BL, Add. ms. 30846, 11th century *in.*, fol. 53r

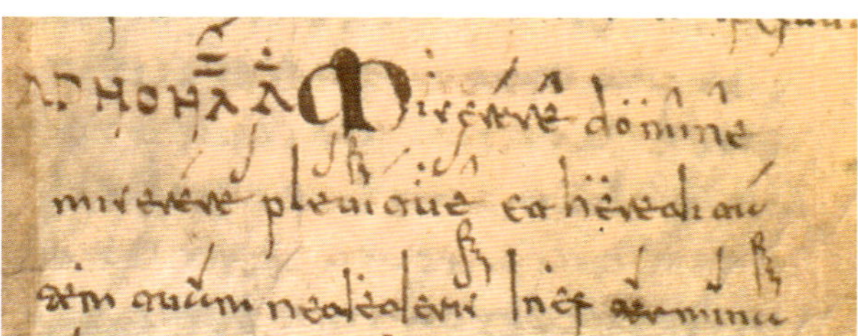

16. Madrid, RAH, Cod. 60, 9th century *ex.* (11th century for the commentary and perhaps for the added notation), fol. 50r

hand intervened, reminiscent of the Rioja codices (see Silos, AM, Cod. 6) (figs. 18 and 19).

Additions inserted in codices with a range of different contents offer some representative samples of a style more typical of a quick note than a positioned melodic copy (figs. 20 and 21).

One particular case can be seen in the Madrid inventory, BN, ms. 10029, one of the oldest examples with Visigothic notation.[61] Together with a limited inventory of neumatic signs of unelaborated *ductus* (fol. 159r), the

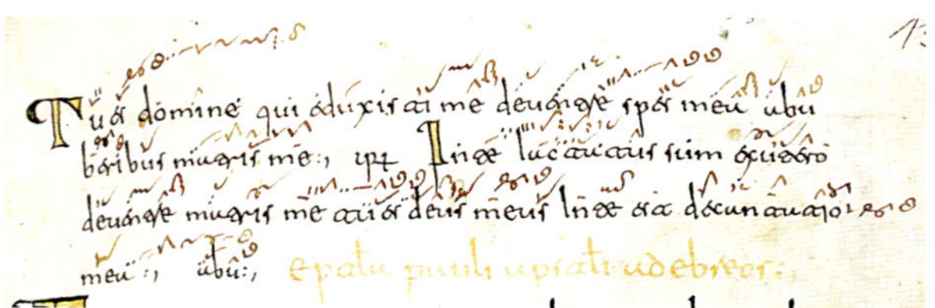

17. Toledo, BC, 35-6, 10th century *ex.*-11th century *in.*, fol. 133r

same codex contains a cryptic list of notational signs directly associated with pitch notation (fols. 158v and 55r). The grave accent *(tractulus)* and the acute accent *(virga)* can be traced back to the tradition of the readings

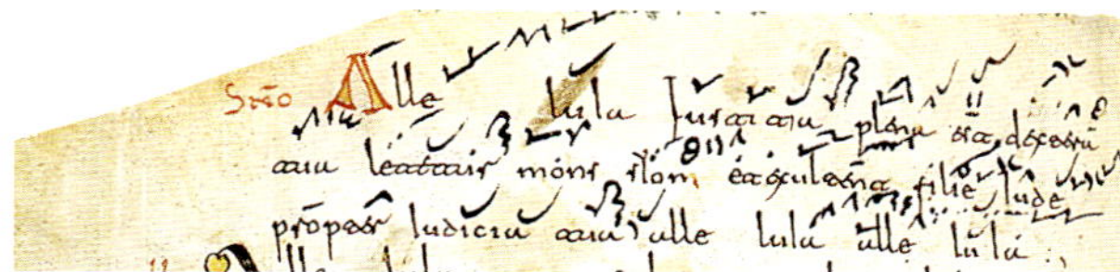

18. Toledo, BC, 35-6, 10th century *ex.*-11th century *in.*, fol. 151v, *Alleluia*

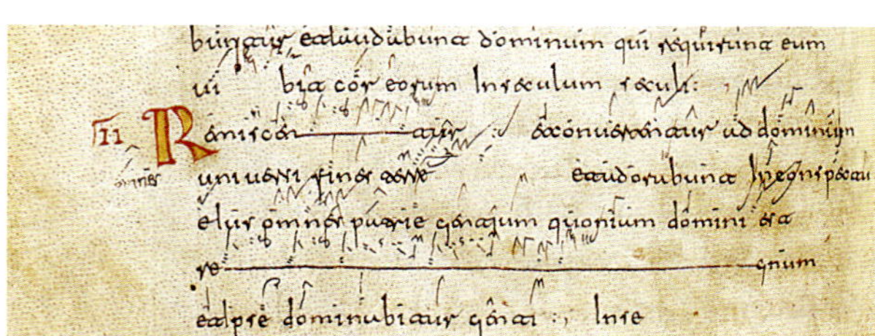

19. Toledo, BC, 35-6, 10th century *ex.*-11th century *in.*, fol. 168v

or semitoned poems.[62] The addition to fol. 4 in London, BL, Add. ms. 30845, is a similar case of the correlation between the selection of accentual neumatic signs and the style of recitation (figs. 22, 23, 24, and 25).

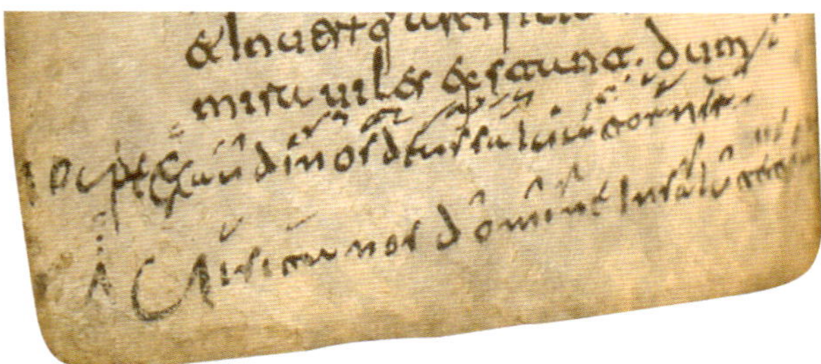

20. Madrid, RAH, Cod. 60, 9th century *ex.* (notation and commentary, 11th century), fol. 50r (lower margin)

The notational signs of fols. 54v-55r suggest that the text had a declamatory, quantifying and accentual function (figs. 26, 27 and 28).

21. El Escorial, RB, a.I.13, 10th century, add. fol. 197r

These examples demonstrate the existence of another kind of inventory associated with literary genres or specific compositional styles, such as the recitation or cantillation of the liturgical texts. These signs correspond to a style of syllabic recitation, which was adjusted to the textual prosody using two basic elements, acute and grave accents, represented by the *punctum* and *virga,* or *punctum* (.) and *tractulus* (-), respectively, as well as by ekphonetic signs (Madrid, BN, ms. 10029,

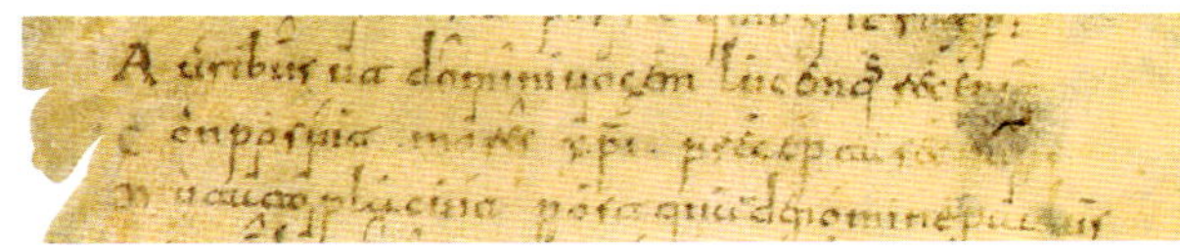

22. Biblioteca Nacional de España, ms. 10029, 10th c. *ex.*-11th c. *in.*, fol. 159r

23. Biblioteca Nacional de España, ms. 10029, 10th c. *ex.*-11th c. *in.*, fol. 158v

24. Biblioteca Nacional de España, ms. 10029, 10th c. *ex.*-11th c. *in.*, fol. 55v, *Disticon philomelaicum.* A limited inventory of neumatic forms, basically *virga* y *tractulus,* with the insertion of rounded signs

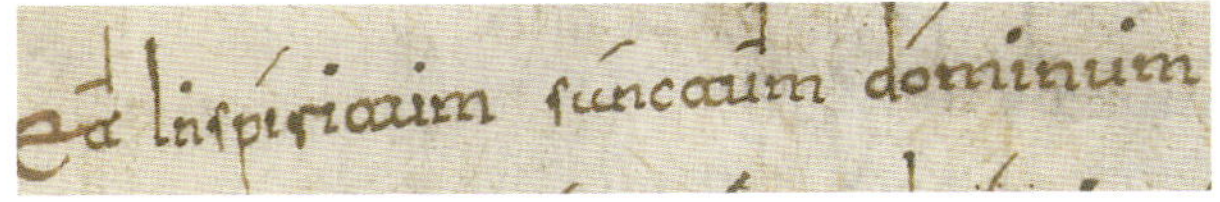

25. London, BL, Add. ms. 30845, 11th century *med.,* fol. 4r

fol. 54v).[63] Finally, it is worth noting the diversity of graphic variants for the *tractulus* and the *punctum* in the example from Córdoba, AC, ms. 123, a phenomenon also observed by Philipps for the composite neumes of the Antiphonary of León,

26. Biblioteca Nacional de España, ms. 10029, 9th c. *ex.*-10th c. *in.*, fol. 55r

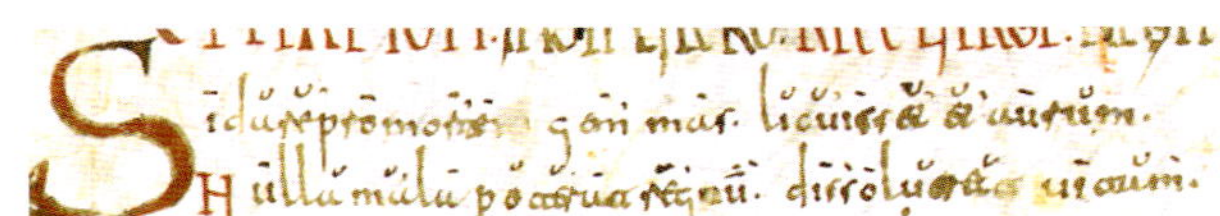

27. Biblioteca Nacional de España, ms. 10029, 9th c. *ex.*-10th c. *in.*, fol. 54v

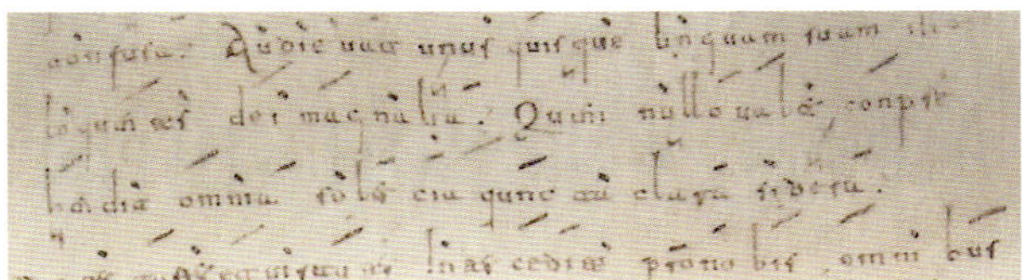

28. Córdoba, AC, ms. 123, 10th century *ex.*-11th century *in.*, fol. 208

which might signal some rhythmic or expressive differentiation.[64]

The only way to define the immanent significance of the neumes in the different Visigothic sources, to determine the styles typical of the different copying centers, and to date precisely the evolutionary phases of the notation is to compare their morphology. Any interpretation of the graphic variations should bear in mind that there is no reason why an a priori relationship should exist between these and some specific melodic or rhythmic function; there may also be variants that reflect the copyist's own individual character or the different phases in the evolution of the notation.[65] For greater clarity, I illustrate the phenomenon with some signs with unusual strokes taken from the Silos manuscripts. See the marked final stroke of the *torculus* in the case of BL, Add. ms. 11695, the way the pen is supported at the end the drawing and the angular profile of the neumes in Silos, AM, Cod. 6, the uniquely drawn *climacus* in Silos, AM, Cod. 5, and the particular shape of the *podatus flexus* in BL, Add. ms. 30845 (figs. 29, 30, 31, and 32).

To conclude: seen from the perspective of the classification of the Spanish repertory and its melodic structures, a distinction can be made between certain clearly differentiated traditions, as demonstrated by, inter alia, Wagner and Randel,[66] from the point of view of musical paleography, but definitive arguments are still lacking to allow any nuanced typological characterisation to be made. We do not have sufficient criteria to allow us to attribute precisely a type or particular feature of the

29. London, BL, Add. ms. 11695, 10th century *ex.*, fol. 1r

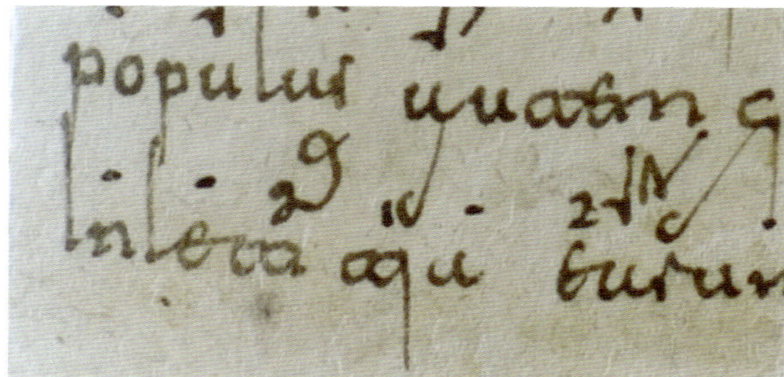

30. Silos, AM, Cod. 6, 11th century *med.*, fol. 26r

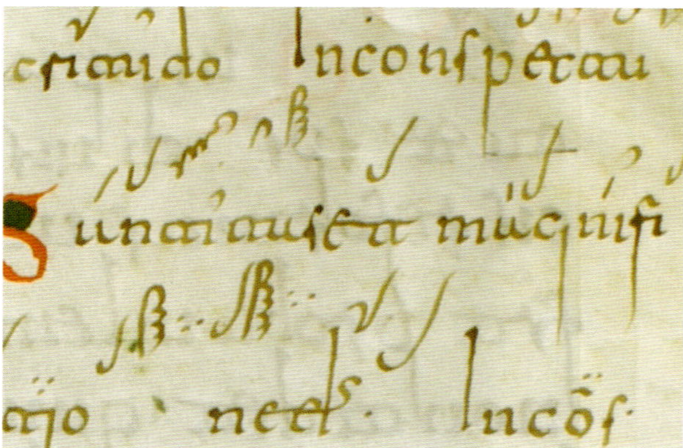

31. Silos, AM, Cod. 5, 11th century *med.*, fol. 40r

notational morphology to a specific cultural area or production center. Proof of this can be seen in the examples in diagram 1 that still have no specific geographic or cultural attribution. Likewise, the absence of criteria within the morphological analysis of the notation that are capable of distinguishing the dates of sources precisely requires us

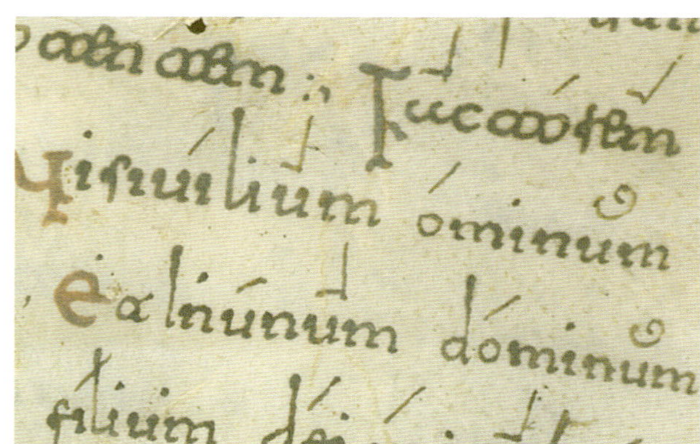

32. London, BL, Add. ms. 30845, 11th century *med.*, fol. 4r

to consider additional arguments from the paleography of texts, codicology, or related to the contents. Nonetheless, in a preliminary analysis, the study of the *ductus* of the notation allows us to establish formal subsets that delimit somewhat more than the generic north-south division, as well as to arrive at considerations about the genesis of the manuscripts, specifically, the copying center from which they came and their intended destination.[67] Through close analysis of the diversity of graphic variants in each codex—some of which are shown in the examples above—it will be possible to identify the different styles of the center or copyist in question, and the cultural context and economic situation of the centers where these codices were copied.

From a joint examination of the Visigothic sources from the northern tradition, one may deduce that they do not constitute a monolithic block but can be broken down or classified into subsets according to the *ductus*, the morphology, and the greater or lesser wealth of their inventory of neumes, as well as by their cultural and chronological context. A timeline of northern and southern groups of Visigothic notation is given in diagram 2, although the absence of examples in Visigothic notation from the south prior to the 11th century creates an asymmetry that might give rise to erroneous conclusions. For this reason, it is important to remember here that despite this shortfall, the scientific community assumes the same age for both notational traditions.[68]

In drawing up a classification of the different notational subgroups, we need to make a detailed analysis of the specific morphology of each example, in other words, an analysis of the progressive mutation of each of the graphic signs and the particular features of each source and the center or cultural sphere from which they come. As we have seen, in the case of southern notation, this sequence extends across a broad stretch of time, extending well into the 13th century. The difference between the careless notational script of the 13th century Toledan examples (Toledo, BC, 35-3, and Museo de los Concilios y de la Cultura Visigoda, 1325 and 1326), where the outlines of the neumes are barely drawn, and the fragment from Coimbra (AU, IV-3.ª-Gav. 44), with clearly drawn notation (11th century *in.*) is illustrative of the diachronic evolution of southern notation. The progressively more cursive *ductus*, the reduced diversity of graphic variants, the absence of special signs that appear in some specimens from the northern peninsula, as well as the careless strokes and inexact calculation of the space provided for inserting the melismas are some of the most characteristic aspects of this group of sources (fig. 33).[69]

With regard to the second system used in the Iberian Peninsula, Catalonian notation, just some of the characteristic aspects are summarized, based on the studies by Moll, Mas and Garrigosa, and the classical studies by Sablayrolles, Sunyol, and Anglès.[70] The selection of manuscripts shown in diagram 2 highlights two points: in Catalonia, the Carolingian script was adopted before it was in the rest of the Peninsula, whereas Aquitainian notation penetrated at a relatively late date, with the examples preserved from the end of the 11th century in this notation being considered exceptional. Catalonian and Aquitainian notational systems coexisted from the beginning of the 12th century, when the former lost its previous predominance. The historical explanations are given.[72]

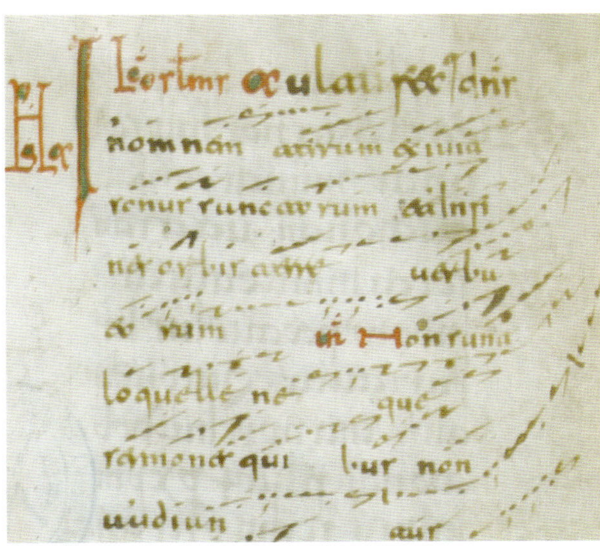

33. Museo de los Concilios y de la Cultura Visigoda, 1325-1, Frag.[71]

One particular feature of Catalonian notation is the diachronic evolution to be seen at least in a limited group of graphic signs, albeit not in all of them. Its development can be divided into four phases over a period of time stretching from the 9th century *ex.*, when the first documents preserved have been dated, to the 12th century *ex.* or 13th century *in.*, when it was finally abolished. These phases are essentially defined by a greater economy of signs, more precision in the graphic representation as a result of the segregation of the neumes, an increasingly stronger diastematic awareness and a change in the axis of the script.[73] Among the first examples with archaic Catalonian notation are the fragment from Tarragona (Tarragona, AHA, 22/1) from the 9th century *ex.*;[74] the antiphon of the consecration of the church in the Castle of Tona contained in an example dating from 889 (Barcelona, BC, parchment 9135 2-VIII-2), and the Barcelona fragment, also with pre-Catalonian or archaic Catalonian notation (Barcelona, BC, M. 1408-3), from the 10th century *in.*, from a previous date to the first examples of Visigothic notation represented by the Antiphonary of León (León, AC, ms. 8) and the fragments from the Antiphonary of Silos (Paris, BNF, N. A. L. 2199, fols. 14-16) (figs. 34 and 35).[75]

The presence of particular graphic forms such as the looped neumes or the singular *quilisma,* the script axis, the presence of the *virga* in an isolated position, and, finally, the diversity of variants for the same notational sign, correspond to the initial stage of Catalonian notation.

In addition to these examples in archaic Catalonian notation, there is another broad series mostly comprising fragments, some of which contain only some notational signs.[76] Diagrams 1 and 2 contain a selection

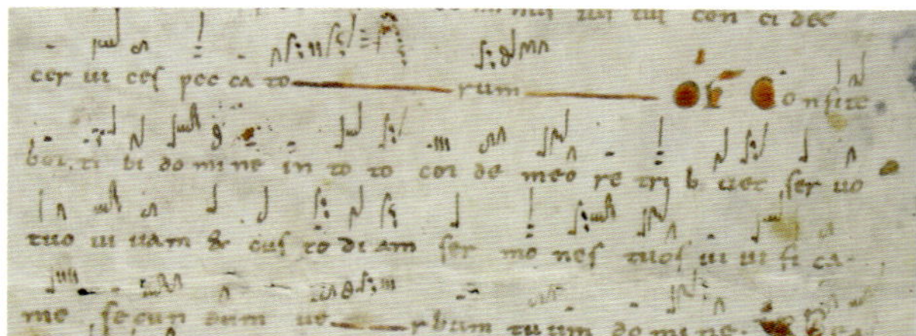

34. Barcelona, BC, M. 1408/3, 10th century *in.*, recto and verso

35. Barcelona, BC, parch. 9 135 2-VI-2 (illegible), year 889

of representative witnesses to the different evolutionary phases of Catalonian notation, to which we might add the two following examples:

A representative example from an early stage of Catalonian notation can be found in the fragment of an Antiphonary from Vic, ABEV, ms. 122/1 and 2, from the 10th century *med.* from Brull (Olsona) (fig. 36).

The miscellaneous codex of Ripoll (Barcelona, ACA, Ripoll 4) dated to the second half or end of the 11th

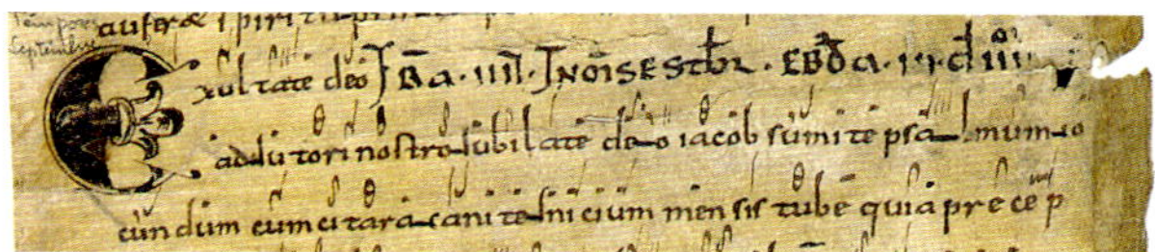

36. Vic, ABEV, ms. 122, 10th century *med.*, fol. 1v

century, gives a careful notation arranged diastematically on a drypoint line, corresponding to the ruling of the writing frame (fig. 37).

The codex of Lleida, AC, Roda 16 is unusual in that it has not been set to music entirely. In some pieces only the *finalis* contain Catalonian notation *in campo aperto* (see fol. 124v), where the reduction in graphic variants, the growing diastemacy, although still not explicit, and the greater precision in drawing the neumatic signs indicates a phase characteristic of the 11th century *in.* A slight levogyrate inclination can be seen on some folios. On fol. 123v, a second hand has notated a short melody in Aquitainian notation (figs. 38, 39, and 40).

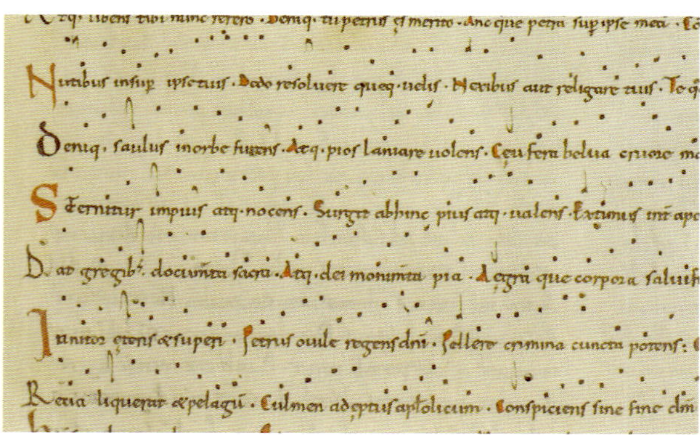

37. Barcelona, ACA, Ripoll 40, 11th century *med./ex.*, fol. 63v

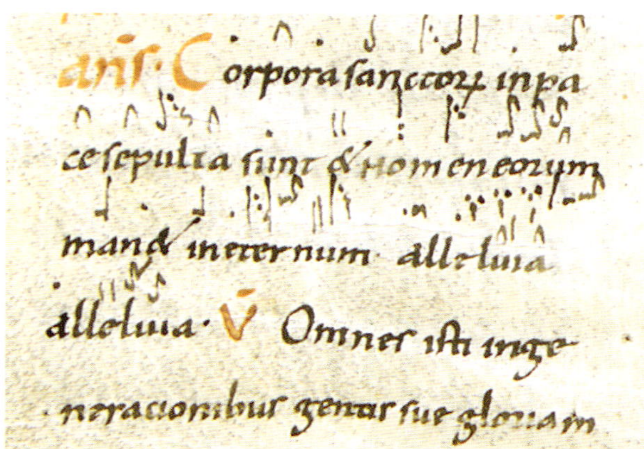

38. Lleida, AC, Roda 16. Sacramentary, Ritual and Pontifical, 11th century *in.* Around 1018, fol. 124v (Catalonian notation *in campo aperto*)

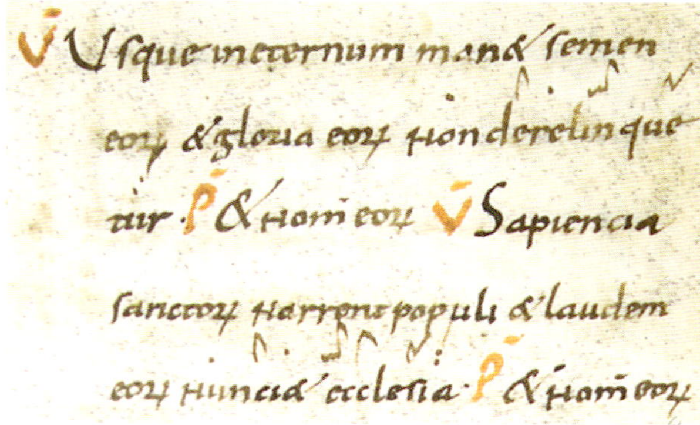

39. Lleida, AC, Roda 16, fol. 124v

40. Lleida, AC, Roda 16, fol. 123v

The example from Barcelona, ACA, Ripoll 106, also from the 11th century *in.,* written in Carolingian script with Catalonian notation *in campo aperto,* features a more angular morphology, no looped neumes, the survival of some linked shapes and a clearly diastematic intention. An additional example of this typology can be found in Paris, BNF, Lat. 933.

The sacramentaries of Vic, ABEV, ms. 66, copy from 1036, and ms. 67, copy from ca. 1050, show a notation *in campo aperto* of a limited inventory, given the genre and function of the pieces set to music (see Vic, ABEV, ms. 67, fol. 44v) (fig. 41).

41. Vic, ABEV, ms. 66, year 1050, fol. 82v

The example of Montserrat, BM, ms. 72,[77] dated to the 12th century *med.,* in Carolingian script with Catalonian notation on drypoint line, belongs to the final phase in the development of Catalonian notation. The segregation of the elements, disappearance of the isolated *virga*, angular drawing of the neumes, use of *custos*, real diastemacy supported on the drypoint line and perceptible in the drawing of the composite neumes place it in the final stage of local notation, before its definitive replacement by Aquitainian notation. As in the series of representative examples from the northern Peninsula mentioned earlier, in this example there are also two coexisting systems of notation: Catalonian and Aquitainian. The intervention of a second hand to insert the Aquitainian notation dates from after 1160 (fig. 42).

42. Montserrat, BM, ms. 72, 12th century *med.*, p. 322

Finally, a representative example is given of thick-stroked Catalonian notation, which, despite its late date—first half of the 12th century—is drawn *in campo aperto* although a certain attempt at diastemacy can be observed (fig. 43).

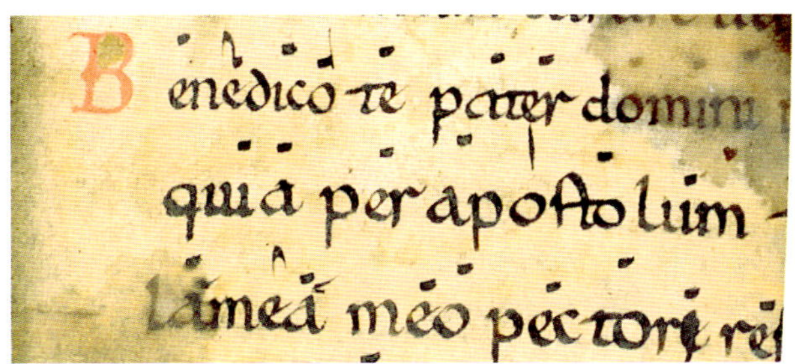

43. Vic, ABEV, ms. 123/3, 12th century. Fragment from the antiphonary of the office of St. Agatha

This selection of representative examples of the different typologies of notation reflects the nuanced process of adopting Carolingian culture over a period of nearly four centuries, from the 10th to the 13th century, a process that began with the change of script and culminated with the adoption of the Aquitainian notation between the 11th century *ex.* and the 12th century *ex.* As the earlier representative cases illustrate, the defining aspects of the various phases in the development of notation consist of a progressive stylisation of the script, the abandonment of unifying signs and the associated *scandicus*, the progressive trend towards diastemacy, and an increasingly marked irregularity in the angle of writing. While examples dating from the 9th century *ex.* to the 11th century *in.* display a wide variety of neumatic forms, manuscripts from the 11th *med.* to the 12th century see a reduction in graphic diversity, accentuating angular features, distinguishing between thick and fine strokes and tending towards an increasingly pronounced diastemacy, progressively adopting the drypoint line and the *custos* as tonal references.

The list of sources given in diagram 2, further amplified with those mentioned, shows a greater degree of complexity for the Catalonian area, resulting not only from the greater number of sources preserved but also from the prolonged survival of local notation and of the multiple forms coexisting with the new forms of notation, Aquitainian and square. This corroborates the idea of a transitional process that was very different from that of other locations in the Peninsula where the notational model was replaced much more suddenly, even when the liturgical reform occurred later.[78]

With regard to the codices of the transition period, which, as we have seen, are of exceptional value for any study of the process of Franco-Roman reformation on the Peninsula, two strictly differentiated groups may be identified, based on the chronology and morphology of the notation: the sources from the area of Catalonia and the sources from the rest of the Peninsula. Nonetheless, the Visigothic element survived in both, essentially in the script, whereas in the notation, the Aquitainian neumes replaced the Visigothic in a process that was sometimes gradual but more often sudden, or led to scenarios of coexistence with local notation, as was the case of Catalonia.[79] Two exceptions within this section are the antiphonary BL, Add. ms. 30850, and the breviary Add. ms. 30847, both from Silos, where the local systems survive in both script and notation, although the latter already began to reflect influences of Aquitainian notation which merit closer study. The reduction in the variety of signs, and the progressive angularity of the *ductus* are some of the factors indicating a transitional stage away from Visigothic notation, in which it is possible to identify not only elements typical of inventories from diverse cultural areas on the Peninsula but also phenomena of contact with the Aquitainian notation (fig. 44).

44. London, BL, Add. ms. 30847, 11th century *ex.*, fol. 15v

In the case of Silos, different models clearly coexist: the copy of the Franco-Roman repertory in Visigothic script and notation in the antiphonary BL, Add. ms. 30850, from the 11th century *ex.*, and in the breviary BL, Add. ms. 30847, as well as copy in Visigothic script and Aquitainian notation in the breviary, BL, Add. ms. 30848, 11th century *ex.* The two examples, BL, Add. ms. 30850 and Add. ms. 30848, which appear to be traceable to a common source (listed in Hesbert's corpus as St. André d'Avignon; *CAO* 5, 435), despite being of the same provenance and having been made within a short time of each other, display different script systems (figs. 45 and 46).[80]

45. London, BL, Add. ms. 30848, 11th century *ex.*, fol. 112v

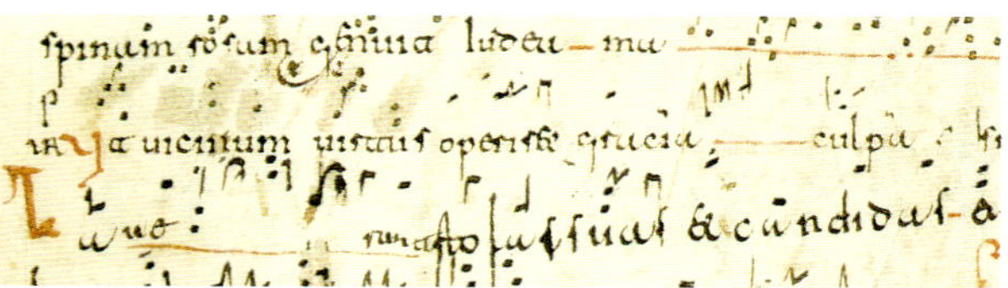

46. London, BL, Add. ms. 30850, fol. 239v

On the one hand, this suggests that experts from different copying centers were working at the same time; on the other hand, it indicates that the process of copying the new repertory was not systematic. The notation of Silos, London, BL, Add. ms. 30847, gives an additional example of the Visigothic transitional notation with a *ductus* close to that of Aquitainian notation in certain signs. The same is true of the Antiphonary of Silos, London, BL, Add. ms. 30850.[81] The latter also includes an inventory of mixed notational signs typical of both the eastern and the western regions of the Peninsula, which is reflected, inter alia, in the use of significative letters, *oriscus,* and *trigon*.

Another type of phenomenon equally characteristic of the period of transition is the translation of certain melodic pieces from one type of notation to another. Here we refer back to the examples from the Rioja area (Madrid, RAH, Cod. 56, and Silos, AM, Cod. 4).[82] One additional example of the specialists from different copying centers working together can be seen in the Roman missal, Madrid, RAH, Cod. 18, an example of excellent workmanship in both the Visigothic positioned script of a liturgical character, free from any Carolingian influence despite its late date, and in the perfect design of the Aquitainian notation, the work of an expert, probably ultra-Pyrenean, hand (fig. 47).[83]

The *Liber comicus* of Silos, Paris, BNF, N. A. L. 2171, dated around 1067, is further evidence of the coexistence of script systems in the initial phase of the reform.

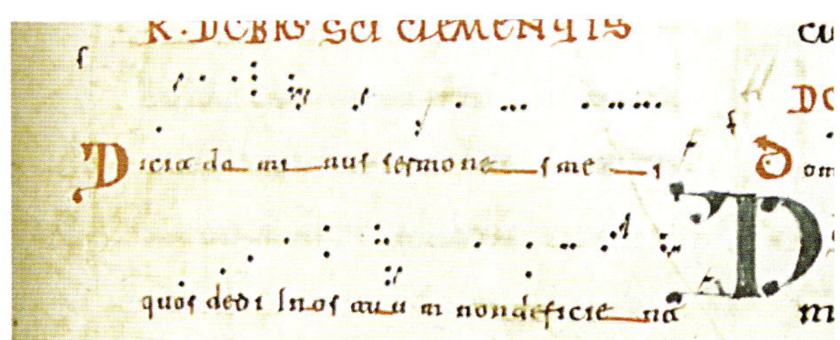

47. Madrid, RAH, Cod. 18, 11th century *ex.*, fol. CCLXV

As we saw with reference to Catalonian notation, equally diverse models can be seen in the Catalonian area of the transitional phase towards the system of Aquitainian notation, which penetrated from the beginning of the 12th century. I offer here only the paradigmatic case of Lleida, AC, Roda 18, in Carolingian script with Visigothic reminiscences, where the Catalonian notation coexists with the Aquitainian, and refer back to the examples shown in diagram 2 and described in the second part of this publication (fig. 48).

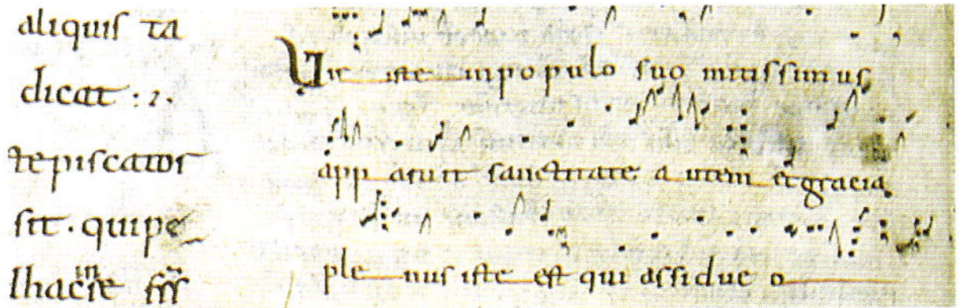

48. Lleida, AC, Roda 18, fol. 194v

The Roda codex also contains some folios in which Aquitainian notation *in campo aperto* was inserted after the original Catalonian notation had been scraped. The manuscripts from Vic, ABEV, ms. 105; Lleida, AC; Roda, 11; Paris, BNF, Lat. 933, and Paris, BNF, N. A. L. 495,[84] in Carolingian script and witnesses to the coexistence of Catalonian and Aquitainian notation constitute representative samples of the transitional phase in Catalonia. One singular case is that of the fragment of breviary from Montserrat, BM, 790/III, from the 12th century, in which the Catalonian and Aquitainian neumes alternate within the same piece of music. Nonetheless, it should be remembered that the Catalonian system of notation is a closed system, unaffected by the morphologies of transition, as Mas and Garrigosa have shown.[85] According to these authors, the only phenomenon of contact is to be found at a late date towards the last third of the 12th century, and only in the field of diastemacy, although, as we have seen in the example of Barcelona, ACA, Ripoll 40 (11th century *med.-ex.*), this is already pronounced. In the context of Catalonia, therefore, the term "transition" is understood more in the sense of coexistence of systems than of mutation from one system to another.

Included in this group are the later fragments from the Archivo Capitular of Santiago de Compostela and Orense in Visigothic script, although with clear Carolingian influence and Aquitainian notation, a reflection of the conservatism typical of the Compostela periphery.[86] Finally, the fragment from Coimbra, AU, IV-3.ª S.-Gav. 44 (20), in Visigothic script and Aquitainian notation, and the two cases cited earlier, Madrid, RAH, Cod. 56 and Silos, AM, Cod. 4,[87] in which the original Visigothic notation of some pieces has been scraped and replaced with Aquitainian notation, are representative samples of the different procedures used in the transition to the use of a new repertory of scripts.

The third notational system applied in the Iberian Peninsula—which coexisted with the aforementioned systems for nearly three centuries (from the 10th through the 13th centuries)—is Aquitainian notation.[88] Aquitainian notation, because of its unequivocal sense of tonal representation, proved to be a perfect system for disseminating the monophonic repertory. It includes a series of characteristics that are worth reviewing: 1) the use of the *punctum* as a basic sign of tonal representation, except in the *torculus* and the *pes stratus*, the latter being a sign limited to manuscripts of Galician and Franco-Roman origin; 2) the angle of script, vertical for the descent and oblique for the melodic ascent; 3) the diastemacy, that is, the graphic representation of the melodic intervals, using a line traced in drypoint in the interlineal space and the regular use of a *custos* of tonal significance at the end of the baseline, irregularly applied to the Portuguese manuscripts; 4) the use of the *quilisma*, an ornamental neume in an ascending sequence, with a particular form distinguishing it from the family of the French and German pitch notations, and 5) the knowledge of the semitone sign, also shown for Visigothic notation, and represented using different signs: semicircular *virga*, *virga cornuta*, *porrectus* or quilismatic *scandicus.*[89]

Aquitainian notation also shows different evolutionary stages from notation *in campo aperto* to lined drypoint notation, a red-colored line or various lines of tonal significance, common from the second half of the 11th century.

The different models used to explain the phenomenon of the more or less drastic abolition of Visigothic notation and its replacement by Aquitainian notation are still not entirely satisfactory, and it is not possible to demonstrate almost any specific interaction between the two systems, except for the isolated cases mentioned earlier of Aquitainian notation influencing Visigothic and Catalonian notation. Questions still arise as to now each of the different cultural areas reacted to the imposition of the new rite and with it the new notational system. It is wellknown that the replacement of one type of notation by another required specialists from centers in southeastern France, well accustomed to this type of script, as shown in the *Emilianense* codices (from San Millán de la Cogolla), Madrid, RAH, Cod. 18, and the additions to Madrid, RAH, Cod. 56, both works of extreme perfection, which may be attributed to a foreign hand. If we take separately the group of Catalonian sources, which, as we have said, belong to a very different historical context,[90] the sources representing each of the combinations listed here suggest a series of unknown factors awaiting an explanation. First, it is surprising that whereas in some areas we have evidence of script systems coexisting, in others there is no record of this happening. There may be a number of reasons related both to material factors, that is the lack of sources from the transitional period for determined areas, and formal factors, in other words, the possibility that the copying procedures were different in each center. The copies may have been the work of Spanish specialists, of ultra-Pyrenean specialists or even the result of collaboration between the two. In this respect, the cases of Aragón and of Navarre are paradigmatic, with not a single source extant that reflects the combination of script systems that was seen to exist in other areas of the Iberian Peninsula. In both territories, the first examples preserved of the new rite were copied in Carolingian script and Aquitainian notation (see diagram 2: Aragón, Navarre), although it is not possible to specify whether the copyists are local or come from centers in southern France, even if in many cases the elaborate *ductus* suggest the latter.[91] On the other hand, there are sufficient examples from Castile attesting to different procedures and intermediary stages in the change of rite on which specialists from both sides of the Pyrenees worked, as is illustrated in the section on the transitional codices.

No conclusive theory may be advanced to explain this situation, but one might posit the possible relationship between the geopolitical situation of these territories and the formal particularity of the sources copied during the transition process. As mentioned at the beginning of this article, the enduring opposition to the reformist movement amongst some circles of the clergy and nobility, the conservatism of some copying centers and the particular network of connections with centers in southeastern France make each manuscript a unique and immediate reflection of the context in which it was created.

This leads us to one of the most important questions in the study of Aquitainian notation in Spain: the lack of strictly paleographic musical criteria that would enable us to attribute a manuscript to a given area. As Huglo has written, the graphic differences in Aquitainian notation between a manuscript from an Iberian center and an ultra-Pyrenean one are practically impossible to appreciate.[92] Ultimately, the sign of the *custos* and the quilisma might, in isolated cases, offer useful indicators. Nor does the illumination of the manuscripts provide a sufficient criterion to distinguish between sources from centers on either side of the Pyrenees.[93] Nonetheless, the extensive collection of extant codices and fragments from the Franco-Roman repertory is a sufficiently large source of data to enable the reconstruction of activity at Iberian copying centers. From the point of view of music paleography, the difficulty lies in establishing solid criteria that can classify the entire group by local or regional traditions.[94] In this regard, the latest offering from Alvarenga on a supposed morphology specific to the Aquitainian notation in Portuguese manuscripts is revealing.[95] His theory, which contradicts the view supported by Corbin, confirms the absence of viable criteria for geographic attribution of the different morphologies of Aquitainian notation.[96] On the other hand, it is possible to establish a chronological sequence of the sources, based on the morphology of the signs and their semantic value, as Nelson (1996) shows for the case of the Zamora sources and Rodríguez Suso (1993) shows for the sources from the Basque Country.

In the absence of historical documents, other than legends and official chronicles which recount the most ordinary and functional aspects involved in learning the new repertory and assimilating the new forms of script, it is the liturgical-musical sources that, when compared meticulously, may be able to resolve these issues. There are more examples that reflect a full assimilation of the new notational system than those dealt with earlier: Visigothic notation(s), Catalonian notation and transitional notations. In the Catalonian area, it is possible to distinguish between different periods and morphologies of Aquitainian notation, as well as the existence of combinatory models, examples of which are given in the section on the transitional codices.[97]

An example of the introduction of the new rite and of the use of Aquitainian notation in Portugal in diagram 2 is the Missal of Mateus, Braga, AD, Add. ms. 1000, and various fragments of varying typology from the diocese of Braga, AD, fragms. 210 and 244; Coimbra, Lisbon, IAN, Torre do Tombo, Frag. Cx. 20, no. 14 and Porto, BPM, Santa Cruz 76 and 83.[98] Toledo preserves two office antiphonaries, BC, ms. 44-1 and ms. 44-2, which are of entirely Franco-Roman workmanship in terms of their contents and the morphology of their script and notation, which was also copied from French models and closely affiliated with the models introduced—via Cluny-Moissac—in the dioceses of Coimbra, Braga, and Lamego,[99] an issue addressed extensively by Steiner (figs. 49 and 50).[100]

With regard to some Aragonese sources of the Franco-Roman rite copied in an advanced phase of the

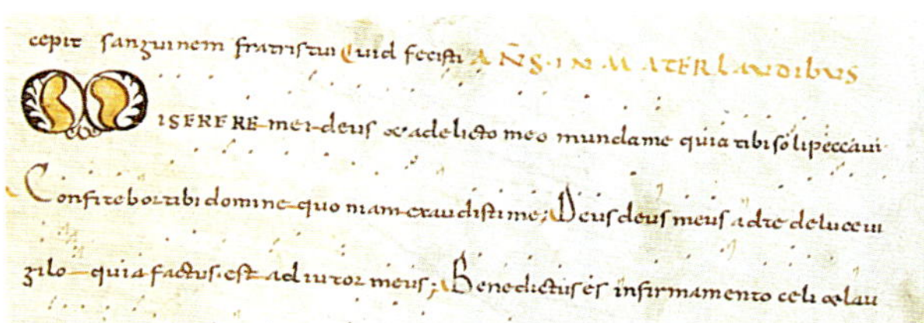

49. Antiphonary. Toledo, AC, 44-1, 11th century *ex.*, fol. 50r

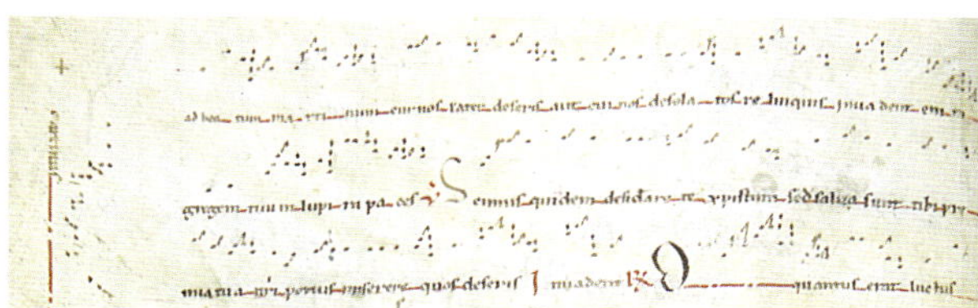

50. Antiphonary. Toledo, AC, 44-2, 12th century *in.*, fol. 156v

reform, such as the Antiphonary of Santa Cruz de la Serós (Jaca, AM, w./o. s.) and the breviaries from the Monastery of San Juan de la Peña (El Escorial, ms. L.III.3, ms. L.III.4, ms. Q.III.10), we again see the lack of strictly paleographic criteria for attributing their origin with any certainty to a center on either side of the Pyrenees.[101] Manuscripts would have been imported from southeastern France for use by the monastic, cathedral and parish centers in the Iberian Peninsula to meet the needs that arose during the first phase of the reform, as some of the examples selected show: the Huesca hymnary, Huesca, AC, Cod. 1, and the tropary-prosary, Huesca, AC Cod. 4, the latter made up of some sections of diverse ultra-Pyrenean provenance.

Diagram 2 shows a large number of examples belonging to this group, which represent the different phases in the assimilation of Carolingian script and Aquitainian notation on the Peninsula. Once again, we return to the question of the location of the center where the copyists worked: were they Iberian, were they foreign specialists integrated into the Spanish communities, or were the codices imported?

In addition to the manuscripts mentioned in the section on transitional codices, the examples that follow below include some of the most characteristic morphologies of the Aquitainian notation represented in Iberian sources, not all of which were only partially included in the aforementioned diagram (figs. 51, 52, 53, 54, 55 and 56).

51. Antiphonary. Frag. Huesca, AHP, Protocolos Notariales, 12030/35. Notation over a line in drypoint, 11th century *ex.*-12th century *in.*, fol. recto

52. Evangeliary. Avila, AC, w./o. s. Notation over a line in drypoint, 12th century *ex.*-13th century *in.*, fol. 5r

53. Gradual. Braga, AD, Frag. 82. Notation over a line colored in red, 12th century *ex.*

54. Prosary-Tropary. Vic, ABEV, ms. 105. Notation over a line colored in red and other lines in lead. Clef, 12th century (2nd half), fol. 59v

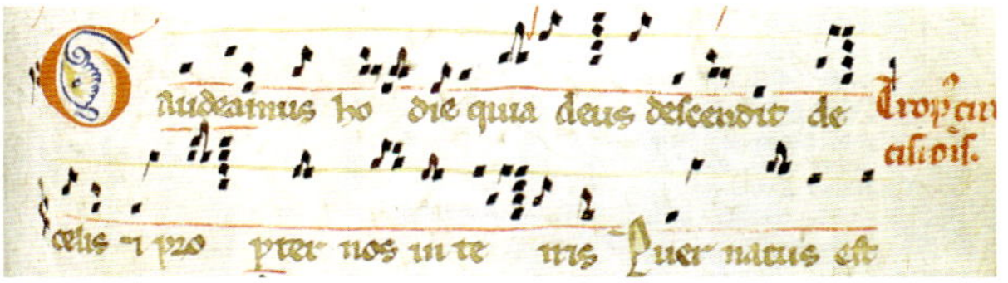

55. Prosary-Tropary. Vic, ABEV, ms. 106. Aquitainian notation over two lines. Clef, 13th century, fol. 43r

56. Sacramentary from Fitero. Pamplona, ARGN, K. 6. Aquitainian notation over four lines, 12th century *ex.*-13th century *in.*, fol. 57r

Diversity of contexts

An exploration of the different notational systems shows the diversity of contexts or spaces in which both melodic notes and complete pieces, with or without literary text, are inserted, as well as isolated notational signs with different functions. The following is a list of the most common contexts:

1) Musical notation adapted to texts not initially intended for receiving it in sources that are not strictly of musical-liturgical type.
2) *Melodiae*, with or without text, inserted in sources of different typology, not necessarily musical-liturgical.
3) Notational signs with functions other than that of tonal representation: reference marks and cryptography.

1) The selection shown in diagrams 1 and 2 includes some typologies with contents that are not strictly musical-liturgical, in which a contemporary or later hand has added notational signs. Here we should mention the Bibles of Cardeña (Burgos, AC, w./o. s.) and Silos (Cracow, Czartorysky Library, ms. 3.118); the homiliary (Córdoba, AC, ms. 1, and Sheffield, Galleries & Museums Trust, ms. 31); the sacramentary (Vic, ABEV, ms. 67), the lectionary (Lleida, AC, Roda 14), the miscellaneous codex (Madrid, BN, ms. 10029), the orationale (London, BL, Add. ms. 30852), and the fragment of a *Liber horarum* (El Escorial, a.I.13, fols. 196-197,[102] among others (fig. 57).

The manuscript Madrid RAH, Cod. 27 contains an annotated Alleluia on fol. 50r, and Madrid, RAH, Cod. 60, also contains inserts with musical notation

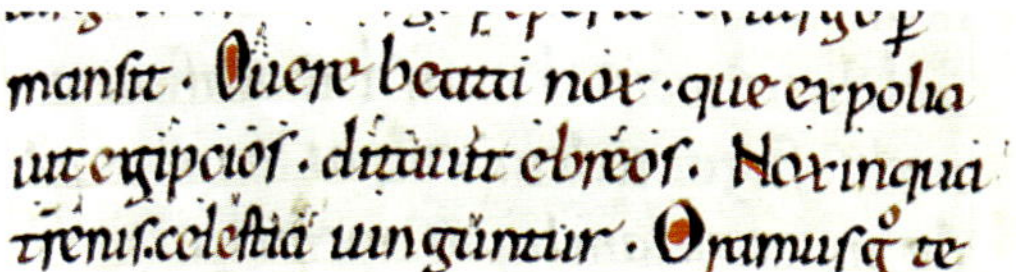

57. Sacramentary. Vic, ABEV, ms. 67, 11th century *med.*, fol. 44v. Written in Ripoll or Vic by a scribe from Ripoll

on fols. 28v-29r and 48v-50. Similarly, the *Orationale*, London, BL, Add. ms. 30852, contains additions on various folios with musical notation.[103] The homiliary, London, BL, Add. ms. 30853, not dealt with here, also includes musical notes in Carolingian script and Aquitainian notation (fol. 175v, lines 2-3; fol. 222v, lines 5-10) in a very careful stroke, using *custos*. In fol. 65r, lines 14-15, and before the *Sermo in vigilia Pasche*, a text has been inserted with northern Visigothic notation in a very careful stroke, in keeping with the general *ductus* of the codex.

2) With regard to the *melodiae*, linked or not to a text, and inserted in spaces that were not originally planned for this purpose, we offer two additional examples for illustrative purposes (figs. 58 and 59).

The folios added at the end of the Antiphonary of Silos, London, BL, Add. ms. 30850, which form part of a tonary, are of special interest. The annotations in fol. 239v suggest that melodic notes

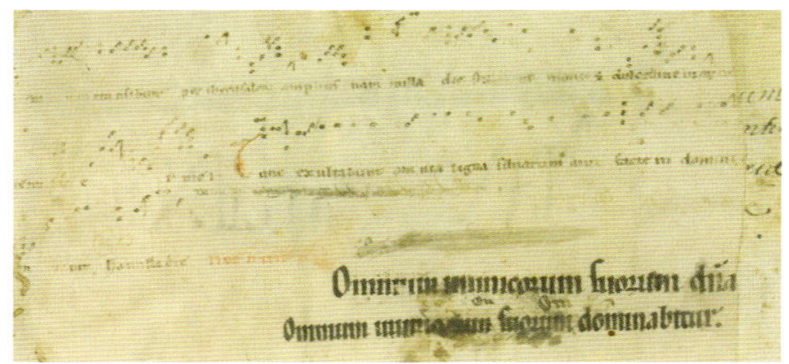

58. Ildephonsus. *De Virginitate Vitae Sanctorum.* El Escorial, RB, a.II.9, 10th century *ex.*-11th century *in.*, fol. 1r

59. *Codex miscellaneus.* El Escorial, RB, a.I.13, 10th century, fol. 197r

were intended to help singers learn a repertory that would have still been unfamiliar to Spanish communities. Similar examples can be found in the following manuscripts: Paris, BNF, N. A. L. 2170, fol. 210v, a *Benedicamus* added in the left margin in Aquitainian script with notation, nine lines; fol. 236v, a responsory for St. Martial added over a scraped text, in Visigothic notation with a notable Aquitainian influence. In the left margin a series of test neumes are notated, and in the right-hand column, there is a short illegible text with notation. The orationale, London, BL, Add. ms. 30853, contains in fol. 261r a long four-line *melodia* in Aquitainian notation with a very fine stroke, but no text. The manuscript Madrid, RAH, Cod. 30, contains a singular addition of neumatic signs that is difficult to interpret (fig. 60).

The same codex contains numerous melismas inserted in the margins, a common phenomenon in the Visigothic sources (fig. 61).

Except in the latter case of prolongation of a melodic discourse outside the writing frame, there may be two reasons for the series of neumes written in such different contexts as these, in many cases

60. *Liber misticus.* Madrid, RAH, Cod. 30, 10th century *ex.*, fol. 96r

61. Madrid, RAH, Cod. 30, fol. 114v. A melisma in the left-hand margin refers to the Alleluia at the end of the folio

making use of blank spaces in a codex that was not specifically designed for notation: 1) an attempt of a new type of notation and 2) a hastily written series of neumes, possibly intended for teaching purposes or to help singers retain an unfamiliar or not widely disseminated melody. Such inserts are found especially in the period of transition towards the new liturgical usage and should therefore be interpreted within the framework of the learning process and of the recasting of the repertory. In this case, the inserts document the vitality of a process of transformation, with Spanish and ultra-Pyrenean specialists interacting.

3) There are also cases of notational signs added for nonmusical purposes, either as reference marks or as marks to indicate the insertion of glosses in the margin,[104] or in isolation with a meaning that is not always possible to decipher.

A broad inventory of notational signs with a cryptographic meaning has also been documented in the writing of notarial deeds and in historical documents. Brou was the first to draw attention to the extravagant use of neumes in sources from the northern Iberian Peninsula from the 10th century on, a usage that was to continue until roughly the 13th century.[105] On the Iberian Peninsula, as Azevedo Santos points out, three systems of "substitutory" cryptographic script were known, one of which used notational signs.[106] The notaries themselves used this inventory to sign their names, but that was not the only purpose: we can also find other cases of the use of neumes with a cryptic meaning, for example, in the glosses from San Millán de la Cogolla (fig. 62).

More frequently, notational signs are used as reference marks (figs. 63, 64, and 65).[107]

The selection of examples offered here also reflects a diversity of functions for the neumatic signs, depending on the context to which they belong: for musical purposes, as reference marks for the glosses, and for

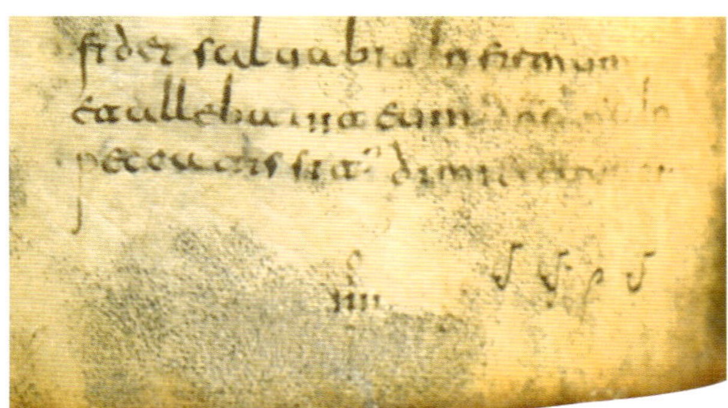

62. *Sanctorum Cosmae et Damiani passio, missa et orationes.* Madrid, RAH, Cod. 60, 9th century *ex.*, fol. 65v

cryptographic purposes, documented in notary deeds and other kinds of sources, as we saw in the case of Madrid, RAH, Cod. 60.[108] We can thus deduce the conventional and arbitrary value of the inventory of neumatic signs. However, the most surprising thing is their graphic diversity and, thus, the exhaustive knowledge that the copyists must have had of notational signs, as

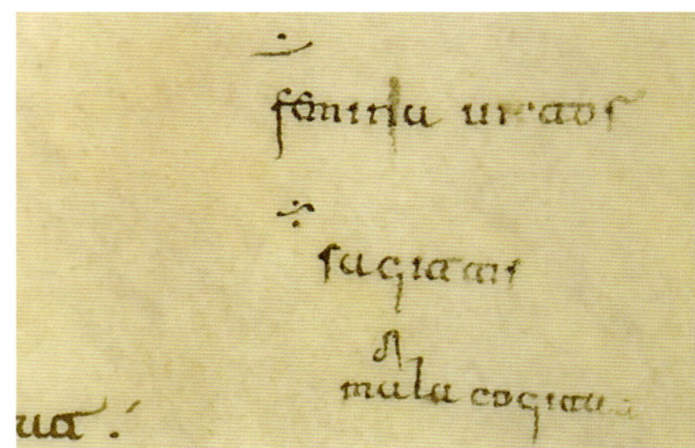

63. Ildephonsus. *De virginitate Vitae Sanctorum.* El Escorial, RB, ms. a.II .9, 10th-11th centuries, fol. 78r. The inventory of reference signs include, in addition to the notation, punctuation and melodic repetition signs

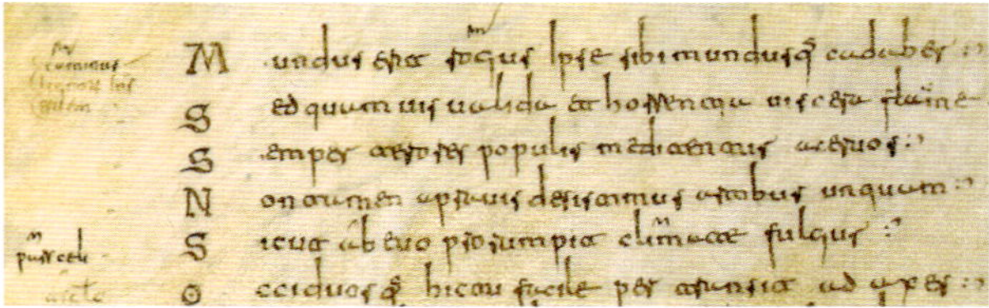

64. *Anthologia hispana (Azagra Codex).* Biblioteca Nacional de España, 10th century *in.* (11th century *in.*, Mundó), ms. 10029

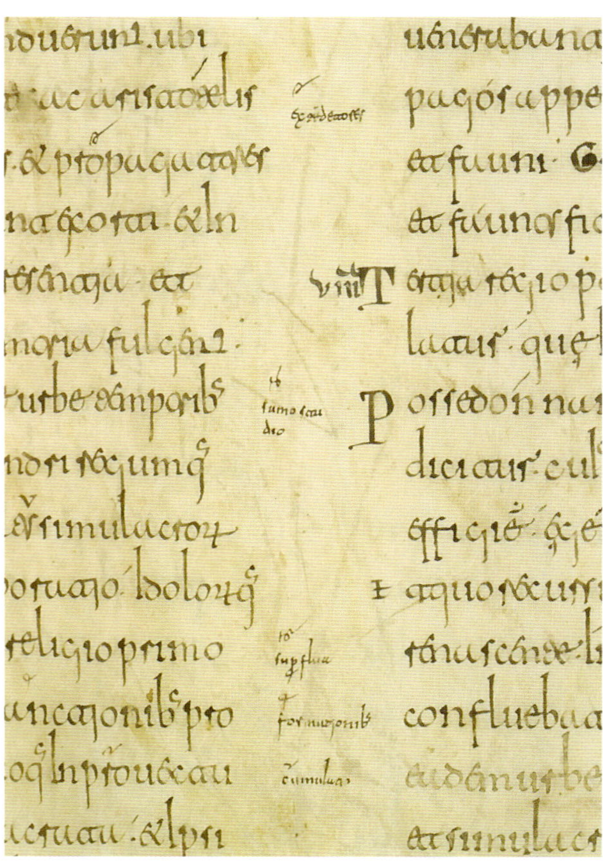

65. *Passionarium.* El Escorial, RB, ms. b.I.4, Cardeña, 11th century, fol. 4r

the selected examples show. Both notaries and copyists of liturgical codices show themselves to have possessed an absolute mastery of the drawing of neumes; we must therefore assume that there were expert calligraphers who did not necessarily know the musical contents but were capable of drawing the melodic repertory of the musical-liturgical manuscripts. This suggests that the code of notational signs was accessible to a broad spectrum of specialists and was not restricted exclusively to the musical-liturgical sphere. This leads us back to the question of whether the insertion of the neumes in the liturgical sources was the work of specialists in music, that is of a *notator*, with an expertise in using this code (as some authors have argued), or whether this work was performed by copyists who were experts in using different script codes, an explanation that appears more plausible in light of the materials analysed. This would tend to cast doubt on the thesis that in the process of preparing musical-liturgical sources, a copyist worked on the text and a *notator* on the melodies. In any case, it seems worth drawing attention to the inventory of the aforementioned notational signs inserted in codices whose content was not strictly musical-liturgical, to complement the study of the variants, functions, and phases of Visigothic notation on the northern Iberian Peninsula.

Diversity of periods: Anachronisms

Diagram 2 allows us to draw a series of conclusions relating to different areas of inquiry. Seeing these sources, one is initially surprised by the great number of different script systems from the various areas or cultural nuclei on the Peninsula, and the wealth of combinatory models, not only during the period of transition but even before the official date of the liturgical reform and the imposition of its formal structures.[109] Second, it is possible to see a clear chronological asymmetry. This asymmetry suggests a scenario of fragmentation, in which each example relates to geographical areas that formed part of a singular network of relations with Iberian and ultra-Pyrenean centers. These apparent anachronisms are therefore indicators of historical traditions that are specific to each area and each center.

As we have seen, the case of Catalonia is particularly complex because of the early fusion of liturgical practices and script forms. The blurring of boundaries in a very early period and the cultural permeability that this involved was reflected both in the formal and the structural fields of the sources. Less evident is the process of transition in the area of the High Pyrenees, from which scarcely any musical-liturgical examples have been preserved, even though the interactions with the ultra-Pyrenean centers were many over the course of time. In the area of Navarre, we scarcely have an empirical base, and it is impossible to reconstruct the process of transition from the musical-liturgical sources preserved, given also the nonexistence of sources from such relevant centers as the monasteries of San Salvador de Leyre and Santa María de Irache. One exceptional case in this regard is Santa María la Real de Nájera, to whose musical culture we have access via a small but significant set of sources, whereas no example whatsoever is extant for Pamplona. In this context, the southern Peninsula can be seen as an isolated area, with a single center of culture, Toledo, which was in turn closely linked to the diocese of Braga, from which hardly any examples of the old Spanish rite are extant. To a great extent, our only access to the scientific and cultural milieu of the southern Peninsula is through the activity of the Mozarabic communities displaced towards the north. A good example of their refined mastery of writing techniques can be seen in the Antiphonary of León, AC, ms. 8, a copy of a model from Beja. The map of the Spanish rite and the period of transition to the Franco-Roman liturgy on the Iberian Peninsula is therefore incomplete in various areas, covering a little less than half the total area of land of the strip surrounding the Camino de Santiago, bounded to the south by the changing frontier of the reconquest, with a small island confined to Toledo, the only center representing what is known as the southern tradition.

Even though the base materials do not reflect the whole but only fragments of the liturgical history of the period in question, a detailed analysis enables us to reconstruct partially the process of transition from the Spanish and Catalonian-Narbonnaise traditions to the Franco-Roman ones, operating around an east-west axis of penetration: Catalonia,[110] Aragón and Navarre at almost the same time (1071), Castile and León-La Rioja somewhat later (ca. 1076), Toledo (ca. 1086) and, in association with Toledo, the northern area of Portugal (1080). The westward advance was delimited by two centers: the Monastery of Ripoll and the diocese of Coimbra-Braga. The asymmetries we have mentioned in the field of the script systems therefore reflect a particularised adoption of the new rite in the different areas. Wherreas the oldest testimonies of Carolingian script date from the 9th century and of the Catalonian notation from the 9th century *ex.* (Document of Tours), both systems confined to the Catalonian-Narbonnaise area, the first contacts with Carolingian script in Portugal came around 1050, while Aquitainian notation began to be adopted in the last decade of the 11th century and the first testimonies of the new rite date from no earlier than 1081.[111] The geographic position vis-à-vis the Pyrenean border and the frontier of the advancing reconquest symbolise the impact of the reform promoted by Cluny and implemented through the corresponding network of connections between the Iberian Peninsula and the communities of southeast France.

Some conclusions

Although the official chronology of liturgical reform in the different regions of the Iberian Peninsula, with the exception of Catalonia, places it in the last third of the 11th century (1063-1080), the diversity and overlapping of script systems and the anachronistic survival of the Visigothic form or part of it for almost another four centuries reflects varied and individual dynamics in the adoption of the new rite. Initial resistance, seen in the political area in the first frustrated delegation by Hugo Candidus in 1065, was reflected by the conservatism of the scripts used in manuscripts for a long stretch of time. This conservatism affected both the forms of graphic representation and the structural aspects alluded to earlier. Given the great variety of models and the chronological asymmetry reflected in the sources, it is difficult to apply a single theoretical framework to explain the process of transition in the different areas of the Peninsula. A study of the corpus of manuscripts shows the vitality of a process of transition that led to diverse scenarios with no uniform and systematic format, in either the formal or the structural field, with a combination of script systems and of Visigothic and Franco-Roman forms, derived in each case from the diverse origins of the exemplars and of their respective interactions, as the varied classification of the sources shows. Each example therefore represents an individual case, part of a singular cultural identity with a particular interpretation of the inventory of neumatic signs.

We still need to resolve such elementary questions as that of the various evolutionary phases of Visigothic notation between the 10th and the 14th centuries, explaining its characteristics from a paleographic and semiological view. Such an analysis would involve a comparative study of the sources to identify the morphologies and significance(s) particular to each neume, in both an absolute and a relative sense, in other words, particular to a specific manuscript or group of manuscripts of common features. From there one might identify more precisely the phenomena of contact between the different notational systems and define, in the same sense as in the paleography of texts, the specific characteristics of each geographical and cultural area. In this respect, particular attention needs to be paid to the ruling method used in the codices, given that, as we have seen, the introduction of Carolingian techniques preceded the adoption of Carolingian script, which in turn preceded the notation, offering proof of a process of infiltration of the Carolingian element at three levels and in a staggered chronological sequence: 1) codicological—preparation of the page, ruling method; 2) paleographic—script (primarily the systems of abbreviation); and 3) paleographic—notation.[112] At the same time, although there is evidence of the qualitative difference in the notated exemplars—we should remember the distinction between the rurally produced manuscripts and those from the royal chancellery or from politically, economically, and culturally relevant monastic centers—.We need to explain the substantial differences in the greater or lesser degree of complexity in their respective notational and melodic systems. Likewise, other questions remain as to the complex process of adapting the new Aquitainian system of notation and about the copyists involved in producing the vast number of manuscripts required to provide the communities with the new books of worship. Another issue that remains to be resolved is that of the exemplars that were circulating in the Peninsula; a more advanced classification is required, organized by areas or traditions from the paleographical and musical point of view, a goal which, as we have seen from the latest research in Portugal, is debatable. With regard to dating, doubts also remain as to some manuscripts dated to different periods, sometimes several centuries apart.

Nonetheless, thanks to recent contributions from leading specialists, a series of criteria for the paleography of music have been identified that will allow a specific set of Iberian sources from the Catalonian-Narbonnaise area to be dated. Likewise, progress has been made with regard to Aquitainian notation, not only in extending the inventory of sources but also in defining the chronological sequence and geographical distribution. In the case of Visigothic notation, however, a series of criteria pertaining strictly to the paleography of music must be defined that will allow us to establish a reliable chronological sequence.[113] A plausible response is still lacking for the phenomenon explained here of the temporal anachronisms or asymmetries reflected by some sources during the process of adopting the new rite. How can one explain the copies of the *Liber misticus* (London, BL, Add. ms. 30845 and 30846), in Visigothic script and notation, the latter partially inserted, with a careless *ductus*, created in the 11th century *med.* when the process of reform was already fully active?

The questions posed in this chapter show the complexity of the study of Spanish notations and confirm the need to design useful tools for the analysis of musical paleography and to include historical and cultural considerations, contexts that are of great value for understanding the process of liturgical transition on the Iberian Peninsula.

NOTES

[1] As we shall explain later, the process of assimilating Carolingian culture began much earlier in the Catalonia-Narbonne area than in the rest of the Iberian Peninsula. The first examples in Carolingian script and Catalonian notation are from the last quarter of the 9th century (see Biblioteca de Cataluña, parchment 9135; Biblioteca de Cataluña, ms. 1408-3, and Tarragona, ms. 22/1), whereas Aquitainian notation only appeared from the 12th century on. The 13th century marked the final phase of copying liturgical and musical specimens in Visigothic script and/or notation and is dealt with briefly here.

[2] I thank Professor Anscari M. Mundó, Miquel S. Gros, and Michel Huglo, as well as my colleagues Màrius Bernadó, Miguel C. Vivancos, and Susan Boynton for their valuable guidance and their stimulating dialogue throughout the writing of this study.

[3] Having considered the issue of the transition from one rite to another, we have undertaken a study of different formal objects using the disciplinary approach and methodological models of scholars of the subject. One of the most important recent historical and artistic studies is by Rose Walker. *Views of Transition. Liturgy and Illumination in Medieval Spain.* London: British Library, 1998. Walter continues the research begun by Meyer Schapiro. "From Mozarabic to Silos". In *idem. Romanesque Art.* London: George Braziller, Inc., 1977, 28-101 (Spanish edition, *idem.* "Del mozárabe al románico en Silos". In *idem. Estudios sobre el románico.* Madrid: Alianza Forma, 1985, 37-119) analyses the relationship between text and image in the corpus of Visigothic codices before, during, and after the change in rite. From a strictly historical perspective, there are several works on the process of liturgical reform from the 10th to 12th centuries: Marcelin Defourneaux. *Les Français en Espagne aux XIème et XIIème siècles.* Paris: Presse Universitaires de France, 1949, 17-49; Charles Julian Bishko. "Liturgical Intercession at Cluny for the King-Emperors of León". *Studia Monastica* 3 (1961): 53-76; Anscari M. Mundó. "Moissac, Cluny et le mouvement monastique de l'Est des Pyrénées du xème au XIIème siècle". *Annales du Midi* 75 (1963): 551-573 and *Moissac et l'occident au XIe siècle. Actas del Coloquio Internacional de Moissac, 3-5 de mayo de 1963.* Toulouse: Edouard Privat, 1964, 229-251; Pierre David. *Études historiques sur la Galice et le Portugal du VIe au XIe siècle.* Coimbra: Instituto de Estudos Históricos, 1947; Justo Pérez de Urbel. *Los monjes españoles en la Edad Media.* 2nd ed. Madrid: Ancla, 1954.

[4] Some specimens, such as the fragment of an antiphonary from the 11th century, in the guard leaf of the *Codex miscellaneus,* Madrid, BN, ms. 11556 (see Agustín Millares Carlo, et al. *Corpus de códices visigóticos.* Las Palmas de Gran Canaria: UNED, Centro Asociado de Las Palmas de Gran Canaria, 1999. Vol. 1: 122) the provenance of which is still the subject of debate: St. Zoilus of Carrión, province of Palencia (according to Brou, Vives, Brockett, and Janini) and St. Zoilus of Córdoba (according to Moll Roqueta), could contribute to making up this documentary shortfall. See Louis Brou and José Vives. *Antifonario visigótico de la Catedral de León.* Barcelona: Centro de Estudios e Investigación San Isidoro (CSIC-CECEL), 1959. Vol. 1: 44-45 (Monumenta Hispaniae Sacra: Serie Litúrgica 5, no. 2. Facsímiles musicales 1); José Janini. "Los fragmentos visigodos de St. Zoilus of Carrión". In *Liturgica.* Montserrat: Abbey of Montserrat, 1966. Vol. 3: 73-83 (Scripta et Documenta: 17); Clyde W. Brockett. *Antiphons, responsories and other chants of the mozarabic rite.* New York: The

Institute of Mediæval Music, 1968, 43; Jaime Moll Roqueta. "Nuevos hallazgos de manuscritos mozárabes con neumas musicales". *Anuario Musical* 5 (1950): 12, n. 2.

[5] Ismael Fernández de la Cuesta. *Historia de la música española.* Vol. 1, *Desde los orígenes hasta el Ars nova.* Madrid: Alianza, 1983. *Idem.* "Mozárabe, Canto". In Emilio Casares Rodicio, coord. and dir. *Diccionario de la música española e hispanoamericana.* Madrid: SGAE, 2000. Vol. 7: 848-851.

[6] Ismael Fernández de la Cuesta. *Manuscritos y fuentes musicales en España: Edad Media.* Madrid: Alpuerto, 1980.

[7] José Janini. *Manuscritos litúrgicos de las bibliotecas de España.* Vol. 1, *Castilla y Navarra;* vol. 2, *Aragón, Cataluña y Valencia.* Burgos: Aldecoa, 1977 (vol. 1) and 1980 (vol. 2) [Publicaciones de la Facultad de Teología del Norte de España (Sede de Burgos): 38].

[8] Don Michael Randel. *The Responsorial Psalm Tones of the Mozarabic Office.* Princeton, New Jersey: Princeton University Press, 1969. The pioneering work in this area—from whose conclusions Randel dissents—is by Peter Wagner. "Untersuchungen zu den Gesangstexten und zur responsorialen Psalmodie der altspanischen Liturgie". In *Gesammelte Aufsätze zur Kulturgeschichte Spaniens.* Münster: Aschendorff, 1930. Vol. 2: 67-113 (Spanische Forschungen der Görresgesellschaft: 1).

[9] I use the term *geographical and cultural area* to refer not merely to the physical space, but to a cultural space that is associated—with a greater or lesser *degree of freedom*—to a specific political and institutional framework. For a distinction between the *physical* and *historical* categories in reference to a geographical space, see José Antonio Maravall Casesnoves. "De los nombres de España y de sus partes" and "España la mayor y España la menor. El plural 'Las Españas'. Otras formas de expresión en relación con la diversidad territorial peninsular". In *idem. El concepto de España en la Edad Media.* 4th ed. Madrid: Centro de Estudios Constitucionales, 1997, 54-79. For our purpose, territorial denominations are useful labels for identifying categories that refer to *cultural* spaces, each of the features that are sufficiently uniform to distinguish it from the others, even though this may not always coincide with a given political identity.

[10] With regard to the expression "production centers" as opposed to *Scriptoria,* see the Introduction

[11] García Turza, working from a philological perspective, supports a multidisciplinary approach to further a systematic understanding of the sources. Ruiz Asencio, talking about the usefulness of meticulously comparing the different monographs, highlights the urgent need for a methodology based on reliable criteria for dating and attributing the sources to a *scriptorium* or, at least, to a specific geographical-cultural framework. Finally, Mundó suggests a statistical-comparative method for dating manuscripts. See Claudio García Turza, coord. *Los manuscritos visigóticos: estudio paleográfico y codicológico.* Vol. 1, *Los códices riojanos datados.* Logroño: Fundación San Millán de la Cogolla, 2002, 10-11; José Manuel Ruiz Asencio. "Hacia una nueva visión de las glosas emilianenses y silenses". In César Hernández Alonso, ed. *Las glosas emilianenses y Silenses.* Critical edition and facsimile. Burgos: Ayuntamiento de Burgos, 1993, 83-118; José Manuel Ruiz Asencio. "Códices pirenaicos y riojanos en la biblioteca de Silos en el siglo XI". In José A. Fernández Flórez, dir. *Silos. Un milenio. Actas del Congreso Internacional sobre la Abadía de Santo Domingo de Silos.* Vol. 2, *Historia.* Santo Domingo de Silos: Monastery of Silos, University of Burgos, 2003, 177-210 (Studia Silensia: 26).

[12] We have already referred to this question in the general introduction to this work. See the section "Sources. Geographical range. Centers of production" (pp. 33 and subsq.).

[13] See Anscari M. Maria Mundó and Jesús Alturo. "Problemática de les escriptures dels períodes de transició i de les marginals". *Cultura Neolatina.* 58 (1998): 129. The article by Ludwig Vones in this work refers specifically to the problem described here (see pp. 43 and subsq.).

[14] Here it is worth remembering the early subordination of the Catalonian bishoprics to the protection of Rome, which was partly motivated by a desire for independence from the Narbonnaise archdiocese, a process that some authors date to the end of the 9th century (ca. 892). See Manuel Riu y Riu. "La organización eclesiástica". In Ramón Menéndez Pidal, ed. *Historia de España.* Vol. 7**, *La España cristiana de los siglos VIII al XI.* Madrid: Espasa Calpe, 1999, 636-639. Other authors, however (Miquel S. Gros), date Catalonian independence from Narbonne later (ca. 971).

[15] See the studies by Julio Valdeón ("Castilla y León"), Juan Carrasco ("Navarra") and Josep Mª. Salrach ("Condados catalanes y corona de Aragón"). In Juan Carrasco, et al. *Historia de las Españas medievales.* Barcelona: Crítica, 2002, 141-239.

[16] For the relationship between San Millán and Silos, see José Manuel Ruiz Asencio. "Códices pirenaicos y riojanos...". Op. cit. Vol. 2: 177-210; Miguel C. Vivancos. *Glosas y notas marginales de los manuscritos visigóticos del Monasterio de Santo Domingo de Silos.* Santo Domingo de Silos: Monastery of Silos, 1996 (Studia Silensia: 19); *idem.* "Circulación de manuscritos en la Edad Media. El caso de San Millán y Silos". In Maciej Bielawski and Daniël Hombergen, dirs. *Il monachesimo tra eredità e aperture. Actas del Simposio Testi e Temi nella Tradizione del Monachesimo Cristiano for the 50th anniversary of the Monastic Institute*

of St. Anselm. Rome: Pontificio Ateneo S. Anselmo, 2004, 785-802 (Studia Anselmiana: 140). On the statistics for the Silos collections, see Anne Boylan. "Manuscript illumination at Santo Domingo de Silos (xth to xiith centuries)". Pittsburgh: University of Pittsburgh, 1990 (Order Number 9209579).

[17] Both cases have been studied by Manuel C. Díaz y Díaz. *Códices visigóticos en la monarquía leonesa*. León: Centro de Estudios e Investigación San Isidoro (CSIC-CECEL), 1983; *idem. Libros y librerías en la Rioja altomedieval.* Logroño: Gobierno de La Rioja, Instituto de Estudios Riojanos, 1979; and *Coloquio sobre Circulación de Códices y Escritos entre Europa y la Península en los Siglos* VIII-XIII. *Actas.* Santiago de Compostela: University of Santiago de Compostela, 1988.

[18] Many specialists have spoken of the difficulties of trying to situate, geographically and chronologically, the corpus of musical-liturgical manuscripts, especially sources in the Spanish tradition. A number of research projects are currently underway in the fields of paleography, codicology, and textual criticism which, it is hoped, may resolve these questions. The publication currently under preparation, coordinated by Díaz y Díaz, Velazquez Soriano, and Ruiz Asencio and entitled *Códices visigóticos* [Turnhout: Brepols. (In press.)] will provide a new list of all extant Visigothic codices. A new catalog of the *Fragmentos de códices visigóticos* is being drafted by Pardo, Ostos, and Del Camino. A recent project, directed by García Turza (op. cit.) with sponsorship from the Fundación San Millán de la Cogolla offers, in a monograph, an analysis of different Visigothic codices; the first volume in the series is Claudio García Turza. It was precisely García Turza who highlighted the lack of a "rigorously reliable methodological support" that could resolve the chronological attribution of the ca. 350 preserved Visigothic manuscripts. The statement applies equally to geographical and paleographic-musical classification.

[19] It is important to note that the identifying labels used in paleographic studies denote, or rather *build*, areas that do not always have an exact historical equivalent. It makes sense from a paleographic perspective to speak of the "Rioja" or "Pyrenees" areas, even if the term does not match geopolitical and institutional units of the period. Hence, the term *Pyrenean* in diagram 1 on these pages encompasses some of the manuscripts taken from the groups of Catalonia, Navarre, and Aragón. We have based our terminological criteria on the cited works by Ramón Menéndez Pidal; José Antonio Maravall Casesnoves; and Juan Carrasco. I am particularly interested in the latter's minimalist chronological and geopolitical classification, covering the period between the 8th and 10th centuries, and embracing the territories of Al-Andalus, the Kingdom of Asturias and León, the kingdom of Pamplona, the county of Aragón, and the Catalonian counties, and also the particularly agitated period with many political changes, between the 11th and 13th centuries, the period dealt with in this chapter. During this time, the political nuclei comprised, on the one hand, the kingdom of Almoravide and Almohade taifas, and, on the other, the kingdom of Navarre and the two great leaders of the advancing Reconquest, Aragón and Castile.

[20] Manuel C. Díaz y Díaz, basing himself on the borders of the kingdom of León in the times of Ferdinand I in the 11th century *med.,* also includes the collections of Silos and San Millán in his list. See Manuel C. Díaz y Díaz. *Códices visigóticos...* Op. cit., 466, n. 360. The diagram, nonetheless, stresses the independence of the subsets within the generic term of *Castile and León*.

[21] There are only a few extant examples of the Spanish rite in Portugal, some with notation from the north and others with notation from the southern part of the Peninsula. However, in addition to the one included in diagram 1 and three fragments from Lamego (Episcopal Palace) of Castilian origin which we were unable to reproduce for this publication, we should also mention two new fragments from Bragança and Viseu (no. 105, *Actas do Concílio XIII de Toledo;* and no. 403, *Decretos do Concílio de Calcedónia*) included in Isabel Vilares Cepeda and Teresa Duarte Ferreira, scientific and technical coordinators. *Inventario dos códices iluminados até 1500*. Lisbon: Ministério da Cultura, Biblioteca Nacional, Inventario do Património Cultural, 2001. Vol. 2: 68-69, 215-216.

[22] See sheet, part 2, p. 300.

[23] See Julio Valdeón. "Castilla y León". In Juan Carrasco, et al. Op. cit., 143 *et passim.*

[24] See Joaquim Garrigosa i Massana. *Els manuscrits musicals a Catalunya fins al segle* XIII*. L'evolució de la notació musical.* Lleida: Institut d'Estudis Ilerdencs, 2003, 370 (Col·lecció Emili Pujol: 2; Màrius Bernadó, dir.).

[25] Boylan sees the following codices as coming from the *scriptorium* at Silos: London, BL, Add. ms. 30847, 30848, 30850, 30853 (only the penitential) and 11695, Paris, BNF, N. A. L. 235 (fols. Av-B), 2177 and 2170 (*Vita of Saint Martial);* however, Vivancos distinguishes four stages of activity at the *scriptorium* at Silos, including the following manuscripts, included in diagram 1. From the first stage (10th century *in.*): Cracow, Czartorysky Library, ms. 3.118; Paris, BNF, N. A. L. 2170; and London, BL, Add. ms. 30852. From the third stage (first half of the 11th century): Silos, AM, Cods. 3, 5 and 7; and from the fourth stage (second half of the 11th century): Salamanca, BGU, ms. 2668; and London, BL, Add. ms. 30847,

30848, 30850 and 11695. The origin of the three *misticus* has yet to be determined: London, BL, Add. ms. 30844, 30845, 30846, and Salamanca, BGU, ms. 2637 (in the latter case, opinions are divided between San Millán and Silos). For the bible, Cracow, Czartorysky Library, ms. 3.118, no hypothesis has yet been offered on its origin. Ruiz Asencio attributes the following manuscripts to the Pyrenean and Rioja areas: from La Rioja, probably, Silos, AM, Cod. 5; from Nájera, Silos, AM, Cods. 6, 7 and 3; from the kingdom of Pamplona, BL, Add. ms. 30852. Finally, Vezin attributes the codex London, BL, Add. ms. 30849 to an Iberian monastery, though he is unable to specify any particular center. He speculates that it may have been copied from an ultra-Pyrenean model. The Santo Domingo de Silos codex, BL, Add. ms. 30852, is of Aragonese origin according to Díaz y Díaz, whereas Anne Boylan thinks it is from Cardeña (op. cit.). For further information, see Miguel C. Vivancos. Op. cit., 62-67; José Manuel Ruiz Asencio. "Códices pirenaicos y riojanos…". Op. cit. Vol. 2: 177-210; and Jean Vezin. "El códice British Library add. 30849 y la introducción de la carolina en España". In José A. Fernández Flórez. Op. cit., 211-222.

[26] See Manuel C. Díaz y Díaz (p. 93).

[27] Garrigosa includes it, with sound reasoning, among the Catalonian manuscripts, given the see of Huesca's links to the see of Tarragona. See Joaquim Garrigosa i Massana. Op. cit.

[28] See Susana Zapke. "Monodie und virtuelle Polyphonie in Aragón". In Bruno Bouckaert and Eugeen Schreurs, eds. *Musical Life in Collegiate Churches in the Low Countries and Europe. Chant and Polyphony*. Leuven-Peer: Alamire Foundation, 2000, 399-412 [The Di Martinello Music Collection (KULeuven, University Archives): Yearbook of the Alamire Foundation 4].

[29] It would be helpful to draw up an inventory of copy specimens from ultra-Pyrenean centers in order to examine typological differences with Iberian specimens, in both formal and structural approach. On trans-Pyrenean relations, from which the listed manuscripts result, see Manuel C. Díaz y Díaz. "La circulation des manuscrits dans la Péninsule Ibérique du VIIIème au XIème siècle". *Cahiers de Civilisation Médiévale* 12 (1969): 219-241.

[30] See p. 251

[31] See the examples of disputed origin: London, BL, Add. ms. 30852; Madrid, BN, ms. 10029 (Toledo 14-22); Madrid, BN, ms. 10001 (Toledo 35-1); Salamanca, BGU, mss. 2668 and 2837; Silos, AM, Cod. 5 and Paris, BNF, N. A. L. 2199; Sheffield Galleries & Museums Trust, ms. 31; Cracow, Czartorysky Library, ms. 3.118.

[32] On some of the literary and theoretical sources, see the article by Michel Huglo. "La tradición de la *Música Isidori* en la Península Ibérica", in this work.

[33] The third part of this article gives some representative samples of these later specimens. The list is as follows: Toledo. Madrid, BN, ms. 10110, olim Toledo, BC, 35.2. *Liber misticus.* 13th-14th centuries. [Millares 171.] Toledo, BC, ms. 35-4. *Varia officia et missae.* 12th-13th centuries (Mundó sets the date between 1192-1208). Visigothic script-Visigothic notation from the south. [Millares 322.] Toledo, BC, ms. 35-5. *Varia officia et missae.* 13th century *med.* Visigothic script-Toledo notation. [Millares 323.] Toledo, Museo de los Concilios y de la Cultura Visigoda. Fragment of *Liber misticus.* no. 1.325-1. 13th century. Visigothic script and Visigothic notation from the south. Spanish repertory. [Millares 330.] Toledo, Museo de los Concilios y de la Cultura Visigoda. Fragment of *Liber comicus*, no. 1326. 13th century. Visigothic script and Visigothic notation from the south. Spanish repertory. [Millares 332.] Toledo, Museo de los Concilios y de la Cultura Visigoda: *Hymnarium*, no. 1325-2. 13th century Visigothic script-Visigothic notation from the south. Spanish repertory. [Millares 331.] Cincinnati (Ohio, USA). *Liber misticus.* 12th to 13th centuries. [Millares, 10th century, 34.]

[34] Inter alia, the following, not included in the diagram, are paradigmatic: Tarragona, AHA, ms. 22/1, *Liber misticus,* 9th century *ex.* (880, Alturo i Perucho), Carolingian rustic script and Catalonian archaic notation, and Barcelona BC, 1408-3, antiphonary of the mass, 10th century *in.* (900, Mundó), Carolingian rustic with reminiscences of Visigothic and Catalonian archaic notation. Mundó defines the script as "notarial Carolingian rustic" to distinguish it from the Carolingian of the county curia and from that of the monastic or cathedral clerics. See Anscari M. Mundó. "Un fragment molt antic de litúrgia romana a Catalunya. Excursus I: Nous manuscrits amb notació catalana arcaica; Excursus II: El "Missal Místic o Mixt" a Catalunya". In *II Congrés Litúrgic de Montserrat* (1966). Montserrat: Abbey of Montserrat: 1967. Vol. 3: 180, and *idem* and Jesús Alturo i Perucho. Op. cit., 121-148. The term "Catalonian" used for this period is not entirely exact, and we should consider using the term *pre-Catalonian*, coined by D'Abadal i de Vinyals. See Ramón D'Abadal i de Vinyals. "Nota sobre la locución *Marca Hispánica*". *Boletín de la Real Academia de Buenas Letras de Barcelona* 27 (1957-1958): 157-164; *idem.* "La Pre-Catalunya (segles VIII-IX i XI)". In Ferrán Soldevilla, dir. *Historia dels Catalans.* Barcelona: Ariel, 1970. Vol. 2: 601-992 and Ramón Menéndez Pidal, ed. Op. cit. Mundó applies the terms *pre-Catalonian* and *archaic Catalonian* to the script systems. See Anscari M. Mundó. *Ibidem,* 188.

[35] Diagram 2 uses the word *transition** with an asterisk when other script systems hve been inserted in later additions.

[36] The term *transition* is not employed here with the same meaning as in Lowe, who limits it exclusively to Visigothic sources dated between 894 and 945. See Elias A. Lowe. *Studia palaeographica. A contribution to the History of early latin Minuscule and to the Dating of Visigothic mss.* Munich, 1910 and *idem. Codices latini antiquiores. A Palaeographical Guide to Latin Manuscripts Prior to the Ninth Century.* Vol. 9, *Hungary, Luxembourg, Poland, Russia, Spain.* Oxford: Clarendon Press, 1966. Rather, I use it, like Millares Carlo, Vezin, Ruiz Asencio, and Díaz y Díaz, to refer to the period between the second half of the 11th century and well into the 12th century, the period of greatest activity in copying Franco-Roman models. Here we should not forget the phenomenon identified by Ruiz Asencio, whereby the Carolingian abbrevative system was adopted prior to the official replacement of Visigothic by Carolingian script in the kingdom of Castile-León, in Aragón and in La Rioja. See José Manuel Ruiz Asencio. "Hacia una nueva visión..." Op. cit., 101 and subsq. See also Jean Vezin. Op. cit. This is of substantial relevance in identifying the concept of transition with paleographic rigor.

[37] We have not specified the different systems of Visigothic script, because this lies outside our area of expertise. We might, however, differentiate between various stages, indicating the progressive adoption of Carolingian practices, first in the ruling method, then in the system of abbreviations, and later on again in the assimilation of the particular graphic forms. In Portugal, Visigothic script survived well into the 12th century (1172). Azevedo Santos dates the beginning of transition Visigothic in Portugal to the 11th century *med.* (1054-1172). The process was to take 118 years, during which time it spread from Pendorada, north of the Duero, to Pedroso. See Maria José Azevedo Santos. *Da visigótica à carolina a escrita em Portugal de 882 a 1172.* Lisbon: Fundação Calouste Gulbenkian, Junta Nacional de Investigaçao Científica e Tecnológica, 1994, 276-279 (Textos Universitarios de Ciències Sociais e Humanas).

[38] The case of the Bibles requires additional clarification. Obviously these are not examples of *transition* conceived *ex professo* to disseminate the new repertory, but Visigothic examples that continued in use and to which melodies in Aquitainian notation were added for certain parts of the repertory, essentially the Song of the Sybil and the *Lamentations of the prophet Jeremiah.* These cases of additions in Aquitainian notation (see diagrams 1-3) with a *T* followed by an asterisk.

[39] See Alexandre Olivar. "Les Supervivències litúrgiques autòctones a Catalunya en els manuscrits dels segles XI-XII". In *II Congrès Litúrgic de Montserrat.* Montserrat: Abbey of Montserrat, 1967. Vol. 3: 21-89; and Josep Romà Barriga. *El Sacramentari, Ritual i Pontifical de Roda.* Barcelona: Fundació Salvador Vives Casajuana, 1975.

[40] I am referring here strictly to the formal aspect, and not the structural aspect, that is, the configuration and combination of forms in the Spanish, Catalonian-Narbonnaise and Franco-Roman rites, where the symbiosis of materials is equally perceptible.

[41] Note that the catalog numbers given in Millares Carlo do not always coincide with those currently used in the archives. This is the case of the Braga fragment.

[42] Unfortunately it was not possible to consult the three Braga fragments mentioned here, which are currently filed under different catalog numbers to those given in Millares Carlo's corpus. I would like to thank the director of the Arquivo Distrital de Braga, Maria da Assunçao Vasconcelos, for her kind help.

[43] See François Avril, et al. *Manuscrits enluminés de la Péninsule Ibérique.* Paris: Bibliothèque Nationale de France, 1983, 20.

[44] Jean Vezin. "Observations sur l'emploi des réclames". *Bibliothèque de l'École de Chartes* 125 (1967): 17; Manuel C. Díaz y Díaz. "La circulation des manuscrits...". Op. cit., 234, n. 108; *idem. Libros y librerías...* Op. cit., 55-62.

[45] My thanks to Michel Huglo for this information. On the manuscript in question, see Roger Reynolds. "Baptismal Rite and Paschal Vigil in transition in medieval Spain: a new Text in visigothic script". *Medieval Studies* 55 (1993): 257-272.

[46] My thanks to Professor Ruiz Asencio (University of Valladolid) for informing me of its existence.

[47] My thanks to Miquel Saints Gros (Archivo de Vic) for having told me of the existence of the two fragments. See Ana Suárez González. "Dos supervivientes visigóticos (Zamora, AHP, Frags. 15 and 202)". In *Miscel·lània litúrgica catalana.* Barcelona: Societat Catalana d'Estudis litúrgics e Institut d'Estudis Catalans, 2006. Vol. 14: 119-137; and Kathleen Nelson. *Medieval Liturgical Music of Zamora.* Ottawa: The Institute of Medieval Music, 1996, 76, 83, 84, 93 and 241 (Wissenschaftliche Abhandlungen: 67).

[48] Nonetheless, studies of musical paleography in the context of Iberian notations have come a long way, with significant developments since the 1980s. Referential contributions have been made by Maur Sablayrolles. "À la recherche des manuscrits grégoriens espagnols: *Iter hispanicum". Sammelbände der Internationalen Musik Gesellschaft* 13, no. 4 (July-September 1912): 509-531; Casiano Rojo, and Germán Prado. *El canto mozárabe: estudio histórico-crítico*

de su antigüedad y estado actual. Barcelona: Biblioteca de Cataluña, 1929; Grégoire M. Sunyol. *Introduction à la paléographie musicale grégorienne.* Paris: Société de Saint Jean l'Évangéliste, Desclée, 1935 (French translation, *idem. Introducció a la paleografia musical gregoriana.* Montserrat: Abbey of Montserrat, 1925); Anscari M. Mundó. "Un fragment molt antic...". Op. cit. Vol. 3: 173-191; *idem.* "Consideracions paleogràfiques a l'entorn de la monodia litúrgica medieval en l'obra d'Higini Anglès". *Recerca Musicològica* 9-10 (1989-1990): 5-14 *(Actes del Congrès Internacional "Higini Anglès i la musicologia hispànica").* Herminio González Barrionuevo. "Presencia de signos adicionales de tipo melódico en la notación 'mozárabe' del norte de España". *Revista de Musicología* 9, no. 1 (1986): 11-27 [edition in French, "Presénce de signes additionnels de type mélodique dans la notation 'mozarabe' du nord de l'Espagne". *Études Grégoriennes* 23 (1989): 141-151]; *idem.* "La grafía del 'sálicus' en la notación 'mozárabe' de tipo vertical". *Revista de Musicología* 12, no. 2 (1989): 397-410; *idem.* "Dos grafías especiales del 'scándicus' en la notación 'mozárabe' del norte de España". *Revista de Musicología* 13, no. 1 (1990): 11-79; *idem.* "Los códices 'mozárabes' del archivo de Silos: aspectos paleográficos y semiológicos de su notación neumática". *Revista de Musicología* 15, nos. 2-3 (1992): 403-472 *[La música en la abadía de Silos. Trabajos del I Simposio de Musicología Religiosa (Burgos, Silos, marzo de 1991)]*; *idem.* "Relación entre la notación 'mozárabe' de tipo vertical y otras escrituras neumáticas". *Studi Gregoriani* 11 (1995): 5-12; Jaume Moll Roqueta. Op. cit., 11-14; *idem.* "La notación visigótico-mozárabe y el origen de las notaciones occidentales". In *Liturgia y música mozárabes. Ponencias y comunicaciones presentadas al I Congreso de Estudios Mozárabes: Toledo 1975.* Toledo: Instituto de Estudios Visigótico-Mozárabes de San Eugenio, 1978, 257-272 (Serie D 1); *idem.* "Per una tipologia de la notació catalana". *Butlletí de la Societat Catalana de Musicologia* 2 (1985): 9-22—Spanish translation in *idem.* "Para una tipología de la notación catalana" *Revista de Musicología* 9, no. 2 (1986): 339-409—; Josiane Mas. "La notation catalane". *Revista de Musicología* 11, no. 1 (1988): 11-30; Susana Zapke. "Estudios de semiología comparada en base a dos antifonarios altoaragoneses SJP y SCS". In Eliseo Serrano Martín, ed. *Muerte, religiosidad y cultura popular, siglos XIII-XVIII.* Zaragoza: Institución Fernando el Católico, 1994, 509-517; *idem.* "Procesos asimilativos del nuevo repertorio francorromano en el norte de la Península". *Revista de Musicología* 16 (1993): 2257-2267; *idem. El Antifonario de San Juan de la Peña (siglos X-XI): estudio litúrgico-musical del rito hispánico.* Zaragoza: Institución Fernando el Católico, 1995; Nancy Phillips. "Notationen und Notationslehre von Boethius bis zum 12. Jahrhundert". In Thomas Ertelt and Frieder Zaminer, eds. *Geschichte der Musiktheorie.* Darmstadt: Wissenschaftliche Buchhandlung, 2000. Vol. 4: 293-623 (especially the separate "Spanische Neumen" in pages 442-457); and Joaquím Garrigosa i Massana. Op. cit.

49 Cases in which attributions of origin have not been positively established are indicated by a question mark. When the indication of provenance has a generic significance (i.e. referring to a province or diocese), this is shown in parentheses. Specimens of trans-Pyrenean origin are shown underlined in italics.

50 I am not referring here to the *ductus* of the script, but to the specific drawing of the notational signs. It would be difficult to find such notable differences for the letter *a* between two Visigothic codices, as we see in the drawing of a *torculus* or *scandicus*. The individual ingredient is stronger in the field of notation, although this observation needs to be qualified and can only be demonstrated empirically.

51 The oldest testimonies of Spanish sources with musical notation go back to the 10th century, 900 or even to a somewhat earlier date, around 850. See Anscari M. Mundó. "Un fragment molt antic...". Op. cit. Vol. 3: 186 and subsq.; and Michel Huglo. "La notation wisigothique est-elle plus ancienne que les autres notations européennes?" In Emilio Casares, Ismael Fernández de la Cuesta and José López-Calo, eds. *España en la música de Occidente. Actas del congreso internacional celebrado en Salamanca, 29 de octubre-5 de noviembre de 1985.* Madrid: INAEM, Ministerio de Cultura, 1987. Vol. 1: 19-26.

In comparison with other types of European notation, Visigothic notation could therefore claim an earlier stage, with a gestation phase in or around the 7th century pertaining to the context of the scientific culture promoted by St. Isidore of Seville. As for Catalonian notation, the transmitter of the Catalonian-Narbonnaise liturgical tradition and Septimania, there are various interpretations as to its origin, based either on Visigothic notation (Stäblein, Wagner), the notation of accents, or on the Visigothic and Aquitainian notations, seen in this case as a phenomenon of hybridization (Sablayrolles, Sunyol, Anglès, Ferretti). See Josiane Mas. "La tradition musicale en Septimanie. Répertoire et tradition musicale". In Edouard Privat, ed. *Liturgie et musique (IXe-XIVe s.).* Toulouse: Privat, 1982, 282-285 (Collection d'Histoire religieuse du langue doc au XIIIe et au début du XIVe siècles: Cahiers de Fanjeaux 17); Bruno Stäblein. *Schriftbild der einstimmigen Musik. Musikgeschichte in Bildern.* Vol. 3, part 4. Leipzig: VEB Deutscher Verlag für Musik, 1975: 33-34, 214-217; Peter Wagner. "Neumenkunde. Paläographie des liturgischen Gesanges". In *idem. Einführung in die gregorianischen Melodien.* Leipzig: Breitkopf and Härtel, 1912. Vol. 2: 259 and subsq.; Maur Sablayrolles. Op. cit; Grégoire M. Sunyol. Op. cit., 23-29; Higini Anglès. *La música a Catalunya fins al segle XIII.* 2nd ed. Barcelona: Biblioteca de Cataluña, Universidad Autónoma de Barcelona, 1988, 193-201; Paolo Maria Ferretti. *Le codex 903 de la Bibliothèque Nationale de Paris (XIe siècle). Graduel de St. Yrieix.* Tournai: Abbey of St. Pierre de Solesmes, 1925 (Paléographie Musicale: 1). Vol. 13: 107 and subsq.

[52] With the exception of Old Catalonia, the official change-over to the new rite came at the end of the 11th century (Council of Burgos, 1080) and the decree on the replacement of Visigothic by Carolingian script was passed at the Council of León in 1090. Nonetheless, Carolingian elements had begun to filter in well before this time, with some authors calling for a public decree that would definitively impose a unified system of script throughout the Peninsula.

[53] In other words, the influence of the Carolingian system was felt in the area of script and even earlier in the material preparation of the codex (as Vivancos notes for some examples from Silos) than in the field of notation. See Miguel C. Vivancos. Op. cit., 66. Nonetheless, the inverse case, survival of the Visigothic script—with varying degrees of Carolingian influence—in combination with Aquitainian notation, is documented in sources from the musical-liturgical transition dating from until well into the 12th century. See, among others, the sheets with the fragments from Orense, Santiago de Compostela and Coimbra [IV-3.ª-Gav. 44 (20)], and San Millán (RAH, Cod. 18) and Silos (BL, Add. ms. 30848) in the second part of this work.

[54] Two main classifications have been proposed for the rich inventory of signs contained in Visigothic notation: a typological and chronological grouping (Grégoire M. Sunyol. Op. cit.) and classification of the signs in accordance with the different sources (Casiano Rojo, and Germán Prado. Op. cit.). The former distinguishes between square, cursive, and liquescent forms, a classification that is based on the chironomic origin of the neumes, and which goes back to the classification proposed by Cardine for the notation of Saint Gall and Metz; the latter groups the variants of each sign by their particular use in each source. Although Rojo y Prado's list is incomplete, his methodological proposal is more workable than the former. See a summary on the current state of the question in Nancy Phillips. Op. cit., 442-456.

[55] In defining *ductus*, we use Elisa Ruiz García's definition, the speed and way of forming the graphic signs in the act of writing. A distinction is drawn between black lettered *ductus (litterae positae)* and cursive *ductus (litterae cursiuae).* In the first case, each sign is drawn in isolation with independent strokes, requiring the quill to be raised each time; in the second case, the letters are linked to one other, and, to the extent possible, the *escriptorio* instrument is not raised from the page.

[56] The generalisation regarding the more or less accentuated drawing of the neumes needs to be qualified, because it is equally necessary to differentiate between virtuoso and less experienced copyists, and between the output of economically well-off and culturally relevant manuscript copying centers on the one hand and peripheral centers on the other. Mundó suggests that there was a hierarchy with regard to the generic concept of the *copyist.* See Anscari M. Mundó. "Un fragment molt antic...". Op. cit. Vol. 3: 183-184.

[57] Gregori M. Sunyol's theory as to the phases of Visigothic notation has been discounted. The Toledo codices do not represent a prior phase to those of the examples from the north. See *idem.* Op. cit., 317 and subsq., 331-352.

[58] For an illustration of the codices cited, see the respective catalographical sheets in the second part of the work.

[59] One very interesting fragment because of its startling analogy with the notation of the Antiphonary of San Juan de la Peña is Madrid, RAH, ms 9/4579, fragment of a strip of antiphonary, 10th century *ex.* to 11th century *in.* My thanks to Miquel S. Gros for drawing my attention to this. See Francesc Xavier Altès i Aguiló. "El retall testimonial d'un full d'Antifoner visigòtic (siglos X-XI) procedent de l'antic arxiu de la Seu de Roda d'Isàvena (Madrid, RAH, ms. 9/4579)". In *Miscel·lània Litúrgica Catalana* 9 (1999): 33-50.

[60] See Elisa Ruiz García. *Catálogo de la sección de códices de la Real Academia de la Historia.* Madrid: Real Academia de la Historia, 1997, 220.

[61] The dating continues to be the subject of debate. Janini and Serrano and Ruíz García place it around the 10th century, whereas Mundó attributes it to the 11th century. See José Janini, José Serrano, and Anscari M. Mundó. *Manuscritos litúrgicos de la Biblioteca Nacional de Madrid.* Madrid: Dirección General de Archivos y Bibliotecas, 1969, 128-129. See sheet ms. 10029 in the second part of this work; Elisa Ruiz García, see pp. 312.

[62] See Isidorus Hispalensis. *De ecclesiasticis officiis.* Turnhout: Brepols, 1989 (Corpus Christianorum: Series Latina 113). 2, 11, 2: ML 83, 791.

[63] Brockett indicates two types of notational inventories, which he places in the following chronological order: 1. ekphonetic notation, for which he does not offer specific

examples; and 2. *accent-notation,* viewed as the genesis of the Visigothic and Catalonian notations (Clyde W. Brockett. Op. cit.).

[64] Nancy Phillips. Op. cit. Vol. 4: 450.

[65] Here I am not referring to the evident differences in significance to be seen in certain morphologies, such as the two used for the *scandicus* and studied by various authors quoted earlier Rojo y Prado, Sunyol, Moll and, exhaustively, by Herminio González Barrionuevo. "Dos grafías especiales del 'scandicus'...". Op. cit., 11-79; *salicus*, see *idem.* "La grafía del 'salicus' en la notación 'mozárabe' de tipo vertical". *Revista de Musicología* 12, no. 2 (1989): 397-410, but to signs that correspond to one particular copyist. We agree with Barrionuevo's conclusion in his study of the Silos codices; see *idem.* "Los códices 'mozárabes' del archivo de Silos...". Op. cit. 403-472. Levy also touched on this aspect, concluding that the different graphic typologies did not affect the musical substance; see Kenneth Levy. "Old-Hispanic chant in its European context". In Emilio Casares, Ismael Fernández de la Cuesta, and José López-Calo, eds. *España en la música de Occidente. Actas del congreso internacional celebrado en Salamanca, 29 de octubre-5 de noviembre de 1985.* Madrid: INAEM, Ministerio de Cultura, 1987. Vol. 1: 3-14.

[66] See Peter Wagner. "Der mozarabische Kirchengesang und seine Überlieferung". In *Gesammelte Aufsätze zur Kulturgeschichte Spaniens.* Münster: Aschendorff, 1928. Vol. 1: 102-141 (Spanische Forschungen der Görresgesellschaft: 1); *idem.* "Untersuchungen zu den Gesangstexten...". Op. cit. Vol. 2: 67-113; Don M. Randel. *An Index to the Chant of the Mozarabic Rite.* Princeton, New Jersey: Princeton University Press, 1973; *idem. The Responsorial Psalm Tones...* Op. cit.

[67] Based on the morphology of the notation and the workmanship of the manuscript itself, we can distinguish between examples from culturally dominant centers and those that come from peripheral centers. As Vivancos demonstrated in the case of the different phases of the Silos *scriptorium*, the specific position of the copying center and its economic and political situation are essential factors that condition the material workmanship of the codices. Compare two contemporary codices: Silos, AM, Cod. 4, from San Prudencio de Monte Laturce, and Silos, AM, Cod. 5, from an unknown center in Rioja. See Miguel C. Vivancos. Op. cit., 62-67.

We can also separate different manuscripts according to the person/destination for whom/which they were copied, with the royal codices—for example, Santiago de Compostela, BXU, ms. 609 (Res. 1)—at the top of the ladder and copies made for small rural churches at the bottom.

[68] Grégoire M. Sunyol's theory as to the three phases of Visigothic notation and the greater age of the Toledo tradition over that of the northern Peninsula has therefore been ruled out. See *idem.* Op. cit., 317 and subsq., 331-352.

[69] On an archetype common to both types of notation, north and south, of Carolingian origin (Levy) and on the influence of the Arabic element on the *ductus* of the southern notation (Stäblein), see Kenneth Levy. Op. cit. Vol. 1: 6; see also Bruno Stäblein. Op. cit., 34 and 214.

[70] The term "Catalonian", which, as I have already said, is not entirely accurate historically, has been accepted as a technical term and was coined by Maur Sablayrolles in 1906: "Un viatge a través dels manuscrits gregorians espanyols". *Revista Musical Catalana-Butlletí de l'Orfeó Català* 3 (1906): 91, 131, 149, 177, 200, 221; 4 (1907): 4, 23, 48, 116, 139, 161, 208, 231; 5 (1908): 4, 203, 227; 6 (1909): 9, 95, 132, 172; Grégoire M. Sunyol. Op. cit.; Josiane Mas. "La notation catalane". Op. cit., 11-30. Jaume Moll Roqueta. "Per una tipologia...". Op. cit., 9-22. The geography of this notational system comprises the Catalonian bishoprics and counties of Vic, Barcelona, Manresa, Girona, and Urgell, as well as the area of Andorra and trans-Pyrenean Catalonia: Arles sur Tech, Elna, Vallespir. In other words, its origin is limited to the area of Narbonne, from where the two oldest examples with Cat Catalonian alan notation come: Paris, BNF, Lat. 1796 and 933 (which have not been included in this study due to the Bibliothèque Nationale de France's refusal to grant permission to reproduce them). On trans-Pyrenean Catalonia, see Anscari M. Mundó. "Moissac, Cluny...". Op. cit., 551-570 and in *Moissac et l'occident...* Op. cit. The first list of Catalonian sources from the 10th to the 13th centuries was produced by Higinio Anglès. Op. cit., 134-180. For a complete list, see Joaquím Garrigosa i Massana. Op. cit.

[71] It has not been possible to determine the folio, given the impossibility of consulting the original.

[72] See p. 192.

[73] On the possible common origin of Catalonian and Visigothic notations in what is known as *accent notation,* see Anscari M. Mundó. "Un fragment molt antic...". Op. cit. Vol. 3: 188 (corroborated by Huglo in a quote from the article). On the possible phenomena of contact from the comparative inventory of graphic signs and the study of its mutations, see the synthesis by Josiane Mas. "La notation catalane". Op. cit. 28. Garrigosa offers a corresponding comprehensive view of all of the formal elements that characterize this evolution; see Joaquim Garrigosa i Massana. Op. cit., 347-366.

In chronological order, the main representatives of the Catalonian notation are: Barcelona, UAB, ms. 33/10, 10th century *in.-med.;* Copenhagen, Universitetsbibliotek 1927, AM. 795, 4th, 10th century; Solsona, Archivo diocesano, Frag. 19, 10th century *med.;* Montserrat, Archivo de la Abadía de Montserrat, Parchments of Bages, no. 9, year 949; Vic, ABEV, Frag. VIII/23, 10th century *med.;* Vic, ABEV, Frag. I/6, 10th century *med.;* Vic, ABEV, ms. 122/1-2, 10th century *med.;* Vic, ABEV, ms. 66, year 1038; Montserrat, Archivo de la Abadía de Montserrat, Parchments of Bages, no. 1.102, year 982; Lleida, AC, Roda 16, 11th century *in.;* Barcelona, ACA, Ripoll 59, 11th century *in.;* Barcelona, ACA, Ripoll 74, 11th century *in.;* Vic, ABEV, ms. 66, 11th century *in.;* Barcelona, ACA, Ripoll 74, 11th century; Antiphonary for Matins of Le Tech, Paris, BNF, Lat. 14301, 11th century *med.;* Copenhagen, Det Kongelige Bibliotek, Ny Kgl., 1794, 11th century; Vic, ABEV, ms. 103, 11th century *ex.;* Paris, BNF, Lat. 5304, 11th century *med.;* Barcelona, ACA, Frag. 86, 12th century *in.;* Girona, AD, ms. 45, 12th century *in.;* Barcelona, BC, ms. 1805, to 12th century *med.-ex.;* Paris, BNF, Lat. 891, 12th century *ex.;* Barcelona, ACA, Frag. 35 bis, 12th century *med.;* Vic, ABEV, Frag. V/2, 12th century *med.;* Ripoll, AHC, ms. 2, olim A. 4, 12th century *ex.* In Emilio Casares Rodicio, et al. *Diccionario de la música española e hispanoamericana*. Madrid: SGAE, 2000, erroneously cites Vic, ABEV, ms. 61, a book of sermons from the end of the 14th century.

[74] Studied by Anscari M. Mundó. *Ibidem.* Vol. 3: 173-191.

[75] On the dating of the Antiphonary of León, see the article by Díaz y Díaz in this work, pp. 93. The Parisian fragments of the Antiphonary of Silos were dated by Gros around the 9th century *ex.* to the 10th century *in.* See Miquel S. Gros. "Les fragments parisiens de l'antiphonaire de Silos". *Revue Bénédictine* 74 (1964): 324-333. See also Louis Brou. "Notes de paléographie musicale mozarabe". *Anuario Musical* 10 (1955): 23.

[76] Barcelona (ACA, parch. Guifred I, 12), year 904; Barcelona (ACA, Frag. 1), 10th century *in.*; Barcelona (BC, ms. 2101), 10th century *in.;* Barcelona (BU, ms. 602), 10th century *in.;* Barcelona, ACA, Frag. 1, olim Codex Varia VIII), 10th century *in.* (Catalonian *in campo aperto*) and Montserrat Montserrat, Archivo de la Abadía de Montserrat, Parchments of Bages, no. 215, 10th century *ex.* (Catalonian *in campo aperto*). We give the datings corresponding to the notation; the manuscript from which they are taken may precede the insertion of this notation. The selection is based on the groups gathered by Anscari M. Mundó. "Un fragment molt antic...". Op. cit. Vol. 3: 188-190; and Joaquím Garrigosa i Massana. Op. cit., 310-347.

[77] See Joaquim Garrigosa i Massana. *Ibidem,* 156; Alexandre Olivar. "Serie de benedictiones lectionum en el Cod. Montserratensis 72". *Ephemerides Liturgica*e 62 (1948): 230-234; and Higini Anglès. Op. cit. 140.

[78] In this regard, see Manuel Riu y Riu. "L'esglesia catalana al segle x". In *Symposium Internacional sobre els Orígens de Catalunya (segles VIII-XI).* Barcelona: Generalitat de Cataluña, 1991-1992. Vol. 1: 161-189; Miquel S. Gros. "Los ritos de la Tarraconense y Narbona" (introduction to the catalog of José Janini. *Manuscritos litúrgicos...* Op. cit. Vol. 2: 7-17; *idem.* "El ordo romano-hispánico de Narbona para la consagración de iglesias". *Hispania Sacra* 19, no. 38 (1966): 321-401; and Josiane Mas. "La tradition musicale en Septimanie...". Op. cit., 269-286.

[79] An example of this can be seen in the breviary of uncertain provenance, London, BL, Add. ms. 30849, where the script is Visigothic throughout, with Carolingian influences, whereas the notation is Aquitainian on drypoint line, proof that the Spanish copyist was in the process of learning the recently introduced Carolingian script.

[80] See Michel Huglo. "La Pénétration des manuscrits aquitains en Espagne". *Revista de Musicología* 8, no. 2 (1985): 255.

[81] A detailed study is needed of the phenomena of contact between the Visigothic notation and the Aquitainian, which we can only illustrate here with some isolated examples. The breviary, London, BL, Add. ms. 30847, only contains notation up to fol. 85. Two hands have intervened, one more careful than the other (example of the first: fol. 60; and of the second: fol. 68v). The notation appears to have been added at a later date in darker ink. The *differentiae* are written in the margin of the page.

[82] See sheets in pp. 260 and 282. For a study of the melodies of the Spanish rite with possibility of transcription, see Casiano Rojo, and Germán Prado. Op. cit., 73-81, facs. 12-14.

[83] See Paolo Maria Ferretti. Op. cit. Vol. 2, pl. 89. Jean Vezin. "Un calendrier franco-hispanique de la fin du XIe siècle". *Bibliothèque de l'École des Chartes* 121 (1963): 5-15.

[84] The *Prosarium-Troparium* of Girona, Paris, N. A. L. 495, is the latest example of the coexistence of notational systems, with the Catalonian and square notations alternating on four-line staff and clef, and the latter being inserted after the original had been scraped off: fol. 3v, fol. 4, fols. 15v-16, fols. 49-49v, fols. 51, 52, 53, 54, 55, 56, fols. 58v-66 (from line 5 on), fol. 70, fols. 89v-90, fol. 91v, fols. 94-94v, fol. 96, fol. 97, fol. 98 (one line) and fol. 114. Fols. 118-119 also contain notes in notations from different periods.

[85] "... la notación catalana es mostra com una notació amb una definició explícita, sense que es pugui parlar de notació de transició ni d'adaptació momentània a cap altra família". Joaquím Garrigosa i Massana. Op. cit., 384-390; and Josiane Mas. "La notation catalane". Op. cit. 21-24.

[86] From the last quarter of the 11th century, Santiago de Compostela enjoyed a direct link to new trends on account of its position at the end of the routes of pilgrimage (the *Camino* de Santiago). According to Díaz y Díaz, the survival of the old script is inconceivable. Only the periphery, Orense and Braga, was to prove more conservative and less receptive. See Manuel C. Díaz y Díaz. *Códices visigóticos...* Op. cit., 466.

[87] Cod. 4 has inserts in Aquitainian notation on the following folios: 9, 13, 14, 75v, 144, 181v, 205v, 209v, 213v, 235v, 267, 275v, 319v, and 344v.

[88] The first area of penetration of Carolingian culture was Catalonia, followed by Navarre, with the official introduction of the new rite in the Monastery of San Salvador de Leyre in 1067, and Aragón, historically linked to Tarragona, where it was established in the Monastery of San Juan de la Peña in 1072. The situation in Castile was more diverse, with a somewhat later transition culminating in the Council of Burgos, held in 1081. The spread of the new rite and its script forms, as well as the process of transition in the different areas of the Iberian Peninsula, have been widely studied. Here we refer to the most representative studies: Solange Corbin. *Essai sur la musique religieuse portugaise au Moyen Âge (1100-1385).* Paris: Les Belles Lettres, 1952; Ismael Fernández de la Cuesta. "La irrupción del canto gregoriano en España. Bases para un replanteamiento". *Revista de Musicología* 8, no. 2 (1985): 239-248; Michel Huglo. "La pénétration des manuscrits...". Op. cit., 249-256; José Francisco Rivera Recio. "La Iglesia mozárabe". In Ricardo García Villoslada, dir. *Historia de la Iglesia en España.* Madrid: Biblioteca de Autores Cristianos, 1982, Vol. 2-1: 275-285; Carmen Rodríguez Suso. *La monodia litúrgica en el País Vasco.* 3 vols. Bilbao: Bilbao Bizkaia Kutxa, 1993 (Biblioteca Musical del País Vasco); Kathleen Nelson. Op. cit.; Pedro Romano Rocha. "Influjo de los antifonarios aquitanos en el oficio divino de las iglesias del noroeste de la Península". In *Estudios sobre Alfonso VI y la reconquista de Toledo. Actas del II Congreso Internacional de Estudios Mozárabes (Toledo 1985).* Toledo: Instituto de Estudios Visigótico-Mozárabes, 1990. Vol. 4: 27-45; Susana Zapke. "Die fränkisch-römische Überlieferung in Aragonien (Nordspanien)". In László Dobszay, ed. Papers Read at the Meeting of the International Musicological Society Study Group *Cantus Planus*: Eger (Hungary), September 1993. Budapest: Hungarian Academy of Sciences, Institute for Musicology, 1995, 353-366.

[89] On the semitone sign, see Paolo Maria Ferretti. "Étude sur la notation aquitaine d'après le Graduel de Saint-Yrieix". In *idem,* op. cit; Marie-Nöel Colette. "La notation du demi-ton dans le manuscrit Paris, BNF, Lat. 1139 et dans quelques manuscrits du sud de la France". In Claudio Leonardi and Enrico Menesto, eds. *La tradizione dei tropi liturgici. Atti dei convegni sui tropi liturgici. Parigi (15-19 ottobre 1985)-Perugia (2-5 settembre 1987) organizzati dal Corpus Troporum sotto l'egida dell'European Science Foundation.* Spoleto: Centro italiano di studi sull'alto medioevo, 1990, 297-311 (Biblioteca del Centro per il collegamento degli studi medievali e umanistici nell'Università di Perugia 3).

[90] Among the oldest examples of Aquitainian notation used in Catalonia, which come from ultra-Pyrenean centers, are the fragment from Tarragona, AHA, ms. 22/1, dating from 880; the fragment from the 11th century *med.,* Barcelona, BC, ms. 1408-5a; Paris, BNF, N. A. L. 557; and Barcelona, ACA, Ripoll ms. 74 from the 11th century *in.*

[91] See Susana Zapke. *Fragmentos litúrgico-musicales de la Edad Media en archivos de Aragón. Siglos* XI *ex.-*XIII *ex.* Huesca: IEA, DGA, 2007.

[92] Michel Huglo. "La pénétration des manuscrits...". Op. cit., 256.

[93] The case of the Visigothic manuscripts is somewhat similar, with the circulation of specialists between the different production centers blurring any specific identifying feature from a particular center.

[94] Even after querying codicologists and paleographers specialising in the corpus of liturgical manuscripts from southern France, we have not been able to define valid criteria for attributing the sources. Nor has it been possible to determine a relationship of possible characteristics typical of the Iberian centers from the point of view of the illumination of the first liturgical-musical manuscripts of the Franco-Roman rite, dated between the end of the 11th century and the beginning of the 12th century. Everything appears to indicate that in this stage of the reform, the Iberian manuscript centers that were producing and copying the Franco-Roman rite failed to develop their own style. The overly sudden transition did not allow gradual assimilation; instead the urgent need to provide new song books hardly left enough of a margin if time for the development of a separate style, at least from the formal point of view, which is the area that concerns us here.

[95] See João Pedro d'Alvarenga. "Breves notas sobre a representação do meio-tom nos manuscritos litúrgicos medievais portugueses, ou o mito da 'notação portuguesa'". In *idem* and Manuel Pedro Ferreira, eds. *Actas do Colóquio Internacional Monodia Sacra Medieval, Lisboa-Évora, 2-5 de Junho, 2005*. (In press.)

[96] Solange Corbin. Op. cit., 251.

[97] If its Catalonian origin is confirmed, the first example of Aquitainian notation in Catalonia would be the fragment Barcelona, BC, ms. 1451-8 from ca. 1100. One example of Aquitainian notation on four colored lines with bass clef is the Antiphonary of Tarragona, AHA, 20/15 from the 12th century *ex.,* not included in our selection.

[98] A considerable number of fragments of codices of Franco-Roman repertory is preserved in Portugal. The recent catalogs of the Biblioteca Nacional de Portugal, the Biblioteca del Monasterio de Santa Cruz de Coimbra, and the Biblioteca Municipal do Porto give access to an extensive corpus, representing the scenario of change in Portugal. See bibliography.

[99] See Pedro Romano Rocha. Op. cit.; *idem. L'office divin au Moyen Âge dans l'église de Braga: Originalité et dépendences d'une liturgie particulière au Moyen Âge.* Paris: Fundaçâo Calouste Gulbenkian, 1980. On the fragments of Lamego and their connections with Toledo see Manuel Pedro Ferreira. "Three Fragments from Lamego". *Revista de Musicología* 16, no. 1 (1993): 457-476 *[Actas del XV Congreso de la Sociedad Internacional de Musicología: Culturas Musicales del Mediterráneo y sus Ramificaciones (Madrid, 3-10 de abril de 1992)].*

[100] See Ruth Steiner. "Introduction". In Ronald T. Olexy, et al. *Cantus. An Aquitainian Antiphoner: Toledo, Biblioteca Capitular, 44.2. A Cantus Index.* Ottawa: The Institute of Mediæval Music, 1992, vii-xxi (Wissenschaftliche Abhandlungen: 55/1).

[101] No information whatsoever is available for the area of Aragón on the copyists, with no colophons extant or mentions in this regard in the musical-liturgical sources. See the monograph on the former and the comparative analysis with the breviaries from San Juan de la Peña. See Susana Zapke. *Das Antiphonar von Sta. Cruz de la Serós, XII. Jh.* Neuried: Ars Una, 1996.

[102] Janini only mentions fols. 196v-197r. Fol. 196r also contains the addition of a short melodic sequence in Visigothic notation, inscribed outside the writing frame. José Janini. *Manuscritos litúrgicos...* Op. cit. Vol. 1: 79.

[103] Fol. 3r, lines 15-16 *(confitebor)*; fol. 3v, lines 6-7 *(confitebor),* line 21 *(ego in);* fol. 4r, lines 8-10, intercolumn (RS *Confitebor tibi Dno.*), lines 20-22, intercolumn *(alla.),* fol. 12v, line 12 *(Missus est Gabriel),* fol. 13, lines 14-15, intercolumn *(Angelus Domini*), fol. 42v, line 19 (RS *Ego in laboribus*), fol. 43v, lines 18-19 (RS *Infixus sum*), fol. 48, lines 11-12, intercolumn *(Vincenti dabo);* fol. 48v, lines 8-10 *(quare.),* fol. 93v, lines 8-9 and 19-22, long insert of musical notation, fol. 100, line 10 *(A Hec dicit).* The remaining folios contain varied notational signs such as reference marks to the glosses.

[104] On the reference marks, see Louis Brou. Op. cit., 31-34; Miguel C. Vivancos. Op. cit., 92-96; Jean Vezin. "Observations sur l'emploi...". Op. cit., 17.

[105] Louis Brou. *Ibidem,* 31-32.

[106] María José Azevedo Santos. Op. cit., 110-111.

[107] For a list of notational signs used as reference marks in the Silos codices see: Miguel C. Vivancos. Op. cit., 94-96. We might add to this list the *Codex regularum,* London, BL, Add. ms. 30055, fols. 194v-221v, mentioned by Louis Brou. Op. cit., illus. VIII, no. 2, and the orationale, London, BL, Add. ms. 30853, which also contains an extensive inventory.

[108] This phenomenon was observed for the first time by J. Forada and Castán. "Signaturas escritas con caracteres considerados hasta aquí como neumas o signos musicales". *El Arte en España* 6 (1867): 105-109; as well as by Agustín Millares Carlo. *Tratado de paleografía española.* Madrid: Espasa Calpe, 1983; and Grégoire M. Sunyol. Op. cit., 199, among others. One example of a notarial document with the insertion of cryptographic script based on notational signs can be found in the Archivo Histórico Nacional, Sahagún, 606 P, a notarial subscription inscribed in a document of sale, dated 18 September 1082.

[109] Remember that this was after the Council of León (1090) when the replacement of Visigothic script by Carolingian script was officially declared, although the latter had been in use on the Iberian Peninsula since the 9th century.

[110] The date of adoption of the Franco-Roman rite in Catalonia is the subject of some debate. The tendency among chroniclers and historians was to place it in a late period, after the reform in Aragón. Paul Kehr offers various arguments that suggest that it penetrated at an earlier date, somewhere around 1050: *Papsturkunden in Spanien. Vorarbeiten zur Hispania pontificia.* 2 vols. Berlin: Weidmannsche Buchhandlung, 1926-1928 (ND Göttingen 1970. Abh. Gött. NF 18/2, 22/1).

The replacement of the Spanish rite by a rite linked to the metropolis of Narbonne in the Catalonian church during the 9th century involved a hiatus in relations with the see of Toledo, partly motivated by the Saracen threat, and a progressive association with the March of Gócia i Septimania. See Higini Anglès. Op. cit., 26-34, and Miquel S. Gros. "La liturgie narbonnaise témoin d'un changement rapide de rites liturgiques". In *Liturgie de l'église particulière et liturgie de l'église universelle. Conférences Saint-Serge 1975*. Rome: Edizioni Liturgiche, 1976, 127-152; *idem*. "Los ritos de la Tarraconense...". Op. cit., 7-17. On the survival of Spanish forms in the Catalonian-Narbonnaise liturgy, see Alexandre Olivar. "Survivances wisigothiques dans la liturgie catalano-languedocienne". In Edouard Privat, ed. Op. cit., 157-172.

[111] Maria José Azevedo Santos. Op. cit., 260-262; and José Mattoso. "Data da introduçao da liturgia romana na diocese de Braga". In *idem*. *Religião e Cultura na Idade Média Portuguesa*. Lisbon: Imp. Nacional-Casa da Moeda, 1982, 91-102. Also published in *idem*. *Obras completas*. Vol. 9. Lisbon: Imp. Nacional-Casa da Moeda, 2002. See also *idem*. "Monges e clérigos portadores de cultura francesa em Portugal (séculos XI e XII)". In *idem*. *Portugal Medieval: novas interpretaçoes*. Lisbon: Imp. Nacional-Casa da Moeda, 1985, 481-509.

[112] See Salamanca, BGU, ms. 2668, London, BL, Add. ms. 30851; and Paris, BNF, N. A. L. 2171, 2169 and 2179. In Carolingian ruling, each folio is ruled on the hair side, a procedure which was not usual in the oldest Visigothic codices.

[113] In textual paleography, Lowe's methodology, as applied to the Visigothic corpus, is still a splendid tool. See Elias Avery Lowe. *Studia palaeographica...* Op. cit. Studies such as those by Azevedo Santos and Ruiz Albi on the transition from Visigothic to Carolingian script have provided valuable contributions for dating the sources precisely. A similar theoretical and methodological template to that proposed for textual paleography would serve as a basis for further progress in the area of musical paleography. See Maria José Azevedo Santos. Op. cit.; see also Irene Ruiz Albi. "La distinción gráfica de 'TI/TJ' en los documentos visigóticos del archivo de la catedral de León". In *Orígenes de las lenguas romances en el reino de León. Siglos IX-XII*. León: Centro de Estudios e Investigación San Isidoro (CSIC-CECEL), Caja España de Inversiones. Archivo Histórico Diocesano, 2004, 439-456.

Bibliography

ABADAL I DE VINYALS, Ramón d'. "Nota sobre la locución *Marca Hispánica*". *Boletín de la Real Academia de Buenas Letras de Barcelona* 27 (1957-1958): 157-164.

—."La Pre-Catalunya (segles VIII-IX i XI)". In Ferrán Soldevilla, ed. *Historia dels Catalans*. Barcelona: Ariel, 1970. Vol. 2: 601-992.

ALTÈS I AGUILÓ, Francesc Xavier. "El retall testimonial d'un full d'Antifoner visigòtic (s. X-XI) procedent de l'antic arxiu de la Seu de Roda d'Isàvena (Madrid, Academia de la Historia, ms. 9/4579)". In *Miscel·lània litúrgica catalana* 9 (1999): 33-50.

ALVARENGA, João Pedro d'. "Breves notas sobre a representação do meio-tom nos manuscritos litúrgicos medievais portugueses, ou o mito da 'notação portuguesa'". In *idem* and Manuel Pedro Ferreira, eds. *Actas do Colóquio Internacional Monodia Sacra Medieval, Lisboa-Évora, 2-5 de Junho, 2005*. (In press.)

ANGLÈS, Higini. *La música a Catalunya fins al segle XIII*. 2nd edition. Barcelona: Biblioteca de Cataluña, 1988.

AVRIL, François, Jean-Pierre ARIEL, Mireille MENTRÉ, Alix SAULNIER, and Jolanta ZAŁUSKA. *Manuscrits enluminés de la Péninsule Ibérique*. Paris: Bibliothèque Nationale de France, 1983.

BARRIGA, Josep Romà. *El sacramentari, ritual i pontifical de Roda*. Barcelona: Fundació Salvador Vives Casajuana, 1975.

BISHKO, Charles Julian. "Liturgical Intercession at Cluny for the King-Emperors of León". *Studia Monastica* 3 (1961): 53-76.

BOYLAN, Anne. *Manuscript Illumination at Santo Domingo de Silos (Xth to XIIth centuries)*. Pittsburgh: University of Pittsburgh, 1990 (Order Number 9209579).

BROCKETT, Clyde W. *Antiphons, Responsories and other Chants of the Mozarabic Rite*. Vol. 13. New York: The Institute of Mediæval Music, 1968.

BROU, Louis. "Le joyau des antiphonaires latins". *Archivos Leoneses* 8 (1954): 7-114.

—. "Notes de paléographie musicale mozarabe". *Anuario Musical* 10 (1955): 23-44.

CARRASCO, Juan, Josep Mª. SALRACH, Julio VALDEÓN, and Mª. Jesús VIGUERA. *Historia de las Españas medievales*. Barcelona: Crítica, 2002 (Historia medieval).

COLETTE, Marie-Noël. "La notation du demi-ton dans le manuscrit Paris, BNF, Lat. 1139 et dans quelques manuscrits du sud de la France". In Claudio Leonardi and Enrico Menesto, eds. *La tradizione dei tropi liturgici. Atti dei convegni sui tropi liturgici. Parigi (15-19 ottobre 1985)-Perugia (2-5 settembre 1987) organizzati dal Corpus Troporum sotto l'egida dell'European Science Foundation*. Spoleto: Centro italiano di studi sull'alto medioevo, 1990, 297-311 (Biblioteca del Centro per il collegamento degli studi medievali e umanistici nell'Università di Perugia 3).

COLETTE, Marie-Noël, Marielle POPIN, and Philippe VENDRIX. *Histoire de la notation: du Moyen Âge à la Renaissance*. Paris: Minerve, 2003.

Coloquio sobre circulación de códices y escritos entre Europa y la Península en los siglos VIII-XIII. 16-19 de septiembre de 1982. Actas. Santiago de Compostela: University of Santiago de Compostela, 1988.

Corbin, Solange. *Essai sur la musique religieuse portugaise au Moyen Âge (1100-1385).* Paris: Les Belles Lettres, 1952.

David, Pierre. *Études historiques sur la Galice et le Portugal du VIe au XIe siècle.* Coimbra: Instituto de Estudos Históricos, 1947.

Defourneaux, Marcelin. *Les Français en Espagne aus XIe et XIIe siècles.* Paris: Presses Universitaires de France, 1949.

Díaz y Díaz, Manuel C. "Los prólogos del *antiphonale visigothicum* de la Catedral de León (León, Arch. Cat., 8)". *Archivos Leoneses* 8 (1954): 226-257.

—. "La circulation des manuscrits dans la Péninsule Ibérique du VIIIème au XIème siècle". *Cahiers de Civilisation Médiévale* 12 (1969): 219-241.

—. *Libros y librerías en La Rioja altomedieval.* Logroño: Gobierno de La Rioja, Instituto de Estudios Riojanos, 1979.

—. *Códices visigóticos en la monarquía leonesa.* León: Centro de Estudios e Investigación San Isidoro (CSIC-CECEL), 1983.

Durán Gudiol, Antonio. *La Iglesia de Aragón durante los reinados de Sancho Ramírez y Pedro I (1062?-1104).* Rome: Iglesia Nacional Española, 1962.

—. "La Santa Sede y los obispados de Huesca y Roda en la primera mitad del siglo XII". *Anthologica Annua* 13 (1965): 35-134.

Fernández de la Cuesta, Ismael. *Manuscritos y fuentes musicales en España: Edad Media.* Madrid: Alpuerto, 1980.

—. *Historia de la música española.* Vol. 1, *Desde los orígenes hasta el Ars Nova.* Madrid: Alianza, 1983.

—, ed. *Antiphonale silense (British Library, Add. ms. 30850).* Madrid: Sociedad Española de Musicología, 1985.

—. "La irrupción del canto gregoriano en España. Bases para un replanteamiento". *Revista de Musicología* 8, no. 2 (1985): 239-248.

—. "El canto viejo-hispánico y el canto viejo-galicano". *Revista de Musicología* 16 (1993): 438-456.

—. "Mozárabe, Canto". In Emilio Casares Rodicio, coord. and dir. *Diccionario de la música española e hispanoamericana.* Madrid: SGAE, 2000. Vol. 7: 848-851.

Ferreira, Manuel Pedro. "Three Fragments from Lamego". *Revista de Musicología* 16, no. 1 (1993): 457-476 *[Actas del XV Congreso de la Sociedad Internacional de Musicología: Culturas Musicales del Mediterráneo y sus Ramificaciones" (Madrid, 3-10/IV/1992)].*

Ferretti, Paolo Maria. *Le codex 903 de la Bibliothèque Nationale de Paris (XIe siècle). Graduel de St. Yrieix.* Tournai: Abbey of St. Pierre de Solesmes, 1925 (Paléographie Musicale: 1). Repr. of 1925 edition, *ibidem.* Vol. 13. Solesmes: Abbey of St. Pierre de Solesmes, 1992 (Paléographie Musicale: 1).

Forada y Castán, J. "Signaturas escritas con caracteres considerados hasta aquí como neumas o signos musicales". *El Arte en España* 6 (1867): 105-109.

García Turza, Claudio, coord. *Los manuscritos visigóticos: estudio paleográfico y codicológico.* Vol. 1, *Los códices riojanos datados.* Logroño: Fundación San Millán de la Cogolla, 2002.

Garrigosa i Massana, Joaquim. *Els manuscrits musicals a Catalunya fins al segle XIII. L'evolució de la notació musical.* Lleida: Institut d'Estudis Ilerdencs, 2003 (Col·lecció Emili Pujol: 2; Màrius Bernadó, dir.).

González Barrionuevo, Herminio. "Presencia de signos adicionales de tipo melódico en la notación 'mozárabe' del norte de España". *Revista de Musicología* 9, no. 1 (1986): 11-28. [Published in French, "Presénce de signes additionnels de type mélodique dans la notation 'mozarabe' du nord de l'Espagne". *Études Grégoriennes* 23 (1989): 141-151.]

—. "La grafía del 'sálicus' en la notación 'mozárabe' de tipo vertical". *Revista de Musicología* 12, no. 2 (1989): 397-410.

—. "Dos grafías especiales del 'scándicus' en la notación 'mozárabe' del norte de España". *Revista de Musicología* 13, no. 1 (1990): 11-79.

—. "Los códices 'mozárabes' del archivo de Silos: aspectos paleográficos y semiológicos de su notación neumática". *Revista de Musicología* 15, nos. 2-3 (1992): 403-472 *[La música en la Abadía de Silos. Trabajos del I Simposio de Musicología Religiosa (Burgos-Silos, marzo de 1991)].*

—. "Relación entre la notación 'mozárabe' de tipo vertical y otras escrituras neumáticas". *Studi Gregoriani* 11 (1995): 5-12.

Gros, Miquel S. "Les fragments parisiens de l'antiphonaire de Silos". *Revue Bénédictine* 74 (1964): 324-333.

—. "El ordo romano-hispánico de Narbona para la consagración de iglesias". *Hispania Sacra* 19, no. 38 (1966): 321-401.

—. "La liturgie narbonnaise témoin d'un changement rapide de rites liturgiques". In *Liturgie de l'église particulière et liturgie de l'église universelle. Conférences Saint-Serge 1975.* Rome: Edizioni Liturgiche, 1976, 127-154.

—. "Los ritos de la Tarraconense y Narbona". In José Janini. *Manuscritos litúrgicos de las bibliotecas de España*. Vol. 2, *Aragón, Cataluña y Valencia*. Burgos: Aldecoa, 1980, 7-17 [Publicaciones de la Facultad de Teología del Norte de España (Sede de Burgos): 38].

HUGLO, Michel. "La tradition musicale aquitaine: répertoire et notation". In Edouard Privat, ed. *Liturgie et musique (IXe-XIVe s.)*. Toulouse: Privat, 1982, 253-68 (Collection d'Histoire religieuse du langue doc au XIIIe et au début du XIVe siècles: Cahiers de Fanjeaux 17).

—. "La pénétration des manuscrits aquitains en Espagne". *Revista de Musicología* 8, no. 2 (1985): 249-256.

—. "La notation wisigothique est-elle plus ancienne que les autres notations européennes?" In Emilio Casares, Ismael Fernández de la Cuesta and José López-Calo, eds. *España en la música de Occidente. Actas del congreso internacional celebrado en Salamanca, 29 de octubre-5 de noviembre de 1985*. Madrid: INAEM, Ministerio de Cultura, 1987. Vol. 1: 19-26.

—. "Bilan de 50 annees de recherches (1939-1989) sur les notations musicales de 850 a 1300". *Acta Musicologica* 62, fasc. 2/3 (May-December 1990): 224-259.

ISIDORUS HISPALENSIS. *De ecclesiasticis officiis*. Turnhout: Brepols, 1989 (Corpus Christianorum: Series Latina 113).

JANINI, José. "Los fragmentos visigodos de San Zoilo de Carrión". *Liturgica*. Vol. 3: Montserrat: Abbey of Montserrat, 1966, 73-83 (Scripta et Documenta: 17).

—. "Liturgia: Liturgia Romana". In *Diccionario de historia eclesiástica de España*. Madrid: CSIC, Instituto P. Enrique Flórez, 1972. Vol. 2: 1320-1324.

—. *Manuscritos litúrgicos de las bibliotecas de España*. Vol. 1, *Castilla y Navarra;* vol.2, *Aragón, Cataluña y Valencia*. Burgos: Aldecoa, 1977 (vol. 1) y 1980 (vol. 2) [Publicaciones de la Facultad de Teología del Norte de España (Sede de Burgos): 38].

JANINI, José, José SERRANO, and Anscari M. MUNDÓ. *Manuscritos litúrgicos de la Biblioteca Nacional de Madrid*. Madrid: Dirección General de Archivos y Bibliotecas, 1969.

KEHR, Paul. *Papsturkunden in Spanien. Vorarbeiten zur Hispania pontificia*. 2 vols. Berlin: Weidmannsche Buchhandlung, 1926-1928 (ND Göttingen 1970. Abh. Gött. NF 18/2, 22/1).

—. "Das Papsttum und die Königreiche Navarra und Aragón bis zur Mitte des 12. Jahrhunderts". Berlin: Akademie der Wissenschaften, 1928. (Abhandlungen der Preußischen Akademie der Wissenschaften zu Berlin: Philosophisch-Historische Klasse 4).

LEVY, Kenneth. "Old-Hispanic chant in its european context". In Emilio Casares, Ismael Fernández de la Cuesta and José López-Calo, eds. *España en la música de Occidente. Actas del congreso internacional celebrado en Salamanca, 29 de octubre-5 de noviembre de 1985*. Vol. 1. Madrid: INAEM, Ministerio de Cultura, 1987.

LOWE, Elias Avery. *Studia palaeographica. A Contribution to the History of early latin Minuscule and to the Dating of Visigothic mss.* Munich, 1910.

—. *Codices latini antiquiores. A Palaeographical Guide to Latin Manuscripts Prior to the Ninth Century.* Vol. 11, *Hungary, Luxembourg, Poland, Russia, Spain*. Oxford: Clarendon Press, 1966.

MARAVALL CASESNOVES, José Antonio. *El concepto de España en la Edad Media*. 4th ed. Madrid: Centro de Estudios Constitucionales, 1997.

MAS, Josiane. "La tradition musicale en Septimanie. Répertoire et tradition musicale". In Edouard Privat, ed. Op. cit., 269-286.

—. "La notation catalane". *Revista de Musicología* 11, no. 1 (1988): 11-30.

MATTOSO, José. "Monges e clérigos portadores de cultura francesa em Portugal (séculos XI e XII)". In *idem. Portugal Medieval: novas interpretaçoes*. Lisbon: Imp. Nacional-Casa da Moeda, 1985, 481-509 (Temas Portugueses).

—. "Data da introduçao da liturgia romana na diocese de Braga". In *idem*, ed. *Religião e Cultura na Idade Média Portuguesa*. Lisbon: Imp. Nacional-Casa da Moeda, 1982, 91-102. (2nd ed., Lisbon: Imp. Nacional-Casa da Moeda, 1997). Work also included, in *idem. Obras completas*. Vol. 9. Lisbon: Imp. Nacional-Casa da Moeda, 2002.

MENÉNDEZ PIDAL, Ramón, ed. *Historia de España*. Vol. 7 **, *La España cristiana de los siglos VIII al XI. Los núcleos pirenaicos (718-1035). Navarra, Aragón, Cataluña*, dir. José María Jover Zamora. Madrid: Espasa Calpe, 1999.

MILLARES CARLO, Agustín. *Tratado de paleografía española*. Madrid: Espasa Calpe, 1983.

MILLARES CARLO, Agustín, Manuel C. DÍAZ Y DÍAZ, Anscari M. MUNDÓ, José Manuel ASENCIO, Blas CASADO QUINTANILLA and E. LECUONA RIBOT, eds.*Corpus de códices visigóticos*. 2 vols. Las Palmas: UNED, Centro Asociado de Las Palmas de Gran Canaria, 1999.

MOLL ROQUETA, Jaume. "Nuevos hallazgos de manuscritos mozárabes con neumas musicales". *Analecta Musicologica* 5 (1950): 11-14.

—. "La notación visigótico-mozárabe y el origen de las notaciones occidentales". In *Liturgia y música mozárabes.*

Ponencias y comunicaciones presentadas al Primer Congreso de Estudios Mozárabes: Toledo 1975. Toledo: Instituto de Estudios visigótico-mozárabes de San Eugenio, 1978, 257-272 (Serie D 1).

—. "Per una tipologia de la notació catalana". *Bulletí de la Societat Catalana de Musicología* 2 (1985): 9-21. Translated into Catalonian in *idem.* "Para una tipología de la notación catalana". *Revista de Musicología* 9, no. 2 (1986): 399-409.

MORRIS, Charles W. *Foundations of the Theory of Signs.* Chicago: University of Chicago Press, 1979 (1st ed., 1938).

MUNDÓ, Anscari M. "El commicus palimsest Paris lat. 2.269. Amb notes sobre liturgia i manuscrits visigòtics a Septimania i Catalunya". In *Liturgica.* Montserrat: Abbey of Montserrat, 1956. Vol. 1 (1956): 151-275 (Scripta et Documenta: 7).

—. "Moissac, Cluny et les mouvements monastiques de l'Est des Pyrénées du Xe au XIIe siècle". *Annales du Midi* 75 (1963): 551-573; and also appears in *Moissac et l'occident au XIe siècle. Actas del Coloquio Internacional de Moissac, 3-5 de mayo de 1963.* Toulouse: Edouard Privat, 1964, 229-251.

—. "La datación de los códices litúrgicos visigóticos toledanos". *Hispania Sacra* 18, no. 35 (1965): 1-25.

—. "Un fragment molt antic de litúrgia romana a Catalunya. Excursus I: Nous manuscrits amb notació catalana arcaica; Excursus II: El Missal Místic o Mixt a Catalunya". In *II Congrés Litúrgic de Montserrat* (1966). Montserrat: Abbey of Montserrat: 1967. Vol. 3: 173-191.

—. "Consideracions paleogràfiques a l'entorn de la monodia litúrgica medieval en l'obra d'Higini Anglès". *Recerca Musicològica* 9-10 (1989-1990): 5-14 (Actes del Congrès Internacional Higini Anglès i la musicologia hispànica).

MUNDÓ, Anscari M., and Jesús ALTURO I PERUCHO. "Problemática de les escriptures dels períodes de transició i de les marginals". *Cultura Neolatina* 58 (1998): 129.

NELSON, Kathleen. *Medieval Liturgical Music of Zamora.* Ottawa: Institute of Mediæval Music, 1996 (Wissenschaftliche Abhandlungen: 67).

OLEXY, Ronald T., Keith FALCONER, Lila COLLAMORE, Richard RICE, and Ruth STEINER. *An Aquitainian Antiphoner: Toledo, Biblioteca Capitular, 44.2. A Cantus Index.* Ottawa: Institute of Mediæval Music, 1992 (Wissenschaftliche Abhandlungen: 55/1).

OLIVAR, Alexandre. "Serie de benedictiones lectionum en el Cod. Montserratensis 72". *Ephemerides Liturgicae* 62 (1948): 230-234

—. "Les supervivències litúrgiques autòctones a Catalunya en els manuscrits dels segles XI-XII". In *II Congrès Litúrgic de Montserrat.* Montserrat: Abbey of Montserrat, 1967. Vol. 3: 21-89.

—. "Survivances wisigothiques dans la liturgie catalano-languedocienne". In Edouard Privat, ed. Op. cit., 157-172.

PÉREZ DE URBEL, Justo. *Los monjes españoles en la Edad Media.* 2 vols. 2nd ed. Madrid: Ancla, 1954.

PHILLIPS, Nancy. "Notationen und Notationslehre von Boethius bis zum 12. Jahrhundert. Nordspanische Neumen". In Thomas Ertelt and Frieder Zaminer, eds. *Geschichte der Musiktheorie.* Vol. 4. *Die Lehre vom einstimmigen liturgischen Gesang.* Darmstadt: Wissenschaftliche Buchgesellschaft, 2000, 445-451.

RANDEL, Don Michael. *The Responsorial Psalm Tones of the Mozarabic Office.* Princeton, New Jersey: Princeton University Press, 1969.

—. *An Index to the Chant of the Mozarabic Rite.* Princeton, New Jersey: Princeton University Press, 1973.

REYNOLDS, Roger. "Baptismal Rite and Paschal Vigil in Transition in Medieval Spain: A new Text in visigothic script". *Medieval Studies* 55 (1993): 257-272.

RIU y RIU, Manuel. "L'esglesia catalana al segle X". In *Symposium Internacional sobre els Orígens de Catalunya (segles VIII-XI).* Barcelona: Generalitat de Cataluña, 1991-1992. Vol. 1: 161-189.

—. "La organización eclesiástica". In Ramón Menéndez Pidal, ed. Op. cit., 636-639.

RIVERA RECIO, José Francisco. "La Iglesia mozárabe". In Ricardo García Villoslada, dir. *Historia de la Iglesia en España.* Vol. 2-1. Madrid: Biblioteca de Autores Cristianos, 1982.

ROCHA, Pedro Romano. *L'Office divin au Moyen Âge dans l'église de Braga: Originalité et dépendences d'une liturgie particulier au Moyen Âge.* Paris: Fundaçâo Calouste Gulbenkian, 1980.

—. "Les Sources languedociennes du Bréviaire de Braga". In Edouard Privat, ed. Op. cit., 185-207.

—. "Influjo de los antifonarios aquitanos en el oficio divino de las iglesias del noroeste de la Península". In *Estudios sobre Alfonso VI y la reconquista de Toledo. Actas del II Congreso Internacional de Estudios Mozárabes (Toledo 1985).* Toledo: Instituto de Estudios Visigótico-Mozárabes, 1990. Vol. 4: 27-45.

RODRÍGUEZ SUSO, Carmen. *La monodia litúrgica en el País Vasco (fragmentos con notación musical de los siglos XII al XVIII).* 3 vols. Bilbao: Bilbao Bizkaia Kutxa, 1993 (Biblioteca Musical del País Vasco).

ROJO, Casiano, and Germán PRADO. *El canto mozárabe: estudio histórico-crítico de su antigüedad y estado actual.* Barcelona: Biblioteca de Cataluña, 1929.

RUIZ ALBI, Irene. "La distinción gráfica de '*TI/TJ*' en los documentos visigóticos del archivo de la Catedral de León". In *Orígenes de las lenguas romances en el reino de León. Siglos IX-XII.* León: Centro de Estudios e Investigación San Isidoro (CSIC-CECEL), Caja España de Inversiones, Archivo Histórico Diocesano, 2004. Vol. 2: 439-456.

RUIZ ASENCIO, José Manuel. "Hacia una nueva visión de las glosas emilianenses y silenses". In César Hernández Alonso, José Fradejas Lebrero, Gonzalo Martínez Díez and José Manuel Ruiz Asencio, eds. *Las glosas emilianenses y silenses. Critical edition and facsímile.* Burgos: Ayuntamiento de Burgos, 1993, 83-118.

—. "Códices pirenaicos y riojanos en la biblioteca de Silos en el siglo XI". In José A. Fernández Flórez, dir. *Silos. Un milenio. Actas del Congreso Internacional sobre la Abadía de Santo Domingo de Silos.* Vol. 2, *Historia.* Santo Domingo de Silos: Monastery of Silos, University of Burgos, 2003, 177-210 (Studia Silensia: 26).

RUIZ GARCÍA, Elisa. *Catálogo de la Sección de Códices de la Real Academia de la Historia.* Madrid: Real Academia de la Historia, 1997.

SABLAYROLLES, Maur. "Un Viatge a través dels manuscrits gregorians espanyols". *Revista Musical Catalana-Butlletí de l'Orfeó Català* 3 (1906-1909).

—. "Une notation neumatique intéressante". *Rassegna Gregoriana* 8 (1909): 405-414.

—. "À la Recherche des manuscrits grégoriens espagnols. *Iter hispanicum*". *Sammelbände der Internationalen Musik Gesellschaft* 13, no. 4 (July-September 1912): 509-531.

SANTOS AZEVEDO, Maria José. *Da visigótica à carolina a escrita em Portugal de 882 a 1172.* Lisbon: Fundaçao Calouste Gulbenkian, Junta Nacional de Investigaçao Científica e Tecnológica, 1994 (Textos Universitarios de Ciências Sociais e Humanas).

SHAILOR, Barbara. "The Scriptorium of San Sahagún: A Period of Transition". In Bernard F. Reilly. *Santiago, Saint-Denis and Saint Peter. The Reception of the Roman Liturgy in León-Castile in 1080.* New York: Fordham University Press, 1985, 41-61.

SCHAPIRO, Meyer. *Romanesque Art.* London: George Braziller, Inc., 1977. (Translated into Spanish, *idem. Estudios sobre el románico.* Madrid: Alianza Forma, 1985.)

STÄBLEIN, Bruno. *Schriftbild der einstimmigen Musik.* Leipzig: VEB Deutscher Verlag für Musik, 1975. Vol. 3, no. 4: 9-16, 33-34, 214-217 (Musikgeschichte in Bildern).

SUÁREZ GONZÁLEZ, Ana. "Dos supervivientes visigóticos (Zamora, AHP, fragmentos 15 and 202)". In *Miscel·lània litúrgica catalana.* Barcelona: Societat Catalana d'Estudis litúrgics e Institut d'Estudis Catalans, 2006. Vol. 14: 119-137.

SUNYOL Grégoire M. *Introduction à la paléographie musicale gregorienne.* Paris: Société de Saint Jean l'Évangéliste, Desclée et Cie., 1935. (Translation into Catalonian, *idem. Introducció a la paleografia musical gregoriana.* Montserrat: Abbey of Montserrat, 1925.)

VEZIN, Jean. "Un calendrier franco-hispanique de la fin du XIe siècle". *Bibliothèque de l'École des Chartes* 121 (1963): 5-15.

—. "Observations sur l'emploi des réclames dans les manuscrits latins". *Bibliothèque de l'École des Chartes* 125 (1967): 5-33.

—. "El códice British Library 30849 y la introducción de la carolina en España". In José A. Fernández Flórez, dir. Op. cit., 211-222.

VILARES CEPEDA, Isabel, and Teresa A. S. DUARTE FERREIRA, coords. *Inventario dos códices iluminados até 1500.* Vol. 1, *Distrito de Lisboa;* vol. 2, *Distritos de Aveiro, Beja, Braga, Bragança, Coimbra, Évora, Leiria, Portalegre, Porto, Setúbal, Viana do Castelo e Viseu. Apêndice. Distrito de Lisboa.* Lisbon: Ministério da Cultura, Biblioteca Nacional, Inventario do Património Cultural, 2001.

VIVANCOS, Miguel C. *Glosas y notas marginales de los manuscritos visigóticos del Monasterio de Santo Domingo de Silos.* Santo Domingo de Silos: Monastery of Silos, 1996 (Studia Silensia: 19).

—. "Circulación de manuscritos en la Edad Media. El caso de San Millán y Silos". In Maciej Bielawski and Daniël Hombergen, dirs. *Il monachesimo tra eredità e aperture. Actas del Simposio Testi e Temi nella Tradizione del Monachesimo Cristiano para el cincuenta aniversario del Instituto Monástico de San Anselmo.* Rome: Pontificio Ateneo S. Anselmo, 2004, 785-802 (Studia Anselmiana: 140).

WAGNER, Peter. "Neumenkunde. Paläographie des liturgischen Gesanges". In *idem,* ed. *Einführung in die gregorianischen Melodien. Ein Handbuch der Choralwissenschaft.* Vol. 2. Leipzig: Breitkopf and Härtel, 1912.

—. "Der mozarabische Kirchengesang und seine Überlieferung". In *Gesammelte Aufsätze zur Kulturgeschichte Spaniens.* Münster: Aschendorff, 1928. Vol. 1: 102-141 (Spanische Forschungen der Görresgesellschaft: 1).

—. "Untersuchungen zu den Gesangstexten und zur responsorialen Psalmodie der altspanischen Liturgie". In *ibidem,* 1930. Vol. 2: 67-113.

WALKER, Rose. *Views of Transition. Liturgy and Illumination in Medieval Spain*. London: British Library, 1998.

ZAPKE, Susana. "Procesos asimilativos del nuevo repertorio francorromano en el norte de la Península". *Revista de Musicología* 16 (1993): 2257-2267.

—. "Manuscritos litúrgico-musicales de la Diócesis de Jaca-Huesca fuera de Aragón". In Francisco Bolea y Marta Pujol, eds. *Signos: arte y cultura en el Alto Aragón medieval*. Huesca: Diputación Provincial de Huesca, 1993, 133-136, 300.

—. "Estudios de semiología comparada en base a dos antifonarios altoaragoneses SJP y SCS". In Eliseo Serrano Martín, ed. *Muerte, religiosidad y cultura popular, siglos XIII-XVIII*. Zaragoza: Institución Fernando el Católico, 1994, 509-517.

—. "Die fränkisch-römische Überlieferung in Aragonien (Nordspanien)". In László Dobszay, ed. *Ponencias de la sexta reunión del International Musicological Society Study Group Cantus Planus: Eger (Hungría), septiembre de 1993*. Budapest: Hungarian Academy of Sciences, Institute for Musicology, 1995, 353-366.

—. *El Antifonario de San Juan de la Peña (siglos X-XI): estudio litúrgico-musical del rito hispánico*. Zaragoza: Institución Fernando el Católico, 1995.

—. *Das Antiphonar von Sta. Cruz de la Serós, XII. Jh.* Neuried: Ars Una, 1996.

—. "Antes del gregoriano el viejo canto hispano. Sobre la actividad de monjes y clérigos aragoneses en la Edad Media". In *Actas de las Primeras Jornadas de Canto Gregoriano, noviembre 1997*. Zaragoza: Institución Fernando el Católico, 1997, 45-91.

—. "Monodie und virtuelle Polyphonie in Aragón". In Bruno Bouckaert and Eugeen Schreurs, eds. *Musical Life in Collegiate Churches in the Low Countries and Europe. Chant and Polyphony*. Leuven-Peer: Alamire Foundation, 2000, 399-412 [The DiMartinello Music Collection (KU-Leuven, University Archives): Yearbook of the Alamire Foundation 4].

—. *Fragmentos litúrgico-musicales de la Edad Media en archivos de Aragón. Siglos XI* ex.-*XIII* ex. Huesca: IEA, DGA, 2007.

PART TWO

Catalog of Manuscripts

Introduction to the Second Part

The information given in the eighty-nine descriptive catalographical sheets is intended to enable initial identification of the manuscript. The particular features of each manuscript are set out in the transcription and the one-page commentary. The folios have been selected both on the grounds of formal criteria—notation, illumination, combination of script systems— and for structural features —i.e. elements related to the singularity of the repertoire—.

The model of catalographical sheets is based on the description protocols proposed by Andrew Hughes —*Manuscripts for Mass and Office. A Guide to their Organization and Terminology.* Toronto: University of Toronto Press, 1982 (2nd ed., 1995) —and Elisa Ruiz García— *Introducción a la codicología.* Madrid: Fundación Germán Sánchez Ruipérez, 1988 (2nd ed., 2002).

Typological classification of the manuscripts is based on the following studies by Michel Huglo: *Les livres de chant liturgique.* Turnhout: Brepols, 1988 (Typologie des sources du moyen âge occidental: 52); and "Liturgische Gesangsbücher". In Ludwig Finscher, ed. *Die Musik in Geschichte und Gegenwart.* Kassel: Bärenreiter; Stuttgart: Metzler, 1996. Vol. 5: 1411-1437.

The various typologies are quoted in English, except for manuscripts whose traditional name, as set out in the inventories and catalogs of reference, is known in Latin and would seem unfamiliar in translation (e.g. *Liber misticus, Liber ordinum*).

In specific cases, different dates proposed by different authors are included. When different dates are attributed to different sections of the manuscript, the corresponding folios are specified.

This is followed by the name of the institution where the manuscript is currently held with the respective catalog number. If a previous catalog number exists, this is shown in brackets, preceded by olim.

Given that in many cases it is difficult to reconstruct the iter of the manuscript, we have given the provenance, which is deemed to be the place where it was previously used and/or kept. We only specify the place of origin of the manuscript in cases of absolute certainty. Speculative provenance and/or origin are indicated with a question mark, followed by name of the author attributing this location to the manuscript. Here the *membra disiecta* pose a particular problem and in this case we have limited ourselves to indicating the archives in which they are now held.

The first body of text gives a short physical description of the manuscript (support, binding, composition of the page, materials, type of script and notation), and key decorative elements. All information has been checked against the original, occasionally revealing discrepancies with catalogs currently in use.

The entry on the general contents summarizes, especially in the case of miscellaneous examples, the basic sections for initial identification of the manuscript.

The full-page folio is transcribed, respecting as faithfully as possible the original text and using the following criteria: transcription of literary incipits, with or without musical notation; complete transcription of the rubrics and chant pieces, with the resolved abbreviations shown in rounded script; illegible or reconstructed parts of the text given in square brackets; transcription in capital letters of the nomina sacra; and transcription of Greek orthography in modern Latin.

The bibliography gives a selection of most representative specific publications. At the beginning, where applicable, we give the text or facsimile editions of the manuscript in question.

The map shows all the sites of provenance and/or origin of the manuscripts described in the specification sheets.

The eighty-nine manuscripts described in the catalographical sheets are classified typologically on the basis of the notation systems known in the Iberian Peninsula between the 9th and 12th centuries: Visigothic (northern and southern), Catalonian and Aquitainian notation. The manuscripts are in turn grouped in chronological order in the corresponding areas or cultural centers in the Iberian Peninsula from which they come. This order is shown in diagram 2, in the chapter on notation systems (see the article by Susana Zapke, pp. 201-203).

Production Centers in the Iberian Peninsula and the South of France

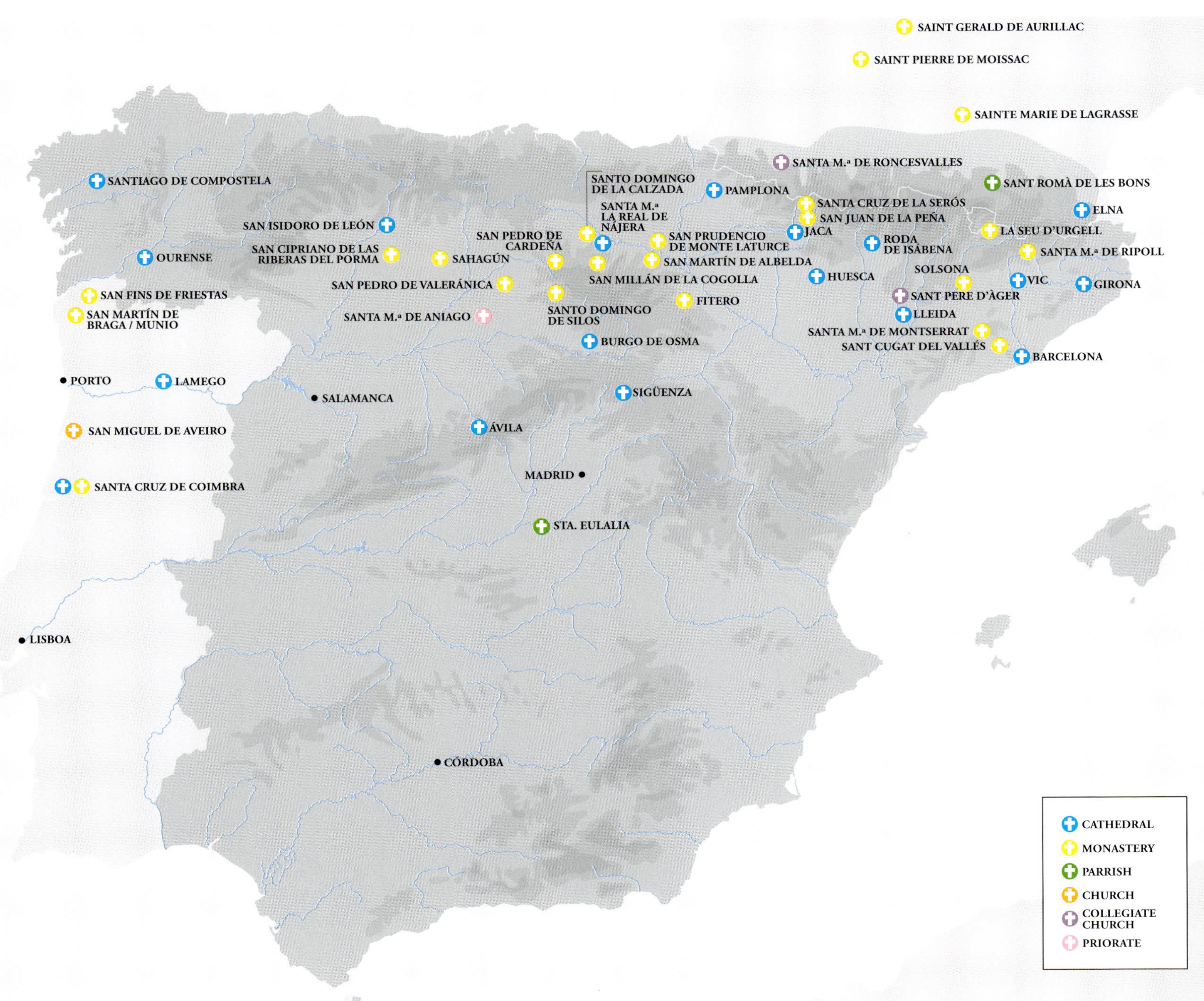
SAINT GERALD DE AURILLAC
SAINT PIERRE DE MOISSAC
SAINTE MARIE DE LAGRASSE
SANTA M.ª DE RONCESVALLES
SANT ROMÀ DE LES BONS
SANTIAGO DE COMPOSTELA
SANTO DOMINGO DE LA CALZADA
PAMPLONA
SANTA CRUZ DE LA SERÓS
ELNA
SANTA M.ª LA REAL DE NÁJERA
SAN JUAN DE LA PEÑA
SAN ISIDORO DE LEÓN
LA SEU D'URGELL
SAN PEDRO DE CARDEÑA
SAN PRUDENCIO DE MONTE LATURCE
JACA
RODA DE ISÁBENA
SANTA M.ª DE RIPOLL
OURENSE
SAN CIPRIANO DE LAS RIBERAS DEL PORMA
SAHAGÚN
SAN MARTÍN DE ALBELDA
SOLSONA
HUESCA
VIC
GIRONA
SAN FINS DE FRIESTAS
SAN PEDRO DE VALERÁNICA
SAN MILLÁN DE LA COGOLLA
SANT PERE D'ÀGER
FITERO
SAN MARTÍN DE BRAGA / MUNIO
SANTA M.ª DE ANIAGO
SANTO DOMINGO DE SILOS
LLEIDA
SANTA M.ª DE MONTSERRAT
BURGO DE OSMA
SANT CUGAT DEL VALLÈS
BARCELONA
PORTO
LAMEGO
SALAMANCA
SIGÜENZA
SAN MIGUEL DE AVEIRO
ÁVILA
MADRID
SANTA CRUZ DE COIMBRA
STA. EULALIA
LISBOA
CÓRDOBA
CATHEDRAL
MONASTERY
PARRISH
CHURCH
COLLEGIATE CHURCH
PRIORATE

Antiphonary (fragmentum)

10TH CENTURY *IN.* / 9TH-10TH CENTURIES (GROS) (FOL. 15R)

BIBLIOTHÈQUE NATIONALE DE FRANCE, PARIS, N. A. L. 2199, 14-16.
PROVENANCE: MONASTERY OF SANTO DOMINGO DE SILOS (BURGOS), BUT PROBABLY WRITTEN IN LEÓN.
The parchment, despite its present condition, seems to be well prepared and of good quality; the fragment consists of three leaves, foliated in a modern period along with the rest of the fragments that appear in the folder; because of the trimming of the fragments, it is impossible to determine the size of the leaves, although the codex may have measured approximately 350 × 225 mm; the writing frame measures 278 × 200 mm; one column, limited by a single vertical line on each side; the horizontal prickings may have run along the outer margin; 16 lines; ruling in drypoint, but it is impossible to determine how it was done; Visigothic minuscule, written by a single hand; northern Visigothic notation.

General contents: Fragments of an antiphonary according to Spanish liturgical use, the most important of which are housed in Paris, but there are others in the archive at the Monastery of Santo Domingo de Silos (AMS, musical fragment 26 and in AMS, Cod. 1) and in the Bible of Silos, presently in Cracow, Czartorysky Library, ms. 3.118. The antiphonary must have suffered an early deterioration since the pieces from Silos and Cracow serve to reinforce the binding. A significant number of manuscripts were used in this way at Silos in the 15th century. There are six fragments preserved in the Bible, but they are so diminutive in size that they contribute nothing to understanding such an important antiphonary; musical notation appears in all of them, and only in two cases are there isolated words, one of which is the from the service for the Ascension. The Silos fragments from Codex 1 are bigger because they served as guard leaves. One of them appears to have been detached from the cover and is preserved separately as musical fragment 26; the other one is still attached to the back cover and is in a poor state of preservation. Two diminutive fragments reinforce a couple of the quires.

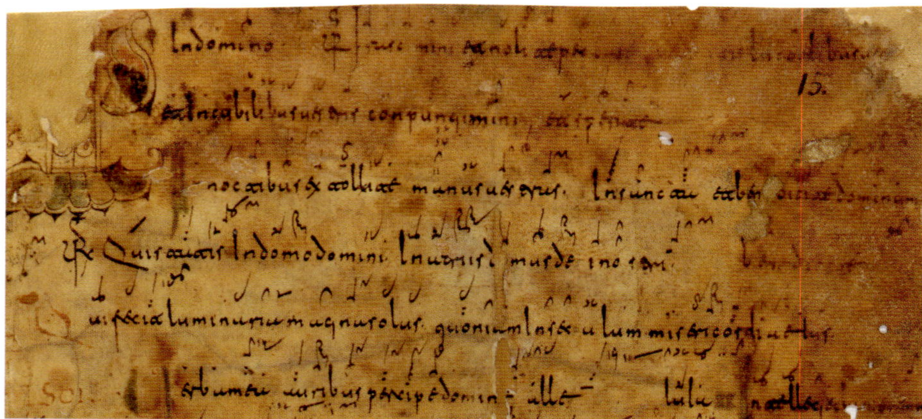
Detail of fol. 15r

Leaf shown: 15r
in Domino...
UERSUS. Irascimini et nolite peccare [que dici]tis in cordibus ues[tris] et in cubilibus uestris conpungimini. Et sperate. In noctibus extollite manus uestras in sancta et benedicite Dominum. UERSUS. Qui statis in domo Domini in atriis d[o]mus Dei nostri benedicite. Qui fecit luminaria magna solus quoniam in seculum misericordia eius. SONO. Uerba mea auribus percipe Domine alleluia, intellege clamorem meum rex meus et Deus meus quoniam ad te orabo alleluia. SONO. Custodi me Domine ut pupillam oculi [s]ub umbra alarum tuarum, exaudi Deus iustitiam meam alleluia. II. Prote[ges] me a facie impiorum qui me afflixerunt inimici mei circum[dederunt] animam meam. Exaudi Deus. SONO. Deus precinxit me uirtutem et posuit inmaculata uiam meam alleluia. II. Dextera tua Domine [susc]epit me et disciplina tua ipsa me docebit alleluia. SONO. Custodi animam meam Domine libera me alleluia alleluia alleluia. II. Dirige me in ueritate tua et doce me quia tu es Deus meus salbator meus te expectabi tota die alleluia.

Considerable space was left between the lines for the musical notation, which is characterized by an elaborate *ductus*, with fine strokes and a clear vertical orientation, typical of manuscripts from the northern part of the Peninsula. A rich variety of forms are used in the neumes.

BIBLIOGRAPHY
EDIT. FÉROTIN 1912, 890-892. GROS 1964a, 324-333. DÍAZ Y DÍAZ 1983, 461, 469-470. FLORES ARCAS 1990, 69-75. ZAPKE 1995a, 82. VIVANCOS 1996, 56, 104, 311. MILLARES CARLO ET AL. 1999, 1: 171. RAMOS 2006, 432-434.

Miguel C. Vivancos

In domino Ꝟ Irascimini et nolite peccare ... in cubilibus

uestris conpungimini et ...

... noctibus extollite manus uestras in sancta et benedicite dominum

Ꝟ Qui statis in domo domini in atriis domus dei nostri

... qui fecit luminaria magna solus quoniam in seculum misericordia eius

Verbum meum auribus percipe domine alle luia intellege

rex meus et deus meus quoniam ad te orabo alleluia

Custodi me domine ut pupillam oculi sub umbra alarum tuarum et ...

... tuarum me alle luia Ꝟ Protege me a facie impiorum qui me

adflixerunt inimici mei ... animam meam ... expandistis

... et precinxisti me uirtutem et posuisti inmaculatam uiam meam alleluia

Ꝟ Erudiuit me dominus ... ipsa me ... et disciplina

ipsa me docebit alle luia Custodi animam meam domine

... alleluia alle luia alleluia Ꝟ Dirige me in ueritate tua et doce me

quia tu es deus meus salvator meus ... alle luia

Cum ...

Antiphonary

10th Century *med.* (fol. 50r)

Archivo Capitular, León, ms. 8.
Provenance: Monastery of San Cipriano de las Riberas del Porma (?) (León), Beja (?) (Díaz y Díaz).
Well-preserved parchment; Spanish full binding; leaves: 306; modern foliation in ink and with Arabic numerals situated in the upper right margin; the leaves measure 330 × 240 mm; one 17-line column for the antiphonary and a variable number of columns and lines in the prologues (additional fols. 20-27, two columns); 32 lines; ruled in drypoint; liturgical style Visigothic minuscule of excellent quality; alternating modules depending on the character of the text, larger for texts with notation; a rich and abundant variety of initials with anthropomorphic, botanical and lacework motifs; historiated initials; two figures that may depict the codex's scribe, Teodemundo, and its recipient, the abbot Ikilano (fol. 1v); independent miniatures serve to illustrate the subject matter (fol. 50r inter alia); the scribes are Teodemundo (Bishop of the diocese of Salamanca until 960?) and Arias (fols. 20-27); northern Visigothic notation skillfully written and with an extraordinarily rich variety of forms; additional expressive symbols; represents the same typology as Santiago de Compostela, BXU, ms. 609 (Res. 1); Salamanca, BGU, ms. 2668; Zaragoza, BGU, M-418; and Madrid, RAH, Cod. 30.

General contents: *Oficium de Letania* (fol. 1r); an epigram dedicated to the abbot Ikilano (fol. 1v); *Incipit Cyclus XXXV annorum* (fol. 2r); *Incipit prologus in libro antiphonarium* (fol. 2v); *Item admonitio cantoris sub metro eroico elegiacum dictatm qualiter letiferam pestem vane glorie refugiat et cor mundum labiaque in Deum...* (fol. 3r); *Anuntiationes festivitatum* (fol. 3v); prose *Sublimius diebus* (fol. 4); *Sacrum in diem Sancti Iacobi apostoli VIII Kalendas Augusti* (fol. 5r, with notation); the cross of Oviedo (fol. 5v); Legend: *Llibrum Ikilani Abbati* (fol. 6r); Mozarabic calendar (fols. 6v-19v); three additional introductory quires, several hands of the 10th and 11th centuries *med.* (fols. 20-27); the codex's date of composition (fol. 26r); *Incipit liber Antiphonarium de toto anni circulo. A festivitate Sancti Aciscli usque in finem* (fols. 28v-206v, fragmentary); *Ordo psallendi in diem Sancti Aciscli* (fol. 29r); *Ordo beatissimi Iuliani aepiscopi quem dedit in eclesia ubique fuerit* (fol. 116v).

Leaf shown: 50r
Officium in diem Sanctae Eolalie ad vesperum IIII idus. decembris. [Saint Eulalia of Mérida, 10 December] *Vespertinum Dominus inluminatio mea et salus mea. Versus Dominus defensor vite mee a quo trepidabo.* II. *Benedic anima mea Domino.* III. *Benedic anima mea Domino.* IIII. *Qui redimet. Sono Alleluia. Ingredere.* II. *Alleluia. Intra in ortum. Antiphona. Columba speciosa perfecta. Versus Adstitit regina. Antiphona. Inter medios cleros. Versus Quem Iacob. Ymnus Germine nobilis. Versus Speciem et.* Alle [-luia, lengthy melisma in the right hand margin].

The most complete antiphonary of purely Spanish liturgical use, with a total of 500 responsories with verses, from León, it stands out for its rigor in tonal organization, and for its range of notational signs. Other northern codices, such as from La Rioja, Salamanca, San Millán and Santiago, share the same psalmodic schema. The Visigothic repertoire uses seven psalmodic formulas for the responsorial verses, adapted to the textual prosody. For the antiphons, the schema is more varied, without strictly adhering to textual prosody except in the intonation formulas. Two of the three anonymous prologues to the Antiphonary of León allude to how the antiphons and responsories are to be performed. Extensive melismas in the margins of the leaves are a characteristic phenomenon of Spanish ritual codices. The use of a notable variety of special expressive signs, extensively described by Dom Brou, is another peculiarity in the codex's sophisticated notational system. The biblical sources are cited in the right margin: *In psalmo XXVI, In psalmo CII, In cantica canticorum, in psalmo LXVII,* besides the generic abbreviation *ibi.*

Detail of fol. 198v

Bibliography

Edit. Facs. *Antiphonarium Mozarabicum* 1928. Prado 1928, 219, 224, 227. Wagner 1928, 121. Rojo and Prado 1929. Anglès 1935, 9. Domínguez Bordona 1935, 153-163. Edit. Férotin 1952, 913 and subsq. Brou 1954, 7-114. Díaz y Díaz 1954, 226-257. Pérez de Urbel 1954, 115-144. Brou and Vives 1959. Millares Carlo 1961, 26-27. Randel 1969, 10-52. Fernández de la Cuesta 1980, 58-59. Guilmain 1981, 309-401. Randel 1985, 229-238. González Barrionuevo 1986, 11-27. Gómez Pallarés 1987, 25-48. Huglo 1987, 1: 19-26. Levy 1987, 1: 3-14. Viñayo 1990, 61-63. *Las edades del hombre* (Martín) 1991, 87-89. Huglo 1993, 477-490. González Barrionuevo 1995, 5-112. Zapke 1996, 120, 249.

Susana Zapke

OFFICIUM IN DIEM SCE EOLALIE AD UPRU iiii ids dec

PS D ominus inluminatio mea — et sa — lus me a quem timebo. VR Dominus defensor vite mee — a quo trepidabo.

S B enedic anima mea domino et omnia interiora mea nomini sancto e — ius. quem

S B enedic anima mea domino et noli oblibisci omnes retributiones e — ius. q

S Q ui redimet de interitu vitam meam — qui coronat te in misericordia et misericordia.

SN A lle — luia. Ingredere in domum matris tue et requiem capito — rum ut egrediaris filia Sion et pulcre agnos eos alle — luia alle — luia.

S A lle — luia. Inventa invocatum meum sponsum meum filia Iherusalem flores enim ut geminavit in terra cresce lux dicit dominus donec adspiret dies et amoveantur umbre alle

C olumba speciosa perfecta ut sol et gemis precincta caput meum plenum et rore celi et crines guttis noctium. VR Adstitit regina

L Inter medios cleros pinne columbe deargentate alle luia et supra scapulas eius in viriditate auri allelluia alle luia. VR Gaudent in celo. L Celestis nobilis. VR Specie tua

Inspecu

ibi

Inspecu

ibi

ibi

Incuncta eu cun ac cont

Ibi

Ibi

Inps lx

alle

Alvarus Paulus (Opera et alia opuscula)

10TH CENTURY *EX.*-11TH CENTURY *IN.* (FOL. 208R)

BIBLIOTECA CAPITULAR, CÓRDOBA, MS. 123.
PROVENANCE: UNKNOWN (PROBABLY FROM LEÓN AND NOT FROM CÓRDOBA AS SOME AUTHORS HAVE MAINTAINED. FOR PART C, WITH MUSICAL NOTATION, THE AREA OF SAHAGÚN-ESLONZA, WHERE THERE WERE CONTACTS WITH MOZARABIC EMIGRANTS AND THE INFLUENCE OF FRENCH TRENDS, HAS BEEN SUGGESTED AS A POSSIBLE CENTER OF PRODUCTION).
The parchment is in a precarious state of preservation; old binding with leather over walnut tree boards with polychrome remnants; 221 leaves (fragmentary); modern foliation in pencil with Arabic numerals in the upper right margin; the leaves measure 240 × 160 mm; the writing frame measures 180 × 120 mm; one column justified with double vertical lines on both sides; horizontal prickings in the right margin; the number of lines varies from 23 to 25; ruled in drypoint over the recto of the first leaf and the verso of the second leaf; Visigothic minuscule with a rather careless *ductus*; use of the *ti* and *tj* ligatures; an addition in Carolingian script from the 12th century on fol. 9v; use of catchwords at the end of the quaternion; several scribes, varying from part to part and even within the same part, consistent northern peninsular Visigothic notation with meticulous strokes.

General contents: The first part (fols. 1-164) was written by a single scribe named *Sisuertus presbyter* (fols. 91r, 100r and 121r). It contains the works (incomplete) of Álvaro de Córdoba: poems, *confessio* (fol. 9v), a poem added in 12th century Carolingian script, *de lucifero*, an epistolary (fols. 25v-121v), a brief illustrasted table of contents (without title, fols. 122r-164v), which ends suddenly. The second part (fols. 165-207) contains interrogations with quotes from Junilius Africanus, Fulgentius and Isidore, as well as the abbot Esperaindeo; a penitential (fol. 178); *De genealogiis* (fol. 196v); St. Augustine's sermon on the lost tree (fol. 198r); a brief table of contents of Enoch (fols. 199v-207); the beginning of the Creed (fol. 207v), partially scraped with an abrupt ending. The third part (fols. 208-221v) appears to have been an independent codicological unit. Additional pieces appear with musical notation on a leaf that was left blank (fol. 208r), dated around the 11th century *ex.* (Díaz y Díaz).

Leaf shown: 208r
[FRAGMENT OF THE OFFICE OF PENTECOST. PROSES]
The first 10 lines are a continuation of the prose *Orbis conditor regressus est in sinu Patris... carismatum dona. Repleti sunt... Ihesu redemptor bone da nobis quod petimus in secula.* Amen. *ARIANI METRA.* VERSUS DE SANCT*IS. Alma sollemnitas... Iudicantes duodecim tribus Israhel alleluia.*

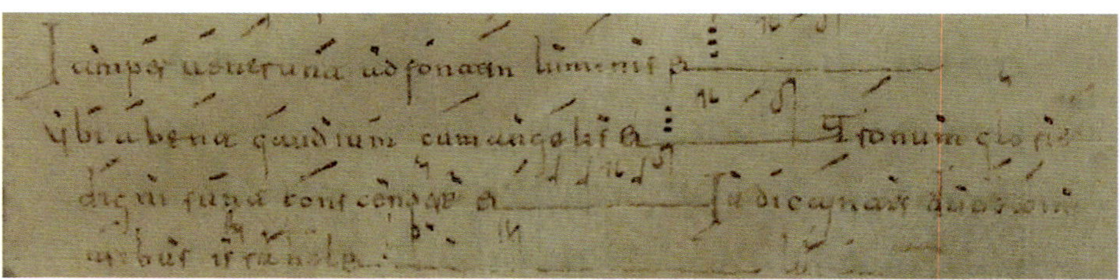
Detail of fol. 208r

The Archivo Capitular de Córdoba preserves a complete copy of this volume, copied in the 17th century (ms. 124). Some initial notes and letters illustrate the history of the manuscript in the 16th and 17th centuries. The presence of the two proses, with Visigothic notation, confirm the circulation of this type of repertoire in the Peninsula at a very early period, and in the form of separate quires which would ultimately be integrated into one unique manuscript with varied content, liturgical or of some other nature, as is the case with this copy. Other examples attest to the same procedure, such as the *Distinctio vocabulorum* (Barcelona, ACA, Ripoll 76), which includes a prose to St. Nicholas on fol. 77v (13th century); or the *Liber scintillarum* of *Bede* (Barcelona, ACA, Ripoll 199), which contains a prose and trope for the Sanctus (12th century) on fols. 170v-172r, or even the Antiphonary of León (León, AC, ms. 8), in which a prose from the 11th century was added on fol. 1v. The manuscript from Córdoba contains one of the few examples preserved in the Peninsula of proses disseminated in Visigothic script and notation. A manuscript from Silos, London, BL, Add. ms. 30850, contains the same piece in the flyleaves, the prose *Alma sollemnitas.* Fol. 8v presents the incipit of the *lectio de assumptio Sancte Marie sermo beati Hieronimi presbiteri ad Paulam et ad virgines sub ea degentes.* Finally, the beautiful binding of this copy should be noted because it is one of the few preserved from this era. Earlier and just as exceptional is the binding of the *Capitulare Evangelarium* from the Archivo Capitular de Girona (ms. 2), dated to the first half of the 11th century.

BIBLIOGRAPHY
ARTILES 1932, 201-291. LECLERCQ 1949b, 327-338. BROU 1951, 27-41; 1955, 29. FERNÁNDEZ DE LA CUESTA 1980, 59. DÍAZ Y DÍAZ 1983, 370-374. MILLARES CARLO 1983, 44-45. CASTRO 1991, 48. MILLARES CARLO ET AL. 1999, 1: 44-46.

Susana Zapke

... domi nu. Repleti sunt spiritu sancto
ceperunt loqui variis linguis. Apostoli ... magna
facta ... voce conveniunt multi ... mente
confusa. Audiebat unusquisque linguam suam illos
loquentes dei magnalia. Quem nullo valet conspi-
... omnia sol ... cum ... clara sidera.
Post ascensionem ... in ascendit ... promissionibus omnibus
a domino ... digni accipere ... celestia ...
... sancto. Ihesu redemptor bone da nobis
quod ... in secula. ... ANTIPHONA? ... RA
VIR PSCIS Alma sollemnitas domini gloriosique martiris
... Resplendet hec ... coronati ...
domini ... Fulgentia aurea ... gloriosi ...
Tenentes decretum domini ... Per ... principum
... gloria ... premia ... Et ... dis ...
... propter ... claritatem ... Et ...
... ad ... luminis ...
Ubi habent gaudium cum angelis ... sonum glorie
digni ... consequi ... dignatus ...
... in secula ...

Psalterium et Liber canticorum (Diurnal of Ferdinand I)

1055 (ERA 1093) (FOL. 212V)

BIBLIOTECA GENERAL UNIVERSITARIA, SANTIAGO DE COMPOSTELA, MS. 609 (RES. 1).
PROVENANCE: MONASTERY OF SAHAGÚN (DÍAZ Y DÍAZ). RELATED TO LA RIOJA AND EASTERN CASTILE *(LIBER CANTICORUM)* AND TO THE CAROLINGIAN KINGDOM. LEÓN (LÓPEZ-CALO).
Excellent parchment, perfectly preserved (restored); modern binding with leather, Mudejar style, with leather straps (1973); 224/225 + 2 leaves (an error appears after fol. 199, which is remedied by numbering it 199bis); defects between fols. 4 and 5 and between fols. 134 and 135; modern foliation in pencil, Arabic numerals in the upper right margin; several errors; the leaves measure 310 × 220 mm; the writing frame measures 220 × 110 mm; one column justified with double vertical lines on both sides; prickings no longer visible; 22 to 34 lines; ruled in drypoint; Visigothic minuscule; use of *ti* and *tj* ligatures; full-page miniatures on fols. 1, 6, 7, 207v and 208v; the initial of each psalm is decorated with an elaborate drawing, some with anthropomorphic and zoomorphic motifs; verse initials are marked in gold; the titles of each psalm and didascalias are in red; scribes, Pedro and an illuminator, Fructuoso: *Petrus erat scriptor, Fructuosus denique pictor* (fol. 208v); Visigothic notation from the northern peninsula with exquisitely elaborated strokes and a considerable wealth of graphic signs and neumatic combinations; all the notation appears to have been written by a single hand.

General contents: Title page and calendar (fols. 1r-4r); dedication: *Florus Isidoro abbati* (fols. 4v-5v); Psalter (fols. 7r-206r): *In nomine Domini incipit liber psalmorum, Beatus vir qui timet Dominum* (Incipit, fol. 7); includes Old Testament chants and, at the end, some prayers, one of them with a litany (fol. 198v); the text corresponds to the *vetus hispana;* the deaths of various kings of León (fol. 207v); the *attestatio: Sancia, cev uolvit quod sum, Regina peregit, era milena novies dena quoque terna; Petrus erat scriptor, Fructuosus denique pictor* (fol. 208v); *Ordo ad medivm noctis* (fol. 209r); the section with notation begins (fol. 210r): *Ordo ad celebrandum nocturnos* (fol. 215v); *Responsoria ad nocturnos dominicales* (fol. 216r).

Leaf shown: 212v
[Continuation of the *RESPONSORIUM Per diem clamavi et nocte coram te*]
... an galli cantum, an mane. VERSUS *Dominus Iesus Christus.* RESPONSORIUM *Uigilate et orate.* VERSUS *Uidete, nequando adgrauetis corda.* RESPONSORIUM *Anima mea desiderat te, deus.* VERSUS *Sicut cerbus desiderat* RESPONSORIUM. *Uigila, domine, super oues gregis tui.* VERSUS *Custodi nos, domine.*

This codex, which was written at the order of Queen Sancha as a gift for her husband, King Ferdinand I, reflects the implicit intention of strengthening the dynasty of

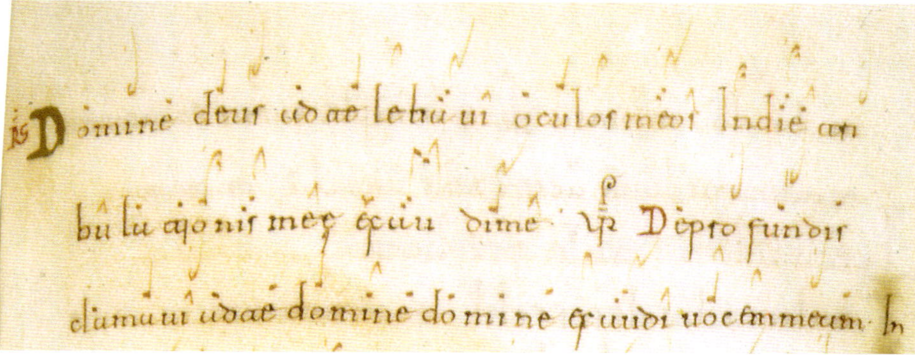
Detail of fol. 213r

León and enhancing its dignity. The lower inscription on fol. 208v confirms that the queen ordered this copy. Fol. 6r (presently 3r) includes a full-page *ex libris* with a labyrinth that is deciphered as follows: FREDINANDI REGIS SUM LIBER. Another inscription reads: FREDINANDI REGIS NECNON ET SANCIA REGINA SUM LIBER. Both inscriptions reveal that the codex was intended for the King and that, as such, it was conceived for private use, a type of manuscript of which very few copies have survived. Leaf 6v (presently fol. 3v) includes a miniature that represents the King, the Queen and an additional figure, perhaps the scribe, an abbot, or maybe even a noble (Sicart).

The notation reveals clear diastematic tendencies despite being *in campo aperto*, but this apparent diastematic tendency does not facilitate even an approximate transcription of the melodies. The notation presents an elaborate *ductus* of regular design, comparable to that in the codices from the Riojan tradition. It is one of the most beautiful examples of Spanish notation from the northern part of the Peninsula.

BIBLIOGRAPHY

EDIT. FACS. *LIBRO DE HORAS DE FERNANDO I DE LEÓN* 1995. FÉROTIN 1901, 374-387; 1912, 931-936. ROJO AND PRADO 1929, 24. MILLARES CARLO 1963, 71. RANDEL 1969, 6, 138-139, 240-241, 270-271. JANINI 1977, 246. SICART 1981, 21-44. LÓPEZ-CALO 1982, 17-23. DÍAZ Y DÍAZ 1983, 279-292. PARDO 1998, 117-119. MILLARES CARLO ET AL. 1999, 1: 176-177.

José López-Calo

RS Domine deus uitae leuaui oculos meos in die an
bulationis mee ecce dñe. V. De pro fundis
clamaui uitae domine domine exaudi uocem meam. In

RS Pectauaus sum nocte cum cor de meo anxiaretur
et spiritus meus et dixi numquid in aeternum
re pellet deus. V. Timor et tremor uenerunt
super me et contexerunt me tenebre. Et dixi

RS Animum meum certa lum peccare cogitau de subiau neu
atuns posicione et de aeternu aos manau ibi
enim non que rinaus penitaen tia nec luctum
fuerunt luctime dum atm pus haber conuertere
clama et dic deus meus miserere mei. V.
Quaerebatis a anima mea et quaere me conautbas
speru in domino. Clama

O tu domino annae lucem et orum a tibi
mi sere aut et om nia que peccaueris abeo dubia

Orationale

9TH CENTURY *EX.* (FOL. 93V)

BRITISH LIBRARY, LONDON, ADD. MS. 30852.
PROVENANCE: MONASTERY OF SANTO DOMINGO DE SILOS (BURGOS).
Inadequately prepared, poor-quality parchment which uses the edges of the skin; 15th century binding, leather over boards; 1 + 115 + 3 leaves; 18th century foliation in the upper right margin; the leaves measure 320 × 260 mm; the writing frame measures 242 × 190 mm; two columns, double vertical justification on all leaves; the vertical prickings are visible on the edge and the horizontal prickings between the columns; 22 lines, except for fols. 7-38 which have as many as 26; ruled in drypoint on the exterior of the first bifolium placed over the second, and on the interior of the fourth placed over the third; almost continuous Visigothic minuscule with a wide and thick stroke; two hands, one for fols. 7-38; northern Visigothic notation; it should be noted that in its present state, there are several lacunae.

General contents: Prayers from the Spanish liturgy for the entire liturgical year, although there are some lacunae. On fols. 96v, 97v, 98r and 99r there are some judicial notes and formulas written quite carelessly by a semi-cursive Visigothic minuscule hand from the end of the 9th century or the beginning of the 10th. An almost unintelligible, yet quite interesting note, appears on fol. 97v, written with ink lighter than the rest with some distinguishing characteristics that may indicate a different scribe: *Sancta Trinitas qui est in celo et quatuor aubangelio quia salba meo kaballo colore bago. Sante Damiane, Sante Gensiale, Sante Marsiale in frena [fronte?] oceus carer quia non poissan meu caballo benaso* (?). Because the paleness of the ink and the near illegibility of the letters prevent a more precise reading, this interpretation is mere conjecture.

Leaf shown: 93v
... *mira per Filium uirtute coruscans, liuera in brachio tuo quos eius redemisti sanguine sacro; ut quodquod in morte Filii tui consepulti sumvs, infinita cum eo letitia exultemus. ALIA* [in the margin: *Absorta est mors in uictoria. UERSUS. Deus deorum Dominus*] *Christe Deus a quo mors in uictoriam... ALIA* [in the margin: *Alleluia. Redemit nos Dominus et benedixit nos. UERSUS. Benedixit domus Aaron. RESPONSUM. Letamini in Domino. UERSUS. Omnes gentes plaudite manibus*] *Christe Dei Filius cuius morte... AD MATUTINUM* [in the margin: *Fructificemus Deo. UERSUS. Quam rectus est sermo Domini*] *Fac nos Deus Pater... ALIA* [in the margin: *Nos omnes redemti sumus. UERSUS. Quoniam ipsius est mare*] *Nos omnes qui tuo Christe redempti sumus sanguine pretioso quesumus ut tante pietatis pretioso liuerati non.*

The musical notation is reserved for the antiphons, written in a smaller section apart from the prayers but by the same hands responsible for the main text. Because of the limited amount of space available, especially for antiphon melodies written between the columns, and the reduced size of the letters used for the chant texts, the notation is at times invisible and totally lacking in skill and precision.

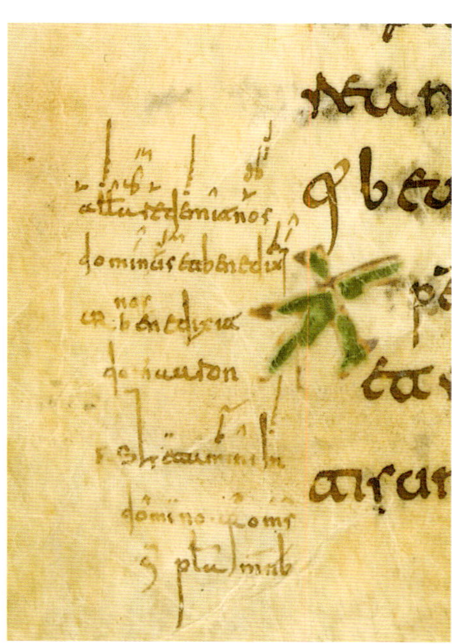

Detail of fol. 93v

BIBLIOGRAPHY

VIVES 1945, 1-24. EDIT. VIVES 1946.
MILLARES CARLO ET AL. 1999, 1: 88.

Miguel C. Vivancos

mitti per filium tuum auge
scotur cunctis nostris. huius in bru
chio tuo quo revelante
demundati sanguine tuo.
y(et) quod quod in morte fi
lii tui conse pultisumus.
in firmitate cum eo letitia
exaltemur. ALIA. Xpe
re tu qui mortis in uictoriu(m)
absorta uita. qui mortis uic
toriam simul et aculeum
destruens. magnum mun
do redemptionis presidium
contulisti. da nobis ua
cationum mortis ut sua
profectibus insultantes
ut festiua gaudium te
neamur perduci quando
q(ue) beatiores. ALIA.
Xpe di filius cuius morte
et resurrectione redemp
ti sumus. benedictio nob(is)

et confirmatio cordium n(ost)ro(rum)
resurrectionis tue po
tentia. ut alnate resur
rectionis n(ost)re misterium
agnoscamus. et futu
re beatitudinis gau
dia cupiamus. AD M
Fac nos d(omi)ne p(er) ... lau
fructificare tibi. ua
eluratu nat umrimur
quem ex mortuis susci
tasti. xpi resurrectio fili
tui quod suscitando
nos tu unde deuicit
ut diuitate. peruenire
nos faciat ad eternae
hereditate. ALIA.
Nos omnes quia tu Xpe re
demptor sumus sangui
ne p(ro)tectiono quesumus
ut tu nos pietate
protectio ... uitanon

Liber ordinum

10TH CENTURY *EX.* (FOL. 24R)

REAL ACADEMIA DE LA HISTORIA, MADRID, COD. 56.
PROVENANCE: MONASTERY OF SAN MILLÁN DE LA COGOLLA (LA RIOJA).
(FOL. AV-I: "... *QUI LOCUM ISTUM SANCTI EMILIANI CONFESSORIS CONSECRASTI...*", IN THE PRAYER *VIAM SANCTORUM OMNIUM.*)
Good-quality white parchment; modern binding; 155 leaves, numerous lacunae; modern foliation, with mistakes, in ink with Arabic numerals in the upper right margin; the leaves measure 250 × 175.5 mm; the writing frame measures 170 × 95 mm; one column justified with double vertical lines on both sides; horizontal prickings in the right margin, vertical prickings in the upper margin; 18 to 19 lines; ruled in drypoint with odd leaves over even ones; stylish liturgical Visigothic minuscule; stems with beveled tips; consistent use of the *tj* ligature before a vowel; two writing modules, a larger one for the liturgical texts and a smaller one for the rites; cartouches with a colored background; superimposed initials with Carolingian influence; primary initials filled in with anthropomorphic and zoomorphic motifs (fishes), and exquisite initials decorated with interlace over the entire leaf; numerous marginal notes and additional pieces with Visigothic notation framed in red; catchwords or compound catchwords; the scribe, *Dominicus*; northern Visigothic notation of beautiful artistry. Some leaves are scraped; on the following leaves, the text is replaced by Aquitainian script: fols. 24r, 26r, 30v, 31v, 32r, 32v, 33, 33v, 34r, 35r, 37r, with very small letters and very thin strokes, requiring a magnifying glass for an accurate reading. Numerous pieces lack notation; a *custos* is employed in the pieces with Aquitainian notation.

General contents: ... *Item antifone secundum Romanos* (fol. 0r). with remains of Visigothic notation*; Item antifone ad lignum adorandum* (fol. 0v)*; Exorcismum olei* (fol. 1r)*; Exorcismum incensi* (fol. 4r); ordines and benedictions (up to fol. 26v); preces (fol. 27r-v); office of the dead (fols. 24r-27r*).* Scrapings and subsequent additions of Aquitainian notation; exp. ... *Ex concilio Toletano VIIo era IIIa ubi et Toletum dicit* (fol. 37v); exp. ... *eruit victo serpente beatorum animas Hebrei tunc* ... (fol. 46v)*; Ordo missarum botibarum de sacerdote* (fols. 53v-55v); COLOPHON: *Dominicus scribtor memorare tu sacrificiorum offertor in infirmitate subiacens a mole meorum peccatorum obprimens presuiter vocor sed indignum nomine fungor queso me adesse memor* (i.m.) (fol. 123r); *Missa IIIa plurales* (fols. 125-128v); *Ordo misse omnimode* (fols. 134v-141v); EXP. ... *loquebatur discipulis suis dicens* ... The *lectio* from the Gospel of St. Matthew for the *Missa de tribulatis* (fol. 155v), which begins on fol. 146r.

Leaf shown: 24r
Domine exaudi orationem. Benedictus Dominus Deus meus. Miserere mei Dominus
Quod sidistalerit aliquantis permosi recitentur [add.: salutat.... ptbero]
RESPONSORIUM *Ecce ego viam universe*
VERSUS. *Dies quibus pere [mna]. Seculorum* [outside the writing frame] *Oremus... nima. Inter agmina beatorum*
CONPLETURIA *Suscipe Domine animam servi tui.*

There are, in addition to Cod. 56, two copies of the *Liber ordinum* in Spain: Silos, AM, Cod. 4 and Silos, AM, Cod. 3. Cod. 56 includes rites that are exclusively episcopal, such as the *ordo* for blessing the chrism on the feast of Sts. Cosmas and Damian and the burial ritual for a Bishop. The particular interest of this manuscript is that it brings together two versions (although the differences between them are minimal) of the texts of the common of *ordo missae.* The first one coincides with the *Liber ordinum* from San Prudencio de Monte Laturce, Silos, AM, Cod. 4. On some leaves the original Visigothic notation has been scraped off to be replaced by Aquitainian notation, noting in the right margin the modal cadence of the piece. There are other places in the codex where the neumes have been scraped and the new notational system has been introduced. Use of a drypoint line in the interlinear space where the original notation was replaced. There are other passages that have been erased, substituting not only the melodies, but also the texts, with Visigothic script.

The transcribed series corresponds to the funeral rite with 16 antiphons, three Responsories and two litanies. The *Liber ordinum*, Silos, AM, Cod. 4, substitutes

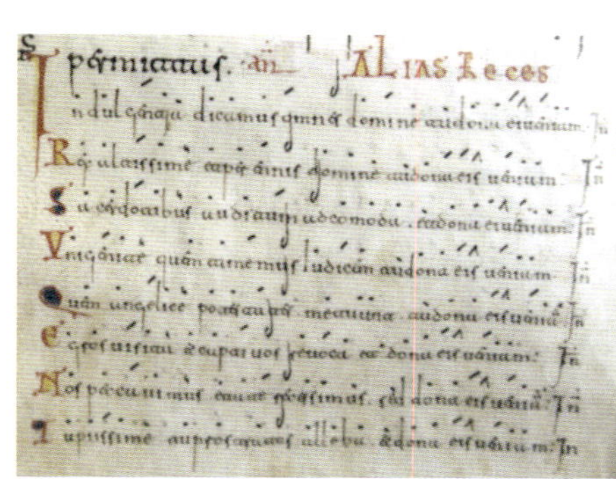

Detail of fol. 27v

Visigothic notation for Aquitainian. This copy brings together a unique series of supplication litanies from the Old Spanish rite endowed with a melodic version that differs from other sources (fols. 27r-v). The *Liber ordinum* is a clear example of the transitional phase and of the coexistence of musical notation systems.

BIBLIOGRAPHY

PÉREZ DE URBEL 1908, 503. FÉROTIN 1912. PRADO 1928, 234-237. ROJO AND PRADO 1929, 12-13, 13b, 34. ROJO 1930, 307. BROU 1952, 57-76. HUGLO 1955, 361-383. MENÉNDEZ PIDAL 1958, 7-19. PINELL 1965, 109-164. RANDEL 1969, 64-68, 76. JANINI 1977a, 162. GROS 1978, 50-55. FERNÁNDEZ DE LA CUESTA 1980, 37. VIVANCOS 1996, 104. RUIZ GARCÍA 1997, 315-317. *SANCHO EL MAYOR Y SUS HEREDEROS* 2006, 1: 81-82 (SÁENZ PASCUAL).

Susana Zapke

osculum pacis. Si quis explanat uale fuerit post oppressione ...
nis incipiunt cum quos sequentes psalmos. III psalmo

III D(omi)ne quid multiplicati
IIII Cum inuocarem exaudiuit
VIIII Confitebor tibi d(omi)ne
XII Usquequo d(omi)ne obliuisceris
XVII Diligam te d(omi)ne uirtus mea
XXII D(omi)n(u)s regit me et nihil mihi
XXIIII Ad te d(omi)ne leuaui animam
XXVII Ad te clamaui d(eu)s meus
XXVI D(omi)n(u)s inluminatio mea
XXVIIII Exaltabo te d(omi)ne q(uonia)m
XXX In te d(omi)ne speraui non
XXXVIIII Expectans expectaui
XLI Sicut ceruus desiderat ad
LIIII Exaudi d(eu)s orationem meam
LXX In te speraui d(omi)ne non con
Miserere mihi d(omi)ne q(uonia)m conculcauit
Miserere mei d(eu)s miserere mei q(uonia)m in te
Exaudi d(eu)s deprecationem meam
Quam amabilia sunt
Inclina d(omi)ne aurem tuam
D(omi)ne d(eu)s salutis mee per diem
D(omi)ne exaudi orationem meam
Benedic anima mea d(omi)no et om(ni)a
Benedic anima mea d(omi)no d(omi)ne d(eu)s
Paratum cor meum d(eu)s paratum
Dilexi q(uonia)m exaudiet d(omi)n(u)s
Credidi propter quod locutus
Ad d(omi)n(u)m cum tribularer
Leuaui oculos meos in montes
Letatus sum in his que dicta
Confitebor tibi d(omi)ne in toto
D(omi)ne probasti me et cognouisti
Eripe me d(omi)ne ab homine malo
Uoce mea ad d(omi)n(u)m clamaui

D(omi)ne exaudi orationem meam. Benedictus d(omi)n(u)s d(eu)s meus. Miserere mihi d(eu)s s(e)c(un)d(u)m ma[illegible]
Quibus decantatis [illegible] per ordinem [illegible] psalmis per ordinem
Completis quoque [illegible] fuerint ... hunc
responsum. R(esponsorium) C(redo) ... cunctis lucere
...dormium cum ... meis ... plus ... non ...
... mei domine ... de regno tuo. V(ersus) D(eu)s quibus ... Secula
... parati ... non ... tua ...
patrum meorum ... Oratio. ... fr(atr)ibus
... beatorum. ... conlocare dign(e)t(ur). Explicit.

Suscipe d(omi)ne animam serui tui illius de seculo reuer-
tentem ad te. Emitte angelos tuos s(an)c(t)os
in obuiam illius. Et uiam iustitie demonstra
ei. Aperi ei portas iustitie. Et repelle
ab eo principes tenebrarum. Agnosce
d(omi)ne depositum fidelem quod tuum
est. Suscipe d(omi)ne creaturam tuam
non ex diis alienis creatam, sed a te
solo deo uiuo et uero. Quia non est alius
d(eu)s preter te et non est secundum opera tua.

Bible

10th Century *ex.* (fol. 70r)

Czartorysky Library, Cracow (Poland), ms. 3.118.

Provenance: Monastery of Santo Domingo de Silos (Burgos) although it does not seem to have been written there.

Good-quality, well-prepared parchment; 20th century binding; 1 + 216 + 1 leaves; 18th century foliation in the upper right margin in ink, modernized in the upper left column on some of the damaged leaves; numbers 70 and 206 are repeated; the leaves measure 366 × 270 mm; the writing frame measures 298 × 205 mm; two columns, justified with double vertical lines at the edges and a single line between the columns; vertical prickings cannot be seen; the horizontal prickings run along the outside margin; 37 lines; ruled in drypoint placing odd leaves over the even ones with the quire folded; very consistent Visigothic minuscule; one can barely discern the distinction between *ti* and *tj;* a single scribe wrote the entire manuscript; abundant commentary in the margins, almost always in the scribe's hand; thematic observations, clarification or exegetical notes, critical notes that indicate Biblical variants, liturgical indications and lexicographical comments; Aquitainian notation that appears in the Book of *Lamentations* and, without text, on fols. 2 and 37; on fol. 68v, using the same notation, two *Ite missa est* have been added.

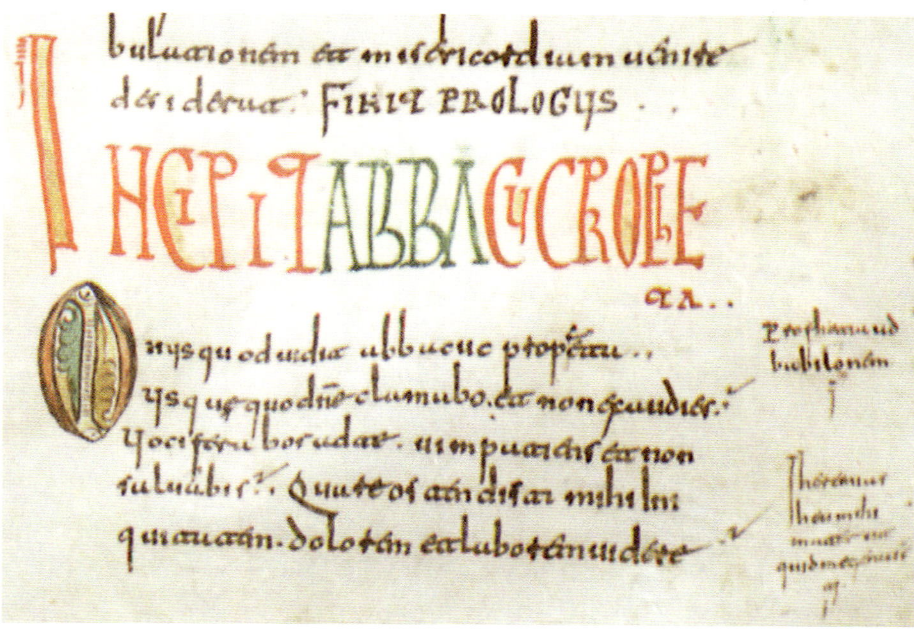

Detail of fol. 134r

General contents: A Bible that comprises the books of the four major prophets, the twelve minor prophets, Tobít, Esdras, Nehemiah, Esther, Judith and the first and second book of the Maccabees. The complete Bible must have been divided into three volumes. The first one may have been dedicated to the Historical Books and the third to the Sapiential Books and the New Testament.

Leaf shown: 70r

Trenos Iheremie prophete ubi ciuitas sue ruina quadruplici planxit alfabeto. Et factum est… Aleph. Doctrina. Quomodo sedet sola… Beth. Confusio. Plorans plorabit… Gimel. Retributio. Migrauit Iudas… Deleth. Timor. Uie Syon lugent… He. Uiam. Facti sunt… Uau. Et ille. Egressus est… Zay. Ducte. Recordata est… Heth. Pauor. Peccatum peccauit… Teth. Exclusio. Sordes eius… Ioth. Desolata. Manum suam… Caph. Curuati sunt. Omnis populus… Lameth. Cor siue seruo. O uos omnes… Mem. Uiscera alibi ex ipsis. De excelso misit ignem in ossibus [*Lamentationes* 1, 1-13].

The codex was sold in Paris along with the rest of the codices from Silos in 1878, but was acquired by the Polish prince Czartorysky, and considered lost until the end of the 20th century, when it was studied for the first time and was revealed to be from Silos.

As in other Spanish Bibles, the *Lamentations* are notated, but in this case the original has been scraped off and rewritten in Aquitainian notation. It would be quite interesting if it could be confirmed that this corresponds to an Old Spanish melody. The notator wrote some words in the margin (fol. 71v) in Carolingian minuscule, which was typical around the end of the 11th century. The diastematy is far from perfect because of the lack of space available for the neumes. In the upper margin of the leaf shown, a melody was copied that may well have been a recitation formula for the *Lamentations*. The notation makes consistent use of a *custos,* with a pronounced final stroke. The melody is basically syllabic, except at the beginning and end of each verse.

Bibliography

Vivancos 1996, 103-108.

Miguel C. Vivancos

TRENOS ID HEREMIE PROPHETE UBI EXILIUM ASSUEPUINA.

QUADRUPLICI PLANCTU PER ALFABETO.

Et factum est postquam
in captivitatem reduc
tus est Israhel et Hierusalem deserta est
sedit Hieremias flens et plan
xit lamentationem hanc in Hierusalem
et dixit. ALEPH. doctrina.
Quomodo sedet sola civitas plena
populo facta est quasi vidua domina
gentium princeps provinciarum facta
est sub tributo. BETH. confusio.
Plorans ploravit in nocte et lacrime
eius in maxillis eius non est qui conso
letur eam ex omnibus caris eius.
Omnes amici eius spreverunt eam et fac
ti sunt ei inimici. GIMEL. retributio.
Migravit Iudas propter afflictionem et
multitudinem servitutis habitavit
in gentibus nec invenit requiem.
Omnes persecutores eius adprehenderunt
eam inter angustias. DELETH. timor.
Vie Sion lugent eo quod non sint qui ve
niant ad sollemnitatem. Omnes por
te eius destructe sacerdotes eius ge
mentes virgines eius squalide
et ipsa oppressa amaritudine.
Facti sunt hostes eius in ca- HE. [illegible]
pite inimici illius locupletati sunt
quia Dominus locutus est super eam propter
multitudinem iniquitatum eius parvuli
eius ducti sunt captivi ante fa
ciem tribulantis. VAU. [illegible]
Et egressus est a filia Sion omnis decor eius

facti sunt principes eius velut arietes
non invenientes pascua et abierunt
absque fortitudine ante faciem
subsequentis. ZAI. ducat.
Recordata est Hierusalem dierum afflictio
nis sue et prevaricationis omnium
desiderabilium suorum que habuerat
a diebus antiquis cum caderet populus
in manu hostili et non esset auxilia
tor. Viderunt eam hostes et deriserunt
sabbata eius. HETH. pavor.
Peccatum peccavit Hierusalem propterea instabilis
facta est. Omnes qui glorificabant
eam spreverunt illam quia viderunt
ignominiam eius. Ipsa autem gemens
et conversa retrorsum. TETH. exclusio.
Sordes eius in pedibus eius nec recorda
ta est finis sui. Deposita est vehe
menter non habens consolatorem.
Vide Domine afflictionem meam quoniam
erectus est inimicus. IOTH. devolu[...]
Manum suam misit hostis ad omnia
desiderabilia eius quia vidit gentes
ingressas sanctuarium suum de quibus
preceperas ne intrarent in ecclesiam tuam.
CAPH. curvati sunt.
Omnis populus eius gemens et querens pa
nem dederunt pretiosa queque pro
cibo ad refocilandam animam.
Vide Domine et considera quoniam facta sum
vilis. LAMETH. [illegible]
O vos omnes qui transitis per viam attendi
te et videte si est dolor sicut do
lor meus quoniam vindemiavit me ut lo
cutus est Dominus in die furoris sui.
MEM. viscera [illegible]
De excelso misit ignem in ossibus

Liber misticus

10TH CENTURY *EX.* (975-1000, GROS) (FOL. 105R)

REAL ACADEMIA DE LA HISTORIA, MADRID, COD. 30.
PROVENANCE: MONASTERY OF SAN MILLÁN DE LA COGOLLA (LA RIOJA).
Good-quality parchment with a very white tone; in a very poor state of preservation because of water damage and various effects of the passage of time; restoration with paper grafts on leaves 113, 182, 187, 189, 190, 217-230; lacks binding; 230 leaves (with lacunae and damage); modern foliation in pencil with Arabic numerals centered in the lower margin; another modern foliation that does not coincide with the aforementioned, in pencil and smaller in size, in the upper right margin; catchwords at the end of each quire consisting of one or two words situated in the lower margin of the leaf; the leaves measure 380 × 275 mm; the writing frame measures 245/250 × 180 mm; one column, justified with triple vertical lines; there are very marked horizontal prickings in the right margin, and the vertical prickings are imperceptible; 25 lines; ruled in drypoint with the quire open; liturgical Visigothic minuscule; stems end with pronounced beveled tips, the letters have rounded profiles influenced by Carolingian minuscule; consistent use of the *tj* ligature before a vowel; decoration brutally eliminated; rubrics with interlocked letters; some initials are polychrome with interlace and zoomorphic motifs; the first letters of the verses, psalms and the beginning of the *repetenda* are filled in with red; the manuscript was written by a single scribe; very elaborate northern Visigothic notation written over the line that corresponds to the ruling of the writing frame; tendencies towards diastematy; pronounced curves in the forms of the *clivis,* the round *podatus,* the *climacus* and compound neumes formed from the *podatus;* marked accentuation of the final stroke on the *torculus* and the stems of the *podatus* and its associated compound neumes; alternating thin and thick strokes; the use of special signs (small lines over the neumes); consistent use of two signs under the text to indicate the *repetenda;* the same signs in the antiphonaries of San Juan de la Peña and León; an additional sign, abbreviations with contractions, *p* and *semp.* for *semper* (fol. 34r, text line 10: *semper;* fol. 65r, text line 5); some pieces lack notation (*Psallendum* fol. 194v).

General contents [THE POOR STATE OF PRESERVATION DOES NOT ALLOW IDENTIFICATION OF ALL THE CONTENTS]: Advent (end of the Mass of St. Acisclus and fellow martyrs) until the beginning of Lent *(Officia et Missae);* [fragmentary] *Deus pater omnipotens qui est fons et origo totius…* (fol. 1r); Mass of St. Eulalia (fol. 226r); oratio: *O quam suabes quum sonsone te Christe fideles…* (fol. 230v); *perveniamus ad gaudia repromissa, amen* [fragmentary].

Leaf shown: 105r
[AD MISSAM]
[SACRIFICIUM: Ingressus est Daniel]
… *dicens benedicite Domino.* II. *Confortavit me similitudo filii hominis.* III. *Venit Micahel princeps angelorum militie. In locum.* VESPERTINUM *Iubilate.* ANTIPHONA *Ecce Dominus noster.* VERSICULUS *A solis ortu.*

The *Liber misticus* gathers the various formularies, for office as well as Mass, of the liturgical calendar. None of the preserved *liber misticus* transmit their

Detail of fol. 65r

content in its entirety. The most complete copies, together with the Aemilianense (RAH, Cod. 30), are Silos (BL, Add. ms. 30844, 30845, 30846 and Silos, AM, Cod. 6), Toledo (BC, 35-5, 35-6 and 35-7) and Madrid (BN, ms. 10110), also from Toledo. In Portugal only a fragment, which has disappeared, was preserved in the Archivo Capitular de Santa Cruz de Coimbra. The *Sono*, seen in two verses of the leaf shown here, is a chant similar to the *Vespertinum*. Distinctly melismatic in style and responsorial in structure, it can comprise two or more verses with a more melismatic style than the verses of Responsories. The melisma written in the right margin corresponds to the last verse of the *Sono,* called *Laude,* a vocalization over the *alleluia,* in the style of a lengthy *jubilus*. It is a chant typical of the Spanish rite and is also written in the margin in other manuscripts, such as those of León, San Juan de la Peña and Silos. On the first line outside the writing frame is written a brief melisma that is independent of the melody of the longer melisma.

BIBLIOGRAPHY

FÉROTIN 1912. JANINI 1977a, 154. FERNÁNDEZ DE LA CUESTA 1980, 35. EDIT. GROS 1984, 111-224. HUGLO 1987, 1: 19-26. RUIZ GARCÍA 1997, 219-220.

Susana Zapke

dicens benedicite domino & confitemini ei allelluia ..

II Confortauit me similitudo filii hominis & dixit daniel

uenit autem annuntiare tibi & ego sum micahel princeps ma

gnus & dixi ad eum quomodo potest seruus domini

loqui cum domino suo & locutus est dicens .. benedi

III Ecce micahel princeps angelorum in militie et de

precatus est deum pro filiis istrahel ut saluarentur

omnes qui scripti sunt in libro uite & respondit mihi

angelus daniel claude sermonem & signa librum

usque ad xpistum ducem & edificetur ihrusalem & unguatur

sanctus sanctorum .. In lo cum.

Jubilate .. A Ecce dominus noster ipse fortem uelociter

ueniet & non erit deficiens neque laborans .. a solis ortu

Antiphonary (fragmentum)

10TH CENTURY *EX.* (FOL. 1R)

BRITISH LIBRARY, LONDON, ADD. MS. 11695.
PROVENANCE: MONASTERY OF SANTO DOMINGO DE SILOS (BURGOS), ALTHOUGH IT DOES NOT SEEM TO HAVE BEEN WRITTEN THERE.
The parchment is well prepared and of good quality; 19th century Beatus of Silos binding (where the fragments are inserted); the remains of the antiphonary are composed of four leaves; foliation from the 18th century in the upper right margin; the leaves measure 375 × 236 mm; the writing frame measures 296 × 221 mm; one column justified with triple vertical lines on both sides; the prickings are negligible; 15 lines; ruled in drypoint with the quire folded and the odd numbered leaves placed over the even numbered ones; very clear and elegant Visigothic minuscule; a single scribe; northern Visigothic notation.

General contents: The leaves of the antiphonary were bound with the commentary by Beatus of Liébana on the Apocalypse.

Leaf shown: 1r
... *bunt te. Deo* gratias. *Transibimu.* Laudes. *Alleluia. Gaudete iusti in Domino rectos decet laudatio.* SACRIFICIUM. *Regnum et potestas et magnitudo regni dabitur populo sanctorum alleluia. II. Consurget Micael princeps magnus et salbabitur omnis qui inuentus fuerit in libro scriptus et qui ad iustitiam erudiunt multos fulgebunt quasi stelle in perpetuas eternitates. Pertransibunt plurimi et multiplex erit scientia populo* sanctorum. VESPERTINUM. *Iubilate Domino omnes gentes quia ecce ueniet salbator omnium Deus.* VERSUS. *Letentur celi et exultet terra. Quia ecce.*

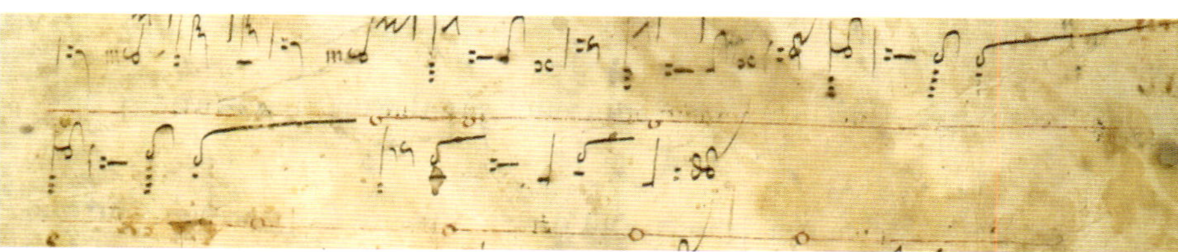

Detail of fol. 1r

The composition of the Beatus commentary was concluded in 1091 by the scribes Domingo and Muño, but the decoration was not finished until 1109 by the prior Pedro. The four antiphonary leaves must have been incorporated into the Beatus commentary at a very early date, possibly as soon as the latter was completed, from a codex that was already in a deteriorated state and from which it was desirable to preserve its most decorated leaves: the cross of Oviedo (fol. 2v) serves as the antiphonary title page; the anagram VPR over the entire page (fol. 4r), undoubtedly the beginning of the *vespertinum* for the feast of St. Acisclus, the first of the liturgical cycle, followed on the verso of the same leaf by the word LUX, also over the entire page, the first word of the first chant of the service of St. Acisclus *(Lux orta est iustis);* another cross of Oviedo (fol. 3v) which closes the antiphonary; and finally the fol. 1, which contains the end of the service of St. Romain and the beginning of the first holiday of the Advent, which is the only one that contains musical notation. On fol. 2r, possibly when it was incorporated into the Beatus, a representation of Hell was painted which bears no relation whatsoever to the antiphonary in which the leaves originated.

This fragment constitutes the remains of a magnificent antiphonary from the Spanish liturgy of which, unfortunately, the leaf shown is the only one with musical notation to have survived. It is characterized by its outstanding artistry; the *ductus* is quite conventional and elaborate, vertically arranged as is typical of manuscripts from the northern part of the Peninsula. It is worth noting the marked lengthening of the final stroke of the *pes* within compound neumes, a detail that may convey a rhythmic value, simply be a peculiar trait of the scribe or may even represent an attempt to fill in a poorly calculated space. The graphic variety of the neumes reveals the complexity of the notational system of the Spanish liturgy and the expertise of the scribe of this antiphonary. It is worth pointing out that in the lengthy *iubilus* over the final syllable of the word *eternitates* (lines 7-9), the line in red presents a series of circles that may be purely ornamental.

BIBLIOGRAPHY

DÍAZ Y DÍAZ 1983, 399-400. MILLARES CARLO ET AL. 1999, 1: 83-84. VIVANCOS 2003, 24-27.

Miguel C. Vivancos

Alle luia
Regnum et potestas et magnitudo regni dabitur populo
sanctorum alle luia
N° 98.

Liber hymnorum (fragmentum)

11TH CENTURY *IN.* (FRONT COVER PASTEDOWN)

REAL ACADEMIA DE LA HISTORIA, MADRID. FILE COD. 118 [A1; A2; B.], ADD. MS. COD. 14, PASTEDOWN ON THE FRONT COVER.
PROVENANCE: MONASTERY OF SAN MILLÁN DE LA COGOLLA (LA RIOJA).
The parchment is in a very precarious state of preservation and, to a considerable extent, illegible; lacks binding; 1 folium with stub; lacks foliation; the leaves measure 350 × 215 mm; the writing frame measures 273 × 174 mm; two columns justified with double vertical lines on either side and four vertical lines in the intercolumn; imperceptible prickings; 27 lines; ruled in drypoint; direct stamp on the rough section; Visigothic minuscule of considerable beauty, typical of the liturgical codices from the San Millán scriptorium; headings in red; miniatures of an angel pouring from a glass and of two other figures; written by a single scribe; without notation.

General contents: The fragment comes from a *Liber hymnorum* of the Visigothic rite. Hymns of St. Cucuphas, *in primitiis*, St. Cyprian, the beheading of St. John the Baptist, St. Michael the Archangel and the Sts. Faustus, Januarius and Martial.

Leaf shown: [Front cover pastedown] [… End of the hymn: *Urbis magister Tasciae* in honor of St. Cyprian of Carthage] […] *verbis docens Esperiam / Tu doctor in terra pius / Deo patri* [VERSUS] *Posui adiutorium super.*
IMNUS IN DECOLLATIONE SANCTI IOHANNIS Hic Ihoannes mire natus / Hunc tori vino repletus / Hic Dei precessit unum / Nuntiat redemptionem / Hunc rogemus abditorum / Arceat iram [superni] / Gloria Deo patri sit [VERSUS] *Educ Domine de carcere [animam]*
IMNUS IN DIE SANCTI MICAELIS ARCANGELI.

Although devoid of musical notation, this fragment of an 11th century hymnary (front cover pastedown, Cod. 14 from the 13th century) is unusual because it contains a portion of the rich hymn repertoire of the Old Spanish liturgy: the beheading of St. John (24:12), St. Michael (29:12) and the Sts. Faustus, Januarius and Martial (13:10). The fragment illustrates the configuration of the calendar, as well as the Spanish *Liber hymnorum.* Comparisons with other sources have revealed the archaic composition of the present copy. There are few remaining examples from the Spanish rite of hymns accompanied by notation since, as in the present case mostly just the text is preserved. There are two exquisite inhabited initials for the hymns of St. John (fol. recto) and St. Michael (fol. verso), which show the majestic artistry of this codex. An anagram interpreted as *Metro domni Ildefonso,* that is, "a poem by St. Ildephonsus", appears between the columns at lines 8-10, indicating the authorship of the hymns. The back cover pastedown of Cod. 14 is a leaf from a *Liber horarum* (monastic *ordo*), in which the anticipated notation was for some reason not added; this pastedown is from the same period, and possibly written by the same scribe (see the Responsories *Peculiaris vigilia.* Cod. 14 [RAH, Folder V. Cod. 118]). It is one of the rare copies, among a total of five codices and two fragments, that transmit the liturgy of the hours according to the monastic *ordo* of the Old Spanish rite, and it is the only one to represent the monastic liturgy at San Millán. This fragment contains part of the *peculiaris vigilia,* a further development of the *ordo ad medium noctis* (Saint Domingo de la Calzada, *Ordo ad nocturnos*). Both fragments, the *Liber hymnorum* and the *Liber horarum,* may have come from the same manuscript, although the latter reflects the monastic *ordo*, the former reflects the cathedral *ordo.*

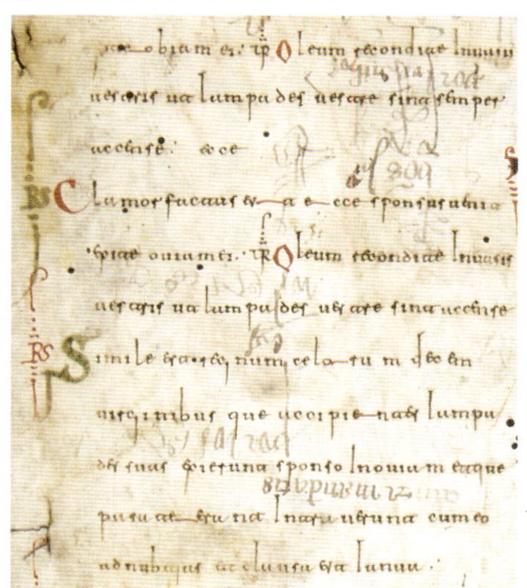
Detail of *Liber horarum* (rear pastedown)

BIBLIOGRAPHY
LOWE AND HARTEL 1887, 501. PÉREZ PASTOR 1908, 481. GARCÍA VILLADA 1923, 106. PÉREZ DE URBEL 1926, 5-21, 113-139, 209-245, 305-320. MILLARES CARLO 1932, 462. LECLERQ 1949, 91-118. PINELL 1957, 409. DÍAZ Y DÍAZ 1958, 656. MILLARES CARLO 1961, 337-444. PINELL 1964, 195-230; 1965, 122. DÍAZ Y DÍAZ 1991, 193-196. RUIZ GARCÍA 1997, 136.

Susana Zapke

uerbis docens et pretium ·
Tu doceas in actu prius
et imitaris in celestibus
quod predicas tu dogmate
sue nos attingere ppferen ·

De eo post. Positus ad uesperum sup

Ymn(us) In decollatione sci
Iohannis :

Hic Iohannes mire
nimis destruli
...scetu · unice
iudicem prophetauis
quam sta Inde edictis
preuia nascendo xpm
preuia et mortuum ·

Hunc adori uino repleatus
sanguinem lubet sui ·
qui se stuprum cedit
audax coniugalis criminis
sed factum summa coronu
laureatus glorium ·

Hic dei preseruatio unu mire
nitum filium ·
et tempore quo subsequente
pretro uterque preuia
mortis et precursor ipse
morte primus occidit ·

Nunquam sec[illegible] non
esse xpm [illegible]
uiaule muni [illegible] xpm
mortuum [illegible] xpm
probru dixit posse
mundi colligere

Hunc rogamus ab[illegible]
corda mentis [illegible]
ua scelus [illegible]
motus [illegible]
confessa [illegible]
quum p[illegible]

Atque [illegible]
pub[illegible]
patris ben[illegible] quum
sicut [illegible] donec
et [illegible] beata in
possidere perennem ·

Gloria deo patri sit [illegible]
filio sit p[illegible]
ne[illegible] sanc[illegible]
quid [illegible]
secla seculis am

E ducs ne decurrit

YMNUS IN DIE S(AN)C(T)I MICA
ELIS ARCANGELI

Guardas codice 14

Officia sanctorum

11TH CENTURY *MED.* (FOLS. 51V-52R)

HISPANIC SOCIETY OF AMERICA, NEW YORK, B 2916 (OLIM TOLEDO, BIBLIOTECA DE LA CATEDRAL, 33.2).
PROVENANCE: THE PRIMATE CATHEDRAL OF TOLEDO, BUT ORIGINALLY FROM SAN MILLÁN DE LA COGOLLA (LA RIOJA).
Parchment of varied quality, some parts are discolored by water damage; the binding is probably from the 16th century; 2 + 99 + 2 leaves; modern foliation in ink, corrected in pencil; the leaves measure 193 × 135 mm; the measurements of the writing frame vary; a single column justified with one vertical line on both sides; ruled in drypoint; the number of lines varies between 17 (fols. 1r-37v) and 16 (fols. 64r-99v); liturgical Visigothic minuscule with some subsequent additions; three scribes can be distinguished: fols. 1-78r, fols. 78v-89r and fols. 89v-90v; there are additions in Carolingian minuscule on fols. 1r, 51v-52r, 84r, 84v-85v, and in Gothic on fols. 98v-99r; northern Visigothic notation written by a single hand; Aquitainian notation on fols. 1r, 51v-52r, 84v-85v, and with letters on fols. 98v-99r.

General contents: Old Hispanic offices of St. Martin, St. Emilianus and the Assumption of the Virgin. The readings for the office of St. Martin are taken from the *Vita* de Sulpicius Severus, and those for the office of St. Emilianus come from the *Vita* of that saint by Braulio of Zaragoza.

Leaves shown: 51v-52r
[END OF THE OFFICE OF ST. MARTIN, FOL. 51v]
... nos in quacuumque... contuminet. Per. BENEDICTIO. Dominus Ihesus Christus, qui linguam beatissimi Martini ... In spe et post in re plenissime capiatis. Amen. [In the margin, in 12th century script: *Alleluia. Virga Iesse floruit uirgo Deum et hominem genuit pacem deus in se redidit reconci[li]ans imam summis.*] (fol. 52r) [VESPERTINUM] *OFFICIUM IN DIEM SANCTI EMILIANI PRESBITERI AD UESPERAS. Adesi testimoniis tuis Domine... elegi iudicia tua conmemorabi cum.*

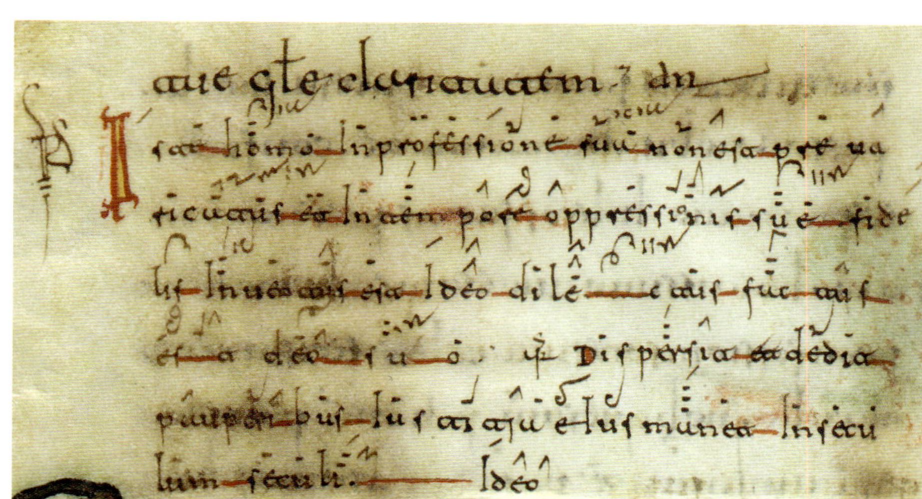
Detail of fol. 25v. Courtesy of The Hispanic Society of America, New York

The manuscript is decorated with polychrome initials comparable to those in other 11th century manuscripts from the scriptorium of San Millán. The script presents certain similarities with that of the *Liber ordinum* from the same monastery (RAH, Cod. 56). The office of St. Emilianus contained in this codex is the most complete copy known, and the office for the Assumption is unique. The subsequent additions reflect the fact that the manuscript was adapted for use after the liturgical reform carried out at the end of the 11th century. The *Alleluia* added on fols. 51v-52r is a 12th century composition. On fol. 98v, a hand from the end of the 12th century or the beginning of the 13th sketched an ascending and descending modal scale with alphabetic notation in the form of an inverted V. This diagram recalls the lambda indicated in the diagrams that illustrate St. Isidore of Seville's text *De musica,* which appears in Castilian manuscripts. A note on fol. 99r indicates the intervals between the notes of the scale.

The manuscript was preserved in the library of the Primate Cathedral of Toledo from the 15th century until at least 1869. Archer Huntington, founder of the Hispanic Society of America, purchased it between 1895 and 1910.

BIBLIOGRAPHY
BOYNTON 2002, 189-215.

Susan Boynton

nos in qua quumque supplantabit· nec mortiferis quo libet modo contami net.· Per Bno

Dns Ihs XPs qui linguam beatissimi martirim et in sui nominis confessione uicatricem· et in laudes suas in uinctione potentiorem fecit confessoris os suum aperiat in confessionibus laudis sue.· Et qui illum abstinenti(a)e fecit legibus gloriosum· uos efficiat penitentie fructibus opulentos.· Ut eam pacem quam ille conciues monitus retinendam predicauit discipulis· uos et nunc in spe et post in re plenissime capiatis.· Am

Allelu — a — Virga iesse — floruit uirgo — deum et hominem genuit

R OFFICIUM IN DIEM SCI EMILIANI PRESBITERI

adis

Adest [illegible] monitis ciuis do mine no [illegible] confundere uia manducatorum [illegible] cu cum cum dilu — [illegible] cor me um [illegible] ueri [illegible] ele gi iudici a [illegible] con me mo tibi. cum. pacem — deus in se — redigite reconcilians in omnia — summus —

Liber psalmorum, canticorum et hymnorum

11TH CENTURY *MED.* (FOL. 118V)

BRITISH LIBRARY, LONDON, ADD. MS. 30851.
PROVENANCE: MONASTERY OF SANTO DOMINGO DE SILOS (BURGOS).
High-quality parchment that is well prepared and has generous margins; 15th century binding in leather over boards; consists of 1 + 202 + 1 leaves; 18th century foliation in the upper right margin but corrected in pencil in the 19th century; the leaves measure 395 × 310 mm; the writing frame measures 273 × 220 mm; two columns justified with double vertical lines in both cases; visible prickings, the vertical ones on the edge and the horizontal ones in the right margin; 25 lines; ruled in drypoint placing odd leaves over the even ones with the quire folded; ordinary Visigothic minuscule, without Carolingian characteristics, written by a single scribe; northern Visigothic notation.

General contents: Psalms, hymns and canticles for the Spanish liturgy, to which a selection of *Liber horarum* is added.

Leaf shown: 118v
mortis perditum reducat, ad uitam Deus. *Iam iam quieti psallite, Patrique laudem dicite, Christumque laudemus pium, simulque* Sanctum *Spiritum. Hec nos redemit Trinitas, cuius perennis gloria in seculum, nescit mori uibens* per *omne seculum. Am*en. UERSUS. *Specie*m. *HYMNUS IN DIEM* SANCTE *MARIE UIRGINIS. A solis ortu cardine, et usq*ue *terre limitem Christum canam*us *princip*em, *natum Maria uirgine... I*TEM *AD MATUTINUM. Fit porta Christi* per *uia, refecta plena* gratia, *transitq*ue *rex et permanet clausa ut fuit per secula... HYMN*US *IN DIE*M SANC*TI TOME APOSTOLI. Festu*m *Christe rex per orbem inluxit almificu*m *in quo.* [In the margin, in 14th century script: *tu primero goço madre Sancta Maria*].

The manuscript's musical notation, reserved for the antiphons and other chants from various offices (written with smaller letters to leave sufficient space for the notation) is clear and precise. Only eight hymn texts are neumed (see Boynton).

This leaf is an example of the use of neumes as references to the numerous glosses added in the margins of the manuscript, a common practice in many of the codices from Silos, although lacking the precision contained in this one. The first part of the manuscript, the Psalter, has been glossed by one or two hands around the middle of the 12th century, in Carolingian script with no Visigothic vestiges. The glosses are mostly synonyms in the Vulgate, but in many other cases they consist of lexicographical or contextual commentaries. In this section, the tie-marks are not neumes. By contrast, the hymnary, glossed by several hands around the end of the 11th century, uses neumes as tie-marks. The vast majority of the glosses provide equivalents in Latin, although there are some words in the Romance vernacular.

BIBLIOGRAPHY

GILSON 1905. DÍAZ Y DÍAZ 1983, 316-317. VIVANCOS 1995, 2; 1996, 113-162. BOYNTON 1999, 244-248. MILLARES CARLO ET AL. 1999, 1: 87-88.

Miguel C. Vivancos

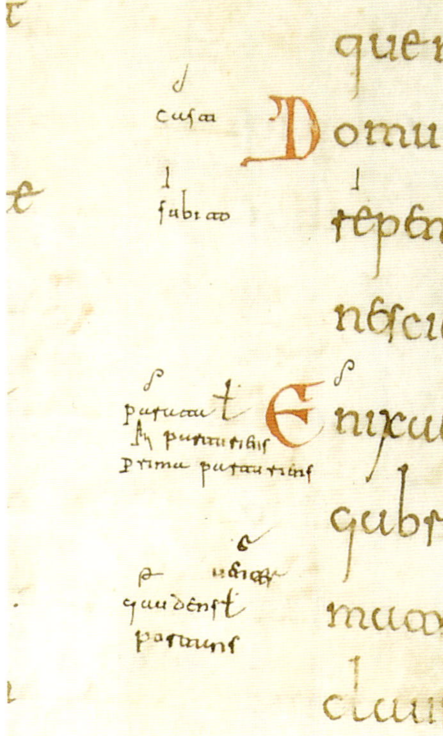

Detail of fol. 118v

mortis perdita reducat
ad uitam mundi.
Iubilum quietem psalliat
puerique laudem diciat.
xpmque laudemus pium.
simulque scm spm.
Hec nos redemit criminis.
cuius perennis gloria in scm
nescia mori uibens per omne
sctm.

Hymnus in diem scę
marie uirginis.

A solis ortus cardine. et
usque terre limitem. xpm
canamus principem.
natum
maria uirgine.
Beatus auctor scti seruile
corpus induit. ut carne
carnem liberans. non perderet
quos condidit
Clausa parentis uiscera
celestis intrat gratia. uenter
puelle baiulat. secreta
que non noberat.
Domus pudici pectoris. templum
repente fit dei. intacta
nesciens uirum. uerbo concepit filium.
Enixa est puer pera quem
gabriel predixerat. quem
matris aluo gestiens
clausus Iohannes senserat.
Fit porta xpi peruia
referta plena gratia
transitque rex et permanet
clausa ut fuit per sctu.
Genus superni numinis.
processit aula uirginis
sponsus redemptor conditor
sue gigans ecclesie.
Honor matris et gaudium.
Inmensa spes credentium.
per atra mortis pocula.
resolbit nostra crimina.

Hymnus in die scti thome apostoli

Feratur xpe rex per orbem
Inluxit almificum. In quo

Liber canticorum et horarum

May 1059 (fol. 155v)

Biblioteca General Universitaria, Salamanca, ms. 2668.
Provenance: This manuscript is thought to have been originally a possession of Sancha, Queen Consort of Ferdinand I, King of León (fol. 1r: *Sancia regina*) and of her daughter, Princess Urraca Fernández. There is evidence that it was kept in the 14th century in the old priory of Santa María de Aniago (Valladolid), which belonged to the Monastery of Silos (fol. 1r: *Iste liber est conventus Sancte Marie de Aniago; quis furatus fuerit in pa[tibulo]. suspendatur, etc. marti pa.*).
Well-preserved parchment; modern binding in blue Morocco leather for Alfonso XIII (monogram inside); 3 + 187 + 4 leaves; modern foliation in ink with Arabic numerals in the upper right margin; leaves measure 212 × 145 mm; text block 140 × 90 mm; one column, justified with double vertical lines on both sides over the entire leaf; clearly perceptible horizontal prickings in the right margin of fols. 8r-15r, and partially visible vertical prickings in the upper margin; 17 to 19 lines (when notation is included), 14 (when only text); ruled in drypoint on the inner and outer leaves of each quire; very consistent Visigothic minuscule with round strokes; links and letters: open *a*, vertical stems on the *d* and the *l* with beveled tips; smaller letters with notation; initials have zoomorphic and interlace motifs; headings in red; scribe: Christophorus (fol. 158: *In XVII kalendas iunias, era TLXLVII, Christophorus indignus scripsit*); intermittent northern Visigothic notation on fols. 144r-175v over the line that corresponds to the ruling for the text block; there are changes in the ink tone and alternating thick and fine strokes, consistent ductus with very limited range of graphic variants and even less diversity than in the manuscripts of León (ms. 8), Santiago (Reserve 1), San Juan de la Peña (M-418) and San Millán (Madrid, RAH, Cod. 30); pronounced tendency towards diastematy.

General contents: *In nomine Domini nostri Iesu Christi incipit liber canticorum de toto circulo anni era T nonagessima septima. Canticum Esaye prophete* (fol. 1v); inc.: *Dominus de Sina veniet et de Seyr ortus est nobis…* (fol. 2r); *In nomine domini Ihesu Christi explicit liber canticorum. Deo gratias* (fol. 141v); *Ordo ad medium noctis* (fol. 141v); *Ordo post nocturnis* (fol. 158v); *Ordo ad celebrandum nocturnis* (fol. 164v); *Ordo nocturnalis in resurectione domini a primo die pasce usque ad pentecosten* (fol. 173v); colophon: *Explicit liber canticorum et orarum, Deo gracias, amen. In xvii^o^ kalendas junias era TLXLVII^a^. Christophorus indignus scripsit mementote* (fol. 159v)*; Quiquunque vult salvus esse…* (fol. 176r); *Confessio: Confitebor domino Deo, sancta Maria… Omnia peccata mea quecumque peccavi ego misera et peccatrix Sancia* (overwritten *Urracka*)… (fol. 179r); *Hec est letania, id est, rogaciones* (fol. 180v).

Leaf shown: 155v
[nocturnos feria sexta]
Benedictus es Domine. Miserationes Deus miserere Deus VIa. Feria.
Responsorium *Misereatur nobis* / Versus *Inluminet Dominus* / Responsorium *De die in die* / Versus *Deus Israhel. Benedictus* / Responsorium *Exaudi me Domine quoniam benigna.*

According to Vivancos, the codex can be attributed to the initial phase of the *scriptorium* at Silos during the abbacy of St. Dominic, 1042-1073. It is purely Visigothic in style, without Carolingian influence. In the right margin, level with the tenth line, one can read *et bene,* which refers to the repetition in the responsory. The responsories are sung to melodies based on four modes, with formulaic melodic patterns for reciting the verses. In the transcription, the formulas correspond to the tones F, E and B. From a musical point of view there are notable coincidences with Salamanca, ms. 2668, and Santiago de Compostela, ms. 609 (Res. 1). The configuration of the neumes within the writing space suggests a diastematic tendency, a characteristic that does not always appear in the notation of the Old Spanish rite. Another noteworthy element is a peculiar confession formula on fol. 178r, presumably alluding to Queen Doña Sancha and her daughter Urraca.

Detail of fol. 156r

Bibliography

Ewald 1883. Férotin 1901, 62. Wagner 1928, 102-142. Rojo and Prado 1929, 23-24. Wagner 1930, 67-113. Domínguez Bordona 1933, 474, no. 1138, fig. 395. Whitehill 1934, 95-122. Sunyol 1935, 647. Pinell 1954, 146; 1955, 97-98. Millares Carlo 1963. Brockett 1968, 51-53. Randel 1969, 6, 39-49; 1973, xix. Janini 1977, 239. Fernández 1980, 166-167. Martín 1991, 89-90. Mentré 1994, 270. Vivancos 1996, 57, 65-66, 200, 306. Millares Carlo et al. 1999, 1: 174-175. *Ex-libris universitatis* 2000, no. 15. *Maravillas de la España medieval* 2001, 232-234. Lilao and Castrillo 2002, 1065-1066.

Susana Zapke

benedictus es domine. Ps. miseratione

Deus miserere deus miserere deus mise rere deus miserere deus miserere deus miserere ds miserere.. Yia FRA

Ps. Misereatur nobis et benedicat nos de us..

V. Inluminet dominus vultum suum super nos et

Ps. De die in die benedictus dominus ..

V. Deus israhel ipse dabit virtutem et fortitudinem plebis sue . benedic

Ps. Exaudi me domine quoniam benigna

Saint Ildephonsus, De virginitate Sanctae Mariae

12 October 1059 (fol. 40r)

Archivo del Monasterio de Santo Domingo de Silos (Burgos), Cod. 5.
Provenance: La Rioja (?).
Sometimes known as *Lectiones et oficia*; crude and poorly prepared parchment which uses the outer edges of the skin; 15th century binding in leather over boards; 89 leaves; 18th century foliation in the upper right margin in ink, but number 43 is omitted; the leaves measure 275 × 190 mm; the writing frame measures 201 × 133 mm; one column, justified by double vertical lines on both sides; vertical prickings visible very near the edge; the horizontal prickings run along the outer margin; 21 to 23 lines; ruled in drypoint with the quire open placing the first bifolium over the second and the fourth over the third; Visigothic minuscule written by an inexperienced scribe who constantly varies the size of the letters and commits numerous mistakes in the transcription; the scribe is Blasco; northern Visigothic notation; the neumes are deformed by a notation scribe who may not have understood their melodic significance; the texts that are accompanied by musical notation have a reduced letter size to leave sufficient room for the notation.

General contents: *De virginitate Sanctae Mariae,* by St. Ildephonsus (fols. 1r-36r); *Sermo de Sancte Marie* (fols. 436r-439v); *Officium de Sancti Martini episcopi* (fols. 40r-82v); *Inuentio uel dedicatio Sancti Micaelis arkangeli* (fols. 83r-90v).

Leaf shown: 40r
Officium de Sancti Martini episcopi ad uesperum. *Confessio et pulcritudo in conspectu Domini. Uersus. Santitas et magnificetia in sanctifitione eius. In cons. Sono. Dispersit et dedit pauperibus alleluia, iustitia eius manet in eternum alleleluia. II. Cornu eius exaltabitur in gloria allelu[ia]. Laudes. Beatus qui cogitat de pauperem in die mala salbabit eum Dominus et custodiet. Uersus* [torn]. *Beatus uir qui non habiit in consilio impiorum alleluia sed in lege Domini fuit uoluntas eius alleluia alleluia. Uersus. Gloria et diuitie. Set.*

The few notated pieces in this manuscript are from the office of St. Martin of Tours. Although the notation is clear, it is rudimentary with a very limited variety of signs, employing predominantly rounded forms. There are abundant ties for the compound neumes. Numerous syllables lack notation.

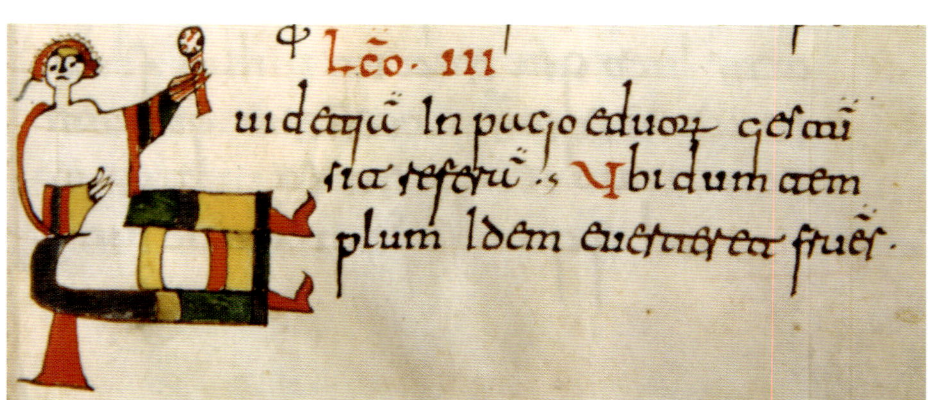

Detail of fol. 61r. Initial *Q*

Bibliography

Díaz y Díaz 1983, 473-475. González Barrionuevo 1992, 403-472. Vivancos 1995, 20. Millares Carlo et al. 1999, 1: 181-182. Ruiz Asencio 2003, 193-197.

Miguel C. Vivancos

OFFM DSCI MARTINI EPSCPI ALR

Confessio et pulcritudo in conspectu

domini. ip Sanctitas et magnifi

centia in sanctificatione eius. In cos

SNO Dispersit dedit pauperibus

alleluia. Iustitia eius manet in seculum

alleluia. V Cornu eius exal

tabitur in gloria alleluia

tr. Beatus qui cogitat de paupere in die mala

liberabit eum dominus et custodiet. ip

Beatus vir qui non abiit in consilio impiorum

alleluia sed in lege domini fuit voluntas eius

alleluia alleluia. R Gloria et... sec

Antiphonary

11TH CENTURY *EX.* (FOL. 239V)

BRITISH LIBRARY, LONDON, ADD. MS. 30850.
PROVENANCE: MONASTERY OF SANTO DOMINGO DE SILOS (BURGOS).
A well-prepared parchment of excellent quality; 20th century binding; comprises 1 + 241 + 1 leaves; 18th century foliation in the upper right margin. The numbers 52, 132, 154, 157 and 222 are repeated; corrected in pencil in the 19th century; the leaves measure 330 × 244 mm; the writing frame measures 231 × 196 mm; one column justified with a double vertical line in the interior margin and a triple vertical line on the outside margin; vertical prickings are visible at the edge and horizontal prickings in the right margin; 15 lines; ruled in drypoint, leaf by leaf on the grain side; very consistent Visigothic minuscule, with no apparent Carolingian characteristics; one scribe for the entire manuscript except for some additions; northern Visigothic notation with Aquitainian influence; some chants with modal indications and melodic intonation formulas.

General contents: A Franco-Roman Antiphonary for monastic use preserved in its entirety to which some offices have been added, similar to the one at Santo Domingo de Silos, and the remains of a tonary in Carolingian minuscule (fols. 235-241), but almost completely scraped and rewritten.

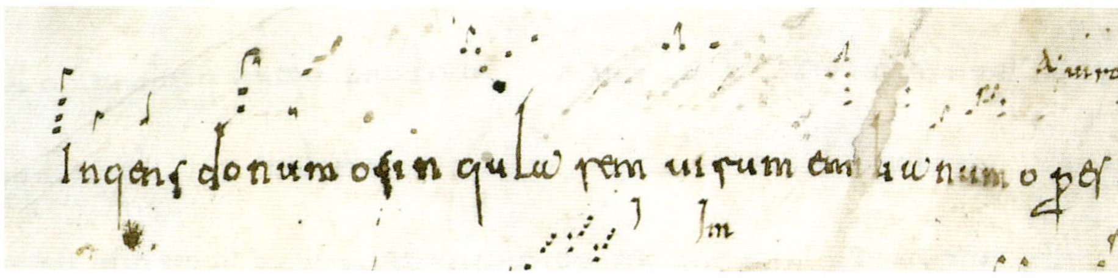

Detail of fol. 239v

Leaf shown: 239v
Ingens donum o singularem uirum Emilianum, o prestantisimum eius animum. RESPONSORIUM. *Beatissimi uiri a Deo electi sanctissimi Dominici hodierna die sollemniter celebremus sollemnia, cuius intercessio ueneranda refulget.* VERSUS. *Beate hac gloriosyssime Dominice pater ora pro nobis pium et redemptorem nostrum. Hodier.* DE SANCTA *MARIA.* RESPONSORIUM. *Stirps Gesse...* VERSUS. *Uirgo Dei genitrix...* RESPONSORIUM. *Ad nutum Dominum...* VERSUS. *Ut uicinum...* Responsorium. *Lauerunt stolas...* Versus. *Isti sunt... [G]loria Patri...*

Although the antiphonary is written in Visigothic minuscule and Spanish notation, it follows the Roman monastic *cursus* which corresponds to the time when the Spanish liturgy had been replaced by the Franco-Roman. Considerable space is left between the lines for the musical notation, which is clear and precise. The melodies come from the Gregorian repertoire. The leaf reproduced here is one of those remaining from a Carolingian prosary, of which the remains can be seen on the right side of the page. The note in Visigothic minuscule says: "Episcopus karnotensis eglesie Sancte Marie nomine Iuo", referring to Ivo de Chartres, Bishop from 1090 to 1116, which suggests that the tonary comes from there and was incorporated into a recently completed antiphonary in the Silos collection around that time. It is difficult to define the different typologies in the notation of the tonary, although they present some influence from Brittany. At a subsequent date, these leaves were reused at the Monastery of Silos for its own pieces, among which was the office, almost in its entirety, of the abbot St. Dominic, deceased in 1073. In this case, as in the rest of the codex, the notation is Visigothic, even though the repertoire is Gregorian with local variations. Finally, in the leaf's upper and lower margins there are numerous annotations in Aquitainian notation, mostly initia and terminations, which are considered to be among the first examples of this notation written in the Peninsula.

BIBLIOGRAPHY

EDIT. CAO 1965, VOL. 2. EDIT. FACS. FERNÁNDEZ DE LA CUESTA 1976, 233-256. DÍAZ Y DÍAZ 1983, 316. FERNÁNDEZ DE LA CUESTA 1985. ZAPKE 1996, 247, 250, 255, 281-360. MILLARES CARLO ET AL. 1999, 1: 87. VIVANCOS 2002, 63-84. ASENSIO 2003, 482-487.

Miguel C. Vivancos

Clamaui clam... Mentem sanctam Seruite domino

laudate dnm Dominum est cons...

Gloria seculorum amen.

Omnes Factus Inplorauerit

A uiro iniquo

Ingens donum est singularem uirum cum ... o per amcissimum eius unum

RS Beatissimi uiri adeo electi sanctissimi dominici

hodiernum diem sollemnizat celebremus sollempn...

cuius intercessio ... effulsit

V Eia — hunc gloriosissime dominice ora pro nobis

pium ... nostrarum hodie ... mente sanctam

Gloria patri et filio et spiritui sancto.

Gloria patri et filio et spiritui sancto.

Iuxta

Gloria amen

Sacerdotes Inuenimus compete

RS Stirps Iesse — uir — gam produxit uirgaque florem

et super hunc florem requiescit spiritus almus

V Virgo dei genitrix uirgo est flos filius eius

RS Adoremus — dominum nostrum diuinitatis honore sicut

spinam rosam genuit Iudea mariam

... uicinorum uirtutis operis gratia culpa sicut

RS Isti ... lauerunt stolas suas et candidas eas fecerunt

in sanguine agni. V Isti sunt

qui uenerunt ex magna tribulatione et lauerunt stolas suas. In san...

Gloria patri et filio et spiritui sancto In sanguine

... in manu mea

Omnis terra Sicut populi Sicut oculi

In necessitatibus Deus in nomine Iudicante

Dixit dominus Gloria seculorum amen

Reminiscere Reformat Misericordia

In uoluntate

Vidimus Videns dns Magnam gloria

Ab occultis meis Tecum iudicium dominus

Acceptabis Exultabit filia Erubescant

Hierusalem R Resnoster Ecce agnus

Gloria ...

Gloria seculorum amen. Alleluia alleluia alleluia alleluia

In omnem terram Omnes gentes ... alleluia alleluia alleluia alleluia alleluia

alleluia alleluia alleluia

Gloria seculorum amen.

Quinque prudentes intrauerunt ad nuptias.

Christi uirgo alleluia alleluia alleluia

alleluia alleluia

Breviary

11TH CENTURY *EX.* (FOL. 15V)

BRITISH LIBRARY, LONDON, ADD. MS. 30847.
PROVENANCE: MONASTERY OF SANTO DOMINGO DE SILOS (BURGOS).
Good-quality, well-prepared parchment; 20th century binding; comprises 2 + 186 + 2 leaves, foliated in the upper right corner in the 18th century; numbers 69, 76, 134 and 183 are repeated and 149 and 151 are omitted; new foliation in pencil from the 19th century; the leaves measure 333 × 211 mm; the text block measures 233 × 140 mm; one column justified with a simple vertical line on each side; the vertical prickings are visible at the edge; the horizontal prickings run along the right margin; 25 lines; ruled in drypoint, one bifolium at a time on the hair side; Visigothic minuscule with no evident Carolingian characteristics, written by a single scribe throughout the manuscript; northern Visigothic notation with obvious Aquitainian influence oriented around the drypoint line that corresponds to the ruling of the text block.

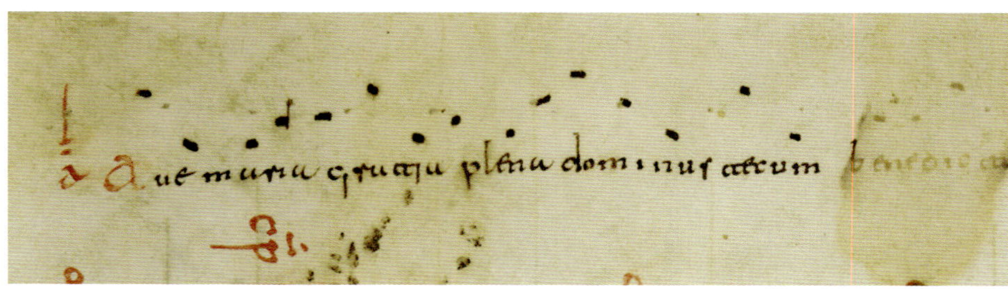

Detail of fol. 15v

General contents: A Roman monastic breviary that in its present state covers the period from the second Sunday of Advent until the Wednesday of the fourth week of Lent.

Leaf shown: 15v
Et aspera in uias planas. Ueni Domine et noli tardare, alleluia. Seuouae. ANTIPHONA. *Dominus ueniet, occurrite illi dicentes: magnum principium et regni eius non erit finis; Deus fortis, dominator, princeps pacis, alleluia, alleluia. Seuouae.* ANTIPHONA. *Omnipotens sermo tuus Domine a regalibus sedibus uenit, alleluia. Seuouae.* [G]*loria seculorum amen.* CAPITULA. *Confortate manus dissolutas et genua deuilia rouorate; dicite pusillanimis: confortamini et nolite timere.* Deo gratias. RESPONSORIUM. *Festina. Vox clara.* ORATIO. *Excita* Domi*ne potentia.* PER *OMNES ORAS DIEI* CAPITULA. *Qui uenturus est ueniet et non tardauit, iam non erit timor in fini*bus *no*stri*s quonia*m *ipse est saluator no*ster*.* Deo gratias. ORATIO. *Preces populi tui* quesumus *Domi*ne *clementer exaudi, ut qui de aduentu Filii tui unigeniti* secundum *carne*m *letantur, in seculo cum uenerit in magestate sua premiu*m *eterne uite percipiant.* Per *eundem... I*TEM *AD UESPERVM.* CAPITULA. *Gaudete in* Domi*no semp*er, *iterum dico: gaudete. Modestia* uestra *nota sit omnibu*s *hominibu*s; Domi*nus prope est.* Deo gratias. ORATIO. *Excita* Domi*ne potentia ut supra. I*TEM *PER OMNES EBDOMAS DE ADUENTUM* DOMI*NI USQUE AD NATALE* DOMI*NI.* CAPITULA. *Gaudete in* Domi*no.* CAPITULA. *Nolite ante tempu*s *iudicare.* [Vertical, in the margin: ANTIPHONA. *Aue Maria gratia plena Dominus tecum benedicta tu in mulieribus alleluia. Benedictus* Domi*nus* Deu*s* I*s*ra*hel. Seuou ae.* In the lower margin, in a Gothic cursive: *In Dei nomine et eius gratia. In Dei nomine et eius gratia*].

To include musical notation, the text ruling was left blank over the pieces that were supposed to be notatedand their texts were written in letters of smaller size. This format is discontinued after fol. 85. In comparison to that of other contemporary manuscripts, the notation does not present an excessive diversity of graphemes. The antiphons are accompanied by their corresponding psalmic terminations. There is a preponderance of the *punctum* with respect to other graphemes and, in these cases, there is a noticeable intention of diastematy, highlighted by the fact that the notation uses the lines of the text ruling as its point of reference. The melodies are from Franco-Roman repertoire, as in the model from which this manuscript was copied, and represent the period of transition from the Spanish liturgy to the Franco-Roman.

BIBLIOGRAPHY

DÍAZ Y DÍAZ 1983, 315. WALKER 1998, 49 *ET PASSIM.* MILLARES CARLO ET AL. 1999, 1: 87.

Miguel C. Vivancos

et aus peru Inuia plunas ueni domine et noli tardare alle

luia . Seuouae . a Dominus ueniet occurrite illi di

centes magnum principium et regni eius non erit finis deus

fortis dominator princeps pacis alleluia alleluia . Seuouae .

a Omnipotens sermo tuus domine a regalibus sedibus ueniet alle

Gloria seculorum amen

luia . Seuouae . cp Confortate manus dissolutas et genua debilia roborate dicite pusillanimis confortamini et nolite timere . dg . RS Festina . V op durū

or Excita dne potentiam . Domi otus diei . cp Qui uenturus est ueniet et non tardabit iam non erit timor in finibus nostris quoniam ipse est saluator noster . dg .

or Preces populi tui quesumus dne clementer exaudi ut qui de aduentu filii tui unigeniti secundum carnem letantur in secundo cum uenerit in maiestate sua premium eterne uite percipiant . per eundem . Ad uesperum .

cp Gaudete in dno semper iterum dico gaudete modestia uestra nota sit omnibus hominibus dns prope est . dg .

or Excita dne potentiam . ut . In per omnes ebdomadas de aduentum dni usque ad natale dni .

cp Gaudete in dno . cp Nolite ante tempus iudicare

In dei nomine zelestia In dei nomine zelestia

a Aue maria gratia plena dominus tecum benedicta tu in mulieribus alleluia . Benedictus dns ds israhel . Seuouae .

Liber ordinum

May 18, 1052 (fol. 229v)

Archivo del monasterio de Santo Domingo de Silos (Burgos), Cod. 4 (olim Codex A vel B).
Origin: Monastery of San Prudencio de Monte Laturce (La Rioja).
Superbly prepared parchment with wide margins; 19th century binding; 3 + 346 + 3 leaves; foliation in ink in the upper right margin from the 18th century, in which numbers 9 and 171 are repeated; in the lower left-hand margin, there is modern foliation in pencil without errors which usually follows the old numeration; the leaves measure 293 × 215 mm; the writing frame measures 195 × 139 mm; one column justified with double vertical lines on both sides; visible vertical prickings very close to the edge; the horizontal prickings run along the right margin so close to the edge that in many cases they have disappeared due to trimming; 26 lines on fols. 4-7, 20 in the rest of the manuscript; ruled in drypoint placing odd leaves over the even ones with the quire folded; very well formed Visigothic minuscule, clear, firm and large with a thick stroke, common among manuscripts for liturgical use; the scribe is Bartolomé, until fol. 342r; the remainder of the manuscript was copied by two hands quite similar to Bartolomé but of inferior quality; very abundant, and quite meticulous, northern Visigothic notation; the texts with neumes use smaller letters to leave sufficient room for the notation.

General contents: Calendar (fols. 1r-3r); *Orologium* (fol. 4r); declaration of festivities (fols. 4v-5r); *In nomine Domini. Incipit liber ordinvm ex patrvm ordine collectvm in vnvm. Incipivnt brebes eiusdem* (fols. 6r-7v); *Item alium ordinem* (fols. 7v-8v); *In nomine domini nostri Ihesv Christi. Incipit liber ordinum de ordinibvs eclesiasticis* (fols. 8v-332r); *Ordo ad talamum benedicendvm* (fols. 332r-v); *Ordo nubentvm* (fols. 332v-338v); *Missa de hostibus* (fols. 339r-343v); *Item missa uotiba de anniuersario defuncto* (fols. 343v-344v).

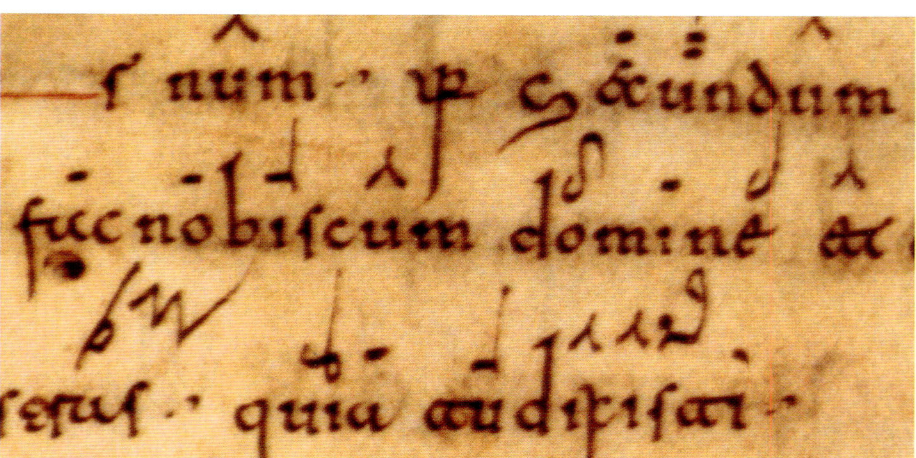

Detail of fol. 342r

Leaf shown: 229v
… melius est uotum… Psallendum. Uota mea Domino reddam in atriis domus Domini. Uersus. Disrupisti uincula mea tibi sacrificabo hostiam laudis. In a. Alium Psallendum. Disrumpe Domine uincula peccatorum meorum ut sacrificem tibi hostiam laudis. Uersus. Tribulationem et dolorem inueni et nomen Domini inuocabi, obsecro Domine liuera animam meam. Ut. Epistola Pauli apostoli ad Romanos.

From a musical point of view, this manuscript is extremely important not only for the excellent quality of the notation but also for containing in the margin of fol. 144r a copy of three antiphons of the *Mandatum* in Aquitainian notation while preserving the Spanish neumes in the body of the text. Therefore, these are among the few pieces in the Spanish repertoire that can be transcribed precisely. In the margin of fol. 181v is the Responsory *Stola uite,* from the office of St. Dominic of Silos. It is worthy to note other *probationes* of Aquitainian notation. The unusual form of the *clivis* of the second scribe (fol. 342r), drawn with two almost curved strokes joined at their vertex, is also noteworthy. The *psallendum* chants transmitted here are responsorial in style, characterized by a more elaborate melodic development.

Bibliography

Edit. Férotin 1904. Rojo and Prado 1929, 71, 80-81 *et passim.* Díaz y Díaz 1979, 76-79. Asensio 1991, 35-42. Edit. Janini 1991. González Barrionuevo 1992, 403-472. Vivancos 1996, 385-387; 2002a, 201-225; 2006, 122-124.

Miguel C. Vivancos

melius est uotum non uouere.
quam post uotum promissa
non reddere. Ne dederis os tuum
ut peccare facias carnem tuam.
neque dicas coram angelo ~~angelo~~.
non est prouidentia. Ne forte
iratus ds super sermone tuo dissipet
cuncta opera manuum tuarum.
Ubi multa sunt somnia plurime
uanitates et sermones innumeri. tu uero dm time. PSL.

Uota mea domino reddam
in atriis domus domini
VR. Dirupisti uincula mea
tibi sacrificabo hostiam laudis. Inu

ALIUS PSL. Disrumpe domine uincula peccatorum
meorum ut tibi sacrificem tibi hostiam
laudis. VR. Tribulationem et dolorem
inueni et nomen domini inuocaui. O obsecro
domine libera animam meam. ut

EPISTOLA PAULI APOSTOLI AD ROMANOS.

Liber horarum (fragmentum)

10TH CENTURY *EX.*-11TH CENTURY *IN.* (FOL. 2R)

ARCHIVO CAPITULAR, SANTO DOMINGO DE LA CALZADA (LA RIOJA), W./O. S. (OLIM D. NO. 4).
PROVENANCE: MONASTERY OF SAN MARTÍN DE ALBELDA (RUIZ ASENCIO).
The parchment is in a very precarious state of preservation; the external leaves 1r and 2v are illegible; the ink is smeared from humidity; used as the binding for another volume; subsequent inscription: "Libro de muchas donaciones hechas por diversas personas a esta iglesia de Señor Sancto Domingo de la Calçada en el qual se contienen muchas antigüedades"; one bifolium; lacks foliation indications; the leaves measure 275 × 210 mm; the writing frame measures 210 × 130 mm; one column justified with double vertical lines on both sides; in the present state of the fragment the prickings are negligible; 22 lines; ruled in drypoint; Visigothic minuscule of excellent artistry; primary initials are filled in with blue, orange and green ink; secondary initials are in red ink; common abbreviations and punctuation signs; distinguishes between the *ti* and *tj* ligature; written by a single scribe; northern Visigothic notation *in campo aperto*, alternating thick and thin strokes; the *ductus* is less elaborate than in other northern Visigothic codices; the ink of the notation is darker than that used for the text.

General contents: Part of the *Officium ad nocturnos*.

Leaf shown: 2r
[AD NOCTURNOS]
[RESPONSORIUM Benedicam Domino]
VERSUS *In Domino laudabitur anima mea.* RESPONSORIUM *Adiutor et liberator meus.* VERSUS *Exaudi orationem meam.* YMNUS *Tu rex redemtor omnium qui cuncta. Nocturnis horis surgimus. Ut turba quicquid demonum. Ne ipsa plebs nequissima. At nunc gementes poscimus* CONPLETURIA *Splendor indeficiens lucis eterne.*

The Archivo Capitular de Santo Domingo de la Calzada preserves, in addition to three leaves belonging to a cartulary in Visigothic script two other fragments from codices that are also Visigothic and of disputed provenance. The first explicit mention of these fragments appears in an article by María Luisa Povés (1952). Here, only a leaf from the second fragment is reproduced because it contains northern Visigothic notation. The other fragment, which is also composed of one double leaf, is from a Psalter in Visigothic minuscule typical of the north of the peninsula and dated between the 10th century *ex.* and the 11th century.

Based on paleographic and codicological characteristics, Ruiz Asencio suggests Albelda as this fragment's place of origin, and Miguel C. Vivancos points out a certain affinity with Cod. 5 from Santo Domingo de Silos.

The fragment reproduced here presents a series of characteristics which approach the typology of a *liber horarum,* a book devoted to the hours of the monastic office, or the typology of a *liber misticus,* a volume which contains the repertoire of the office and the Mass of the entire liturgical calendar rather than the characteristics of a breviary as indicated by Povés in the above-mentioned article. The two transcribed responsorial verses represent tones B and C of the Spanish modal system from the tradition from La Rioja, according to Randel's classification. In tone B, which is bipartite in structure, the first syllable is accompanied by a *punctum,* whereas the second intonation—not adjusted to the textual accent—consists of a *scandicus* with four elements, depending on the length of the text. The final cadence consists of two elements. Tone C is characterized by a bipartite structure and a final cadence with three elements. The intonation adjusted to the textual accent is similar to

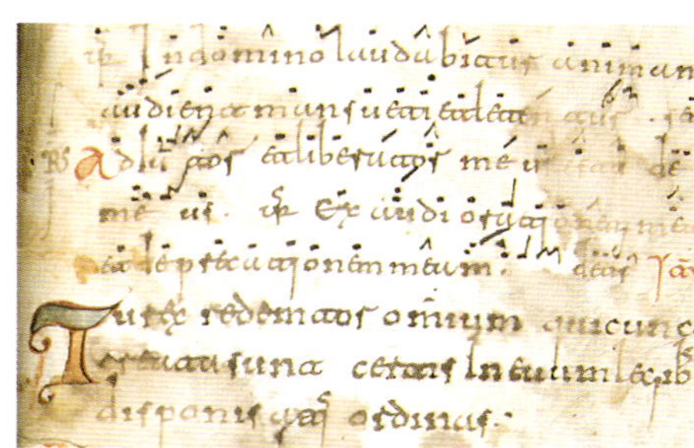

Detail of fol. 2r

that of tone B. The second intonation is adjusted to the last textual accent. The final cadence consists of three elements. There is a possible affiliation with the fragment of the Psalter from the Archivo de la Real Chancillería de Valladolid (Parchment Collection, Folder 1, no. 3) and with the fragment from Valbanera (Bible, Folder. 1, no. 3).

BIBLIOGRAPHY

EDIT. *RH* 1892-1921, 2: 681, 699. MENÉNDEZ PIDAL, 1919, 113. MILLARES CARLO 1931, 134; 1932, 454. POVÉS 1952, 517-520. PINELL 1964, 213. RANDEL 1969, 78, 110-111, 124-125. MILLARES CARLO ET AL. 1999, 1: 177-178.

Susana Zapke

R. In domino laudabitur anima mea
audiant mansueti et letentur. alleluia.
V. Adiutor et liberator meus esto deus meus. R. Exaudi orationem meam
et deprecationem meam. ... Ymn.

Tu Christe redemptor omnium quicumque
tempora certis in tuis legibus
disponis et ordinas.

Nocturnis horis surgimus ut
in quo pandimus nostri oris organum
et laudamus hymnis dulcibus.

Ut acturba quicquid damnosum corripiat
usque proprio puniendo cursu omnia
et dominatione confisus.

Ne ipsa plebs nequissima invicatrix
cunctis criminis nos ad perhenne
incendium secum cremandos deferat.

At nunc gementes poscimus auximdi
potentiam ut nos ab omni liberos
reddas citius piaculo. Psallat. Capitula

Splendor indeficiens lucis aeterne
sanctifica nobis a tenebris noctis ostende.

Antiphonary (fragmentum)

10TH CENTURY *EX.* (FOL. 8R)

BIBLIOTECA GENERAL UNIVERSITARIA, ZARAGOZA, M-418.
PROVENANCE: MONASTERY OF SAN JUAN DE LA PEÑA (HUESCA).
ORIGIN: SANTA MARÍA LA REAL DE NÁJERA (DÍAZ Y DÍAZ).
Very poorly preserved parchment; damage, wax and water stains render the texts partially illegible; in the upper and lower margins, the fragment was cut in order to thread a strip through it when the fragment was used in the 16th century as a binding for the *Historia de los santos Voto y Félix*, by a monk of San Juan de la Peña known as Macario; an eight-leaf fragment (fragmentary with interspersed lacunae) from an original of around 300 leaves; the leaves measure 348 × 270 mm; the writing frame measures 265 × 175 mm (with variations on several leaves); modern foliation in the upper right margin; one column ruled with triple vertical boundary lines on both sides; 16 lines; horizontal prickings in the outer left margin of the verso leaves; the vertical prickings are imperceptible; ruled in drypoint on the hair side with the quire open; exquisitely formed Visigothic minuscule in black ink written with a quill with a symmetricaltip; very upright stems with a beveled tip; syllables with a melisma are separated by a ruling line colored red; magnificent initials with anthropomorphic and interlace motifs, such as the main initial R; copied by a single hand; *Probationes calami* and subsequent annotations from the 12th and 17th centuries; beautifully drawn northern peninsular Visigothic notation, adiastematic and *in campo aperto*, with a great variety of graphic forms, as well as special signs indicating repetition and others with expressive meaning.

General contents: St. Vincent, office and Mass (fols. 1r-3v); St. Thyrsus and companions (fols. 4r-v); St. Agatha, office (fols. 4v-5v); St. Agatha, Mass (fols. 5v-6r); St. Dorothy, office and Mass (fols. 6r-v); Chair of St. Peter, Mass (fol. 7r); Sts. Emeterius and Celedonius, office and Mass (fols. 7v-8r); Sunday "ad carnes tollendas" (fol. 8r-v).

Leaf shown: 8r
*[ALLELUIATICUM. OFFICIUM IN DIEM SANCTORUM EMETERI ET CELEDONI, AD VESPERUM.]... iniquitas obduravit. VERSUS Beati inmaculati. RESPONSORIUM Viri sancti germinate. Versus Germinate iusti. Sicut. DE PSALMO Da nobis let*itiam. *DE CANTICO Letitia. BENEDICTIONES Omnes sancti serbi. Sono Beati qui cus*todiunt. *ad missam. PRELEGENDUM Splendore repleti. PSALLENDUM Da nobis auxilium. VERSUS In Deo faciemus. In tribulatione. Laudes Alleluia. Gaudete iusti. SACRIFICIUM Hec dicit Dominus. OFFICIUM IN DOMI*NICO *ANTE CARNES TOLLENDAS [AD VESPERUM]. VESPERTINUM Sacrificate sacrificium vespertinum.*

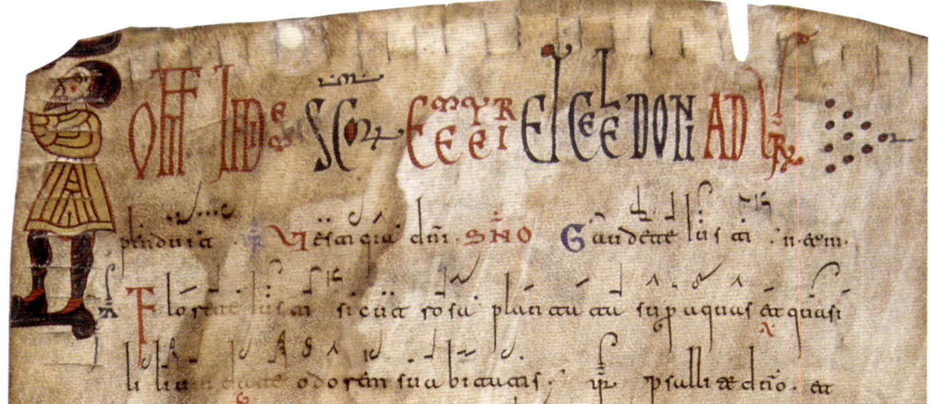

Detail of fol. 7v

The Visigothic codices transmit the office and Mass repertoire in a single volume. The order of Mass is identical for the *ordo monasticum* and the *ordo cathedralis,* whereas the cursus of the office in the *ordo monasticum* includes more pieces. The Mass of the Visigothic rite was closely connected to the hours of the divine office, which explains why liturgical books, include the offices *ad vesperum, ad matutinum* and *ad missam*. The office of the martyrs Emeterius and Celedonius from Calahorra (March 3), which is complete in San Juan de la Peña and typical in the Spanish rite's calendar of saints' days, does not appear in the Antiphonary of León, perhaps due to the rule of not celebrating the calendar's festivities during Lent. It is impossible to obtain a reliable transcription of the melodies given the lack of a tonal reference and an unambiguous interpretation of the notational signs. Rather, these seem to reflect an oral tradition in which graphic visualization, far from offering a literal transcription, served as a mnemonic aid for learning the melodies.

With respect to the tonal system, before the octoechos, the Spanish tradition is based on a structure of four or five tonal formulas that articulate the whole of its melodic repertoire. Santa María la Real de Nájera is the place of origin; San Juan de la Peña is not (Díaz y Díaz).

BIBLIOGRAPHY

UBIETO ARTETA 1950, 191-204. BROU 1952a, 35-65. RANDEL 1973; 1985, 229-238. EDIT. FACS. *ANTIPHONALE HISPANIAE VETUS* 1986. HUGLO 1987, 1: 19-26. ZAPKE 1992, 155-183; 1994, 509-517; 1995b; 2002a, 5: 1556; 2002b, 5: 1556-1557. *SANCHO EL MAYOR Y SUS HEREDEROS* 2006, 2: 588-589 (GALTIER MARTÍ).

Susana Zapke

Liber ordinum

JANUARY 1039 (FOL. 168R)

ARCHIVO DEL MONASTERIO DE SANTO DOMINGO DE SILOS (BURGOS), COD. 3 (OLIM CODEX B).
ORIGIN: MONASTERY OF SANTA MARÍA LA REAL OF NÁJERA (?) (LA RIOJA).
Rather coarse and poorly prepared parchment, often using the edge of the skin; 15th century binding, leather over boards; 1 + 173 + 1 leaves; 18th century foliation in ink appears in the upper right margin; the number 119 is repeated four times and the numbers 32, 52, 80-89, 91, 115, 117, 125, 127 and 167 are omitted; the leaves measure 250 × 180 mm; the writing frame measures 190 × 133 mm; one column justified with double vertical lines on both sides; only in some cases are the prickings visible; the vertical ones have disappeared as a result of trimming; the horizontal ones run along the right margin very close to the edge; 20 lines, with some exceptions; ruled in drypoint with unfolded quires, placing the first bifolium over the second and the fourth over the third; Visigothic minuscule which broadens considerably with a point at the upper end of the stems; its appearance is, in general, messy and gives the impression that it was written in haste; the scribe was Juan, at least for fols. 7-179 (although fols. 90-106 appear to be written by another scribe); northern Visigothic notation; the result is less than graceful and, at times, deformed, with a tendency towards curvature; the compound neumes are somewhat imprecise; the notated texts are written in letters of reduced size to leave sufficient space for the neumes.

General contents: Calendar (fols. 1r-6v); *Liber ordinum* (fols. 7r-179v); *Officium de adsumtio Sancte Marie* (fols. 180r-201v). On fol. 106v, added in a note in Visigothic minuscule, are some quantities of cereal, measured in *almudes*, that some individuals received or delivered. All the names are Mozarabic.

Leaf shown: 168r
... *et* spiritu*s tui sancti infusione benedicas Christe.* P*OST* PR*IDIE: Benedic* Domin*e huic ostie in onorem tui* nomin*is oblate et summentiu*m *ex ea sanctifica mente*m *et purifica uoluntatem. Amen.* A*D* ORATIONEM*: Malo*rum *nostro*rum, *f*ratre*s d*ilectissi*mi, memores, lacrimosas preces* Domin*i dirigam*us *ad aures; quo mundati a uitiis liuere ad eu*m *proclame*mus *e terris:* Pater. B*E*NEDICTI*O: Ch*ristu*s Domi*nu*s qui est uita mortaliu*m *auferat a uob*is *om*ne*s maculas delicto*rum. Amen. *Induat uos decore uirtutu*m *et donet uob*is *consortiu*m *angelo*rum. *Ut probauiles fide et opere inmaculati perueniatis ad eterna*m *hereditate*m. A*D* UESPERUM. O*RDO DE COTIDIANO INFRA EBDOMADA IIª* FERIA. *Usque ad uesperum quam magnificata sunt opera tua* Domin*e.* ANTIPHONA. *Adimplentis letitia cum uultu tuo Domine.* U*E*RSU*S. Delectationes.* ANTIPHONA. *Adimplenor* [sic] *letitia alleluia cum uultu tuo Domine alleluia.* [In the margin: U*E*RSU*S. Ut cognoscam*us]. *Inmense celi conditor, qui mixta ne confundere, aqua fluenta diuidens, celum dedisti limitem.*

The notation here, limited to the antiphons of the office for the evening prayers, presents the characteristics that have already been pointed out, which show that this is the work of a musical scribe with limited skills.

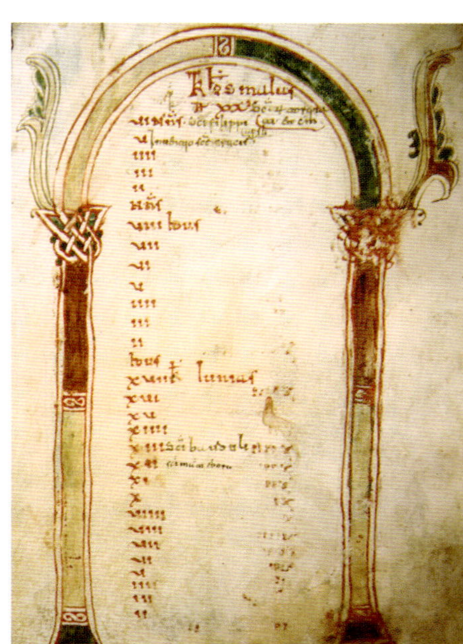

Detail of fol. 1r (May calendar)

BIBLIOGRAPHY
FÉROTIN 1904. JANINI 1981a. DÍAZ Y DÍAZ 1983, 471-473. GONZÁLEZ BARRIONUEVO 1992, 403-472. MILLARES CARLO ET AL. 1999, 1: 180. RUIZ ASENCIO 2003, 202-205.

Miguel C. Vivancos

et sps tui sci infusione benedicat. Xpe PS PRDE

Benedic dne hunc ostie in honorem tuum nris oblatam. et sumentia quum ecce scifica mane. et purifica voluntatem. amen. AD ORONEM

Dolor eror frm dltm manorer lacrimosus precor dne dirigunt ad aures. Quo mundum a magis lugere a deum proclamant securis. pr BNO

Xps dns quem ita vitam mortalium assumpsit a nos omnes maculis delictorum. amen. Induat vos decore instantiam. et donet vos consortium angelorum. Ut probabiles fide et opere immaculatam perveniatis ad regna tua hereditate.

AD ORDO DE COTIDIANO INFRA EBDOMADA II F.

Uiquique adu... quam magnificata sunt opera tua dne.

A. Adimpleatur laude cum cantatio domine. ps Delectasti me.

A. Adimpleatur laude alleluia cum cantatio domine alleluia.

Inmense celi conditor. qui mixta ne confundere aqua fluenta dividens. celum dedisti limitem.

Liber misticus

11TH CENTURY *MED.* (FOL. 25R)

ARCHIVO DEL MONASTERIO DE SANTO DOMINGO DE SILOS (BURGOS), COD. 6.
ORIGIN: MONASTERY OF SANTA MARÍA LA REAL OF NÁJERA (?) (LA RIOJA).
Traditionally known as the *Breviarium gothicum,* although strictly speaking it is a *liber Misticus*; paper (quite probably the first in Europe) and parchment, generally of good quality and well prepared; 20th century binding; consists of 1 + 157 + 1 leaves; 18th century foliation, in ink, in the upper right margin; numbers 6, 118 and 125 are repeated; the leaves measure 195 × 145 mm; the writing frame measures 148 × 92 mm; one column justified with a single vertical line on both sides; the paper leaves are not ruled; the vertical prickings are visible on the edge; the horizontal prickings run along the outside margin; the number of lines varies from 14 to 16; ruled in drypoint placing odd leaves over the even ones with the quire folded; large Visigothic minuscule, quite consistent, with no trace of Carolingian influence; at least two scribes, one for the paper leaves (fols. 1-37) and another for the leaves in parchment (fols. 38-154); northern Visigothic notation exhibiting similarities to that of the Antiphonary of León, especially on the parchment leaves; the texts that appear with neumes use smaller letters to leave sufficient room for the notation.

General content: *Missa de sanctis* (fols. 1r-4v); *Officium de uno iusto* (fols. 4v-16r); *Officium de uno confessore* (fols. 16r-25r); *Officium de uirginibus* (fols. 25r-36v); *Officium de una uirgine* (fols. 36v-37v); *Officia* from ten Sundays *de cotidiano* (fols. 38v-154v).

Leaf shown: 25r
OFFICIUM DE UIRGINIBUS AD UESPERUM. In noctibus extollite manus uestras in sancta et benedicite Domino. UERSUS. Qui statis in domo Domini in atriis domus Dei nostri. Et. SONO. Alleluia. Iustitia plena est dextera tua, letetur mons Sion et exultent filie Iude propter iudicia tua alleluia alleluia. ANTIFONA. Ut columbe mansuete plaudebant sibi de alis suis et gloriabuntur in itinere suo, populus autem gaudebat gaudio magno in letitia earum. UERSUS. Letentur mons Sion.

In this manuscript, all of the pieces to be sung in the various offices are notated with clarity and a skillful configuration of the neumes.. On occasions, the neumes exceed the writing frame and run into the margin (as in other Visigothic codices), as seen on this leaf with the word *benedicite* on the third line. The *ductus* of the notation is not very meticulous: it is inclined to the right and the stems of the neumes are noticeably prolonged.

BIBLIOGRAPHY

EDIT. FERNÁNDEZ DE LA CUESTA 1965. DÍAZ Y DÍAZ 1983, 475-476. GONZÁLEZ BARRIONUEVO 1992, 403-472. MILLARES CARLO ET AL. 1999, 1: 182. RUIZ ASENCIO 2003, 197-200.

Miguel C. Vivancos

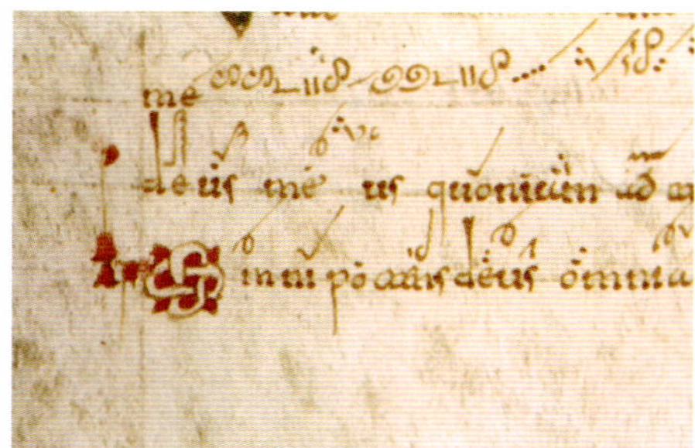

Detail of fol. 38v (parchment folio)

offertorium de virginibus. ad v[espe]r[a]s

Hic innocatabus et colligat munus
uestratis in sunctum et benediciat
domino. V. Quis scandit ... tis in domo domini in iu[s]tis, domus dei inostri: et

Sño Alle luia luia. Lutata qui plenum est a
dextera tua cum letatis mons sion exsultatione
filie iude propter iudicium tuum.
allelu ia alle luia. R.

Ut a columbe mansuete plaudebunt sibi
deum lusus et gloriam bunt in carne suo
populus unatum gaudebit gaudio magno
in letatia qui eorum: V. Letatur mons...

Liber horarum

11TH CENTURY *MED.* (FOL. 1R)

ARCHIVO DEL MONASTERIO DE SANTO DOMINGO DE SILOS (BURGOS), COD. 7.
ORIGIN: MONASTERY OF SANTA MARÍA LA REAL OF NÁJERA (?) (LA RIOJA).
Also known as *Horae diurnae et nocturnae;* parchment with wide margins, well prepared, although on occasion it uses the outer edges of the skin; 15th century binding in leather over boards; 1 + 141 + 1 leaves; 18th century foliation in ink in the upper right margin, skips number 88; the leaves measure 243 × 166 mm; the writing frame measures 139 × 99 mm; one column justified with double vertical lines on both sides; the vertical prickings are visible and run along the middle of the margins; the horizontal prickings run along the outer margin at a fair distance from the edge; 16 lines; ruled in drypoint with the quire unfolded and the first bifolium over the rest; quite consistent Visigothic minuscule which is thickened considerably with a point at the upper edge of the stems; no Carolingian influence is noted; a single scribe for the entire manuscript; northern Visigothic notation; the texts that contain neumes have reduced the size of the letters to leave sufficient room for the notation.

General contents: *Officium de infirmis* (fols. 1r-12r); *Officium de defunctis* (fols. 12r-23r); *Officium episcoporum seu presbiterorum defunctorum* (fols. 23r-30v); *Incipit prologus* (fol. 31r-v); *Liber horarum* (fols. 32r-141v).

Leaf shown: 1r
*et propitius adtribuat consortiu*m *beatorum. Adq*ue *ita uos eripiat semp*er *a malo ut custodiat uos et conserbet semp*er *in bono.* OFFICIUM *DE INFIRMIS AD UESPERUM*. *Exaudi nos Deus salbator noster. Sono. Sana Domine omnes langores.*

This manuscript was designed to include notation for the melodies by reducing the size of the letters of the pieces to be sung,

Detail of fol. 92v

even though neumes were added only in a few places (specifically on fols. 1r-v; 7r; 12v; 13r; 15v; 16r-v; 17r; 28r-29v; 109v). The notated pieces, which are not abundant, were neumed for the most part by the text scribe. On this leaf the text and music are written by the same hand, and, although a good scribe, he does not seem to have been an expert in notation (he appears to be the same scribe as in Cod. 6). The neumes, which incline to the right, also indicate a notable lack of expertise. In the right margin of fol. 1, the note "buelto con psalterio" appears, the name by which the manuscript is designated in a 13th century Silos library catalog.

BIBLIOGRAPHY

EDIT. FLORES ARCAS 1997. DÍAZ Y DÍAZ 1983, 477. GONZÁLEZ BARRIONUEVO 1992, 403-472. VIVANCOS 1995, 22. MILLARES CARLO ET AL. 1999, 1: 182-183. RUIZ ASENCIO 2003, 200-202.

Miguel C. Vivancos

...ri sepulturis adcaelestia coronatu
...

Adgloriam uos ceptam tamparuulo
uitam adducat uos et conserbet
semper inbono.

OFFM DE LHTR MISAD ...

Exaudi nos deus
salutaris noster
SHO S...
...mine omnia ...

Cap. 6

Bible

10TH CENTURY *IN.* / 9TH-10TH CENTURIES (MILLARES CARLO) (FOL. 236V)

ARCHIVO CAPITULAR, BURGOS, W./O. S.
PROVENANCE: MONASTERY OF SAN PEDRO DE CARDEÑA (BURGOS).
The parchment is well preserved; leather binding over boards; 397 leaves; modern foliation in pencil in the upper right margin for both the recto and verso; the leaves measure 470 × 330 mm; two columns justified with double vertical lines on both sides and a triple vertical line between the columns which spans the entire leaf; the prickings are imperceptible; 52 lines; ruled in drypoint; Visigothic minuscule with liturgical characteristics; the primary initial of each book is richly decorated and painted red, yellow and green; worthy of special mention are fols. 54-170 for their beautiful artistry; fol. 312r contains two decorated arches with arabesque motifs; the secondary initials and rubrics are in red, alternating with initials filled in with a greenish blue; decorative elements with zoomorphic, anthropomorphic, botanical and arabesque motifs; there are catchwords at the foot of the page consisting of one or more words; the work of a single hand; Visigothic notation, partially applied to the *Lamentations of Jeremiah;* accent notation (Brockett, 1968).

General contents: Completely preserved Bible, except the final chapters of the Apocalypse (chaps. 12-22 and fols. 306-312). It begins with the words *Incipiunt capitula del Génesis*… and ends with the words *et mulier fugit in solitudinem ubi habet locum paratum a Deo, u tibi pascat illam diebus mille ducentos sesaginta* (Apoc. 12:6) from the Apocalypse of John. It also contains the Prefaces of St. Jerome to the books of Sacred Scripture and some prologues whose author cannot be determined.

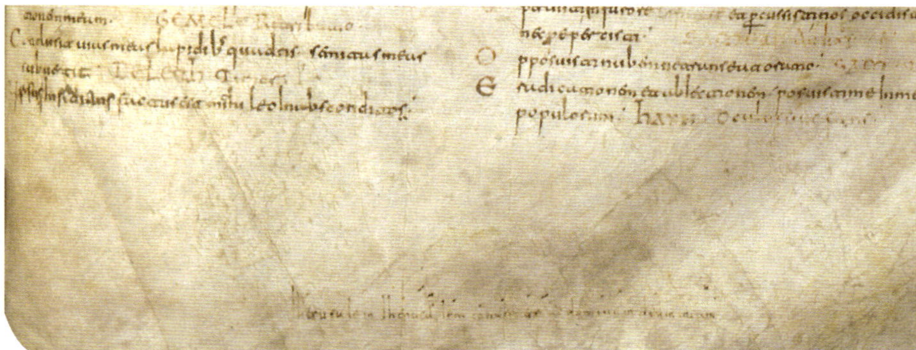

Detail of fol. 237r

Leaf shown: 236v
[LAMENTATIONS OF JEREMIAH. CHAPTER I, 11-22. CHAPTER II, 1-15]
ecclesiam tuam. CAPH. CURUATI SUNT. Omnis populus... LAMETH. COR SIUE SERUO. O uos omnes... MEM. UISCERA ALIBI EX IPSIS. De excelso... NUN. UICUS VEL PASCUA EORUM. Uigilavit iugum... SEMECH. AUDIENS SIUE FIRMAMENTUM. Abstulit omnes... HAYN. OCULUS SIUE FRONS. Idcirco ego plorans... PHE. ERRAUIT. Expandit Syon... SADE. CONSOLATIO. Iustus est Dominus... COPH. ASPICE. Uocabi amicos meos... RES. CAPUD. Uide Domine... SEN. ULNUS SUPER UULNUS. Audierunt quia... THAU. ERRAUIT SIUE CONSUMMAUIT. Ingrediatur omne... INCIPIT SECUNDO. ALEPH. DOCTRINA. Quomodo obtexit... BETH. CONFUSIO. Precipitauit Dominus... GEMEL. RETRIBUTIO. Confregit in ira... DELET. TIMOR. Tetendit archum... HE. UIAM. Factus est Dominus... UAU. ET ILLE. Et dissipavit... ZAY. DUCTE. Reppulit Dominus... HETH. PAUOR. Cogitavit Dominus... TETH. EXCLUSIO. Defixerunt in terra... IOTH. DESOLATA. Sederunt in terra... CAPH. CURUATI SUNT. Defecerunt pre lacrimis... LAMECH. COR SIUE SERUO. Matribus suis... MEM. UISCERA ALIBI EX IPSIS. Cui comparabo te... NUN. UICUS VEL PASCUA EORUM. Prophete tui... SAMECH. AUDIENS SIUE FIRMAMENTUM [Lam 1, 11-22; 2, 1-15].

There are three extant Visigothic copies of the Bible that are practically complete and that include musical notation in the *Lamentations of Jeremiah.* The Bible of Cardeña is, although not unique, a special case of melodies being inserted in a nonmusical codex. There are parallel phenomena in the Visigothic Bible (ms. 31, Biblioteca Histórica de la Universidad Complutense de Madrid) dated to the 9th century and in the Bible from Silos preserved in Cracow (Czartorysky Library, ms. 3.118). Other fragments worthy of mention: the Bible of Oña (Silos, AM, w./o. s.) and Salamanca (Archivo de los Sacerdotes Operarios Diocesanos w./o. s.). This practice is not exclusively Spanish; it is also found documented in other traditions. The melodic design is in recitative style, mostly syllabic except for some brief melismatic passages on the letters that precede each verse and on the final cadences. The Cardeña melody coincides with the versions that appear in the Antiphonary of Silos (AM 9) and in the Lectionary of Girona.

BIBLIOGRAPHY
ANDRÉS 1912, 101-164. ROJO 1917. PRADO 1928, 229-231. ROJO, 1930b, 312. LUDWIG 1971, 127-131. FERNÁNDEZ DE LA CUESTA 1983, 105. DÍAZ Y DÍAZ 1983, 300; 1984, 31-41. MANSILLA 1990, 50-53. RIBAY 1992, 511-564. HARDIE 1993, 912-942; 1998, 370-389.

Susana Zapke

236v

celestium matrum. CAPH Curuatio

Omnis populus eius gemens et querens panem. dederunt pretiosa quaeque pro cibo ad refocillandam animam. Vide domine et considera quoniam facta sum uilis. LAMECH Cor siue [illegible]

O uos omnes qui transitis per uiam. attendite et uidete si est dolor sicut dolor meus. quoniam uindemiauit me ut locutus est dominus in die furoris sui. MEM Viscera uel ibi ex ipsis.

ii De excelso misit ignem in ossibus meis et erudiuit me. expandit rete pedibus meis. conuertit me retrorsum. posuit me desolatam. tota die merore confectam. NUN Piscis uel pascuum eorum.

Vigilauit iugum iniquitatum mearum in manu eius. conuolutae sunt et inpositae collo meo. infirmata est uirtus mea. dedit me dominus in manu de qua non potero surgere. SEMECH Adiutorium siue firmamentum.

Abstulit omnes magnificos meos dominus de medio mei. uocauit aduersum me tempus ut contereret electos meos. torcular calcauit dominus uirgini filiae Iuda. AIN Oculus siue fons.

iii Idcirco ego plorans et oculus meus deducens aquam. quia longe factus est a me consolator conuertens animam meam. facti sunt filii mei perditi. quoniam inualuit inimicus. PHE Errorem

Expandit Sion manus suas. non est qui consoletur eam. Mandauit dominus aduersum Iacob in circuitu eius hostes eius. facta est Hierusalem quasi polluta menstruis inter eos. SADE [illegible]

Iustus est dominus. quia os eius ad iracundiam prouocaui. Audite obsecro uniuersi populi. et uidete dolorem meum. Virgines meae et iuuenes mei abierunt in captiuitatem. COPH Aspice.

fini Vocaui amicos meos. et ipsi deceperunt me. sacerdotes mei et senes mei in urbe consumpti sunt. quia quaesierunt cibum sibi ut refocilarent animam suam. RES Caput.

Vide domine quoniam tribulor. uenter meus conturbatus est. subuersum est cor meum in memet ipsum quoniam amaritudine repleta sum. foris interficit gladius et domi mors similis est. SEN [illegible]

Audierunt quia ingemesco ego. et non est qui consoletur me. Omnes inimici mei audierunt malum meum. laetati sunt quoniam tu fecisti. Adduxisti diem consolationis. et fient similes mei. THAU [illegible] siue consummatio

Ingrediatur omne malum eorum coram te. et uindemia eos sicut uindemiasti me propter omnes iniquitates meas. multi enim gemitus mei et cor meum maerens.

INCIPIT SECUNDO. ALEPH Doctrina

Quomodo obtexit caligine in furore suo dominus filiam Sion. proiecit de caelo in terram inclitam Israhel. et non est recordatus scabelli pedum suorum in die furoris sui. BETH Domus.

Praecipitauit dominus nec pepercit omnia speciosa Iacob. destruxit in furore suo munitiones uirginis Iuda. deiecit in terram. polluit regnum et principes eius. GIMEL Retributio.

Confregit in ira furoris omne cornu Israhel. auertit retrorsum dexteram suam a facie inimici. et succendit in Iacob quasi ignem flammae deuorantis in gyro. DELETH Timor.

ii Tetendit arcum suum quasi inimicus. firmauit dexteram suam quasi hostis. et occidit omne quod pulchrum erat uisu in tabernaculo filiae Sion. effudit quasi ignem indignationem suam. HE Ista.

Factus est dominus uelut inimicus. praecipitauit Israhel. praecipitauit omnia moenia eius. dissipauit munitiones eius. et repleuit in filia Iuda humiliatum et humiliatam. VAU Et ille.

Et dissipauit quasi hortum tentorium suum. demolitus est tabernaculum suum. obliuioni tradidit dominus in Sion festiuitatem et sabbatum. et obprobrio in indignatione furoris sui regem et sacerdotem. ZAI Ducat

iii Repulit dominus altare suum. maledixit sanctificationi suae. tradidit in manu inimici muros turrium eius. uocem dederunt in domo domini sicut in die sollemni. HETH Fauor.

Cogitauit dominus dissipare murum filiae Sion. tetendit funiculum suum et non auertit manum suam a perditione. luxitque antemurale. et murus pariter dissipatus est. TETH Exclusio.

Defixae sunt in terra portae eius. perdidit et contriuit uectes eius. regem eius et principes eius in gentibus. Non est lex. et prophetae eius non inuenerunt uisionem a domino. IOTH [illegible]

fini Sederunt in terra. conticuerunt senes filiae Sion. consperserunt cinere capita sua. accincti sunt ciliciis. abiecerunt in terram capita sua uirgines Hierusalem. CAPH Curuati sunt.

Defecerunt prae lacrimis oculi mei. conturbata sunt uiscera mea. effusum est in terra iecur meum super contritione filiae populi mei. cum deficeret paruulus et lactans in plateis oppidi. LAMECH Cor siue [illegible]

Matribus suis dixerunt ubi est triticum et uinum. cum deficerent quasi uulnerati in plateis ciuitatis. cum exhalarent animas suas in sinu matrum suarum. MEM Viscera [illegible]

Cui comparabo te. uel cui assimilabo te filia Hierusalem. Cui exaequabo te et consolabor te uirgo filia Sion. Magna est enim uelut mare contritio tua. quis medebitur tui. NUN Piscis uel pascuum eorum.

Prophetae tui uiderunt tibi falsa et stulta. nec aperiebant iniquitatem tuam ut te ad paenitentiam prouocarent. Viderunt autem tibi adsumptiones falsas et eiectiones. SAMECH Adiutorium siue firmamentum.

Anthologia hispana (Azagra Codex)

9th-10th Centuries / 11th Century *in.* (Mundó) (fol. 158v)

Biblioteca Nacional, Madrid, ms. 10029 (olim Toledo 14.22 and HH. 134).
Provenance: The Primate Cathedral of Toledo. Produced in a Mozarabic environment. Pyrenean (Mundó).
Poor-quality parchment with defects in the mounting and in a terrible state of preservation; tan leather binding over boards; 3 + 1 + 159 + 3 leaves; these leaves are subsequent complementary additions; modern foliation in pencil; the leaves measure 235/240 × 155/160 mm; the writing frame measures 185/170 × 100/120 mm; one column justified with double vertical lines on either side; prickings are occasionally visible in the form of a small oblique incision; 26/27 lines depending on the section; ruled in drypoint by means of a direct impression on the hair side; a) Visigothic minuscule, slightly inclined to the left, of a small module, archaic and of southern origin; b) Visigothic minuscule of northern origin, straight, of a small module, with well-developed vertical bars; c) Visigothic minuscule, rounded and of larger module; uses the *tj* group before a vowel; several scribes for the text and the notation; northern Visigothic notation *in campo aperto*; few variations in the neumes; poor-quality *ductus*.

General contents: Compilation of literary works, of considerable value because it contains several poetic compositions for which there are few extant witnesses. The majority of the authors are Spanish: Eugenio de Toledo, Álvaro de Córdoba, Martín de Dumio, etc. Few peninsular manuscripts have been preserved that contain texts of this kind. This manuscript contains three neumed texts: a) *Carmen philomelaicum,* Eugenio de Toledo, with the incipit: *Vox, filomela, tua metrorum carmina uincit* (fol. 55v); b) *Carmen poenitentiale Vincentii,* with the incipit: *Deus miserere mei, Deus miserere mei* (fol. 141v); and c) an untitled anonymous poem: *Inclite parentis alme Christe pignus* (fol. 158r).

Leaf shown: 158v
*Meminere enim debes / Confusus procul a nostro / Usque diem illum / Gloria carmen resonat. Imperat omni*potens*: Procul, o procul effuge demon / Ne somnum turbes / Crucis alme fero signum / Hic pater et Verbum / Lubricus inc ammis* [Traube: *anguis*] */ Sit celle Dominus / Exorcidio uos omnes / Crucis alme fero / Quam telluris spatia* [Last stanza on fol. 159r: *Per diem salbasti nos, Domine, in nocte custodi nos, Ihesu. Chri*ste].

The manuscript was acquired by Miguel Ruiz Azagra, minister of the emperor Rudolph II, in Valladolid. Upon the minister's death, a canon of the Cathedral of Toledo, Juan Bautista Pérez, requested that it be donated by the heirs; as a result, the manuscript was incorporated into the extensive library of the metropolitan see in 1587. The anonymous text which begins on fol. 158r, *Inclite parentis alme Christe, pignus unicu,* is a composition inspired by the *Versus supra lectum* by Eugenio de Toledo. It is a poem made up of ten stanzas of three verses each, which begs Christ for help to endure temptation and rebukes the devil with formulas reminiscent of exorcism: *Fuge prorsus, fuge, demon, esto tuis particeps / Usque diem illum magni uerique iudicii.* The Damasian epigram continues on fol. 159r with notation: *Iam dudum Saulus,* where the neumes present greater diversity and elaboration. It should also be mentioned that there is a series of prayers with Visigothic notation that Prado and Meyer dated to the 9th century. The *Liber ordinum* of Silos, AM, Cod. 4, and *Liber ordinum* of San Millán, Madrid, RAH, Cod. 56 transmit the same repertoire. The

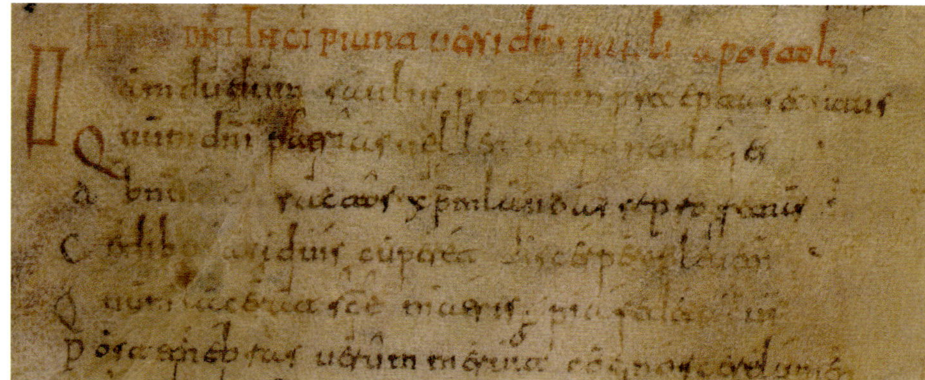

Detail of fol. 159r. Biblioteca Nacional de España

fact that Visigothic notation is included in some of the texts is unique inasmuch as it is not originally a musical codex. The notation presents a simple morphology, with an abundance of simple forms and, in essence, a syllabic melodic formula. The neumes have mostly angular lines, with the exception of the *podatus,* which to some degree evokes ekphonetic signs and prosodic accents.

Bibliography

Meyer 1914. Prado 1928, 225. Díaz y Díaz 1958-1959, 198-202, 206, 236-237, 312-313, 321, 376, 462, 464, 482, 485-487, 505, 507, 509, 632 and 671. Riou 1963-1964, 309. Jiménez Delgado 1968, 277-332. Gil Fernández 1973, 2: 690-691. Vendrell 1979, 655-705. Díaz y Díaz 1983, 51, 232, 258, 264, 265 y 267; 1991, 58, 114, 172, 293-295, 300. Millares Carlo et al. 1999, 1: 117-118.

Elisa Ruiz García

Meminere enim debes pretium tibi dedicatum in tantis
membra xpi atque fugam arripe. sicut nobis ipse xps
precatus ut docuit dicta.
Confusus procul unde recedas cenobio in quo te nos
munitos crucis signum ualide. fuge protinus fuge
demon tetris tartari particeps.
Usque diem illum magnum uerique iudicii cum sanctos
quos tu tantum ausus es coniungentur angelis tuisque
condemnatus inferno uasto.
Et tu carmen sermone patri uatque filio spiritu qui semper
gratia coniunctus aequalitate. qui cum deo patre
perfectusque trinitatis.
Imperat omnipotens procul o procul effuge demon ne fraude
nostram possis adire aciem.
Nec somnium aut bis nec mortis uinculo ministrante
nec fallax animum sordidet ipse meum.
Crucis alme sacro signum fuge demon.
Hic operatur et uerbum uel sancti spiritus gloria unus ubique deus
celsus et omnipotens.
Lubricus in cunctis fugiat in tantum princeps pe
... ne noceat ... dicatur deo. Crucis alme.
Sit hac cella dominus sanctis nam ... pie benignus ita placeat
xpo fulgeat ...
Et ... uos omni demonum ... omnis
angeli ... fugiat abhinc. Crucis alme sig.
Quam ...

Liber canticorum (fragmentum)

10TH CENTURY *IN.* / 11TH CENTURY (MILLARES CARLO) (FOL. 175V)

BRITISH LIBRARY, LONDON, ADD. MS. 30844.
PROVENANCE: MONASTERY OF SANTO DOMINGO DE SILOS (BURGOS), ALTHOUGH IT DOES NOT SEEM TO HAVE BEEN WRITTEN THERE.
Mediocre parchment both in quality and preparation; 15th century binding, leather over boards; the fragment consists of five leaves, foliated in the upper right margin in the 18th century; the leaves measure 325 × 290 mm; the writing frame measures 279 × 221 mm; two columns, justified with double vertical lines on the edges and a single line in the intercolumn; the vertical prickings are visible on the edge; the horizontal prickings run along the edge of the outer margin; 27 lines; ruled in drypoint, although it is impossible to determine how the ruling was carried out; Visigothic minuscule written by a single hand; northern Visigothic notation; the five leaves preserved of this *Liber canticorum* are the remains of a quaternion, which has lost the entire first bifolium and the fourth leaf.

General contents: The leaves in the *Liber canticorum* (fols. 173-177) have been bound together with a *Misticus* which, in its present state, is quite disordered, with numerous lacunae. It begins with the Feast of St. Mary which incorporates the opusculum *De virginitate Sanctae Mariae,* by San Ildephonsus of Toledo, divided into lessons, and ends with the Feast of the Chair of St. Peter. It is written in two columns; room was left for musical notation in the sections that needed it, but it was never added. The *Misticus* is from the second half of the 11th century.

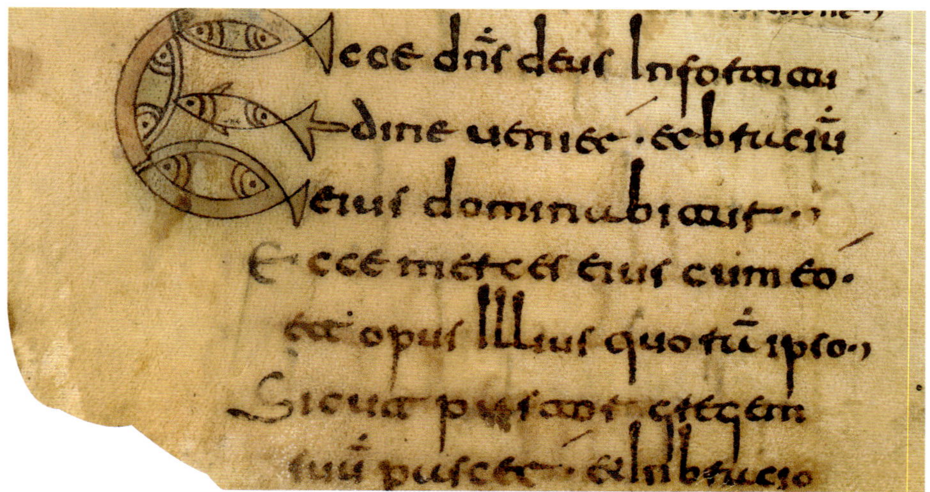

Detail of fol. 175v. Initial *E*

Leaf shown: 175v
Uere fenum est populus. Etsiccatum est fenum et cecidit flos, uerbum autem Domini Dei nostri stabit in eternum. Super montem excelsum ascende tu qui euangelizas Syon, exalta in fortitudine uocem tuam qui euangelizas Iherusalem; exalta et noli timere, dic ciuitatibus Iuda: ecce Deus uester [Is 40:7-9]. *VII.* CANTICUM ESAYE PROPHETE. ANTIFONA. *Ecce Dominus Deus in fortitudine ueniet et bracium eius dominabitur; ecce merces eius cum eo et opus illius quoram ipso. Sicut pastor gregem suum pascet et in bracio [suo] congregabit agnos [et in si]nu suo leuab[it; fetas i]pse portabit. [Quis mensus est pugillo] aquas et celos palmo ponderabit? Quis adpendit tribus digitis molem terre et librabit in pondere montes et colles in statera? Quis adiubabit spiritum Domini aut quis consiliarius eius fuit et ostendit illi? Quum quo iniit consilium, et instruxit eum, et docuit eum semitam iustitie, et erudibit eum scientia, et uiam prudentie hostendit illi? Ecce gentes quasi stille situle et quasi momentum statere reputati sunt; ecce insule quasi puluis exiguus. Et Liuanus non sufficiet ad succidendum et animalia eius non sufficient ad olocaustum. Omnes gentes quasi non sint, sic sunt* [Is 40:10-17].

The remains of *Liber canticorum* which follows Spanish liturgical use, has musical notation that uses thick strokes and is limited to antiphons that precede each canticle, standing out for its simplicity since the melodies are mostly syllabic.

BIBLIOGRAPHY
DÍAZ Y DÍAZ 1983, 402. WALKER 1998, 49, 53 *ET PASSIM*. MILLARES CARLO ET AL. 1999, 1: 85-86.

Miguel C. Vivancos

Vere fenum est populus; sic
catum est fenum et ceci
dit flos. uerbum autem
domini dei nostri stabit in
eternum.

Super montem excelsum
ascende tu qui euange
lizas Sion. exalta in
fortitudine uocem tuam
qui euangelizas Hierusalem.
exalta et noli timere.
dic ciuitatibus Iuda
ecce deus uester. VIII

[illegible] propheta

Ecce dominus in fortitudine ueniet
et brachium eius cum dominatione.

Ecce dominus deus in fortitu
dine ueniet. et brachium
eius dominabitur.

Ecce merces eius cum eo.
et opus illius coram ipso.

Sicut pastor gregem
suum pascet. et in brachio
suo congregabit agnos
et in sinu suo leuabit.
fetas ipse portabit.

aquas. et celos palmo
ponderabit.

Quis adpendit tribus digitis
molem terre et librabit
in pondere montes. et
colles in statera.

Quis adiubabit spiritum domini
aut quis consiliarius eius
fuit. et ostendit illi.

Cum quo iniit consilium
et instruxit eum et docuit eum
semitam iustitie. et
erudibit eum scientiam. et uiam
prudentie ostendit illi.

Ecce gentes quasi stille
situle et quasi momentum
statere reputate sunt.

Ecce insule quasi pulbis
exiguus. et libanus non
sufficiet ad succidendum.
et animalia eius non
sufficient ad olocaustum.

Omnes gentes quasi non sint
sic sunt

Liber misticus

10TH CENTURY *EX.*-11TH CENTURY *IN.* (FOL. 182V)

BIBLIOTECA CAPITULAR, TOLEDO, 35-6.
PROVENANCE: THE PRIMATE CATHEDRAL OF TOLEDO. PROBABLY OF NORTHERN PENINSULAR ORIGIN.
Well-preserved parchment; binding with boards lined with dry tanned leather, 16th to 17th centuries; 199 leaves (fragmentary); modern foliation with Arabic numerals in the upper right margin; the leaves measure 309 × 205 mm; the writing frame measures 230 × 135 mm; one column justified with triple vertical lines that run the entire leaf; horizontal prickings are partially visible in the margins of the leaf, but the vertical prickings are imperceptible; 23 lines (with variations); ruled in drypoint with the quire folded, placing the odd leaves over the even ones; Visigothic minuscule with very meticulous and fine strokes; smaller letters are used for the texts with notation; contemporary corrections and subsequent corrections from the 11th to the 12th centuries; primary initials in black, red, green and yellow, some with zoomorphic motifs; headings in red and alternating red, black, green and yellow. The text is the work of a single scribe, whereas the notation is the work of several scribes in different phrases; monogram, fol. 124r: *Ildefonsi;* partial northern Visigothic notation, not particularly refined; black and ocher inks, modulations in thickness of the stroke; additions of melismas in the margins; *ductus* related to those of Silos and San Millán de la Cogolla.

General content: Begins with an incomplete Easter Week and a structure similar to the Bobbio Missal from the 8th century. After the octave of Easter is, strictly speaking, a *Liber misticus.* It exhibits formal similarities with the Antiphonary of León, *Ordo psallendi de octavas Paschae,* which correspond to the Visigothic Antiphonary archetype [fragmentary]. Mass *Post pridie,* Easter Monday; the offices of the octave of Easter (fol. 1r); *Ordo psallendi in primo dominico post octavas pasce hasta el Domingo IIIIº* (fols. 36v-58r); *Ordo psallendi in diem sancte Crucis* (fol. 65r); *Ordo psallendi in diem Ascensiones* (fol. 84v); *Ordo psallendi de subsequenti Dominico post ascensiones Domini* (fol. 99r); *Ordo exeuntes letanias apostolicas* (fol. 102r); [lacunae: fols. 101v-102r, two leaves are missing; fols. 103v-104r, two leaves are missing]; the office of the Pentecost [the beginning is fragmentary] (fol. 104r); *Ordo sanctorum Adriane et Natalie* (fol. 114v); *Ordo psallendi in nativitate Sancti Iohannis baptiste* (fol. 123v); *Ordo psallendi in diem sanctorum Petri et Pauli* (fol. 140r); *Ordo psallendi in diem sanctarum Iuste et Rufine* (fol. 151r); *Ordo in diem sancti Cristofori* (fol. 160v)*; Ordo psallendi de primitiis* (fol. 165v); *Ordo psallendi in diem sancti Cucufati* (fol. 175v); *Ordo psallendi in diem sancti Felices* (fol. 182v); *Ordo psallendi in diem sanctorum Iusti et Pastoris* (fol. 192r) [fragmentary].

Leaf shown: 182v
ORDO PSALLENDI IN DIEM SANCTI FELICIS AD VESPERUM

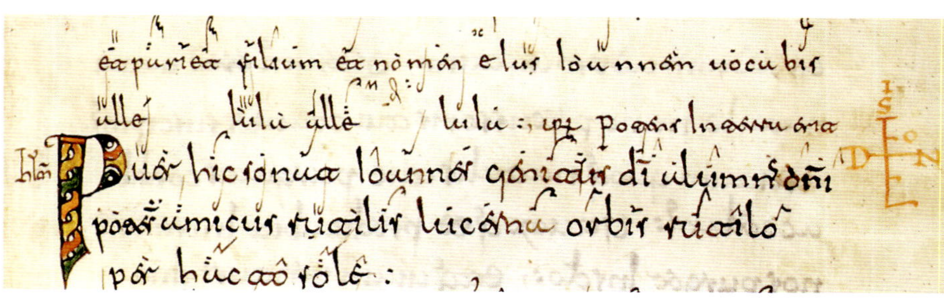
Detail of fol. 124r. Monogram: *Ildefonsi*

[VESPERTINUM] *Gloria et honore choronasti;* [ANTIPHON] *Gloriam et magnum. II. Vitam petit; Sono Alleluia. Beatus vir. II. Gloria et divitie;* ANTIFONA *Felix qui pronus est;* VERSUS *Beatus qui intelligit;* ALLELUIA *Felix qui ex abundantia;* VERSUS *Potens in terra.* *HYMNUS Fons Deus vite perennis.*

According to Mundó, this manuscript is the oldest Visigothic codex (10th to 11th centuries) from Toledo. Férotin, Rojo and Prado and also Anglès dated it between the 9th and 10th centuries, whereas Millares Carlo situates it in thse 10th century *in.* The split "i" as the abbreviation for "in", as well as the abbreviation for *quibus*, with a split b, indicate a later date. Comparison with Toledo, BC, 35-5 (13th century) and Toledo, BC, 35-2 (Madrid, BN, ms. 10110, olim. Toledo, BC, 35-2, 13th to 14th centuries) shows the development of Visigothic script and notation over time. There is a copy from the year 1753 (BN, Madrid, ms. 13053) carried out at the order of father Burriel. The vertical notation and its thin strokes are typical of codices from the north of the peninsula, although Mundó suggests that the manuscript originated in Toledo. The *ductus,* by no means meticulous, suggests a certain degree of haste in the copying process. Although it was foreseen that the text would be accompanied by notation, many of the pieces, such as the long melisma at the beginning of the second verse of the *Sono,* have none. The inclusion of melismas in the margins is characteristic of Visigothic codices; they clearly demonstrate the articulation of the melody through the reiteration of neumatic formulas or sequences.

BIBLIOGRAPHY

FÉROTIN 1912, 738-754. ROJO AND PRADO 1929, 19. MILLARES CARLO 1935, NO. 25, 47-48. ANGLÈS 1938, 1-68. MILLARES CARLO 1961, 337-444. MUNDÓ 1965, 19. PINELL 1965, 106. JANINI AND SERRANO 1969, 163-164. JANINI 1977a, 102-103. GROS 1978, 45-64. JANINI 1983, 151-229. ANGLÈS 1988, 144, 167, 180, 186.

Susana Zapke

ORDO DE L[IBR]O IN DIEM S[AN]C[T]I FELICIS AD VESPERUM

Gloria et honore coronasti eum domine :,

Gloriam et magnum decorem posuisti super caput eius :, dne

II Vitam petiit et tribuisti ei longitudinem dierum. dne :,

SNO Alle luia. Beatus uir qui timet dominum alleluia

In mandatis eius cupiet nimis alle luia alle luia :,

II Glo ria et diuitie in domo

eius et iustitia eius manet in seculum seculi alle luia :,

Felix qui pronus est ad misericordiam benedicetur de panibus suis

dedit pauperibus :, ypt Beatus qui intelligit :,

Felix qui ex habundantia sua cibo sponte largitus pau

perum de opere suo recipiet fructum laboris alle luia :, ypt Potentia

ym Fons deus uite perennis lux origo luminis aspice

plebem cunctam fletu summi martiris

excipe uotum precantum sume laudum carminis :,

Ex tu felicis almi pangimus insignia tu resolue

uincla lingue dans sonore cantica ut ualeat

rite queamus promere magnalia :,

Iste numque cesare urbis munera mundi

ulis discipline dum studeret litteris utrumque

famosa fabra tergo quando decora :,

Audiens placet fidelis mox letanda per uana

Homiliary

11TH CENTURY *IN.* (FOL. XIIIR)

COLLECTION OF THE GUILD OF ST. GEORGE, SHEFFIELD GALLERIES & MUSEUMS TRUST. SHEFFIELD (GREAT BRITAIN), MS. 31 (OLIM RUSKIN MUSEUM 7).
PROVENANCE: UNKNOWN.

The parchment varies in thickness and is well-preserved; modern 19th century binding; 273 leaves (fragmentary); two foliations; the original comprises 289 leaves, and a modern hand numbered the leaves again, reaching the number 273; the original state comprised a total of 305 leaves; the original foliation, located in the center of the recto leaves, is written in red ink in Roman numerals; the leaves measure 335 × 470 mm; the writing frame measures 230 × 345 mm; two columns justified with double vertical lines on both sides and between the columns; the prickings are partially visible, the horizontal prickings are in the right margin; 41 lines (with some variations); ruled in drypoint; liturgical Visigothic minuscule of excellent artistry; abundant primary initials *I* (the incipit) with exceptional interlace decoration: on fol. CXXXv, the explicit covers the entire page of the first part and the incipit covers the entire page of the second part: *F* (*Fides*): fol. LXXXIX, *In quinquagesima Sermo Iohannis Episcopi*); each homily is preceded by a polychromatic initial decorated with interalce motifs reminiscent of the decoration found in another series of Spanish manuscripts from the 11th century (London, BL, Add. ms. 30850, Add. ms. 30851 and Add. ms. 30853) and specifically of the decoration found in the Antiphonary of León, with respect to the ornamental motifs as well as the type of ink, mostly yellow followed by green and red; written by a single scribe; beautifully drawn Visigothic notation *in campo aperto,* with a vertical axis typical of the northern part of the peninsula.

General contents: Winter part: *Ex huius nobis lectionis verbis* (fol. 10r) until fol. 130r. Summer part: *Explicit liber Homeliarum partis prime. Incipit partis secunde liber omeliarum ex ipsorum etenim doctoribus magnorum magne studium diligentie constructum. Amen Deo gratias.* (fols. 130v-288v in the original numbering): *In celo credimus percipiendum. Nam sunt nonnulli qui christianitatis nostre* (Homily 32 in Gospel: *PL LXXVI:* 1232-7C).

Leaf shown: XIIIr
[End of the *Sermo beati Agustini de Adventu Domini*]
[Versos of the *Iudicii signum* from the Song of Sybil] *Audite qui dixerit. Iudicii signum.*
FERIA III (TERTIA) ANTE NATALE DOMINI. Lectio Sancti Evangeli secundum Lucam. In illo tempore missus est angelus Gabriel… OMILIA EIUSDEM LECTIONIS BEATI BEDE PRESBYTERI.

The Sheffield Homiliarium offers a clear example of a transitional codex, a copy of a Carolingian model in Visigothic script and notation. The degree to which this manuscript coincides with the models of Paul the Deacon and Charlemagne is almost absolute, except on three occasions which have to do with the order of the content and the presence of a total of seven original homilies. It only includes two brief homilies by St. Isidore and is completely lacking homilies by the Spanish bishops, even those included in the 11th century Homiliarium from Toledo. Therefore, the scribe had a Carolingian model that he scrupulously copied, preserving the typically Spanish script, notation and illumination, in addition to taking certain liberties such as extending the incipit text of the second part. The only case of the vertical type of Visigothic notation included in the Homiliarium is applied to the *Iudicii signum* verses from the Song of Sybil. It is an extremely simple syllabic recitation in which only two notational signs are used: the *punctum* and two types of the *podatus.* The texts come from St. Augustine's *De civitate Dei* (XVIII, 23: *PL XLI:* col. 579), and from the pseudo-Augustinian sermon *Vos inquam convenio, o Iudei,* designated for the last week of Advent. The initials of what is a total of 27 verses (plus the

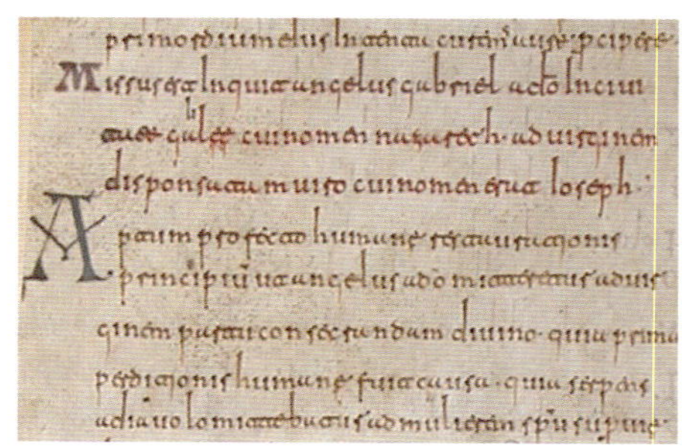

Detail of fol. XIIIv. Collection of the Guild of St. George, Sheffield Galleries & Museums Trust

introduction: *Audite qui dixerit*) make up the acrostic in Greek: *Iesus Creistos tev Dnios Seoter.* As is the case with Vic, ABEV, Frag. XI/1, the 17th verso reads *volvetur* instead of *solvetur,* and the 18th reads *deiciet* instead of *reiciet*. Also see Homiliarium of Córdoba, AC, ms. 1.

BIBLIOGRAPHY

QUARITCH 1862, 4: 185. LECLERCQ 1948, 198-214. BROU 1949, 147-191. ÉTAIX 1959, 213-224. DÍAZ Y DÍAZ 1983, 351. WALKER 1998, 86. MILLARES CARLO ET AL. 1999, 1: 172-173.

Susana Zapke

tia nos iuste damnetis iudicatis ecce inquam conuin
cimus nos ad quod teneris. Demonstrauimus enim nos
decantantes testimonium Christo fuisse perlatum qui in
ueritatis non accepit eum mundus enim per linguas
inimicorum suorum. Nonne quando ille potentissimus fu
cundissimi incendium caminum in illum noua progenies
caelo demittitur alto dicebat Christo testimonium
perhibebat. Indubitanter hoc uenturum nisi illos
decantantibus dominus sanctis in medio ignis ardentium
Illi illi regem quis sanctorum superbie cupientem
perdomuit nabuchodonosor regem scilicet
babilonis non praetermittam. Dic nabuchodonosor
quid in fornace quo tres uiros ligatos inter
misisti dic quid tibi fuerit reuelatum. Nonne
inquit tres uiros misimus in fornace ligatos et
uiuunt dicit? Uere rex. Ecce inquit uideo ego quattuor
uiros solutos deambulantes in medio ignis
et corruptio nulla est in eis et aspectus quarti
similis filio dei. Quaeso alienigena unde tibi hoc quis
tibi adnuntiauit filium dei. Quae lex quae propheta
adnuntiauit filium dei? Nondum quidem in mun
do nascitur, et similitudinem nascentis agnoscis
unde tibi hoc quis tibi suggessit adnun
tiare nisi quia sicut diuinitus ignis ille lu
minauit ut qui illic apparebat ecce
praesentis inimici iudaei sic dicens testimonium filio
dei. Sed quia in ore duorum uel trium testium stat omne
uerbum sicut ipse dominus suum contumacibus
confitetur in lege uestra scriptum est quia duorum
hominum testimonium uerum est etenim decantantibus
dignis testibus introducitis testimonium
ueritatis et omni pugnare sufficit testis. Quid sibilla
uaticinando etiam de Christo clamauerit in medium
proferam ut ex uno lapide utrorumque frontes percu
tiantur iudaeorum scilicet atque paganorum atque suo
gladio sicut goliath Christi omnes percutiantur inimi
ci.

Audite quid dixerit.

Iudicii signum tellus sudore madescet
E caelo rex adueniet per saecla futurus
Scilicet in carne praesens ut iudicet orbem
Unde deum [illegible] incredulus atque fidelis
C[elsum …]
Sic animae cum carne aderunt quas iudicat
Cum iacet incultus densis in uepribus orbis
Reicient simulacra uiri cunctam quoque ga[zam]
Exuret terras ignis pontumque polumque
Inquirens taetri portas effringet auerni
Sanctorum sed enim cunctae lux libera carni
Tradetur sontes aeterna flamma cremabit
Occultos actus retegens tunc quisque loquetur
Secreta atque deus reserabit pectora luci
Tunc erit et luctus stridebunt dentibus omnes
Eripitur solis iubar et chorus interit astris
Uoluetur caelum lunaris splendor obibit
Deiciet colles ualles extollet ab imo
Non erit in rebus hominum sublime uel altum
Iam aequantur campis montes et caerula ponti
Omnia cessabunt tellus confracta peribit
Sic pariter fontes torrentur fluminaque igni
Et tuba tum sonitum tristem dimittet ab alto
Orbe gemens facinus miserum uariosque labores
Tartareumque chaos monstrabit terra dehiscens
Et coram hic domino reges sistentur ad unum
Reccidet e caelo ignisque et sulphuris amnis

Haec de Christi natiuitate passione et resurrectione atque
secundo eius aduentu ita dicta sunt ut si quis
in graeco capita horum uersuum discernere uoluerit
inueniat Ihesus Christos Theu Soter quod in latinum
translatis eisdem uerbis apparet praeter quod
graecus linguarum proprietas non udeo potuit
obseruari. Credo iam uos o inimici iudaei tantis
testibus ita obrutos confutatosque esse ipsa ueri
tate ut nihil ultra repugnare nihil quaerere
debeatis

FER IIII ANTE NATALE DNI

Lectio sci euangli secundum lucan.

In illo tempore missus est angelus gabriel
a deo in ciuitatem galileae cui nomen nazareth
ad uirginem desponsatam uiro cui nomen erat
ioseph de domo dauid et nomen uirginis mariae. et reliqua.

OMELIA EIUSDEM LECTIONIS BEATI BEDE PRESBITERI

Liber misticus

11TH CENTURY *IN.* (FOL. 53R)

BRITISH LIBRARY, LONDON, ADD. MS. 30846.
PROVENANCE: MONASTERY OF SANTO DOMINGO DE SILOS (BURGOS).
Good-quality parchment; 15th century binding, leather over boards; comprises 1 + 175 + 1 leaves, numbered in the upper right margin in the 18th century, but numbers 90 and 121 are repeated; the leaves measure 295 × 235 mm; the writing frame measures 212 × 182 mm; part (A) of the codex has two columns, framed by double vertical lines on the outside and a single line between the columns; other quires (part B) have one column with a single vertical boundary line on both sides; vertical prickings are visible at the edge; the horizontal prickings run along the right margin; the number of lines varies from 21 to 24; ruled in drypoint with the odd leaves placed over the even ones and the quire folded in part A; in part B the quire is not folded and the first bifolium is placed over the second, whereas the fourth is placed over the third; Visigothic minuscule; some words in Arabic were written by the same scribes (fols. 8, 15v, 24, 52v, 58v, 100 and 169); there are basically two scribes: one for part A which covers leaves 1-7; 13; 25-56; 75-87; and another for part B, responsible for leaves 8-12; 14-24; 57-74; and 88-175; leaves 132r-135v, which contain a *Sermo de cotididie* (sic), are from a subsequent hand; fol. 175 was left blank for part of the recto and all of the verso and this space was used by another hand to copy the Passion of St. Julian. The complexity of the manuscript's composition leads one to think that scribe B found the leaves of scribe A, the remains of a *liber misticus* that was incomplete for whatever reason, and used them to complete his work. In fact, in some cases (fols. 13, 56v) he scraped off the parts of A that did not interest him, and he left other parts of his own leaves blank (fols. 24v, 74v) so that they would fit in better with those of part A; the musical notation is typical of the northern part of the Peninsula.

General contents: Goes from Easter Monday to Pentecost.

Leaf shown: 53r
Dominus Iesus Cristus qui es testis fidelis, primogenitus mortuorum et princeps regnum terre, ipse dilexit nos et labit nos a peccatis nostris sanguine suo, alleluia. UERSUS. *Qui ambulat.* ORATIO. *Domine Ihesu Christe qui es testes fidelis, primogenitus mortuorum, laba nos a conlubionibus uniuersis ut qui dudum nos labasti in sanguine tuo, nunc quoque nos interminabilibus iustifices indulgentie donum, ut per te abeamus uitam per quem uocati sumus ad gratiam. Amen.* LAUDES. *Christus Iesus qui cum in forma Dei esset non rapinam arbitratus est esse se equalem Dei, set semetipsum exinaniens formam serbi accepit, umiliabit se usque ad mortem, mortem autem crucis. Ydeo Dominus Iesus Cristus in gloria est Dei Patris, alleluia.* UERSUS. *Christus Iesus surgens a mortuis iam non moritur, mors illi non dominabitur. Ideo.* DE CANTICO. *Ad prendam Domine ascendisti, requiescens accubuisti ut leo ex uirtute tua suscitatures.* UERSUS. *Ludate* [sic] *lau.* LAUDES. *Laudate Dominum de celis, alleluia.* UERSUS. *Lauda.* QUERE RETRO CONPLETURIA. DE *II* FERIA AD VESPERVM. VESPERTINUM. *Letetur celi et exultet terra.* [In the margin: UERSUS. *Mobeatur ma[re] et plenitud[o] eius. Et*]. UERSUS. *Gaudebunt campi et omnia que in eis sunt. P. Et ex.* ANTIPHONA. *Pater glorie suscitabit Iesum Cristum a mortuis et conlocabit eum et potestatem et uirtutem et dominatio super omnem nomen quod nominauitur.* UERSUS. *Notum fecit Dominus.*

Both parts of the manuscript were supposed to include musical notation; the texts to be notated were written in letters of reduced size. Nevertheless, except for a handful of cases, and always with a hand different from those of the scribes (as in the leaf shown), the notation was never added. Even here, the scribe copied a verse in the margin showing considerable inexperience in the writing of neumes. The notation is unusually large and somewhat inclined to the right.

BIBLIOGRAPHY
EDIT. JANINI 1976-1979. DÍAZ Y DÍAZ 1983, 404-405. WALKER 1998, 49 *ET PASSIM.* MILLARES CARLO ET AL. 1999, 1: 86-87.

Miguel C. Vivancos

Detail of fol. 53r

Dominus Ihesus Cristus qui
est testis fidelis primo genitus
mortuorum et princeps regnum terre ipse dilexit nos
et lauit nos a peccatis nostris in sanguine suo alle luia.

Domine Ihesu Christe qui es testis
fidelis primogenitus
mortuorum laua nos a
conluuionibus uniuersis:
ut qui dudum nos lauisti
in sanguine tuo nunc
quoque nos in eo mirabiliter
efficies in dulcedine
donum: Ut pace abeunti
cum per quam uocati sumus
ad gloriam. Amen.

et ... labia ... usque
ad mortem ... cum eis ...
dominus Ihesus Cristus in gloria est dei patris alle luia.

Xpistus Ihesus surgens a mortuis iam non moritur mors
illi non dominabitur ...

AC Ad prandium domini ascendisti requiescatis accubuisti
ut leo expurgisceris a mortuis suscitatus. Et lauda...

L Laudate dominum de celis ... Et laus.
QUERE RETRO:

DIE TERTIA AD VESPERUM

...

Gaude bona campi ... omnia que in eis sunt: ...

Plesum ... ...

... ...

... ... super om-
nem nomen quod nominatur ...

Liber misticus

11TH CENTURY *MED.* (FOL. 4R)

BRITISH LIBRARY, LONDON, ADD. MS. 30845.
PROVENANCE: MONASTERY OF SANTO DOMINGO DE SILOS (BURGOS).
The parchment is of mediocre quality; 15th century binding in leather over boards; comprises 1 + 161 + 1 leaves, foliated in the upper right corner in the 18th century, but the numbers 54, 127 and 132 are repeated and the numbers 63-66 are omitted; the leaves measure 370 × 265 mm; the writing frame measures 289 × 187 mm; two columns justified with double vertical lines in every case; vertical prickings are visible at the edge; the horizontal prickings, in the majority of the quires, run along the center of the second column; the number of lines varies from 27 to 31; written principally by two scribes; the first, rather careless, was responsible for fols. 8-121, which he wrote in a light ochre ink. The scribe responsible for the musical notation, who used a considerably darker ink, took the time to redo the stems and downward strokes. The second scribe, responsible for fols. 121-150, is somewhat more meticulous than the first; a different hand copied fols. 150-152, and another on fols. 152-159. Finally, a fifth scribe finished the codex, copying fols. 1-7 and 160-161. Fols. 91-94 form a binion with the Mass of the Assumption of the Virgin, added between quires x and xi of the *liber misticus* in the 11th century. Leaf 4 was an addition, as was leaf 84, a piece of parchment with notated liturgical formulas. The notation is northern Visigothic.

General contents: Offices of Quiricus, Jerome, Adrian and Natalia, John the Baptist, Pelagio, Zoilo, Peter and Paul, Christopher, Justa and Rufina, Esperato and Marina, *Officium de primitiis,* Cucuphas, Felix, Justus and Pastor, Mamas, Lawrence, *Sacratio Sancti Martini,* Assumption of St. Mary, Ginés, Augustine, Cyprian, Euphemia, Michael, Faustus and Januarius and Martial, Cosmas and Damian, Servandus and Germain, Vincent and Sabina and Cristeta, Martin, Emilianus, *Translatio Sancti Saturnini, Officium de letanias canonicas,* Bartholomew.

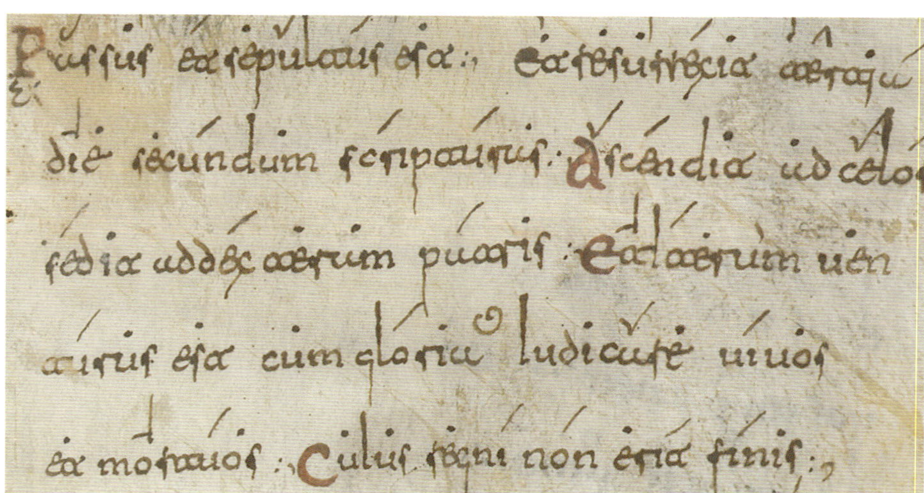

Detail of fol. 4r

Leaf shown: 4r
Credo in unum Deum patrem omnipotentem, factorem celi et terre, uisiuilium ominum [sic] *et inuisiuilium. Et in unum dominum Ihesum Cristum, filium Dei unigenitum, ex Patre natum ante homnia secula, Deum de Deo, lumen de lumine, Deum uerum de Deo uero, genitum non factum, cumsubstantialem Patris per quem omnia facta sunt. Qui propter nos homines et propter nostram salutem descendit de celis. Et incarnatus est de Spiritu Sancto et* [sic] *Maria uirgine et homo factus est. Crucifixus etiam por nouis sub Pontio Pilato, passus et sepultus est. Et resurrexit tertia die secundum scripturas. Ascendit ad celos, sedit ad dexteram Patris et iterum uenturus est cum gloria iudicare uiuos et mortuos, cuius regni non erit finis. Et in Spiritum Sanctum dominum et uiuificantem, qui ex Patre et Filioque procedit, qui cum Patre et Filio simul adorandum et cumglorificandum, qui locutus est* per *prophetas. Et unam sanctam catholicam et apostolicam eclesiam. Confiteor unum babtismum in remissione peccatorum et expecto resurrectionem mortuorum et uitam futuri seculi. Amen.*

The manuscript has musical notation written in darker ink than the text; occasionally the neumes spill into the margins. The leaf shown is a piece of parchment added to the codex in the second half of the 11th century, with Visigothic minuscule and notation, but with the peculiarity of including some rhythmic signs represented by the letters *a (augete)* and *t* (*tenete,* only on the verso), in a highly cursive script under the relevant syllables *(Deum, et homo, passus).* There are also two unusual rounded signs for the *torculus* and the *scandicus.* On the verso of the leaf there is the *laus* which begins: *Quem cuncta laudant,* followed by another which begins: *Nulla laude.*

BIBLIOGRAPHY

EDIT. JANINI 1976-1979. DÍAZ Y DÍAZ 1983, 403-404. WALKER 1998, 49 *ET PASSIM.* MILLARES CARLO ET AL. 1999, 1: 86.

Miguel C. Vivancos

Credo in unum deum patrem 4
omnipotentem. Factorem
celi et terre. Uisibilium omnium
et inuisibilium. Et in unum dominum
Ihesum christum filium dei unigenitum.
Et ex patre natum ante omnia secula.
Deum de deo lumen de lumine deum uerum
de deo uero. Genitum non factum cum
substantialem patris per quem omnia
facta sunt. Qui propter nos homines
et propter nostram salutem descendit
de celis. Et incarnatus est de spiritu sancto
ex maria uirgine. Et homo factus est.
Crucifixus etiam pro nobis sub pontio pilato.
Passus et sepultus est. Et resurrexit tertia
die secundum scripturas. Ascendit in celos
sedet ad dexteram patris. Et iterum uen
turus est cum gloria iudicare uiuos
et mortuos. Cuius regni non erit finis.
Et in spiritum sanctum dominum et uiuifi
cantem. Qui ex patre et filio procedit.
Qui cum patre et filio simul adorandum
et conglorificandum. Qui locutus est
per prophetas. Et unum sanctum catho
licum et apostolicum ecclesiam.
Confiteor unum baptismum in remissione
peccatorum. Et expecto resurrectionem
mortuorum. Et uitam futuri se
culi amen.

Liber misticus

11TH-12TH CENTURIES (FOL. 45R)

BIBLIOTECA CAPITULAR DE TOLEDO, 35-7 (OLIM 30.29; 35.40. SINCE 1808, 35-7).
PROVENANCE: PARISH OF SANTA EULALIA (TOLEDO).
Well-preserved parchment; modern binding in simple parchment over boards (20th century); 122 leaves; the beginning and end are fragmentary; lacunae between fols. 70v-71r (one leaf); fols. 72v-73r (one leaf); fols. 74v-75r (one leaf); modern foliation in ink with Arabic numerals in the upper right margin; the leaves measure 305 × 240 mm; the text block measures 220 × 170 mm; two columns justified with one vertical line at both outer edges and between the columns, but when the text is notated, it is generally arranged in one column; horizontal prickings for the space between the columns; the vertical prickings are imperceptible; 25 lines; ruled in drypoint placing the even leaves over the odd ones; Visigothic minuscule from the end of the 11th century or beginning of the 12th century; uncial M that opens toward the right; the O has a central point; the r has an artificial point; additions in Visigothic cursive from the end of the 13th century (fols. 41v, 54r, 55v, 87r); the scribe is Sebastianus (fol. 54r); horizontal Visigothic notation of the style from Toledo with consistent strokes, typical of a later period.

General contents: The *Libellus* of St. Mary with seven *missae* or lessons of the office taken from the *De Virginitate* of St. Ildephonsus. An *Ordo ad commendandum* (fols. 44r-45v), interspersed with other chants, is followed by the office of the Assumption of the Virgin and a selection of offices and Masses from the Christmas cycle to the *Apparitio Domini.* [Fragmentary. Three quires are missing.] *Officium in diem Sanctae Mariae* (fols. 1r-35r); *Ordo ad commendandum corpora defunctorum* (fol. 44r); *Ad Accedentes* [= Sequentia]. *Alme virginis festum* (fol. 45r); *Officium in Adsumptio sancte Marie* (fol. 45v); *In Nativitate Sancte Mariae* (fol. 54r, added in the 13th century); *Finit liber de dicta sancta Maria mater Domini vel adsumptio eius* (fol. 55r); *Officium in diem Nativitatis Domini* (fol. 55r); one leaf, originally blank, with added antiphons (fol. 55v); *Officium in diem Sancti Stephani* (fol. 73r); *Officium in diem Sancti Iohannis Apostoli* (fol. 86v); *Officium in diem Circumcisionis Domini* (fol. 94v); *Officium in diem Apparitionis Domini* (fol. 112r). [Fragmentary. At least one quire is missing.]

Leaf shown: 45r
[ORDO AD COMMENDANDUM CORPORA DEFUNCTORUM]
[*Item* ad *missa Canticu*m *angelo*rum *Gloria in excelsis Deo,* fol. 44v.]
Domine Deus... Cum sancto spiritu in gloria Dei patris amen.

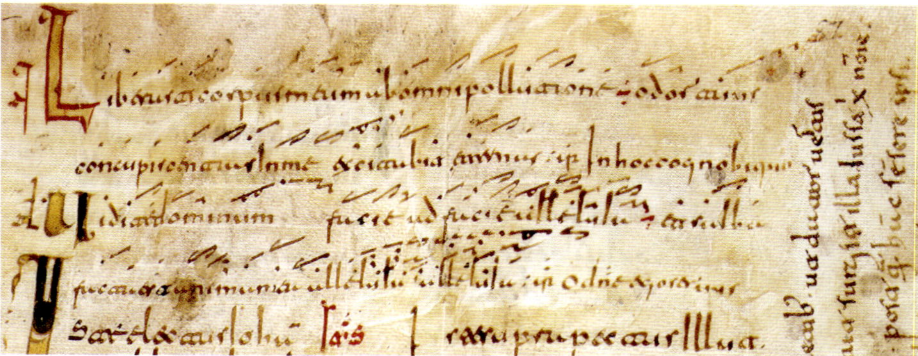

Detail of fol. 87r

*I*TEM *PROLOGUS.*
Ymnus trium puerorum. Angelus Domini simul descendit. Deo gratias.
*A*D *ACCEDENTES Alme virginis festum advenit gaudete omnes simul in unum. Alle.*
Tellus polusque maria et aque que sunt supra in celis. E.
Aerus nos venit cunctos liberare gratis omnes gaudeamus. E.

This codex exhibits a certain similarity with the codices BC, 35-1 and 35-3, which are also from the parish of Santa Eulalia in Toledo where they were used until the 14th century. 35-7 served as a model for the Mozarabic editions of Cardinal Cisneros during the 15th century. In 1753, a complete copy of the manuscript was prepared (Madrid, BN, ms. 13060, fols. 1r-117r). In 1755 the Jesuit researcher Burriel hired the calligrapher Palomares to undertake a reproduction on parchment that is still preserved as ms. II/483, in the biblioteca del Palacio Real de Madrid. The fol. 145r shows a sequence with the unique heading "ad accedentes, Alme virginis", which ends with an "alleluia" for which the melisma ascends the right margin. This is the latest known copy used in the Mozarabic parishes of Toledo.

BIBLIOGRAPHY

FÉROTIN 1912, COLS. 738-754. MILLARES CARLO 1935, NO. 26. ANGLÈS 1938, 1-68. BROU 1951, 33-35, ILLUS. XII. MILLARES CARLO 1963, NO. 176. MUNDÓ 1965, 14-15. PINELL 1965, 109-164, NO. 101, NO. 147 AND NO. 179. RANDEL 1969, 7, 85; 1973, 482-485. JANINI 1977, 103-104; 1978, 161-177. GROS 1978, 45-64. JANINI 1983, II: 233-273, ILLUS. III, fol. 50r. MUNDÓ 1983, 175-196. GONZÁLVEZ 1985, 157-185.

Susana Zapke

Domine deus rex celestis. deus pater omnipotens. Domine fili unigenite ihesu christe. Domine deus agnus dei filius patris. Qui tollis peccata mundi miserere nobis. Qui tollis peccata mundi suscipe deprecationem nostram. Qui sedes ad dexteram patris miserere nobis. Quoniam tu solus sanctus. Tu solus dominus. Tu solus altissimus ihesu christe. Cum sancto spiritu in gloria dei patris amen.

ITEM PROLOGUS

Hymnus trium puerorum. Angelus domini simul descendit cum azaria et sociis eius in fornace. Et excussit flammam ignis de fornace et fecit medium fornacis quasi ventum spiritum roris flantem. Et non tetigit eos omnino ignis neque contristavit neque quicquam molestie intulit. Tunc illi tres quasi ex uno ore hymnum dicebant et magnificabant et benedicebant domino de fornace dicentes:

AD ACCEDENTES

Alme virginis festa in mundum venit a quo gaudeat omnes simul in unum alle

stellas poli quem nunc nuntiat aqui terrena super ... celis

... nostra venia cunctos liberet et tueatur omnes qui credimus

Psalterium, Liber canticorum, Liber hymnorum

12TH-13TH CENTURIES / 9TH CENTURY (MILLARES CARLO) (FOL. 82R)

BIBLIOTECA NACIONAL, MADRID, MS. 10001 (OLIM MS. 35.1).
PROVENANCE: THE PRIMATE CATHEDRAL OF TOLEDO.
ORIGIN: A) TOLEDO (DOMÍNGUEZ BORDONA, MUNDÓ, KLEIN); B) LEÓN (ENCISO, MILLARES CARLO, DÍAZ).
Poor-quality parchment; binding in leather that has turned yellowish on the board; there are still traces of metal clasps; four protruding ribs on the spine; 172 leaves; the two front guard leaves belong to a *liber misticus* (mass of the 5th Sunday in Advent and part of the office of Christmas), fol. 141, palimpsest, add. 12th century); late Roman foliation in ink *(psalterium)* and Arabic foliation in ink in the rest; modern foliation in pencil; the leaves measure 335/340 × 255 mm; the text block measures 275 × 190 mm; the quaternions show catalog numbers in Roman numerals followed by the abbreviation for *quaternio (Q);* two columns justified by a double line on each side; prickings are hardly visible; 29 lines; ruled in drypoint with a direct impression onto the hair side; Mozarabic-type Visigothic minuscule; the texts with notation have smaller writing; the *ti* ligature before a vowel does not show the sibilate spelling; highly characteristic ligature between the letters *an,* typical of cursive writing; one main hand signed by Mauro (fol. 75v) and a second one, very similar to the previous one, that intervenes in the *Psalterium;* the copy seems to have been produced for a presbyter called Abundancio (fol. 75v); dating: a) 10th century *med.*; b) 12th to 13th centuries (Mundó); horizontal Visigothic notation *in campo aperto,* characteristic of codices from the northern peninsular tradition; careless strokes, making it difficult to define the profile of the various neumes and giving the impression that the copying of the melodies was carried out rather hastily; on the other hand, the notation in the leaves added at the beginning of the codex (fols. 1-2v: *Liber misticus*) is beautiful and precise; the spelling is clearly defined, and the writing axis runs vertically, characteristic of the tradition in the north of the Peninsula; the fragment reproduced here clearly shows the difference between both kinds of notation, thanks to the scraping and addition of three lines, in the right column, of fol. 2r, in southern or horizontal notation.

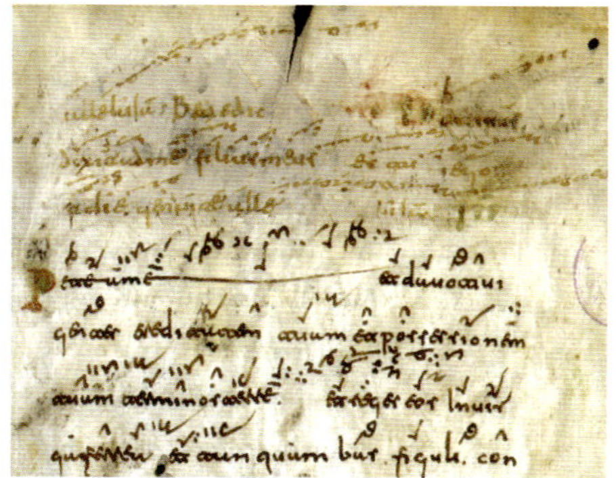

Detail of fol. 2r. Biblioteca Nacional de España

General contents: the body of the manuscript contains a *liber psalmorum,* a *liber canticorum,* and a *liber hymnorum.* The organization of its contents suggests a connection with the kingdom of León through certain poetic compositions, for example, a hymn in honor of Santiago; however, from a paleographic point of view, it shows influences from the cultural sphere of Toledo.

Leaf shown: 82r (fol. 165r, pagination in ink) Fragment of the Gospel according to St. Luke (1:46-55) and another fragment from the Book of Isaiah (45:8-9). The first one, which contains the *Magnificat,* is number 14 in the series. It is preceded by the antiphon: "Fecit mici magna qui potens est / et sanctum nomen eius et miseri- / cordia eius in omni progenie". The second hymn, number 15 in the series, begins with the verse: "Rorate celi desuper et nubes pluant iustum". As in the previous case, it is preceded by the antiphon: "Aperiatur terra et germinet salba- / torem et iustitia oriatur simul".

The manuscript was possibly in a Mozarabic parish church in Toledo for a long period. Both antiphons are introduced by zoomorphic initials in a typically Mozarabic style and are provided with Visigothic notation from the south of the Peninsula. The texts are two classical hymns that form part of the Spanish liturgical tradition. The Jesuit Andrés Marcos Burriel, commissioned a copy of the Psalter (Madrid, BN, 13050) and the Hymn book (Madrid, BN, 13056) in 1754.

BIBLIOGRAPHY
DOMÍNGUEZ BORDONA 1933: 1, NO. 671. ENCISO 1941-1942, 307; 1943, 189-211. DÍAZ Y DÍAZ 1959, 340, 341, 343-366, 538-539, 541-543, 545, 547, 551-552, 554, 634, 639, 641, 654-655, 661-662 AND 669. MILLARES CARLO 1963, NO. 84. MUNDÓ 1965, 14. RANDEL 1969, 7. FERNÁNDEZ DE LA CUESTA 1980, 83. DÍAZ Y DÍAZ 1983, 156, 324-325, 426-427. GONZÁLVEZ 1997, 770, 772. WALKER 1998, 115. MILLARES CARLO ET AL. 1999, 1: 112-113.

Elisa Ruiz García

populo meo. plurimum faciet
lex et eligit et lapides:
Et leuabit signum ad populos
ecce dominus audiat in fecit a
ub ex extremis terre:
Dicite filie Sion ecce salu
uator tuus ueniet ecce
merces eius cum eo. et opus
illius coram ipso:
Et uocabunt eos populus sanctus
redempti a domino. tu
uero uocaberis ciui
tas quesita et non
derelicta: XIIII:

Canticum ex euangelio secundum lucam:

Fecit mihi magna qui potens est
et sanctum nomen eius et misericordia
eius in progenie et progenie
et generatione:

Magnificat
animam mea
dominum et exultauit
spiritus meus in deo salu
tari meo:
Quia respexit humili
tatem ancille sue
ecce enim ex hoc beatam
me dicent omnes generati
ones. Quia fecit mihi
magna qui potens est et sanc
tum nomen eius. et mi
sericordia eius in proge
nies et progenies timen
tibus eum:
Fecit potentiam in brachio
suo dispersit superbos mente
cordis sui:
Deposuit potentes de sede et
exaltauit humiles:
Esurientes repleuit bonis
et diuites dimisit inanes:
Suscepit israhel puerum suum
memorari misericordie sue
sicut locutus est ad pa
tres nostros abraham et semi
ni eius usque in seculum: XV:

Canticum esaie prophete:

Aperiatur terra et germinet saluatorem
et iustitia oriatur simul:

Rorate celi desuper
et nubes pluant iustum
Aperiatur
terra et germi
net saluato
rem et iustitia oriatur
simul. ego dominus creaui eum.
Ve qui contradicit fictori
suo testa de samiis terre

Antiphonary (fragmentum)

11TH CENTURY *IN.* (FOL. 1R)

ARQUIVO DA UNIVERSIDADE, COIMBRA, IV-3.ª-GAV. 44 (22), X *EX.*-XI *IN.*
PROVENANCE: CATHEDRAL OF COIMBRA (PORTUGAL).
Well-preserved parchment, despite having been damaged on all its margins; it was used as binding material; fol. 1v has a darker color due to being in direct contact with the wood on the covers when it was used as a guard leaf for a 14th century missal; the fragment was discovered at the end of the 1920s; one leaf; it has no foliation; the leaf measures 272 × 218 mm; the text blockmeasures 267 × 171 mm; one column is justified by a double vertical line on both sides; horizontal prickings are partially visible in the left margin; vertical prickings cannot be seen; 25 lines (20 with text); ruled in drypoint; liturgical Visigothic minuscule without any Carolingian influence and in two sizes, the texts provided with notation being smaller; initials in red and black, fine interlace motif in the initial *X* in "Christus"; in the *D* in "Dominus" on fol. 1v there are still strokes in green ink; written by a single hand; Visigothic notation angled to the right, of the type known as *horizontal*, resembilng the notation in manuscripts from Toledo; the neumes are not written diastematically, despite the fact that they are in a broad space between the lines that results from having left blank one of every two lines of the text block ruling.

General contents: Vespers office for the Saturday before the third Sunday in Advent. Leaf verso: End of the Completuria, rubric "Ad Matutinum", incipit of the hymn *Eterne rerum* and the first antiphon of the *matutinum Erit Dominus sicut ros.*

Leaf shown: 1r
Antiphon *Ero quasi ros Israel* Versus *Quoniam Iacob elegit sibi Dominus* Hymnus *Christi caterva* Versus *Veni Domine et noli tardare* Completuria *Christe Ihesu Dei Filius admirabilis.*

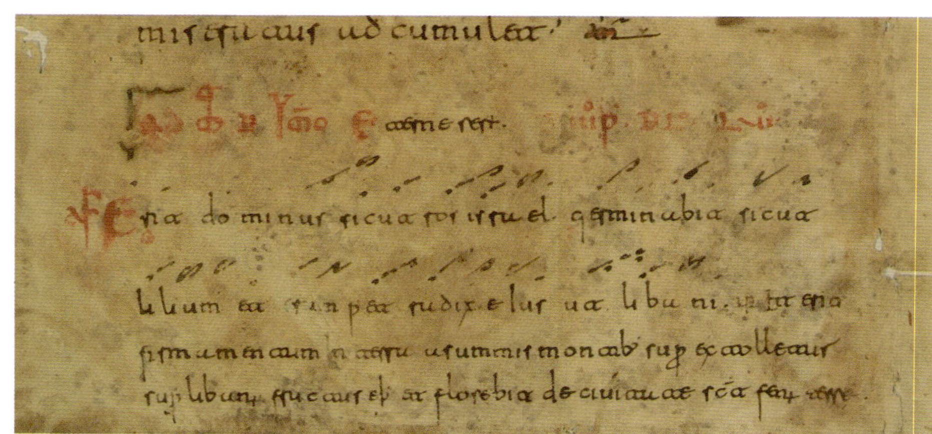

Detail of fol. 1v

This is one of the few witnesses of the Spanish rite to have survived in Portugal; it is beautiful yet crude.

It is worth mentioning the resemblance of the *ductus* in the notation to that in some codices from Toledo, especially Toledo 35-7, although in the Coimbra fragment the neumes are more clearly defined. Certain spellings appear that are common to those in Visigothic notation in the south of the Peninsula, such as the compound neumes, the *scandicus* with three notes or *salicus*, and the signs for a melody to be repeated (two dots framing an oblique line under *et,* on the third line, and a *G* under *ego* on the fourth line). Given the clear similarity with Toledo, as far as the morphology of the notation is concerned, some authors point out that the codex might have been brought in during the reconquest of Coimbra (1064) by King Ferdinand I the Great (1037-1065). The possibility that it might have originated in the see of Coimbra itself cannot be ruled out either (Corbin, Brou). Rojo and Prado, Corbin, Brou, Millares Carlo, and Ruiz Asencio all agree regardingthe date of the fragment.

BIBLIOGRAPHY

ROJO AND PRADO 1929, 39. VASCONCELOS 1929, 245-273. MILLARES CARLO 1931, 133. CORBIN 1952b, 173. BROU 1955, 29. MILLARES CARLO 1963, 13-14. PINELL 1965, 134. DÍAZ Y DÍAZ 1983, 369-370. FERNÁNDEZ DE LA CUESTA 1983, 115. QUEIRÓS 1993. FERREIRA 1993, 16/1: 458. MILLARES CARLO ET AL. 1999, 1: 43. QUEIRÓS 2000, 140.

Maria José Azevedo Santos
Marco Daniel Duarte

A[ntiphona]. Iso quasi flos fructus est — dicit dominus alleluia

quia ex me fructuatus est lux in ueritatem et alleluia

et odor eius sicut odor libani et quasi oliba

gloria eius ego gaudium et di — rigam

illum alleluia alle — luia. V. Quoniam Iacob elegit sibi

dominus et Israhel in possessionem sibi. Et odor. Gloria. Ant. Spiritus sanctus eum

PR. Veni domine et noli tardare

Xpe Ihesu Dei filius admirabilis cui nullus
in terris filior dei uel equalis est aut
uel similis. Excita potentiam tuam
et ueni ut saluos facias nos.
Ad te domine precem nostram dirigimus, ut
medelam quam pollicitus es requirentibus
dignenis prerogare conuersis.
Ac sic nos quorum moderamine discipline
corrigis, ut clementiam tuam in ira non
auferas. Nec prophanetur terrarum tuum
cultum ob admissa facinora, sed temperetur
ultio miseratione superna.
Talis te tantum quod displiceat ubique.

Collectaneum

10TH CENTURY (900, ALTURO) (FOL. 92V)

ARCHIVO DE LA CORONA DE ARAGÓN, BARCELONA, RIPOLL 106.
PROVENANCE: MONASTERY OF SANTA MARÍA DE RIPOLL (GIRONA).
Well-preserved parchment with an ivory tone; modern binding in parchment (19th century); 140 leaves; foliation in pencil with Arabic numerals in the upper right margin; the leaves measure 265 × 225 mm; the writing frame measurements vary depending on the sections that make up the codex; the leaves measure 215 × 170 mm; the horizontal prickings are recognizable in the right margin; the vertical prickings are imperceptible; one column that varies from 18 to 32 lines in different parts of the manuscript; the ruling is imperceptible; liturgical Carolingian minuscule; additions with 11th century *in.* writing; primary initials in red and brown, headings with letters filled in with red ink; some initials are also filled in with red ink in the body of the text; several hands; Catalonian notation *in campo aperto* with a noticeable tendency toward diastematy and subsequent additions (10th century *med., ex.* / 11th century) by different hands on some leaves.

General contents: A miscellaneous codex that includes various patristic texts and other texts of a scientific nature, with some tables for calculating the Christian calendar. On the back: *Artis metrica Bedae. Soliloquiorum S. Agustini.* The following notated fragments are included: 1. *Domine in virtute tua* (fol. 26v). 2. *Iudicii signum* (fol. 92v). 3. *Alleluia. Cantantibus organis* (fol. 92v). 4. *Sana, Domine, omnes languores nostros* (fol. 114v). 5. *Iste confessor Domini sacratus* followed by the antiphon *Deus deorum Dominus lucutus est* (fol. 114v). 6. *Himnum in natale apostolorum*: *Christe splendor glorie laudes* (fol. 140).

Leaf shown: 92v
METRUM IRETREAM SIBILLE MIRIFICE PROBATUERIT DE ADVENTUM DOMINI PRIMO ET SECUNDO ET CONSUMACIONE SECULI. Ivdicii signum tellus sudorem madescit [sic].
HIC DE PRIMO ADVENTUM DOMINI. In manus inquid infidelium.
[ADDED AT THE BOTTOM OF THE PAGE] *Alleluia. Cantantibus organis Celcilia* [sic] *virgo soli Domino decantabat dicens fiat cor meum et corpus meum... inmaculatum ut non confundar.*

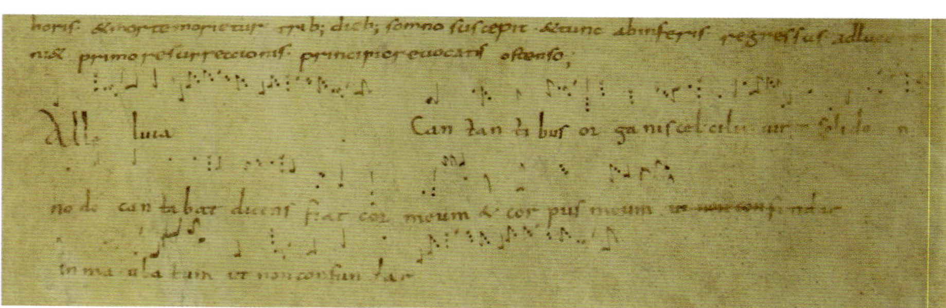
Detail of fol. 92v

The copy of the Song of Sybil verses of the *Iudicii signum* on fol. 92v represents one of the first testimonies of the Middle Ages and one of the oldest of all those related to the Spanish March, the historical nucleus of Catalonia. The verses are copied here, exceptionally, in an oblong manner, making maximum use of the space available. A well-known fragment of Lactantius on the passion, death and resurrection of Christ follows the verses. At the bottom of the page, in a space that was originally left blank, a later hand added the antiphon *Alleluia. Cantantibus organis,* with adiastematic Catalonian notation. The same hand wrote down the melody of the first verse of the Song of the Sybil, a total of 14 neumes. The limited interlinear space that was available must have dissuaded the scribe from continuing his work.

BIBLIOGRAPHY
BEER 1907-1908, 54, 59-66. ANGLÈS 1935, 134-136; 1941, 14. CORBIN 1952, 5-6. DONOVAN 1958, 166-167. GARRIGOSA 1994, 226-227. GÓMEZ MUNTANÉ 1997, 11-12. GARRIGOSA 2003, 65-66.

Maricarmen Gómez

sex tertii ... tempora euidenter demonstrat ; Tunc filii et ante legem et
ut sub legem tercium sub gratia ; Igitur ipse annus senarionumero continetur
habens enim dies ccc. lxv. ; Sexies quippe sexageni fiunt ccc. sexies remanent
festo dies v. ; Quinque dies secta sunt menses tamen ... si et illud queras per dies
peretorum sex faciunt ; Ecce quam ... medie aduuauit de senarii numeri perfectionem et si nouissimum uolui tamen quam ... reddis rationem ; UERSUS UER-

SIBILLE MIRIFICE PROBANT DE ADUENTU DOMINI PRIMO ET SECUNDO ET CONSUMMACIONE SECULI

Iudicii signum tellus sudore madescet
E caelo rex adueniet per secla futurus ; Scilicet ut in carne presens ut iudicet orbem ; Unde
deum cernent incredulus atque fidelis ; Celsum cum sanctis eui iam termino in ipso ; Sic anime
cum carne aderunt quas iudicat ipse ; Cum iacet incultus densis in uepribus orbis
reicient simulacra uiri cunctam quoque gazam ; Exuret terras ignis pontumque polumque ; Inquirens tetri portas effringet auerni ; Sanctorum sed enim cuncte lux libera carni ; Tradetur sontes aeterna flamma cremabit ; Occultus actus retegens tunc quisque loquetur
secreta atque deus reserauit pectora luci ; Tunc erit et luctus stridebunt dentibus omnes ; Eripitur solis iobar et chorus interit astris ; Voluetur caelum lunaris splendor obibit ;
Deicit colles ualles extollet ab imma ; Non erit in rebus hominum sublime uel altum ; Iam equantur campis montes cerula ponti omnia cessabunt ; Tellus confracta peribit sic pariter
torrentur ; flumina que igni ; Sed tuba tum sonitum tristem dimittet ab alto ; Orbe
gemens facinus miserum uariosque labores tartareumque chaos monstrauit terra dehiscens
et quoram hic domino reges sistentur ad unum recidet e caelo ignis que et sulphuris amnis

In manus inquid infidelium postea ueniet dabunt LIBRI DE PRIMO ADUENTU DOMINI
autem deo alapas manibus incestis et inpurato hore expuent uenenatos sputos ; Dabit uero
ad uerbera simpliciter sanctum dorsum et colapos accipiens tacebit ne quis agnoscat quod
uerbum aut unde uenit ut inferis loquatur et chorona spinea choronetur ad cibum autem
fel et ad sitim acetum dederunt in ospitalitatis hanc monstrabunt mensam ; Ipse enim insipiens tuum dominum non intellexisti medentem mortalium mentibus sed spinis choronasti et
orridum fel miscuisti templi uero scindetur et medio die nox erit ; Tenebrosa nam in tribus
horis et morte morietur tribus diebus somno suscepit et tunc ab inferis regressus ad lucem ueniet primo resurreccionis principio reuocatis ostenso ;

Alleluia Cantantibus organis cecilia uirgo soli do-
mino decantabat dicens fiat cor meum et corpus meum inmaculatum ut non confundar

Liber glossarum et t[...]logiarum

10th-11th Centuries (Alturo) / 11th Century *(post quem* 1020, Mundó) (fol. 4r)

Archivo de la Corona de Aragón, Barcelona, Ripoll 74.
Provenance: Monastery of Santa María de Ripoll (Girona).
Parchment; modern binding in parchment (19th century); 158 leaves; modern foliation in pencil, fols. 1-158; fols. 89v, 95v and 140v are blank; the leaves measure 297/358 × 245 mm; the writing frame varies considerably throughout the codex; the abundance of defects in the parchment imply numerous irregularities in the leaves' measurements and format; some leaves have one column, and others have two; the first part comprises the tonary, justified with double vertical lines from top to bottom on both sides; on some leaves the horizontal prickings are visible in the right margin; throughout the manuscript the number of lines varies; in the first section which corresponds to the tonary, there are 23 to 24 lines of text with its corresponding musical notation; in other sections it is common to have two columns and 30 lines; ruled in drypoint; Carolingian minuscule; capitals in red and black ink; initials and headings in red ink or with red ornamentation; several scribes were involved; numerous subsequent additions on several pages were left blank due to defects in the parchment; the different original units (fols. 1-16, 17-140 and 141-158) were grouped together at an early date; apparently, it was copied around 1020 by the monk Guifredo; Mundó recognizes the hand of this scribe who also worked on the Ripoll Bible currently preserved in the Biblioteca Apostolica Vaticana (Lat. 5729), in the tonary section (Mundó 1994: 144); Catalonian notation *in campo aperto.*

General contents: Manuscript with miscellaneous scholastic content. It is identified by various formulas: *Liber glossarum et [e]timologiarum, Liber glossarum et tonologiarum, Liber glossarum et timologiarum.* On the initial leaves of one copy of the *Etimologías* by St. Isidore, a scribe from the 11th century took on the task of copying a small tonary. The musical notation (Catalonian neumes) only appears in the first section of the codex (fols. 1-5v), a tonary (intonations in eight tones of the *Gloria patri,* introits, graduals, *alleluias,* offertories and communions), and on the leaves added at the end. There are also additions made by another, later scribe on some blank leaves (fols. 97v-98v, 102r), various erotic Latin poems in goliardic style dated to around the end of the 12th century (known as *Carmina Rivipullensia*) without musical notation, and other poems, notes and quotations (fols. 103v, 153v, 154r, 157v, 158r-v). Also on fols. 157v-158, which were originally left blank, various musical pieces were subsequently added (Responsories and *alleluias*) in Aquitainian and Catalonian notation. Fol. 1r contains various *probationes pennae* with neumes.

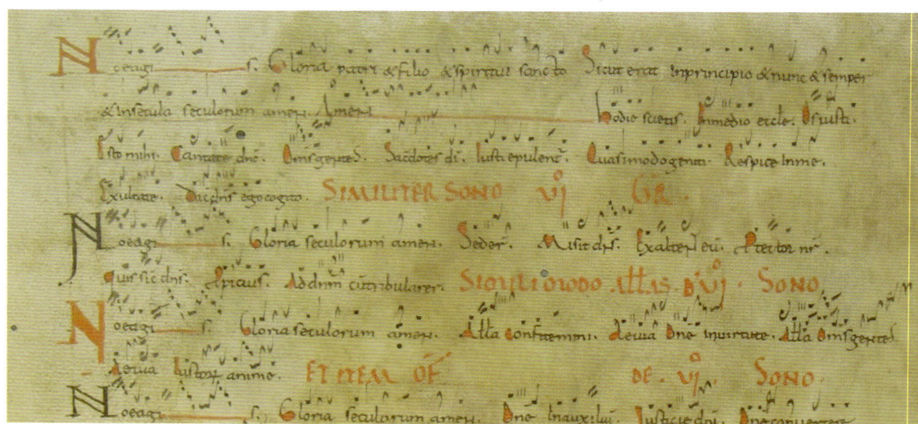

Detail of fol. 4r

Leaf shown: 4r
Corresponding intonations at the fifth tone. According to Alturo (1996), the codex must have been copied between 980 and 1000. In this codex the term *sonus* is used to refer to the tones *(tonus)*, as occurs in contemporary tonaries from the south of France. Despite the evidence of a certain degree of dependence on Aquitainian models, in Michel Huglo's opinion, the tonary from Ripoll has a distinctive character.

Bibliography

Bofarull 1823, 164. Sablayrolles 1909, 408-414. Beer 1910, 10, 74-75. Sablayrolles 1911, 302-303; 1911-1912, 210-211. García Villada 1915, 580-584 [39-43]. Nicolau d'Olwer 1923, 10-13, 24 (Facs.) 108. Llauró 1927, 331-338; 1928, 4: 271-341. Millares Carlo 1932, 246. Nicolau d'Olwer 1932, 240-249. Anglès 1935, 11, 134, no. 1, fig. 26; 1941, 4. Sunyol 1935, 365. *Le graduel romain* 1957, 31. Olivar 1967, 28, no. 18. Huglo 1971, 160-161. Anglès 1975, 282, 289-290. Rico 1976 [1994: 107-176]. Fernández de la Cuesta 1980, 73. Janini 1980, 43. Moll 1986, 404, 406. Ibarburu 1987, 282-283. Mas 1988, 20, 22. Garrigosa 1994, 224-225, 281, no. 283. Alturo 1996, 67-91. Bernadó 1999, 452. Gómez Muntané 1999, 137. Sargatal 1999, 432, no. 19. Garrigosa 2000, 34, no. 18, 46. Gómez Muntané 2001, 33, 34, 160. Mundó 2002, 80, 82. Garrigosa 2003, 62-64.

Màrius Bernadó

v Eterna corona glo ET INDE AN(S) QUI SIC INFLECTUNT XIIII SONO.

Noeagis Gloria patri & filio & spiritui sancto Sicut erat in principio & nunc & semper & in
secula seculorum amen. Rorate celi. Emitte. Post partum virgo. Seculorum amen. Ecce rex venit
da mercede. Posuisti dne. Seculorum amen. Intuens in caelu. Homo erat. Sem ist. So eculoru am.
Ex egipto. In mandatis ei. Seculorum amen. Rubum que viderat. Ambulabunt. Innouabant.
Seculorum amen. Sion renouaberis. Amor. In camino ignis. INCIPIUNT OFFICIA D[E] V SONO.

v Noeoeane Gloria patri & filio & spiritui sancto Sicut erat in principio & nunc & semper
& in secula seculorum amen Amen Loquebar. Dne refugium. Dne lux tua media. Me expectat.
Letare. Exaudi dns. Ecce dns aduenia. Miserere mi. Amen. Circumdederunt. ET SIMILITER D[E] V S[ONO] GR

Noeoeane Gloria seculorum amen. Ex sion. Benedictus. Videront. ET SIMILI MODO DE
Noeoeane Gloria seculorum amen. Alleluia Beatus uir. Alleluia Diligam. ALL(ELUI)AS V SONO
Alleluia memento dno. ITEM OF DE V SONO

Noeoeane Gloria seculorum amen. Reges tarsis. Iubilate. Benedic anima mea. ET
Noeoeane Gloria seculorum amen. Seruite dno. Intellege. EODEM MODO D[E] COM[PLETURIIS] V S.
In mandasti. Pacem meam. Ultimo festiuitatis. Non uos relinquam. Dico ubi. Panem de celo. Voce mea.
Iustus dns. Quis dabit. Aduersum me. Letabimur. Qui mihi ministrat. Domus mea. Unam peti.

ET RESPONSI QUI EODEM MODO INFLECTUNT V. SONO

Noeoeane Gloria patri & filio & spiritui sancto Sicut erat in principio & nunc & semper & in secula
seculorum amen. Obsecro dno. v Qui regis. Caedi sue ua... in ciuitate. Ecce ueni & dns. v Ec dnabit

ET INDE AN(S) QUI SIC FLECTUNT COM ES. A V SONO

Noeoeane Gloria patri & filio & spiritui sancto Sicut erat in principio & nunc & semper & in secula
seculorum amen. Letamini. Montes & omnes. Solute templu hoc. Aduenientes patro. Spe insuperabile.
Transactu puericia. Beata augusta. Iulianus fr. INCIPIUNT OFFICIA D[E] VI SONO

Miscellany

Second half of the 11th Century or *ex.* (fol. 63v)

Archivo de la Corona de Aragón, Barcelona, Ripoll 40.
Provenance: Monastery of Santa María de Ripoll (Girona).
Common title (12th century): *Translatio Sancti Stephani. Ecclesiasticus ordo ad Karolum. Epistule Hincmari ad Karolum* (fol. 1r). Title on the spine (19th century): *Translatio S. Estef. Cap. Caroli Magni.*
Parchment; modern binding in parchment (19th century); 65 leaves; modern foliation from fol. 1 to fol. 65; fols. 3v, 4r, 8r-v, 11r, 53r and 63v are blank; the leaves measure 360 × 300 mm; the writing frame measurements vary; two columns except for the first leaves (1v-33r), which are additions made by a subsequent scribe, and fol. 63v, which has long lines; prickings no longer visible; 40 lines of text throughout the majority of the leaves, in the main body of the manuscript; fol. 63v has 17 lines of text and music and 8 of text without musical notation; fol. 64 is written in two columns justified with a double vertical line on both sides, with 40 lines; on fol. 64v, at the end of the second column, two lines of neumes appear without text; in spite of having been prepared for it, fol. 65v was never notated; ruled in drypoint; Carolingian minuscule; initials alternate red and black ink, rubrics in red, various scribes; the main body of the codex, copied around 1020, is the work of the monk Guifredo; Catalonian notation oriented around drypoint lines traced for the ruling of the text.

General contents: *Liber Domini Ansegisi abbatis quem composuit ad Dominum Ludovicum et Lotarium eius filium imperatores [= Capitularium Caroli Magni et Ludovici Pii libri IV / collecti a Ansegiso abbate]. Liber quintus [= Capitularium regum franchorum liber primus / collectus a Benedicto levita]. [Et alia capitularia et opuscula].*
Summary of contents:
1. *De beato Stephano protomartire Christi qualiter corpus eius venerandum ab Iherosolimis Constantinopolim sit translatum XVIIIº kalendas ianuarii / Arnallus Scolasticus* (the addition of a subsequent scribe; fols. 1v-3r).
2. *Promissio Odonis regis* (the addition of another scribe somewhat later; fol. 4v).
3. *[Capitularia regum franchorum]* (fols. 5r-7v).
4. *Liber domni Ansegisi abbatis quem composuit ad domnum Ludovicum et lotarium eius filium imperatores [= Capitularium Karoli Magni et Ludovici Pii libri IV / Ansegiso abbate]* (fols. 9r-26v), followed by two tables of capitula of Charlemagne and Louis the Pious (fols. 26v-27v).
5. *Liber quintus [= Capitularium regum franchorum Liber primus / Benedicto levita]* (includes introductory verses, prefaces and the table of contents of the fifth book; fols. 27v-48v).
6. *[Capitularia regum franchorum]* (fols. 49r-52v).
7. *Sacrum Carthaginense concilium dicit. Quisquis episcoporum ad primates aecclesiae…* (fols. 53v-54v).
8. *[Epistola ad Carolum regem: Ecce domine sicut hic dilectus…] / [Hincmari Rhemensis]* (fols. 55r-62r).
9. *[Epistola ad Carolum regem: Ecce domine sicut hic dilectus frater…] / [Hincmari Rhemensis]* (fols. 62r-63r).
10. *Versus in natale apostolorum Petri et Pauli* (fol. 63v).
11. *Versus in honore Sancti Michaelis archangeli* (fols. 64r-v).

The final guard leaf is a folio (fol. 65r-v) with the episcopal *ordo* for the dedication of churches from the second half of the 11th century, without musical notation. The only musical notation found in the entire codex is that for two hymns, one dedicated to St. Peter and St. Paul (*Tempora fulgida nunc rutilant*, fol. 63v) and the other to St. Michael (*Splendida nempe dies rutilat*, fol. 64v). The notated portion of the manuscript is completely independent of the remainder of the codex.

Leaf shown: 63v
UERSVS IN NATALE APOSTOLORUM PETRI ET PAVLI. TEMpora fulgida nunc rutilant annua commoda iam remeant. Area frugibus aucta bonis fert noua gaudia ruricolis frondibus undique compta suis. Festa dies hodie renitet…

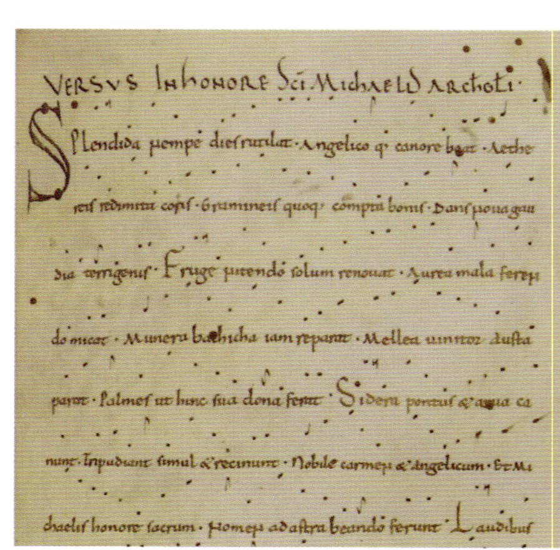

Detail of fol. 64r

These two hymns, with clear Visigothic affinities, are unique to Ripoll.

Bibliography

Viage literario viii, 1803-1852, 43. Bofarull 1823, 147. Ewald 1881, 386. Sablayrolles 1906-1909, 151. Beer 1907-1908, 98, 112. García Villada 1915, 559-560 [18-19]. Anglès 1932, 282. Nicolau d'Olwer 1932, 201, 209. Anglès 1935, 140, no. 8. Moragas 1961, 591-598. Olivar 1967, 28. Rico 1976 [1994, 107-176]. Fernández de la Cuesta 1980, 72. Ibarburu 1987, 278, 291-292. Garrigosa 1994, 221, 227, no. 278. Gómez Muntané 2001, 36. Mundó 2002, 80, 82. Garrigosa 2003, 58-59.

Màrius Bernadó

UERSUS IN NATALE APOSTOLORUM PETRI ET PAULI.

TEMpora fulgida nunc rutilant · Annua commoda iam remeant · Arua frugibus aucta bonis · Fert noua gaudia ruricolis · Frondib.

Festa dies hodie renitet · Petrus in aethere cum radiat · Paulus in astrea regna micat · Quo deus arbiter ad superum · Adiecit hac die collegium undiq. conspicuum

Agmine primus apostolico · Petrus in orbe dũt merito · Claviger inclitus insuper · Iura refert pia xpicolis · Soluit et alligat in populis ·

Ferrea uincula quem metuunt · Nec laquei retinere queunt · Carceris ostia sponte patent · Demonis agmina cuncta pauent · Nilq. sui retinere ualet ·

Ianitor aeternis ipse manet · Pastor et ipse gregis renitet · Cui pascua in recta suos · Pascere doctus ouando greges · Scandere sidera donat oues ·

Simonis omnia prestigia · Voce fugantur apostolica · Infernus haud cohibere ualet · Quem Petrus inde redire iubet · Tenta celica quique tenet ·

Paulus in orbe dedit monita · Dogmata preclue salutifica · Montibus unde salus rediit · Quomodo cuncta potens tribuit · Noxia queq. ualens repulit ·

Discipulis deus auctor ait · Quem fore me referunt homines · Vosq. mei pietate greges · Dicite quid sup hoc placeat · Quisq. fide de hoc pie quid sapiat ·

Petrus abhinc cui pura fides · Eminet aucta sup proceres · Primus ad hec uenerandus ait · Filius es patris ingeniti · Xpistus unicus ipse dei ·

Mox pius auctor ad hec fruito · Munera contulit ista suo · Vere beatus et ipse manes · Farre quod indice uera refers · Qui dominans sup astra sedet ·

Atq. libens tibi nunc refero · Denique tu petrus es merito · Hanc que petra sup ipse meam · Construo funditus aecclesiam · Quam sine fine tenendo regam ·

Nutibus insup ipse tuis · Dedo resoluere queq. uelis · Nexibus aut religare tuis · Te quoque clauibus aethereis · Munero quis tua fit super S

Denique Saulus in orbe furens · Atq. pios laniare uolens · Ceu fera belua cruore madens · Lumine territus aethereo · Sternitur orbus ipse solo ·

Sternitur impius atq. nocens · Surgit abhinc pius atq. ualens · Extimus inter apostolicos · Qui fuerat uenientio coros · Primus inde instruit ecclesias

Dat gregibus documenta sacra · Atq. dei monimenta pia · Aegra que corpora saluificat · Funeraq. somata uiuificat · Atq. animas pie purificat ·

Ianitor ętens et superi · Petrus ouile regens dni · Pellere crimina cuncta potens · Celsaque gaudia restituens · Vt uelit omnia semper agens ·

Retia liquerat et pelagi · Culmen adeptus apostolicum · Conspiciens sine fine dominum · Cuius ouanter ad imperium · Confugit omne genus hominum ·

Hi simul ergo duo proceres · Saluificos recreando greges · Martirio subiere poli · Quos nero traxit ad interitum · Demonis esca pater scelerum ·

Petrus enim subeundo crucem · Paulus et ense ferendo necem · Sic simul astrea regna petunt · Celica premia semper habet · Atq. dominum sine fine uidet ·

O bone pastor adesto tuis · Petre beate fauens famulis · Serto uiuamina plena bonis · Da ueniam scelerum miseris · A uariis libare malis

Suscipe carmina nostra libens · Respice nos pius atq. potens · Vt paradisus in astra uirens · Nos capiat sibi semper habens · Quam manet auctor et omni parens.

Hec quoque pocula nec non cibos · Sanctifica recreando tuos · Corpora quis hic foueas · Purificesq. potens animas · Nos quoque prospere possideas

Docto et alme tuere tuos · Paule beate fouens famulos · Da quoque mente subire poli · Quo uideant sine fine dominum · Teq. sui teneant socium ·

Euge beate ualensq. petre · Paule pop[ulo]q. me semper aue · Celica quos tenet aula dei · Angelici simul et cunei · Aetereiq. fouent populi ·

Virtus honorq. sit ingenito · Lausq. decus genito dno · Spiritui quoque paraclito · Gloria perpes et imperium · Sit sine tempore perpetuum Amen ·

Sacramentary, Ritual and Pontifical

11TH CENTURY (CA. 1000-1018) (FOL. 122R)

ARCHIVO CAPITULAR, LLEIDA, RODA 16 (OLIM MS. 14. NEW SHELFMARK: RC 0036).
PROVENANCE: CATHEDRAL OF RODA DE ISÁBENA (HUESCA). IT WAS PROBABLY COPIED IN THE *SCRIPTORIUM* OF LA SEU D'URGELL AND WAS PART OF A COLLECTION OF BOOKS DONATED TO RODA IN 1018, THE YEAR THE CHURCH WAS NEWLY CONSECRATED AFTER ITS DESTRUCTION, WHICH TOOK PLACE IN 1006 AT THE HANDS OF AL-MANSUR'S SON, THE GENERAL ABD-AL-MALIK.
The parchment is in a good state of preservation despite its continuous use; bound with wooden covers and a leather spine; 221 leaves (12 + 209); the first 12 leaves come from a 12th century lectionary; there are defects and leaves that have been reused after being scraped; foliation in ink with Arabic numerals in the central body of the volume (fols. 1-209); once the preliminary leaves that correspond to the lectionary were added, a new corresponding numbering was added in pencil (fols. 1-221); the leaves measure 330 × 240 mm; the writing frame measures 230 × 150 mm; fols. 205 and 206 correspond to an old interspersed quire of much smaller size *(Ordo super eum qui ab infidelitate ad ueram fidem et catholicam uoluit reuertere* and *benedictio uasorum);* two columns justified with double vertical lines; the horizontal prickings are visible in the outside lateral margin; 23 lines; ruled in drypoint; Carolingian minuscule; a larger module is used for the euchological texts and the headings than for the notated chants; the text is in dark brown or black ink and the headings are in red, occasionally they are highlighted in black; very simple initials in black and red ink highlighted with yellow and red strokes; some initials present floral decorations; worthy of special mention is the initial of *Te igitur* which represents the image of Christ on the cross; basically, the body of the manuscript was written by a single hand, characterized by a consistent and steady stroke; a second contemporary hand and a third hand from a somewhat later date took on various additions and corrections; archaic Catalonian notation reminiscent of Visigothic notation.

General contents: This manuscript comprises an important collection of ordines for the purpose of administering the sacraments and for other liturgical rituals. It also includes a Roman canon and an interesting collection of episcopal blessings for Mass. The liturgical structure and its texts follow the characteristic standards of the Catalonian-Narbonnaise liturgy, and contain elements from the Old Spanish liturgy. One of its peculiarities is the presence of antiphons with musical notation for the consecration of a church. Its notation gives good evidence of the coexistence of Visigothic notational procedures with newer elements.

Leaf shown: 122r
[*ANTIPHONAE IN DEDICACIONE ECCLESIE*]
Fundamenta templi huius sapiencia sua fundauit ea...

From a liturgical point of view, the manuscript is of particular interest for its combination of Visigothic formularies with other formularies of Franco-Roman origin. Because of various changes of catalog number, some scholars have referred to this manuscript as Roda 14. At some point, it was catalogued as manuscript 14 of the Archivo Capitular de Lleida, without taking into account the Roda manuscript numbers, leading to many errors of identification in various studies and repertories.

Detail of fol. 124v

BIBLIOGRAPHY

ESPAÑA SAGRADA XLVII, 327-331 (MANUEL ABAD Y LASIERRA); *VIAGE LITERARIO,* 1803-1852, 15: 175-177. ALTISENT 1926, 523-551. DOMÍNGUEZ BORDONA 1933, 194, NO. 330, FIG. 181. ANGLÈS 1935, 150, NO. 19, FIG. 36. GUDIOL 1955, 116, FIG. 105. RIUS 1957, 161-210. BOHIGAS 1960, 89-90, FIG. 32, 130a. *EL ARTE ROMÁNICO* 1961, 93. GROS 1964, 101. BARRIGA 1965, 3-58. GROS 1966, 321, 323-324. BARRIGA 1967, 205-224. OLIVAR 1967, 40. GAMBER 1968, NO. 1575. BARRIGA 1974; 1975, 36-37; 1978, 11-41. JANINI 1980, 149, NO. 562. FERNÁNDEZ DE LA CUESTA 1980, 130. BOHIGAS 1985, 111. GROS 1989, 134-135. *CATALUNYA ROMÀNICA XVI,* 1996, 441 (JORDI BOIX), 442-443. RODRÍGUEZ SUSO 1998, 178, 194-195. *ARS SACRA* 2001, 137-138. GÓMEZ MUNTANÉ 2001, 33. GARRIGOSA 2003, 147-148, NO. 193, 331-332. *SANCHO EL MAYOR Y SUS HEREDEROS* 2006, 50-54 (FRANCESC FITÉ).

Màrius Bernadó

ANs IN DEDICACIONE

Fundamenta templi ecclesie huius sapiencia sua fundauit eam in qua dominum celi conlaudant angeli si ruent uenti & fluent flumina non possunt mouere umquam fundata enim est supra petram. ANs

Ecce hodor filii mei sicut hodor agri pleni quem benedixit dominus. A Sanctificauit dominus tabernaculum suum quia hec est domus dei in qua inuocetur nomen eius de quo scriptum est & erit nomen meum ibi dicit dominus. A Unxit te dominus deus tuus oleo leticie pre consortibus tuis. P Eructauit.

Mane surgens iacob erigebat lapidem in titulum fundens oleum desuper uotum uouit domino uere locus iste sanctus est & ego nesciebam. INCIPIT ORDO ECCLESIE CŌSECRANDE

Inprimis faciant uigilias ipsa nocte ante reliquias in loco mundissimo canentes psalmodiā nocturnos ut matutinis laudib' de plurimorum scōrum. In crastinū uero annunciat pontifex ad populū quorum reliquie martirum ut scōrum ibidem conseruant. ut in cuius honore eccla ueneratur.

ORDO AD SACRANDAM IN DIE AECCLAE NOUE.

Prius enī antequā ingrediatur pontifex in aeccla illuminent duodecim candele p circuitū eccle & induat se uestimentis sacris. & exeant omnes extra ecclam tantū duobus clericis remanentibus & claudit hostiū aeccle. Tunc incipit ep̄s cū omi

Lectionary, Homiliary of the Office

11TH CENTURY *EX.* (FOL. 196V)

ARCHIVO CAPITULAR, LLEIDA, RODA 18 (NEW SHELFMARK: RC 0035).
PROVENANCE: CATHEDRAL OF RODA DE ISABENA (HUESCA).
Parchment; binding with wooden covers and leather spine; 231 leaves; incomplete at the end; modern foliation in pencil (fols. 1-231); the leaves measure 350 × 245 mm; the writing frame measures 265 × 190 mm; two columns; imperceptible prickings; 25 lines; ruled in drypoint; Carolingian minuscule which, according to Mundó, contains some reminiscences of the Visigothic *ductus*; text in brownish-black ink; initials in red, black and yellow ink, some slightly decorated; the texts with musical notation are written in smaller letters; although various scribes intervene, the majority of the manuscript is by the same scribe who presents similarities and common characteristics with the scribe in charge of copying the Pontifical of Roda (Lleida, AC, Roda 16); various hands, sometime after, were in charge of making additions to the codex; Catalonian and Aquitainian notation over the line that corresponds to the writing frame ruling; occasional presence of *custos*.

General contents: Lectionary comprising only the *Sanctorale* beginning with the feast of St. Stephen. Includes the Sanctorale cycle, as well as the offices of the Common of Saints (after fol. 206r). The feasts of the Virgin, of the foremost martyrs and of only a few confessors (St. Martin, St. Brice and St. Nicholas) also appear, as well as some acts of saints and various sermons. The most noteworthy of these is the sermon for the feast of St. Vincent, patron of the church of Roda de Isabena, a text written by St. Justus, Bishop of Urgell (6th century).

The notated section is composed of various antiphons, responsories and hymns located on fols. 90v, 194v-199v, 208v-211r and 216r-229r, mainly for the chants of the *commune sanctorum* and the office of Matins. This manuscript is noteworthy for its combination of Catalonian notation (fols. 194v-196, 208v-211r and 216r-229r) and Aquitainian notation (fols. 90v and 197v-199v) in the same codex. On fols. 196v-197r, the original Catalonian notation was scraped off and replaced with Aquitainian notation.

Leaf shown: 196v
[*IN NATALE SANCTI NICOLAI*]

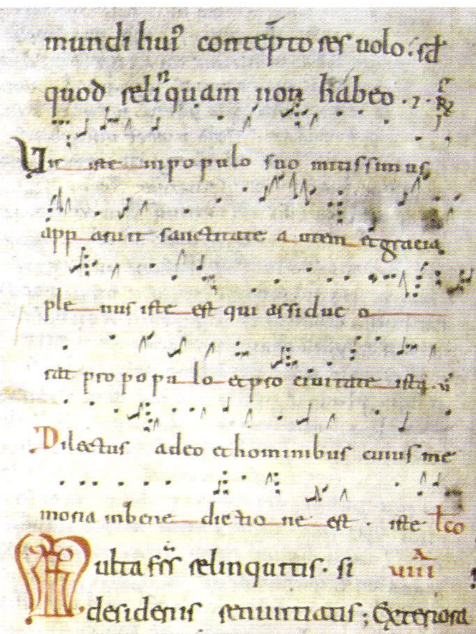

Detail of fol. 194v

[Antiphona] *O pastor eterne o clemens [et] bone custos qui dum devoti gregis preces atenderes voce...*
[Antiphona] *Adoremus regem seculorum in quo vivit nicholaus...*
[Antiphona] *Nobilissimis siquidem natalibus ortus velut lucifer nicholaus emicuit.*
[Antiphona] *Postquam domi puerilem decursat etatem...*
[Antiphona] *Pudore bono repletus dei famulus sum[p]tibus datis stupri nefas prohibuit...*

Despite the fact that the bulk of the text is of Roman origin, the insertion of local elements and remnants of the Spanish rite are detectable. On the basis of its structure and chronology, this manuscript is one of the first witnesses to the adoption of new Franco-Roman liturgical practices in a diocese that was, in principle, reluctant to vary its liturgical customs and abandon its Spanish practices. The manuscript contains the offices of nine lessons for the Sanctorale. According to some authors, it is a homiliary in which several lessons from the second and third nocturnes present a single continuous patristic text (Olivar 1996).

BIBLIOGRAPHY

VILLANUEVA 1821, 13-14, 219-221; 1851, 173-175. ANGLÈS 1935, 150. DÍAZ Y DÍAZ 1958-1959, NO. 10: 5. OLIVAR 1967, 40. BARRIGA 1975, 36-37; 1978. FERNÁNDEZ DE LA CUESTA 1980, 130. JANINI 1980, 149-150. CASTILLÓN 1994, 138. OLIVAR 1996, 67. *CATALUNYA ROMÀNICA XVI*, 1996, 441. *ARS SACRA* 2001, 138-139, NO. 88. GARRIGOSA 2003, 148.

Màrius Bernadó

Tunc scs andreas uoce magna dix;
Dne ihu xpe magister bone. iube me de ista cruce non deponi. nisi ante spm meu susceperis; Et cum hoc dixisset. uidentib; cunctis splendor nimi' sic fulgur de celo ueniens. ita circum dedit eum. ut penitus p ipso splendore. oculi eum non possent humani aspicere; Cumq; permansisset splendor fere dimidie hore spacium. abscedente lumine. emisit spm. simul cum ipso lumine pgens ad dnm.

Egeas u arrept' a demonio. ante qua peruenir& ad domu sua. in uia in conspectu omiu a demonio uexat' expirauit. Fr u ei'. tenens corp' sci andree euasit. Qd & matrona queda potentissima xpo amabilis nme maximilla. accipiens corpu aromatib; reuerent condidit in sepulcro. S; emergentib; annis. sacratissima ei' ossa uigesimo constantini impris anno. ab achaia constantino poli translata s. Regnante ihu xpo dno nro. q uiu regn in s s secula.

O pastor eterne o clemens & bone custos qui dum deuoti gregis preces attenderes uoce lapsa de celo presuli sanctissimo dignum episcopatu nicholaum ostendisti tuu in famulum + e u o u a e.

Adoremus regem seculorum in quo uiuit nichola us honor sacerdotum Venite.

Nobilissimis siquidem natalibus ortus ulut lucifer nicholaus emicuit. + e u o u a e. Postquam domi puerilem decursat etatem cunctis mundi licuit spretis oblectacionibus xpisti se iugo subiciens documentis sanctis suum prebuit auditum. a e u.

Pudoris bono repletus dei famulus sum tibus d...il stupri nefas prohibuit a e.

Psalter, Hymnary and Rhymed Office of Saint Raymond

1191 (FOL. 153V)

ARCHIVO CAPITULAR, LLEIDA, RODA 11 (NEW SHELFMARK: RC 0029).
PROVENANCE: CATHEDRAL OF RODA DE ISÁBENA (HUESCA).
Heavily worn parchment, restored long ago with reinforcements on the leaves; binding with old oak boards and leather spine; 211 leaves (damaged); 16 leaves added at the beginning numbered in pencil and 195 leaves with modern numbering in ink which runs in parallel, without matching, to another foliation, also modern, in pencil; the leaves measure 290 × 200 mm; the text block measures 210 × 135 mm; text in a single column; prickings cannot be seen; 21 lines; when the musical notation appears, it is quite variable; ruled in drypoint; Carolingian minuscule script; richly illuminated initials in red ink, and occasionally with blue and green ink; rubrics in red ink; written by various scribes; the preliminary leaves contain additions by several hands of the 12th century; the last few leaves in the body of the codex (fols. 185v-194) present additions by various scribes from the 13th century; Catalonian and Aquitainian notation oriented around the drypoint line; occasional presence of a *custos*.

General contents: The front guard leaf is a fragment of an office lectionary from the 12th century. The 15 preliminary leaves contain various liturgical texts, many of them with music: marriage ritual with Hispanic formulas (fols. 1-2); hymn for Saint John the Baptist: *Precursor Christi nam et magnum…* (fol. 2v); lessons for the office during the Holy Triduum, with Aquitainian notation (fols. 3-4); hymn for St. Peter: *Quesumus miser omnipatrator…* (fol. 5); farsed epistle of the prophet Isaiah, with Aquitainian notation (fol. 6); calendar of Roda (fols. 6v-9); various proses copied by different hands (fols. 9v-12v); gospels and Kyrie, with Catalonian notation (fol. 13v); lessons for the office of the dead (fols. 14-15v).

The main body of the codex consists of a ferial Psalter (fols. 1-121), which includes responsories with Catalonian neumatic notation, various canticles (fols. 122-127) and a collection of hymns (fols.127v-145) without musical notation. This is followed immediately by a section in another contemporary hand (fols. 146-152), containing a *vita* of St. Raymond, Bishop of Roda between 1104 and 1126, written by the canon Elías, and the rhymed office of the same St. Raymond (fols. 152v-161) with musical notation. There follow various offices of the *commune sanctorum* (fols. 161v-184) and on various added leaves (fols. 185v-194), some texts about St. Raymond (news of the transfer) and two Roda chronicles, as well as other texts. In some blank folios (fols. 145v and 152r), scribes from the 16th century added copies of epistolary documents.

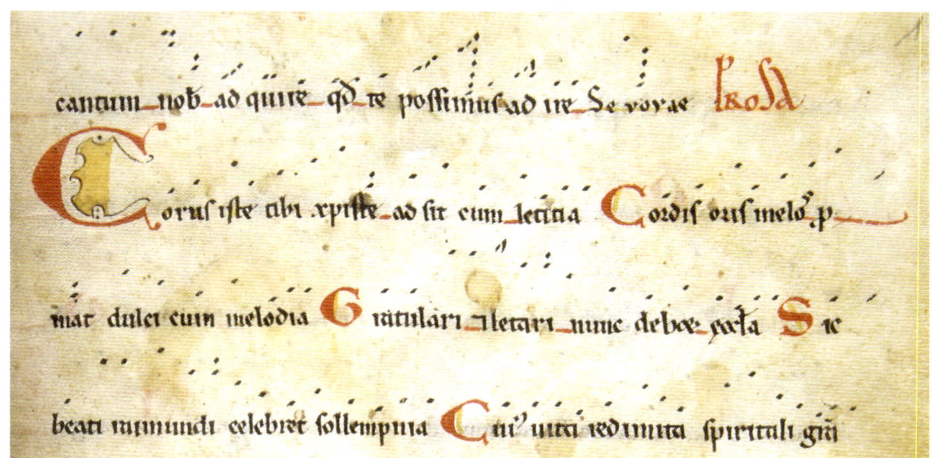

Detail of fol. 167

Leaf shown: 153v
[RHYMED OFFICE OF ST. RAYMOND]
Beatus igitur Raimundus vir vite venerabilis barbastrensis episcopus regali prosapia originem duxit…
[Resp.] *Magna prole sanctus Raimundus iure beatus…*
Observations: In the lower margin of fol. 185v the date the codex was copied is shown: *Factu sest hoc in anno ab incarnatione domini Mº Cº XCº Iº. In honore domini nostri Iesu Christi et beate Marie et sancti Raimundi episcopi.*

BIBLIOGRAPHY

ESPAÑA SAGRADA, XLVI, 247-256. *VIAGE LITERARIO*, 1803-1852, 15, 177-178, AND APPENDICES LIII, LVII, LVIII, LIX AND LX. *AH XVI* 1894, 84, 85, 245, 246. *AH XVII* 1894, 169-172. SABLAYROLLES 1911-1912, 425. ANGLÈS 1931, xvii; 1935, 148-150. GUDIOL 1955, 134. DÍAZ Y DÍAZ 1959, NOS. 914, 915, 1.097, 1.100, 1.101, 1.104, 1.131, 1.183, 1.186. BOHIGAS 1960, 54-55, FIG. 17, 130b. *EL ARTE ROMÁNICO* 1961, 93, NO. 158. OLIVAR 1967, 40, NO. 118. BARRIGA 1975, 37; 1978, 11. FERNÁNDEZ DE LA CUESTA 1980, 129. JANINI 1980, 144-146. PEÑAS GARCÍA 1983, 17. CASTILLÓN 1994, 138. BOIX 1996, 441. PLANAS 1996, 441-442; 2001, 132-133, NO. 83. GÓMEZ MUNTANÉ 2001, 48. GARRIGOSA 2003, 146, 463. *SEU VELLA* 2003, 238-239.

Màrius Bernadó

annis doctrina fotus primum fuit inde remotus milicie mores

cuit atque labores. V. his uir A De inde uolente deo uacuus sensu pue

rili in melius creuit metit ex que seminat fruit. R. Quare A Mundi

fluxa uidens quasi stercora terrea ridens quod nichil est spuit sub xpi

lege quieuit. V. Dne deo mil. V. Iustum deduxit et. Lc. Prima

Beatus igitur Raimundus uir uite uenerabilis barbastrensis eps regali prosapia originem duxit. et durbano opido oriundus fuit. Ab infancia litteris traditus fuit inde subtractus armiger extitit. Post hec inspirante sibi diuina gratia relicta huius mundi milicia. ad litterarum redit studia. et sic doctrine memor apostoli. euacuauit que erant paruuli.

Magna p le satus Raimundus uir be atus en ha R.

[illegible] mutans amana queque refutans Pe r uigil in se [illegible]

Sacramentary

11TH CENTURY (1041-1043) (FOL. 43R)

ARCHIVO Y BIBLIOTECA EPISCOPAL, VIC (BARCELONA), MS. 67 (LXX).
ORIGIN: MONASTERY OF SANTA MARÍA DE RIPOLL (GIRONA).
The parchment is well preserved; modern binding, 19th century *in.,* boards covered with black leather; 221 leaves; 19th century *in.* foliation in black ink with Arabic numerals, intermittent in the upper right margin and in pencil in the same location; the leaves measure 295 × 220 mm; the writing frame measures 210 × 170 mm; one column justified with triple vertical lines on both sides; the vertical prickings are only visible on some leaves in the upper and lower margins; the horizontal prickings are invisible because the codex was trimmed for binding; 19 (fols. 1r-97r), 25 (fols. 97v-99v), 20 (fols. 100r-139v) and 19 lines (fols. 140r-221v); ruled in drypoint on the flesh side of each bifolium; large (5 mm tall) Carolingian minuscule script with thick strokes; the scribe, Solomon, was a monk at Ripoll, *scriptor*, between 1041 and 1043, of some documents belonging to the Bishop-abbot Oliba de Vic (deceased in 1046); his name is not explicitly noted in the manuscript, but the identification of Solomon as the scribe can be is deduced by comparison with other documents; even though the text, as determined by the script, may belong to the Ripoll *scriptorium*, the monk Solomon may have written it in the Vic *scriptorium* to be used in the chapel of the above-mentioned Bishop Oliba's episcopal residence; Catalonian notation in red ink at the beginning and then black ink with a very fine stroke on fols. 42v-45; subsequent to the production of the codex, the neumes were added in the space between the lines, *in campo aperto.*

Detail of fol. 44r

General contents: A mixed Sacramentary which is mostly Gregorian but with Gelasian texts from the Anianian supplement. The manuscript begins with the Mass *ordo* and the Roman canon (fragmentary); followed by the Masses at the end of the Christmas cycle and the rest of the Temporale, and ends with the Advent Masses. The Christmas Eve Mass includes the *ordo* from the Catalonian-Narbonnaise tradition. Leaves 97v-99v contain the Temporale cycle and some votive Masses. After leaf 100r, the text begins with the calendar of saints' days, votive Masses, the Masses of the *Commune sanctorum* and the Mass for the dead. The ending on fol. 210v: "Explicit liber sacramentorum" is followed by a brief presbytery ritual written by the same scribe (after fol. 211r there is a brief monastic ritual), with a text containing commendations for the souls of the dying a benediction for various locations in the monastery a canonical benediction from the Anianian supplement, and assistance for the ailing, last rites and burial.

Leaf shown: 43r
Leaves 42v-45r contain the end of the Good Friday Synaxis with the Lord's Prayer, the Eucharistic Communion of all the participants and the rubric ordering the cleansing of the church's altar. This is followed by the Easter Vigil rite, which begins at midday the hour of Sext on Holy Saturday, with the vesting of the altars by placing the top and front altar cloths. The Vigil begins at three in the afternoon, the hour of None with the lighting of the new fire by rubbing silica stones and rock crystal. The candelabrum is lit, and the prayer of the blessing of the new light is recited. All this is carried out in the church's sacristy. This is followed by the *laus cerei,* which must be sung by the deacon. Finally, on fol. 45r, the *laus cerei* ends, followed by the blessing of the incense and the first prayers that accompany the vigil's Bible readings. The *Sacramentarium Rivipullense* is of the utmost importance for the information it offers on the ancient rites of the archdiocese of Narbonne, on which the diocese of northern Catalonia depended until the year 1150 when Tarragona was permanently restored. It is also the oldest Sacramentary of monastic origin from the old archdioceses of Narbonne and Tarragona. The notation was added subsequently; this type of liturgical book generally is not designed to include melodies. The notation presents a simple melodic structure of syllabic style.

BIBLIOGRAPHY

VILLANUEVA 1894, 320-331. FERRERES 1929, xcv-xcix. GUDIOL 1934, 89-90. OLIVAR 1953, cv. EDIT. OLIVAR 1964. GAMBER 1968, 421, NO. 824. JANINI 1977, 317. GROS 1997-1998, 347-355. GARRIGOSA 2003, 233-234, NO. 362.

Miquel S. Gros

Qua ppt adstantes uos frs karmi . adtam
miri sci huius luminis claritatē . una
mecum queso dei omptis mi̅sdam inuoca
te . Ut qui me nō meis meritis intra le
uitarum numerū dignatus ē aggregare .
luminis sui gratiam infundendo . cerei hui⁹
laudē implere pficiat . P eundem dnm
nrm ihm xpm filiū suū . qui cū eo uiuit
& regnat ds . p omia scla sclor . R . AM .
Dns uobiscū . R . Et cū spū tuo . Sur
sū corda . Habemus ad dnm . Gras
agam⁹ dno dō nro . R . Dignū & iustū ē .
VERE QUIA dignum & iustū est . Te in
uisibilē dm̄ omptm patrē filiūq; tuū
unigenitum dnm nrm ihm xpm cū scō
spū . toto cordis ac mentis affectu . & uo
cis ministerio psonare . Qui pnob tibi
aetno patri . ade debitū soluit . & uete
ris piaculi caucionē . pio cruore detersit .

Breviary (fragmentum)

11TH CENTURY *EX.* (FOL. R)

ARCHIVO Y BIBLIOTECA EPISCOPAL, VIC (BARCELONA), FRAG. XI/I.
PROVENANCE: CATHEDRAL OF VIC (BARCELONA).
Poorly preserved parchment (especially the verso); no binding; a detached leaf is used as binding material; lacks foliation; the leaves measure 298 × 240 mm at the widest part (the edges are deteriorated); the writing frame measures 280 × 220 mm; two columns; the prickings between the columns on the recto have been gone over with ink; 36 lines on recto and verso; liturgical Carolingian minuscule; brown ink on the recto, with initials that alternate red and brown ink; some initials in the body of the text are filled in with red; on the verso, black ink is used with secondary initials and headings in red ink; the work of a single hand on the recto, a different hand on the verso; Catalonian notation *in campo aperto* with some degree of diastematy despite the small space set aside for it, and with a rounded profile on the recto; the neumes are oriented around the line of the ruling for the writing frame on the verso, where some small oblique lines are visible as well; the quill has a rather angular tip.

General contents: Because of the poor condition of the leaf, of which only the recto is clearly legible, it is impossible to determine with precision the contents of this manuscript. The verses of the *Iudicii signum* of the Song of the Sybil are reproduced here with music, from the fourth verse on, in which part of the original acrostic in Greek majuscule can be recognized: [IES]VCS CREISTOS TE(V)S UIOC[Y]NIOS (?) (S)EOTER (Jesus Christ God Lord Savior). The 17th verse replaces the first word, *volvetur,* with *solvetur,* and the following verse replaces *deiciet* with *reiciet,* which reduces the integrity of the acrostic. The three verses that are missing at the beginning must have been copied on the previous leaf. After the verses from the Song of the Sybil, the *Sermo de symbolo* (in an abbreviated version of which the verses constitute an integral part) continues until the end. The verso of the leaf contains responsories for Matins on Christmas Day, with prosulas or *verbetas* accompanied by neumatic notation. This notation is of the same type as that used for the *Iudicii* verses, although it is oriented around a line drawn in drypoint (alternate lines ruled for the text are left blank). Despite of the leaf's extreme state of deterioration, it is possible to read the complete text of the *verbeta* reproduced in the smaller image (fol. verso): "Olim prophetae predixere nasciturum Christum ex virgine, sicut David in psalmo refert." The printed breviaries from the dioceses of Vic and Barcelona also contain this series of *verbetas*, proof of continuity in the recitation of these pieces during Christmas celebrations. See *Breviarium vicense* (Lyon, 1557), Vic, ABEV, Hemeroteca w/o s., fols. 104-108 and *Breviarium barcinonense* (Barcelona, 1560), Vic, ABEV, XVI/1569, fols. 22-26.

Leaf shown: r
Vnde deum cernent incredulus absque fidelis. Celsum cum sanctis / Sic anime cum carne / Cum iacet in cultus / Reicient simulacra viri / Exuret terra signis / Inquirens tetri portas / Sanctorum set enim / Tradentur fontes eterna/ Occultos actus retegens / Secreta atque Deus / Tunc erit et luctus / Eripitur solis vibar / Solvetur celum / Reiciet colles valles / Non erit in rebus / Iam equantur campis / Omnia cessabunt tellus / Sic pariter fontes torrentur / Et tubatum sonitum / Orbe gemens facinus miserum / Tartareumque cahos monstrabit / Et coram hic Domino reges / Recidet e celo ignisque.

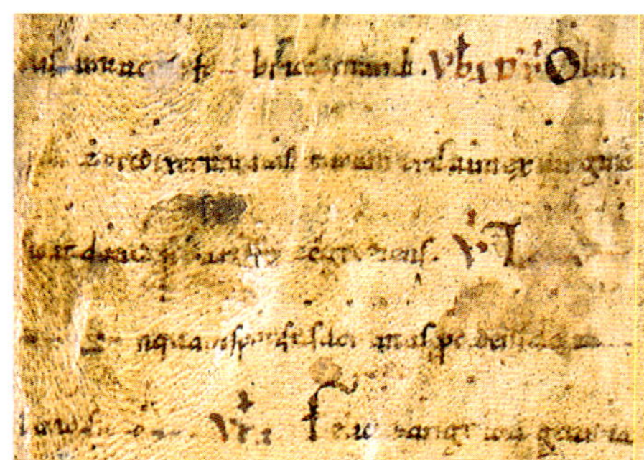

Detail of fol. v

Although the transcription of the version of the Song of the Sybil transmitted in this manuscript is problematic because of its clearly adiastematic notation, it is one of the oldest preserved versions with musical notation. After the last verse, the first word of the refrain is repeated, which may indicate that it was repeated after an undetermined number of verses, although no definitive conclusion is possible in this regard.

BIBLIOGRAPHY
ANGLÈS 1935, 170. JANINI 1975, 22. GÓMEZ MUNTANÉ 1997, 2: 13. GARRIGOSA 2003, 273.

Maricarmen Gómez
Susana Zapke

Cant Sibille

XI, 1

Unde deum cernent incredulus absque fidelis
Celsum cum sanctis eui iam termino in ipso
Sic anime cum carne aderunt quos iudicat ipse
Cum iacet incultus densis in uepribus orbis
Reicient simulacra uiri cunctam quoque gazam
Exuret terras ignis pontumque polumque
Inquirens tetri portas effringet auerni
Sanctorum sed enim cuncte lux libera carni
Tradentur sontes eterna flamma cremabit
Occultos actus retegens tunc quisque loquetur
Secreta atque deus reserabit pectora lucis
Tunc erit et luctus stridebunt dentibus omnes
Eripitur solis iubar et corus interit astris
Soluetur celum lunaris splendor obibit
Deiciet colles ualles extollet ab imo
Non erit in rebus hominum sublime uel altum
Iam equantur campis montes et cerula ponti
Omnia cessabunt tellus confracta peribit
Sic pariter fontes torrentur fluminaque igni
Et tuba tum sonitum tristem dimittet ab alto
Orbe gemens facinus miserum uariosque labores
Tartariumque chaos monstrabit terra dehiscens
Et coram hic domino reges sistentur ad unum
Recidet e celo ignisque et sulphuris amnis. Iudicii.

Haec de Christi natiuitate, passione et resurreccione atque secundo eius aduentu ita dicta sunt, ut si quis in greco capita horum uersuum discernere uoluerit, inueniet ihs xps. Io krev. botek. quod et in latinum translatis eisdem uersibus apparet, preter quod grecorum literarum proprietas non adeo potuit obseruari. Credo iam uos, o inimici iudei, tantis testibus ita obrutos et confutatos, que est ipsa ueritate, ut nec ultra repugnare nec querere debeatis. Sed de celesti igitur natiuitate queritur. Forte Iohannes beatissimus accedat.

Et archana nobis reuelet mysteria, et indicat quid erat, et ubi erat, et qualis erat, et quando erat, et quid agebat, et ubi uenit, et qualiter uenerit, et qua causa uenerit. Dic sancte Iohannes quid erat. In principio erat uerbum.
Dic et ubi erat. Et uerbum erat apud deum.
Dic et qualis erat. apud. Et deus erat uerbum.
Et quid agebat. Omnia per ipsum facta sunt.
Ubi uenit. In propria. Et quare uenit.
Ut peccata tolleret mundi. Et uerbum caro factum est et habitauit in nobis. Satis arbitror, o inimici iudei, natiuitatis Christi ubique testimonia patuisse, et uestram superbiam confutandam, et nostram gloriam cumulandam. Lucas beatissimus medicus et euangelista secundum carnem Christi natiuitatis explicat sacramentum. Factum est in quid dum essent ibi impletum est tempus ut pareret. Et nos igitur dulcissimi fratres in te uersucias iudeorum abentes presidia ueritatis suscipiamus natum Christum. Qui nos nascendo, moriendo et ressurgendo redimit et celi ianue uite aditum reserauit. Amplectamur fidei brachiis sacra cunabula. Ueneremur Christum in paruulum in presepe mentibus castis, moribus dignis, et non tam carnali quam spirituali gaudio diem natiuitatis domini celebremus. Et si meritis impares sumus, iungamur nos uocibus angelicis et fide alacri mente deuota dicamus omnes pariter: Gloria in excelsis deo et in terra pax hominibus bone uoluntatis. Quia natus est nobis hodie saluator mundi qui est Christus dominus in ciuitate Dauid. Cui est honor et gloria, uirtus et potestas per infinita secula seculorum. AMEN.

Prosary, Tropary

12th Century *in.* (fol. 58v)

Archivo y Biblioteca Episcopal, Vic (Barcelona), ms. 105 (olim CXI).
Provenance: Scriptorium of Cathedral of Vic.
Dating: Quires I-VI (fols. 1-46), 12th c. *in.*; quires VII-VIII (fols. 47-62), 12th c. *ex.*; quires IX-X (fols. 63-77), 12th c. *in.*; quire XI (fols. 78-85), 13th c. *in.*
Parchment; 19th century *in.* full modern binding covered with black leather and clasps of chamois leather strips; title label with the old catalog number (CXI) and inventory number (no. 7.614); 85 leaves; modern foliation, in ink, with Arabic numerals that only indicate the 10s; a second hand corrected the mistakes in pencil; the leaves measure 215 × 140 mm; the text block measures 175 × 105 mm; one column justified with double vertical lines on both sides that span the entire leaf; there are no visible prickings in quires I-VI; in quires VII-XI, there are 43 tiny punctures in the center of the leaf, almost hidden by the fold; quires I-VI have in most cases, 22 lines; quires VII-VIII have in most cases, 12 lines; quires IX-X have in most cases, 22; quire XI has 16; ruled in drypoint, every other leaf on the hair side; Carolingian minuscule from various periods with traces of the Visigothic system in quires I-VI and IX-X; the major and minor initials in quires I-VI are in red ink or in red combined with black; quires IX and X have the major initials are in red and the minor initials are in black and the rubrics in red; quires VII, VIII and XI have the major and minor initials in red; a rustic garland with geometric ornamentation decorates the beginning of the text of fol. 60r; several scribes from different periods; quires I-VI were elaborated by a principal scribe and three secondary scribes (fols. 8r-v; 9v-10v; 35v-36r, 37r-v, 39r-v); the same principal scribe was in charge of quires IX-X; quires VII-VIII were commissioned to a single scribe, although the blank leaves were used by another scribe from a subsequent period to add the texts of fols. 58v-62v (quire VIII) and of fols. 63r and 70v-71 (quires IX-X); quire XI was written by one scribe; there is also the intervention of subsequent hands from the 13th century or even later that added texts in the margin (fols. 32v and 33v) or rubrics (fol. 58v); varied notation from several periods; quires I-VI have Catalonian notation *in campo aperto;* quires IX-X have Aquitainian notation; in quires VII-VIII, XI and in additions in quires IX-X, there is Aquitainian notation on three lines, with the f-clef and the c-clef and on fols. 78-85, Aquitainian notation on a four-line staff (13th century).

General contents: [Fragmentary]; a tropary-prosary organized like a gradual (fols. 1-42); chants from the *Ordinarium missae* with and without tropes (fols. 42v-46v: Kyrie, fols. 42v-43v; Sanctus with osanna prosulas, fols. 44-45v; Kyrie (add.), fols. 45v-46v); collection of tropes from the *Ordinarium* and *Proprium missae* and proses (fols. 47-58: Kyrie with and without tropes, fols. 47-52; trope ofthe Gloria, fols. 52v-54; tropes from the introit of the feast of Mary's Assumption, fols. 54v-55; trope of the Gloria, fol. 55v; Sanctus with prosula from the osanna, fol. 56r-v; prose for the feast of the Invention of the Holy Cross, fols. 56v-58r); liturgical dramas and *Versus* for Holy Thursday (add., fols. 58v-63r: *Eamus mirram emere*, fols. 58v-60; *Rex in acubitum*, fols. 60-62; *Audi iudex mortuorum*, fols. 62-63v); collection of proses and tropes from the *Ordinarium* and from the *Proprium missae*, from *Versus* (add.) and antiphons (fols. 63v-77v); collection of proses, a farced epistle, *Exultemus resonemus*, and Kyrie trope (fols. 78-85v); [fragmentary].

Leaf shown: 58v
[Liturgical drama for Easter Sunday]
Verses pascales de iii Mariis
*Eamus mirra*m *emere cu*m *liquido aromate Ut valeam*us / *unge*re *corpus datu*m *sepulture Omnipote*ns *pat*er *altissime* / *angelor*um *rector mitissime quid facient iste miseri-* / *me Dic*xit a*ngel*us *Heu quant*us *e*st *noster dolor* / *Amissimus eni*m *solatium Ih*esu*m Ch*ristum *Marie filium* / *iste nobis erat subsidium Heu Set eamus ung-* / *uentu*m *emere quo possimus corp*us *inungere non* / *amplius poscet putrescere Heu Dic tu nobis* / *mercator iuvenis hoc unguentu*m *si tu vendide-* / (fol. 59) *[-ris].*

The codex is heterogeneous due to the additions from before the 13th century. The oldest nucleus (quires I-VI) has two parts. One with, the tropes of chants for the Proper of the Mass, for the Gloria, and proses, in the order of the liturgical year. The second part contains the chants of the Ordinary, specifically the Kyrie and the Sanctus, with and without tropes. The most recent quires incorporate tropes from the Proper and from the Ordinary, proses, liturgical dramas, processional verses, antiphons and even a farced Easter epistle. These additions, which altered the arrangement of the original manuscript, were to update the repertoires. The text shown belongs to one of the most beautiful liturgical dramas of Easter Sunday. After the second stanza, *Omnipotens pater*,

Detail of fol. 58v

the melody adopts the form of a traditional ballad with a descending melisma over the exclamation *Heu*. The use of decasyllabic verse, with two hemistiches, underscores the melody's popular character.

Bibliography

Viage literario, 1803-1852, 6: 74-93; 194: 320-331. Sablayrolles 1905, 201-202, 222-223. Gudiol 1923-1927, 120-122. Anglès 1931, xix; 1935, 145, no. 15, facs. nos. 33-34, 62-63. Prado 1941, 100, 106-110. Donovan 1958, 74 and subsq. Husmann 1964, 97-98. Fernández de la Cuesta 1970, 213. Janini 1980, 328. Bellavista 1981, 132-133. Castro 1991, 61-74, 271-276. Dronke 1994, 83-108. Castro 1997, 124-134. Gros 1999, 44-56.

Eva Castro Caridad

Versus pascales de III Mariis

Eamus mirram emere cum liquido aromate. Ut valeamus

ungere corpus datum sepulture. Omnipotens pater altissime

angelorum rector mitissime quid facient iste miseri

me. Dicit angelus. Heu quantus est noster dolor

Amisimus enim solatium Ihesum Christum Marie filium

iste nobis erat subsidium. Heu. Set eamus ungu

entum emere quo possimus corpus inungere non

amplius posset putrescere. Heu. Dic tu nobis

mercator iuvenis hoc unguentum si tu vendideris

Lectionary

11TH CENTURY *MED.* (FOL. 112V)

BIBLIOTHÈQUE NATIONALE DE FRANCE, PARIS, LAT. 5304.
PROVENANCE: MOISSAC FOR FOLS. 1-60 AND CATALONIA (ELNA?) FOR THE REST. ACQUIRED IN 1678 BY JEAN-BAPTISTE COLBERT. IN 1732 IT WAS IN THE ROYAL LIBRARY.
Parchment; 17th century binding, in leather, with Colbert's coat of arms; 267 leaves; modern foliation in pencil in the middle of the upper margin; the leaves measure 455 × 310 mm for fols. 1-60, and 455 × 325 in the rest of the manuscript; the writing frame measures 355 × 210 mm for fols. 1-60 and 380 × 245 mm in the rest of the manuscript, with slight variations; two columns justified with double vertical lines on both sides; prickings are visible throughout; 40 lines for fols. 1-60, 26-32 lines in the rest of the manuscript; ruled in drypoint; Carolingian minuscule; several scribes; Catalonian notation *in campo aperto.*

General contents: Legendary (fols. 1-60); *Leccionarium officii (pars hiemalis)* (fols. 61-163); *Lectionarium officii* (fols. 164-267).

Leaf shown: 112v
scriptum est quod... omnes Christi percutiantur inimica. Audite quid dixerit. Iudicii signum: tellus sudore madescet... Tartarerumque chaos monstrabit terra deiscens. Et coram hic Domino reges sistentur ad unum. Recidet e celo ignisque et sulfuris amnis.

This copy is from Elna, the episcopal see in the dominion of Roussillon at the border between the eastern Pyrenees and the Languedoc-Roussillon region. Geographically it is located in the area known as Northern Catalonia, a territory under the sovereignty of the Catalonian counties of Roussillon. The Cathedral of Elna was built in the 10th century.

The lectionary is a liturgical book typical of the monastic and cathedral rite. In this copy, the sermon *Contra iudeos, paganos et arianos,* sometimes called *Sermo de symbolo,* erroneously attributed to St. Augustine (*PL XLII:* cols. 1117-1130, *praes.* col. 1126), follows the version of the Song of the Sybil. In this manuscript, the sermon is the sixth lesson for Christmas Matins.

The Song of the Sybil comprises 27 hexameters, as was already found on two occasions in St. Augustine's *City of God* (XVIII, 23). Unlike other manuscripts, this one does not use the first verse as a refrain. The stanzas consist of two verses that alternate the same melody with two recitatives in this case A and D. Each stanza is marked with the initial letter in reddish orange in which the acrostic "IESUS CREISTOS TEUS DOMINIOS SEOTER" appears. The song begins with the formula "Audite quid dixerit", a typical expression in manuscripts from the Iberian Peninsula. The Catalonian neumes that appear in darker ink were incorporated at a later date. Huglo dates the neumes in the second half of the 11th century (see Étaix 1981, 351, no. 13).

Additional examples of the Song of the Sybil appear in Córdoba, AC, *Homiliary,* ms. 1; Vic, ABEV, *Breviarium*, Frag. XI/I; and Sheffield Galleries & Museums Trust, *Homiliary,* ms. 31.

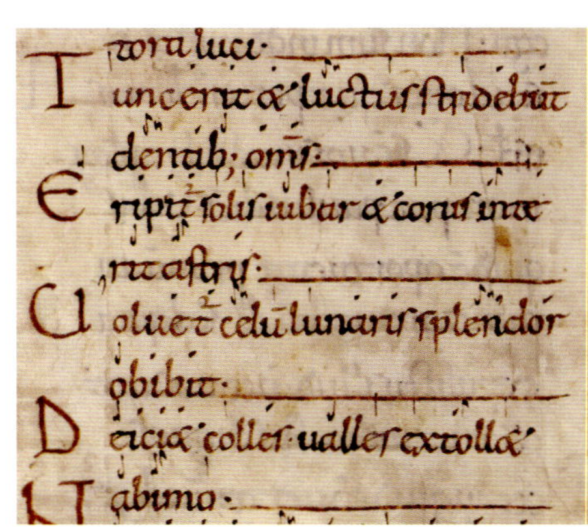

Detail of fol. 112v

BIBLIOGRAPHY

ANGLÈS 1935, 288-302, 292-293, NO. 4, FIG. 76. CORBIN 1952b, 1-10, 6. ÉTAIX 1981, 333-399, 351, 353 [1994, 453-518, 471, 473]. AMIET 1982, 139-154. AVRIL ET AL. 1982, 30-31, NO. 35, ILLUS. 13 [= FOLS. 134v, 66, 156, 82v], 45-46, NO. 41, *PL XXII, XXIII* [= 168v, 258v]. MAS 1982, 269-286, 278-279. SEVESTRE 1982, 269-283. ZALDÍVAR 1993, 190-195. GÓMEZ MUNTANÉ 1996-1997. CASTRO 1997, 273-301. GÓMEZ MUNTANÉ 2001, 70-82; 2002, 35-69. FRAÏSSE 2003, 27-30. COLETTE 2004, 165-176.

Shin Nishimagi

scriptum est . quod duorum homi
num testimonium sit uerum .
etiam ex gentibus tercius te
stis introducatur . ut testi
monium ueritatis ex omni
parte roboretur . Quid autem
sybilla uaticinando de
xpo clamauerit in medium
proferam ? ut ex uno lapi
de utrorumque frontes percu
tiantur . iudeorum scilicet atque
paganorum . atque suo gladio
sic golias omnes xpi percutian
tur inimici . Audite quid
dixerit .

Iudicii signum tellus sudore
madescet .
E celo rex adueniet per secla
futurus .
Scilicet in carne presens ut
iudicet orbem .
Unde deum cernent increduli
atque fideles .
Celsum cum scis cum iam termi
no in ipso .
Sic anime cum carne aderunt
quas iudicat ipse .
Cum iacet incultus densis in
uepribus orbis .
Reicient symulacra uiri cunc
tam quoque gazam . spoliumque ;
Exuret terras ignis pontumque ;
Inquirens tetri portas effrin
get auerni .
Sanctorum sed enim cunctae lux libe
ra carni .
Tradentur sontes eterna flama
cremabit .
Occultos actus retegens tunc
quisque loquetur .
Secreta atque deus reserabit pec
tora luci .
Tunc erit et luctus stridebunt
dentibus omnes .
Eripitur solis iubar et corus inter
rit astris .
Uoluetur celum lunaris splendor
obibit .
Deiciet colles ualles extollet
ab imo .
Non erit in rebus hominum sub
lime uel altum .
Iam equantur campis montes et
cerula ponti .
Omnia cessabunt tellus confrac
ta peribit .
Sic pariter fontes torrentur
fluminaque igni .
Et tuba tunc sonitum triste demit
tet ab alto .
Orbe gemens facinus miserum
uariosque labores .
Tartareumque chaos monstra
bit terra dehiscens .

Collectarium, Ritual

11TH CENTURY *EX.* (FOLS. 1-154, FOLS. 163-272) / 12TH CENTURY (FOLS. 155-162, FOL. 205V)

BIBLIOTHÈQUE NATIONALE DE FRANCE, PARIS. LAT. 933.
PROVENANCE: ABBEY OF SAINTE MARIE DE LAGRASSE, DIOCESE OF CARCASSONNE. CHARLES-MAURICE LE TELLIER, ARCHBISHOP OF REIMS, RECEIVED IT FROM THE ABBEY OF LAGRASSE AND DONATED IT TO THE FRENCH ROYAL LIBRARY IN 1700.
Parchment; modern binding in brown leather with the monogram of Louis XVIII; 1 + 272 leaves; modern foliation in ink with Arabic numerals in the upper right margin; the leaves measure 225 × 181 mm (fols. 155-162: 220 × 150 mm); the writing frame measures 151 × 141 mm (fols. 155-162: 175-118 mm); one column justified on both sides with double vertical lines that cross the entire leaf and double horizontal lines at both edges; the litanies are written in double columns and distributed throughout various parts of the manuscript; the horizontal prickings are partially perceptible on some leaves; the vertical prickings are evident; 18 lines (fols. 155-162: 28 lines); ruled in drypoint; Carolingian minuscule; headings in red with an orange tone; three main scribes and numerous subsequent additions; Catalonian notation *in campo aperto* (fol. 112r, fol. 205v).

General contents: The manuscript comprises a collectar (fols. 3r-96v) and a ritual (fols. 119v-272r) that includes an *ordo* for the consecration of a church, evidently written by a scribe from Italy (fols. 155r-162v).

Leaf displayed: 205v
[in pec]tore, inter scapulas... Ceteri vero dicant: ANTIPHONA *Sana Domine... Si fuerit in LXXa dicatur hec:* ANTIPHONA *Sana me Domine... ALIA* ANTIPHONA *Dominus locutus est... Dum canitur imponite manus, imponant sacerdotes manus super egrotum. Dominus erigit elisos... Prius uero quam incipiat unguere sacerdos, dicat.*

Although this manuscript is not peninsular, it includes an *ordo* for the anointing of the sick from the Spanish liturgy, which is also found in the Sacramentary of Cathedral of Vic from the 11th century (ABEV, ms. 66), in the *Liber* misticus of Combret, from the end of the 11th century (Paris, BNF, N. A. L. 557), and in the Pontifical of Vic, from the 11th century *ex.* (ABEV, ms. 104), as well as in other manuscripts. Abbreviated versions of this *ordo* are found in the *Liber ordinum minor* from Silos and in the Sacramentary from Ripoll (Barcelona, ACA, Ripoll 67). The four antiphons appear in all of these sources and even in the antiphonary from

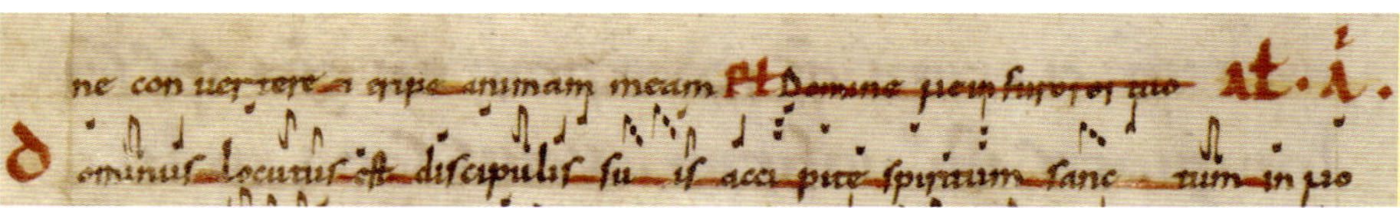

Detail of fol. 205v

the Cathedral of León. In this manuscript, the antiphon *Sana me Domine,* typical of Septuagesima because it has no alleluia, is not notated. We include a manuscript from southeast France (from the Abbey of Sainte Marie de Lagrasse, situated not far from Carcassonne and barely 29 kilometers from Narbonne) so as to provide a paradigmatic example of the circulation of the repertoire in both directions: from the Spanish environment to the French one and vice versa. Narbonne, a Visigothic center since the year 461, constituted an important center of influence over southern France and Catalonia. We find, therefore, vestiges of the Old Spanish liturgy in manuscripts that come from the south of France, such as—obviously in a much greater proportion because of the liturgical-musical reform—from the French repertoire in the manuscripts from the Iberian Peninsula. The interaction between liturgical traditions was more extensive in the area around the border, on both sides of the Pyrenees, as demonstrated by the organization of the liturgical manuscripts.

BIBLIOGRAPHY
DELISLE 1868, 305. LAUER 1939, 330-331. MARTIMORT 1956, 306-307, NOS. 4-5, 318. GY 1960, 454, 456, 461. JANINI 1965, 385-409. MARTIMORT 1982a, 25-49; 1982b, 51-80. MAS 1982, 269-286.

Shin Nishimagi

tore · int scapulas · in manib' · in pedib' · intus & foris

In nñe patris · & filii · & sps sci · regnantis in dicens ·
scta sctor · accipe sanitatē corporis · & remissio
nem omnium peccator · A · ceteri ū dicant · A ·

Sana domine om-nes languores nostros alle-luia redime de interitu uitam nostram alle-luia al-le-luia P̄s Domine ne
in furore tuo arguas me neq; in ira tua corripias me Totum cū Gta.

Si fuerit in lxx · dicant hec · A · Sana me domine
turbata sunt ossa mea & anima mea turbata est ualde tu domi
ne con uertere & eripe animam meam P̄s Domine ne in furore tuo at · A ·

Dominus locutus est discipulis su-is acci-pite spiritum sanc-tum in no
mine meo demoni-a e-i ciente & sup in firmos imponite manus uestras
& be-ne ha-bebunt P̄s Deus deorum R̄ Dominus locutus est Dū ca
nit imponite man' · imponant sacerdotes Dominus erigit man' sup
elisos dominus soluit compeditos do-mi-nus sanat in firmos egro
P̄s Qui sanat contritos corde & alligat contritiones eorum Gloria patri & filio tum ·
R̄ Dominus erigit Prius ū quam incipiat unguere
sacerdos · dicat

Prosary, Tropary

12TH CENTURY *IN.* (FOL. 46V)

BIBLIOTHÈQUE NATIONALE DE FRANCE, PARIS, N. A. L. 495 (REGISTER NO. 8283).
PROVENANCE: CATHEDRAL OF GIRONA.
Parchment; modern binding; 120 leaves [additional bifolium (fols. 1-2) + 15 original quires, of which the first 14 are made up of quaternions and the last one by a ternion (fols. 3-119)]; modern foliation in Arabic numerals in the upper right corner, which ends with the number 119 because of the error in the foliation of 113bis,; the leaves measure 166 × 109 mm; the text block measures 114 × 71mm; one column justified by a vertical line, traced in drypoint, on both sides; prickings cannot be seen; 16 lines, though on fols. 14v-15v, 17, 43v and 49v, they fluctuate between 8 and 18; ruled in drypoint, with odd leaves placed over even ones; clear and quite well-written Carolingian minuscule script; rubrics in red; major and minor initials in red; red coloring of the line over which the melismas are written; copyists, two main scribes, one of whom copied the tropary (fols. 3-49) and the other the prosary and chants of the Agnus (fols. 50-117); two 13th century scribes, of whom one added the Kyrie *Sume pater* (fols. 14v-15v) and the other the prosula of the Osanna *Celeste preconium* (fol. 49). The additional bifolium at the beginning (fols. 1-2) and the blank leaves at the end of the codex (fols. 118-119) were used by several scribes from the 14th to the 16th century to copy responsories, antiphons, documents and prayers; Catalonian notation, some pieces without notation; in some cases, the Catalonian notation was replaced by square notation on a staff.

General contents: Antiphons and responsories (fols. 1-2; add.); [fragmentary]; tropes of the Kyrie (fols. 3-16v); Gloria with prosulae of the *Regnum* (fols. 17-43v); Sanctus with prosulae of the Osanna (fols. 44-49v); *Secencia cum prosa* (fol. 50); prosary with tropes from the *Proprium* of the introit, offertory and communion and of the *Ordinarium* of the Gloria and Sanctus (fols. 51-115); *Agnus Dei* (fols. 116-117v).

Detail of fol.10r

Leaf shown: 46v
[PROSULAS FROM THE *SANCTUS*: *OSANNA DULCIA SUNT CANTICA* AND *OSANNA PATRIS VERBIGENA*]
[o]rganica. a. Trinum *et* unum... Suscipe cum agmina. a. Angeloru*m* carmina. a. Dicat *nunc* osanna. a. In excelsis.
Osanna patris verbigena. Osa*n*na. [V]oce pura clemens… a. ecclesia tua… a.

The codex is currently incomplete because an indefinite number of quaternions have been lost from the beginning. The musical repertory is divided into two parts corresponding to the two principal hands due to the use of different exemplars. The first section included the tropes of the *Ordinarium*, arranged according to the order of performance in the mass, and the second, the prosary, which opens with an archaic composition, the sequence "Alleluia. Ecce puerpera", and is organized in the manner of a Gradual, including, on some especially solemn feast days, tropes forthe *proprium* and the *ordinarium*, copied according to the liturgical order of performance. An unusual feature of this codex is the repertory of the prosulae of the Osanna, both because of the unusual way it was copied, as on some occasions the prosulae are joined to both exclamations in the base text of the Sanctus and not just to one of them, and because they preserve pieces that are unique in the European context, as is the case of *Osanna patris verbigena*.

BIBLIOGRAPHY
AH XLVII: 343, 369. ANGLÈS 1935, 150-151. HUSMANN 1964, 145. MUNDÓ 1966, 108. HUGLO 1978, 55-65. CASTRO 1991, 113-123, 280-282. GÓMEZ MUNTANÉ 2001, 47. GARRIGOSA 2003, 186.

Eva Castro Caridad

pganuca. A . Trinum et unum laude

mus omnes in hac aula. Susci

pe cum agmina. A Angelorum car

mina. A Dicat nūc osanna. A

In excelsis.

OSANna patris uerbigena. Osana

oce pura clemens exaudi carmina. A

ecclesia tua que boant agmina. A

Breviary (fragmentum)

12TH CENTURY *IN.* (FOL. 5R)

BIBLIOTECA DE LA ABADÍA DE MONTSERRAT (BARCELONA), MS. 822.
PROVENANCE: UNKNOWN.
Parchment; modern binding in parchment; six leaves equivalent to three bound bifolia for those in which the inner bifolium of the quire has disappeared; modern foliation; the leaves measure 230 × 185 mm; one column justified with double vertical lines on both sides; 26 lines, varying on pages with notation; ruled in drypoint; Carolingian minuscule; notated texts are written in letters of smaller size; black ink for the text and red ink for the rubrics, which are filled in with yellow ink; vermilion or black initials with vegetal decoration highlighted in yellow or blue; written by a single scribe; Catalonian notation *in campo aperto*.

General contents: Various offices from the Sanctorale for the month of December, among which St. Leocadia, St. Eulalia, St. Paul of Narbonne, St. Lucy and St. Thomas stand out. The manuscript contains the text of the matins readings and of the antiphons and responsories, for which only the intonation is given.

Leaf shown: 5r
Orante sancta Lucia apparuit ei beata Agatha... ANTIPHONA. *Lucia virgo quid ad me petis... ANTIPHONA. Soror mea Lucia virgo Deo devota... ANTIPHONA Benedico te pater Domini mei Ihesu Christi... ANTIPHONA. Per te Lucia virgo civitas siracusana... IN EVANGELIO ANTIPHONA. In tua pacientia possedisti animam... ANTIPHONA. Ego rogavi Dominum... ORATIO. Exaudi nos... REQUIRE RETRO. IN S. THOME. SUPER VENITE: Regem apostolorum Dominum. SUPER NOCTURNOS. In omnem terram. INCIPIT DE MIRACULIS BEATI*

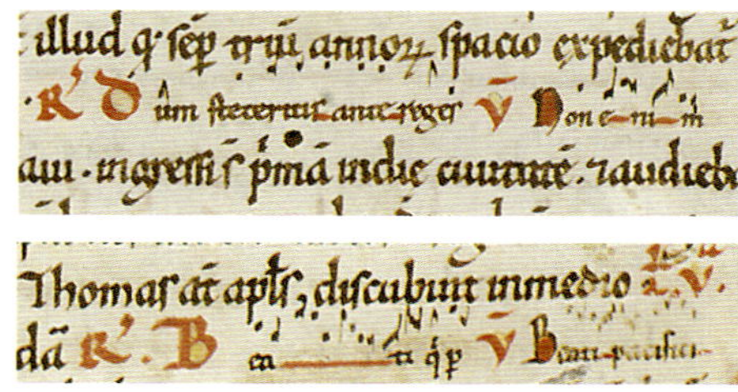

Detail of fol. 5v

THOME APOSTOLI... Beatvm Thomam... RESPONSORIUM. Ecce ego. LECCIO II. Igitur cum sepe... RESPONSORIUM Tollite iugum LECCIO III. Erat enim..

The acquisition of this fragment and its incorporation into the abbey's collection were made public in *Analecta Montserratensia* 3 (1919). It has been commonly identified under the name of *Responsoriale*. It is another example of the combination of Carolingian script and the persistence of Catalonian notation at an advanced period: the beginning of the 12th century.

BIBLIOGRAPHY

SUNYOL 1925, 234; 1935, 371-373, FACS. 114. ANGLÈS 1935, 414, NO. 4. *EL ARTE ROMÁNICO* 1961, 142. OLIVAR 1967, 46, NO. 150; 1969, 90-92. *ABAT OLIBA* 1971, 44. MUNDÓ 1973, 105-113. OLIVAR 1977, 206. FERNÁNDEZ DE LA CUESTA 1980, 143-144. JANINI 1980, 164. MAS 1982, 285. IBARBURU 1987, 278. GARRIGOSA 2003, 165.

Màrius Bernadó

O rante sancta lucia apparuit ei beata agatha consolabatur ancillam xpi. A. Lucia uirgo qd ad
me petis qd ipsa poteris prestare continuo matri. Euouae. A. Soror mea lucia uirgo deo deuota qd
ad me pe- tis qd ipsa poteris prestare continuo matri. Euouae. A. Benedico te pat dn̄i mei ihesu
xpi qr p filium tuum ignis extinctus est a latere meo. A. Per te lucia uirgo ciuitas siracusana
decorabitur ad dn̄m ihm xpm. Sc̄o4 am̄. IN EVG. A. In tua patientia possedisti animā tuā
lucia mr xpi odisti q in mundo ē & corruscas cum ange- lis sanguine pprio inimicum subisti.
A. Ergo roga- tu dn̄m ihm xpm ut ignis iste n̄ dn̄et m̄ sed credentib' in domi- no timo- rem auferre patr nus.
Or. Exaudi nos ds̄ salutaris nr̄. RO. KL. IN S THOME. SVF VENITE.
R. Regem aplo4 dn̄m. Sup nc̄. In omnem terrā. ECCE TAE. Incipit de miraculis
bi thome apli. ut qlit ad martiru coronā dn̄o puen̄ tribuerit. XII K. Ian.
BEATV thomā cū reliqs discplis ad officiū aptat electū. ipsūq
a dn̄o didimū q interptat geminū uocitatū. fides euglica narrat.
Q' p dn̄icę glā ascensionis taddeū unū ex lxx discplis ad abga
rū regē edissenę ciuitatis trāsmisit. ut eū ab infirmitate
curaret. iuxta ūbū q ei a dn̄o scriptū ē. Qd taddś ambienter
impleu. ita ut ueniens imposito regi crucis signaculo. ab omi
eū languore sanaret. Thomas aūt apls xpi. morabat in ihrlm. R. Ecce ego
Iḡr cū sepe a dn̄o cōmoneret ut dixim' bāt thomas ut parter. LC. II.
citerioris indie uisitaret. ulł q̄si ionas a facie dn̄i fugiens differret imple
re q̄ sibi diuinit̄ pcipiebant. apparuit ei dn̄s inuisu noctis dicēs. Ne time
as thoma descende in india. Ego enī uadā tecū inde delinqm. s; glifi
cabo te ibi. implebisq certamē bonū cfess' me corā hoīb' tre illi'. & exind
assumā te cū gła. & statuā te cū frib' tuis in regno mō. Nā scito qr opo
rtet te ibi multa pati pp̄ter me. ut cognoscant oś te docente. qr ego sū ds̄.
Erat enī his dieb' ierosolimis qdā negociator. R. Tollite iugū. LC. III.
aban nōie. q a rege indie missus fuerat. ut hoīe in artificio structure sciēt

Liber responsorialis (fragmentum)

12TH CENTURY *IN.* (FOL. 2V)

BIBLIOTECA DE LA ABADÍA DE MONTSERRAT (BARCELONA), MS. 794-I.
PROVENANCE: THE COVERS OF A VOLUME FROM AN UNIDENTIFIED PARISH NEAR THE CITY OF SOLSONA (LLEIDA). IT BECAME PART OF THE ABBEY'S LIBRARY IN 1946.
Poorly preserved parchment, having served as a cover for other documents; one bifolium that preserves only the original lower margin; lacks foliation; the bifolium measures 210 × 310 mm; the leaf that comes closest to being preserved in its entirety measures 210 × 185 mm; the text block measures 145 mm in width; one column; the prickings are no longer visible; 12 lines on fol. 1v, possibly one or two more in its original state; the drypoint ruling is almost invisible late Carolingian minuscule, more common among notarial manuscripts than liturgical ones; comes from a rural scriptorium; Catalonian notation *in campo aperto* with an evident tendency towards diastematy and a consistent *ductus*.

General contents: The bifolium comes from a nocturnale of the divine office with responsories to be sung after the lessons of matins. From this series, on fol. 1r-v, only seven responsories from the *Officium in sancta Trinitate* are preserved. These responsories traditionally appear at the end of the responsories from the Temporale and before the beginning of the first Sunday of Advent. On fol. 2r-v, three responsories from the *Officium in dedicatione ecclesiae,* situated at the end of the responsories from the Common of the Sanctorale. The last responsory is followed by the verbeta *Per quem cives angelorum*.

Leaf shown: 2v
The first line is illegible.
[RESPONSORIO] *[O quam metuendus] est locus iste,* vere non est aliud nisi domus. *V*ERSUS *Vere Dominus est. P*SALMUS *Vere. Gloria Patri.* VERB*ETA [Per quem cive]s angelorum et sanctorum, ad etera [conscendu]nt et regrediunt. Hic ad superos pergunt [celestia]. Hic inveniunt egri*

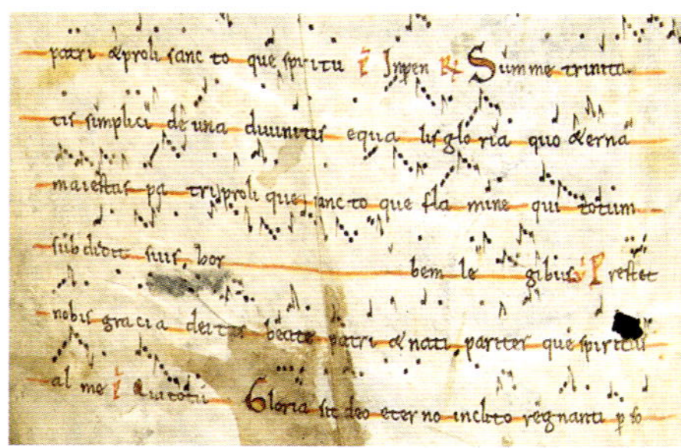

Detail of fol. 2r

medicamen et por[tam]. Per quem omnes conscendere cristicole, Cristo ... am meruere. Ut exaudiens servulorum [preces, ap]periat ianuam venie. Qui est portas [celi, i]dest sacer, auctor sue ecclesie. Hac de...

In this fragment, the verbeta *Per quem cives angelorum* appears with more verses than in the Antiphonary of Sant Feliu de Girona, ms. 591, and in the Bonastre edition (p. 322). This should make it possible to improve the critical edition of the text and music by reconstructing part of the original model. The fragment's responsories, with a certain degree of consistency, follow the order established in the above mentioned Antiphonary of Sant Feliu de Girona, nos. 234-246 and 579-595.

BIBLIOGRAPHY

OLIVAR 1967, 44; 1969, 76; 1977a, 193. JANINI 1980, 162. MAS 1988, 21. MARQUÉS AND GROS 1995, 177-326. MUNDÓ 1997, 450. GARRIGOSA 2003, 162, 220.

Miquel S. Gros

est locus iste uere non est hic aliud nisi domus

portas celi ℣ Vere dominus est

go nesciebam ℟ vere Gloria patri

sancto sicut erat in principio nunc

angelorum et sanctorum

et egre diuntur Hic ad superos perueniunt

Hic inueniunt egri medicamen

Per quem omnes conscendere crist Cristo

m moruere exaudi seruulorum

eriat ianuam ueniente portas

o est sacer auctor sue ecclesie Hac de

[B]enedicat nos deus ℟ Regme ℟ Bene

dictus dominus deus israel qui facit mirabilia

solus et benedictum nomen maiestatis eius in eternum

num ℣ Reple bitur maiestate eius omnis terra fia

fiat ℟ Et bene ℟ Quis deus magnus sicut deus no

ster tu es deus qui facis mira

tam fecisti in populis uirtutem tuam redemisti in bra

chio tuo populum tuum ℟ Tu es ℣ Magnus dominus

et magna uirtus eius et sapiencia eius non

est numerus ℣ Magnus dominus et laudabilis

nimis et magnitudinis eius non est finis

Miscellany

12TH Century *med.;* 2ND hand, *ex.* (p. 206)

Biblioteca de la Abadía de Montserrat (Barcelona), ms. 72.
Provenance: Church of Sant Romà de les Bons, Encamp Parish (Principality of Andorra). Copied in the Cathedral of La Seu d'Urgell.
Parchment; binding in goffered leather on boards, probably carried out towards 1806 by a craftsman from La Seu d´Urgell; 362 pages; modern foliation in ink (pp. 1-362); the leaves measure 241 × 150/155 mm; the text block measures 165 × 120 mm in the initial quires and 115 × 185 mm starting from the eighth; one column in a continuous line, except on the calendar pages (pp. 1-6) and on a leaf with litanies (pp. 155-156), in two columns; prickings are visible in the margins; number of lines varies depending on whether there is musical notation or not; when this appears, there are generally 11-13 lines of text; ruled in drypoint on the hair side; Carolingian minuscule script; in the texts with musical notation, the letter size is smaller; brown ink for the text and red ink in the headings, highlighted in turn with yellow ink strokes; initials in vermilion or black with ornamental features highlighted in yellow, in the final quires; some initials display zoomorphic or vegetal motifs; there are lowercase letters to help the rubricatorin his work with the initials and indications between the lines for the texts with rubrics; numerous errors and omissions; the manuscript was written by several scribes; from p. 341 onwards (office of St. Roman) a second scribe intervenes, the same one that copied the 1805 manuscript from the Biblioteca de Cataluña; Catalonian notation on the line that corresponds to the ruling of the text block; *custos,* occasionally in red ink.

General contents: *Liber misticus* (mass lectionary, antiphonary of the mass, votive sacramentary and rituale). Calendar (pp. 1-6), full breviary (pp. 7-102), sacramentary with votive masses (pp. 103-126), lectionary of the mass (pp. 127-141), blessing and sprinkling of water (pp. 142-144), *Ordo ad catecuminum faciendum* (pp. 144-149), blessing of the Paschal candle on Holy Saturday (pp. 151-154), celebration of the liturgy of the Easter vigil with the litanies of the saints, blessing of the water and baptism (pp. 155-162), *ordo* for marriage (pp. 163-168), sacramentary of the mass with the principal feasts (pp. 168-178), *ordo defunctorum* (pp. 178-203), offices of the Common of the Saints (pp. 205-274), antiphonary of the mass (pp. 274-295), *Lamentations* (pp. 295-300), epistles (pp. 301-308), *benedictio lectionum* (pp. 318-319), Gospels (pp. 320-324), mass and passion of St. Romain (pp. 326-340), responsories and antiphons of the office of St Romain (pp. 341-344) and missal fragment (pp. 345-356). Musical notation on pp. 7-102 (sung portions of the breviary), pp. 151-154 *(Exultet),* pp. 203-300 (troped Kyrie, offices of the Sanctoral, antiphonary of the mass and *Lamentations*), pp. 320-324 (Gospels with genealogies and intonations of the *Te Deum*), pp. 341-344 (responsories and antiphons dedicated to St. Romain) and pp. 345-356 (missal fragment that includes the sung portions of feast days such as St. John the Baptist, All Saints, Purification, Trinity, etc.).

Leaf shown: p. 206
[Responsoria in nataliciis evangelistarum]
In uisione dei uidi et ecce uentus turbinis ueniebat… Versus. *De medio autem eius… Psalmus. Et ex medio. Responsorium. Quatuor facies uni erant et quatuor penne uni pedes…* Versus. *Sub pennis eorum… Psalmus. Et scintille. Responsorium. Quatuor animalia ibant et reuertebantur…* Versus. *Erat autem quasi… [Psalmus] Et erat. Gloria et honor deo sit consolatori…*

Miscellany composed of a mass lectionary, an antiphonary of the mass, and a *Liber misticus* with elements of a breviary and a votive sacramentary combined with a sacramental rituale. The manuscript was probably copied in the *scriptorium* of the Cathedral of La Seu d´Urgell and was donated to the parish church on the occasion of its consecration in 1164. The codex entered the Abbey of Montserrat in 1911.

Its most interesting distinctivefeature is its provenance; it belonged to a small rural church which was consecrated by the Bishop Bernat Roger of Urgell in the year 1164. The manuscript, together with two other complementary liturgical codices (an antiphonary of the mass and a lectionary), was kept until the 19th century *ex.* in the place in which it was used and for which it was probably copied. This is a good example of a particular type of codex that

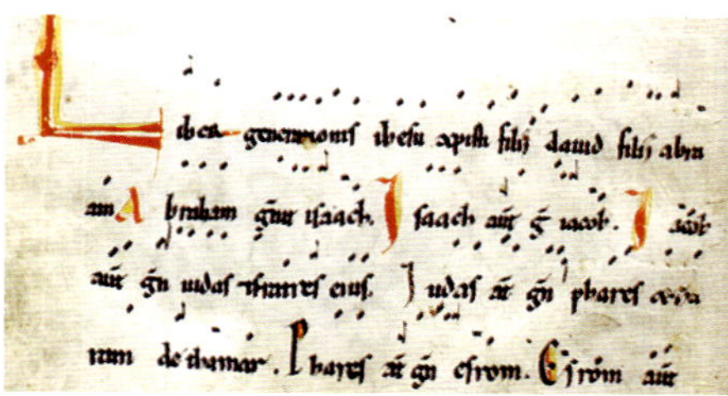

Detail of p. 322

is unique to this liturgical and geographic area of Catalonia, the *Liber misticus* or mixed book, of which some other more or less fragmentary copies have survived.

Bibliography

Albareda 1917, 98-99. Sunyol 1929, 54-65. Anglès 1931, xviii; 1932, 281. Anglès 1935, 140; 1941, 15, no. 8, facs. 6. Sunyol 1935, 373-382. Olivar 1948, 230-234; 1953, cvii-cviii. *Le Graduel Romain* 1957, 75. Franquesa 1958, 20. Mundó 1958, 9. Olivar 1967, 42; 1969, 40-43. Salmon 1967, 58, 108, 111, 115. Bellavista 1976, 29-38. Olivar 1977a, 15-16; 1977b, 44. Bellavista 1979. Fernández de la Cuesta 1980, 132-133. Janini 1980, 157-158. Peñas 1983. Peñas García, 1983, 19, 35, 147-151. Gy 1990, 82; 1991, 28. Olivar 1991, 12. *Catalunya Romànica VI,* 468-469. Huglo 1996, col. 1427. Mundó 1997, 449-450. Garrigosa 2003, 156-157, 456. Altés 2005, 47-277.

Màrius Bernadó

In uisione dei in di(e) et ecce uentus turbinis ueniebat ab aquilone et nubes q(ue) magna et ignis inuoluens et splendor eius in circuitu eius. Et ex medio eo(rum)
similitudo quatuor animalium et aspectus hominis e- rat in eis.
De medio q(ue) autem eius quasi species electri hoc est de medio i- gnis.
Et ex medio. R. Quatuor facies uni erant et quatuor penne uni pedes
uituli
eo- rum pedes recti planta pedis eo(rum). Et scintille quasi aspectus e-
ris cande- ntis. Sub pen- nis eorum manus homi nis in quatuo r pa-
rtibus. Et scintille. R. Quatuo r anima- lia i- bant et reuertebantur in similitudine fulgoris corusca- ntis. Et era t in medio splendor
igni s e- t de i- gne fulgor egre- diens. E- t cum
a- utem qua si uisio discurrentis in me dio quatuor a- nimalium. Et cum
Gloria et ho nor deo sit consolatori sed et luun(?) nunc semper et in eterna secula.

In natalis apostolorum ant(iphon)es super psalmos ad uesperos. Hoc est preceptum meum. E(uouae). Iuues apostolorum. R. Tollite

Prosary, Tropary

12TH CENTURY *EX.* (FOL. 35R)

BIBLIOTECA DE LA ABADÍA DE MONTSERRAT (BARCELONA), MS. 73.
PROVENANCE: DIOCESE OF URGELL (MUNDÓ). NOT OF SPANISH ORIGIN (ANGLÈS). TOULOUSE REGION (CASTRO).
The parchment is in a relatively good state of preservation; binding from ca. 1919; 65 leaves; lacunae between fols. 38 and 39, 47 and 48, 50 and 51, 61 and 62, and 63 and 64; foliation in the upper right margin, by Mundó (ca. 1966); the leaves measure 205 × 140 mm; the writing frame measures 160 × 100 mm; one column justified with vertical lines on both sides; visible horizontal prickings in the right margin; imperceptible vertical prickings; 16 lines; ruled in drypoint, placing odd leaves over the even ones; clear and fairly well-executed Carolingian minuscule; the long and wavy *i* and the *a* with ascenders in the form of a peak date the codex to the second half of the 12th century; the characteristics of the *g* and the *f*, as well as the *st* ligature, are similar to those used in contemporary codices of Catalonian origin as well as those from the south of France; rubrcis in red; major and minorinitials in red; the line marking the separation between words is also colored in red; written by a single hand; late Aquitainian notation oriented around the line colored in red that corresponds to the ruling of the text block; consistent use of a *custos*.

General contents: [Fragmentary] tropes of the Kyrie (fols. 1-12); Gloria (fols. 12-17), with prosulas from the *Regnum* (fols. 13-14v); prosary (fols.17-59v); Sanctus with prosulas for the Osanna (fols. 60-63v); addition with proses for Pentecost (fols. 64-65); [fragmentary].

Leaf shown: 35r
[PROSE FOR EASTER SUNDAY]
Alia. Victime paschali laudes immolent ch*ristiani... Agnus redemit oves... Mors* et *vita duello... Dic nobis Maria... Angelicos testes sudarium... Credendum est.*

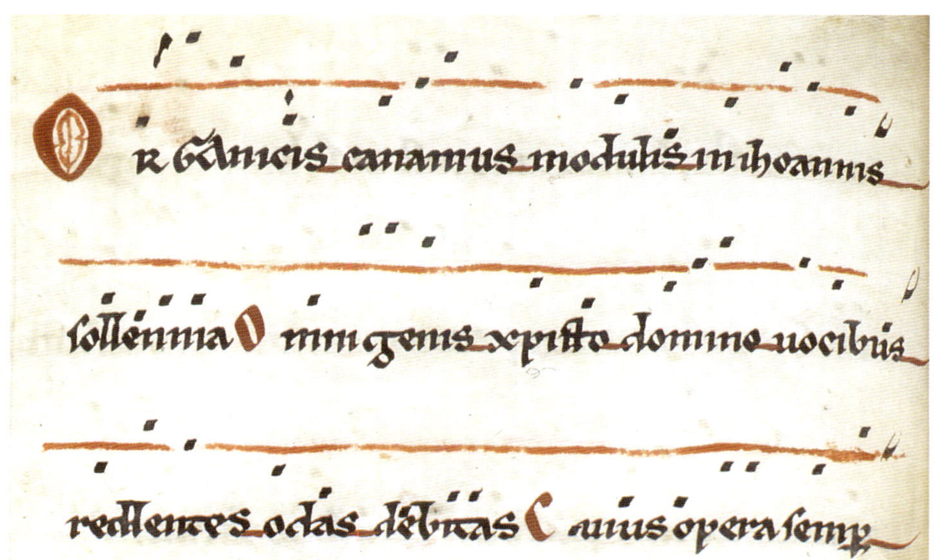

Detail of fol. 23v

The repertoire of this manuscript includes three proses for the Easter Mass: *Fulgens preclara* (fol. 32v; *AH LIII:* no. 35), *Victime paschalis* (fol. 35, *AH LIV:* no. 7) and *Clara gaudia* (fol. 35v, *AH LIII:* no. 38). The prose on the leaf shown here was one of the most widely disseminated ones in the Middle Ages for the celebration of Easter. The dialogue structure of the piece's final stanzas led some churches to present the prose on Easter Sunday as a mimetic performance that represented the dialogue between the apostles and Mary Magdalene. As can be seen, the text copied in the Montserrat manuscript presents a common variant, the reading *paschali* instead of the original *paschalis*. The melody of this piece is in a syllabic style fittingthe textual prosody and a strophic form typical of proses from the classic period. The manuscript is divided into groups of chants for the Ordinary of the Mass, in order of liturgical performance, including the prosary (Kyrie, Gloria, proses and Sanctus).

BIBLIOGRAPHY

ALBAREDA 1917, 3-99. *MONTSERRAT* 1919, 338-339. SUNYOL 1925, 173. ANGLÈS 1931, 1: xviii; 1935, 156, 412. TAXONERA 1954, 16. MUNDÓ 1957, 93. DONOVAN 1958, 208-209. HUSMANN 1964, 93. MUNDÓ 1966, 101-142. OLIVAR 1969, 44-46. FERNÁNDEZ DE LA CUESTA 1980, 133. JANINI 1980, 158. CASTRO 1991, 189-197.

Eva Castro Caridad

alia

Victime paschali laudes immolent xpistiani

Agnus redemit oues xpistus innocens patri recon-

ciliauit peccatores Mors et uita duello conflixere

mirando dux uite mortuus regnat uiuus Dic

nobis maria quid uidisti in uia sepulcrum xpi

uiuentis et gloriam xpisti resurgentis Angelicos

testes sudarium et uestes Surrexit xpistus spes

mea precedet suos in galileam Credendum est

Antiphonary for Mass

12TH CENTURY *EX.* (FOL. 134V)

BIBLIOTECA DE CATALUÑA, BARCELONA, M. 1147.
PROVENANCE: COLLEGIATE CHURCH OF SANT PERE D'ÀGER, LA NOGUERA (LLEIDA).
Modern binding in parchment; 163 leaves; incomplete at the beginning and the end; modern foliation in pencil; the old foliation has been lost because of defects on the sides and the upper and lower margins practically throughout the entire manuscript; the leaves measure 225 × 145 mm; the writing frame has irregular dimensions; a single column justified with horizontal prickings visible in the right margin, whereas the vertical prickings are in the upper margin; 9/12 lines, although there are many leaves with 11 lines of text containing musical notation; ruled in drypoint; Carolingian minuscule; black and red ink; two principal hands: the first was in charge of copying from fol. 8v until fol. 71v and the second hand, from fol. 95 until the end; it seems that additional hands, also from the 12th century, intervened on the preliminary leaves (fols. 1r-8r) and between fol. 72r and fol. 94v; Aquitainian notation; until fol. 20v, the ruling line is marked with black ink (exceptionally highlighted with yellow ink); after fol. 21r, the ruling is in drypoint and, occasionally, there is no line; consistent use of a *custos*.

General contents: A calendar (fragmentary) and various pieces added much later, such as the trope *Clangat cetus iste letus,* fol. 5r, and a farced epistle with musical notation, fol. 6r (fols. 1-8r); the complete cycle of antiphons for Mass (Gradual), from the first Sunday of Advent, including the entire *Proprium de tempore* and the *de sanctis* (fol. 8v-fol. 162v). Fol. 163, in a very poor state of preservation, contains various antiphons for Palm Sunday. On some leaves the musical notation was never added.

Detail of fol. 134v

Leaf shown: 134v
[A PROCESSIONAL ANTIPHON FOR PERFORMANCE AFTER THE EVENING MASS ON THE FEAST OF ST. PETER]
(A*NTIPHONE* PROCESS[*I*]ONAL[*ES*])
Dum duceretur petrus apostolus ad crucem repletus gaudio magno dixit non sum dignus ita esse in cruce sicut dominus meus qui de spiritu sancto conceptus est me autem…

During the restoration process (1965), three fragments with Catalonian notation from the 11th century were found in the spine where they were used to reinforce the binding. The codex has lost a good portion of its lateral and lower margins to rodents. The text is nevertheless reasonably complete. As a characteristic note, it is worth pointing out that the offertories in this manuscript have several versicles.

BIBLIOGRAPHY

VIAGE LITERARIO, 1803-1852, 9: 148-149. ANGLÈS 1931, xvii: 132. ANGLÈS 1932, 282; 1935, 152, 156, NO. 23, FIG. 39; 1941, 16. OLIVAR 1967, 31. BELLAVISTA 1976, 427-452; 1977, 189-232. FERNÁNDEZ DE LA CUESTA 1980, 65. JANINI 1980, 75-76. OLIVAR 1992, 78. GRATACÓS 1994, 136. MUNDÓ 1997, 449. BERNADÓ 1999, 452. GARRIGOSA 2000, 37; 2003, 93-94, 462.

Màrius Bernadó

tu am. Unus confortatus e st Tu espe

A processional

trus Dum duceretur pe trus apo stolus ad

crucem repletus gaudio magno dixit non

su m dignus ita esse in cruce sicut do minus

me us qui de spu san cto conceptus est me au

tem de limo tre i pse formauit ita crux

mea capud meum in terra debet ostendere

at illi uerterunt crucem et pedes eius sursum

confixerunt manus aero deorsum. cum esset

Musica cum rethorica

11TH CENTURY *IN.* (CA. 1018-1046; 1040, MUNDÓ) (FOL. 24V)

ARCHIVO DE LA CORONA DE ARAGÓN, BARCELONA, RIPOLL 42.
PROVENANCE: MONASTERY OF SANTA MARÍA DE RIPOLL (GIRONA).
Parchment; modern binding in parchment (19th century); 113 leaves (paper guard leaves at the beginning and the end); modern foliation from fol. 1 to fol. 113, with a note inserted on fol. 42; between fols. 4 and 5, three are missing because they were cut; the leaves measure 319 × 246 mm (fols. 1-5); 346 × 255 mm (fols. 6-41 and 43-113); 85 × 210 mm (fol. 42); the writing frame measurements vary: 227 × 162 mm (fols. 1-4), 260 × 190 mm (fols. 5-110v); one column except for fols. 72-95 and 108v-109v (where there are two columns); prickings visible in the margins; 33 lines (fols. 1-4), 46-50 lines (fols. 5-58), 34 lines (fols. 59-110) and 39 lines (fols. 111-113); ruled in drypoint; Carolingian minuscule; display script in red and black ink, including botanical and animal ornamental motifs; initials and headings in red or highlighted with strokes in red ink; numerous diagrams in red ink; the majority of the codex was copied by one scribe in the 11th century; there are some additions by other scribes; alphabetic notation, Aquitainian over a line drawn in drypoint (fol. 5r), Daseian (fol. 39r and subsq.).

General contents: Compilation of various music theory treatises. Compiled by the monk Oliva († 1065). Includes a prologue in verse addressed to the monk Pedro, future abbot of Ripoll. The codex consists of two sections that are clearly distinguished, although they have been together since the original compilation in the 11th century. The first part (fols. 1-5) comprises the following:
1. [*Breviarium de musica*] by Oliva.
2. [*Vita Philippi apostoli*].
3. *Versus monocordi* by Oliva.
4. *Diapente et diatesseron simphonie... Ecce modus primus...*
5. *De Guidonis musica:* extract from the treatise *Micrologus*—chap. XIII, 12-21—by Guido of Arezzo.

The second part (fols. 6-113) comprises:
1. *Prosopopeia. Sede sedens diva comes, abbas, praesul Oliva...*
2. *De institutione musica* by Boethius (fols. 6v-38v), an inserted diagram (fol. 42v).
3. *Liber enchyriadis de musica [Musica enchiriadis].*
4. *Scolica enchiriadis de arte musica.*
5. *Commemoratio brevis de tonis et psalmis modulandis.*
6. [*Mensura monochordi secundum tetrachorda Enchiriadis*] *(Incipit: Super unum concavum lignum...)*
7. *Ecce modorum sive tonorum...*
8. *Liber de armonica institutione* by Hucbaldi de St. Amand.
9. *Aforismus artis musicae.*
10. *[Nova expositio] A prima specie diapason.*
11. *Ecce modorum sive tonorum.*

Detail of fol. 24v

12. *[Alia musica].*
13. *Littere designantes directim nervos.*
14. *De tonis.*
15. *Qualiter metiatur monocordus.*
16. *Retorica est beni dicendi scientia...:* extract from *Etimologías* (II, 1-4) by St. Isidore of Seville.
17. *De inventione retorice artis [cum commento Grillii]* by Cicero.
18. *Principia rhetorices* by pseudo-Augustine.
19. *Preexercitamina* by Priscian.

Leaf shown: 24v
[TEXT AND DIAGRAMS FOR THE *DE INSTITUTIONE MUSICA* BY BOETHIUS].

The codex constitutes a magnificent testimony to the flourishing musical life of the 11th century during the abbacy of Abbot Oliva. Together with the works attributed to Oliva (a monk of the same name who was a contemporary of the abbot), the copy comprised the treatises mentioned above.

BIBLIOGRAPHY

VIAGE LITERARIO, 1803-1852, 8: 57-58. BOFARULL 1823, 164. BEER 1910, 11, 70-72, 87. GARCÍA VILLADA 1915, 20-21. NICOLAU D'OLWER 1923, 23. ANGLÈS 1927, 158-159; 1932, 167-170. NICOLAU D'OLWER 1932, 209-210. ANGLÈS 1935, 64-66, 136, 258. DÍAZ Y DÍAZ 1958-1959, NOS. 783-785. BOHIGAS 1960, 45, 47, 129b. HUGLO 1971, 58, NO. 4, 60, NO. 1, 63, NO. 5, 67, 426. ANGLÈS 1976, 1401-1411. GÜMPEL 1977, 260-286; 1978, 57-61. UTTERBACK 1979, 283-296. IBARBURU 1987, 278, 290-291. BOWER 1988, 212, NO. 6. MUNDÓ 1989-1990, 8. MERKLEY 1992, 82. GARRIGOSA 1994, 222, 278, 279. BERNADÓ 1999, 453. CASTIÑEIRAS 1999, 437. GARRIGOSA 1999, 234, 236-237; 2000, 28-29. GÓMEZ MUNTANÉ 1999, 137-138; 2001, 33-34. MUNDÓ 2002, 80, 82. GARRIGOSA 2003, 59-60, NO. 8, ILLUS. IX, 451. GÜMPEL 2004, 23-57.

Màrius Bernadó

scilicet comparat' ad a eundē a duob: semisq. transcendit Sitq. haec differentia f scilicet duo & s. Rursus eadē e differentia b numerū metiat' octies decies semis. fient cc xl s. quod sit g. Igit' g comparat' ad b eodē f differentia sunt minores; Subtracto igit' f abeo qđ ē a atq. b. facti s. d atq. e. Maiorē igit' tenent p portionē int' se d atq. e quā a atq. b. sed d atq. e eandē p portionē int' se retinent quā xviiii s ad xviii s a. igit' ad b minorē retinent p portionem quā xviiii s ad xviii s. quod oportebat ostendere; cclui. ccxliii. xiii. cclui s. ccxl s. iis. XX^I MF.

Videtur tamen eadem p portio cclvi ad ccxliii maior ēē abea quā continent xx & xviiii. sint eni a b c idē qui superius descripti sunt. Metiat' igit' c differentia a omniū uicies. fient cclx qui sint d. Qui comparati ad id qđ ē a eundem quaternario transcendunt hic sit f. rursus idem c metiat' b decies nouies fient ccxlvii hic sit e. Qui comparati ad b eodē f transcendunt. d Igit' numerus a numerum & e numerus numerum b eodē f transcendunt. Adiecto igit' f his qui sunt a atq. b facti sunt d atq. e. Maior igit' ē p portio eo[rum] qui sunt a atq. b quā eo[rum] qui sunt d atq. e. sed d atq. e uicies ac decies nouies multiplicat' c numerus efficit. Maior igitur ē p portio eo[rum] qui sunt a atq. b qui scilicet semitonium continent. quā ea que ē xx ad xviiii. LXII. MCDX.

Demonstratum igit' ē semitonium minus maiorem quidem habere p portionem quā xx ad xviiii. minorem uō quam xviiii s ad xviii s. Nunc idem minus semitonium commati comparem'; quod ē ultimum auditu subiacens: ultimaq. p portio.

SEMITONIUM MINUS MAIUS QUIDEM ĒĒ TRIBUS COMMATIBUS MINUS VERO QUATTUOR

Igit' demonstrandū p ponimus semitoniū min' maius quidem ēē commatibus tribus minus uō quattuor. quod hinc facillime possis agnoscere. Sint tres nūi ita dispositi ut int' se p portionem contineant diapason & eā que d'r sex tonorum. Sit eni a ccclxii cxliiii. Intendant' igit' ad b quidem quinq. toni continui. & sit b cccclxii cccxcii ad c aut' diapason consonantia referat' & sit c dxxiiii cclxxxviii ad d aut' sex toni intendant' sitq. d dxxxi cccclxi. his ita positis & constitutis manifestū ē int' c atq. d comma constitui eo[rum]q. differentiā ēē vii cliii. Id aut' sit k. Remittantur igit' duo toni abeo qđ ē b ad id qđ ē e & sit e ccclxxiii ccxlviii. Rursus ab eo quod ē e intendo diatesseron quod ē f cccc xcvii delxiiii. Cū igitur int' e atq. b duo sint toni int' e atq. f diatesseron. Int' b igit' atq. f minus semitonium reperit'. Sublatis eni diatesseron consonantia duob: tonis sit reliquum semitonium minus quod inprimis numeris constare p dixi cclvi & ccxliii. Quos eosdē numeros similiter nongenties quadragies quatq. multiplices. b atq. f

Lectionary (Temporale)

12TH CENTURY (FOL. 14R)

ARCHIVO CAPITULAR, LLEIDA, RODA 14 (NEW SHELFMARK: RC 0032).
PROVENANCE: CATHEDRAL OF RODA DE ISÁBENA (HUESCA).
Parchment; considerable damage, on occasions appropriately restored in past centuries; early binding in oak, although restored, and leather spine; 152 leaves; incomplete at the beginning; modern foliation in pencil (fol. 19 is repeated); the leaves measure 375 × 250 mm; the text block measures 300 × 180 mm; two columns justified with double vertical lines on both sides and one between the columns; the prickings are not visible; 39 lines; ruled in drypoint; Carolingian minuscule script; text in red ink and rubrics in red with occasional decorative motifs in blue ink; illuminated interlace initials with fantastic animals, some of which were never painted; written by several scribes; staffless Aquitainian notation; consistent use of a *custos*.

General contents: Office lectionary that includes only the *temporale*. It contains some homilies in the form of lessons. The musical notation is limited to the lessons of the *Holy Triduum (Lamentations of the prophet Jeremiah),* which appear on fols. 12-14v. On fol. 149v, at the end of the first column, appears the inscription *Finit est liber. Deo gratias*, and a catchword that refers to the following two pages, which contain somewhat later additions.

Leaf shown: 14r
[LAMENTATIONS OF THE PROPHET JEREMIAH]
SABBATHO SANCTO LECTIO I.
Aleph. Qvomodo obscuratum est aurum mutatus est color obtimus dispersi sunt lapides…

The musical notation was added to a codex that, in principle, was not intended for notation. As in other codices that are not strictly liturgical-musical, the *Lamentations of the prophet Jeremiah* were provided, in some cases later, with musical notation (see Córdoba Homiliary, Sheffield Homiliary and Cardeña Bible).

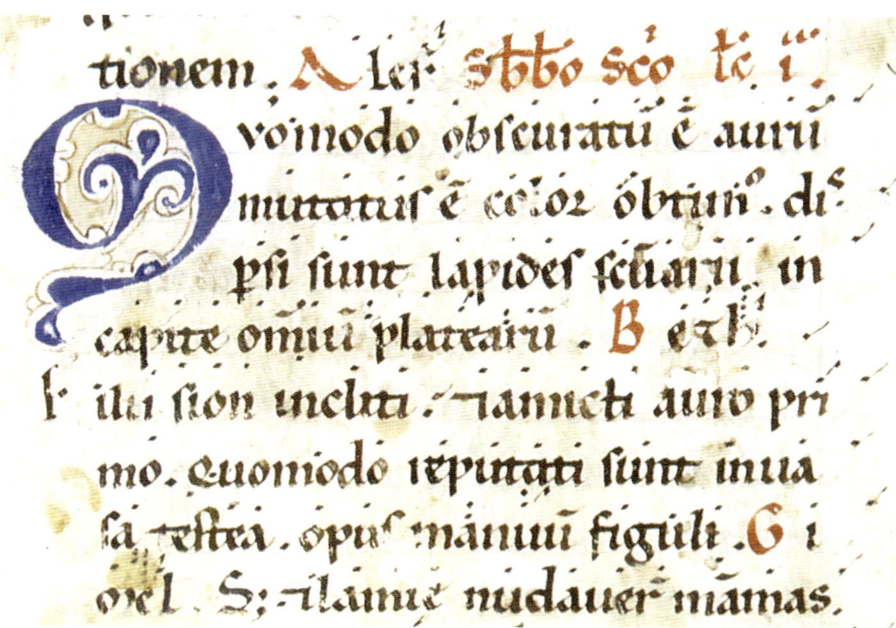

Detail of fol. 14r

BIBLIOGRAPHY

VIAGE LITERARIO, 1803-1852, 15: 175. ROJO 1917. ANGLÈS 1935, 167. *EL ARTE ROMÁNICO* 1961, 93. OLIVAR 1967, 41. BARRIGA 1975, 37; 1978, 11. FERNÁNDEZ DE LA CUESTA 1980, 130. JANINI 1980, 148. MUNDÓ 1994, 141. CASTILLÓN 1994, 138. BOIX 1996, 441. *ARS SACRA* 2001, 135-136. GARRIGOSA 2003, 146-147.

Màrius Bernadó

reverentia. Et quidem cum esset filius dei, didicit ex his quae passus est obedientiam, et consummatus factus est omnibus obtemperantibus sibi causa salutis eternae, appellatus a deo pontifex iuxta ordinem melchisedech. viiij

De quo nobis grandis sermo et interpretabilis ad dicendum, quoniam inbecilles facti estis ad audiendum. Etenim cum deberetis magistri esse propter tempus, rursum indigetis ut vos doceamini quae sunt elementa exordii sermonum dei, et facti estis quibus lacte opus sit non solido cibo. Omnis enim qui lactis est particeps, expers est sermonis iusticie, parvulus enim est. Perfectorum autem est solidus cibus, eorum qui pro consuetudine exercitatos habent sensus ad discretionem boni ac mali. Quapropter intermittentes incoationis Christi sermonem, ad perfectionem feramur. Non rursum iacientes fundamentum penitentie ab operibus mortuis et fidei ad deum, babtismatum doctrine, impositionis quoque manuum ac resurrectionis mortuorum et iudicii eterni. Et hoc faciemus siquidem permiserit deus. Impossibile est enim eos qui semel sunt inluminati, gustaverunt etiam donum celeste, et participes sunt facti spiritus sancti, gustaverunt nichilominus bonum dei verbum virtutesque seculi venturi, et prolapsi sunt, renovari rursus ad penitentiam, rursum crucifigentes sibi met ipsis, et ostentui habentes filium dei. Terra enim sepe venientem super se imbrem bibens et generans herbam oportunam

exercitatos

illuminati

illis a quibus colitur accipit benedictionem a deo. Proferens autem spinas ac tribulos, reproba est et maledicto proxima, cuius consummatio in combustionem. Alef. Sabbato sancto lectio i.

Quomodo obscuratum est aurum, mutatus est color optimus, dispersi sunt lapides sanctuarii in capite omnium platearum. Beth. Filii Sion incliti et amicti auro primo, quomodo reputati sunt in vasa testea, opus manuum figuli. Gimel. Sed et lamie nudaverunt mamas, lactaverunt catulos suos, filia populi mei crudelis quasi strutio in deserto. Deleth. Adhesit lingua lactantis ad palatum eius in siti; parvuli petierunt panem et non erat qui frangeret eis. Lamech. ii.

Non crediderunt reges terre et universi habitatores urbis, quoniam ingrederetur hostis et inimicus per portas Ierusalem. Mem. Propter peccata prophetarum eius et iniquitates sacerdotum eius, qui effuderunt sanguinem iustorum in medio eius. Nun. Erraverunt ceci in plateis, polluti sunt in sanguine; cumque ingredi non possent, tenuerunt lacinias suas. Lamech. Recedite polluti, clamaverunt eis, recedite, abite, nolite tangere; iurgati quippe sunt et commoti dixerunt inter gentes: non addet ultra ut inhabitet in eis. Lc iii.

Oratio Ieremie prophete.

Recordare domine quid acciderit nobis; intuere et respice obprobrium nostrum. Beth. Hereditas nostra versa est ad alienos, domus nostre ad extraneos

Collectanea

12TH CENTURY *MED.* (FOL. 183R)

ARCHIVO CAPITULAR, LLEIDA, RODA 8 (NEW SHELFMARK: RC 0022).
PROVENANCE: CATHEDRAL OF RODA DE ISÁBENA (HUESCA).
Well-preserved parchment; original binding in oak boards covered with goat skin; cords sewn over; there is a metal button on the front cover for closing; 227 leaves; modern foliation in pencil in Arabic numerals in the upper right corner; the leaves measure 153 × 96 mm; one column justified with double vertical lines; horizontal prickings in the right margin, vertical prickings in the upper margin; 22 lines (fol. 183r) that vary in number depending on the different sections or the manuscript (12 lines on fol. 224r); ruled in drypoint using different systems depending on the section; Carolingian minuscule; rubrics in black (fols. 181r-183v), rubrics in red with yellow profile and syllable separation lines underlined in red and yellow (fol. 224r), and rubrics in red without underlining (fol. 224v); the artistry in the quires with notated chants is extremely simple; many hands intervened in the different sections that compose the manuscript; Aquitainian notation oriented around the line corresponding to the ruling of the text block and also without a line; consistent use of a *custos*.

General contents: Miscellany manuscript containing a series of proses with Aquitainian notation in various sections, from different manuscripts.
In sapientia disponens omnia (fols. 181r-182v); *Amor patris et filii* (fols. 183r-v); *Fulgent nova per orbem gaudia* (fol. 223v); *Alleluia sub throno Dei audivi. PROSA IN NATALE SANCTORUM INNOCENTIUM. Urbis nove Iherusalem laudem dicat* (fols. 224r-227v).

Leaf shown: 183r
[Trope of the *BENEDICAMUS*]
Amor patris et filii / verus splendor auxilii.

Detail of fol. 224r

The quires that contain notated chants attest to the insertion of tropes and proses in miscellanies, given the functional character of this compilation. The decoration of the manuscript and the artistry itself are usually, as is the case here, quite modest. Fols. 181r-183v, written by a different scribe, present a *ductus* that is much more meticulous than in the rest of the manuscript. The reduced format of this manuscript can be attributed to to its use by a soloist. The fact that there exist loose leaves containing tropes and proses from miscellanies reflects the circulation of this type of repertoire and its integration into very diverse contexts, as well as a certain lack of system when it came to assigning them a specific place within the liturgical-musical repertoire. The theory about the existence of *libelli* (Huglo) or a set of one, two or a maximum of three quires that would function independently by gathering this type of piece, explains its subsequent insertion in a miscellaneous codex. It is surprising to see such an extensive space provided for the inclusion of the notation on fols. 224-227. Anglès assumed that the addition of a second voice was foreseen, something that cannot be confirmed, and suggested a possible relationship with codices from Saint Martial of Limoges.

BIBLIOGRAPHY
VIAGE LITERARIO, 1803-1852, 15: 172-173. *RH,* 1892-1921, 1004. ANGLÈS 1931, xvii. ANGLÈS 1935, 158-160, NO. 26/2. OLIVAR 1967, 40. HUGLO 1978, 55-65. JANINI 1980, 142-143. CASTRO 1991, 48. GARRIGOSA 2003, 144-145.

Susana Zapke

Amor patris ⁊ filii uerus splendor auxilii
totius spes solacii indeficiens piorum lux ⁊ premium iustorum sublevator perditorum omnis for-
titudinis omnis altitudinis ⁊ beatitudinis donator
omnis sanctitudinis amator omnipotens propi-
cius omnipotens innoxius iustius carius hones-
tius quo nichil est potentius quo nichil est
nil melius illuminator cordium per quem aperte
hominum ueniunt ad auxilium. Fons ingenii
dator premii medicina uicii spiritus consilii
agilis humilis hac inseparabilis promptus et

Hymnary

11th Century *ex.* (fol. 17v)

Archivo Capitular, Huesca, Cod. 1 (olim 1).
Provenance: Abbey of Saint Pierre of Moissac, Tarn-et-Garonne (France).
Good-quality parchment that is generally well preserved; some losses resulting from wear in the lower margin; leaves 34 and 43 have tears that were repaired at an unknown date; modern binding (20th century); 1 + 56 + 1 leaves; it currently comprises seven quires; the chapel master of Huesca, Celestino Vila, took the second one with him when he was transferred to fill the same post at the Cathedral of Granada; the Benedictine Dom Mauro Sablayrolles had the occasion to see and photograph seven of the eight leaves in 1905; these photographs are preserved with the number 166 in the Musical Archive of the Solesmes Monastery and are reproduced in the facsimile edition; modern foliation in pencil in the upper right margin in Arabic numerals; the quaternions are also numbered in pencil and in Arabic numerals; the leaves measured 227 × 138 mm; the writing frame measures 185 × 123 mm; one column justified with a double vertical line on both sides; there are diagonal prickings at the upper edges of the justification lines, but only on the outside and central bifolia of each quaternion; 10 lines; ruled in drypoint placing the first bifolium over the second and the fourth over the third; Carolingian minuscule, slightly inclined to the right, with few abbreviations; rubrics in orangeish red as well as the initials, some of which are bordered in black; on leaf 2r there is an illuminated initial with geometric decoration and interlace in red, orange and black; in the interior of the letter there is a fantastical animal on a green background; the text was written by a scribe from the second half of the 11th century; a 12th century scribe, using darker ink, wrote the glosses, which sometimes obscure the neumes and a hymn on fol. 1v; Aquitainian notation oriented around the line that corresponds to the ruling of the text block; consistent use of a *custos.*

General contents: Dominical hymns: fols. 2-7. Ferial hymns: fols. 7v-8 (the second quaternion is missing). Temporale: fols. 9-32v. Sanctorale: fols. 33-47. Commune: fols. 47v-56.

Leaf shown: 17v
Tu regis alti ianua et porta lucis fulgida...
Ave Maris stella...

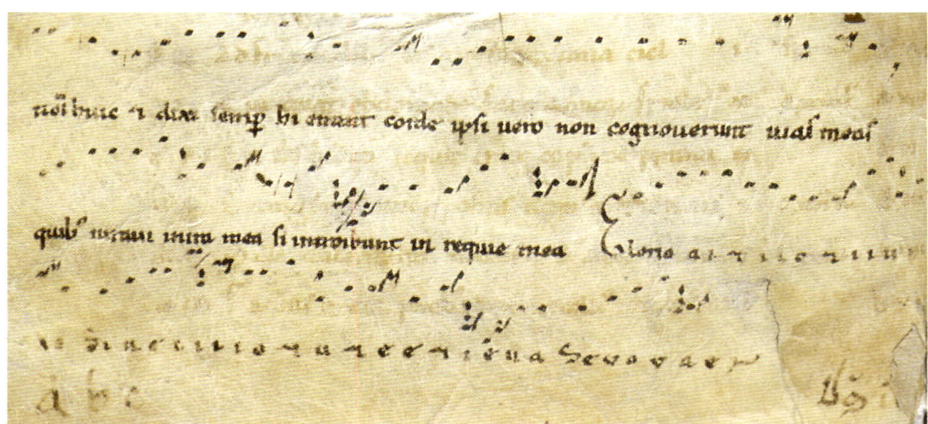

Detail of fol. 1v

The leaf shown contains the last stanza from the hymn *Quem terra pontus* and two and a half stanzas from the hymn *Ave Maris stella*, both for the Feast of the Purification of Mary. Because these are predominantly syllabic melodies, few neumes appear and the simplest ones are the most common. A comparative study of the variations on the same melody applied to different hymns, as well as research on the frequent use of hypermetric verses, can contribute information of great interest for the performance of Gregorian chant. It is also worth emphasizing the presence of some melodies that are extant in no other source. Almost all of the hymns are annotated by a 12th century scribe. Those without glosses were surely out of use at the time they were written down. The scribe who wrote the glosses made some corrections in the original text, refining blurred letters or rewriting stanzas that were difficult to read. The musicologist Moragas has clearly established the relationship of this codex with that of Saint Peter of Moissac, dated to the 10th century, although more recent studies have demonstrated that it belongs to the second half of the 11th century. Surely, the Huesca hymnary was imported as a consequence of the liturgical renovation that occurred in Aragón in the seventh decade of the 11th century. In 1130 the manuscript was already in the Archivo Capitular de Huesca. Finally, we should point out that fol. 1v transmits psalm 94, the invitatory for the office of matins, included at a later date.

Bibliography

Edit. Facs. *Hymnarium Oscense* 1988. Sablayrolles 1906-1909, 233 and subsq.; 1911-1912, 427 and subsq.; Domínguez Bordona 1933, I: 132. Anglès 1935, 184-186. Durán Gudiol 1953, 293-322. Moragas 1956, 277-293. Szövérffy 1971. Gutiérrez 1989, 23-60. Zapke 1996, 236-240. Boynton 1999, 248-251; 2001, 1-26; 2003, 105-106, 124; 2004, 301-329.

M.ª Dolores Barrios Martínez

f. es
Tu regis alti ianua et porta lucis fulgida

f. maria
uita data per uirginem gentes redemptę

cũ plausu laudante
plaudite Gloria tibi dñe. HYMNUM

salue sc̄ti o sc̄a
AVE MARIS STELLA dei mater alma

recipies illã salutẽ
atque semper uirgo felix cęli porta Sumens

f. ab archangelo confirmã
illud aue gabrihelis ore funda nos in pace

conuertens f. peccatricis dissligã offer
mutans euę nomen Solue uincla reis pro

f. a nob
fer lumen cęcis mala nostra pelle bona

f. nobis cui es mat
cuncta posce Monstra te esse matrem su

recipiat f. suã matrẽ f. nrã f. ipse xp̄s filius preulit
mat per te precem qui pro nobis natus tulit

Prosary, Tropary

12TH CENTURY *IN.* (FOL. 86R)

ARCHIVO CAPITULAR, HUESCA, COD. 4.
PROVENANCE: CATHEDRAL OF SAN PEDRO (HUESCA).
Well-preserved parchment; modern binding in dark crimson cloth subsequent to 1953; gilded letters on the spine: *Prosarium-Troparium, saec.* xii. *Sign.* 4; 152 (1 + 150 + 1) leaves; modern foliation in pencil and Arabic numerals, in the upper right margin until fol. 153; errors on some leaves; Arabic numerals on the first twenty quires; the leaves measure 242 × 147 mm; the upper margin was trimmed in the process of binding; the text block measures 175 × 100 mm; one column justified with a double vertical line on both sides from top to bottom; the horizontal prickings are partially visible in the left margin; 18 lines (24 on fol. 1v; 22 on fols. 152v, 149v, 140v and 141; 19 on fol. 5; 20 on fols. 11 and 34; 16 on fols. 30v and 56v; and 16 on fol. 56v); ruled in drypoint using various systems, placing odd leaves over the even ones; Carolingian minuscule; larger letters in the prosary; 11th century Carolingian script (fol. 54v); guard leaves with 13th century Gothic script; headings in red except on fols. 16v-17r where they are in blue; red initials with simple artwork; four different hands; one, for the greater part of the prosary and two others that were contemporary with the principal scribe and contributed additions to the manuscript; fol. 11r-v (scribe 2); add. fols. 18r-19v (scribe 3); fols. 121v-122v (scribe 4 for the *ductus,* more advanced than the other two); there are corrections by the same scribes in the text as well as in the notation; Aquitainian notation with thick strokes around a drypoint line that corresponds to the ruling of the text block; heighting carefully indicated; regular use of a *custos*.

General contents: Structured as in a sacramentary, divided into Masses of the Temporale, the Sanctorale and the Common of Saints. The feast for the dedication of the church (fol. 59v) is situated in the Sanctorale that goes from December to November. *Benedicamus* (fol. 1r), add. 13th century; *Leccio Ysaie prophete* (fol. 1v), farced epistle (add.); prosary (fols. 2r-121v); introductory tropes (fols. 123r-v); tropes of the Kyrie (fols. 123r-138r); prose *S. Crucis* (fol. 139r), add.; tropes of the *Gloria* (fols. 141v-143r) and the *Sanctus* (fols. 144r-149v); prose *Sci. Iacobi* (fol. 150r), add.; prose *Octavas Pascua* (fol. 152v), add.

Leaf shown: 86r
[IN VINCULA SANCTI PETRI. CONCLUSION OF THE *PROSA LAUDES CHRISTO SOLVAT]*
... Hac die plebs leta laudibus iungat pneumata. Qua noster acerba pastor evasit vincula. Clara permerita sordida dilue nostra Petre facinora. Potestate data maxima et prece pia a Christo impetra. Ut nos sua clementia illa det frui vita. Qua regnabunt in patria iusti semper florida. Per eterna vivens secula. ALIA. *Festivum psallat nunc*

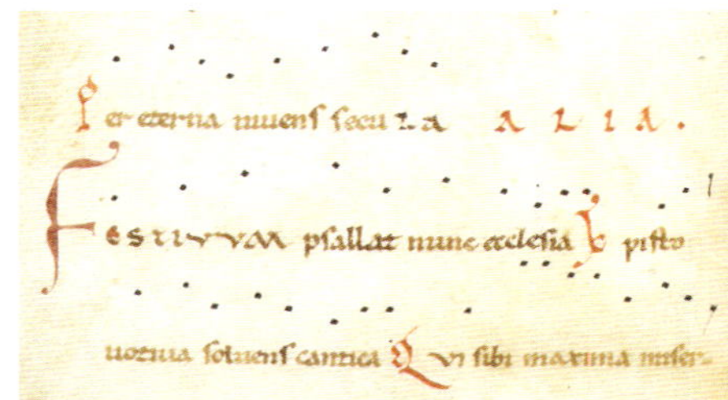

Detail of fol. 85v

ecclesia. Christo votiva solvens cantica. Qui sibi maxima misertus est gratia.
Cum Petrum a dira eductu in custodia. Restituit ad roboranda fidelium agmina. Que presulis exinanita fuerant absentia. Cuius demum preclara virtute animata. Sumunt arma fidei currentes spaciosa. Orbis itinera spurcissimis ritibus dedita. Atque simulacris tunc pro dolor vanis consecrata. Datoque signo cohors beatissima temptat prelia gnaviter herilia nec morte nec vita cedere nescia.

This manuscript is outstanding for its abundant repertoire of unique pieces, proses and tropes from the *proprium* as well as from the *ordinarium* (fols. 13r, 25v, 30v, 36r, 38, 73, 83v and 88v). Its organization is complex because it does not have a single model. The prose *Festivum psallat* from the office *In vincula Sci. Petri*, patron of Aragón—prefaced by the rubric "Alia" and considered to be a unicum (*AH XXXIV:* no. 258; RH, 26.586)—, has an exceptional text based on an account of the reconquest of Huesca en 1096. This detail, together with the installation of the second Bishop of Huesca, Esteban, in 1099, offers a terminus *post quem* for dating the codex. It is common to resort to accounts and protocols in the composition of liturgical texts. The melodic structure is syllabic and follows the textual prosody.

BIBLIOGRAPHY

AH XLVII. AH XLIX. ARCO Y GARAY 1911, 294-301; 1929, 485-533. ANGLÈS 1931, 1: 108. DURÁN GUDIOL 1953, 293-322. SZÖVÉRFFY 1956, 87-110. DONOVAN 1958, 56 AND SUBSQ. HUSMANN 1964. JONSSON 1975. SZÖVÉRFFY 1971. JANINI 1980, 119-124. HUGLO 1986, 13-22; 1990, 139-144. CASTRO 1991, 141-154, 284-291. ZAPKE 1996, 117. GÓMEZ MUNTANÉ 2001, 45-53.

Susana Zapke

tus est gratia C um petrum adira eductum
custodia R estituit ad roboranda fidelium agmina Q ue presulis exinanita fuerant absentia
C uius demum preclara uirtute animata S u-
munt arma fidei currentes spaciosa O rbis itinera spurcissimis ritibus dedita A tque simulacris tunc pro dolor uanis consecrata D atoque
signo cohors beatissima temptat prelia grauiter
ter bellica nec morte nec uita cedere nescia

Breviary, Matutinary

12TH CENTURY *MED.* (FOL. 14R)

ARCHIVO CAPITULAR, HUESCA, COD. 2.
PROVENANCE: CATHEDRAL OF SAN PEDRO (HUESCA).
Well-preserved, good-quality parchment; modern binding in maroon leather; the spine has a gilded inscription: Breviarium saec. xi. Sign. 2; 194 leaves (the end is fragmentary); modern foliation, in ink, in Arabic numerals, in the upper right margin; numeration in pencil in the lower margin of a total of 23 quires; the leaves measure 340 × 230 mm; the writing frame measures 240 × 153 mm; one column justified with a vertical line on both sides that covers the entire leaf; horizontal prickings are visible in the right margin, the vertical prickings are imperceptible; 30 lines; ruled in drypoint and on some leaves with a lead point, placing the odd leaves over the even ones; Carolingian minuscule with very elaborate strokes; the text is written in three sizes for, respectively, the readings, the notated chants and and the rubrics concerning the order of the readings; the chants are indicated by a sign that appears in a red frame within and outside of the text block; the decoration is based principally on distinctive initial letters, with the exception of the beautiful polychrome initials with vegetal, zoomorphic and geometric motifs that are framed with colored backgrounds (fol. 3r: A; fol. 21v: P; fol. 22r: H; fol. 131v: A; fol. 156v: D; fol. 163v: B); major initials are highlighted in red and minor initials in black, in a variety of sizes; the first initial of the series of responsories is larger in size, with red or red and black ink, adorned with simple flourishing; one-or two-word catchwords are framed in red on some leaves; exceptionally without a frame (fols. 123v, 161v); written by a single scribe; scraping, corrections and additions on some leaves (fol. 169v); Aquitainian notation on a the line that corresponds to the ruling of the text block; rigorous annotation of the the differentiae and perfect allocation of the space set aside for the notation; consistent use of a custos.

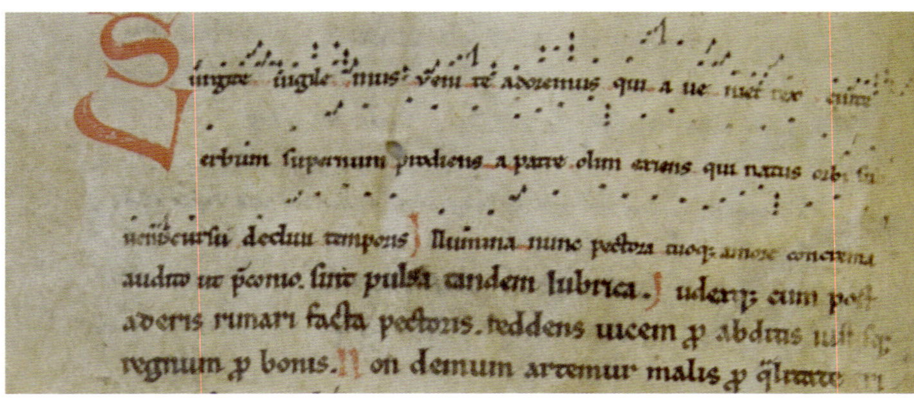

Detail of fol. 2v

General contents: Roman canonical Breviary-Matutinary *Dominica I de Adventu* (fol. 2r); Song of the Sybil (fol. 31r-v); the genealogies of Christ according to Matthew (fols. 37v-38v); the Temporale until the 21st Sunday (fol. 185v); *Lamentaciones* (fols. 121r-122r); antiphons *per ebdomadam post Pentecostes*; *Antífonas ad Magnificat* (fol. 194v). [Fragmentary.]

Leaf shown: 14r
Rubric in red. 11 lines

[THIRD SUNDAY OF ADVENT].
ANTIPHONA *O Sapientia que ex hore. Seae*
ANTIPHONA *O Adonai et dux. Seae*
ANTIPHONA *O Radix iesse qui stas. Seae*
ANTIPHONA *O Clavis David et sceptrum domus. Seae.*

The uniqueness of this codex, which was intended for use by the regular canons and structured with nine readings for the most relevant feasts and three for the rest, is reflected in its mixed typology: breviary, antiphonary, nocturnale and capitulary-collectary. The series of Advent antiphons on fol. 14r form the Greek acrostic *(Ero) cras* that continues on fol. 14v *(Ero)*. The melody is the same throughout the series of antiphons. Cod. 2 contains on fols. 37v-38v the genealogy of Christ according to Matthew, using the same *stemma* as the Sacramentary, Evangeliary, Madrid, BN, ms. 9719 (year 1162), copied in Aragón on the basis of a model from the regular canons of Toulouse. This detail, among others, opens up the possibility that both are based on the same model The same melody appears in Huesca, AC, Cod. 2, Madrid, BN, ms. 9719 and Pamplona, AC, Evangeliary, w./o. s. The three versions are in the first mode with an identical cadence over the key words in the text and a sequence of three phrases that articulate the mode, through successive repetitions.

BIBLIOGRAPHY

ARCO Y GARAY 1911, 294-301; 1929, 485-533. DURÁN GUDIOL 1953, 293-322. HOFFMANN-BRANDT 1971, 2. JANINI 1980, 118. PEÑAS GARCÍA 1983, 47-69.

Susana Zapke

diligitis eam: gaudete cum ea gaudio. universi qui lu-
getis super eam. ant. Dñs omps. Añe. O sapientia. xvi. kl.
januarii incipiuntur et sic in vesperis añ. vigilia nt dñi finiuntur. Ratio.
Sic enim frequentioribus vocibus magis movetur animus. ad preparandum diligentius
venienti dño hospitium: ita assidua renovatione et repetitione cantus dñice adventus sollicitius incitamur ad curam nostre preparationis in adventu dñi salvatoris. In laudibus añe que añ nativitatem per totam unam ebdomadam finiuntur: ea feria incipiantur ut usque
in vigilia nulla non fuerit dñica. que suas etiam proprias habet per ordinem mutatur dies. quo
non continuatim cotidie dicantur. Ratio. Et per hoc frequentius incitamur ad pur-
gationem mentium: et preparandum in nobis deo dignum habitaculum. Verum de his ferialibus
añis est una que numquam dicitur: nisi in nt sci thome apli. idest quinta die añ nt dñi. scilicet aña. Nolite timere. Et tunc post matutinum ad commemorationem dñi adventus dicitur.

A. O sapientia que ex ore altissimi prodisti attingens a fine usque ad finem fortiter suaviterque disponensque omnia veni ad docendum nos viam prudentie. S e a e.

A. O adonai et dux domus israhel qui moysi in igne flamme rubi apparuisti et ei in syna legem dedisti veni ad redimendum nos in brachio extento. S e a e.

A. O radix iesse qui stas in signum populorum super quem continebunt reges os suum quem gentes deprecabuntur veni ad liberandum nos iam noli tardare. S e a e.

A. O clavis david et sceptrum domus israhel qui aperis et nemo claudit claudis et nemo aperit veni et educ vinctum de domo carceris sedentem in tenebris et umbra mortis. S e a e.

Antiphonary (fragmentum)

12TH CENTURY *EX.* (FOL. V)

ARCHIVO HISTÓRICO PROVINCIAL, HUESCA, 12030/36.
PROVENANCE: UNKNOWN. USED FOR BINDING THE PROTOCOL OF NOTARY JUAN BONET (MENOR), JACA, 1589, SHELFMARK 9325.
Brownish-yellow parchment in a precarious state of preservation; used as binding material; one leaf; no foliation; the leaf measures 353 × 359 mm; the text block measures 300 × 230 mm (fragmentary); one column justified with a double vertical line on both sides; prickings invisible; 21 lines (the last line of text is damaged); very even and careful Carolingian script; historiated initial measuring 120 × 80 mm, in red, blue, ochre (two tones), black and green inks; superimposed letters; rubrics and abbreviations of the chants in red and—perhaps only exceptionally in this folio—in black (Line 1); historiated major initial in red, blue, ochre and black inks; minor initials in blue and red; or smaller ones in black ink with some pigment, both with simple interlace line colored in red, marking the separation of the syllable; work of a single scribe; Aquitainian notation oriented around a drypoint line, following the ruling of the text block consistent use of a *custos*.

Detail of fol. r. Antiphonary. Frag. Huesca, AHP, Protocolos Notariales, 12030/36

General contents: *[DOM. QUADRAGESIMA].*

Leaf shown: v
[DOM. II QUADRAGESIMA AD NOCTURNOS]
[INVITATORIUM] *Ploremus coram*
Venite
*HY*MNUS ET *A*NTIFONA*S* ET *V*ERSUS *UT SUP*RA
[RESPONSORIUM] *Tolle arma tua pharetram et archum*
VERSUS *Cumque venatu aliquid*
*R*ESPONSORIUM *Surge pater comede*
VERSUS *Manus quidem manus*
*Quo*modo
*R*ESPONSORIUM *Ecce odor filii mei sicut.*

Liturgical manuscripts that had fallen out of use were commonly employed to bind notarial documents from the 15th to 17th centuries. Approximately 80 fragments from liturgical-musical codices of the 12th to14th centuries that were reused for this purpose are preserved in the Archivo Histórico Provincial in Huesca. Unfortunately, hardly any of the damaged codices have been reconstructed. In some cases, however, concordances in paleography and content have made it possible to put together a few folios that probably originally came from the same manuscript. The fragment reproduced here is the only one from the Huesca archive with a historiated initial, *T,* of remarkable workmanship. No other comparable miniatures from this period are known of in collections in Aragón. The responsory *Tolle arma tua* is taken, although not literally, from Gen. 27, 3-4; 19-20; 22; 27. The scene takes place in two planes, depicting literally the Bible story in which Jacob, counseled by his mother, cheats his father Isaac into giving him his blessing. Isaac, from his deathbed, calls on his firstborn son Esau to take up his weapons and go out and hunt some venison to make a savory meal, so that he can bestow his blessing on him. The upper scene depicts the moment when Isaac, blind and sick, touches his children to recognize the firstborn. The lower scene depicts the hunt, with the two kids that Rebecca, Isaac's wife, has told Jacob to bring. The illumination of the initial suggests a Romanesque language and iconography, and this is reflected in the naturalistic composition of the scene, the depiction of the clothes of the characters, the facial features and the polychrome. The fragment almost certainly comes from an exceptionally fine document, of which only this single leaf remains.

BIBLIOGRAPHY
ZAPKE 2007.

Susana Zapke

OLE ARMA TUA pharetram e t
a rchum et affer de uenatione tua u t co me dam
Et benedicat ti bi anima me a V Cumque ue
natu aliquid attulisset fa c michi inde
medam Et be R Surge pa ter co mede de uenatio ne fi li i tu i Quo
modo tam cito inuenire potuisti fi li uoluntas dei fuit pa ter ut cito michi occur
reret quod uo le bam V Ma nu s quidem manus sunt esa u lo quela a utem
iacob est R Ecce o dor filii mei sicut o do r a gri pleni
quem benedi xit domi nus crescere te fa ci at de us me u s sicut are nam

Antiphonary (fragmentum)

12TH Century *ex.* (fol. 21v)

Archivo del Monasterio de Santa Cruz de la Serós, Jaca, w./o. s.
Provenance: Monastery of Santa Cruz de la Serós (Jaca).
Poorly preserved, yellowing parchment; abundant wax, water, and dirt stains, tears and losses, especially in the lower margin; many leaves have inopportune restorations and sewing; lacks binding; 63 leaves (fragmentary with interspersed lacunae); modern foliation in pencil in Arabic numerals in the upper right margin; there is a mistake in the ordering of the quires; leaves 1 and 2 should be situated after fol. 32 but not together; the leaves measure 360 × 255 mm (fragmentary); the text block measures 260 × 185 mm; one column justified with a vertical line on both sides; the prickings are not visible; 24 lines; ruled in drypoint placing odd leaves over the even ones; Carolingian minuscule with consistent strokes; different size letters for the rubrics and the text; rubrics in red; a line colored in red to mark the separation of the syllables; a variety of major initials with vegetal, zoomorphic, anthropomorphic and interlace motifs, some framed on a colored background; red, blue, ochre, green and black ink; minor initials in black, red and yellow with stylized flourishing; written by a single hand with subsequent additions (fols. 8r, 12r, 19v and 23r) and fragments with modern restoration in Carolingian script (fols. 1r-v, 4r, 20r, 20v, 37r-v, 38r and 39v); Aquitainian notation oriented around the drypoint line that corresponds to the ruling of the text block; four red-colored lines on fol. 15r; consistent use of a *custos*.

General contents: Part of the Sanctorale from St. Sebastian to the Common of St. *In natale Sci. Sebastiani* (fols. 3r-v); *Commemoratio Sce. Agnes* (fol. 4r); *Commemoratio Sci. Fructuosi* (fol. 4r); *In Natale Sce. Agathe* (fols. 12r-14v); *In Cathedra Sci. Petri* (fols. 14v-15v); *Transitus Sci. Benedicti* (fols. 15v-16v); *Translatio Sci. Indalecii ep.* (fols. 21v-21r); *Translatio Sci. Martini* (fol. 22v); *Sca. Maria Magdalena* (fols. 23r-26r); *Transfiguratio Domini* (fol. 28r); *In assumptione Sce. Marie* (fols. 1r-2v, mistakenly numbered; they should be situated after fol. 31v); *In decollatione Sci. Joannis Baptistae* (fols. 33v-36r); *In Nativitate Sce. Mariae* (fols. 36r-39r); *In Exaltatione Sce. Crucis* (fols. 39v-41r); *Sci. Nicolai* (fols. 44r-45r); *Sce. Leocadie, Sce. Eulalie* (fol. 45r); *In Natale Sce. Lucie* (fols. 45r-46r); *Expectatio Sce. Marie* (fol. 46r); *Commune Sanctorum* (fols. 46r-61v); [*Sci. Martini*] (fols. 62r-63v).

Leaf shown: 21v
[In translatione Sci. Indalecii ep.]
… End of the antiphon *ad Magnificat Post primitive ecclesie.*
Invitatorium Presens ut psalmus monet Indalecius. Psalmus *Venite.* Ymnus *Iste confesor.* *In I Nocturno* Antiphona *Vir sanctus Indalecius.* Psalmus *Beatus vir.* Antiphona *Septem Christi discipuli.* Psalmus *Cum inuocarem.* Antiphona *Iam Ihesu Christo Domino.* Psalmus *Verba mea* Antiphona *A Petro septem traditis.* Psalmus *Domine dominus.* Antiphona *Confesor Indalecius.* Psalmus *In Domino.* Responsoria *Cetus apostolicus Christi.*

This is the only musical-liturgical manuscript preserved in the archive of the Monastery of Santa Cruz de la Serós and the oldest antiphonary preserved in Aragón that contains a Franco-Roman repertoire from the Aquitainian tradition. It is of particular interest because of its blending of diverse traditions: vestiges of the Old Spanish rite, a repertoire representing the Aquitainian tradition and a repertoire transmitting both local and regional traditions, typical of the cultural environment from which it came. Unique pieces and singular structures highlight the exceptional character of this manuscript. The rhymed office for the translation of St. Indalecio (fols. 21r-v) is a peculiar case of the creation of a newly minted local cult after the suppression of the Spanish rite. His relics were transferred to the Monastery of San Juan de la Peña on 28 March 1084. The texts are based on the Cluniac monk Ebrethmo's chronicle, written in the 11th century and made known in 1735 by Echéverz, a monk from the aforementioned monastery. The expansion of the Sanctorale at this stage of the transition reflects the will to forge a local hagiographic identity when faced with the infiltration of Aquitainian and Cluniac cults. Exceptionally, the antiphons of the office of St. Indalecio, which follow the order of the eight modes, signal the *Differentia* with the abbreviation *ae.* Initial V. Office of the Assumption of the Virgin.

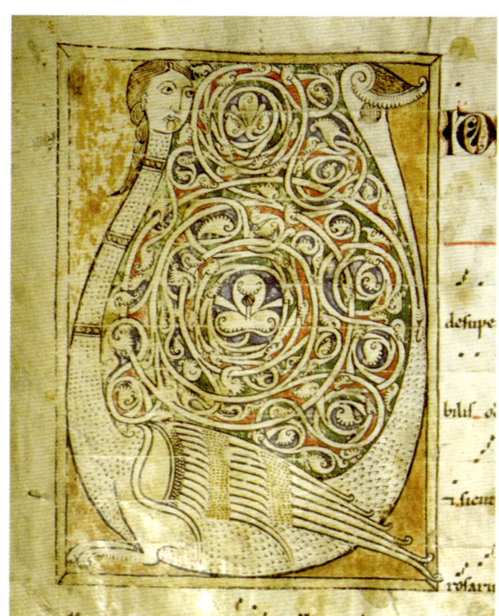

Detail of fol. 1r. Initial *V*

Bibliography

Arco y Garay 1913, 431-455; 1929, 485-533. Vives 1964, 495-508. Ubieto Arteta 1966. Oliván 1974. Zapke 1992, 181-198; 1993, 300; 1995, 353-366; 1996, 152-164. Gómez Muntané 2001, 58.

Susana Zapke

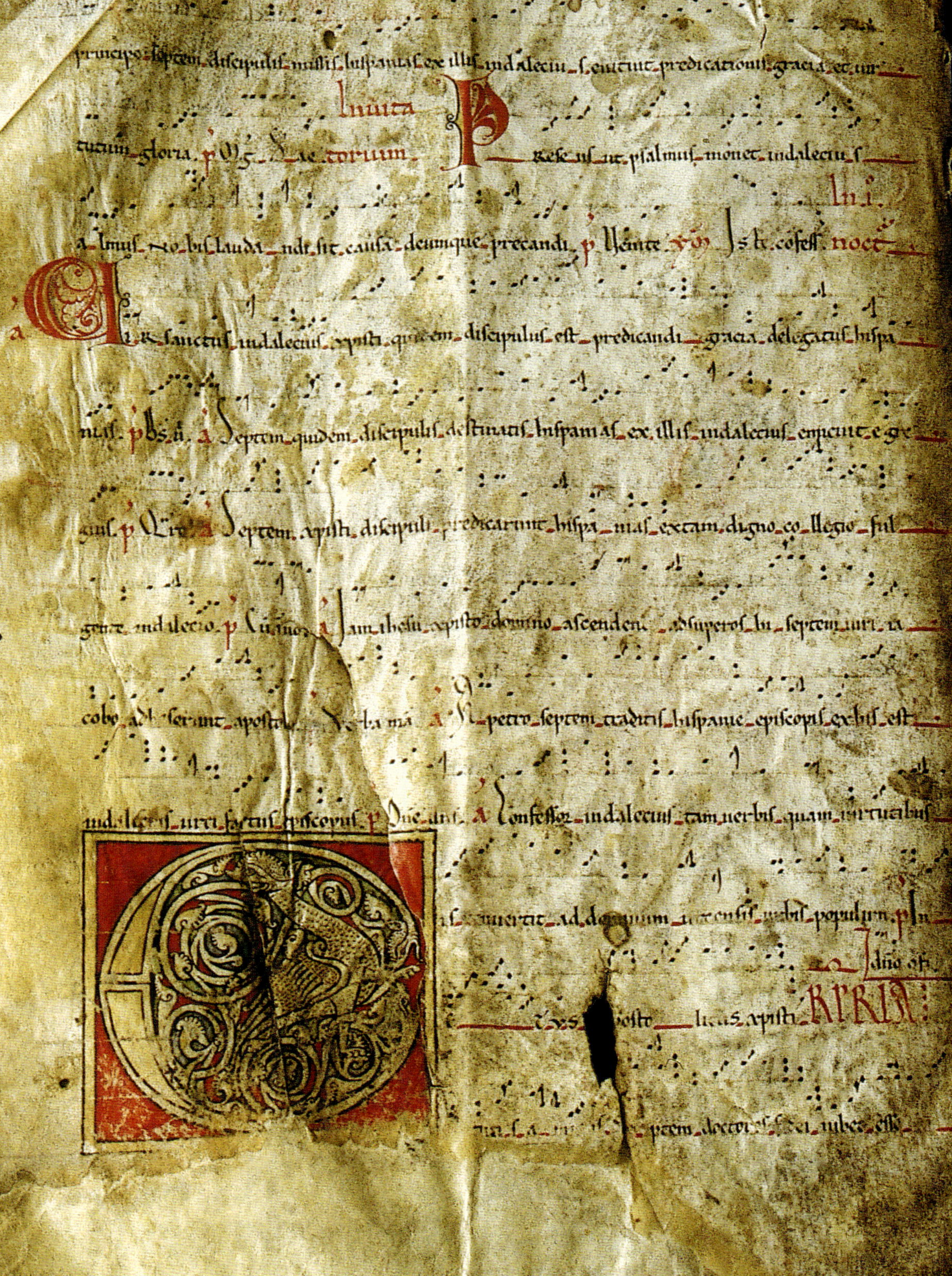

principio septem discipulis missis hispanias ex illis indalecius sortitur predicationis gracia et uir-

tutum gloria. Inuitatorium. P[resens] ut psalmus monet indalecius s-

a ... laudandus sit causa deumque precandi. ... cofess. noct.

A Alme sanctus indalecius xpisti quidem discipulus est predicandi gracia delegatus hispa-

nias. A Septem quidem discipulis destinatis hispanias ex illis indalecius eripuit e ge-

ntis. A Septem xpisti discipuli predicarunt hispanias ex tam digno collegio ful-

get indalecio. A Iam ihesu xpisto domino ascendente ad superos hi septem uiri a ia-

cobo ... apostolo ... A ... petro septem traditis hispanie episcopis ex his est

indalecius uiri factus episcopus. A Confessor indalecius tam uerbis quam uirtutibus

... conuertit ad dominum ... populum

... KYRIE

... septem doctores ...

Breviary

12TH CENTURY *EX.* (FOL. 90R)

REAL BIBLIOTECA DE SAN LORENZO, EL ESCORIAL, MS. L.III.3 (BELONGED TO THE LIBRARY OF THE COUNT-DUKE OF OLIVARES).
PROVENANCE: MONASTERY OF SAN JUAN DE LA PEÑA (HUESCA) (?).
Well-preserved parchment; binding from the 17th century *ex.* (El Escorial); 172 leaves (fragmentarys); modern foliation in pencil in Arabic numerals in the upper right corner; the leaves measure 240 × 160 mm; the text block measures 180 × 125 mm; one column justified with a double vertical line on both sides; horizontal prickings are partially discernible in the right margin; 31 lines; ruled in drypoint; Carolingian script; initials and capitals in blue and red; headings in red; the ink is light brown for the text and black for the notation, suggesting that there may have been two scribes or phases of production; in some cases the text has been gone over in the same ink used for the notation; one scribe for the sanctorale (fols. 23v-171r) and a different hand for the psalter added in the 13th century (fols. 1r-22v); contemporary corrections and erasures; Aquitainian notation in very fine strokes on a drypoint line following the ruling of the text block; on some leaves (e. g. fol. 55r), the line has been gone over in black; consistent use of a *custos*.

General contents: Roman monastic breviary. *Psalterium per hebdomadam dispositum*, fols. 1r-22r (fragmentary); *Proprium Sanctorum (Sci. Stephani-Sci. Thome apost.)* fols. 23r-160r; *Commune Sanctorum* (up to *in natale plurimum martyrum*), fols. 161r-172r.

Leaf shown: 90r
[SCI. IOHANNIS BAPTISTE]... *apparuit [continuation of the ANTIPHONA Ingresso Zacharia templum]. P*SALMUS. *Mag*nificat. *O*RATIO. / *INVITATORIUM Regem precursoris Dominum* / *P*SALMUS. *Venite* / *HYM*NUM *Ut queant laxis* / *IN I.* NOCTURNO. ANTIPHONA. *Priusquam te formarem* / PSALMUS. *Beat*us *v*ir / ANTIPHONA *Ad omnia que mittam* / PSALMUS. *Qua*re *fre*muerunt / ANTIPHONA *Ne timeas et facie* / PSALMUS. *Cu*m *in*vocare*m* / ANTIPHONA *Misit Dominus* / PSALMUS *Ver*ba *mea* / ANTIPHONA *Ecce dedi* / PSALMUS. *Domi*ne *Domi*nus / ANTIPHONA *Dominus ab utero* / PSALMUS *In* Domi*no* / VERSUS *Pr. q.* ...
*L*ECCIO *I. Sollempnitates* / *R*ESPONSORIUM *Fuit homo missus a Deo.*
*L*ECCIO *I. Sollempnitates* / *R*ESPONSORIUM *Fuit homo missus a Deo.*

Detail of fol. 90r

Beautifully written codex with notation and script that show the work of an expert hand, possibly French. A comparison with the breviary, possibly also from La Peña, El Escorial, RB, ms. L.III.4, and the Antiphonary of Santa Cruz de la Serós, Jaca, w./o. s., a nearby Benedictine monastery, shows that identical models were in circulation. At the same time, however, there are some singular differences in the structure of the masses. Of particular interest are the Offices of the Nativity and the Translation of St. Indaletius, a locally venerated saint whose relics were transferred to the Monastery of San Juan de La Peña on 28 March 1084 (fols. 74r-77v; 81v-83r). Also noteworthy are the feast days of Sts. Nunilo and Alodia (fol. 139v) and a number of saints from the Spanish tradition. The composition of the sanctorale shows an interaction among various traditions: Spanish, Roman and French (or to be more precise, Aquitainian). Following the forced replacement of the Spanish rite with the Franco-Roman rite, the creation of new hagiographic cults, such as St. Indaletius, shows that there was some desire to establish a local identity, in contrast to the mass penetration of Cluniac, Aquitainian and Roman hagiography.

BIBLIOGRAPHY
ANTOLÍN 1910-1923, 3: 25. JANINI 1977a, 99-100. ZAPKE 1993, 133-134; 1996, 116, 154, 156, 206-221, 241.

Susana Zapke

apparuit ei Gabriel angelus stans a dextris alta — ris incensi. ℣ Magnificat.

Oratio. Presta quesumus omnipotens deus ut familia tua v. s. Invitatorium.

Regem precursoris dominum — venite — adoremus ℣ Venite.

Hymnus. Ut queant laxis. In .i. nocturno antiphona. Priusquam te formarem in utero novi te et antequam

exires sanctificavi te ℣ Beatus vir. Antiphona. Ad dominum que mitto te dicit dominus

ibis ne timeas et que mandavero tibi loqueris ad eos ℣ Quam admirabile. Antiphona. Ne ti-

meas a facie eorum quia ego tecum sum dicit dominus ut eruam te ℣ Cum invocarem.

Antiphona. Misit dominus manum suam et tetigit os meum et prophetam in gentibus de-

dit me dominus ℣ Verba mea. Antiphona. Ecce dedi verba mea in ore tuo ecce consti-

tui te super gentes et regna ℣ Domine dominus. Antiphona. Dominus ab utero vocavit

me de ventre matris mee recordatus est nominis mei ℣ In domino confido. ℣ Priusquam te formarem.

Sollempnitatem nobis diversorum martyrum fratres karissimi. Lectio .i.

Suite presentis occasio et suscepta ab eis pro Christo nimie passio consecravit. Multimoda namque veterum relatione didicimus non nullos martyrum prostratos gladio igni alios concrematos quam plures bestiarum dilaceratos dentibus innumeros etiam variis tormentorum cruciatibus affectos sperata sui corporis morte aeterne fidei testimonium reddidisse.

℟ Fuit homo missus a deo cui nomen Iohannes erat hic venit in testimonium ~~ut testimonium~~ perhiberet de lumine

Breviary

12TH CENTURY *EX.* (FOL. 7V)

REAL BIBLIOTECA DE SAN LORENZO, EL ESCORIAL, MS. L.III.4 (BELONGED TO THE LIBRARY OF THE COUNT-DUKE OF OLIVARES).
PROVENANCE: MONASTERY OF SAN JUAN DE LA PEÑA (HUESCA) (?).
Well-preserved parchment; 17th century *ex.* binding. (El Escorial); 99 leaves (fragmentary); modern foliation in pencil in Arabic numerals in the upper right margin; the leaves measure 244 × 165 mm; the writing frame measures 190 × 120 mm; one column justified with a double vertical line on both sides; imperceptible prickings; 31 lines; ruled in drypoint; odd leaves placed over the even ones; Carolingian minuscule script; initials and headings in red; written by a single hand; Aquitainian notation, small in size with very fine strokes; consistent use of a *custos.*

General content: Roman monastic breviary. *Proprium Sanctorum.* Incomplete, covering the period from *V Idus Januarii. Natale sanctorum Premium et Feliciani* to *II. Kalendas Octobris. Natale Sancti Hieronymi presbiteri.*

Leaf displayed: 7v
[IN NATALE SCI. IOHANNES BAPTISTA] End of the *Leccio* VIII.
*R*ESPONSORIUM *Inter natos mulierum* / *V*ERSUS *Hic venit in testimonium / Gloria Patri / PROSA Preparator veritatis lucerna / SECUNDUM LUCHAM In illo tempore.*

Detail of fol. 7v

This codex is very similar to the Breviary of the Real Biblioteca de El Escorial, ms. L.III.3 in both form and content, which suggests that the two came from the same place—the Benedictine Monastery of San Juan de La Peña. The even, meticulous strokes of both the notation and the script are the work of an expert, possibly of French origin, who would have been entrusted with the task of copying the codex for the use of the community at La Peña. The importance given to the Offices of St. John the Baptist, with the prose *Preparator veritatis lucerna eximia* followed by the octave, offers another clue to the possible provenance of the codex. The Spanish sanctorale is partially maintained with feasts such as that of St. Zoilus and Companions, St. Justa and St. Rufina, St. Eugene and St. Salvius. Finally, it is worth noting the series of tropes in the ordinary of the mass that are exclusive to Spanish sources, and which are partially represented in the Prosary-Tropary of Huesca, AC, Cod. 4, e.g. *"Cunctipoteus genitor"* (fol. 262v). There are also several tropes of southern origin which are only found in a few Spanish sources: *Adest summa atque precelsa* (fol. 267), also found in Toledo, BC, 35-10 and Huesca, AC, Cod. 4.

BIBLIOGRAPHY

ANTOLÍN 1910-1923, 3: 26. JANINI 1977a, 100. ZAPKE 1993, 133.

Susana Zapke

errantibus et non ageret ut id putaretur. sed iam
quod putabant acciperet ad honorē suum augendum.
S; absit hoc a fideli amico sponsi ut se pro illo absponsa
diligi uellet. Confessus ē se non ēē quod non erat ne p(er)
deret q(uo)d erat. Venit ḡ sup(er)bos docere humilitatē annun-
ciare pe-

Inter-natos-mulie-rum-non-surrexit-maior- R. nitencie.

iohanne-bap-tista-Qui-uiam-domi-no-preparauit-in-here-

mo. V. Hic-ue-nit-in-testimonium-ut-testimoniu-

m-perhiberet-de-lumine-Qui-uiam-Glo-ria-

patri-et-filio-et-spiritui-sancto-Qui-uiam-domino- Prosa.

P. R. ēparator-ueritatis-lucerna-eximia-Audi-pie-uenerantes-te-a-[illegible]-

Qui-in-uentre-matris-iacens-habuisti-gaudia-Resentiendo-[illegible]-xpistum-

in-uentris-angustia-Intra-petens-ut-[illegible]-fugeres-affamina-Neque-

uino-nec-sicera-soluisti-ieiunia-Herba-cibus-aqua-potus-et-terra-cubilia-

erant-tibi-deuoto-[illegible]-desideria-In-heremo. Secundum Lucham.

In illo t(em)p(o)r(e). Elisabeth impletum est tempus pariendi:
et peperit filiū. Et audierunt uicini et cognati eius.
quia magnificauit d(omin)us misericordiam suā cum illa, et
congratulabantur ei. Et reliqua.

Verbum in p(er)fectionis sacra scriptura in bonorū tantum actu uel obitu ponere consueuit. quorū uitam

Sancti Gregorii Magni dialogorum libri IV, Vita Sanctae, Euphrosynae

12TH CENTURY *EX.* (FOL. 119V)

REAL BIBLIOTECA DE SAN LORENZO, EL ESCORIAL, Q.III.10.
PROVENANCE: MONASTERY OF SAN JUAN DE LA PEÑA (HUESCA) (?).
Well-preserved parchment; 17th century *ex.* binding (El Escorial); 127 leaves (last quire, 15th century added, fols. 122-127); modern foliation in pencil in Arabic numerals in the upper right corner and on the left of the verso folio; the leaves measure 248 × 160 mm; the text block measures 180/200 × 125 mm; one column justified on both sides with double vertical lines; horizontal prickings in the right margin; vertical prickings no longer visible; 18 lines; ruled in drypoint; Carolingian script; written by a single hand; Aquitainian notation oriented around a drypoint line following ruling of the text block given the ample space reserved for the notation, the diastematy is particularly accentuated; consistent use of a *custos* at the end of the base line.

General contents: *Liber dialogorum beati Gregorii.*
Additions at the beginning and end of liturgical pieces with Aquitainian notation: prose, *Benedicta semperque sit Trinitas* (fol. 2r); tropes of the agnus, *Agnus Dei. Fons indeficiens pietatis* (fol. 2v); Prose for St. Martin, *Precelsa dies adest ac veneranda* (fols. 119v-120r).

Leaf shown: 119v
In festo Sci. Martini (add.)
Precelsa dies adest ac veneranda / Gaudeat fors apostolica / Vinana nec ne / Hunc quia mortis vira tremunt / Verbo laudit etera et referat potencia / Hunc cum ioanne / Dum secus mare / Vocat digna fatis / Sanctus nauta / Regna terrae ac / Serens mundo.

As is often the case with liturgical and theological codices, pieces with musical notation are found in the blank spaces or added later as a leaf or even as complete quires that have no direct relation to the contents of the codex to which they have been added. In this case, the blank spaces have been used to notate a prose honoring St. Martin, which ends on fol. 120r. In a later hand of the 15th century, a rubric "In festo sancti Martini" has been added. The repertoire of proses, used as para-liturgical pieces, is often inserted into unusual spaces, as this example shows. The melodic structure is A BB CC DD, meaning that except for an initial verse and another final one, each with its own melody, the other verses follow a parallel structure.

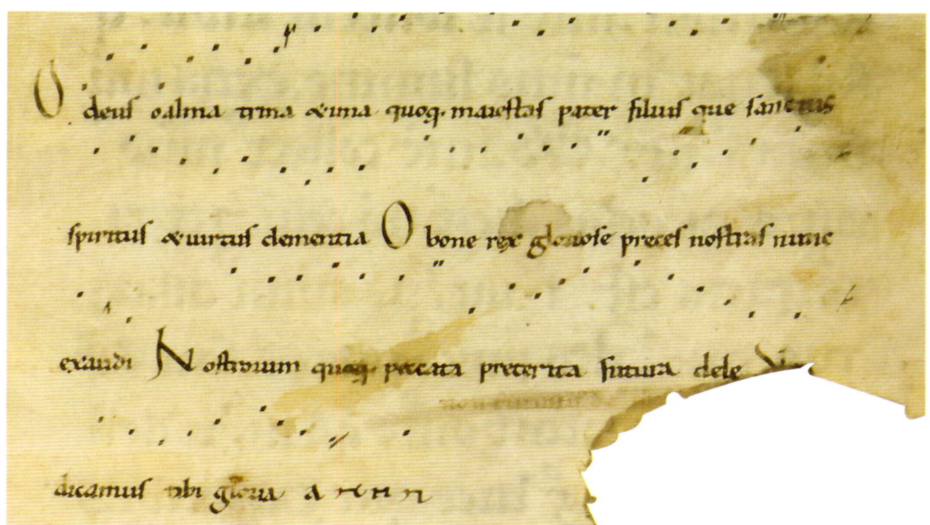
Detail of fol. 120r

BIBLIOGRAPHY
ANTOLÍN 1910-1923, 3: 427-428.
FERNÁNDEZ DE LA CUESTA 1980, 115.
CASTRO 1991, 48. ZAPKE 1993, 133.

Susana Zapke

f. 119v

In festo sancti martini

Precelsa dies adest ac ueneranda Gaudeat sors apostolica ac in die sancta perenni leticia Vizana nec ne ma-
rica sancti uiri digna preferunt preconia iacobi precellen-
tissima Hunc quia mortis uira tremunt uirtute diuina Uerbo clausit ostia et reserat potencia Hunc cum ioanne diua dex-
tem Dum secus mare firmat uestigia Uocat digna satis cle-
mencia celestis regni dictat gloria Sanctus nauta nauim
et recia linquens ac sua prorsus omnia Regna terris ac
maria uisitat uite uernula Secessus mundo [illegible] dum

Sacramentary, Evangeliary

1162 (FOL. 209R)

BIBLIOTECA NACIONAL, MADRID, MS. 9719 (OLIM EE. 26).
PROVENANCE: ARAGÓN.
Well-preserved parchment; 18th century binding in green leather with gilded iron; ex libris Gregorio Mayans and Siscar; 214 leaves; modern foliation in pencil in the upper right corner; the leaves measure 310 × 190 mm; the writing frame measures 228 × 114 mm; one column justified with double vertical lines on both sides; the prickings are not visible; ruled in drypoint; 27/28 lines; Carolingian script; written by a single hand; Aquitainian notation over a line that corresponds to the ruling of the text block consistent use of a *custos*.

General contents: Computus table (fol. 1v) and a calendar from Zaragoza, added in the 14th century (fols. 2-7); Sacramentary (fols. 8v-111v); Evangeliary (fols. 112-214).

Leaf shown: 209r
[GENEALOGY OF CHRIST ACCORDING TO MATTHEW]
Dominus uobiscum. Et cum spiritu tuo. Inicium sancti euangelii secundum Mattheum. Gloria tibi domine. Liber generationis ihesu Christi filii Dauid filii Abraham ... Achaz autem genuit (ex.).

This copy reflects the moment when Aragón adopted the Sanctorale that was characteristic of the centers in the south of France after the Spanish rite was replaced by the Franco-Roman rite, as is demonstrated by the presence of the feasts for St. Martial (Limoges), St. Saturninus (Toulouse) and St. Gerald (Aurillac). The Sanctorale also includes other saints associated with the area around Toulouse such as St. Exuperius and St. Hilary, Bishop of Toulouse. The votive Masses indicate the commemoration of St. Saturninus. The calendar from Zaragoza (fols. 2-7) was subsequently added in the 14th century. The melody of the genealogy according to Matthew from ms. 9719, fol. 209r-v, can be considered, with some variations, identical to that of Huesca, Archivo Capitular, Cod. 2. Both manuscripts offer variations of the same melody and present more complex melodic structures than those transmitted by other Spanish sources, such as, for example, the versions from El Escorial (RB, ms. I.II.13, 14th century) or from Toledo (BC, 35-19, fol. 136, 13th century, written in Castile).

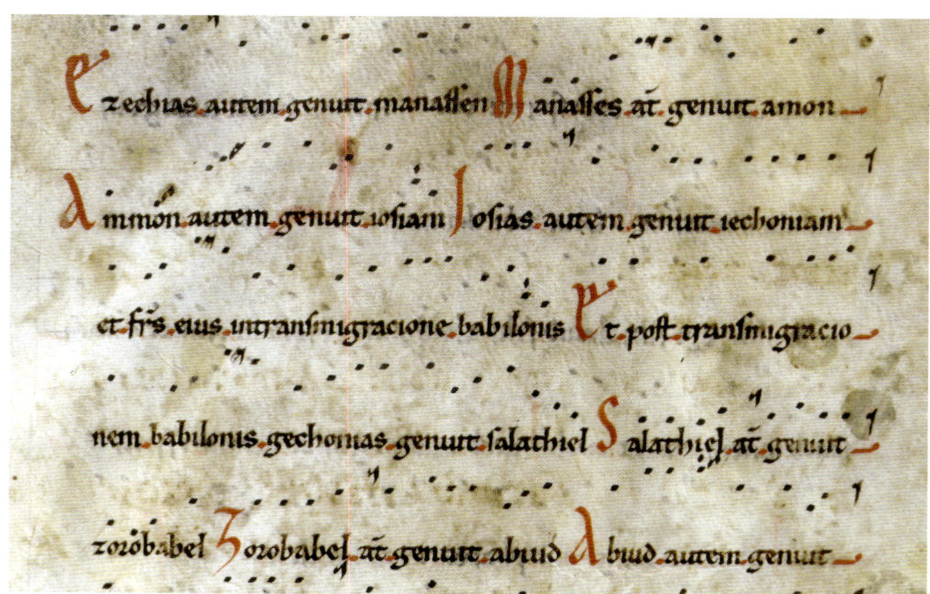

Detail of fol. 209v. Biblioteca Nacional de España

BIBLIOGRAPHY
DOMÍNGUEZ BORDONA 1933, 2: 288. ANGLÈS AND SUBIRÁ 1946, 53-54. CORDOLIANI 1955, 194. GARCÍA ALONSO 1958, 10-11. JANINI AND SERRANO 1969, 116-118. DELCLAUX 1973, 126-127. PEÑAS GARCÍA 1983, 47-69. HERNÁNDEZ APARICIO 2002, 125-126.

Susan Boynton

Dominus uobiscum Et cum spiritu tuo Initium sancti euangelii secundum matheum Gloria tibi domine Liber generacionis ihu xpi filii dauid filii abraham Abraham genuit ysaach Isaach autem genuit iacob Iacob autem genuit iudam et fratres eius Iudas autem genuit phares et zaram de thamar Phares autem genuit esrom Esrom autem genuit aram Aram autem genuit aminadab Aminadab autem genuit nahason Nahason autem genuit salmon Salmon autem genuit booz de rahab Booz autem genuit obeth ex ruth Obeth autem genuit iesse Iesse autem genuit dauid regem Dauid autem rex genuit salomonem ex ea que fuit urie Salomon autem genuit roboam Roboam autem genuit abiam Abias autem genuit asa Asa autem genuit iosaphat Iosaphat autem genuit ioram Ioram autem genuit oziam Ozias autem genuit ioatham Ioatham autem genuit achaz Achaz autem genuit ezechiam

Homiliary

953 (FOL. 327V)

ARCHIVO CAPITULAR, CÓRDOBA, MS. I (OLIM 72).
PROVENANCE: SAN PEDRO DE VALERÁNICA MONASTERY, BURGOS (MILLARES CARLO).
Well-preserved parchment; leather binding over boards; 456 + 1 leaves; modern foliation in pencil with Arabic numerals in the upper right margin; the leaves measure 450 × 330 mm; the writing frame measures 362 × 246 mm; three columns justified with double vertical lines on the edges and one line on each side of both intercolumnar spaces, spanning the entire leaf; the prickings are barely perceptible except for isolated punctures in the margins and between the columns; 39 lines; ruled in drypoint; liturgical Visigothic minuscule with excellent penmanship; rubrics in red; primary and secondary initials filled in with yellow, red, green and blue ink, with very simple decoration; corrections to the text by a different hand; the scribe was Florentius; quires of eight leaves without catchwords; Aquitainian notation *in campo aperto,* probably added around the 11th century *med.,* presents some peculiar ligatures with rounded strokes.

Detail of fol. 328r

General contents: Homilies and readings for the entire liturgical year. The last two leaves contain *Fulgentius, De fide Incarnationis Filii Dei ad Scarilam.*

Leaf shown: 327v
Column a, line 1: … *Iudeis falsis testibus contradicis.*
Column c, line 8: *Quid Sibilla vaticinando etiam de Xristo clamaverit in medium proferamus, ut ex uno lapide utrorumque frontes percutiantur iudeorum scilicet atque paganorum, atque suo gladio sicut Golias Xristi omnes percutiantur inimici. Audite qui[d] dixerit: Iudicii signum tellus sudorem madescet...*
Orbe...

This homiliary, probably copied in Valeránica, includes the sermon by pseudo-Augustine from the 11th chapter with the verses by the Sybil accompanied by neumatic point notation with a pronounced diastematic tendency, which allows an approximate reconstruction of the melody it represents. Although it is one of the oldest versions of the Song of the Sybil, the neumes were added between lines after Florentius completed copying the manuscript in 953 at the age of thirty-five. The script is Visigothic but the notation is Aquitainian, a typology characteristic of the musical manuscripts that replaced those of the Old Spanish liturgy once the latter was abolished. The combination of Visigothic script and Aquitainian notation has raised and continues to raise questions about the date in which the notation was added, which, in principle, was not before the second half of the 11th century.

The tradition of the Song of the Sybil extends throughout the southwest of France and the Iberian Peninsula, from Catalonia to Portugal. There are also examples in Italy, which is proof of the cultural interaction that existed during the Middle Ages. The oldest copy with musical notation, dated to the 10th century, is from the area around Limoges. The melody of the chant presents a psalmodic structure with refrain. In some copies, two melodies alternate, but the model based on one unique melody generally predominates.

Polyphonic versions were composed in the 15th and 16th centuries. In Catalonia this form extended from the 10th to the 15th centuries in a monophonic version, and later in a polyphonic version. This chant was maintained in the Cathedral of León until the 16th century.

BIBLIOGRAPHY

CLARCK 1920, 31, 231. ANGLÈS 1935, 289, 300. CORBIN 1952a, 5-6. DONOVAN 1958, 65, 166. GARCÍA, CANTELAR AND NIETO 1976, 3. GÓMEZ MUNTANÉ 1996, 1: 11. COLETTE 2004, 165-176.

Maricarmen Gómez
Susana Zapke

Iudei si falsis testibus contradicitis.
et hoc ut dicam. sed unaquaque Xpm ui-
derit quicumque uidet ipse uenit
excelsus humilis in splendore dis-
persuasionis sue cum uenit ut a
baptizaretur. qui nullum habe-
bat omnino peccatum. quid res-
pondes. quem cognoueris. quale
testimonium protuleris. audiunt
inimici qui audire nolunt.
Ecce inquid agnus dei. ecce qui tollit
peccata mundi. et cetera.
Tu ad me uenis baptizari. ego a te
debeo baptizari. agnouit seruus
dominum. agnouit uinculis origina-
lis peccati obligatus ab omni genere
peccati liberum. agnouit preco
iudicem. agnouit creatura crea-
torem. agnouit paranimphus
sponsum. Nam et hec uoce locutus est. qui habet sponsam sponsus est. Amicus autem sponsi
stat et audit eum et gaudio
gaudet propter uocem sponsi.
Sufficiunt uobis ista o Iudei.
sufficiunt uobis tanta testi-
testimonia ex lege uestra et ex gen[t]-
ium [(?)]. An adhuc inpudentia
nimia audebitis dicere quod
alienigenas ut nationis
homines Xpo deberent testimonium perhibere. Sed si hoc
dicitis respondit quidem ille
uobis. Non sum missus nisi ad oues
que perierunt domus Israhel.
Sed sicut uos in actibus apostolorum
increpat Paulus. uobis oportebat primum adnuntiare
uerbum dei. sed quia repulistis

illud a uobis et dignos uite eterne
iudicastis ecce in gentia conuerti-
mus ad gentes. Demonstramus
etiam nos ex gentibus testimonium
Xpo fuisse prolatum. quem uates
non tacuit clamando etiam per
linguas inimicorum suorum. Nonne
quando ille poeta facundissimus
inter sua carmina iam noua
progenies celo dimittitur alto
dicebat. Xpo testimonium perhibebat. Indubium hoc uenit a
nisi alios ex gentibus idoneos testes
in medio introducam. Illum illum
regem qui usum super tuum capti-
uando perdomuit. nabuchodonosor regem scilicet babilonis
non pretermittam. Dic nabuchodonosor quid in fornace quo tres
uiros iustos iniuste miseris dic
dic quid tibi fuerit reuelatum.
Nonne inquid tres uiros misimus
in fornace ligatos. et aiunt ei.
uere rex. ecce inquit uideo ego
quattuor uiros solutos deambulantes in medio ignis et corruptio
nulla facta in eis. et aspectus quarti
similis filio dei. O alienigena unde tibi hoc. quis tibi adnuntiauit
filium dei. que lex. que prophetia adnuntiabit filium dei. Nondum
quidem mundo nascitur et similitudo nascentis a te cognoscitur.
Unde tibi hoc. quis tibi ista adnuntiabit. nisi quia sicut diui-
nus ignis inluminauit ita qui
illic aptuat captiuum te tenebat
inimici Iudei sic diceres testimonium filio dei. Sed quia in ore

duorum uel trium testium stat omne uerbum.
sicut ipse dominus iusum conuincit
confusionis. In lege uestra scriptum
est quia duorum hominum testimonium uerum sit. etiam ex gentibus
tertius testis in medio ducatur ut
testimonium ueritatis ex omni
parte roboretur. Quid sibilla
uaticinando etiam de Xpo clamauerit in medium proferamus.
ut ex uno lapide utrorumque frontes
percutiantur Iudeorum scilicet
atque paganorum. atque suo gladio
sicut Golias Xpi omnes percutiantur
inimici. Audite quid dixerit.
Iudicii signum tellus sudore madescit.
E celo rex adueniet per secla futurus.
Scilicet in carne presens ut iudicet orbem.
Unde deum cernent incredulus atque fidelis
Celsum cum sanctis eui iam termino in ipso.
Sic anime cum carne aderunt quas iudicat ipse.
Cum iacet incultus densis in uepribus orbis.
Reicient simulacra uiri cunctam quoque gazam.
Exuret terras ignis pontumque polumque.
Inquirens tetri portas effringet auerni.
Sanctorum sed enim cuncte lux libera carni.
Tradetur sontes eterna flamma cremabit.
Occultos actus retegens tunc quisque loquetur.
Secreta atque deus reserabit pectora luci.
Tunc erit et luctus stridebunt dentibus omnes.
Eripitur solis iubar et chorus interit astris.
Voluetur celum lunaris splendor obibit.
Deiciet colles ualles extollet ab imo.
Non erit in rebus hominum sublime uel altum.
Iam equantur campis montes et cerula ponti.
Omnia cessabunt tellus confracta peribit.
Sic pariter fontes torrentur fluminaque igni.
Et tuba tum sonitum tristem [illegible]
Orbe gemens facinus miserum uariosque labo-
res.

Liber comicus

11TH CENTURY *MED.* (CA. 1067) (P. 18)

BIBLIOTHÈQUE NATIONALE DE FRANCE, PARIS, N. A. L. 2171.
PROVENANCE: MONASTERY OF SANTO DOMINGO DE SILOS (BURGOS).
Parchment; modern binding (20th century); purchased at public auction in Paris, Hôtel Drouot, 1 June 1878; 18th century foliation in ink in the upper right margin; pages are numbered, but numbers 70-89 were skipped and 485 and 486 were repeated; 1 + 478 pages (thus there are 239 leaves); the leaves measure 360 × 260 mm; the writing frame measures 245 × 190 mm; two columns justified with double vertical lines on both sides; visible prickings close to the edge in the right margin; the number of lines vary between 30 to 39 on pp. 1-34, and there are 25 on the subsequent pages; ruled in drypoint with the quire open on the outside of the first bifolium over the second and on the inside of the fourth over the third; Visigothic minuscule; a single scribe execpt for some additions; Aquitainian musical notation added on pp. 18, 19, 21, 43, 400, 404, 436; on the Sanctus on p. 18 the *custos* is applied.

General contents: The codex begins with some fragments of the *Evangelium Nicodemi* and some *Interrogationes de fide catholica* (pp. 1-18), which were added once the majority of the manuscript had been finished; the *Comicus* begins on p. 20 with some computational pieces and a calendar. *In nomine Patris et Filii et Spiritus Sancti. Incipit liber comincum de toto circulo anni* (p. 35).

Leaf shown: p. 18
Exurge Domine non preualeat homo. Seculorum *a*men. *Cantabo Domino qui bona tribuit michi.* Seculorum *a*men. *VIA FERIA AD PRIMAM***.** *Conserua me Domine quoniam in te speraui.* Seculorum *a*men. *IIA FERIA AN*TIPHONA *AD UESPERAS. Sepe expugnauerunt me a yuuentute mea.* Seculorum *a*men. *IIII FERIA AN*TIPHONA *AD UESPERAS. Laudate nomen Domini.* Seculorum *a*men. *IIIA FERIA IN LAUDIBUS. In excelsis laudate Deum.* Seculorum *a*men. *Sanctus, sanctus, sanctus, Dominus Deus Sabaoth, pleni sunt celi et terra gloria tua. Osana in excelsis. Benedictus qui uenit in nomine Domini. Osanna in excelsis.*

It is possible to distinguish at least four scribes in the various notated additions

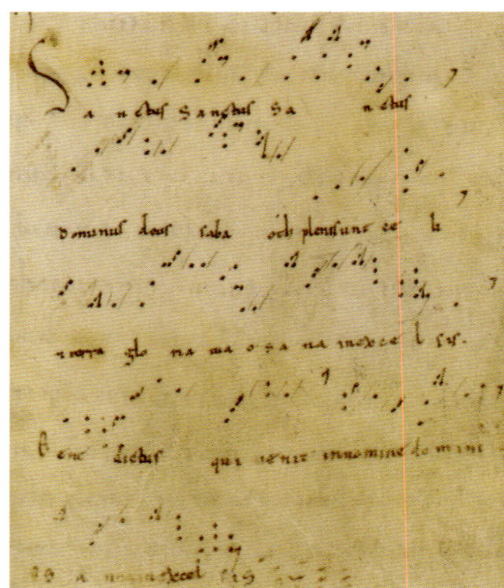

Detail of p. 18

to the manuscript; one of these, on p. 436, is accompanied by the text "Rome ducti armonica cuius qualitatis apostole". The six antiphons on p. 18 are from the office in ordinary time according to the Roman cursus, written in Carolingian minuscule during the first half of the 12th century. The neumes are oriented around lines and each antiphon is accompanied by the psalm-tone formula "Seculorum amen". The only other manuscript that also contains these six antiphons is the Aquitainian Antiphonary (Toledo, BC, 44-1, fols. 31v, 34r, 32r). Another antiphonary (Toledo, BC, 44-2, fols. 193r, 34r, 33r) contains five of them, lacking only *Laudate nomen Domini*; the antiphonary from the Monastery of Vallombrosa (Florence, Biblioteca Laurenziana, Conv. Sopp. 560, fols. 52v, 53v, 55r, 52r, 48v) also contains five of them, lacking *Saepe expugnaverunt*. The Sanctus, written by the same scribe, is a variation of the melody designated number 112 by Thannabaur.

BIBLIOGRAPHY

MORIN 1893. VIVES AND FÁBREGA 1949, 339-380. PÉREZ DE URBEL AND GONZÁLEZ 1950-1955. THANNABAUR 1962, 164. AVRIL ET AL. 1982, 20-22, NO. 28, *PL.* 8, 9. DÍAZ Y DÍAZ 1983, 454-456. BOYLAN 1992, 59-102, 60-62, 71, 78-79, 82. *SCRIPTORIUM SILENSE* 1995, x-xi. VIVANCOS 1996, 255-263. MILLARES CARLO ET AL. 1999, 1: 168-169; 1999, 2: 240.

Shin Nishimagi

Quo tempore adnuntiabit Gabriel
angelus sancte Marie aduentum Christi. R.
In mense agusto. Quo tem-
pore ascendit spiritus in sancte Marie uel concepit ea Christum.
R. XI kalendas apriles. Et quando babtizatus fuit a Iohanne.
R. annis XXX. Et quando conprehensus fuit a iudeis. R.
XI kalendas apriles. Abitabit cum discipulis suis dies XL
et post dies XL demonat oliberti ... discipulos
suos die lob... nonas madias ascendit ad celis. Quomodo
... milex abuit nomen qui de lancea percussit Christum in
latus quando exibit sanguis et aqua R. Longinus.
Quantas miliatas diuiserunt uestimentum Christi R. IIII.
Quantos discipulos abuit Christus R. LXX duos et ipsi autem
fuerunt ... Qui primum dixit ... R. sacerdotus.
Qui primum epistola ... R. sanctus Iacobus. Qui primo monumentum
accepit ante dilluuium R. Abel. Qui primo monumentum
... accepit post ... R. sanctus Ste-
phanus. Qui primum obtulit panem et uinum
in sacrificium. R. Melchisedech sacerdotum.
Qui primum eclesia edificabit. R. sanctus Petrus in An-
tiocie ciuitate. Quale eclesia prima facta est.
R. sancta Sion quando dominus cenam apostolis edificabit.
... nomine Christianorum consecratum in Antiocia
ciuitate.

Finit deo gratias.

ANTIFANAS

Exurge domine non preualeat homo; Sae.

Cantabo domino qui bona tribuit mihi; Sae.

Conserua me domine quoniam in te speraui; Sae. (marg.: ... ad prima)

Sepe expugnauerunt me a iuuentute mea; Sae. (marg.: ... ad ...)

Laudate nomen domini; Saecu... (marg.: ... ad uesperas)

In excelsis laudate deum; Sae. (marg.: ...)

Sanctus Sanctus Sanctus dominus deus sabaoth pleni sunt celi et terra gloria tua osanna in excelsis.

Benedictus qui uenit in nomine domini.

Osanna in excelsis.

Breviary

11TH Century *ex.* (fol. 112v)

British Library, London, Add. ms. 30848.
Provenance: Monastery of Santo Domingo de Silos (Burgos).
A well-prepared parchment of good quality; 15th century binding in Eláter over boards; comprises 1 + 279 + 1 leaves; 18th century foliation in the upper right-hand margin; numbers 181, 235 and 240 are repeated and numbers 17 and 205 are omitted; the leaves measure 375 × 268 mm; the writing frame measures 273 × 199 mm; it is arranged in two columns justified by a double vertical line throughout; prickings are visible, the vertical ones at the edge, and the horizontal ones in the right margin; 32 lines; ruled in drypoint, bifolium by bifolium, on the grain side; Visigothic minuscule with no apparent Carolingian characteristics, the work of a single scribe; Aquitainian notation *in campo aperto*, from several scribes; no *custos*.

General contents: A monastic breviary according to the Roman rite. In its present state, the codex comprises the period from the first Sunday of Advent until the office of the Common of Martyrs: *In Nomine Domini. Incipit Brebiarium de toto circulo. Incipit Officium de adventu Domini* (fol. 3). The manuscript has the added interest of containing a calendar, written by the same scribe responsible for the codex, but unfortunately it is incomplete because in its present state, it lacks the section for the period from September through December, and the first leaf, with the months of January and February, is in a poor state of preservation. Nevertheless, detailed study may provide information on the origin of the codex that served as the model for this manuscript and, consequently, shed light on the implementation of the Roman liturgy at Silos. Together with the most commonly known saints in the West, many of the saints in this manuscript are typical from Spain, as well as other feaststhat clearly come from across the Pyrenees, such as that of St. Potamius, St. Martial, the Translation of St. Martin and the Translation of St. Benedict.

Detail of fol. 112v

Leaf shown: 112v
... famulis tuis ut resurrectionis gratiam consequamur. II feria. Antiphona. *Adoremus Dominum qui nos redemit per crucem. Uenite. In die magno... Ad uesperum. Si quis...* Oratio. *Tua nos... III* feria. *Tempus meum... Ad I[a].* Antiphona. *Uos ascendite... Ad uesperum. Quidam autem... IIII* feria. *Oues mee... Ad I[a]. Multa bona... Ad uesperum. Circumdantes iudei... U* feria. *Magister dicit... Ad uesperum. Desiderio... VI* feria. *Adpropinquabat... Ad uesperum. Principes sacerdotum... Sabbato. Nemo tollit... Officium in ramis palmarvm. Ad vespervm.* Capitulum. *Hoc enim... Circumdederunt me... Quoniam triuulatio... Sed tu.* Ymnus. *Uexilla. Uersus. Dederunt...* Antifona. *Clarifica me... Magnifi*cat. *Seculor*um. *Am*en. *Oratio. Omn*ipoten*s* sem*p*iterne *D*eu*s...*

The notated texst are written in letters of reduced size to leave sufficient space for the neumes. This manuscript transmits the new Franco-Roman repertoire that was implemented after the suppression of the Spanish rite. The texts, as well as the notation, represent the new liturgical usage. The fact that the Aquitainian notation is disposed *in campo aperto,* although with a clear diastematic orientation and without a *custos,* may imply that it was notated a Spanish scribe during the initial stage of copying codices from beyond the Pyrenees. It is also interesting to point out the multiple additions of *differentiae* in the right margins and beween the chants (fols. 47-48). In the leaf shown, the same scribe added an antiphon for the invitatory, in an unusual way: the text breaks off at a right angle.

Bibliography

Díaz y Díaz 1983, 315. Walker 1998, 49 *et passim.* Millares Carlo et al. 1999, 2: 87.

Miguel C. Vivancos

similes eius uas electum ego eum [illegible]
consequamur. &. IIs. A. A [illegible]

In die magno festiuitatis stabat Ihesus et clamabat dicens: qui sitit ueniat ad me et bibat. Bened. Ad Vesp. Si quis sitit ueniat et bibat et de uentre eius fluent aque uiue. Magnif.

Tu nos misericordia Dei et ab [illegible] subtrahe ne uetustas [illegible] expurget et accipiat sancte nouitatis efficiat. &. IIIs.

Tempus meum nondum aduenit tempus autem uestrum semper est paratum. Bened. Ad Vesp. A. Vos ascendite ad diem festum hunc ego non ascendam quia tempus meum nondum aduenit. Ad Vesp. Quidam autem Iudei dicebant quia bonus est alii autem dicebant non sed seducit turbas. Magnif. IIIIs.

Oues mee uocem meam audiunt et ego dominus agnosco eas. Bened. Ad.

Multa bona opera operatus sum uobis propter quod opus uultis me occidere. Ad Vesp. Circumdederunt Iudei dominum dicebant quousque animam nostram tollis si tu es Christus dic nobis palam. Magnif. Vs.

Magister dicit tempus meum prope est apud te facio pascha cum discipulis meis. Bened. Ad Vesp. Desiderio desideraui hoc pascha manducare uobiscum antequam patiar. Magnif. VIs. A. Appropinquabat autem dies festus et querebant principes sacerdotum quomodo Ihesum interficerent sed timebant plebem. Bened. Ad Vesp.

Principes sacerdotum consilium fecerunt ut Ihesum occiderent dicebant autem non in die festo ne forte tumultus fieret in populo. Magnif. Sabbato.

Nemo tollit animam meam sed ego pono eam et iterum sumo eam. Bened.

OFFICIUM IN RAMIS PALMARUM

Hoc enim sentite in uobis quod et in Christo Ihesu qui cum in forma Dei esset non rapinam arbitratus est esse se equalem Deo. AD VESPERUM.

Circumdederunt me uiri mendaces sine causa flagellis ceciderunt me sed tu domine defensor uindica me.
Quoniam tribulatio proxima est et non est qui adiuuet. Sed tu.
Vexilla regis prodeunt. Hymnus.

Clarifica me pater apud temetipsum claritatem quam habui priusquam mundus fieret. Magnif. [illegible]

Omnipotens sempiterne Deus qui humano generi [...]

Missal, Tropary

12TH CENTURY *EX.* (FOL. 267R)

BIBLIOTECA GENERAL UNIVERSITARIA, SALAMANCA, MS. 2637.
PROVENANCE: MONASTERY OF SAN MILLÁN (?), MONASTERY OF SANTO DOMINGO DE SILOS (?).
Parchment of varying quality in a good state of preservation, with the exception of a few leaves; modern binding in Spanish covers (19th century); spine title label: *Missale;* 1 + 267 + 1 leaves (lacunae and quires back to front); old foliation in Roman numerals in black ink, at the center of the upper margin, up to 258; errors of omission and repetition; the last two quires arre unfoliated; modern foliation, from fol. 259, in pencil in Arabic numerals in the upper right corner; inversion of Q. XXXIII (fols. 251-258); the leaves measure 345 × 235 mm; the text block measures 265 × 175 mm; two columns justified by double vertical lines on both sides and triple vertical lines between the columns, spanning the entire leaf; the horizontal prickings are barely perceptible, and the vertical prickings are partially perceptible in the upper margin; on fol. 192r both are clearly visible; 32 lines; ruled in drypoint with the quire folded, with odd pages placed over the even ones; Carolingian script with Gothic features, in fine, even strokes; redline separating the words; rubrics in red; major initials in red, blue, purple and yellow (fol. 2r, half page, with strapwork and zoomorphic motifs); minor initials in bright blue and black; written by a single scribe, although a change in size and penmanship can be seen in the letters from fol. 134v on; additions: fol. 75v, add.; prose of St. Marina, 12th century *ex.*; fol. 17v, add. prayers, 15th century; Aquitainian notation oriented around a line following the ruling of the text block; consistent use of a *custos*.

General contents: *Incipit liber missarum per anni circulum dicendarum. Incipiunt antiphone processionales dicende per adventum domini in diebus dominicis* (fol. 1st); inc.: *Missus est [a] angelus Gabriel a Deo in civitate Nazaret…* (fol. 1st); *Proprium de tempore (dominica I in adventu-dominica XXIV post Pentecostes)* (fols. 2r-167v); *In dedicatione ecclesiae* (fol. 167v); *Proprium de sanctis* (fols. 168v-233r); *Commune sanctorum* (fols. 233r-235v); *Missae votivae* (fols. 235v-245r); *Ordo cum sponsus venerit ad ecclesiam…* (fol. 245r); *Cum introyret sacerdos in domum infirmi…* (fol. 246r); *Pro defunctis* (fol. 250r); *Benedictiones* (fol. 260r); *Exorcismi* (fol. 261v); *Troparium* (mut.) (fols. 262v-267v).
COLOPHON in code: *hbm fbnhtp lhbrp dhffrtf phscf mbghstrp = iam finito libro diferte [forsan] pisce magistro* (fol. 265v).

Leaf shown: 267r
[END OF THE PROSE *NATO CANUNT*]
… nunc letentur omnia nati per exordio. Solus qui creavit omnia. Ipse sua pietate solvat / (add.: Solus qui). Alia. Adest ymma atque precelsa annuata.
Ex virginea carne... Hic est ille... Pax refulsit... Processit stella... Viscera maris... Iam per tempora... Vera lucerna... Resipiscat saballiana… Que latrantur inter... Non de Deo esse... Dicit ita ad hec contra... Pace superba... Homo natus est... Vera lucerna salus... Pacis inclita nobis... Perpes intonizari... Ut nativitas eius... Pace cum prospera... Melodum carmina... Amen.

The document contains the most extensive sanctorale contained in any Roman missal extant on the Iberian Peninsula. The sanctorale shows a clear Frankish influence, though it preserves some cults from the Spanish sanctorale. There are notable correspondences with earlier manuscripts from Silos (London, BL, Add. ms. 30848 and Add. ms. 30849). The title *Alia* on the leaf displayed here is a commonly used heading referring to a *prosa*. The melody, which is essentially syllabic, requires only the *punctum, clivis, pes* and a few quilismatic signs for its graphic representation. In the verse *Solus qui* (left-hand column, line 2), neumatic groups are separated by an oblique line. The *Solus qui* is a later addition and completes the text that the first scribe had forgotten to include. *Probationes calami* on the lower margin. In fol. 75v (see detail), a prose to St. Marina (18 July) has been added (ca. 12th century *ex.*) on a blank leaf. This cult was celebrated in most Spanish sanctorales in the 9th and 10th centuries.

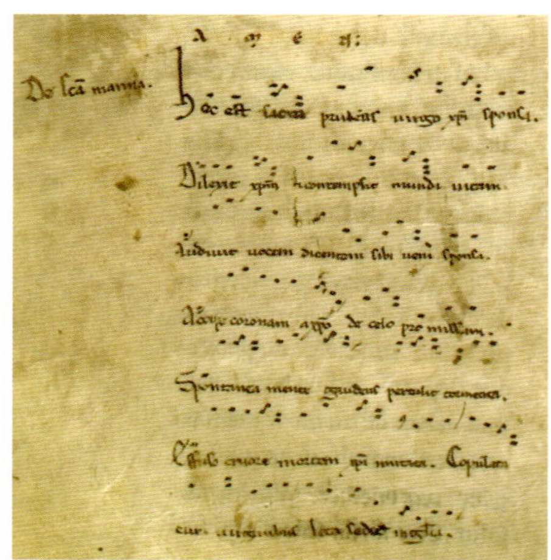

Detail of fol. 75v

BIBLIOGRAPHY

CLUGNET ET AL. 1905. PRADO 1941, 102, 106-108. JANINI 1977a, 236-239. FERNÁNDEZ DE LA CUESTA 1980, 167-168. JANINI 1981b, 135-140. CASTRO 1991, 167-173, 292-295. WALKER 1998, 159-160, 196-203, 245-248. LILAO AND CASTRILLO 2002, 1007-1008.

Susana Zapke

nunc letentur omnia nati per exordia Solus
qui creauit omnia S olus qui trier Ipse sua pietate saluat omnia
peccata nostra amen

ALIA

Nd est ymnia atque precelsa annuata festa
qua salus uenit interra E x uirginea carne trolus
clara ut fatur magnus propheta H ic est ille
qui cuncta mundi uenit soluere agnus crimina
P ax re fulsit in ymnia in altis gloria sonat ti
nulla P rocessit stella maris lucida porta
clausa parit maria V iscera maris tumet lac
tea intacta absque uirga grauida J am pertem
porum ecce puerperum genuit emanuel regem in
secula perpetua regens celestia regna agmina
V era lucerna deum oraculis prophetarum pronus
sum in superna cunabula gignit prolem uirgo
sacra oppima R esipiscat saballiana heretici cozu
mendax lingua Q ue latrantur inter graphia
scolari dicens nunc quid ita N on de deo esse
natum set deuirili semine ortum pande stupenda
D icit ita ad hec contra sors xpistiana irridens
ista satis prebicula P ace superba iudea que
pugnas aduersus xpistum ira tumida H omo
natus est inea olim ut dicit scriptura mistica
dogmata V era lucerna salus et uictoria illi sit
et gracia omnia per secla qui nasci dignatur
hodie interra P acis inclita nobis det ut omnia
que sunt patris et et sua premia eternam auerni
latrinam confringens ianuam P erpes intonizari
sancta queat inaula tua nos ipse de lectat V t
natiuitatis eius incarnati deluat semper nostra
probitat P ace cum prospera decantemus nunc
mente pura M elodum carmina psallentes ipsi
L uoce clara amen

Missal

11TH CENTURY *EX.*-12TH CENTURY *IN.* (*POST QUEM*, 1090, TRANSLATION OF ST. FELIX, 6 NOVEMBER) (FOL. XV)

REAL ACADEMIA DE LA HISTORIA, MADRID, COD. 18.
PROVENANCE: MONASTERY OF SAN MILLÁN DE LA COGOLLA (LA RIOJA).
White parchment of average quality in a precarious state of preservation; old binding with boards; 15 + 350 leaves (fragmentary); modern foliation in pencil with Arabic numerals in the upper right-hand margin until fol. 17 (II, Roman numerals) and from fol. 318 until fol. 350; foliation in Roman numerals from fol. 16, fol. 317 is not numbered; the leaves measure 380 × 250 mm; the writing frame measures 270 × 165 mm; two columns justified with double vertical lines at the outer edges and a triple vertical line in the center, the lines are deeply marked; practically all of the horizontal prickings are visible, the vertical prickings are only perceptible on some leaves; 31 lines; ruled in dry point; very beautiful liturgical Visigothic minuscule (fols. 1r-v, 2ra-3vb and 6r-12v) for sections A, B and E; the letter size is reduced for the texts provided with musical notation; consistent use of the *tj* group before a vowel; major initials of Visigothic origin, there are other Carolingian style initials with monochromatic filling; anthropomorphic initials (fol. 13r), one of them represents the *Agnus Dei* inscribed in a tondo and held by two inverted angels; several scribes from different periods; expert Aquitainian notation with a very fine stroke over the line that corresponds to the writing frames ruling; very pronounced diastematic arrangement and consistent indication of the *Differentiae*; an occasional sign *p* to the left of the neumes (fol. LXIIv, lines 6, 7 and 9 in the offertory *Precatus est Moyses*); scrapings and corrections on some leaves (fol. XLVIII); consistent use of *custos*.

General contents: Five parts. PART A: *Calendarium* (fols. 1r-v). 11th century Visigothic minuscule. A guard leaf from the codex preserved under Cod. 118. PART B: a bifolium in Visigothic minuscule with *Martyrologium Hieronymianum*. [fragmentary] *Cirilli Sauri et [ilegible]nis Pelagie et alios III.* Day XI before the calends of August (fol. 2ra); [...] *et obitum Odoari episcopi Bracara era DCCCXXIII* [...] Day II before the calends of November (fol. 3vb). PART C: *Missae* (fols. 4r-v), 12th century transitional Carolingian script. PART D: one leaf in pure Carolingian script. A 13th century-addition related to the dominical letters, according to the initials of the twelve words used. *[Tabula ad totam rationem computi]* (fol. 5r); *[Tabula computi]* (fol. 5v); *Altitonans Dominus divina gerens bona extat gratuito celi fere antea dona fideli* (fol. 5va). PART E: Gothicizing Carolingian script. *[Calendarium]* (fols. 6r-12v); *[Annotationes computi]* (fols. 12ra-12vb]; add. neumed sequence (fol. 12vb); *[Orationes et missae]* (fols. 13ra-350ra). Prayer to St. Thomas of Canterbury, 11th century (fol. 350r); *Missa de incarnatione, nativitate, pasione, morte* in Visigothic minuscule. *Missa Conceptio sancte Marie*, in Carolingian script (fol. 350va).

Leaf shown: XV
... adventus sui. BENEDICTIONES *Benedictus es Domine Deus patrum nostrorum et laudabilis et gloriosum in secula.* VERSUS. *Et benedictus nomen glorie tue quod est sanctum. Et lau. Seuouae.* VERSUS *Benedictus es in templo. Et la. Benedictus es qui sedes. Et lau.* Versus *Benedictus es qui sedes super cherubim. Et lau.* VERSUS *Benedictus es qui ambulas super. Et lau. Benedicant te omnes. Et lau. Benedicant te celi terra mare et omnia. Et lau. Gloria patri. Sicut erat in principio. Et lau. Benedictus es. Tractus Qui regis Israhel intende. Seuouae. Versus Qui sedes super cherubin. Versus Excita Domine potentiam tuam. Anno quintodecimo. Lucam.*

It is the only work of this genre with Visigothic minuscule and Aquitainian notation, one of the most indicative examples of the transitional process, promoted by the monastic centers in the south of France. It comprises texts read by the officiating priest and additional chants and readings for Mass. There are two scribes from two different cultural and geographic contexts, a common phenomenon in the copying of imported manuscripts during the first phase of the reform. The Spanish scribe makes use of his accustomed Visigothic minuscule. A monk from a French center employs Aquitainian notation. The imbalance between the space foreseen to insert the neumes and the space actually used is omnipresent. The persistence of the Spanish tradition, reflected in the Mozarabic calendar and martyrology (fols. 1r-5v), and calendar (fols. 6r-11v), reveals the will to maintain one's own usage when faced with the new rite. Other reminiscences are observed in the structures of the mass, with characteristics that bring to mind the *missae et officia* of the Spanish rite. The persistence of this tradition is consistent with the reluctant attitude at the Abbey of San Millán.

Detail of fol. 2vb

BIBLIOGRAPHY
VEZIN 1963, 5-25. JANINI 1977, 150-153. DÍAZ Y DÍAZ 1979, 200-202. HUGLO 1982, 253-268. MILLARES CARLO 1983, 1: 183, 333. HUGLO 1985, 249-256. HILEY 1993, 602. RUIZ GARCÍA 1997, 149-152. WALKER 1998, 149-161, 163-164, 165-168, 170, 179, 182-184, 245-248. MILLARES CARLO ET AL. 1999, 2: 126.

Susana Zapke

aduentus sui.

B NONES

Benedictus es domine deus patrum nostrorum et laudabilis et gloriosum in secula. V Et benedictum nomen glorie tue quod est sanctum. Et laud. Seuouae V Benedictus es in templo sancto glorie tue. Et lau. Benedictus es qui sedes super tronum deitatis tue. Et laud. V Benedictus es qui sedes super cherubim intuens abissos. Et laud. V Benedictus es qui ambulas super pennas uentorum et super undas maris. Et laud. Benedicant te omnes angeli et sancti tui. Et laud. Benedicant te celi terra mare et omnia que in eis sunt. Et laud. Gloria patri et filio et spiritui sancto. Sicut erat in principio et nunc et semper et in secula seculorum amen. Et laud. Benedictus es.

TRACT Qui regis israhel intende qui deducis uelut ouem Ioseph. Seuouae V Qui sedes super cherubim appare coram Effraim et Beniamin et Manasse. V Excita domine potentiam tuam et ueni ut saluos facias nos.

Anno quinto decimo LUCAM

Mass Antiphonary, Tropary

12TH CENTURY *IN.* (FOL. 83V, CLXV)

REAL ACADEMIA DE LA HISTORIA, MADRID, COD. 51.
PROVENANCE: MONASTERY OF SAN MILLÁN DE LA COGOLLA (LA RIOJA).
Poor-quality parchment; yellowish tone; only the front board remains from the original binding; 170 leaves (fragmentary); there are remains of an irregular foliation in Roman numerals (the present fol. 1 corresponds to LVIIII); additional modern foliation in pencil with Arabic numerals; there are errors, lacunae and transposed bifolia; the leaves measure 280 × 175 mm; the writing box measures 160 × 100 mm; one column justified with double vertical lines on both sides; imperceptible prickings; 20-22 lines; ruled in drypoint; Carolingian script with small letters; painted miniatures with intense colors and others in black ink with fine strokes and southern French influence; some decorated initials in Romanesque style; numerous miniatures missing; three hands: A (fols. 1r-254r), B (fol. 254v) and C (fols. 255r-270v); Aquitainian notation with fine strokes over the drypoint line of the ruling of the text block; consistent use of a *custos*.

General contents: Temporale [fragmentary]; prose *Iubilate Deo omnis* (*Sabb. in vigilia Pasce*, fol. 50v); Wednesday, the first week of Lent (fols. 59r-181r); *In die sanctus pasce. Antifone ad processionem* (fol. 119v); *Missa de sancta trinitate* (fol. 160r); prose *O alma trinitas* (*Sci. Emiliani,* fol. 149r); *Dominica XXIII post Pentecostes* (fol. 180r); Sanctorale from Sts. Tiburcius and Valerian (14 April) until St. Andrew (fols. 182-228v); *In die sance trinitatis* (fol. 229r); *Sanctus... Hosanna* (add.) (fol. 231v); tropes, Ordinary of the Mass (fols. 232r-247v); prose. *Carmina plebs* (fol. 243v); *Al. Sanctus...* (fol. 244r). Prose. *Te laudant agmina* (fol. 244v); *Al. Sanctus…* (fol. 244v). Prose. *Laudes deo ore pio* (fol. 245r); *Al.* Sanctus... Prose. *Patris sapientia* (fol. 245r); *Al. Sanctus...* Prose *Ossana salvifica tuum* (fol. 245v); *Al. Sanctus.* Prose. *Clangat hodie vox* (fol. 246r); *Al. Sanctus...* (fol. 246v). Prose. *Fidelium turma iubilet voce* (fol. 247r); *Agnus Dei*. Prose. *In nativitate Domini* (fol. 247v).

Leaf shown: 83v, CLXV
[PAINTED MINIATURE]
Cunctipotens fons residet sic iuve superno (above the miniature).
Confitebimur ei quia fecit. VERSUS. *Benedicamus patrem et filium. Seuou.* Amen. VERSUS. *Benedicite omnia opera Domini Domino.* GRADUALE. *Benedictus es Domine.* VERSUS *Benedicite Deum.* LAUDES. *Alleluia.*

The codex was copied from a monastic exemplar from the south of France. The Romanesque miniature on the leaf shown, for the mass of the temporale after the first

Detail of fol. CII. Initial *D*

Sunday after the Octave of Pentecost, is unique in the codex because of its coloring and its elaborate artistry. The iconographic style, typically Romanesque, recalls other codices produced at San Millán around the end of the 11th century. The *maiestas Domini* motif comprises a haloed Christ blessing with his right hand and in his left a book. The mandorla is framed by a vegetal motif and a tetramorph. Two seraphs, looking upward, encircle it. This copy combines an antiphonary for the Mass (gradual) and a presentation typical of other codices such as Salamanca BGU, ms. 2637 and Toledo BC, 35-10, and demonstrates the entrance of proses and tropes into the Peninsula's repertoire. The tropes follow the order of the Mass: Kyrie (in tonal order, as in Huesca, ms. 4), Gloria, Sanctus and Agnus. There follows the prosary, of which only part of the first composition is preserved (fol. 247v: *Alleluia. Psalle iam turba*). The order is common in Spanish codices from the eastern-northeastern, transitional and southern areas. The Sanctorale coincides notably with that of Cod. 18 from San Millán (Madrid, RAH), although the latter contains more local feasts.

BIBLIOGRAPHY

DOMÍNGUEZ BORDONA 1929, 184, NO. 36; 1933, 212-213, NO. 367, FIG. 201. PRADO 1941, 100, 106-110. MUNDÓ 1966, 111. JANINI 1977a, 158-160. CASTRO 1990, 243-263; 1991, 158-165. RUIZ GARCÍA 1997, 295-296. *SANCHO EL MAYOR Y SUS HEREDEROS* 2006, 2: 688-689 (SÁENZ PASCUAL).

Susana Zapke

Cuncta potens solio residet sic iure superno.

CONFITEBIMUR EI quia fecit nobiscum misericordiam suam

℣ Benedicamus patrem et filium Secundum dan ℣ Benedicite omnia opera domini domino

GR Benedictus es domine qui intueris

abyssos et sedes super cherubin ℣ Benedicite

deum celi quia fecit nobiscum miseri-

cordiam suam ℣ ALLELUIA

Antiphonary

12TH CENTURY *EX.* (FOL. 86V, CXXII)

REAL ACADEMIA DE LA HISTORIA, MADRID, COD. 45.
PROVENANCE: MONASTERY OF SAN MILLÁN DE LA COGOLLA (LA RIOJA)
Poor-quality parchment, brownish-grey in color; modern binding in beige (1961); 98 leaves (fragmentary); two old foliations using the Roman system (one in the center of the recto, one in the center of the verso) beginning on fol. XXIIII (fol. 1), and another modern one, in pencil and in Arabic numerals; the leaves measure 310 × 205 mm; the text block measures 210 × 140 mm; one column justified by a vertical line on both sides; prickings in the form of circular holes on the outside margin; 24 lines; ruled in drypoint; Gothicizing Carolingian script; written by a single scribe; Aquitainian notation in an expert hand oriented around the drypoint line of the text block ruling; consistent use of a *custos* in light brown ink, probably inserted by a later scribe.

General contents: Antiphonary for Mass: temporale (fols. 1-86) from the fifth Sunday after Epiphany; concluding with the 23rd Sunday from Pentecost and the dedication of the church. The sanctorale (fols. 86v-98v) runs from St. Sylvester, Pope, to the Annunciation of Mary.

Leaf shown: 86v, CXXII
Beginning of the sanctorale: 31 December, Mass of St. Sylvester (with the introit for the Holy Popes).

Siluestri pape officium. Sacerdotes tui *domine induant iusticiam et* sancti tui *exultent propter Dauid seruum tuum* non *auertas faciem tuam Christi tui* PSALMUS. *Memento domine Dauid.* ORATIO. DA QUESUMUS OMNIPOTENS UNIUS CONFESSORIS. EPISTOLA. PLURES FACTI SUNT. [GRADUAL] *R. Ecce sacerdos magnus qui in diebus suis placuit* deo. VERSUS. *Non est inuentus similis illi qui conseruaret legem excelsi.* ALLELUIA. VERSUS *Inueni Dauid seruum meum.*

Detail of fol. 87r

The formula is the same as that of the Gregorian model for the Office of St. Sylvester. The alternative offertory, *Veritas mea. Versus Posui adiutorium* is also found in the Office of St. Martial. The illumination, with decorated initials (some historiated) suggest that the manuscript dates from around 1200. This manuscript contains features which became typical of the Northern Iberian tradition once the process of liturgical reform had become consolidated and the new Franco-Roman repertoire had been assimilated in the 12th century. The sanctorale includes the feasts of St. Scholastica (fol. 96) and St. Benedict (fol. 98).

BIBLIOGRAPHY

JANINI 1977a, 157-158. FERNÁNDEZ DE LA CUESTA 1980, 36. CASTRO 1991, 158. DOMÍNGUEZ BORDONA 1993, 212. RUIZ GARCÍA 1997, 279-280. SILVA 1999, 61-63. *SANCHO EL MAYOR Y SUS HEREDEROS* 2006, 2: 690-691 (FERNANDO GALVÁN FREILE).

Susan Boynton

Silvestri pape officium.

SACER DOTES tui domine induant iustiam et sancti tui exultent propter david servum tuum non avertas faciem christi tui. V Memento dne d. Sexcta et

Oro Da qs omps deus conf. Epl'a Plures facti sunt.

R Ecce sacerdos magnus qui in diebus suis placuit deo. V Non est inventus similis illi qui conservaret legem excelsi. Alleluia.

V Inveni david servum meum

Missal (fragmentum)

12TH CENTURY *IN.* (FOL. V)

ARCHIVO CAPITULAR, SANTIAGO DE COMPOSTELA, FRAG. 1.
PROVENANCE: PROBABLY FROM THE CATHEDRAL OF SANTIAGO DE COMPOSTELA.
The parchment is in a poor state of preservation because it formed part of the guard leaves of a 16th century volume; it is part of a missal; two loose leaves, somewhat trimmed around the margins; the leaves measure 340 × 220 mm; the writing frame measures 285 × 160 mm; two columns justified with a vertical line on both sides and in the intercolumn; imperceptible prickings, perhaps due to the use that was made of the manuscript; 37 lines for each column; ruled in drypoint; liturgical Visigothic minuscule; use of the *ti* and *tj* groups; initials in red and black with simple decoration; one scribe; Aquitainian notation over the line that corresponds to the writing frame ruling; consistent use of *custos*.

General contents: Frag. 1 contains the Sanctorale Masses: St. John the Baptist, St. Peter, St. Paul, St. Martial, St. Eparchius.

Leaf shown: v
Contains part of an office of Matins. The end of a *lectio*: ... *uocabulo christiano se non posse simul mamone, hoc est, diuitiis, Christoque seruire...*
Sed qui seruit mamonae, ille ubique seruit... Ideo dico uobis nolite solliciti esse animae uestre quid manducetis neque corpori uestro quid uestiamini...
ANTIPHONA *Nolite solliciti esse dicentes* / ANTIPHONA *Considerate lilia agri quomodo crescunt. Magn.*

A footnote on the fragment in red ink with contemporary handwriting: "Estaba como hoja de guarda en el *Libro de Subsidio* (año 1500), no. 652".
This fragment is part of an extensive collection of medieval fragments, the majority of them with musical notation, from the 12th to the 14th centuries, that were used as wrappers for notarial protocols or guard leaves for old books, then recovered during the 1930s.

It is an interesting and characteristic testimony of the transition phase from the Spanish to the Franco-Roman rite, introduced in the Peninsula through monastic centers in the south of France. This codex was copied in two phases and by two hands; while one Spanish scribe, accustomed to Visigothic script, copied the texts, a second scribe, probably of French origin, wrote the melodies in Aquitainian notation.

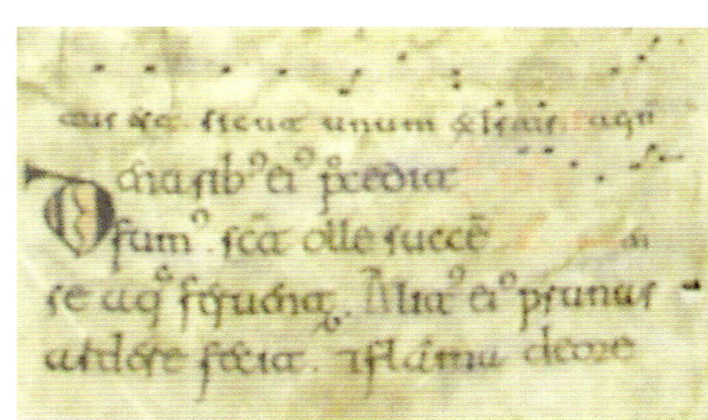

Detail of fol. v

BIBLIOGRAPHY

JANINI 1961, 148-151; 1977a, 246.
MILLARES CARLO 1983, 339; 1999, 1: 176.

José López-Calo

...ruseat uocabulo xpiano se
nō posse simul mamone hoc
ē diuitiis xpo seruire. Beatum
n dixit q hr̄ diuitias. sed q seruit
diuitiis. Qui eni diuitiarū seruus ē. diuitias custodit ut seruus.
Qui autē seruitutis excussit iugū
distribuit eas ut dn̄s.

Sed q seruit mamone. ille
utiq; seruit q reb; istis terrenis
merito sue puersitatis ppo-
situs princeps huius sc̄li a dn̄o dicitur. Ergo aut unū odiet. et
alterū diliget. ut fieri debebit.
Odiet scilicet diabolm̄. diliget dm̄.
aut uni adherebit. et alterū
contempnet. Adherebit scilicet
diabolo cū qrit eius capulsa seculi.
et contempnet autē dm̄. Non dixit
odiet sed sicut solent minus ei
pro ponere cupiditatib; suis
q de bonitate eius ad impuni
tatē sibi blandiunt. Quib; p Sa
lomonem dr̄. Fili ne adicias
peccatū. et dicas miseratio
dī magna ē.

Ideo dico ubis nolite sollici
ti esse anime uestre qd manducetis.
neq; corpori uestro qd uestiamini.
Ergo qd omnib; natura tribuit.
iumentis et bestiis hoib; qq; com
mune ē huius cura penitus li
berabim. sed pcipit nob. ne
solliciti sim qd comedamus.
Ergo in sudore uultus ppriam
nob parē. labor exercendus ē.
sollicitudo tollenda. Non e

plus q̄m uestimentū. Admonet
ut meminerim multo ampli-
us nob dm̄ dedisse qd nos facit
et composuit ex anima et corpe. q̄m
ē alimentū uel uestimentū. ut in
telligas eū qui dedit uitā mul
to facilius escā esse daturū. Si
militer eū q corp dedit. multo
facilius daturū esse uestimentū.
Quo loco quer solet utrū ad uitā
cib iste aut pertineat cū uita incor
porea sit. Iste autē cib corporeus.
sed uitā hoc loco positam nimi
positam nouerim. cui sustentacu
lū ē alimentū iscaud corpei.

Nolite solliciti esse dicentes
quid manducabimus aut quid bibemus
scit enim pater uester celestis quid
uobis necesse sit ...
Considerate lilia agri quomodo
crescunt non laborant neque nent
dico autem uobis quoniam nec Sa
lomon in omni gloria sua coopertus
est sicut unum ex istis ...

Tractatib; ei proedit ...
Istum scēt olle succē ...
se ag fcucng. Ama ei pruinas
ardore facit. inflama ...

Estaba como hoja ... guarda en el Libro de ... 652

Breviary (fragmentum)

12TH CENTURY *IN.* (FOL. A1R)

ARCHIVO CAPITULAR, OURENSE, FRAG. 3.
PROVENANCE: CATHEDRAL OF OURENSE (?).

The parchment is somewhat deteriorated because it was used as a cover for notarial protocols during the 16th century; a note on fol. a1r dated 1565 preceded by "prima paga"; part of an extensive collection of fragments brought together by the archivist priest Emilio Duro Peña; consists of two loose leaves sewn with thread, probably in the 16th century; modern foliation in pencil in the upper right margin (fol. a1r-v; fol. a2r-v); the leaves measure 320 × 220 mm (fragmentary); the writing frame measures 269 × 190 mm; two columns (260 × 85 mm) justified with a vertical line on both sides and between the columns; imperceptible prickings, 32 lines; ruled in deeply etched drypoint; Visigothic minuscule (fol. a1r-v) and Carolingian minuscule (fol. a2r-v) for the text; for the sections accompanied by music (fol. 1r), Visigothic minuscule with alternating red and blue initials and Carolingian script, but with clear Visigothic tendencies as in the rest of the leaves; at least two scribes; Aquitainian notation featuring thick strokes with perfect diastematy, oriented aound the line for the ruling of the text block; the notation seems to have been written by a single hand; use of *custos.*

General contents: *[IN FESTIVITATE TRANSLACIO SANCTI IACOBI APOSTOLI]* (fol. 1r-v); *In die sancti Silvestri et sancte Colunbe* (fol. a2v).

Leaf shown: a1r
[*In festivitate translacio sancti Iacobi apostoli* (30 December)].
[End of the matins antiphon]*: ... carens fidei ira commotus nexuit eum dicens uidebo si te soluet Iacobum* / [PSALMUS] *Exaudi* / VERSICULUS (?) *Adnunciaverunt opera.* [LECTIO IIII]. *Ex anime vero corpus discipuli furtim arripientes...* RESPONSORIUM. *Facta autem in turba sedictione dictum* / VERSUS *In fontem et iustum hoc radium ueritatis.* [LECTIO III]. *Igitur tanto ac tali subnixi patrono...*

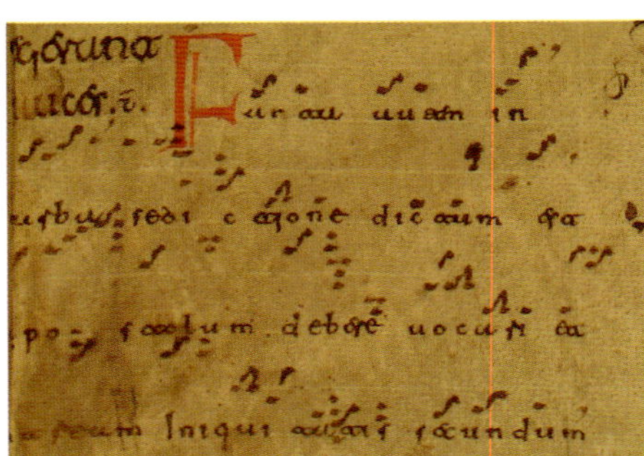

Detail of fol. a1r

These sewn fragments have the notable characteristic of combining two systems of writing: Visigothic on the leaf's recto and Carolingian on the verso. The musical notation, however, is by the same hand throughout the fragment. There is an odd melodic addition from a subsequent period in square notation on a staff in the right margin.

BIBLIOGRAPHY

DURO 1961, 204. MILLARES CARLO 1983, 335; 1999, 1: 152. REY 2002, 35.

José López-Calo

1565

[illegible] ... Adnuntiauerunt opera.

... tumme uero corpus depti
... sutam cumplentes magisteri
... corpus summo cum labore
... pactam foratnatione adlectam
... deuetunt non autem sibi pa
... tuum inuenerunt quem ascen
... dentes alto pelago ... ominantia
... ique repente die ... pueri
... tunc famulique ... solum
... ...
... tum ... ... copio
... ...
... ... munere.
... ideo ... ...
... conspicuauerunt ... nec
... ...
... nunc ... ...
... absque illi ... ...

Furor autem in ... ...

Ciuitas plebs nostra ... iudicate
Gloriosi ... ...
li subnixi patrono ... ad ducem
ad certam suis usibus profuturam
animos intendunt quemque
suo mutati requiescendi locum
domini per ... explorare per
campaniam. Itaque itinere ad
... directo ... ma
rone lupanie nomine ...
ferme quinque miliariis ab urbe
... suctuarum compor
tant atque deponunt loculum.
Quis cum illi fundi possessor
haberetur ... quorundam
conpunctorum ... com
plunt seque ... compo
nentes effici uehementissime
atque ... ... gerunt.
Ocnum quippe feminam ... a
... collocutum ... per
ordinem ... sibi ipsi
... quodam ... delu
brum! ubi adorandum ... ...
... simulacrum atque illic
... quoque ... ...
te frequentabat phanum.

Breviary (fragmentum)

12TH CENTURY *MED.* (FOL. V)

ARCHIVO CAPITULAR, SIGÜENZA (GUADALAJARA), W./O. S.
PROVENANCE: CATHEDRAL OF SIGÜENZA (?).
Yellowed parchment in very poor state of preservation; the recto leaf is partially illegible; there are perforations in the left and right margins from its later use as material for binding 15th to 16th century notarial protocols; one leaf has no traces of foliation; the leaves measure 510 × 320 mm; the writing frame measures 430 × 270 mm; two columns justified by double vertical lines on both sides and double vertical lines between the columns; no traces of prickings can be seen; 42 lines; ruled in drypoint; Gothicizing Carolingian minuscule script; initials in red and black; rubrics in red; smaller letters for the notated texts; numerous abbreviations in the texts without notation; annotations added later in the right margin of the verso leaf in a script of the 15th and 16th centuries; Aquitainian notation with a consistent stroke oriented around the line that corresponds to the ruling of the text block; consistent use of a *custos*.

General contents: Fragment of a notated breviary containing part of the *Lamentations of the prophet Jeremiah.*

Leaf shown: v
[LAMENTATIONS OF THE PROPHET JEREMIAH], left column starting from line 18 in the text.
IN I° NOCTURNE ANTIPHON *Astiterunt reges terre*
[PSALMUS] *Quare fre*muerunt
ANTIPHONA *Diviserunt sibi vestimenta*
PSALMUS *De*us *De*us *me*us *res*pice
[ANTIPHONA] *Insurrexerunt in me*
[PSALMUS] *Do*minu*s illuminatio*
VERSUS *Diviser*unt *sibi vestimenta me*a
Aleph. Quomodo obtexit caligine
Teth. Precipitavit Dominus
Destruxit in furore
Gimel. Confregit in ira
Iherusalem, Iherusalem convertere
[RESPONSORIUM] *Omnes amici mei*
VERSUS Inter iniquos proiecerunt me
LECTIO II
Deleth. Tetendit arcum suum
He Factus est Dominus
Precipitavit omnia.

Codices that had fallen into disuse were commonly reused for binding from the 15th century onwards. The large number of these *membra disiecta* reflects a lack of appreciation for the legacy of the Middle Ages which, combined with the Tridentine reform and the obsolescence of Aquitainian notation, led to the deterioration and dispersion of a significant number of codices, just as had happened in the case of the Hispanic repertoire. The fragment reproduced here, which very probably comes from a full breviary, contains part of the office of vigils for Maundy Thursday. In the Burgo de Osma lectionary (AC, 78A) and in the breviaries in the Archivo Capitular in Huesca (AC, Cods. 2, 3 and 7) the characteristic *Oratio Jeremiae* of Holy Saturday is missing. We cannot confirm whether this is also the case in the Sigüenza manuscript, because only a fragment survives. The recitation of the *Lamentations* is based on a simple melody, predominantly syllabic and divided into three sections: *Initium*, Tenor—mediant cadence—and final cadence, which make it possible to adapt the structure to a varied selection of texts. Unlike the disposition of the text in the Sigüenza manuscript, the sequence of texts is not always in alphabetical order. Each lesson ends with the refrain "Jerusalem, Jerusalem, convertere ad Dominum Deum tuum" (see text line 10, right column). The Responsory, with its corresponding verse, performed by a

Detail of fol. r

soloist, goes deeper into the meaning of the lesson for Holy Saturday (*Omnes amici*, text lines 11-15, right column). In the Sigüenza fragment—which differs, in the part that has survived, from the abovementioned manuscripts from Huesca and Burgo de Osma—the melodic formula in the F mode and the tenor on A, is the same in all the lessons. Silos, Cod. 9 also contains the the tone for the *Lamentations* (fols. 63-67) with a recitation formula different from the one in the Sigüenza fragment.

BIBLIOGRAPHY
UNPUBLISHED.

Susana Zapke

Qui pro nostro ad misso scelere hodie das in escham omnibus populis Kyrie. iii. Domine miserere. Christus factus est.
Traditur pastor mundi per manus miseri iude infidis
iudeis ad crucifigendum ut nos a morte eripi valeremus
gracias persolvientes Kyrie. Christe. Kyrie. In nupcis. A.
Calicem salutaris accipiam et nomen domini invocabo
R. Credidi. Cum his qui hoderunt pacem eram pacificus
cum loquebar illis impugnabant me gratis. A. Ad dominum cum trib-
bulare [illegible] eripe me [illegible] iniusto
ab hominibus iniquis libera me domine. Custodi me a laqueo quem statuerunt michi et ab scandalis ope-
rantium iniquitatem. Domine clamavi. Considerabam
ad dexteram et videbam et non erat qui cognosceret me. Voce mea.

In vesperis. V. Ad vesperum. Dicitur. Postea dicitur sonitu tabule ita respondo ut sacerdos possit dicere versus ad [illegible] incipiendam antiphonam.

Cenantibus autem accepit ihesus panes A.
et benedixit et fregit dedit discipulis suis. Magnificat.

Et ita conpleta oratio ad splendum. Et diaconus dicat Benedicamus domino.

Astiterunt reges terre et principes conve- In I. N.
nerunt in unum adversus dominum et adversus christum eius. Quare fremuerunt. Diviserunt sibi vestimenta
mea et super vestem meam miserunt sortem. A. Dominus [illegible]
[illegible] surrexerunt in me testes iniqui et mentita est iniquitas sibi. Dominus illuminatio. Diviserunt sibi vestimenta [illegible]

Aleph. Quomodo obtexit caligine in furore suo dominus
filiam sion proiecit de celo in terram inclitam israel [illegible]
non est recordatus scabellum pedum suorum in die furoris sui. Ierusalem. Beth. Precipitavit dominus [illegible]
ria speciosa iacob. Destruxit in furore [illegible]
virginis iuda deiecit in terram [illegible]
cipes eius. Gimel. Confregit in ira furoris sui [illegible]
cornu israel avertit [illegible]
[illegible] et succendit in iacob [illegible]
devorantis in gyro. Ierusalem [illegible]

Omnes amici mei [illegible] dereliquerunt
me et prevaluerunt insidiantes michi tradidit me quem
diligebam. Et terribilibus oculis [illegible] plaga [illegible]
tiens aceto potabant me. Inter [illegible]
proiecerunt me et non pepercerunt anime mee.

Daleth. Tetendit arcum suum quasi [illegible] Lecc.
inimicus firmavit dexteram suam quasi hostis et
occidit omne quod pulcrum erat visu in tabernaculo filie
sion effudit quasi ignem indignationem suam. Heth.
Factus est dominus velut inimicus precipitavit [illegible]
Ierusalem. Precipitavit omnia [illegible] dissipavit munitiones [illegible]

Evangeliary

12TH CENTURY *EX.* (FOL. 4V)

ARCHIVO CAPITULAR, BURGO DE OSMA (SORIA), MS. 94.
PROVENANCE: UNKNOWN.
Well-preserved parchment; parchment binding; incomplete manuscript, missing 80 leaves; the beginning is fragmentary, intermediate lacunae and an addition from the end of the 13th century (fols. 79r-80r); modern foliation in pencil in Arabic numerals in the upper right corner; the leaf measures 295 × 129 mm; the text block measures 245 × 120 mm; one column justified with a vertical line on both sides that spans the entire leaf; the prickings are invisible; 26 lines; ruled in drypoint placing odd leaves over the even ones; Carolingian script with fine and consistent *ductus*, red and yellow initials, rubrics marked in red, catchwords at the bottom of the page; several hands and subsequent additions; Aquitainian notation oriented around the drypoint line that corresponds to the ruling of the text block consistent use of a *custos* with various forms.

General contents: Incomplete Temporale (fols. 1r-63r); genealogy of Christ according to Matthew (fols. 4r-5r); genealogy of Christ according to Luke (fols. 7v-8v); lacunae (fols. 58r-59r, *Dominicas VII-XI post Pentecost*); Gospels for the Sanctorale (fols. 64r-65v, incomplete); Gospels for the the Common of Saints (fols. 65v-73r); dedication of the church (fol. 73v); mass for the11,000 virgins and Gospels for the feast of the apostles Phillip and James (fols. 79r-80r, addition from the 13th century).

Leaf shown: 4v
[GENEALOGY OF CHRIST ACCORDING TO MATTHEW]
*[Dominus vobiscum. Et cum spiritu tuo. Initium sancti] evangelii secundum Matheum. Gloria tibi Domine. Liber generationis Ihesu Christi filii David filii Abraham. Abraham autem genuit Isaac. Isaac autem genuit Jacob. Jacob autem genuit Iudam et fratres eius. Iudas autem genuit Phares et Zaram de Thamar. Phares autem genuit Esrom. Esrom autem genuit Aram. Aram autem genuit Aminadab. Aminabad autem genuit Naason. Naason autem genuit Salmon. Salmon autem genuit Booz de Raab. Booz autem genuit Obeth ex Ruth. Obeth autem genuit Iesse. Iesse autem genuit David regem. David autem rex gen*uit *Salomon*em *ex ea q*uae *fuit Urie. Salomon autem genuit Roboam. Roboam autem genuit Abiam. Abias autem genuit Asam. Asa autem genuit Iosaphat. Iosaphat a*utem *genuit Ioram. Ioram autem genuit Oziam. Ozias autem genuit…*

Detail of fol. 8r

The Gospel according to Matthew exhibits a very simple layout from a literary point of view as well as from a formal point of view. The genealogy of Christ follows the stereotypical formula "X autem genuit Y", recited at Christmas and on the Nativity of the Virgin. This formula appears in evangeliaries, lectionaries and breviaries, as well as in other types of liturgical sources. The melodies are fundamentally syllabic, with a cadential formula in the tonic of the corresponding mode. The melodic sequence comprises groups of three phrases, with their respective cadences, that are repeated in the same order. Spanish codices dated between the 11th and 15th centuries present a total of 24 melodic formulas. The Burgo de Osma version is in the seventh mode and agrees with with that found in the evangeliaries of Roncevaux, Museo de la Colegiata, w./o. s., Huesca, AC, Cod. 7, Girona, ms. 13 and El Escorial, RB, ms. I.II.13. In comparison with other versions, the melodic formula of Burgo de Osma is characterized by a style that is less of a recitation, somewhat more adorned, and that endows the syllabic units with brief melodic phrases. The singularity of this evangeliary is also reflected in its abundance of Spanish saints, proof of a persistent underlying autonomy.

BIBLIOGRAPHY

ROJO ORCAJO 1929, 174. SUNYOL 1929, 17; 1935, 223, 264. JANINI 1977a, 39. PEÑAS GARCÍA 1983, 16, 27-28, 30-31, 77-82. *LAS EDADES DEL HOMBRE* 1991, 78 (MARTÍN).

Susana Zapke

euangelij secundum matheum Gloria tibi domine

Liber generationis ihu xpisti filii dauid filii abraham.

Abraham autem genuit ysaac Ysaac autem genuit iacob Ia

cob autem genuit iudam et fratres eius Iudas autem genuit

phares et zaram de thamar Phares autem genuit esrom Es

rom autem genuit aram Aram autem genuit aminadab Ami

nadab autem genuit naason Naason autem genuit salmon.

Salmon autem genuit booz de raab Booz autem genuit obeth.

ex ruth Obeth autem genuit iesse Iesse autem genuit dauid

regem. Dauid autem rex gen salomonē ex ea q̄ fuit urie Salomon

autem genuit roboam Roboam autem genuit abiam Abias

autem genuit asam Asa autem genuit iosaphat Iosaphat au

genuit ioram Ioram autem genuit oziam Ozias autē genuit

Evangeliary

12TH CENTURY *EX.*-13TH CENTURY (FOL. 70R)

MUSEO DE LA REAL COLEGIATA DE SANTA MARÍA, RONCEVAUX (NAVARRE), W./O. S. (CURRENTLY BEING CATALOGUED).
PROVENANCE: UNKNOWN.
Parchment bound with beautiful silver covers from the same period as the codex; recently restored and bound with parchmen that at the same time is separated from the body of the codex, in a separate quire, leaves with music: 70-77; 1 + 94 + 1 leaves; modern foliation in Arabic numerals is missing on most leaves, and as a result of the new ordering of the leavesis no longer of any use from fol. 69 onwards; the leaves measure 270 × 190 mm; one column for fols. 1v-3v and 91v-93v; two columns on the rest, justified with a double vertical line on both sides and a triple vertical line between the columns; prickings cannot be seen; 7 lines on fols. 1v-3v and 91v-93v with text set to music; 12 lines in each column on fols. 70-77, also provided with text and music; 28 lines on the leaves that only contain text; ruled in drypoint on fols. 1v-3v and 91v-93v, even leaves are placed over odd ones; Carolingian script; initials are mainly in red, although they are also in blue or combine both colors; large historiated initial at the beginning of the Gospel narratives, fol. 4r; rubrics in red; probably written by a single scribe; Aquitainian notation, thick strokes on a graphite line on fols. 1v-3v and 91v-93v, which has disappeared in some places; neumes are smaller and well executed around a drypoint line on fols. 70-77; consistent use of a *custos*.

General contents: Texts with musical notation: four versions of the genealogy of Christ according to St. Matthew (fols. 1v-3v; 74-75; 75-75v and 76v-77); and a genealogy of Christ according to St. Luke (91v-93v). There are also the following fragments of the Gospels: St. John 1:1-7 (fol. 70r-v) and 14:23-31 (fols. 72v-73); St. Mark 16:1-7 (fols. 71v-72) and 16: 14-20 (fol. 72r-v); St. Luke 20:38-42 (fol. 74); and St. Matthew 5:1-12 (fol. 76). Texts from St. Matthew 2:1-12 and St. Luke 2:22-32 (fols. 70v-71v). The musical notation was never added, although the manuscript was prepared for it. Text with musical notation: gospels for the masses from the first Sunday in Advent to the XXVI Sunday after Pentecost (fols. 4-77v); the Proper of Saints, from January to December, fols. 78-88v); Common of Saints (fols. 89-91). There follow the gospels for the dedication of the church, veneration of the Holy Cross, veneration of St. Michael and finally the *In agenda defunctorum*.

Leaf shown: 70r
GOSPEL ACCORDING TO St. JOHN 1:1-7. *Dominus uobiscum. Inicium sancti euangelii secundum Iohannem. In principio erat uerbum. Et uerbum erat apud deum et deus erat uerbum. Hoc erat in principio apud deum. Omnia per ipsum facta sunt et sine ipso factum*

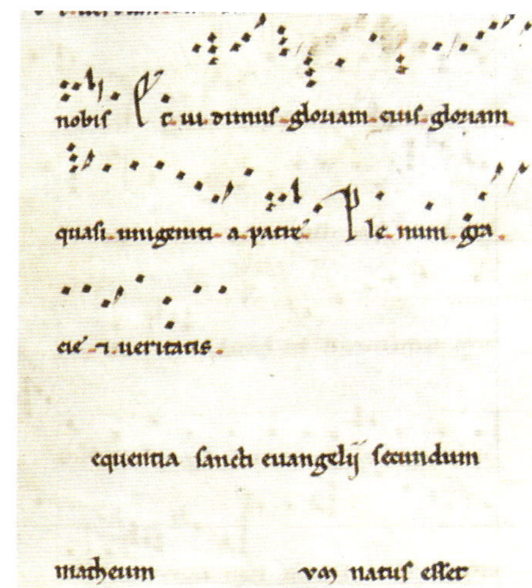
Detail of fol. 70v

est nichil. Quod factum est in ipso uita erat. Et uita erat lux hominum. Et lux in tenebris lucet et tenebre eam non comprehenderunt. Fuit homo missus a deo cui nomen erat iohannes. Hic uenit in testimonium ut testimonium perhiberet de lumine ut omnes crederent per illum. Non erat ille lux set ut testimonium perhiberet de lumine. Erat lux uera que illuminat omnem hominem uenientem in hunc mundum. In mundo erat et mundus per ipsum factus est et mundus eum non cognouit. In propria uenit et sui eum non receperunt...

Fol. 70r contains the gospel for mass on Christmas Day. This is a recitative whose melodic-literary structure consists of 15 musical phrases that invariably end in a cadence on the tonic (G) of the mode; the textual units are almost always grammatically complete; four different melodic elements—some of which are fairly melismatic—follow, or are always naturally combined to form the different parts of the phrase. A preference for certain elements is apparently due to the interest in highlighting the expressive contents of the text with music. This may be the case at the words *Et lux in tenebris lucet* or *Erat lux uera que illuminat.* The neumes are meticulously drawn; there are numerous liquescences and quilismas and the size of the virgae varies in compound neumes, marking the extent of the intervals. This text is also found with music in the Evangeliary, Madrid, BN, glass case 20.6, beautifully illuminated (11th to 12th centuries), which exhibits a similar organization of the phrases within a predominantly syllabic style.

BIBLIOGRAPHY
ANGLÈS 1970, 126. FERNÁNDEZ DE LA CUESTA 1980, 161. PEÑAS GARCÍA 1983, 20, 31, 47-69, 83-93, 99, 179-206; 1995, 21, 23; 2004, 22, 33-36.

M.ª Concepción Peñas García

Dominus vobiscum Initium

sancti evangelii secundum iohannem

In principio erat verbum Et verbum

erat apud deum et deus erat verbum

Hoc erat in principio apud deum

Omnia per ipsum facta sunt et sine ipso

factum est nichil Quod factum est

in ipso vita erat Et vita erat lux ho

minum Et lux in tenebris lucet et

tenebre eam non comprehenderunt Fuit

homo missus a deo cui nomen erat iohannes

Hic venit in testimonium ut testimonium

perhiberet de lumine ut omnes crederent

per illum Non erat ille lux set ut testi

monium perhiberet de lumine Erat

lux vera que illuminat omnem homi

nem venientem in hunc mundum

In mundo erat et mundus per ipsum factus

est et mundus eum non cognovit In

propria venit et sui eum non receperunt

Quot quot autem receperunt eum dedit

eis potestatem filios dei fieri his qui

credunt in nomine eius Qui non

ex sanguinibus neque ex voluntate carnis

Evangeliary

12TH CENTURY *EX.* (FOL. 108V)

ARCHIVO CAPITULAR, PAMPLONA (NAVARRE), W./O. S.
PROVENANCE: UNKNOWN.
Parchment bound with magnificent gold silver 16th century covers; two seals in use; 117 (3 + 114) leaves; modern foliation in Arabic numerals in the middle of the lower margin of the recto leaf; the leaves measure 260 × 160 mm; the text block measures 200 × 100 mm; one column justified with a double vertical line on both sides, two columns for fols. 5r-16v; prickings cannot be seen; text provided with notation: 14 lines on fol. 111v; 10 on fols. 108v and 109; 6 on fol. 109v and 3 on fol. 112r; in the texts without musical notation, the ruling includes 29 lines; ruled in drypoint, two lines for the musical notation on fols. 108v-110r and one for the notation on fols. 111v-112r; Carolingian script; initials in red or combining red with yellow, blue and green; rubrics in red; written by a single scribe, except for the declaration on fol. 113v; Aquitainian notation oriented around the line that corresponds to the ruling of the text block; consistent use of a *custos.*

General contents: Texts with music: genealogy of Christ according to St. Matthew (fols. 108v-109v) and *Sancti Spiritus* sequence (fols. 111v-112r). Texts without music: incipit of the chapters from the Gospels of Matthew, Mark, Luke and John, followed by the preface of St. Jerome (fols. 5r-12v) in four parallel columns, with a numerical list of the chapters that coincide in the four Evangelists; in three columns, those by Matthew, Mark, Luke and those by Matthew, Luke and John; in two columns, those by Matthew and Luke (fols. 13r-16r). The Gospel stories, including the prologues, occupy fols. 16v-108r. Some parts are missing in the Gospel texts: from chap. 26, v. 65 (fol. 50r) of Matthew up to chap. 5, v. 33 of Mark; from chap. 11, v. 8 of Mark (fol. 58v) up to chap. 10, v. 8 of Luke. There are references to the other three Gospel texts in red in the margins of the stories by each Evangelist.

Leaf shown: 108v
[GENEALOGY OF CHRIST ACCORDING TO ST. MATTHEW].
Dominus uobiscum. Et cum spiritu tuo. Inicium sancti euangelii secundum matheum. Gloria. Liber generationis ihesu Cristi filii dauid filii abraham. Abraham genuit ysaach ysaach autem genuit iacob, iacob autem genuit iudam et fratres eius. Iudas autem genuit phares et zaram de thamar. Phares autem genuit esrom esrom autem genuit aram. Aram autem genuit [a]minadab. Aminadab autem genuit naason. Naason autem genuit salmon.

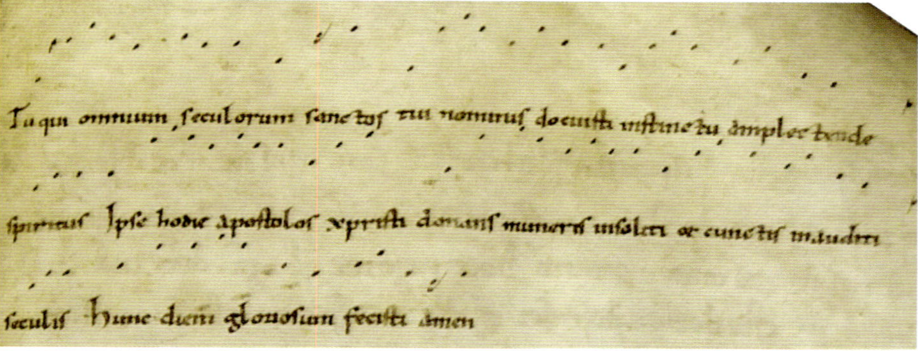

Detail of fol. 112r

Salmon autem genuit booz de raab. Booz autem genuit obeth ex ruth. Obeth autem genuit iesse. Iesse autem genuit dauid regem. Dauid autem rex genuit salomonem ex ea que fuit urie... (The genealogy ends on fol. 109v.)

The genealogy that begins the Gospel story of Saint Matthew is a literary text with little dramatic content that is restricted to a short repetitive formula "A genuit B" applied to the 42 generations from Abraham to Christ. This leaf ends with one of the three phrases that go beyond the repetitive formula and divide the genealogy into another three parts (14 + 14 + 14) stressed musically by using a cadence. What stands out in this fragment are the predominance of the syllabic style, its extensive melodic range and the small groups of neumes that are appropriately placed at one of the most important moments in the text, thereby enhancing its expressiveness. The melody consists of seven phrases separated by the same cadence on the tonic of the first mode. The phrases essentially combine two single elements in various ways. This melody is similar to the version contained in ms. 9719, Madrid, BN, and in Cod. 2, Huesca, AC, both from the 12th century. Other versions that are musically further removed from this can be found in Roncevaux, Tortosa, Toledo and El Escorial. The genealogy of St Matthew was sung on specific feast days during the liturgical year: Christmas and the Nativity of Mary.

The copy contains on fol. 113v a sworn statement dated 1228.

BIBLIOGRAPHY

HERNÁNDEZ ASCUNCE 1964, 146. ANGLÈS 1970, 127,130. FERNÁNDEZ DE LA CUESTA 1980, 154. PEÑAS GARCÍA 1983, 19, 31, 48, 57-69; 2004, 22, 37.

M.ª Concepción Peñas García

Dominus vobiscum. Et cum spu tuo. Initium sancti evangelii

secundum matheum. Gl'a. Liber generationis ihu

x͡pi filii david filii abraham. Abraham genuit ysaach

ysaach autem genuit iacob. iacob autem genuit iudam et fr̄s ei'

Iudas autem genuit phares et zaram de thamar. Phares aūt

genuit esrom. esrom autem genuit aram. Aram aut̄ genuit

Aminadab. Aminadab autem genuit naason. Naason autem genuit salmon. Salmō

autem genuit booz de raab. Booz autem genuit obeth ex ruth

Obeth autem gen̄t iesse. Iesse autem gen̄t david regem

David autem rex genu[it] salomonem ex ea que fuit

urie

Missal, Sacramentary

12TH CENTURY *EX.* (FOL. 56V)

ARCHIVO REAL Y GENERAL DE NAVARRA, PAMPLONA, CODICES AND CARTULARIES, K. 6.
PROVENANCE: CISTERCIAN MONASTERY OF FITERO (NAVARRE).
ORIGIN: A) TOLEDO (DOMÍNGUEZ BORDONA, MUNDÓ, KLEIN); B) LEÓN (ENCISO, MILLARES CARLO, DÍAZ).
Parchment in good condition; modern binding (20th century); 117 leaves; 13th century addition on fol. 1r; early foliation in the lower right corner, intermediate gaps; modern notes in pencil with Arabic numerals in the upper right corner: 4 (4bis) is duplicated and number 27 is missing (the foliation skips from number 26 to 28); the leaves measure 310 × 225 mm; the text block measures 215 × 100 mm; one column; prickings cannot be seen; 18 lines when there is only text, 9 when the text is notated, and a variable number of lines when both formats are combined; staff lines colored in red; Gothic script; large illuminated I initials represent Christ on fol. 1v, in this case in a dedicatory scene; the Annunciation, fol. 6r; Epiphany, fol. 7r; Christ entering Jerusalem, fol. 24r; monk at prayer, fol. 26r; Christ raised from the dead appears to Mary Magdalene, fol. 32r; Ascension, fol. 36v; Pentecost, fol. 38v; Christ Pantocrator, fol. 41r; St. Augustine, fol. 52r; priest exhorting people to pray, fol. 59v; Flagellation, fol. 60r; stoning of St. Stephen, fol. 64v; the Purification, fol. 70v; Assumption, fol. 78r; two beautiful initials with interlace, fols. 83v and 92r; other initials follow in red, blue or both colors combined; rubrics in red and black, sometimes framed in red, are inserted in the text or in the margins; written by a single scribe; square notation with Aquitainian features on a four-line staff in red ink; the letters *c* and *F*, in various positions, serve as clefs on fols. 56v-60r and 62v-63r; *custos* at the end of the line.

General contents: Mass of St. Edmund of Canterbury (fol. 1r). Temporale, from the 1st Sunday in Advent to the 25th Sunday after Pentecost (fols. 1v-49v). *Incipit ordo ad induendum vestimentis sacerdotalibus;* apologias attributed to St. Ambrose and St. Augustine (fols. 49v-60r), followed by the order of Mass. The prefaces for Pentecost, the Holy Cross, the Holy Trinity, the Apostles, Quadragesima, Easter, Ascension, Christmas, the Apparition of the Lord, the Purification, Annunciation and Nativity of Mary, and the Common (fols. 56v-62r) have musical notation. The Lord's Prayer in the canon of the mass is on fols. 62v-63v, also with musical notation. The incomplete Sanctorale starts with St. Stephen the protomartyr and breaks off on fol. 72; the gap runs from the cathedra of St. Peter to St. Germanus (31 July) (fols. 64v-96v). St. Malachy, Bishop († 1148) stands out on fol. 92v, whose feast day was established in the Cistercian Order in 1191. In the margin of fol. 94v is indicated the Mass for St. Edmund of Canterbury, canonized in 1247, referring to the beginning of the book, on fol. 1r, where it was added in the 13th century. Both Masses help to establish the date of the codex. The Sanctorale ends in the vigil of St. Andrew. The Masses for December and the Common of Saints are missing. Fols. 97r-117r contain votive Masses, with gaps. The Mass for the Dead, the *Missa pro tribulatione et temptatione*, *Fac mecum* and the Mass of the Holy Spirit are complete. The manuscript ends with the *Missa pro furto ecclesiae*: *Concede... te miserante celeri satis...*, incomplete.

Leaf shown: 56v
PREFACIO DE NATIVITATE DOMINI
Eterne Deus. Quia per incarnati uerbi misterium noua mentis nostre oculis lux tue claritatis infulsit. Ut dum uisibiliter deum cognoscimus per hunc inuisibilium amorem rapiamur. Et ideo cum angelis et archangelis cum tronis et dominationibus cumque omni milicia celestis exercitus hymnum glorie tue canimus sine fine dicentes.
Eterne Deus. Quia cum unigenitus.
DE APPARITIONE DOMINI.

Proper preface for Christmas: liturgical recitative with a simple syllabic melodic line that corresponds to the more primitive style now called *ferial tone.* After the acclamation, the piece starts directly with the tenor in *recto tono*, C, without the intonation, A (as is also the case in the preface for the Holy Trinity, fol. 59r). The melody consists of three repeated phrases, each divided into two

Detail of fol. 58v

parts, the first of which, because of the requirements of the text, occurs three times inthe last phrase: *Et ideo...* The remaining prefaces of the codex provide the same melody. The C clef is always on the third line of the staff. This melody is the same as the one sung to the *Exultet* in codices 104 (12th to 13th centuries) and 102 (13th century), fols. 103r-107r and 47r-50r, of the Biblioteca Provincial de Tarragona, and in the Evangeliary from the Monastery of Santa María in Vallbona de les Monges (Lleida), Archivo del Monasterio, ms. 1.

BIBLIOGRAPHY

DOMÍNGUEZ BORDONA 1958, 76, 77.
HERNÁNDEZ ASCUNCE 1964, 146. JANINI 1972, II: 1323; 1977a, 225-226. SILVA 1988, 23-59. GOÑI GAZTAMBIDE 1999.
PEÑAS GARCÍA 2004, 21, 30-32.

M.ª Concepción Peñas García

Dominus ds̄ suscipiat sac̄ficiū de ore tuo ⁊ de manib⁹ tuis. ad utilitatē scē̄ sue eccl̄ie. ⁊ ad salutē oī ppl̄o xp̄iano. ⁊ ad remediū oīū fidelīū defūctorꝝ. Prefacio de natiuitate domini.

Eterne deus Quia ꝑ incarnati uerbi misteriū nova mentis nostre oculis lux tue claritatis infulsit. Ut dum uisibiliter deum cognoscimus ꝑ hunc ī uisibilium amore rapiamur. Et ideo cum angelis ⁊ archangelis cum tronis ⁊ dn̄ationib⁹ cumq; omni milicia celestis exercit⁹ hymnum gl̄ie tue canim⁹ sine fine dicentes.

De apparitione dn̄i.

Eterne deus Quia cum unigenit⁹

Antiphonary

11TH CENTURY *EX.* (FOL. 139V)

BIBLIOTECA CAPITULAR, TOLEDO, 44-1.
PROVENANCE: CENTRAL AQUITAINE, SAHAGÚN OR TOLEDO. SCRIBES FROM THE SOUTH OF FRANCE.
Good-quality parchment, the first eight leaves are deteriorated by time and use, but the preservation is relatively acceptable in the rest of the manuscript; the quire that comprises fols. 113-120 is also in a poor state of preservation; 18th century binding in simple parchment; title label: *Antiphonario de Coro* ms. 44.1; 186 leaves (fragmentary); a five-leaf quire with an index of the codex's liturgical content, added in the 18th century by order of Archbishop Lorenzana (1775), precedes the antiphonary; modern foliation in red ink in the upper right corner; there are errors on fols. 139-150; the leaves measure 369 × 260 mm; the writing frame measures 260 × 175 mm; one column justified by a double vertical line on both sides; Aquitainian notation over the line that corresponds to the writing frame ruling; the prickings are imperceptible; 18 lines; ruled in drypoint two at a time on the grain side; Carolingian minuscule with beautiful calligraphy, typical of 11th century southern France, with clear brown ink; the paleographical characteristics only partially coincide with those described by Dufour for the *scriptorium* at Moissac in his monograph; catchwords in the lower margin of the last leaf of each quaternion; three scribes, one of whom may have been a proofreader; subsequent additions; Aquitainian notation *in campo aperto* carefully executed by an expert hand; leaves 5r-6v, 61v, 90r, 91r, 112r-114v, 121v, 123r (partially), 125v-127v (partially), 130v, 160v and 170r and a number of other isolated liturgical pieces lack notation.

General contents: fol. 1r (... *auferetur de femore eius*), leaves are missing from the liturgical time of the Advent. The temporale and the santoral remain fused until fol. 161v, where the Common of Saints begins. It finishes with the fragmentary fol. 186v (... *et enarrate omnia mirabilia eius*). The most significant saints are: fol. 89: *Horiencius* (sic, for *Orencius*) (the Bishop of Auch); fol. 151v-154v: Saturninus (of Toulouse), the most outstanding of all, with octave.

Leaf shown: 139v
[OFFICE OF ST. CECILIA]
... *sanctum nomen homnino* [second part of the antiphon *Nos scientes*]. PSALMUS *Exultate iusti.* ANTIPHONA *Tunc Ualerianus perrexit...* PSALMUS. *Deus noster ref[ugium]*. ANTIPHONA *Cecilia famula tua domine...* PSALMUS *Fundamenta.* ANTIPHONA *Venit sponsa Christi haccipe coronam...* PSALMUS *Cantate Domino.* ANTIPHONA *Hec est uirgo prudens que uenientes sponso...* PSALMUS *Dominus regnauit exul[tet].* ANTIPHONA *Ista est speciosa.* ANTIPHONA *Triduanis ad Dominum popossit...* RESPONSORIUM *Uirgo gloriosa semper euangelium Christi gerebat...* VERSUS *Cilicio Cecilia membra domabat...* antiphona *Ad conlo[quis diuinis].* RESPONSORIUM *Cantantibus organis Cecilia uirgo soli Domino...* VERSUS *Biduanis hac triduanis ieiunisis* [sic]... F*iat Domine.* RESPONSORIUM *Domine Iesu Christe pastor bone...* VERSUS *Nam sponsum que quasi leonem... Cecilia.* RESPONSORIUM *Cecilia intra in cubiculo horantem inuenit... nimio terrore.*

Used at the beginning of the implementation of the Franco-Roman rite at the Cathedral of Toledo after the city was reconquered (1085) and Catholic worship was restored in the cathedral (1086), the antiphonary 44-1 documents the establishment in the Cathedral of Toledo of the new liturgical repertoire as a result of the consecration of the church and the appointment of the French monk Bernard de Sédirac, Abbot of Sahagún, as the new Archbishop. Hugo of Cluny suggested to the new prelate that he bring professed monks from his order, so as to establish communal living and celebrate the divine office. Jiménez de Rada refers to an initial introduction of the new rite at the cathedral, established with a group of monks brought in from Sahagún and reinforced with groups of priests recruited from various places throughout the south of France in successive phases. Local priests, some monks from Sahagún and others from the south of France made up the initial cathedral chapter, which was quite international. According to Rocha, the codex stands out for its hybrid character,

Detail of fol. 123v

both monastic and secular, perhaps in response to the mixed composition of the Cathedral of Toledo chapter itself. The liturgical evidence suggests a dependence on the south of France and, more specifically, on the region of Aquitaine. The sanctoral includes St. Orens of Auch. It was in his Cluniac Abbey that the future Archbishop of Toledo had professed during his youth. The Easter week schema coincides completely with that in the Antiphonary of Albi and closely resembles those of Auch and Toulouse.

BIBLIOGRAPHY

EDIT. FACS. MADRID, BN MÚSICA MS. 813. JIMÉNEZ DE RADA 1793. RIAÑO 1887, 32. ANGLÈS 1931, 48. RIVERA RECIO 1966-1976, 13-29. JANINI AND SERRANO 1969, 278. DUFOUR 1972. JANINI 1977a, 179. FERNÁNDEZ VALVERDE 1989, 6: 252-253. ROCHA 1990, 27-45. GONZÁLVEZ 1997, 77-84. RUBIO 2004.

Ramón Gonzálvez Ruiz

sanctum nomen homi- ni non negare non possumus. P Exultate iusti. A Tunc ualerianus
perrexit ad antestitem et signum quod acceperat inuenit sanctum urbanum. P Dñr ref
A Cecilia famula tua domine quasi ouis tibi argumentosa deseruit. P Fundamta
A Venit sposa xpisti accipe coronam quam tibi dominus preparauit in eternum. P Cantate do.
A Hec est uirgo prudens que uenientes sponso abtulit lampadas suas et introiuit
cum eum ad nubcias. P Dñus regnauit exul. A Ista est speciosa. A Triduanis ad
dominum poposcit inducias ut domum meam ecclesiam consecrarem. R P A
VIRGO gloriosa semper euangelium xpisti gerebat in pectore et non die
bus neque noctibus uocabat a conloquiis diuinis et oratione
V Cilicio cecilia mēbra domabat deum geminibus exorabat. R Conlo. R Cantantibus
organis cecilia uirgo soli domino decantabat dicens fiat domine cor meum
et corpus meum inmaculatum ut non confundar. V Biduanis hac triduanis
ieiuniis orens suā dño pudicicia commendabat dicens fiat dñe. R Domine iesu
xpiste pastor bone suscipe seminum fructus quos in cecilia seminasti seminator
casti consilii cecilia famula tua domine quasi apis tibi argumentosse deseruit
V Nam sponsum que quasi leonem ferocem accepit ad te quasi agnum mansue
tissimum destinauit. Cecilia. R Cecilia intra in cubiculo orantem inuenit ceci
lia eum stantem angelum domini quem uidens ualerianus nimio terrore

Tropary, Sequentiary, Prosary, Prosulary

11TH CENTURY *EX.* (FOL. 32V)

BIBLIOTHÈQUE NATIONALE DE FRANCE, PARIS, N. A. L. 1871.
PROVENANCE: ABBEY OF SAINT PIERRE OF MOISSAC, TARN-ET-GARONNE (FRANCE).
Parchment; modern binding (ca. 2004). The last known owners were an antique dealer from Montauban, F. Danjou, around 1840; the canon Morelot of the Cathedral of Dijon; and finally the Bibliothèque Nationale de France, which bought it from a Parisian antique dealer in 1903; 2 leaves: A-D + 178; modern foliation in ink in the upper right margin in Roman numerals; the leaves measure 285-295 × 180-185 mm; the writing frame measures 230-250 × 130-140 mm; one justified column; visible horizontal prickings in the outer margin of the leaf; 12-14 lines; ruled in drypoint; Carolingian minuscule; eight scribes, but three of them stand out; Aquitainian notation oriented around a line that corresponds to the ruling of the writing frame, without any modal significance; consistent use of a *custos.*

General contents: Tropes (fols. 1r-76r); sequences (fols. 76v-87r); proses (fols. 88r-170v); *prosulae* (fols. 171r-178v).

Leaf shown: 32v
*[... silentium in celo] quasi media hora... Ad com*munionem. *Auctorem omnium... Laudibus alternis...*

Detail of fol. 32v

In this manuscript, after the tropes for the feast of the archangel St. Michael (fols. 31r-32v), on fols. 32v-33r, there are four tropes for the introit on the feast St. Gerald, patron of Aurillac († 909), celebrated on 13 October: *Laudibus alternis* (*AH XXXVI-XXXVII:* no. 41; Weiß, 270-271, no. 255), *Astrigera resonet* (*AH CX:* no. 240; Weiß, 258-259, no. 245), *Concrepet alma cohors* (*AH CX:* no. 239; Weiß, 262-263, no. 248) and *Concinat in Domino* (*AH CX:* no. 238; Weiß, 260-262, no. 247). The rubric for the feast is omitted, although space was reserved for it. In this manuscript, the arrangement of the tropary is repeated in the prosary, and the proses for St. Gerald appear on fols. 160r-161v.

Bannister has pointed out that the feast of St. Gerald is the object of particular veneration in Moissac (see Bannister, 564). Nonetheless, these four tropes are also found in various Aquitainian manuscripts. It is worth noting that Bernard, Archbishop of Toledo (1086-1125), brought from Moissac a monk named Gerald to carry out the liturgical reform, and named him cantor of the Cathedral of Toledo. This may be why the office of St. Gerald appears in the antiphonary of the Cathedral of Toledo (Toledo, Biblioteca Capitular, 44-2, fols. 149v-152r). Years later, Gerald was ordained Archbishop of Braga (1095-1109).

BIBLIOGRAPHY
EDIT. FACS. *TROPAIRE-SÉQUENTIAIRE-PROSAIRE-PROSULAIRE DE MOISSAC,* 2006. DAUX 1901, 36-37. BANNISTER 1903, 554-593, 564. BLUME 1906, 36-37, 110, N.° 41, 238-240. HUSMANN 1964, 147-148. WEISS 1970, 258-263, 270-271, N.° 245, 247-248, 255. DUFOUR 1972, xix, 5, 8-9, 17, 33-34, 39, 42, 66-67, 76, 149-150. *LES TROPAIRES-PROSAIRES* 1985, 32 (GY). WALKER 1998, 194-195. AVRIL ET AL. 1989, 223, NO. 324. CASTRO 1990, 250. COLETTE 1990, 297-311; 2005.

Shin Nishimagi

quasi media hora et septem angeli stantes erant in conspectu dei et date sunt illis

septem tube et uenit alius angelus. Stetit Ut adoleret eum super altare aureum quod

est ante tronum Et ascen In conspectu. AD COM

Auctorem omnium in eternum laudantes regnantem Benedicite P Benedicite

omnes uirtutes domini d Hymnum

LAUDIBUS ALTERNIS nunc et uox uinnula tur mae M

tuas ingemina per sol uere de bita regi O siusti AT

ASTRIGERA resonet que rite boemata scandit geral

di festum diuina uoce caterua O siusti Cuius

in exemplo meruit pie ui uere xpisto E t lingua Mortalium dum cor da suis

se ce rnit ab arius L ex dei A edi ficans alios ue rbi decore

super in I n corde P N oli emulari AT

CONCELEBRET alma cohors xpisti nunc corde geraldo Musicae uox cuius

Antiphonary

12TH CENTURY *IN.* (FOL. 215V)

BIBLIOTECA CAPITULAR, TOLEDO, 44-2 (OLIM 29.12 AND 30.12).
PROVENANCE: AQUITAINE (MOISSAC, AURILLAC, TOULOUSE), SAHAGÚN OR TOLEDO.
The parchment is in a precarious state of preservation; binding in parchment (18th century); 220 leaves; modern foliation in the upper right corner of the leaves; the leaves measure 393 × 264 mm; one column justified with double vertical lines on both sides, the column covers the entire leaf; imperceptible prickings; 26 lines; ruled in drypoint, individually on each leaf; Carolingian minuscule; catchwords at the end of each quire; more than three scribes; Aquitainian notation oriented around the line that corresponds to the ruling of the text block ruling; consistent use of a *custos.*

General contents: *Dominica prima in adventu Domini. Ad vesperas...* (fol. 1r). Followed by the temporale fused with the Sanctorale. *In die nativitatis ihs xpi (In) vitatorium...* (fol. 17v). *In natale sancti Hylarii* (fol. 37r). *In festivitate sancte Scolastice* (fol. 56v). *In natale sancti Benedicti* (fol. 57r). *Feria quinta* [in the margin: *in nocte cene Domini*] (fol. 85r). *In natale sancti Medardi* (fol. 119v). *Sancti Mauricii* (fol. 142). *In vigilia sancti Geraldi* [from Aurillac, 13 October] (fol. 149v). *Dominica XXXIIII* [post Pentecost] (fol. 212r). *Venite exultemus Domino...* [in several tones] (fols. 213v-220v).

Leaf shown: 215v
[D]*eu*[m pl]*o*[r]*e*[m]*v*[s]... *Hodie si uocem... Qvadraginta annis... Gloria... De* Sanct*i Iacobi.* In*vitatorius. Venite omnes christicole... Venite exultemus... Qvoniam Deus... Qvoniam ipsivs est... Hodie si uocem eius...* [p]*a*[tr]*e*[s v]*e*[str]*i* [pr]*o*[b]*a* (fol. 216r: [v]*e*[r]*u*[nt]).

This is one of the oldest manuscripts with chants from the divine office that contains music that can be transcribed into modern notation. It is the first of a series of musical antiphonaries that disseminated the use of the Franco-Roman rite in many churches throughout Castile and Portugal. The manuscript represents the second stage of the process of introducing the Franco-Roman liturgical repertoire to the church

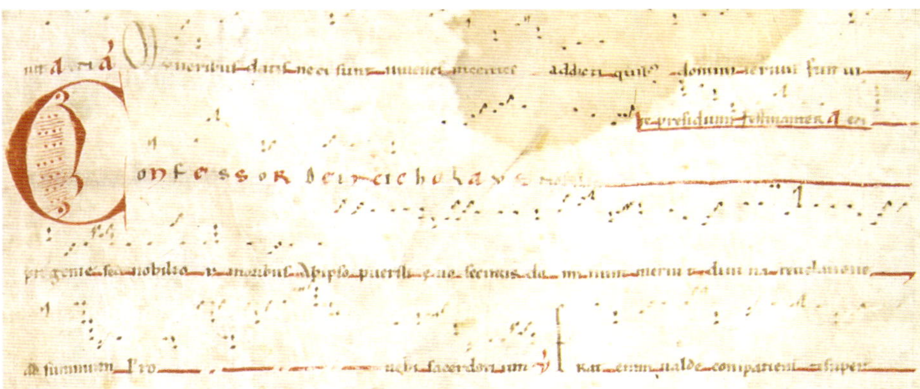

Detail of fol. 168r

of Toledo. This antiphonary, as well as the antiphonary Toledo 44-1, was copied in a French *scriptorium*, which is seen not only in the expert tracing of the letters and notation, but also in the configuration of the Sanctorale. Although its structure follows the monastic *cursus,* it should be noted that some passages are reminiscent of the Roman *cursus.* With respect to its modal organization, there are two recitation tones in the responsories; whereas the body of the Responsory—sung by the choir—recites on the note re, the verse—performed by the soloist—recites on the note fa. This peculiarity was to last until the edition of the *Intonarium Toletanum* from Cisneros (Alcalá de Henares, 1515). Fols. 213v-220v contain several melodic versions of Psalm 94, *Venite exultemus Domino,* which accompanies the antiphon for the invitatory at Matins.

BIBLIOGRAPHY

EDIT. FACS. MADRID, BN MÚSICA MS. 813. RIAÑO 1887, 43. JANINI AND SERRANO 1969, 278. ANGLÈS 1931. RIVERA RECIO 1976, 20-25. JANINI 1977a, 179-180. ROCHA 1980. OLEXY 1980. ROCHA 1982, 185-207. FICKETT 1983. HUGLO 1985, 249-256; 1995, 251-252. ROCHA 1990, 27-45. OLEXY ET AL. 1992. GONZÁLVEZ 1997, 82-84. STEINER 1999, 59-79. COLLAMORE 2000. RUBIO 2004.

Ramón Gonzálvez Ruiz

Hodie si

uocem

Quadraginta annis

Gloria

De s. iacobi. Vit.

Venite omnes christicole ad adorandum christum regem eternum cuius apostolum suum mirabiliter decorauit iacobum

Venite exultemus

nam deus

Quoniam ipsi est

Hodie si uocem eius

Antiphonary (fragmentum)

11th Century *med.* (fol. 2r)

Arquivo da Universidade, Coimbra, IV-3.ª S.-Gav. 44 (20).
Provenance: Benedictine Monastery of San Fins de Friestas (archdiocese of Braga). Originally from Braga or environs (Díaz y Díaz).
Poorly preserved parchment with wrinkles, spots and a deteriorated top region which has damaged both the text and the music; several prickings; very faded ink; it was used as the cover of a cartulary at the Monastery of San Fins de Friestas; bifolium; lacks foliation; the leaves measure 380 × 225 mm; the writing frame measures 310 × 165 mm; one column vertically justified on both sides; 30 lines (15 are text); ruled in drypoint; Visigothic minuscule from around the middle of the 11th century (Díaz y Díaz); initials in red and black; a single scribe for the text and possibly a different scribe for the notation; Aquitainian notation over the line that corresponds to the ruling of the writing frame; consistent use of a *custos*.

General contents: Antiphons for Thursday evening, the better part of the canonical hours for Friday, and Responsories and antiphons for Sunday.

Leaf shown: 2r
Antiphona *Cantemus Domino gloriose. Ps*almus. *Laudate. Seculorum, amen. Ad Bened*ictus. *Ant*iphona *In sanctitate serviamus Domino Ps*almus *Benedictus Ad Vesp*eram. *Ant*iphona. *Et ominis mansuetudinis eius memento Ant*iphona *Ecce quam bomun Ant*iphona *Quoniam in eternum* [Psalmus] *Laudate Ant*iphona *Hymnum cantate nobis* [Psalmus] *Super flu*[mina] *Ad Magn*ificat *Fecit michi Deus meus magna Feria Vj.* [In]*VIT. Dominum qui fecit nos venite adoremus. Venite.*

The fragment is difficult to read because of its use as the cover of a cartulary for the Monastery of San Fins de Friestas that was ordered by the primate Don Diego de Sousa in 1528. It was discovered and described by Vasconcelos together with other fragments from the same collection. According to Díaz y Díaz the writing dates from the middle of the 11th century. In our opinion the codex dates between the end of the 11th century and the beginning of the 12th. It is a characteristic example of the transition from the Spanish to the Franco-Roman rite at the Braga diocese.

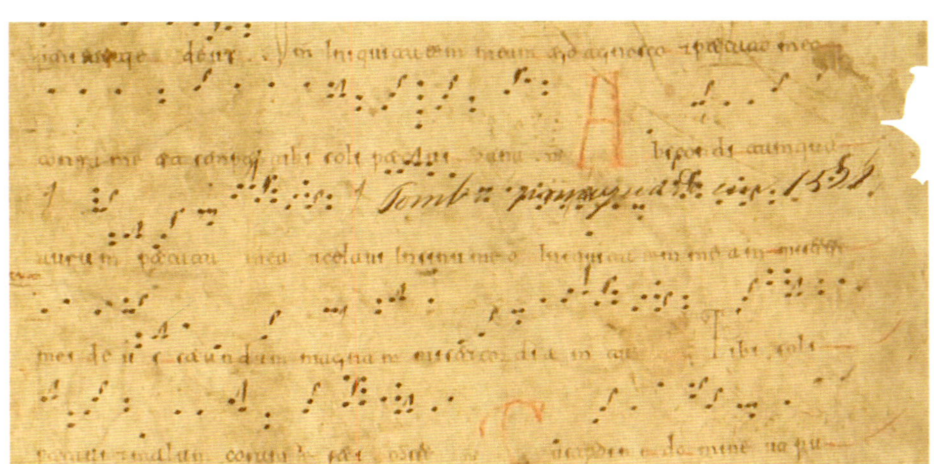
Detail of fol. 1r

Between lines 4 and 6, there is a 24-mm orifice that was there from the beginning, as evidenced by the careful arrangement of the scribe's text and notation. The Aquitainian notation, copied by a different hand and with darker ink than that of the text, shows a sharp diastematic tendency. Corbin erroneously mentions the presence of a red colored line.

The fragment is listed as no. 46 in the Fragment Inventory of the Arquivo da Universidade de Coimbra. It probably belonged to the same codex as another fragment from the same archive listed in the inventory as no. 11.

Bibliography

Vasconcelos 1928, 553-569. Corbin 1952b, 174. Díaz y Díaz 1983, 369. Costa 1992, 85-86. Queirós 1993-1994, 333; 1997, 540-542. Millares Carlo et al. 1999, 1: 43-44. Vilares 2001, 2: 79.

Maria José Azevedo Santos
Marco Daniel Duarte

ae. Dne dignatus ... [illegible] R[egnavit] dominus praecinctus

fortitudinem cum decore ... cultus ... paratus ... [illegible]

ae. ... exultate omnes quia ... deo ... iubilemus ... [illegible]

laudamus nomen eius ... B[enedicamus] domino

... [illegible] ... ae. ...

... [illegible] ... laudate dominum ...

... perios omnes laude dominum quia ... [illegible]

... [illegible] ...

... [illegible] ...

C[antemus] domino gloriose ... magnificatus est

annunciate eius ... laudate deum ...

annunciate eius ... serviamus domino et liberabit nos

adventu nostris. Benedicam ... ae ... omnes ...

audientis eius. Mandavit ... ae ... quia ...

iocundum habitare fratres ... ae ... [illegible]

misericordia eius. ... ae ... [illegible]

... [illegible] ...

quia posuit ... nomen eius ...

D[ominum] qui fecit nos venite adoremus ... [illegible]

deo adiutori nostro ... [illegible] ... omnia ...

... [illegible] ... dominum ...

... [illegible] ...

Antiphonary (fragmentum)

1172-1200 (FOL. 1V)

INSTITUTO DOS ARQUIVOS NACIONAIS, TORRE DO TOMBO, LISBON, FRAG., CX. 20, NO. 14.
PROVENANCE: CHAPTER ARCHIVE OF THE CATHEDRAL OF COIMBRA (PORTUGAL).
Parchment in a reasonable state of preservation; it was used as binding material; one bifolium; lacks foliation; the leaves measure 395 × 273 mm; the text block measures 195 × 293 mm; one column is justified by a double vertical line on both sides that spans the entire leaf; horizontal prickings are visible in the right margin; vertical prickings cannot be seen; 30 lines (15 with text) + 1 (add.); ruling in lead; Carolingian script; alternating initials in red, black or in red and black; written by a single scribe; Aquitainian notation oriented around a line colored in red that corresponds to the ruling of the text block; no *custos*, except at certain points where they have been added later (lines 5, 25, and 29).

General contents: Invitatory psalm (Psalm 94).

Leaf shown: 1v
(...) *semper et in secula seculorum amen.*
Venite exultemus Domino
Venite exultemus Domino iubilemus
[Venite exultemus Domino] (add.).

A meticulously prepared codex with the distinctive feature that all the lines with modal significance have been gone over in red and that *custos* are not used at the end of the line. The notation contains small oblique lines to separate groups of neumes (lines 5, 13, and 27). The later addition of a line "Venite exultemus Domino", in carelessly executed Carolingian script, reproduces the same melody as the final "Venite exultemus Domino", so that meaning of this later annotation is unclear; it may have been intended merely to provide a simple writing exercise. The codex is from the period in which the Roman liturgy was already firmly established in the diocese of Coimbra, which formed part of the ecclesiastical province of Braga; a process that occurred during the episcopates of Crestonio (1092-1098) and Mauricio (1099-1108). It seems that it was in the period in which these prelates were in office that the Mozarabic rite was abandoned because of the influence of Cluny.

Detail of fol. 2v

BIBLIOGRAPHY

VILARES 2001, 2: 232.

Marco Daniel Duarte

semper ⁊ in secula seculoꝝ Amen. Venite exultemus domino iubilemus
deo salutari nr̃o p̄ocupemus faciem eius in confessione ⁊ in psalmis iubilem⁹ ei.
Qm̃ ds̄ magnus dn̄s ⁊ rex magnus sup̄ omnes deos. Qm̃ nō repellet dn̄s plebem
suam q̄a in manu ei⁹ sunt omnes fines terre ⁊ altitudines montium ipse conspicit.
Qm̃ ipsius est mare ⁊ ipse fecit illud ⁊ aridam fundauer̄ man⁹ ei⁹. Venite adorem⁹
⁊ procidamus ante deum ploremus coram domino qui fecit nos. Quia ipse est dn̄s
deus noster nos aũt pp̄ls eius ⁊ oues pascue eius. Hodie si uocem eius audieritis
nolite obdurare corda ur̃a. Sicut in exacerbatione scd̄m diem temptationis in deserto
ubi temptauerunt me patres uestri probauerunt ⁊ uiderunt opera mea. Quadraginta
annis proxim⁹ fui generationi huic ⁊ dixit semp̄ hi errant corde ipsi uero non cognouer̄
uias meas quib⁹ iuraui in ira mea si introibunt in requiem meam. Gl̄a patri ⁊ filio
⁊ spiritui sc̄o. Sicut erat in principio ⁊ nunc ⁊ semp̄ ⁊ in secula seculoꝝ Amen.

Venite exultemus domino iubilemus deo salutari nostro preocupemus faciem eius in
confessione ⁊ in psalmis iubilemus ei. Quoniam deus magnus dominus ⁊ rex magnus
sup̄ omnes deos. Quoniam non repellet dn̄s plebem suam quia in manu eius sunt omnes

Venite exultemus domino iubilemus deo salutari nostro preocupemus

Mateus missal

1130-1150 (FOL. 8R)

ARQUIVO DISTRITAL, BRAGA, MS. 1.000.
PROVENANCE: MATEUS PARISH CHURCH, BRAGA DIOCESE (CURRENTLY VILA REAL DIOCESE). ORIGINALLY FROM LIMOGES.
Well-preserved codex that includes a plenary missal from which the first few leaves have been lost and to which a local calendar has been added; binding in leather, of which hardly any fragments have survived, on chestnut boards; 223 leaves; modern foliation in Arabic numerals, fol. 8r is not numbered; the leaves measure 165 × 265 mm; the text block measures 120 × 210 mm; one column is justified by a double vertical line on both sides that spans the entire leaf; vertical prickings are perceptible on some leaves (fol. 8r) in the upper and lower margin; 32 lines (11 with text); ruled in drypoint; Carolingian script; major initials with interlace, zoomorophicand vegetal motifs in red, blue and yellow ink; minor initials in black or red ink or both; a single scribe wrote the entire missal, except for the last three leaves, which are from a different hand; Aquitainian notation oriented around the line colored in red that corresponds to the ruling of the text block; consistent use of a *custos.*

General contents: the first part (fols. 1r-7r) contains a calendar of Braga, added to the original codex; the missal begins on fol. 8r; this folio contains one of the Christmas epistles provided with notation, added later but in the same period as the original codex; on fol. 7v two texts were added at a later date: the Gospel of the Resurrection, according to St. Mark (Mark 16:1-7), with notation, and the prayers for the feast day of St. Vincent, the martyr, without notation.

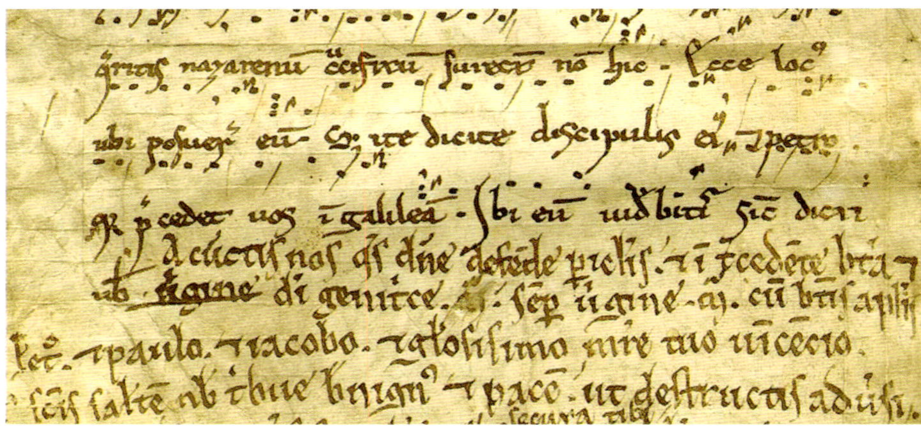

Detail of fol. 7v

Leaf shown: 8r
Lectio epistole beati Pauli apostoli ad Titum. Karissimi...
Reading of the Epistle of St. Paul to Titus, from the Christmas liturgy.

The leaf is an addendum to the original codex that starts on fol. 8v with the mass of the first Sunday in Advent (fol. 8r: writing frame: 108 × 216 mm).

Meticulously prepared codex, copied in a *scriptorium* in Limoges, essentially reflecting liturgical uses at the centers of St. Peter of Moissac and Figeac, with some formulas that are characteristic of St. Martial of Limoges. The missal contains some musical notation added later. It constitutes important evidence of the influence of the monks of Cluny in spreading the Roman liturgy to the western most part of the peninsula. The transcribed leaf includes an epistle provided with notation for one of the most solemn celebrations in the liturgical calendar: Christmas. A century later, a passage from the Easter Gospel was added (fol. 7v). We do not know for what church the missal was intended, but we do know that in 1421 it was found in the parish church of Saint Martin of Mateus, which at that time formed part of the diocese of Braga and now belongs to Vila Real diocese: "Este livro he da igreja da camara de Sam Martinho de Mateus e custou III mil VI centos reais. Era de Christo de mil III centos XXI anos".

The calendar included at the beginning of the codex was added later, ca. 1176. Because it is a manuscript of French origin, it is of great value as a document of the reform of the Braga liturgy promoted by Cluny through the mediation of various centers in the south of France.

BIBLIOGRAPHY
DAVID 1944, 319-358. CORBIN 1952b. EDIT. BRAGANÇA 1975. NASCIMENTO 1978-1979, 325-327. FREIRE 1980, 653-657. ROCHA 1990, 4: 27-45. FERREIRA 1993, 16/1: 463. ALVARENGA 2005.

Marco Daniel Duarte

ectio eplē beati pauli apostoli ad titum. K mi Gaudeamus noua

cum letitia Apparuit gratia saluatoris nrī dei omnibus homini

bus erudiens nos Fulget dies hodierna Nata luce sempiterna

Noua dies noua letitia Nouus agnus noua lux sollempnia

Noua decet gaudia Noua laudet cantica Ut abnegantes impie

tatem et secularia desideria sobrie et iuste et pie uiuamus in hoc seclo

Quisquis necter sed reatum Gaude tamen tanto natum Fit enim

sub peccato redditur liber sancto libertate spiritu Et exaltet mentium

[illegible] uoce sonitu Expectantes beatam spem et aduentum glorie magni dei

saluatoris nrī ihū xpī Speciali gaudio toto Caritati uincta toto Suo de

sempiterno filio Qui dedit semetipsum pro nobis ut nos redimeret ab omni ini

quitate Copulet ecclesia conubio Viduata dn̄o Et gratis gaudet gaudio

Et mundaret sibi populum acceptabilem sectatorem bonorum operum Omnis etas [illegible]

[illegible] pre laudet Hec loquere et exortare in xpō ihū dn̄o nrō Virgo par

[illegible] prudentie Noua [illegible] [illegible] [illegible] Parte [illegible]

[illegible] me

Gradual (fragmentum)

12TH CENTURY *MED.* (FOL. 1V)

ARQUIVO DISTRITAL, BRAGA, FRAG. 49.
PROVENANCE: UNKNOWN.
The parchment is reasonably well preserved, despite having been damaged in the upper margin, which compromises the reading of the text; there is a wrinkle that covers the entire length of the page without affecting the text or the notation; used as binding material for a volume related to the documentation from the Meadela parish (Viana do Castelo); one leaf; lacks foliation (on the recto side appears the indication "49", which corresponds to the catalog number); the leaf measures 255 × 298 mm; the writing frame measures 200 × 277 mm; two columns justified on the right margin with a double vertical line in lead point, while in the left margin the justification is invisible; the prickings cannot be seen; 34 lines (17 of which are text) for both columns (the left column includes two rubrics explaining the liturgical action; Carolingian script with Gothic tendencies; red initials; written by a single hand; Aquitainian notation in darker ink and a different quill on the line that corresponds to the ruling of the text block, colored in red; consistent use of a *custos*.

General contents: Gradual. Rite of the Adoration of the Cross from the Good Friday liturgy.

Leaf shown: 1v
VERSUS *Quid ultra debui facere tibi* [continuation of the hymn] *Improperia (Popule meus, quid feci tibi?)*]. *Agios. Sanctus* [ANTIPHONA] *Ecce lignum crucis. Venite adoremus* PSALMUS *Beati inmaculati.* [ANTIPHONA] *Ecce lignum* [ANTIPHONA] *Crucem tuam adoramus Domine* PSALMUS *Deus misereatur* ANTIPHONA *Adoramus crucis signaculum* [ANTIPHONA] *O admirabile precium cuius* ANTIPHONA *O crux splendidior* ANTIPHONA *O CRUX ADMIRABILE SIGNUM.*

A very carefully prepared codex and another example of the witnesses to the new Franco-Roman rite copied from models that come from the south of France.

Throughout the chant of the *Improperia* and after that of the *Ecce lignum crucis… Venite adoremus,* the rubrics related to the rite of the Presentation and the Adoration of the Cross are inserted in red ink with smaller letters.

Because the only preserved leaf is the one shown here, it is not known where this office appeared in the consecutive order of the celebrations that comprised the plenary missal of which the fragment is an extract; it most likely formed part of the liturgical Lent-Easter sequence, and was probably not situated at the end, in the appendix to the manuscript, as occurred in older books that included the *Improperia* chant. The sequence of both pieces assures us that, in this codex, the liturgical action of Good Friday was completely structured: beside the sections that explain how the rites were carried out, the chant of the *Improperia* was followed by the various antiphons designated for the rite of the Adoration of the Cross. The fact that the different prayers uttered at the moment of the great *preces* before the Presentation of the Cross, which appear on the leaf's recto, and that these were also accompanied by minor indications that were pronounced by the deacon: *Oremus, Flectamus genua, Levate; Oremus, Pro iudeis non flectatur genua* (fol. 1v), confirms our certainty.

Although in the tradition of the Church, chant is closely associated with the solemn Good Friday prayers, as can be seen in the Missal of Mateus, fol. 109r-v, and in the fact that the above-mentioned prayers appear with the title *Orationes que dicende sunt in Iherusalem*, the leaf barely presents music in the part that corresponds to the moments of the Presentation and the Adoration of the Cross.

Detail of fol. 1r

BIBLIOGRAPHY
CORBIN 1952b, 198-193; 1960.

Marco Daniel Duarte

ure crucem de feren-
tes canẽ-
tes ita

Quid ultra debui facere
tibi et non feci ego quidem plantavi te vineam
meam speciosissimam et tu facta es michi nimis
amara aceto namque sitim meam potasti et lancea
perforasti latus salvatori tuo Vt supra Agios
Ischiros
Sanctus

Modo sit locum honorifice
preparatum ante altare et
discooperta crux ab illis qui eā
tenent inquoent excelsa cont̄ pslm

Ecce lignum crucis in quo salus mundi pepe-
ndit venite adoremus Ps. Beati immaculati

Totum dicatur cum repetitione. Ecce lignum et ponant eam cum magna reverē-
tia in locum honorifice compositum. Postea deosculetur ab episcopo et clericis sive a populo
cum reverentia timentes dominum venientes
duo et duo flexis genibus ante crucē incli-
nato vultu in terra sub silencio dicens hanc
orationem ante crucē. Domine ihesu christe

R. Ecce lignum

Crucem
tuam adoramus domine et sanctam resurrectionem
tuam laudamus et glorificamus ecce enim propter crucem venit gaudium in universo mundo Ps. Deus misereatur

A. Adoramus crucis signaculum per quem salutis sump-
simus sacramentum in qua dominus noster quasi in
statera se ipsum precium nostrum pensavit ut
vita vendita fieret mors captivam in quo nec nul-

finxit et contra fortem fortiorem totus mundus triu-
phatorem ostendit hoc tamen plus est mirabile quia
quem totus mundus proficere et in uno stans stipi-
te seu rsum victor suppleuit O admirabile precium cuius pondere captivitas rede-
mpta est mundi tartarea confracta sunt claustra inferni aperta sunt nobis ianua regni A. O crux splendidior cunctis
astris mundo celebris hominibus multum amabilis sanctior universis que sola fuisti digna
portare talentum mundi dulce lignum dulces
clavos dulcia ferens pondera salva presentem
catervam in tuis iugiter laudibus congregata A.
O crux admirabile signum in quo dominus noster
dei filius est suspensus pro nostrorum pondere
criminum mortis dampnavit supplicium et sanguis
eius effusus est in precium nostre salutis

Gradual (fragmentum)

12TH Century *med.* (fol. 1v)

Arquivo Distrital, Braga, Frag. 243.
Provenance: Unknown.
Parchment in a reasonable state of preservation with marks, creases and perforations; all the margins have been damaged, and the text has been affected in the upper margin; used as binding material; one bifolium; modern notation in Arabic numerals in the upper left margin which cannot be attributed to foliation; the leaf measures 207 × 303 mm; the text block measures 170 × 295 mm; one column; imperceptible prickings; 25 lines (13 of text); no ruling can be distinguished; Carolingian script; zoomorphic and vegetal motifs in the major initials with interlace filling; minor initials alternate in red, black and red and blue; written by a single scribe; Aquitainian notation on a red line, following the ruling of the text block; no *custos.*

General contents: *Sabbato Quatuor Temporum in Quadragesima; Domenica vacat.* (Second Sunday of Lent.)

Leaf shown: 1v
[continuation of the verse: ... ego ad te Domine, fol. 1r]... adiutorio inter mortuos liber traditus sum et non egrediebar Presa *Intret* Communione *Domine Deus meus in te speram libera me* Dome*nica vacat* *R*esponsorium Graduale *Tribulaciones cordis* Off*ertorium Meditabor in mandatis* Communione Intellige *Officium Reminiscere miserationum* Tractus *De necessitabus meis Aliud Officium. Domine dilexi decorem domus et locum* [h]*abitationis glorie tue* Psalmus *Iudica me Domine* *R*esponsorium Graduale *Proba me Domine.*

Detail of fol. 2v

A meticulously written codex, with the genres of the chants indicated in red. The composition of fol. 1v is an essential source for studying the introduction of the Roman liturgy, through the order of Cluny, in the extreme west of the Iberian Peninsula. The folio contains the celebrations of Ember Saturday, in Lent, and the Dominica *vacans* for which the scribe wrote only the notated incipits of the chants. There follows a list of pieces from the Cluniac tradition, also collected in the Missal of Mateus from 1130-1150 and which were in use in the diocese of Braga from the second half of the 12th century. The texts making up this *Aliud Officium,* proposed for celebrating the Dominica *vacans,* of which we only currently preserve those of the introit and gradual (both based on Psalm 25), are the same as those found in the Missal of Mateus (fol. 64r): in the Gradual of St. Michel de Gaillac (fol. 41r-v); in the Gradual of Toulouse (fol. 50r-v) and in the Gradual of St. Aredius (fol. 85r). The Gradual therefore offers a choice of *Aliud Officium* for this particular Sunday.

The aesthetic emphasis given to this office is not typical of most graduals and contrasts with the reserved treatment given to the rite that appears first in that only the initia are written, and it is more typical of the *Dominica vacans* in Lent. On the other hand, it is not surprising that the entire notated text is provided precisely for the liturgical formularies that are less common and more closely associated with one particular tradition. The leaf displayed here contains two decorated initials, a *D* and an *O* (fols. 1v and 2v, respectively), which are artistically and technically quite similar. The initial of *Domine* contains zoomorphic motifs: two fantastic animals, facing each other, their claws resting on the curvature of the letter. The miniature forms part of an irregular polygon with a red and blue background with a trace of yellow. The initial *O* (fol. 2v), in *Oculi* (the first word of the introit for the third Sunday of Lent), is filled with labyrinthine interlace which has unfortunately been damaged.

Bibliography

Bragança 1975, 187-188. Vilares 2001, 2: 46-47.

Marco Daniel Duarte

Intret
Domine deus
Dnica uacat
Tribulationes cordis
Meditabor in mandatis
Intellige
Reminiscere miserationum
De necessitatibus meis
officium
Probame domine

Antiphonary (fragmentum)

12TH CENTURY *EX.* (FOL. 1V)

ARQUIVO DISTRITAL, BRAGA, FRAG. 244.
PROVENANCE: UNKNOWN. ENVIRONS OF THE DIOCESE OF BRAGA.
Parchment in reasonable state of preservation, despite numerous marks, creases and tears, which do not affect the text; used as binding material; one folio; lacks foliation; the leaf measures 305 × 420 mm; the text block measures 245 × 320 mm; one column is justified by a double vertical line on both sides running the entire length of the leaf; prickings cannot be made out (the dotted line in the right margin comes from the stitching for later uses); 26 lines (13 of text); ruled in lead; Carolingian script; alternating initials in red, sepia or red and sepia; written by a single hand; Aquitainian notation on a red-colored line, following the ruling of the text block; consistent use of a *custos*.

General contents: *In natale Sci. Stephani protho martir* (fol. 1r).

Leaf shown: 1v
[Continuation of the antiphon *Surrexerunt autem*] ... *et spiritui qui loquebatur* PSALMUS *Cum invocarem. Amen* VERSUS *Posuisti Domine super Stephanus autem* VERSUS *Surrexerunt autem quidam de signagoga* PRESA *facie* RESPONSORIUM *Surrexerunt quidam de signagoga disputantes cum Stephano* PRESA *et non poterant resistire* VERSUS *Commoverunt itaquem plebem et concunrent* PRESA *et non* RESPONSORIUM *Cum esset plenus Spiritu Sancto beatus Stephanus* PRESA *et Ihesum stantem* VERSUS *Exclamans voce magna dixit ecce video* PRESA *et Ihesum* IN *II*º NOCTURNO ANTIPHONA *Commoverunt plebem seniores* PSALMUS *Verba mea* ANTIPHONA *Videbant omens Stephanum.*

A continuation of the Office of Matins of St. Stephen, celebrated as part of the Christmas Octave. Carefully written codex. There is a fairly large illuminated capital *S* (Stephanus) with zoomorphic motifs and minor botanical detail on a blue background. The spaces between the ends of the *S* have been used to draw a wolf devouring its prey (top) and a plant (bottom). The metaphor refers to the persecution and death of St. Stephen, who according to the Acts of the Apostles—which provide the readings for the Office of St. Stephen—was the first Christian martyr.

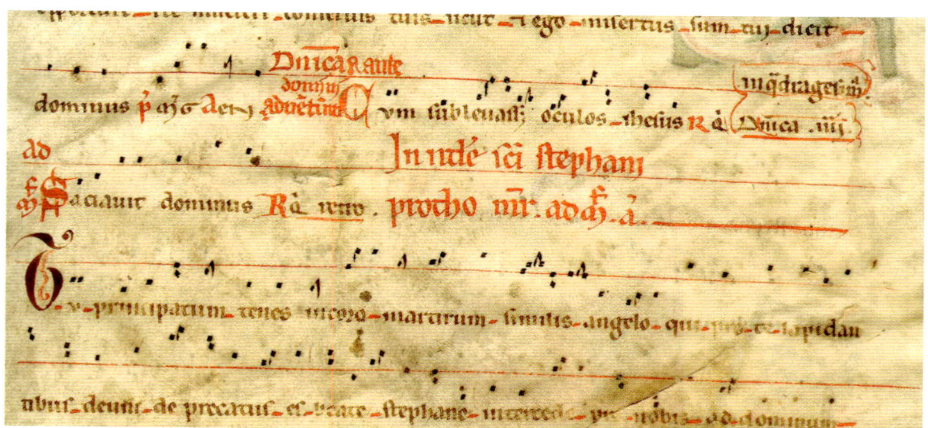

Detail of fol. 1r

BIBLIOGRAPHY

VILARES 2001, 2: 46.

Marco Daniel Duarte

et spiritui qui loquebatur ℟ Cum inuocarem (?) ... ℣ Posuisti domine super

Stephanus autem plenus gratia et fortitudine faciebat

prodigia et signa magna in populo ℣ Surrexerunt autem

quidam de synagoga que appellatur libertinorum et cirenensium disputantes

cum Stephano ℟ Facie ... R Surrexerunt quidam de synagoga disputantes Sancta Com

cum Stephano ℟ Et non poterant resistere sapientie et spiritui qui loquebatur

℣ Commouerunt namque plebem et concurrentes rapuerunt eum et adduxerunt

in concilium ℟ Et non R Cum esset plenus spiritu sancto beatus Stephanus

intendens in celum uidit gloriam dei ℟ Et [illegible] stantem a dextris dei

℣ Et clamans uoce magna dixit ecce uideo celos apertos ℟ Et [illegible] A Com

mouerunt plebem seniores iudeorum et scribe et concurrentes rapuerunt Ste

phanum et duxerunt eum in concilium [illegible] ℟ Verba ma[illegible] A Uidebant

omnes Stephanum qui erant in concilio et intuebantur uultum eius tamquam

Gradual (fragmentum)

12TH Century *ex.* (fol. 2v)

Arquivo Distrital, Braga, Frag. 210.
Provenance: Unknown.
Poorly preserved parchment, with stains, wrinkles perforations, and damage to the text and musical notation due to the trimming of the margins; used as binding material for a volume related to the documentation from São Mamede de Lindoso (Viana do Castelo); one bifolium; lacks foliation; the leaves measure 202 × 321 mm; the text block measures 170 × 277 mm; the text is in two columns; the prickings are not visible; the column on the left has 30 lines (15 of which are text); the column on the right has 30 lines (25 of which are text); traces of lead point ruling are perceptible on some of the leaves; Gothic script; alternating initials in red, black, or red and black, some with modest archaic filigree and little artistic expertise; a single scribe; Aquitainian notation oriented around a red colored line that corresponds to the ruling of the text block; at the beginning of the pieces there are indications of the recitation tones B, F; consistent use of a *custos*.

General contents: Gradual.

Leaf shown: 2v
[Continuation of Mass]
In natale unius martiris
Versus *implebem suam et super sanctos* *Psalmus Benedixisti Domine Aliunde* *Iudicant sancti gentes Psalmus Exultate iusti Aliunde Iustus ut palma florebit* *Psalmus Bonum est Aliumde Iusti epulentur* *Psalmus Exsurgat Deus Aliunde Gloria et honore coronasti... Istus non conturbabitur* *Psalmus Noli emulari.*

After the psalms of the Gradual in the leaf transcribed come the biblical readings that correspond to the mass for the Common Martyrs: the Latin word *Sapientie* corresponds to the Old Testament reading extracted from the Book of Ben Sira *(Liber Sapientiae Iechosuae, Filii Sirach,* also known as *Eclesiasticus liber)* and the New Testament reading is taken from the 2nd Epistle to Timothy. The following leaf (fol. 2r) contains the two *versus alleluiatici*, as is common in the services intended for this celebration.

The leaf has colorful, yet crude, ornamentation in the initials of the liturgical pieces. All of the decorated capitals are several lines high, and the initial I, reiterated four times, is 10 lines high (the beginning of the second column). The fragment contains a note indicating that it was used as binding for the documentation referring to São Mamede de Lindoso, next to which appears the reference "caja 289, no. 6".

Bibliography
Unpublished.

Marco Daniel Duarte

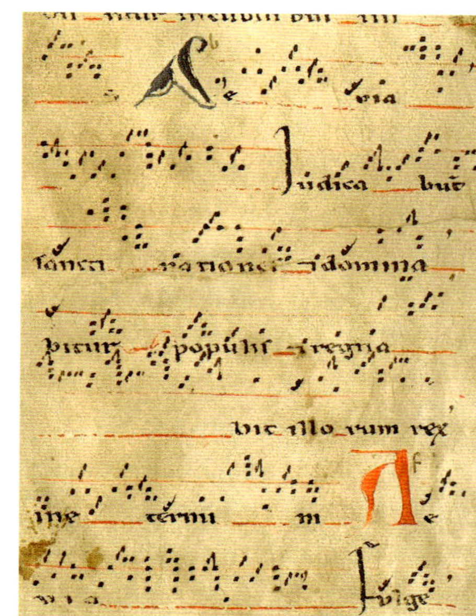

Detail of fol. 1r

implebem suam et super factos ...

meos qui confitentur ad ipsum. p Bn...

dixisti dñe Glā S e a e alłā.

Iudicant sancti gentes et dominantur

populus regnabit dominus deus illorum

in perpetuum. p Exultate iusti. Glā S e a e alł.

Iustus ut palma florebit sicut cedrus

libani multiplicabitur ... eius

in domo dñi in atriis domus dei nri

p Bonum est. Glā S e a e alłum.

Iusti epulentur et exultent in conspectu

dei delectentur in letitia. p Exurgat ds

Gloria et honore. alł. Glā S e a e

coronasti eum et constituisti

eum super opera manuum tuarum

Iustus non conturbabitur quia dominus

firmat manum eius tota die

miseretur et commodat et semen eius in bene

dictione erit meritum conservabi-

tur. p Noli emulari. Glā S e a e ōi.

Presta qs ops ds ut q b. N.

martiris tui natalicia colimus a

cunctis malis imminentibus eius interces-

sione liberemur. p Sapientie.

Beatus uir qui in sapientia morabitur et in

iustitia meditabitur et in sensu

cogitabit circumspectionem dei. Ciba-

bit illum dñs pane uite et intellectus et a-

qua sapientie salutaris potabit illum. Et fir-

mabitur in illo et non flectetur et continebit

illum et non confundetur et exaltabit illum apud

proximos suos. Et in nomine eterno heredita-

bit illum dñs ds nr. Ad thimotheum.

Karissime. Memor esto dnm ihm

xpm resurrexisse a mortuis ex

semine dd secundum euangelium meum in quo

laboro usque ad uincula quasi male

operans. Sed uerbum dei non est alligatum. Ideo

sustineo propter electos. ut et ipsi salutem

consequantur que est in xpo ihu cum gloria celesti.

Evangeliary

12TH CENTURY *EX.* (FOL. 210V)

BIBLIOTECA PÚBLICA MUNICIPAL, PORTO, SANTA CRUZ 76, GENERAL NO. 350.
PROVENANCE: MONASTERY OF SANTA CRUZ, COIMBRA.
Complete codex on white parchment, soiled by use, stitched tears and leaves reconstituted with remnants of parchment; early binding (wooden boards covered in tanned leather); 1 + 226 + 1 folios; modern foliation in pencil in Arabic numerals and in the first quires, in ink, in Roman numerals; there are repetitions in the numbering and incorrect correspondences; dimensions of the codex, 150 × 240 mm; the text block measures 90 × 175 mm; one column; 20 lines; horizontal prickings on the external margins; ruled in lead; Gothic script with notes in Gothic cursive; various initials decorated with latticework, zoomorphic and vegetal motifs and interlace in red black, green, red, yellow and blue inks; some leaves with Aquitainian notation oriented around the line following the ruling of the text block: fols. 75v, 88r, 96v, 97r, 104r, 104v, 105r, 210v, 225r-226v; consistent use of a *custos*.

General content: Evangeliary for the annual liturgical cycle.

Leaf displayed: 210v
IN NATIVITATE SANCTE MARIE
INICIUM SANCTI EVANGELII SECUNDUM MATHEUM

Liber generationis Ihesu Christi filii David filii Abraham. Abraham genuit Isaac Ysaac autem genuit Iacob…

The leaf displayed contains the Gospel reading for the Mass of the Feast of the Nativity of the Virgin Mary. The presentation of the Gospel reading and the three first lines, corresponding to the genealogy of Jesus Christ up to the patriarch Jacob, are notated.

The melody is notated only for the first verses. This contrasts with Spanish examples, where the notation is generally applied to the entire text.

Until recently, Aquitainian notation in manuscripts from Portugal was thought to have a morphology and identity of its own, differentiating it from the Aquitainian notation found in codices from elsewhere on the Iberian Peninsula and also dependent on French models (Corbin). However, this thesis has recently been challenged (Alvarenga) by a comparative analysis of a corpus of five Portuguese codices dated between the end of the 12th century and the beginning of the 14th. The debunking of the notion of "Portuguese notation" is supported by an analysis of the morphology of the various neumatic elements, with special attention to the particular form of of the inclined *punctum* signifying a semitone.

BIBLIOGRAPHY

BIBLIOTECA PÚBLICA MUNICIPAL DO PORTO 1879, 34. AVÉ-MARIA 1932, 10: 67-68. MADAHIL 1942, 49. CORBIN 1952b, 192-193, 251. COLETTE 1987. MIRANDA 1996, 244 AND SUBSQ. NASCIMIENTO AND MEIRINHOS 1997, 321-322. ALVARENGA 2005.

Marco Daniel Duarte
Susana Zapke

Detail of fol. 210v. Initial *L*

Nichil optimum Egidij abbatis. xvj

Qui uos audit Justi epi. xviij

Nolite arbitrari Marcelli mr. Sign xxiiij

uult Eucherij epi. Sunt lubi xvij

IN NATIVITATE sce Marie

Jnicium sci euglij secdm matheum

Liber generationis ihesu xpi.

.I.

filij dauid filij abraham. Abra

ham genuit isaac. Ysaac autem genuit iacob. Jacob aut. genuit iudam et fris eius. Judas autem genuit phares et zaram de thamar. Phares aut. genuit esrom. Esrom aut. genuit aram. Aram aut. genuit aminadab. Aminadab aut. genuit naason. Naason

Pontifical

12TH CENTURY *EX.* (FOL. 24V)

BIBLIOTECA PÚBLICA MUNICIPAL, PORTO. SANTA CRUZ 83, GENERAL NO. 1.134.
PROVENANCE: MONASTERY OF SANTA CRUZ, COIMBRA.
Codex with restored binding; two types of parchment of different thickness; 145 leaves; three types of foliation, with inconsistencies: numbering in ink in Arabic numerals, from the beginning of the 19th century, annotated by José d'Ave-Maria (last librarian of the Monastery of Santa Cruz), other recent numbering in Arabic numerals in pencil on fols. 1-135, and a third, in ink, on the last folios of the codex (fols. 136-145); dimensions, 155 × 224 mm; the text block measures 100 × 175 mm; one column is justified with a vertical line on both sides running the entire length of the leaf; 22 lines (11 of text); horizontal prickings on the external margins; vertical prickings on the top and bottom of the folio; ruled in drypoint; Gothicizing Carolingian script; various initials decorated in red; written by a single scribe; multiple leaves with Aquitainian notation on a line following the ruling of the text block; consistent use of a *custos*.

General contents: Pontifical for the liturgical use by the Bishop, probably from the Cathedral of Braga. Reveals influences from southern France. Contains some nonliturgical documents at the end of the codex: *Divisio Wambae* [ms. *Chronologia Regum Gothorum ab Athanarico ad Wambam* (fol. 142r-v), *Epistula Regi Alfonso III et cunctis episcopis*, era DCCCLVIII (fol. 143r) and *Epistula Regi Alfonso III*, era DCCCL (fol. 143r-v), both letters from Pope John VIII (872-882) and *Privilegium Ovetensis Ecclesiae* (fols. 143v-145r)].

Leaf shown: 24v
[Continuation of the hymn *Redemptor, sume carmen temet concinentium*. Procession of the Holy Oils. Holy Thursday chrismal mass.]
... una spes mortalium audi voces proferentum donum pacis premium. VERSUS *Arbor feta alma luce hoc sacrandum* VERSUS *Stans ad aram Versus Consecrare tu dignare* VERSUS *Ut novetur* VERSUS *Lota mente sacro* VERSUS *Corde natus ex parentis* VERSUS *Sit.*

The text contains errors in the transcription of the hymn, such as *laudem* instead of *lucem* (line 22) and *consorcio* instead of *consortibus* (ibid.).

There are more pontificals than any other type of liturgical document preserved in Portugal, with a total of five extant manuscripts: two from the 12th century, two from the 13th century and one from the 15th century. In each case, the liturgical contents are arranged differently and all follow the Southern French model of pontifical rather than the Roman one. The Pontifical of Braga, ms. 1.134, is considered to be the one of greatest interest. Very probably copied for the Archbishop of Braga, it contains the celebration of three local saints: St. Martin, St. Fructuosus and St. Gerald, as well as a specific reference to the diocese of Braga in the Bishop's consecration rite. Together with the Missal of Mateus, the 12th century Braga Pontifical is one of the most representative sources with the greatest impact on the configuration of the Braga rite. Its association with Toulouse has been partially demonstrated, although it also contains features that are characteristic of the Norman tradition, revealing a complex and fascinating scenario of liturgical interactions in the see of Braga (Bragança 1977).

However, the Braga Pontifical is above all exceptional from a historical perspective; it is unique in the West in terms of the original structure and the rites it contains.

Detail of fol. 24v

BIBLIOGRAPHY

BIBLIOTECA PÚBLICA MUNICIPAL DO PORTO 1879, 37. AVÉ-MARIA 1932, 10: 70-72. MADAHIL 1942, 51. DAVID 1947, 539-554. CORBIN 1952b, 188. BRAGANÇA 1977, 309-398. COLETTE 1987. BRAGANÇA 1994, 173-194. SANTO ANTÓNIO EM SANTA CRUZ 1995, 39. NASCIMIENTO AND MEIRINHOS 1997, 337-339. ALVARENGA 2005.

Marco Daniel Duarte

una spes mortalium audi uoces proferentium donum pacis

premium V. Arbor feta alma luce hoc sacrandum protulit

fert hoc prona presens turba saluatori seculi V. Stans ad

aram immo supplex infulatus pontifex debitum persoluit

omne consecrando crismate V. Consecrare tu dignare rex per-

hennis patrie hoc oliuum signum uiuum iura contra demonum

V. Ut nouetur sexus omnis unctione crismatis ut medetur sau-

ciata dignitatis gloria V. Lota mente sacro fonte aufugan-

tur crimina uncta fronte sacro sancto influunt ut cris-

mate V. Corde natus ex parentis aluum implens uirginis

presta laudem claude mortem crismatis consorcio V. Sit

Breviary (fragmentum)

1176-1200 (FOL. 1R)

ARQUIVO DISTRITAL, AVEIRO. FRAGS. W./O. S. [BOOK OF PARISH RECORDS, NO. 1, 1570-1573].
PROVENANCE: PARISH CHURCH OF SAN MIGUEL DE AVEIRO (?).
Parchment in a poor state of preservation, with stains, perforations, scratches and tearing in the margins, that make it impossible to read the entire text; it was used to bind a book of baptisms dated between 1570 and 1573; one leaf; it has no foliation; the leaf measures 445 × 280 mm; the text block measures 320 × 224 mm; two columns; prickings no longer visible; 38 lines (20 with text) for the left column; 50 lines (46 with text) for the right column; the ruling cannot be seen; Carolingian script in two sizes, smaller for the notated chants; initials in alternating red and black, illuminated initials letters in yellow, red and green; written by a single scribe; Aquitainian notation; consistent use of a *custos.*

General contents: Breviary; Saturday and Sunday offices *infra octavam Nativitatis.*

Leaf shown: 1r
... vidimus gloriam eius gloriam quasi unigeniti a Patre ANTIPHONA *Christus Deus noster* ANTIPHONA *Virgo verbo concepit* ANTIPHONA *Virgo sacra* [et] *virilis ignara* ANTIPHONA *Ecce iam venit plenitudo* ANTIPHONA *Virgo Dei genitrix* ANTIPHONA *Salus eterna mundo apparuit* ANTIPHONA *Ecce de quo Ihoannes.* *HYM*NUS *Christe redemptor.* *DOMENICA INFRA* O*CTA*BAS. *R*ESPONSORIUM *Angelus ad pastores.*

The fragment was used to bind parish documents or notarial acts, which can be seen in the folds, accretions and scratches on the parchment. It formed part of a beautiful example of the Franco-Roman rite, although its style is typical of a rural center, and is a copy of a model that doubtless came from the South of France. The parchment has no ruling or reference line for the notation, which is nevertheless perfectly diastematic. In the part with the Office of Lauds, the leaf contains two illuminated capital letters: a smaller *N*, with vegetal motifs and a more developed *A*, with a zoomorphic motif. The larger initial is for the responsory for the Sunday office after the Christmas Octave and seems to have been left unfinished, judging from the blank spaces that have not been painted.

BIBLIOGRAPHY

VILARES 2001, 2: 24.

Marco Daniel Duarte

Detail of fol. 1v

a dñi in gloriam eius gloriam quasi unigeniti

a patre. S a A Spiritus deus noster in quo diuinitatis est plenitudo carnis nostre infirma suscipiens nobis natus est homo a evia S a e.

A Virgo uerbo concepit uirgo permansit uirgo peperit regem omnium regum. S a A Virgo sacra uirilis ignara consorcii spiritu sancto fecundata ineffabiliter mundi parturiuit auctorem. S a A Ecce iam uenit plenitudo temporis in quo misit deus filium suum in terris. S a A Virgo dei genitrix quem totus non capit or[illegible] sa se ciausis uiscera factus homo uera fides genuit purgauit crimina [illegible] di et tibi uirginitas inuiolata permanet. S a.

A Salus eterna mundo apparuit et hominem perditum ad celestia regna reuocauit. S a.

A Ecce de quo iohannes dixit xpistus natus est in israhel et regni eius non erit finis. S a

Sbbo infra octab cantantur oraña uespa sic in aliis diebus. psalmi scilicet atque uersus. et ad magnificat an.

laudate

S Benedictus qui uenit [illegible] loquebantur

Omnipotens sempiterne deus dirige actus nostros in beneplacito tuo ut in nomine dilecti filii tui mereamur bonis operibus habundare. Qui tecum. S Xps natus est nobis uenite

Hym Xpe redemptor. Congruentes. Beatus uir. Quare fremuerunt. Domine quid. Domine ne in furore. Gla patri. Domine deus meus. Domine dominus noster. In domino confido. Gla patri. Saluum me fac. Dixit insipiens. Domine quis habitabit. V. Tanquam sponsus.

Natiuitatem Dnica infra Oct dñi nostri ihu xpi secundum carnem [illegible] ita euangelista aptissime demonstrat. ut hostenderet eum ex spiritu sancto et maria uirgine natum propter hereticorum astuciam qui negant dñm hominem suscepisse. Sed ideo dñs noster uirginem sibi requisiuit ospicium habitandi ut nobis ostenderet in casto corpore dñm habitare debere. Ad hoc enim deus suscepit hominem in se. ut et nos suscipiamur in nobis sicut ipse dixit. Manete in me et ego in uobis. O sacramentum et celeste misterium in natiuitate dñi. Concepit uirgo ante quam sponsum habeat. parit autem quam nubat. Et quod ad laudem pertinet nomini dñi. et mater et uirgo peperit. uirgo post partum illibata permansit. Quem cum portare timuit cui pareret adorauit. Quem cum pepisset minor erat mater quam filius. R

Angelus ad pastores ait annuncio uobis gaudium magnum quod erit omni

Breviary

11TH CENTURY *EX.* (FOL. 294R)

BRITISH LIBRARY, LONDON, ADD. MS. 30849.

PROVENANCE: MONASTERY OF SANTO DOMINGO DE SILOS (BURGOS), ALTHOUGH IT WAS NOT WRITTEN THERE.

Well-prepared parchment of good quality; 15th century binding in leather over boards; comprises 1 + 308 + 1 leaves, foliated in the upper right-hand margin in the 18th century, but it begins on fol. 5; corrected in pencil; the leaves measure 324 × 208 mm; the writing frame measures 236 × 152 mm; two columns (fols. 5-83, 85-87, 97-142, 183-231, 240-274, 276-308), delimited by two vertical lines on the edges and three in the intercolumn, and one column (fols. 84, 88-96, 143-182, 232-239), delimited by a double vertical line on all sides; the vertical prickings are visible on the edge; the horizontal prickings run along the inner and outer margins; the number of lines varies between 29 and 34; ruled in drypoint leaf by leaf on the hair side; consistent and well-traced Carolingian minuscule, yet it has many Visigothic minuscule characteristics in the ductus, ligatures, and abbreviations; a single scribe copied the entire manuscript, except the additions; Aquitainian notation; a calendar precedes the breviary (fols. 1-4), also by a 12th century scribe, but it nevertheless belongs to a missal that follows the Roman monastic cursus; it must have been added to the codex in a modern period. The breviary must have been written for a cathedral or collegiate church by a Spanish scribe had not yet forgotten his training in the Visigothic script, even though he was able to write a consistent Carolingian script of high quality. A valuable piece of information for the chronology of the codex appears on fol. 232r; the leaf's recto seems to have been scraped for rewriting, in Carolingian minuscule without Visigothic influences, the third nocturn of Matins for the 22nd Sunday after Pentecost; the same scribe, rather carelessly, wrote an *annus currens:* "MCa XXa IIIIa"; because it is in the feminine, it is logical to conclude that it refers to an era, therefore corresponding to the year 1086; if the leaf was rewritten that year, the manuscript must have been existed before that date.

General contents: A Roman canonical breviary that, in its present state, comprises the period from the first Sunday of Advent until the office of the Dedication of a Church.

Leaf shown: 294r
Beatus uir qui in sapientia. CAPITULUM. RESPONSORIUM. *Sanctus Uincencius. Deus tuorum.* *VINCENTII. Sacram huius diei sollempnitatem humili celebremus deuotione qua inuictus Christi martir Uincencius tiranno deuicto insignem uictorie palmam celo gaudens intulit. Sevovae. Adesto* Domine *supplicationibus...* *IN I NOC*TURNO. ANTIPHONA. *Sanctus Uincentius a pueritie literarum traditus, superna sibi prouidente clementia, gemina sciencia efficacissime claruit.* Beatus *uir ae.* ANTIPHONA. *Sanctitate quoque insignis diaconi arce suscepta, uices pontifices diligenter exequebantur.* Quare. ANTIPHONA. *Valerius igitur episcopus et leuita Uincentius spe fruendi uictoria diuinitus subnixi in confessione deitatis*

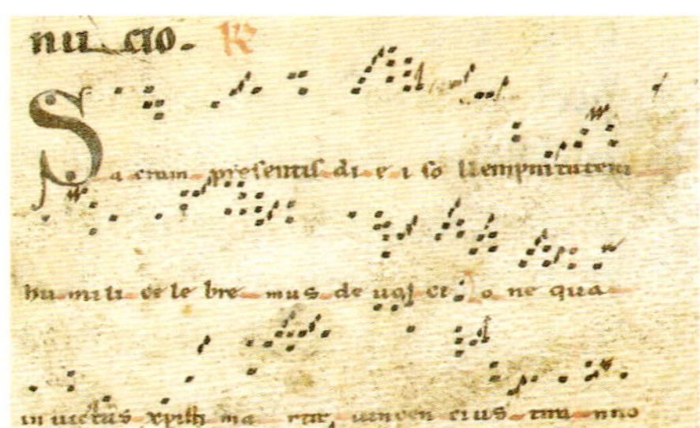

Detail of fol. 294r

alacriter cucurrerunt. Domine *quid multipli.* Versus. *Posuisti.* Lectio *I. Cvm igitur...* RESPONSORIUM. *Sacram presentis diei sollempnitatem humili celebremus deuocione qua inuictus Christi martir Uincencius tiranno deuicto insigne uictorie palmam celo gaudens intulit.* Versus. *Peracto passionis sue uenerando triumpho angelorum ciuibus commitatur.* Lectio *II. Ad Datianus iudex sanctos Dei primo Ualeriani sub carce.*

The breviary was prepared to receive musical notation that was never added.

The music it contains belongs to an appendix added around the middle of the 12th century in Carolingian script and Aquitainian notation with the offices and St. Vincent, martyr, Common of Evangelists, Common of Virgins, St. Mary Magdalen and the Invention of the Holy Cross. The pieces that were supposed to be notated are written in smaller letters, but there is also a blank line to provide more space for the neumes. The offices follow the Roman canonical schema, as does the rest of the breviary. The calendar on fols. 1-4, also by a 12th century scribe, nevertheless belongs to the Roman monastic *ordo*.

BIBLIOGRAPHY

WALKER 1998, 49 *ET PASSIM*. VEZIN 2003, 211-222.

Miguel C. Vivancos

Beatus uir qui in sapientia. Cpl.

R. Sanctus uincencius. Deus tuorum. Vicentii.

Sacratam huius diei sollempnitatem humili celebremus deuotione qua inuictus Christi martir Vincencius tiranno deuicto insignem uictorie palmam celo gaudens intulit. Euouae.

Adesto domine supplicationibus nostris omnipotens deus ut qui ex iniquitate nostra reos nos esse cognoscimus beati uincentii martiris tui intercessione liberemur. P. In .i. noc. turno

a. Sanctus uincentius apuerície litterarum tradi tus superna sibi prouidente clementia gemina sciencia efficacissime claruit. Ps. Beatus uir. a. Sanctitate quoque insignis diaconi arce suscepta uices pontifices diligenter exequebantur. a. Valerius igitur episcopus et leuita uincentius spe fruendi uictoria diuinitus subnixi in confessione deitatis alacriter cucurrerunt. Domine quid multiplicati. v. Posuisti. Lc. i.

Cum igitur apud cesaraugustam ciuitatem ut multorum sinceritas et signata ueritatis uerba testantur: datiano quodam preside gentili et sacrilego adonante et principibus suis. diocleciano et maximiano seuiendi in christianos sorte occasio cecidisset. et ei oblatum diu prophane crudelitatis rabies aspiraret: episcopos ac presbiteros ceterosque sacri ordinis ministros spiritu nequitie exagitatus rapi precepit. Protinus ergo ualerius episcopus et uincentius archidiaconus fidei soliditate et spe fruendi uictoria subnixi. in confessionem deitatis alacriter cucurrerunt. Tanto namque feliciores se esse predixi futuros credentes quanto acriora tormentorum supplicia pia longanimitate certassent euincere. Unde certaminis ac penarum dilatio remunerationis eius uidebatur dispendium.

R. Sacratam presentis diei sollempnitatem humiliter celebremus deuotione qua inuictus christi martir uincencius tiranno deuicto insigne uictorie palmam celo gaudens intulit. V. Per acta passionis sue ueneranda triumpha angelorum ciuibus commiscetur.

Lc. ii.

Adductis datianus iudex sanctis dei primo ualerium sub carce

Bibliography of the Catalog of Manuscripts

L'Abat Oliba i el seu temps: exposició documental de manuscrits i objectes. Barcelona: Archivo de la Corona de Aragón, 1971.

ALBAREDA, Anselm M. "Manuscrits de la biblioteca de Montserrat". *Analecta Montserratensia* 1 (1917): 3-99.

ALBAROSA, Nino, Heinrich RUMPHORST, and Alberto TURCO, eds. *Il cod. Paris Bibliothèque Nationale de France Lat. 776 sec. XI Graduale di Gaillac*. Paduva: La Linea Editrice, 2002 (Assoziazione Internazionale Studi di Canto Gregoriano: Codices Gregoriani 3).

ALTÉS I AGUILÓ, Francesc Xavier. "El llibre místic de Sant Romà de les Bons (Andorra) (Biblioteca de la Abadía de Montserrat, ms. 72)". *Miscel·lània Litúrgica Catalana* 13 (2005): 47-277.

ALTISENT, Joan Baptista. "Pontifical de Roda (siglo XI): notes i transcripció". *Analecta Sacra Tarraconensia* 2 (1926): 533-551.

ALTURO I PERUCHO, Jesús. "La Glossa VI del manuscrit 74 de Ripoll: un epítom isidorià incorporat al *Liber glossarum*". *Faventia* 18, no. 2 (1996): 67-91.

—. "La cultura literaria". In Pere de Palol, dir. *Del romà al romànic: història, art i cultura de la Tarraconense mediterrània entre els segles IV i X*. Barcelona: Enciclopèdia Catalana, 1999, 431-434.

ALVARENGA, João Pedro d'. "A representação do meio-tom nos manuscritos litúrgicos medievais portugueses, ou o mito da 'notação portuguesa'". In João Pedro d'Alvarenga and Manuel Pedro Ferreira, eds. *Actas do Colóquio Internacional Monodia sacra medieval. Lisboa-Évora, 2-5 de Junho, 2005*. (In press.)

AMIET, Robert. "Les livres liturgiques et le calendrier du diocèse d'Elne". In *Liturgie et musique (IXᵉ-XIVᵉ s.)*. Toulouse: Privat, 1982, 139-154 (Collection d'Histoire religieuse du langue doc au XIIIᵉ et au début du XIVᵉ siècles: Cahiers de Fanjeaux 17).

Andorra Romànica. Andorra: Patrimoni Artístic Nacional y Barcelona: Fundació Enciclopèdia Catalana, 1989.

ANDRÉS, A. "La Biblia de Cardeña". *Boletín de la Real Academia de la Historia* 60 (1912): 101-164.

ANGLÈS, Higini. "Die mehrstimmige Musik in Spanien vor dem XV Jahrhundert". In *Beethoven-Zentenarfeier: Internationaler Musikhistorischer Kongress*. Vienna: Universal Edition, 1927, 158-163.

—. "La música a veus anterior al segle XV dins l'Espanya". *Revista Musical Catalana* 24 (1927): 138-144.

—. *El còdex musical de Las Huelgas: música a veus dels segles XIII-XIV.* 3 vols. Barcelona: Biblioteca de Cataluña, 1931.

—. "La musique en Catalogne à l'époque romane. L'école de Ripoll". In *La Catalogne à l'époque romane. Conférences faites à la Sorbonne en 1930*. Paris: Librairie Ernest Leroux, 1932, 157-179 (Université de Paris. Institut d'Art et d'Archéologie-Bibliothèque d'Art Catalan. Fondation Cambó 2).

—. *La música a Catalunya fins al segle XIII*. Barcelona: Biblioteca de Cataluña, 1935.

—. "La música medieval en Toledo hasta el siglo XI". In *Gesammelte Aufsätze zur Kulturgeschichte Spaniens*. Münster: Aschendorff, 1938, 1-68 (Spanische Forschungen der Görresgesellschaft: 1/2).

—. *La música española desde la Edad Media hasta nuestros días. Catálogo de la Exposición Histórica celebrada en conmemoración del primer centenario del nacimiento de Felipe Pedrell*. Barcelona: Biblioteca Central, 1941.

—. *Historia de la música medieval en Navarra*. Pamplona: Institución Príncipe de Viana, 1970.

—. "El *Breviarium de Musica* del Monjo Oliva (segle XI)". In José López-Calo, ed. *Hygini Angles: Scripta Musicologica*. Rome: Edizioni de Storia e Letteratura, 1976. Vol. 3: 1401-1411.

ANGLÈS, Higinio, and José SUBIRÁ. *Catálogo musical de la Biblioteca Nacional de Madrid.* Vol. 1, *Manuscritos*. Barcelona: Instituto Español de Musicología, CSIC, 1946.

Antifonario visigótico mozárabe de la Catedral de León. Facsimile edition. Vol. 1, Barcelona: Centro de Estudios e Investigación San Isidoro (CSIC-CECEL), 1959; vol. 2, Madrid: CSIC, Instituto P. Enrique Flórez, 1953-1954 (Monumenta Hispaniae Sacra: Serie Litúrgica 5, no. 2. Facsímiles musicales 1).

Antiphonale hispaniae vetus (s. X-XI). Facsimile edition. Zaragoza: Institución Fernando el Católico, 1986. ANTOLÍN, Guillermo. *Catálogo de los códices latinos de la Real Biblioteca de El Escorial.* 5 vols. Madrid: Imprenta Helénica, 1910-1923.

ARCO Y GARAY, Ricardo. "El Archivo de la Catedral de Huesca". *Revista de Archivos, Bibliotecas y Museos* 25 (1911): 294-301.

—. "El Monasterio de Santa Cruz de la Serós". *Linajes de Aragón* 4 (1913): 431-455.

—. "Archivos históricos del Alto Aragón". *Universidad* 7 (1929): 485-533.

El arte románico: exposición organizada por el Gobierno Español bajo los auspicios del Consejo de Europa (Barcelona-Santiago de Compostela, 10 julio a 10 octubre 1961). Barcelona: Ministerio de Asuntos Exteriores, Dirección General de Relaciones Culturales, 1961.

ARTILES RODRÍGUEZ, José. "El códice visigótico de Álvaro de Córdoba". *Revista de Archivos, Bibliotecas y Museos* 9 (1932): 201-291.

ASCASO, M. V. "Un ritual litúrgico alto-medieval: el Prosarium-Troparium de la Catedral de Huesca". In *Memoria de licenciatura*. Zaragoza: Faculty of Philosophy and Letters of the University of Zaragoza, 1986.

ASENSIO, Juan Carlos. "Las antífonas *Ad lotionem pedum* en la antigua liturgia hispana". *Glosas Silenses* 6 (1991): 35-42.

—. *El canto gregoriano: historia, liturgia, forma*. Madrid: Alianza, 2003.

AVÉ-MARIA, José de. *Bibliotheca Manuscripta Monasterii S. Crucis Colimbricensis*. In A. G. da Rocha Madahil, ed. "Os códices de Santa Cruz de Coimbra". *Boletim da Biblioteca da Universidade de Coimbra* 8 (1927): 379-420; 9 (1928): 192-229, 352-383; 10 (1932): 55-105; 11 (1933): 50-96.

AVRIL, François, Jean-Pierre ANIEL, Mireille MENTRÉ, Alix SAULNIER, and Yolanta ZAŁUSKA. *Manuscrits enluminés de la péninsule ibérique*. Paris: Bibliothèque Nationale de France, 1982.

AVRIL, François, Léo BARBE, Michel BARRÈRE, et al. *De Toulouse à Tripoli: la puissance toulousaine au XIIe siècle, 1080-1208: [Catalogue de l'exposition, Toulouse] Musée des Augustins, 6 janvier-20 mars 1989.* Toulouse: Musée des Augustins, 1989.

BANGO TORVISO, Isidro Gonzalo, dir. *Maravillas de la España medieval: tesoro sagrado y monarquía. Catálogo de la exposición Real Colegiata de San Isidoro, León, 18 de diciembre de 2000 al 28 de febrero de 2001.* Vol. 1, *Estudios y catálogo.* Valladolid: Junta de Castilla y León, Caja España, 2001.

—, dir. *Sancho el Mayor y sus herederos: el linaje que europeizó los reinos hispanos.* (Exhibition catalog.) 2 vols. Pamplona: Fundación para la Conservación del Patrimonio Histórico de Navarra, 2006.

BANNISTER, Nenry Marriott. "Un tropaire-prosier de Moissac". *Revue historique de littérature religieuse* 8 (1903): 554-593.

BARRIGA, Josep Romà. "La consagración episcopal en el Pontifical de Roda". *Analecta Sacra Tarraconensia* 38 (1965): 3-58.

—. "El ritu del baptisme al Pontifical de Roda (Osca)". *II Congrès Litúrgic de Montserrat*. Montserrat: Abbey of Montserrat, 1967. Vol. 3: 205-224.

—. *El Sacramentari, Ritual i Pontifical de Roda*. Lleida: Cátedra de Cultura Catalana Samuel Gili i Gaya, Institut d'Estudis Ilerdencs, 1974.

—. *El Sacramentari, Ritual i Pontifical de Roda (Cod. 16 de l'Arxiu de la Catedral de Lleida, c. 1000).* Barcelona: Fundació Salvador Vives Casajuana, 1975.

—. "El manuscrit 18 de l'Arxiu de la Catedral de Lleida: *Leccionari*, per a l'ofici, del segle XI, provinent de Roda". *Miscel·lània Litúrgica Catalana* 1 (1978): 11-41.

Beer, Rudolf. *Die Handschriftenschätze des Klosters Santa Maria de Ripoll.* Vienna: Alfred Hölder, 1907-1908 [Sitzungsberichte der Kais. Akademie der Wissenschaften in Wien: Philosophisch-Historische Klasse 155/3 (part 1) and 158/2 (part 2)].

— *Los manuscrits del Monastir de Santa María de Ripoll.* Barcelona: Casa de Caritat, 1910.

Bellavista, Joan. "L'Antifoner de la Missa de l'església de Sant Pere d'Àger (M. 1147 de la Biblioteca de Catalunya a Barcelona)". *Revista Catalana de Teologia* 1 (1976): 427-452.

—. "Un còdex litúrgic del segle dotzè procedent de Sant Romà de les Bons". *Quaderns d'Estudis Andorrans* 1 (1976): 29-38.

—. "L'Antifoner de la Missa de Sant Pere d'Àger: el santoral (M. 1147 de la Biblioteca de Catalunya a Barcelona)". *Revista Catalana de Teologia* 2, no. 1 (1977): 189-232.

—. *L'Antifoner de missa de Sant Romà de les Bons.* Andorra: Casal i Vall, 1979 (*Monumenta Andorrana:* 6).

—. "La litúrgia a Catalunya en els segles de transició de l'Alta a la Baixa Edat Mitjana". *Revista Catalana de Teologia* 6, no. 1 (1981): 127-156.

Bernadó, Màrius. "La cultura musical i els espectacles escènics". In Pere de Palol, dir. *Del romà al romànic: Història, art i cultura de la Tarraconense mediterrània entre els segles IV i X.* Barcelona: Enciclopèdia Catalana, 1999, 450-453.

Blume, Clemens, and Henry Marriott Bannister, eds. *Analecta hymnica medii aevi XLIX, Tropi Graduales. Tropen des Missale im Mittelalter. II. Tropen zum Proprium Missae.* Leipzig: O. R. Reisland, 1906.

—. *Analecta hymnica medii aevi XLVII, Tropi Graduales. Tropen des Missale im Mittelalter. I. Tropen zum Ordinarium Missae.* Leipzig: O. R. Reisland, 1905.

Bofarull, Próspero de. "Catálogo de los códices manuscritos... pertenecientes al suprimido monasterio de... Ripoll (1823)". Fernando Valls y Taverner, ed. "Códices manuscritos de Ripoll". *Revista de Archivos, Bibliotecas y Museos* 35 (1931): 5-15 and 140-175.

Bohigas, Pedro. *La ilustración y la decoración del libro manuscrito en Cataluña: contribución al estudio de la historia de la miniatura catalana.* 3 vols. Barcelona: Asociación de Bibliófilos de Barcelona, 1960.

Bower, Calvin M. "Boethius' *De institutione Musica.* A Handlist of Manuscripts". *Scriptorium* 42 (1988): 205-251.

Boylan, Ann. "The Library at Santo Domingo de Silos and its Catalogues (XIth-XVIIIth centuries)". *Revue Mabillon* New Series 3, 64 (1992): 59-102, parts 60-62, 71, 78-79 and 82.

Boynton, Susan. "Eleventh-Century Continental Hymnaries Containing Latin Glosses". *Scriptorium* 53 (1999): 200-251.

—. "Glosses on the Office Hymns in Eleventh-Century Continental Hymnaries". *The Journal of Medieval Latin* 11 (2001): 1-26.

—. "A Lost Mozarabic Liturgical Manuscript Rediscovered: New York, Hispanic Society of America, B2916, olim Toledo, BC, 33.2". *Traditio* 57 (2002): 189-219.

—. "Orality, Literacy, and the Early Notation of the Office Hymns". *Journal of the American Musicological Society* 56 (2003): 99-168.

—. "The Didactic Function and Context of Eleventh-Century Glossed Hymnaries". In Andreas Haug, Christoph März and Lorenz Welker, eds. *Der Lateinische Hymnus im Mittelalter: Überlieferung-Ästhetik-Ausstrahlung.* Kassel: Bärenreiter, 2004, 301-329 (Monumenta Monodica Medii Aevi: Subsidia 4).

Bragança, Joaquim O. "Pontifical de Braga do século XII". *Didaskalia* 7 (1977): 309-398.

—. "A sagração dos reis portugueses". *Didaskalia* 24 (1994): 173-194.

—, ed. *Missal de Mateus (Manuscrito 1000 da Biblioteca Pública e Arquivo Distrital de Braga).* Lisbon: Fundaçao Calouste Gulbenkian, 1975.

Brockett, Clyde W. *Antiphons, Reponsories and other Chants of the Mozarabic Rite.* Brooklyn, New York: Institute of Mediæval Music, 1968 (Musicological Studies: 15).

Brou, Louis. "Un nouvel homiliare en écriture wisigothique. Le codex Sheffield "Ruskin Museum" 7". *Hispania Sacra* 2, no. 3 (1949): 147-191.

—. "Séquences et tropes dans la liturgie mozarabe". *Hispania Sacra* 4, no. 7 (1951): 1-15.

—. "Fragments d'un antiphonaire mozarabe du monastère de San Juan de la Peña". *Hispania Sacra* 5, no. 9 (1952): 35-65.

—. "Notes de paléographie musicale mozarabe". *Anuario Musical* 7 (1952): 51-76.
—. "Le joyau des antiphonaires latins". *Archivos Leoneses* 8, no. 5 (1954): 7-114.
—. "Notes de paléographie musicale mozarabe". *Anuario Musical* 10 (1955): 23-44.
—. "Fragments d'un antiphonaire mozarabe du monastère de San Juan de la Peña". In *Antiphonale hispaniae vetus (s. x-xi)*. Facsimile edition. Zaragoza: Institución Fernando el Católico, 1986, 53-62.
Calle González, Benjamín. *Catálogo de música y documentos musicales del Archivo Catedral de Lérida.* Lleida: Dilagro, 1984.
Canal, José de la. *España Sagrada.* Vol. 46, *De las Santas Iglesias de Lérida, Roda y Barbastro en su estado antiguo.* Madrid: Imprenta de los Herederos de D. José del Collado, 1836.Castillón, Francisco. "Catálogo del de Lleida. Fondos de Roda de Isábena". *Aragonia Sacra* 9 (1994): 133-192.
Castiñeiras, Manuel A. "Ripoll i les relacions culturals i artístiques de la Catalunya altmedieval". In Pere de Palol, dir. *Del romà al romànic: Història, art i cultura de la Tarraconense mediterrània entre els segles iv i x.* Barcelona: Enciclopèdia Catalana, 1999, 435-442.
Castro, Eva, ed. "Le long chemin de Moissac a S. Millán (Le troparium de la Real Acad. Hist., Aemil 51)". In Claudio Leonardi and Enrico Menesto, eds. *La tradizione dei tropi liturgici. Atti dei convegni sui tropi liturgici. Parigi (15-19 ottobre 1985)-Perugia (2-5 settembre 1987) organizzati dal Corpus Troporum sotto l'egida dell'European Science Foundation.* Spoleto: Centro italiano di studi sull'alto medioevo, 1990, 243-263 (Biblioteca del Centro per il collegamento degli studi medievali e umanistici nell'Università di Perugia: 3).
—. *Tropos y troparios hispánicos.* Santiago de Compostela: University of Santiago de Compostela, 1991.
—. *Teatro medieval.* Vol. 1, *El drama litúrgico.* Barcelona: Crítica, 1997.
Catalogue of the reserved and most valuable portion of the Libri collection, containing one of the most extraordinary assemblages of ancient manuscripts and printed books ever submitted for sale. London: Bernard Quaritch, 1862.
Chevalier, Ulysse. *Repertorium Hymnologicum. Catalogue des chants, hymnes, proses, sequences, tropes en usage dans l'Eglise latine depuis les origines jusqu'à nos jours.* 6 vols. Louvain-Brussels: Polleumis and Centerick, 1892-1921.*RH*
Clarck, Charles Upson. "Collectanea Hispanica". *Transactions of the Connecticut Academy of Arts and Sciences* 24 (1920): 1-243 and 70 illus.
Clugnet, L., E. Blochet, I. Guido, H. Hyvernat, F. Nau, and F. M. E. Pereira. *Vie et office de Sainte Marine. Textes latins, grecs, coptes, arabes, syriaques, éthiopiens, haut-allemand, bas-allemand et francais.* Paris: Librairie A. Picard, 1905 (Bibliothèque Hagiographique Orientale: 8).
Colette, Marie-Noël, ed. "La notation du demi-ton dans le manuscrit Paris, BNF, Lat. 1139 et dans quelques manuscrits du sud de la France". In Claudio Leonardi, and Enrico Menesto, eds. *La tradizione dei tropi liturgici. Atti dei convegni sui tropi liturgici. Parigi (15-19 ottobre 1985)-Perugia (2-5 settembre 1987) organizzati dal Corpus Troporum sotto l'egida dell'European Science Foundation.* Spoleto: Centro italiano di studi sull'alto medioevo, 1990, 297-311 (Biblioteca del Centro per il collegamento degli studi medievali e umanistici nell'Università di Perugia: 3).
—. "Le chant de la Sibylle: composition, transmission et interprétation". In Monique Bouquet and François Morzadec, eds. *La Sibylle. Parole et représentation.* Rennes: Presses universitaires de Rennes, 2004, 165-176.
—. "Le graduel de Gaillac (BNF, Lat. 776) et le tropaire de Moissac (BNF, N A. L. 1871). Deux manuscrits aquitains contemporains (3e quart du xie siècle)". In O. Legendre and J.-B. Lebigue, eds. *Les manuscrits liturgiques, cycle thématique 2003-2004 de l'IRHT.* Paris: IRHT, 2005 (Ædilis: Actes 9). Disponible en: http://aedilis.irht.cnrs.fr/liturgie/03_1.htm.
—. *Tropaire-Séquentiaire-Prosaire-Prosulaire de Moissac (troisième quart du xie siècle). Manuscrit Paris, Bibliothèque Nationale de France, N. A. L. 1871.* Paris: Societé Française de Musicologie, 2006.
Collamore, Lila. "Aquitainian Collections of Office Chants: A Comparative Survey". Unpublished doctoral thesis, Catholic University of America, Washington, 2000.
Corbin, Solange. "Le *Cantus Sibyllae*: origine et premiers textes". *Revue de Musicologie* 31 (1952): 1-10.
—. *Essai sur la musique religieuse portugaise au Moyen Âge (1100-1385).* Paris: Les Belles Lettres, 1952.
—. *La deposition liturgique du Christ au vendredi saint. Sa place dans l'histoire des rites et du théatre religieux: analyse de documents portugais.* Paris: Les Belles Lettres, 1960.

CORDOLIANI, A. "Inventaire des manuscrits de comput eclésiastique conservés dans les bibliothèques de Catalogne". *Hispania Sacra* 4, no. 8 (1951): 359-384.

—. "Les manuscrits de comput ecclésiastique des Bibliothèques de Madrid". *Hispania Sacra* 8, no. 15 (1955): 177-208.

COSTA, Avelino de Jesus da. "Fragmentos preciosos de códices medievais". In *idem. Estudos de cronologia, diplomática, paleografia e histórico-linguísticos.* Porto: Sociedade Portuguesa de Estudos Medievais, 1992.

"Crònica del Santuari. 1919. III. Cultura. Arxiu [Adquisicions:] A. Manuscrits". *Analecta Montserratensia* 3 (1919): 338-339.

DAUX, Camille, ed. *Tropaire-Prosier de l'Abbaye Saint-Martin de Montauriol.* Paris: Librairie A. Picard, 1901(Bibliothèque liturgique: 9).

DAVID, Pierre. "Le Missel de Mateus: notes historiques et liturgiques". *Biblos* 20 (1944): 319-358.

—. *Études Historiques sur la Galice et le Portugal du VIe au XIIe siècle.* Paris: Les Belles Lettres, 1947.

DELCLAUX, Federico. *Imágenes de la Virgen en los códices medievales de España.* Madrid: Ministerio de Educación y Ciencia, Dirección General de Bellas Artes, Patronato Nacional de Museos, 1973.

DELCOR, Mathias. "Le scriptorium de Ripoll et son rayonnement culturel. État de la question". *Les Cahiers de Saint-Michel de Cuxà* 5 (1974): 45-64.

DELISLE, Léopold. *Le cabinet des manuscrits de la Bibliothèque Nationale.* Vol. 1. Paris: Imprimerie Imperiale, 1868.

DÍAZ Y DÍAZ, Manuel C. "Los prólogos del *antiphonale visigothicum* de la Catedral de León (León, Arch. Cat., 8)". *Archivos Leoneses* 8 (1954): 226-257.

—. *Index Scriptorum Latinorum Medii Aevi Hispanorum.* 2 vols. Salamanca: University of Salamanca, 1958-1959 (Analecta Salmanticensia: 13).

—. *Códices visigóticos en la monarquía leonesa.* León: Centro de Estudios e Investigación San Isidoro (CSIC-CECEL), 1983.

—. "Primitivos escriptorios burgaleses". In Saturnino López Santidrián, ed. *El factor religioso en la formación de Castilla: simposio organizado por el Excmo. Ayuntamiento de Burgos y la Facultad de Teología en el MC aniversario de la ciudad (884-1984).* Burgos: Aldecoa, 1984, 31-41 [Publicaciones de la Facultad de Teología del Norte de España (Sede de Burgos): 50].

—. *Libros y librerías en la Rioja altomedieval.* Logroño: Gobierno de La Rioja, Instituto de Estudios Riojanos, 1991.

DOMÍNGUEZ BORDONA, Jesús. *Catálogo de la exposición de códices miniados españoles.* Madrid: Sociedad de Amigos del Arte, 1929.

—. *Manuscritos con pinturas: notas para un inventario de los conservados en colecciones públicas y particulares de España.* 2 vols. Madrid: Centro de Estudios Históricos, 1933.

—. "Exlibris mozárabes". *Archivo Español de Arte* 11 (1935): 153-163.

—. "Miniatura". In *Ars Hispaniae: historia universal del arte hispánico.* Vol. 18. Madrid: Plus Ultra, 1958, 15-242.

DONOVAN, Richard B. *The Liturgical Drama in Medieval Spain.* Toronto: Pontifical Institute of Medieval Studies, 1958 (Studies and Texts: 4).

DREVES, Guido Maria, ed. *Analecta hymnica medii aevi XVI, Hymnodia Hiberica. Spanischen Hymnen des Mittelalters.* Leipzig: O. R. Reisland, 1894.

—, ed. *Analecta hymnica medii aevi XVII, Hymnodia Hiberica. Liturgische Reimofficien aus Spanischen Brevieren.* Leipzig: O. R. Reisland, 1894.

DRONKE, Peter, ed. *Nine medieval Latin plays.* Cambridge: Cambridge University Press, 1994.

DUFOUR, Jean. *La Bibliothèque et le scriptorium de Moissac.* Ginebra, Paris: Librairie Droz, 1972 (Hautes études médiévales et modernes: 15).

DURÁN GUDIOL, Antonio. "Los manuscritos de la Catedral de Huesca". *Argensola* 4, no. 16 (1953): 293-322.

DURÁN GUDIOL, Antonio, Ramón MORAGAS, and Juan VILLAREAL. *Hymnarium oscense (s. XI).* Vol. 1, *Edición facsímil.* Vol. 2, *Estudios.* Zaragoza: Institución Fernando el Católico, 1988.

DURO PEÑA, Emilio. "Los códices de la Catedral de Orense". *Hispania Sacra* 14, no. 27 (1961): 185-212.

Las Edades del Hombre: La música en la Iglesia de Castillla y León. (Exhibition catalog.) Valladolid: Junta de Castilla y León, 1991.

Las Edades del Hombre: Libros y documentos en la Iglesia de Castilla y León. (Exhibition catalog.) Valladolid: Junta de Castilla y León, 1990.

Elorza, Juan Carlos, ed. *El Scriptorium silense y los orígenes de la lengua castellana.* (Exhibition catalog.) Valladolid: Junta de Castilla y León, 1995.

Enciso, Jesús. "El estudio bíblico de los códices litúrgicos mozárabes". *Estudios Bíblicos* 1 (1941-1942): 291-313.

—. "El breviario mozárabe de la Biblioteca Nacional (olim Toledo 35.1)". *Estudios Bíblicos* 2 (1943): 189-221.

Étaix, Raymond. "Homiliaires wisigothiques provenant de Silos à la Bibliothèque Nationale de Paris". *Hispania Sacra* 12, no. 23 (1959): 213-224.

—. "Quelques homéliaires de la region catalane". *Recherches Augustiniennes* 16 (1981): 333-398.

Evans, Paul. *The Early Trope Repertory of St. Martial de Limoges.* Princeton, New Jersey: Princeton University Press, 1970 (Princeton Studies in Music: 2).

Ewald, Paul. "Reise nach Spanien in Winter von 1878 auf 1879". *Neues Archiv der Gesellschaft für ältere Deutsche Geschichtskunde* 6 (1881): 219-398.

—. *Exempla scripture visigoticae.* Heidelberg: G. Koester, 1883.

Ex-libris universitatis: el patrimonio de las bibliotecas universitarias españolas (Exhibition catalog.) *Santiago de Compostela, septiembre-octubre 2000).* Madrid: CRUE, 2000.

Falconer, Keith. "The Modes Before the Modes: Antiphon and Differentia in Western Chant". In Peter Jeffery, ed. *The Study of Medieval Chant: Paths and Bridges, East and West. In Honour of Kenneth Levy.* London: Boydell and Brewer, 2000, 131-145.

Fernández de la Cuesta, Ismael, ed. *El "Breviarium gothicum" de Silos. Archivo monástico, ms. 6.* Madrid, Barcelona: CSIC, 1965 (Monumenta Hispaniae Sacra: Serie Litúrgica 7).

—. "Notas paleográficas al Antifonario silense del Museo Británico (Add. ms. 30850)". In *Homenaje a fray Justo Pérez de Urbel.* Santo Domingo de Silos: Monastery of Silos, 1976. Vol. 1: 233-256 (Studia Silensia: 3).

—. *Manuscritos y fuentes musicales en España: Edad Media.* Madrid: Alpuerto, 1980.

—. *Historia de la música española.* Vol. 1, *Desde los orígenes hasta el Ars Nova.* Madrid: Alianza, 1983.

—. *Antiphonale Silense (British Library, Add. ms. 30850).* Madrid: Sociedad Española de Musicología, 1985.

Fernández Valverde, Juan, ed. *Rodríguez Jiménez de Rada: historia de los hechos de España.* Madrid: Alianza, 1989.

Férotin, Màrius. "Deux manuscrits wisigothiques de la bibliothèque de Ferdinand I roi de Castille et de León". *Bibliothèque de l'Ecole des Chartes* 62 (1901): 374-387.

—. *Le Liber ordinum en usage dans l'Église wisigothique et mozarabe d'Espagne du cinquème, au onzième siècle.* Paris: Librairie Firmin-Didot, 1904 (Monumenta Ecclesiae Liturgica: 5).

—. *Le Liber Mozarabicus Sacramentorum et les manuscrits mozarabes (reimpr. de l'édition de Paris 1912 et bibliographie générale de la liturgie hispanique, préparées et présentées par A. Ward y C. Jonson).* Rome: CLV Edizioni Liturgiche, 1995 (Monumenta Ecclesiae Liturgica: 6).

Ferreira, Manuel P. "Three Fragments from Lamego". *Revista de Musicología* 16, no. 1 (1993): 457-476. *[Actas del XV Congreso de la Sociedad Internacional de Musicología Culturas Musicales del Mediterráneo y sus Ramificaciones (Madrid, 3-10 de abril de 1992)].*

Ferreres, Juan Bautista. *Historia del Misal Romano.* Barcelona: Eugenio Subirana, 1929.

Fickett, Martha. "Chants for the Feast of Saint Martin of Tours". Unpublished doctoral thesis, Catholic University of America. Washington, 1983.

Fité, Francesc, and Josefina Planas, eds. *Ars Sacra. Seu Nova de Lleida. Els tresors artístics de la Seu Nova de Lleida.* Lleida: Ayuntamiento de Lleida, 2001, 138-139.

Flores Arcas, Juan Javier, ed. "La liturgia de la dedicación de iglesias según los manuscritos de Silos". In *El románico en Silos. IX centenario de la consagración de la iglesia y claustro, 1088-1988. [Actas del Congreso Internacional, Burgos-Silos, 25-29 septiembre 1988].* Santo Domingo de Silos: Monastery of Silos, 1990, 69-75 (Studia Silensia: 1).

—. *Las horas diurnas del Liber horarum de Silos (Cod. Silos, Arch. Monástico, 7).* Santo Domingo de Silos: Monastery of Silos, 1997 (Studia Silensia: 21).

Flórez, Enrique. *España Sagrada.* Vol. 11, *Contiene la vida y escritos, nunca publicados hasta hoy, de algunos varones ilustres cordobeses, que florecieron en el siglo nono*. Madrid: Antonio Marín, 1753.

Fraïsse, Chantal. "Culture monastique au début du XIe siècle. Le cas du scriptorium de Moissac". In Quitterie Cazes, ed. *L'art du Sud de la création à l'identité (XIe-XXe siècle): Actes du 126e Congrès des sociétés historiques et scientifiques, Section archéologie et histoire de l'art, Toulouse, 2001*. Paris: Éditions du CTHS, 2003.

Franquesa, Adalbert M. "El ritual tarraconense". In *Liturgica.* Vol. 2. Montserrat: Abbey of Montserrat, 1958, 249-298 (Scripta et Documenta: 10).

Freire, José Geraldes. "A edição do "Missal de Mateus" por Joaquim O. Bragança". *Bracara Augusta* 34, fasc. 78 (1980): 653-657.

Gamber, Klaus. *Codices Liturgici Latini Antiquiores.* 2 vols. Friburgo: Universitätsverlag, 1968 (Spicilegii Friburgensis: Subsidia 1).

García Alonso, Ireneo. "La administración de sacramentos en Toledo después del cambio de rito (siglos XII-XIII)". *Salmanticensis* 5 (1958): 3-79.

García Villada, Zacarías. "Formularios de las bibliotecas y archivos de Barcelona". *Anuari de l'Institut d'Estudis Catalans* 4 (1911-1912): 533-552.

—. *Bibliotheca Patrum Latinorum Hispaniensis.* Vol. 2, *Nach den Aufzeichnungen Rudolf Beers, bearbeitet und herausgegeben von Zacharias García, S. J.* Vienna: In Kommission bei Alfred Hölder, 1915 (Sitzungsberichte der Kaiserlichen Akademie der Wissenschaften in Wien: Philosophisch-Historische Klasse 169).

—. *Paleografía española.* Madrid: Junta para Ampliación de Estudios, Centro de Estudios Históricos, 1923.

García y García, Antonio, Francisco Cantelar Rodríguez, and Manuel Nieto Cumplido. *Catálogo de los manuscritos e incunables de la Catedral de Córdoba*. Salamanca: Pontifical University, 1976.

Garrigosa, Joaquim. *Catálogo de manuscritos e impresos musicales del Archivo Histórico Nacional y del Archivo de la Corona de Aragón.* Madrid: Dirección General de Bellas Artes y Archivos, Dirección General de Archivos Estatales, 1994.

—. "Música i litúrgia". In Marina Miquel, and Margarida Salas, coords. *Temps de monestirs: els monestirs catalans entorn l'any mil.* Barcelona: Pòrtic-Generalitat de Cataluña, Departamento de Cultura, 1999, 232-241.

—. "Monodia litúrgica i profana". In José Aviñoa, dir. *Història de la Música Catalana, Valenciana i Balear.* Vol. 1, *Dels inicis al Renaixement*. Barcelona: Edicions 62, 2000.

—. *Els manuscrits musicals a Catalunya fins al segle XIII. L'evolució de la notació musical.* Lleida: Institut d'Estudis Ilerdencs, 2003 (Col·lecció Emili Pujol: 2).

Gil Fernández, Juan. *Corpus scriptorum muzarabicorum.* Madrid: Instituto Antonio de Nebrija, 1973 (Manuals and annexes from *Emerita*: 28).

Gilson, J. P. *The Mozarabic Psalter (British Museum, Add. ms. 30851).* London: Harrison and Sons, 1905 (Henry Bradshaw Society: 30).

Gómez, Maricarmen. *El Canto de la Sibila.* Vol. 1, *León y Castilla*. Madrid: Alpuerto, 1996.

—. *El Canto de la Sibila.* Vol. 2, *Cataluña y Baleares*. Madrid: Alpuerto, 1997.

—. "La Catalunya carolíngia: de música i litúrgia". In *Catalunya a l'època carolíngia: art i cultura abans del romànic (segle IX i X): 16 desembre 1999-27 febrer 2000, Museu Nacional d'Art de Catalunya*. Barcelona: Diputación de Barcelona-Museo Nacional de Arte de Cataluña, 1999, 135-138.

—. *La música medieval en España.* Kassel: Reichenberger, 2001 (DeMusica: 6).

—. "El Canto de la Sibila: orígenes y fuentes". In Maricarmen Gómez, and Màrius Bernadó, eds. *Fuentes musicales en la Península Ibérica (ca. 1250-ca. 1550). Actas del Coloquio Internacional, Lleida, 1-3 de abril de 1996.* Lleida: University of Lleida-Institut d'Estudis Ilerdencs, 2002, 35-69.

Gómez Pallarés, Juan. "Sobre manuscritos latinos de cómputo en escritura visigótica". *Hispania Sacra* 39, no. 79 (1987): 25-48.

González Barrionuevo, Herminio. "Presencia de signos adicionales de tipo melódico en la notación "mozárabe" del norte de España". *Revista de Musicología* 9, no. 1 (1986): 11-27.

—. "La grafía del *sálicus* en la notación "mozárabe" de tipo vertical". *Revista de Musicología* 12, no. 2 (1989): 397-410.
—. "Dos grafías especiales del "scándicus" en la notación "mozárabe" del norte de España". *Revista de Musicología* 13, no. 1 (1990): 11-79.
—. "Los códices "mozárabes" del archivo de Silos: aspectos paleográficos y semiológicos de su notación neumática". *Revista de Musicología* 15, nos. 2-3 (1992): 403-472 *[La música en la Abadía de Silos. Trabajos del I Simposio de Musicología Religiosa (Burgos-Silos, March 1991)]*.
—. "Relación entre la notación "mozárabe" de tipo vertical y otras escrituras neumáticas". *Studi Gregoriani* 11 (1995): 5-12.
—. "The Persistence of the Mozarabic Liturgy in Toledo after A. D. 1080". In Bernard F. Reilly, ed. *Santiago, Saint-Denis and Saint Peter. The Reception of the Roman Liturgy in León-Castille in 1080.* New York: Fordham University Press, 1985, 157-185.
—. *Hombres y libros de Toledo, 1086-1300.* Madrid: Fundación Ramón Areces, 1997.
Goñi Gaztambide, José. *Libros, bibliotecas y escritores medievales navarros.* Pamplona: Mintzoa, 1999.
Gros, Miquel S. "Les fragments parisiens de l'antiphonaire de Silos". *Revue Bénédictine* 74 (1964): 324-333.
—. "Las órdenes sagradas del Pontifical ms. 104 (CV) de la Biblioteca Capitular de Vic". *Hispania Sacra* 17, nos. 33-34 (1964): 99-133 *[Miscelánea en memoria de dom Mario Férotin (1914-1964)]*.
—. "El ordo romano-hispánico de Narbona para la consagración de iglesias". *Hispania Sacra* 19, no. 38 (1966): 321-401.
—. "El *ordo missae* de la tradición hispánica". In *Liturgia y música mozárabes: ponencias y comunicaciones presentadas al I Congreso Internacional de Estudios Mozárabes (Toledo 1975).* Toledo: Instituto de Estudios Visigótico-Mozárabes de San Eugenio, 1978, 45-64.
—. "El *Liber misticus* de San Millán de la Cogolla: Madrid, Real Academia de la Historia, Aemil. 30". *Miscel·lània Litúrgica Catalana* 3 (1984): 111-224.
—. "Noves dades sobre el Sacramentari de Ripoll". *Boletín de la Real Academia de Buenas Letras de Barcelona* 46 (1997-1998): 347-355.
—. *Els tropers prosers de la Catedral de Vic: estudi i edició.* Barcelona: Societat Catalana d'Estudis Litúrgics, Institut d'Estudis Catalans, 1999 (Biblioteca Litúrgica Catalana: 2).
Gudiol, Josep. *Catàleg dels llibres manuscrits anteriors al segle* XVIII *del Museu Episcopal de Vich.* Barcelona: Imprenta de la Casa de Caritat, 1934.
—. *La pintura mig-eval catalana. Els Primitius.* Vol. 3, *Els llibres il·luminats.* Barcelona: S. Babra, 1955.
Guilmain, Jacques. "On the chronological development and classification of decorated initials in latin manuscripts of tenth-century Spain". *Bulletin of the John Rylands University Library of Manchester* 63, no. 2 (1981): 309-401.
Gümpel, Karl-Werner. "Musica cum Rhetorica: die Handschrift Ripoll 42". *Archiv für Musikwissenschaft* 34 (1977): 260-286.
—. "Spicilegium rivipullense". *Archiv für Musikwissenschaft* 35, no. 1 (1978): 57-61.
—. "Portugal and Spain". In Christian Meyer, Elzbieta Witkowska-Zaremba, and Karl-Werner Gümpel, eds. *The Theory of Music from the Carolingian Era up to c. 1500. Descriptive Catalogue of Manuscripts. (vol. 5: Parts Czech Republic, Poland, Portugal and Spain) [Répertoire International des Sources Musicales, Serie B, Band III, 5].* Munich: G. Henle, 1997.
—. "Das *Breviarium de musica* und die *Versus monochordi* des Mönchs Oliba von Ripoll". In Michael Bernhard, ed. *Quellen und Studien zur Musiktheorie des Mittelalters III [Symposium Musiktheorie im Mittelalter. Quellen-Texte-Terminologie, Musikhistorisches Kommission der Bayerische Akademie der Wissenschaften, Munich, July, 25-28, 2000].* Munich: H. C. Berg, 2001, 87-119 (Musikhistorischen Kommission: Bayerische Akademie der Wissenschaften 15).
—. "El *Breviarium de Musica* i els *Versus Monocordi* del monjo Oliba de Ripoll". *Miscel·lània Litúrgica Catalana* 12 (2004): 23-57.
Gutiérrez, Carmen Julia. "El Himnario de Huesca: nueva aproximación". *Anuario Musical* 49 (1989): 23-60.
Gy, Pierre-Marie. "Collectaire, rituel, processionel". *Revue des Sciences Philosophiques et Théologiques* 44, no. 3 (1960): 441-469.

—. "Typologie et ecclésiologie des livres liturgiques". *La Maison-Dieu* 121 (1975): 7-21; reprinted in: Pierre-Marie G. *La Liturgie dans l'histoire*. Paris: Editions Saint-Paul-Cerf, 1990, 75-89.

—. "The Different Forms of Liturgical *Libelli*". In Gerard Austin, ed. *Fountain of Life: In Memory of Niels K. Rasmussen, OP*. Washington, DC: Pastoral Press, 1991, 22-34.

HARDIE, Jane M. "*Lamentations* in Spanish sources before 1568: Notes towards a geography". *Revista de Musicología* 16, no. 2 (1993): 912-942 *[Actas del XV Congreso de la Sociedad Internacional de Musicología, "Culturas musicales del Mediterráneo y sus ramificaciones" (Madrid, 3-10 de abril de 1992)*. Vol. 2].

—. "*Lamentations* Chant in Spanish Sources: A Preliminary Report". In Bryan Gillingham, and Paul Merkley, eds. *Chant and its Peripheries: Essays in Honour of Terence Bailey*. Ottawa: Institute of Mediæval Music, 1998, 370-389 (Musicological Studies: 72).

HERNÁNDEZ APARICIO, Pilar. *Inventario general de manuscritos de la Biblioteca Nacional de Madrid*. Vol. 14, *9501-10200*. Madrid: Biblioteca Nacional de España, 2002.

HERNÁNDEZ ASCUNCE, Leocadio. "La música sacra en la historia pampilonense". *Príncipe de Viana* 7, no. 22 (1964): 144-176. XIe

HESBERT, René Jean. *Corpus Antiphonalium Officii*. Vol. 2, *Manuscripti "cursus monasticus"*. Rome: Herder, 1965.*CAO*

HILEY, David. *Western Plainchant: A Handbook*. Oxford: Oxford University Press, 1993.

HOFFMANN-BRANDT, Helma. "Die Tropen zu den Responsorien des Officium". *Inaugural-Dissertation der Philosophischen Fakultät der Friedrich-Alexander-Universität*. Erlangen, Núremberg: Friedrich-Alexander University, 1971.

HUGLO, Michel. "Les *Preces* des graduels aquitains empruntées à la liturgie hispanique". *Hispania Sacra* 8, no. 16 (1955): 361-383.

—. *Les tonaires: Inventaire, analyse, comparaison*. Paris: Societé Française de Musicologie, 1971.

—. "Tradition orale et tradition écrite dans la transmission des mélodies grégoriennes". In Hans H. Eggebrecht, and Max Lütolf, eds. *Studien zur Tradition in der Musik: Festschrift Kurt von Fischer zum 60. Geburtstag*. Munich: Emil Katzbichler, 1973, 31-42.

—. "On the origins of the troper-proser". *Journal of the Plainsong and Medieval Music Society* 2 (1979): 11-18.

—. "La tradition musicale aquitaine. Répertoire et notation". In *Liturgie et musique (IXe-XIVe s.)*. Toulouse: Privat, 1982, 253-268 (Collection d'Histoire religieuse du langue doc au XIIIe et au début du XIVe siècles: Cahiers de Fanjeaux 17).

—. "La pénétration des manuscrits aquitains en Espagne". *Revista de Musicología* 8, no. 2 (1985): 249-256.

—. "Les *Libelli* de Tropes et les premiers Tropaires-Prosaires". In Ritva Jacobson, ed. *Pax et sapientia. Studies in Text and Music of Liturgical Tropes and Sequences. In Memory of Gordon Anderson. (Corpus Troporum.)* Stockholm: Almqvist & Wiksell, 1986, 13-22 (Acta Universitatis Stockholmiensis: Studia Latina Stockholmiensia 29).

—. "La notation wisigothique est-elle plus ancienne que les autres notations européennes?". In Emilio Casares, Ismael Fernández de la Cuesta, and José López-Calo, eds. *España en la música de Occidente. Actas del congreso internacional celebrado en Salamanca, 29 de octubre-5 de noviembre de 1985*. Madrid: INAEM, Ministerio de Cultura, 1987. Vol. 1: 19-26.

—. "Centres de composition des tropes et cercles de diffusion". In Claudio Leonardi, and Enrico Menesto, eds. *La tradizione dei tropi liturgici. Atti dei convegni sui tropi liturgici. Parigi (15-19 ottobre 1985)-Perugia (2-5 settembre 1987) organizzati dal Corpus Troporum sotto l'egida dell'European Science Foundation*. Spoleto: Centro italiano di studi sull'alto medioevo, 1990, 139-144 (Biblioteca del Centro per il collegamento degli studi medievali e umanistici nell'Università di Perugia: 3).

—. "Recherches sur les tons psalmodiques de l'ancienne liturgie hispanique". *Revista de Musicología* 16, no. 1 (1993): 477-490 *[Actas del XV Congreso de la Sociedad Internacional de Musicología, "Culturas musicales del Mediterráneo y sus ramificaciones" (Madrid, 3-10/IV/1992)]*.

—. "Liturgische Gesangbücher". In Ludwig Finscher, ed. *Die Musik in Geschichte und Gegenwart*. Kassel: Bärenreiter; Stuttgart: Metzler, 1996. Vol. 5: 1411-1437.

HUSMANN, Heinrich. *Tropen-und Sequenzenhandschriften [Répertoire International des Sources Musicales, Serie B, Band V, 1]*. Munich, Duisburg: G. Henle, 1964.

IBARBURU, M. Eugenia. "L'escriptori de Santa Maria de Ripoll i els seus manuscrits". In Antoni Pladevall i Font, ed. *Catalunya Romànica X, El Ripollès*. Barcelona: Enciclopèdia Catalana, 1987, 276-281 [334].

Indice preparatorio do catalogo dos manuscriptos, com reportório alphabetico... fasc. 1: mss. Membranaceos (Catalogo da Biblioteca Pública Municipal do Porto). Porto: Biblioteca Pública Municipal do Porto, 1879.

JANINI, José. "Notas sobre libros litúrgicos hispánicos". *Hispania Sacra* 14, no. 27 (1961): 148-151.

—. "Los fragmentos de Sacramentarios existentes en Vich". *Hispania Sacra* 18, no. 36 (1965): 385-409.

—. "Liturgia: Liturgia romana". In Quintín Aldea, Tomás Marín, and José Vives, eds. *Diccionario de historia eclesiástica de España*. Madrid: CSIC, Instituto P. Enrique Flórez, 1972. Vol. 2: 1320-1324.

—. "La colección de fragmentos litúrgicos de Vic". *Analecta Sacra Tarraconensia* 48 (1975): 3-32.

—. *Manuscritos litúrgicos de las Bibliotecas de España*. Vol. 1, *Castilla y Navarra*. Burgos: Ediciones Aldecoa, 1977 [Publicaciones de la Facultad de Teología del Norte de España (Sede de Burgos): 38].

—. "Officia Silensia. Liber misticus". *Hispania Sacra* 29 (1976): 325-381; 30 (1977): 331-418; 31 (1978-1979): 357-483.

—. "Las piezas litúrgicas del Toledo 35-7 editadas por Ortiz". *Escritos del Vedat* 8 (1978): 161-167.

—. *Manuscritos litúrgicos de las Bibliotecas de España*. Vol. 2, *Aragón, Cataluña y Valencia*. Burgos: Ediciones Aldecoa, 1980 [Publicaciones de la Facultad de Teología del Norte de España (Sede de Burgos): 38, no. 2].

—. *Liber ordinum sacerdotal (Cod. Silos Arch. Monástico, 3)*. Santo Domingo de Silos: Monastery of Silos, 1981 (Studia Silensia: 7).

—. "La misa hispánica de santa Marina". *Anales Valentinos* 7 (1981): 135-140.

—. *Liber missarum de Toledo y libros místicos*. Toledo: Instituto de Estudios Visigótico-Mozárabes, 1983.

—. *Liber ordinum episcopal (Cod. Silos Arch. Monástico, 4)*. Santo Domingo de Silos: Monastery of Silos, 1991 (Studia Silensia: 15).

JANINI, José, Ramón GONZÁLVEZ, and Anscari M. MUNDÓ. *Manuscritos litúrgicos de la Catedral de Toledo*. Toledo: Instituto Provincial de Investigaciones y Estudios Toledanos, 1977.

JANINI, José, José SERRANO, and Anscari M. MUNDÓ. *Manuscritos litúrgicos de la Biblioteca Nacional de Madrid*. Madrid: Dirección General de Archivos y Bibliotecas, 1969. JIMÉNEZ DELGADO, J. "Juvenco en el códice matritense 10029". *Helmantica* 19 (1968): 277-332.

JIMÉNEZ DE RADA, Rodrigo. "De rebus Hispaniae". In Francisco Antonio de Lorenzana, ed. *Patrum Toletanum Opera*. Vol. 3. Madrid, 1793.

JONSSON, Ritva, dir. *Corpus Troporum I. Tropes du propre de la messe 1. Cycle de Noël*. Stockholm: Almqvist & Wiksell, 1975 (Acta Universitatis Stockholmiensis: Studia Latina Stockholmiensia 21).

LAUER, Philippe. *Catalogue général des manuscrits latins*. Vol. 1. Paris: Bibliothèque Nationale de France, 1939.

LE ROUX, Raymond. "Aux origines de l'Office festif: Les antiennes et les psaumes des Matines et les Laudes pour Noël et le 1er Janvier". *Études grégoriennes* 4 (1961): 65-170.

LECLERCQ, Jean. "Tables pour l'inventaire des homiliaires manuscrits". *Scriptorium* 2 (1948): 198-214.

—. "Textes et manuscrits de quelques bibliothèques d'Espagne". *Hispania Sacra* 2, no. 3 (1949): 91-118.

—. "Un tratado sobre los nombres divinos en un manuscrito de Córdoba". *Hispania Sacra* 2, no. 4 (1949): 327-338.

Les tropaires-prosaires de la Bibliothèque Nationale: Catalogue de l'exposition organisée à l'occassion du troisième Colloque International sur les tropes (Paris, 16-19 Octobre 1985). Paris: Bibliothèque Nationale de France, 1985.

LEVY, Kenneth. "Old-hispanic chant in its european context". In Emilio Casares, Ismael Fernández de la Cuesta, and José López-Calo, eds. *España en la música de Occidente. Actas del congreso internacional celebrado en Salamanca, 29 de octubre-5 de noviembre de 1985*. Madrid: INAEM, Ministerio de Cultura, 1987. Vol. 1: 3-14.

—. *Gregorian Chant and the Carolingians*. Princeton, New Jersey: Princeton University Press, 1998.

Libro de horas de Fernando I de León. Studies by Manuel C. Díaz y Díaz, and Serafín Moralejo; transcription of the text by M.ª Virtudes Pardo Gómez, and M.ª Araceli García Piñeiro. *Ed. facs. do manuscrito*

609 (Res. 1) da Biblioteca Universitaria de Santiago de Compostela. Santiago de Compostela: Testimonio Editorial, Consejería de Educación y Ordenación Universitaria, 1995.

Lilao Franca, Óscar, and Carmen Castrillo González. *Catálogo de manuscritos de la Biblioteca Universitaria de Salamanca.* Vol. 2, *Manuscritos 1680-2777.* Salamanca: University of Salamanca, 2002.

Lowe, Gustav, and Wilhelm von Hartel, eds. *Bibliotheca Patrum Latinorum Hispaniensis.* Vol. 1. Vienna: Alfred Hölder, 1887.

López-Calo, José. *La música medieval en Galicia.* A Coruña: Fundación Pedro Barrié de la Maza, Conde de Fenosa, 1982.

Llauró, Joan. "Los Glosarios de Ripoll". *Analecta Sacra Tarraconensia* 3 (1927): 331-389; 4 (1928): 271-341.

Ludwig, Peter. "*Lamentations* dans quelques manuscrits bibliques". *Études Grégoriennes* 12 (1971): 127-131.

Madahil, António Gomes da Rocha. "Inventário do mosteiro de Santa Cruz de Coimbra à data da sua extinção em 1834". *O Instituto* 101 (1942): 445-573.

Mansilla, Demetrio. *Catálogo de los códices de la Catedral de Burgos.* Madrid: CSIC, Instituto P. Enrique Flórez, 1952.

Marqués, Josep M., and Miquel S. Gros. "L'antifonari de Sant Feliu de Girona. Girona: Museu Diocesà, ms. 45". *Miscel·lània Litúrgica Catalana* 6 (1995): 177-326.

Martimort, Aimé-Georges. "Un sacramentaire de la region de Carcassone des environs de l'année 1100". In *Mélanges en l'honneur de Monseigneur Michel Andrieu.* Volumen fuera de serie de *Revue des Sciences Religieuses.* Strasbourg: Palais Universitaire, 1956, 305-326.

—. "Répertoires des livres liturgiques du Languedoc antérieurs au Concile de Trente". In *Liturgie et musique (IXe-XIVe s.).* Toulouse: Privat, 1982, 51-80 (Collection d'Histoire religieuse du langue doc au XIIIe et au début du XIVe siècles: Cahiers de Fanjeaux 17).

—. "Sources, histoire et originalité de la liturgie catalano-languedocienne". In *Liturgie et musique (IXe-XIVe s.).* Toulouse: Privat, 1982, 25-49 (Collection d'Histoire religieuse du langue doc au XIIIe et au début du XIVe siècles: Cahiers de Fanjeaux 17).

Mas, Josiane. "La tradition musicale en Septimanie. Répertoire et tradition musicale". In *Liturgie et musique (IXe-XIVe s.).* Toulouse: Privat, 1982, 269-286 (Collection d'Histoire religieuse du langue doc au XIIIe et au début du XIVe siècles: Cahiers de Fanjeaux 17).

—. "La notation catalane". *Revista de Musicología* 11, no. 1 (1988): 11-30.

Menéndez Pidal, Gonzalo. "Sobre el escritorio emilianense en los siglos X a XI". *Boletín de la Real Academia de la Historia* 143 (1958): 7-19.

Menéndez Pidal, Ramón. *Documentos lingüísticos de España.* Vol. 1, *Reino de Castilla.* Madrid: Junta para Ampliación de Estudios e Investigaciones Científicas. Centro de Estudios Históricos, 1919.

Mentré, Mireille. *El estilo mozárabe: la pintura cristiana hispánica en torno al año 1000.* Madrid: Encuentros, 1994.

Merkley, Paul. *Modal Assignment in Northern Tonaries.* Ottawa: Institute of Mediæval Music, 1992.

Meyer, Wilhelm. *Die Preces der mozarabischen Liturgie.* Berlin: Weidmannsche Buchhandlung, 1914 (Abhandlungen der königlichen Gesellschaft der Wissenschaft zu Göttingen: Philologisch-historische Klasse NF 15/3).

Millares Carlo, Agustín. *Contribución al "corpus" de códices visigóticos.* Madrid: Tipografía de Archivos, 1931.

—. *Los códices visigóticos de la catedral toledana. Cuestiones cronológicas y de procedencia.* Madrid: Real Academia de la Historia, 1935.

—. "Manuscritos visigóticos. Notas bibliográficas". *Hispania Sacra* 14, no. 28 (1961): 337-444.

—. *Manuscritos visigóticos: notas bibliográficas.* Barcelona, Madrid: CSIC, Instituto P. Enrique Flórez, 1963 (Monumenta Hispaniae Sacra: Subsidia 1).

—. *Tratado de paleografía española* (3rd ed., in collaboration with José Manuel Ruiz Asencio). 3 vols. Madrid: Espasa Calpe, 1983.

Millares Carlo, Agustín, Manuel C. Díaz y Díaz, Anscari M. Mundó, José Manuel Ruiz Asencio, Blas Casado Quintanilla, and E. Lecuona Ribot, eds. *Corpus de códices visigóticos.* Vol. 1, *Estudio*, vol. 2, *Álbum.* Las Palmas de Gran Canaria: Gobierno de Canarias, UNED, Centro Asociado de Las Palmas de Gran Canaria, 1999.

Millenum: Història i art de l'Església catalana (Barcelona, del 3 de maig al 25 de juny de 1989). (Exhibition catalog.) Barcelona: Generalitat de Cataluña, 1989.

Miranda, Maria Adelaida. "A Iluminura Românica em santa Cruz de Coimbra e Santa Maria de Alcobaça. Subsídios para o estudo da iluminura em Portugal". Unpublished doctoral thesis, Lisbon: Faculty of Social and Human Sciences of the Universidade Nova de Lisboa, 1996.

Moines de Solesmes. *Le Graduel Romain.* Vol. 2, *Les sources.* Ed. Michel Huglo. Solesmes: Abbey of Saint-Pierre, 1957.

Moll, Jaime. "Per a una tipologia de la notació catalana". *Butlletí de la Societat Catalana de Musicologia* 2 (1985): 9-21.

—. "Para una tipología de la notación catalana". *Revista de Musicología* 9, no. 2 (1986): 399-409.

Moragas, Beda. "Contenido y procedencia del Himnario de Huesca". In *Liturgica.* Vol. 1. Montserrat: Abbey of Montserrat, 1956, 277-293 (Scripta et Documenta: 7).

—. "Transcripció musical de dos himnes". In *Miscelánea en homenaje a Monseñor Higinio Anglés.* Barcelona: CSIC, 1961. Vol. 2: 591-598.

Morin, Germain, ed. *Liber comicus sive lectionarius missae, quo Toletana ecclesia ante annos mille duocentos utebatur.* Maredsous: Monastery of S. Benedicti, 1893 (Anecdota Maredsolana: 1).

Mundó, Anscari M. *Els manuscrits de Montserrat.* Montserrat: Abbey of Montserrat, 1944.

—. *Librorum liturgicorum Cathalauniæ s.* IX *ad* XVI *in Bibliotheca Abbatiae Montisserrati exhibitio (Occasione VI Conventus Internationalis Studiorum Liturgiæ, diebus 9 ad 13 septembris an. Dni. 1958).* Montserrat: Abbey of Montserrat, 1958.

—. "Manuscrits i miniatures romànics a Barcelona". *Serra d'Or* 3, no. 10 (1961): 15-19.

—. "La datación de los códices litúrgicos visigóticos toledanos". *Hispania Sacra* 18, no. 35 (1965): 1-25 *[Miscelánea en memoria de dom Mario Férotin (1914-1964)].*

—. "El proser-troper Montserrat 73". In *Liturgica.* Vol. 3. Montserrat: Abbey of Montserrat, 1966, 101-142 (Scripta et Documenta: 17).

—. "Un fragment molt antic de litúrgia romana a Catalunya. Excursus I: Nous manuscrits amb notació catalana arcaica; Excursus II: El Missal Místic o Mixt a Catalunya". In *II Congrés Litúrgic de Montserrat (1966).* Montserrat: Abbey of Montserrat, 1967. Vol. 3: 173-191.

—. "Sermó inèdit sobre sant Pau de Narbona atribuït al bisbe Oliva de Vic". In *Narbonne. Archéologie et histoire.* Vol. 2, *Narbonne au Moyen Âge. XLVe Congrès de la Fédération historique du Languedoc méditerranéen et du Roussillon (Narbonne, 14, 15 et 16 avril 1972).* Montpellier: Fédération historique du Languedoc méditerranéen et du Roussillon, 1973, 105-113.

—. "Notas para una historia de la escritura visigótica". In *Bivium. Homenaje a Manuel C. Díaz y Díaz.* Madrid: Gredos, 1983, 175-196.

—. "Consideracions paleogràfiques a l'entorn de la monodia litúrgica medieval en l'obra d'Higini Anglès". *Recerca Musicològica* 9-10 (1989-1990): 5-14 *(Actes del Congrès Internacional Higini Anglès i la musicologia hispànica).*

—. "La cultura artística escrita". In Antoni Pladevall i Font, ed. *Catalunya Romànica I, Introducció a l'estudi de l'art romànic català. Fons d'art romànic català del Museu Nacional d'Art de Catalunya.* Barcelona: Enciclopèdia Catalana, 1994, 133-162.

—. *Les Bíblies de Ripoll: Estudi dels mss. Vaticà, Lat. 5729 i Paris, BNF, Lat. 6.* Vatican City: Biblioteca Apostolica Vaticana, 2002 (Studi e testi: 408).

Nascimento, Aires Augusto. "Missal de Mateus". *Evphrosyne: Revista de Filologia Clássica* Nova Serie, 11 (1978-1979): 325-327.

Nascimento, Aires Augusto, and José Francisco Meirinhos, coords. *Catálogo dos Códices da Livraria de Mão do Mosteiro de Santa Cruz de Coimbra na Biblioteca Pública Municipal do Porto.* Porto: Biblioteca Pública Municipal do Porto, 1997.

Nicolau d'Olwer, Lluís. "L'escola poètica de Ripoll en els segles x-xiii". *Anuari de l'Institut d'Estudis Catalans* 6 (1915-1920) [1923]: 3-84.

—. "La littérature latine au xe siècle". In *La Catalogne à l'époque romane. Conférences faites à la Sorbonne en 1930.* Paris: Librairie Ernest Leroux, 1932, 181-195 (Université de Paris. Institut d'Art et d'Archéologie-Bibliothèque d'Art Catalan. Fondation Cambó: 2).

—. "La littérature latine au XIe siècle". In *La Catalogne à l'époque romane. Conférences faites à la Sorbonne en 1930*. Paris: Librairie Ernest Leroux, 1932, 197-223 (Université de Paris. Institut d'Art et d'Archéologie-Bibliothèque d'Art Catalan. Fondation Cambó: 2).

—. "La littérature latine au XIIe siècle". In *La Catalogne à l'époque romane. Conférences faites à la Sorbonne en 1930*. Paris: Librairie Ernest Leroux, 1932, 225-249 (Université de Paris. Institut d'Art et d'Archéologie-Bibliothèque d'Art Catalan. Fondation Cambó: 2).

OLEXY, Ronald T. "The Responsories in the 11th Century Aquitainian Antiphonal Toledo, Bibl. Cap. 44-2". Unpublished doctoral thesis, Catholic University of America, Washington, 1980.

OLEXY, Ronald T., Joseph METZINGER, Keith FALCONER, Lila COLLAMORE, and Richard RICE. *An Aquitainian Antiphoner: Toledo, Biblioteca Capitular, 44.2: Printouts from an Index in Machinereadable from Cantus Index*. Ottawa: Institute of Mediæval Music, 1992 (Musicological Studies: 55, no. 1).

OLIVÁN BAYLE, Francisco. *Los monasterios de San Juan de la Peña y Santa Cruz de la Serós*. Zaragoza: Talleres Editoriales El Noticiero, 1974.

OLIVAR, Alejandro. "Serie de *benedictiones lectionum* en el Cod. Montserratensis 72". *Ephemerides Liturgicae* 62 (1948): 230-234.

—. *El Sacramentario de Vich: estudio y edición*. Madrid, Barcelona: CSIC, Instituto P. Enrique Flórez, 1953 (Monumenta Hispaniae Sacra: Serie Litúrgica 4).

—. *Sacramentarium Rivipullense*. Madrid, Barcelona: CSIC, Instituto P. Enrique Flórez, 1964 (Monumenta Hispaniae Sacra: Serie Litúrgica 7).

—. "Les supervivències litúrgiques autòctones a Catalunya en els manuscrits dels segles XI-XII". In *II Congrés litúrgic de Montserrat*. Montserrat: Abbey of Montserrat, 1967. Vol. 3: 21-89.

—. *Els manuscrits litúrgics de la Biblioteca de Montserrat*. Montserrat: Abbey of Montserrat, 1969 (Scripta et Documenta: 18).

—. *Catàleg dels manuscrits de la Biblioteca del Monestir de Montserrat*. Montserrat: Abbey of Montserrat, 1977 (Scripta et Documenta: 25).

—. "Els manuscrits andorrans conservats a la Biblioteca de Montserrat". *Quaderns d'Estudis Andorrans* 2 (1977): 43-47.

—. *Catàleg dels manuscrits de la Biblioteca del Monestir de Montserrat. Primer suplement*. Montserrat: Abbey of Montserrat, 1991 (Scripta et Documenta: 41).

—. "La litúrgia a Catalunya ara fa mil anys". In *I Symposium Internacional sobre els origens de Catalunya (segles VIII-XI)*. Barcelona: Comissió del Mil·lenari de Catalunya, Generalitat de Cataluña, 1992. Vol. 2: 75-84.

—. "Nou panorama de la investigació de la història de la litúrgia a Catalunya". *Miscel·lània Litúrgica Catalana* 7 (1996): 45-105.

OTTOSEN, Knud. *The Responsories and Versicles of the Latin Office of the Dead*. Aarhus: Aarhus University Press, 1993.

PADRES BENEDICTINOS DE SILOS. *Antiphonarium mozarabicum de la Catedral de León*. León, 1928.

PARDO GÓMEZ, María Virtudes. *Catálogo de manuscritos da Biblioteca Xeral*. Santiago de Compostela: University of Santiago de Compostela, 1998.

PEÑAS GARCÍA, Concepción. *La música en los evangeliarios españoles*. Madrid: Sociedad Española de Musicología, 1983.

—. *Catálogo de los fondos musicales de la Real Colegiata de Roncesvalles*. Pamplona: Gobierno de Navarra, Departamento de Educación, Cultura, Deportes y Juventud, 1995.

—. *Fondos musicales históricos de Navarra. Siglos XII-XVI*. Pamplona: Universidad Pública de Navarra, 2004.

PÉREZ PASTOR, Cristóbal. "Índice por títulos de los códices procedentes de los monasterios de San Millán de la Cogolla y San Pedro de Cardeña". *Boletín de la Real Academia de la Historia* 53 (1908): 469-512.

PÉREZ DE URBEL, Justo. "Origen de los himnos mozárabes". *Bulletin Hispanique* 28 (1926): 5-21, 113-139, 209-245, 305-320.

—. "Antifonario de León. El escritor y la época". *Archivos Leonenses* 8 (1954): 115-144.

PÉREZ DE URBEL, Justo, and Atilano GONZÁLEZ RUIZ-ZORRILLA, eds. *Liber commicus*. 2 vols. Madrid: CSIC, 1950-1955 (Monumenta Hispaniae Sacra: Serie Litúrgica 2-3).

PINELL, Jordi M. "Las *missae*, grupos de cantos y oraciones en el oficio de la antigua liturgia hispana". *Archivos Leoneses* 8 (1954): 145-185.

—. "El *Liber horarum* y el *Misticus* entre los libros de la antigua liturgia hispana". *Hispania Sacra* 8, no. 15 (1955): 85-105.
—. "El oficio hispano-visigótico". *Hispania Sacra* 10, no. 20 (1957): 385-427.
—. "Fragmentos de códices del antiguo rito hispánico. I-II: Las guardas del Emilianense 14". *Hispania Sacra* 17, nos. 33-34 (1964): 195-230 *[Miscelánea en memoria de dom Mario Férotin (1914-1964)]*.
—. "Los textos de la antigua liturgia hispánica". In Juan Francisco Rivera Recio, ed. *Estudios sobre la liturgia mozárabe*. Toledo: Publicaciones del Instituto Provincial de Investigaciones y Estudios Toledanos, 1965, 109-164.
PLADEVALL I FONT, Antoni, dir. *Catalunya Romànica VI, Alt Urgell, Andorra*. Barcelona: Enciclopèdia Catalana, 1992.
—. *Catalunya Romànica XVI, La Ribagorça*. Barcelona: Enciclopèdia Catalana, 1996.
—. *Catalunya Romànica XVII, La Noguera*. Barcelona: Enciclopèdia Catalana, 1994.
—. *Catalunya Romànica XXVI, Tortosa i les Terres de l'Ebre. La Llitera i el Baix Cinca. Obra arquitectònica dispersa i restaurada*. Barcelona: Enciclopèdia Catalana, 1997.
POVÉS, M. Luisa. "Los fragmentos de códices visigóticos de la Catedral de Sto. Domingo de la Calzada". *Revista de Archivos, Bibliotecas y Museos* 58 (1952): 517-520.
PRADO, Germán. *Manual de liturgia hispano-visigótica o mozárabe*. Madrid: Voluntad, 1927.
—. "Mozarabic melodies". *Speculum* 3 (1928): 218-238.
—. *Cantus lamentationum pro ultimo triduo hebdomadae majoris justa hispanos codices*. Paris: Desclée, 1934.
—. "El Kyrial español". *Analecta Sacra Tarraconensia* 14 (1941): 97-128.
QUEIRÓS, Abílio. "Missal Medieval da Sé de Coimbra". Unpublished doctoral thesis, Coimbra: Faculty of Letters of the University of Coimbra, 1993.
—. "Inventário dos fragmentos litúrgico-musicais existentes no A. U. C. (1.ª parte)". *Boletim do Arquivo da Universidade de Coimbra* 13-14 (1993-1994).
—. "Inventário dos fragmentos litúrgico-musicais existentes no A. U. C. (2.ª parte)". *Boletim do Arquivo da Universidade de Coimbra* 15-16 (1997).
—. "Fragmento de um códice litúrgico-musical da Sé de Coimbra (século X-XI)". In *Semente em Boa Terra. Raízes do Cristianismo na Diocese de Coimbra. Do século IV a 1064*. Coimbra: Gráfica de Coimbra, 2000, 138-140.
RAMOS RIOJA, María Teresa. "Fragmentos musicales del archivo del Monasterio de Santo Domingo de Silos". In Miguel C. Vivancos, ed. *Catálogo del archivo del Monasterio de Santo Domingo de Silos*. Santo Domingo de Silos: Monastery of Silos, 2006 (Studia Silensia: 39).
RANDEL, Don M. *The Responsorial Psalm Tones of the Mozarabic Office*. Princeton, New Jersey: Princeton University Press, 1969.
—. *An Index to the Chant of the Mozarabic Rite*. Princeton, New Jersey: Princeton University Press, 1973 (Princeton Studies in Music: 6).
—. "El antiguo rito hispánico y la salmodia primitiva en Occidente". *Revista de Musicología* 8, no. 2 (1985): 229-238.
REY OLLEROS, Manuel. *La música medieval en Ourense*. Vol. 1, *Pergaminos musicales del archivo catedralicio*. Ourense: Xunta de Galicia, Consejería de Cultura, 2002.
RIAÑO, Juan F. *Critical and Bibliographical Notes on Early Spanish Music*. London: Bernard Quaritch, 1887.
RIBAY, Bernard. "Les *Lamentations de Jeremie* du *Breviarium notatum* de Silos". *Revista de Musicología* 15, nos. 2-3 (1992): 511-564 *[La música en la Abadía de Silos. Trabajos del I Simposio de Musicología Religiosa (Burgos, Silos, marzo de 1991)]*.
RICO, Francisco. *Signos e indicios en la portada de Ripoll*. Barcelona: Fundación Juan March, 1976; reproduced in *idem*. *Figuras con paisaje*. Barcelona: Galaxia Gutenberg-Círculo de Lectores, 1994, 107-176.
RIOU, Yves. "Les manuscrits neumés des poèmes d'Eugène II de Tolède". *Annuaire de l'École Pratique des Hautes Études* (1963-1964).
RIUS SERRA, J. "Bendiciones episcopales en un manuscrito de Roda". *Hispania Sacra* 10, no. 19 (1957): 161-210.
RIVERA RECIO, Juan Francisco. *La iglesia de Toledo en el siglo XII (1086-1208)*. 2 vols. Rome, Toledo: Instituto Español de Historia Eclesiástica, IPIET, 1966-1976.

ROCHA, Pedro Romano. *L'office divin au Moyen Âge dans l'église de Braga: Originalité et dépendences d'une liturgie particulier au Moyen Âge*. Paris: Fundação Calouste Gulbenkian, 1980.

—. "Les sources languedociennes du Bréviaire de Braga". In *Liturgie et musique (IXe-XIVe s.)*. Toulouse: Privat, 1982, 185-207 (Collection d'Histoire religieuse du langue doc au XIIIe et au début du XIVe siècles: Cahiers de Fanjeaux 17).

—. "Influjo de los antifonarios aquitanos en el oficio divino de las iglesias del noroeste de la Península". In *Estudios sobre Alfonso VI y la Reconquista de Toledo. Actas del II Congreso Internacional de Estudios Mozárabes (Toledo 1985)*. Toledo: Instituto de Estudios Visigótico-Mozárabes, 1990. Vol. 4: 27-45.

RODRÍGUEZ SUSO, Carmen. "L'évolution modale, dans les antiennes de l'*ordo* wisigothique pour la consécration de l'autel". *Études grégoriennes* 26 (1998): 173-204.

ROJO, Casiano. *Cantus lamentationum, apud hispanos usurpatus quem ex codice Silensi saeculo XIII conscripto nunc primum iuris publici fecit*. Bilbao: Elexpuru, 1917.

—. "The Gregorian Antiphonary of Silos and the Spanish Melody of the *Lamentations*". *Speculum* 5, no. 3 (1930): 306-323.

ROJO, Casiano, and Germán PRADO. *El canto mozárabe: estudio histórico-crítico de su antigüedad y estado actual*. Barcelona: Biblioteca de Cataluña, 1929.

ROJO ORCAJO, Timoteo. *Catálogo descriptivo de los códices que se conservan en la Santa Iglesia Catedral de El Burgo de Osma*. Madrid: Tipografía de Archivos, 1929.

RUBIO SADIA, Juan Pablo. *Las órdenes religiosas y la introducción del rito romano en la Iglesia de Toledo. Una aportación desde las fuentes litúrgicas*. Toledo: Instituto Teológico de San Ildefonso, Instituto de Estudios Visigótico-Mozárabes, 2004.

RUIZ ASENCIO, José Manuel. "Códices pirenaicos y riojanos en la biblioteca de Silos en el siglo XI". In José A. Fernández Flórez, dir. *Silos. Un milenio. Actas del Congreso Internacional sobre la Abadía de Santo Domingo de Silos*. Vol. 2, *Historia*. Santo Domingo de Silos: Monastery of Silos, University of Burgos, 2003, 177-210 (Studia Silensia: 26).

RUIZ GARCÍA, Elisa. *Catálogo de la Sección de Códices de la Real Academia de la Historia*. Madrid: Real Academia de la Historia, 1997.

SABLAYROLLES, Maur. "Un viatge a través dels manuscrits gregorians espanyols". *Revista Musical Catalana* 3 (1906): 91-94, 131-132, 149-151, 177-183, 200-203, 221-226; 4 (1907): 4-9, 23-37, 48-51, 116-121, 139-142, 161-166, 208-211, 231-236; 5 (1908): 4-6, 203-206, 227-230; 6 (1909): 9-15, 95-99, 132-139, 172-180.

—. "Une notation neumatique intéressante". *Rassegna Gregoriana* 8 (1909): 405-414.

—. "Une notation grégorienne espagnole". In *Al maestro Pedrell: Escritos heortásticos*. Tortosa: Orfeó Tortosí, 1911, 301-306.

—. "À la recherche des manuscrits grégoriens espagnols: Iter hispanicum". *Sammelbände der Internationalen Musik Gesellschaft* 13 (1911-1912): 205-247; 401-432; 509-531.

SAINZ DE BARANDA, Pedro. *España Sagrada*. Vol. 47, *De la Santa Iglesia de Lérida en su estado moderno*. Madrid: Imprenta de la Real Academia de la Historia, 1850.

SALMON, Pierre. *L'Office divin au Moyen Âge: Histoire de la formation du bréviaire du IXe au XVIe siècle*. Paris: Cerf, 1967 (Lex orandi: 43).

Santo António em Santa Cruz. Códices do Mosteiro de Santa Cruz de Coimbra no Tempo de Santo António (Roteiro da Exposição da BPMP no VIII Centenário do Nascimento de Santo António 26 de Setembro a 8 de Dezembro de 1995). Porto: Biblioteca Pública Municipal do Porto, 1995.

SARGATAL, Ramon. "L'ensenyament a l'escola monàstica de l'alta edad mitjana". In Marina Miquel, and Margarida Salas, coords. *Temps de monestirs. Els monestirs catalans entorn l'any mil*. Barcelona: Pòrtic-Generalitat de Cataluña, Departamento de Cultura, 1999, 206-217.

SERDÀ, Lluís. "La introducció de la litúrgia romana a Catalunya". In *II Congrés Litúrgic de Montserrat*. Montserrat: Abbey of Montserrat, 1967. Vol. 3: 9-19.

Seu Vella: L'esplendor retrobada. (Exhibition catalog.) Lleida: Departamento de Cultura, Generalitat de Cataluña, Fundació La Caixa, 2003.

SÉVESTRE, Nicole. "La tradition mélodique du Cantus Sibyllae". In Danielle Buschinger, and André Crepin, eds. *La représentation de l'antiquité au Moyen Âge: Actes du colloque des 26, 27 et 28 mars 1981, Université de Picardie, Centre d'Études Médiévales*. Vienna: K. M. Halosar, 1982, 269-283 (Wiener Arbeiten zur germanischen Altertumskunde und Philologie: 20).

SICART, Ángel. *Pintura medieval: la miniatura*. Santiago de Compostela: Fundación Sánchez Cantón, 1981.

SILVA Y VERÁSTEGUI, Soledad de. *La miniatura medieval en Navarra*. Pamplona: Gobierno de Navarra, Departamento de Educación y Cultura, 1988.

—. *La miniatura en el Monasterio de San Millán de la Cogolla: una contribución al estudio de los códices miniados en los siglos XI al XIII*. Logroño: Instituto de Estudios Riojanos, Gobierno de La Rioja, 1999.

STÄBLEIN, Bruno. "Lamentatio". In Friedrich Blume, ed. *Die Musik in Geschichte und Gegenwart*. Kassel: Bärenreiter, 1960. Vol. 8: 133-142.

STEINER, Ruth. "Directions for chant research in the 1990's: the impact of chant data bases". *Revista de Musicología* 16, no. 2 (1993): 697-705 *[Actas del XV Congreso de la Sociedad Internacional de Musicología, "Culturas musicales del Mediterráneo y sus ramificaciones" (Madrid, 3-10/IV/1992)*. Vol. 2].

—. "The Twenty-two Invitatory Tones of the Manuscript Toledo, Biblioteca Capitular, 44-2". In Malcolm Cole, and John Koegel, eds. *Music in Performance and Society: Essays in Honor of Roland Jackson*. Warren, Michigan: Harmonie Park Press, 1997, 59-79 (Detroit Monographs in Musicology/Studies in Music: 20).

SUNYOL, Gregori M. *Introducció a la paleografia musical gregoriana*. Montserrat: Abbey of Montserrat, 1925.

—. "Els Cants de la Genealogia de Jesucrist". *Vida Cristiana* 17 (1929): 54-65.

—. *Introduction à la paléographie musicale gregorienne*. Paris: Société de Saint Jean l'Évangéliste, Desclée, 1935.

SZÖVÉRFFY, Joseph. "Huesca et les hymnes de Saint Pierre". *Hispania Sacra* 9, no. 17 (1956): 87-110.

—. *Iberian Hymnody: Survey and Problems*. Worcester, Mississippi: Classical Folia Editions, 1971.

TAXONERA, Marc. *La biblioteca y el archivo de Montserrat*. Montserrat: Abbey of Montserrat, 1954.

THANNABAUR, Peter Josef. *Das einstimmige Sanctus der römischen Messe in der handschriflichen Überlieferung des 11.-16. Jahrhunderts*. Munich: Walter Ricke, 1962 (Erlanger Arbeiten zur Musikwissenschaft: 1).

UBIETO ARTETA, Antonio. "El libro de san Voto". *Hispania Sacra* 3, no. 5 (1950): 191-204.

—. *Cartulario de Santa Cruz de la Serós*. Valencia: Anubar, 1966.

UTTERBACK, Kristine T. "*Cum multimodi curiositatis*: A Musical Treatise from Eleventh-Century Catalonia". *Speculum* 54, no. 2 (1979): 283-296.

VASCONCELOS, António de. "Fragmentos preciosos de dois códices paleográfico-visigóticos". *Biblos* 4 (1928): 553-569.

—. "Fragmentos dum códice visigótico". *Biblos* 5 (1929): 245-273.

VENDRELL PEÑARANDA, Manuela. "Estudio del Códice de Azagra". *Revista de Archivos, Bibliotecas y Museos* 82 (1979): 655-705.

VEZIN, Jean. "Un calendrier franco-hispanique de la fin du XIème siècle (Madrid, Acad. Hist. 18, fols. 6-11v)". *Bibliothèque de l'École des Chartes* 121 (1963): 5-25.

—. "El códice British Library add. 30849 y la introducción de la carolina en España". In José A. Fernández Flórez, dir. *Silos. Un milenio. Actas del Congreso Internacional sobre la Abadía de Santo Domingo de Silos*. Vol. 2, *Historia*. Santo Domingo de Silos: Monastery of Silos, University of Burgos, 2003, 211-222 (Studia Silensia: 26).

VILARES CEPEDA, Isabel, coord. *Inventário dos códices iluminados até 1500*. 2 vols. Lisbon: Ministerio de Cultura, Biblioteca Nacional, 2001.

VILLANUEVA, Jaime. "Códices e incunables de la Catedral de Vich". *Boletín de la Real Academia de la Historia* 25 (1894): 320-331.

—. *Viage literario a las Iglesias de España*. 22 vols. Madrid, Valencia: Real Academia de la Historia, 1803-1852.

VIVANCOS, Miguel C. *Glosas y notas marginales de los manuscritos visigóticos del Monasterio de Santo Domingo de Silos*. Santo Domingo de Silos: Monastery of Silos, 1996 (Studia Silensia: 19).

—. "*Liber ordinum* de San Prudencio de Monte Laturce (AMS 4)". In Claudio García Turza, coord. *Los manuscritos visigóticos: estudio paleográfico y codicológico*. Vol. 1, *Códices riojanos datados*. Logroño: Fundación San Millán de la Cogolla, 2002, 201-225.

—. "Officia propria Sancti Dominici de Silos ex veteribus codicibus collecta". *Ecclesia Orans* 19 (2002): 63-84.

—. "Consideraciones históricas y codicológicas en torno al Beato de Silos". In *Beato de Liébana. Códice del Monasterio de Santo Domingo de Silos*. Facsimile edition. Barcelona: Moleiro, 2003, 11-69.

Vives, José. "El oracional mozárabe de Silos". *Analecta Sacra Tarraconensia* 18 (1945): 1-24.

—. *Oracional visigótico*. Madrid: CSIC, Instituto P. Enrique Flórez, 1946 (Monumenta Hispaniae Sacra: Serie Litúrgica 1).

—. "Tradición y leyenda en la hagiografía hispánica". *Hispania Sacra* 17, nos. 33-34 (1964): 495-508.

Vives, José, and Ángel Fábrega. "Calendarios hispánicos anteriores al s. xiii". *Hispania Sacra* 2, no. 4 (1949): 339-380.

Wagner, Peter. "Der mozarabische Kirchengesang und seine Überlieferung". In *Gesammelte Aufsätze zur Kulturgeschichte Spaniens*. Münster: Aschendorff, 1928. Vol. 1: 102-142 (Spanische Forschungen der Görresgesellschaft: 1).

—. "Untersuchungen zu den Gesangstexten und zur responsorialen Psalmodie der altspanischen Liturgie". In *Gesammelte Aufsätze zur Kulturgeschichte Spaniens* (Spanische Forschungen der Görresgesellschaft: Serie 1). Münster, Aschendorff, 1930. Vol. 2: 67-113.

Walker, Rose. *Views of transition. Liturgy and Illumination in Medieval Spain*. London: British Library, 1998.

Weiss, Günther, ed. *Introitus-Tropen*. Vol. 1, *Das Repertoire der südfranzösischen Tropare des 10. und 11. Jahrhunderts*. Kassel: Bärenreiter, 1970 (Monumenta Monodica Medii Aevi: Subsidia 3).

Whitehill, Walter Muir. "A Catalogue of Mozarabic Liturgical Manuscripts containing the Psalter and *Liber canticorum*". *Jahrbuch für Liturgiewissenschaft* 14 (1934): 95-122.

Yarza, Joaquín. "Iconografía de la crucifixión en la miniatura española". *Archivo Español de Arte* 47 (1974): 13-38.

Zaldívar, Álvaro. "El Canto de la Sibila: una aportación oscense al drama litúrgico medieval". In *Signos: arte y cultura en el Alto Aragón medieval (Huesca, 26 junio-26 septiembre de 1993)*. Huesca: Gobierno de Aragón, Diputación Provincial, 1993, 190-195.

Zapke, Susana. "El oficio de san Indalecio en el Antifonario de Santa Cruz de la Serós, siglos xi-xii". *Aragonia Sacra* 6 (1991): 181-198.

—. "Estructura melódica de la Salmodia responsorial del rito hispano, ejemplificada en el Antifonario de San Juan de la Peña". *Nassarre* 8, no. 1 (1992): 155-183.

—. "Manuscritos litúrgicos de la Diócesis de Jaca-Huesca fuera de Aragón". In *Signos: Arte y cultura en el Alto Aragón Medieval (Huesca, 26 junio-26 septiembre de 1993)*. Huesca: Gobierno de Aragón, Diputación Provincial, 1993, 133-135.

—. "Estudios de semiología comparada en base a dos antifonarios altoaragoneses SJP y SCS". In Eliseo Serrano Martín, ed. *Muerte, religiosidad y cultura popular. Siglos xiii-xviii*. Zaragoza: Institución Fernando el Católico, 1994, 509-517.

—. *El Antifonario de San Juan de la Peña (siglos x-xi): estudio litúrgico musical del rito hispano*. Zaragoza: Institución Fernando el Católico, 1995.

—. "Die fränkische-römische Überlieferung in Aragón (Nordspanien)". In László Dobzay, ed. *International Musicological Society Study Group Cantus Planus. Papers Read at the 6th Meeting (Eger, Hungary, 1993)*. Budapest: Hungarian Academy of Sciences, Institute for Musicology, 1995. Vol. 1: 353-366.

—. *Das Antiphonar von Sta. Cruz de la Serós, xii. Jh*. Neuried: Ars Una, 1996.

—. "Mozaraber". In Hans Dieter Betz, Don S. Browning, Bernd Janowski, and Eberhard Jüngel, eds. *Religion in Geschichte und Gegenwart. 4. Auflage*. Tübingen: Mohr Siebeck, 2002. Vol. 5: 1556.

—. "Mozarabische Liturgie". In Hans Dieter Betz, Don S. Browning, Bernd Janowski, and Eberhard Jüngel, eds. *Religion in Geschichte und Gegenwart. 4. Auflage*. Tübingen: Mohr Siebeck, 2002. Vol. 5: 1556-1557.

—. *Fragmentos litúrgico-musicales de la Edad Media en Archivos de Aragón. Siglos xi ex.-xiii ex.* Huesca: Instituto de Estudios Altoaragoneses, Diputación General de Aragón, 2007.

Appendices

Glossary

This glossary aims to help nonspecialists understand the liturgical and musicological terminology used in this book. At no time have we aimed to offer a comprehensive definition of these terms, which in many cases would require much greater precision; however, we have tried to make it easier to understand a text that inevitably is full of technical terms and a liturgical vocabulary that is inaccessible to the general public. We have basically included here liturgical and musicological terms used in certain parts of the book. Given the difference between the Roman and Hispanic liturgies, rites of which the codices described here form a part, we have tried to distinguish between the terms commonly used in each of them, as on occasions the same word has different meanings in one rite or the other. To make it easier to identify them, the words marked with an asterisk are the ones that are typical of the Hispanic liturgy.

Ad accedentes*. Characteristic chant in the communion rite for Mass; it generally begins with the words of Psalm 33:9: "Gustate et videte quam suavis est Dominus".

Ad commixtionem*. Prayer recited quietly by the priest when mixing a portion of the host and the wine consecrated during mass. It usually ends with a *Trisagion*-style ovation.

Ad completorium. Last of the canonical hours, performed before retiring for the night.

Ad confractionem*. Responsorial antiphon that accompanies the breaking of the bread during Mass on feast days; it can be repeated up to three times, or several different antiphons can be sung. It is sometimes called *Laudes ad confractionem.*

Ad orationem dominicam*. Eighth variable prayer in the Mass; it comes before the chant of the Lord's Prayer.

Ad pacem*. Fourth variable prayer in the Mass, recited before the kiss of peace.

Adiastematy. See Diastematy. Characteristic quality of a notation system that does not differentiate between different pitches and places the notational signs at a single level.

Advent. *(Lat. adventus)* Liturgical period lasting four weeks before Christmas that heralded the celebration of the birth of Christ.

Agnus Dei. Song of praise added to the Mass by Pope Sergius towards the year 680. The term comes from John 1:29. It is the remains of certain preces that originated in the East that spread in the West in the 7th century *ex.* This chant was sung by the clergy and the congregation, which responded with the litany *miserere nobis.*

Agyos*. See Trisagion.

Alia*. Second variable prayer during Mass; it is recited by the priest to ask God to accept the congregation's prayers and offerings.

Alleluia. Chant performed by a soloist to which the choir provides a response. It is one of the characteristic pieces during Mass that function as songs of praise and precede the reading of the Gospel. During Lent, Advent, or the office of the dead, it is replaced by the *Tractus* (see

TRACTUS). Characteristic of the Alleluia is the placing of the *iubilus* (see IUBILUS) on the final *a* of the *alleluia,* a melisma that is usually long and florid.

ALLELUIATICUM*. Antiphon with alleluias sung in response that is characteristic of the Sunday morning office, except during Lent.

ALLISIO INFANTUM*. Name of the feast day of the slaughter of the Holy Innocents; it is held on 8 January.

ANTIPHON. *(Gr. Antiphonos)* Chant consisting of one or two verses, taken from the Bible or created independently, which precedes the psalm and forms part of both the mass and the divine office. The melody shows a more elaborate design in the latter case (see ANTIPHONS, MARIAN). The mode of the antiphon, which can be recognized from the final cadence, establishes in turn the choice of psalm tone The abbreviation *Euouae (seculorum Amen)* refers to the psalmodic cadence (*differentia*).

ANTIPHONA AD COMMUNIONEM. Antiphon sung during communion, with a complex melodic structure, which is generally accompanied by some verses from the psalms.

ANTIPHONA AD PACEM*. Antiphon sung at Mass during the kiss of peace with text that is usually taken from the Gospel of St. John 14:27: *Pacem relinquo vobis.*

ANTIPHONARIUS. Liturgical book that contains the pieces sung in the divine office except for the hymns. In its original form, the *Graduale*, the book of the Mass, it was called *Antiphonale missarum* as opposed to *Antiphonale offici*.

ANTIPHONARIUS*. Collection of chants for the mass and the festive cathedral office, following the order of the calendar starting with the feast of St. Acisclus (17 November), to which common and votive pieces are added, all with musical notation.

ANTIPHONS, MARIAN. Series of antiphons in praise of the Virgin sung at the end of each office depending on the liturgical period. They are as follows: *Alma redemptoris mater, Ave regina caelorum, Regina caeli laetare,* and *Salve regina.*

APPARITIO DOMINI*. Name given to the feast of the Epiphany celebrated 6 January.

BENEDICTIO*. Blessing in the Mass or office, always variable, generally divided into three parts and always performed before the communion rite during Mass.

BENEDICTIONES*. Antiphon that accompanies the canticle *Benedictus es Domine Deus* (Dn 3:52-90), often performed during the morning office.

BIBLE*. Strictly speaking, the Bible is not a liturgical book, because the biblical pericopes for each celebration are included in lectionaries. However, there are some Bibles that include an indication of the liturgical festivals in their margins next to the passages to be read on these. Others indicate Old Testament canticles. From a musicological perspective, the ones that are especially interesting are those copies in which musical notation is added to the *Lamentations*, which are typical of the offices during Easter.

BREVIARY, PLENARY. Liturgical book that contains all the formulas and rites of the divine office; it did not exist before the 11th century.

CANTILLATION. Type of basic recitation of biblical texts characterized privileging text over melody. The recitation is based on the prosody and syntactic structure of the text to stress its meaning while always avoiding an emphasis on elaborate melodic patterns.

CANTOR. From the 10th century onwards, the priest or monk responsible for teaching the chant-repertoire and conducting the choir or schola was known as a *cantor*.

CAPITULUM or *Capitula:* Short reading from the Holy Scriptures.

CARNES TOLLENDAS*. See DOMINICA DE CARNES TOLLENDAS.

CATCHWORD. Note at the end of a leaf or bifolium, or at the end of a quaternion, with the first word or words on the next leaf, to ensure the correct order of the manuscript.

CHANT, GREGORIAN. Monophonic chant in Latin used by the Church of Rome. It is named after Pope Gregory the Great, who decreed a new liturgical order in 600 that would end up replacing local traditions such as the Gallican or Hispanic rites. Only the Ambrosian tradition was able to survive the effects of the reform.

Clamor*. Response-type of solemn chant during Mass, joined to the *Psallendum* on major feasts. It is also found in the offices of sext and none and in the office of the dead.

Collecta. First variable prayer during Mass, said before the Epistle

Comicus*. Hispanic liturgical lectionary that includes the three readings during mass: *Prophetia* (or reading from the Old Testament), an Epistle (or reading from the New Testament), generally called *Apostolus* as it is taken from the letters of St. Paul, and a Gospel reading. None of these readings usually has musical notation, although there are cases in which neumes have been written above the text of the Passion.

Commune sanctorum. Set of pieces dedicated to those saints who do not have an office of their own. The structure of the pieces varies depending on the saint's status (apostle, martyr, Bishop confessor, non-Bishop confessor, virgin, etc.).

Completas. See *Ad completorium*.

Completuria*. Last variable prayer during Mass, but not always to be found in all manuscripts, especially in the oldest ones; the term also designates the prayer at the end of each hour of the office.

Cursus. See *usus*. Selection of chants, readings, and prayers that define a specific Latin rite.

Custos. Sign at the end of a melodic melody line marking the pitch at which the following line begins. The *custos* is a crucial element characteristic of the system of Aquitainian notation, demonstrating its clear diastematic conception. It was introduced into the Peninsula in the 11th century, the period in which the reform of the liturgy began.

Dextrogirous. See levogyrous. Script in which the axis tilts towards the right.

Diastematy. See Adiastematy (*Gr. diástema:* interval). Specific quality of a notational system that can graphically represent different pitches.

Differentia. Cadential formulas for each psalm tone that reinforce the link with the repetition of the antiphon after the doxology. Tonaries (see Tonary) include the complete list of these cadences, sometimes grouped in the different genres to which they belong. The tonaries in the Aquitainian tradition arrange these cadences according to tones from 1 to 8.

Dominica de carnes tollendas*. First Sunday in Lent. In the Hispanic liturgy, Lent began on the first Sunday, not the previous Wednesday, so that the Lenten fast began on the Monday that followed the first Sunday.

Doxology. Prayer formula praising *(doxa)* God, the Holy Trinity, or the saints. Lesser doxology: *Gloria Patri...* sung at the end of the psalms. Greaterdoxology: *Gloria in excelsis Deo* in the laudes (Ambrosian rite) or during mass according to the Roman *cursus*.

Ductus. Rate of speed and way of producing graphic signs during the act of writing. There is a difference between slow *ductus (litterae positae)* and cursive *ductus (litterae cursivae)*. In the first case, the signs are drawn separately with separate strokes, which forces the scribe to raise the quill with each gesture; in the latter, the letters are joined together, and, to the extent possible, the scribe avoids raising the writing tool from the surface of the page.

Dyptichum*. See Nomina offerentium.

Epiphany. Feast celebrated in the West on 6 January that commemorates the three manifestations of the Lord: to the Gentiles through the Magi, to the Jews through baptism, and to his disciples through the miracle at the Wedding in Canaan.

Episema. Additional sign added to neumes to show special rhythmic or melodic features.

Evangeliarium. Liturgical book that contains the gospel readings for each day of the year.

Feria. Any day of the week that is neither Saturday nor Sunday, starting with Monday or feria II.

Graduale. Roman liturgical book that contains the chants at Mass, also called *antiphonarium missae* to distinguish it from the *antiphonarium* containing the pieces for the office. The responsorial chant that together with the Tractus (see TRACTUS) shows a high degree of melodic development is also known by this name. This is a chant performed by a soloist from the steps of the altar, which is the origin of its name. The melodies of graduals are classified in groups according to the tone that they are assigned based on the final note. The most common group of this kind of chant belongs to the fifth mode, with an ending on F.

HOMILIARIUS. Liturgical book that contains homilies or lessons for the third nocturn at matins.

HOMILIARY, RESPONSORIAL. The first trace of this type of book, which was not widespread, is found in the great homiliaries of the night office, which included the incipit of the responsory to be sung at the end of each reading. Later on, homiliaries were to provide the complete responsory, so that they became like a kind of breviary.

HOURS, LITURGICAL. Sung offices made up of psalms, hymns, and readings that are spread over the day following the classical names for how the hours are divided up. (See PRIME, TERCE, SEXT, NONE, VESPERAE, AD COMPLETORIUM, LAUDES, AND VIGILIAE.)

HYMNARIUS. Liturgical-musical source that contains the repertoire of hymns.

HYMNUM. Liturgical-poetical-musical form in which each strophe is sung to the same melody. The first definition of a hymn is attributed to St. Augustine *(Enarrationes in psalmos)*. Apart from hymnaries, which are the most fundamental source for compilations of the repertoire of hymns, these chants can be found in antiphonaries, Psalters, breviaries, and other liturgical-musical books.

ICTUS. Term coined by Dom Mocquereau to refer to a vertical mark that points out the beginning of a rhythmic sequence.

IMPROPERIA. The chant of the reproaches, so called in reference to Christ's words of reproach for the people who had betrayed him, is characteristic of the celebration of Good Friday and is recited just after the antiphon *Ecce lignum crucis*. The chant includes a series of invocations in Greek and Latin sung in alternation by soloists and the choir.

IN CAMPO APERTO. This applies to notation that does not specify pitch; an example is Visigothic notation. Aquitainian notation, on the other hand, uses a line to demarcate the range in which the melody is sung.

INLATIO*. Fifth variable prayer during Mass, in the form of the preface of the Roman Mass It is generally very long and ends with the chant of the *Sanctus* sung by the entire congregation.

INTERVAL. *(Latin: Intervallum)*. Tonal space between two pitches.

INTONATION. Melodic formula for the beginning of a chant.

INTROITUS. *Antiphona ad introitum*. Introductory chant of the Mass, accompanying the passage of the priest towards the altar, it consists of an antiphon, a psalm, the doxology *Gloria patri* and the repetition of the antiphon.

IUBILUS. See ALLELUIA. Term that refers to the melisma on the final syllable of the *alleluia*.

KYRIE. A song of praise in Greek repeated three times, followed by the invocation, *Christe eleison,* also repeated three times, which ends with another three *Kyrie eleison*. They are sung during Mass and on many other occasions, and the invocations sung at the former had highly developed melodies.

LAMENTATIONES. Lessons for the Office of Darkness or *Tenebrae*, from the Book of Jeremiah in the Old Testament, which were recited on a specific tone called *tonus lamentationum* in the first nocturnal office of matins during the *Holy Triduum* (Maundy Thursday, Good Friday, and Holy Saturday). Each lesson ends with the verse *Jerusalem*. During the Middle Ages, there was a wide variety of *tonus lamentationum* inthe various traditions. The melody is syllabic and consists of a beginning (*initium* or *intonatio*), a recitation range *(tenor)*, an inflection *(mediatio),* and an ending (*terminatio* or *differentia*).

LAUDES. Canonical hour performed each day at dawn after the night office.

LAUDES*. Responsorial chant with alleluia that concludes the Liturgy of the Word after the homily during Mass (outside Lent).

Laudes ad confractionem*. See Ad confractionem.

Legendum*. Or *Legendus.* Name given to the first two readings during mass (*prophetia* and *apostolus*).

Lent. Liturgical period from Ash Wednesday up to and including the morning of Maundy Thursday, which prepares for the celebration of the Easter triduum.

Levogira. See dextrogirus. Script in which the axis slants to the left.

Libellus. Format used to transmit the liturgical repertoire before the codex. Together with the *Rotullus*, the *Libellus* constitutes the first written record for new repertoire and generally consists of a single quaternion.

Liber canticorum*. Book that includes the canticles from the Old Testament according to the liturgical order in which they were recited in the office, with their own antiphon, generally set to music. Normally the *Liber canticorum* forms a unit with the *Liber psalmorum* and the *Liber hymnorum.*

Liber horarum*. Plenary book that contains the diurnal and nocturnal hours of the divine office according to the *ordo cathedralis* or monastic order, with notation for the chants.

Liber hymnorum*. Collection of proper hymns for the liturgical seasons and the feast days of the Lord and the saints. Usually at least the first strophe is notated. Normally the *Liber hymnorum* forms a unit with the *Liber canticorum* and the *Liber psalmorum.*

Liber missarum*. Also known as *Manuale.* It brings together the various prayers of the Mass in a single book. Only one codex from Toledo with these characteristics has survived, but it is frequently mentioned in documents.

Liber orationum*. Also known as *orationale.* It includes the prayers for the festal cathedral office, accompanied by their corresponding antiphon, which is often provided with musical notation.

Liber ordinum*. Plenary book that includes all the pieces required to perform sacraments and blessings, to which a large number of votive masses have been added. There is a *Liber ordinum maior* for bishops and a *liber minor,* suitable for the performance of sacraments and sacramentals by priests. Many of the chants have musical notation.

Liber precum*. Collection of penitential prayers for the office and Mass, usually called *Miserationes* because almost all of them begin with the word *Miserere.* No copies of this book have survived, but it is frequently mentioned by documentary sources and would definitely have contained musical notation.

Liber psalmorum*. Book containing the Old Testament psalms according to the liturgical order in which they are recited in the office, accompanied by the psalmic prayers and their corresponding antiphons and verses, generally set to music. The *Liber psalmorum* usually forms a unit with the *Liber canticorum* and the *Liber hymnorum.*

Liber sermonum*. Also called a homiliary, it includes the patristic homilies for Sundays and feasts that are read in the office and during Mass.

Litaniae. Series of invocations, sung in alternation by the choir and congregation, addressed directly to God through the saints. Letania major refers to the Rogations procession that takes place on St. Mark's Day (25 April). Letania minor refers to the Rogations procession that takes place on each of the three days before the feast of the Ascension.

Lucernarium*. See Oblatio luminis.

Manuale*. See Liber missarum.

Martyrologium. Catalog of saints recognized by the Church that includes a short piece of information or *elogium* about each one celebrated on each day of the year. It is read communally after the office of Prime.

Matins. See Vigiliae.

Matutinarium*. Responsorial antiphon that accompanies the canticle in the morning office during Lent.

Melisma. Series of neumes that form a melodic pattern of variable length on a vowel.

Melody, standard. This refers to melodies that can be adapted to various texts by making minimum adjustments involving variations in the number of syllables.

Miserationes*. See Preces.

Missa*. First variable prayer during Mass, making reference to the liturgical occasion (feast of the day), it is generally fairly long and is recited by the priest at the beginning of the eucharistic liturgy. It is sometimes called *Oratio admonitionis.* The term also designates the group of three psalms, with antiphons and prayers and a responsory that forms part of the morning office.

Missa omnimoda*. Common votive Mass, not linked to any special occasion, at which prayers are said for the entire Church.

Missa secreta*. Fixed part of the canon of the Mass that includes the words of the Eucharistic institution; the term *secreta* refers to the mysterious nature of these words, which were heard by the faithful with great reverence. They were not said at a volume that the congregation could not hear, although it is possible that as time went by, they were spoken very quietly.

Missale. Liturgical book that contains the ceremonies, prayers, and readings for the celebration of mass.

Misticus*. Plenary book that in its entirety was to cover four volumes, with pieces from the office and the Mass. Many of these are usually accompanied by musical notation.

Mode. In the sphere of sacred monophony, a concept that refers to the structure of both tonal and rhythmical material, as well as to the intervals between pitches. The Gregorian repertoire has a total of eight modes, divided into four authentic modes and four plagal ones, which are derived from the former.

Monody. Chant for one voice part.

Neumatic. Referring to neumes. When a neume is long, it is said to be structured in various neumatic elements.

Neume. (*Gr. pneuma:* breath) From the 7th century onwards, a textless melisma (vocalise). Amalarius called a group of three long melismas *neuma triplex*; from the 12th century onwards, it referred to a sign representing the pitches of a melody. The first recorded testimony of *tabulae neumarum* or *nominae notarum* are from the 11th and 12th centuries.

Nocturn. One of the two or three groups of psalms and readings that make up the night office of vigils (Matins).

Noenoeane-Noeagis. The tonaries in the Byzantine liturgy used this meaningless series of syllables with a mnemonic function to illustrate the various melodic formulas employed in chants.

Nomina offerentium*. List of names of saints, of members of the clergy, of offerers, of the entire congregation, and of the dead that the priest or deacon, and on some occasions the cantors, recite during mass after the *Alia* prayer. It is sometimes called *Dyptichum* or *Dypticha.*

None. The last of the little canonical hours; it used to be performed after midday, although from the late Middle Ages onwards, it was usually joined to sext after the conventual Mass.

Notation. System of signs for the graphic representation of music.

Notation, Aquitainian. See Dot notation. It is characterized by the almost exclusive use of dots to represent tones and by its diastematic nature (see Diastematy) It makes use of a custos (see Custos) and of a line that was originally imaginary but later matched the lines of the writing frame, as tonal references. The name *Aquitainian notation* refers to its main zone of influence in Aquitaine, a region located in the southwest of modern France. The oldest evidence for this type of notation dates back to the 10th century.

Notation, Catalonian. Notation typical of the Catalonian-Narbonne rite that spread in Catalonia, an area that was to adopt the new Gallo-Roman rite before the rest of the Peninsula. It forms part of the family of notation with accents, and it includes a great variety of graphic signs and special neumes, and an early form of diastematy. The oldest evidence for this kind of notation dates back to the 11th century, and its use expanded in various more developed forms until well into the 12th century.

Notation, Dot. See Aquitainian notation. The notation from southwest France is sometimes called dot notation or superimposed dot notation. It is usually known as *Aquitainian notation*.

Notation, Hispanic. See Visigothic notation. Notation used to transmit the Hispanic rite. Its adiastematic profile and *in campo aperto* notation make it practically impossible to transcribe any of the repertoire. The great variety of marks and additional signs shows that the notational language of the old Hispanic rite achieved high levels of sophistication. Replaced by Aquitainian notation from the 11th century onwards as part of the liturgical-musical reform, the continuity of the Hispanic rite was reduced, and nowadays it is impossible to reconstruct the melodies in its repertoire, except in certain isolated cases in which the Visigothic neumes were scraped off and replaced by Aquitainian notation. There are two different styles or types of this notation: vertical, typical of centers in the North of the Peninsula, and horizontal, characteristic of the south and more specificially of the codices in Toledo and the old Portuguese dioceses of Braga and Coimbra.

Notation, Visigothic. See Hispanic notation.

Oblatio luminis*. Opening rite of the evening office, comparable to the *lucernarium* in other liturgies, which consists of the deacon lighting a lamp.

Octoechos. A system of eight modes, or musical structures, around which the entire repertoire of sacred monophony is arranged. The differences between each mode are based on the final note and the dominant, which is also called the *psalmodic tenor*. The term, which was common in the Byzantine repertoire, is open to a certain degree of uncertainty because it can refer not only to the eight modes but also to the arrangement of the Psalter in eight-week cycles.

Offertorium. Also called by some sources the *Antiphona ad offertorium*. Chant that accompanies offerings during Mass. Originally its structure was longer and more complex, like the structure of a responsorial chant. From the 12th century onwards, the number of verses was reduced. Neumatic phrases and melismas play an important role in both the body of the offertory and in its verses, but does not reflect is genre, for it is traditionally considered antiphonal.

Officium festivum*. Proper office for days when there is a special celebration of a mystery of Christ or the feast of a saint and for those days on which the office has a special form, with psalms, canticles, and particular readings, as occurs on Sundays and certain weekdays in Lent or during the Easter period.

Officium de quotidiano*. Office for those days on which no specific feast day is celebrated.

Oratio admonitionis*. See Missa.

Oratio dominica*. The Lord's Prayer, which the officiating priest recites alone at Mass, while the congregation responds to each invocation with *amen*.

Ordo cathedralis*. A series of services comprising the evening and morning offices and the celebration of the Eucharist, arranged in the same way in all churches, including those in monasteries. Terce, sext, and none are included only on penitential days.

Ordo monasticus*. Series of offices particular to monasteries (in contradistinction to the *ordo cathedralis*), which included the following offices: *Ad medium noctis; Peculiaris vigilia; Ordo in nocturnos; Ordo post nocturnos; Ordo peculiaris (Aurora); Prima et Secunda; Tertia; Quarta et Quinta; Sexta; Septima et Octava; Nona; Decima, Undecima et Duodecima; Completa (Ordo ante Completas, Ad Completa, Post Completa);* and *Ante lectulum*. Not all these hours were recited in the choir; some were prayed by monks in private.

Passionarium*. Book that includes the passions or lives of the saints for use in the office or during Mass.

Pontificale. Liturgical book containing the ceremonies for performing the sacraments that were reserved for bishops and the blessings and other liturgical ceremonies that were under the purview of bishops.

Post nomina*. Third variable prayer in the Mass concluding the recitation of the *Nomina offerentium.*

Post pridie*. Seventh variable prayer in the Mass, following the words of Eucharistic institution and usually including an invocation to the Holy Spirit, or epiclesis.

Post Sanctus*. Sixth variable prayer during Mass, actually the conclusion of the *Inlatio;* because its ending was sung, it often appears in manuscripts with musical notation.

Preces*. Chants that replace the laudes in Masses celebrated during Lent. As a solemn entreaty and invitation to prayer, *preces* also appear in the evening office at Lent and at funerals, and are sometimes called *Miserationes.*

Prelegendum*. Chant at the beginning of the Mass, similar to the introitus in the Roman liturgy.

Prime. See liturgical hours. The first of the four little hours of the divine office, to which the *officium capituli* is added with the reading of the martyrology and other preces.

Processionale. Liturgical book, also known as *Liber processionum* or *Processionarium,* that includes the prayers and chants performed in processions.

Proprium sanctorum. Part of the liturgical calendar that includes the feast days of the saints.

Proprium de tempore. Part of the liturgical calendar that includes the celebrations particular to each day, except for the celebrations in the calendar of saints' days.

Prosa. Trope adapted to an extended melisma, *melodia,* or *sequentia* at the beginning of the *alleluia.* It is known as *prosa* in Romance-language areas and as *sequentia* in Germanic-language areas.

Prosula. Prosella. Prosellus. Diminutive of *prosa* that refers to a trope (see Trope) with a simple structure. The term refers to the tropes of the *Kyrie*, *Gloria*, *Sanctus,* and *Agnus Dei* and can also be adapted to the *alleluia* and to the end of the offertory.

Psallendum*. Chant performed during Mass after the *Prophetia;* also the antiphonal chant in the festal morning office that was sung with a psalm, while the faithful walked in procession to the baptistry or to a martyr's tomb.

Psalterium. Book of the Old Testament that includes 150 poems or psalms attributed mostly to King David. As a liturgical book, the *psalterium* includes the psalms arranged in the order in which they are recited in each office and day of the week.

Quinquagesima. Sunday before Ash Wednesday, that is, fifty days before Easter.

Repetenda. Sign written in various ways (two dots tracing an oblique line and a figure like a capital *G*) placed under the text to show where the melody is repeated.

Responsorial. Musical practice in which the soloist's voice alternates with the choir.

Responsorium. Melismatic chant in the office or mass after a reading. The responsory is followed by the verse at the end of which the responsory is taken up again at a point called repetenda (see Repetenda) or *presa,* which is pointed out by a specific graphic sign.

Rotullus. Rolled-up parchment fragment with varying liturgical content. It seems to have been used as a primitive writing medium to spread repertoire before it was definitively and more elaborately integrated into a codex. Along with the *libellus*, the *rotullus* is considered to be a predecessor of the codex.

Rubric. Written text in red ink that refers to practical indications for the officiating priest.

Sacramentarium. Liturgical book that includes the canon and variable prayers of the Mass but that never includes sung pieces or readings.

Sacrificium*. Responsory that accompanies the presentation of offerings during Mass; similar to the offertory in the Roman liturgy.

Sanctorale. List of feast days of saints celebrated according to the liturgical calendar.

Sanctus. Chant that follows the recitation of the preface, the text of which text comes from the Prophet Isaiah (6:3); this refers to the hymn of the Seraphim in the temple of Jerusalem that invites the Church on earth to join the Church on high. The literary structure establishes the melody that consists of a sequence of short phrases and characteristic cadential formulas. The more elaborate melodic developments are preserved in the troped *sanctus*, in which each musical ornament falls on the word Hosanna.

Sanctus*. Song of praise with text from Is 6:3 and Mt 21:9, sung by the congregation at Mass as a colophon to the *Inlatio.* The *trisagion* at the beginning of Mass is sometimes also called *Sanctus*.

Septuagesima. The Sunday before Sexagesima Sunday, or the third Sunday before Ash Wednesday.

Sequentia. See Prosa. A characteristic term used in Germanic-language areas to refer to a type of poetic-musical composition identical to *prosa*.

Sexagesima. The Sunday before Quinquagesima Sunday, or the second Sunday before Ash Wednesday.

Sext. See Hours, Liturgical. The third of the four little hours of the office, to be sung at midday, although it ended up being recited after the end of Mass.

Sono*. Chant, usually with a complex melody, that is characteristic of the Sunday morning office, which probably accompanied the rite of censing the altar and church. On certain feast days, it was also recited during the evening office.

Terce. Third of the four little hours of the office; it was normally sung just before the mass.

Threni*. Chant that replaces the *Psallendum* in Masses during Lent, with a text usually but not always taken from the book of *Lamentations,* which is the origin of the name. It is often called *Trinos,* which is a corruption of the Hebrew word.

Tonale (Tonarius). List of psalm tones with their respective cadences (see Differentiae) illustrated by certain liturgical examples.

Tractus. Chant between lessons that replaces the *alleluia* in penitential periods; the tract includes several verses, after which it repeats the first part. The verses are based on a standard melody. This is a responsorial chant sung by a soloist; a reading from the Gospel followed its performance.

Trisagion*. Song of praise to the Holy Trinity that was sung only on major feasts with text that could be in Latin only or in both Latin and Greek. Sometimes the *trisagion* is called the *Agyos* or *Sanctus,* but it is not to be confused with the chant that follows the *Inlatio* (see Inlatio).

Troparium. Liturgical-musical collection containing the trope repertory. There are no rules regarding the structure and selction of texts for this type of liturgical source, so wide variety of types exists. The origins of the tropary (older than the prosary) date back to the 9th century, and it began to decline around the 12th century. This type of repertoire is usually found in mixed sources: *Troparium-Prosarium* or *Troparium-Prosarium-Procesionale*.

Tropus. Insertion or addition to a liturgical chant that may appear as a melisma or accompanied by a text, as a prelude, interlude, or postlude. With regard to their origin, context, and function, it is possible to distinguish between the following types: adapted, developed, interpolated, framed, complementary, and substitutional tropes. The classification adopted recently has been based on criteria concerning the genesis of tropes and distinguishes between melogenous (based on a melody), logogenous (based on a text), and meloform tropes. The word *trope* was originally understood to be a synonym of *melisma* or *neume*, as medieval sources themselves demonstrate.

Usus cathedralis. See Usus monasticus. *Usus* or *ordo cathedralis* refers to the liturgical cursus followed by a cathedral or collegiate community.

Usus monasticus. See Usus cathedralis. *Usus* or *ordo monasticus* refers to the liturgical cursus followed by a monastic community. It differs from the *ordo cathedralis* in how the liturgy of the office is arranged, whereas the Mass follows an almost identical format.

Verbeta. Term limited to Catalonian manuscripts, referring to tropes that are generally like short sung *proses* at matins on the most solemn feast days. The melody can be identical in all the verses or change every two verses.

Versiculus. Short prayer that consists of a phrase and its reponse or *responsum,* often taken from the book of psalms.

Versus. Verse that is sung in the office after the hymn, or the middle part of any responsorial chant that is not repeated.

Vespertinum*. Responsorial chant of the evening office, accompanying the rite of the *oblatio luminis.*

Vigiliae. Name given to the night office of matins until the end of the Middle Ages.

List of Abbreviations

ARCHIVES AND LIBRARIES

ABEV: Archivo y Biblioteca Episcopal de Vic
AC: Archivo Capitular (Córdoba, Santiago, Ourense, etc.)
ACA: Archivo de la Corona de Aragón (Barcelona)
AD: Arquivo Distrital (Braga)
AHA: Archivo Histórico Archidiocesano (Tarragona)
AHP: Archivo Histórico Provincial (Huesca, Zamora)
AM: Archivo Monástico (Silos, Sta. Cruz de la Serós)
ARCH: Archivo de la Real Chancillería (Valladolid)
ARGN: Archivo Real y General de Navarra (Pamplona)
AU: Arquivo Universitario (Coimbra)
BC: Biblioteca Capitular (Toledo)
BC: Biblioteca de Cataluña (Barcelona)
BGU: Biblioteca General Universitaria (Zaragoza, Salamanca)
BL: British Library (London)
BM: Biblioteca Monástica (Montserrat)
BN: Biblioteca Nacional (Madrid, Lisbon)
BNF: Bibliothèque Nationale de France (Paris)
BNM: Biblioteca Nazionale Marciana (Venice)
BPM: Biblioteca Pública Municipal (Porto)
BU: Biblioteca Universitaria (Leiden)
BXU: Biblioteca General Universitaria (Santiago de Compostela)
HS: Hispanic Society of America (New York)
IAN: Instituto dos Arquivos Nacionais (Torre do Tombo, Lisbon)
RAH: Real Academia de la Historia (Madrid)
RB: Real Biblioteca (El Escorial)
UL: University Library (Cambridge)

REFERENCE WORKS

AH: Analecta hymnica medii aevi
LU: Liber Usualis
PG: Patrologia Graeca
PL: Patrologia Latina
JL: Regesta Pontificum Romanorum

List of Manuscripts, Dated Manuscripts and Printed Sources

MANUSCRIPTS

Apt, Biblioteca Basilica de Sta. Ana, ms. 17
Apt, Biblioteca Basilica de Sta. Ana, ms. 18
Autun, Bibliothèque Municipale, ms. Séminaire 28
Aveiro, Arquivo Distrital de Aveiro, Fraga. w./o. s. [Parochial books no. 1, 1570-1573]
Ávila, Archivo Capitular, ms. w./o. s.
Barcelona, Archivo Capitular, ms. w./o. s.
Barcelona, Archivo de la Corona de Aragón, Frag. 1
Barcelona, Archivo de la Corona de Aragón, Frag. 35 bis
Barcelona, Archivo de la Corona de Aragón, Frag. 36
Barcelona, Archivo de la Corona de Aragón, parch. Guifredo I, 12
Barcelona, Archivo de la Corona de Aragón, Ripoll 40
Barcelona, Archivo de la Corona de Aragón, Ripoll 42
Barcelona, Archivo de la Corona de Aragón, Ripoll 74
Barcelona, Archivo de la Corona de Aragón, Ripoll 76
Barcelona, Archivo de la Corona de Aragón, Ripoll 106
Barcelona, Archivo de la Corona de Aragón, Ripoll 151
Barcelona, Archivo de la Corona de Aragón, Ripoll 199
Barcelona, Archivo Diocesano, Frag. w./o. s.
Barcelona, Biblioteca de la Abadía de Montserrat, ms. 72
Barcelona, Biblioteca de la Abadía de Montserrat, ms. 73
Barcelona, Biblioteca de la Abadía de Montserrat, ms. 794-1
Barcelona, Biblioteca de la Abadía de Montserrat, ms. 822
Barcelona, Biblioteca de Cataluña, M. 1147
Barcelona, Biblioteca de Cataluña, M. 1408-3
Barcelona, Biblioteca de Cataluña, M. 1408-5a
Barcelona, Biblioteca de Cataluña, M. 1408-9a
Barcelona, Biblioteca de Cataluña, M. 1451-8
Barcelona, Biblioteca de Cataluña, M. 1805
Barcelona, Biblioteca de Cataluña, M. 2101
Barcelona, Biblioteca de Cataluña, parch. 9135, 2-VIII-2
Barcelona, Biblioteca General, Universidad Autónoma de Barcelona, ms. 33/10
Benevento, Biblioteca Capitular, ms. 34
Benevento, Biblioteca Capitular, ms. 35
Benevento, Biblioteca Capitular, ms. 40
Berlín, Staatsbibliothek Preussischer Kulturbesitz, ms. Latin fol. 445
Berlín, Staatsbibliothek Preussischer Kulturbesitz, ms. Philipps 1831
Braga, Arquivo Distrital, Frag. 23 (olim Registro Geral, Caixa Frag. 244, 1)
Braga, Arquivo Distrital, Frag. 49
Braga, Arquivo Distrital, Frag. 82
Braga, Arquivo Distrital, Frag. 210
Braga, Arquivo Distrital, ms. 1000
Braga, Arquivo Distrital, Registro Geral, Caixa Frag. 280, 3
Braga, Arquivo Distrital, Registro Geral, Caixa Frag. 284, 12
Bruselas, Real Biblioteca, ms. II 4856
Burgo de Osma, Archivo Capitular, ms. 78A
Burgo de Osma, Archivo Capitular, ms. 94
Burgos, Archivo Capitular, ms. w./o. s.
Burgos, Archivo del Monasterio de Santa María la Real, Códice de Las Huelgas, ms. w./o. s.
Cambridge, University Library, add. 5905
Coimbra, Archivo de la Universidad, IV-3.ª S.-Gav. 44 (20)
Coimbra, Archivo de la Universidad, IV-3.ª-Gav. 44 (22)
Copenhagen, Det kongelige Bibliotek, Ny Kgl., 1794
Copenhagen, Universitetsbibliotek, 1927, AM. 795, 4.º
Córdoba, Archivo Capitular, ms. 1
Córdoba, Archivo Capitular, ms. 123
Cracow, Biblioteca Czartorysky, 3.118
El Escorial, Real Biblioteca de San Lorenzo, &.I.3
El Escorial, Real Biblioteca de San Lorenzo, &.I.14
El Escorial, Real Biblioteca de San Lorenzo, &.J.2
El Escorial, Real Biblioteca de San Lorenzo, &.J.3
El Escorial, Real Biblioteca de San Lorenzo, a.I.13
El Escorial, Real Biblioteca de San Lorenzo, a.II.9

El Escorial, Real Biblioteca de San Lorenzo, b.I.4
El Escorial, Real Biblioteca de San Lorenzo, b.I.10
El Escorial, Real Biblioteca de San Lorenzo, b.I.11
El Escorial, Real Biblioteca de San Lorenzo, b.I.12
El Escorial, Real Biblioteca de San Lorenzo, I.d.1
El Escorial, Real Biblioteca de San Lorenzo, I.II.13
El Escorial, Real Biblioteca de San Lorenzo, L.III.3
El Escorial, Real Biblioteca de San Lorenzo, L.III.4
El Escorial, Real Biblioteca de San Lorenzo, P.I.6
El Escorial, Real Biblioteca de San Lorenzo, P.I.7
El Escorial, Real Biblioteca de San Lorenzo, P.I.8
El Escorial, Real Biblioteca de San Lorenzo, Q.III.10
El Escorial, Real Biblioteca de San Lorenzo, R.III.9
El Escorial, Real Biblioteca de San Lorenzo, T.II.24
El Escorial, Real Biblioteca de San Lorenzo, T.II.25
Florence, Biblioteca Medicea Laurenziana, Conv. Sopp. 560
Florence, Biblioteca Medicea Laurenziana, ms. LXXXVI.3
Girona, Archivo Capitular, ms. 2
Girona, Museo Diocesano, ms. 45
Huesca, Archivo Capitular, Cod. 1
Huesca, Archivo Capitular, Cod. 2
Huesca, Archivo Capitular, Cod. 4
Huesca, Archivo Capitular, Cod. 7
Huesca, Archivo Histórico Provincial, 12030/36
Jaca, Archivo del Monasterio de Santa Cruz de la Serós, w./o. s.
Karlsruhe, Badische Landesbibliothek, ms. 504
Lamego, Arquivo da Câmara Eclesiástica, Palacio Episcopal, 3 Frags.
Leiden, Universidad, Vossianus Lat. Fol. 74
León, Archivo Capitular, Frag. III
León, Archivo Capitular, ms. 8
León, Archivo Capitular, ms. 22
Lisbon, Biblioteca Nacional, Alcobaça 446
Lisbon, Biblioteca Nacional, Frag. w./o. s.
Lisbon, Instituto dos Arquivos Nacionais, Torre do Tombo, Frag. Cx. 20, doc. 1, Casa Forte, módulo 2, Gav. 3
Lleida, Archivo Capitular, Roda 8
Lleida, Archivo Capitular, Roda 11 (new shelfmark RC 0029)
Lleida, Archivo Capitular, Roda 14 (new shelfmark RC 0032)
Lleida, Archivo Capitular, Roda 16
Lleida, Archivo Capitular, Roda 18
London, British Library, Add. ms. 11695
London, British Library, Add. ms. 30844
London, British Library, Add. ms. 30845
London, British Library, Add. ms. 30846
London, British Library, Add. ms. 30847
London, British Library, Add. ms. 30848
London, British Library, Add. ms. 30849
London, British Library, Add. ms. 30850
London, British Library, Add. ms. 30851
London, British Library, Add. ms. 30852
London, British Library, Add. ms. 30853
Madrid, Biblioteca Histórica de la Universidad Complutense, ms. 31
Madrid, Biblioteca Nacional, ms. 289
Madrid, Biblioteca Nacional, ms. 9719
Madrid, Biblioteca Nacional, ms. 10001
Madrid, Biblioteca Nacional, ms. 10008
Madrid, Biblioteca Nacional, ms. 10029
Madrid, Biblioteca Nacional, ms. 10110
Madrid, Biblioteca Nacional, ms. 11556
Madrid, Biblioteca Nacional, ms. 13050
Madrid, Biblioteca Nacional, ms. 13053
Madrid, Biblioteca Nacional, ms. 13056
Madrid, Biblioteca Nacional, ms. 13060
Madrid, Biblioteca Nacional, ms. 19421
Madrid, Biblioteca Nacional, glass case 14.3
Madrid, Biblioteca Nacional, glass case 20.6
Madrid, Biblioteca del Palacio Real, ms. 483
Madrid, Real Academia de la Historia, Cod. 14, Folder V, Cod. 118
Madrid, Real Academia de la Historia, Cod. 18
Madrid, Real Academia de la Historia, Cod. 22
Madrid, Real Academia de la Historia, Cod. 25
Madrid, Real Academia de la Historia, Cod. 27
Madrid, Real Academia de la Historia, Cod. 30
Madrid, Real Academia de la Historia, Cod. 45
Madrid, Real Academia de la Historia, Cod. 51
Madrid, Real Academia de la Historia, Cod. 56
Madrid, Real Academia de la Historia, Cod. 60
Madrid, Real Academia de la Historia, Cod. 76
Madrid, Real Academia de la Historia, Cod. 118
Madrid, Real Academia de la Historia, ms. 9/4579
Milan, Biblioteca Ambrosiana, Cod. M. 12 sup.
Modena, Biblioteca Capitular, ms. 7
Modena, Biblioteca Capitular, O.I.17
Montecassino, Archivo de la Abadía, Cod. 99
Montecassino, Archivo de la Abadía, ms. Lat. 7530
Montpellier, Archive de l'Hérault, ms. 58 H 6
Montpellier, Bibliothèque de l'École de Médecine, ms. H 159
Montpellier, Bibliothèque de l'École de Médecine, ms. 20
Montpellier, Bibliothèque de la ville, ms. 6
Montserrat, Archivo de la Abadía, Parchments of Bages, no. 9
Montserrat, Archivo de la Abadía, Parchments of Bages, no. 215
Montserrat, Archivo de la Abadía, Parchments of Bages, no. 1.102
Montserrat, Biblioteca de la Abadía, 790/III
Montserrat, Biblioteca de la Abadía, 1254/IV
Montserrat, Biblioteca de la Abadía, ms. 72

Montserrat, Biblioteca de la Abadía, ms. 73
Montserrat, Biblioteca de la Abadía, ms. 794/I
Montserrat, Biblioteca de la Abadía, ms. 822
Munich, Staatsbibliothek, Clm 14429
New York, Hispanic Society of America, B 2916
New York, Hispanic Society of America, HC 380/897
Ohio, University Heights, John Stamitz Collection, ms. w./o. s.
Ourense, Archivo Capitular, Frag. 3
Palma de Majorca, Museo Diocesano, ms. w./o. s.
Pamplona, Archivo Real y General de Navarra, Codices and Cartularies, K.6
Pamplona, Museo Capitular, w./o. s.
Paris, Bibliothèque Mazarine, ms. 689
Paris, Bibliothèque Nationale de France, grec 2093
Paris, Bibliothèque Nationale de France, Lat. 778
Paris, Bibliothèque Nationale de France, Lat. 793
Paris, Bibliothèque Nationale de France, Lat. 887
Paris, Bibliothèque Nationale de France, Lat. 891
Paris, Bibliothèque Nationale de France, Lat. 903
Paris, Bibliothèque Nationale de France, Lat. 909
Paris, Bibliothèque Nationale de France, Lat. 933
Paris, Bibliothèque Nationale de France, Lat. 1086
Paris, Bibliothèque Nationale de France, Lat. 1118
Paris, Bibliothèque Nationale de France, Lat. 1120
Paris, Bibliothèque Nationale de France, Lat. 1137
Paris, Bibliothèque Nationale de France, Lat. 1139
Paris, Bibliothèque Nationale de France, Lat. 1646
Paris, Bibliothèque Nationale de France, Lat. 2832
Paris, Bibliothèque Nationale de France, Lat. 2855
Paris, Bibliothèque Nationale de France, Lat. 3827
Paris, Bibliothèque Nationale de France, Lat. 5302
Paris, Bibliothèque Nationale de France, Lat. 5304
Paris, Bibliothèque Nationale de France, Lat. 7530
Paris, Bibliothèque Nationale de France, Lat. 8093
Paris, Bibliothèque Nationale de France, Lat. 14301
Paris, Bibliothèque Nationale de France, Lat. 16819
Paris, Bibliothèque Nationale de France, N. A. L. 235
Paris, Bibliothèque Nationale de France, N. A. L. 495
Paris, Bibliothèque Nationale de France, N. A. L. 557
Paris, Bibliothèque Nationale de France, N. A. L. 1154
Paris, Bibliothèque Nationale de France, N. A. L. 1177
Paris, Bibliothèque Nationale de France, N. A. L. 1871
Paris, Bibliothèque Nationale de France, N. A. L. 2169
Paris, Bibliothèque Nationale de France, N. A. L. 2170
Paris, Bibliothèque Nationale de France, N. A. L. 2171
Paris, Bibliothèque Nationale de France, N. A. L. 2177
Paris, Bibliothèque Nationale de France, N. A. L. 2199
Paris, Bibliothèque Nationale de France, N. A. L. 2772
Paris, Bibliothèque Nationale de France, N. A. L. 2773
Paris, Bibliothèque Nationale de France, N. A. L. 15163
Porto, Biblioteca Pública Municipal do Porto, Santa Cruz 17, ms. 21
Porto, Biblioteca Pública Municipal do Porto, Santa Cruz 76, general no. 350
Porto, Biblioteca Pública Municipal do Porto, Santa Cruz 83, general no. 1134
Ripoll, Archivo Histórico Comarcal, ms. 2
Rome, Biblioteca Apostolica Vaticana, ms. Lat. 5729
Rome, Biblioteca Apostolica Vaticana, ms. Urb. Lat. 602
Roncevaux, Museo de la Real Colegiata de Santa María, ms. w./o. s.
Salamanca, Archivo de los Sacerdotes Operarios Diocesanos, Frag. w./o. s. (Bible)
Salamanca, Biblioteca General Universitaria, ms. 2637
Salamanca, Biblioteca General Universitaria, ms. 2668
Saint Gall, Stiftsbibliothek, ms. 231
Saint Gall, Stiftsbibliothek, ms. 232
Saint Gall, Stiftsbibliothek, ms. 233
Saint Gall, Stiftsbibliothek, ms. 235
Saint Gall, Stiftsbibliothek, ms. 237
Saint Gall, Stiftsbibliothek, ms. 913
Saint Gall, Stiftsbibliothek, ms. 1399 a.1
Santiago de Compostela, Archivo Capitular, *Codex Calixtinus*
Santiago de Compostela, Archivo Capitular, Frag. 1
Santiago de Compostela, Biblioteca General Universitaria, ms. 609 (Res. 1)
Santo Domingo de la Calzada, Archivo Capitular, ms. w./o. s.
Sheffield, Collection of the Guild of St. George, Sheffield Galleries & Museums Trust, ms. 31
Sigüenza, Archivo Capitular, Cod. 20
Sigüenza, Archivo Capitular, Frag. w./o. s.
Silos, Archivo del Monasterio de Santo Domingo de Silos, Cod. 1
Silos, Archivo del Monasterio de Santo Domingo de Silos, Cod. 3
Silos, Archivo del Monasterio de Santo Domingo de Silos, Cod. 4
Silos, Archivo del Monasterio de Santo Domingo de Silos, Cod. 5
Silos, Archivo del Monasterio de Santo Domingo de Silos, Cod. 6
Silos, Archivo del Monasterio de Santo Domingo de Silos, Cod. 7
Silos, Archivo del Monasterio de Santo Domingo de Silos, Cod. 9
Silos, Archivo del Monasterio de Santo Domingo de Silos, Frag. mus. 26
Silos, Archivo del Monasterio de Santo Domingo de Silos, w./o. s. (Bible)
Solsona, Archivo Diocesano, Frag. 19
Tarragona, Archivo Histórico Archidiocesano, ms. 20/15
Tarragona, Archivo Histórico Archidiocesano, ms. 22/1
Tarragona, Biblioteca Provincial, ms. 102

Tarragona, Biblioteca Provincial, ms. 104
Toledo, Biblioteca Capitular, 10-5
Toledo, Biblioteca Capitular, 14-22 (see Madrid, Biblioteca Nacional, ms. 10029)
Toledo, Biblioteca Capitular, 15-10
Toledo, Biblioteca Capitular, 15-11
Toledo, Biblioteca Capitular, 35-1 (see Madrid, Biblioteca Nacional, ms. 10001)
Toledo, Biblioteca Capitular, 35-2 (see Madrid, Biblioteca Nacional, ms. 10110)
Toledo, Biblioteca Capitular, 35-3
Toledo, Biblioteca Capitular, 35-5
Toledo, Biblioteca Capitular, 35-6
Toledo, Biblioteca Capitular, 35-7
Toledo, Biblioteca Capitular, 35-10
Toledo, Biblioteca Capitular, 35-19
Toledo, Biblioteca Capitular, 44-1
Toledo, Biblioteca Capitular, 44-2
Toledo, Museo de los Concilios y de la Cultura Visigoda, no. 1325-1/2
Toledo, Museo de los Concilios y de la Cultura Visigoda, no. 1326
Tortosa, Archivo Capitular, ms. 135
Valbanera, Archivo del Monasterio, Frag. Fold. 1, no. 3
Valenciennes, Bibliothèque Municipale, ms. 384-385
Valenciennes, Bibliothèque Municipale, ms. 399
Valladolid, Archivo de la Real Chancillería, Frag. w./o. s.
Vallbona de les Monges, Archivo del Monasterio de Santa María, ms. 1
Venice, Biblioteca Nacional Marciana, ms. 232 (4257)
Verona, Biblioteca Capitolare, ms. 89
Vic, Archivo y Biblioteca Episcopal, Frag. I/6
Vic, Archivo y Biblioteca Episcopal, Frag. V/2
Vic, Archivo y Biblioteca Episcopal, Frag. V/40
Vic, Archivo y Biblioteca Episcopal, Frag. VIII/23
Vic, Archivo y Biblioteca Episcopal, Frag. XI/I
Vic, Archivo y Biblioteca Episcopal, ms. 66
Vic, Archivo y Biblioteca Episcopal, ms. 67
Vic, Archivo y Biblioteca Episcopal, ms. 105
Vic, Archivo y Biblioteca Episcopal, ms. 106
Vic, Archivo y Biblioteca Episcopal, ms. 122/1-2
Vic, Archivo y Biblioteca Episcopal, ms. 123/3
Vienna, Österreichische Nationalbibliothek, Cod. 683 (olim Cpv 683)
Vienna, Österreichische Nationalbibliothek, Cod. 2503
Zamora, Archivo Histórico Provincial, Frag. no. 15
Zamora, Archivo Histórico Provincial, Frag. no. 202
Zaragoza, Biblioteca General Universitaria, M-418

DATED MANUSCRIPTS

Homiliario. Córdoba, AC, ms. 1, year 953
Liber canticorum et horarum. Salamanca, BGU, ms. 2668, May of 1059
Liber ordinum. Silos, AM, Cod. 3, January of 1039
Liber ordinum. Silos, AM, Cod. 4, 18 May 1052
Lleida, AC, Roda 11 (new shelfmark: RC 0029), year 1191
Psalterium et Liber canticorum (Diurno de Fernando I).
Sacramentario, Evangeliario. Madrid, BN, ms. 9719, year 1162
Salterio, himnario y oficio rimado de san Raimundo.
San Ildefonso, De virginitate Sanctae Mariae. Silos, AM, Cod. 5, 12 October 1059
Santiago de Compostela, BXU, ms. 609, Res. 1, year 1055 (era 1093)

PRINTED SOURCES

Vic, Archivo y Biblioteca Episcopal, Hemeroteca Vic, Impr. w./o. s. (Lyon 1557)
Vic, Archivo y Biblioteca Episcopal, Impr. XVI/1569 (Barcelona 1560)

List of Scribes

Arias (Antifonario. León, AC, ms. 8)
Bartolomé (*Liber ordinum*. Silos, AM, Cod. 4)
Blasco (*San Ildefonso, De virginitate Sanctae Mariae*. Silos, AM, Cod. 5)
Cristophorus (*Liber canticorum et horarum*. Salamanca, BGU, ms. 2668)
Dominicus (*Liber ordinum*. Madrid, RAH, Cod. 56)
Ericone
Florentius (Homiliario. Córdoba, AC, ms. 1)
Fructuosus (*Psalterium et Liber canticorum*. Santiago de Compostela, BXU, ms. 609, Res. 1)
Guifredo (*Códice misceláneo*. Barcelona, ACA, Ripoll 40), (*Liber glossarum*. Barcelona, ACA, Ripoll 74)
Mauro (*Psalterium, Liber canticorum, Liber hymnorum*. Madrid, BN, ms. 10001)
Petrus (*Psalterium et Liber canticorum*. Santiago de Compostela, BXU, ms. 609, Res. 1)
Salomón (Sacramentario. Vic, ABEV, ms. 67)
Sebastianus (*Liber misticus*. Toledo, BC, 35-7)
Teodemundo (Antifonario. León, AC, ms. 8)

Index of Personal Names

Place Names Index

Typological Index of Manuscripts

Photographic Credits

© Archivo Capitular, Ávila (José Ramón San Sebastián, Nature & Travel): p. 222 (52).
© Archivo Capitular, Burgo de Osma (Fernando Alvira): pp. 392-393.
© Archivo Capitular, Burgos, Cabildo Metropolitano (Antonio Gutiérrez): pp. 294-295.
© Archivo Capitular, Catedral de Huesca (Fernando Alvira): pp. 146 (1), 149 (3), 354-355, 356-357, 358-359.
© Archivo Capitular, Córdoba: pp. 104 (2), 166 (2), 213 (28), 254-255, 372-373.
© Archivo Capitular, León (Imagen M.A.S): pp. 95 (1), 211 (12), 252-253.
© Archivo Capitular, Lleida (Fernando Alvira): pp. 216 (38), 216 (39), 216 (40), 219 (48), 320-321, 322-323, 324-325, 350-351, 352-353.
© Archivo Capitular, Ourense (José López-Calo): pp. 388-389.
© Archivo Capitular, Santiago de Compostela (José López-Calo): pp. 386-387.
© Archivo Capitular, Sigüenza (Fernando Alvira): pp. 390-391.
© Arquivo da Universidade de Coimbra: pp. 118 (2), 210 (3), 312-313, 406-407.
© Archivo del Monasterio de Santo Domingo de Silos: pp. 214 (30; 31); (Ángel Alonso Cuevas): pp. 276-277, 282-283, 288-289, 290-291, 292-293.
© Archivo Histórico Archidiocesano de Tarragona: p. 17 (1).
© Archivo Histórico Provincial de Huesca (Markwardt Zapke): pp. 221 (51), 360-361.
© Archivo Real y General de Navarra, Pamplona: pp. 222 (56), 398-399.
© Archivo Capitular, Santo Domingo de la Calzada (Fernando Alvira): pp. 284-285.
© Arquivo Distrital de Aveiro: pp. 424-425.
© Arxiu i Biblioteca Episcopal, Vic (Fernando Alvira): pp. 167 (3), 216 (36), 217 (41; 43), 222 (54; 55; 57), 326-327, 328-329, 330-331.
© Biblioteca Capitular, Toledo: p. 61(1); (Fernando Alvira): pp. 127 (1), 134 (3), 209 (1; 2), 210 (4; 5), 212 (17; 18; 19), 221 (49; 50), 300-301, 308-309, 400-401, 404-405.
© Czartorysky Library, Cracow (Poland): pp. 262-263.
© Biblioteca de Cataluña, Barcelona: pp. 45 (2), 216 (34; 35), 346-347.
© Biblioteca de la Abadía de Montserrat: p. 18 (2); (Fernando Alvira): pp. 217 (42), 338-339, 340-341, 342-343, 344-345.
© Biblioteca General Universitaria, Zaragoza (Fernando Alvira): pp. 211 (11), 286-287.
© Biblioteca Nacional, Lisbon: p. 78.
© Biblioteca Nacional de España. The photographs were prepared in a photografic laboratory at the Biblioteca Nacional de España: pp. 70 (2), 210 (7; 8), 211 (9), 213 (22; 23; 24; 26; 27), 224 (64), 296-297, 310-311, 370-371.
© Biblioteca Pública Municipal do Porto: pp. 420-421, 422-423.
© Biblioteca Xeral Universitaria, Santiago de Compostela: pp. 256-257.
© Bibliothèque Nationale de France. Cliché Bibliothèque Nationale de France: pp. 179 (3), 250-251, 332-333, 334-335, 336-337, 402-403.

About the Authors

Maria José Azevedo Santos earned a doctorate in Medieval History at the University of Coimbra (1989) and is professor of Paleography and Diplomatics, a member of the Institute of Paleography and Diplomatics and a researcher at the Center of History of Society and Culture at the same university. Head of the Arquivo da Universidade de Coimbra and elected member of the International Latin Paleography Committee, she has devoted most of her research and teaching to medieval Latin and Portuguese paleography, diplomatics and codicology, fields in which she has given lectures and seminars at prestigious European universities and scientific institutions (Universidad Autónoma de Barcelona, the universities of Alcalá de Henares, León, Salamanca, Louvain la Neuve, and the Czech Academy of Sciences). She has written numerous pioneering publications in a field of study in which there is a paucity of tradition of research in Portugal, such as *De la visigótica a la carolina. La escritura en Portugal de 882 a 1172* (1994), directed by Manuel C. Díaz y Díaz, with which she earned her doctorate and which is the first Portuguese work on medieval Latin diplomatics and paleography.

M.ª Dolores Barrios Martínez graduated in arts from the University of Zaragoza, is head of the Archivo General de la Diputación Provincial de Huesca, and runs the Archivo Capitular of Huesca. Director of the Remembrance Collection of the Study Institute of Upper Aragón, she specializes in medieval history and has published several works on the history of Aragón: *Libro del Castillo de Sesa* (1982), *Una explotación agrícola del siglo XIII (Sesa, Huesca*) (1983), *Mujeres aragonesas del siglo XI* (2004), and *Documentos de Montearagón (1058-1205)* (2004).

Màrius Bernadó studied music at the Barcelona Conservatory and graduated in Philosophy and Art History (specialising in Music) from the Universidad Autónoma de Barcelona and in Liturgy from the Faculty of Theology of Catalonia. A lecturer in the History of Music at the University of Lleida, he works primarily on 15th-16th century plainsong, especially through the study of liturgical documents. He runs the DeMusica collection of the Reichenberger publishing house and has published, among other articles, "Sobre el origen y la procedencia de la tradición himnódica hispánica a fines de la Edad Media" and "Adaptación y cambio en repertorios de himnos durante los siglos XV and XVI: algunas observaciones sobre la práctica del canto mensural en fuentes ibéricas". In collaboration with Maricarmen Gómez Muntané, he edited the *Actas del Coloquio Internacional Fuentes Musicales en la Península Ibérica (ca. 1250-ca. 1550).*

Susan Boynton studied musicology at Yale University, earned a doctorate in Musicology at Brandeis University, an MA in Medieval Studies at Yale University, and a diploma in Medieval Studies at the Catholic University of Louvain-la-Neuve. An associate professor in the Department of Music at Columbia University, her main areas of research are Medieval Latin hymnaries, hymn glosses, monastic *consuetudines* and liturgical usage at the abbeys of Farfa and Cluny. Among her publications are "A Lost Mozarabic Liturgical Manuscript Rediscovered. New York, Hispanic Society of America, B2916, olim Toledo, Chapter Library, 33.2" (2002), "Orality, Literacy, and the Early Notation of the Office Hymns" (2003), "The Didactic Function and Context of Eleventh-Century Glossed Hymnaries" (2004), "The Theological Role of Office Hymns in a Ninth-Century Trinitarian Controversy" (2005) and *Shaping a Monastic Identity. Liturgy and History at the Imperial Abbey of Farfa, 1000-1125* (2006). She is currently writing a book on Andrés Marcos Burriel's study of the Visigothic manuscripts in the Cathedral of Toledo.

Eva M.ª Castro Caridad has a doctorate from the University of Santiago de Compostela and is professor of Latin Philology there. Her doctoral thesis, supervised by professor Manuel C. Díaz y Díaz, focused on the study of the liturgical tropes in the mass that have survived in Hispanic manuscripts, research that earned her the Extraordinary Doctorate Award. She has done research at Stockholm and Cambridge universities. Her work has focused on religious poetry, especially liturgical poetry, and Medieval Latin dramas, fields in which, among others, the following publications stand out: *Tropos y troparios hispánicos* (1991), *Teatro Medieval 1: El drama litúrgico* (1997), and *Dramas escolares latinos (siglos XII-XIII)* (2001).

Manuel Cecilio Díaz y Díaz has a doctorate in Classical Philology from the University of Madrid and doctorates honoris causa from the universities of Lisbon, Salamanca, León and Coimbra. He has lectured in Latin Philology at the universities of Valencia (1953), Salamanca (1956), and Santiago de Compostela (1968-1989), where he is a professor emeritus. A National Research Prize winner (1998), he has published, among other works, *Libros y librerías en la Rioja altomedieval* (1979), *Códices visigóticos en la monarquía leonesa* (1983), and *Manuscritos visigóticos del sur de la Península* (1995).

Marco Daniel Duarte is a graduate and doctoral student in the History of Art in the Faculty of Arts at the University of Coimbra and is a corresponding member of the Portuguese Academy of History and a member of the Department of Liturgy and Sacred Music of the diocese of Guarda. He has been awarded a scholarship by the Portuguese Ministry of Science, Technology and Higher Education Foundation for Science and Technology. His area of specialization is religious art, especially in the fields of iconography and iconology. Among his most important publications are *Cunhar e tecer as cortes de Leiria de 1254* (2006) and *Arte sacro en Fátima. Una peregrinación estética* (2006).

Maricarmen Gómez Muntané studied Music at the Liceo Conservatory and Musicology at Göttingen University and earned a doctorate in Philosophy and Letters at the University of Barcelona. She has lectured on Early Music at the Universidad Autónoma de Barcelona since 1997 and has been visiting professor at Princeton University (1989-1990), at the University of North Texas (1996) and at the École Normale Supérieure in Paris (2003); Director-at-Large of the International Society of Musicology (1987-1997) and has collaborated on numerous international studies. Her publications include *La música en la casa real catalanoaragonesa 1336-1432* (1979), which won the National Musicology Prize (1977), *El Llibre Vermell de Montserrat* (1990), *El Canto de la Sibila* (1996, 1997), *La música medieval en España* (2001), and *El Cancionero de Uppsala* (2003). She is currently preparing a critical edition on the musical genre of the *ensalada*.

Ramón Gonzálvez Ruiz graduated in Ecclesiastical History and Theology from the Gregorian University in Rome, obtained a diploma in archival studies from the Vatican University, and earned a doctorate in Medieval History at the Universidad Complutense de Madrid. Emeritus archivist canon at the Cathedral of Toledo and director of the Royal Academy of Fine Art and Historical Sciences of Toledo, he is professor in the History of the Church at the San Ildefonso Theological Institute in Toledo, professor at the University College of Toledo and a corresponding member of the Royal Academy of History (Madrid) and Real Academia de Bellas Artes de Sant Jordi (Barcelona). His main research area is the medieval history of the Church of Toledo, focusing especially on subjects linked with books, culture, the Mozarabic liturgy and ethnic-religious minorities. He is the author of *Hombres y libros de Toledo* (1997) and *"Blas Ortiz y su mundo". La Catedral de Toledo 1549, según el doctor Blas Ortiz, Descripción Graphica y Elegantissima de la S. Iglesia de Toledo* (1999), and has also supervised and coordinated *La Biblia de san Luis de la Catedral de Toledo* (2003, 2004) and *Cuatro estudios sobre la imprenta incunable de Toledo* (2006). He is currently preparing a book titled *Historia de la Iglesia de Toledo.*

Miquel Sants Gros Pujol studied Liturgy and Gregorian Chant at the Advanced Liturgy Institute at the Catholic Institute in Paris, at the École des Chartes and at the Gregorian Chant Institute also in Paris. A Presbyter in the Bishopric of Vic, he is currently head of the Archivo-Biblioteca Episcopal in the city and diocese of Vic and chairman of the Catalonian Society of Liturgical Studies, a branch of the Institute of Catalonian Studies. His main research area is the liturgical history of the Catalonian/Narbonne tradition, a subject on which he has published widely. He has also edited *Els tropers prosers de la Catedral de Vic* (1999).

Barbara Haggh graduated in Germanic Philology from the University of Nebraska-Lincoln, earned a doctorate in Musicology from the University of Illinois-Urbana, and lectures on Musicology in the School of Music at the University of Maryland. She has been awarded scholarships by the American Council of Learned Societies (ACLS), International Research and Exchanges

(IREX), National Endowment for the Humanities (NEH), American Philosophy Society, the British Academy, the Catholic University of Louvain, the Leverhulme Trust and the Free University of Brussels, and her research fields focus on Carolingian theory, early notational systems, the cultural background of Paris in the 13th century, and lost or little-studied musical repertoires: offices of the saints, late plainsong, urban music, and music on manuscript fragments. She has written more than fifty articles on medieval sacred monody, the theory of music, urban music, and the Burgundian order of the Golden Fleece. She has edited the earliest office in honor of St. Isabel of Hungary, and published several books of essays on medieval sources and musicology, as well as editing a volume in honor of Herbert Kellman on subjects ranging from Norman poetry to the music of Piazzolla. At the moment she is preparing a monograph on the 9th century treatise, *Musica disciplina;* several studies on medieval Marian office; and a study on two *ordinarium* missals from Ghent and Dijon, as well as an article, together with Michel Huglo, on the manuscripts of the Sainte-Chapelle in Paris.

Michel Huglo a PhD at the University of Paris IV (Sorbonne) (1969), earned a doctorate in Musicology at the University of Paris X (Sorbonne, 1981), and is main researcher emeritus at the National Center for Scientific Research (CNRS) in Paris, which awarded him the Silver Medal for research (1987). Senior research professor of Musicology in the Department of Musicology and Ethnomusicology at the School of Music of the University of Maryland and corresponding member of the American Musicological Society (1997), he has been a scientific researcher for the CNRS since 1962 and head researcher since 1972, founder of the Musicology section at the Text History and Research Institute (IRHT) in Paris (1976), and professor of Medieval Musical Paleography at the École Pratique des Hautes Études (Paris IV Sorbonne) (1973-1986) and of Latin Paleography with regard to musical sources at the Free University of Brussels (1974-1987). Visiting Professor at the University of Vienna (1990) and New York University (1993), and Visiting Mellon Professor at the Institute for Historical Study at Princeton University (1990-1991), he has also been made a doctor honoris causa by the University of Chicago (1991). He has written more than two hundred articles on the history and sources of Gregorian chant, the theory of medieval music, and the primitive *organum;* among his most important publications are the edition of *Le Graduel Romain 2: Les sources*, and inventories of processionals and of manuscripts of music theory in the Middle Ages.

Gunilla Iversen has a doctorate in Classical Philology, is professor of Latin and Head of the Latin Department at the University of Stockholm, and head of the international research project Sapientia and Eloquentia: Meaning and Function in the Poetry, Music and Drama of the Medieval Latin Liturgy, and in Biblical Commentaries". She is a specialist in Latin poetry in the medieval liturgy and is the editor of *Studia Latina Stockholmiensia*, has edited several volumes in the *Corpus Troporum* series, and is currently preparing the edition of tropes of the *Gloria in excelsis*. She is the author of numerous studies on Latin poetry in the Middle Ages, Hildegard of Bingen, and Catullus; one of her most important publications is *Chanter avec les anges. Poésie dans la messe médiévale: interprétations et commentaires* (2001).

José López-Calo has a degree in Arts from the University of Granada and earned a doctorate in History at the University of Santiago de Compostela and in Musicology at the Pontifical Institute of Sacred Music in Rome. A Jesuit priest and professor emeritus of the History of Music at the University of Santiago de Compostela, he is the author of numerous works and articles especially devoted to music in Spanish cathedrals, and he coedited the *Diccionario de la música española e hispanoamericana* (10 vols., 1999-2002). Among his best-known works are several catalogs of cathedral archives, such as the *Catálogo del Archivo de Música de la Catedral de Ávila* (1978) and the catalog of the Archivo Capitular of Valladolid (in press), as well as historical monographs on the Middle Ages and the 17th century, especially *La música en la Catedral de Granada* (1963); *La música en la Catedral de Palencia* (1980); *La música medieval en Galicia* (1982); *Historia de la música española. Siglo XVII* (1983); *La música en Galicia* (1988); and *La música en la Catedral de Burgos* (2003).

Shin Nishimagi has a doctorate in Musicology and is a postdoctoral researcher at the École Pratique des Hautes Études (4th Section) in Paris. He has studied Musicology at Waseda University in Tokyo and has been a Research Fellow of the Japan Society for the Promotion of Science for Young Scholars. His main research field is the study of manuscript sources, especially medieval liturgical-musical ones.

M.ª Concepción Peñas García is a lecturer in Music at the Universidad Pública de Navarra. Her main research areas are the history of sacred peninsular monophony and musical pedagogy. She won the National Musicology prize in 1982 for a study of music in Spanish evangeliaries. A great expert on the liturgical tradition of the popular repertoire in the kingdom of Navarre, among her numerous publications are *La música en los evangeliarios españoles* (1983), *Catálogo de los fondos* *musicales de la Real Colegiata de Roncesvalles* (1995), *Música y tradición en Estella* (2000), *Los cantorales de Cisneros. Estudio y presentación del Cantoral* (2004), and *Fondos musicales históricos de Navarra. Siglos XII-XVI* (2004).

Elisa Ruiz García earned a doctorate in Classical Philology at the Universidad Complutense de Madrid. She lectures on Paleography and Diplomatics at the Complutense and has been a professor of Greek at the INEM. Her main areas of research deal with the semiotic and anthropological aspects of written culture, codicology, the history of books and libraries, and the relationship between written culture and religiosity in the 15th century. Her publications include *Manual de codicología* (1988); *Hacia una semiología de la escritura* (1992); *Catálogo de la Sección de códices de la Real Academia de la Historia* (1997); *Los libros de Isabel la Católica. Arqueología de un patrimonio escrito* (2004); and *Libro de horas de los retablos. Ms. Vitr. 25.3 de la Biblioteca Nacional* (2005).

Miguel Carlos Vivancos Gómez is a monk at the Monastery of Santo Domingo de Silos (Burgos). He is a graduate in Theological Sciences of the Faculty of Theology of Northern Spain (See of Burgos) and earned a doctorate in History at the University of Valladolid. He has been archivist and librarian at the Monastery of Silos and has published numerous works on medieval documents, the codicology and paleography of mainly Visigothic manuscripts, and various subjects related to monastic history. His main publications include *Documentación del Monasterio de Santo Domingo de Silos (954-1254)* (1988); *Glosas y notas marginales de los manuscritos visigóticos del Monasterio de Santo Domingo de Silos* (1996); *Las glosas silenses* (2001); *Biblia de san Luis. Catedral Primada de Toledo* (2002); and, in collaboration with Fernando Vilches, *La regla de San Benito. Traducción castellana del siglo XV para uso de los monasterios de San Millán y Silos* (2001).

Ludwig Vones has a doctorate in Medieval History from the University of Cologne and is a lecturer there in Medieval History. His main research areas are the medieval history of France and the Iberian Peninsula, the history of the papacy in the Middle Ages, especially in Avignon; cultural and religious exchange in the Iberian Peninsula and the Western Mediterranean; the development and spread of heretical trends and the history of the Staufens and other late-medieval dynasties. He is currently running the Iberia Pontificia-Provincia Tarraconensis research project, which focuses on identifying the relations between the Holy See and the dioceses and churches in the ecclesiastical province of Tarraconense until 1198, with a special emphasis on Catalonia. He is the author, among other publications, of *Die 'Historia Compostellana' und die Kirchenpolitik des nordwestspanischen Raumes 1070-1130. Ein Beitrag zur Geschichte der Beziehungen zwischen Spanien und dem Papsttum zu Beginn des 12. Jahrhunderts* (1980); *Geschichte der Iberischen Halbinsel im Mittelalter, 711-1480. Reich-Kronen-Regionen* (1993); and *Kirchenreform zwischen Kardinalkollegium, Kurie und Klientel* (1998).

Susana Zapke graduated in Romance Philology and Musicology at the University of Cologne and earned a doctorate in Musicology at the University of Hamburg. She studied piano and double bass at conservatories in San Sebastián, Bayonne and Freiburg. She is a lecturer in Musicology at the universities of Cologne, Stuttgart, Salamanca and Vienna and has been working as a researcher for the BBVA Foundation since 2003. From 1993 to 1998, her research focused on western sacred monophony within the framework of the habilitation project promoted by the Deutsche Forschungsgemeinschaft (DFG) and the Lise-Meitner-Programm (Ministry of Science and Research, Düsseldorf). Her main fields of research include 9th-12th century liturgical-musical sources (with a special emphasis on the Visigothic rite, the transition to the Roman rite and the new genres of medieval Latin lyric poetry), 15th-16th century poetic-musical compositions and the change in formal and aesthetic models in the early decades of the 20th century (modernism, second Viennese school). She has published *Falla. Entre la tradición y la vanguardia* (1999) and the Spanish version of Constantin Floros' book *Alban Berg-Hanna Fuchs. Un amor epistolar* (2005), and her other publications include *El Antifonario de San Juan de la Peña, siglos X-XI* (1995), *Das Antiphonar von Santa Cruz de la Serós, XII Jh.* (1996) and *Fragmentos litúrgico-musicales de la Edad Media en archivos de Aragón* (2007). She is currently preparing a study of Schönberg's literary works in the context of modernist thought.

ehina nu scu

ethina & mortuum

uncationi unio repleatis

sanguinem iubet tui

quia te sacrificium cedia

audux conlucgulis criminis

sed sacrum summa coronu

lauritatis glorium

Hic dei presb. gesia unu iuuen

nuaum filium

tempore quo subrequia

tua